SUCCESS WITH WORDS

Reader's Digest

SUCCESS WITH WORDS

A GUIDE TO THE AMERICAN LANGUAGE

Prepared in Association
With Peter Davies

The Reader's Digest Association, Inc., Pleasantville, New York/Montreal

STAFF FOR SUCCESS WITH WORDS

Project Editor: David Rattray
Text and Production Editor: Joyce O'Connor
Art Associate: Ken Chaya
Associate Editor: Suzanne E. Weiss
Copy Editor: Diana Marsh
Research Associate: Leslie Jean Simmons
Contributing Proofreader: Kendra K. Ho
Editorial Consultant: Eileen Myles

Contributing Staff

Prof. William Bauer, University of New Brunswick (grammar); Bruce Bohle (sports, political terms); Dr. Craig Carver, Managing Editor, *Dictionary of American Regional English* (U.S. dialects); Prof. Jerry R. Craddock, University of California, Berkeley (Portuguese words, Spanish words); Ormonde de Kay (poetic genres); Fran Duncan (Special Assistant to Peter Davies); Stuart Berg Flexner, Editor in Chief, Random House Dictionaries (slang); Alma Graham, Senior Editor, McGraw-Hill Publishing Co. (gender treatment); Prof. J. Murray Kinloch, University of New Brunswick (Canadian English); Eve Kirk (style, literary usage, citations); Prof. John Major, Dartmouth College (Chinese words, Japanese words); Danelle McCafferty (trademarks, theater terms); Carolyn Rattray (citations); William Sabin, Editor in Chief of Business Books, Professional and Reference Book Division, McGraw-Hill Publishing Co. (etiquette of style, legal terms, publishing terms); Rt. Rev. Edward Randolph Welles, Fourth Bishop of West Missouri (Bible, citations)

Library of Congress Cataloging in Publication Data
Main entry under title:

Success with words.

1. English language—United States—Usage—Dictionaries. 2. English language—Usage—Dictionaries. I. Reader's digest. II. Davies, Peter, 1940–
PE2835.S9 1983 427'.973 82-62542
ISBN 0-89577-168-3

Printed in the United States of America

INTRODUCTION

What precisely is Standard English? Dan Rather's speech or William F. Buckley's—or Billy Graham's? The usage of *Time* magazine or of the Congressional Record? Considering the variety that exists within English as spoken in North America alone, just whose standard is *the* standard? What authority makes it standard, and where does that authority come from?

Standard English is defined by scholars as the "prestige dialect" of our language. A Mark Twain or a Will Rogers can achieve humorous effects by deliberate and pointed use of nonstandard idioms. But the radio and television news is always delivered in a formal, generalized Standard English with little or no distinctive regional flavor. Business letters, legal arguments, scientific descriptions, magazine articles, and ceremonial speeches are also written in Standard English. Mastery of this prestige dialect is a key to success in most of the most prestigious activities of our world.

Who determines exactly which idioms do or do not qualify as Standard English? An unofficial consensus exists that recognizes certain idioms as standard and certain others as definitely nonstandard, but leaves many others as uncertain or debatable. Is it correct to split an infinitive? to write *different than* or *the reason is because*? Is *flaunt* misused for *flout*, or *infer* for *imply*? Are the words *hopefully* and *finalize* acceptable? Does *disinterested* mean 'not interested' or 'not motivated by self-interest'?

These questions remain because Standard English is not defined or fixed by any official authority. It emerges from a common consent that leaves plenty of room for disagreement and plenty of room for change. It does not exist in a vacuum but is part of the huge pattern of variety that makes up the English language worldwide.

Problems of Usage

In this book we have taken a fresh look at usage problems within Standard English—specifically, Standard American and Canadian English. To complete the picture, we had to go into the relationship between North American English and other leading varieties of English. This led to a consideration of many of the seemingly endless possibilities that the language offers. We are not handing down judicial rulings on usage. That method has often been tried, sometimes with great insight and power of conviction. Its most brilliant expositor was H. W. Fowler, whose classic *Dictionary of Modern English Usage* (1926) is a model of the prescriptivist method. Our approach is different. We prefer to look carefully at what the language itself is doing; that is, at how people are in fact using it. This is the true basis of the term *usage*. Some usages are better than others—better because they are clearer, more effective, more pleasing, more sensitive, or sometimes better merely because a consensus of influential people prefers them. Some issues are head-on collisions, with admired writers and speakers irreconcilably opposed on both sides. Other matters turn out to be so complicated that few people, if any, dare take a hard and fast line on them.

Citations and Recommendations

In order to make our discussions realistic, to reflect what is really going on in the language, we have collected a large number of real examples, or citations, both of disputed or debatable usages and of usages that are merely interesting in one way or another. We have concentrated on the printed word, which is the most accessible source of well-thought-out usage. Although we have centered our attention on current and familiar Standard American and Canadian English, we have also included much material from classics of literature, from historical sources, and from writings published elsewhere in the English-speaking world. In all cases of dispute we discuss the issues and give an opinion, generally with a recommendation. Our recommendations are sometimes two- or three-pronged, reflecting various levels and social contexts: the usually formal language used at a job interview is not necessarily the same as the informal language of an exchange between friends over the cafeteria table. Because it is generally helpful, often essential, to know the kind of person whose usage is being discussed, we cite familiar people and sources—names that you will recognize immediately so that their style or background can easily be identified. That a usage occurs in *Time* magazine is one kind of information; that it appears in the writing of a Nobel-prize-winning novelist like William Faulkner is another. We thus quote both admired literary authors of the past and present and well-known personalities from all walks of life—Jane Austen, George Washington, Thomas Wolfe, Margaret Mitchell, Winston Churchill, Jack Nicklaus, Mary McCarthy, S. J. Perelman, Harpo Marx, Martin Luther King, Jr., William C. Westmoreland, James A. Michener, to name a few at random. Likewise, we quote extensively from current newspapers and magazines, including *Reader's Digest.*

The frequent appearance of some sources and authors does not represent any intentional editorial bias. It happens that some writings lend themselves to useful excerpts much more than others. However, the decision to make particular use of *Reader's Digest* was a deliberate editorial choice, and an important one. *Reader's Digest* usage symbolizes the kind of standard North American English usage on which we center our recommendations—not the usage of a literary elite nor of some self-identified upper class; not the artificial usage of the old-fashioned schoolteacher, but the middle-of-the-road, effective, varied American usage of the most widely familiar kind. We don't, however, confine ourselves to the styles of English that appear in *Reader's Digest*, multifarious as they are; we have simply kept the *Digest* in mind as a general guide and norm.

The Scope of English

Anyone who takes an interest in the English language cannot fail to be impressed by its immense bulk and variety, the results of a long and far-flung history. The speech of North America has fascinatingly distinct forms, from New Brunswick to New England to Georgia and from New York City to Toronto to San Francisco. Further variations are seen in the rest of the English-speaking world, from India to Jamaica and from Liverpool to Brisbane. Within a single community the lawyer speaks differently from the plumber;

the farmer from the preacher. The sheer number of available words in English is staggering. No one can know them all, but ordinary people have much larger vocabularies than they think they have. Besides the universal everyday "core" vocabulary of 15,000 words or so, most of us also have a command of various specialized terminologies—the language of jobs, hobbies, sports, activities and interests of all kinds. Then, too, there is the diverse and ever-expanding word stock that each of us acquires through reading.

This book is intended to reflect and to explore some of the inexhaustible richness of our language. It is deliberately miscellaneous, but it takes as a central theme what might be called the hard-core issues of usage—questions over which experts wrangle, purists lay down the law, and average speakers hesitate. Our recommendations offer resolutions of the issues insofar as they can be resolved. But in the end you, the reader of this book, must be the final arbiter of how to use your own language. We can only offer information and suggestions for you to adopt as you see fit.

Note. Throughout this book, cross-references to main entries are set in SMALL CAPITALS.

Special Topics

The kinds of entries we have described so far relate to individual words or pairs or groups of similar words. The book also contains entries that deal with general problems, topics, and matters of interest, many of which cover specialized vocabularies or entire categories of language.

Literature and Style. This book provides exhaustive coverage of the topics that traditionally appear in rhetoric books, such as figures of speech and literary forms and styles. There is a summary entry at FIGURES OF SPEECH containing cross-references to such individual topics as ANTITHESIS, IRONY, METAPHOR, PUN, and SIMILE. Related entries include CLICHÉ, EUPHEMISM, JARGON, SLANG, and VOGUE WORDS; FALLACY; and BURLESQUE, LAMPOON, and SATIRE.

The Etiquette of Style. In this book you will find a wide coverage of stylistic etiquette, especially as it is observed in the usage of business and publishing. Among these entries are CAPITALIZATION, DIACRITICS, FORMS OF ADDRESS, NUMBER STYLE, PLURALS, POSSESSIVES, PUNCTUATION, and WORD DIVISION.

Sports. Herein you will also find entries on the specialized terminologies of sports, including BASEBALL, BASKETBALL, FOOTBALL, HOCKEY, HORSE-RACING, and HORSES AND HORSEMANSHIP terms, with special attention to idioms that have entered the mainstream of general usage.

Gender Treatment. One of the most serious issues confronting modern usage is the cluster of problems relating to gender. For some, it is still appropriate to say *Everyone has his secret ambition,* intending to include both women and men. For others, such usage has ceased to be acceptable. The chief entries are at DEAR SIR OR MADAM; EVERYONE . . . HE; FEMALE-GENDER WORD FORMS; HE OR SHE; MAN; -MAN; MISS, MRS., MS.; PARALLEL STYLE; SHE; THEY; and WOMAN, LADY, GIRL.

Varieties of English. Our central picture is of Standard American English as a preeminent member of the great family of the dialects of English. We have placed it in true perspective by describing also the other dialects, national branches, and historical stages of the language. The value of this supporting coverage can be seen in two ways. First, it is intrinsically fascinating to explore the almost endless variety of speech that the English-speaking peoples have developed since the Angles and Saxons first settled on the island of Britain and their descendants went out and colonized the world. Second, an awareness of the other dialects and branches is an essential element in understanding the nature of Standard American English and Canadian English and what distinguishes them from their siblings elsewhere.

The historical background begins with the entry OLD ENGLISH and continues with MIDDLE ENGLISH and ELIZABETHAN ENGLISH. The major modern national branches and varieties are described at AMERICAN ENGLISH, AUSTRALIAN ENGLISH, BRITISH ENGLISH, CANADIAN ENGLISH, and SCOTTISH ENGLISH.

North American Dialects. Our coverage of the dialects of North America is detailed. We are proud to be able to present the first comprehensive description ever printed in one book of every regional dialect of the United States and Canada. The mosaic formed by these speech varieties is surveyed at REGIONAL DIALECTS OF AMERICAN ENGLISH and at CANADIAN ENGLISH. Each dialect also has its own entry, including a list or lists of characteristic features and vocabulary. Each American dialect has a map.

Every regional variety that has been fully observed by scholars is included, from the NEW ENGLAND DIALECT to the GULF SOUTHERN, from the VIRGINIA PIEDMONT to the PACIFIC NORTHWEST. We also investigate ALASKAN, HAWAIIAN, and PUERTO RICAN speech; CANADIAN FRENCH, CENTRAL AND PRAIRIE CANADIAN, NEWFOUNDLAND ENGLISH, and the BRITISH COLUMBIA DIALECTS; even the urban dialects of NEW YORK CITY, BOSTON, CHICAGO, and SAN FRANCISCO. Particular attention has been given to the nonregional but highly characteristic speech of Black Americans, at the entry BLACK ENGLISH. Also included are general articles on REGIONAL DIALECT, SOCIAL DIALECT, URBAN DIALECT, and PIDGIN AND CREOLE LANGUAGES, plus separate entries on such special speech varieties as BONAC, BOONTLING, CHINOOK JARGON, GULLAH, JAMAICAN ENGLISH, LOUISIANA FRENCH, and PENNSYLVANIA GERMAN-ENGLISH. In addition, we provide entries on individual words, sets of synonyms, and other features that are especially interesting because of their regional variety. Thus, there are entries on COTTAGE CHEESE, DOUGHNUT, and HEADCHEESE, each of which has different synonyms in different parts of North America—a reflection of local culture often going back to settlement times. There is an entry covering the word *greasy*, with its two pronunciations, /**grē**-sē/ and /**grē**-zē/, by which you can often tell where a person was born and raised; and there are others on such dialectal gems as YOU-ALL, CATERCORNER, and the phenomenon of *r*-lessness—the nonpronunciation of postvocalic *r* in parts of New England, New York, and the South (at R-LESSNESS, INTRUSIVE R).

Etymology. Some modern educators and linguists have held that etymology, the history of individual words, is irrelevant and can even confuse people striving to grasp current meanings and usages. We don't agree. To people seriously interested in their own language, word histories when properly presented and understood are intriguing in themselves and often provide an essential key to perceiving shades of meaning or to resolving problems of usage. But, as we point out in the entry ETYMOLOGY, origins don't *control* ongoing usage. Nonetheless, throughout this book we have brought in etymology wherever it seemed helpful or worthwhile.

The Sources of the English Vocabulary. This book provides comprehensive coverage of the entire array of sources from which English has built up its now vast vocabulary. Much of our inherited word stock can be traced back to ancestral INDO-EUROPEAN, and there is further coverage of inherited words at OLD ENGLISH and MIDDLE ENGLISH. There are also separate entries on virtually every major language from which English has borrowed words, each giving representative lists and often other information, such as how to pronounce foreign words. The source languages that English has drawn on most freely are covered at FRENCH WORDS, GREEK WORDS, and LATIN WORDS. There are also entries for AFRICAN, AFRIKAANS, ARABIC, AZTEC, CARIBBEAN, CHINESE, DUTCH, EGYPTIAN, GERMAN, HUNGARIAN, INDIAN (AMERICAN), INDIAN (INDIA), INNUIT, IRISH, ITALIAN, JAPANESE, MALAY, NORSE, PERSIAN, PORTUGUESE, RUSSIAN, SANSKRIT, SCANDINAVIAN, SOUTH AMERICAN, SPANISH, TURKISH, WELSH, and YIDDISH words.

Pronunciation. Pronunciation being a major concern of usage, we have devised a system for rendering it that is both phonetically accurate (though simplified) and easy to read. The table on the following pages presents this system.

Even now we have not definitively described the contents of this book, which contains an open-ended assortment of entries that you may enjoy as you browse, from ACRONYMS to BACK-FORMATIONS, from COGNATES to FOLK ETYMOLOGY, from NEWSPEAK to SPOONERISM, from SHIBBOLETH to TONGUE TWISTERS. This wide-ranging miscellany, as well as the more systematic categories we have summarized, is devoted to our guiding principle: Success with words is not to be sought in a rigid and unquestioning cultivation of rules but will follow naturally from a lively *INTEREST* in language.

PRONUNCIATION KEY

The following pronunciation symbols have been used throughout this book and are highly compatible with systems found in current dictionaries and other reference works. The only nonalphabetic character is ə, known as the *schwa,* representing the unstressed neutral vowel that is the commonest vowel sound in English. Our approach to pronunciation has generally been "prescriptive"—that is, reflecting the most widely accepted standard for a given word or sound, though not necessarily all possible acceptable variations of it. The exception to this occurs in regional speech entries (*Coastal Southern dialect, Northern dialect,* etc.) and in entries dealing with linguistic matters (as *pidgin and creole languages*). There the approach is "descriptive"—that is, reflecting the actual or usual pronunciation without regard to the accepted standard. Wherever it has been necessary to combine individual sym-

Symbol	Example
Vowels	
/ä/	father, card
/ă/	hat, rabbit
/ā/	gate, gain
/â/	care, fair, wear
/à/	*French* chat, *General Southern* time; *between* /ä/ *and* /ă/
/ĕ/	bed, head
/ē/	free, cede
/ê/	burn, heard, girl, word
/ə/	away, enemy, circus, wisdom, famous
/ë/	*French* feu, *German* Goethe; *like saying* /ā/ *with lips pursed*
/ĭ/	hit, middle
/ī/	bite, ice
/î/	fear, here, spirit
/ŏ/	pot, cotton
/ō/	coat, open, snow
/ô/	caught, law, dog, *French* coq, *German* doch
/ò/	*British* glass, can't, *New York City and Coastal Southern* car, calm, father; *close to* /ô/ *and* /ä/
/o͝o/	hood, could
/o͞o/	root, suit, blue
/ŭ/	mother, cut, tough
/ü/	*French* duc, *German* über, *Scottish* bluid; *like saying* /ē/ *with lips pursed*
/ou/	plow, loud
/oi/	coin, toy

bols in order to describe a sound (as in General Southern *plow* /**plăo͞o**/), each symbol retains its own separate pronunciation as given in the table. Three final considerations: (1) Although many words in English have both primary and secondary stresses, we give only the primary, in boldface type, as: *rationale* /răsh-ə-**năl**/. Syllables are separated by hyphens. (2) The "glottal stop"—a speech sound made by quickly closing the glottis and then releasing it with a short burst of air—is rendered with an apostrophe followed by a hyphen, as: *nothing* /**nŭ**'-n/. This sound can be heard in certain dialects of English and in such languages as Hawaiian. (3) In a few words the consonants *l* and *n* are treated as one syllable, without a preceding vowel; in these words the apostrophe is used to separate the syllable, as: *metal* /**mĕt**'l/; *sudden* /**sŭd**'n/.

Symbol	Example
Consonants	
/b/	**b**ell, ru**bb**er
/ch/	**ch**op, ri**ch**, hi**tch**
/d/	**d**ay, ma**dd**er
/f/	**f**ox, **ph**antom, rou**gh**
/g/	**g**row, be**gg**ar
/h/	**h**ope
/j/	**j**ump, **g**em
/k/	**k**ite, **c**rew
/KH/	*Scottish* lo**ch**, *Yiddish* **ch**utzpah; *like saying* /k/ *with a forceful breath*
/l/	**l**amp, ba**ll**ot
/m/	hu**m**, su**mm**er
/n/	**n**ote, wi**nn**er
/N/	*French* bo**n**; *a nasal sound*
/ng/	wi**ng**, si**ng**ing
/p/	**p**in, fli**pp**er
/r/	**r**ide, bo**rr**ow
/s/	**s**afe, to**ss**, **c**ircle
/sh/	**sh**ine, **s**ure, offi**c**ial
/t/	**t**op, cha**tt**er
/th/	**th**in, tru**th**
/*th*/	**th**is, bro**th**er
/v/	**v**ine
/w/	**w**ax
/y/	**y**am, on**i**on
/z/	**z**eal, ro**s**e, **x**ylophone
/zh/	mea**s**ure, bei**g**e

A

a, an. The original form of the indefinite article in Old English was *an* = 'one.' Later, *an* was reduced to *a* before most words starting with a consonant. The choice between *a* and *an* is made by pronunciation, not spelling. Words beginning with a consonant sound take *a;* words beginning with a vowel sound take *an: a unit; a $1 bill; an honor.*

Special Cases. *An* is sometimes used before words with an unstressed first syllable beginning with the sound /h/ or /y/: *an historic moment; an unique achievement.* This is often thought to be peculiarly British, but it also occurs in the United States. To most Americans it now seems archaic or affected, while to others it seems elegant.

◊ ***Recommendation.*** If in doubt, use *a* before all consonant sounds and *an* before all vowel sounds.

a-. The English prefix *a-* is historically a reduced form of the preposition *on.*

(1) It occurs in adverbs and adjectives such as *abed* = 'in bed,' *afoot* = 'on foot,' and *ashore* = 'on shore.' These are all old words; it is no longer possible to use the prefix to form new words of this type.

(2) It also occurs with verbs, forming a special kind of present tense meaning 'in the state or process of (doing or being something)':

> Gather ye rosebuds while ye may,
> Old Time is still a-flying. . . .
>
> —Robert Herrick,
> *To the Virgins to Make Much of Time*

This use of the prefix was once part of the standard language, but is so no longer. It is still in active use among country people in England and Scotland, but is dying out there, too. It is interesting that this old prefix is at present in much wider use in the United States than it is in Britain. It is still used in most regions of the country from New England to the South, but is probably commonest in the Southern and South Midlands speech areas.

> "I haven't been a-huntin' in thirty years."
>
> —from Crawford Feagin,
> *Variation and Change in Alabama English*

It is reported from several regions that this prefix is now used chiefly by older and less educated people. This can be taken as evidence that the usage is in the process of dying out in America as well as in Britain. Even so, it will no doubt remain familiar, since it is embedded in so much literature, both British and American. It is also very much alive in popular music, as in Bob Dylan's *The Times They Are A-changin'.*

abbreviations. ***General Use.*** In private and informal writings people abbreviate words and names in any way they find useful and understandable. In print and formal writing there are rules and conventions for the thousands of possible abbreviated forms, to avoid confusion and prevent overuse. The first rule is, When in doubt, spell it out. This applies to all general writing such as fiction, history, news, and formal letters. Abbreviations are much more heavily used in technical and business writing. But certain terms are always or usually abbreviated in ordinary prose as well.

Periods, Spacing, Capitalization. The present trend is toward simplicity. Periods have been eliminated in many cases, and spaces within groups of initials are often closed up. Capitalization generally follows the same style as the fully written words. The forms given below are recommended forms, not necessarily the only acceptable ones.

Personal Names. When initials are used for given names, each is followed by a period and a space: *John F. Kennedy; O. J. Simpson.* Prefixed names retain their prefixes: *Nicholas de B. Katzenbach.*

Titles, Ranks, Academic Degrees. These titles are almost always abbreviated: *Mr.; Mrs.; Ms.; Dr.; Esq.* The titles *Reverend* and

Honorable are spelled out if used with *the* but are otherwise abbreviated: *the Reverend Martin Luther King, Jr., Rev. Martin Luther King, Jr.; the Honorable John C. Culver, Hon. John C. Culver.*

Official and service titles are generally spelled out in full if the surname is used alone and abbreviated if the full name is used: *Governor Rockefeller, Gov. Nelson A. Rockefeller; Commodore Perry, Cmdre. Matthew C. Perry.*

Academic degrees are abbreviated with periods and without spaces:

B.A. = Bachelor of Arts
B.S. = Bachelor of Science
D.D. = Doctor of Divinity

Groups. Many terms are commonly abbreviated in names of business firms:

Assoc. = Associates
Bros. = Brothers
Co. = Company
Corp. = Corporation
Inc. = Incorporated
& Co. = and Company

Names of numerous governmental and international agencies, nonprofit organizations, political groups, private and public companies, and academic institutions are now frequently given as initials without periods or spaces:

CIA = Central Intelligence Agency
HUD = (Department of) Housing and Urban Development
IBM = International Business Machines
MIT = Massachusetts Institute of Technology

Countries. In general the names of countries should not be abbreviated in formal writing. An exception is the Union of Soviet Socialist Republics, usually abbreviated to U.S.S.R. Some other national names are sometimes abbreviated, usually with periods:

U.K. = United Kingdom (Britain)
D.D.R. = German Democratic Republic, East Germany (German *Deutsche Demokratische Republik*)

See also UNITED KINGDOM; UNITED STATES.

Geographical Elements. If the name of an island, mountain, or river contains the word *island, isle, mount, mountain,* or *river,* it should be spelled out in formal writing: *Baffin Island; the Isle of Wight; Mount Rushmore; the Ogeechee River.* On maps and in gazetteers and other reference works these elements are abbreviated to *Is., Mt.,* and *R.* In the names of cities and other places, terms such as *Fort, Port,* and *Mount* should always be spelled out: *Fort Lauderdale; Mount Vernon.* In place names the word *saint* may be either spelled out or abbreviated *St.: Saint Louis, St. Louis.*

Points of the Compass. When used as regular nouns and adjectives in formal writing, *north, northern, northwest, northwesterly,* etc., should always be spelled out: *Rain closed in from the north. She was born in northern Illinois. The room had a northwesterly exposure.* In writing that is heavily concerned with topography, the points of the compass may be abbreviated: *a tall tree bearing SSW; a property line that runs NE for 100 feet.*

Names of regions containing compass points should preferably be spelled out, but may informally be abbreviated with periods: *West Africa, W. Africa.* But names of cities should always be spelled out: *North Little Rock; West Palm Beach.*

Time. The abbreviations for *ante meridiem* (before noon) and *post meridiem* (after noon) are given in small capitals with or without periods or in lower-case letters with periods: A.M., AM, P.M., PM; a.m., p.m.

The names of the weekdays and the months are spelled out in ordinary writing. In dates, lists, etc., they may be abbreviated with periods (*May, June,* and *July* are not usually abbreviated):

Sun. Mon. Tues. Wed. Thurs. Fri. Sat.
Jan. Feb. Mar. Apr. Aug. Sept. Oct. Nov. Dec.

In highly condensed listings or tables all may be abbreviated without periods:

Su M Tu W Th F Sa
Ja F Mr Ap My Je Jl Ag S O N D

Time zones are written in capitals without space or periods:

EST = Eastern Standard Time
MDT = Mountain Daylight Time (that is, Daylight Saving Time in the Mountain zone of the United States)
GMT = Greenwich Mean Time

Units of Measurement. The traditional units such as inches, acres, ounces, gallons, and pounds should be spelled out in nontechnical writing. Metric units such as centimeters, hectares, liters, and grams may be given in full but are now more often abbreviated in both technical and nontechnical writing.

Latin Notations.

aet. = *aetatis*, 'at the age of'

cf. = *confer*, 'compare'

e.g. = *exempli gratia*, 'for example'

et al. = *et alii, et aliae*, 'and the others (people)'

etc. = *et cetera*, 'and the rest (things), and so forth'

et seq. = *et sequentes, et sequentia*, 'and the following (people or things)'

fl. = *floruit*, 'flourished'

ibid. = *ibidem*, 'in the same place'

id. = *idem*, 'the same'

i.e. = *id est*, 'that is'

inf. = *infra*, 'below'

loc. cit. = *loco citato*, 'in the place or context cited'

loq. = *loquitur*, 'speaks'

MS, MS. = *manuscriptum*, 'manuscript'

n.b. = *nota bene*, 'note well'

op. cit. = *opere citato*, 'in the work or book cited'

Q.E.D. = *quod erat demonstrandum*, 'which was to be demonstrated'

q.v. = *quod vide*, 'which see'

sc. = *scilicet*, 'namely'

sup. = *supra*, 'above'

s.v. = *sub verbo*, 'under the word'

v. = *vide*, 'see'

viz. = *videlicet*, 'namely'

See also C., CA.

abhor. This powerful word is from Latin *abhorrēre* = 'to shrink away from something, shuddering with revulsion.' The English meaning is 'to regard with loathing, disapprove of extremely':

> I knew he [a Masai chief] abhorred the Kikuyu and their hospital as deeply as he did the white man.
> —Shirley MacLaine, *Don't Fall Off the Mountain*

> . . . on the air, there are a lot of things he [TV host Phil Donahue] can no longer let pass. He especially abhors affronts to women and feminism.
> —William Brashler, *Reader's Digest*

The adjective *abhorrent* means 'detestable, extremely unpleasant':

> The prospect of ordering more people out of their homes was abhorrent to him.
> —John G. Fuller, *Reader's Digest*

abide. The verb *abide* has two past forms: *abode*, which is now old-fashioned, and *abided*, the usual choice today. Its original meanings, 'to wait for, remain, reside (in a place),' are archaic. The commonest current meaning is 'to put up with, tolerate,' usually but not always used negatively:

> "I won't abide anything in my campaign that smacks of racism, segregation, or apartheid," King declared.
> —*Boston Herald American*

> Public schools abide mediocre students [and] put 18-year-olds who can't decide what to wear in the morning into independent-study groups. . . .
> —Suzanne Britt Jordan, *Reader's Digest*

Abide by means 'to conform to, acquiesce in, fulfill':

> We argued that—to guarantee that both nations abided by SALT I—each should open its territory to inspection teams from the other.
> —Melvin R. Laird, *Reader's Digest*

The original sense of the verb is preserved in the adjective *abiding* = 'lasting':

> The Yugoslavs . . . and the Russians share a range of abiding affinities—cultural, linguistic, and religious.
> —David A. Andelman, *Atlantic Monthly*

ability, capacity. Used of human qualities, these two words overlap but have different implications. *Ability* is the more general; it can mean any kind of power to perform. More particularly, a *person of ability* is typically one who has both natural aptitude or talent and the experience to use it skillfully for practical achievement. *Capacity* literally means 'the quality of being able to contain or receive.' Referring to human attributes, it lies more in the area of character and natural aptitude than in that of experience and acquired skill. A *person of capacity* is one who is able to respond effectively to new or varied demands and situations.

abode. See ABIDE.

aborigines, aboriginal. ***Origin.*** The *Aborīginēs* /ăb-ə-rĭj-ə-nēz/ were an ancient people who lived near Rome before the Romans. The name appears to be from the Latin phrase *ab orīgine* = 'from the beginning'; but since it was always used as a proper noun, it is probably a version of the tribe's real name, altered by the Romans to mean 'the people here since the beginning.'

Uses. The plural noun *aborigines* is now used to refer to primitive peoples in various parts of the world. The adjective *aboriginal* means 'being the earliest known (inhabitants) in an area.' In Southeast Asia, for example, the non-Malay, non-Indo-Chinese peoples living in mountainous and remote sections are so called:

> [Malaysia] . . . where naked Stone Age aborigines still hunt with blowpipes and worship rocks.
> —Christopher Lucas, *Reader's Digest*

In North America both terms are occasionally applied to Indians, Innuit (Eskimos), or other pre-Columbian peoples:

> Where else but from Nantucket did those aboriginal whalemen, the Red-men, first sally out in canoes to give chase to the Leviathan?
> —Herman Melville, *Moby-Dick*

> Black American alder . . . was widely used by the aborigines of North America for its astringent properties.
> —M. Grieve, *A Modern Herbal*

Australian Use. Much the commonest use of the word *aborigines* is in Australia, where the pre-European peoples are now always, and officially, called the *Aborigines.* Although the singular form *Aborigine* exists, *Aboriginal* or *Aboriginal person* is preferred for an individual.

> Probably the best-known is Evonne Goolagong Cawley, the tennis player, who is not a full aborigine.
> —Fox Butterfield, *New York Times*

Here "a full Aboriginal" would have been the better phrase. The shortened form *Abo* /ăb-ō/ is considered derogatory.

Australian Aboriginal Words. The Australian Aborigines, who were the sole inhabitants of the island-continent for as much as 40,000 years, spoke about 230 different languages. Some of the words that have been borrowed from them into English are:

boomerang = 'flat, curved throwing weapon, some types of which return to the thrower'

budgerigar /bŭj-ə-rĭ-gär/ = 'small, brightly colored parakeet'

corroboree /kə-rŏb-ə-rē/ = 'ceremonial and religious gathering with music and dance'

dingo = 'Australian wild dog'

kangaroo = 'marsupial animal with long hind legs for leaping'

koala = 'bearlike, tree-living marsupial animal'

wallaby = 'marsupial animal related to the kangaroo but smaller'

wombat = 'bearlike, burrowing marsupial animal'

See also AUSTRALIAN ENGLISH.

about. There are two fairly recent American idioms using the word *about*. They were at first regarded as informal, suitable only for spoken use, but are now acceptable in formal writing also.

(1) *about* = 'involved with, interested in, devoted to':

> In the end Jackson State is about death, and death is not something on which we like to focus.
> —Joseph Rhodes, Jr., *New York Times*

> Historically, the Populist Party was about the redistribution of economic power.
> —Arthur M. Schlesinger, Jr., *New York Times*

(2) *not about to* = 'emphatically unwilling to (do something)':

> Had I done so, I would have surrendered the civilian control of your government to the military, and I was not about to do that.
> —Harry Truman (quoted), *Reader's Digest*

> The importer is not about to absorb the tariff himself, so instead passes it along to the buyer. . . .
> —Steve Saft, *National Fisherman*

> No members of Russia's rubber-stamp parliament are about to question KGB operations.
> —Marvin Stone, *U.S. News & World Report*

above. Although basically an adverb or a preposition, *above* has long been used in legal and business writings as an adjective meaning 'previously mentioned in this document,' and especially 'appearing higher up on this page': *considering the above allegations. We refer to the above diagram.* The noun phrase *the above* is also used, as in multiple-choice tests: . . . (*d*) *none of the above.* Some critics feel that it's grammatically unacceptable to make an adverb into an adjective or noun like this. They would correct the examples to: *considering the allegations (cited) above;* (*d*) *none of the choices (offered) above. We refer to the diagram (shown) above.*

Furthermore, for ordinary writing, especially of a literary kind, the use of *above* in any of these ways, regardless of part of speech, may sometimes seem overformal or stiff. It can be avoided by rewriting the sentence. For example, *After the above experiences, I felt sure* . . . could become *After these experiences.* . . .

> The problem with writing your autobiography is that you feel a reluctance to include puffs like the above.
> —Veronica Lake, *Veronica*

This, though harmless, could just as well be changed to "puffs of this kind" or "puffs like this one."

◇ ***Recommendation.*** These are questions of style, not correctness. First, there is nothing grammatically wrong with using *above* as an adjective or as a noun, even if conservatives may prefer to use it only as an adverb or preposition. Second, if you like to use *above* to mean 'just mentioned,' or *the above* to mean 'what I've just mentioned,' you are fully entitled to do so.

absolute phrases. Generally, all phrases in a sentence must be bonded into the grammatical structure of the sentence. There is a notable exception in English—the absolute participial phrase. This is a floating phrase that contains a subject and a participle functioning as a verb, and is not locked onto any element in the rest of the sentence:

> . . . and Elizabeth at that instant moving towards them, he was struck with the notion of doing a very gallant thing.
> —Jane Austen, *Pride and Prejudice*

Here the phrase "Elizabeth . . . moving towards them" is independent of everything else. It has the same force as a clause with a conjunction and a finite verb, as "while Elizabeth was moving towards them." Further examples:

> His letter ignored, Matos went on a hunger strike.
> —David Reed, *Reader's Digest*

The absolute phrase here contains a past participle ("ignored") and also functions like a full clause. Such phrases can occur anywhere in a sentence:

> Before long, the chipmunk ran up, his cheeks bulging.
> —Randall Jarrell, *The Bat-poet*

When the subject of an absolute phrase is a pronoun, it is put in the subjective, or nominative, case: *He having gone on ahead, the rest of us followed one by one.* But absolute phrases with pronouns as subjects, though correct, are now felt to be awkward or old-fashioned. The preceding phrase would usually be recast as either a dependent clause, *Since he had gone on ahead,* or an independent clause, *He went on ahead, and the rest of us followed.* While absolute phrases of the kind described here are standard and definitely correct, dangling phrases, which contain no subject of their own and do not fit into the sentence structure, are not. See DANGLING PHRASES.

abysmal. The word *abysm* is an old variant of *abyss* = 'bottomless pit, endless void' (see ABYSS, ABYSSAL). It is now archaic or obsolete, but its adjective, *abysmal,* is used to mean 'as low as possible, bottomlessly low, deplorably bad':

> Snow was these people's ally. For it was their protection and their shelter from abysmal cold.
> —Farley Mowat, *Reader's Digest*

> . . . the abysmal ignorance of many alleged archaeologists who can only be described, if uncharitably, as fantasy buffs.
> —Glyn Daniel, *Scientific American*

abyss, abyssal. It was formerly believed that beneath the earth was a bottomless pit or an infinite empty space called the *abyss;* the word is from Greek *abyssos* = 'bottomless' (*a-* = 'lacking' + *byssos* = 'bottom'). This pit was often thought to be the same as hell. The word *abyss* is now used to mean 'any vast or endless space' or 'the deepest levels of the ocean.' Figuratively, it is used of a condition of utter destruction or a scene of misery and hopelessness:

> But if we fail, then the whole world, including the United States, including all that we have known and cared for, will sink into the abyss of a new Dark Age. . . .
> —Winston Churchill, speech (1941)

The adjective *abyssal* means only 'of or relating to the deepest levels of the ocean':

> We were dragging at the edge of the continental shelf where the bottom begins its sharp plunge to the abyssal plains.
> —Jack Rudloe, *Reader's Digest*

academe, academia, academy. ***Origin.*** Plato's school at Athens, the *Akadēmeia,* was named for the garden in which it met. The garden itself got this name because it was sacred to a hero called *Akadēmos.* The school, which was founded in about 385 B.C. and lasted until the 6th century A.D., is sometimes regarded as the first university. The Greek word *Akadēmeia* becomes in Latin *Acadēmia* and in English *academia* /ăk-ə-**dē**-mē-ə/ or *academy.* The hero-name *Akadēmos* becomes in English *Academe* /**ăk**-ə-dēm/, used by John Milton in a poetic reference to Plato's school: "See there/The olive grove of Academe."

Uses. *Academe* was used, echoing Milton's line, by Mary McCarthy in the ironical title of her novel about university politics, *The Groves of Academe* (1952). Since that time *academe* (usually written with a small *a*) has become a widely used journalist's term for 'the world of universities':

> . . . a letter signed by seven middle-aged male professors. They proposed that academe henceforward set as its "goal" the hiring of specified proportions of women.
> —Andrew Hacker, *New York Times*

> . . . branding it "ignorant rubbish." . . . Even by the kick-'em-and-gouge-'em standards of academe, this was rough stuff.
> —William A. Davis, *Boston Globe*

As the quotations suggest, this use is generally somewhat scornful. Scholars have objected to it on the grounds that it is based on a misunderstanding of Milton's line and Mary McCarthy's echo of it, both referring to the hero from whom Plato's school derived its name and not to the school itself.

The proper term for 'the world of universities' is *academia* (sometimes capital *A*):

> 'Twasn't too long after this vast federal largesse was set in motion that academia's euphoria began evaporating.
> —Malcolm S. Forbes, *Forbes*

> When business and academia discuss this loss of our cutting edge, they decry causes elsewhere—government, taxes, unions.
> —Fred M. Hechinger, *Reader's Digest*

Academy has several distinct senses: (1) 'Plato's school itself, and Platonic philosophy generally'; (2) 'an official society of artists, scientists, etc., such as the American Academy of Arts and Sciences' (membership in such an academy being a high professional honor); (3) 'a specialized school or college, such as the United States Naval Academy at Annapolis' (which trains officers for the navy); (4) 'a private secondary school'; (5) sometimes, with *the*, 'the world of universities':

> It looks like the office of a junior professor. And indeed, Bobby's rumpled, diffident manner reminds one of the academy.
> —Doug Ireland, *New York*

◇ ***Recommendation.*** *Academe* is best used with clear reference to *Akadēmos*, who can be regarded as a kind of patron saint of universities. As a term for 'the academic world,' *academia* is preferable. All of the uses of *academy* given above are standard.

academic, academician. The adjective *academic* means (1) 'of or relating to universities and higher learning':

> . . . a raging academic storm. The issue: can apes really master the essence of human language—the creation of sentences?
> —*Time*

(2) 'of only theoretical interest, not practical or likely to happen':

> Archibald Cox . . . stated that he was studying whether or not he could indict me before an impeachment had taken place. Having said this, he hastened to add that, of course, such a study was only academic.
> —Richard Nixon, *R.N.*

The noun *academic* means 'university teacher or scholar':

> . . . it's the government agencies, private industry, academics and others who use the census statistics to do in-depth analyses.
> —*Smithsonian*

The noun *academician* primarily means 'member of an official academy or honorific society of scholars, artists, or scientists':

> Nobody, of course, expects [the Russian Academy of Sciences] to take a bold stand in support of Mr. Sakharov. But surely the Academicians can muster the moral courage to avoid expelling him.
> —*New York Times*

But this word is now increasingly used to mean 'university scholar or teacher':

> . . . artists and academicians mingled with politicians and high society in the inner circle of the Kennedys.
> —*U.S. News & World Report*

> To an academician, Vietnam may have been no more than a "symptom." . . .
> —Philip Geyelin, *The Atlantic*

◇ ***Recommendation.*** All the uses of *academic* given above are standard and correct. *Academician* is best used in its primary meaning, 'member of an official academy.' Its use to mean 'university scholar or teacher' is undesirable. For this sense *academic* is the better choice.

Acadian. See CAJUN; CANADIAN FRENCH.

accent. (1) Bostonians do not ordinarily notice each other's Boston accents, and Southerners do not talk about the Southern accent.

The British are convinced that they alone have no accent. *Accent* is any pronunciation of a language that is noticeably different from the listener's own pronunciation. Such pronunciation differences between speakers of separate nations, regions, and social classes are among the features that define dialects. See DIALECT.
(2) In the pronunciation of an individual word, accent is emphasis on a syllable. This emphasis may be achieved either by *stress* (that is, greater intensity) or by *pitch* (that is, relative level). In English, stress accent is basic. Nearly every word has a primary stress, and many also have one or more secondary stresses. The pronunciations in this book show only the primary stress, given in boldface type; for example: the noun *accent* is pronounced /**ăk**-sĕnt/, the verb /**ăk**-sĕnt/ or /ăk-**sĕnt**/. In languages such as Chinese, pitch accent is basic; every syllable is pronounced at one of several pitch levels, like musical tones, and these differences in pitch govern the meanings of the words.
(3) *Accent* also means a mark, such as (´) or (`), added to an individual printed or written letter to give it a particular pronunciation. See DIACRITICS.

accept, except. These two verbs, which in many people's speech are pronounced the same, are occasionally confused. To *accept* is to receive or agree to: *We accept your kind invitation.* To *except* is to make an exception of, exclude: *No one will be excepted from taking the test.*

acclimate, acclimatize. Both mean 'to accustom (someone or something), or to become accustomed, to new conditions': *They tried to acclimate the boys to their new surroundings. Tommy quickly became acclimatized to the routine.* They are equally correct; the choice between the two is a matter of individual preference. *Acclimatize* is pronounced /ə-**klī**-mə-tīz/. *Acclimate* may be pronounced either /**ăk**-lə-māt/ or /ə-**klī**-mət/.

accomplice. See COHORT.

accuse. While the verb *charge* is properly followed by *with* (*They charged him with fraud*), the verb *accuse* should be followed by *of.* This applies whether the word is used in the formal legal sense or in a nontechnical situation.

> No witness could announce his distress more vividly than to accuse his tormentor with being ineffectual.
> —Louis Nizer, *My Life in Court*

◇ ***Recommendation.*** *Accuse . . . with* is a definite breach of idiom. It's easy to avoid and should be avoided.

accused, alleged. The adjective *accused* is properly applied to a person against whom a formal legal charge (neither proved nor disproved at that point) is made. It should not identify the person as if he or she had been convicted. A man who is on trial for murder is often, in newspapers for example, referred to as *the accused murderer;* the correct formula is *the accused man* or *the man accused of the murder.*

The adjective *alleged,* on the other hand, has less force than *accused. Alleged* means 'said to be (true, or of a certain character), but not necessarily so.' *Alleged* casts explicit doubt on whether the allegation is true. It is thus proper to refer to a man accused of murder as *the alleged murderer.* Referring to things, the word has the same implication of doubt; *the alleged murder* leaves open the question of whether a murder has occurred at all.

> Lee Harvey Oswald, accused assassin of President John F. Kennedy . . .
> —*Boston Globe*

◇ ***Recommendation.*** Although *accused assassin* is widely used, we regard it as an error. *Alleged assassin* is correct.

acerb, acerbic. These are two forms of one adjective, from Latin *acerbus* = 'sharp, harsh, sour.' The pronunciation is /ə-**sêrb**/, /ə-**sêr**-bĭk/. The meaning is 'bitingly severe, bitterly critical,' and there is no difference between *acerb* and *acerbic:*

> . . . the acerb "Point Counterpoint" debate between conservative James J. Kilpatrick and liberal Shana Alexander.
> —Irwin Ross, *Reader's Digest*

> H. L. Mencken, perhaps the most acerbic of our literary critics, once wrote, "As for Conrad's *Lord Jim*, I would not swap it for all the children born in Trenton, N.J., since the Spanish War." —A. L. McLeod, *New Jersey Monthly*

The noun *acerbity* can mean 'biting severity' or 'sharpness and harshness.' It's used with a nice precision in the following:

> . . . everything in the desert either stings, stabs, stinks or sticks. You will find the flora here as venomous, hooked, barbed, thorny, prickly, needled, saw-toothed, hairy, stickered, mean, bitter, sharp, wiry and fierce as the animals. Something about the desert inclines all living things to harshness and acerbity.
> —Edward Abbey, *Reader's Digest*

Achilles' heel. An old metaphor, but still a popular one, for a single vulnerable point in an otherwise strong position. It refers to the Homeric hero Achilles; his mother, the nymph Thetis, was said to have made him invulnerable by dipping him in the river Styx. But in doing so she held him by one heel, which was not immersed and therefore remained vulnerable. Achilles was later mortally wounded in this heel, by Paris in some versions of the story and by Apollo in others. The apostrophe in the name is sometimes dropped but is better kept:

> Agricultural enterprise is the Achilles heel of the Soviet system.
> —George F. Kennan, *American Diplomacy 1900–1950*

> But the Basque region remains the political Achilles' heel for the center-right Government of Prime Minister Adolfo Suarez.
> —Jonathan Kandell, *New York Times*

acolyte. In the Roman Catholic and Episcopal churches *acolytes* are assistants who perform minor parts of the ritual or services. The word is also used figuratively of any attendant at a ritual or mystery:

> The world flocks in to witness the mystery of London enacted once a year in the ceremonial thoroughfare called the Mall and on Horse Guards Parade. The sidewalks are thick with foreigners; the guardsmen stand like acolytes at the shrine. —Jan Morris, *Reader's Digest*

> The faith of sophisticates goes to large electronic machines with computer printouts or cathode-ray tube terminals, attended by white-coated acolytes. —Adam Smith, *Esquire*

acquiesce /ăk-wē-**ĕs**/. The literal meaning (now obsolete) is 'to rest contented (in a place or state).' The current meaning is 'to tacitly accept something, go along with something,' and the correct preposition is *in*. The same applies to the noun *acquiescence*.

> For various reasons I had to acquiesce in the situation and accept the fact that no major reorganization reform or voluntary fiscal restraint would come from Congress during my first term.
> —Richard Nixon, *R.N.*

> It is the government's seeming acquiescence in these land seizures, in part, that has produced the cries that Mexico is going communist.
> —Carl T. Rowan and David M. Mazie, *Reader's Digest*

acronyms. A true acronym is a word formed from the initial letters of a phrase. This method of coining new words is a real linguistic innovation of the 20th century and seems to have originated spontaneously in the military jargon of the First World War. One of the earliest lasting examples is *Anzac* = 'Australian or New Zealand soldier,' which formed itself from Australian and New Zealand Army Corps, title of the force that landed on Gallipoli in April, 1915. Anzac is to this day a word of serious patriotic power in Australia and New Zealand. The Second World War produced new acronyms that were consciously formed by officials as code words, among them *radar,* from *ra*dio *d*etecting *a*nd *r*anging, and *Pluto,* from *p*ipe *l*ine *u*nder *t*he *o*cean, a device used in the invasion of Normandy.

The acronym remains a favorite with the military, but it is now also used with abandon by academics, bureaucrats, corporations, children, and all other classes of word coiners, in all countries that use any form of alphabet. Structurally, there are three kinds of acronyms: pure acronyms, which are formed from initial letters only; hybrid acronyms like *radar,* which use more than just the initials; and syllabic acronyms, like *Delmarva,* from *Del*aware, *Mar*yland, and *V*irgini*a*.

It must also be pointed out that there is an ethical distinction among acronyms. Honest acronyms emerge, either by pure chance or with a little discreet assistance, from genuinely preexisting phrases. Counterfeit acronyms, or retroacronyms, are formed by simply choosing some snappy or appropriate term and devising a phrase to which it can (falsely) be attributed. We recognize a small number of honorable exceptions such as *WAVES,* which we like to pretend really did emerge from *W*omen *A*ppointed for *V*oluntary *E*mergency *S*ervice. But the backward or cheating approach has now become dangerously common and threatens the integrity of true acronym formation. We can only deplore such obvious pseudocoinages as *ORACLE,* said to represent *O*ptimum *R*ecord *A*utomation for *C*ourts and *L*aw *E*nforcement, a system used in Los Angeles. And we point to the sad fact that transparent fakes like *PACE* are claimed by several dozen rival organizations or systems, such as *P*erformance *a*nd *C*ost *E*valuation; *P*recision *A*nalog *C*omputing *E*quipment; and *P*rogram to *A*dvance *C*reativity in *E*ducation.

Selection of Noteworthy Acronyms. The following list typifies the increasing variety found among acronyms. Of interest are terms whose meanings cannot be determined from the words of origin (*Bren* gun, *MIG*) and words from languages other than English (*flak, Fiat*). Some acronyms are written in capital letters (*CORE, NATO*); others are written as lower-case words (*bev, quasar*); still others may go either way (*MIRV/Mirv, WASP/Wasp*).

Amex = *Am*erican Stock *Ex*change

ARVN /**är**-vĭn/ = 'the South Vietnamese army' (U.S. military term in the Vietnam War): from *A*rmy of the *R*epublic of *V*iet *N*am

asdic, ASDIC = 'British sonar in World War II': from *A*nti-*S*ubmarine *D*etection *I*nvestigation *C*ommittee (which sponsored it)

awol /**ā**-wôl, A.W.O.L. (individual letters pronounced)/ = *a*bsent *w*ith*o*ut *l*eave

Basic English = 'simplified form of English intended for international use': from *B*ritish, *A*merican, *S*cientific, *I*nternational *C*ommercial English

bev = 'unit of energy, one billion electron-volts': from *b*illion *e*lectron-*v*olts

Bren gun = 'British light machine gun': from the two places where it was first manufactured, *Br*no, Czechoslovakia, and *En*field, England

CINCPAC /**sĭngk**-păk/ = *C*ommander *in* *C*hief, *Pac*ific

CINCUSAFE /**sĭngk**-yo͞o-sāf/ = *C*ommander *in* *C*hief, *U*nited *S*tates *A*ir *F*orces, *E*urope

Clarnico /**klär**-nĭ-kō/ = *Clar*k, *Ni*chols, and *Co*ombes (firm of confectioners)

Cobol, COBOL /**kō**-bŏl, -bôl/ = *co*mmon *b*usiness-*o*riented *l*anguage (type of computer language)

CORE /kôr/ = *C*ongress *o*f *R*acial *E*quality

DARE = *D*ictionary of *A*merican *R*egional *E*nglish

Elas = 'National People's Army of Liberation' (forming the Greek word for Greece): from Greek *E*thnikos *L*aikos *A*pelefterikos *S*tratos

ERIC = *E*ducational *R*esources *I*nformation *C*enter (a service of the U.S. Office of Education)

Fiat /**fē**-ət, **fē**-ät/ = 'type of Italian-made automobile': from *F*abrica *I*taliana *A*utomobili, *T*orino (name of the manufacturer, located in Turin)

flak = 'bursting antiaircraft fire': from German *Fl*ieger*a*bwehr*k*anone = 'antiaircraft gun'

Gestapo /gə-**stä**-pō/ = 'German secret police, 1933–45': from German *Ge*heime *Sta*ats*po*lizei = 'secret state police'

GIGO /**gĭg**-ō/ = garbage *in*, garbage *out* (a slogan of computer programmers)

JAMA = *J*ournal of the *A*merican *M*edical *A*ssociation

Maphilindo /**măf**-ĭ-**lĭn**-dō/ = 'name of a proposed union of South Pacific countries': from *Ma*laysia, the *Phil*ippines, and *Indo*nesia

MIG = 'Soviet fighter aircraft': Russian, from the names of its designers, Artem *Mi*koyan and Mikhail *G*urevich

MIRV, Mirv /**mêrv**/ = 'American missile with separately controlled warheads': from *m*ultiple *i*ndependently targeted *r*eentry *v*ehicle

MOMA, Moma /**mō**-mə, **mä**-mə/ = *M*useum *o*f *M*odern *A*rt (New York City)

NATO /**nā**-tō/ = *N*orth *A*tlantic *T*reaty *O*rganization

NOW = *N*ational *O*rganization for *W*omen

OGPU /**ŏg**-p**o͞o**/ = 'former name of the Soviet foreign intelligence agency': Russian, from Obiedinennoye Gosudarstvennoye Politicheskoye Upravlenie = 'combined state political administration'

OPEC /**ō**-pĕk/ = *O*rganization of *P*etroleum-*E*xporting *C*ountries

Pakistan /**păk**-ĭ-stăn/ = 'name of a Muslim country northwest of India': Urdu *Pakistan* = 'holy country,' also representing *P*unjab, *A*fghan provinces, *K*ashm*i*r, *S*ind, and Baluchi*stan*

PERT = *P*rogram *E*valuation and *R*eview *T*echnique (a system of management analysis)

Qantas /**kwän**-təs/ = *Q*ueensland *an*d Northern *T*erritories *A*erial *S*ervices (an Australian airline)

quasar /**kwā**-zär, -sär/ = 'distant object emitting radio waves': from *quas*i-stell*ar* radio source

UNESCO, Unesco /yo͞o-**nĕs**-kō/ = *U*nited *N*ations *E*ducational, *S*cientific, and *C*ultural *O*rganization

WASP, Wasp = *w*hite *A*nglo-*S*axon *P*rotestant

◇ ***Recommendation.*** Honest acronyms are the best acronyms.

acute accent. See DIACRITICS.

A.D., B.C. The abbreviation A.D. stands for Latin *Anno Domini* = 'in the year of the Lord,' meaning 'in the (specified) year after the birth of Jesus Christ.' Traditionally and logically, A.D. is put before the date and can only be used with individual years, not with centuries or periods. The letters B.C. stand for 'Before Christ.' They are logically put after the date and can be used with centuries or other periods as well as with years. In formal writing these differing usages are still observed: *Augustus was born in 63 B.C. and died in A.D. 14.*

The plaque left on the moon by the Apollo astronauts reads, "Here men from the planet Earth first set foot Upon the Moon July 1969 AD." An indignant letter to the *Los Angeles Times* called this a "grammatical error," pointing out that it should have read "July, A.D. 1969." But for reasons of convenience and common sense, many writers now dispense with the distinction:

> . . . in the generally disturbed times of the first centuries B.C. and A.D. . . .
> —T. G. E. Powell, *The Celts*

◇ ***Recommendation.*** In highly formal contexts, and where only one or two dates are mentioned, the traditional rule should be followed. In historical and other writings where dates and periods before and after Christ are frequently cited, it is acceptable to put A.D. as well as B.C. after the date and to use both with centuries and periods as well as with years: *in the 3rd century A.D.*

adage. See PROVERB.

adamant. The *adamant* was a stone or metal believed by medieval alchemists to be impenetrably hard (from Greek *adamant-* = 'untamable, unbreakable'). The word is now used chiefly as an adjective referring to persons; the meaning is 'absolutely firm on a particular matter, refusing to compromise, inflexible':

> Dell'Aqua had used all his diplomatic skill but Kiyama had been adamant and had refused to commit himself or change his position.
> —James Clavell, *Shōgun*

> Provinces such as Alberta, which has most of the country's oil and gas, and Newfoundland, which is the poorest province but which has prospects of oil wealth offshore, are adamant about controlling this wealth for their own benefit. —*New York Times*

adapt, adept, adopt. (1) To *adapt* is to reshape something for a new situation or changed purpose:

> A legitimate attempt to adapt TV programming to changing American tastes and lifestyles . . .
> —Arnie Katz, *Video*

Of persons, the verb can be reflexive, hence transitive (*adapt oneself*), but is now most often used intransitively:

> Bobby also deserves a pat on the back for the way he has adapted himself generally [in school].
> —Albert Norris (quoted), Arthur M. Schlesinger, Jr., *Robert Kennedy and His Times*

> I gradually adapted to Harvard Military Academy regimen—bar sporadic transgressions. . . .
> —J. Paul Getty, *As I See It*

The old form of the noun, *adaption,* is now little used. The standard form is *adaptation.* (2) Originally, an *adept* was an alchemist, someone who had attained complete knowledge of the secret science of alchemy. As a noun *adept* now means 'person versed in secret knowledge or following some philosophy'; as an adjective, 'having secret knowledge or following a philosophy':

> Peter, a philosophy minor, was an adept of the Kantian ethic; he had pledged himself never to treat anyone as a means.
> —Mary McCarthy, *Birds of America*

> They knew how to respond to the approach of God because they had known him all along, not because they were particularly adept in occult lore.
> —Thomas Howard, *Christianity Today*

But much more often nowadays the adjective *adept* means simply 'skillful, able to do something well':

> He was notably adept at figures and his quickness at mental arithmetic had turned him, in his youth, into a sort of one-man parlor game.
> —Brendan Gill, *Here at The New Yorker*

> We, who spoke no Russian, were provided with a crew who spoke no English. Everyone became very adept at sign language.
> —Mike Douglas, *My Story*

(3) *Adopt* basically means 'to take for oneself, choose.' The chief specific uses are 'to take (a child) legally into one's family' and 'to take up (an attitude, idea, plan, etc.)':

> As Maude of Merrill Lynch suggests, there's no rush to adopt such a policy.
> —William C. Bryant, *U.S. News & World Report*

> Paul Mellon and Michel Fribourg have adopted aristocratic life-styles in the European manner, maintaining numerous residences and following the expected pursuits of their class. . . .
> —Jacqueline Thompson, *The Very Rich Book*

In the strictest sense, foster parents are the *adoptive* not *adopted* parents of their foster children.

ad baculum. See FALLACY.

ad captandum. See FALLACY.

adduce. This verb means 'to bring forward (facts or arguments) as part of a discussion or legal case':

> This question occurred to Judge Boyle because of a variety of facts adduced at the inquest.
> —John Barron, *Reader's Digest*

> Hamilton first laid down principles of public economy and then adduced arguments to support them.
> —Samuel Eliot Morison, *The Oxford History of the American People*

adept. See ADAPT, ADEPT, ADOPT.

ad hominem. Short for Latin *argumentum ad hominem* = 'argument to the man,' that is, argument by personal attack. See FALLACY; INVECTIVE.

ad invidiam. See FALLACY.

ad nauseam. This adverbial phrase, from Latin, means 'to the point of causing nausea, to a disgusting or wearying extent':

> His nasal mutter was imitated by laymen, his favorite endearments, such as "My dove," "My little chickadee," and "My glowworm" . . . were repeated ad nauseum.
> —Robert Lewis Taylor, *W. C. Fields*

The spelling *ad nauseum,* as in the example quoted, is an error.

adopt. See ADAPT, ADEPT, ADOPT.

ad populum, ad verecundiam. See FALLACY.

adverse. See AVERSE, ADVERSE.

advise, advice. In business and politics the verb *advise* is used to mean 'inform.' This usage is disliked by those who feel that *advise* should only mean 'to give counsel.' But the usage is fully established in its own sphere, where it means not merely 'to inform casually,' but 'to give formal and official notice of something':

> A letter . . . promptly advised us that A-P-A Transport Corp. . . . had purchased 500 tickets to that event. We stand corrected.
> —Michael Aron, *New Jersey Monthly*

> Three months ago, President Carter advised his Cabinet that he expected to resolve the remaining disarmament difference personally with Soviet leader Leonid Brezhnev.
> —Jack Anderson, *Hampshire Gazette*

The noun *advice,* especially in the plural, is similarly used to mean 'official information, notification.' In the following quotation "advices" appears as a deliberately overformal word, brought into a light essay as a small touch of humor:

> Maine sends about a million Christmas trees out of the state every year, according to my latest advices.
> —E. B. White, *Home-coming*

◇ ***Recommendation.*** The use of *advise* to mean 'inform' and of *advice* to mean 'information' is standard and correct in formal and official contexts. It is somewhat unsuitable to ordinary and informal language.

adviser, advisor. Both spellings are widespread and correct. Newspapers usually prefer *adviser.* A counselor of students is nearly always spelled *adviser.* Fortunetellers for some reason prefer *advisor.*

aegis /ē-jĭs/. The original *aegis* was a mysterious and awe-inspiring object wielded by the Greek god Zeus and his daughter Athena. Thought to be a goatskin cape or shield, it could raise thunderstorms and was used by the gods to protect their favorites and terrify their enemies. In English *aegis* means 'protecting strength' and is almost always used with *under*:

> Kissinger, under Nelson Rockefeller's aegis, moving quickly from the campus

> to the inner circles of the Nixon White House . . .
> —James Wooten, *Dasher*

> The Pacific Territory is the last of 11 trusteeships administered under the aegis of the United Nations Trusteeship Council. —Bernard Weinraub, *New York Times*

Aegis is now sometimes used in the weakened sense 'administration, sponsorship':

> Game shows and talk shows, the main types of original programming produced outside the network aegis . . .
> —Richard Zoglin, *Atlanta Constitution*

aerie. This is the traditional term for an eagle's or a hawk's nest, typically built high up on a crag or at the top of a tall tree. The word comes from Medieval Latin *aeria,* which has the same meaning. The preferred American spelling is *aerie,* but *aery* is also used. The usual pronunciation is /**âr**-ē/ rhyming with *dairy,* but some prefer /**ĭr**-ē/ as in *weary,* /**ăr**-ē/ as in *marry,* or even / **ĭr**-ē/ as in the first syllables of *irrigate.* The preferred British spelling is *eyrie* or *eyry,* also occasionally used in the United States:

> . . . the pinnacle on which the wedge-tailed eagles' eyrie was set . . .
> —*Canberra Times*

The word is also used of a human home or of accommodations in a high place:

> For a while I was assigned to a tower, a lovely aerie with three windowed walls. —Edwards Park, *Smithsonian*

> The private elevator opens into Mr. Friedman's brilliant blue-and-white executive aerie, with sunlit patio on one side and a greenhouse on the other.
> —Francis X. Clines, *New York Times*

◇ ***Recommendation.*** Unless you have other preferences, spell this word *aerie* and pronounce it to rhyme with *dairy.*

aesthetic, esthetic, etc. The spelling *esthetic* is equally correct, but *aesthetic* is somewhat commoner in the United States (and is the only British spelling). The American pronunciation is /ĕs-**thĕt**-ĭk/, but some Americans use the British /ēs-**thĕt**-ĭk, ĭs-/.

(1) The adjective *aesthetic* (or *esthetic*) primarily means 'relating to human perception of beauty.' Secondarily it means 'satisfying one's perception of beauty,' and '(of persons) having a developed taste for beauty':

> High speed films have long enabled photo-journalists to stop fast action in dim light, but they have had to pay a high aesthetic price . . . the dense particles of silver . . . show up on enlarged prints as an unsightly graininess.
> —*Discover*

> Such a Japanese feast is an esthetic happening that leaves me stunned with pleasure.
> —Christopher Lucas, *Reader's Digest*

> Nowhere is the Chieftains' aesthetic success more evident than in concert.
> —Scott Isler, *Rolling Stone*

> [Roone Arledge] combines aesthetic qualities with a toughness that is utterly concealed by a low-key, mild personality. . . .
> —Howard Cosell, *Cosell*

Likewise the adverb:

> Esthetically, the Colorado River system lifts the heart and staggers the mind. —*Reader's Digest*

> The most aesthetically demoralizing thing about New Jersey is that wilderness of tank farms along the turnpike.
> —*New Jersey Monthly*

(2) The noun *aesthetic* (or *esthetic*) means 'a principle or theory of beauty.' *Aesthetics* (or *esthetics*) is 'the philosophy of beauty':

> The Siegel vision and the Siegel aesthetic were already sweeping Las Vegas like gold fever.
> —Tom Wolfe, *The Kandy-Kolored . . . Baby*

> TV-movies are elementarily functional creations; questions of aesthetics are almost irrelevant.
> —Tom Shales, *Panorama*

(3) An *aesthete* (or *esthete*) is a person who cultivates the appreciation of beauty, especially in art. The word is now negative, implying 'arty, effete person':

> The characters I had heard were central in [Colette's work]—salon habitués, polylingual aesthetes, expressionist dancers, lesbians—don't especially draw me. . . .
>
> —Benjamin DeMott, *Atlantic Monthly*

> . . . a couple of middle-aged aesthetes trained on corned-beef and Dr. Brown's Celery Tonic were ill equipped to ascend the slopes of Kanchenjunga. . . .
>
> —S. J. Perelman, *Westward Ha!*

affect, effect. Although these verbs are related, they are never synonymous.

Effect means 'to give effect to, be a cause of, bring about (a result, purpose, action, etc.)': *The war effected a great change in American values.*

Affect is used, first, of causative conditions and events; it means 'to act upon, have some influence on': *Both diet and exercise affect blood pressure. The news affected her strongly.* Secondly, *affect* is used of persons, meaning 'to cultivate, go in for (a mannerism, style, practice, etc.)': *He affects the rugged outdoor look.* It can also mean 'to project a false impression of having (an attitude, belief, etc.)': *I affected interest in the plan.*

affinity. The original meaning of *affinity* is 'relationship by marriage' (as opposed to *consanguinity* = 'relationship by blood'). But it also means 'family relationship in general, kinship.' The word has taken on a range of figurative meanings, used with several different prepositions.

(1) *affinity with* or *between* = 'likeness of temperament, sympathy':

> Most of the Prince's friends . . . were rich men who loved pleasure; and among them the Prince discovered a special affinity with Jews.
>
> —Philip Magnus, *Edward VII*

> Intensely nationalistic and Moslem, Somalia . . . is apt to feel a stronger ideological affinity with the Arab states than with predominantly Christian Ethiopia.
>
> —John Darnton, *New York Times*

> There was between them a natural affinity of spirit: they enjoyed the same pleasures, laughed at the same jokes, agreed in their opinions, respected each other's judgments.
>
> —David Cecil, *A Portrait of Jane Austen*

> Not since the days of grand designers Roosevelt and Churchill has there been such a natural affinity between American and British leaders.
>
> —William Safire, *New York Times*

(2) *affinity to* = 'underlying similarity, natural or structural resemblance': *In Caribbean music we hear an unmistakable affinity to African music. Moon rocks, it turns out, have a basic affinity to certain Earth rocks.*

(3) *affinity for* = 'quality of combining well, based on compatibility':

> Not without reason called l'herbe royale, these versatile herbs [basils] have a great affinity for tomatoes, fish and egg dishes. . . .
>
> —Irma S. Rombauer and Marion Rombauer Becker, *The Joy of Cooking*

(4) *affinity for* = 'sympathetic attraction, liking based on a feeling of being similar':

> From the moment of their first acquaintance, Fields had felt an especial affinity for Dickens, in some of whose characters he saw strong traces of himself.
>
> —Robert Lewis Taylor, *W. C. Fields*

> Show people and fighters always seemed to have a great affinity for each other.
>
> —Harpo Marx, *Harpo Speaks*

(5) *affinity for* = 'ability to perform well in an activity, based on natural instinct rather than training':

> He started at the bottom, but quickly demonstrated a flair for business in

general and an affinity for the oil business in particular.
—J. Paul Getty, *As I See It*

He has vowed to be an activist anchorman when he succeeds Walter Cronkite in 1981, claiming an affinity for the "cutting edge" of breaking events.
—Ron Powers, *The Newscasters*

Is there a natural affinity for any single game by any single nation, or is the distinction purely a matter of tradition?
—William F. Buckley, Jr., *Execution Eve*

Today, Pelé regards his affinity for the game as fated. "I believe it was a gift of God," he says. "I was born for soccer, just as Beethoven was born for music."
—Warren R. Young, *Reader's Digest*

There are critics who claim that the uses of *affinity* with *to* and *for* are incorrect. But as the quotations show, the word is used in these ways by a wide range of writers.

◇ ***Recommendation.*** All of the uses shown above are legitimate. Use *affinity* with any preposition that seems natural.

affixes. *Affixes* are linguistic fragments that are attached to words or word elements and modify meaning or function. In English they are attached either at the beginning of the word (*prefixes*) or at the end (*suffixes*). Some languages also have *infixes*, which are inserted in the middle; these are rare, however, in English.

In this book we distinguish between affixes and *word elements*. Affixes have only modifying force, as *dis-* = 'not-' or *-ation* = 'state or quality of.' Word elements have their own meanings like nouns and adjectives, as *micro-* = 'small' or *-ology* = 'science.' See WORD ELEMENTS.

English Affixes. (1) *Inflectional endings.* The inflectional endings have purely grammatical functions. English once had a large array of inflections but has discarded all except a few. The chief ones are:

-s *or* **-es,** forming the plural of most nouns

-s, written with an apostrophe, forming the possessive (and sometimes the plural) of nouns

-er, -est, forming the comparative and superlative, respectively, of adjectives

-s *or* **-es,** forming the third person singular of the present tense of verbs

-d *or* **-ed,** forming the past tense and past participle of most verbs

-ing, forming the present participle and verbal noun of verbs

(2) *Other native affixes.* Among the other affixes inherited from Old English and still in use are:

be- (1) = 'around, completely': *beset; besmear; beloved* (2) forming verbs: *befriend*

-dom = 'state, condition, rank': *serfdom; martyrdom; kingdom*

-en (1) forming verbs: *darken; strengthen* (2) forming adjectives: *flaxen; wooden*

-er, forming agent nouns: *singer; digger*

-ful = 'full of, apt to': *wonderful; meaningful; helpful*

-hood = 'state, condition': *childhood; livelihood*

-ish = 'belonging to, like, somewhat': *English; fiendish; biggish*

-less = 'lacking': *nameless; helpless*

-ly (1) forming adverbs: *sadly; beautifully; meaninglessly* (2) forming adjectives: *womanly; yearly*

-ness = 'state, quality': *happiness; blackness; thankfulness*

-ship = 'state, quality, rank': *friendship; generalship; professorship*

-some, forming adjectives: *awesome; lonesome*

-ster, forming agent nouns: *spinster; teamster*

un- = 'not': *unwise; unharmed; unconvincing*

-ward = 'in the direction of': *backward; northeastward; homeward*

-wise, forming adverbs: *otherwise; crabwise; counterclockwise*

-y, forming adjectives: *mighty; twisty*

Latin and Greek Affixes. The great majority of current English affixes have been borrowed from Latin and Greek, often through French.

(1) Among the Latin-derived suffixes are:

-able, -ible: *demonstrable; tangible*
-age: *marriage; postage*
-al: *presidential; regal*
-an: *human; median; Roman*
-ance, -ence: *endurance; obedience*
-ant, -ent: *patient; vacant*
-ar: *lunar; singular*
-ary: *solitary; temporary*
-ate: *fortunate; refrigerate*
-ess: *patroness; shepherdess*
-ile: *fragile; prehensile*
-ine: *canine; saturnine*
-ite: *favorite; finite*
-ive: *creative; festive*
-ment: *movement; temperament*
-or: *favor; honor; horror*
-ose, -ous: *bellicose; spacious*
-tion: *creation; demolition; solution*
-tude: *fortitude; solitude*

(2) Some Latin prefixes are:

ab- = 'away from': *abduct; absent*
ad- = 'toward': *adduce; admit*
com-, con- = 'together, completely': *combine; confuse*
de- = 'down, off, un-': *descend; decapitate*
dis- = 'apart, un-': *distend; disorient*
ex- = 'out of, un-': *excess; excommunicate*
in-, im- = (1) 'in, into': *intrude; impel* (2) 'not, un-': *indecent; impure*
non- = 'not': *nondescript; nonentity*
per- = 'through, completely': *percolate; permutation*
pro- = 'for, forward, before': *proceed; propose*
re- = 'again, back': *regress; renovate*
sub- = 'under, less than': *submerge; substandard*
super- = 'over, beyond': *superintend; supernatural*
trans- = 'across, through': *transpose; transpire*

(3) Among the Greek-derived suffixes are:

-ac: *cardiac; insomniac*
-asm: *enthusiasm; spasm*
-ast: *enthusiast; gymnast*
-ic: *cryptic; Hellenic; skeptic*
-ics: *hysterics; politics*
-ism: *barbarism; magnetism*
-oid: *spheroid; Caucasoid*

(4) Some Greek-derived prefixes are:

a-, an- = 'lacking in, un-': *achromatic; amoral; anonymous*
ana- = 'up, again': *analyze; Anabaptist*
apo- = 'from, off': *apogee; apostate*
cata- = 'down, completely': *cataract; catalogue*
dia- = 'through, completely': *diameter; diagnosis*
epi- = 'on, in, at': *epitaph; epidemic*
hyper- = 'beyond, more than': *hyperbole; hypertension*
hypo- = 'under, less than': *hypodermic; hypotension*
meta- = 'with, after, changed': *metaphysics; metamorphosis*
para- = 'beside, along': *parallel; parameter*
peri- = 'around, about': *perimeter; peripatetic*
syn-, sym- = 'with, together': *synchronize; sympathy*

aficionado /ə-fē-sē-ə-**nä**-dō, ə-fĭsh-ə-/. This synonym for 'enthusiast, fan' comes from the world of bullfighting and was popularized largely by Ernest Hemingway. In Spanish *aficionado* means 'serious devotee,' from *aficionarse* = 'to be devoted to,' from *afición* = 'devotion, affection.' The plural of *aficionado* is *aficionados;* the feminine form is *aficionada,* plural *aficionadas.*

> I had a wonderful day and have since become an aficionado of American football.
> —David Niven, *The Moon's a Balloon*

I should admit at the outset that I am anything but a science-fiction aficionada.
—Molly Haskell, *Village Voice*

African words. (1) For the special category of African words that have come into American English via Black English, see BLACK ENGLISH; GULLAH.

(2) Words from the Afrikaans (Dutch) language of South Africa are given separately at AFRIKAANS WORDS.

(3) Below is a selection of other words that have been adopted into English at various times from the many languages of Africa. Exact sources are given when known. Most of these words come from the huge Niger-Congo family of languages (including Bantu) and were picked up by European travelers or colonists in Africa.

banana = 'well-known fruit of a large tropical plant or tree': the word arrived in English in the reign of Queen Elizabeth I, brought (via Spanish and Portuguese) from Wolof or Mandingo *banäna*

baobab /bā-ō-băb/ = 'massive-trunked tree of central Africa': exact source unknown

basenji /bə-sĕn-jē/ = 'smooth-coated, nonbarking central African dog': from Bantu *ba-senji* = 'natives, native dogs'

bongo = 'central African antelope with spirally curved horns': exact source unknown

chimpanzee = 'primate ape of the equatorial African forests': from Kongo *chimpenzi*

***cola** = (1) 'seed of a West African tree' (2) 'carbonated soft drink'

***dashiki** /dä-shē-kē/ = 'loose, brightly colored, African-inspired shirt'

gnu /nyōō, nōō/ = 'large, oxlike antelope of southern Africa' (also known as *wildebeest*): from the Bushman language

juju = (1) 'West African magical object or amulet' (2) 'magical power or spell': from Hausa *djudju* = 'fetish, spirit'

mamba = 'poisonous snake of southern Africa': from Zulu *im-amba*

mumbo jumbo = originally 'name of a West African deity,' later (in English) 'meaningless ritual or language': probably from Mandingo *mama-dyumbo*, a religious term

okapi /ō-kä-pē/ = 'central African animal related to the giraffe but shorter': exact source unknown

***okra** /ō-krə/ = 'mucilaginous pods of a semitropical African plant'

quagga /kwäg-ə, kwăg-ə/ = 'zebralike horse of southern Africa, striped in front and on top, now extinct': probably from Hottentot

raffia = 'fiber of a Madagascan palm tree, used for weaving, binding, etc.': from Malagasy

samba = 'Brazilian dance derived from West African sources': from Portuguese, from African

tsetse /tsĕt-sē, tsēt-, sĕt-, sēt-/ = 'African fly that transmits cattle infections': from Tswana

yam = 'tuber of a tropical plant, a staple food in West Africa': via Spanish and Portuguese, from Mende *nyambi*

*Appears as separate entry

Afrikaans words. The Afrikaans language is descended from the colonial Dutch spoken by Dutch settlers of the Cape of Good Hope, with influences from Low German, Malay, and African languages. Its speakers are called *Afrikaners.* Listed below are the chief English words that have been borrowed from Afrikaans. Several, such as *springbok* and *wildebeest*, are easily recognized as containing "cousins" of English words, the effect of the close family relationship between English and Dutch. *Baas* may also seem familiar, since the Dutch word from which it comes has been separately borrowed in America as *boss.* For this and other Dutch borrowings see DUTCH WORDS.

aardvark /ärd-värk/ = 'large anteater': Afrikaans *aardvark, erdvark* = 'earth-pig,' from *aarde, erde* = 'earth' + *vark* = 'pig'

apartheid /ə-pärt-hīt, -hāt/ = 'official segregation of races in South Africa': Afrikaans *apartheid* = 'separateness,' from *apart* =

'separate' + *-heid* = suffix equivalent to the English suffix *-hood*

baas = 'sir, master': Afrikaans *baas* = 'master'

bush = 'uncleared country, wilderness': Afrikaans *bosch, bos* = 'forest'

commando = 'soldier of special forces trained in swift raiding tactics': Afrikaans *kommando* = 'unit of mounted, light-armed militia in the Boer army in the war of 1899–1902'

eland /ē-lənd/ = 'large antelope with twisted horns': Afrikaans *eland,* from Dutch *eland* = 'elk, stag'

kraal /kräl/ = 'stockaded village of South African blacks': Afrikaans *kraal* = (1) 'stockaded village' (2) 'livestock enclosure'

laager /lä-gər/ = 'temporary protective encampment': Afrikaans *laager, laer* = 'defensive circle of wagons used by the Boers,' from German *lager* = 'camp, lair'

rand = 'basic monetary unit of South Africa': Afrikaans *rand* = 'shield'

spoor = 'the trail of an animal, including tracks, scent, droppings, etc.': Afrikaans *spoor* = 'trail, track'

springbok = 'small gazelle that characteristically leaps up sharply in the air': Afrikaans *springbok* = 'spring(ing) buck,' from *spring* = 'to spring, jump' + *bok* = 'buck, deer'

veld, veldt /vĕlt, fĕlt/ = 'grassland': Afrikaans *veld* = 'grassland,' originally 'field'

wildebeest /wĭl-də-bēst, vĭl-/ = 'oxlike antelope' (also known as *gnu*): Afrikaans *wildebees* = 'wild beast'

Afro-American. This term is used of black American culture and history:

> The belief that slavery shattered the Afro-American family is not new. . . .
> —Herbert Gutman, *New York Times*

> Far and away the leader of these composers was the Afro-American musical genius Scott Joplin (1868–1917).
> —Rudi Blesh, *Scott Joplin*

See also BLACK ENGLISH.

again, against. ***Pronunciation.*** The standard American pronunciations are /ə-gĕn/, /ə-gĕnst/. On the Atlantic coast, especially in parts of New England, southeastern Virginia, and northeastern North Carolina, the pronunciations /ə-gān/ and /ə-gānst/ are sometimes used; but elsewhere in the United States these are usually considered affected. The pronunciations /ə-gĭn/, /ə-gĭnst/ are widespread in rural areas but are usually considered uncultivated. In Britain /ə-gān/, /ə-gānst/ and /ə-gĕn/, /ə-gĕnst/ are equally standard.

Regional Uses. In the Southern and Midland speech regions of the United States, both words are used in expressions of time to mean 'before' or 'by the time that':

> "We will get there agin he does."
> "Hit'll rain ag'in morning."
> "I'll have this sewing done against dinner time."
> —from *Dialect Notes*

> I aimed to give you yore pick of em ag'in you got married.
> —Alberta Hannum, *Thursday April*

> Shannon Budd is raising him a new house against winter come.
> —Maristan Chapman, *Happy Mountain*

aged. As an adjective used of humans or other creatures and meaning 'very old,' or as a noun meaning 'old people,' the word is pronounced /ā-jĭd/: *an aged grandmother; a home for the aged.* Used to mean 'so many years old,' it is pronounced /ājd/: *a man aged 40.* Used of wine or food that has been kept for a certain length of time to mature, it is also pronounced /ājd/.

agenda. This was originally a Latin plural meaning 'things to be done.' It is now a standard singular noun with its own regular plural *agendas.* The meaning is either 'list of items to be considered at a meeting' or 'program of political goals to be attained':

> John Kennedy had set that agenda for his successor: tax reduction, the civil

rights bill, federal aid to education. . . . —Doris Kearns, *Lyndon Johnson and the American Dream*

The United States has a broad agenda of specific arms control regulations proposals. —Alexander Haig (quoted), NBC news program

aggravate, aggravation. The basic meaning of the verb *aggravate* is 'to make (a trouble) graver or more serious, make worse':

> . . . a whole host of diseases caused or aggravated by stress . . .
> —Charles and Bonnie Remsberg, *Reader's Digest*

> . . . fearful that these costly new rules will further aggravate today's high rate of inflation.
> —*U.S. News & World Report*

In law, a crime is called *aggravated* if it is worse than the simple form of the crime; if, for example, other offenses or unusual violence is involved:

> . . . awaiting trial on charges of aggravated burglary, aggravated battery and two counts of kidnapping.
> —*Savannah Morning News*

The secondary meaning of *aggravate* is 'to irritate or anger.' This sense has often been condemned by the experts, but it has been in wide use for many years:

> Hard down out of that! . . . don't aggravate me—I won't have it.
> —Herman Melville, *Moby-Dick*

> You just don't aggravate yourself, and try to get along and do the things you have to do today.
> —George Burns, *Reader's Digest*

The noun *aggravation* can follow either the basic or the secondary meaning of the verb; it is now much used to mean 'serious social pressures and harassment':

> If you walk through life showing the aggravation you've gone through, people will feel sorry for you, and they'll never respect you.
> —Dick Gregory, *Nigger*

> A woman M.B.A. should have a strong constitution—she's going to have to take a lot of aggravation.
> —Patricia Runewitsch (quoted), *New York Times*

Regional Uses. In the South and its western settlement areas, *aggravate* is often pronounced /ăg-ər-vāt/ or /ăg-ə-vāt/. The word has undergone some fanciful variations:

aggrafret = *aggra(vate)* + *fret*
aggravex = *aggra(vate)* + *vex*
aggravoke = *aggra(vate)* + *(pro)voke*

> Him and his army! I'll war him, I will: he ain't never seen no war like what I can aggravoke.
> —William Faulkner, *The Wishing Tree*

◇ ***Recommendation.*** The use of *aggravate* to mean 'irritate, anger' and of *aggravation* to mean 'irritation, harassment' is standard and correct.

aging is the preferred U.S. spelling:

> . . . the aircraft providing this lead are almost all aging B-52s. . . .
> —*Reader's Digest*

The British spelling *ageing* also sometimes occurs in the United States.

agree. When the meaning is 'to consent to or accept (someone else's plan, idea, etc.),' the preposition is *to: I agree to your proposal.* When the meaning is 'to come to a mutual acceptance of (a plan, idea, etc.),' the preposition is *on: They finally agreed on an interpretation.* When the meaning is 'to have the same opinion as (someone else),' the preposition is *with: He agreed with her about violence on television.*

ain't. *Ain't* probably originated as a contracted form of *am not,* but it is also used for *are not* and *is not* and for *have not* and *has not.* It occurs chiefly in the speech of country and working-class people, in both England and the United States.

Ordinary use of *ain't* has long been singled out as a mark of uneducated speech. Generations of schoolteachers have worked to train children who learn *ain't* at home or from their peers to suppress it in their speech and written work. The teachers have succeeded to some extent, but *ain't* still survives.

It has been argued that some uses of *ain't* are more defensible than others; that its use for forms of *be (am not, are not, is not)* is more justifiable than its use for forms of *have (have not, has not)*. In particular, some have felt that *ain't I?* is reasonable, since the alternatives are unsatisfactory in one way or another; this issue is discussed separately at AREN'T I? In effect, however, all meanings of *ain't* are equally under the ban.

Most people throughout the English-speaking world avoid *ain't* themselves, but all know it and understand its social implications when they hear or read it. Not only is *ain't* a living word in the speech of millions of unpretentious people, it is also a self-conscious device used by people who do not usually include it in their conversation.

Uses. The actual usage of *ain't* thus falls into two categories: all-purpose rural and working-class use, and limited middle-class and upper-class use. *Ain't* often occurs with the double negative, frequently with an emphatic effect: *They ain't never changed.* Almost certainly, the speakers who continue to use *ain't* in daily conversation have been taught that it is "bad grammar." Speaking to an educated stranger, some would probably suppress it, and few would use it in a business letter or clearly formal situation.

But the underlying and widespread defiance of the schoolmarm's best-known language rule is best illustrated by an anecdote from *Reader's Digest:*

> It had been a stimulating convention, and all the way to the airport the three educators talked about verbal fluency, sentence combining and student responses to literature. As one of them paid for the cab ride, the driver peered at him curiously. "What are you guys?" he inquired, "English teachers?" Assured that they were, he smiled broadly, leaned out the window and shouted, "Ain't, ain't, ain't!"
> —Bill Lemley

It is well known that middle- and upper-class people in many places use *ain't* among themselves, especially in intimate and relaxed conversation, but totally suppress it in front of outsiders. This may be commoner in the American South than elsewhere, but it also persists, for example, among the more old-fashioned country gentry in England, who are sufficiently class-confident to ignore or even relish "bad grammar" and keep on using *ain't.*

This feeling about *ain't* is also the basis of some specialized or pointed uses, as for achieving a down-home, folksy effect and for emphasis, especially with the double negative. Al Jolson's famous ad-lib "You ain't heard nothin' yet, folks!" is one example. Another is a remark by Winston Churchill that a portrait he disliked made him look "half-witted, which I ain't." Some others:

> Fate is what life gives to you. Destiny is what you do with it. If you are five-four, you ain't ever going to be six-two. —Bill Gove, *Reader's Digest*

> [Geraldine] Page, now appearing Off-Broadway in a Strindberg repertory, plays a wealthy and powerful political patroness [in an episode of *Kojak*]. Strindberg it ain't, but Page it most assuredly is.
> —Katie Kelly, *New York Post*

The definitive analysis is provided by Will Rogers:

> Maybe *ain't* ain't right, but I notice lots of folks who ain't sayin' *ain't* ain't eatin'.

à la. This French expression is used primarily in cooking. It is short for *à la mode (de)* = 'in the manner (of)':

tomates à la provençale = 'tomatoes in the manner of Provence' (that is, sautéed with herbs and garlic)

crabe à la Mornay = 'crab in the Mornay style' (that is, with a cheese sauce; named in honor of the statesman Philippe de *Mornay,* 1549–1623)

Hence, in general usage *à la* means 'in the fashion of, in the way proposed by, under the system of, etc.' The accent is usually retained, though the expressions *a la carte* and *a la mode* are commonly used without it:

> We can seek a formula that will neutralize South Vietnam à la Mansfield and De Gaulle but any such formula will only lead in the end to the same results as withdrawing support.
>
> —Lyndon Johnson (quoted), Doris Kearns, *Lyndon Johnson and the American Dream*

> As examples ranging from Germany to Hong Kong make clear, lowering taxes à la Kemp-Roth increases economic activity.
>
> —Malcolm S. Forbes, Jr., *Forbes*

Alaskan English. Alaska as a speech region is essentially an extension of the PACIFIC NORTHWEST DIALECT. Many of the forces that influenced the speech of the Pacific coast states, such as the influx of settlers to the mining, logging, and fishing industries, have also influenced Alaskan English. The early settlers of this least populous state came primarily from the North, the Midlands speech area, and the West, but a broader wave of regional speech has recently flowed into the state with the development of the Alaska oil pipeline.

Although Alaska is not a distinct dialect area on its own, it has many words and phrases unique to it. Most of these have to do with the cold climate and harsh terrain or are borrowings from the languages of the Aleuts and Innuit and from CHINOOK JARGON. The name Alaska itself comes from the Aleut *alakshak* = 'peninsula.' See also INNUIT (ESKIMO) WORDS.

The following is a list of some of the terms distinctive to or especially common in Alaska.

ahikio = 'type of utility sled' (from Innuit)

banana belt = 'the warmer parts of Alaska'

banya = 'steam bath or sauna'

black diamond = 'hematite cut and polished for jewelry'

breakup = 'the time when the ice on rivers and the ocean breaks up, spring'

bunny, boots = 'large, inflatable rubber boots worn against extreme cold'

burn *or* **berm pile** = 'a pile of trees, stumps, and brush cleared from the land'

bush = 'any remote area accessible only by boat or plane'

cabin fever = 'irritability as a result of living in close quarters for an extended period of time'

cache = 'log huts or boxes on stilts used to store food and supplies out of the reach of animals'

chuck = 'inlet, harbor'

fish camp = 'temporary or semipermanent habitation along a river or the ocean'

freeze-up = 'the time of year when seaports are icebound and all bodies of water are frozen'

glaciering = 'ice formed from water that overflows the tops and banks of streams as they freeze solid'

gussuck (derogatory) = 'a white person'; used by the Innuit

haul road = 'unpaved road used to truck goods and supplies to remote areas'

ice bridge = 'bridge across a river made by spraying water to form layers of ice'

iron dog = 'snowmobile'

kupiak = 'coffee' (from Innuit)

kuspuk = 'long, hooded Innuit dress' (from Innuit)

marine highway = 'the state's ocean-ferry system'

mush = (1) 'to travel by dog sled' (2) 'to travel on foot over snow'

musher, dog musher = 'one who drives a sled-dog team'

muskeg /mŭs-kĕg/ = 'swampy area covered with vegetation'

outside = 'anywhere except Alaska'

parka /pär-kē/ = 'hooded coat or jacket'

pulka /pŭl-kə/ = 'utility sled' (from Innuit)

ruff = 'the fur edging on the hood of a parka or coat'

snow berm = 'the ridge of snow graded up by a plow'

snow-go = 'snowmobile'

squaw candy = 'dried or smoked salmon'

stack robber = 'device fitted on stovepipes to radiate heat'

stateside = 'the continental United States'

taku wind = 'a strong wind from the Taku River valley'

tillicum = (1) 'person, friend' (2) 'people'

toolies = 'a wild, remote area'

utilidor = 'insulated box that houses water and sewer pipes'

visqueen = 'thin plastic sheeting' (from a trade name)

wanigan /**wän**-ĭ-gən/ = (1) 'small building mounted on runners or wheels so that it can be easily moved' (2) 'an addition to a mobile home'

albeit. This conjunction means 'even though' or 'although admittedly.' The preferred pronunciation is /ôl-**bē**-ĭt/, but /ăl-**bē**-ĭt/ is also sometimes used.

> A new civilization had arisen with startling rapidity, a civilization in which the Indian was expected to take a part, albeit it was to a great extent an exploited and unhappy one.
> —J. T. Adams, *The Epic of America*

> In the U.S. the Pill's side effects, a genuine albeit not a large risk, are cutting steadily into its popularity.
> —Philip Morrison, *Scientific American*

Algonquin, Algonquian. A small Indian tribe living in and around the Ottawa Valley in Canada was originally named *Algonquin* or *Algonquian* (sometimes also spelled *Algonkin* or *Algonkian*). The people are now usually called the *Ottawa*. Their language belongs to a very large group of languages, the speakers of which once dominated most of eastern and midwestern North America—among them, Arapaho, Blackfoot, Cheyenne, Cree, Fox, Massachuset, Micmac, Ojibwa, and Shawnee. The family of languages, or any member of it, is called *Algonquian* (sometimes spelled *Algonkian*).

algorithm, algorism. Now becoming widely familiar in the language of computer programming, these formerly obscure words refer to a mathematical procedure that performs a specific task within a program. They happen to commemorate one of the great contributions of the medieval Islamic world to mathematics. Muhammad ibn-Mūsa al Khwārizmi, generally regarded as the inventor of algebra, was born in about A.D. 780 in the city of Khwarizm (now called Khiva, in Uzbek, U.S.S.R.). He was called Al-Khwarizmi = 'the man of Khwarizm,' and his book on algebra became known in Europe in a Latinized form of this name, *Algorismus*. This, becoming *algorism* in English, came to be used to mean 'arithmetic done with Arabic numerals' or 'any arithmetical calculation.' In the 17th century the word was wrongly associated with Greek *arithmos* = 'number' (as in *arithmetic*), and so was altered to *algorithm*, which has now become the prevailing form, especially in computer terminology; but some still prefer the older form *algorism*.

alibi is originally a Latin adverb meaning 'elsewhere.' In law, to make a *plea of alibi* is to claim to have been elsewhere when a deed was done; from this legal usage *alibi* became a noun meaning 'plea or proof of having been elsewhere.' As any lawyer or reader of crime fiction knows, false but plausible alibis are often sworn to by friends of the accused. This is the origin of the slang use of *alibi* to mean 'any lame or unconvincing excuse,' immortalized by Ring Lardner's ballplayer Alibi Ike, who had an excuse for everything:

> "He's got the world beat," says Carey afterwards. "I've known guys that had an alibi for every mistake, but this baby can't even go to bed without apologizin'."
> —Ring Lardner, *Haircut and Other Stories* (1915)

This use has often been condemned as sloppy and tending to confuse the legal and correct sense of the word. But it is now used by respectable writers in formal contexts:

> "Socialism" is your alibi for rejecting the real progress capitalism has made,

the leveling you abhor, if the truth were told.
—Mary McCarthy, *Birds of America*

Although "computer error" has become the number one alibi for the fact that nothing seems to work well anymore, nobody suggests anything but a computer cure. —*Geo*

◇ ***Recommendation.*** This use remains controversial. For some, it is now fully established as standard, if somewhat informal. For others, it is still considered slang. The choice is yours.

alleged. See ACCUSED, ALLEGED.

allegory. *Allegory* is the most elaborate of a family of literary forms in which the characters, events, or setting of a story is understood to represent something else. In an allegory, for example, a character may be intended to represent the principle of virtue; the setting may stand for purgatory; or the train of events may symbolize the mystery of death and rebirth. Thus, an allegory is a kind of extended metaphor, telling two stories at once: the surface narrative and a more meaningful subtext.

Other members of the allegory family are parable, FABLE, and MYTH. In everyday usage the distinctions between these terms are often blurred. But differences nevertheless exist, and they are worth preserving for the sake of precision.

Ideally, an allegory should be fairly long and complex in structure, and the elements in the surface narrative should, for the most part, represent concepts rather than things. This is well illustrated in the great medieval French allegory *Le Roman de la Rose* (The Romance of the Rose), in which the hero encounters characters with such names as Reason, Danger, and Slander (and is at one point struck in the heart by three arrows named Hope, Sweet Thoughts, and Soft Looks) while searching for the Rose, the symbol of his fair lady's love. Similarly, in the greatest of English allegories, John Bunyan's *Pilgrim's Progress* (1678), the hero, Christian, meets, among others, Mr. Worldly Wiseman, Hopeful, and the Giant Despair as he makes his way through such places as Vanity Fair and the Slough of Despond toward the Desired Country of spiritual reward.

Although the full-blown allegory was one of literature's dominant forms from Ovid's day until well into the 18th century (by which time it was primarily used as a vehicle for satire, as in *A Tale of a Tub* by Jonathan Swift), it is no longer much in fashion, seeming overcontrived and ponderous to modern tastes.

This is less true of the junior members of the family. The *parable*, a short, simple tale illustrating some basic spiritual truth, has been a common means of inspirational instruction since at least Biblical times. The best-known parables are those of Jesus Christ—the good Samaritan, the prodigal son, the sower, the lost sheep, and so on.

Another relative of allegory is *fable*. Fables are as short and simple as parables, but they tend to be less uplifting, since typically their purpose is to illustrate human folly. Another distinctive feature of fables is that some or all of the characters in the narrative are animals with human attributes—Aesop's Ant and Grasshopper, for example, or even our own Br'er Rabbit.

Finally, there is *myth*. Here we refer only to the secondary meaning of the term. Originally, of course, myths were the opposite of allegories in that they were intended to be understood literally, not figuratively. But in retrospect, when people no longer took them at face value, myths could be regarded as allegorical representations of ideas and events—of the creation, the turn of the seasons, the triumph of love over death, and so on. Plato was one of the first to make this secondary application of the term. As defined by him, a myth was a short allegorical story illustrating a philosophic concept.

Allegory and its various cousins have one element in common: a laudable but potentially dangerous tendency to make complicated matter easier to understand and more attractive, by means of analogy. Ideas are given a personal identity, complex events get put into everyday contexts, abstractions are turned into things. Such simplification can be helpful, but it can also be very misleading. We may accept allegory—or fable, parable, or myth—as poetry, but we should be wary when it is offered to us as proof.

alliteration. While rhyme is the repetition of the sound of whole words or syllables, usually at the ends of lines of verse, alliteration is the repetition of initial vowels or consonants, as *arms and armor; dawn of day; hearth and home.* Poets have cultivated alliteration as a form of word music, often preferring it to rhyme. The best effects are achieved not by simple repetition but by subtle echoes:

> Out of doubt, out of dark, to the day's rising,
> I came singing in the sun, sword unsheathing,
> To hope's end I rode and to heart's breaking:
> Now for wrath, now for ruin and a red nightfall.
>
> —J. R. R. Tolkien, *The Lord of the Rings*

The foregoing is a conscious imitation of the alliterative form predominant in Old English poetry.

> In Xanadu did Kubla Khan
> A stately pleasure dome decree:
> Where Alph, the sacred river, ran
> Through caverns measureless to man
> Down to a sunless sea.
>
> —Samuel Taylor Coleridge, *Kubla Khan*

Here each line ends with a pair of alliterating words, but the effect is not obvious because the rhymes (*decree* and *sea, ran* and *man*) are more conspicuous than the alliteration. Whether Coleridge did this consciously is impossible to say, but it certainly plays its part in the sound texture of the poem.

> This be the verse you grave for me:
> Here he lies where he longed to be;
> Home is the sailor, home from sea,
> And the hunter home from the hill.
>
> —Robert Louis Stevenson, *Requiem*

The final series of words beginning with *h* might almost symbolize the poet's last breaths.

Lesser poets, and writers of comic verse, have made crude but still effective use of alliteration. A tyrannical English schoolmaster, Dr. Bethel of Eton, was immortalized by one of his former pupils:

> Didactic, dry, declamatory, dull,
> Big burly Bethel bellowed like a bull.

Totally alliterative poems have been composed as feats of ingenuity. The supreme example of this strange genre is B. Poulter's "Siege of Belgrade," written about 1817:

> An Austrian army, awfully arrayed,
> Boldly by battery, besieged Belgrade;
> Cossack commanders cannonading come,
> Dealing destruction's devastating doom;
> Every endeavor engineers essay,
> For fame, for fortune, fighting furious fray;
> Generals 'gainst generals grapple—gracious God!
> How honors Heaven heroic hardihood!
> Infuriate, indiscriminate in ill,
> Kindred kill kinsmen, kinsmen kindred kill!
> Labor low levels loftiest, longest lines,
> Men march 'mid mounds, 'mid moles, 'mid murderous mines;
> Now noisy, noxious, noticed nought
> Of outward obstacles opposing ought:
> Poor patriots, partly purchased, partly pressed,
> Quite quaking, quickly "quarter, quarter," quest;
> Reason returns, religious right redounds,
> Suvarov stops such sanguinary sounds.
> Truce to thee Turkey—triumph to thy train!
> Unjust, unwise, unmerciful Ukraine!
> Vanish vain victory, vanish victory vain!
> Why wish ye warfare? Wherefore welcome were
> Xerxes, Ximenes, Xanthus, Xavier?
> Yield, ye youths! Ye yeomen, yield your yell!
> Zeno's, Zapater's, Zoroaster's zeal,
> And all attracting—arms against acts appeal.

Among the criticisms that might be made of this curiosity is that it does not use the true alliteration of sounds but opts for the merely graphic alliteration of letters, matching up "Austrian" and "army," etc. One might also mention that the letter *j* is left out and that long parts of the piece don't make sense. It remains a monument to alliteration mania.

In prose, crude alliteration was long cherished by old-fashioned orators and boosters. In Sinclair Lewis's novel *Babbitt* (1922) Zenith is a growing Midwestern city:

> All of them displayed celluloid buttons the size of dollars and lettered "We zoom for Zenith." Martin Lumsen's little boy Willy carried a tasseled banner inscribed "Zenith the Zip City—Zeal, Zest and Zowie—1,000,000 in 1935."

Alliteration has been devalued; it is now used in an almost self-mocking way, as a feeble substitute for eloquence, expected to raise laughs or groans:

> It is . . . easy for those seeking my job to come up with flashy, instant solutions to everything from potholes to pot, from pornography to pollution.
> —Abraham Beame (quoted), *New York Times*

all of. The original and still basic construction of *all* with nouns is *all the time; all the people.* Before personal pronouns, it is used with *of: all of us; all of them.* It is now also, primarily in American English, used with *of* before nouns: *all of the time; all of the people.* Because this is a relatively new construction, uncommon before the 20th century, some conservative critics feel it is undesirable, and many editors will generally eliminate the *of.*

◇ ***Recommendation.*** This is entirely a matter of personal idiom. Such constructions as *all of the time* and *all of the people* are fully established as correct American English. The more traditional forms—*all the time; all the people*—are of course equally correct.

allow. (1) With impersonal subjects in the sense 'to make possible (a conclusion, etc.),' *allow* is used either with *of* or as a simple transitive verb: *The data seem to allow (of) two conflicting interpretations.*
(2) Used with personal subjects, meaning 'to permit,' *allow* is only a transitive verb taking a direct object and should not be used with *of: My grandmother never allowed such outrageous behavior.*
(3) Used with personal subjects, meaning 'to concede verbally, admit,' *allow* is used with a direct object, very often a clause introduced by *that.*

> Elizabeth allowed that he had given a very rational account of it.
> —Jane Austen, *Pride and Prejudice*

(4) There is also a dialectal use, meaning 'to give it as one's opinion, suppose.' This is sometimes used, for mildly satirical effect, with *as how:*

> Nixon allowed as how the best way to knock Romney down in the polls was to remove his winner status by beating him in New Hampshire.
> —William Safire, *Before the Fall*

> A bit of Happy Talk ensued, in which anchorman Daly (in the role of Dr. Interlocutor) allowed as how he didn't care about the weather. . . .
> —Ron Powers, *The Newscasters*

The effective meaning here is 'sagely made a trite or obvious observation.'

all right. Following the examples of *almost, already,* and other words that once were phrases beginning with *all,* it is natural enough that *all right* should ultimately become a single word. After all, it is spoken as a single word, and the written form *alright* does often occur. This form may eventually establish itself, but for the time being most authorities agree that *alright* is unacceptable in formal writing.

allude, allusion. Properly, *allude to* means 'to mention or convey (something) in an indirect fashion':

> A particularly sticky area is an affair—alluded to, not dramatized—between a

high-school student and one of her teachers.

—David Jacobs, *Panorama*

An *allusion* is an indirect mention, often a reference to a well-known saying or fact without quoting exactly or spelling it out:

> Apart from dark allusions to the coming of age of Orwell's Big Brother, many Britons are profoundly uneasy about Foot's elevation [to the leadership of the Labor party].
>
> —J. D. Douglas, *Christianity Today*

In the following passage the writer makes an allusion to the proverbial book title *How to Win Friends and Influence People:*

> There is no more effective way of losing friends and alienating people than by knowing more about language than they do, particularly the language which they themselves speak and write. —Thomas Pyles, *Essays*

Both noun and verb are often used loosely to mean simply 'mention,' without any sense of indirectness.

◊ ***Recommendation.*** The simpler words *refer, mention,* and *reference* may often be preferable to *allude* and *allusion*—unless indirectness is an important part of the meaning. Note also that a common slip is to confuse *allusion* with *illusion;* the latter means 'misconception, mistaken idea.'

alma mater, alumna, alumnus. These Latin expressions are based on the same metaphor. Your school or college is your *alma mater* = 'nourishing mother' because she gave you intellectual nourishment, and you are thus her *alumna* = 'foster daughter' or *alumnus* = 'foster son.' The Latin words *alma* and *alumna, alumnus* are based on the root *al-* = 'to nourish, feed a child.' The plural of the feminine form *alumna* is *alumnae* /ə-**lŭm**-nē/; of the masculine form *alumnus* it is *alumni* /ə-**lŭm**-nī/:

> . . . the more than 12,000 Harvard and Radcliffe alumni-alumnae, relatives and friends . . . —*Boston Globe*

alms /ämz/. This noun, meaning 'gift of money to the poor,' can be construed as singular or plural; both Biblical citations below are from the King James Version:

> [He] asked an alms. —Acts 3:3

> When thou doest alms, let not thy left hand know what thy right hand doeth.
>
> —Matthew 6:3

> For alms are but the vehicles of prayer.
>
> —John Dryden, *The Hind and the Panther* (1687)

already. (1) The adverb *already* = 'beforehand, as early as this,' is now entirely distinct from the phrase *all ready* = 'fully prepared': *Have you eaten lunch already? We were all ready to eat lunch.*

(2) The slang use of *already*, expressing impatience (approximately 'for goodness' sake!'), as in *all right already,* is a translation of German or Yiddish *schon* = 'already, indeed, after all.'

alright. See ALL RIGHT.

also is an adverb, originally meaning 'altogether so, in just the same way.' It now means simply 'in addition, furthermore, besides.' It is tending to become a conjunction with the force of 'and furthermore': *Standard features include power steering and power brakes, also bucket seats.* This seems a natural enough development but is resisted by most authorities.

◊ ***Recommendation.*** In speech and informal writing the use of *also* to mean 'and' is acceptable. In all formal usage it is better used only as an adverb.

alternate, alternative. (1) The adjective *alternate* means 'arranged or occurring with first one and then the other, succeeding by turns': *legal parking each day on alternate sides of the street; alternate inflation and deflation of the economy.*

(2) The adjective *alternative* basically means 'being one of two choices,' or 'offering a sec-

ond choice': *We have two alternative ways to go. There is an alternative approach to the problem.* Both the noun and the adjective are also often used of more than two choices: *We have several alternatives.*

◇ ***Recommendation.*** Although some conservatives still prefer to restrict *alternative* to a choice between two things, it is fully correct and standard to use it also of a choice among several.

(3) The noun *alternate*, especially in politics, means 'person who substitutes for another.' As a result the adjective *alternate* has taken on the meaning 'substitute' and has thus encroached on the basic meaning of *alternative: The bridge is under repair, and the alternate route takes 20 minutes.*

◇ ***Recommendation.*** The use of *alternate* to mean 'offering a second choice, substitute' is now too well established to be classed as an error. But the best usage is to keep the two words separate, using only *alternative* for 'substitute' and keeping *alternate* to mean only 'succeeding by turns.'

(4) *Alternative* is now also widely used in a range of political, cultural, and economic senses, meaning approximately 'opposed to the political establishment, offering a revolutionary life style, innovative, unorthodox.'

> In the 1970s, Gorda [California] attracted people seeking alternative life styles. —*New York Times*

> American alternative energy policy has to date given priority to gasohol, coal liquefaction and the development of oil shales. . . . —Edwin Kiester, *Geo*

> Sprung from the alternative nightclub scene in London, this five-man band . . .
> —David Livingstone, *Maclean's*

altogether. The adverb *altogether*, meaning 'entirely' or 'including everyone or everything,' is distinct from the phrase *all together*, meaning 'all at one time, all in unity': *These charts look altogether too complicated to use. It's encouraging to see so many of the team's fans all together.*

altruistic. See DISINTERESTED.

alumna, alumnus. See ALMA MATER, ALUMNA, ALUMNUS.

ambiance, ambience. The word is from French *ambiance* = 'surroundings, environment.' In English it may be spelled *ambiance* or *ambience*. The meaning is 'social atmosphere, environment':

> Underground Atlanta . . . is once again the heart of the city's dining and entertainment area in gaslight ambience.
> —*Reader's Digest*

> Imagine a dizzily high-class ambiance of ermine, sable and mink, gowns by Dior and Saint Laurent.
> —*Reader's Digest*

ambivalence, ambivalent. The noun *ambivalence* means 'simultaneous mixture of opposite feelings' or 'tendency to alternate between opposite feelings':

> Diplomats, reporters, and administrators alike, whether admiring or repelled, were all fascinated by the baffling ambivalence of Johnson's behavior: the mixture of primitive conduct with the exercise of imperial power, the commingling of cruelty and compassion, the suggestion of a wildness not fully tamed.
> —Doris Kearns,
> *Lyndon Johnson and the American Dream*

The adjective *ambivalent* means 'having opposite feelings' or 'alternating between opposite feelings':

> Sometimes the man is more certain than his partner that he wants no other children, or is less ambivalent about cutting off his biological ability to produce a child.
> —Joan Rattner Heilman,
> *Reader's Digest*

amenity. This word is used much more widely in Britain than in the United States.

The pronunciations /ə-měn-ə-tē/ and /ə-mēn-ə-tē/ are both correct. The basic meaning is 'pleasantness, agreeableness.'

(1) In the plural, used of places, the word means 'civilized comforts and conveniences,' ranging from public parks to plumbing:

> In many instances we try to adopt the way of life of the country we are visiting . . . giving up most of the conveniences and amenities we usually regard as essential. —*Sierra*

> A mild, healthful place with a fine water supply, it enjoyed the most advanced amenities of that day, right down to an ingenious system of drains. —James A. Michener, *The Covenant*

(2) Used of social life, *amenity* means 'the pleasantness of civilized living and good manners':

> Existence then was characterized by a blend of qualities that gave it a peculiar amenity. —David Cecil, *A Portrait of Jane Austen*

In the plural it usually means 'formal politeness, conventional civilities observed without warmth':

> After brief amenities, Kuznetsov, speaking flawless English, said that the Soviets were not interested in the domestic political problems of the United States. . . . —Charles Colson, *Born Again*

> Amenities were carefully observed between the Attorney General [Kennedy] and the director [J. Edgar Hoover]. —Arthur M. Schlesinger, Jr., *Robert Kennedy and His Times*

America, American. The name *America* was coined in 1507 by a German map maker, from *Americus* Vespucius, the Latinized form of *Amerigo* Vespucci, the Italian navigator who reached the New World seven years after Columbus. Theoretically, *America* should still mean the whole of the New World. But in current English it is almost never so used. North America and South America together can be called *the Americas;* but *America* by itself is only used to mean the United States of America, and *American* as a noun means only a U.S. citizen.

This situation sometimes causes uneasy feelings, as if it were arrogant for the United States to have taken over the name of the entire hemisphere. The style manual of the *Reader's Digest,* for example, urges editors "to substitute *the United States* when that is what the author means" but concedes that "there is no way to get around using *American* as a noun or adjective referring to a citizen of the United States, even though the word properly belongs to citizens of all nations of the Americas."

While it is always a good thing to be sensitive to such issues, there is no need for Americans of the United States to apologize for this usage. *The United States of America* is the nation's only formal name, but it is too long for any but formal use. *America* is merely a shortened form of it, not an arrogant claim to represent the New World. The British have always been content to use it in this way. In fact, in the whole of the English-speaking world, it is hardly possible (however logical it might seem) to call a Canadian or a Brazilian an American. Instead, the term is often used in distinguishing U.S. Americans from their neighbors in North America or the Western Hemisphere:

> Canadians would like to claim Vinland as theirs because of the Saga references to maple trees. . . . Americans, on the other hand, would also like to claim Vinland as theirs. . . . —Magnus Magnusson, *Vikings!*

The adjective *American* is slightly different. While it usually refers to the United States, as *American English, American politics,* it can also refer to the Americas as a whole, as *American Indians, American mammals.*

◇ ***Recommendation.*** In formal political contexts, *United States* (*of America*) is preferable to *America* or *American.* In most general situations, *America* and *American* are universally acceptable as references to the United States and its people. (See also UNITED STATES.)

American English. Almost as soon as British settlers arrived in America, a new variety of English was born. The coming together of several British dialects in one place was itself a new situation that altered the sound and form of the English spoken in the New World. The relative isolation of American speech from British speech soon made the differences even greater.

The famous British critic and lexicographer Samuel Johnson was the first to refer to this new variety as the "American dialect" (1756). But for Johnson this was hardly a flattering term. Most British writers of the time held that the language in America was a corruption of the "correct" speech of London. Even John Adams held this view when he proposed in 1780 that Congress establish an academy for "refining, improving, and ascertaining [that is, setting or fixing] the English language." He did not mean the language of America.

It was not until 1789 that the outspoken Noah Webster, the dean of American dictionary makers, defended the independence of American speech on patriotic grounds: "The reasons for American English being different than English English are simple: As an independent nation, our honor requires us to have a system of our own, in language as well as government." Thomas Jefferson, whose writings had long been attacked for their American "barbarisms," confidently predicted in 1816 that "an American dialect will be formed." In fact, his prediction was already well on its way to being realized.

American English differs from British English in numerous ways. The most important of these are the borrowing of words from other languages; the general use in American speech of certain archaic and dialectal British terms; and the widespread coinage of new American words and phrases.

Word Borrowings. Nearly every language adopts words from other languages. English has been a notorious word borrower and is richer because of it. After the Norman Conquest, for example, the English language absorbed thousands of French words. Likewise, the language in America has supplemented its word stock with many terms from the cultures and nationalities that have come in contact with it.

American Indian Words. Many Indian terms were adopted by the settlers, especially as they encountered unfamiliar plants and animals. Most of these words entered the language in the 17th and early 18th centuries. See INDIAN WORDS (AMERICAN INDIAN).

French Words. The French were among the earliest explorers and settlers of America and consequently contributed a unique though small body of words to American English. Some of these are regionalisms characteristic of Louisiana and the surrounding area (see GULF SOUTHERN DIALECT; LOUISIANA FRENCH). Others are words that the French in America adopted from Indian or other languages, which then passed into American English. Some of these are borrowed from Canadian (see CANADIAN ENGLISH). For a fuller discussion of words from French see FRENCH WORDS.

Dutch Words. The Dutch were among the first settlers in the New World, and they contributed a handful of important words to American English. See DUTCH WORDS.

Spanish Words. Terms from Spanish form the largest group of loanwords in American English. In part this is due to the continuing influence of Mexican culture. Because the Spanish had established a hacienda culture throughout much of the West, many of these borrowings are an important part of the dialects of that region. See PACIFIC SOUTHWEST, ROCKY MOUNTAIN, SOUTHWESTERN, and WESTERN dialects. See also SPANISH WORDS.

German Words. German loanwords entered American English from immigrant speakers rather than from a conquered colonial rival. For more information see GERMAN WORDS; PENNSYLVANIA DUTCH; PENNSYLVANIA GERMAN-ENGLISH.

West African Words. The West African languages brought by blacks in the 18th century have also contributed to the uniqueness of the American vocabulary. See AFRICAN WORDS; BLACK ENGLISH; GULLAH.

Archaic and Dialectal British Terms. The English colonists brought with them three main dialects from the mother country. Most of the Puritans spoke the East Anglian dialect of the southern and southeastern counties of England; a majority of the Quakers brought the Midland English dialect. Later, the third major dialect, the Ulster dialect, arrived with the influx of Scotch-Irish colonists. Many of the words and phrases of these dialects gained general currency in America while remaining dialectal in England.

In some cases the British words current in the 17th and 18th centuries simply died out in later British speech but continued to be used in American speech. Certain of these archaic terms have reentered the British English vocabulary from American English.

Selected Vocabulary. The following is a list of terms that are or were dialectal or obsolete in England but remained generally current in America:

andiron = 'one of a pair of supports for the logs in a fireplace'

bug = 'insect'; in Standard British it means 'bedbug'

cabin = 'poor or rough dwelling'

***catercorner** = 'in a diagonal or oblique position'

chore = 'routine task or job'

clodhopper = 'country bumpkin'

copious = 'plentiful, abundant'

cordwood = 'wood piled in cords and usually used for fuel'

cross-purpose = 'an unintentionally opposing purpose'

deck = 'pack of cards'

din = 'noise'

drool = 'to salivate and dribble'

druggist = 'a dispenser of medicines, pharmacist'; in British English *chemist*

fall = 'autumn'

flapjack = '*pancake'

greenhorn = 'inexperienced person, novice, newcomer'

guess = 'to suppose'

loan = 'to lend'

molasses = 'thick syrup obtained when sugar is refined'

offal = 'waste, byproduct of a process'

ornate = 'adorned, ornamented'

polliwog = 'tadpole'

pond = 'a small, natural or artificial body of water'; in England it means 'artificial body of water'

progress = 'to advance or develop'; readopted in England after 1800

quit = 'to stop'

ragamuffin = 'someone in dirty, ragged clothes'

raise = (1) 'to breed' (2) 'to rear' (3) 'to grow'

reckon = 'to suppose'

shoat = 'young weaned pig'

sick = 'ill'

squirt = 'small, usually annoying person'

stock = 'cattle'

trash = 'refuse, garbage'

underpinning = 'basis, support'

*Appears as separate entry

Coined Words and New Uses. American English is a prolific coiner of new words and usages, many of which have been adopted by English speakers around the world. New coinages are created in several ways, and some special vocabularies are direct expressions of the American pioneer experience. (1) *Tall talk.* Not until well into the 19th century did a genuinely home-grown American consciousness begin to make itself felt. America's eyes turned westward, and an aggressive, self-confident, uncouth, daring spirit found its embodiment in folk heroes like Andrew Jackson, Daniel Boone, and Davy Crockett. It also found its expression in the *tall talk* of the backwoods, the speech of men who bragged they could "lick their weight in wildcats and chaw off the ear of a grizzly." A typical example of tall talk is found in this passage from one of the many anonymous books attributed to Davy Crockett:

> I jocosely asked the ragged hunter, who was a smart, active young fellow, of the steamboat and alligator breed, whether he was a rhinoceros or a

hyena, as he was so eager for a fight with the invaders. "Neither the one, nor t'other, Colonel," says he, "but a whole menagerie in myself. I'm shaggy as a bear, wolfish about the head, active as a cougar, and can grin like a hyena, until the bark will curl off a gum log. There's a sprinkling of all sorts in me, from the lion down to the skunk; and before the war is over you'll pronounce me an entire zoological institute, or I miss a figure in my calculation. I promise to swallow Santa Anna without gagging, if you will only skewer back his ears, and grease his head a little."

—*Life of David Crockett* (1865)

Selected Vocabulary. This kind of exuberant talk also created a picturesque vocabulary of preposterous words. Though most of these have little or no currency today, some still live in certain regional dialects. Here are some of the best examples of tall-talk expressions:

absquatulate = 'to go away'
blustiferous = 'blustery, violent'
***bodacious** = (1) 'complete' (2) 'remarkable'
breadbasket = 'stomach'
catawampus, cattywampus = (1) 'fierce, savage' (2) 'askew, awry'
cavort = 'to prance, frisk'
circumsurround = 'to encircle, surround completely'
clamjamfry = 'nonsense, rubbish'
clodpolish /**klŏd**-pōl-ĭsh/ = 'awkward' (from *clodpole*)
cohogle = 'to confuse, confound'
conbobberation = 'commotion, confusion'
creature comfort = '*whiskey'
dadshamed = 'confounded, damned'
darnation = 'damnation'
dashy trashy = 'trifling, worthless'
dedodgment = 'exit'
exflunctify = 'to use up or wear out'
explaterate = 'to explain, talk'
explicitrize = 'to censure'
flagratious = 'flagrant'
flambergast = 'to flabbergast, astonish'
flipperty-gibbet = 'at once'
flugens = 'interjection expressing strong feelings'
flummuck = 'to outdo, overcome'
gemornetty = 'interjection expressing surprise'
giraffed = 'deceived, humbugged'
grandiferous = 'extremely well'
helliferocious = 'extremely ferocious'
honeyfuggle = 'to cheat'
hornswoggle = 'to deceive, bamboozle'
in cahoots = 'in league with, conspiring with'
killniferously = 'fondly'
lickspittle = 'contemptible person, bootlicker'
locumsgilly = 'to overcome'
mollagausauger = 'brutish or bullying fellow'
monstracious = 'huge, monstrous'
monstropolous = 'monstrous'
obflisticate = 'to do away with, obliterate'
odoriferous = 'excited, wrought up'
overscrumptious = 'overparticular, fussy'
peedoodles = (1) (noun) 'nervousness' (2) (adjective) 'jittery'
pestiferous = 'pesky'
puckerstopple = 'to embarrass'
rambunctious = 'wild, uncontrolled'
rampoose = 'to go on a rampage'
ripsniptiously = 'in a fiery, lively manner'
sevagerous = 'very savage'
sharp-set = 'hungry'
shy = 'trial, chance'
singecate = 'violent-tempered person'
sizzled = 'drunk'
skirmudgeon = 'rascal'
slang-whanger = 'orator'
slooney = 'worthless person, nincompoop'
sockdologer = 'a heavy blow'
sumtotalize = 'to sum up'
suspicion = 'very small amount'
swipey = 'drunk'
teetotaciously = 'completely, totally'
wrap-rascal = 'hunting shirt'

*Appears as separate entry

(2) *Language of the frontier.* Though the mainstream of American English flowed from east to west with the push of civilization, there was also a countercurrent that flowed from the fringes of the frontier back to the East. The language of the Wild West has left its unmistakable mark on American

speech. The words and phrases of Western work and play have created much of the distinctiveness of the Western dialects as well (see PACIFIC SOUTHWEST DIALECT; WESTERN DIALECT). One favorite Wild West pastime that has given American English quite a sizable body of words is gambling and card playing. Here are some of the commoner expressions:

ace *or* **something up one's sleeve** = 'means of cheating, an advantage kept in reserve, usually illegitimately'
ace in the hole = 'secret but legitimate advantage'
blue-chip (stock) = 'the best money stock paying good dividends'
bluff = 'to pretend to have an advantage or strength, fool or deceive'
break even = 'to make gains and losses that balance exactly'
call one's bluff = 'to challenge someone to carry out his or her threat'
cards stacked against one = 'circumstances being such that one is at a disadvantage'
cash in one's chips = 'to die'
deal = 'any transaction or arrangement'
dealing from the bottom of the deck = 'taking unfair advantage'
deal (one) in = 'to include (someone) as a participant'
deal (one) out = 'to exclude (someone) as a participant'
duck = 'to back out or default'
feed the kitty = 'to contribute to a fund'
finesse = 'to proceed with tact and cleverness'
follow suit = 'to do what someone else has done'
for openers = 'as a beginning action in an activity'
go (someone) one better = 'to outperform or excel'
hit the jackpot = 'to have a stroke of good luck'
in hock = 'in debt' (from the game of faro, the *hocketty card* being the last card in the faro box)
in the chips = 'wealthy, financially secure'
load the dice = 'to take unfair advantage'
long suit = 'something at which one excels'
pass the buck = 'to shirk one's responsibility' (literally 'to pass or forgo one's deal')
play both ends against the middle = 'to lessen the potential of a loss by making counterbalancing bets, investments, etc.'
play one's ace = 'to use one's best resource'
poker face = 'a face that does not express thoughts or feelings'
***renege** = 'to fail to keep a promise or an obligation'
shoestring = 'a barely adequate amount of capital' (from faro)
square deal = 'honest transaction'
stack the deck = 'to arrange a situation secretly for cheating'
string along = (1) 'to follow or accept trustingly' (2) 'to fool or deceive (someone)'; in gambling it means 'to continue play'
when the chips are down = 'when matters reach a decisive point'

*Appears as separate entry

(3) *Compounds, affixes, and functional shifts.* One of the two commonest types of new coinages is an extension of or an addition to the meaning of an established word, like *apartment* or *folder*. The other is the invention of a new word altogether *(cocktail, gerrymander, highfalutin)*. New words in American English are usually invented either by linking two existing English nouns (as in *Sun Belt, bookstore, handlebar mustache*) or by combining Latin or Greek roots and affixes, as in *automobile* and in H. L. Mencken's *ecdysiast* (= 'stripteaser').

American English is especially fond of compounding words; for example, the *Dictionary of Americanisms* lists more than 135 words compounded with *corn* (*corn basket, corn bread, cornhusker, corn liquor,* etc.) and more than 100 compounded with *yellow*. American English also tends to coin and use more freely nouns compounded from a verb plus a preposition or other particle; for example, *blowout, brushoff, buildup, checkoff, checkup, fallout, feedback, knockout, lockout, payoff, runaround, run-in, setup, showdown,* and *workout.*

Here are some examples of how American English freely uses prefixes and suffixes to create new words:

anti-: *antifederalist; antislavery; antisecession; anti-brain-truster; antifreeze; anti-Prohibition*

de-: *debunk; dehorn; demoralize; demote; detassel*

-ee: *escapee; draftee; trainee; addressee; evacuee; pollee*

-ette: *usherette; drum majorette; dinette; kitchenette*

-ist, -ician, -or: *receptionist; cosmetologist; cosmetician; beautician; mortician; electrician; realtor*

-ite: *socialite; laborite*

* **-ize:** *itemize; demoralize; burglarize; slenderize; winterize; hospitalize; Americanize*

-ster: *gangster; speedster*

*Appears as separate entry

American English also takes greater liberties with grammatical categories. New words are frequently created by shifting the function of an existing word. Nouns are used as verbs: to *audition;* to *author* a book; to *captain* a team; to *chair* a meeting; to *contact;* to *date;* to *park;* to *package;* to *program;* to *pressure* someone; to *radio* a message; to *service;* to *solo;* to *vacation.* Verbs are used as nouns: a big *push;* a good *buy;* an *assist;* an athletic *meet;* a *release.* Adjectives are used as nouns: *briefs; casuals; comics; formals; funnies; a commercial* (= 'advertisement'); *hopefuls; uppers; lovelies; Reds.*

Finally, American English is fond of phrases used as adjectives: *portal-to-portal* pay; *door-to-door* service; *on-the-spot* conference; *on-site* inspection; *off-the-record* speech; *out-of-town* district; *down-the-line* support; *round-the-clock* watch.

Selected Vocabulary. The following is a small offering of American coined words. Many have become international. The list taken as a whole thematically reflects aspects of American history and character.

abolitionist
affiliate = 'to associate'
affiliation
Afro
alumnus See ALMA MATER, ALUMNA, ALUMNUS.
anesthesia
apartment = 'a usually rented residence of several rooms'
appendectomy, appendicitis
appreciation = 'an increase in value'
armory = 'place where arms are manufactured'
assemblyman
Atomic Age
automobile
baby-sit
baking powder
balding
ballpark
ballyhoo
basketball
bazooka
be-bop
belittle
Bermuda shorts
bifocals
billion = 'a thousand million'
bindery
bleachers
blizzard
bloomers
blowhard
blurb
bobsled
bogus
bookstore
boom = 'an increase in the economy, population, etc.'
* **boondocks**
* **boondoggle**
boost = 'to lift from below,' hence 'to promote'
bootleg
bootlick
bourbon
boyfriend
brainstorm
branch = 'creek'
bromide = 'platitude'
* **buffalo**

bugaboo
bulldozer
burglarize
burgle
bushwhacker
buzz saw
cable
cablegram
caboodle = 'the whole lot'
campus
can = 'sealed metal container for food'
carpetbagger
casket = 'coffin'
chain saw
checkers = 'a board game'
cheerleader
chewing gum
claim = 'piece of land for mining or settling'
class = 'students of the same academic grouping'
cloudburst
cobbler = 'fruit-pie dessert'
cocktail
coed, coeducation
complected
conferee
confidence man
congressional, congressman
conniption
conscript (verb)
* **contact** (verb)
corn = 'Indian corn or maize'
corner (verb)
corsage
cosmic ray
cowcatcher
cracker-barrel
crackerjack
crank = 'eccentric person'
craps = 'gambling dice game'
crazy bone
credit card
creek = 'small *stream'
crook = 'criminal'
crosscut saw
crush = 'infatuation'
currency = 'money'
custom-made
cut corners
deadhead
dean = 'college administrator'
demoralize
demote
department store
dicker
dishrag
district attorney
dive = 'disreputable establishment for drinking or entertainment'
divide = 'mountains forming a watershed between two river systems'
dock = 'wharf, pier'
donate
doodle (verb)
dope, dopey
down = 'to swallow'
downtown (adverb and noun)
drink = 'a body of water'
drugstore
dry = 'opposed to the sale of liquor'
dry goods
dude
duplex
editorial, editorialize
efficiency expert
elective = 'nonrequired academic course'
electric chair
electrician
electrocute
elevator
emigrant
equal rights
escalator
everglade
eye-opener = 'a drink of alcohol, usually in the morning'
faculty = 'the teaching staff of a college or university'
fan = 'enthusiastic devotee'
feature = 'to display or highlight'
fedora
feel like = 'to have a desire or inclination for (doing something)'
feisty
Ferris wheel
fink
firebug
firecracker
firewater
fish story

*Appears as separate entry

fix = (1) (noun) 'a situation' (2) (verb) 'to prepare (food)'
fizzle = 'to fail'
flophouse
flunk = 'to fail an examination or a school course'
folder = 'cover for holding loose papers'
fraternity = 'male college organization'
free-for-all
freewheeling
freeze = 'to remain motionless'
freezer
freight = 'transported goods'
fresh = 'impudent'
freshman
frypan
fudge
full-blooded
fumigator
fundamentalist
furlough
gabfest
galoot
gangster
gas = (1) 'gasoline' (2) 'pretentious talk'
gasoline
gat = 'pistol'
genocide
gerrymander
get-up = 'initiative'
ghostwrite
Gibson girl
gimmick
gin mill = 'low-class saloon'
girlfriend
glare ice = 'ice having a glassy surface'
G-man
go-ahead = 'ambition, spirit'
goatee
goldarn(ed)
goldbrick = (1) (noun) 'a bar of gold' (2) (verb) 'to swindle' (3) (verb) 'to shirk'
gold digger = 'a woman whose aim is to obtain money from the men she associates with'
gold standard
gooey
goose bump See GOOSE FLESH.
gopher
gorilla
go-to-meeting
grab bag
grade = (1) (noun) 'the degree of slope in a road' (2) (verb) 'to smooth up or level' (3) (noun) 'a year course in elementary school' (4) (noun) 'a mark given as an estimate of academic achievement'
graduate school
graft = 'to obtain money dishonestly'
graham = 'of whole-wheat flour'
grain belt
grammar school
gramophone
grand = 'one thousand dollars'
grass roots
greenback
grit = 'obstinate courage, determination'
grouch
grouchy
groundhog
grubstake
gubernatorial
gulch
gully = 'to erode'
gumshoe
gun = 'pistol'
gym
half-breed
halitosis
hamburger
handlebar mustache
hangover = 'the aftereffect of drinking excessive alcohol'
hard-shelled
hash house
haymaker = 'violent blow'
hayride
haywire
haze = 'to embarrass, humiliate'
* **headcheese**
headline = 'newspaper caption'
heeled = 'wealthy'
hellbent
highball
highbrow
highfalutin
high school
hijack, hijacker
hillbilly
hindsight
hitch = (1) (noun) 'period of time' (2) (verb) 'to harness (an animal), yoke, tie up'

hitchhike
hitch (up) = 'to marry'
hobo
hoedown
holdup
homebody
homemade
homestead
homestretch
homogenized milk
honky-tonk
hoodlum
hookup = 'a connection of apparatus, resources, etc.'
hoopla
Hoosier
hootchy-kootchy
horse sense
horse thief
hot dog
humdinger
hunky-dory
husky = 'strong, vigorous'
hustle = (1) (noun) 'drive, energetic effort' (2) (verb) 'to exert oneself briskly'
hydrant
hydraulic
icebox = 'refrigerator'
ice cream
ice storm = 'freezing rain'
immigrant
inaugural
Indian file = 'single file'
Indian summer
inflation = 'overexpansion (of money and prices)'
insider = 'anyone who has confidential information or influence'
installment plan
intern
interurban
itemize
jackknife
jackpot
jalopy
jamboree
jaywalk
jazz
jeep
jell = (1) 'to congeal' (2) 'to take shape or become definite'
jerkwater
jinx
jitters
joint = 'establishment of low repute'
josh = 'to joke, banter'
joy ride
jumbo
jumping-off place
junior = 'third-year high school or college student'
junior college
junk dealer
junket = 'pleasure trip taken by an official at government expense'
junk shop
junkyard
kangaroo court
katydid
kazoo
keister, keester
keno
kerosene
Kewpie doll
kibitz, kibitzer
killdeer
know-how
lame duck
land grant
landslide
lemon = 'worthless person or thing'
lengthy
libber
lickety-split
Linotype
lipstick
loan shark
* **lobby** = 'to promote specific legislative action'
* **locate** (verb)
location
loco
log cabin
logger
lollapalooza
* **lollygag**
lordy
lousy
lowbrow
lowdown
lumberjack

*Appears as separate entry

lunatic fringe
lunkhead
lynch
mail order
malted milk
maple syrup
martini
maverick
medicine man
memorize
merger
midway
Midwest
mimeograph
miscegenation
mixer = 'social gathering'
mockingbird
morgue
moron, moronic
mortician
mosey
motorcade
movie
mucilage
muscle (verb)
notions = 'small articles or wares'
odometer
* **O.K., okay**
oleomargarine
organized labor
Ouija board
outdoors
outfit (noun)
overalls
overcoat
pack = 'to carry'
painkiller
palooka
panhandle, panhandler
parade ground
parking meter
parkway
patent leather
pathfinder
peanut
peanut butter
pep
pep talk
phone
phonograph
phony
physical education
pixilated
pocketbook
poison ivy
poker = 'betting card game'
poker chips
policyholder
polio
pooch
pool = 'fund'
poolroom
poplar
poppycock
* **porch** = 'covered gallery, veranda'
postage
postgraduate
pragmatist
praline
predicate (verb)
preempt
probation
probe = 'to conduct an investigation'
prom
proofreader
prorate
prosecuting attorney
prospect (verb)
prospector
public domain
pussyfoot
quarantine (verb)
racketeer
raft (verb)
rail-splitter
rain barrel
rally (noun)
range = 'area of uncultivated land'
rapid = 'fast-moving section of a stream'
rapid transit
rapist
rattlesnake
razz
razzle-dazzle
realtor
recess = 'school playtime'
referendum
reform school
refrigerator
release (noun)
relocate See LOCATE.
rendition

reservation = 'tract of land set aside for use and occupancy of Native Americans'
restroom
resurface
revamp
revolver
rifle
rig
ritzy
roach
roadster
rookie
root beer
roughhouse
roundup
route (verb) See ROUT, ROUTE.
rowdy
ruckus
runway
safe-deposit
sagebrush
scalawag
school district
schooner
scrawny
scrimshaw
scrumptious
seaboard
senior = 'fourth-year high school or college student'
senior citizen
sex appeal
shack
sharecropper
shenanigan
shindig
ship (verb)
shortchange
shotgun
showboat
shuck
shyster
sideburns
sidekick
sideshow
sidetrack
sidewalk
sissy
skulduggery
skyrocket
skyscraper
slapstick
sleuth
slingshot
smart aleck
smidgen
snowplow
snowshoe
soda jerk
sophomore
sourdough
speak-easy
spellbinder
spelling bee
splurge
spring fever
standoff
steamboat
stenographer
stickup
stooge
stool pigeon
straw boss
straw poll or **vote**
stump = 'to confuse, baffle'
stunt
sundae
swamp (verb)
tacky
tattletale
T-bone steak
teddy bear
telegram
telephone
tenderfoot
tenderloin
tenement house
thermos
thumbtack
ticker tape
tidewater
tie-up
timberline
tinhorn
tintinnabulation
tintype
tornado
torpedo
* **tote**
tractor
transfer (noun)

*Appears as separate entry

transient (noun)
truant officer
truck farm
tucker = 'to tire'
tuna
tutti-frutti
tuxedo
two-by-four
typewriter
typo
underbrush
underdog
unicycle
upcountry
upgrade
upholster
upstate
urinalysis
vacation
valedictorian
veteran = 'ex-serviceman'
weasel (verb)
whippoorwill
white-collar See BLUE-COLLAR, WHITE-COLLAR.
whiz
whole-hog
whoopee
wisecrack
witch hazel
witness stand
woodsy
woozy
Yankee
yellow journalism
yep
zoot suit

amid, amidst. These variants, both meaning 'in the middle of, surrounded by,' are equally correct; *amid* is the more usual choice.

amok, amuck. The common phrase *run amok* literally means 'to go on a murderous rampage.' For the origin, see MALAY WORDS. Figuratively, the phrase means 'to go out of control, act irresponsibly and disastrously':

> Maladjusted people who feel humiliated still occasionally wreak havoc on society by running amok.
> —Charles and Cherry Lindholm, *Science Digest*

> The nation's first attempt at socialized health care has run amok.
> —Dan Thomasson and Carl West, *Reader's Digest*

The phrase is sometimes used like *run afoul of* = 'to run into trouble with,' and *amok* by itself is sometimes used as if it meant 'crazily full of, awash':

> The Bonomi's Cabinet ran amok of Italy's traditional political chaos.
> —Charles L. Mee, *Meeting at Potsdam*

> True, the afternoon soaps are full of problems, but they are problems (amnesia, abortion, infidelity) that do not seem like real problems to the rich, whose lives are often happily amok with abortion and infidelity anyway.
> —Stephen Birmingham, *Panorama*

◇ ***Recommendation.*** The latter two uses quoted are mistakes. *Run amok* means much the same as *go berserk*, literally or figuratively. The older spelling *amuck* is preferred in Britain. *Amok* is now clearly the prevailing American form.

among, amongst. *Amongst* is now a less-used variant of *among*, but it is still correct and by no means old-fashioned. See also BETWEEN, AMONG.

ampersand. The sign & or *&*, meaning 'and,' is now seldom used in print or formal writing, such as business correspondence, except sometimes in the names of companies—*Smith & Wesson; A & P*—and in a few abbreviated expressions such as *R & R* = 'rest and recuperation' and *R & D* = 'research and development.' One noteworthy use of it is by *Rolling Stone* magazine in the term *rock & roll*, a style that neatly avoids the ugly abbreviation *'n'*. It is always permissible, and often desirable, to write *and* instead of using the ampersand, even in business names: *Smith and Wesson; rock-and-roll.*

In private letters and other personal writings, ampersands of various shapes are widely used.

amphibology, sometimes also *amphiboly,* is an ambiguity that arises from the syntactic or grammatical structure of a phrase or sentence. *For sale, Irish wolfhound, eats anything, very fond of children* is, for example, an amphibology that might give a prospective buyer pause. Amphibology is usually simply the result of sloppy writing, as in *It was an antique French writing desk such as might have been used by a lady of the court of Louis XIV with bowed legs,* or sometimes mere lack of punctuation, as in the familiar road sign *Slow Children Ahead.* But it can also be used deliberately to mislead. The ancient oracles were famous for their ability to phrase their predictions so ambiguously that no matter what happened, they could always claim to have been right. Similarly, the philosopher Immanuel Kant cited the example of an amphibolous pledge made by King Francis I to the Holy Roman emperor Charles V: "What my brother Charles wishes, that I wish also." What each wanted, notes Kant, was to annex the independent city of Milan.

Related to amphibology is EQUIVOCATION, in which ambiguity arises from using an individual word in more than one sense. See also FALLACY.

an. See A, AN.

anaphora. See TAUTOLOGY AND PLEONASM.

anchor, anchorman, etc. The noun *anchor* has evolved a curious spread of meanings.
(1) The original (human) *anchor* is the rear man or woman, often the heaviest, in a tug-of-war team; metaphorically, the anchor at the end of the rope.
(2) Hence, in other sports the *anchor* or *anchorman* is the team member, often the strongest or most skilled, who competes last, as on a relay team in swimming or track.
(3) At the U.S. Military Academy at West Point and elsewhere, *anchor* is an ironic term for the person who graduates in last place.

> The traditional "Anchor Man" not only holds his diploma but a bag of 696 dollar bills from classmates.
> —*New York Times*

(4) In broadcasting, the *anchor* or *anchorman, anchorwoman,* or *anchorperson* is the senior member of a news-reading team; this use preserves both the sense of 'heavyweight' and that of 'last player,' since the anchor typically puts himself or herself on last to wind up the program. There is now also *co-anchor,* a word that seems slightly strained and is untrue to the metaphor, and the verb *anchor* = 'to act as anchor for (a program)':

> [Mary Richardson] WNAC-TV's first ever full-time anchorperson . . . Co-anchor of the evening news on Sacramento's KCRA-TV for the last two years . . . —*Boston Globe*

(5) In the retailing business an *anchor* is the biggest outlet in a chain or the biggest store in a shopping center:

> . . . eager to sign a contract with East Bay Development Corp. of Reading to develop the tract, with a K-Mart store as anchor tenant.
> —*Springfield* (Mass.) *Morning Union*

and. (1) *Uncoordinated series.* In a series like *a, b, and c,* the items listed should be equivalent grammatically; that is, they should all be nouns or noun phrases, or all verbs or verb phrases, etc. Uncoordinated sentences often occur:

> . . . he was glad to see that most of the space people were open, helpful, and had a sense of humor. —*Forbes*

◇ ***Recommendation.*** The example shows a definite error of sentence structure. It should be rewritten "were open and helpful and had a sense of humor."

(2) *And who. And* can be used to link two parallel phrases or two parallel clauses, but it should not be used to link a phrase with a

clause. This typically occurs with noun phrases that are followed by relative clauses:

> . . . a distant cousin called Thomas Knight, a landowner with property both in Kent and Hampshire and who lived in a big mansion, Godmersham Park near Canterbury.
>
> —David Cecil, *A Portrait of Jane Austen*

> Robert Kunzig, a Pennsylvania political ally of Minority Leader Hugh Scott, and who had been made head of the General Services Administration, felt . . .
>
> —William Safire, *Before the Fall*

◇ ***Recommendation.*** The simplest form of the rule is that *and who* should only follow a previous *who* clause (or more than one of them); the same applies to *and which.* The examples can be rewritten in several ways: (a) by making two parallel clauses: "a landowner who owned property . . . and who lived in . . . ," "Kunzig, who was an ally . . . and who had been . . ."; (b) by making two parallel phrases: "a landowner with property . . . and living in . . . ," "Kunzig, an ally of . . . and a man who had been . . ."; (c) by removing the *and:* "a landowner with property . . . who lived in. . . ." But this would not work in the second example, since *who* would then attach itself to a wrong antecedent ("Scott" instead of "Kunzig").

(3) *And/or.* This device originated as a legalism, which has been widely adopted in business and then in general usage. It is also widely condemned by stylists.

> . . . should prepare to send Eisenhower one or more American divisions and/or all the French divisions which he was capable of receiving . . .
>
> —Winston Churchill, *Triumph and Tragedy*

> Commander after commander was removed and/or shot at his orders.
>
> —Harrison E. Salisbury, *The Unknown War*

Critics dislike *and/or* because it forms a word with the nonverbal device of a slash mark and because it seems an ugly evasion of proper sentence structure: according to them, *A and/or B* should be written out either *A and B, or either* (*of them*) or *A or B, or both* (*of them*). Note, however, that neither of these solutions would work at all smoothly with the examples quoted. The critics would retort, "Then rewrite the whole sentence from scratch."

◇ ***Recommendation.*** We confess to feeling that *and/or* is a legitimate innovation that often demonstrates its efficiency both in speech and in writing. But conservative feeling against it is strong. Be prepared for trouble if you use it in highly formal contexts.

anecdote. An *anecdote* is a short account of an interesting or amusing incident. In the social sciences, the adjective *anecdotal* is now widely used to mean 'based only on reports of individual occurrences, not on adequate statistical evidence':

> In the past, many doctors have given anecdotal evidence that the practice of defensive medicine is rising. But the AMA poll . . . is one of the few studies to have documented the trend on a statistical basis.
>
> —Lawrence K. Altman, *Reader's Digest*

anent /ə-nĕnt/. This old preposition means 'concerning, about.' Still standard in Scottish legal usage, it is sometimes used elsewhere to achieve a certain mock-literary effect:

> Professor Bennett is quite correct in his remark anent the wariness of English educators.
>
> —Thomas Pyles, *Reform in Latin Pronunciation*

> But Mencken did not stick his neck out anent *kibosh*'s parentage.
>
> —Leo Rosten, *The Joys of Yiddish*

Angle, Anglia, Anglican. In the 5th century A.D. a Germanic people of the small district of Angul on the coast of Schleswig, Germany, who were called the *Engle* or, in Latin, *Angli*, crossed the North Sea and settled in the old Roman province of Britain. They are known to historians as the *Angles,* and the parts of Britain settled by them and their relatives the Saxons became known as *Anglia* (see also ENGLAND, ENGLISH). One of the kingdoms they created in Britain was called *East Anglia;* this name still survives as the unofficial name of the eastward bulge of the country containing the counties of Norfolk and Suffolk.

In Medieval Latin the word *Anglicanus* meant 'belonging to the English,' and the English church was called *Anglicana ecclesia,* in English 'Anglican church.' After the Protestant Reformation *Anglican* was kept as the title of the Church of England, whose members can be called *Anglicans.*

Anglo. This new word has been extracted from *Anglo-Saxon. Anglo* is used to refer to people of English, or English-speaking, descent, especially in places where they are not a majority:

> There is a feeling among the "Anglos," as the English-speaking Canadians are called, that they have by default let the "Francos," or the French-speaking minority, dominate a debate that is critical to Canada's future.
> —Dusko Dodler, *Boston Globe*

> . . . a Canadian customs agent spoke for his Anglo countrymen this morning. "Let 'em go," he said [referring to the Quebecois].
> —William K. Stevens, *New York Times*

> The illegal immigrant from Mexico has more right than any other illegal immigrant alien who comes from across the ocean, because the Anglos stole Texas, Oklahoma, Colorado, New Mexico, Arizona, Nevada etc. from Mexico during the Manifest Destiny period.
> —Raymond Morantes (letter), *Time*

Anglo-Indian words. See INDIAN WORDS (INDIA).

Anglo-Saxon. After the fall of the Roman Empire, Britain was invaded and settled by the Germanic Angles and Saxons. Their language (from about A.D. 700 to about 1100) is now most usually known as *Old English.* Collectively, the people themselves and their Old English–speaking descendants are called the *Anglo-Saxons.* When *Anglo-Saxon* is used in a modern context, it means 'English' or 'of English descent,' without specific reference to the original Angles and Saxons. See also ENGLAND, ENGLISH; OLD ENGLISH.

animism. See PERSONIFICATION.

antagonist comes from Greek athletics, meaning 'a struggler-against, an opponent in a struggle such as wrestling' (from *anti-* = 'against' + *agōn* = 'struggle, contest'). Hence, it also means 'opponent, enemy in general.' The word may look like an exact opposite of *protagonist,* but etymologically it isn't. For the reasons see PROTAGONIST.

anthropomorphism. See PERSONIFICATION.

anticipate. Properly, to *anticipate* an event, a move, or a situation is to foresee it and respond to it by taking some action ahead of time:

> For any commander, trying to anticipate the enemy's moves is an essential preoccupation.
> —William C. Westmoreland, *A Soldier Reports*

> He studies the pitcher, trying to block out all distractions, and making mental pictures of what he anticipates the pitch will be.
> —Dave Anderson, *Reader's Digest*

To anticipate a person or persons is to forestall them, do something or get somewhere before they do:

> Epicureanism . . . anticipated the Jews and Christians in divorcing doctrine from local sovereignties.
> —Moses Hadas, *Hellenistic Culture*

But this verb is now often used to mean merely 'expect,' or even 'intend, plan,' with no sense of response or preparatory action:

They anticipate the Lucas [restaurant] to be successful enough to begin a chain of "theme" restaurants with a theater theme.

—Krys Keller, *Savannah Morning News*

I anticipate sending to the Congress early in the spring a set of further proposals. . . .

—Jimmy Carter (quoted), *New York Times*

◇ ***Recommendation.*** The use of *anticipate* should include a sense of foreseeing and responding to events or the actions of others. If only expectation or intention is meant, as in the last two examples above, the simpler *expect* or *intend* is the better choice.

antithesis. The word *antithesis* (plural *antitheses*) means 'complete opposite, direct contrast': *Nazism was the antithesis of all that was best in German culture.* As a figure of speech, *antithesis* is defined as 'contrasting ideas expressed in adjacent words, clauses, or sentences.'

The ideal antithesis is perfectly balanced:

Sex has become one of the most discussed subjects of modern times. The Victorians pretended it did not exist; the moderns pretend that nothing else exists.

—Fulton J. Sheen, *Peace of Soul*

Nothing so lifts a soldier's morale as getting a letter from home, and nothing so depresses him as reading it.

—Thornton Wilder (quoted), Harpo Marx, *Harpo Speaks*

A specially balanced antithesis may be formed from a precise inversion of terms:

America did not invent human rights. . . . Human rights invented America.

—Jimmy Carter, farewell speech (1981)

But many antitheses are not perfectly balanced and are no less effective for that. For example, the famous "Millions for defense, but not one cent for tribute" probably falls just short of perfect symmetry because the word "tribute" is not the logical opposite of "defense." The ancient Greek rhetoricians identified several subcategories of antithesis, both balanced and unbalanced. For instance, metaphorical antitheses, such as *an iron fist in a velvet glove,* they called *antitheton.* (Some expressions that seem to be antitheses—such as "That's one small step for a man, one giant leap for mankind," said by astronaut Neil Armstrong on the moon, July 20, 1969—are actually complementary terms in logic.) One of the oldest and most effective tricks in rhetoric is *accumulated antithesis,* or the piling of one antithesis on top of another until a desired effect has been achieved. A modern example of accumulated antithesis is George Bernard Shaw's marathon denunciation of the English middle class in act 3 of *Man and Superman.* Here is a short extract from this famous tirade:

They are not moral: they are only conventional. They are not virtuous: they are only cowardly. . . . not dutiful, only sheepish; not public spirited, only patriotic; not courageous, only quarrelsome; not determined, only obstinate; not masterful, only domineering; not self-controlled, only obtuse; not self-respecting, only vain; not kind, only sentimental. . . .

See also FIGURES OF SPEECH.

antonym, a word whose meaning is the opposite of another's, as opposed to a SYNONYM. *Right* and *wrong, sweet* and *sour,* and the like are pairs of antonyms.

anxious. The primary meaning of *anxious* is 'distressed in mind,' especially 'deeply worried about the outcome of some situation':

. . . the residents, many of whom have built their own homes and never plan to leave, were naturally anxious to find out just what the state intended to do with their hard-earned property.

—*New Jersey Monthly*

But *anxious* is quite often used in the positive sense 'keenly wishing (for or to do some particular thing),' without any suggestion of distress or worry:

> I've brought along someone I know you're anxious to meet.
> —Dorothy L. Sayers, *Gaudy Night*

> Lady Bird had invested most of her inheritance in a radio station, and they were both anxious to expand into television.
> —Sam Houston Johnson, *My Brother Lyndon*

Some critics disapprove of this use, claiming that *anxious* should always connote distress, leaving *eager* as the positive word. This simply ignores the facts of usage. In practice, *anxious* is used positively just as often as negatively. The noun *anxiety*, on the other hand, usually has the negative sense 'severe worry':

> There is nothing so degrading as the constant anxiety about one's means of livelihood.
> —W. Somerset Maugham, *Of Human Bondage*

As a term in psychology, *anxiety* refers to a state of acute fear without objective cause.

◇ ***Recommendation.*** It is a mistake to try to force usage to be neatly logical. *Anxious* means either 'worried' or 'eager,' while its noun *anxiety* almost always means only 'severe worry.'

any. There is a common construction combining a superlative adjective with a phrase in which *any* modifies a singular noun whose sense seems to be plural.

> We boast that we belong to the nineteenth century and are making the most rapid strides of any nation.
> —Henry David Thoreau, *Walden*

> Argentina . . . has the biggest middle class of any country in Latin America.
> —David Reed, *Reader's Digest*

> Divorced women have the lowest household incomes of any group of women surveyed. —*Ms.*

Some believe that this construction is unacceptable and should be rewritten, either by changing *any* to *all* and making the noun it modifies plural—"the biggest middle class of all countries in Latin America"—or by making the adjective a comparative with *any other* "more rapid strides than any other nation," etc.

◇ ***Recommendation.*** The construction isn't easy to analyze, but it's firmly established as a natural idiom of the language. Rewrite it if you prefer, but it's standard and correct as is.

anymore is an adverb used in negative sentences, meaning 'now, still':

> . . . he says he doesn't want to do it anymore.
> —Lloyd G. Smith, *Reader's Digest*

Any more is a two-word adjectival phrase meaning 'additional, further' and should not be written solid, as in the following:

> . . . saw his scholastic grades drop to a point which precluded anymore extra-curricular activities.
> —*Boston Herald American*

anyplace, someplace. These two adverbs are Standard American English, but they are still distinctly less formal than *anywhere* and *somewhere*.

anyways, anywheres. These two adverbs are dialectal and nonstandard variants of *anyway* and *anywhere*.

aphorism /ăf-ə-rĭz-əm/ = 'memorable definition of a principle or pithy statement of some insight':

> . . . Samuel Butler's well-known aphorism that a chicken is only an egg's way of making another egg.
> —Albert Rosenfeld, *Smithsonian*

> [Jimmy Carter] had forgotten Rickover's favorite aphorism—show me a good loser and I'll show you a loser.
> —James Wooten, *Dasher*

> The memorable aphorism of an Irish-American girl who, looking over some revealed hanky-panky of a local politi-

> cian, sighed: "The whole truth about any of us would shock all the rest of us."
> —Alistair Cooke, *The Americans*

See also APOTHEGM; MAXIM; PROVERB.

apocalypse /ə-pŏk-ə-lĭps/. The Apocalypse (from the Greek word for 'revelation') is another name for The Revelation of Saint John the Divine, the last book in the New Testament, describing Saint John's vision of the end of the world. An *apocalypse* is any inspired revelation, especially a vision of the end of the world. The word is now also popularly used of any scene of utter destruction:

> Guatemala's 39-Second Apocalypse [title of an article about an earthquake in which 23,000 people were killed]
> —Scott Seegers, *Reader's Digest*

> Two decades of cold war accompanied by the feared possibility of a nuclear apocalypse . . . —Doris Kearns, *Lyndon Johnson and the American Dream*

The adjective *apocalyptic* means 'prophesying the end of the world, believing in an apocalypse,' or merely 'prophesying doom':

> The group [The Children of God] is highly apocalyptic, considering the world . . . doomed to early destruction. —George W. Cornell, *Reader's Digest*

> Commentators and correspondents talked in apocalyptic terms and painted the night's events in terms of an administration coup aimed at suppressing opposition. —Richard Nixon, *R.N.*

apocryphal /ə-pŏk-rĭ-fəl/. The Apocrypha (Greek for 'hidden writings') are various books included in the Greek and Latin versions of the Old Testament but rejected from the Jewish and Protestant versions as not genuine. The adjective *apocryphal* thus means 'unfounded, spurious':

> They called him "Dugout Doug" and circulated apocryphal stories about his life of luxury behind the lines.
> —William Manchester, *American Caesar*

apostrophe. See POSSESSIVES.

apothecary, boutique, bodega. *Apothecary* is the old-fashioned word for 'pharmacist.' A *boutique* is a small specialty store, typically selling gifts or chic clothes and accessories. A *bodega* is a Hispanic grocery. The three words have a common origin. The Greek word *apothēkē* meant 'putting-away place, storehouse for merchandise' (*apo* = 'away' + *thē-* = 'put'). It was borrowed into Latin as *apothēca* = 'warehouse, store.'
(1) From Latin *apothēca* came the Latin word *apothēcārius* = 'storekeeper,' later especially 'keeper of a store of medicinal drugs, pharmacist.' This was borrowed into Middle English as *apothecary*.
(2) Greek *apothēkē* was also borrowed into Provençal as *botica* and thence into Old French as *boutique* = 'shop.' In Modern French *boutique* specifically means 'small shop' and was borrowed into English in the sixties.
(3) Latin *apothēca* was inherited in Spanish as *bodega* = 'store,' especially 'wineshop' or 'grocery.' In the last sense it has recently been brought into American English:

> Like many industrious Puerto Ricans, Pete came to this country and opened up a small bodega.
> —Dennis Smith, *Report From Engine Company 82*

apothegm. An *apothegm* /ăp-ə-thĕm/ is a terse, witty statement expressing a general truth. The following saying, attributed to Charles XII of Sweden, is an apothegm: "The sword does not jest." See also APHORISM; MAXIM; PROVERB.

apparatchik. This noun, pronounced /ăp-ə-rä-chĭk/, is from Russian *apparatchik* = 'party worker,' from *apparat* = 'apparatus,' the Stalinist term for the political machine of the Soviet Communist party. It is now chiefly used by political commentators in the mildly sarcastic sense of devoted worker for any political organization:

. . . the young Labor apparatchiks at present mishandling the country.
—Bob Ellis, *The Bulletin* (Sydney, Australia)

Under the new chairmanship of Ted Kennedy, however, the Office of Technology Assessment . . . has become the happy hunting ground for Kennedy apparatchiks.
—William Safire, *New York Times*

apposition. Two nouns or noun phrases referring to the same person or thing, and placed together in a sentence without any connecting words, are said to be *in apposition.* The *appositive* words can be positioned in various ways: *The author Sinclair Lewis was there. Sinclair Lewis, Nobel-Prize-winning author of* Babbitt, *was there.*

Titles, a special type of appositive, can be placed before a personal name without a comma and without an article: *General Marshall, General of the Army George C. Marshall, Secretary Marshall, Secretary of State Marshall.* The current style of treating any personal label as if it were a title was apparently originated by *Time* magazine. This is now widely done with occupational terms that are not titles:

Interviewer Frost . . .
—*Newsweek*

Art Historian and Picasso Expert David Rubin . . .
—*Time*

Real titles are also expanded into descriptive phrases but still used as if they were titles:

Black ambassador to Finland Carl Rowan . . . —Doris Kearns, *Lyndon Johnson and the American Dream*

The same style is also followed with family terms:

He heavily rewrote the final version with advice from wife Rosalynn.
—*Time*

Elizabeth Taylor, resplendent in purple, with husband John Warner at her side . . . —*New York Times*

It is carried to its fullest extremes with identifying tags for certain newsworthy or notorious characters:

. . . attempted Presidential assassin Sara Jane Moore . . . —*Time*

Symbionese Liberation Army kidnap victim Patricia Hearst . . .
—*Reader's Digest*

Note. This stylistic device was invented by journalists to achieve a certain brisk effect. However, it saves little or no space, and it never occurs in natural speech, although radio and television news writers have picked it up from print journalism. It is far from obligatory even in journalism. Each of the foregoing examples can easily be rearranged into the normal style for apposition: "David Rubin, the art historian and Picasso expert"; "with her husband, John Warner, at her side" or "with John Warner, her husband, at her side"; "Patricia Hearst, who was kidnapped by the Symbionese Liberation Army." See also ATTRIBUTIVES.

appreciate. The basic meaning is 'to understand the value of': *He appreciated the offer for what it was worth and no more.* There is a range of derivative meanings, some of which have been disapproved of by usage experts.

(1) 'to have an informed understanding (of)':

He appreciated that new forces were bursting the crust of the old social and political order.
—Philip Magnus, *Edward VII*

The Confederates tended to see the campaign in conventional terms, and failed to appreciate the devastating effects of Sherman's skilled maneuvers.
—Burke Davis, *Sherman's March*

(2) 'to evaluate critically':

But that is like appreciating an oration solely for the musical qualities of the speaker's voice.
—Alexander Eliot, *Atlantic Monthly*

(3) 'to know the true worth of, and value highly':

> The Bohemians adored Mozart, and . . . he wrote his greatest opera for them, fired by the unique experience of being wholly appreciated for the only time in his creative life.
> —Marcia Davenport, *Mozart*

> I have eaten these tubers boiled, creamed, fried and roasted, and have appreciated them all these ways.
> —Euell Gibbons, *Stalking the Wild Asparagus*

(4) 'to be grateful for':

> I would appreciate a correction of the small piece which mentions that I and other commissioners accepted discounts on room rates at Resorts International Hotel. . . .
> —letter, *New Jersey Monthly*

The last sense is widely used in polite and everyday expressions of thanks: *I appreciate your taking the trouble. Appreciate that.*

◇ ***Recommendation.*** All of these uses are widely used and entirely legitimate.

a priori. The term *a priori* (Latin, 'in advance') refers to a kind of reasoning in which preestablished definitions or principles are used to justify conclusions made about a present question. In other words, a priori reasoning assumes that since proof of a contention has been made at some earlier time, there is no need to go through it all again. People who like to win arguments would be well advised never to let their opponents use a priori reasoning. See also FALLACY.

apriorism. See FALLACY.

apt. The basic meaning of *apt* is 'fit for something, well qualified for something.' Of things, it means 'appropriate': *an apt reply to a tough question.* Of people, it means 'quick to learn': *the aptest student I ever had.* But the commonest use of the word is with verbs in the infinitive, meaning 'likely to (do something).' Within this usage there are two levels. In the first, *apt* means 'inherently inclined (to act in a certain way)':

> A man apt to promise is apt to forget.
> —Thomas Fuller, *Reader's Digest*

> Intensely nationalistic and Moslem, Somalia . . . is apt to feel a stronger ideological affinity with the Arab states than with predominantly Christian Ethiopia.
> —John Darnton, *New York Times*

In the second level of this usage, *apt* means merely 'likely, because of circumstances (to act in a certain way or undergo certain action)':

> If the Court decision accelerates such research, society is apt to benefit.
> —*New York Times*

> The rare prosecutor who does not [resign when his party loses the presidency] is apt to be forced out.
> —Irwin Ross, *Reader's Digest*

> Anything he gets into is apt to get out of hand. —*Reader's Digest*

Some authorities would like to restrict the use of *apt* to the first of these two levels, the meaning 'inherently inclined,' preferring *liable* or *likely* when the probability does not result from the nature of the subject but from other factors.

◇ ***Recommendation.*** The use of *apt* to mean merely 'likely' is an established idiom. *Likely* or *liable* may well be chosen instead, but *apt* is equally correct. See also LIABLE; LIKELY.

Arab, Arabian, Arabic. *Arab* is the proper name of the Semitic people who originated in Arabia, the large peninsula of southwestern Asia between the Persian Gulf and the Red Sea, and who are now spread through much of the Middle East and North Africa. The correct pronunciation is /ăr-əb/; the old-fashioned pronunciation /ā-răb/ is now considered substandard and impolite. *Arab* as a noun may mean an Arab person or a horse of the type bred by the Arabs that is ancestral to thoroughbreds. As an adjective *Arab* is used mostly in the political sense: *the Arab League; Arab oil policies.*

The original homeland of the Arabs is also known as the *Arabian Peninsula.* The adjective *Arabian* is used mostly in the geographical and cultural sense: *the Arabian desert; Arabian storytelling.*

Arabic is the language of the Arabs. *Arabic* as an adjective refers chiefly to language and to the *Arabic numerals* (the figures 1 through 9, with 0), which were imported by the Arabs to the West. (The system actually began in India, and the Arabs refer to it as the Indian system, just as we call it the Arabic.)

Arabic words. The civilization of the Arabs has made deep contributions to European civilization, and this fact is very clearly reflected by the many important words we have borrowed from the Arabic language. Most did not come directly into English but were borrowed through Turkish, Italian, Spanish, and French. In the selection below, note how many of the words relate to science and technology and to sophisticated products, objects, and comforts of civilized life. This Arab influence began in the early Middle Ages and has gone on for centuries. Of the words listed below, the following were fully established in English before the year 1600: *admiral, alchemy, alcohol, algebra, alkali, artichoke, azimuth, azure, caliber, carat, caraway, cipher, cotton, elixir, hashish, henna, jar, lute, magazine, mohair, monsoon, nadir, saffron, tariff,* and *zenith.* The rest, including *carafe, coffee,* and *zero,* have been added during the past 400 years.

admiral = 'naval commander in chief,' originally *amyrel of the sea*: French *amiral,* from Arabic *'amir-al-(bahr)* = 'commander of the (sea),' from *'amir* = 'prince, commander'

alchemy = 'the medieval science of chemistry': Arabic *al-kīmīyā* = 'the art of transmuting (metals)'

alcohol = 'spirit distilled from wine'; distilling was invented by alchemists, and *alcohol* originally meant 'fine powder of antimony,' later 'pure spirit or essence of anything,' later 'distilled spirit': Arabic *al-kohl* = 'the antimony'

alcove = 'recess in a room': Spanish *alcoba* = 'curtained recess for a bed,' from Arabic *al-qobbah* = 'the vault'

alfalfa = 'a plant used for animal fodder': Spanish *alfalfa,* from Arabic *al-fasfaṣah* = 'the best fodder'

algebra = 'form of symbolic arithmetic': Arabic *al-jebr* = 'the reuniting,' in full 'the science of reuniting and making equations'

alkali = 'hydroxide of sodium, potassium, etc.,' originally 'ashes of soda': Arabic *al-qalīy* = 'the ashes'

artichoke = 'thistlelike plant with edible flowers': Italian *arcicioffo,* Spanish *alcarchofa,* from Arabic *al-kharshōf* = 'the artichoke'

assassin = 'political murderer,' originally 'member of the Assassins, a society of hashish-eating Arabs dedicated to killing Europeans in the time of the Crusades': Arabic *ḥashshāshīn* = 'hashish-eaters,' from *ḥashīsh* = 'hashish'

azimuth = 'angular measurement used in astronomy and navigation': Arabic *as-sumūt* = 'the compass-bearings,' from *samt* = 'direction'

azure = 'clear blue': Spanish *azur* or *azul,* from Arabic *al-lāzaward* = 'the lapis lazuli' (a blue gemstone)

caliber = 'inside measurement of a tube': Arabic *qalīb* = 'mold for casting metal objects'

carafe = 'glass wine pitcher': French *carafe,* Italian *caraffa,* from Arabic *gharaffa* = 'pitcher'

***carat** = 'unit of weight of gems' and **karat** = 'degree of purity of gold': from Arabic *qīrāt* = 'weight of four grains'

caraway = 'aromatic seeds of a plant': Arabic *karawyā* = 'caraway'

cipher = (1) 'the symbol for zero' (2) 'a secret code': Arabic *sifr* = 'zero'

coffee = 'beverage made from the beans of an Arabian shrub': Dutch *koffie,* Turkish *kahve,* from Arabic *qahwah* = 'coffee'

cotton = 'cloth made from the soft fiber of the cotton shrub': Arabic *qoton* or *qutn* = 'cotton'

elixir = 'all-healing medicine': Arabic *al-iksir* = 'the medicine'

hashish = 'extract of the hemp plant used as a drug': Arabic *ḥashīsh* = 'hemp'

henna = 'extract of an Egyptian plant used as a reddish dye for hair': Arabic *ḥinnā'* = 'henna plant'

Islam = 'the religion founded by the prophet Mohammed': Arabic *islām* = 'submission (to God)'

jar = 'glass or ceramic vessel': French *jarre,* from Arabic *jarrah* = 'large urn'

lute = 'deep-bodied wooden stringed instrument': French *lut,* from Arabic *al-ūd* = 'lute,' literally 'the wood'

macramé = 'lacework of knotted string': French *macramé,* Turkish *makrama,* from Arabic *miqramah* = 'kind of cloth'

magazine = (1) 'storehouse' (2) 'periodical paper': French *magasin* = 'storehouse,' from Arabic *makhāzin* = 'storehouses'

mohair = 'fabric made from the shiny wool of the Angora goat': Italian *moccaiaro,* from Arabic *mukhayyar* = 'choice cloth, mohair'

monsoon = 'seasonal wind and rain system in the Indian Ocean': Dutch *monssoen,* Portuguese *monção,* from Arabic *mausim* = 'season (of the monsoon)'

* **Moslem, Muslim** = 'believer in Islam'

muslin = 'fine cotton cloth': French *mousseline,* Italian *mussolina,* from Arabic *mūṣlin* = 'cotton fabric made in Mosul' (city in Iraq)

nadir = 'astronomic point opposite to the zenith': Arabic *naẓīr as-samt* = 'opposite the zenith,' from *naẓīr* = 'opposite'

saffron = 'spice and yellow dye obtained from a crocus': Medieval Latin *safranum,* from Arabic *za'farān* = 'saffron'

sherbet = (1) 'cool fruit-juice drink' (2) 'sweet water-ice': Turkish *sherbet,* from Arabic *sharbah* = 'sherbet drink'

sirocco = 'hot south wind in the Mediterranean': Italian *scirocco,* from Arabic *sharuq* = 'east wind in North Africa (from the Sahara)'

sofa = 'soft upholstered seat,' originally 'platform with cushions and carpets': Arabic *suffah* = 'cushioned dais'

tariff = 'schedule of taxes to be paid on imported goods': Spanish *tarifa,* Turkish *ta'rifa,* from Arabic *ta'rif* = 'published information, schedule'

zenith = '(in astronomy) the highest point on the celestial sphere': Spanish *zenit,* from Arabic *samt ar-ra's* = 'direction over the head,' from *samt* = 'direction'

zero = 'the numerical quantity 0': Italian *zero,* from Arabic *sifr* = 'zero'

*Appears as separate entry

Arcadia, Arcadian, Arcady. *Arcadia* is a region in Greece, in the center of the Peloponnesus. In classical antiquity it was rural and backward, and there were no cities there. It was thought of, especially by poets, as a place of idyllic peace, where shepherds still lived the archaic simple life. *Arcadia,* also in English *Arcady* /**är**-kə-dē/, is still used as a poetic metaphor of rural paradise:

> I hied me off to Arcady—
> The month it was the month of May. . . .
> —Louise Chandler Moulton, *Arcady*

The adjective *Arcadian* means 'idyllically rural':

> They turned into an intersecting street, narrower but more shady and even quieter, with a golden Arcadian drowse. . . .
> —William Faulkner, *Sartoris*

> From Srinagar a brief reconnaissance, by bus or taxi, takes you to regions of Arcadian beauty and simplicity.
> —Ernest O. Hauser, *Reader's Digest*

> . . . by the year 1832 some of the Arcadian innocence and simplicity characteristic of the three previous decades had, in fact, been lost.
> —H. E. Maude, *History of Pitcairn Island*

archaeology, archeology. U.S. preferences, among scholars and in newspapers and magazines, are rather evenly divided between these two spellings. The present writer's personal preference is *archaeology.*

archaic = 'ancient, old-fashioned.' We use this label for words and forms that were once in common use but are now retained only in specialized or limited use. Examples: in the liturgical language of the church, *ye* for *you, brethren* for *brothers;* in legal terminology, *oyer and terminer* = 'power to hear and determine criminal cases'; in old-fashioned poetry, *My country, 'tis of thee. . . .*

archipelago. The preferred plural is *archipelagoes.* The preferred pronunciation is /är-kə-**pĕl**-ə-gō/, but /är-chə-/ and /är-chē-/ are also used and are equally correct. The word is from Italian *arcipelago,* in which the syllable *-ci-* is pronounced /-chē-/. This was the Medieval Italian term for the Aegean Sea, literally meaning 'the chief sea': *arci-* = 'chief' (equivalent to English *arch-* as in *archbishop*) + *pelago* = 'sea.' By the 17th century the word was used in English to indicate any sea that, like the Aegean, is full of islands. It now almost always means a group of islands, especially a very numerous group: *the Bismarck Archipelago.*

arctic. The constellations of the Great Bear and the Little Bear dominate the region of the north celestial pole, above the north polar region of the earth. The Great Bear was already known to the Greeks as *arktos* = 'bear,' and the adjective *arktikos* = 'belonging to the bear' thus meant 'around the North Pole.' In Latin this became *arcticus,* sometimes dropping the *c* to become *articus.* This form was borrowed into English in the Middle Ages as *artic.* Centuries later it was realized that the original word had a *c* (or Greek *k*) before the *t,* and the spelling *artic* was corrected to *arctic* and its pronunciation to /**ärk**-tĭk/. But to this day the pronunciation /**är**-tĭk/ comes naturally to many people. They can legitimately claim that it is so old a variant that it doesn't count as a mistake.

aren't I. Here is a quandary of everyday usage. *I'm doing the best I can, am I not?* is too formal or fancy for most people. The logical contracted form *amn't,* pronounced /**ăm**-ənt/, exists in some dialects, notably in Irish, but is unknown to most other people. The form *ain't* is universally familiar and commonly used but is widely felt to be uneducated (see AIN'T). This leads many people to say *aren't I,* but this too is condemned by grammarians on the grounds that the declarative forms *I are* and *I aren't* cannot be used.

◇ ***Recommendation.*** The grammarians have gone too far on this one. We recommend *aren't I* (as in *I'm doing my best, aren't I?*) as a perfectly reasonable solution for anyone who doesn't like the other alternatives.

artful. This adjective and its adverb *artfully* have an interesting range of meanings, in which admiration and disapproval can be blended in varying proportions. At one end of the scale the *art* that a person or deed displays can be 'dissembling skill, guile'—a rather old-fashioned sense of the word. At the other end, the *art* involved can be 'legitimate skill in achieving a certain effect neatly or smoothly':

> I saw John Dean's testimony on Watergate as an artful blend of truth and untruth. . . . —Richard Nixon, *R.N.*

> "I'm an artful man, Jack" [said the Skipper], "an' I, generally speaking, get my own way. I couldn't live with my missus peaceable if it wasn't for management."
> —W. W. Jacobs, *Many Cargoes*

> Though Johnston was a master of defensive strategy, Sherman slipped past the rebel force, maneuvering his army of 100,000 with a mobility new to modern warfare, constantly enveloping the enemy, threatening Johnston's rear, artfully flanking and countermarching over a broad front.
> —Burke Davis, *Sherman's March*

> *Thirty Minutes* is itself a series of finely perceived, artfully arranged vignettes.
> —R. Z. Sheppard, *Time*

as. (1) In the construction *A is as good as or better than B,* the second *as* is often left out:

> Mr. Truman, whose sense of timing was as good or better than any stand-up comedian I've heard . . .
> —Merle Miller, *Plain Speaking*

Correctly, "as good as or better than."

> I'm in as good or better physical condition than any senior golf player in the world.
> —Tommy Bolt, *The Hole Truth*

This needs reconstruction: "as good physical condition as any player—or better."

> "The education of young people in science is at least as important, maybe more so, than the research itself," Dr. Seaborg said. —*New York Times*

This also needs reconstruction: either "as important as, maybe more important than, the research" or "as important as the research, or maybe more so."

◇ ***Recommendation.*** Dropping the second *as* in a comparison is a definite mistake, and a very common one. It typically results from a change of mind in midsentence. In speech, the only way to avoid it is to see it coming and keep the second thought until the end of the sentence. In writing, such sentences should be revised.

(2) It used to be taught that the comparison *A is as good as B* when put into the negative must become *A is not so good as B*. This rule need no longer be taken seriously. Whichever you prefer, *not as good as* or *not so good as*, is correct.

(3) *As* is sometimes used to mean 'since, because.' Some usage experts dislike this, feeling that it is a weak method of referring to a reason and also that it is apt to be mistaken for *as* meaning 'when':

> As grandpa wanted to capture this colony of bees, he next set up a hive on the sawed-off stump.
> —Euell Gibbons, *Stalking the Wild Asparagus*

> The spirit of Grant Rice's resolution is still in effect, as the club's business has always been conducted with a minimum of formality.
> —Clifford Roberts, *The Story of the Augusta National Golf Club*

◇ ***Recommendation.*** This usage is a matter of personal idiom. Provided that there is no ambiguity, it is perfectly acceptable.

(4) *As far as X (is concerned).* In this construction the verb of the clause, *is concerned,* is often left out. It could be argued that when this happens, *as far as* is simply being used as a prepositional phrase meaning 'as for X (but no further than X)':

> Now, as far as Mrs. Meir—here's the essence of what happened.
> —Richard Nixon (quoted), *New York Times*

> As far as any investigation of members of Congress, however, I am not familiar with that at all. . . .
> —Jimmy Carter (quoted), *New York Times*

◇ ***Recommendation.*** Perhaps *as far as* really is turning into a prepositional phrase meaning 'as for,' but more time is needed for it to establish itself. For the time being it is not acceptable in formal speech or writing; the full construction, including the verb *is concerned,* is still preferable.

(5) See LIKE.

askance. The phrase *to look askance* literally means 'to look sideways,' a piece of body language implying suspicion or doubt. In the following quotation an American father is thinking of introducing Chinese Communist discipline to his children:

> "In all the photographs, Chinese kids are neat. They are calm and smiling. They are even *obedient.*"
> Liz [his wife] looked askance.
> —Thomas Bolton, *Reader's Digest*

More often the phrase is used figuratively to mean 'view with suspicion or doubt':

> But the medical establishment looks askance at holistic medicine.
> —Adam Smith, *Esquire*

assay. See ESSAY, ASSAY.

assistant. See COHORT.

athwart /ə-thwôrt/. The basic meaning of this preposition is 'across, from side to side of':

> And as he stood so, with afternoon [that is, sunshine] slanting athwart the southern end of the porch . . .
> —William Faulkner, *Sartoris*

Another meaning is 'across someone's path,' with the implication that trouble is expected:

> Sometimes her efforts at frugality and careful planning ran athwart Sara.
> —Joseph P. Lash, *Eleanor and Franklin*

In nautical usage *athwart* or *athwartships* means 'at right angles to the length of the vessel.'

atrophy. The pronunciation is /ăt-rə-fē/. The word is from Greek *atrophos* = 'unfed, not nourished': *a-* = 'not' + *troph-* = 'to nourish.' In biology it means 'the wasting away of tissue from disuse, lack of nutrition, age, etc.' The verb is used figuratively to mean 'degenerate, lose vigor, or disappear entirely, especially from lack of support, relevance, etc.,' or 'cause to degenerate':

> Nixon was chiefly engaged in winding down such of [Johnson's programs] as he could not let atrophy. . . .
> —William J. Miller, *Reader's Digest*

> The fact is, the treaty has been a disaster already. It has atrophied our defense effort: the B-1 bomber canceled, the Trident missile-submarine program delayed, cruise-missile development hobbled. . . .
> —Melvin R. Laird, *Reader's Digest*

attributives. Any noun may be used, like an adjective, to qualify another noun: *forest floor; hurricane warnings; the communications industry; missile deployment.* Here *forest, hurricane, communications,* and *missile* are nouns used attributively. This use of nouns to serve as adjectives is now increasing enormously. It occurs not so much in natural speech as in the daily written usage of the modern world, especially in business, technology, and government and in media coverage of the general scene:

> . . . heavy air-conditioner use . . .
> —*Des Moines Register*

> He took the UMass provost job.
> —*Boston Globe*

> . . . third-world agriculture developments . . .
> —*Chicago Tribune*

> . . . business equipment flexibility . . .
> —*Forbes*

> . . . population density adjustments . . .
> —*Business Week*

This stylistic development is a very powerful trend in the use of the English language. Until fairly recently, such phrases as these would have been structured with adjectives and prepositions: "heavy use of air conditioners"; "took the job as provost of UMass"; "agricultural developments in the third world"; "flexibility in business equipment"; "adjustments in the density of population."

Generic terms for people in their various functions in modern society now form a notable class of attributives:

> consumer goods (in universal use)

> . . . taxpayer discontent . . .
> —*New York Post*

> . . . investor worries . . .
> —*Florida Times-Union*

> . . . the chances of patient survival . . .
> —*Reader's Digest*

> . . . buyer interest . . .
> —*Business Week*

> . . . lawyer incompetence . . .
> —*Newsweek*

◇ ***Recommendation.*** In the contexts of business, technology, reportage, etc., this attributive style is so widely used that it cannot be seriously criticized and is clearly a permanent part of the future of the English language. But such major changes in a language come slowly. This innovation is not yet acceptable in writing that strives for traditional formality. While many individual expressions such as *consumer goods* and *consumer affairs* have become established phrases that cannot be rearranged, the best prose style will not use attributive nouns indiscriminately. Compare APPOSITION.

au. This French preposition, pronounced /ō/, occurs in a number of borrowed phrases, such as *au courant* /ō ko͞o-räN/ = 'in the stream, up to date'; *au fait* /ō fā/ = 'to the point, in touch'; *au fond* /ō fôN/ = 'at bottom.' It also occurs in numerous culinary terms such as steak *au poivre* /ō pwävr/ = 'with pepper.'

auger, augur. These two unrelated nouns are occasionally confused because of their very similar spellings and their identical pronunciation /ô-gər/.

(1) auger. This is an old-fashioned carpenter's tool for boring holes, consisting of a steel shank with a spiral bit set at right angles in a wooden handle. The word is one of those that have lost an initial *n* by influence of the indefinite article; it was originally *nauger*, but by a mistake that became permanent, *a nauger* turned into *an auger*. Other examples of this shift are *adder* and *apron*, which were originally *nadder* and *napron*. The carpenter's auger has now mostly been replaced by the bitbrace and the drill, but the word remains in use for various other tools, such as the sink auger or plumber's snake, used to clear blocked pipes, and power tools used to bore holes in the ground.

(2) augur, augury. The *augurs* were official Roman diviners. Their function was to read omens (in the shapes described by flights of birds, the appearance of animal entrails, etc.) relating to the success of state enterprises. On several historical occasions their readings were disregarded with disastrous consequences. The modern substitute for these divinations is statistics:

> The morning after the state votes, the big-money contributors, the earnest cause people, the political professionals, all poke through the results, like ancient Roman augurs picking through bird entrails to divine the will of the gods.
>
> —Theodore H. White, *Reader's Digest*

Hence the verb *augur* = 'to be a sign of the future, portend (for good or bad)':

> One of the younger McKinley's pleasures was listening to classical music—which augurs well for the continuation of Texaco's long-standing sponsorship of the Metropolitan Opera radio broadcasts. —*Fortune*

> Many school districts . . . are strengthening their negotiating approach in ways that augur even tougher bargaining in the future. —*Business Week*

The noun *augury* /ôg-yə-rē/ means 'an indication of the future,' often used in a playfully superstitious sense:

> Haldeman called the new appointees together . . . in a large meeting room of the Hotel Pierre in New York—the Sapphire Room, a happy augury, I thought.
>
> —William Safire, *Before the Fall*

aura. The plural is preferably *auras*, sometimes *aurae* /ôr-ē/. The basic *aura* is a subtle air that seems to emanate from a person and can be sensed by others:

> . . . there was something wild and desperate about Frank, an aura of trouble.
>
> —Colleen McCullough, *The Thorn Birds*

> His lady laughed, not in the same ribald tone as before but still a sound musky with sexual aura.
>
> —Walter F. Murphy, *The Vicar of Christ*

A place may also generate an aura:

> He could hear the wind moaning and it lent an aura of menace to the darkened room.
>
> —G. Gordon Liddy, *Out of Control*

The aura of a human activity, work of art, etc., is the mood or atmosphere it projects, whether naturally or artificially:

> And indeed almost any Wodehouse plot has the aura of the musical comedy theatre. . . .
>
> —David A. Jasen, *P. G. Wodehouse*

> [Walter Cronkite] has given the news an aura of solidity.
> —George Reedy, *Panorama*

auspices, auspicious. *Auspices* /ô-spə-sēz/, now always plural, are signs or indications of coming fortune (from Latin *auspicium* = 'bird-observation, divination of the future by watching the flights of birds'). Auspices are, unless otherwise stated, usually favorable:

> The auspices, at least for Byron's immortality, improved. . . . Just before they sailed again, Byron was handed a poetic tribute by the mighty Goethe himself. . . .
> —Elizabeth Longford, *Byron*

The commonest current meaning of this noun is 'benevolent patronage, sponsorship,' chiefly in the phrase *under the auspices of:*

> . . . become involved in an existing "study-and-action group," either under the auspices of a single church or in connection with Christians of different churches . . . —*Christianity Today*

In the next quotation, *auspices* is used half humorously to mean 'commercially motivated sponsors':

> It is my opinion that in such circumstances the journalist should feel free to accept the round-trip fare. . . . But once again—he must know that he will feel free to write as he sees the situation, without any inhibition deriving from the auspices.
> —William F. Buckley, Jr., *Execution Eve*

The adjective *auspicious* /ô-spĭsh-əs/ means either 'marked by favorable omens' or 'fortunate, prosperous, encouraging':

> The senior advisers of His Imperial Highness were asked to choose an auspicious day for such a . . . ritual.
> —James Clavell, *Shōgun*

> He . . . planned to present this [bottle of champagne] to us on the auspicious occasion of his fourth child's birth.
> —Thomas A. Dooley, *The Edge of Tomorrow*

> Granted that I began my [art] collecting at an auspicious time.
> —J. Paul Getty, *As I See It*

Australian English. To an American ear "broad Australian" sounds like the cockney of London, and cultivated Standard Australian sounds like cultivated Standard British. In fact, broad Australian is not derived from cockney but from a mixture of Southern and Midland British accents. In broad Australian *bait* appears as /bīt/, while *last* appears as /lăst/ as in Standard American, not as /läst/ as in Standard British. There are other differences, too subtle to describe here.

Although Australia is as big as the contiguous United States, Australian English has never formed any regional dialects. But it has a large quantity of unique vocabulary, some borrowed from the Aborigines, some surviving from words that have died out in Britain, but most developed from the resources and history of the Australian people.

Selected Vocabulary.

beauty! = 'excellent! great!'
billy = 'metal vessel for making tea'
bludger = 'shirker, freeloader'
bushranger = 'outlaw robber'
capsicum = (everyday word for) 'bell pepper'
chook = 'chicken'
cocky = 'small farmer'
dinkum = 'genuine, sincere'
fossick = (1) 'to pick over old mineral diggings' (2) 'to rummage'
galvo = 'galvanized sheet iron'
good day! /gə-dā, gə-dī/ = 'good morning! hello!'
greenie = 'environmental activist'
grog = 'any alcoholic drink, typically beer'
interstate (adverb) = 'out of state'
knock back = 'to reject'
mateship = 'affectionate solidarity among Australian men'
migrant = 'immigrant'
ocker = 'young Australian man with no pretensions to culture'
offsider = 'assistant, sidekick'
outback = 'backcountry, desert'

paddock = 'any field or enclosure, up to thousands of acres in size'
Pom, Pommy = 'English person'
port = 'suitcase'
push = 'cliquey social group'
ropeable = 'angry'
run = 'grazing land, ranch'
sheila = 'Australian woman'
squatter = 'gentleman rancher'
station = 'ranch'
stockman = 'cowhand'
stubbies = 'short shorts'
stubby = 'small glass of beer'
tucker = 'food'
whinge = 'to complain irritatingly'

Other than names of native plants and animals, very few Australian words have been taken into American English. Among those few are:

****finalize*** = 'to make (a decision, plans, etc.) final'
larrikin = 'wild young man'
wowser = 'puritanical person'

*Appears as separate entry

For a selection of Australian Aboriginal words in English see ABORIGINES, ABORIGINAL.

author. Journalists writing about writers sometimes use this noun as a verb:

> He went on to author best-selling books that blended bittersweet childhood memories with his effervescent humor.
> —Earl Wilson, *Reader's Digest*

◇ ***Recommendation.*** The verb *author* undeniably exists, but *write* is better.

authoress. Most women now regard the term *authoress* as demeaning. We recommend *author* in all cases. See also FEMALE-GENDER WORD FORMS.

averse, adverse. (1) *Averse*, always used of persons, means 'opposed' and is properly followed by *to:*

> He was naturally averse to change for its own sake.
> —George Mead, *Saturday Evening Post*

But because the word comes from Latin *āversus*, literally meaning 'turned away (from),' it has been argued that it should be followed by *from*, and some reputable writers still adhere to this rule:

> Sir Edward Grey was strongly averse from making any formal protest. . . .
> —Philip Magnus, *Edward VII*

◇ ***Recommendation.*** The idea that origins can or should control idiom is an *etymological fallacy* (see ETYMOLOGY). *Averse to* is correct, and *averse from* is pedantic.

(2) *Adverse* (from Latin *adversus* = 'turned toward, opposed') means 'acting against, unfavorable, detrimental' and is almost always used of circumstances, feelings, or statements, not of persons: *adverse trends; making adverse comments.* In the following it is probably a mistake for *averse:*

> We accepted only some minor items, but were not adverse to buying things as cheaply as possible.
> —Clifford Roberts, *The Story of the Augusta National Golf Club*

◇ ***Recommendation.*** Use *averse* only of people and *adverse* only of things.

aversion. When meaning 'strong dislike,' *aversion* is correctly followed by *to* or *for:*

> . . . though Silianov, the writer, disgraced himself by showing an effeminate aversion to cutting his prisoners' throats.
> —Eric Ambler, *The Schirmer Inheritance*

Aversion is also occasionally used to mean 'something or someone detested':

> Metal cleats are one of my pet aversions because I think they are hard on ropes.
> —Henry Garrett Smith, *The Marlinspike Sailor*

avoid, evade. These two words share the meaning 'to keep or get away (from someone or something),' but with different effect. *Avoid* is the simpler verb, with no particular implications as to motive or circumstances. *Evade* carries overtones of cunning, often of irresponsibility or even guilt. Thus, to avoid a person may be altogether prudent, but to evade a person seems shifty. This contrast carries over to the nouns *avoidance* and *evasion; tax avoidance* is making permissible arrangements not to incur tax or to minimize it, while *tax evasion* is nonpayment of tax that is due—the former legal, the latter illegal. See also ESCHEW.

awful, awesome. These two words once meant much the same thing, but they have diverged until they are almost entirely distinct—a process called *differentiation.*
(1) *Awful* originally meant 'causing awe, worthy of deep and reverential fear.' It was applied to God, to great spiritual experiences, and to majestic spectacles of nature:

> The awful shadow of some unseen Power
> Floats though unseen among us. . . .
> —Percy Bysshe Shelley, *Hymn to Intellectual Beauty* (1816)

> How awful to feel himself there . . . an atom amidst the infinity of nature!
> —F. D. Maurice, *Prophets and Kings of the Old Testament* (1853)

This sense of *awful* can now hardly be used, except with deliberately archaic flavor. In the 19th century *awful* was widely used in a series of slang senses, 'monstrous, very bad, frightful'; it was applied to anything, however trivial—*an awful child; awful weather*—and eventually became a mere intensifier meaning 'great, considerable': *an awful crowd of people; an awful waste of time.* These meanings have largely driven out the original one. The commonest current meanings of *awful* range from 'terrible, frightful' through 'deplorable, wretched' to 'considerable, large (in amount)':

> The more awful you make war, the sooner it will be over. War is hell, at the best.
> —William Tecumseh Sherman

> Soon everyone would be holding out, refusing to decide until the President called. You can imagine how impossible that would be when I tell you the awful difficulty we had at a much lower level.
> —Henry Hall Wilson (quoted), Doris Kearns, *Lyndon Johnson and the American Dream*

> I've been to 58 campuses, taught more than 500 classes, answered more than 5000 questions and, in the process, learned an awful lot about American youth.
> —Gerald R. Ford, *A Time to Heal*

The adverb *awfully* is now used in the even narrower range of meanings from 'deplorably' to 'very':

> . . . can Mr. Hammarskjold go to Budapest? Even if he makes it, he will arrive awfully late.
> —E. B. White, *The Points of My Compass*

> He has tried awfully hard in the past few years to stretch his liberal conscience. . . .
> —Alistair Cooke, *The Americans*

(2) As *awful* lost its original reference to real awe, *awesome* became available to fill the gap. It is now almost always used in the following range of meanings: 'amazingly vast'; 'appallingly grave'; 'frighteningly powerful'; 'impressive and large-scale'; 'impressive, remarkable in any way':

> Deep beneath the surface of the north Pacific Ocean, nearly as deep in places as Mount Everest is high, runs the great Aleutian trench. An awesome gouge in the earth's crust . . .
> —Leonard Bickel, *Reader's Digest*

> The Soviet Union has built up the most awesome military machine mankind has ever seen.
> —Sam Nunn (quoted), *Time*

> . . . securing an awesome 32% share of the North American tractor market.
> —Bob Tamarkin, *Forbes*

Aztec words. The chief language of the Aztec Empire in Mexico, destroyed by the

Spanish in 1519, was Nahuatl /nä-wät'l/. It is still spoken by millions of Mexicans descended from the Aztecs. A number of English words come from Nahuatl, nearly all of them borrowed through Mexican Spanish.

avocado = 'pear-shaped fruit of the avocado tree of Central America': Spanish *avocado* = 'advocate,' a distortion of *aguacete* = 'avocado,' from Nahuatl *ahuacatl* = 'testicle,' hence 'avocado'

axolotl /ăk-sə-lŏt'l/ = 'a salamander of Mexico and the Southwestern United States': Nahuatl *axolotl* = 'water spirit, axolotl'

cacao /kə-kä-ō, -kā-ō/ = 'seed or bean of the cacao tree of Central America, from which chocolate is made': Spanish *cacao*, from Nahuatl *cacahuatl* = 'cacao beans'

chicle /chĭk'l/ = 'gummy juice of the sapodilla tree, the chief ingredient of chewing gum': Spanish *chicle*, from Nahuatl *chictli*

chili = 'a hot pepper, the fruit of a Central American pepper plant': Spanish *chili* or *chile*, from Nahuatl *chilli*

chocolate = 'drink or candy made from cacao beans': Spanish *chocolate*, from Nahuatl *xocolatl* = 'bitter water, unsweetened drink made from cacao beans'

coyote /kī-ō-tē, kī-ōt/ = 'a small wolf of western North America': Spanish *coyote*, from Nahuatl *coyotl*

mescal /mĕs-kăl/ = 'a cactus of Mexico and the Southwestern United States, the source of peyote': Spanish *mescal*, from Nahuatl *mexcalli*

mesquite /mĕs-kēt/ = 'a shrub of Mexico and the Southwestern United States, with pods that are used as cattle feed': Spanish *mesquite*, from Nahuatl *mizquitl*

ocelot /ŏs-ə-lŏt/ = 'a large spotted wildcat of South and Central America and the Southwestern United States': French *ocelot*, from Nahuatl *ocelotl* = 'jaguar'

B

Babbitt. The hero of Sinclair Lewis's novel *Babbitt*, published in 1922, was George Babbitt, a realtor in the Midwestern city of Zenith. His name has become an allusive term for the American businessman as a social type, thought (by those who use the term) to personify such qualities as smugness and philistinism.

> I can think of no clergyman in any great American city today whose public dignity and influence are much above those of an ordinary Class I Babbitt.
> —H. L. Mencken, *Prejudices*

> He is a stock character: the man who "spends his life riding to and from his wife," the eternal Babbitt whose sanctuary is the club locker room, whose ideas spring ready-made from the illiberal press.
> —Phyllis McGinley, *Reader's Digest*

> . . . CBS News, which for years had operated in the deep red, causing it to be scorned by the corporate Babbitts as a constant drain on network profits . . .
> —Gary Paul Gates, *Air Time*

The abstract nouns *Babbittism* and *Babbittry* are also used:

> I tried to convince myself that I had fled America in 1925 to escape its Babbittism, Coolidgeism, puritanism, its Prohibition and the pathetic "booster" atmosphere of the Chamber of Commerce and Rotary.
> —William L. Shirer, *Midcentury Journey*

> The memorabilia are an interesting mix of Hemingway macho and Sinclair Lewis babbittry.
> —Francis X. Clines, *New York Times*

After these outpourings of scorn, it's worth remembering that George Babbitt himself was not the mere bland conformist that his name now suggests. He could be good company, he didn't lack romantic aspirations or even rebellious tendencies, and he was a highly effective public speaker.

back-formations. The term *back-formation* was coined by Sir James Murray (1837–1915), editor of the great *Oxford English Dictionary.* It means 'a word formed by reversing a normal process of word formation.' The typical back-formation in English is made by removing an affix from an existing word; the new shorter word then looks like the base of the previously existing longer word, but in fact it's the other way round. The noun *editor* = 'one who prepares books for publication' came into English in the 17th century; later the verb *edit* = 'to do what an editor does' was formed by removing the suffix *-or.* Most English back-formations are verbs formed by reducing nouns or adjectives. They are often initially created through ignorance or as a joke.

> He spoke with a certain what-is-it in his voice, and I could see that, if not actually disgruntled, he was far from being gruntled.
>
> —P. G. Wodehouse, *The Code of the Woosters*

Gruntled, unfortunately, has never caught on; but back-formations often become real words, although they continue to be regarded as undesirable or frivolous. Thus, ENTHUSE, a back-formation from *enthusiasm,* is found useful and reasonable by some but is disapproved of by others. *Burgle,* humorously coined from *burglar* by W. S. Gilbert (of Gilbert and Sullivan fame), is now accepted as Standard British but seems quaint in America, where *burglarize* is preferred (the British think *burglarize* is weird or hilarious). But back-formation is clearly an established if minor process of word coinage in English, since several dozen such words have become universally accepted and are no longer even noticed as anything special. A selection follows.

Back-formation	**Derived from**
automate	*automation*
baby-sit	*baby sitter*
diagnose	*diagnosis*
emote	*emotion*
greed	*greedy*
jell	*jelly*
laze	*lazy*
liaise	*liaison*
orate	*orator*
peddle	*peddler*
peeve	*peevish*
reminisce	*reminiscence*
sculpt	*sculptor*
televise	*television*

backlog. This American word is at least 300 years old; its literal meaning is 'large log placed at the back of a fireplace.' The backlog both sustains the fire when it is not being regularly tended and keeps an active fire to the front of the fireplace, allowing heat to radiate into the room instead of up the chimney. In the days before central heating, fire making was an art, as the following quotations suggest:

> In the cavernous fireplace burns a great fire, composed of a huge green back-log, a large green forestick, and a high cob-work of crooked and knotty refuse-wood.
>
> —Sylvester Judd, *Margaret* (1845)

> The fire was built according to architectural principles known to those days. First came an enormous back-log, rolled in with the strength of two men, on top of which was piled a smaller log. . . . —Harriet Beecher Stowe, *Oldtown Folks* (1869)

Regional Variations. In parts of the South, especially the South Midland and Gulf Southern speech regions, the usual term is *backstick. Base-log, banking-log, night-log,* and *draft-log* are also used, but not quite as often.

If there is a backlog in a fireplace, it is reasonable to expect a *forelog;* and this term is in fact used in New England for a smaller log put at the front of the fire. Another term, used in both New England and the Midland speech region, is *forestick*, as in the first quotation above.

Figurative Use. The first figurative use of *backlog* meant 'reserve supply, accumulation of some useful resource.' Later the word became more general; its usual current meaning is 'any accumulation, as of unfinished work, unused resources, etc.':

> The backlog of refugees worsens daily as thousands flee . . . Vietnam.
> —*U.S. News & World Report*

Hence also the verb *backlog:*

> . . . family courts are backlogged with long and painful battles. . . .
> —*Newsweek*

back of, in back of. These prepositions, both meaning 'behind' and both universally familiar, are Standard American English.

> In back of the plateau were the mountains. . . .
>
> . . . Back of the rolling country we were going through we saw the mountains. . . .
> —Ernest Hemingway, *The Sun Also Rises*

Nonetheless, a strong prejudice against both forms persists, and many will not accept them as standard formal usage, insisting on *at the back of* or else *behind* (these in Standard British are the only possible forms).

◇ ***Recommendation.*** We think it's high time that *back of* and *in back of* were fully accepted as standard in all levels of American usage, even if many people prefer to use *behind.* But we are bound to recognize that full acceptance has not yet occurred. We support those who use (*in*) *back of* regardless of disapproval; but the disapproval exists, and the disapprovers are entitled to their feelings.

bad, badly. (1) *Bad* is often used as an adverb meaning 'intensely, very much,' in expressions like *It hurts bad* and *We don't need the money as bad as that.* This use is very widespread, and in that sense is a natural part of the language. It has never been accepted as standard and is unacceptable in any formal context.
(2) *Badly* is often used as a kind of adjective with the verb *feel. I felt badly* may mean either 'I felt sick' or 'I felt sorry.' The preferred standard form for these meanings is *I felt bad.*

◇ ***Recommendation.*** These two well-known uses of *bad* and *badly* should be avoided in formal standard usage.

balance. In bookkeeping *balance* means, first, 'equality between the debit and the credit in an account'; secondly, it means 'difference between the debit and the credit,' and especially 'favorable difference, surplus of credit.' Hence, the word *balance* is often used metaphorically to mean 'amount remaining from anything, remainder.'

> . . . when Tommy Bassett wired for me to come to Lake Keuka, New York, for the balance of the summer . . .
> —Hoagy Carmichael, *Sometimes I Wonder*

This metaphorical usage is condemned by some critics, on the grounds that the literal idea of balance, one amount weighed against another, is no longer present.

◇ ***Recommendation.*** Idioms cannot be restrained by literal-minded logic. There is nothing wrong with using *balance* to mean 'remainder.'

bale, baleful. *Bale,* in the sense of 'evil, trouble, misery' is now archaic and quite rare. Here is a 100-year-old literary use of the word in this sense:

> No themes are so human as those that reflect for us, out of the confusion of life, the close connection of bliss and bale, of the things that help with the things that hurt. . . .
> —Henry James, *What Maisie Knew*

The adjective *baleful* is in much wider use. It literally means 'bringing evil results':

> The Munich agreement had its baleful consequences throughout Central Europe.
> —Anthony Eden, *The Reckoning*

> The influence of the modern medical school on liberal-arts education in this country over the last decade has been baleful and malign, nothing less.
> —Lewis Thomas, *The Medusa and the Snail*

In this sense there is often little difference between *baleful* and the rarer word *baneful* (see BANE, BANEFUL).

Baleful is also often used of human facial expressions, looks, eyes, etc., meaning 'threatening, malevolent, grim':

> . . . detecting the projectionist's baleful eye fixed on me . . . I twisted my features into a sickly placatory grin and sank back. . . . —S. J. Perelman, *The Road to Miltown*

> The President, not smiling, growled, "Good morning," and everyone who witnessed the baleful look directed at the Chief of Staff thought to himself, "Better him than me."
> —William Safire, *Before the Fall*

balk, balky. A holdover from the days of horse travel, the verb *balk*, used of a horse, means 'to stop and refuse to go on,' or 'to shy at an object or obstacle.' Used of humans, it means 'to refuse to act as hoped':

> The Senate . . . has already passed such a bill at least twice but the House has balked. —*Forbes*

To balk at means 'to refuse, recoil from':

> If the union balked at O'Neil's demands, General Tire would simply close its plant. . . .
> —Trevor Armbrister, *Reader's Digest*

> . . . the Soviet invaders are attacking guerrillas with deadly nerve gases that even Adolf Hitler balked at using.
> —Jack Anderson, *Savannah Morning News*

The adjective *balky* means 'inclined to refuse to act as hoped, uncooperative':

> Why has Congress been so balky then on major White House proposals?
> —*U.S. News & World Report*

balkanize. This verb means 'to divide (a country or region) into small sections that fight among themselves.' The noun is *balkanization*. The reference is to the Balkan Peninsula of southeastern Europe, which historically has been divided into small, weak countries and dominated by major powers:

> . . . fears that Carter's program might "balkanize" the nation by spurring divisive regional conflicts were not materializing. —*Newsweek*

> They would cite Canada's problems with the province of Quebec as the type of balkanization of a country that they deplore.
> —William J. Leary, *Boston Herald American*

balm, balmy. The noun is pronounced /bäm/. *Balm* (or *balsam*) is an aromatic resin exuded from certain trees. Hence, the word *balm* is used to mean 'soothing or healing ointment' and, figuratively, 'soothing or healing influence':

> Sleep that knits up the ravel'd sleave of care,
> The death of each day's life, sore labor's bath,
> Balm of hurt minds. . . .
> —Shakespeare, *Macbeth*

(There is also an herb of the mint family called *balm* or *lemon balm*.)

The adjective *balmy* /**bäm**-ē/ means 'fragrant with balm, soothing.' When used of weather it means 'deliciously mild and fragrant' or merely 'pleasantly warm':

> The weekend's balmy temperatures would end by Monday, when a cold front would move in. . . .
> —*Atlanta Constitution*

Not related to *balm* is the slang adjective *balmy* meaning 'crazy':

> He was a nut. I don't know if he was balmy about his wife, but he was about that. —Rex Stout, *All in the Family*

This *balmy* is a variant of *barmy* = 'frothy, effervescing like beer,' from *barm* = 'froth.'

banal, banality. Until recently the adjective *banal*, as a borrowed French word, was usually pronounced /bə-**năl**/ or /bə-**näl**/. By now the anglicized pronunciation /**bā**-nəl/ is probably preferred by Americans. Both versions are still correct. The meaning is 'boringly commonplace, lacking in interest or originality, dreary and hackneyed':

> She had a horror of common or banal objects, or ones that were often copied, with fashionable motifs; if a piece of furniture was to please her it must be unique of its sort. . . .
> —Nancy Mitford, *Madame de Pompadour*

> Shrimp-colored gladioli were limp and faded in their dime-store vases, the most banal of green plants were set in plastic pots covered with gold foil. . . .
> —Mimi Sheraton, *New York Times*

> Donahue . . . doesn't sing, tell jokes, cue the band, fall into banal chatter.
> —William Brashler, *Reader's Digest*

> The swearing-in ceremony was brief, and after a few gratuitous and banal remarks about courage and dedication by city officials I was given the three-inch chrome maltese cross that is the badge of a firefighter.
> —Dennis Smith, *Report From Engine Company 82*

The noun *banality* means either 'the quality of being banal' or 'something that is banal':

> The once understandable method of choosing a President has been converted into a permanent political race in which banality, bluster, and media-manufactured events substitute for constructive debate.
> —Robert MacLeish, *Atlantic Monthly*

> God, how he despised the aggressive young men of the electronic media. They learned nothing from day to day. They just flitted from flower to flower, intoning resonant banalities.
> —Spiro T. Agnew, *The Caulfield Decision*

bane, baneful. *Bane* is an Old English word literally meaning 'death, cause of death, poison' (as in names of poisonous plants such as *henbane*).

> Rum . . . is, in my opinion, the bane of morals and the parent of idleness.
> —George Washington, letter (1788)

It is now most often used in less severe senses, of persons or things that cause serious trouble or mere annoyance:

> The Eastern European fishing fleet [was] long the bane of American fishermen. . . . —Tony Muldoon, *National Fisherman*

> No text on soldierly discomforts would be complete without mention of the cootie, or body louse. This little devil was the bane of military life right up to World War II, when DDT came along.
> —Bill Mauldin, *Smithsonian*

> Miss Weyhauser had a small brother of nine, and he became the bane of my existence—a really horrid little boy.
> —David Niven, *The Moon's a Balloon*

The comparatively rare adjective *baneful* literally means 'fatal, poisonous,' hence 'very harmful, destructive':

> Let me now warn you in the most solemn manner against the baneful effects of the spirit of party.
> —George Washington, *Farewell Address* (1796)

See also BALE, BALEFUL.

banshee. In Gaelic folklore the *banshee* is a female spirit who warns of a coming death in a family by wailing at night near the house:

> [Scarlett] was Irish enough to believe in second sight, especially where death

premonitions were concerned, and in his wide gray eyes she saw some deep sadness which she could only interpret as that of a man who has felt the cold finger on his shoulder, has heard the wail of the Banshee.
—Margaret Mitchell, *Gone With the Wind*

Figuratively, a banshee is a screaming person or a person so distraught as to be virtually screaming, or anything that makes loud wailing noises:

"I've just found out about these magazines and films, and I've become a raving banshee over it," says . . . a Manhattan lawyer and psychiatrist who has been barnstorming around the country in a crusade against the abuse of minors. —*Reader's Digest*

Sirens are sounding. The whole city, it seems, is possessed by the howling of banshees.
—Studs Terkel, *Talking to Myself*

barbarians. "Civilized" people have various ideas about "barbarians." In Homer's day *barbaroi* meant simply 'unintelligible people, non-Greek speakers,' and the Greeks did not regard them as inferior, only as foreign. Later, as Greek civilization became more splendid and exclusive, Aristotle had the cultural arrogance to define barbarians in general, including highly civilized peoples such as the Persians, as 'slaves by nature.' The Romans inherited a measure of this view but were less snobbish about it, and willing to incorporate barbarian peoples fully into their empire. With a capital *B* the word is now chiefly used of the European and Asian peoples who broke up the Roman Empire and later warred against medieval Europe: Goths, Vandals, Huns, Tartars, etc. The modern view of barbarians ranges from the comic-book (they were hairy and always fighting) to the anthropological (barbarians are halfway between "primitive savagery" and "full civilization"), and from the Christian, disapproving (they were cruel, immoral, and filthy) to the romantic, admiring (they were vigorous, heroic, and creative).

(1) The noun and adjective *barbarian* can be used with any of these underlying images in mind. Besides its basic European meaning of 'non-Greek, non-Roman,' it is also used as a translation of Chinese and Japanese terms meaning 'European or American, regarded as uncivilized and inferior':

There was China—the greatest empire in the world, a vast, sophisticated realm whose leaders scorned the "red faced barbarians." . . .
—Marvin Harris, *Cannibals and Kings*

In a cultural-political sense *barbarian* means 'member of a people that have abandoned civilized and humane principles':

. . . in the Hitler time I saw what collective barbarians the Germans could become . . . the German people became possessed of an evil spirit, which brutalized them and degraded them so that they justly earned—and deserved—the hatred of every other people in Europe.
—William L. Shirer, *Midcentury Journey*

Applied to individuals, *barbarian* often means primarily 'ruthlessly cruel person':

Even such thorough-going barbarians as Hitler, Stalin and Tojo, who had no qualms about murdering prisoners of war or oppressing civilian populations under belligerent occupation . . .
—Alex McColl, *Soldier of Fortune*

In a purely cultural sense *barbarian* means 'unsophisticated, nonartistic person':

The difference between being a barbarian and a full-fledged member of a cultivated society is in the individual's attitude toward fine art.
—J. Paul Getty, *As I See It*

(2) The adjectives *barbaric* and *barbarous* are largely synonymous and interchangeable, but there are some differences of emphasis and overtone between them.

Barbaric typically means 'bloody, willing to commit crimes that civilized countries define as atrocities':

The Communist offensive of 1972 had unleashed that barbaric strain of North Vietnamese brutality that so marked the conduct of the Vietnam War.
—Richard Nixon (quoted), *New York Times*

It can also mean merely 'uncouth, ill-mannered, nasty':

In a few moments Robert came over and said that he could well understand why she might think football barbaric, but it did mean a lot to Jack.
—Arthur M. Schlesinger, Jr., *Robert Kennedy and His Times*

I think shopping is barbaric—all those people pushing stuff on you that you don't want or need.
—Rosalind Russell, *Life Is a Banquet*

Barbaric can also have the connotation 'richly magnificent in a somehow uncivilized manner,' especially 'overdecorated to the point of bad taste':

They had found a highly organized society [in Mexico] of barbaric splendor. . . .
—J. T. Adams, *The Epic of America*

Barbarous is used in much the same senses as *barbaric.* It can also mean 'atrocity-committing':

The Enemy [British], persisting in that barbarous line of Conduct they have pursued during the course of this War, have lately most inhumanly executed Captain Joshua Huddy of the Jersey State Troops. . . .
—George Washington, letter (1782)

. . . receiving reliable information of the barbarous and inhuman treatment to which Jews were being submitted in German-occupied Europe . . .
—Anthony Eden, *The Reckoning*

It can also mean 'culturally uncivilized':

It taught the young Tsar what he had already suspected—that imperial Russia was still a semi-Oriental state with a barbarous history and a lack of true contact with the currents of science, literature, art and medicine that were sweeping over the European continent in this post-Renaissance era.
—Martin L. Gross, *Book Digest*

Barbarous can also mean 'overdecorated to the point of bad taste':

. . . the barbarous taste of our time and country, which had loaded the walls of the room with furniture and the furniture with bric-a-brac . . .
—Ambrose Bierce, *The Man and the Snake* (1891)

Barbarous has a further specialized use referring to language: 'unrefined, incorrect, full of errors':

It was these homely, pragmatic aphorisms which endeared this uncouth American [Benjamin Franklin] to the French; in his barbarous way he spoke their language.
—James A. Michener, *Chesapeake*

. . . she would chatter in some barbarous mixture of Chinese and English.
—Pearl S. Buck, *Hearts Come Home*

(3) The nouns *barbarism* and *barbarity* are also largely synonymous and interchangeable, but they too differ to some extent in emphasis or overtone.

Barbarism most often means 'state of uncivilized culture,' either of a people that have never attained civilized status or of a civilized people that have declined or collapsed:

With or without a thermonuclear war (and one may be forced out of the hatred and pressures that surround a collapsing society), barbarism looms.
—Isaac Asimov, *Science Past—Science Future*

It can also mean 'the practice of committing atrocities':

At the time, the Allied command appears to have been very little disturbed by this barbarism [systematic reprisals against the Italian peasantry].
—Farley Mowat, *And No Birds Sang*

Referring to language, *barbarism* is used to mean 'gross error, breach of good usage.' This is a somewhat snobbish use, an ivory tower term applied by perfectionists to other people's mistakes. In the following quotation, it is amusing that the speaker himself has made two errors: first, there is nothing inherently wrong with using a noun as an adjective, and secondly, the example he mentions is that of a *verb* used as an adjective:

> As has been the recent custom, I had circulated a "discuss list," if you'll forgive the literary barbarism of using a noun as an adjective.
> —Walter F. Murphy, *The Vicar of Christ*

There is a further, linguistic use of the word *barbarism*, now rather old-fashioned. See BARBARISMS.

Barbarity, like *barbarism*, can mean simply 'uncivilized state':

> . . . patience . . . not only to tolerate the discomforts of such a wretched place but what is more to fight the barbarity, ignorance, idolatry, and vices which seem scarcely human but rather those of irrational animals.
> —Peter Forbath, *The River Congo*

More often, *barbarity* means 'inhumanity, the committing of atrocities':

> If the people raise a howl against my barbarity and cruelty, I will answer that war is war and not popularity-seeking. If they want peace, they and their relatives must stop war.
> —William Tecumseh Sherman, letter (1864)

barbaric, barbarous, barbarity. See BARBARIANS.

barbarisms. In the days when Latin and Greek were a dominant part of education, classicists held that English words based on Latin or Greek words should be formed exactly by the rules of Latin or Greek word formation. A word that violated these rules was called a *barbarism*. For example, the English word *coloration*, formed from two Latin elements, was condemned because in Latin the suffix *-ātiō(n)-* could not be added directly to the noun *color* to form an abstract noun like *colorātiō(n)-*. Also classed as barbarisms were hybrid words, formed from a Latin word added to a Greek word or from either added to an English word. Thus, *speedometer*, formed from English *speed* with Greek *meter*, was labeled a barbarism, and so was *television*, formed from Greek *tele-* with Latin *vision*. This view was based on a pedantic misunderstanding of the nature of living languages. There are indeed "rules" of word formation in Modern English, and in every language, but they aren't governed by such artificial restraints. Unmistakably, *coloration*, *speedometer*, and *television* are acceptable and have been correctly formed by the real rules of English formation. The attempt to dismiss them as barbarisms was part of the last stand of the classical elitists in their long-lasting effort to make English dependent on Greek and Latin (especially Latin). See also GREEK WORDS; LATIN WORDS.

barrio. The pronunciation is **/bär-ē-ō/**, the plural *barrios*. The word means 'Hispanic district in a U.S. town or city.' It was first used in the Southwestern United States. In Spanish the word *barrio* means simply 'any ward or section of a city':

> And above the grey dust-bitten shanties of the Mexican barrios and the roadside barbecue shacks . . .
> —Edna Ferber, *Giant*

> Most came from seedy Chicano *barrios* in East Los Angeles. . . .
> —Nathan M. Adams, *Reader's Digest*

Barrio, often *El Barrio*, is now also used to mean 'the world of city-dwelling Hispanic people in the United States':

> The law is directly implicated in the creation and the continuation of the nation's ghettos and barrios and the conditions in them.
> —Haywood Burns, *New York Times*

> The exhibition, in the words of the museum's director, Jack Agueros, "both forecasts and summarizes the Latin American presence in North America; it presages the role of El Barrio in the cultural life of the Latin community." —*New York Times*

bar sinister, bend sinister. These two expressions are often used to mean 'sign or implication that someone was born out of wedlock.' The usage springs from a vague belief that the terms referred to heraldic devices identifying bastard sons of kings or lords. Technically, both expressions are wrong. *Bar sinister* is an impossible term in heraldry; a *bar* is a broad horizontal strip across the middle of a shield, and *sinister* means 'on or toward the left or oriented in the opposite direction from the usual'; since the bar is always horizontal, it can never be sinister. A *bend* is a broad diagonal strip running from top left to bottom right (when you are looking at the shield from the front); a *bend sinister* thus runs from top right to bottom left (again, when viewed from the front) and is a device that exists on many coats of arms—but is never an indication of bastardy.

Both expressions have been garbled from *bendlet sinister* and *baton sinister*, the actual devices that in English heraldry have been used on the arms of bastard sons (the *baton* being reserved for royal bastards). The *bendlet* is a narrow diagonal strip half the width of a bend, and the baton is the same thing with both ends cut off; both normally run from top left to bottom right, so that the bendlet sinister and the baton sinister slope the other way. The duke of Monmouth, for example, was the eldest of King Charles II's bastards and was not ashamed to display his bastardy on his shield, with a baton sinister over the royal arms.

◇ ***Recommendation.*** Few people but heralds and historians can be expected to care deeply about these details. To refer to illegitimacy as the bar sinister or the bend sinister is technically a mistake but hardly a disaster. On the other hand, anyone who has taken the trouble to read through the above explanation now knows that either bendlet sinister or baton sinister is the correct allusion.

baseball terms. Despite its debt to cricket and rounders, baseball has a language largely its own—one that has changed little over the century in which "the great American game" has flourished. The sport itself is such a thicket of technicality that no one has ever devised a satisfactory one-sentence definition of it without using technical terms. Not surprisingly, a number of baseball terms have been absorbed into the general vocabulary.

(1) Terms specific to baseball but also occasionally applied to nonbaseball situations:

assist = 'a defensive play that leads to a putout'; for example, an infielder's handling of a ground ball followed by a throw to a baseman, or an outfielder's throw to a baseman

balk = 'pitcher's act of failing to deliver a pitch promptly after beginning the motion to do so; when there are opponents on base, an illegal hesitation that permits the opposing base runner or runners to advance a base'

battery = 'the pitcher and the catcher of one team, considered as a pair'

batting average = 'statistical measure of a batter's capability, figured by dividing the number of hits made by the batter by the number of times at bat'

bean ball (slang) = 'pitch that comes close to the batter's head or that hits the head'

bloop = 'to hit (the ball) in the air safely but not squarely'

brush back = 'to force (a batter) away from home plate with a pitch close to the batter's person'; used of a pitcher contending with a batter crowding home plate

bullpen = (1) 'area adjoining the outfield, where relief pitchers prepare themselves for play by warming up' (2) 'a team's relief pitchers'

bunt = (1) (verb) 'to hit (the ball delivered by the pitcher) without swinging the bat' (2) (noun) 'ball that rolls slowly in the infield because of such contact with the bat'

bush league (slang) = 'a minor league'

change-up, change, change of pace = 'pitch whose speed in flight is markedly less than that of most pitches, calculated to throw the batter off stride'

choke (up) = 'to grip (the bat) high on the handle, at a point near the center of the bat's length rather than at the normal point near the end'

cleanup = 'place in the batting order of the player who bats fourth' (so called because the player in that place, normally a good hitter, is often in a position to drive home teammates who are base runners, or "to clean the bases")

count = 'number of balls and strikes accumulated by a batter'

curve, curve ball = 'pitch thrown so that it travels on a curved course to the batter'

delivery = 'pitch'

double = 'hit that permits a batter to reach second base safely'

double-header, double bill = 'two games played, usually by the same teams, on one day's program, with a brief interval between games'

down = 'out, retired'

dugout = 'either of two partially excavated areas that house members of teams not in action on the playing field'

first base = 'first of the three bases in the circuit traveled by a base runner on the way to home plate'

fly ball, fly = 'ball batted in a high arc, especially when hit to the outfield'

force in = 'to cause (a run) to score by walking a batter when the bases are all occupied by base runners'; used of a pitcher

foul territory = 'that part of the playing field outside the foul lines, including the area behind home plate'

foul tip = 'ball, barely touched by a swung bat, that has no forward movement from home plate'

fungo = 'fly ball hit in pregame practice to an outfielder by a coach, who tosses the ball into the air and bats it'

ground ball, grounder = 'batted ball that travels by bouncing or rolling over the turf rather than soaring in an arc'

hit = 'batted or bunted ball that enables a batter to reach a base safely without benefit of an error or a fielder's choice'

hole = 'area of the rear part of the infield, between the stations of the shortstop and third baseman'; used in the expression *go into the hole* = 'to field a ground ball hit in the hole'

home plate, home = 'five-sided piece of hard rubber, embedded so as to be flush with the ground, beside which the batter stands and to which a player runs after reaching third base in order to score'

home run, homer (informal) = 'longest hit, which permits a batter to make a complete and uninterrupted circuit of the three bases and to score, usually the result of the ball's clearing an outfield barrier'

infield = (1) 'inner part of the playing field, within which home plate, the pitcher's box, and the three bases are located' (2) 'the four infielders'

infielder = 'any of four defensive players stationed in the infield: first baseman, second baseman, third baseman, shortstop'

inning = 'one of the nine periods of play that make up a regular game, during which each team has a turn at bat and which is concluded when three players of each team have been put out'

knuckle ball, knuckler = 'breaking pitch noted for the unpredictability of its course, thrown by gripping the ball with the knuckles or fingernails'

line drive, liner = 'ball batted sharply in the air but on a low course that approximates a straight line rather than an arc'

loaded = '(of bases) fully occupied by base runners'

major leagues, the majors = 'the two professional leagues (American and National) having the highest caliber of play'

minor leagues, the minors = 'the professional leagues whose caliber is below that of the major leagues'

mitt = 'protective leather covering for the hand, heavier than a glove and worn by the catcher and first baseman'

mound = 'pitcher's box'

no-hit game, no-hitter = 'game in which one team gets no hits'

on = 'on base'

on base = 'having reached a base safely'

on deck = 'next at bat, following the present batter'

out = (1) (adjective) 'opposite of safe, that is, denied the right to occupy a base or home plate, as when a batter strikes out, hits a fly ball that is caught or a ground ball and is tagged out before reaching first base, or when a base runner attempting to advance on the bases is tagged out' (2) (noun) 'the result of such a play'

outfield = (1) 'outer part of the playing field extending between the perimeter of the infield and the field's outer limits' (2) 'the three outfielders'

outfielder = 'any of three defensive players in the outfield: right fielder, center fielder, left fielder'

pinch hitter = 'player who takes a teammate's turn at bat'

pitch = (1) (verb) 'to function as pitcher' (2) (noun) 'ball thrown by the pitcher'

pitcher = 'player of the team not at bat who throws the ball toward opposing batters'

pop fly, pop-up = 'short fly ball that descends in the infield or just beyond it'

put out = 'to cause (a batter or base runner) to be out'

retire = 'to put out (a batter, base runner, or side)'

right field = 'part of the outfield behind the area of first base and to the right of center field as viewed from home plate'

run = (1) 'product of a base runner's complete circuit of the three bases, concluding with a touch of home plate' (2) 'basic unit of measure in scoring a game, counting one point for each such circuit'

safe = '(of a batter or base runner who has arrived at the base or home plate ahead of a fielder's throw or who has escaped a fielder's attempt to tag the runner) having reached a base or home plate without being put out'

score = 'to reach home plate safely, thereby producing a run'

screwball = 'breaking pitch whose break is opposite in direction to that of a curve'

second base = 'second of the three bases in the circuit traveled by a base runner on the way to home plate'

shoestring catch = 'catch of a fly ball made at shoe-top level, when the ball has descended almost to the turf'

shortstop = 'infielder stationed about midway between second base and third base'

shut out = 'to keep (an opposing team) scoreless, especially for an entire game'; used of a pitcher

shutout = 'complete game in which one team is held scoreless'

single = 'hit that permits a batter to reach first base safely'

sinker = 'pitched ball that suddenly descends from a straight course as it nears the batter'

slide = 'base runner's act of dropping to the ground and going into a base feet first or headfirst, as a means of evading a fielder's tag or of upsetting a fielder'

spitball = 'pitched ball, now illegal, whose eccentric flight is caused by the pitcher's application of saliva or sweat to the ball'

squeeze play = 'bunt attempted or executed so as to bring a runner on third base to home plate safely'

steal = 'to advance to and reach (a base) safely while a teammate is at bat, but not as a result of the batter's having hit the ball or walked, or of a wild pitch, passed ball, or error by a defensive player'; used of a base runner

strike = (1) 'pitch within the strike zone, at which a batter does not swing'; also called *called strike* (2) 'result of a batter's swinging and missing a pitch or hitting the ball into foul territory, where it drops without being caught on the fly by a defensive player'

strike out = (1) 'to be put out as a result of accumulating three strikes, provided that the third does not come from hitting a foul, which merely extends the turn at bat'; used of a batter (2) 'to retire (a batter) by recording three strikes under the same conditions'; used of a pitcher

switch hitter = 'batter whose batting stance varies according to the pitcher faced and who therefore bats left-handed against a right-handed pitcher and right-handed against a left-handed pitcher'

Texas leaguer = 'short fly ball that drops in the outfield for a hit'

third base = 'last of the three bases in the circuit traveled by a base runner on the way to home plate'

triple = 'hit that permits a batter to reach third base safely'

walk = (1) (noun) 'base on balls' (2) (verb) 'to receive a base on balls'; used of a batter (3) (verb) 'to grant (a batter) a base on balls'; used of a pitcher

wild = (1) '(of a pitcher) incapable of throwing strikes consistently' (2) '(of a thrown ball) beyond the reach of an intended receiver of the ball'

wind up = 'to make preliminary bodily movements, especially of the arms and legs, as part of the process of throwing the ball'; used of a pitcher

World Series = 'postseason games played between the best team in each major league to determine the championship of American professional baseball'

(2) Some terms or expressions that have come into the general vocabulary:

big-league = 'first-rate, outstanding'

bush-league, bush = 'second-rate, provincial'

can't *or* **won't get to first base** (slang) = 'unable or unlikely to make even a decent start on something'

foul ball = 'someone or something to be deplored or censured'

have two strikes on *or* **against (one)** = 'to be at a great handicap even before starting a venture'

home run = 'something excellent or remarkable'

new ball game = 'new competitive situation in which changed circumstances have matched the contestants more evenly and thus put the outcome in doubt'

off base (informal) = 'inaccurate, wide of the mark'

out in left field (slang) = '(of a person) incompetent or inept so as to be out of touch with a situation, or (of a situation, suggestion, etc.) not practical or pertinent'

pinch hitter = 'person who takes the place of another in an emergency'

screwball = 'person whose characteristic behavior is eccentric' (suggested by the course of such a pitched ball)

strike out = 'to fail completely and usually ignominiously'

throw (one) a curve = 'to deal deceptively or unfairly with someone, put at a disadvantage by surprising'

wild pitch = 'irrational or irresponsible act'

basketball terms. Of all major sports, basketball is the most truly American in origin and roots, though its inventor, Dr. James Naismith, was born and educated in Canada. The game, introduced in 1891, is now played worldwide in more than 100 countries. Its vocabulary is its own; little of the basketball terminology heard regularly inside gymnasiums and sports arenas has entered our everyday language.

assist = 'to pass the ball from one player to a teammate who then scores a field goal'

backboard = 'vertical surface to which the basket is attached and from which the ball often rebounds'

back court = 'a team's defensive area, that half of the court containing the basket the team is defending'

back-court man = 'a guard'

backliner = 'a guard'

basket = 'field goal'

blocking = 'foul committed by a defensive player in obstructing the legal path of an offensive opponent through contact'

boards (informal) = 'backboards considered as an area of play'; used typically in the expression *controlling the boards* = 'controlling the rebounding balls by gaining possession of them'

bucket (slang) = 'field goal'

center = 'offensive player whose functions include participating in the center jump'

charging = 'foul by an offensive player in running forcefully into a defensive opponent who has legal possession of the ball'

corner man = 'forward'

dribble = 'to bounce the ball continuously on the court surface while running, as a means of controlling or advancing the ball'

fast break = 'offensive technique for advancing the ball at great speed to the goal being defended by the opposing team in an attempt to prevent them from making an effective defense'

field goal = 'successful shot into the basket during regular play, which scores two points'

forward = 'either of two players who, together with the center, make up the principal offensive unit of a team'

foul = 'any of several rules infractions, but usually a personal foul' See also *technical foul*, below.

foulline = 'free-throwline'

foul out = 'to leave the remainder of the game as a penalty for having committed the maximum number of personal fouls allowed by the rules'

foul shot = 'free throw'

free throw = 'penalty shot awarded to a fouled player, allowing the player to toss the ball into the basket defended by the opponents without hindrance, and worth one point if successful'

free-throw line = 'line 15 feet from the backboard of the basket defended by the opponents, behind which a player stands when attempting a free throw'

goal tending = 'illegal interference by a defensive player with the flight of the opponents' ball when it is on a descending path above the rim of the basket or on or within the rim'

guard = 'either of a team's two defensive players, whose primary job is to impede opponents' attempts to score points'

hook shot = 'an attempt to score a field goal in which the shooter releases the ball with the hands over the shoulder while facing slightly away from the basket'

jump shot, jumper = 'an attempt to score a field goal in which a player releases the ball at the peak of an upward jump'

layup = 'an attempt to score a field goal with a shot made from a jumping position alongside or under the basket, the backboard serving as a rebounding surface'

personal foul = 'rules infraction involving illegal bodily contact with an opponent, as in blocking, holding, pushing, or tripping'

press = 'form of defense that seeks to hinder offensive opponents by aggressive but legal means, such as close guarding'; a *full-court* or *all-court press* is employed over the entire court, and a *half-court press*, only after the offensive team has entered the opponents' half of the court

rebound = 'ball that remains in play after an unsuccessful attempt to score a field goal and after the ball has bounded off the backboard or basket rim'

set shot = 'an attempt to score a field goal with a shot from a stationary position, usually employing both hands of the shooter'

shoot = 'to throw the ball toward the basket in an attempt to score'

steal = 'to gain possession of the ball by a skillful defensive maneuver'

technical foul = 'infraction of a technical rule, or a penalty for a player's unsportsmanlike behavior' See *personal foul*, above.

three-point play = 'field goal plus a subsequent successful free throw by a player fouled in the act of scoring the field goal'

traveling = 'illegal movement by a player in possession of the ball, as a result of failure to dribble the ball while moving'

violation = 'infraction of rules, less serious than a foul, such as traveling or stepping outside the boundaries of the court'

bastard. See ILLEGITIMATE CHILD.

B.C. See A.D., B.C.

beat. The standard past participle is *beaten*, but the old variant participle *beat* remains in good, though slightly informal, use, especially in the sense 'defeated.'

> Everybody thought for sure I was beat, and I wasn't too sure myself how it would turn out that time.
> Harry Truman (quoted), Merle Miller, *Plain Speaking*

> I'm used to having half the audience come to see me get beat, regardless of who my opponent is.
> —Muhammad Ali, *The Greatest*

because. See 'CAUSE.

because of. See DUE TO.

begging the question. In everyday usage this term is often applied to any argument that seems to be deliberately avoiding the point at issue. But such a loose definition could apply equally to a whole family of argumentative irrelevancies. Question begging—or, as the ancient logicians called it, *petitio principii*—refers to a specific kind of evasion in which the arguer justifies his or her position with the very point being debated. If, for example, we argued that telepathy cannot exist because direct thought transference between individuals is impossible, or we insisted that a newspaper story must be true because the paper wouldn't print it if it weren't, we would be begging the question in the strict sense of the term. For more see FALLACY.

behalf. There is a shadowy rule that *on behalf (of)* means merely 'acting as the agent of, representing,' while *in behalf (of)* means 'acting in the interests of, supporting.' The trouble is that someone "representing" another will usually be also "supporting" that person. In both of the following typical quotations it can be argued that *on behalf* is correct since legal representation is meant, and that *in behalf* is correct since support and advocacy are meant.

> Three of the four defendants chose not to testify in their own behalf.
> —John Leonard, *New York Times*

> A class action is a suit begun by one or more persons not only on their own behalf but also on behalf of all other persons similarly situated.
> —Walter F. Murphy, *The Vicar of Christ*

Probably the only context where *on behalf of* clearly does not imply support is in formal legal and parliamentary usage when no argument is going on: *Speaking on behalf of the chairman, who could not attend, he declared the committee in session.*

Another difficulty with this rule is that it's hard to remember. Highly skilled writers, striving for correct and effective usage, hesitate about it and make opposite decisions. Following are two passages from the same page of a book describing a debate in the U.S. Senate, and two passages from consecutive pages of a biography of President Jimmy Carter—both books very competently written.

> Culver tells him that Stennis is going to announce his acceptance of the amendment and Goldwater then agrees to speak in its behalf. . . .

> . . . John Chafee . . . speaks on behalf of Culver's amendment.
> —Elizabeth Drew, *Senator*

> Carter became chairman of the 1974 Democratic Campaign Committee, a usually thankless and rather lackluster job that requires . . . dozens of fund-raising speeches on behalf of Democratic Congressional candidates. . . .

> . . . He was remembering, perhaps . . . the large chunk of Lance's life that had been spent in his behalf in those long-ago days. . . .
> —James Wooten, *Dasher*

In any case, there is simply no consensus about this rule. Some writers seem to take care to use *in behalf of* strictly to mean 'in support of,' and others are content to use *on behalf of* indiscriminately:

> The essence of liberalism is the use of government to intervene on behalf of people. —Leon Shull (quoted), *New York Times*

> . . . he toyed with the idea of canceling any demonstration in his behalf. . . . —Bill Moyers, *Listening to America*

◇ ***Recommendation.*** Lawyers and strict constructionists will no doubt go on trying to discriminate between *on behalf of* and *in behalf of.* In general usage the rule is unnecessary and unenforceable. *On* and *in* are equally satisfactory.

behest. This is an old word meaning 'a command.' It is now used as a fancy synonym both for 'command' and for 'urging, strong suggestion':

> The Persian Empire was cemented by its couriers, who rode tirelessly over roads at the behest of the Great King. —Isaac Asimov, *Science Past—Science Future*

> It was at my father's behest that I took boxing lessons, and at my mother's that I studied the piano. —J. Paul Getty, *As I See It*

> At one point the most famous black athletes in America gathered in Cleveland, at the behest of Jim Brown and Bill Russell, to meet with Ali and attempt to persuade him to accept some kind of compromise with the Army. —Howard Cosell, *Cosell*

behoove. The verb *behoove* is now used only in the construction *it behooves* with a personal object followed by an infinitive. The entire construction means 'it is necessary or appropriate or advantageous for (the person) to do (something).' *Behoove* is a highly formal word, in modern usage verging on the pompous:

> Gentlemen . . . it behooves us, standing together eye to eye and shoulder to shoulder as fellow-citizens of the best city in the world, to consider where we are both as regards ourselves and the common weal. —Sinclair Lewis, *Babbitt* (1922)

> I believe it would behoove divorce-ridden America to learn of the devotion to family that exists amongst the primitive people. —Thomas A. Dooley, *The Edge of Tomorrow*

> While a commander must avoid overcontrol, it behooves him to know what goes on at least two echelons of command below him. —William C. Westmoreland, *A Soldier Reports*

The past tense of *behoove* is *behooved:*

> Vivian Dubois considered very carefully what it behooved him to do next. —Agatha Christie, *A Pocketful of Rye*

being. The conjunctional phrases *being as, being how, being that* = 'considering that, since, because' are widespread in dialectal and informal use. Such constructions as *We missed the start of the movie, being as we got caught in traffic* would be unacceptable in writing and in more formal speech.

bellwether. *Wether* is the Old English word for 'male sheep.' One traditional method of herding sheep was to choose a dominant male, put a bell on him, and allow him to lead the flock. Thus, *bellwether* became a metaphor for a leader whom "the herd" will follow blindly. In modern U.S. politics a bellwether is a person or group regarded as a trend indicator:

> . . . two industries that the U.S. has always regarded as bellwethers: steel and autos . . . —*Business Week*

But the word is also sometimes used of a more positive leadership role:

> A commander clearly is the bellwether of his command and must display confidence and resolution. —William C. Westmoreland, *A Soldier Reports*

bend sinister. See BAR SINISTER, BEND SINISTER.

beside, besides. *Beside* is now only a preposition, meaning 'by the side of, alongside' or 'in comparison with': *Who is that standing beside you in the photograph? Beside the battleship the cutter looked fragile and unseaworthy. Besides,* however, is both an adverb meaning 'in addition, furthermore' and a preposition meaning 'in addition to' and 'except for': *You haven't cleaned your room; besides, you still have to do your homework. Besides ballet, Beth teaches folk and Renaissance dancing.*

bet. The standard past tense and past participle are *bet. Betted* is also acceptable for either, but it is now becoming rare.

better than. This expression is often used to mean 'more':

> You know, I've been in this business for better than 35 years, and I've never heard of this company.
> —quoted in *New York Times*

> Roughly speaking, that means that better than one family in five is a boat owner.
> —Fox Butterfield, *New York Times*

> Currently inflation is running at better than 13 percent annually. . . .
> —Dave Whitney, *Florida Times-Union*

◇ ***Recommendation.*** Some people reject this usage simply because "more" is not necessarily "better." It is a slightly informal idiom but is widespread and perfectly legitimate. It should be used sparingly in formal writing and like any idiom should not be pushed too far. In the third quotation above, the idiom is unsuitable to the context, but it may have been chosen deliberately, for ironical effect.

bettor, better. For 'one who bets' these spellings are equally correct. *Bettor,* the more formal version, is favored by the authorities, including race-track stewards and dictionaries. The betting public, however, generally prefers *better:*

> Americans seem to have an insatiable appetite for casino gambling—last year bettors lost $2 billion in Nevada. . . .
> —John Mervin, *Forbes*

> He and Horace Bane and Joe the Barber and nameless other two-dollar betters . . .
> —Studs Terkel, *Talking to Myself*

between, among. The traditional rule is that *between* is used for relationships of two and *among* for relationships of three or more. But *between* is also used with more than two when the relationship is considered to link each individual to each of the others. Such situations are usually debatable. The result is that some people will use *between* in cases where others will insist on *among.*

> The contrast between the three nations now laying claim to large stretches of the continent was a fascinating one.
> —J. T. Adams, *The Epic of America*

> At one of the recent economic summit conferences between myself and the other leaders of the Western world . . .
> —Jimmy Carter (quoted), *New York Times*

> . . . the latest in a series of sporadic negotiations among the British, the Guatemalans, and the Belizeans . . .
> —Linda Charlton, *New York Times*

> In 1975, he negotiated the compromise among Cesar Chavez, the Teamsters, and the growers.
> —David S. Broder, *Atlantic Monthly*

◇ ***Recommendation.*** If in doubt, use *among* for relationships involving more than two. But *between* is also justified when the relationship is structured to link each member mutually with every other.

between you and I. See ME.

bi-, semi-. In adjectives referring to periods of time, the basic rule is that *bi-* means 'two' and *semi-* means 'half.' But the rule is not at all consistently followed.

(1) *Biweekly* primarily means 'once every two weeks' and *bimonthly* primarily means 'once every two months.' But they are all too often used to mean 'twice a week' and 'twice a month'; for these meanings the better choice is *semiweekly* and *semimonthly*.

(2) *Semiannual* likewise is the better term for 'twice a year.' Unfortunately, *biannual* also, when it is used, means 'twice a year.' The preferred term for 'once every two years' is *biennial* (from Latin *biennium* = 'period of two years').

◇ ***Recommendation.*** The usage of these terms is in serious disarray and can cause real confusion. We strongly recommend the following exclusive uses:

semiweekly = 'twice a week'
biweekly = 'every two weeks'
semimonthly = 'twice a month'
bimonthly = 'every two months'
semiannual = 'twice a year'
biennial = 'every two years'

We advise abandoning *biannual* entirely.

Bible. The English language owes a continuing debt to the Holy Bible, above all to the King James Version of 1611. Ever since Christianity was introduced into Britain, the Scriptures have been translated over and over into the developing language of the people. King James I, an enthusiastic theologian who came to the English throne in 1603, gave ardent support to the idea of a new version of the Bible by naming a translation committee in 1604. These chosen scholars undertook their task with certain advantages. It was a time when English genius and the English language were in flower. The Book of Common Prayer with its beautiful language had recently come into use. The earlier Bible versions of John Wycliffe (1382), William Tyndale (1525–35), and Miles Coverdale (1535), together with the Great Bible (1539–68) and Bishops' Bible (1568), had prepared the way well for the new one.

Finally completed and published in 1611 as the "Authorized Version," this Bible came to be known in America as the King James Version (KJV). The Epistle Dedicatory, addressed by the translators to King James by way of a preface to the new Bible, stated in part that "out of the Original Sacred Tongues, together with comparing of the labours, both in our own, and other foreign Languages, of many worthy men who went before us, there should be one more exact Translation of the holy Scriptures into the *English Tongue*. . . . And now at last, by the mercy of God, and the continuance of our labours, it being brought unto such a conclusion . . . we hold it our duty to offer it to Your Majesty . . . as to the principal Mover and Author of the work. . . ." Other words in this statement expressed anxiety about the reception of the new version. The translators did not dream of the preeminent place it would attain in "the *English Tongue*."

We have much company in claiming that the King James Version has never been surpassed or equaled in the years since it appeared. There have been newer translations that were more precise, literal, or accurate in detail, but none has approached the vigor, beauty, or majesty of the KJV. It has been a shaping influence on our language for nearly 400 years. An English professor at Princeton University in the 1920s began his course by stating: "The three greatest creations in English are the King James Version of the Holy Bible, the works of William Shakespeare, and the Book of Common Prayer. Of these the King James Version has had the most enduring influence over the centuries and in the present." Recently, a Roman Catholic theological scholar wrote: "For liturgical usage, one might well ask if the *King James Version* has ever been excelled."

Millions of copies of the KJV continue to roll off the presses year by year, among them the large, handsome Washburn College Bible (1979), with color illustrations from art collections throughout the world. If imitation is the sincerest form of flattery, the appearance, also in 1979, of The New King James Bible New Testament ("It makes the King James even better") is further evidence of the continuing influence of the KJV.

Enduring Language From the King James Bible. This is a selection of familiar idioms, expressions, and sayings. The archaic grammar or words do not prevent most of these selections from being understood. They are given in order of Biblical appearance, with definitions and explanations where necessary.

the fat of the land = 'the best available food and other luxuries'
And ye shall eat the fat of the land.
—Genesis 45:18

milk and honey
A land flowing with milk and honey.
—Exodus 3:8

my people
Let my people go.
—Exodus 5:1

bricks without straw = 'a task deliberately made impossible'
Ye shall no more give the people straw to make brick.
—Exodus 5:7

the fleshpots = 'comfort, abundance'
Would to God we had died by the hand of the Lord in the land of Egypt, when we sat by the fleshpots.
—Exodus 16:3

the stars in their courses = 'destiny'
The stars in their courses fought against Sisera.
—Judges 5:20

**shibboleth*
Say now Shibboleth: and he said Sibboleth: for he could not frame to pronounce it right.
—Judges 12:6

after one's own heart
A man after his own heart.
—1 Samuel 13:14

the mighty
How are the mighty fallen.
—2 Samuel 1:25

by the skin of one's teeth = 'by the narrowest margin'
I am escaped with the skin of my teeth.
—Job 19:20

*Appears as separate entry

the root of the matter = 'the basic cause, essential aspect'
Seeing the root of the matter is found in me.
—Job 19:28

out of the mouths of babes and sucklings = '(insight often comes) from ordinary people'
Out of the mouth of babes and sucklings hast thou ordained strength.
—Psalm 8:2

green pastures
He maketh me to lie down in green pastures.
—Psalm 23:2

the valley of the shadow of death
Yea, though I walk through the valley of the shadow of death, I will fear no evil.
—Psalm 23:4

runneth over
My cup runneth over.
—Psalm 23:5

strength to strength
They go from strength to strength.
—Psalm 84:7

threescore years and ten
The days of our years are threescore years and ten.
—Psalm 90:10

heap coals of fire on = 'to achieve a moral victory over (someone) by returning good for bad'
If thine enemy be hungry, give him bread to eat . . . For thou shalt heap coals of fire upon his head.
—Proverbs 25:21–22

a time for every purpose
To every thing there is a season, and a time for every purpose under the heaven.
—Ecclesiastes 3:1

cast bread on the waters = 'to do a generous deed, or make an investment, without counting on a return'
Cast thy bread upon the waters: for thou shalt find it after many days.
—Ecclesiastes 11:1

a drop in the bucket = 'a trivial contribution or factor'
The nations are as a drop of a bucket.
—Isaiah 40:15

eye to eye = 'in perfect agreement'
They shall see eye to eye.
—Isaiah 52:8

the salt of the earth = 'the most admirable kind of people'
Ye are the salt of the earth: but if the salt have lost his savor, wherewith shall it be salted?
—Matthew 5:13

hide one's light under a bushel = 'to be reluctant to show one's achievement or ability'
Neither do men light a candle, and put it under a bushel [a large bin or vessel], but on a candlestick; and it giveth light unto all that are in the house.
—Matthew 5:15

turn the other cheek = 'to accept trouble or harm without retaliation'
Resist not evil: but whosoever shall smite thee on thy right cheek, turn to him the other also.
—Matthew 5:39

pearls before swine = 'something valuable wasted on the unappreciative'
Neither cast ye your pearls before swine.
—Matthew 7:6

wolf in sheep's clothing
Beware of false prophets, which come to you in sheep's clothing, but inwardly they are ravening wolves.
—Matthew 7:15

a house divided
If a house be divided against itself, that house cannot stand.
—Mark 3:25

in one's right mind = 'sane and sensible'
Clothed, and in his right mind.
—Mark 5:15

worthy of his hire
The laborer is worthy of his hire.
—Luke 10:7

riotous living
Wasted his substance with riotous living.
—Luke 15:13

the scales fall from one's eyes = 'one suddenly understands'
Immediately there fell from his eyes as it had been scales.
—Acts 9:18

respecter of persons
God is no respecter of persons.
—Acts 10:34

no mean = 'considerable'
I am . . . a Jew of Tarsus . . . a citizen of no mean city.
—Acts 21:39

a law unto oneself = 'independent'
These, having not the law, are a law unto themselves.
—Romans 2:14

wages of sin
The wages of sin is death.
—Romans 6:23

the powers that be
The powers that be are ordained of God.
—Romans 13:1

through a glass darkly = 'obscurely'
For now we see through a glass, darkly; but then face to face.
—1 Corinthians 13:12

to suffer fools gladly
For ye suffer fools gladly, seeing ye yourselves are wise.
—2 Corinthians 11:19

a thorn in the flesh = 'a chronic source of irritation'
And lest I should be exalted above measure through the abundance of the revelations, there was given to me a thorn in the flesh, the messenger of Satan to buffet me.
—2 Corinthians 12:7

fall from grace = (1) 'to cease to live religiously' (2) 'to lose someone's favor'
Ye are fallen from grace.
—Galatians 5:4

inner man = 'the stomach, the appetite'; now used jocularly, except in Biblical context

To be strengthened with might by his Spirit in the inner man.

—Ephesians 3:16

labor of love

Remembering without ceasing your work of faith, and labor of love, and patience of hope in our Lord Jesus Christ.

—1 Thessalonians 1:3

filthy lucre

Not greedy of filthy lucre.

—1 Timothy 3:8

the root of all evil

The love of money is the root of all evil.

—1 Timothy 6:10

multitude of sins

Charity shall cover the multitude of sins.

—1 Peter 4:8

The King James Bible and Literary Style. From colonial times until the 20th century, the King James Bible was the only book in many American households. To millions it was the sole available model of high literary style. Here is an example of the sonorous cadences for which the King James Version is justly celebrated. Of this passage the famous 19th-century critic George Saintsbury wrote, "I know no more perfect example of English prose rhythm."

Set me as a seal upon thine heart,
as a seal upon thine arm: for love *is* strong as death;
jealousy *is* cruel as the grave: the coals thereof *are* coals of fire,
which hath a most vehement flame.
Many waters cannot quench love,
neither can the floods drown it. . . .

—Song of Solomon 8:6–7

Modern Translations. The two oldest existing Bible manuscripts are Codex Sinaiticus (discovered by Konstantin von Tischendorf of Germany in St. Catherine's Monastery on Mount Sinai in 1844, given to Czar Alexander II in 1859, and sold to the British Museum by the Soviet government in 1933) and Codex Vaticanus (now in the Vatican Library). Von Tischendorf prepared these two invaluable resources for publication in 1867, thus making them accessible for the first time to the scholarly world. With these newly available manuscripts plus other discoveries, and using new scientific methods, scholars everywhere undertook to improve existing Bible translations.

The main reason new translations have been necessary is, of course, that so many words no longer carry the same meanings as they did 400 years ago. For example, in various passages in the King James Version you will find *prevent* in the sense of 'precede,' *reprove* for 'decide,' and *conversation* for 'behavior.' No mere handful of words is thus affected, but a formidable list, enough to generate a garbled understanding of many passages. The King James may still be the best, but even the most highly educated person of today would be unwise to use it without a scholarly commentary and notes.

Steps were taken in 1870 in England to revise the Authorized Version while retaining its style. This Revised Version (RV or ERV) was published beginning with the New Testament in 1881. While the RV made improvements in accuracy and consistency, it lost the loveliness and vitality of the KJV and failed to take its place.

The present century has seen a number of fresh translations. New Testament versions by James Moffatt (1913), Edgar Goodspeed (1923), Ronald Knox (1944), and J. B. Phillips (1947–58) are some of the most attractive.

The past 30 years have witnessed among others the publication of the Revised Standard Version (RSV, 1952), The Amplified Bible (AB, 1964), The Jerusalem Bible (JB, 1966), The New English Bible with Apocrypha (NEB, 1970), The New American Bible (NAB, 1970), The New American Standard Bible (NASB, 1971), The Living Bible (LB, 1971), Good News Bible (GNB, 1976), Good News Bible with Deuterocanonicals/Apocrypha (GNB, 1978), the New International Version of the Holy Bible (NIV, 1978), and The Reader's Digest Bible (1982).

The scholars of the non–Roman Catholic churches in the United States began work on the Revised Standard Version in 1930; the New Testament was published in 1946, the Old in 1952. The revision continues. An "Ecumenical Edition" with Apocrypha/Deuterocanonical Books was issued for Eastern Orthodox, Roman Catholic, and Anglican use in 1973. Forty million copies of the RSV are currently in print.

The Amplified Bible was produced under the oversight of the Lockman Foundation. Its readership has been largely limited to the evangelical community.

The major Roman Catholic version is The Jerusalem Bible. This is the English equivalent of the French Bible de Jérusalem, translated not from the Latin but instead from the Hebrew and Greek. The helpful critical notes throughout take account of decisions and implications of the Second Vatican Council. The 28 principal collaborators on the JB have achieved a high degree of beauty and readability.

The New English Bible is a fresh translation from the original texts rather than a revision of earlier translations. The project began in 1946, when the Presbyterian church of Scotland invited British Anglicans, Baptists, Methodists, and Congregationalists to join in creating the new Bible. The work of the NEB scholars was reviewed by literary advisers to achieve a delicate sense of English style.

Another Roman Catholic version is the spare, contemporary New American Bible, translated under the auspices of the Catholic Biblical Association of America.

The New American Standard Bible, fa-

Comparison of Leading Bible Translations

	King James Version	Revised Standard Version	Jerusalem Bible
Genesis 4:9	And the LORD said unto Cain, Where *is* Abel thy brother? And he said, I know not; *Am* I my brother's keeper?	Then the LORD said to Cain, "Where is Abel your brother?" He said, "I do not know; am I my brother's keeper?"	Yahweh asked Cain, "Where is your brother Abel?" "I do not know," he replied. "Am I my brother's guardian?"
Numbers 6:24–26	The LORD bless thee, and keep thee: the LORD make his face shine upon thee, and be gracious unto thee: the LORD lift up his countenance upon thee, and give thee peace.	"The LORD bless you and keep you: The LORD make his face to shine upon you, and be gracious to you: The LORD lift up his countenance upon you, and give you peace."	'May Yahweh bless you and keep you. May Yahweh let his face shine on you and be gracious to you. May Yahweh uncover his face to you and bring you peace.'
Psalms 19:1	The heavens declare the glory of God; and the firmament showeth his handiwork.	The heavens are telling the glory of God; and the firmament proclaims his handiwork.	The heavens declare the glory of God, the vault of heaven proclaims his handiwork. . . .
Isaiah 55:2	Wherefore do ye spend money for *that which is* not bread? and your labor for *that which* satisfieth not? hearken diligently unto me, and eat ye *that which is* good, and let your soul delight itself in fatness.	"Why do you spend your money for that which is not bread, and your labor for that which does not satisfy? Hearken diligently to me, and eat what is good, and delight yourselves in fatness."	Why spend money on what is not bread, your wages on what fails to satisfy? Listen, listen to me, and you will have good things to eat and rich food to enjoy.

vored by many fundamentalist Protestants, is a formal, evangelical translation. It was also sponsored by the Lockman Foundation.

One man, Kenneth Taylor, an evangelical Protestant, produced The Living Bible. It is an idiomatic paraphrase, saying "what the writers . . . meant" in "different words than the authors used." The sale of 24 million copies in the first decade attests its popularity.

The United Bible Societies' Good News Bible (subtitled The Bible in Today's English Version), with its conversational language, is quite easy to read. A special New Testament edition for Eastern Orthodox Bible study and a complete GNB with Roman Catholic imprimatur have been issued.

The translators and editors of the New York International Bible Society's New International Version were motivated by "concern for clear and natural English" and sought "to avoid obvious Americanisms on the one hand and obvious Anglicanisms on the other." They have created a lucid, literary version.

Comparison of Seven Leading Versions. All translators are faced with fascinating choices of words, idiom, and style. Exceptionally fascinating are the efforts and successes of the modern Biblical translators to modernize or improve on the King James Version. So that you can sample the details yourself, we have selected ten short passages (five from the Old Testament and five from the New Testament) and set out the King James Version, followed by the versions arrived at by six of the leading modern translations.

New English Bible	New International Version	Good News Bible	The Living Bible
Then the LORD said to Cain, 'Where is your brother Abel?' Cain answered, 'I do not know. Am I my brother's keeper?'	Then the LORD said to Cain, "Where is your brother Abel?" "I don't know," he replied. "Am I my brother's keeper?"	The LORD asked Cain, "Where is your brother Abel?" He answered, "I don't know. Am I supposed to take care of my brother?"	But afterwards the LORD asked Cain, "Where is your brother? Where is Abel?" "How should I know?" Cain retorted. "Am I supposed to keep track of him wherever he goes?"
The LORD bless you and watch over you; the LORD make his face shine upon you and be gracious to you; the LORD look kindly on you and give you peace.	"The LORD bless you and keep you; the LORD make his face shine upon you and be gracious to you; the LORD turn his face toward you and give you peace."	May the LORD bless you and take care of you; May the LORD be kind and gracious to you; May the LORD look on you with favor and give you peace.	'May the Lord bless and protect you; may the Lord's face radiate with joy because of you; may he be gracious to you, show you his favor, and give you his peace.'
The heavens tell out the glory of God, the vault of heaven reveals his handiwork.	The heavens declare the glory of God; the skies proclaim the work of his hands.	How clearly the sky reveals God's glory! How plainly it shows what he has done!	The heavens are telling the glory of God; they are a marvelous display of his craftsmanship.
Why spend money and get what is not bread, why give the price of your labour and go unsatisfied? Only listen to me and you will have good food to eat, and you will enjoy the fat of the land.	"Why spend money on what is not bread, and your labor on what does not satisfy? Listen, listen to me, and eat what is good, and your soul will delight in the richest of fare."	"Why spend money on what does not satisfy? Why spend your wages and still be hungry? Listen to me and do what I say, and you will enjoy the best food of all."	Why spend your money on foodstuffs that don't give you strength? Why pay for groceries that don't do you any good? Listen and I'll tell you where to get good food that fattens up the soul!

cont.	King James Version	Revised Standard Version	Jerusalem Bible
Micah 6:8	He hath showed thee, O man, what *is* good; and what doth the LORD require of thee, but to do justly, and to love mercy, and to walk humbly with thy God?	He has showed you, O man, what is good; and what does the LORD require of you but to do justice, and to love kindness, and to walk humbly with your God?	—What is good has been explained to you, man; this is what Yahweh asks of you: only this, to act justly, to love tenderly and to walk humbly with your God.
Luke 11:2–4	Our Father, which art in heaven, Hallowed be thy name. Thy kingdom come. Thy will be done, as in heaven, so in earth. Give us day by day our daily bread. And forgive us our sins; for we also forgive every one that is indebted to us. And lead us not into temptation; but deliver us from evil.	"Father, hallowed be thy name. Thy kingdom come. Give us each day our daily bread; and forgive us our sins, for we ourselves forgive every one who is indebted to us; and lead us not into temptation."	'Father, may your name be held holy, your kingdom come; give us each day our daily bread, and forgive us our sins, for we ourselves forgive each one who is in debt to us. And do not put us to the test.'
John 16:33	In the world ye shall have tribulation: but be of good cheer; I have overcome the world.	"In the world you have tribulation; but be of good cheer, I have overcome the world."	"In the world you will have trouble, but be brave: I have conquered the world."
Galatians 3:28	There is neither Jew nor Greek, there is neither bond nor free, there is neither male nor female: for ye are all one in Christ Jesus.	There is neither Jew nor Greek, there is neither slave nor free, there is neither male nor female; for you are all one in Christ Jesus.	. . . and there are no more distinctions between Jew and Greek, slave and free, male and female, but all of you are one in Chris[t] Jesus.
Colossians 4:6	Let your speech *be* always with grace, seasoned with salt, that ye may know how ye ought to answer every man.	Let your speech always be gracious, seasoned with salt, so that you may know how you ought to answer every one.	Talk to them agreeably an[d] with a flavor of wit, and try to fit your answers to the needs of each one.
Revelation 20:12	And I saw the dead, small and great, stand before God; and the books were opened: and another book was opened, which is *the book* of life: and the dead were judged out of those things which were written in the books, according to their works.	And I saw the dead, great and small, standing before the throne, and books were opened. Also another book was opened, which is the book of life. And the dead were judged by what was written in the books, by what they had done.	I saw the dead, both grea[t] and small, standing in front of his throne, while the book of life was opened, and *other books opened* which were the record of what they had done in their lives, by which the dead were judged.

New English Bible	New International Version	Good News Bible	The Living Bible
God has told you what is good; and what is it that the LORD asks of you? Only to act justly, to love loyalty, to walk wisely before your God.	He has showed you, O man, what is good. And what does the LORD require of you? To act justly and to love mercy and to walk humbly with your God.	No, the LORD has told us what is good. What he requires of us is this: to do what is just, to show constant love, and to live in humble fellowship with our God.	No, he has told you what he wants, and this is all it is: *to be fair and just and merciful, and to walk humbly with your God.*
"Father, thy name be hallowed; thy kingdom come. Give us each day ur daily bread. And for- ive us our sins, for we oo forgive all who have one us wrong. And do ot bring us to the test."	'Father, hallowed be your name, your kingdom come. Give us each day our daily bread. Forgive us our sins, for we also forgive everyone who sins against us. And lead us not into temptation.'	'Father: May your holy name be honored; may your Kingdom come. Give us day by day the food we need. Forgive us our sins, for we forgive everyone who does us wrong. And do not bring us to hard testing.'	"Father, may your name be honored for its holiness; send your Kingdom soon. Give us our food day by day. And forgive our sins—for we have forgiven those who sinned against us. And don't allow us to be tempted."
In the world you will ave trouble. But cour- ge! The victory is mine; have conquered the vorld.'	"In this world you will have trouble. But take heart! I have overcome the world."	"The world will make you suffer. But be brave! I have defeated the world!"	"Here on earth you will have many trials and sorrows; but cheer up, for I have overcome the world."
here is no such thing as ew and Greek, slave nd freeman, male and emale; for you are all ne person in Christ esus.	There is neither Jew nor Greek, slave nor free, male nor female, for you are all one in Christ Jesus.	So there is no difference between Jews and Gentiles, between slaves and free men, between men and women; you are all one in union with Christ Jesus.	We are no longer Jews or Greeks or slaves or free men or even merely men or women, but we are all the same—we are Christians; we are one in Christ Jesus.
et your conversation be lways gracious, and ever insipid; study how est to talk with each erson you meet.	Let your conversation be always full of grace, seasoned with salt, so that you may know how to answer everyone.	Your speech should always be pleasant and interesting, and you should know how to give the right answer to everyone.	Let your conversation be gracious as well as sensible, for then you will have the right answer for everyone.
could see the dead, reat and small, standing efore the throne; and ooks were opened. hen another book was pened, the roll of the ving. From what was ritten in these books e dead were judged pon the record of their eeds.	And I saw the dead, great and small, standing before the throne, and books were opened. Another book was opened, which is the book of life. The dead were judged according to what they had done as recorded in the books.	And I saw the dead, great and small alike, standing before the throne. Books were opened, and then another book was opened, the book of the living. The dead were judged according to what they had done, as recorded in the books.	I saw the dead, great and small, standing before God; and The Books were opened, including the Book of Life. And the dead were judged according to the things written in The Books, each according to the deeds he had done.

biennial. See BI-, SEMI-.

bifurcation. See FALLACY.

Billingsgate. For more than 300 years the London fish market at *Billingsgate* has been proverbial for 'elaborate foul language':

> Youth is beginning to ask why the lowest common denominator must rule, and why we must go straight from Watergate to Billingsgate.
> —Robert Moses (quoted), *New York Times*

billion. In the United States, Canada, and most of the rest of the world a *billion* is a thousand million. But in Britain, Germany, and a few other countries a *billion* is a million million. The word is in any case a less than satisfactory coinage, since in most people's speech it does not sufficiently contrast with *million*. Thus results an irritating if inevitable habit of broadcasters, of emphasizing the first syllable with massive explosive stress every time they mention the word.

bimonthly, biweekly. See BI-, SEMI-.

black, colored, negro. In the time of slavery all three terms were in respectable use. After the Civil War black people generally preferred to be called *colored* or *Colored (people)*. From about the turn of the century *negro* or *Negro* was preferred. Since the civil rights movement of the 1960s *black* or *Black* has become the standard term. It is often spelled with a capital, but the present tendency is to use small letters for *black, white,* and other color terms applied to people. The capital is always used in such terms as *Black Studies* and *Black English*. Some prefer that the word *black* not be used as a noun; the alternatives are *black* or *Black person* (*people, man, woman,* etc.) or *Black American*. See also BLACK ENGLISH.

◇ ***Recommendation.*** Unless you have special preferences, use *black* (small *b*) for both noun and adjective.

Black English. In the 1960s, while the civil rights movement was making the word *black* a symbol of racial pride, language specialists were beginning to pay serious attention to the speech of black Americans, especially in cities such as Detroit and New York. Previously, most people (both black and white) had thought of black speech as ungrammatical and substandard. It is now increasingly understood that Black English is an ethnic American DIALECT, with its own consistent rules of grammar and pronunciation and with roots in the languages of West Africa. For more on the status of Black English see SOCIAL DIALECT.

Origins. In general, Black English originated in the South during the period of slavery and later spread to the North and throughout the United States. What kind of language was it, and how did it originate? There are two schools of thought among the language specialists. One holds that it is simply a variety of Southern speech that developed over the years in much the same way as the white Southern dialects such as Virginia Piedmont. The other view is that Black English has evolved from a creole language based on African origins. The latter view, that Black English is "an Africanized form of English," is the one followed here.

The West Africans who were brought to this country as slaves spoke many different languages, such as Wolof, Hausa, Twi, Ibo, Kongo, and Gola. These are separate languages, but there is a family resemblance among many of them; they share both structural features and many words that are recognizably the same. The slavers often systematically separated people taken from the same tribes in order to prevent them from communicating. And in America, the slaves were at first unable to communicate with their white owners; but this soon became a matter of survival. They were thus forced to develop a *pidgin*, a simplified language that mostly substituted English words for native words but kept much West African structure and many African terms—especially words that were similar in several of the different languages. (See PIDGIN AND CREOLE LANGUAGES.)

In the succeeding generations of slaves born on plantations in America, this African-English speech mixture was strongly influenced by the speech of white slave owners; over time, it gradually adopted more and more of the features of English grammar and vocabulary and thus became a *creole* language. This early form of Black English can still be heard in the present-day creole of Jamaica and other Caribbean countries. It also survives in the Gullah creole spoken by blacks on the coast and Sea Islands of South Carolina and Georgia. (See GULLAH.)

Later, the American creole of the plantations acquired even more features of white speech and thus became the dialect now called Black English, which is unique among American dialects in some of its grammar, pronunciation, and vocabulary. To this day, the gap between Black English and Standard American English continues to narrow.

This version of the origin of American Black English remains controversial and is hard to prove or disprove because of the lack of early records. But a truly balanced view of Black English must take into account not only its African sources but also the patterns of segregation in American society since the abolition of slavery. A dialect is created or maintained when some speakers of a language are separated either geographically or socially from the rest. The long-lasting social and cultural separation of black Americans from the general white population must be recognized as profoundly influencing the special features of Black English.

Black English Today. Not all black Americans speak Black English. There are many whose speech is indistinguishable from that of their white neighbors. Moreover, many are proficient at both Black and Standard English, being able to switch styles at will, depending on the situation and company. The new awareness that Black English is a distinct dialect, and not just poorly used English, has had its greatest impact on education. Readers and textbooks in Black English have been developed, but not without much opposition and controversy. In 1979 a Federal judge in Ann Arbor, Michigan, handed down a decision requiring teachers of black children to have some knowledge of their dialect.

Black English is not identical throughout the United States. Some expressions are regional to the South or to the urban North. And many Black English words have over the past 300 years become familiar to whites and have passed into the general vocabulary of American English and international English.

The following sections give selected examples of some of the special grammar, pronunciation, and vocabulary used by most Black English speakers.

Grammar. (1) *The verb* be. In Standard English, when *be* is the main verb of a sentence, it appears in one of its five inflected forms: *is, am, are, was, were.* In Black English, the form *be* can be used as the main verb: *I be in school. He be angry at me.* Sometimes it appears as *bees* or *be's: The soup bees bad.* These uses of *be* and *bees,* however, are usually reserved to indicate something that occurs over and over again or habitually. If the situation does not recur, *be* is usually omitted entirely: *He a mean dude. He running to school.* Thus, *The soup bees bad* means 'The soup's bad every day.' But *The soup bad* means 'The soup's bad today.' Further examples of habitual *be:*

> "They be slow all the time."
> "She be late every day."
> "I see her when I bees on my way to school."
> "By the time I go get my momma, it be dark." —from Geneva Smitherman, *Talkin and Testifyin*

(2) *Multiple negation.* Double negatives such as *He doesn't know nothing* have been around since Shakespeare's time, though this usage is not accepted in Standard English. In Black English, double, triple, and quadruple negatives are common and follow a consistent grammatical pattern:

> "It ain nobody I can trust" = 'I can trust no one'
> "It ain nobody I can't trust" = 'I can trust everyone'
> "Wasn't no girls could go with us" = 'None of the girls could go with us'

"Wasn't no girls couldn't go with us" = 'All of the girls could go with us'
—from Geneva Smitherman, *Talkin and Testifyin*

(3) Possessives. In Standard English the possessive is indicated by an apostrophe and *s*, but in Black English the *'s* is often omitted. Only the order of the words indicates the possessive: *the girl glove. It be Herbert boat.*

Pronunciation. (1) Consonants at the ends of words are frequently dropped. Thus *bed, desk, hand, cost, wasp* may be pronounced /bĕ/, /dĕs/, /hăn/, /kŏs/, /wäs/.
(2) Initial /th/ is often pronounced /d/, so that *the, them, they, that* appear as /də/, /dĕm/, /dā/, /dăt/. But note that initial /th/ is not changed; *thing* never appears as /dĭng/.
(3) When /th/ occurs at the end of a word, it is often pronounced /f/: *with, mouth, tooth* become /wĭf/, /mouf/, /to͞of/.
(4) When /r/ occurs after a vowel, especially at the end of a word, it usually disappears; *during, more, door* are pronounced /**do͞o**-ĭng/, /mō/, /dō/. (This feature also occurs in some white dialects; see R-LESSNESS, INTRUSIVE R.) The omission of final /r/ has led to the merging of some words, so that one word fills the functions of two original words. In Black English *you* /yō/ can mean 'you' or 'your,' and *they* /dā/ can mean 'they' or 'their': *It is you book. It is they book.*
(5) Like /r/, the sound /l/ is usually omitted when it follows a vowel; *help, self, will* become /hĕp/, /sĕf/, /wĭ/. Sometimes final /l/, especially in words of more than one syllable, becomes /ə/; *steal* is /**stē**-ə/, *nickel* is /**nĭk**-ə/.
(6) The sound /ĭng/ is often pronounced /ăng/; *thing* appears as /thăng/, *sing* as /săng/.
(7) As in the white speech of many parts of the South, the sound /ī/ is usually pronounced /ȧ/ and /oi/ is usually pronounced /ō-ə/; *side, nice, time* become /sȧd/, /nȧs/, /tȧm/, and *boy, joy* become /**bō**-ə/, /**jō**-ə/.

Vocabulary. (1) This is a selection of words and phrases that are or have been in wide use in Black English, although not necessarily among all speakers. Some terms have also been current in white (Southern) dialect or in general American slang:

ace = 'best friend'
airish (chiefly Southern and Midland) = 'inclined to put on airs'
bad = 'very good, stylish'
bad eye = 'threatening glance'
bad mouth = 'malicious gossip': *She's putting the bad mouth on him.*
before-day (chiefly Southern) = 'the time just before dawn'
behind a dime (chiefly Coastal Southern) = 'at all'; used in expressing distrust: *I wouldn't trust him behind a dime.*
blood = 'fellow black'
bo dollar (chiefly Southern) = 'silver dollar'
bogart = 'to bully or act in a forceful manner'
boogaloo = (1) 'to dance' (2) 'to fool around'
boot = 'black person, usually male'
boss = 'excellent'
bringdown = 'anyone or anything that is depressing'
bro = 'black male, brother'
buck-eyed = 'having protruding eyes'
burn = (1) 'to shoot' (2) 'to cook food' (3) 'to cheat (someone)'
buzhies /**bo͞o**-zhēz/ = 'bourgeois, middle-class black people'
call (the) hog(s) (chiefly Southern and Midland) = 'to snore'
Charles, Charlie, Chuck = 'a white man'
cheese-eater = 'toady, apple polisher'
chicken-eater (chiefly Coastal Southern) = 'preacher, especially black Southern Baptist preacher'
chinch = 'bedbug'
chunk = 'to throw'
citizen = 'conventional white person'
clean = 'stylishly dressed'
conk = 'head'
cool out = 'to calm down'
cop = (1) 'to obtain' (2) 'to steal'
cop on (someone) = 'to talk derogatorily about'

crack one's side(s) *or* **a rib** (chiefly Coastal Southern) = 'to laugh very hard'

creep = (1) 'to cheat (on a friend)': *He's trying to creep on her.* (2) 'to leave, depart'

crib = 'house, apartment'

cuff, cuffee = 'black person'

dap = 'dapper, stylishly dressed'

dead cat on the line (chiefly Southern) = 'suspicious or fishy situation'

deadly = 'excellent'

dig = (1) 'to understand' (2) 'to pay attention to, look at' (3) 'to like'

do = (1) 'hairdo' (2) 'party, social affair'

dozens, dirty dozens = 'elaborate game in which participants insult one another's relatives, especially their mothers, the loser being the first person to give in to anger'

dude = 'male person'

duking /dōōk-ĭng/ = 'fighting'

dusk dark (chiefly Gulf Southern) = 'dusk'

eat cheese = 'to ingratiate oneself, apple polish'

elites /ē-līts/ = 'bourgeois black people'

excusing (of) (chiefly Coastal Southern) = 'except (for), not counting'

eyeball = 'to look at'

fan = 'to show off, flaunt oneself'

fat cat = 'wealthy person'

fat-mouth = 'to talk too much'

fine = '(of a woman or man) beautiful'

fixin' to = 'ready to, intending to'

flew coy = 'became coquettish'

flipped-out = 'crazy'

fly = '(of clothes) stylish'

fo' *or* **fore day** = 'the time just before dawn'

fold someone's ears = 'to give advice, talk impressively'

footstool = 'stooge, dupe'

forget it = 'emphatic phrase expressing negation, denial, refutation'

four-and-one = 'payday, Friday'

fox = 'beautiful woman'

foxy = '(of a woman) beautiful'

frail eel = 'good-looking woman'

freeze on (someone *or* **something)** = 'to ignore'

front = 'to put on airs'

front street = (1) 'straightforward or honest' (2) 'vulnerable to attack'

funky = (1) 'smelly' (2) 'very good or beautiful'

gall shirt (chiefly Southern) = 'shirt-length undergarment'

gam = 'to brag, show off'

gangster = 'to take over forcibly'

gatemouth = 'gossiper'

gators = 'alligator shoes'

Georgia ham = 'watermelon'

get down = (1) 'to do something in a more intense way' (2) 'to put soul into one's dancing'

get (something) together = 'to organize, start'

get with it = 'to be in fashion or in the spirit of what is happening'; usually used as a command

gig = 'job'

gig around = 'to work at a number of jobs'

girl = 'term of address used between black women'

give (one) some slack = 'to show restraint'; used as a plea for sympathy or understanding

glimming = 'seeing'

goat hair = 'bootleg liquor'

got a thing going = 'engaged in a goal-directed or purposeful activity'

grapes = 'wine'

gray, gray boy = 'white, white person'

grease = (1) (noun) 'black person' (2) (verb) 'to eat'

grip = 'to beg or plead'

grit = 'to eat'

grits = 'food in general'

grunt = 'meal, dinner'

gum-beating = 'talking'

gunpowder = 'gin'

hack = (1) 'anger, annoyance' (2) 'white person' (3) 'prison guard'
hame = 'job, vocation'
hammer = (1) 'female, girl' (2) 'a man's girlfriend'
hammer man = 'authoritarian figure'
handkerchief head = 'Uncle Tom'
hand (one) one's hat = 'to urge a person to leave'
hang = 'job, gig'
hang loose = 'to remain relaxed or calm'
hang-up = 'problem, preoccupation'
hard leg = (1) 'a man' (2) 'an ugly woman'
hat up = 'to go away, depart'
have a thing about = 'to be obsessed or preoccupied with a person or idea'
hawk = (1) (noun) 'cold wind' (2) (verb) 'to pursue or watch closely'
head rag (chiefly General Southern) = 'cloth worn on the head'
heavy = (1) 'nice, enjoyable' (2) 'stylish, attractive'
hide = 'drums'
high yellow *or* **yella** = 'light-skinned black person'
hinkty = 'snobbish'
hog = 'Cadillac'
hood = 'one's neighborhood'
humbug = 'fight, brawl'
hustlers don't call showdowns = 'beggars can't be choosers'
hype = 'scheme, deception, phony situation'
iced, be = (1) 'to be rejected or refused by someone' (2) 'to be imprisoned'
ice potato = 'white potato'
igg (General Northern) = 'to ignore, disregard, reject'
ignorant oil = 'wine, whiskey'
ink = 'cheap wine'
jack = (1) 'a male' (2) 'money'
jackleg (General Southern) = 'lay or unprofessional preacher or lawyer'
jack up = (1) 'to rob or steal' (2) 'to beat up'
jam back = 'to dance'
jibs = (1) 'lips' (2) 'buttocks'
jick head = 'drunkard'
jim = 'male person'
jive = (1) (noun) 'talk, slang, insincere talk' (2) (verb) 'to lie or deceive'
jive cat = 'insincere person'
jivetime = (1) 'insincere, not serious' (2) 'dishonest, deceptive' (3) 'stupid, ignorant'
Joe Sad = 'person without friends, unpopular person'
jones = (1) 'fixation, compulsive attachment' (2) 'drug habit'
joy-juice = 'wine, whiskey'
jump = (1) 'a dance' (2) 'a fight'
junk (General Southern) = (1) 'worthless or foolish talk'; usually used in the phrase *junk talk* (2) 'narcotics'
juvey = 'reform school'
keen, king (Southern and Midland) = '(of shoes) having sharply pointed toes'
kicks = (1) 'shoes' (2) 'thrills'
killout = 'a fascinating person or an extremely exciting situation or thing'
kitty = 'Cadillac'
know what's happening = 'to be able to take care of oneself, be street-wise'; not the same as *What's happening?* (see below)
kong = 'homemade whiskey'
konk = (1) 'the human head' (2) 'grease'
kopasetic = 'excellent'
lame = (1) (noun) 'unsophisticated person' (2) (adjective) 'not fashionable, dull or boring' (3) (adjective) 'stupid, ignorant'
later (Northern and Midland) = 'goodbye, farewell'
lay bread on = 'to lend or give money'
lay dead = (1) 'to wait, do nothing' (2) 'to hide'
lay it on = 'to explain fully and candidly'
lay on = 'to give'
lay up = 'to relax, take it easy'
lean on = 'to hit, beat up'
least = 'dull person or situation'
leg = 'female'

let it rip = 'don't bother, skip it'
letter from home = 'watermelon'
liberate = 'to steal'
lid = 'hat'
light up (someone) = 'to hit or strike'
like (man) = 'expression used as a form of punctuation or an exclamation'
line = 'price of an item'
lines = 'money'
lip = 'defense lawyer'
lip off = 'to talk back, verbally rebel'
Little Eva = 'loudmouthed white girl'
long green *or* **bread** = 'a great deal of money'
machine = 'automobile'
main man = (1) 'favorite friend' (2) 'one's hero' (3) 'a woman's boyfriend'
make haste (General Southern) = 'to hurry'
make it = 'to go away, leave'
Man, the = (1) 'policeman' (2) 'any white authority figure'
mean = (1) 'good or best' (2) 'honest' (3) 'strong'
mellow = (1) (noun) 'friend, pal': *What's happening, mellow?* (2) (noun) 'lover' (3) (adjective) 'attractive or stylish; agreeable, nice'
mellow-back = 'fashionably dressed'
member = 'fellow black person'
mess with = 'to annoy, bother, harass'
mink = (1) 'attractive woman' (2) 'girlfriend'
Miss Ann = 'white woman'
Mister Charlie = 'white man'
moldy = 'out of style'
my man = 'friendly term of address from one male to another'
my people = 'group to which one belongs'
nab = 'policeman'
nail = 'a man'
natural = 'Afro haircut'
neck-breaking it = 'moving swiftly'
Negro = 'an Uncle Tom'
nice = 'feeling good': *I'm nice today.*
nickel = 'five dollars, five-dollar bill'
nod = 'hair'
nose (wide) open = 'in love, infatuated or strongly influenced by': *She sure got your nose open.*
not ready = 'naïve, unaware person'
nowhere = (1) 'unacceptable, unsatisfactory' (2) 'strange, unusual'
numb = 'dumb, stupid'
nut role = 'stupidity or craziness pretended for a purpose': *I played the nut role on him and got my way.*
ofay = 'white man'
off = (1) 'to beat up (someone)' (2) 'to kill': *Did they really off him last night?*
O.G. = 'Old Girl, mother'
oil = (1) '*whiskey' (2) 'graft, bribe'
on time = 'quite appropriate'
oreo = 'black person with white-oriented attitudes, Uncle Tom'
out of sight = 'excellent, outstanding'
outside baby *or* **child** (Southern and Midland) = '*illegitimate child'
paddy = 'white person'
peck = 'to eat'
peep = 'to see with great understanding, see through (a deceitful action or effort)'
piano = 'spareribs'
pies = 'the eyes'
pill = 'a basketball'
pin = 'to stare, see'
pixie = 'processed or straightened hair style'
pluck = 'wine'
plumb = 'serious mistake'
poke = 'roll of money'
popped = 'arrested, apprehended'
pounds = 'money'
prat = 'to play coy, pretend to refuse'
pressed = 'well-dressed'
process = 'straightened hair style on a black male'
program = 'life style, method of operation'

*Appears as separate entry

punk out = 'to back out of a situation after promising one's participation or services'

quit the scene = (1) 'to leave' (2) 'to die'

raggedy = 'poor, destitute, shabby'

raghead = 'black male who wears a scarf on his head to protect an expensive hair style'

raise = (1) (noun) 'parents, guardians': *My raise won't like it.* (2) (verb) 'to go, move': *Let's raise, man!*

rap = (1) (verb) 'to talk, converse' (2) (noun) 'speech, address'

red-bone = 'light-colored black woman'

rep = 'reputation'

ride = 'automobile'

rip off = 'to steal'

rooster = 'a man'

rough = 'attractive, stylish'

running (something) down = 'explaining an issue, relating a situation'

same ol' same ol' = 'routine thing or situation'

satchel-mouth = 'person with a large mouth'

saw = 'landlord or landlady of a cheap rooming house'

scarf, scoff = 'to eat'

scene = (1) 'event or happening' (2) 'place of an event' (3) 'predicament'

scratch = 'money'

scream on (someone) = 'to rebuke, tell off'

scribe = 'a letter'

seed = (1) 'baseball' (2) 'son or daughter'

set = 'party or dance'

shack = 'home, apartment'

shades = 'eyeglasses, especially sunglasses'

shaking = 'event, happening, news'

sheen = (1) (noun) 'automobile' (2) (verb) 'to drive a car'

shiv = 'knife, razor'

short = 'automobile'

shucking and jiving = (1) 'fooling, lying' (2) 'being lazy, procrastinating' (3) 'dancing'

sides = 'phonograph records'

signifying = 'dozens'

sister = 'fellow black woman'

skimmer = 'hat'

skin = 'the hand'

skin, give (one) some = 'to exchange hand slaps with a person as a form of greeting or affirmation, slap five'

sky piece = 'hat, beret'

slack = (1) 'money' (2) 'break, chance, opportunity'

slap five = 'to slap another's palm as a greeting'

slide = (1) (noun) 'pants pocket' (2) (verb) 'to go or leave'

snag = 'ugly or unrefined female'

snake = 'sneaky person'

solid = 'good, desirable'

soul = 'pride in or emotional attachment to Afro-American culture or the black heritage and experience'

soul brother = 'another black male'

soul food = 'Southern-style cooking done by black Americans'

soul sister = 'another black female'

sounding = 'dozens'

space (out) = 'to go or leave'

squeeze = 'girlfriend or boyfriend'

stepinfetchit = 'an Uncle Tom'

stompers = (1) 'shoes' (2) 'feet'

stone = 'expression used as an intensifier'; for example, *stone fox* = 'very beautiful girl'

straight = (1) 'permissible' (2) 'nice or friendly' (3) 'real, genuine'

strung out = (1) 'in love, deeply infatuated' (2) 'addicted to drugs'

sugar hill = (1) capital *S*, *H* 'middle-class neighborhood in Harlem' (2) 'red-light district'

swag = 'stolen goods'

tack = 'clever or smart man'

tall money = 'wealth, a great deal of money'

T.C.B. = 'taking care of business, doing what is necessary to perform effectively or skillfully'

tell it like it is = 'to explain honestly and completely, be frank and candid'

terrible = 'stylish, good, fine'

thing /thăng/ = (1) 'hobby, interest, or occupation' (2) 'talent or skill'

ticky = 'particular, fussy'

tight cheeks *or* **jaws** = 'very angry, incensed'

toast = 'good, fine'

together = (1) 'composed, calm' (2) 'aware' (3) 'fashionable' (4) 'pleasurable'

Tom = 'Uncle Tom'

tore up = (1) 'unhappy' (2) 'drunk'

tough = 'very desirable, attractive'

Uncle Tom = 'self-effacing black person who tries to make a favorable impression on whites'

uncool = 'not appealing or pleasurable'

uptight = (1) 'angry, tense, ill at ease' (2) 'feeling good'

uptown = (1) 'stylish' (2) 'wealthy'

vines = 'clothes'

wail = 'to sing or play a musical instrument with emotion or fervor'

walk heavy = 'to carry oneself in a self-glorifying or conceited manner'

waste = 'to beat severely, injure'

What's going down? = 'What's new? What's the situation?'; used as a form of greeting

What's happening? = 'Hello, how are you?'

where it's at = (1) 'the truth of a situation' (2) 'that which is stylish or fashionable'

where one is coming from = 'what one means in saying something, one's point of view'

with it = (1) 'fully aware' (2) 'in agreement with' (3) 'socially adept, stylish'

woofing = 'threatening by bluffing'

wrinkles = 'chitterlings'

yeasting = 'exaggerating'

You ain't sayin' nothin' = 'Your opinion is worthless'

zap = 'to move quickly'

zonked = (1) 'drunk' (2) 'high on drugs'

(2) This is a selection of Black English words, all of African origin, that have been borrowed into white speech at various levels: into Southern dialect (as *cooter, poor joe*); into general American slang (as *hip, tote*); or into Standard and international English (as *banjo, jazz, yam*):

banjo = 'stringed instrument with a diaphragm of stretched vellum'

boogie, boogie-woogie = (1) 'percussive style of jazz piano playing of the 1940s' (2) 'jitterbug-type dance done to this music': from, or related to, Hausa *buga* or *bugi* and Mandingo *buga* = 'to beat drums'; current West African English *bogi* or *bogi-bogi* = 'to dance'

* **buckaroo** (Western) = 'cowboy' (also possibly from Spanish *vaquero*)

chigger = 'small red biting larva of a mite': from Wolof *jiga* = 'insect'

cooter (General Southern, especially Coastal Southern) = 'tortoise, turtle'

* **goober** (Southern and Midland) = 'peanut'

* **gumbo** = (1) '*okra' (2) 'soup or stew made with okra'

hep, hip = 'alert, knowledgeable'

jazz = 'musical style originated by blacks in New Orleans'

jitter = 'to tremble, shake' and **jitterbug** = 'a fast dance of the 1940s'

jive = (1) (verb) 'to talk misleadingly' (2) 'a jazz style of the 1930s'

* **juke** (chiefly Southern) = 'to carouse' and **jukebox** = 'coin-operated phonograph'

Obeah /ō-bē-ə/ = 'form of magic'

pinder (chiefly Coastal Southern) = 'peanut'

poor joe (chiefly Coastal Southern) = 'great blue heron' (a FOLK ETYMOLOGY from Gullah *pojo*, from Vai *pojo* = 'heron')

* **tote** = 'to carry'

voodoo = 'Caribbean religion using sorcery'

yam = 'tuberous root of an African plant'

zombie = 'reanimated corpse in voodoo, deity in Obeah'

*Appears as separate entry

(3) For some vocabulary of an American creole language related to Black English, see GULLAH. For some other English words of African origin, see AFRICAN WORDS.

Examples. Selected transcriptions of actual speech illustrating Black English usage.

(1) Southern:

> De sojers come gallopin' up to de house, dey horses feets clickin' on de ice. Dey th'owed de reins over de hitchin' post an' come trompin' up on de po'ch. . . . De bigges' one bow to Mammy like she was lady an' ax her if dey could have some supper an' spen' de night. Mammy tole him . . . to jus' make deyse'fs at home.
>
> —interview (1938) with an 80-year-old former plantation slave, from George P. Rawick (ed.), *The American Slave: A Composite Autobiography*

(2) Northern:

> "I know where a restraun' is locate' on eighteen street . . . on de lef' han' si' an' you cou' buy foo'."
>
> —from Bengt Loman, *Conversations in a Negro American Dialect*

> "Dem dudes alway be doin day thang." (eighth-grade student)

> "Hur' up, the bell ranging." (fourth-grade student)

> "Doin the civil right crisis, we work hard." (college student)
>
> —from Geneva Smitherman, *Talkin and Testifyin*

blame. The basic meaning of the verb *blame* is 'to hold (someone or something) responsible for (a fault or trouble)': *blame the government for inflation; blamed ice and low visibility for the accident.* The construction is now often turned around, so that *blame* comes to mean 'to put responsibility for (trouble) on (someone or something)': *blame inflation on the government; blamed the accident on ice and low visibility.* This construction was for some time generally regarded as bad grammar, but it is now increasingly used and increasingly accepted:

> The most popular position to take on Vietnam . . . was to bug out and blame it on Johnson and Kennedy.
>
> —Richard Nixon (quoted), *New York Times*

> Radical feminists blame the oppression of women on such deep-seated institutions as the patriarchal family and the capitalist economic system.
>
> —John Talbot, *Smithsonian*

◇ ***Recommendation.*** The construction *to blame* (trouble) *on* (something or someone) must now be recognized as standard; but some people continue to dislike it and prefer to avoid it in favor of *to blame* (someone or something) *for* (trouble).

blends. It is often found convenient to run two words together, squeezing out some syllables or elements, to form a compacted new word. Lewis Carroll, who coined several (such as *chortle,* from *chuckle* + s*nort*), called them *portmanteau words,* after the compartmented Victorian suitcase into which clothes were crammed. Such words are now more often known as *blends.* This method of word formation (like ACRONYMS) has greatly increased in popularity during the 20th century and is one of the characteristic features of today's vocabulary. Some examples:

belletrist = 'literary aesthete': from *bel*les *lettres* + *-ist*
bit = 'single character in binary-based computer language': from *b*inary + dig*it*
Breathalyzer = 'apparatus for testing alcoholic content of blood via breath': *breath* + an*alyzer*
* **brunch** = *br*eakfast + l*unch*
Chunnel = *Ch*annel + t*unnel* (name of a proposed tunnel under the English Channel)
gasohol = *gas* + alc*ohol*
guestimate = *guess* + *estimate*
laundromat = *laundr*y + auto*mat*
Medicare = *medic*al + *care*
motel = *mot*or + hot*el*
sexploitation = *sex*ual + ex*ploitation*

smog = *sm*oke + f*og*
Spanglish = *Span*ish + Eng*lish* (see also PUERTO RICAN SPEECH)
vash = *v*olcanic *ash*
workaholic = *work* + alc*oholic* (with a change of *o* to *a*)
workfare = *work* + wel*fare*

*Appears as separate entry

blickey. See BUCKET, PAIL, BLICKEY.

blond, blonde. ***Origin.*** These words come directly from French, *blond* being the masculine form and *blonde* the feminine form meaning (adjective) 'having fair hair and usually fair skin and blue or gray eyes' or (noun) 'fair-haired person.'

Uses. In English it is traditional to use *blond* when the word applies to a male, to males and females collectively, or to impersonal nouns such as *hair* or *complexion,* keeping *blonde* only for females: *a blond boy; a blonde girl. Both schoolchildren had blond hair. He was a blond. She is a blonde. They are both blonds.*

This rule is not rigid. The adjective *blonde* is sometimes used of skin, hair, etc., when the person referred to is female:

> Miss Albertson, whose small build and tousled short blonde hair give her a somewhat waifish look . . .
> —Eleanor Blau, *New York Times*

But many feminists now object to unnecessary sex markings of English nouns and adjectives on the grounds that such distinctions usually discriminate against women. The word *blonde* is especially resented, since it frequently has sexual overtones; a woman described as a blonde is assumed to be sexually attractive unless it is stated otherwise, while the same is not necessarily assumed of a man called a blond. In general, the form *blonde* now occurs less than it used to, but as the second quotation below shows, there is still some confusion or hesitation:

> . . . she noticed a striking young blond at the end of the bar. . . . "She's a regular here. . . ."
> —Bob Talbert, *Reader's Digest*

> . . . Sachs' wife, Marja, a blond Finn taller than any man in the room, and another blond woman. At his own end, there was a blonde in buckskin. . . .
> —John Vinocur, *New York Times*

◇ ***Recommendation.*** Those who prefer to continue using *blonde* (adjective and noun) for females are entitled to do so. But when the adjective refers to hair or complexion, even though belonging to a female, *blond* is now definitely preferred. Those who accept the feminist arguments against sex-discriminating terms will use *blond* in all situations. For those who are simply in doubt this is also the best solution.

blue-collar, white-collar. These two terms originated in the United States in the 1920s. A *white-collar worker* was a male office worker who typically wore a suit and a shirt with a white detachable collar. A *blue-collar worker* was one who wore work clothes instead of a suit; his shirt was often blue. This color coding of working attire has changed, but the two terms are firmly established throughout the English-speaking world:

> I'm a plumber's son from Brookline, Massachusetts, so I come from about as blue collar a background as you can come from, and I'm grateful for that.
> —Lenny Baker (quoted), *New York Times*

White-collar has recently extended its range:

> Mobsters are experts in a wide array of criminal pursuits ranging from gambling, loan-sharking and drug pushing to sophisticated white-collar crimes such as bankruptcy, fraud and investment schemes.
> —*U.S. News & World Report*

bodacious. This favorite adjective of the cartoon character Snuffy Smith is a regionalism commonly used in the midlands, the South, and the Ozarks. It is probably a blend of *bold* and *audacious* (there is a British dialect word *boldacious*). It means 'thorough, complete': *He's a bodacious fool;* or 'unabashed, unceremonious, brazen':

> Admiral Sims . . . uttered sacrilegious sentiments about air power and was not struck down, but the bodacious blurt did him no good with his brother Navy men. —*Time*

As an adverb, *bodacious* or *bodaciously* means 'thoroughly, completely': *She's so bodacious unreasonable when she gets mad;* or 'boldly, unceremoniously':

> I 'lowed maybe you'd been took prisoner and carried bodaciously off!
> —Joel Chandler Harris, *Tales of the Home Folks*

> "He picked her up bodaciously, and carried her off."
> —from *Dialect Notes*

> Hit jist wears a person's patience bodaciously out.
> —Rebecca Hyatt, *Marthy Lou's Kiverlid*

bodega. See APOTHECARY, BOUTIQUE, BODEGA.

Bonac /**bŏ**-nək/. This is the local name for the rural speech of East Hampton, Long Island, New York. The speakers are sometimes called *Bonackers*. *Bonac* is shortened from the name of a small saltwater inlet, Accabonac Creek. With the increasing urbanization of the area, this colorful vestige of folk speech is rapidly disappearing.

Pronunciation. In some details Bonac very closely resembles New York City and New England speech. Specifically, /r/ is quite frequently dropped after vowels; *beard*, for example, is pronounced /bēəd/ by Bonackers. This /r/ is also frequently added to words ending in a vowel sound, especially when followed by a word beginning with a vowel. For example, the sentence *I saw it* is usually pronounced /ī sôr ĭt/.

The /ou/ sound in words like *house* and *cow* usually becomes /ĕo͞o/: /hĕo͞os/, /kĕo͞o/. The /â/ sound in words like *vary* and *Sarah* is often pronounced /ă/: /**văr**-ē/, /**săr**-ə/. The /ă/ sound in words like *bad* and *path* is usually pronounced /āə/ or /āyə/: /bāəd/, /pāyəth/.

Vocabulary. (1) Bonac shares much of its vocabulary with the dialects of the region, specifically the NEW YORK CITY, HUDSON VALLEY, and NEW ENGLAND dialects. But Bonac also has many terms of its own. Here is a sampling:

clam the tide out = 'to be the last guest, or one of the last, to leave a party'

downstreet = 'upstreet'

dreen = 'stream that empties into a creek or bay' (variant of *drain*)

heft = 'weight'

It'll drink *or* **eat** = 'It's drinkable or edible': *"Don't drink that beer; I just dropped it." "It'll drink."*

Long Island hurry = 'stew of potatoes and salt'

neutral ground = 'grass strip between the sidewalk and the street'

prit near = 'almost'

samp = 'dish made of white corn kernels, navy beans, and ham hocks or salt pork' (from an Algonquian word for 'corn mush')

say somethin' = 'to talk a lot': *She can say somethin', can't she?*

sea poose = 'an outward-moving whirlpool in the surf, dangerous to bathers' (from an Algonquian word for 'stream')

skip = 'no meal': *We had skip for lunch.*

ugly = 'in a bad mood': *I'm ugly today.*

upstreet = 'into the business section of any of the major villages': *I'm goin' upstreet* [or *downstreet*] *for a few minutes.*

up the Island = 'toward New York City'

weather = 'good weather': *We'll work tomorrow if there's weather.*

(2) Many of the terms characteristic of eastern Long Island speech are nautical or fishing terms and are also used by speakers in other areas of the northeastern coast. Some of these are:

dragger = 'trawler'

mash = 'mesh of a net'

open (**oysters, clams,** etc.) = 'to shuck or shell'

opening shop = 'place where workers shuck shellfish'
sharpie = 'flat-bottomed skiff, now usually with an outboard motor'
Sputnik grass = 'long tubular seaweed' (so called because it reappeared locally about the time the Russians launched the Sputnik satellite)
striper = 'striped bass'
weakfish = 'sea trout'

bona fide, bona fides. Both terms come from legal Latin. *Bona fides* means 'good faith.' *Bona fide* is its ablative form, meaning 'in good faith.'

Pronunciation. *Bona fide* has been so much assimilated into English that in the United States it is now usually pronounced as if it were a single adjective spelled *bonafied:* /**bō**-nə-fīd/ or /**bŏn**-ə-fīd/. But some prefer pronouncing it with four syllables, as in Latin: /**bō**-nə **fī**-dē/ or /**bŏn**-ə **fī**-dē/.

In the case of *bona fides,* the Latinate pronunciation with four syllables is still usual: /**bō**-nə **fī**-dēz/ or /**bŏn**-ə **fī**-dēz/; and the phrase is customarily given in italics.

Uses. *Bona fide* is originally adverbial: *He made the offer bona fide.* It is now often adjectival: *I thought it was a bona fide offer.* Used this way, the term is sometimes hyphenated: *bona-fide.* The legal meaning is 'in good faith, without intent to deceive.' In common usage *bona fide* now often means simply 'genuine, real':

> Cuba claims that only 82 of these are bona-fide American citizens.
> —James Reston, *Reader's Digest*

> I was not sure whether the CIA actually had any bona fide reasons to intervene with the FBI.
> —Richard Nixon, *R.N.*

Bona fides is a noun phrase meaning 'good faith, sincerity':

> . . . he had given dramatic evidence of . . . his political bona fides.
> —Robert Rhodes James, *Churchill: The Politician*

But *bona fides* is now often mistaken for a plural noun, as if it were spelled *bonafides* and meant 'credentials.' The uses below are thus in error.

> [Question by CIA:] "How were Oswald's *bona fides* established?"
> —*Reader's Digest*

> Their bona fides are not at issue.
> —*Business Week*

◇ ***Recommendation.*** If in doubt, pronounce *bona fide* /**bō**-nə fīd/ and *bona fides* /**bō**-nə **fī**-dēz/. Italicize only the latter. Do not use *bona fides* as a plural noun meaning 'credentials.'

bonnyclabber. See CLABBER.

boon. The noun *boon* is not related to the adjective *boon.* The noun, from Old Norse *bōn* = 'prayer,' originally meant 'favor, request.' This use is archaic:

> . . . upon my feeble knee
> I beg this boon, with tears not lightly shed.
> —Shakespeare, *Titus Andronicus*

The word is now used to mean 'remarkable benefit, blessing':

> Marta was a boon to Mother—"She's the best help we have ever had," she said.
> —Rumer Godden, *The Kitchen Madonna*

> Not everyone on the American side thinks the closure [of Alaskan halibut fisheries to Canadian fishermen] will be an unqualified boon to the U.S.
> —Terry Johnson, *National Fisherman*

The adjective *boon* is from Old French *bon* or *bone* = 'good' and means 'good, kind, convivial.' It is now used only in the cliché phrase *boon companion,* which strictly speaking should mean 'good fellow, hearty, convivial person' but in practice most often means merely 'close friend':

> I concede that as an orchid man Theodore may be as good as he thinks he is, but as a boon companion—a term I

once looked up because Wolfe told me it was trite and shouldn't be used—you can have him.
—Rex Stout, *All in the Family*

boondocks, boonies. *Boondocks* was picked up by the U.S. Army fighting against Filipino nationalist guerrillas in the Spanish-American War (1898). Much of the fighting took place in rough hill country and heavy jungle, which in Tagalog (the chief language of the Philippines) is called *bundok* = 'mountain, hill country.' American soldiers borrowed this word from their enemies as *boondocks*, which has become a permanent part of the language, meaning 'backcountry, undeveloped rural areas, the sticks.' It can be singular or plural:

> "We can appreciate the work the Carters had to do coming from a boondocks like Plains," [said Elmer Carlsen, a wealthy Iowa farmer,] refraining from referring to his hometown, Audubon, Iowa (pop. 2,907) as a boondocks.
> —Albin Krebs, *New York Times*

During the Vietnam War, GI's applied the word to the difficult jungle terrain in which much of that war was fought, using especially the shortened form *boonies*. This form has also passed into the language as a general term for 'undeveloped country':

> He eventually moved Deere out of its 90-year-old musty headquarters in downtown Moline to the nearby boonies. . . . —*Forbes*

boondoggle. This peculiar term is a legacy of the New Deal. It is said to have been coined in 1925, from unknown origins, by a scoutmaster named Robert Link. He gave the name to the braided leather lanyard that Boy Scouts wore around the neck; these lanyards could be handmade by scouts as a simple do-it-yourself project. In the 1930s Federal agencies such as the Works Progress Administration were set up by President Franklin D. Roosevelt to create jobs for the armies of unemployed. The more pointless of these make-work projects were labeled *boondoggles* by the opposition, and the word has become a permanent part of the political vocabulary meaning 'an expensive government project mounted for purely political reasons':

> But that's just what the Appropriations Committee of the House of Representatives did a few days ago in following its time-encrusted custom of endorsing a string of flagrantly extravagant and senseless boondoggles disguised as navigation, irrigation, flood control, power or recreation projects, every one of them economically indefensible and environmentally destructive.
> —John B. Oakes, *New York Times*

boonies. See BOONDOCKS, BOONIES.

Boontling /**bo͞ont**-lĭng/. This is the name of an extraordinary made-up "language" spoken in Mendocino County, California, from about 1880 to 1920. *Boont* is the nickname for Boonville in Anderson Valley, and *ling* is an abbreviation of *lingo*. *Boontling*, then, is the lingo of Boonville. Although only a few old-timers remember it today, it had during its greatest currency more than 1,000 words and phrases and nearly 300 specialized personal and place names. In its heyday there were about 500 people living in or around Boonville who could speak it to some extent.

Boontling was probably created by a group of young men of the area as a kind of secret tongue for a privileged few. But the jargon soon spread from this initial group and became the cant of the entire area, a linguistic game that could be used in various situations to exclude non-Boonters.

Selected Boontling Terms.

apple-head = 'a girl, especially one's girlfriend'

arkin' tidrick /**är**-kĭn **tĭd**-rĭk/ = 'wreck, automobile collision'

backdated chuck = 'backward, naïve, or stupid person'

bahl /bäl/ = 'good, of excellent quality'

bahler = 'anyone or anything of excellent quality': *The grannyhatchet was a*

bahler = 'The big antlered buck deer was a dandy.'
bahlness = 'very attractive woman'
barl /bärl/ = 'to shoot a gun'
barney man = 'cowboy'
batter = 'bachelor'
beark /bârk/ = 'overactive, aggressive person' (from *bearcat*)
bee jay = 'to repeat oneself'
belhoon /bĕl-**hōōn**/ = 'dollar'
big book = 'the Bible'
blooch /blōōch/ = 'to chatter aimlessly' (from *blue jay*)
blue tail = 'rattlesnake'
bohoik /bō-**hoik**/ = 'to laugh loudly and energetically'
branch = (1) 'to leave' (2) 'to turn one's attention elsewhere'
bright lights = 'a city'
briney = (1) 'the ocean' (2) 'the coastal area'
buckey = 'nickel'
buckeye = 'to loaf, avoid hard work'
bulrusher = '*illegitimate child'
can-kicky /kăn-**kĭk**-ē/ = 'angry, disgusted'
chapport /**chă**-pōrt/ = 'to challenge to a fight'
chipmunk = (1) (verb) 'to hoard' (2) (noun) 'hoarder or collector'
chuck = 'dull or ignorant person' (from *chucklehead*)
chuckish = 'dull-witted, stupid'
codgy /**kŏ**-jē/ = 'old, somewhat senile'
codgyhood = 'old age'
collar-jumpy = 'irritable, nervous'
croakins = 'funeral'
deek = 'to look or examine'
deem = 'dime'
dehigged /dē-**hĭgd**/ = 'without money, broke'
dish = 'to cheat (someone)'
doolsey /**dōōl**-sē/ = (1) (noun) 'candy' (2) (adjective) 'sweet'
dreek = (1) 'to beat or whip' (2) 'to overcome or overwhelm'
dubs /dŭbz/ = 'two of anything'
dumplin' dust = 'flour'
ear-settin' /îr-**sĕt**-ĭn/ = 'a scolding or reprimand'
earth = 'truth': *That's earth* = 'That's the truth.'
eelst = 'an old man, any old male' (from *old stag*)
ex = 'to vote'
featherleg = 'belligerent person, know-it-all'
frattey /**frăt**-ē/ = 'wine'
frattey shams = 'grapevines'
fuzzeek /fŭ-**zēk**/ = 'peach'
glimmers = 'eyeglasses'
gorm /gōrm/ = 'to eat'
greeley = (1) 'newspaper' (2) 'reporter or editor'
greeney = 'tantrum or fit'
hair buryin' = '*shivaree'
hairk /hârk/ = 'haircut'
harp = 'to talk, especially to talk Boontling'
heese = 'a school, especially a high school'
hig = (1) (noun) 'dollar' (2) (verb) 'to lend or give money'
higgery = 'a bank'
higgy = 'wealthy'
high gitter /hī **gĭt**-ər/ = 'an alcoholic'
high heel = 'policeman or sheriff'
hob /hŏb/ = (1) 'shoe' (2) 'dance'
hoot on = 'to ridicule or deride'
huger /**hyōō**-jər/ = 'anything of large size'
iron moshe /mōsh/ = 'locomotive or train'
jape = 'to drive'
jeffer /**jĕf**-ər/ = 'a fire'
jenny = 'to tattle'
jimhead = 'confused or deranged person'
lip-splittin' /lĭp-**splĭt**-ĭn/ = 'fist fight'
lock = 'to marry'
log-lifter /lŏg-**lĭft**-ər/ = 'heavy rainstorm'
low desk = (1) 'to conduct business' (2) 'to keep records'

*Appears as separate entry

lurk = 'lunch'
milky = 'foggy'
neeble = 'bad, inferior, defective'
nonch /nŏnch/ = 'objectionable, bad, taboo'
Old Dusties = 'hell'
otto /ŏt-ō/ = 'to work hard'
peerl /pêrl/ = 'to rain or drizzle'
pike = 'to travel or walk'
pleeble = 'to play baseball'
reel = 'family relative'
ridgy = (1) 'old, decrepit' (2) 'backwoodsy, backward'
roger /rŏj-ər/ = 'big storm'
rooje /ro͞oj/ = 'to cheat'
rout = 'to scold harshly'
seertle /sêrt'l/ = (1) (noun) 'a fish, especially a salmon' (2) (verb) 'to fish'
shag = 'to stumble or move awkwardly'
shams /shămz/ = 'foliage, brush'
shavin' knocker = 'youngster'
shy = (1) 'to leave' (2) 'to stop doing something'
skee = '*whiskey'
skiddley = 'doubtful, worrisome'
slug = 'to sleep'
sol /sŏl/ = 'the sun'
string = 'to kill or maim'
teebowed /tē-bōd/ = 'deaf, hard of hearing'
teedee /tē-dē/ = 'today'
teleef /tĕ-lēf/ = 'telephone'
tidrick /tĭd-rĭk/ = 'party, meeting, gathering'
tongue-cuppy /tŭng-kŭp-ē/ = 'sick, nauseated'
toobs /to͞obz/ = 'twenty-five cents'
turkey neck = 'to gawk or stare'
tweed = 'child'
wess = 'to fib or exaggerate'
whittlin' = 'politics, politicking'
yabbelow /yă-bə-lō/ = 'to talk or chatter'
yibe /yīb/ = 'yes'
yink /yĭngk/ = 'young man'
zeese = 'coffee'

*Appears as separate entry

boot. This word, not related to *boots* meaning 'footwear,' originally meant 'advantage, benefit.' As a noun it now only occurs in the phrase *to boot,* meaning 'as an extra, on top of everything else,' typically used in a flourish of indignation:

> I never did understand . . . an old man like that and a five-star general to boot, why he went around dressed up like a nineteen-year-old second lieutenant.
> —Harry Truman (quoted), Merle Miller, *Plain Speaking*

> Suddenly we believed that by offering equal opportunities we could make everybody happy, forgive everybody who failed, and expect gratitude to boot.
> —Suzanne Britt Jordan, *Reader's Digest*

The verb *boot,* meaning 'to be of advantage, help,' is entirely archaic.

> Alas! What boots it with uncessant care
> To ply the homely slighted shepherd's trade?
> —John Milton, *Lycidas*

But the last word must be left to the American artist James McNeill Whistler, who as a reluctant and undisciplined cadet at West Point in the 1850s was reprimanded for having dirty boots and insouciantly replied, "What boots it?" Not long after, he left the service.

born, borne. The general-purpose past participle of the verb *bear* is *borne.* In the sense of 'to give birth to,' the active past participle is *borne: She had borne two children.* In the same sense, the passive past participle is *borne* if the act or fact of childbearing is meant, especially if the mother is referred to explicitly: *Two children had been borne by her.* When it is the biographical fact of entering the world that is basically meant, *born* is used: *He was born in Kentucky.*

The adjective meaning 'being so by birth, native, natural, naturally disposed, etc.,' is *born* in every case: *a Canadian-born artist. James is a born musician. Elizabeth seemed born to succeed.*

born again. In evangelical Christianity, being *born again* is a crucial experience of spiritual rebirth in which an individual's faith and eventual salvation are affirmed.

> Except a man be born again, he cannot see the Kingdom of God.
> —John 3:3

From 1976, when President Jimmy Carter and many of his supporters were nationally publicized as born-again Christians, the term was taken up by journalists in a sarcastic sense to refer to anyone converted to a new political creed or point of view:

> Like so many other money managers these days, he's strictly a born-again Graham and Dodd man, a believer in "risk aversion," a devotee of undervalued securities, a plain old bargain hunter. —Geoffrey Smith, *Forbes*

> The goal of a balanced federal budget is almost universally acclaimed. Are these born-again economizers sincere?
> —James Kilpatrick, *Florida Times-Union*

Boston urban dialect. Boston is the influential focal area of the eastern New England dialect. It dominates this region both culturally and linguistically. Unlike many URBAN DIALECTS, most notably that of New York City, upper-class Boston speech has traditionally enjoyed almost nationwide prestige. Boston has three main subdialects.

Greater Boston Area. The most prevalent subdialect is used by speakers of most social levels living outside the central area. With minor variations, this Greater Boston area subdialect is essentially the same as the eastern New England dialect.

Brahmin. A minority subdialect is spoken by the upper or so-called Brahmin class. This durable local aristocracy should not be confused with the larger class of educated and economically prosperous speakers. It is not uncommon for a member of an eminent Brahmin family who speaks this subdialect to have neither wealth nor a college degree. Some of the distinctive pronunciation features of this subdialect:

(1) *Glass* is usually pronounced /glȧs/; but *half, aunt, past* are often pronounced with /ä/: /häf/, /änt/, /päst/.
(2) The /ō/ sound of words like *home* and *ago* is frequently pronounced /ou/: /houm/, /ə-**gou**/.
(3) The /r/ sound is frequently dropped and replaced with /wə/. For example, *four, sure* are frequently pronounced /**fô**-wə/, /**shōō**-wə/.
(4) Words like *suit, new, due* are often pronounced with a /yōō/ sound: /syōōt/, /nyōō/, /dyōō/.

Central City Area. A third subdialect is spoken in the central city area, including South Boston, East Boston, Charlestown, and South Cambridge. Speakers of this subdialect frequently use these pronunciation features:

(1) *Washed* is usually /wȯsht/.
(2) The /r/ sound is usually added to words ending in a vowel or vowel sound if they are followed by a word beginning with a vowel. For example, *law* is pronounced /lôr/ in the phrase *law and order.*
(3) *Loam* is often /lōōm/.
(4) *Chimney* is often /**chĭm**-lē/.
(5) Words like *library, strawberry* are pronounced with the final syllable /brē/: /**lī**-brē/, /**strä**-brē/.
(6) *Bottle*, and less often *battle* and *kettle*, are pronounced with a glottal stop: /**bŏ**'-l/, /**bă**'-l/, /**kĕ**'-l/. This is especially common among persons of Irish descent, though this may be coincidental.

Several important changes in Boston speech have recently been observed. Doubtless these new features will spread outward from Boston and affect the New England dialect as a whole.

(1) The partial pronunciation of /r/ after vowels, or the use of *r*-colored vowels, is increasing, especially in words which have /ėr/, such as *girl, thirty*. This is less true of words with the other vowels preceding /r/, such as *hear, care, shore, poor*.
(2) The intrusive, or extra, /r/ is decreasing. For example, in the phrase *the shah of Iran, shah* was almost always pronounced /shär/. Studies show that this tendency to add /r/ is decreasing.
(3) The /ȧ/ sound in words like *past, glass, grass* is becoming /ă/, the way it is most often pronounced in the General Northern dialect.

bottom line. In an age dominated by business preoccupations, it is natural enough that an accountant's term for the last figure on a balance sheet should pass into fashionable usage. *Bottom line* has clearly taken over from predecessors such as *final analysis,* and now means anything from 'inescapable implication' or 'unavoidable result' to 'ultimate version' or 'summary of a complex situation':

> He [the president of a record company] has been extolled as a commercial genius who can smell a hit across a county, and reviled as a heartless dictator who thinks only of the bottom line.
> —James Lincoln Collier, *Reader's Digest*

> The bottom line of the "partnership" [between big business and government in Japan] is a loss of freedom, first economic and then personal.
> —William Safire, *New York Times*

> There is a bottom line here, however, that has not yet consolidated; the operation against Zaire from Angola would certainly not have been launched without Cuban backing, and that means, ultimately, Soviet backing.
> —*National Review*

> Abruptly the psychiatrist looked up at Chris.
> "Well, it's terribly complicated," he told her, "and I've oversimplified outrageously."
> "So what's the bottom line?" Chris asked.
> "At the moment," he told her, "a blank. She needs an intensive examination by a team of experts. . . ."
> —William Peter Blatty, *The Exorcist*

boughten. This adjective, which means 'purchased in a store, rather than homemade or home-grown' is a dialect term in both England and America. In England it is used almost exclusively in the southwest:

> Boughten bread ain't got near the heart in't as that as we makes a'twom [at home].
> —from Joseph Wright, *English Dialect Dictionary*

In the United States *boughten* is used in the Northern and North Midland dialects. It is most commonly heard in the term *store-boughten bread* (also known as *baker's bread*). *Boughten* is also used with reference to anything that is not home-grown:

> The flowers in Willoughby's rather lavish arrangements were what Matild called "boughten."
> —Agnes Light, *Light in the Sky*

> No boughten tomatoes, however fresh from the "vine-ripened, home-grown" bin at the market, can touch a tomato grown by me in my own patch.
> —Celestine Sibley, *Reader's Digest*

This 'not home-grown' sense has been humorously extended in the expression *boughten teeth* (= 'dentures, false teeth'). In the Southern and Midland dialects *bought* is the usual term.

boulevard. This word, meaning 'broad city street, typically tree-lined and landscaped for walkers,' commemorates a chapter in the evolution of cities and a well-taken opportunity in the use of planning space. By 1800 many of the old cities of Europe had expanded outside their original walls. In Paris and elsewhere the walls had long been used by the citizens as walks; when the walls themselves were pulled down, the city authorities took the opportunity of keeping the space so gained to make broad streets, usefully encircling the inner city, with parklike walks on both sides. The Old French word *boloart* = 'city wall, rampart' was borrowed from Dutch *bolwerc* = 'bulwark, rampart.' *Boloart* became in Modern French *boulevard;* and when the ramparts were pulled down, the word remained as the name of the walks. By the 1870s *boulevard* /**bo͞o**-lə-värd/ was also an English word meaning 'broad tree-lined street,' a feature much used in the laying out of American cities such as Washington and Los Angeles. For a comparable story in city planning see MALL.

boutique. See APOTHECARY, BOUTIQUE, BODEGA.

bracero. The pronunciation is /brə-**sâr**-ō/, the plural *braceros*. The word is from Mexican Spanish *bracero* = 'laborer,' literally 'man who works with his arms,' from *brazo* = 'arm.' *Bracero* is the official term for a Mexican laborer who has been admitted to the United States for temporary seasonal work in agriculture or industry, especially under the Bracero Program, lasting from World War II until 1966.

brackets. See PUNCTUATION.

bring, take. These two basic verbs are contrasted in standard usage according to the position that the speaker has in mind: *bring* means 'to convey (something) toward' that position, *take* means 'to convey (something) away from' that position. In the simplest situations, the position is the speaker's actual position. Speaker standing outside: *Bring it out of the house. Take it into the house.* Speaker inside: *Bring it into the house. Take it out of the house.* In some dialects *bring* can be used in other ways: a person inside the house can say, *Bring it outside.* This is nonstandard. When the speaker's actual position is irrelevant, as in most third-person narrative, there is usually an implicit position or point of view that governs the choice between *bring* and *take*. *She brought the groceries home.* (The narrator's point of view is the vicinity of home.) *She took the groceries home.* (The narrator's point of view is the vicinity of the store, or simply a remote, undefined perspective, looking on from neutral ground or as it were from the sky.)

brinkmanship. See GAMESMANSHIP.

Brit. The ancient Celtic inhabitants of Britain were called *Britons* or *Brits*. These terms are only historical, but the name Brit has recently been re-created by shortening *British*. It is used especially by the Australians:

> There is a historic mistrust between the Boer and the Brit in South Africa.
>
> —*Brisbane Courier-Mail*

It is now also used by Americans. In the following quotation, a CIA agent in Hong Kong is briefing the head of British intelligence:

> "Technically, Chinese junks are forbidden to sail between Victoria Island and Kowloon Point, sir, but the last thing the Brits want is a hassle with the mainland over rights of way. Sorry, sir."
>
> "Not at all," said Smiley politely. "Brits we are and Brits we shall remain."
>
> —John Le Carré, *The Honourable Schoolboy*

As the quotation indicates, the term is not liked by the British themselves.

Britain. This is the ancient and geographical name of the large island off western Europe, and also the usual name of the nation comprising this island and Northern Ireland.
(1) The name *Britain* (Latin *Britannia*) is of Celtic origin. The Celtic inhabitants were called the *Brits* or *Britons* (see BRIT). Their ancient language, of which Welsh is a continuation, is known as *British Celtic*.
(2) Britain, Ireland, and the numerous small islands around them are *the British Isles*.
(3) When England, Wales, and Scotland were united, the resulting nation was named *Great Britain*, not as a boast but to indicate that the whole island was united for the first time. *Britain* or *Great Britain* remains the usual name for the country as a whole. Its formal political title, especially when stressing the inclusion of Northern Ireland, is the UNITED KINGDOM. *England* is often loosely used for *Britain* (see ENGLAND, ENGLISH).
(4) The people of Britain collectively are the *British* or *Britons*. Briton is correct but is not now much used by the people themselves. *Britisher*, probably an American coinage, is also not much used.

British Columbia dialects. The settlement history of British Columbia differs from that of the rest of Canada. Most of British Columbia's settlers were already Canadians when they set out on their move westward. Many of the original settlers of British Columbia came from Ontario and the Maritime Provinces. A number came from the United Kingdom; their influence is probably strongest in the south of Vancouver Island and in the Okanagan Valley. U.S. influence is probably less marked in British Columbia than elsewhere in Canada, although it is still strengthened by the north-south trading routes in this part of the country. (See map at CANADIAN ENGLISH.)

General Features. Many speech characteristics are shared by all, or almost all, British Columbians; as in other provinces, there is a solid core of agreement that might be said to constitute common British Columbia usage. However, Greater Vancouver, southern Vancouver Island, the Okanagan region, and the Kootenay region probably each have some elements of a separate dialect. But the distinction between one dialect and another lies in the proportionate, not the exclusive, possession of these elements. For example, the pronunciation of *tomato* as /tə-**mā**-tō/ is heard in southern Vancouver Island as well as in the Okanagan region and in the Kootenay region; but in southern Vancouver Island only 24 percent of one surveyed group used this pronunciation, while in the Kootenay region 92 percent of the corresponding group used it.

Pronunciation. Common usage in British Columbia gives *progress* as /**prō**-grĕs/, *leisure* as /**lĕ**-zhər/, and *soot* as /sŏŏt/. The word *which* is pronounced with /w/, not /hw/. The words *ant* and *aunt* are both pronounced /ănt/; *cot* and *caught* are both /kŏt/; *greasy* /**grē**-sĭ/ rhymes with *fleecy* /**flē**-sĭ/, and *missile* /**mĭs**'l/ rhymes with *thistle* /**thĭs**'l/. In the Greater Vancouver area, however, some of the older speakers do not rhyme the last three pairs. In this same area the words *Mary*, *merry*, and *marry* are rapidly coming to sound exactly alike; this is also true in the Kootenay region and probably elsewhere in British Columbia as well. The dialect of the Greater Vancouver area is probably most clearly marked by its failure to distinguish such pairs as *spear it* and *spirit*, both pronounced /**spîr**-ĭt/, and by the frequency with which "glides" occur after slack vowels: *is* often sounds like /ĭəz/, *pull* like /pŏŏəl/, and so on. The dialect of southern Vancouver Island is particularly noteworthy for the high percentage of younger speakers who use the vowel /ä/ at the beginning of *apricot* (83 percent, as opposed to 75 percent in the Okanagan region and 69 percent in the Kootenay region). Similarly, while 80 to 90 percent of southern Vancouver Island informants used /ä/ in *calm*, in other parts of British Columbia this pronunciation was favored by only 60 to 80 percent.

Grammar and Syntax. In these two levels of language British Columbia shows almost nothing that is distinct from usage elsewhere in Canada. As a past tense of *dive*, the form *dove* is rather more common than it is elsewhere. British Columbians *visit* their neighbors more often than they *visit with* them. And in Greater Vancouver at least, the older speakers tend to get sick *in* rather than *at* or *to* the stomach. It is difficult to draw any firm conclusion from these items, as *dove* is more usual in American than in British English; *visit* is commoner in British English; and sick *in* the stomach may well reflect Australian speech patterns. Among younger speakers, here as elsewhere, dialect lines are becoming blurred with the increasingly pervasive influence of the mass media.

Vocabulary. In the common usage of British Columbia, American influence shows up strongly in the vocabulary. The leaves turn red in the *fall;* the seed of a cherry is the *pit;* and letters are delivered by the *mailman.* However, children in southern Vancouver Island eat *chips,* and their mainland contemporaries eat *French fries;* island children play on a *seesaw,* but as one travels east the American term *teeter-totter* becomes progressively more popular, achieving a 95 percent use in the Kootenay region. Similarly, the younger speakers in the latter region seem to be abandoning the Canadian *chesterfield* in favor of *couch* and to be moving toward adoption of the American *shades* over the Canadian *blinds.* But no clear trend emerges, since the same young people are adhering firmly to the Canadian *kerosene* over the American *coal oil.*

Considered as a whole, the vocabulary of British Columbia shows remarkable richness and variety. Many words show the influence of Amerindian languages, usually through the medium of CHINOOK JARGON, a Chinook-based pidgin used on the Pacific coast in the 19th and early 20th centuries. Other influences are identified below.

(1) Terms from Tlingit, Chinook, Chahalis, and coast Salish:

hootchinoo /hōō-chē-nōō/ = 'crude, home-made liquor'
salal /sə lăl/ = 'a small evergreen shrub, *Gaultheria shallon*'
skookum /skōō-kəm/ = 'big, strong'
sockeye = 'a species of Pacific salmon, *Oncorhynchus nerka*'

(2) Terms reflecting the environment:

candlefish = 'a small fish, *Thaleichthys pacificus*, oily enough to be lit and used as a candle or torch'
devil's club = 'a shrub of western Canada, *Oplopanax horridus*'
kokanee /kō-kə-nē/ = 'a dwarf landlocked salmon, *Oncorhynchus nerka kennerlyi*'
steelhead = 'a species of Pacific trout, *Salmo gairdnerii*'
wolf-willow = 'any of several shrubs, especially the silverberry'

(3) Terms from history and legend:

Gastown = 'Vancouver' (from "*Gassy* Jack" Deighton, once a popular innkeeper there)
grease trail = 'any trail leading to the interior of the province'
mile house = 'early inn'
potlatch = (1) 'gift' (2) 'occasion of gift giving'
quarter section = 'land area of 160 acres'
Sasquatch /săs-kwăch/ = 'wild hairy monster of Indian lore'
section = 'one square mile'

(4) Terms from the lumbering, mining, and fishing industries:

bar = 'gold-bearing ridge of sand or gravel in or beside a stream'
bar diggings = 'gold-mining operations in a bar'
boom dozer, boom scooter, dozer boat, log bronc = 'boat used to assemble logs into booms and control them once they are in'
bulldoze = 'to blast with explosive'
bull pen = 'area where logs are assembled for forming into booms'
coho = 'a species of Pacific salmon, *Oncorhynchus kisutch*'
cutthroat trout = 'a species of trout, *Salmo clarkii*, with red streaks below the jaw'
dog salmon = 'a species of Pacific salmon, *Oncorhynchus keta*'
dry diggings = 'gold claims away from the bed of a stream'
grilse = 'immature salmon'
high-lead system /hī-lēd/ = 'system of yarding logs that uses only one spar tree'
miners' meeting law = 'law of the early gold-mining communities'
paystreak = 'profitable deposit of gold-bearing gravel'
skyline system = 'system of yarding logs that uses two spar trees'

(5) Slang terms:

bush salmon = 'deer bagged by a poacher'
crummy = 'boxcar used as a passenger coach'; related to *crumb* = 'body louse'
donkey puncher = 'operator of a donkey engine'
hurdy, hurdy-gurdy = 'dance-hall girl, frequenting gold-rush saloons'
pit-lamp = 'to hunt deer illegally, with a light'
Rocky Mountain deadshot = 'pancake'

British English. The people of England tend to find the American term *British English* amusing—or annoying. "We *are* the English," they are apt to explain with long-suffering logic. "What we speak is *the English language*." But the term *British English* is unavoidable, and justified. American English, Australian English, British English, Canadian English, and others now exist as vigorous national varieties that are neither diverging to become separate languages nor converging to form a homogenized World English. Twentieth-century British English is just one of the family, not its progenitor.

Like the others, it is an altered form of the English of the 17th and 18th centuries. Like the others, it has made its own innovations; and although it preserves some features that the others have lost, the same is true of each of the others. The shared language and literature keep the English-speaking peoples in close contact, and they influence one another; but their histories, environments, and characters differ deeply, and it is natural that their speech should differ. British has a certain special prestige as the senior member of the group, but no international authority. (SCOTTISH ENGLISH is dealt with separately; this entry covers the English of England.)

Dialects and Standard English. In 13th-century England there was no standard language. Every locality spoke its own highly distinct dialect, and people from different parts of the one small country could not easily communicate. Government was little centralized, and its business was conducted more often in French and Latin than in native English.

From about 1350 the king's government, based in London and Westminster, grew in authority and made increasing use of English. The London dialect, just one variety of the Midland group of dialects, began to gain prestige. As the speech of the court and the language of government, it had become by Shakespeare's time the national standard, the chief medium of literature and print, and the preferred dialect of the upper classes. It thus began to replace the local dialects, while absorbing some of their features. The process has continued down to the present day. The old dialects still exist but are spoken only by a few, mostly old, people in rural districts. Nearly everyone now speaks Standard British or a modified version of it. There are thus two levels of regional speech in England, the true dialects and Standard British. The true dialects, which are clearly dying out, differ strongly in grammar as well as in pronunciation and vocabulary; they would be largely incomprehensible to speakers of Standard British or Standard American. Standard itself has regional variations of vocabulary and accent, taken over from the true dialects.

Received Standard and Modified Standard. *Received Standard* is the traditionally most prestigious form of Standard British, associated with the old public schools (see *public school* under section 7 of Vocabulary, below), the universities of Oxford and Cambridge, and the official announcers of the British Broadcasting Corporation (BBC). Forms of Standard that contain regional or non-upper-class features can be called modified Standard.

In George Bernard Shaw's play *Pygmalion* and its musical version, *My Fair Lady*, Received Standard is the speech taught by Professor Henry Higgins to the cockney flower girl Eliza Doolittle. Until recently this speech form, especially its accent, was considered almost essential to social success. This rigidly snobbish attitude has now softened somewhat. Forms of modified Standard are heard almost everywhere, and a certain amount of regionalism and even lower classism has its own cachet, rather like the wave of ethnic pride that has been sweeping America.

As an example of modified versus Received, the vowel sound in words like *path* and *laugh* is /ä/ in Received Standard but /ă/ or /ŭ/ in the modified Standard of the North. Similarly, the vowel sound in *up* and *some* is /ŭ/ in Received but /o͞o/ in the North. In the speech of Prince Charles, who of course speaks Received Standard, *up the path* would be /ŭp *th*ə päth/. John Lennon, born and brought up in Liverpool, spoke a Northern type of modified Standard; in his natural speech (before being influenced by American), *up the path* would probably have been /o͞op *th*ə pŭth/. These two types of pronunciation are both variations of Standard British English. Some of these differences are obvious, others quite subtle.

British and American. American English originated from the Standard English of the 17th and 18th centuries, with various features of the old regional dialects all recombined and reshaped in America. Today's British has lost some features that American has kept, kept some that American has discarded, and made many innovations of its own. At the level of grammar there is not much difference between the two varieties. Their pronunciations differ markedly and their vocabularies and nuances of idiom even more so. There are a number of different spellings. Individual American usages and words can often be traced to their origins in British dialects. *Gotten*, retained in Standard American, has been almost entirely eliminated from Standard British but survives tenuously in some of the dialects. On the other hand, the adjectival *boughten* = 'bought in a store rather than homemade' does not exist in either standard language but survives dialectally in certain regions in both countries (see BOUGHTEN).

Oscar Wilde's description of Britain and America as "two great countries divided by a common language" contains truth as well as wit. They have never had much genuine trouble understanding each other, but they have a long history of being irritated with each other. British purists have felt that uncouth Americanisms were corrupting their language; American language patriots have claimed that British was effete and that the future was theirs anyway. Up to about 1900, Standard American was probably more influenced by Standard British than British was by American, but throughout this century the current has been powerfully reversed. On balance, modern British has borrowed far more American words than American has borrowed from British (not counting, of course, the common word stock that American inherited). In both cases the borrowings are more extensive than either side realizes. Some words or expressions are well known to be Americanisms or Briticisms and are resisted or welcomed accordingly; but others are never noticed until they have become so fully established that they are felt to have been native all along.

British contributions to the vocabulary of sports include *badminton*, *golf*, and (*lawn*) *tennis*, and more recently *Rugby*, *soccer*, *squash*, and *gamesmanship*. In clothing there are *cardigan*, *raglan sleeves*, *Wellington boots*, *trench coat*, and *miniskirt*. In politics there are ESTABLISHMENT, MANDARIN, *iron curtain*, *Big Brother*, and *the corridors of power*. *Breathalyzer*, *CAT scan*, *cable television*, *Hovercraft*, and *kiss of life* are British inventions and coinages, as are *brain drain*, *bungalow*, *chortle*, *tabloid*, *Parkinson's Law*, and *smog*. More surprising, perhaps, is the category of slang and informal language, in which American English is generally far more colorful and inventive than British. But *bonkers*, *cop* = 'policeman,' GAY, *mod*, *posh*, *spoof*, and *swank* are all Briticisms fully established in American, and *perks* – 'fringe benefits' and TRENDY are recent additions. BRUNCH is a good example of the thoroughly naturalized alien; British by origin, the word was borrowed into American in the 1920s, died out in Britain, and is now widely perceived as an Americanism.

There are many more Briticisms in American than these, but they are vastly outnumbered, and outweighed in prominence and usage, by Americanisms that have become part of British—even disregarding the hundreds of names of plants and animals and things peculiar to America. One example of prevailing American influence is that disputed usages such as *hopefully* = 'it is to be hoped that' and *alibi* = 'excuse' tend to become widespread in British soon after their emergence in American (see HOPEFULLY; ALIBI).

It is this sort of thing, of course, that especially outrages British purists. However, American purists denounce these usages with equal fury and equal lack of success. It is remarkable that most of the situations considered to be serious usage issues, such as the use of *whom* (see WHO), the SPLIT INFINITIVE, the placement of ONLY, the status of AIN'T, and the meaning of DISINTERESTED, are in fact treated identically in Britain and America. The same deviations occur; conservatives condemn them, permissivists justify them, and a large percentage of British and American speakers pay no attention to them one way or the other.

At the same time, there are many clear differences between British and American "correct" usage and in the preferences of everyday idiom. In British English, *I've got an uncle who* is a normal and natural equivalent of American *I have an uncle who*. British *I should think so* contrasts with American *I would think so.* There are also complex differences, hard to pin down, in the use of *shall* and *will* (see SHALL, WILL). British constructs collective nouns as plurals (*The Cabinet are meeting tonight*) more readily than American. But British tends to resist the free formation of phrasal verbs like *visit with, head up,* and *plan on;* these are perfectly possible in British, but many people perceive them as American and much prefer plain *visit, head,* and *plan.*

There are strongly marked differences in the use of some prepositions. (*In*) *back of* does not occur in British; it can only be *at the back of* or *behind* (see BACK OF, IN BACK OF). *Outside of* can occur but is much less frequent than it is in American. *Out the window* and *out the door* also occur but are considered to be careless or nonstandard; the only approved forms are *out of the window, out of the door.* There are also numerous individual differences of expressive idiom, as that a British candidate *stands for* Parliament, while an American candidate *runs for* office.

Individual differences between British and American English are further explored in the following sections on pronunciation, spelling, and vocabulary. The total difference is not really profound. The two peoples speak the same language, but they speak it in different styles. They can almost infallibly identify each other from speech. Few Americans can imitate any of the forms of British well enough to escape detection in Britain, and vice versa. There are too many nuances. Such differences, trivial in themselves, seem to amount to a cultural defense mechanism. It is extremely convenient to be part of the English-speaking world. But national cultures such as those of Australia, Britain, and Canada can still resist losing their identities under American dominance. One effective way of doing this is through language. It is thus safe to predict that the national varieties of English will persist. British English in particular has shown that it is fully capable of living with American influence—grumbling about it but in the end absorbing and Briticizing it—without losing any of its own distinctiveness.

Pronunciation. The most conspicuous single difference between Received Standard British and Standard American pronunciation is in the treatment of the vowel in words like *path, pass, dance,* and *ask.* In Shakespeare's time this vowel was short /ă/. Southern British changed it to long /ä/ in the 18th century, and this became Received Standard. Standard American retains the older /ă/. But note that Northern British also keeps this vowel as short, while eastern New England and Coastal Southern speech often have /ä/.

The second most obvious British-American difference is the Standard British loss of /r/ in words like *far, hard,* and *mother.* Here again, Standard American has kept the older form, still pronouncing /r/ in these words. And here again Northern and other regional forms of British also keep /r/, while the eastern New England dialect and some forms of Southern often lose it. (See also R-LESSNESS, INTRUSIVE R.)

Two further systematic British differences are the treatment of the endings *-ary/-ory* and *-ile.* While American generally pronounces the suffix *-ary/-ory* with a secondary stress on the first syllable, British gives this syllable no stress or eliminates it entirely. *Dictionary,* in American /**dĭk**-shə-nĕr-ē/, becomes British /**dĭk**-shən-ə-rĭ/ or most often /**dĭk**-shən-rĭ/. Likewise *military* /**mĭl**-ĭ-trĭ/, *preliminary* /prə-**lĭm**-ən-rĭ/, and *library* /**lī**-brə-rĭ/ or more often /**līb**-rĭ/. With the adjectival ending *-ile,* on the other hand, the situation is reversed. British English gives this syllable a full "spelling" pronunciation, with secondary stress, while American English generally leaves it unstressed. *Docile, fragile,* and *futile,* in American usually /**dŏs**-əl/, /**frăj**-əl/, /**fyo͞ot**'l/, are in Standard British always /**dō**-sīl/, /**frăj**-īl/, /**fyo͞o**-tīl/.

Another more or less consistent difference is in the treatment of stress in many words borrowed from French and still perceived as French. American tends to put the stress on the last syllable, British tends to bring it forward. *Ballet, croquet,* in American /bă-**lā**/, /krō-**kā**/, are in British /**băl**-ā/, /**krō**-kā/.

Most other British differences from American are less systematic or are confined to individual words. A selective listing follows.

ate usually /ĕt/, sometimes /āt/
been usually /bēn/, sometimes /bĭn/
* **bona fide** /**bō**-nə **fī**-dĭ/
buoy /boi/
clerk /kläk/
Derby, derby /**dä**-bĭ/
Don Juan /dŏn **jo͞o**-ən/
Don Quixote /dŏn **kwĭk**-sət/
dynasty /**dĭn**-əs-tĭ/
* **either** usually /**ī**-*thə*/, often /**ē**-*thə*/
fillet (= 'boneless slice of meat or fish') /**fĭl**-ĭt/
frontier /**frŭn**-tĭ-ə/
herb /hĕb/
leisure /**lĕzh**-ə/
lieutenant /lĕf-**tĕn**-ənt/
magazine /măg-ə-**zēn**/
medicine usually /**mĕd**-sən/, sometimes /**mĕd**-ĭ-sĭn/
mustache /mə-**stäsh**/
mythology /mī-**thŏl**-ə-jĭ/
* **neither** usually /**nī**-*thə*/, often /**nē**-*thə*/
nephew usually /**nĕv**-yo͞o/, often /**nĕf**-yo͞o/
* **pariah** /**păr**-ē-ə/
patriot /**păt**-rĭ-ət/
premier /**prĕm**-ĭ-ə/
primer (= 'introductory book') /**prī**-mə/
process /**prō**-sĕs/
produce (verb) /prə-**dyo͞os**/
produce (noun) /**prŏd**-yo͞os/
progress (noun) /**prō**-grĕs/
provost /**prŏv**-əst/
quinine /kwĭ-**nēn**/
research /rĭ-**sĕch**/
schedule /**shĕd**-yo͞ol/
solder /**sōl**-də/
squirrel /**skwĭr**-əl/
tomato /tə-**mä**-tō/
trait /trā/
vase /väz/
vitamin /**vĭt**-ə-mĭn/
zenith /**zĕn**-ĭth/

*Appears as separate entry

Some place names used in both countries have markedly different British and American pronunciations. Those ending in *-ham* (Old English *ham* = 'homestead') are in British always reduced to /-əm/: *Birmingham* /**bêrm**-ĭng-əm/. Names of counties ending in *-shire* are in Received Standard pronounced with /-shə/: *Hampshire* /**hămp**-shə/; in modified Standard the final syllable often becomes /-shîr/ or /-shīr/. Pronunciations of many other British place names depart from their spellings in often unpredictable ways, as the following sample shows:

Berkeley /**bäk**-lĭ/
Berkshire /**bäk**-shə/
Bideford /**bĭd**-ĭ-fəd/
Blenheim /**blĕn**-ĭm/
Fowey /foi/
Gloucester /**glŏs**-tə/
Hereford /**hĕr**-ə-fəd/
High Wycombe /hī **wĭk**-əm/
Keighley /**kēth**-lĭ/
Leicester /**lĕs**-tə/
Loughborough /**lŭf**-bə-rə/
Marlborough /**môl**-bə-rə/
Norwich /**nŏr**-ĭj/
Salisbury /**sôlz**-bə-rĭ/
Thames /tĕmz/
Warwick /**wä**-rĭk/
Worcester /**wo͝os**-tə/

The element *Saint*, both in names of saints and in place names, is usually pronounced /sənt/, and usually spelled *St: St Ives* /sənt **īvz**/.

Spelling. British spelling is slightly more archaic than American. The American situation is due largely to the efforts of Noah WEBSTER, who succeeded in putting over a few sensible reforms that have not been followed by the British. The total of differences is not large, but unfortunately it is also not consistent.

Many abstract nouns that in American end in *-or*, in British end in *-our: arbour, armour, behaviour, candour, clamour, colour, favour, flavour, harbour, labour, neighbour, rigour, splendour*, and others; but British has *error, horror, pallor, stupor*, etc., and American usually has *glamour*. Both have *-or* for agent nouns such as *author, doctor, collaborator, tractor;* but it is always *saviour* in British, and often in American, especially as an appellation of Jesus Christ: *the Saviour.*

British has *-re* where American has *-er* in *centre, goitre, mitre, spectre*, etc., but American hesitates between *theater* and *theatre;* and both have *acre, lucre*, and *mediocre*. British has *metre* = 'measure of length' but *meter* = 'instrument for measuring.'

British has *-ce* where American has *-se* in *defence* and *offence*. In verbs with unstressed final syllables ending in *l*, British illogically doubles the *l* in inflections and agent nouns: *levelled, levelling; travelled, travelling, traveller*. For the verb ending *-ize*, British prefers *-ise* but also uses *-ize*: *visualise; realise; capsize*.

Some other spelling variants:

British	*American*
aeon	**eon**
anaemic	**anemic**
cheque	**check** *or* **cheque**
disc	**disk** *or* **disc**
draught	**draft**
encyclopaedia *or* **encyclopedia**	**encyclopedia** *or* **encyclopaedia**
enquire	**inquire**
fulfil	**fulfill**
gaol *or* **jail**	**jail**
grey *or* **gray**	**gray**
haemorrhage	**hemorrhage**
kerb = 'edge of a sidewalk'	**curb**
manoeuvre	**maneuver**
mediaeval *or* **medieval**	**medieval**
mould	**mold**
moulder	**molder**
moustache	**mustache**
omelette	**omelet** *or* **omelette**
plough	**plow**
programme	**program**
pyjamas	**pajamas**
skilful	**skillful**
sulphur	**sulfur**
tyre = 'tread on a wheel'	**tire**
vice = 'clamping tool'	**vise**

Vocabulary. The following terms are selections of British English that either do not occur in American English at all or differ from American terms in form, meaning, range of meanings, or usage.

(1) Topographical terms:

beck (in the North) = 'stream'

county = 'any of the traditional territorial units of Britain, by which local government was formerly organized, such as Kent, Devonshire, Suffolk, or Lancashire'; in British usage the word *county* is never put after the name (as in *Suffolk County*, New York). The correct British form is simply *Suffolk*, or, more elaborately, *the county of Suffolk*. (In Irish usage *county* is put before the name but lower-cased: *county Mayo*.)

dale (in the North) = 'river valley between hills'

down (in the South) = 'hill' and **downs** = 'undulating chalk uplands, generally treeless and grassy'

eyot /āt/ = 'island or islet in the river Thames'

fell (in the North) = 'hill' and **fells** = 'rough wilderness upland, generally treeless'

fen = 'low marshy land subject to flooding' and **the Fens** = 'large areas of fen in Cambridgeshire and Lincolnshire, now drained'

heath = 'a tract of rough wilderness land, often grown with shrubs including heather'

moor = (1) 'a tract of rough wilderness land, much the same as a heath' (2) 'such a tract kept as a shooting preserve'

river In British usage the word *river* is generally put before, not after, the name: *the river Thames; the river Trent; the river Nile.*

shire = 'a county, especially one that has a name ending in *-shire*' See Pronunciation, above.

(2) Animals and plants:

bug = 'bedbug'; has been used in dialects to mean 'insect in general,' as in Standard American, but not in Standard British

cock = (1) 'male domestic fowl, rooster' (2) 'any male bird'; in British usage not felt to be subject to taboo

daisy = 'small plant with white or pink-tinged flowers that close up at night, often growing as a weed in lawns'

robin = 'sparrow-sized European bird with a red breast'; resembles the much larger American robin only in having a red breast (although both birds happen to belong to the thrush family)

vine = 'grapevine'; not used of climbing plants in general, as in the United States

(3) Food and drink:

biscuit = 'any cracker or cookie'

bitter = 'the basic English draft beer, uncarbonated, strongly flavored with hops, and drunk cool, not chilled'

candy floss = 'cotton candy'

chips = 'fried pieces of potato, usually cut larger than French fries'

cider = 'hard cider'

cookery book = 'cookbook'

corn = 'any cereal grain, especially wheat'

cornet = 'ice-cream cone'

courgette /ko͞or-**zhĕt**/ = 'variety of squash similar to zucchini'

crisps, potato crisps = 'potato chips'

crumpet = 'round, flat battercake with holes in the top, eaten toasted, with butter'

elevenses = 'midmorning snack'

grill = 'to broil'

hock = 'Rhine wine'

joint = 'large cut of meat for roasting'

kipper = 'a split and smoke-cured herring'

marrow, vegetable marrow = 'variety of squash, often grown very large'

mince = 'ground meat'

prawn = 'crustacean roughly the same size as a smallish American shrimp'

scone /skŏn, skōn/ = 'small white cake made with baking powder, essentially the same as an American baking-powder biscuit'

shrimp = 'crustacean generally much smaller than an American shrimp'

stout = 'very dark beer made with roasted malt'

swede /swēd/ = 'rutabaga'

sweets = 'candy'

toffee = 'candy similar to taffy'

whitebait = 'very small silvery fish, generally no more than two inches long, the young of herrings, sprat, and other species, eaten whole, fried in a light batter'

(4) Domestic terms:

au pair /ō **pâr**/ = 'young woman from a foreign country doing domestic work for an English family in exchange for room and board'

clothes-peg = 'clothespin'

cotton wool = 'absorbent cotton'

dustbin = 'garbage can'

first floor = 'second floor (above the ground floor)'

flat = 'apartment'; does not, as in the United States, imply poor quality

flex = 'electric cord'

gramophone = 'phonograph'

jug = 'pitcher'; the older word *pitcher*, not now in Standard British use, is familiar in Britain only from the King James Bible

methylated spirits = 'denatured alcohol used for fuel, cleaning, etc.'

mews = 'street of carriage houses'

mews house = 'carriage house converted as a residence'

mount = 'picture mat'

nappy = 'diaper'

paraffin = 'kerosene'

pram = 'baby carriage'

rates = 'local property taxes'

reel = 'spool (of thread, wire, etc.)'

secateurs /**sĕk**-ə-tərz/ = 'pruning shears'

second floor = 'third floor (above the ground floor)'

tap = 'faucet'; the standard household word

tin = 'can'; but *can* is now also increasingly used

torch = 'flashlight'

wash up = 'to wash the dishes'

wireless (old-fashioned) = 'radio'; *radio* is now the predominant word

(5) Transportation:

aeroplane = 'airplane'

bonnet = 'automobile hood'
boot = 'automobile trunk'
caravan = 'trailer, mobile home'
carriage = 'railroad car'
flyover = 'highway overpass'
juggernaut lorry (informal) = 'semitrailer'
lorry = 'truck'
minicar, mini = 'automobile smaller than a subcompact'
motor scooter = 'small two-wheeled gas-powered vehicle'
motorway = 'superhighway'
pavement = 'sidewalk'
petrol = 'gasoline'
railway = 'railroad'
return = 'round trip'
roundabout = 'traffic circle'
saloon (car) = 'sedan'
shooting brake = 'station wagon'
silencer = 'muffler'
sleeper = 'railroad tie'
spaghetti junction (informal) = 'multiple superhighway intersection'
subway = 'pedestrian underpass'
truck = 'open railroad freight car'
tube = 'deep subway tunnel of circular cross section, the London subway'
underground = 'subway'
windscreen = 'windshield'
zebra crossing = 'pedestrian crossing marked by white stripes on a black road surface'

(6) Slang and informal terms:

bags I! = 'dibs on!'; children's term used to claim something
banger = 'sausage'
beak = 'magistrate'
bedsit = 'bed-sitting room, one-room lodging'
bloke = 'fellow, guy'
bloody = 'the well-known British all-purpose expletive'; formerly a heavily tabooed word, it had its most famous literary use in George Bernard Shaw's play *Pygmalion* (1912), in which Edwardian audiences were thrilled to hear Mrs. Patrick Campbell as Eliza Doolittle say, "Not bloody likely!" The taboo on *bloody* is now only mild, but has not disappeared.
brolly = 'umbrella'
clobber (chiefly Londoners' slang) = 'clothes'; not related to the American verb *clobber* = 'to beat, defeat'
codswallop = 'nonsense' (first recorded in the early 20th century)
fag = 'cigarette'
fains I! = 'children's ritual call to prevent a certain action by an opponent or teammate'
grotty = 'inferior, nasty' (from *grotesque*)
kip = (1) (verb) 'to sleep' (2) (noun) 'sleep'
nark = 'police informer, paid spy, sneak' (from Romany [Gypsy] *nak* = 'nose,' translating the earlier slang *nose* = 'informer')
nick = (1) (verb) 'to steal' (2) (noun) 'prison'
telly = 'television'

(7) Miscellaneous terms:

aluminium /ăl-yə-**mĭn**-yəm/ = 'aluminum'
bank holiday = 'national legal holiday'
bill = '(in restaurants, etc.) check'
* **billion** = 'one million million'
cashier = 'bank teller'
catapult = 'slingshot'
death duties = 'inheritance taxes'
devilry = 'deviltry'
don = 'an academic'
dustman = 'garbage man'
earth = '(electrical) ground'
faggot = 'bundle of kindling wood'
Father Christmas = 'Santa Claus'; but *Santa Claus* is also used
fire brigade = 'fire department, fire company'
fortnight = 'period of two weeks'
green fingers = 'green thumb'
holiday = 'vacation'
leader = 'editorial in a newspaper'
letter box = 'private mailbox, for incoming mail'
mum, mummy = 'mom, mommy'
note = 'currency bill'
pernickety = 'persnickety'
pillar box = 'public mailbox, for outgoing mail'

post = (1) (noun) 'the public transmission of mail' (2) (noun) 'letters or packages sent by mail' (3) (noun) 'a particular pickup of mail' (4) (verb) 'to send by mail'

preparatory school, prep school (informal) = 'fee-charging school for children from about age 7 to about age 13'

public school = 'fee-charging school for children from about age 13 to about age 18'; the term originally meant 'endowed, non-profit-making school open to the public,' as opposed to 'privately owned school operated for profit'

ring, ring up = 'to telephone (someone)'

rise = 'an increase in pay, a raise'

rowlock /rŏl-ək/ = 'oarlock'

sick = 'feeling nausea'; not used to mean 'ill in general'

spanner = 'monkey wrench'

stalls = 'orchestra seats in a theater'

table = '(in parliamentary usage) to submit (a matter or document) for discussion'

tower block = 'high-rise building'

truncheon = 'policeman's night stick'

* **zed** = 'the letter *z*'

*Appears as separate entry

See also ELIZABETHAN ENGLISH; MIDDLE ENGLISH; OLD ENGLISH; SCOTTISH ENGLISH; U, NON-U.

Britisher. See BRITAIN.

Britons. See BRIT.

brunch. This blend of *breakfast* and *lunch* was invented in England at the turn of the century, probably by fashionable undergraduates at Oxford. Since then *brunch* has become firmly established in the United States and has all but died out in England. Most people in both countries would suppose it to be an Americanism. The word, and the meal, are chiefly in use in big cities and suburbia, where restaurants often offer brunch, and people have it at home on weekends. Some people regard the term with distaste. The journalist Heywood Broun is said to have observed, "There may be some perfectly nice people who use the word 'brunch,' but I prefer not to know about them." This reaction would no doubt apply even more strongly to the fancy extended form *bruncheon* and the verb *brunch*:

> He is being lunched, brunched, wined and dined. . . .
> —Enid Nemy, *New York Times*

buckaroo. A *buckaroo* is a cowboy, otherwise known as a *beef driver, broncobuster, cowhand, cowpoke, cowpuncher, range rider,* and *wrangler. Buckaroo* is the oldest of these terms and is still used in the West:

> Nothing ever did worry that buckaroo as long as his fingers wasn't too cold to roll a cigarette.
> —Harry L. Wilson, *Somewhere in Red Gap* (1916)

> In the 20's and 30's . . . the wing chap came into more and more general vogue. . . . When those buckaroos waddled along as dismounted bipeds with those mammoth contraptions on, they sure looked funny.
> —Jo Mora, *Trail Dust and Saddle Leather* (1950)

Two competing theories explain the word's origin. The most widely accepted one holds that it comes from the Spanish word for 'cowboy,' *vaquero* /vä-**kā**-rō/, the Spanish /v/ sounding similar to the English /b/. Folk etymology altered the pronunciation of the first part of the word to /bŭk/, either as a reference to maleness or to the bucking of a wild horse, and the word became *buckayro* /bŭ-**kā**-rō/:

> "I'll cross-examine her myself, boys," said the Squire. "I can talk what they call 'buckayro' Spanish. It ain't got but thirteen words in it, and twelve of them are cuss words."
> —Jerome Hart, *Vigilante Girl* (1910)

It was later given the fanciful suffix *-aroo* or *-eroo* (as in *floperoo, smackeroo, switcheroo,* etc.). This shifted the stress, resulting in the present pronunciation: /**bŭk**-ə-rōō, bŭk-ə-**rōō**/.

The other theory argues that the word came from the Gullah *buckra,* which means 'white man' (for other Gullah words see GULLAH). This word was carried to the West by black cowboys who used it ironically to refer to Mexican *vaqueros.* Later, the *-aroo* suffix was added.

bucket, pail, blickey, etc. These synonyms for the familiar container show interesting patterns of distribution among country people across the United States.
(1) *Bucket* versus *pail.* Both words are known to everyone, but *pail* is commoner in the North and *bucket* in the Midland speech area and the South. In eastern New England, however, both terms are equally common. In the South, while *bucket* prevails for the basic vessel, *pail* refers to a wooden container that has one long straight handle and is used for milk or water.

Metal or plastic garbage containers, widely used to feed farm animals, are also known by different terms in different parts of the country. *Garbage pail* and *slop pail* are used in every region. *Slop bucket* (like *bucket* itself) is the usual term in the North. *Swill pail* also occurs in the North. *Garbage bucket* occurs almost exclusively in the South.
(2) *Pail.* A fairly recent usage is the verb *pail* = 'to milk': *He went out to pail the cows.* This occurs most often in the North (but not the Northeast) and the North Midland speech area.
(3) *Blickey.* In New Jersey and southeastern New York the word *blickey* is often used instead of *pail* or *bucket.* It was originally a Hudson River valley word, borrowed in colonial times from Dutch *blikje* = 'tin pail.'

buffalo, bison. The original, and true, *buffalo* is one of several mammals belonging to the cattle family and is native to Africa and Asia. The original *bison,* also a member of the cattle family, is the European bison, or wisent, now rare. The famous North American animal that once grazed the Great Plains in million-strong herds belongs to the same genus (*Bison*) as the European bison but is smaller. It is therefore correctly and technically called bison. But from the pioneering days onward it has been known as the buffalo, and that is how most Americans still prefer to think of it.

burlesque. The term *burlesque,* originally an adjective that comes (via French) from Italian *burlesco* = 'mocking, ridiculous,' may be used in English as a noun, a verb, or an adjective. In its primary meaning it refers to humorous ridicule that relies chiefly on exaggeration to achieve its effect. As a technique it may be used in either satire or parody, although it is more often associated with the latter.

But for many people the connotations of the term have been both broadened and slightly skewed by its popular application to a now almost defunct form of theatrical entertainment. For most Americans over 40 years of age the word *burlesque* will probably never be entirely free of associations with that gaudy world in which top bananas delivered double-entendres, well-endowed ladies in G-strings carried such sobriquets as The Queen of Shake, exquisitely bored chorines chewed gum even while they danced, and Irish tenors never failed to sing "A Pretty Girl Is Like a Melody." See also LAMPOON; SATIRE; SPOOF.

bust. The verb *bust* is by origin a dialectal pronunciation of *burst,* meaning 'to break open, split, etc.' It has long been used also as slang in various senses: as a verb, 'to punch,' 'to break (someone) financially,' 'to demote (a soldier) in rank,' 'to arrest'; as a noun, 'a failure,' 'a punch,' 'a drinking spree.' In the economic sense of 'financial collapse,' as in *the cycle of boom and bust,* it has attained the status of a fully standard word. *Bust* has thus evolved a spread of meanings that now coexist at different levels in the spectrum of usage: dialect, slang, and standard.

but. (1) The basic function of *but* is as a conjunction marking contrast. At the beginning of a sentence it is occasionally followed by a comma, indicating a pause for emphasis.

> Merchants were good to the firefighters then, because they expected firefighters to be good in return as they made their annual, semi-annual, or monthly fire inspections. But, the system has changed now.
>
> —Dennis Smith, *Report From Engine Company 82*

◇ ***Recommendation.*** This use of an emphatic comma is disapproved of by most stylists. But the emphatic pause that it represents occurs naturally in speech and is therefore perfectly justifiable in writing. It should not be used too often, and only for definite emphasis.

(2) *But* also functions as a preposition meaning 'except.' When so used, it is followed by the objective case: *No one but him thought of it*—that is, *No one thought of it but (except) him.* However, the nominative (subjective) case is also possible: *No one but he thought of it.* In this construction *but* is seen by some grammarians to function as a conjunction introducing an incomplete clause: *No one thought of it but he (thought of it).*

◇ ***Recommendation.*** *No one but him* and *no one but he* are equally correct.

(3) As an adverb meaning 'only,' *but* is used differently at two levels of usage. The standard usage:

> I knew there was but one man who could secure us that support, the Senator from Illinois, Everett Dirksen.
>
> —Lyndon Johnson (quoted), Doris Kearns, *Lyndon Johnson and the American Dream*

There is also a dialectal usage with a double negative:

> . . . we never set a table because we never had but one fork or spoon each. . . . —Anne Moody, *Coming of Age in Mississippi*

◇ ***Recommendation.*** The standard construction "there was but one man" is correct but now slightly old-fashioned; most people would use *only* instead of *but.* The double negative construction "we never had but one fork" is unacceptable in standard usage but is very widespread in everyday dialectal speech. Each construction is correct at its own level.

(4) *But that* or *but what* is used in certain constructions expressing doubt, as *You can't tell but that* (or *but what*) *it'll be raining this time tomorrow.* These are informal or dialectal constructions. In standard usage *if* or *whether* is used. See WHETHER, IF; see also DOUBT.

(5) For the construction *cannot help but,* see HELP.

buzz words. See VOGUE WORDS.

Byzantine. The preferred U.S. pronunciation is /**bĭz**-ən-tēn/, the preferred British pronunciation /bī-**zăn**-tīn/ or /bĭ-**zăn**-tīn/. The meaning is 'of or relating to the Greek city of Byzantium (now Istanbul), the capital of the Byzantine Empire from A.D. 330 to 1453, or characteristic of its art and architecture.'

The political history of Byzantium is fraught with treacherous and deadly power struggles conducted by emperors, empresses, priests, generals, lords, and officials inside the gorgeously mysterious world of the imperial palace. The word *Byzantine* is thus used figuratively in modern politics to mean 'intrigue-ridden and deadly':

> The eventual departure of Brezhnev undoubtedly will touch off a Byzantine struggle for power inside the Kremlin.
>
> —Jack Anderson, *Boston Globe*

> Zapata was finally trapped in a Byzantine piece of trickery. One of Carranza's federal officers hinted to a prisoner of *Zapatista* sympathies that he might be willing to switch sides. . . .
>
> —William Weber Johnson, *Smithsonian*

> . . . a pattern of Byzantine firings and near-firings that have long kept Gould executives looking over their shoulders. —Paul Ingrassia, *Wall Street Journal*

C

C, the symbol for 100, from Latin *centum* = 'hundred.' See ROMAN NUMERALS.

c., ca. These two forms are abbreviations, used with dates, of Latin *circa* = 'around.' The word is pronounced /**sêr**-kə/. Both abbreviations are sometimes used without the period, and both may be capitalized. *Circa* or its abbreviation is found widely in scholarly writings, reference materials, and the like. In more general usage the words *about* and *around* serve just as well as the Latin form and are preferred by many.

cabal. The pronunciation is /kə-**băl**/, and the word is from French *cabale* = 'political intrigue,' from *cabala* = 'secret Jewish-Christian cult, the cabala'; see CABALA, CABALISTIC. A *cabal* is a covert political alliance or intrigue. The word received a special boost in England in the 1670s when it was noticed that the initials of five of the most powerful politicians—Clifford, Arlington, Buckingham, Ashley, and Lauderdale—formed the word *cabal* as an acronym. These men were then referred to collectively as the Cabal, although actually they formed two rival groups, not a single alliance or party.

Currently, *cabal* is used either of an unofficial and secret group of political allies or of the cause or issue they work for. It is implied that the group operates by underhand methods and has sinister motives for staying hidden:

> The nominating convention . . . fell into the hand of a conspiracy of old guard senators. But the cabal's choice for President was set aside.
> —Thomas Boylston Adams, *Boston Herald American*

> It gives consumers a chance to use a product [the moped] approved by the Legislature and takes away what seems to have been a cabal against it by the Department of Motor Vehicles.
> —Ralph Blumenthal, *New York Times*

cabala, cabalistic. The *cabala* (often capital *C*) is a system of occult Jewish-Christian doctrine originating in the Middle Ages and based on mystical interpretations of the Hebrew Scriptures, or Old Testament. The word is from Hebrew *qabbalah*, which means 'received doctrine.' The preferred spelling is *cabala*, but the spellings *cabbala*, *kabala*, and *kabbala* are also acceptable. The pronunciation is /kə-**bä**-lə/ or /**kăb**-ə-lə/.

The adjective *cabalistic* /kăb-ə-**lĭs**-tĭk/, with similar alternative spellings, basically means 'of or relating to the cabala':

> The most frequently visited tomb [in the old Jewish quarter of Prague] is that of the 16th-century rabbi Judah Low who, according to legend, created the Golem—a herculean artificial man which he brought to life, whenever he needed its services, by inserting in its mouth a cabalistic parchment with the secret name of God.
> —Ronald Schiller, *Reader's Digest*

The word is also used figuratively to mean 'involving magical-seeming formulas':

> Just flash a few rectangles of hard plastic [that is, credit cards] embossed with cabalistic numbers, and you enter the magic world of Buy Now, Pay Later. . . . —*Reader's Digest*

cacao. See COCOA, CACAO.

caddie, caddy. The golfer's help is a *caddie*, the box for tea is a *caddy*. Like most of the genuinely old terminology of golf, *caddie* was originally a Scottish word. In 18th-century Edinburgh it meant an errand boy who could be hired for odd jobs, only one of which was to carry golf clubs. The word is a Scottish borrowing of French *cadet* = 'young soldier, cadet.' *Caddy* comes from the world of colonial British tea plantations; it is from Malay *kati* = 'unit of weight equivalent to about one and one-third pounds.'

cadre. This awkward term is used more in print than in speech. Both its pronunciation and its meanings are tricky.

Origin. The French word *cadre*, originally meaning 'picture frame,' hence also 'framework,' was borrowed from Italian *quadro* = 'square panel, picture.' In the new armies of the French Revolution (1790s) *cadre* became a technical term meaning 'regimental framework or nucleus, permanent group of professional officers and men that can form a regiment by training recruits.' In this sense *cadre* was borrowed into English as *cadre* = 'core personnel of a regiment.' French *cadre* was also borrowed into Russian as *kadr;* this was transferred by Russian revolutionaries from the military to the political sphere and used to mean 'core group of trained revolutionaries, Communist cell' and also later 'individual political worker, member of a cell.' The English word *cadre*, keeping the French military meaning, has also taken on the Russian political meanings.

Pronunciation. In British English *cadre* is treated as an anglicized French word and pronounced /**kä**-drə/. In the United States the preferred pronunciation is now /**kăd**-rē/, but /**kä**-drē/ and /**kä**-drə/ are also used.

Uses. The current meanings of *cadre* are: (1) 'nucleus of trained military personnel' or 'skeleton group of soldiers in the field':

> When moving far from the base camp, a [U.S.] unit would leave behind a small security and house-keeping cadre.
>
> —William C. Westmoreland, *A Soldier Reports*

(2) 'key group of workers in any field':

> Carter and his cadre of aides had little experience in foreign affairs before coming to Washington.
>
> —*Boston Globe*

> Gone are the days when AFL-CIO decision-making was dominated by a like-minded cadre of elderly men. . . .
>
> —*U.S. News & World Report*

(3) 'disciplined group of revolutionary workers, Communist cell':

> Outside it was the standard New York City event—with pickets, the police and puzzled bystanders. . . . The Communist cadre held hand-lettered signs that read: "Long live the U.S.S.R."
>
> —Maurice Carroll, *New York Times*

(4) 'individual Communist political worker' or 'established Communist official':

> Mao succeeded in purging thousands of cadres from the party. . . .
>
> —*Time*

> [In Peking] from the apartment of a diplomat friend one could look directly into an apartment house reserved for middle-ranking cadres. . . . More senior cadres have their own small houses with a bit of garden around, but nobody has ever seen how the top echelon lives. . . .
>
> —Edward N. Luttwak, *Reader's Digest*

Cairo. The capital of Egypt is pronounced /**kī**-rō/. The city in Illinois is pronounced /**kā**-rō/; in Georgia, /**kĕr**-ō/ or /**kā**-rō/.

Cajun /**kā**-jən/ is a French dialect spoken in Louisiana or a speaker of that dialect. The name comes from *Acadian* = 'of Acadia' (now Nova Scotia). The Cajun people are descended from the original French settlers in Nova Scotia who were driven off their land by the British in the mid-1700s. (Their sufferings are described in Longfellow's narrative poem *Evangeline*.) The Cajun language, derived from the Maritime branch of Canadian French, is a much-changed form of French, but it is a dialect, not a creole. The word *bayou* is borrowed from Cajun.

This dialect is only one of the forms of French spoken in Louisiana today. For the others, as well as more on Cajun, see LOUISIANA FRENCH.

Caledonia /kăl-ə-**dō**-nē-ə, -**dōn**-yə/ is the ancient name of the northern part of Britain, recorded by the Roman historian Tacitus. It is used as a poetic and ceremonial name for Scotland. The adjective is *Caledonian.*

calisthenics, callisthenics = 'exercises for beauty and strength.' The idea of such exercises was invented, or reinvented, in the 19th century, and the word was formed from two Greek words: either *kalos* = 'beautiful' or *kallos* = 'beauty' + *sthenos* = 'strength.' The spelling accordingly varies between *cali-* and *calli-*. The American preference is for the former, the British for the latter.

callithump. See SHIVAREE, CALLITHUMP, SKIMMERTON.

callus, callous. The noun *callus* = (1) 'hardened and thickened area of skin' (2) 'defensive psychological hardening' is from Latin *callus* = 'hardened skin.' An example of the second, figurative, sense is:

> The Negro has a callus growing on his soul and it's getting harder and harder to hurt him there.
> —Dick Gregory, *Nigger*

The noun, especially in sense two, is often spelled *callous.*

The adjective *callous* = (1) 'covered with a callus or calluses' (2) 'hardhearted, harsh and merciless' is from Latin *callōsus*, adjective of *callus*. An example of sense two:

> No one who has witnessed or experienced the agony and horror of depression or psychosis would accuse the physician of being callous or punitive in using ECT in such cases.
> —Marshall D. Hogan (letter), *Atlantic Monthly*

An alternative adjective for sense one is *callused,* sometimes spelled *calloused.*

◇ ***Recommendation.*** These variant spellings occur too often, and too widely in respectable writings, to be classed as gross errors. But it is clearly preferable to spell the noun *callus,* with the Latin noun ending *-us,* and to keep *callous,* with the standard adjectival ending *-ous,* for the adjective; the alternative adjective is best spelled *callused.*

can, may. The rule taught to generations of schoolchildren is that *can* expresses possibility but *may* must be used for permission. It is not a really necessary rule. The child who asks *Can I leave the room, please?* is asking permission perfectly clearly and politely. The inevitable correction, *You mean,* "May *I leave the room?*" reinforces the teacher's authority, but it hardly adds anything to comprehension.

◇ ***Recommendation.*** The rule is weakening, but formal standard usage still insists on the distinction between *can* and *may.*

Canadian English. Canadian English is generally much less diversified than either American English or British English. Yet some regional varieties do exist, such as NEWFOUNDLAND ENGLISH; the MARITIMES, RED RIVER, and BRITISH COLUMBIA dialects; and CENTRAL AND PRAIRIE CANADIAN—the last being probably the most influential pattern and the closest thing Canada has to a prestige dialect. Some features that contribute to the regional diversity of Canadian English are these: the voicing of initial fricatives (Newfoundland only); the pronunciation of *vase* as /vās/ (Prince Edward Island only); the pronunciation of *aunt* as /änt/; the use of *bluff* for 'grove of trees'; and the popularity of the pronunciation of the first sound in *apricot* as /ā/. Nonetheless, outside Newfoundland and the Maritime Provinces, Canadian English is remarkably homogeneous and is, for the most part, generally regarded as being an extension of the Inland Northern dialect of U.S. English. In British Columbia the affinity is probably with the U.S. Pacific Northwest dialect rather than the Inland Northern, although, in the present state of knowledge of Canadian English, this remains somewhat speculative. The principal varieties of Canadian English are indicated on the map on page 115. (For the major American English dialects see REGIONAL DIALECTS OF AMERICAN ENGLISH.)

Historically, Canadian English owes much to the English brought northward by the Loyalists during the Revolutionary War period, and at least some of the present diversity in Canadian English reflects the mixed origins of this group. Since Loyalist days,

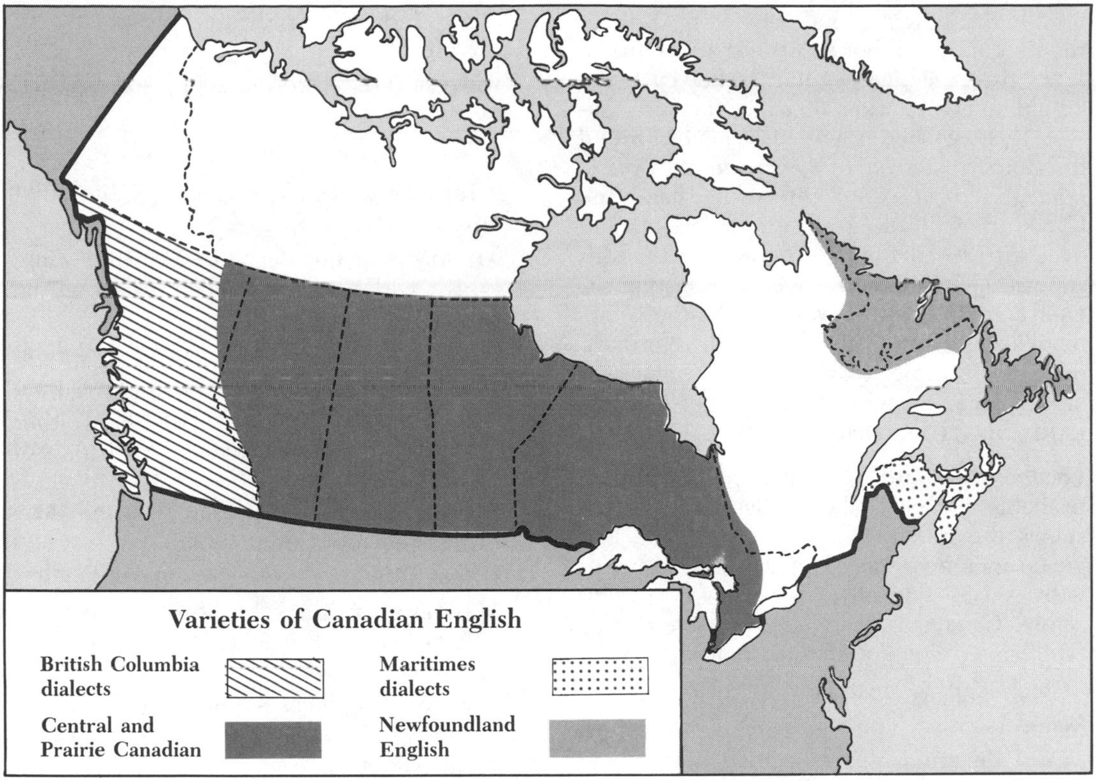

however, there has been continuing influence from the various forms of speech in the British Isles (Scottish and Irish, as well as Standard English) along with inevitable, heavy pressure from the speech of the United States.

Pronunciation. There is no one feature of pronunciation that is unique to Canadian English; rather it is the concurrence of several features that distinguishes Canadian pronunciation from that of American English and British English. The first of these is the pronunciation of /r/. Like most North Americans, Canadians pronounce this sound both before consonants and at the ends of words; *farther* and *father* always sound different from each other, being usually /**fär**-*th*ər/ and /**fä**-*th*ər/, respectively, while *wore* and *woe* are, respectively, /wôr/ and /wō/. Like most Americans north of the Susquehanna River, Canadians rhyme *greasy* /**grē**-sī/ with *fleecy* /**flē**-sī/ and not with *sleazy* /**slē**-zī/. Like most Scots, Canadians pronounce *cot* and *caught* the same way, giving both the sound /ä/. Like many speakers from Virginia, South Carolina, and elsewhere, Canadians have the sound /ī/ in *knives* but a sound like /əī/ in *knife;* so, too, Canadians have /ou/ in *loud* but a sound like /ŭo͞o/ in *out* and *about,* and it is this last sound that leads Americans to accuse Canadians of saying /o͞ot/ and /ə-**bo͞ot**/. In general, Canadians give the word *lever* its British pronunciation /**lē**-vər/ rather than its American pronunciation /**lĕv**-ər/. Canadians tend to pronounce *arctic* as /**är**-tĭk/ and *khaki* as /**kär**-kē/. Among younger Canadians at least, *luxury* is /**lŭg**-zhə-rī/, *congratulate* is /kən-**grăj**-ə-lāt/, and the capital of Canada has been moved to an apparently new city called—and sometimes even spelled!—*Oddawa.*

Grammar and Syntax. When a Canadian looks at his watch at 10:45, he will usually announce that it is *quarter to eleven;* he will stuff his unpaid bills *behind* the clock; if he does not stay *at home,* he will *visit* his neighbor. If the neighbor happens to be British, the neighbor will notice little that is unusual about the Canadian's syntax. If, however, the neighbor is a speaker of U.S. Northern dialect, he may wonder why his Canadian friend did not say *quarter of eleven, in back of, to home*, and *visit with*. On the other hand, the Canadian will often prefer *different than* over *different from* or *different to*. Like his American neighbor, he will live *on*, not *in*, Elm Street. In most ways, then, the Canadian is closer to the speakers of the Northern dialect of American English than to speakers of any other form of the language. (See INLAND NORTHERN and NORTHERN dialects.)

Vocabulary. The Canadian vocabulary is probably the part of Canadian English that shows the greatest independence; the language includes many Canadianisms—words with senses typically, if not always exclusively, Canadian.

(1) Terms reflecting history, politics, etc.:

Clear Grit = 'obstinate liberal'

concession = 'grant of land'

Confederation = 'the uniting of the several provinces to constitute the Dominion of Canada'

Creditiste = 'supporter of the Quebec wing of the Social Credit party'

Durham boat = 'shallow-draft false-keeled river boat'

factory = 'fur-trading post'

Family Compact = 'governing class in Ontario, prior to 1837'

Loyalist = 'person loyal to the British Crown and hence emigrating from the United States to Canada in the 1780s'; in full, *United Empire Loyalist*

Mountie = 'member of the Royal Canadian Mounted (federal) Police'

Red River cart = 'sturdy two-wheeled cart, constructed without nails'

* **riding** = 'electoral division returning usually one member to an elected assembly'

separate school = 'school for children belonging to a religious minority'

separatist = 'advocate of the withdrawal from Confederation of a province or area'

treaty Indian = 'Indian in receipt of treaty money'

walking boss = 'foreman of a series of logging operations'

*Appears as separate entry

(2) Terms referring to regions of Canada and their inhabitants:

Atlantic Provinces = 'the Maritime Provinces and Newfoundland'

Bluenose = 'Nova Scotian'

Cariboo = 'south-central British Columbia'

French Shore = (1) 'the northeastern and western (to Cape Ray) coasts of Newfoundland' (2) 'the western coast of Nova Scotia, from Yarmouth to Digby'

Herring-Choker = 'person from the Maritime Provinces, Maritimer'

Lower Canada = 'the Province of Quebec'

Maritimes = 'the Maritime Provinces: Nova Scotia, Prince Edward Island, and New Brunswick'

Prairie Provinces = 'the Provinces of Manitoba, Saskatchewan, and Alberta'

Spud Island = 'Prince Edward Island'

Upper Canada = 'the Province of Ontario'

(3) Terms referring to nature:

Canada goose = 'a large gray goose, *Branta canadensis*, with black head and neck and white cheek patches'

Canada jay, whiskey jack = 'a gray crestless jay, *Perisoreus canadensis*'

Douglas fir, red fir = 'the largest tree native to Canada, *Pseudotsuga taxifolia*'

groundhog = 'a woodchuck, *Marmota monax*'

malemute = 'sled dog, first bred by Malemute Eskimos'

McIntosh Red = 'eating apple with red skin and white flesh'

splake = 'hybrid game fish of the trout family'

tamarack = 'a larch, *Larix laricina*'

(4) Terms borrowed from the Amerindian languages; see also INDIAN WORDS (AMERICAN INDIAN):

carcajou /kär-kə-jo͞o/ = 'wolverine'

caribou = 'large North American reindeer'

cheechako /chē-**chä**-kō/ = 'inexperienced newcomer'

manitou /**măn**-ə-to͞o/ = 'spirit, deity'

muskeg = 'swamp'

oolichan /**o͞o**-lə-kən/ = 'a small fish of the smelt family, *Thaleichthys pacificus*'

(5) Some Canadianisms have been borrowed from the Innuit and are now mostly shared with American and other branches of English. See INNUIT (ESKIMO) WORDS.

(6) Terms borrowed from French:

Acadian = 'inhabitant of those areas of the Maritime Provinces culturally and linguistically French'

bateau /bă-**tō**, **bă**-tō/ = 'flat-bottomed boat, tapered at both ends'

cache = 'hiding place, storage place'

cariole = 'light, open sled, usually horse drawn'

portage = 'place where both vessel and cargo are carried from one waterway to another'

Siwash (now derogatory) = 'native Indian' (via CHINOOK JARGON from French *sauvage* = 'savage')

snye = 'channel'

Besides borrowing French *words*, Canadian English also borrows French *meanings* and transfers them to already existing English words. Here are two examples of this, especially common in the Province of Quebec, where French is the dominant language.

collective convention = 'collective agreement, labor contract'

modalities = 'details'

(7) Terms showing something of the color and style of Canadian speech (though not peculiar to it):

cellar = 'unlived-in basement'

chesterfield = 'couch'

* **cottage cheese** = 'soft, unripened skim-milk cheese, Dutch cheese'

eaves trough = 'roof *gutter'

firefly = 'nocturnal beetle with a luminescent abdomen, lightning bug'

French fries = 'deep-fried potato slices'

frog run = 'second (and poorer) run of sugar maple sap'

hydro = 'electricity service'

jack = 'to hunt illegally, using a light'

kitty-cornered = 'crosswise, diagonally opposite, *catercorner'

paper bag = 'bag, paper sack'

* **pit** = 'stone of a cherry'

ram pasture = 'men's communal sleeping quarters'

rampike = 'tall, dead tree'

robin run = 'first (and better) run of sugar maple sap'

robin storm *or* **snow** = 'late spring snowstorm, about the time the robins return'

* **shivaree** = 'rough, often mock serenade'

sleigh = 'sled'

soldier bean = 'small, white bean with markings like the outline of a wooden toy soldier'

sugar bush = 'grove of maple trees'

vacation = 'holiday'

*Appears as separate entry

Canadian English Versus British and American Usage. In some of its vocabulary, Canadian English agrees with British practice and is at variance with American, as:

Canadian	*American*
blinds	**shades**
braces	**suspenders**
porridge	**oatmeal, mush**
serviette	**napkin**
tap	**faucet**

In many instances, however, Canadian and American practices agree, while British usage is different; for example:

Canadian	*British*
(automobile terms)	
gas	**petrol**
hood	**bonnet**
trunk	**boot**
(railroad terms)	
baggage car	**luggage van**
conductor	**guard, ticket collector**
ticket agent	**booking clerk**
tie	**sleeper**

(general terms)

apartment	**flat**
cookie	**biscuit**
cotton batting	**cotton wool**
garbage can	**dustbin**
mailman	**postman**
thumbtack	**drawing pin**

Canadian French is the dialect of French spoken by five million Canadians, chiefly in the Province of Quebec. Before the British conquest (1759) and the Louisiana Purchase (1803) French was a serious rival to Spanish and English for the linguistic domination of North America. In recent times some of the most influential leaders in Quebec's government have adamantly maintained that secession from Canada is the only hope of guaranteeing the survival of French Canadian culture and language.

> Independence for Québec now appears as normal, I might say inevitable, as it was for the American states 200 years ago. —René Lévesque, premier of Quebec (quoted), *Winnipeg Tribune* (1977)

Having missed the French Revolution and other upheavals, Canadian French has preserved old features that have been altered in European French; yet the pressure on this island language from the surrounding ocean of English is shown in massive borrowings of words. It is said that a garage attendant in Montreal will accept the request "Checkez-moi les brakes, s'il vous plaît" (Please check the brakes for me). The two chief dialects within Canadian French are Quebecois and Acadian (the latter spoken in the Maritime Provinces). Among Canadian French borrowings in English are *lacrosse, portage,* and *prairie.* See also CANADIAN ENGLISH; LOUISIANA FRENCH.

canard. The pronunciation is /kə-**närd**/. The meaning is 'false rumor,' especially a fabricated story spread deliberately to discredit someone. It comes from an expression in old French thieves' slang, *vendre un canard à moitié,* literally 'to half sell a duck,' referring to some kind of trick in which a swindler pretended to sell someone a duck but avoided delivery. Hence *canard* = 'duck' acquired the additional sense of 'hoax' and especially 'calculated false rumor.' In English it is usually used in political contexts. It is a strong word, accusing one's opponents, or even persons unknown, of deliberate lying, sometimes slander:

> Anyone who knows Stanley Friedman at City Hall knows it is a canard to accuse him of craving a "no-show" job. —Francis X. Clines, *New York Times*

> The laetrilists spread the vicious canard that the American medical "cancer establishment" opposes laetrile because of its vested economic greed. —Daniel S. Martin, *New York Times*

cannot, can't. In formal or emphatic speech people do say /**kăn**-ŏt/ or /kă-**nŏt**/. Mostly they say /kănt/, but if this is written down or put into print, it is often reported as *cannot.* The spelling *can't,* although it would in many instances accurately represent what was said, is still felt to be somewhat informal. The spelling *cannot* may thus signify either the formal pronunciation /**kăn**-ŏt/ or /kă-**nŏt**/ or the much more usual /kănt/.

cannot help but. See HELP.

can't hardly, couldn't hardly. See HARDLY.

Canuck /kə-**nŭk**/. Although the forms *Canack, Cannacker, Canuck, Canuk, Conuck, Kanuck, Kanuk,* and *K'nuck* have all been known from time to time, only *Canuck* is now in use.

Meanings and Usage. (1) = 'any Canadian.' Used by Canadians to Canadians about Canadians, *Canuck* is informal but is not felt to be derogatory. It often has overtones, not unwelcome, of strength and roughness, and it has received the accolade of being adopted into the name of the Vancouver Canucks hockey team. However, several American dictionaries caution their readers that the

word may be offensive, and they may be right to do so, since Canadians might well find the word uncomplimentary if used by non-Canadians.
(2) = 'a French Canadian.' In this sense the word would probably be interpreted as a derogatory usage.
(3) = 'Canadian French.' In this sense the word would almost certainly be felt to be derogatory.
(4) = 'a Canadian horse or pony.' This sense of the word is now obsolete.
(5) = 'anything made in Canada.' The word is neutral in this sense, but this use is rare.
(6) *Jack Canuck, Johnny Canuck* = 'a Canadian soldier.' The usage level of this expression is approximately that of *GI Joe* or *Tommy Atkins.*
(7) = 'an imaginary figure personifying Canada or Canadians, or both.' In this sense the word applies to all Canadians and seems to have overtones of a possibly defiant pride.

◇ ***Recommendation.*** Canadians need no advice from us on the various ways they use this term. We advise non-Canadians to avoid it altogether in the presence of Canadians, unless they are very sure of their company.

Origin. Apart from those content to characterize *Canuck* as being of uncertain origin, lexicographers have propounded at least six theories on the etymology of this word; each will be considered briefly.
(1) The word is from Hawaiian *kanaka* = 'man.' Though not impossible, it does seem improbable that Canadians should have sought in far-distant Hawaii for a word with which to describe themselves.
(2) The word is from *Connaught,* an early French Canadian nickname for immigrants from Ireland. Although this theory is supported (cautiously) by the *Dictionary of Canadianisms on Historical Principles,* it does not explain the final /k/ sound of *Canuck;* moreover, it does not fit very well with the fact that *Canuck* seems originally to have applied especially to a French Canadian.
(3) The word is from the first syllable of *Canada,* or is an "alteration" or "corruption" or "mispronunciation (by Indians) of English *Canadian* or French *canadien.*" Unfortunately, these theories are not really adequate, since they too fail to explain the final /k/ sound.
(4) The word is a blend of the first syllable of *Canada* and the Algonquian noun ending *-uc* (*-uq*). This theory has at least the merit of fully explaining the sound of *Canuck.*
(5) The word is a blend of *Can(ada)* and *(Chin)ook* or is formed from *Canada* by analogy with *Chinook.* Like the preceding, this theory fully explains the sound of *Canuck* but is open to objections based on time and geographical factors.
(6) The word is the English version of *kanuchsa,* the Iroquois word for a resident of a *kanata,* or community. Of all the explanations, this one, referred to by M. H. Scargill in *A Short History of Canadian English,* seems the most probable.

Although the *Dictionary of Canadianisms* gives 1849 as the date of the first appearance of the word in the form *Canuck* and applied to a Canadian, the *Dictionary of American English* (Chicago, 1938) records the form *Kanuck* applied to a French Canadian as early as 1835. This may indeed have been the earliest sense of the word, for even the general term *Canadian* was at first most commonly used to mean a French Canadian: as late as 1832 an English-speaking inhabitant of British North America was referred to as an *American.* It may well have had the meaning 'French Canadian' in Canada and have developed its general meaning 'any Canadian' in the United States.

Johnny Canuck probably "made his first appearance as a cartoon character in . . . 1869. . . . The cartoonist had already translated Johnny into a Western hat and vaguely British field uniform and used him as a symbol for young Canadians, regardless of language" (K. Lefolii, *The Canadian Look—A Century of Sights and Styles*).

Canute. Canute the Great (A.D. c. 994–1035), king of Denmark, Norway, and England, did not, as tradition has it, defy the tide. The original story is that when Canute's advisers suggested he was invincible, he made a symbolic demonstration that he was not by sitting enthroned on the beach as the tide came in and ordering it to stop. That the king actually went through with the charade is considered unlikely by modern historians. In any event, folklore has utterly missed the point, and the unfortunate Canute has become proverbial for mindless defiance of the inevitable—the exact opposite of his intention. The misapprehension is now probably too deeply rooted to be changed, and writers will continue to take Canute's name in vain as in the following:

> Canute-like, defying the incoming tide, America persists in retaining old-fashioned weights and measures when the rest of the world has gone metric.
>
> —*Newsweek*

canvass. ***Origin.*** This word is a 16th-century derivative of *canvas* = 'kind of heavy cloth.' The verb first meant 'to toss (a person) in a canvas sheet as a form of hazing.' Later it came to mean 'beat and buffet' or 'shake out and ventilate (a subject), sift through, discuss thoroughly.' From this arose the political sense 'to go through a place or among people soliciting support for an election.'

Uses. The current American uses of the verb are (1) 'to discuss and scrutinize (a subject)'; (2) 'to personally approach (people) for their votes or cooperation'; (3) 'to examine (votes cast) in an election.' The noun correspondingly means (1) 'discussion'; (2) 'personal solicitation'; (3) 'examination of votes cast.'

> Folkerth had carefully canvassed 50 of the old hardware-store distributors from various areas of the country, seeking their advice.
>
> —Geoffrey Smith, *Forbes*

> Are you a phone-aholic? Ask the manager of a country club if you can canvass for new members in exchange for a free membership. . . .
>
> —Constance Stapleton, *Reader's Digest*

> At the last minute Johnson canceled plans for the speech. A canvass of opinion in Congress had convinced him . . . that the country was in no mood for progressive words on race.
>
> —Doris Kearns, *Lyndon Johnson and the American Dream*

capacity. See ABILITY, CAPACITY.

capitalization. One of the best games going is to consult various style manuals on the rules of capitalization. One authority says *Federal Government;* another says *federal government* or *Federal government.* One approves of *the Mayor of Waukegan;* another endorses *the mayor of Waukegan.* One urges you to write *Board of Directors;* another says the correct form is *board of directors.* At first glance this kind of disagreement among "the authorities" is utterly confusing and even depressing. At second glance, however, it provides the key to understanding the function of capitalization.

Capitalization gives importance, distinction, and emphasis to whatever it touches. This explains why every sentence begins with a capital letter—to emphasize that a new thought has begun; why the simple phrase *oval office* becomes the *Oval Office* when it signifies the seat of presidential (sometimes Presidential) power; why the manufacturers of certain photocopying equipment have trademarked the name Xerox, to prevent it from becoming a generic, undistinguished (and thus lowercased) term for any kind of photocopy. Once capitalization is viewed as a process of assigning special significance to words, it becomes obvious why the authorities are bound to disagree. They tend to assign significance to those things that loom largest in their lives and to de-emphasize things that seem more remote. Thus, government insiders are more likely to write *Federal Government* and *the Mayor* than those outside; people outside a company are less likely to care about its *board of directors* than those who work for the company or own its stock.

In short, one's use of capitalization is likely to vary with one's perspective. Instead of trying to choose the "correct" form, astute writers will recognize that each alternative may have its appropriate uses, depending on the circumstances and the context. Instead of approaching capitalization as a number of flat rules to be mechanically applied, effective writers will view it as a flexible instrument of style that can give special force and vigor to their writing.

The guidelines to capitalization that are given in this entry have been divided into these 15 topics:

1. Proper Nouns	**10. Calendar References, Seasons, and Events**
2. Common Nouns	**11. Ethnic Terms**
3. First Words	**12. Religious Terms**
4. Personal Names	**13. Scientific Terms**
5. Titles With Personal Names	**14. Words With Numbers or Letters**
6. Organizations	**15. Titles of Artistic and Literary Works**
7. Governmental Organizations	
8. Place Names	
9. Compass Points	

1. Proper Nouns. The formal or official names of particular persons, places, or things—in short, proper nouns—are always capitalized because of the distinction these names deserve: *Martin Luther King, Jr.; Winter Park, Florida; General Motors; the Red Cross; Reed College; the Statue of Liberty.* For the same reason, capitalize nicknames and imaginative names that refer to particular persons, places, or things: *Too Tall Jones; the Windy City; the Empire State; the New World; the Big Board; the Sun Belt.*

Also capitalize proper adjectives (forms derived from proper nouns): *Danish* (from *Denmark*); *Faulknerian* (from *Faulkner*); *Dantesque* (from *Dante*). In a few cases it is customary to lower-case the adjective derived from a proper noun: *constitutional; congressional; senatorial* (referring, respectively, to the U.S. *Constitution, Congress,* and *Senate*).

A number of terms that include or consist of the name of a person or place are now considered to have lost their connection with the original name and thus are lower-cased:

ampere	macadam road
boycott	morocco leather
chinaware	platonic love
diesel engine	quisling
klieg lights	watt

While there is general agreement about not capitalizing the terms listed above, the following terms (and others like them) are in a state of transition. Although the items are shown in lower case here, a number of authorities still recommend capitalizing. In such cases you can choose the form you prefer or select one authority and follow that style consistently.

bohemian existence	paris green
danish pastry	pullman car
dutch oven	russian dressing
french fries	scotch whisky
herculean	turkish towel

2. Common Nouns. The fundamental rule is this: Capitalize a common noun when it is part of a proper name but not when it is used alone or in place of the proper name. For example: *Uncle Warren, my uncle; the Ford Motor Company, the company; the Sherry Netherland Hotel, this hotel; the Social Security Act, the act.*

The common-noun element of a proper name, when used in place of the full name, is often referred to as a *short form.* In a few special cases, which will be noted in the following discussion, these short forms are capitalized because they carry the full force of complete proper names. However, these cases are clear exceptions to the fundamental rule given above. Writers who capitalize all types of short forms, beyond the well-established exceptions, run the risk of exhausting the special emphasis that capitalization is intended to convey. When everything stands out, nothing stands out. Our recommendation, then, is this: If you choose to capitalize a common noun when it stands alone, have a good reason for it.

3. First Words. The initial letter of the "first word" should usually be capitalized.

(1) Capitalize the first word of a *sentence* and of any phrase that is used as a sentence:

> Do you believe her story? Not me. Incredible!

Also capitalize the first word of a sentence that is *quoted:*

> I myself heard Jennings say, "There's no chance that I will resign. If they want me out of this office, they'll have to come in with a crane."

(2) Capitalize the first word of an *independent question* within a sentence:

> The question now is, Will funds be appropriated to implement the defense legislation?

When several independent questions follow a common introduction, capitalize the first word of each question:

> Here's what I'd like to know: Who authorized the repaving of the municipal parking lots? When? Were competitive bids sought first? If not, why not?

(3) Capitalize the first word *following a colon* under any of these conditions: (a) if the material preceding the colon is a short introductory word like *Remember* or *Note;* (b) if the material following the colon starts on a new line; (c) if the material following the colon is a quoted sentence or starts with a proper noun, a proper adjective, or the pronoun *I*; (d) if the material following the colon consists of two or more sentences. However, if the material following the colon cannot stand alone as a separate sentence and none of the first three conditions applies, then do not capitalize the first word. (The first sentence in this section is a good example of this rule.)

The only difficult decision about capitalizing after a colon occurs when two independent clauses (in effect, two complete sentences) are brought together within the same sentence with only a colon between them. The decision to capitalize or not depends on the importance assigned to the second clause. If the second clause simply explains or illustrates the idea presented in the first clause, don't capitalize the start of it. (Note: Some business firms and publishers always capitalize this clause as a matter of style.)

> If they accept your terms, it's for only one reason: they need the business.

However, if the second clause is presented as a formal rule or expresses the main thought (and the first clause simply serves to set the situation up), then capitalize the start of the second clause:

> Our new policy on gift matching is as follows: For every dollar that an employee contributes to a college or university, the company will contribute two dollars.

(4) Capitalize the first word of each item displayed in an *outline* or a *list*:

> This book will tell architects of public buildings:
> - How to achieve designs that are economically responsible, yet responsive to community needs
> - How to incorporate open space into designs intended for high-density locales
> - How to create up-to-date facilities in existing structures.

(5) The first word of each line of *poetry* is customarily capitalized:

> In the *Boston Sunday Herald* just three lines
> Of no-point type for you who used to sing
> The praises of imaginary wines,
> And died, or so I'm told, of the real thing. . . .
>
> —Richard Wilbur,
> *To an American Poet Just Dead*

Some poets deviate from this rule for special effect:

> as freedom is a breakfastfood
> or truth can live with right and wrong
> or molehills are from mountains made
> —long enough and just so long
> will being pay the rent of seem
> and genius please the talentgang
> and water most encourage flame . . .
>
> —e. e. cummings, from *Fifty Poems*

4. Personal Names. As a rule, capitalize the first letter of each word in a person's name, as well as any initials used in the name. However, respect individual preferences on this point; the poet quoted above, e. e. cummings, wanted his name treated without capitals at all.

Names with prefixes sometimes pose special problems. In surnames beginning with *O'*, capitalize both the *O* and the first letter following the apostrophe: *O'Malley; O'Rourke.* In surnames beginning with *d'*, *da, de, del, della, di, du, l', la, le, van,* and *von,* individual preferences on capitalization (as well as spacing and spelling) can vary quite widely: *van den Heuvel, Van Den Heuvel, VanDen Heuvel, Vanden Heuvel, Vandenheuvel.*

When a surname begins with an uncapitalized prefix and is used alone in running text, without a title, a first name, or even initials preceding it, it is common practice to capitalize the prefix to prevent a misreading: *General de Gaulle, Charles de Gaulle, C. A. de Gaulle,* but *De Gaulle.*

When a name like *La Salle* (with a space after the prefix) has to be written all in capital letters, write *LA SALLE.* However, if the name is *LaSalle* (with no space after the prefix), write *LaSALLE.*

5. Titles With Personal Names. Capitalize all titles that precede personal names—titles of a personal nature (*Mr., Mrs., Ms., Miss*) as well as titles that indicate rank in an organization or status in a profession (*President, Chairman, Mayor, General, Corporal, Dr., Professor*). Occupational designations that precede a name, such as *attorney, psychiatrist, music critic, neurosurgeon,* are capitalized by some writers and publications (for example, *Time* magazine), but we recommend not capitalizing because these are not really titles. (You might call someone "Dr. Federico," but you wouldn't address him as "Psychiatrist Federico" or "Neurosurgeon Federico.") In short, reserve capitalization for legitimate titles. See APPOSITION; ATTRIBUTIVES.

When these titles follow a personal name or take the place of a personal name, they are not capitalized as a rule. Exceptions are sometimes made, however, for (1) high-ranking national officials: *the President, the Vice President, the Secretary of State* (and other cabinet members), *the Chief Justice* (and other members of the U.S. Supreme Court), heads of Federal agencies, and members of Congress; (2) high-level state officials: *the Governor, the Lieutenant Governor;* (3) heads of state and other international figures: *the Pope, the Prime Minister, the Queen of Denmark.*

6. Organizations. Capitalize the formal names of all types of organizations—business, political, educational, religious, and social: *Poe Box Company; Fourth Ward Democratic Association; Stanford University; First Congregational Church of Newton; Upper Montclair Country Club.* Follow the organization's style when you know it; if you don't, capitalize all words except articles (*the, a, an*), short prepositions (*of, for*), and short conjunctions (*and, or*). Don't capitalize short forms (such as *company* or *association*) except in legal documents or other formal material where the short form is intended to convey the full force of the complete name. Thus, in ordinary material you might write:

> The managers I talked with at the Fox Trucking Company said that the company would not raise its rates during the next 12 months.

In a contract or a letter of agreement, a Fox official would most likely write:

> For a period of 12 months from the date of this agreement, the Company agrees not to increase the rates shown in the attached schedule.

7. Governmental Organizations. Capitalize the formal names of all governmental organizations at the Federal, state, and local level: *the Ninety-ninth Congress; the California Department of Transportation; the Essex County Board of Freeholders.* The word *administration* is often capitalized: *the Reagan Administration, the Administration.* Also capitalize the names of all international organizations: *the United Nations Security Council; the Dominion of Canada; the United Kingdom.*

It is customary to capitalize short forms of key Federal organizations: *the House* (of

Representatives); *the Department* (of Commerce, Labor, etc.); *the Court* (U.S. Supreme Court). However, short forms of state and local bodies are not usually capitalized except by insiders. Thus, you might write to friends in town, urging them to join you in a protest *at the next meeting of the board of education.* Meanwhile the board itself might be issuing this announcement: *At its next meeting the Board of Education will discuss its plan to close the Grove Street School.*

The word *federal* is capitalized when it is part of the formal name of an agency or a piece of legislation: *Federal Trade Commission; Federal Insurance Contributions Act.* It is often lower-cased in other contexts: *federal tax laws; federal regulators; federal government;* in this book, however, we have chosen to capitalize it: *Federal organizations.* The term *government* alone (referring to the U.S. government) is commonly lower-cased except by people in government. However, in a context where the terms *government* and *federal government* have the full force of an official name, they should be capitalized.

8. Place Names. Capitalize the names of places, both natural and man-made: *Mount Rainier; Hudson River; Lake Michigan; Chrysler Building; Logan Airport; Golden Gate Bridge; Pennsylvania Turnpike.* As a rule, however, do not capitalize a short form used in place of the full name: *the mountain; the river; the bay;* etc. In a few special cases, because of longstanding identification of a short form with a specific place, the short form is capitalized. Thus, you might fly out to *the Coast* (referring to the West Coast) or cross *the Channel* (English, of course) on your way over to *the Continent* (of Europe). By the same token, imaginative names clearly identified with a specific place are capitalized: *Back Bay* (Boston); *Bay Area* (San Francisco); *Foggy Bottom* (State Department area of Washington, D.C.); *the Loop* (Chicago); *Nutmeg State* (Connecticut).

Capitalize *city* only when it is part of the official name or part of a well-established imaginative name: *Oklahoma City; Eternal City* (Rome); *city of Detroit.* Similarly, capitalize *state* only when it follows the state name or is part of an imaginative name: *state of Washington, Washington State; Tarheel State* (North Carolina); *the States* (referring to the United States).

9. Compass Points. Capitalize *north, south, east,* and *west* (and related words like *northeast* and *southwest*) when they are part of a proper name (*North Dakota, South America*) or refer to a specific region that is distinctive because of certain social, cultural, or political characteristics: *out West; back East; up North; down South.* However, lower-case these words when they simply indicate location or direction: *located just east of Fifth Avenue; traveled west of the Mississippi.* Thus, you would do the antiques shops on *the West Side* (if that's what that part of town is actually called); otherwise, you would simply do the shops on *the west side of town.*

Similarly, capitalize *northern, southern, eastern,* and *western* (and related words) when they refer to social, cultural, or political aspects of a region: *Southern cooking; Eastern religions; Western governments.* But a shoot-'em-up movie about cowboys is a *western.* However, lower-case these terms when they simply refer to the climate, the geography, or the general location of a region: *southerly breezes; the northern slopes of Mount Washington; the southwestern region of the country.*

10. Calendar References, Seasons, and Events. Capitalize the names of days and months, but lower-case the names of seasons except in the rare instances when they are personified: *Thursday; January; all through the spring and summer; harsh Winter with her bitter winds.*

Capitalize the names of all holidays and religious days: *New Year's Eve; April Fool's Day; Fourth of July, the Fourth; Veterans Day; Ash Wednesday; Holy Week; Passover; Rosh Hashana; Ramadan; Tet.*

Do not capitalize the names of decades and centuries except in imaginative references: *before the sixties; during the nineteen-thirties; in the twenty-first century; the early nineteen hundreds; the Roaring Twenties; the Gay Nineties.*

Capitalize the names of events and the imaginative names given to historical or cultural periods. *Renaissance; Enlightenment; French Revolution; Boston Tea Party; World War I; Great Depression; Prohibition; New Deal; Great Society; Brotherhood Week.*

References to cultural ages are usually capitalized: *Stone Age; Dark Ages; Middle Ages; Elizabethan Age; Age of Reason.* However, more recent references, such as *space age* and *nuclear age,* are often lower-cased unless they appear in the same context with a capitalized reference to age; then, for the sake of consistency, they are capitalized also.

11. Ethnic Terms. Capitalize the names of races, nationalities, tribes, languages, and similar terms referring to ethnic groups: *Caucasians; Negroes; Chicanos; Saudi Arabians; the Sioux; Slavic-Americans.* Designations based on color are customarily lower-cased. See BLACK, COLORED, NEGRO.

12. Religious Terms. Capitalize all references to a supreme being: *God; the Father; the Son; the Holy Spirit; the Lord; the Messiah; Adonai; the Almighty; the Word; the Supreme Being.* The pronouns *he, his,* and *him* used to be capitalized under all circumstances when referring to a supreme being; today these pronouns tend to be capitalized only when there is no specific reference to God nearby: *Trust in the Lord and honor him always. Pray with your heart and He will hear you.*

Capitalize all references to persons revered as especially holy: *Blessed Virgin; Mother of God; the Apostles; John the Baptist; Saint Jude; the Prophet; Buddha.*

Capitalize all references to the Bible and other sacred writings; however, do not underscore or italicize these references:

Apostles' Creed	Psalm 23
Dead Sea Scrolls	Revised Standard Version
Genesis	Scripture
Gospels	Sermon on the Mount
Kaddish	Talmud
King James Bible	Ten Commandments
Koran	
Lord's Prayer	
Old Testament	

The adjective derived from the word *Bible* may by choice be capitalized (as throughout this book); the current trend favors lower case: *biblical scholars.*

Capitalize the names of religions, their members, and their buildings: *Reform Judaism; Anglican; Jehovah's Witnesses; Roman Catholicism; St. John's Episcopal Church* (the formal name of a building); *the only Methodist church in town* (an informal reference to a specific building). The word *church,* when it refers to the total institution, may by preference be capitalized or lower-cased: *the Protestant Episcopal Church; the Baptist church.*

Capitalize references to important religious events: *the Creation; the Fall; the Flood; the Exodus; the Last Supper; the Crucifixion; the Resurrection; the Second Coming.* However, as a general rule lower-case references to religious rites and services: *attend a mass* (but *celebrate the Mass*); *a vesper service; a baptism; a christening; a bar mitzvah; a seder.* The names of certain Christian sacraments are capitalized: *Eucharist; Holy Communion; Anointing of the Sick.*

13. Scientific Terms. In the scientific names of plants and animals, capitalize the name of the genus but not the name of the species (even if derived from a proper name): *Kalmia latifolia* (mountain laurel); *Quercus virginiana* (live oak); *Sus scrofa* (pig); *Monodon monoceros* (narwhal); *Geococcyx californianus* (road runner). In the popular names of plants and animals, capitalize only proper nouns and adjectives: *California laurel; Virginia creeper; Labrador retriever; Brahman bull.*

Names of chemical elements and compounds are lower-cased, but the corresponding symbols are capitalized: *calcium chloride* ($CaCl_2$); *boric acid* (H_3BO_3); *carbon 14.*

14. Words With Numbers or Letters. Capitalize words followed by a number or a letter to indicate sequence: *Room 1303; Gate 12A; Flight 617; Class 7-B.* In literary references, the terms *page, paragraph, line, verse,* and *note* are lower-cased; other such terms are often capitalized: *Volume III; Chapter 4; Section Two; Figure 6-4; Table 8; Appendix B.*

15. Titles of Artistic and Literary Works. Capitalize all words in titles and headings except articles (*the, a, an*), short conjunctions (such as *and, but, or*), and short prepositions (such as *by, for, in, to*). Authorities disagree on how short is "short." We recommend that you capitalize any conjunction or preposition of four or more letters. In that way you can avoid fussy distinctions such as capitalizing *that* as a pronoun and lower-casing *that* as a short conjunction.

> *Who Am I and What Do I Want to Do With My Life?*
> "Energy Legislation Is Not Expected to Survive"

Always capitalize the first and last word of a title, as well as the first word after a colon or a dash within a title. (This guideline applies even to articles, short prepositions, and short conjunctions.)

> *Off the Record: The Private Papers of Harry S Truman*
> "Luciano Pavarotti—A Voice to Be in Awe Of"

Capitalize short words like *on* and *up* only when they serve as adverbs:

> "Moving Up in the Corporation" (*up* as an adverb)
> "Climbing up the Corporate Ladder" (*up* as a preposition)

Authorities disagree on the treatment of hyphenated words in titles. Many capitalize only the first element. We recommend treating each element according to the guidelines given above, for the sake of both consistency and appearance:

> "Spur-of-the-Moment Comments Prove Embarrassing"
> "Twenty-Four Are Chosen for the Play-Offs"

For a specialized use of capitalization see TRADEMARKS.

capitol, capital. The Capitoline Hill, the highest of the hills of ancient Rome, was the site of a temple to Jupiter. This temple, known as the *Capitol*, was the central shrine of the Roman state religion, and to some extent became a symbol of the state itself. Under the Roman Empire other cities also built themselves Capitols. With this classical precedent the building in Washington, D.C., in which the Congress of the United States meets, was named the *Capitol*, and the hill it stands on is *Capitol Hill*. As a metaphor, *Capitol Hill* thus means the Congress itself. The building in which a state legislature meets is often also, unofficially, called a *capitol* (small *c*). The noun *capital* means, among other things, a chief city or a city that is a seat of government. *Capitol* and *capital* are occasionally confused. *Capitol* is a building, *capital* is a city.

carat, karat. Gems are measured in *carats*, gold in *karats*. The two words are ultimately of the same origin (Greek, via Arabic; see ARABIC WORDS). A *carat* is a unit of weight: 200 milligrams of gem. A *karat* is a unit of fineness: 1/24 part of pure gold, so that 24-karat gold is pure gold, while 12-karat gold is 50 percent pure gold and 50 percent alloy. To confuse matters *karat* is often spelled *carat*, even in the jewelry trade.

careen. This verb is originally a technical nautical term, meaning 'to beach a ship, lean her over, and clean and caulk the hull.' A secondary nautical sense is used of a ship under sail, 'to tilt over in the wind':

> . . . the ship casts off her cables; and from the deserted wharf the uncheered ship for Tarshish, all careening, glides to sea.
> —Herman Melville, *Moby-Dick*

In current general use *careen* is used of vehicles, planes, people, etc., to mean 'lurch and sway along, rush ahead swaying from side to side out of control':

> Enthusiastic young Falangists, waving their red and black flags, careen through the streets, loudspeakers blasting their rousing anthem. . . .
> —James M. Markham, *New York Times*

It can also mean 'to zoom along bouncing or ricocheting erratically':

> . . . each hit bad shots that either careened off the wall in the closet and came back into the bedroom, or missed the door altogether. . . .
> —Dan Jenkins, *Dead Solid Perfect*

> . . . the man starts to descend the beautiful, curving staircase. At the first step he slips and falls on his butt. . . . He keeps falling, clumpety-clump. . . . Now, somersaulting down, he careens off the wall at the second landing and keeps falling.
> —John Keasler, *Reader's Digest*

And figuratively it can mean 'to go giddily or crazily bouncing along through life':

> Jimmy Carter had been severely critical of comparable flash-card trips made by his predecessors, with the obvious implication that he wouldn't be caught careening around the world in such extravaganzas once *he* became President.
> —John B. Oakes, *New York Times*

This madcap verb has drawn solemn and disapproving comments from usage experts, who claim that it results from a confusion of (nautical) *careen* with the verb *career* = 'to go wildly along.' Considering the quotations above, we suggest that *carom* (= 'to strike against and rebound') may also have gotten into the act.

◇ ***Recommendation.*** Trying to discourage the use of perfectly legitimate extensions like this one is what earns "usage experts" a bad name. Whatever its parentage, *careen* is a vivid and entirely satisfying word; and despite official disapproval, it is as unstoppable as a patrol wagon of Keystone Kops.

career. See CAREEN.

Caribbean words. The two pronunciations /kăr-ə-**bē**-ən/ and /kə-**rĭb**-ē-ən/ are equally correct. The sea between Central America and the West Indian islands is so named from the Caribs, a warlike people who were widespread in the islands when Columbus arrived in 1492. Their name, first recorded by Columbus himself, means 'brave men' in their own language but is better known to us as the source of our word *cannibal* (see below). We have a number of other words from the Carib languages and also from those of the Taino and other Arawaks, peaceful Indian peoples who were not related to the Caribs and are now extinct in the islands. All the following words were adopted by the Spanish from the Caribs and Arawaks and were borrowed from Spanish into English between 1550 and 1700.

barbecue = 'grill for roasting meat': Spanish *barbacoa,* from Taino *barbacoa* = 'stick framework or platform'

caiman /**kā**-mən, kā-**măn**/ = 'Central American reptile similar to the alligator': Spanish *caimán,* from Carib *caymán*

cannibal = 'human who eats human flesh': Spanish *caníbal* or *caríbal* = 'cannibal,' from *Caniba* or *Cariba,* names of the warlike peoples of Cuba and Haiti, recorded to have been cannibals

canoe = 'light boat propelled by paddles': Spanish *canoa,* from Arawak *canoa* = 'boat carved from a single log or tree trunk'; recorded by Columbus

hammock = 'swinging bed made of netted string, gathered and suspended at both ends': Spanish *hamaca,* from Taino; the hammock was invented by the Arawaks, probably in mainland Central America

hurricane = 'heavy tropical cyclone and storm originating in the Caribbean or nearby parts of the Atlantic': Spanish *huracan,* from Carib *huracan*

maize = 'Indian corn': Spanish *maíz,* from Taino *mahiz*

manatee = 'large, nearly hairless sea mammal of coastal waters of the Gulf of Mexico and the Caribbean': Spanish *manatí,* probably from Carib *manati* = 'breast'

mangrove = 'tropical tree with thickly massed roots that grows in dense clumps on warm coastal mud banks': from Spanish *mangle* (+ English *grove*), from Taino *mangle*

papaya = 'large, yellow melonlike fruit of the papaya tree, of Central America': Spanish *papaya,* from Carib

carom. See CAREEN.

carousal, carrousel. Though both are concerned with merrymaking, these two words are entirely unconnected. A *carousal* /kə-rou-zəl/ or *carouse* /kə-rouz/ is a drinking party, generally of uproarious nature; for the origin of the word see *carouse* at GERMAN WORDS. A *carrousel* /kăr-ə-sĕl/, also spelled *carousel*, is a merry-go-round, a revolving platform with wooden horses and other animals, for riding on to the sound of calliope music; the word is from Italian *carosello* = 'musical horseback ride, mock tournament.'

case. In Old English, nouns, pronouns, and adjectives had numerous forms or word endings to indicate their function in a sentence. These forms are called *cases*. Modern English has eliminated nearly all of the old forms, but some case terminology is still used to describe how certain words relate to the words around them. The chief cases in Modern English are *subjective*, designating the subject of a verb, that is, the "doer" of the action; *possessive*, indicating the relationship of belonging, possession, etc., between particular words; and *objective*, indicating the object of a verb or preposition, that is, the "receiver" of the action or intention.

Most of the personal and relative pronouns have kept their case forms in Modern English: *I, she, he, we, they, who* (subjective); *my, your, his, her, its, our, their, whose* (possessive); *me, her, him, us, them, whom* (objective). The personal pronouns *you* and *it* are the same in the subjective and objective cases. *Her* is the same form in both objective and possessive case, and some pronouns also have absolute forms of the possessive case (*mine, yours, hers, ours, theirs*): *The idea was mine. Yours is the cup on the top shelf. Their voices don't compare with hers. If he needs a car, he can take ours. Would theirs be the winning ticket?*

Like the pronouns *you* and *it*, modern nouns have one basic form for both the subjective and objective function and another for the possessive: *citizen, citizen's (the rights of every citizen, a citizen's duty); birds, birds' (watching the birds build nests, the birds' nests)*. Adjectives have only one form, having lost their case markings entirely.

The classical languages Latin and Greek had a full array of cases, which sometimes affect Modern English through etymology or grammar. The classical cases are *nominative* (the same as English subjective), *vocative*, *accusative* (usually the same as English objective), *genitive* (the same as English possessive), *dative*, and *ablative*. See also GRAMMAR; POSSESSIVES.

caster, castor. A *caster*, literally a thing for casting or sprinkling, is a small bottle, often glass, with a perforated top, used at the table for dispensing salt, sugar, vinegar, etc.; a *caster* can also be a stand for several such containers. Secondly, a *caster* is one of the small solid metal wheels supporting some pieces of furniture and heavy objects; this sense comes from an old use of the verb *cast* = 'to revolve.' Both of these uses of *caster* can also be spelled *castor;* we recommend *caster* for these.

There is a separate word *castor*, which is an old name for the beaver and also a term for a strong-smelling oil extracted from beavers and used in perfumes. Finally, *castor oil*, which is derived from a bean and is used in medicine, was so named because it somewhat resembles the beaver oil.

catalyst. In chemistry a *catalyst* is an agent or substance that causes a chemical reaction without itself being changed by the reaction. This fact, learned by millions in high school science, is striking enough to have become a favorite image applied to human affairs. The customary meaning is 'an unintentional cause of change':

> Catalyst for the crisis is a power struggle between the federal government in Ottawa and leaders of the nation's 10 provinces.
>
> —Gerson Yalowitz, *U.S. News & World Report*

> Thus, Sonny [Werblin], who opposed the merger of the two leagues, was in

> fact the unwitting chief catalyst of the merger.
> —Howard Cosell, *Cosell*

> Forgiveness is a catalyst creating the atmosphere necessary for a fresh start.
> —Martin Luther King, Jr., *Strength to Love*

Hence also the adjective *catalytic* = 'acting as a catalyst' and the verb *catalyze* = 'to act as a catalyst.'

catch. *Caught* is the standard past tense and past participle. But there are several often-used dialectal versions of these forms.

As past tense, *caught* and *catched* were used with almost equal frequency until about the 18th century.

> The reason of this order is, that the wolves the more readily come to bayte [bait] that they may be catched for the general good of the Island.
> —*Records of the Colony of Rhode Island* (1646)

Caught then gradually became the accepted past-tense form, and *catched* was used only in certain dialects. Similarly, *catched* was an early accepted form for the past participle.

> We cleaned ourselves (to get rid of the Game we had catched the Night before).
> —George Washington, *Diaries* (1748)

Today, *catched* is still frequently used, especially among older rural speakers. It is usually pronounced /**kĕcht**/ and sometimes /**kĭcht**/, which is reflected in the informal spelling *ketched*.

> I kin make bug-juice all the rest o' my life an' sell it without being ketched.
> —William Harben, *Abner Daniel* (1902)

In standard speech *catch* also has the variant pronunciation /**kĕch**/.

Cotch(ed) has always been a dialectal form of *catch* in both England and America.

> I got skeared when they was all a-shootin' b'hind me an' I run t' beat all, but I cotch it pretty bad.
> —Stephen Crane, *The Red Badge of Courage*

◇ ***Recommendation.*** *Caught* is now the only standard form for both past tense and past participle.

catchword. See VOGUE WORDS.

catercorner. In the 15th century the English borrowed the French term *quatre* = 'four' and unconsciously altered its spelling and pronunciation to *cater* /**kăt**-ər/. It was used primarily to refer to the four-spot on dice or cards. But by the 16th century *cater* also meant 'to place, move, or go diagonally,' in reference to the diagonal relationship of the opposite corner spots of a cater. It was not until the latter half of the 19th century that *caterways*, *caterwise*, and the commonest term today, *catercorner*, came into use. *Catercorner* means 'crosswise, diagonally' when referring to the direction of a movement, and 'askew, diagonally slanting, out of adjustment' when referring to the position or angle of something. It has various forms:

> It aint easy work, this ere, of talking when a feller's mouth cuts through his face catecornering as mine does.
> —Ann Stephens, *High Life in New York* (1843)

> They had climbed the steep bank now and started across the pasture in what Tom called a "catter-cornering" direction.
> —Alice B. Emerson, *Ruth Fielding at Snow Camp* (1913)

> He leaned against the wall, eying me catacornered, but innocent.
> —*Harper's Magazine* (1893)

Although *catercorner* is used throughout the United States, its variants *catty-corner* and *kitty-corner* are usually confined to specific regional dialects, the former to the Coastal Southern, Pacific Northwest, and Pacific Southwest dialects and the latter to the Northern and Western dialects. *Kitty-cornered* is favored in Canadian English.

In many regions of the United States the Americanism *catawampus* /kăt-ə-**wäm**-pəs/ is synonymous with *catercorner*.

> The old gentleman's cabin is one of the old backwoods sort; two logbuilt rooms and a boarded-up lean-to. The roof-line is a trifle catawampus . . . and the walls are weatherwarped and powdery gray.
> —Charles Wilson, *Backwoods America* (1934)

This high-sounding, fanciful word, often spelled *cattywampus* /kăt-ē-**wäm**-pəs/, is a product of the "tall talk" era in the development of AMERICAN ENGLISH. It also means 'angry, fierce, savage.'

> Where is the wealth and power that should make us fourteen millions take to our heels . . . for fear of being catawamptiously chawed up?
> —Frederick Douglass, speech (1857)

> It sets me plumb catawampus ter hev ter listen ter them blacksmiths.
> —Mary Murfree, *In the Tennessee Mountains* (1884)

Antigodlin, antigogglin, antigoslin, and variants are the General Southern dialect words meaning (as adjectives) 'askew, slanting, awry,' and (as adverbs) 'at angles, crosswise, diagonally.'

> "The news knocked me all anti-goslin." "Your hat is on anti-goslin."
> —from *Dialect Notes* (1915)

> I have heard a farmer complain of a plow hand who got drunk, "Why, he couldn't plow a straight furrow; he went antegoddlin' across the field."
> —*Baltimore Sun* (1940)

Galley-west, found in the Northern dialect, is another related term for 'askew, awry.' It is a variation of the English dialect *colly-west* or *colly-weston* in the idiom *It's all along 'o Colly Weston,* which was used as far back as 1587 to refer to anything that went wrong.

> Your verdict . . . has knocked what little [critical penetration] I *did* have galley-west!
> —Mark Twain, *Letters* (1917)

> He stopped so abruptly that several men banged into him, scattering the dream galley-west.
> —John Cheever, *Falconer*

Some other colloquial terms in the United States meaning 'askew, slanted, awry' are *cockeyed, haywire, hipskeltered, slaunchwise, whopper-jawed,* and *whomper-jawed.*

catholic, Catholic. Greek *katholikos* means 'general, universal, worldwide.' Hence, the adjective *catholic* (with a small *c*) means 'relating to the whole world or the whole human race': *arms control, a matter of catholic importance.* Applied to individual views, sympathies, comprehension, etc., it means 'broad and generous, not limited by sectional preoccupations': *a catholic interest in people and their problems.* The early Christian church, striving for unity, labeled itself *Catholic* in the sense 'universal, worldwide.' Although most often associated with the Roman Catholic church, this title is also retained by several other major Christian traditions, including the Eastern Orthodox and Anglican churches. The noun *Catholicism* refers to the faith and practice of Catholic Christianity. The noun *catholicity* is sometimes used like *Catholicism* but is more often used to mean 'universality, breadth of interest.'

> Hewitt believed that of all the CBS News correspondents only Reasoner had the experience and catholicity to handle the broad range of subjects he envisioned. . . .
> —Gary Paul Gates, *Air Time*

catsup. See KETCHUP.

'cause. In everyday informal speech many if not most people very often pronounce *because,* when unstressed, as /kôz/ or /kŏz/ or /kəz/. In literature, especially children's fiction, this is often rendered *'cause* or *'cos.* No written version, of course, other than a sophisticated phonetic transcription, accurately represents the stream of ordinary speech. Spellings such as *'cause* simply indicate that the speaker is talking in a relaxed manner.

cedilla. See DIACRITICS.

Celtic. Before the Roman Empire the Celts ruled most of western and central Europe. Their name is first recorded, in Greek, as *Keltai,* which became *Celtae* in Latin. In English most people pronounce the word /sĕlt/, but those who study the Celts and their languages prefer to pronounce it /kĕlt/. The spelling *Kelt,* although reflecting the original pronunciation, is now old-fashioned and little used. (There is another word *celt,* meaning 'ancient stone or bronze ax head' and always pronounced /sĕlt/; it has no connection with the Celtic peoples.)

center around. One of the images deeply programmed into us by elementary schooling, and reinforced throughout life, is the circle, with its center, radius, circumference, etc. Somehow the image has thrown up the expressions *center around, center round,* and *center about,* which are often condemned by usage experts. We know that a *center,* of all things, cannot be *around* anything. But the expression keeps on cropping up, and it doesn't seem to cause any trouble or misunderstanding—until the schoolteacher points out its awful illogic. We ought to have said *center on, center in, revolve around, pivot on, orbit around*—anything but *center around.* We feel the truth and force of the teacher's admonition. We resolve to do better. But in unguarded moments these nonsensical expressions will slip out:

> The life of the widow . . . was like one long service to the departed soul; its many annual observances centring about the funeral urn. . . .
> —Walter Pater,
> *Marius the Epicurean* (1885)

> The full and friendly social life, centred round dinner at the fashionable hour of six . . . —David Cecil,
> *A Portrait of Jane Austen*

> Pride in family, place, and tradition were inherent with the man; his realization of their importance grew with the years, until many of his activities became centered about genealogical research. . . .
> —John P. Marquand,
> *The Late George Apley*

> Leonard Lyons' dreams centered around hot borsch and sour cream. . . .
> —Truman Capote,
> *The Muses Are Heard*

> The White House announced the plan—centered around a guaranteed income—explaining that the system would cost only $2.8 billion more. . . .
> —Kenneth Y. Tomlinson,
> *Reader's Digest*

◇ ***Recommendation.*** Relax. The logic of language is not as literal as the logic of the schoolroom.

Central and Prairie Canadian. ***Origin.*** Not all Canadians born between Toronto and the Rockies speak identically, but except for certain linguistic enclaves, such as the Ottawa Valley, Canadian English throughout this area is reasonably homogeneous. (See the map at CANADIAN ENGLISH.) This is natural enough, since the area was populated basically by a westward spread from Ontario. However, this westward spread was augmented by the immigration of groups of settlers from the British Isles and elsewhere; Scots and Irish installed themselves in the Ottawa Valley, for example, while Germans settled in Kitchener, Ontario, and Ukrainians established themselves both east and west of Winnipeg, Manitoba.

Pronunciation. In the linguistic enclaves mentioned above, the speech used by the first generation of immigrants was often their native tongue, frequently supplemented by a very slight knowledge of English. Their sons and daughters were often bilingual, although their English sometimes suffered interference from the original tongue. Thus, pronunciations such as /wĭl-ĭch/ for *village,* /shtŏp/ for *stop,* and /rīs/ for *rise* were not uncommon in the German-settled areas of Saskatchewan. Similarly, it is probably the immigrants' original dialect that accounts for /ă/ rather than /ä/ in *far* and *garden* in the Ottawa Valley. Outside such enclaves, however, the pronunciation of the English in this part of the country is very much that described at CANADIAN ENGLISH.

Grammar and Syntax. The same is largely true of the grammar and syntax of Central and Prairie Canadian. There are occasional interferences from non-English languages, as when the adverb of time wanders in the sentence and the speaker produces *He came yesterday home* or *I'll go tomorrow with him to town.* Particularly in originally Yiddish-speaking areas, the direct object frequently appears first in the sentence, for emphasis: "Lucky father. Two surgeons he's got" (Morley Torgov, *A Good Place to Come From*). In other idioms native Canadians west of Toronto seem to prefer *sick at the stomach* to *sick to the stomach,* which is current east of Toronto and derives from the U.S. General Northern dialect. Likewise, the usual interrogative in this area is *Have you . . . ?* rather than the U.S. Northern *Do you have . . . ?* But apart from these minor variations, the grammar and syntax of Central and Prairie Canadian are very much those described at CANADIAN ENGLISH.

Vocabulary. It is probably in vocabulary that Central and Prairie Canadian is most obviously subdivided. In the following lists of terms, the province in which each term principally circulates appears in parentheses where known.

(1) The influence of the Scottish and Irish settlers is still alive in such words as:

cow byre (Ontario) = 'cow barn or stable'
skelp (Ontario) = 'slap'
snib (Manitoba) = 'latch of a door'
swither (Ontario) = 'to hesitate'

(2) Other words have entered the area from the United States. Some probably came directly north across the middle border, such as:

sun dog (Manitoba) = 'false sun, seen on very cold days'
tote road (Ontario, Manitoba) = 'road to a logging camp'

Some, however, originating in the Midland dialect of the United States, probably followed the more circuitous route of the Loyalists. Among such are:

coal oil (Ontario, Manitoba) = 'kerosene'
overhead (Ontario) = 'barn loft'
side meat (Ontario) = 'salt pork'
slop (Ontario) = 'sour milk'

(3) Many of the words commoner in this dialect area than elsewhere in Canada reflect the country's sociopolitical organization. Here belong:

concession (Ontario) = 'road'
location ticket = 'land title deed'
police village (Ontario) = 'unincorporated village'
reeve (Ontario) = 'chairman of a village or other local governing council'

(4) Other terms reflect Canadian trade, agriculture, etc. Among these are:

barn boss (Manitoba) = 'man in charge of a lumber-camp stable'
coil (Ontario, Manitoba, Saskatchewan) = 'small pile of hay in a field'
dew worm (Ontario, Saskatchewan) = '*earthworm useful as bait'
fire reels (Ontario) = 'fire engine'
garden worm (Saskatchewan) = '*earthworm useful as bait'
hatching-hen (Ontario, Manitoba) = 'broody hen'
saltie (Ontario) = 'sailor on an oceangoing vessel'
stook = 'a grouping of grain sheaves, stack of hay bales'
Winnipeg couch = 'kind of couch that opens out to form a bed'

*Appears as separate entry

(5) Two words reflect prairie features of the landscape:

bluff (Manitoba, Saskatchewan) = 'clump of trees'
slough /slo͞o/ = 'shallow, swampy natural depression'

(6) Some slang terms bear testimony to the Canadian sense of humor:

shinplaster = 'bank note of low denomination'
sodbuster = 'farmer'
stubble-jumper = 'farmer, usually one producing crops rather than livestock'

Finally, it is interesting to note that a few words current in Central and Prairie Canadian have reversed the general trend and have established themselves on the southern side of the Canadian-U.S. border. They include *coal oil, dew worm, stook,* and *shivaree* (see SHIVAREE, CALLITHUMP, SKIMMERTON).

ceremonial, ceremonious. These two words are partly synonymous, in many contexts interchangeable. The difference is that *ceremonious* is the more emphatic. *Ceremonial* is the all-purpose adjective, meaning 'relating to ceremony, merely of the nature of ceremony.' *Ceremonious* means 'fond of ceremony, full of ceremony,' often 'too full of ceremony':

> Traditionally, the Vice President didn't have much to do. His job was chiefly ceremonial, and his impact on legislation was minimal.
> —Gerald R. Ford, *A Time to Heal*

> Everyone who has any knowledge of my manner of acting in public life, will be persuaded that I am not accustomed to impede the despatch or frustrate the success of business, by a ceremonious attention to idle forms.
> —George Washington, letter (1789)

> Here was the incomparable private detective [Nero Wolfe], ironic and ceremonious. . . .
> —Edmund Wilson, *A Literary Chronicle*

chairman. When an adult female heads a committee, what should she be called? Some people prefer the traditional term, *chairman.* Others, noticing the specific intention of *-man,* object.

> On Sunday, the chair was graced by the cool, iron-willed, and witty presence of Anne Saunier, an Ohio paper-company executive, who made a point of briskly correcting speakers who addressed her as "Madam Chairman." ("I'm not a man, and I don't have any plans to become one.")
> —*Ms.* (1978)

In many organizations *chairperson* is now used as a substitute for *chairman.* Sometimes, however, *chairperson* is applied to female officeholders only. A male officeholder is still called a *chairman.* At best, such usage suggests a halfhearted attempt at change. At worst, it turns *person* into a code word for *woman,* suggesting that the *-man* word is the term that bestows real status. Some women, recognizing the status issue, insist on being called *chairman.*

Actually, a simpler solution is available. When we speak, for instance, of *farmhands,* or agricultural laborers who work with their hands, we are using metonymy, a figure of speech in which some feature or quality associated with a thing is substituted for the thing itself. Through the magic of metonymy, *Capitol Hill* means the U.S. Congress, which meets there. *The White House* means the President, who lives there. Similarly, *the chair* can mean the presiding officer who sits there, and this use has been standard since the 17th century. In meetings people not only sit on chairs, but they also address the chair—and the chair may even recognize them. *Chair* has also become a verb; thus, the presiding officer can chair a meeting. So there is no reason why an organization cannot elect a chair or be headed by a chair of the board. That would be fitting, since *board* underwent a similar transformation, from a plank to a council table to the group of administrators who meet around that table.

◇ ***Recommendation.*** *Chair* is a better choice than *chairperson* because it is shorter and because it has been in the language so long. Or, entirely different titles may be used, such as *president* (of an organization), *presiding officer* (at a meeting), *convener* (of a convention), or *coordinator* (of a project or committee). See also FEMALE-GENDER WORD FORMS; MAN; -MAN; PARALLEL STYLE.

chauvinism. In 19th-century France Nicolas Chauvin, an old soldier who had served under Napoleon, became a byword for displays of extreme patriotism. Chauvin was caricatured on the stage, and the term *chauvinisme* = 'superpatriotism' was formed from his name. Borrowed into English as *chauvinism* /**shō**-və-nĭz-əm/, the word still basically means 'extreme patriotism, excessive and warlike devotion to one's country.' Hence also the noun and adjective *chauvinist* and the adjective *chauvinistic:*

> [Hitler] contrived, therefore, a synthetic Aryan "religion" to fuel the chauvinism necessary for his dreams of conquest.
> —Robert L. DeWitt, *The Witness*

> . . . *Patton,* a movie . . . which portrayed the World War II general to be—depending on the viewpoint of the viewer—either a patriot misunderstood by carping critics or a passionate chauvinist incapable of understanding the sensitivities of his troops or the public.
> —William Safire, *Before the Fall*

> Kroc is a chauvinistic apologist for American capitalism. . . .
> —Jacqueline Thompson, *The Very Rich Book*

In the late 1960s the feminist movement coined the term *male chauvinism,* meaning 'unquestioning belief by men that men are superior to women.' This expression (and its derivatives) quickly became so familiar that the idea could be conveyed without including the word *male:*

> [Soviet wives] must also run their households with little help from their generally chauvinist husbands.
> —Jean Knight, *U.S. News & World Report*

> The National Governors Association has a somewhat chauvinistic bent and prefers governors' spouses be seen and not heard.
> —Chris Black, *Boston Herald American*

> Women's libbers are by now doubtless labelling me an archetypal chauvinist. . . . —J. Paul Getty, *As I See It*

At the same time, *chauvinism* and its derivatives have also been applied to excessive devotion to any group, section, or issue:

> Growing up in Iowa and Minnesota imbued Reasoner with a strong and enduring sense of regional pride. He was, in fact, a spirited chauvinist about the Midwest and he often made sweeping claims on behalf of the region, such as his contention that the Midwest was the true home of democracy. . . .
> —Gary Paul Gates, *Air Time*

> The acceptance of black people's right to use ethnic chauvinism as a means of psycho-social liberation. . . . It was black chauvinists who first made this demand. . . .
> —Orlando Patterson, *New York Times*

> Today, however, even the most chauvinist network apologists concede that some children, under certain conditions, will imitate antisocial acts witnessed on the tube.
> —*Reader's Digest*

◇ ***Recommendation.*** Plain *chauvinism* is still 'superpatriotism.' If *male chauvinism* (or any other type) is meant, it is best to specify.

cheap. It is a pity that the negative uses of this honorable word are driving out its literal and original meaning, 'low-priced.' For most people *cheap* now seems to be loaded with bad connotations, from 'shoddy, inferior' and 'sleazy, dingy' to 'miserly' and 'mean and unethical.' Could this be a sign of the times, normal usage in an age when high price is the criterion of value and low price must be apologized for with such euphemisms as *inexpensive* and *affordable*?

Even now some people are still strong-minded enough to use *cheap* in its literal, and surely desirable, sense. This is a mark of confident good usage:

> Special small soufflé dishes are not necessary. Any little fireproof dishes, about 2 inches deep, will do. (Very cheap ones can often be bought at Woolworth's.)
> —Elizabeth David, *Summer Cooking*

> Anyway, the things you can't find here are the cheap things. Like smelts and cod. A fowl is cheaper than a roasting chicken, and you get soup from it too.
> —Mary McCarthy, *Birds of America*

check, meaning 'written order to a bank to withdraw funds from an account,' is spelled *cheque* by the British, reflecting the original French spelling. The British spelling is not entirely unknown in American banking, however, the most eminent example being the *travelers cheques* issued by the American Express Company.

chic. Pronounced /shēk/, this is originally a noun in fashionable French slang, referring to a peculiarly French quality of stylish elegance in women. In English it is used both as a noun meaning 'elegance, style' and as an adjective meaning 'elegant, stylish.'

> In London she had been considered exceptionally well dressed. . . . She now realized that never could she have had, by French standards, the smallest pretensions to *chic*.
> —Nancy Mitford, *The Pursuit of Love*

> For all her chic thinness, she [Holly Golightly] had an almost breakfast-cereal air of health. . . .
> —Truman Capote, *Breakfast at Tiffany's*

Chic has now also become a generalized vogue word of culture, as in *radical chic* = 'fashionable left-wing politics' and *Texas chic* = 'style of dress featuring very expensive Western boots, shirts, ten-gallon hats, etc.' The term is often used with more than a tinge of sarcasm.

> The "angry blacks" March [on Washington] suddenly had been made chic. Suddenly it had a Kentucky Derby image. For the status-seeker, it was a status symbol. "Were you *there*?" You can hear that right today.
> —*Autobiography of Malcolm X*

> Nationalism, once condemned by Liberals as racist, fascist, and crazy, is now respectable, even chic.
> —Heather Robertson, *Today*

> Despite his roots in Greenwich Village insurgency, he [Edward Koch] says he has never been radical or chic. "Chic, me?"
> —*New York Times*

Chicago urban dialect. Metropolitan Chicago is a densely populated area of about 3,700 square miles in northeastern Illinois and northwestern Indiana, nearly one and a half times the size of Delaware. Although it is geographically situated in the Northern dialect area, its speech variety, like that of most major cities, does not fall neatly into the dialect of its general region. Instead, Chicago urban speech is a composite of dialects that have been brought to it, like layers of sediment deposited over time. The foundation or bottom layer is the NORTHERN DIALECT, spoken in its clearest form by native Chicagoans, especially many of the older ones. Above this foundation is a more recent stratum of MIDLAND and SOUTHERN dialect, which is heard most clearly in the speech of the younger inhabitants and which gives this metropolitan dialect a special distinctiveness. And upon this is a superficial layer of generally current American English.

As with all large cities, this composite language is made even more complex and difficult to describe by the strong presence of social and ethnic dialects. By 1850, for example, 20 percent of Chicago's population was Irish. By 1860, the Germans made up the largest number of foreign-born citizens of the city. From about 1870 to 1920, Czech, Italian, Scandinavian, Russian, and Polish immigrants were the dominant groups. Then in the 1930s, black migration from the Southern states numerically overwhelmed this white European melting pot. Shortly after, there was an influx of Latin Americans. This mixture of ethnic speech, together with the differences in the speech of various social groups, makes it almost impossible to speak of a single Chicago dialect.

Central City Versus Suburban Pronunciation. There are several distinctive pronunciation differences between the speech of the 75 communities that traditionally make up the central city of Chicago and that of its outlying metropolitan area, which includes such communities as Highland Park, Elgin, Wheaton, and Joliet.

Some central-city pronunciation features among working-class speakers:

(1) The sound /o͞o/ is used instead of /o͝o/ in words like *room* and *broom:* /ro͝om/, /bro͝om/.
(2) *Precinct* is pronounced /**prē**-sĭn/.

Some pronunciation features among central-city speakers from bilingual ethnic communities:
(1) *Moth, thrashed, with* are often pronounced with /t/: /mŏt/, /trăsht/, /wĭt/.
(2) Words like *either, mother, father* are often pronounced with /d/ instead of /*th*/: /**ē**-dər/, /**mŭd**-ər/, /**fä**-dər/.

Many of the pronunciation features of suburban Chicago speech are also features of the Midland and Southern dialects. This is the case with the remaining features discussed here. The following seven features of suburban speech are also used by young central-city black speakers:
(1) *Beard, ear, pier* are usually pronounced /bērd/, /ēr/, /pēr/.
(2) *Chimney, rinses, since* are pronounced /**chĕm**-nē/, /**rĕn**-səz/, /sĕns/.
(3) *Root, roof* are pronounced /ro͝ot/, /ro͝of/.
(4) *Crop, wasp, on* are pronounced /krôp/, /wôsp/, and /ôn/ (as compared with the Northern dialect's /krŏp/, /wäsp/, /ŏn/).
(5) *Hoarse, mourning* are pronounced /hōrs/, /**mōrn**-ĭng/.
(6) The second syllable of *beautiful, kettle, faucet, mountain* is usually pronounced with /ĭ/ instead of /ə/: /**byo͞o**-tĭ-fəl/, /**kĕ**-tĭl/, /**fä**-sĭt/, /**moun**-tĭn/.
(7) Words like *Tuesday, news, dues* are pronounced /**tyo͞oz**-dā/, /nyo͞oz/, /dyo͞oz/. (See also NEWS, TUNE, DUKE.)

The following seven Midland and Southern dialect features of suburban Chicago speech are also used by older central-city white speakers:
(1) *Gums* is pronounced /go͞omz/.
(2) *Creek* is /krĭk/.
(3) Words like *soot* are pronounced /sŭt/.
(4) *Genuine* is pronounced /**jĕn**-yo͞o-īn/.
(5) *Syrup* is /**sêr**-əp/.
(6) *Mushroom* is /**mŭsh**-ro͞on/ or /**mŭsh**-ə-ro͞on/.
(7) *Yeast* is /ēst/.

Vocabulary. (1) The vocabulary of metropolitan Chicago speech is primarily Northern with a smattering of Midland and Southern terms. Because no extensive lexical study has yet been published, there are only a few words and expressions known to be unique to Chicago speech:

bunk = 'makeshift bed on the floor, pallet'
***doughnut** = 'any kind of sweet roll'
dray = 'sledge, stoneboat'
dry-wall fence = 'fence or wall made of loose rock or stone'
facerboards = 'house siding'
gopher = 'chipmunk'
landing = 'small front *porch'
peach stone = '*pit or seed of a peach'
quilt = 'any kind of blanket'
sill, water, *or* **hose cock** = 'outdoor water outlet or faucet'
stinger = '*dragonfly'

*Appears as separate entry

(2) Words of foreign origin occasionally used in Chicago:

bibbeleskäse /**bĭp**-lĭ-käs/, **smearcase** /**smîr**-käs/, **schmearcase** /**shmîr**-käs/ (German); **smetlak** /**smĕt**-lăk/ (Czech) = '*cottage cheese'
sülze /**zo͞ol**-tsə/ (German); **sulc** /so͞olt/ (Czech); **sylteflesk** /**sĭl**-tə-flĕsk/ (Norwegian) = '*headcheese'

*Appears as separate entry

chili, with plural *chilies,* is the preferred spelling for the hot pepper and the seasoning made from it. Variant spellings are *chile* and *chilli. Chile* is a country on the Pacific coast of South America.

chimera. The Chimera of Greek myth was a fire-breathing female beast, part lion, part goat, and part serpent or dragon. The word *chimera* /kī-**mîr**-ə, kə-/ is now used to mean 'illusion, something imagined to exist that turns out to be nonexistent':

> The chimera of a North-West Passage, guide way to China and the East around or through the north of North America . . .
> —Allan Villiers, *Captain Cook*

> For the next ten years, the number of persons living below the poverty line held steady at about 25 million. But

> that apparent stagnation was a statistical chimera, resulting from the Census Bureau's persistence in measuring only cash income.
> —A. F. Ehrbar, *Fortune*

The adjective *chimerical* /kī-**mĕr**-ə-kəl, kə-**mîr**-/ means 'illusory' or 'full of illusions':

> The Roaring Twenties were a period of the Great American Prosperity which was built on shaky, if not outright chimerical, foundations.
> —J. Paul Getty, *As I See It*

Chinaman, the usual term for a Chinese male during the imperialist era, is now regarded as offensive.

Chinese words. China has been in contact with the West for over 2,000 years, and in that time it has contributed many words to the vocabularies of European languages, including English. Communication has not been continuous, however, so Chinese words have come to the West at different times and under different circumstances. In the long run the Chinese writing system has served to isolate China from the outside world even more effectively than the Great Wall itself. An outline of how Chinese words are spoken and written, and how to write them in English, must therefore precede the story of how and when they came from China to the West.

Writing and Pronunciation. Chinese words are not inherently hard to pronounce, but a number of factors make them seem difficult to English speakers. The most important of these factors are *writing, dialect differences,* and *tones.*

Writing. Chinese is not written with an alphabet but rather with *characters* (also called *ideograms*). These, in their earliest form, were pictures of things or ideas. However, Chinese characters in their present, highly developed form are not a system of picture writing. They are a complex means of conveying ideas, but not pronunciation. While words written in an alphabetical language convey pronunciation in addition to meaning, the pronunciation of each Chinese character must be learned independently of how it is written.

Several systems for converting Chinese into alphabetical form have been devised for English, and systems have been created for French, German, and other languages. Two systems in common use for English have been the Postal system, devised for place names by the British-run Chinese Post Office in the 19th century, and the Wade-Giles system, created by the British linguists Thomas Francis Wade and Herbert A. Giles around the turn of the century. Wade-Giles—or W-G, as scholars call the system for short—describes the sound of Chinese fairly well for speakers of English (but not, for example, for speakers of French) when it is properly used. However, for correctness, Wade-Giles depends on the use of an apostrophe to distinguish between related consonants (for example, *k* pronounced /g/ and *k'* pronounced /k/). These apostrophes are frequently omitted in newspaper usage, making accurate pronunciation impossible.

In 1979 the Chinese government officially announced that it would use exclusively a new system called *Pinyin* (= 'transcription'), and expressed the hope that Pinyin would replace all other systems in use in Western languages. While Pinyin (PY) makes some distinctions that are not readily apparent to English speakers—for example, *ch* and *q* are both pronounced approximately like English /ch/—and while it uses some letters and combinations that look rather strange, the new system allows for an approximate pronunciation of Standard Chinese when its conventions are learned. In some cases, such as the names *Mao* and *Shanghai,* the Wade-Giles and Pinyin systems coincide. The table on pages 138–39 provides a brief pronunciation guide for both systems.

Dialects. About 80 percent of all Chinese speak Standard Chinese, which is commonly known in English as *Mandarin* and in Chinese as (W-G) *Kuoyü*/(PY) *Guoyu* (= 'national language') or *p'u-t'ung-hua*/*putonghua* (= 'common speech'). But along the southeastern coast of China a number of separate dialects are spoken, including Amoy,

Pronouncing Chinese

Symbol: Wade-Giles	Symbol: Pinyin	Pronunciation	Example: Wade-Giles	Example: Pinyin
Vowels				
a	**a**	/ä/	ch'a	cha
ai	**ai**	/ī/	lai	lai
ao	**ao**	/ou/	hao	hao
e	**e**	/ë/	che tse	zhe ze
ei	**ei**	/ā/	shei	shei
i	**i *or* yi**	/ē/	ch'i i	qi yi
ih	**i *after* ch, sh, zh**	/êr/	chih	zhi
o	**o *or* uo**	/ô/	po lo	bo luo
o	**e**	/ë/ *after* h	ho	he
u	**u**	/ōō/	fu	fu
u	**o**	/ŭ/ *before* ng	sung	song
u *after* ss, ts, tz	**i *after* g, s, z**	/ŭ/	tzu	zi
u	**ou**	/ō/ *after* y	yu	you
ü	**ü *after* l**	/ü/	lü	lü
ü	**u *after* j, q, x, y**	/ü/	ch'ü	qu
-ien *or* yen	**-ian *or* yan**	/yĕn/	ch'ien yen	qian yan
Consonants*				
ch	**zh *or* j**	/j/	chou chi	zhou ji
ch'	**ch *or* q**	/ch/	ch'i ch'an	qi chan
hs	**x**	*between* /s/ *and* /sh/; *no English equivalent*	hsing	xing
j	**r**	/r/	jen	ren
k	**g**	/g/	kai	gai

Pronouncing Chinese

Symbol		Pronunciation	Example	
Wade-Giles	Pinyin		Wade-Giles	Pinyin
Consonants*				
k'	k	/k/	k'u	ku
p	b	/b/	pao	bao
p'	p	/p/	p'in	pin
t	d	/d/	ting	ding
t'	t	/t/	t'i	ti
ts	z	/dz/	tsai	zai
ts'	c	/ts/	ts'ao	cao

**In both systems* f, h, l, m, n, ng, s, ss, sh, *and* w *are written and pronounced approximately as in English.*

Fukienese, Taiwanese, Cantonese, and Hakka. These dialects are unintelligible with each other and with Mandarin. Cantonese and Mandarin, for example, are as far apart as Portuguese and French. (A Cantonese and a Mandarin speaker can communicate in writing, however. Remember, Chinese characters have no sound value.) The names of some well-known Chinese are usually given in dialect forms in the West, and many Chinese words in English derive from dialect pronunciations. Here are some examples of familiar Chinese names in both modified Wade-Giles (newspaper) and Pinyin styles.

Wade-Giles	**Pinyin**
Chiang Ching	Jiang Qing
Chiang Kai-shek	Jiang Jieshi
Mao Tse-tung	Mao Zedong
Sun Yat-sen	Sun Yixian *or* Sun Zhongshan *(name by which he is usually known in China)*
Teng Hsiao-ping	Deng Xiaoping

The Postal system of place names was heavily influenced by the dialects. Most newspapers now use Pinyin for all except a handful of familiar place names. Library card catalogues, however, remain in Wade-Giles. The following is a comparison of some Chinese cities and provinces as rendered in the Postal and Pinyin systems.

Postal	**Pinyin**
Chungking	Chongqing
Fukien	Fujian
Hangchow	Hangzhou
Kiangsi	Jiangxi
Shensi	Shaanxi
Soochow	Suzhou
Szechuan	Sichuan

See also PEKING.

Tones. Chinese is a tonal language. The meaning of a spoken word depends not only on its pronunciation but on the tone in which it is spoken—hence the well-known singsong quality of spoken Chinese. Mandarin has four tones—level, high-rising, low-rising, and falling—while some dialects have as many as seven. Technically, then, Romanized Chinese (Chinese written in the Roman alphabet) should also indicate tones. This is done in either of two ways—with special symbols (as in *mā, má, mǎ, mà*) or with superscript numerals (as ma^1, ma^2, ma^3, ma^4).

Each is a completely different word (written with a different character). Thus, *mā* = 'mother'; *má* = 'hemp'; *mǎ* = 'horse'; and *mà* = 'curse.' In ordinary practice, however, tones are almost never indicated, and the foreigner trying to pronounce Chinese must simply forget about them—even if, when you are traveling in China, this might lead to your asking for soup when you were really trying to ask for sugar.

Note. For the rest of this entry, Mandarin forms of words are given in both newspaper-style and Pinyin transliterations, like this: Mao Tse-tung/Mao Zedong.

History. From about 200 B.C. silk was transported along a caravan route, the Silk Road, from China to Syria, for sale throughout the Mediterranean world. The Greeks and Romans knew of the silk country only as a vague place in easternmost Asia. The Romans called the silk people either *Sērēs* (ultimately from Chinese *ssu/si* = 'silk') or *Sinae* (from Chinese *Ch'in/Qin,* the name of the powerful dynasty that unified China in the 3rd century B.C.). Several English words are related to these ancient names:

China = 'name for the country first used in India, and picked up by the English there': (via Hindi and Sanskrit) from Chinese *Ch'in/Qin* = 'name of a ruling dynasty'

serge = 'fine woolen fabric': from French *serge,* from Latin *sērica* = 'silken fabric,' from *Sērēs* = 'the Chinese, the silk people'

silk = 'fabric made from the fibers woven by silkworms': Old English *sioloc,* from Old Slavic *shelku,* ultimately from Chinese *ssu/si* = 'silk'

Sino- = 'Chinese,' as in *Sinologist* = 'Western specialist in Chinese culture'; *Sino-Soviet* = 'relating to China and the Soviet Union': from Latin *Sinae* = 'the Chinese'

The Silk Road became too dangerous for travel by late Roman times. It was reopened in the 13th century under the Mongols, who briefly ruled unchallenged from Hungary to Korea after the conquests of Genghis Khan. Marco Polo went to China along the Silk Road in the 1270s and contributed another European name for China: *Cathay,* from *Kitai,* name of a Mongol tribe that ruled northern China from 907 to 1125.

After about 1500, European navigators opened up the sea route around the Cape of Good Hope and through the Indian Ocean, and this replaced the Silk Road as the main avenue of trade. Travelers compared notes and discovered that the Sērēs and the Sinae were the same people and that Cathay and China were the same place. *China* began to be used as the standard European name for the country and *Chinese* for the people.

Vocabulary. (1) Terms from the China trade:

china = 'porcelain pottery': shortened from *chinaware* = 'pottery from China'

***kowtow** = 'an elaborate bow to the Chinese emperor'

pekoe = 'a high-quality tea made from young, downy leaves': from Amoy dialect *pek-ho* (Mandarin *pai-ho/bai-hao*) = 'white down'

sampan = 'Chinese boat': from Cantonese *san-pan* = 'three boards' (a keel and two thwarts), itself borrowed from Portuguese *champana* = 'skiff'

shantung = 'a finely woven silk fabric, usually with warp and weft of contrasting colors': from *Shantung/Shandong* (a province on the eastern coast)

tea = 'beverage made from the dried leaves of an Asian shrub': earlier English *tay,* (via Dutch) from Amoy dialect *t'e* (Mandarin *ch'a/cha*)

typhoon = 'hurricane in the China Sea or western Pacific Ocean': from Mandarin *t'ai-feng/taifeng* = 'great wind' and the Japanese form of the same word, *taifun*

(2) Pidgin terms. As trade on the southern China coast increased in the 17th, 18th, and 19th centuries, few of the European traders learned Chinese, and not many Chinese learned European languages. They solved their mutual language problem by develop-

*Appears as separate entry

ing pidgin, a simplified trade language that contained elements of Chinese, Malay, Portuguese, and English (see PIDGIN AND CREOLE LANGUAGES). Many of these pidgin terms have been brought into English, and some have become standard expressions:

chopsticks = 'pair of sticks used for eating food': original meaning 'quick-sticks,' from pidgin *chop-chop* = 'quickly,' from Cantonese *kap-kap* (Mandarin *k'uai k'uai*) = 'quickly'

chow[1] = 'large, thickly furred dog with a blue-black mouth and tongue': from a southern China dialect (Mandarin *kou/gou*) = 'dog'

chow[2] = 'food': probably from pidgin *chow-chow* = 'dish of mixed pickles,' from Cantonese (Mandarin *tsa-tsa/zaza*) = 'miscellaneous'

joss = 'a Chinese god,' hence *joss house* = 'Chinese temple'; *joss stick* = 'Chinese incense stick': from pidgin *joss*, from Portuguese *dios* = 'god'

junk = 'Chinese sailing ship': (via pidgin) from Malay *djong* = 'ship'

long time no see (informal) = 'I haven't seen you in a long time': direct translation of the common Chinese greeting *hao-chiu mei-chien/haoju meijian*

look-see (informal) = 'quick look, brief inspection': translation of Chinese *k'an-chien/kanjian*

* **mandarin** = 'high-level civil servant'

pidgin = (1) 'trade language spoken on the southern China coast' (2) 'any trade language formed by simplification of a lingua franca': from a Cantonese pidgin pronunciation of English *business*

soy = (1) 'dark-brown sauce prepared from fermented soybeans' (2) 'soybean, an Asian bean that is a major source of protein': from Cantonese and Japanese *shoyu* = 'soy sauce'

taipan = 'boss, powerful managerial executive among European businessmen in the China trade': from Mandarin *ta-pan/daban* = 'master'

yen = 'strong desire, yearning': from pidgin *yen* = 'craving for opium,' from Mandarin *yen/yan* = 'smoke, opium smoke'

*Appears as separate entry

(3) Social and food terms. From about 1850 many Chinese came to North America to work as coolie laborers, especially in the California goldfields and on the great railroad construction projects in the West. Encountering severe racial discrimination in the labor market, many later migrated to the cities to work in restaurants and laundries, virtually the only places open to them; as cooks, they developed a distinctive Chinese-American cuisine. More terms resulted:

Chinatown = 'Chinese quarter of an American or a European town, typically policed or controlled by its inhabitants'

chop suey = 'small pieces of meat cooked with vegetables and bean sprouts': from Mandarin *tsa-sui/zasui* = 'miscellaneous bits'

chow mein = 'combination of stir-fried vegetables and meat served over fried noodles': from Mandarin *ch'ao-mien/chaomian* = 'fried noodles'

fan-tan = 'card game known in American Chinatowns since the Civil War': from Mandarin *fan-t'an/fantan* = 'barbarian gambling'

litchi, lychee, lichee /lē-chē/ = 'succulent fruit of a Chinese tree, having pearly white flesh and a large seed': from Mandarin *li-chih/lizhi* = 'litchi seed'

lo mein = 'fried noodles with stewed meat, etc.': from Mandarin *la-mien/lamian* = 'hand-stretched (noodles)'

mahjong, mahjongg = 'Chinese game similar to rummy but played with small ivory tiles': from Cantonese *ma chiang* (Mandarin *ma-ch'iao/maqiao*) = 'sparrow warrior' (so named because the shuffling of tiles sounds like sparrows twittering)

moo goo gai pan = 'steamed stew of chicken, mushrooms, and vegetables': from Mandarin *mo-ku chi-p'ien/mogu jipian* = 'tree-mushroom chicken slices'

subgum = 'any of various dishes of mixed ingredients': from Mandarin *shih-chin/shijin* = 'manifold brocade'

tofu = 'custardlike cake made from ground and fermented soybeans': from Mandarin *toufu/doufu* = 'bean curd'

tong = 'Chinese benevolent and cooperative society': from Mandarin *tang/dang* = 'party, faction, association'

won ton = 'soup with dumplings of noodle dough stuffed with various fillers': from Cantonese (Mandarin *hun-t'un/huntun*) = 'Huntun, a mythological being without sensory organs, a symbol of the chaos that preceded the creation of the universe'

(4) Postwar terms. Since World War II, more Chinese words have been added to our vocabulary:

chi /chē/ = 'vital force': from Mandarin *ch'i/qi* = 'breath, essence, material or vital force' (see *ki* at JAPANESE WORDS)

* **gung-ho** = 'extremely or excessively enthusiastic, zealous'

kung fu = 'a technique of unarmed combat related to t'ai chi, karate, and other martial arts': from Mandarin *kung-fu/gongfu* = 'distilled skill'

t'ai chi ch'uan = 'a type of slow calisthenic exercise that is intended to impart unity with the universe, and can also be used as a technique of self-defense': from Mandarin *t'ai-chi ch'uan/taijiquan* = 'ultimate fist, that is, tradition of the Supreme Ultimate or principle of universal unity'

yin-yang = 'female-male, that is, the fundamental dualism of the universe'

*Appears as separate entry

(5) Modern China. Some translated terms from the political rhetoric of the People's Republic of China have become familiar:

barefoot doctor = 'medical or paramedical worker among the masses, working with minimal equipment'

capitalist-roader = 'one who advocates capitalism instead of Communism'

Cultural Revolution (in full, **Great Proletarian Cultural Revolution**) = 'the period of political turmoil in China from 1966 to 1976, marked by the attempt to enforce Maoism'

Gang of Four = 'Chiang Ching/Jiang Qing (widow of Mao Tse-tung/Mao Zedong) and three associates, accused of plotting to overthrow the government in the 1970s'

Great Leap Forward = 'a grass-roots crash program of industrialization sponsored by Mao Tse-tung/Mao Zedong in the 1950s and subsequently abandoned'

paper tiger = 'a ferocious but weak enemy': a folk saying applied by Mao Tse-tung/Mao Zedong to the United States and other forces opposing the Chinese revolution

Chinook jargon /shĭ-**no͝ok**, chĭ-/.

The early trade language of the Pacific Northwest is known as the *Chinook jargon*. It is not jargon at all, however, but a very old pidgin language formerly spoken by the numerous Northwest Indian tribes among themselves and later by European traders and settlers coming in contact with these tribes.

Before the white man arrived, there were a large number of Indian languages in this region, each one extending over a very small territory and differing greatly from the others in the vicinity. The dominant tribes were the Chinook of the upper Columbia River valley, the Nootka of western Vancouver Island, the Chehalis of the Puget Sound area, and the Kwakiutl of northern Vancouver Island and adjacent British Columbia. The jargon originally sprang from the slave trade among these tribes. In order for the traders to communicate with each other, a common language, or pidgin, developed (see PIDGIN AND CREOLE LANGUAGES). This was based primarily on Chinook, but the other languages contributed many words.

Capt. John Meares in 1788 was one of the first Europeans to record a Chinook jargon word. He wrote in his journal that the Nootka chief Callicum upon tasting blood exclaimed "cloosh," actually *kloshe* = 'good' (many of these tribes practiced cannibalism). In the fall of 1805, Capts. Meriwether Lewis and William Clark were addressed in the jargon by the Chinook chief Concomly. Many of the words that Lewis and Clark thought were the Chinook language are recorded in their famous journals.

As contact increased with French Canadian, American, and English explorers and traders, the jargon adopted many new words from their European languages. Many of these words were needed to name the strange new objects that the white people brought with them.

Like most pidgin languages, Chinook jargon has a relatively small vocabulary, approximately 500 words, half being of Chinook origin. Some words are onomatopoeic, such as *chik-chik* = 'wagon, cart, wheel'; *hee-hee* = 'laughter' or 'to laugh'; *lip-lip* = 'to boil'; *kah-kah* = 'crow'; *poo* = 'to shoot'; *tum-tum* = 'heart, spirit.' Many French and English words passed into the jargon relatively unchanged, though the pronunciation systems of the Indian languages altered these borrowings to a degree. For example, /r/ was either changed to /l/ or not pronounced at all. Here are a few of the French Canadian and English words in the jargon:

bloom = 'broom'
Boston = 'an American'
cly = 'to cry'
cosho = 'pig, bacon' (French *cochon*)
Dutchman = 'any white man other than an American, Englishman, or Frenchman'
labootai = 'bottle' (French *la bouteille*)
lekleh = 'key' (French *le clef*)
nose = (1) 'nose' (2) 'point of land' (3) 'bow of a boat'
pan = 'bread' (French *pain*)
sun = (1) 'sun' (2) 'a day'

Like other pidgins, the jargon has a radically simplified syntax and grammar. For example, it uses only singular nouns. The plural is expressed by adding *hiyu* = 'many, much, abundance': *kalakala* = 'bird,' *hiyu kalakala* = 'birds, flock of birds'; *hiyu sheep* = 'flock of sheep.' Only one form of a verb is used in Chinook jargon, regardless of person, number, or tense. Tense is expressed by an adverb of time.

By 1875 some 100,000 persons spoke the Chinook jargon daily. But with the flood of settlers, English became the lingua franca, or common language, among the Indians. By the turn of the century the jargon speakers had dwindled to a few thousand. Today, Chinook jargon is essentially a dead language.

Even so, a few of its expressions survive in English use, especially in ALASKAN ENGLISH, the BRITISH COLUMBIA DIALECTS, and the PACIFIC NORTHWEST DIALECT. The following are most of these surviving terms.

camas, camash = 'an American plant of the genus *Camassia*': from *kamass* = 'edible bulb of a plant of the hyacinth species'

cheechako = 'tenderfoot or inexperienced person': from *chee* = 'new, recent' and *chako* = 'to come'

chinook = (1) 'moist, warm, inland-blowing wind' (2) capital *C* 'a Chinook Indian' (3) capital *C* 'the language of the Chinook'

chuck = 'inlet, harbor': from *chuck* = 'water, river'

high muckamuck = 'important or self-important person, big shot': from *hiya muckamuck* = 'plenty to eat'

klootchman = 'Indian woman': from *klootchman* = 'woman, female, wife'

muckamuck = (1) (verb) 'to eat' (2) (noun) 'food': from *muckamuck* = 'food' or 'to eat, chew'

potlatch = 'festive celebration, great social event': from *potlatch* = 'a gift' or 'to give'; the potlatch was a Northwest Indian festival at which gifts were distributed

Siwash = (1) (derogatory) (noun) 'an American Indian' (2) (verb) 'to camp, rough it' (3) (noun) 'a small provincial college': from *siwash* = 'Indian, savage,' from French *sauvage* = 'wild' or 'a savage'

skookum = (1) (noun) 'evil spirit' (2) (adjective) 'having strength or power' (3) (adjective) 'of good quality, first-rate': from *skookum* = 'strong, powerful, potent'

tillicum = (1) 'person, friend' (2) 'people': from *tillikum* = 'people, tribe, folks, friends, relations'

tyee = (1) 'boss, leader' (2) 'a large chinook salmon': from *tyee* = 'a chief, boss, officer, anything superior'

chutzpah /ho͞ots-pə, ĸʜo͞ots-/. This borrowing from Yiddish means 'extreme gall, breathtaking effrontery':

> Since he was older and less telegenic than the likes of Mudd and Rather, he felt he had to make up the difference in hustle and chutzpah, and he did.
> —Gary Paul Gates, *Air Time*

> . . . demonstrating that he is a con man with unsurpassed chutzpah. Asked if he swindled an uncle out of $50,000, Weinberg quickly denied it. He then added: "It was a cousin." —*Time*

For more borrowings from Yiddish see YIDDISH WORDS.

circa. See C., CA.

circumflex. See DIACRITICS.

clabber. Even though this is the commonest dialect term for curdled sour milk, it is used primarily in the General Southern dialect and in parts of the West. In fact, there is no national or literary term for *clabber*. Instead there are several regional terms. *Clabber* itself comes from the Irish or Gaelic word *clabbar,* which means 'mud' or 'thick.' Clabber has been a part of Southern cuisine for well over a century:

> It was a heavenly place for a boy, that farm of my uncle John's. . . . The sumptuous meals—well, it makes me cry to think of them. Fried chicken, roast pig; wild and tame turkey, ducks . . . squirrels, rabbits, pheasants, partridge . . . biscuits, hot batter-cakes . . . hot corn pone . . . buttermilk, sweet milk, "clabber"; watermelons, muskemelons . . . peach cobbler—I can't remember the rest.
> —Mark Twain,
> *Autobiography* (1897–98)

In New England the usual term for curdled sour milk is *bonnyclabber* or *bonnyclapper.* The first part of this term (*bonny*) also derives from Gaelic and means 'milk':

> The morning's milk turns to curd in the evening. This they call "*bonny clabber,*" and eat it with honey, sugar, or molasses. —Charles Janson,
> *The Stranger in America* (1807)

Lobbered or *loppered milk* is another variant also used in the New England dialect, as well as in the Inland Northern and Hudson Valley dialects.

The Northern dialect version is *clobber* or *clobbered milk. Cruds* and *crudded* or *cruddled milk* are used in most of the North Midland region. Another North Midland term is *thick milk,* which can also be heard in the Hudson Valley dialect. It is a direct translation of the Pennsylvania Dutch term *dickemilch.* See also COTTAGE CHEESE.

cliché. Pity the poor, unloved cliché. Dictionary definitions are contemptuous: "a trite phrase or expression . . . a hackneyed theme or situation" *(Webster's New Collegiate Dictionary).* Experts in usage are dismissive: the lexicographer Eric Partridge described his *Dictionary of Clichés* as being "full of things better left unsaid," phrases that were "so hackneyed as to be knock-kneed and spavined." English teachers and editors are cautionary: "Avoid clichés," they chorus, some going so far as to add, "like the plague." Even Presidents have been hard on clichés:

> Bob Haldeman insisted on "game plans" from Jeb Magruder on everything from publicizing a speech to putting together a clipping book, but the President [Nixon] struck it out of a speech draft, with the admonition to me: "Don't use clichés."
> —William Safire, *Before the Fall*

Some people, indeed, see in the poor cliché not merely an infelicitous turn of speech but a kind of awful creeping social menace:

> It is a kind of brainwashing, and in order to be successful . . . the cliché as stimulus has to be repeated over and over again in order to elicit the thoughtless, mechanical response it sets out to elicit.
> —Anton C. Zijerveld,
> *On Clichés: The Supersedure of Meaning by Function in Modernity*

> There is no bigger peril either to thinking or to education than the popular phrase.
>
> —Frank Binder (quoted), Donna Woolfolk Cross, *Word Abuse*

Given all this opprobrium, it is not surprising that the term *cliché* is almost never used in anything approaching a positive context:

> They [the speeches of Anthony Eden] consist entirely of clichés—clichés old and new—everything from "God is love" to "Please adjust your dress before leaving."
>
> —Winston Churchill

> To this autumn's list of wavering assumptions and disintegrating clichés—Islamic unity, the Solid South, the Phillies-can't-win-in-the-clutch—please add the immutable solidity of the West German economy.
>
> —John Vinocur, *New York Times*

But what, precisely, *is* the object of this universal scorn? What distinguishes the cliché from the thousands of other standard expressions—*How do you do,* for example, or *Take care of yourself*—that saturate our daily speech? If we were to agree that such phrases as *like a bolt from the blue, hook, line, and sinker,* and even *inextricably linked* qualify as clichés, would we necessarily say the same of *bleary-eyed* or *under the impression that* or *strictly speaking*? Are cliché and jargon the same thing? How often does a phrase have to be repeated before it becomes a cliché? Where do we draw the line between cliché on the one hand and idiom and slang on the other? Is *draw the line* a cliché?

Easy as it is to formulate such questions, it is not so easy to produce their answers. Although the cliché has had few more dedicated enemies than *The New Yorker,* when the editor and critic Wolcott Gibbs tried to advise the magazine's copy editors on the subject, his instructions, though excellent, were less than precise:

> Our writers are full of clichés, just as old barns are full of bats. There is obviously no rule about this except that anything you suspect of being a cliché undoubtedly is one and had better be avoided.
>
> —*Theory and Practice of Editing* New Yorker *Articles*

Some writers have argued that one hallmark of the genuine cliché is that it was once a fresh and imaginative coinage—so fresh and imaginative, in fact, that it was repeated until it finally became tiresome:

> Hush little bright line,
> Don't you cry. . . .
> You'll be a cliché
> Bye and bye.
>
> —Fred Allen

This implication of tarnished wit seems to apply to certain clichés: *as cool as a cucumber,* for example, may once have been amusing, and it is remotely possible that *a sea of upturned faces* may at some time have seemed a vivid metaphor. But can we imagine that *bewildering variety, cherished belief, sigh of relief,* and *none the worse for wear* were ever widely admired? Such pat phrases seem to have been around since before any of us can remember, without pedigree or explanation.

It has also been said that the worst clichés are those that are unnecessary, verbose, or essentially meaningless:

> Empire builders though they were, they seemed to think and move in inches, tilling their farms or plantations in serried ranks as they advanced.
>
> —J. T. Adams, *The Epic of America*

There is certainly no logical reason for including "serried ranks" in this passage; it merely adds words without furthering the meaning. Nor is there anything economical in saying, to take another example, *in deadly earnest* rather than *in earnest.* But if logic and economy were the sole criteria of language, we might lose a lot of our good poetry along with our bad clichés. It is often difficult to agree on what is "necessary" in English prose or poetry. In what sense, for instance, is any metaphor necessary?

There is another aspect of the cliché that makes it difficult to define: how it is used. There are times when a cliché can be used so casually, as a kind of throwaway phrase, that it will not seriously offend a listener's sensibilities. But the same cliché, when put on display by an inept user, can be genuinely irritating:

> "For the Pen," said the Vicar; and in the sententious pause which followed I felt I would offer all the gold of Peru to avert the solemn, inevitable . . . "is mightier than the Sword."
> —Logan Pearsall Smith, *All Trivia*

In short, when we set out to define clichés, we must also take into consideration such variables as circumstance of use and even personal taste.

So far, we have been discussing only clichés that are, as a euphemistic cliché would have it, "of a certain age." But in our own era of rapid mass communication, a phrase need not be elderly to become a cliché. VOGUE WORDS, or as they have been more voguishly called, *buzz words*, are contemporary favorites that enjoy a brief period of fashion and then succumb to overkill. There were times in recent memory when it was possible to sound TRENDY by referring to any conceptual boundary as a PARAMETER (in defiance of the word's real meaning); by adding the hyphenated adjectives *-related*, *-oriented*, and *-intensive* to a hundred different nouns; or by speaking authoritatively if not always knowledgeably of *supply-side economics* and *quantum leaps*. Most of these phrases are already old hat, but you would doubtless have no trouble in making up a list of their contemporary counterparts.

Although both current slang and jargon supply many of these instant clichés, the categories of slang, jargon, and cliché are separate (see JARGON; SLANG). In other words, it is possible to use slang and jargon without resorting to clichés. Possible, but not easy, because the demand for fresh vogue words is so intense that ordinary phrases can become clichés almost overnight. As the Hollywood mogul Samuel Goldwyn is supposed to have said about prospective movies, "Let's have some new clichés."

But still we lack a precise definition. We have said that in order to be a cliché a phrase does not have to be the burned-out relic of former wit, nor does it have to be old, verbose, or vacant of meaning. We have said, too, that clichés are not identical with slang or jargon; and we have even considered the possibility that some clichés are not clichés in every circumstance. Is there any other, more inclusive way of identifying clichés? How about frequency of repetition?

Here we come up against one of the oddest, and perhaps most illuminating, facts about clichés. A number of so-called clichés, precisely because they are among the most frequently repeated, may claim to have graduated from the cliché category to the status of idiom (see IDIOM). When we use such phrases, we have no illusions about them. We do not think of them as being imaginative, elegant, pointed, or really much of anything—except quick, efficient, universally recognized and understood ways of conveying those commonplace but necessary thoughts that are the building blocks of all ordinary communication.

By this time it must be clear that the much-maligned cliché is not the simple villain its enemies make it out to be. The very concept of cliché is fuzzy, indistinct at its edges, and shot through with qualifications and variables. Certainly in informal speech, and sometimes even in more formal address, it is virtually impossible to avoid using some clichés. (This entry, for instance—illustrations and examples apart—undoubtedly contains a few.) The editor of the Sunday *Times* of London spoke to this point in some well-taken advice to journalists:

> To enjoin writers never to use a cliché is to anticipate a definition and to seek the impossible. . . . It is impossible to ban them [clichés] because they serve a natural inclination. At best they are a form of literary shorthand, with the attraction of economy. . . . What deskmen can do with clichés in copy is to ration them, and tolerate only the best.
> —Harold Evans, *Newsman's English*

And how can we identify the tolerable best? Alas, there is no rule. "To write good prose," said Somerset Maugham, "is an affair of good manners," and good manners are obviously as much the product of instinct as of precept. But at least we can begin by ridding our minds of such simplistic notions as that all standard phrases are ipso facto clichés, that all clichés are bad, and that all clichés must therefore be avoided absolutely. As with much else in English, the truth is both subtler and more forgiving than that.

climactic, climatic, climacteric. *Climactic,* which means 'being a climax, coming to a climax,' is often used accidentally for *climatic,* which means 'relating to climate.' This occurs frequently in speech and sometimes gets into print. Occasionally too the opposite mistake occurs, and *climatic* is used for *climactic* or *anticlimatic* for *anticlimactic.* These are both definite mistakes.

Climacteric, pronounced either /klī-**măk**-tər-ĭk/ or /klī-măk-**tĕr**-ĭk/ means 'physical and psychological turning point occurring in a middle-aged person's life,' especially the menopause in women and the so-called male menopause in men. The word can also mean 'any critical point':

> "How old is he?" "About sixty." The doctor nodded. "After the climacteric, many manic-depressive patients spontaneously recover."
> —Mary McCarthy, *The Group*

> It was the evening of little Belle's recital, the climacteric of her musical year.
> —William Faulkner, *Sartoris*

clique, a word borrowed from French, is pronounced /klēk/ or else anglicized to /klĭk/. The meaning is 'selfish or snobbish group forming an unofficial club and excluding outsiders from influence, privilege, or power':

> There was a strong vein of elitism in Murrow and his clique. Most of them were well-educated and were drawn more to ideas than to events; they wanted to enlighten as well as inform. And from that vantage point, they viewed [Walter] Cronkite as something of an outsider.
> —Gary Paul Gates, *Air Time*

> That little clique back there has taken great personal satisfaction reviewing my politics instead of my pictures.
> —John Wayne (quoted), *Reader's Digest*

clone, a biological term for plant or animal offspring reproduced asexually from one individual. A *clone* can be a whole "family" of such plants or animals, which are genetically identical, or an individual member of such a family. *To clone* is to produce a clone. The term has recently become well known because of experimental work on cloning mammals and because of widespread rumors in the news media that human clones were being produced. This possibility impressed the journalistic mind so deeply that the word *clone* itself engendered new meanings: 'replica, imitator of someone, unoriginal copy of something':

> Today there are countless clones of [Geraldo] Rivera on TV news staffs around the country: soft-haired, mustachioed, handsome devils with *Latino* surnames, all smouldering with ill-contained outrage on behalf of the downtrodden common man. . . .
> —Ron Powers, *The Newscasters*

> Every year the number of tax guides that come to roost seems to increase. Many are clones of previous books. . . .
> —*The Independent Investor*

The verb *clone* is similarly used to mean 'make an unoriginal copy of':

> Grant's kaffeeklatsch counseling [a TV show offering psychological guidance] has been such a smash that stations around the country have been rushing to clone her. —*Time*

coanchor. See ANCHOR, ANCHORMAN.

Coastal Southern dialect. This is a highly diversified subdivision of the SOUTHERN DIALECT. It is spoken in southeastern Virginia and the lowlands of North Carolina, South Carolina, Georgia (with the Chattahoochee

Coastal Southern dialect

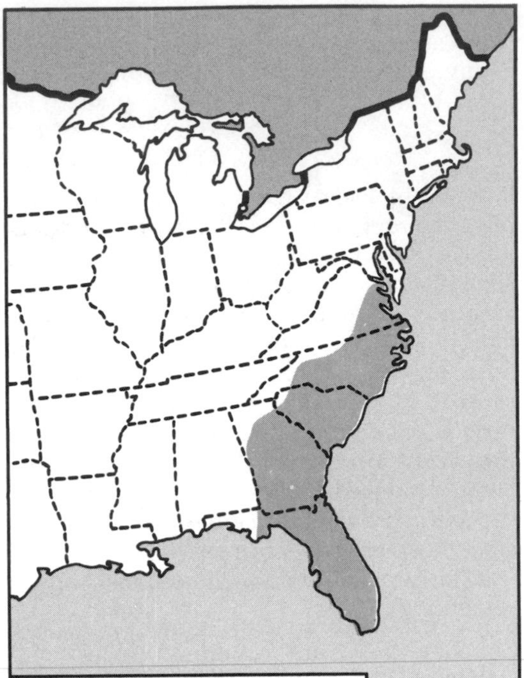

Coastal Southern dialect

River forming the western boundary), and Florida. The region has preserved its colonial speech patterns better than any other section of the Atlantic coast (except perhaps eastern New England). This preservation is due largely to the relative isolation of the area. Expansion inland was slow. The early settlements were kept apart by hostile Indian tribes and by swamps and other difficult terrain, and movement was further hindered by the hot, wet climate. Although this speech area has much internal diversity, there are many characteristics of pronunciation and vocabulary common to the region as a whole.

Pronunciation. Most of the pronunciation features of this speech area are identical with those of the Virginia Piedmont dialect. Other distinctive features of Coastal Southern, however, are too complex to explain here.

Vocabulary. (1) Words shared with the speech of New England:

breeze up = 'to become windy'
creek = 'saltwater inlet'
northeaster, norwester = 'wind blowing from the northeast or northwest'
piazza = 'covered *porch'
spider = 'cast-iron frying pan'

*Appears as separate entry

(2) Terms confined chiefly to the Coastal Southern region:

bloodynoun = 'bullfrog'
catty-corner (also Pacific Northwest, Pacific Southwest) = 'diagonal, *catercorner'
cooter = 'tortoise, turtle'
corn dodgers = 'cornmeal dumplings'
crocus bag *or* **sack** = '*gunnysack'
dope (especially South Carolina, western North Carolina) = 'carbonated soft drink, especially Coca-Cola'
down to a gnat's heel = 'to the last detail'
duck = 'cigar or cigarette butt'
excusing (**of**) (used chiefly by black speakers) = 'except (for), not counting'
fatwood = 'kindling wood'
fussbox = 'fussy person, *fussbudget'
groundnuts, ground peas = 'peanuts'
hopping john = 'stew made with cowpeas, rice, and bacon'
kernel = '*pit (of a peach)'
lay out (**of school**) (also South Midland) = 'to play *hooky'
lightwood /lĭd-əd/ = 'kindling'
liver pudding = 'liver sausage'
lulling = '(of wind) decreasing'
mutton corn = 'sweet corn'
outen (**the light** *or* **fire**) (also North Midland) = 'to turn off, put out'
pinder = 'peanut'
pinto (used chiefly by black speakers) = 'coffin'
poor joe = 'great blue heron' (FOLK ETYMOLOGY from Gullah *pojo*, from Vai *pojo* = 'heron')
potato hill = 'place to store vegetables over winter'
savannah = 'grassland'
shivering owl = 'screech owl'
sick on one's stomach = 'queasy'
turn of wood (also Virginia Piedmont) = 'armload of wood'
whicker = 'whinny'

*Appears as separate entry

(3) Terms used especially in North Carolina:
cookie = '*doughnut'
hickey-horse, hickey-board = '*seesaw'
Sunday baby *or* **child** = '*illegitimate child'
trumpery room = 'storeroom'
whet seed = 'whetstone'

*Appears as separate entry

cocoa, cacao. People have always tended to mix up these two words. *Cocoa* /**kō**-kō/ means 'chocolate or a chocolate beverage such as hot chocolate or chocolate milk.' *Cacao* /kə-**kä**-ō/ is the bean from which chocolate and cocoa butter are produced. The root of both is the Aztec word *cacahuatl* = 'cacao bean.' The word *cocoa* arose when the pronunciations of *cacao* and *coco* (for *coconut*) were confused, sometime during the Spanish colonial period in Latin America.

cognates. The word *cognate* /**kŏg**-nāt/ is from Latin *cō-gnātus,* literally 'born together, linked by birth,' hence 'related by blood, having a common parent or ancestor.'

Cognate Languages. Referring to languages, *cognate* means 'descended from a single ancestral language.' Thus, Italian and Spanish are cognate, both being descended from (that is, being changed forms of) Latin. English and German are cognate, both being descended from the old Germanic language (see GERMANIC). More distantly, Latin and Germanic are cognate, as descendants of the ancestral language INDO-EUROPEAN. It can therefore also be said that, for example, English and Spanish are cognate. Figure 1 diagrams the relationships of these languages.

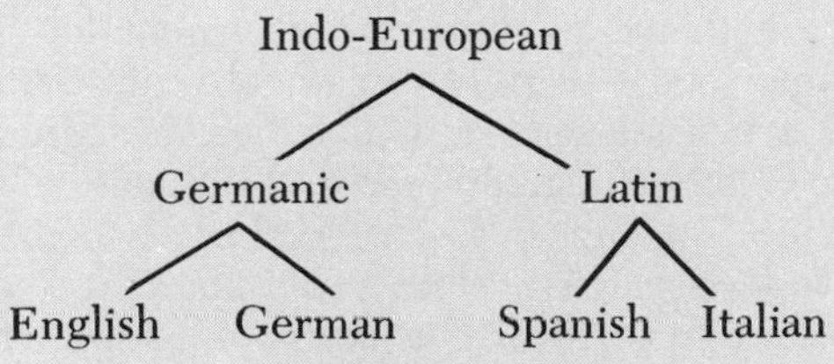

Fig. 1. Cognate Languages †

Cognate Words. Two or more words are called *cognate words* (or simply *cognates*) if they come from one preexisting word. This can happen in several different ways.
(1) *Variants.* Many words have variant forms, differing slightly in spelling or pronunciation. In time, variants may become established as separate words. Eventually, they may move so far apart that the relationship is no longer close or obvious. In Elizabethan English, for instance, the word *metal,* literally meaning 'metallic substance,' could be used figuratively to mean 'the quality of a person's temperament.' It could also be spelled *mettle,* in either meaning. Later, two separate words emerged, one spelled *metal* and the other *mettle.* We now use the two as entirely independent of each other. *Metal*

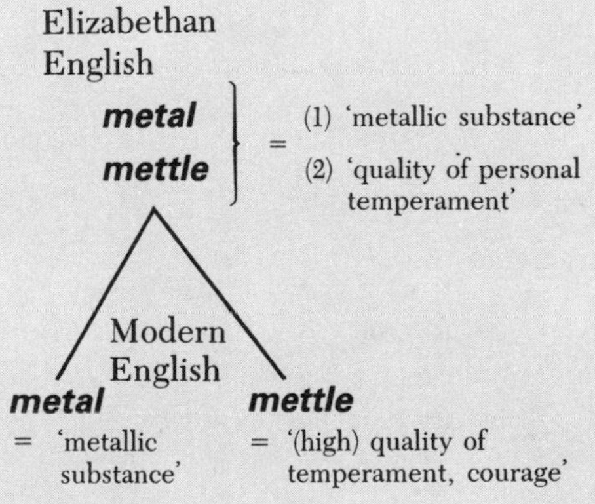

Fig. 2. Variants Becoming Cognates †

and *mettle* are cognates. This development is illustrated in figure 2.
(2) *Separate inheritance.* When a language splits into dialects, which then become separate languages, much of the original vocabulary will be retained in the new languages, usually in altered form. The Latin word *caballus* = 'horse' was thus inherited in Ital-

† Solid lines indicate continuous unbroken inheritance; broken lines with arrows, borrowings from one language into another.

ian as *cavallo,* in Spanish as *caballo,* and in French as *cheval.* These three words are cognate (see figure 3).

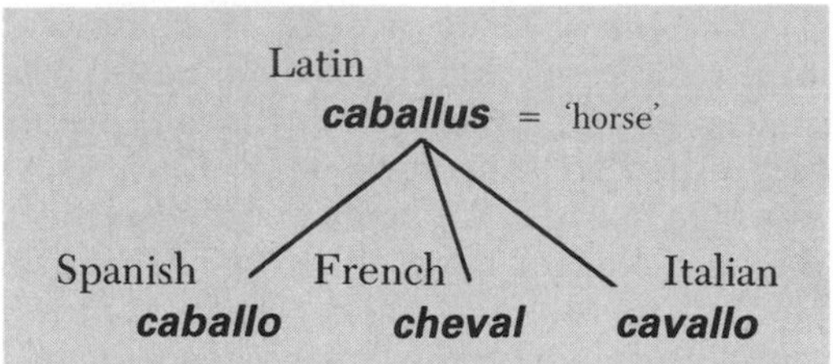

Fig. 3. Cognates by Separate Inheritance †

(3) *Multiple borrowings.* It often happens that a single word is borrowed from one language into two or more others. English *guillotine* and German *guillotine,* both from French, are cognates (figure 4).

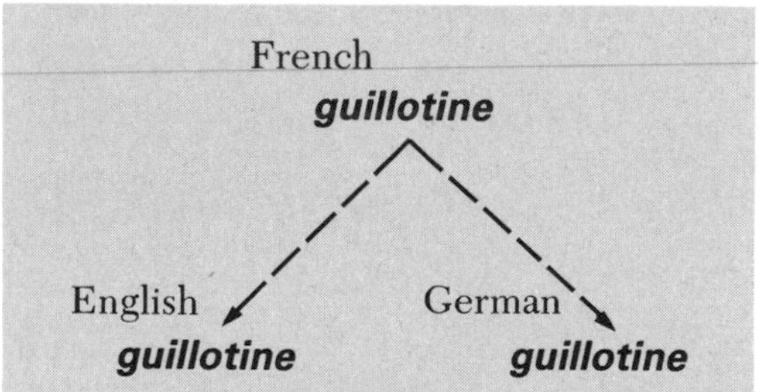

Fig. 4. Cognates by Borrowing †

Some words are borrowed from language to language in complex chains. The Arabic word *qahwah* = 'coffee' was borrowed into Turkish as *kahve.* After 1600 the Turkish word was borrowed into Italian as *caffè,* and from Italian into French and Spanish as *café,* into German as *kaffee,* and into Dutch as *koffie.* From Dutch it was borrowed into English as *coffee.* All of these European words, stemming directly or indirectly from Arabic *qahwah,* are cognates. This multiple borrowing is shown in figure 5.

It also often happens that one word is borrowed, directly or indirectly, into a given language on several occasions, usually in a different form or meaning, or both. French *café* = 'coffee' was also used to mean 'coffeehouse.' In this sense it was borrowed into English as *café.* The English words *coffee* and *café,* of the same origin but with different meanings, are thus cognates (figure 5).

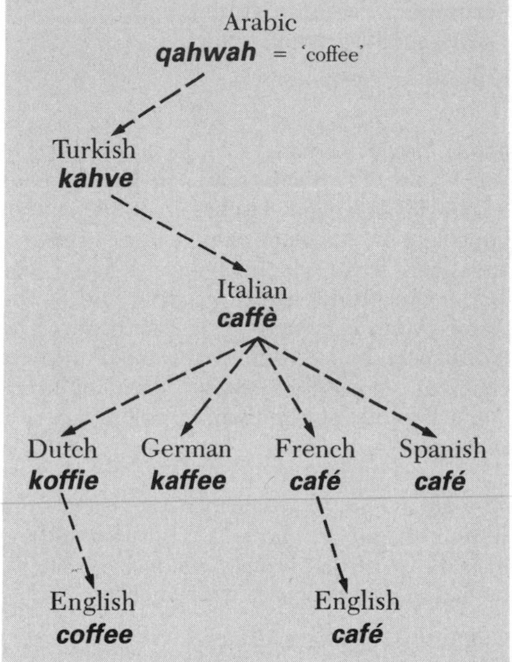

Fig. 5. Cognates by Multiple Borrowing †

(4) *Derivation.* Separate words formed by derivation within a language are also called cognates, such as *northern* and *northerly,* both derived from *north.*

(5) *Permutations.* Pairs or sets of cognates arise in all permutations of the above. The enormously expanded vocabulary of English is full of them. Some examples follow.

Short, Shirt, Skirt. The Germanic word *skurta-* meant 'short' and was also used as a noun to mean 'short undergarment for the upper body, shirt.' As an adjective it became Old English *sceort,* which became Middle and Modern English *short.* As a noun it became Old English *scyrte* = 'shirt,' becoming Modern English *shirt.* The noun also appeared in Old Norse as *skyrta* = 'shirt.' This was borrowed into Middle English as *skirt,* with the meaning changed (for unknown reasons) to 'skirt'; hence Modern English *skirt.*

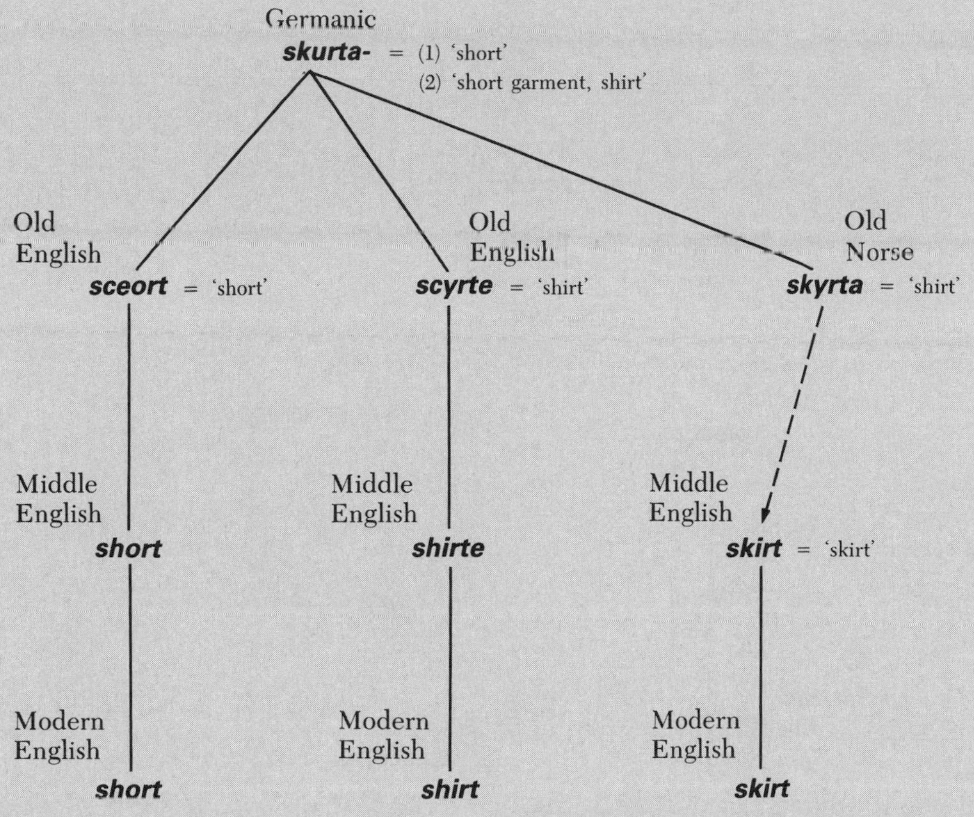

Fig. 6. Short, Shirt, Skirt †

Short and *shirt* are cognates by inheritance; *skirt* is a cognate by borrowing of both. Figure 6 illustrates how these three words are connected.

Bishop, Episcopal. Greek *episkopos* = 'overseer, supervisor' (from *epi-skopein* = 'to oversee, supervise') was used as a title of pastors in the earliest Christian church. It was borrowed into Latin as *episcopus,* becoming a title of a high-ranking priest in charge of a large district or diocese. In an unrecorded Latin variant form *biscopus,* the word was borrowed into Old English (9th century) as *biscop,* becoming *bishop* in Middle and Modern English. The adjective of *episcopus* was *episcopālis* = 'relating to a bishop or bishops.' This was brought into English via Old French as *episcopal. Bishop* is one of many English nouns, lacking adjectives of their own, that have acquired different-looking but cognate adjectives. *Episcopal* is used specifically to designate the various Protestant churches that are governed by bishops. See figure 7 for a diagram of this permutation.

Hospital, Hostel, Hotel. The Medieval Latin word *hospitāle* meant 'lodging, guest house, guest room.' This was inherited in Old French as *ostel, hostel* = 'lodging,' later also 'inn' and 'nobleman's town mansion.' In

† *Solid lines indicate continuous unbroken inheritance; broken lines with arrows, borrowings from one language into another.*

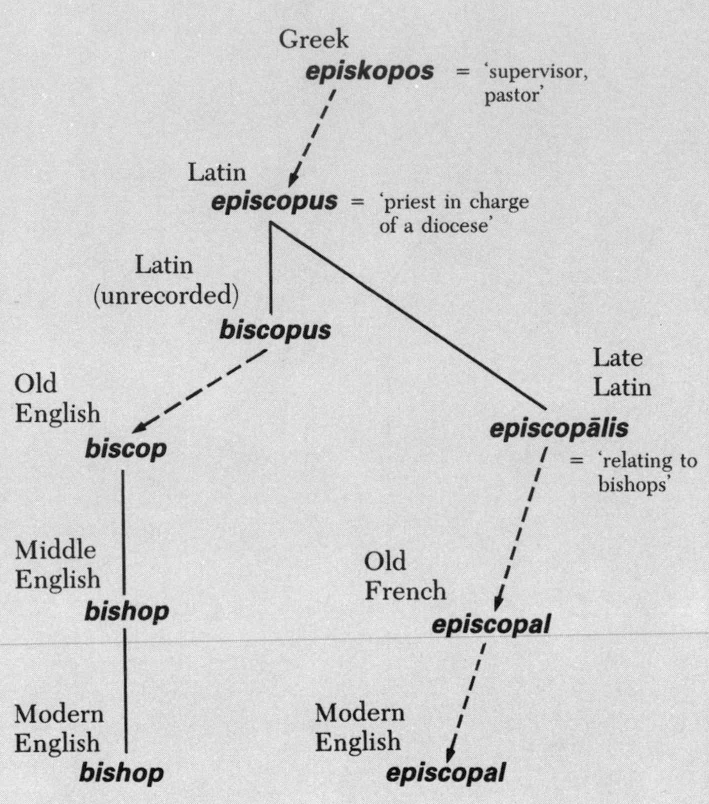

Fig. 7. Bishop, Episcopal †

the first two senses it was borrowed into Middle English as *hostel* = 'inn, lodging for students in a university'; Modern English *hostel* is still used to mean 'cheap lodging for students.' Old French *hostel* became Modern French *hôtel,* used especially to mean 'high-quality inn.' This was borrowed into English (18th century) as *hotel.* Medieval Latin *hospitāle* was separately borrowed into Old French and thence into Middle English as *hospital* = 'guest house,' also 'home for the poor or aged.' In the 16th century the word began to be used of certain charitable houses that cared for the sick, such as St. Bartholomew's Hospital in London. This became the primary sense of the Modern English word only in the 19th century. The three cognate words *hospital, hostel,* and *hotel* are thus three different modern versions of the medieval *hospitāle,* or lodging house (see figure 8).

Night, Nocturnal. The word *night* is inherited from Old English *niht,* Germanic *nakht-,* and ultimately Indo-European *nokwt-* = 'night' (see INDO-EUROPEAN). *Nokwt-* also appears in Latin *noct-, nox* = 'night.' The Latin adjective *nocturnus* = 'happening at night, active at night' was brought into English as *nocturnal.* Thus, our native, inherited noun *night* has the formal adjective *nocturnal,* borrowed from Latin but, as it happens, a cognate too (see figure 9). The same relationship exists between other nouns and their adjectives, among them *father, paternal; mother, maternal; mind, mental;* and *nose, nasal.* The nouns are

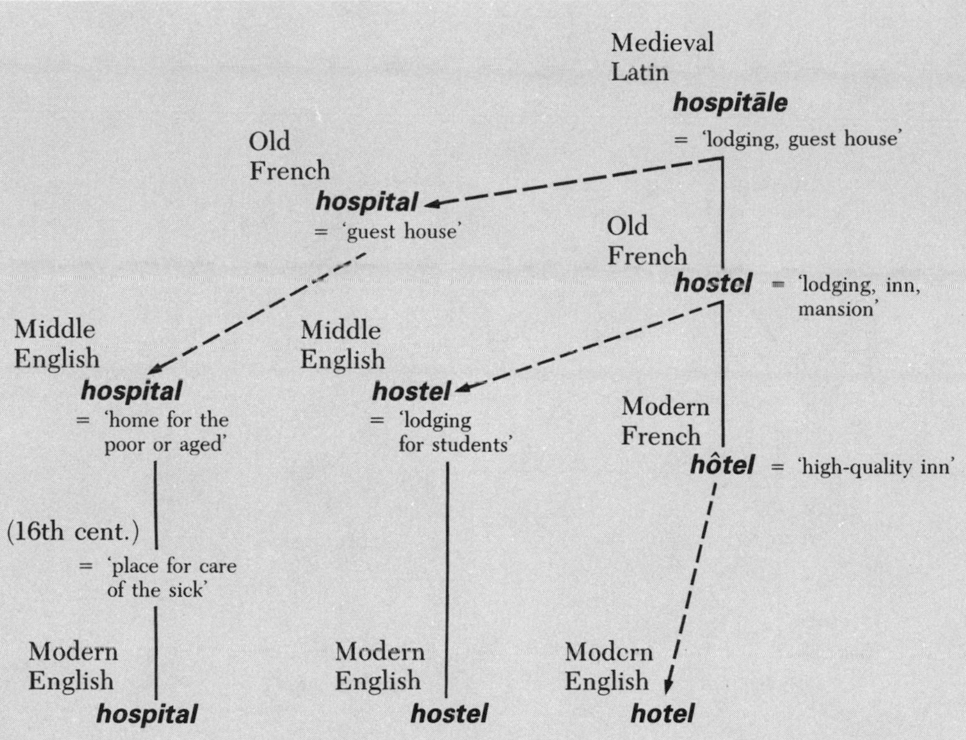

Fig. 8. Hospital, Hostel, Hotel †

all native Old English words inherited from Indo-European. The adjectives are all borrowed from Latin adjectives derived from nouns of the same Indo-European origin.

cohort, a unit of the Roman army forming one-tenth of a legion, containing 300 to 600 men. The word is used to mean 'group of supporters, statistical set of persons born in one year, crowd, squad':

> Reagan's ideological cohorts—men like Nevada Senator Paul Laxalt and North Carolina Senator Jesse Helms—could never accept the know-it-all interloper.
> —*Time*

† *Solid lines indicate continuous unbroken inheritance; broken lines with arrows, borrowings from one language into another.*

> The group coming along behind them, and into the labor force in the Eighties, is the less populous baby-bust cohort.
> —*Fortune*

> As for playing *behind* golfers like Nicklaus and Palmer, well, that was simply a matter of patience—waiting until their cohorts had moved their easy, elephantine meanderings beyond range.
> —George Plimpton, *The Bogey Man*

In the last quotation, the use of "cohorts" aptly plays on the word's military background, since it refers partly to the great crowds of Arnold Palmer fans known as Arnie's Army.

In many other cases where the plural form *cohorts* is used, it is unclear whether the writer means 'various groups of people' or is thinking of *cohort* as 'an individual person':

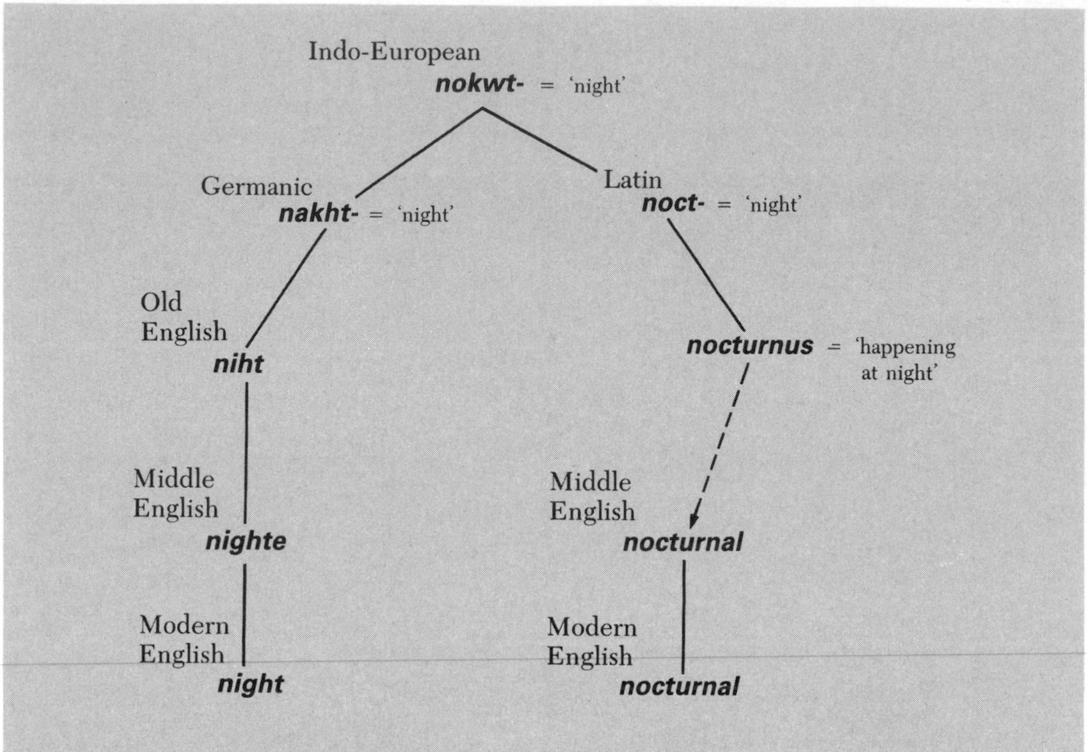

Fig. 9. Night, Nocturnal †

> Meanwhile, Lovett's cohorts had amassed a special fund to hire a strong defense team.
>
> —Kenneth Y. Tomlinson, *Reader's Digest*

Probably as a result of this plural usage, the "singular" form *cohort* is now widely used of individual persons. The meaning ranges from 'assistant, supporter' through 'old friend, crony' to 'accomplice in crime':

> A prim Chinese public-relations girl with a couple of assistants made up the receiving line, and as the guests filed in, the girl and her cohorts came forward frightfully cordially. . . .
>
> —John Le Carré, *The Honourable Schoolboy*

> When he wrote the memorable lyric to "Some Enchanted Evening," he hired a messenger to deliver the script to his crusty cohort, Richard Rodgers. . . .
>
> —Marian Christy, *Boston Globe*

> Marshal Budenny, an old cohort of Stalin, tried . . . to get Stalin to yield.
>
> —Harrison E. Salisbury, *The Unknown War*

◇ ***Recommendation.*** This use of *cohort* to refer to individual persons is now so widespread, especially in journalism, that we can't regard it as an actual mistake. Nevertheless, we recommend avoiding it. There are plenty of clearer terms in all shades of meaning—*accomplice, assistant, confederate,* etc. Keep *cohort* to refer to a group, as in the first three quotations.

cola, kola. This is the seed or nut of a West African tree (genus *Cola*). It contains caffeine

† Solid lines indicate continuous unbroken inheritance; broken lines with arrows, borrowings from one language into another.

and is chewed as a stimulant and digestive. The word is borrowed from Temne, a language of Sierra Leone, and it first appeared in English in the late 18th century. In the 19th century, extract of cola was used in the United States as an ingredient in "tonic" beverages, among them the carbonated drink that became Coca-Cola. Later, competing beverages like Pepsi-Cola appeared on the market, and *cola* eventually was also used as a general term for any similar drink. (See also AFRICAN WORDS; SODA POP; TRADEMARKS.)

coleslaw. This raw cabbage salad, now familiar all over the English-speaking world, is a contribution of the colonial Dutch in America. The word is borrowed from Dutch *koolsla,* meaning 'cabbage-salad,' from *kool* = 'cabbage' + *sla* = 'salad.' *Coleslaw* is often pronounced as if it were spelled *cold slaw* and is sometimes so spelled on restaurant menus; it is occasionally even reduced to *slaw.* This is a good example of FOLK ETYMOLOGY; the word *coleslaw* has no apparent meaning in terms of English, so is distorted slightly to make it partly meaningful.

◇ ***Recommendation.*** Saying *cold slaw* is not a serious mistake. But the word should be spelled *coleslaw.*

collective nouns. A noun denoting a group of persons or animals is basically singular, taking a singular verb and singular pronouns: *The team was at its best* (it is perceived as a unit). But the same noun may often be perceived as plural, taking a plural verb and plural pronouns: *The team are considering their options* (the players are perceived as individuals). In many specific contexts, usage is optional, according to the perceptions and the emphasis of the speaker. The grammatical rule governing plurality is here flexible enough to follow logic. *The team was at its best* may be the fundamental grammatical choice, but *The team were at their best* is equally possible and equally correct. Some other collective nouns that may alternate in this way are *class, crew, crowd, family, flock, herd, jury, orchestra, panel.*

colonel. The mismatch of the spelling *colonel* with the pronunciation /**kêr**-nəl/ can only be explained by etymology. The word originated in 16th-century Italy, where the military organization set much of the pattern for the rest of Europe. The lead company of an infantry regiment was called the *colonella* = 'little column' (from *colonna* = 'column'); hence, the commanding officer, leading the *colonella,* was called the *colonello.* This title was borrowed into French as *coronel;* the alteration of *l* to *r,* especially in a word that originally contained two /l/ sounds, is quite common in French, Spanish, and Italian. In this case the change also made the word seem to be related to *corona* = 'crown,' suitable enough as an emblem for a commanding officer. French *coronel* was then borrowed into English as *coronel,* first recorded in 1548. By 1600 or so, both the French and the English realized that the actual spelling in Italian had *l,* not *r,* and both corrected the word to *colonel.* The official English pronunciation, used by educated people and recorded in dictionaries, then followed the corrected spelling: /**kŏl**-ə-nəl/ or /**kŏl**-nəl/. But in popular use, no doubt including that of common soldiers, the word continued to be thought of as *coronel,* pronounced /**kŏr**-ə-nəl/, eventually /**kêr**-nəl/. The old uneducated pronunciation and the corrected spelling have prevailed. Thus results one of the oddities for which Modern English is notorious.

colored. See BLACK, COLORED, NEGRO.

comma. See PUNCTUATION.

commonwealth. *Weal* or *wealth* was originally 'well-being,' not riches. The *common weal* or *commonwealth* was 'the general well-being, the good of the community.' This archaic meaning is still felt in the resonant political word *commonwealth* = 'a people constituting a state, a sovereign nation.' In 1649 victorious republicans executed the king of England, abolished the monarchy, and named the new state the Commonwealth of England. Although the monarchy was restored in 1660, the idea of commonwealth has remained powerful. In the American Revolution, Virginia, Pennsylvania, Massachusetts, and Kentucky chose to call themselves commonwealths, as they officially are to this day. The Australian federation is the Commonwealth of Australia. After World War II the British government produced the term *Commonwealth of Nations*, hoping that it would induce several dozen ex-colonies to hold loosely together. In 1952 Puerto Rico designated itself a commonwealth. And the word also remains in use for an abstract community of interests, as *the commonwealth of literature*.

compare. The basic rule for the choice between *compare with* and *compare to* still holds up, but it isn't inflexible and it doesn't cover all situations.

(1) *Compare A with B* = 'to place two things of the same general kind side by side to consider their similarities and differences':

> Former Senator Eugene McCarthy gave a series of . . . lectures . . . in which he compared the America of today with the America of Alexis de Tocqueville. —*The New Yorker*

> As we compare disc with tape we note that, at present, tape is the technology with record capability.
> —Bernard Falkoff, *Video*

(2) *Compare A to B* = 'to liken, say that A is like B in some remote or figurative way':

> If I may be allowed to speak figuratively, our Assemblies in Politics are to be compared to the Wheels of a Clock in Mechanics. . . .
> —George Washington, letter (1782)

> In the interview, Mr. Giscard d'Estaing compared persons objecting to Concorde to those who objected to railroads in the last century.
> —*New York Times*

(3) But the past participle *compared* is very often used in sense one, referring to two things of the same kind but stressing only their differences. The preposition *with* would be justified, but *to* is more often used.

> Compared to most *New Yorker* writers and editors, I am gregarious to the point of seeming lunacy.
> —Brendan Gill, *Here at The New Yorker*

> . . . the run-of-the-mill tornado, while destructive in its own right, is mild when compared to the quite rare "maxi" tornado.
> —Warren H. Spencer, *Reader's Digest*

> About the Russians we are wary but not jittery. Compared to us, however, they cannot make their economic system work. . . .
> —Thomas Griffith, *Atlantic Monthly*

(4) *Compare* is also used to mean 'to be equal to, be put on a par with,' often in negative statements. Here *with* is also justified, but *to* is perhaps more often used.

> I have read so often of a child's thrill when visiting the circus for the first time. I believe it does not compare with my enthrallment when walking through the courthouse.
> —Louis Nizer, *My Life in Court*

> . . . turning out a stream of novels and plays that critics were beginning to say did not compare to the early work.
> —Michael J. Arlen, *Passage to Ararat*

> That ignorant misuse of *like* is not to be compared to the conjunctive use that told us about a cigarette that "tastes good like a cigarette should."
> —Theodore M. Bernstein, *The Careful Writer*

◇ ***Recommendation.*** The choice between *compare with* and *compare to* is less simple than the traditional rule suggests. There is room for flexibility. The examples cited are typical of current good usage, but they are not binding.

compatriot. Properly, this word means 'fellow national, person of the same country.' Informally, *compatriot* is sometimes used to mean 'colleague, fellow worker,' or 'peer, member of a peer group, person of similar age and status':

Kissinger told his White House compatriots that the foreign service establishment was taking advantage of Rogers' vanity. . . .
—William Safire, *Before the Fall*

[Children today] seem more mature than I remember my high school compatriots. . . .
—Ken Cruickshank, *Florida Times-Union*

◊ ***Recommendation.*** A use like this is a matter of taste. To some it will seem a perfectly natural extended use, though informal. To others there is something slightly undesirable about it; they wouldn't use it themselves, and if they heard it they might feel that the word was being distorted.

complected. This adjective means 'having a certain color of complexion,' as *dark-complected; light-complected.* It is a back-formation from *complexion.* Although *complected* is a perfectly reasonable, even useful, word, it remains informal or dialectal and is not accepted in formal standard usage. (See BACK-FORMATIONS.)

complement, compliment. A *complement* is literally 'a completing, a filling up.' The word now generally means 'something that completes or perfects, something that goes perfectly with something else':

It is the unknown land which all of us have known and have longed to find in youth. It is the undiscovered complement of all that we have seen and known, the lost half of our dark heart. . . .
—Thomas Wolfe, *The Web and the Rock*

Helen joined the band with Jimmy Rushing's blessing and stayed for the next five years. She was the perfect complement to Rushing, and she and Jimmy became life-long friends.
—John Hammond, *John Hammond on Record*

The verb *complement* means 'to make complete, go perfectly with':

The two complemented one another, Hewitt always looking at the big picture, Curtis zeroing in on the details.
—*Forbes*

The adjective *complementary* means 'filling out or forming a perfect whole, matching without conflict':

Science deals mainly with facts; religion deals mainly with values. They are not rivals. They are complementary.
—Martin Luther King, Jr., *Strength to Love*

The word *compliment* ultimately has the same origin as *complement,* but in an entirely different sense. It literally meant 'a completing or fulfilling of social duties, a polite accomplishment.' *Compliment* now has the narrower meaning 'a polite congratulation, a minor expression of respect or praise.'

compound. This word is often used to mean 'enclosed private estate with a number of buildings,' such as the presidential compound at Camp David, Maryland, or the Kennedy family compound at Hyannisport, Massachusetts. It has a surprising history. In the eastern parts of the old British Empire, *compound* meant 'walled enclosure surrounding a European home, business office, or warehouse.' The word was first used in Indonesia and Malaya, and was borrowed from Portuguese *campon* and Dutch *kampoeng,* which are both versions of the Malay word *kampong* = 'village, group of buildings' or 'district of a town inhabited by a foreign nationality,' such as the Chinese quarter, or *kampong,* in the city of Batavia (now Djakarta). The change of this alien word to the English-seeming form *compound*—somehow implying that a "compounded" or "composite" group of buildings is involved—is a classic example of FOLK ETYMOLOGY. In modern usage *compound* is also found in a context that closely reflects the word's colonial background; an embassy compound is the walled, now often fortified, enclosure around an embassy and its outbuildings.

compound adjectives. A compound adjective is typically a short punchy combination of words such as *time-honored, tax-free, smooth-talking, tongue-tied,* and *straight-from-the-shoulder.* A compound adjective is often called a *unit modifier* because the individual words in a compound adjective function as a unit in the process of modifying a noun. Consider for a moment how a compound adjective differs from two other types of modifiers—coordinate and noncoordinate adjectives.

When two coordinate adjectives precede a noun (as in *a high, dry location*), each adjective modifies the noun in a separate but equal fashion. In effect, the foregoing phrase describes a location that is both high and dry.

When two noncoordinate adjectives precede a noun (as in *high monthly expenses*), the first adjective modifies the combined idea of the second adjective plus the noun. In this case, we're talking about monthly expenses that are high, not expenses that are both high and monthly.

By contrast, when a compound adjective precedes a noun (as in *a high-level decision*), we are not talking about a decision that is both high and level, nor are we talking about a level decision that is high. We are talking about a decision that has been made at a high level in some organization. In short, *high* and *level* work together to modify *decision.*

Compound adjectives are derived from and stand for longer phrases and clauses. Sometimes the words that make up a compound adjective are extracted intact from the longer phrase or clause. For example, *a white-collar worker* is a compact version of *a worker who typically wears a shirt with a white collar while on the job.*

Sometimes, in the process of becoming a compound adjective, the extracted words undergo a small change in form. Thus, *a reconciliation with a short life* becomes *a short-lived reconciliation.* (The *-lived* part of this word is accurately pronounced /līvd/, because it is derived from the noun *life,* not the verb *live;* however, /lĭvd/ is also an acceptable pronunciation.)

Sometimes the extracted words undergo a reversal of word order. Thus, *a salesman who stands there silently, as if someone had tied a knot in his tongue* becomes *a tongue-tied salesman.*

And sometimes the extracted words undergo a change both in form and word order. Thus *a negotiator who speaks softly* becomes *a soft-spoken negotiator.*

From a syntactical point of view, then, the birthing of a compound adjective can be a fairly wrenching experience. A few words are (1) taken out of their normal position in a descriptive word or phrase that naturally follows a noun, (2) often given a little twist with regard to form or word order, or both, and (3) jammed in front of a noun (where they don't normally belong) and made to function as a unit modifier.

As a result, almost every compound adjective has to be hyphenated so that the individual words can be readily grasped as a single concept. However, the very same sequence of words may appear elsewhere in a sentence and not constitute a compound adjective (and hence not require connecting hyphens). This kind of ambiguity produces, with understandable frequency, confusion and frustration. Indeed, one authority—John Benbow, writing in the stylebook of the Oxford University Press—has said: "If you take hyphens seriously you will surely go mad."

The following guidelines have been devised with the aim of reducing the confusion, the frustration, and the possibility of going mad.

Before a Noun. In general, hyphenate the words in a compound adjective that appears before the noun it modifies.

long-range plan	higher-priced suit
three-week vacation	well-known politician
accident-prone son	spaced-out look
law-abiding citizen	up-to-date account
odd-looking hairdo	run-of-the-mill job
old-fashioned hat	hit-and-run driver

There are a few exceptions to the general rule: (1) Don't hyphenate the words in a proper name that serves as a modifier before a noun. The capital letters make it easy to grasp the words in the name as a unit, and the hyphen is unnecessary.

Atlantic City casino	White House staff
Charles Addams cartoon	General Motors car

(2) Don't hyphenate the words in a well-established foreign expression that modifies a noun. The foreign words already stand out as a unit.

ad hoc committee	sotto voce remarks
ex officio member	prima facie evidence

A few foreign expressions used as modifiers are sometimes seen with hyphens: *a bona-fide competitor; a laissez-faire policy.*

(3) Don't hyphenate a well-established compound noun that modifies another noun. Compound nouns like *real estate, social security,* and *income tax* designate ideas or institutions that are readily grasped as a unit.

stock car races	health department rule
high school education	municipal bond offering

By contrast, similar adjective-noun combinations have to be hyphenated because they do not have an independent standing as a well-known compound noun.

high-speed presses	part-time job
blue-ribbon jury	short-term loan

(4) Don't hyphenate a combination consisting of an adverb ending in *-ly* plus a participle: *a nicely furnished room; a rapidly changing situation.* These words are in a normal form and normal word order; they do not represent a unit modifier.

However, hyphenate a combination consisting of an adjective ending in *-ly* plus a participle: *a costly-looking handbag; a friendly-sounding bark.* Moreover, do hyphenate adverb-participle combinations when the adverb does not end in *-ly: a well-known precedent; a long-drawn-out debate; an ever-smiling face; a much-loved uncle.*

Elsewhere in a Sentence. When the words that make up a compound adjective appear elsewhere in a sentence in a normal form and in a normal word order, do not hyphenate them. They are no longer considered compound adjectives.

low-cost housing
housing at a low cost

a three-year lease
a lease running for three years

a $35,000-a-year job
a job paying $35,000 a year

a friendly-looking dachshund
a dachshund with a friendly look

an up-to-date style
a style that is up to date

a soon-to-be-released movie
a movie soon to be released

However, if the words that make up a compound adjective still reflect a change in form or word order when they appear elsewhere in a sentence, hyphenate the words—they are still functioning as a unit modifier.

The following combinations are always hyphenated:

Noun-adjective:
This financial undertaking is risk-free. (This financial undertaking is free of risk.)

Noun-participle:
The negotiations have been time-consuming. (The negotiations have been consuming much time.)

Adjective-participle:
You were nicer-looking before you gained weight. (You looked nicer before you gained weight.)

Adjective-noun + -ed:
His responses reveal how tough-minded he is. (His responses reveal a tough mind.)

Moreover, certain adverb-participle combinations require a hyphen if the participle is not part of the verb.

Her achievements are well known. (No hyphen is needed, since the sentence could read *Her achievements are known.*)

His motives were well-intentioned. (A hyphen is needed, since you could not say *His motives were intentioned.* However, some authorities recommend dropping the hyphen in compounds using *well* and *ill* when they follow the noun.)

Some compound adjectives in the categories just listed are now written as a single word: *carefree* (versus *risk-free*), *hardheaded* (versus *tough-minded*), *wellborn* (versus *well-intentioned*). It will be a happy day for writers and editors when all compound adjectives achieve perfect union. Until that golden age arrives, these guidelines on when to hyphenate may be of some help.

compound nouns. When two or more words are used to name something, the resulting term is a compound noun:

jackpot	jackanapes
jack-tar	jack-in-the-box
jack pine	jack-in-the-pulpit
jack rabbit	jack-of-all-trades
jack salmon	jack-o'-lantern

The words that make up a compound noun do not have to be nouns themselves:

know-how	checkup
make-believe	printout
breakdown	the well-to-do
takeoff	the have-nots

All that matters is that the words make up a unit that functions as a noun. (For the plurals of compounds see PLURALS.)

Some compound nouns are written as separate words, some are hyphenated, and some are written as one word:

back road	time clock
back-formation	time-out
backache	timekeeper
check mark	night court
check-in	night-light
checklist	nightmare
half brother	hair shirt
half-truth	hair-raiser
halftone	hairbrush

As the foregoing examples reveal, there are no consistent patterns here. It would be wonderfully convenient, for example, if you could safely assume that all two-syllable compound words beginning with *work-* or ending in *-off* were spelled as one word. But dictionaries abound with examples to the contrary:

workhorse	layoff
work force	play-off
workshop	standoff
work basket	send-off
workout	takeoff
work-up	write-off

To make matters worse, dictionaries do not agree on how compound nouns should be written—and for an obvious reason: since lexicographers base their spelling decisions on citations culled from published materials, the disagreement merely reflects the diverse practices of working writers.

In a situation like this, all you can do is either accept the authority of one dictionary and follow it faithfully, or sit down and do your own decision making (decisionmaking? decision-making?).

There are only a few guidelines you can fall back on.

(1) If you hit on a word like *decision making* and can't find it in your dictionary, you can treat it as two words.

(2) If you are somewhat more daring, go by way of analogy (a time-consuming but picturesque route). Thus, if you can't find *worksheet (work-sheet? work sheet?)* in your dictionary, look for another word beginning with *work* that has the same number of syllables and patterns of stress, and the same grammatical structure. Once you encounter *workroom* above and *workweek* below the place on the dictionary page where *worksheet* ought to be, you can feel fairly comfortable about spelling *worksheet* as a single word. (Note: *Webster's New World Dictionary* gives *workroom, workweek*, but *work sheet.*)

(3) If you are truly courageous, you will defy a dictionary's mind-boggling variations (for example, *layoff/play-off, workhorse/work force*) and treat like words alike. (If enough writers begin imposing a consistent style on such words, think of the impact on lexicographers' citations.)

Keep in mind that the long-term goal of most compound words (especially those of two syllables) is to become solid. Words like *good-bye* and *by-pass* are now becoming established as *goodbye* and *bypass*. When weighing alternative spellings, avoid the hyphenated form (except in phrases like *jack-in-the-pulpit*); this form is clumsy-looking and the one least likely to survive. When deciding whether to write a compound noun as separate words or as one word, choose the solid form unless the resulting word would produce an odd combination of letters. Yet even here there are exceptions. The older form *week-night* has now become *weeknight*. No one is likely to misread the solid form as *wee knight*, any more than one is tempted to misread *manslaughter* as *man's laughter*.

(4) And when courage fails and you don't want to "sit down and do your own *decision making*," then "sit down and *make a decision*." In short, don't use any compound noun you can't handle comfortably.

compound verbs. A compound verb is derived from two separate words that function as a unit. Compound verbs are either hyphenated or written as one word:

air-condition	grandstand
blue-pencil	blackball
hand-letter	upstage
single-space	downgrade

If a compound verb is hyphenated as an infinitive, all derivative verb forms should also be hyphenated:

> Wouldn't it be nice if we could have all the posters *hand-lettered*?
> I can *hand-letter* the posters very quickly.
> *Hand-lettering* twenty posters seemed like a good idea at the beginning.

When the gerund—the verbal noun ending in *-ing*—stands alone, without referring to an object like *twenty posters* in the third sentence, drop the hyphen:

> Is there a typeface that can create the effect of *hand lettering*?

Don't confuse two-word phrasal verbs (such as *follow up, lay out, lead in,* and *take off*) with corresponding compound nouns that may be hyphenated or written solid (*follow-up, layout, lead-in, takeoff*).

> Let's follow up with the consultant every week.
> Let's aim for a weekly follow-up.

> Please lay out the copy in two columns.
> Please check the layout of the copy.

comprise. The basic and correct meaning of *comprise* is 'to include, be made up of':

> The community comprises mainly Protestants, Catholics and Jews in nearly equal numbers.
> —John T. McQuiston,
> *New York Times*

Note that it is the community that comprises its members, the whole that comprises the parts. But *comprise* is often used in the opposite sense, 'to compose, make up':

> The three American divisions comprised General Truscott's VIth Corps. . . .
> —Winston Churchill,
> *Triumph and Tragedy*

If someone had pointed it out to him, Churchill would certainly have corrected this to "the divisions made up the Corps." Even more often, a passive construction, *is comprised of*, is used to mean 'is made up of' (the result of confusion with *is composed of*):

> The president drew polite applause from the audience comprised of several thousand representatives of cities and towns. . . .
> —*Savannah Morning News*

> . . . while etiquette is surely a factor, acceptable behavior is comprised of a good deal more.
> —Fran Lebowitz,
> *Metropolitan Life*

◇ *Recommendation.* These uses of *comprise* to mean 'compose, make up,' in both the active and the passive voice, are now so widespread that they are recognized in some dictionaries and are regarded by many people as acceptable. However, resulting as they do from confusion with *compose*, and probably also with *consist*, they are no help to clear expression and are unnecessary anyway. We recommend avoiding them and using *comprise* to mean only 'include, be made up of.'

comptroller is an archaic spelling of *controller,* still widely used as a title of corporate financial officers. It is pronounced the same as *controller.*

concensus. Misspelling of CONSENSUS.

conch, a type of large mollusk shell. The better pronunciation is /kŏnk/, with plural *conchs.* But /kŏnch/ with plural *conches* /**kŏn**-chəs/ is not incorrect.

confederate. See COHORT.

confirmatio. Old term for the presenting of evidence supporting one's thesis in a piece of expository writing. See EXPOSITION.

confutatio. Old term for the rebutting of arguments against one's thesis in a piece of expository writing. See EXPOSITION.

congeries. This word looks as if it might be French and possibly plural, but it is actually singular, coming from the Latin singular noun *congeriēs* = 'a heaping together.' There are several pronunciations in respectable use, including /**kŏn**-jə-rēz/, /kən-**jîr**-ēz/, and /kən-**jĕr**-ē-ēz/. The plural is just like the singular: *congeries.* An imaginary singular, *congerie* or *congery,* is sometimes produced. The meaning of *congeries* is 'loose collection, unstructured group':

> The Song of Solomon is neither a unified lyric nor a drama . . . but rather a congeries of lyrics, some twenty-five in number.
> —Moses Hadas, *Hellenistic Culture*

> Except in presidential years, the national parties are little more than loose congeries of ambitious men.
> —Bill Moyers, *Listening to America*

◇ ***Recommendation.*** If in doubt, pronounce this word /**kŏn**-jə-rēz/. Do not use the back-formation form *congerie* or *congery.*

connive. The underlying sense of *connive* is 'to wink at, close one's eyes to something in front of one'; the proper and effective meaning is thus 'to pretend not to notice something being done and do nothing to stop it.' The word is rich with implications about human behavior and motivations, especially in politics. The person who *connives at* a crime or other action has at least a moral or public duty to prevent or oppose it but remains cynically inactive and will later claim to have known nothing about it, or make some other excuse:

> . . . a violent and fanatical anti-foreign movement, in part connived at by the Chinese government, which led to much destruction of foreign property.
> —George F. Kennan, *American Diplomacy 1900–1950*

> . . . the Russophobe French, British and U.S. politicians and industrialists who had connived at the growth and spread of fascism, concealing their real admiration for it beneath the public explanation that it was the only trustworthy "bulwark against communism."
> —Farley Mowat, *And No Birds Sang*

The noun *connivance* similarly means 'the act or fact of conniving, a refraining from taking action':

> With the connivance of Roosevelt a revolution was staged in Panama. . . .
> —J. T. Adams, *The Epic of America*

But *connive* is now often used in the much simpler active sense 'to contrive, conspire, intrigue':

> In one of the shows Alda likes best, Hawkeye connives to send the innocent Radar to Japan for a little "R & R." . . .
> —George Vecsey, *Reader's Digest*

> . . . last year the government expelled Soviet diplomats who connived with local communists in disrupting the economy by strikes.
> —David Reed, *Reader's Digest*

◇ ***Recommendation.*** The use of *connive* to mean 'contrive, conspire, intrigue' is too widespread to be condemned as an error. However, *connive at* can still be used in its original, subtler sense 'to wink at, stand idly by and allow something deplorable to be done.' The understanding and right use of such fine-tuned words is one of the pleasures of language.

consensus. The misspelling *concensus* sometimes occurs, showing that there is a mistaken tendency to associate *consensus* with *census*. In fact, this word contains the Latin word *sensus* = 'feeling, sense'; *consensus* is 'a feeling together, shared opinion, general agreement':

> As a football player Namath came to the pros with more ability to play the quarterback position than any man who has yet lived. This is not my statement alone; it is the consensus of the most expert minds in football. . . .
> —Howard Cosell, *Cosell*

> There is a consensus, too, that a vasectomy is not a good idea if the wife objects to it.
> —Joan Rattner Heilman, *Reader's Digest*

In politics, consensus is the ever-desirable state of agreement on an issue by a majority, typically bipartisan and involving compromise and trade-offs:

> Culver's intention is to accept as many amendments as he can without undermining the purposes of the bill, in order to build the broadest possible consensus behind it.
> —Elizabeth Drew, *Senator*

The adjective is *consensual:*

> Presenting himself to the people as a master technician, a consensual leader who could produce something for everyone without cost to everyone . . .
> —Doris Kearns, *Lyndon Johnson and the American Dream*

◇ ***Recommendation.*** Don't use the phrase *consensus of opinion*. It is both a redundancy and a cliché.

consummate. This word is both an adjective and a verb. The adjective is pronounced /kən-**sŭm**-ət/. Based on Latin *consummātus* = 'all added together, summed up,' it means 'complete, perfect, one-hundred-percent':

> Ross was in awe of him because, for all Irvin's Western background, he seemed so much the consummate Eastern insider.
> —Brendan Gill, *Here at The New Yorker*

Used of persons as practitioners of skill, it means 'very accomplished, exquisitely skillful':

> [Big Minh was] a consummate politician with genuine charisma for the Vietnamese people . . .
> —William C. Westmoreland, *A Soldier Reports*

> From the first arc of his bow, Perlman becomes the consummate virtuoso, simultaneously in command of the music and relaxed enough to let it sing.
> —Annalyn Swan, *Reader's Digest*

The verb *consummate* is pronounced /**kŏn**-sə-māt/ and means 'to bring to completion.' Used of deals, alliances, etc., it means simply 'to complete, achieve':

> The pro-football merger had been consummated. The first Super Bowl game was to be played in January 1967. . . .
> —Howard Cosell, *Cosell*

Of marriage, or of unmarried persons living together, it means 'to complete (the relationship) by the first act of full sexual intercourse':

> . . . he felt that the story would work as well if the young couple's lovemaking was not actually consummated.
> —David Jacobs, *Panorama*

Referring to abstract qualities, *consummate* means 'to bring to the highest level, put the final touch to':

> . . . a man who had not only deserted his wife and child, but had consummated his iniquity by going off to live with another woman.
> —Thomas Wolfe, *The Web and the Rock*

contact. To make new words by turning nouns into verbs is a normal and long-established process in English. In this century it has been done more and more, perhaps especially in American English. The verb *contact* = 'to get in touch with (someone)' first appeared in the 1920s. At that time British purists were beginning to feel seriously threatened by the rising prestige and influence of American English. The verb *contact* was quickly noticed and identified as a new and frightful Americanism. Many Americans, especially of the anglophile literary establishment, followed suit and poured condemnation on the new verb. Other word watchers in both countries accepted it, pointing out that it is an eminently useful word, since it covers all forms of communication—letter, telephone, telex, personal appearance, or any combination of these. The only synonymous alternative is the phrase *get in touch with,* which many people now would regard as less crisp than *contact. Contact* is, in fact, an indispensable word in business, industry, and government; it is also used in everyday speech and is in respectable literary usage in all English-speaking countries, as the following quotations demonstrate:

> Demosthenes emerged and, contacting Darius and his leading satraps, offered . . .
>
> —Mary Renault, *The Nature of Alexander*

> Frau Hoffmann . . . was writing about the women in Hitler's life when I contacted her.
>
> —David Pryce-Jones, *Unity Mitford*

Nonetheless, even though it has been part of the language for more than half a century, the word is still strongly disliked and avoided by an old-fashioned but influential minority.

◇ ***Recommendation.*** The verb *contact* is entirely standard on all levels of usage. Those who dislike it are entitled to avoid it in their own usage, but to penalize or disapprove of someone else for using it is nothing but prejudice.

continual, continuous. (1) Of the two words, only *continuous* refers to continuity through space: *a continuous zone of warm oceanic water; a continuous line of cars. Continual* cannot be used in this sense.
(2) Both adjectives, and their adverbs (*continually, continuously*), refer to continuity through time. In clear contexts many careful writers distinguish between the two, using *continuous* to mean 'going on without a break, unceasing,' and *continual* to mean 'going on repeatedly, occurring at frequent intervals':

> The rains have been almost continuous; water stands everywhere.
>
> —E. B. White, *The Points of My Compass*

> Continual rains flooded the rivers in the army's northward path. . . .
>
> —Burke Davis, *Sherman's March*

These two writers conscientiously signal that the rains did not continue without any break; they were either "continual" or "almost continuous."

> Since about that time, war had been literally continuous, though strictly speaking it had not always been the same war.
>
> —George Orwell, *1984*

Even though there was a change of enemy, the state of warfare continued with no pause.

> There is evidence that marshes behind barrier beaches, especially older ones, can be eroded by continual wave action in a large bay.
>
> —Paul J. Godfrey, *Oceanus 1976*

The wave action does not go on all the time, but it is renewed in various states of wind and tide.

But many activities cannot be so neatly pinned down:

> What is needed now is massive, continual support for smokers who want to stop. . . .
>
> —Gwenda Blair, *Reader's Digest*

Does this mean that gestures of support are to be made at frequent intervals? Or that support is to be generally ongoing in the whole community? The answer is, it could mean one or the other, depending on the writer's frame of mind. Either *continuous* or *continual* could be justified here. Quite possibly, *continuous* was rejected merely because the next word begins with *s*.

> There had been continuous fighting or marching for more than two weeks. . . .
>
> Bruce Catton,
> *A Stillness at Appomattox*

Here the historian is telling us that at every moment throughout the two weeks there was fighting or marching, although obviously the individual soldiers and units had pauses for eating and sleeping. He wishes to emphasize the overall unbearable continuity of stress and exhaustion and therefore chooses the stronger word "continuous."

Furthermore, many good writers ignore the distinction entirely:

> The cicadas sang their grating song with a frenzied energy; it was as continual and monotonous as the rustling of a brook over the stones. . . .
>
> —W. Somerset Maugham,
> *The Force of Circumstances*

Maugham may have tried *continuous and monotonous* and rejected it because of the unpleasing combination of sounds. In any case, the meaning can't be mistaken: the cicadas trilled without ceasing. Likewise, *continuous* and *continuously* are often used of activities that are clearly repeated rather than unceasing:

> Among my family and friends, I was accustomed to a continuous manifestation of high spirits in the form of badinage, laughter, and intermittent bursts of song and whistling.
>
> —Brendan Gill,
> *Here at The New Yorker*

> . . . reports on the scandal had been given to him continuously for nine months. . . .
>
> —Alistair Cooke,
> *The Americans*

◇ ***Recommendation.*** The distinction between *continuous* = 'going on without a break' and *continual* = 'going on repeatedly' is a counsel of perfection. You may like to try to live up to it whenever possible, but you are free to ignore it.

contractions. The contracted forms in commonest use in standard speech are (1) those of the present tense of *be* (*I'm, you're, he's, she's, it's, we're, they're*); (2) those of the auxiliary verb *will* (*I'll, you'll, he'll, she'll, we'll, they'll*); and (3) the negative auxiliaries (*isn't, aren't, wasn't, weren't, won't, can't, couldn't, wouldn't, shouldn't, doesn't, didn't, haven't, hasn't, hadn't, mustn't*). The conservative position is never to use contractions in writing (except when representing speech). Most people use them in informal writings such as personal letters, and many now also use them in business letters, reportage, and creative literature. Judicious use of the contracted forms can give a relaxed and mildly informal tone in all but the most ceremonial contexts. Occasionally, contracted and possessive forms are confused. See IT'S, ITS; POSSESSIVES. See also AIN'T; AREN'T I?

contrary-to-fact condition. This is a common use of the subjunctive. See SUBJUNCTIVE.

cosmopolitan. The Greek Cynic philosopher Diogenes, who despised luxury and believed in living as simply as possible, was asked from what city he came. He answered, "I am a world-citizen," meaning that he regarded nationality as trivial and preferred to be considered simply as a member of the worldwide human race. The word he used was *kosmopolītēs*, from *kosmos* = 'world' + *polītēs* = 'citizen.' It has been revived in the adjective *cosmopolitan*, originally meaning 'reflecting world culture, not restricted by the narrowness of nationalism or chauvinism, not parochial':

> The legislation of this country should become more catholic and cosmopolitan than that of any other.
>
> —Ralph Waldo Emerson,
> *Lectures* (1844)

It is also used to mean 'showing an interesting and tolerant mixture of distinct national cultures':

> Always [St. Petersburg/Leningrad] had been different from the rest of Russia, more cosmopolitan, more European, a mixture of non-Slav peoples, Germans, Swedes, Dutch, English, French and Italian.
>
> —Harrison E. Salisbury, *The Unknown War*

Referring to people, it now often means 'well-traveled, at home in many countries'; as a noun it means 'sophisticated person who travels a lot':

> Today, affluent cosmopolitans flock to the rococo pleasure dome [Maxim's restaurant in Paris] . . . to see and be seen. Rothschilds, Vanderbilts and Mellons, they've dined here by the squadron. Aristotle Onassis called it his "canteen." The Duke and Duchess of Windsor almost lived at No. 16, the Royal Table. The Aga Khan, Prince Rainier and his Grace, Elizabeth Taylor, Salvador Dali and his pet ocelot—name them, they've been here.
>
> —Christopher Lucas, *Reader's Digest*

These glittering jet setters are a far cry from the angry old philosopher who insisted on living in a barrel. But words once coined go into the fluctuating stream of usage, and the coiners own no patents to keep the terms to their original meanings. Even so, a pristine flavor or an underlying truth often lingers. All, in the end, are cosmopolitans and world citizens—Diogenes, Dali, and the rest of us.

cottage cheese. This is the commonest name for the soft, unripened cheese made from soured skim milk. It is now industrially produced, but before refrigeration it was universally made in the home by farmers or anyone who kept even one cow or a few goats. *Cottage cheese* is especially interesting in American English because of the many different terms that have been used for it throughout the older parts of the United States. Many of these terms are still current.

Two widespread terms in New England are *curd cheese* and *sour milk cheese.* The Standard British word, *curds,* can also be heard in New England, while in the Southern dialect this has been shortened to *curd,* though *curds* and *curd cheese* are also used in the South. In addition, the Gulf Southern dialect calls it *cream cheese,* which in most parts of the country means something quite different. In scattered areas cottage cheese is also known as *farmer's cheese* and *clabber cheese,* the latter an extension of the regional term for 'sour milk' (see CLABBER).

Cottage cheese was a favorite food of German and Dutch settlers, and several of its regional names derive from those languages. In the North Midland dialect, for example, *smearcase* /**smîr**-kās/ or *shmearcase* /**shmîr**-kās/ is still a common name. It was originally the Pennsylvania Dutch term *schmierkas,* which means literally 'spread or smear cheese,' because it was often spread on bread or toast.

> Now were deployed before appreciative eyes the callow chicken, the odoriferous onion, and . . . loaf bread flanked by appetizing apple-butter, snowy smear-kase, and dulcet honey.
>
> —*Scribner's Magazine* (1879)

The German *bibbeleskäs,* pronounced in Chicago and other areas as /**bĭp**-lĭ-kās/, and the Czech *smetlak* /**smĕt**-lăk/ are occasionally used in places where German and Czech immigrants settled.

In the Hudson Valley region, which was originally settled by the Dutch, the usual term is *pot cheese*, an alteration of Dutch *pot kees*. The earliest known written use of this word is humorously metaphorical:

> Tell me, thou heart of cork . . . and brain of potcheese, what will you do when Bull sends his boats over to plunder your farms.
>
> —James K. Paulding, *The Diverting History of John Bull and Brother Jonathan* (1812)

Dutch cheese is the term for cottage cheese in the Inland Northern dialect. A rather squeamish Pennsylvania writer wrote in 1829 that

> while standing in the market, I saw a great curiosity, called Dutch cheese. . . . It is made from curds and skimmed milk, and is not very tempting.
>
> —Anne Royall, *Mrs. Royall's Pennsylvania*

council, counsel. These are occasionally confused. A *council* is a meeting for discussion, or a permanent committee or assembly. *Counsel* is the process of discussion or consultation; formal advice resulting from discussion; or any kind of advice. In legal usage a lawyer or group of lawyers giving advice and representing a client in litigation can be called *counsel* (plural as well as singular).

coyote = 'small North American wolf.' The pronunciations /kī-**ō**-tē/ and /**kī**-ōt/ are equally correct.

credible, creditable. *Credible* means 'worthy of belief, believable': *a credible account of her adventures.* The meaning of creditable is 'deserving credit, praiseworthy': *We can count on Vogel to do a creditable job.*

creole languages. See PIDGIN AND CREOLE LANGUAGES.

criterion /krī-**tîr**-ē-ən/ = 'standard for making judgments, measure against which to judge anything' is from Greek (it is related to *critical*). The ending *-on* is that of a Greek neuter singular noun. The plural is *criteria* or, equally correct, *criterions:*

> King Edward's habits were accepted as the criterion of sophisticated European elegance before the lights went out in 1914.
>
> —Philip Magnus, *Edward VII*

> From first to last, he remained an admirable amateur reviewer of plays, and his criterion in judging a particular work was simply the measure of his enjoyment of it. . . .
>
> —Brendan Gill, *Here at The New Yorker*

> We know more today about criteria for analyzing than we did in the past. . . . Our crude criterion for success is whether or not the patient stays in treatment.
>
> —Janet Malcolm, *The New Yorker*

The form *criteria* is now frequently used as a singular:

> Certainly no one in full possession of all his faculties can claim that Oswald didn't fall within this criteria.
>
> —J. Edgar Hoover, *Reader's Digest*

> In Korea's case, the State Dept. was forced to resort to the fourth criteria, which essentially allows the government to grant permission to fish to any nation it decides is deserving.
>
> —*National Fisherman*

> The folk on the bus apply a special criteria to judging national campaigns that really has little to do with personalities or issues.
>
> —Hal Gulliver, *Atlanta Constitution*

◇ ***Recommendation.*** It sometimes happens that the plural of a noun becomes an acceptable singular. This is not such a case. To use *criteria* as singular is a definite mistake. (For more on plural forms of foreign-language words see PLURALS.)

critique /krĭ-**tēk**/ = 'review, critical discussion' is from a French noun meaning 'critical discussion, criticism':

> There are two further points I would make, supplementing the critique of the religious peace movement I made in that article.
>
> —George S. Weigel, Jr., *National Catholic Reporter*

The word is now increasingly used as a verb meaning 'to discuss and review, criticize, evaluate':

> [ABC has] announcers on the course with hand-held mikes who critique the lies and the shots.
>
> —Marlene Floyd, *Golf Digest*

Nixon critiqued the dinner as if it had been a major military battle.
—H. R. Haldeman, *The Ends of Power*

Women have better palates than men because they are constantly critiquing their own cooking.
—Frank J. Prial, *New York Times Magazine*

◇ ***Recommendation.*** Many a noun turns into a perfectly legitimate verb. This one is still being resisted, but we guess it will establish itself. For the time being it's in limbo. Use it if you wish, but be aware that many people dislike it.

crony, originally recorded as university slang in England, means 'close companion, long-time friend':

I came to the Writers' Club the next day and told my cronies that I had met Kava's wife. . . .
—Isaac Bashevis Singer, *Atlantic Monthly*

Journalists use the word insinuatingly of friendships in business and politics, frequently implying that someone is doing questionable favors:

Last year, Johnson and a Las Vegas crony . . . cooked up plans for a 3,000-room joint-venture resort on the outskirts of the city. —*Business Week*

That information is what Rinaldo is said to have passed along to several other presidential hopefuls who also happen to be his present and former cronies in Congress.
—Harvey Fisher, *New Jersey Monthly*

Hence *cronyism* = 'the practice of appointing unqualified friends to public office':

The vice of cronyism is nowhere more clearly demonstrated than in the suspicions aroused by the Bert Lance sale of a portion of his bank shares at a premium price to a prominent Saudi Arabian.
—Wallace M. Cohen (letter), *New York Times*

czar. The Russian form of this word is *tsar,* which is still technically correct when referring to Russian emperors. But *czar,* the Polish spelling, is now more generally used. For the etymology, see RUSSIAN WORDS. Before the Revolution of 1917, the czar or tsar ruled the Russian empire as an absolute autocrat, not as a constitutional monarch. The word has thus become a metaphor for a man wielding exceptionally unrestrained power; especially, a government official given authority that overrides various departments:

But the creation of an overall intelligence czar with Cabinet-level status is being considered favorably. —*Time*

Japan's economic czar Mr. Takeo Fukuda . . . —*The Australian*

At this point, the limits-to-growth crowd can be expected to rush in with armloads of studies calling for a Department of Water, with a czar to determine who will get what water at what price.
—William Safire, *New York Times*

D

dais = 'platform for speakers, etc., in a hall or room.' This word has a variety of pronunciations: /dās/, /dīs/, /**dā**-ĭs/, and /**dī**-ĭs/. We recommend /**dā**-ĭs/.

dangling phrases. A phrase containing a subject and a participle can correctly function as an independent, clauselike part of a sentence; see ABSOLUTE PHRASES. However, a phrase containing a participle but no subject cannot ordinarily stand as an absolute:

> I was shocked a few weeks ago when, having been press-ganged by movie-magazine addicts and chained in front of a television tube, this extraordinary phenomenon revealed itself. . . .
> —Russell Baker, *New York Times*

Here the phrase "having been press-ganged . . . tube" has no subject of its own and is clearly intended as an ordinary participial phrase attached to "I." But since "I" is not the subject of the subordinate clause in which the phrase appears ("when . . . this extraordinary phenomenon revealed itself"), the participle "having been press-ganged" has no legitimate connection in the sentence structure and is thus a *dangling phrase.*

There are generally three ways to eliminate this type of dangler. The first is to give it a subject of its own and turn it into a proper absolute phrase: "when, I having been press-ganged, the phenomenon revealed itself." This would be correct but awkward. Pronouns are now seldom used as subjects of absolute phrases. A better solution is to recast part of the sentence so that the participial phrase has a subject to depend on: "when, having been press-ganged, I witnessed this phenomenon." Best of all, in most cases, is to turn the participial phrase into a clause with a conjunction, a subject, and a predicate: "when, after I had been press-ganged, this phenomenon revealed itself."

Another example:

> On the table beside the bed . . . was a small bunch of flowers in a blue vase. Touching them, they crumbled in her fingers.
> —William Faulkner, *Sartoris*

This could be rewritten "When she touched them, they crumbled" or "She touched them, and they crumbled."

Note that a participial phrase at the beginning of a sentence can generally qualify only the subject of the sentence:

> Being absolutely exhausted by the ride, he decided to go no further that day.
> —J. C. Clifford, *Home From the Hill*

This is correct sentence structure, with the initial phrase properly connected to the subject of the sentence. But very often a sentence is begun with a phrase in anticipation of a suitable subject and is then given a different subject, leaving the phrase to dangle:

> With a neck-cracking jerk the car leaped forward. Never a timorous woman, their speed now seemed to her to be maniacal.
> —Edna Ferber, *Giant*

The second sentence was presumably at first visualized as something like "Never a timorous woman, she now found their speed maniacal." But "speed" actually emerged as the subject of the sentence, and in modern usage an initial phrase like "Never a timorous woman" cannot qualify an indirect object like "her." In the past, however, such usage was acceptable:

> Uncommonly conscientious for a seaman, and endued with a deep natural reverence, the wild watery loneliness of his life did therefore strongly incline him to superstition.
> —Herman Melville, *Moby-Dick*

Here the two opening phrases are considered to go with the object of the sentence, "him." But the convention has changed, and a modern editor would probably correct Melville's prose.

Further examples of phrases that dangle even though the words they modify are expressed in the sentence:

> A sailor of vast experience, this was by no means the first convoy which he had escorted to Murmansk.
> —C. S. Forester, *Saturday Evening Post*

"A sailor of vast experience" belongs with "he." One solution is to reposition the phrase: "This was by no means the first convoy which he, a sailor of vast experience, had escorted to Murmansk." Another involves slightly more revision: "He was a sailor of vast experience, and this was by no means the first convoy which he had escorted to Murmansk."

> Originally carvel planked, Bob elected to strip-plank the hull in rebuilding.
> —*Wooden Boat*

"Originally carvel planked" modifies "hull," not "Bob." To make this clearer, the writer could have revised the sentence in this manner: "In rebuilding, Bob elected to strip-plank the hull, which had originally been carvel planked."

Exceptions. A group of common participles have been found so useful in parenthetical phrases that the rule against danglers has not been applied to them. Among these frequently used participles are *admitting, assuming, barring, considering, counting, depending, excluding, including, leaving, speaking,* and *supposing.*

> Assuming you're right, that's all we can expect to achieve.

> Considering the amount of money involved, it's not worth the trouble.

> Excluding unpaid commitments, the total takings were nearly $400.

> There are, broadly speaking, only two alternatives.

These constitute an established idiom and are considered correct. Some constructions of this kind have been used so much that they have to all intents and purposes become prepositions or conjunctions. See DUE TO; PROVIDED, PROVIDING.

◇ ***Recommendation.*** Dangling phrases are among the commonest errors in modern English sentence structure and are never acceptable, apart from the exceptions noted.

dare. A special idiom governs the usage of *dare* in the third person singular. In most cases the form is, quite regularly, *dares: If she dares to deny your request, show her the letter.* But when followed by an infinitive without *to*, especially when negative and in questions, the form is usually *dare: She dare not ask. Dare he attempt it?* This also applies when the infinitive is left out but implied: *No, he dare not.*

DARE. See DICTIONARY OF AMERICAN REGIONAL ENGLISH.

dash. See PUNCTUATION.

dashiki /dä-**shē**-kē/. This is a loose, buttonless, brightly patterned West African pullover shirt. It was introduced into the United States in the late 1960s. The word is borrowed from Yoruba *danshiki.* (See also AFRICAN WORDS.)

data is the (Latin) plural of *datum* = 'given fact, piece of information.' The word *data* is now used both as a true plural, meaning 'facts, pieces, or organized sets of information,' and as a singular collective noun, or mass noun, meaning 'information.'

> ERDA also points to a number of questions for which, it says, the data are simply not yet available. . . .
> —Allen L. Hammond, *Science*

> Data from these weather satellites have been used for such diverse purposes as . . .
> —Richard D. Lyons, *New York Times*

> Such data supplies the Department of Energy with information. . . .
> —*Smithsonian*

> . . . data shows that a significant portion of the Southeastern Alaska King

> salmon catch originates in the waters of Washington and Oregon.
>
> —*National Fisherman*

◇ ***Recommendation.*** Both of these uses are correct and standard.

deaf. In 1789 Noah Webster wrote:

> *Deaf* is generally pronounced *deef.* It is the universal practice in the eastern states; and it is general in the middle and southern; tho some have adopted the English pronunciation, *def.* The latter is evidently a corruption. . . .
>
> —*Dissertations on the English Language*

Webster was swimming against the tide, even in his own day. The pronunciation /dēf/ still survives in some dialectal speech, but /dĕf/ is now the only standard pronunciation.

dean, doyen. These are cognate forms of the same word—*deien* in Medieval French, *doyen* in Modern French, both descended from Latin *decanus* = 'leader of ten.' *Doyen* is pronounced either /**doi**-ən/ or /dwȧ-yäɴ/. As a church title *dean* is the only form of the word, for the clergyman who heads a cathedral or for one who supervises several parishes within a diocese. *Dean* is also the only form as an academic title, for an officer who supervises a student body, faculty, school of a university, or college.

Both *doyen* and *dean* are used as an unofficial title for the senior ambassador of the diplomatic corps in a particular capital, who speaks or acts for the whole corps on occasions involving problems of protocol, etc.

> The same day, the Netherlands Minister, Baron van Swinderen, doyen of the Diplomatic Corps and a man of unrivalled experience in his profession, asked to see me. . . .
>
> —Anthony Eden, *The Reckoning*

> There are 42 Canadians serving here [Moscow] under Ambassador Robert Ford, the dean of the diplomatic corps.
>
> —Robert Trumbull, *New York Times*

Chiefly *dean,* but sometimes *doyen,* is used of anyone who is preeminent in some profession or field of activity.

> Lieutenant General W. J. Hardee, the dean of American military scholars and author of a text on tactics used by both armies, took command in Macon.
>
> —Burke Davis, *Sherman's March*

> . . . *ex cathedra* pronouncements from Andrew Sarris, the dean of American film critics . . .
>
> —Bruce McCabe, *Boston Globe*

> . . . Walter Cronkite . . . his responsibilities as the doyen of television journalists.
>
> —Gary Paul Gates, *Air Time*

Doyen has the advantage, if it is an advantage, of having a feminine form, *doyenne,* /**doi**-ĕn, doi-**ĕn**/, or /dwȧ-**yĕn**/.

> . . . follow the advice of Mrs. Isabella Beaton, the doyenne of Victorian cooking.
>
> —R. W. Apple, Jr., *New York Times*

Dear Sir or Madam. Traditionally, many business letters have begun with the singular salutation *Dear Sir* or the plural *Gentlemen.* These forms of address made sense in the days when men wrote and received most business letters. Now, however, masculine salutations when the sex of the recipient is unknown seem outdated or inappropriate, as though a speaker looked out at an audience of women and men and addressed them simply as "gentlemen." This doesn't happen on the podium, but it does happen on the page. Businesswomen are weary of receiving letters addressed *Dear Sir.* Writers of sales letters run a particular risk in assuming that all their customers are male. They can quickly alienate half their potential market if they adopt a *Dear Sir* or *you and your wife* approach. A woman reading such a letter may put away her checkbook once she realizes the message isn't directed to her.

◇ ***Recommendation.*** There is as yet no perfect solution to the problem of addressing an unknown recipient, but there are several workable ones.

(1) You can skip a salutation altogether by using memo style.

Director of Marketing
Amalgamated Widget Company
Gary, Indiana
To the Director:

(2) You can also salute a businessperson by title or function.

Dear Director:

(3) You can address an organization or corporation by name, as an entity.

Dear Reader's Digest:
Dear IBM:

(4) You can use an inclusive formal salutation in the singular.

Dear Madam or Sir:
or
Dear Sir or Madam:

(5) Depending on the context, you can adopt an inclusive plural salutation.

Ladies and Gentlemen:

(6) You can fall back on a traditional and serviceable form.

To Whom It May Concern:

Sometimes a telephone call to the place of business will provide the name of a person in a certain position. Then the letter can be safely addressed: *Dear Mr. Fishwick; Dear Ms. Carlson;* etc. (See also FORMS OF ADDRESS; MISS, MRS., MS.; PARALLEL STYLE.)

debacle /dĭ-**bäk′**l, dā-/. This word literally means 'the breaking up of ice on a frozen river' and 'the rush of water, ice, and debris that may follow such an event.' Hence, in old-fashioned military language *debacle* meant 'the sudden breakup and rout of a body of troops.' It now generally means 'any total defeat or disaster':

> . . . the American debacle at home which he saw as the consequence of our intervention in Vietnam.
> —Brendan Gill, *Here at The New Yorker*

> Bush summed up his New Hampshire debacle in a post-primary phone call to Reagan: "Ron, congratulations, sir. You beat the hell out of me." —*Time*

debark, disembark = 'to get out of or unload from a vessel, vehicle, or plane.' Both forms are in use, with *debark* tending to prevail in the armed forces and *disembark* probably preferred by civilians.

debouch. The usual pronunciation is /dĭ-**bo͞osh**/, but some use /dĭ-**bouch**/. The meaning, applied especially to troops, is 'to move out from a confined space into the open':

> . . . a column of horse-drawn wagons which had debouched from the Naoussa road . . .
> —Eric Ambler, *The Schirmer Inheritance*

Used of routes, pathways, rivers, etc., the word means 'to come out into the open':

> . . . a narrow stairway debouching between two stores, beneath an array of dingy professional signs.
> —William Faulkner, *Sartoris*

decimate. Roman commanders sometimes punished mutinous troops by decimating them; that is, by executing one man in ten, the victims being selected by lot. *Decimate* has long been used as a metaphor of heavy slaughter of any kind—in battle, by disease, etc. Except in the original context, no particular proportion is implied. The word now generally means 'to kill or destroy in terrible numbers or quantities':

> We participated in the famous "Turkey Shoot" in the Marianas, during which we decimated the enemy's forces.
> —Gerald R. Ford, *A Time to Heal*

> Speaking of the disease which had decimated the savages around Plymouth

before the Pilgrims landed, a Puritan characteristically noted that "by this means Christ made room for this people to plant."
—J. T. Adams, *The Epic of America*

Soldiers decimated Uganda's wildlife herds.
—David Lamb, *Reader's Digest*

On the plus side, the U.S. regained control of its offshore resources, which were being decimated by heavy-fishing foreign fleets. —*National Fisherman*

de facto, de jure. In legal usage these are Latin adverbial phrases meaning, respectively, 'in fact, actually' and 'in law, legally.' In general usage they are used as adjectives meaning 'actual but not legally recognized' and 'legal, legally defined or recognized':

I'm not especially delighted by our *de facto* apartheid, let alone South Africa's *de jure* species.
—Studs Terkel, *Talking to Myself*

Tokyo's recognition of Peking's *de jure* sovereignty over Taiwan has proved compatible with Taiwan's *de facto* autonomy.
—John K. Fairbank, *New York Times*

Although in these examples both terms are italicized, they—and many other expressions from Latin—are more and more seen in regular (roman) type. As with most Latin terms, several different pronunciations are used. Probably the commonest are the fully anglicized /dĭ **făk**-tō/ and /dĭ **jŏŏr**-ē/. For Latin pronunciation in general see LATIN WORDS; for additional legal usages see LEGAL TERMS.

defect, deficiency. In common usage these two nouns are largely synonymous, but *deficiency* also has an area of use not shared by *defect.* Both usually mean 'imperfection, failure, flaw, fault':

It is a conventional defect of journalism that one so often fails to learn the end of a story. . . . —Brendan Gill,
Here at The New Yorker

Deficiencies in air bags appear in both types of tests.
—Earl and Miriam Selby,
Reader's Digest

The basis for making a choice between the two words is often elusive, but probably *deficiency* is more often chosen when the writer is thinking of the fault as due to a lack. The following quotations, from a much-admired stylist, seem to illustrate this.

And when the U.N. wanted to send observers in [to Hungary in 1956] it received a polite no. This is palpably ridiculous, and it boils down to a deficiency in the Charter. . . .

. . . Among its other defects, the Charter is virtually amendment-proof.
—E. B. White,
The Points of My Compass

Deficiency can also have the more distinct sense 'a falling short, inadequate supply, insufficiency':

Let us suppose you have certain nutritional deficiencies and think perhaps better food might help.
—Adelle Davis,
Let's Eat Right to Keep Fit

de jure. See DE FACTO, DE JURE.

delectable. It is claimed that no two words can be absolutely synonymous—there will always be some reason for using one rather than the other, even if the reason is buried in the speaker's or writer's unconscious. *Delectable* is related to both *delicious* and *delightful,* and is largely synonymous with either. Even so, if only because it is rarer and perhaps because of some quality of its sound, *delectable* has a flavor all its own:

I consider the mango and the papaya two of the most delectable fruits with which God graced an already bountiful world. —Euell Gibbons,
Stalking the Wild Asparagus

I didn't get the impression that I'd swept her off her feet. But I knew quite well she had swept me off mine. It's a strange sort of indescribably delectable elation. —Mike Douglas, *My Story*

ally started allowing ordinary Chinese into the place. —John Fraser, *Book Digest*

demur, demurrer, demurrage. The underlying meaning of *demur* /dĭ-**mêr**/ is 'to delay.' In law, to demur or enter a *demurrer* is to seek to dismiss or delay an action on legal grounds while admitting that the facts alleged may be true. *Demurrage* /dĭ-**mêr**-ĭj/ is the delaying of an unloading ship or other freight carrier beyond the time allowed; the demurrage is also the fee payable for this.

In general use, to demur to a proposition is to raise objections, hesitate, or have doubts, without directly opposing or refusing it:

> . . . I proposed to Zeitlin that Kava write it. At first Zeitlin demurred. "Kava, of all people?" he said. "First of all it would take him a year or two. Secondly, he will make mincemeat out of everybody. . . ."
> —Isaac Bashevis Singer, *Atlantic Monthly*

> In late August I asked for approval of combined American-South Vietnamese air strikes against specific targets in the panhandle, but Washington demurred.
> —William C. Westmoreland, *A Soldier Reports*

dénouement /dā-**nōō**-mäɴ, dā-nōō-**mäɴ**/ in French means 'the untying of a knot.' In English it is now often written without the accent. As a literary term the *dénouement* is the final unraveling or resolution of a plot, and hence in general the often-surprising outcome of a story or sequence of events.

> At the conclusion of all this drama and excitement, the Channel 7 "Eyewitness News" reporter provided the story's true denouement: the suspect was not the real murderer. He was an innocent man.
> —Ron Powers, *The Newscasters*

> The farce of the International Club reached an ironic denouement several months later when the authorities actually started allowing ordinary Chinese into the place. —John Fraser, *Book Digest*

deprecate, depreciate. These words are unrelated but have become confused.

(1) The literal meaning of *deprecate* is 'to pray against (something), wish to prevent or avert.' This is now somewhat old-fashioned but will often be encountered in literature:

> The friends of humanity will deprecate war, wheresoever it may appear. . . .
> —George Washington, letter (1793)

> See how a sleepy child will put off the inevitable departure for bed . . . he is quite worn out, and peevish, and stupid, and yet he implores a respite, and deprecates repose, and vows he is not sleepy. . . .
> —J. S. Le Fanu, *Uncle Silas* (1864)

The usual current meaning is 'to disapprove of (something) and try to prevent it' or generally 'to deplore':

> Knollys and Fisher deprecated all talk in the royal circle about compulsory military training, which they regarded as ridiculous.
> —Philip Magnus, *Edward VII*

> Linguists tend to deprecate popular use of such [nontechnical] works, but not to provide viable alternatives for laymen in need of practical information.
> —J. L. Dillard, *All-American English*

> . . . there are few jobs for women more deprecated in the Moslem world than nursing.
> —Frank J. Prial, *New York Times*

Deprecate is also correctly used in a milder sense, of modestly disclaiming credit or discounting praise, or politely contradicting someone.

> While Freeman, a very modest man, deprecated the idea that he was years ahead of applied police criminology, he was pleased at having anticipated the professionals in dust analysis, examina-

> tion of blood, footprint preservation and other techniques.
> —E. F. Bleiler, *The Best Dr. Thorndyke Detective Stories*

> Depending on his mood and the nature of the audience, Johnson told the story different ways. On some occasions, he tended to deprecate his own role in the mission, insisting that he was not really the one who should have received the Silver Star.
> —Doris Kearns, *Lyndon Johnson and the American Dream*

The adjective *deprecatory* means, first, 'wishing to avert something' and, second, 'politely apologetic.'

> He used to nod many times to her and smile when she came in, and utter inarticulate deprecatory moans when she was going away.
> —William Makepeace Thackeray, *Vanity Fair*

> She would utter on these occasions some pretty and deprecatory remark on the necessity of her troubling him anew. . . . —Thomas Hardy, *The Distracted Preacher*

> Having briefed the company commanders he turned to me with his usual rather deprecatory manner. "I say, Squib . . . perhaps you'd better take the lead yourself."
> —Farley Mowat, *And No Birds Sang*

The participial adjective *deprecating* is used chiefly in the sense of politely contradicting someone, often only implicitly:

> "I'm afraid my doings are very small beer compared with yours." As there was no possible answer to this but a deprecating laugh, Harriet laughed deprecatingly.
> —Dorothy L. Sayers, *Gaudy Night*

We have given so many examples of *deprecate* in its several proper senses because it can be a subtle and useful word. But it is now often used as a synonym of *depreciate*. This was at first a mere mistake, or MALAPROPISM; in the following quotation Thackeray, who knew the correct meaning, shows how a smooth-talking, ill-educated auctioneer misuses it.

> "Don't be trying to deprecate the value of the lot, Mr. Moss," Mr. Hammerdown said. . . . —*Vanity Fair*

As often happens with malapropisms, this one has gained legitimacy by wide usage, and many people are unaware that *deprecate* means anything but 'to belittle, disparage.'

> . . . those who deprecate a director for turning his hand to a commercial or two . . .
> —Mike Harris, *The Australian*

This use is especially common with the compound adjectives *self-deprecating* and *self-deprecatory* and the noun *self-deprecation*, which are now most often used to mean, respectively, 'speaking modestly of oneself' and 'the action of doing this.'

> Despite his giftedness, he is perhaps the most self-deprecatory of journalists.
> —Studs Terkel, *Talking to Myself*

> Yet Henry told others that story about himself, in a self-deprecating way, and you had to like him for it.
> —William Safire, *Before the Fall*

> Indulging in characteristic self-deprecation, Mao said, "These writings aren't anything. There is nothing instructive in what I wrote."
> —Richard Nixon, *R.N.*

(2) *Depreciate* literally means 'to lower the price or value of (something), devalue,' as a government can depreciate a currency. Presently very familiar is the technical use in tax accountancy and business, 'to claim diminished value of (a capital asset) as a charge against taxable income.'

> So Barnes depreciated the auto carrier fleet as rapidly as possible and cut debt to a minimum. . . .
> —James Cook, *Forbes*

The generalized sense of *depreciate* is 'to belittle, speak disparagingly or modestly of':

> He depreciated his capacity either as a zoologist or as an artist, "in nothing am I professionally expert." . . .
> —George Seaver, *Edward Wilson of the Antarctic*

> She knew full well this cake was equal or superior to the standard of her baking, but it was proper to depreciate her skill while accepting the compliment.
> —Bessie Lewis, *To Save Their Souls*

Thus, *self-depreciation* (not *self-deprecation*) is the proper term for 'humble estimation of one's own worth, self-disparagement':

> To her nephew Edward she described her work, with humorous self-depreciation, as "that little bit (two inches wide) of ivory, in which I work with so fine a brush as produces little effect after much labour."
> —David Cecil, *A Portrait of Jane Austen*

◇ ***Recommendation.*** While recognizing that many people now prefer to use *deprecate*, especially in its derivatives, to mean 'disparage,' we recommend the proper and distinct uses of both *deprecate* and *depreciate*. Thus, one should *deprecate* only actions or abstractions, not people.

derby. The premier English flat horse race was founded by the 12th earl of Derby in 1780. It is for three-year-olds and is run more than a mile and a half on Epsom Downs in Surrey. There are other Derbies, such as the French Derby and the Kentucky Derby. The British pronunciation is /**dä**-bĭ/; the American, /**dêr**-bē/. The word is now also used for innumerable stunts and humorous races, including *soapbox derbies, roller derbies*, and *demolition derbies*. The *derby hat*, a round and rigid piece of headgear often with a curved brim, was probably named after the Kentucky Derby, as a promotional idea of American hat makers. Once popular with all classes, it is now little worn except by fox-hunting and show-jumping people and British businessmen. The British generally call it a *bowler*, after the London hatter *Beaulieu* (pronounced /**byo͞o**-lĭ/), who first made it about 1850. But an ultratraditionalist minority call it a *coke*, after William *Coke* (pronounced /ko͝ok/), the man who commissioned the first one from Beaulieu.

derisive, derisory. The fundamental meaning of *derisive* is 'expressing derision, laughing scornfully':

> After the first rush of derisive publicity women's liberation has adopted a suspicious and uncooperative attitude to the press. . . .
> —Germaine Greer, *The Female Eunuch*

Secondarily, it can mean 'ridiculously small, trifling':

> One remembers Washington and his generals and the statesmen buying up, for derisive sums, the land given the soldiery in lieu of pay.
> —John Keats, *Eminent Domain*

Derisory, a rarer word, is used in the same two senses. It would be more convenient if *derisive* were used only in the first sense and *derisory* reserved for the second.

desert, dessert. (1) The verb *desert* = 'to leave, abandon' is pronounced /dĭ-**zêrt**/.
(2) The noun *desert* = 'uninhabited dry wasteland' is pronounced /**dĕz**-ərt/.
(3) The noun *desert* = 'merit,' often in the plural *deserts* = 'what someone deserves,' is pronounced /dĭ-**zêrt**/.
(4) The noun *dessert* = 'last course of a meal' is pronounced /dĭ-**zêrt**/.

Etymologically, (1) and (2) are related: a *desert* is an area that is deserted, abandoned, uninhabited. Terms (3) and (4) are also related, although less directly; the connection is provided by the word *serve*. A person's *desert* is earned by deserving, service, serving. The *dessert* course originally came when the table was cleared—Old French *desservir* = 'to unserve, remove the service, clear the table.'

détente /dā-**tänt**/. This now-familiar word is a vestige of the time when most international diplomacy was conducted in French. *Détente* literally means 'a loosening, slackening,' and specifically 'an easing of tensions between two powers.' It is now most familiarly associated with relations between the United States and the Soviet Union.

> While Washington has worked out a détente with the Soviet Union and has established friendly relations with China, the Korean peninsula remains frozen in a classic cold war.
> —David Reed, *Reader's Digest*

diacritics. The adjective *diacritic* or *diacritical* means 'making a distinction,' and the noun *diacritic* means 'distinguishing mark on a letter.' Diacritics, or *diacritical marks*, are placed on both vowels and consonants. Within the broad category of diacritics are three marks called *accents*, which appear above certain vowels in French and some other languages: the *acute accent*, the *grave accent*, and the *circumflex*. Besides the accents, typical diacritics are the *dieresis* and the *cedilla*. These and other diacritical marks are discussed in this entry.

To a linguist a diacritic is a helpful device to alert readers that a letter so marked may have phonetic value that it doesn't ordinarily possess. For example, the spelling *expose* is normally construed as a two-syllable verb pronounced /ĭk-**spōz**/ and meaning 'to unmask, reveal.' However, when the spelling is *exposé*, the diacritic—an acute accent over the final *e*—transforms the word into a three-syllable noun pronounced /ĕk-spō-**zā**/ and meaning 'a disclosure of something scandalous or even criminal.'

But to many a nonlinguist, especially one pecking away on a conventional typewriter, diacritical marks are fussy bits of pedantry that will subsequently have to be inserted in the typescript by hand and—on balance—little nuisances that aren't worth the trouble. But before dismissing all diacritics, let us take a brief look at where they have come from and where they appear to be going.

Acute Accent. You will typically encounter an acute accent (´) atop the final *e* in a French word that is on its way to becoming thoroughly assimilated into the English language, as in the following:

attaché (case)	fiancé (masc.)
blasé	fiancée (fem.)
café	née
canapé	outré
cliché	passé
consommé	risqué
entrée	sauté

In words such as these the acute accent signals the reader that the final *e* is a distinct syllable (usually stressed and pronounced /ā/) and is not merely the silent *e* that ends so many English words.

This *é* also shows up in a number of other words derived from French; for example, *éclair; éclat; élan; précis*. In these words the acute accent serves simply to establish the phonetic value of the *e*. And in some words, one encounters the acute accent both within and at the end of the word: *décolleté; protégé; résumé;* etc. To be sure, the accent is disappearing from many of these words in English as they lose their French connection. Words like *cafe, divorcee, entree, matinee, melee,* and even *nee* (beloved locution of society news editors) now commonly appear without accents, and dictionaries hold different views on which form is predominant. In such circumstances either adopt one authority and follow it consistently, or make your own decisions on a selective basis. Indeed, of all the words shown above, there is only one for which we urge you to retain the accents: *résumé*. When you are applying for a job, you never know when a prospective employer may judge your spelling ability largely on whether you knew enough to put accents on both *e*'s. (Touché?)

Note that in Spanish words and names the acute accent does not affect vowel quality but indicates a stressed syllable, as in *México* /**mā**-hē-kō/.

Grave Accent /gräv, grāv/. This diacritic (`) typically appears over *a* and *e* in words and phrases of French origin. When such expressions retain at least part of their French coloration, the accents are retained as well:

pièce de résistance = originally 'main course of a meal,' hence 'showpiece, outstanding item'

pied-à-terre = literally 'foot to the ground,' hence 'secondary lodgings, temporary quarters'

vis-à-vis = literally 'face to face,' hence 'as compared with, in relation to'

However, in expressions such as *a la carte* and *a la mode* the accent over the first *a* has practically disappeared. (Voilà!) But see À LA.

Circumflex. This diacritic (ˆ) is still very much in evidence in a number of French words and phrases that are not yet fully assimilated into the English language. It is a French convention usually indicating that in Old French an *s* followed the vowel but has long ago dropped out.

maître d'hôtel = literally 'master of the house,' meaning 'headwaiter'

papier-mâché = literally 'chewed paper,' a material made largely from wastepaper and easily molded

raison d'être = literally 'reason for existence'

table d'hôte = literally 'host's table,' meaning 'complete meal with a fixed price' as opposed to separately priced items ordered from the menu, that is, a la carte

tête-à-tête = literally 'head to head,' hence 'private conversation between two people'

In English the circumflex is now disappearing from the word *fete* (= 'feast') and may soon take leave of *tête-à-tête*. Given these transitional circumstances, either follow one authority without question or make your own style decisions as you go along.

Tilde /**tĭl**-də/. This diacritic (˜) comes to us chiefly through a few Spanish words and names, where the mark appears over the letter *n* to signify /ny/: *riña; niñez*. The word *cabana* no longer retains the tilde in English, and when the words *señor, señorita*, etc., and *mañana* become fully anglicized, they will no doubt lose the tilde too.

Dieresis /dī-**ĕr**-ə-sĭs/. The word (in Greek) means 'separation (of vowel sounds).' The diacritical mark (¨) is placed over a vowel to indicate that the vowel should be pronounced as a separate syllable. However, the dieresis is rapidly passing from the scene. It survives today largely in words of foreign origin, such as *naïve* and *naïveté*, although probably not for long; the forms *naive* and *naiveté* (ultimately, *naivete*) are gaining strength (see NAÏVE). The dieresis is also used in English words like *coöperate* and *reëducate*. But this is a matter of choice. Some publishers prefer to use the hyphen in such words: *co-operate; re-educate*. Probably the majority nowadays regard the problem as self-solving, assuming that most readers perceive *cooperate* and *reeducate* as four-syllable words without any special assistance.

Umlaut /**o͝om**-lout/. The umlaut (¨), in form the same as the dieresis, appears in German words and names on the vowels *a, o*, and *u* and the diphthong *au*. It indicates a shift in pronunciation from the back to the front of the mouth, a process known as *umlaut* (= 'sound mutation'). In Early Modern German the letter *e* served as the sign of this pronunciation shift and was written either atop the letter or immediately after it. Eventually, two dots above the letter replaced the *e*. A well-known survival of the older use of *e* as the umlaut sign occurs in the name of the poet Goethe.

If you are writing German names or words containing umlaut signs in an English-language context, you have a choice. You may transcribe the umlaut sign just as it appears in present-day German, or you may drop it and add *e* after the letter. Thus, *Düsseldorf* may also be written *Duesseldorf; Köln* (Cologne) may be written *Koeln; Göring* (the Nazi leader) may be written *Goering;* and so forth. Do not, however, simply eliminate the sign and write *Dusseldorf; Koln; Goring;* etc.

Cedilla /sĭ-**dĭl**-ə/. This mark (¸) appears in French, Spanish, and Portuguese words and names, beneath the letter *c* only. When *c* is followed by *a, o*, or *u* in these languages, it is regularly pronounced /k/. The cedilla is used to indicate that a *c* in this position is nonetheless pronounced /s/. French *garçon* is /gär-**sōN**/. The place name *Curaçao* is /ko͞or-ə-**sou**/

(hence the English word *curaçao* /kyo͝or-ə-sō, kyo͝or-ə-**sō**/ = 'orange-flavored liqueur').

Haček /**hă**-chĕk/. In English-language contexts this rather rare mark (ˇ) occurs chiefly on the letter *c* in Czech names, indicating that the letter is pronounced /ch/. Such names in English are usually respelled with *ch* or *cz*.

Pronunciation Symbols. In various phonetic systems, as distinct from standard spelling, an array of diacritics is used to indicate precise phonetic values. In the pronunciation system used in this book, the *macron* (¯) placed over a vowel indicates a "long" sound and the *breve* (˘) indicates a "short" sound. Several other conventions are also used. For an explanation of our pronunciation system turn to the front of the book.

dialect. Every speaker of a language speaks a *dialect* of some kind. A dialect is the characteristic speech used by the members of a single regional or social community. The speech of an individual is called an *idiolect.* No given person's speech—with its pronunciation, intonation, word choice, syntax, grammar, etc.—is exactly like another person's speech. But speakers in the same locale or social group nevertheless share a common core of language features, and their idiolects taken together form a dialect. Every dialect has a set of pronunciation and grammatical features and a number of vocabulary items that differentiate it from other dialects. A set of common linguistic features spread out geographically forms a REGIONAL DIALECT. A set of features shared by speakers of a social grouping defines a SOCIAL DIALECT.

A language is a continuous chain of dialects. Adjacent dialects are mutually understandable; but the greater the geographical or social distance between dialects, the less intelligible their speakers become to one another. A New England farmer would have no problem conversing with an Inland Northern farmer and very little difficulty understanding a Gulf Southern farmer. But these three American dialect speakers would have some difficulty understanding their Scottish or South African counterparts, even though they all speak English. Similarly, the social and cultural distance between a black day laborer and a white business executive, both in Detroit, is great enough to make their speech almost mutually unintelligible. (For more information on American speech see REGIONAL DIALECTS OF AMERICAN ENGLISH.)

An upper-class dialect is usually a *prestige dialect.* When it is the dialect spoken in a culturally and economically dominant locality, and when most speakers of a language consider it to be superior to all the other dialects, it becomes a *standard dialect,* or simply the standard form of the language.

dialect, dialectic. *Dialect* (see separate entry) is a variety of language; *dialectic* is a form of discussion or philosophy. Both terms were invented by the Athenian Greeks in the 5th century B.C.

(1) *Dialect.* The classical Greek verb *dialegesthai* meant 'to have a talk among several people, converse' (from *dia* = 'between, among several' + *legesthai* = 'to speak'). From *dialegesthai* was formed the noun *dialektos*, meaning 'speech, conversation, discussion,' and also meaning specifically 'one of the distinct types of Greek speech.' The ancient Greeks were aware that their language had a number of distinct regional varieties—that the Greek of Athens (Attic) was different from the Greek of Sparta (Doric). This is the origin of the English word *dialect.*

(2) *Dialectic.* From the noun *dialektos* in its meaning 'discussion, debate' came the adjective *dialektikos* = 'relating to discussion.' The special term *dialektikē tekhnē* = 'the art of debate' (*tekhnē* = 'art') was coined by Athenian philosophers who had developed debate into a logical method of inquiry, a basic idea that is still powerful today. This term is the origin of the word *dialectic* = 'philosophical discussion, philosophical system.' In the history of Western philosophy this word has been applied to a succession of different influential systems. The dialectic of Socrates, the teacher of Plato, was a rigorous discussion of any subject, such as love or courage, often in the form of a series of questions and answers, designed to arrive at a

true definition. The dialectic of the German philosopher Hegel was a view of human ideas in which an initial idea (*thesis*) generates its opposite (*antithesis*), and the two are transformed into a higher truth (*synthesis*). This is the basis of the dialectics (or dialectic) of Marx and Engels, which is also known as *dialectical materialism* and is the official philosophy of the Communist world.

Derivatives. The adjective of *dialect* is *dialectal* = 'relating to a variety or varieties of language.' The adjective of *dialectic* is *dialectical*, as in *dialectical materialism*. A student of or expert in dialects is preferably called a *dialectologist*. A practitioner of dialectic is a *dialectician*.

dialogue. The spelling *dialog* is also correct, but we prefer *dialogue*. The word means 'conversation between two or more people.' Note that *dia-* does not mean 'two' (it is an originally Greek prefix here meaning 'across, among'). The term for a conversation specifically between two people is *duologue*. *Dialogue*, as in a play or film, can involve any number of people.

Currently, however, *dialogue* has a fashionable use that does stress the idea of just two participants: 'constructive discussion between two parties that have distinctly divergent positions or ideologies, or even between outright enemies, exchange of ideas.'

> Only toward the end of his career, as cordial relations with Roman Catholics became a new phenomenon of the 1960s, did Fry enter into ecumenical contacts with that Christian body, mainly through bilateral Lutheran-Roman Catholic dialogues.
> —Frederick K. Wentz, *Ecumenical Trends*

> Moscow hopes Reagan will soften, too. It suggests: "Ease your hostility, and you will find us ready for *constructive dialogue*."
> —*U.S. News & World Report*

> . . . British officials . . . sought to continue a dialogue with the gunmen in a search for a bloodless solution.
> —*Savannah Morning News*

Perhaps inevitably, this has generated a verb meaning 'to engage in dialogue':

> It is my hope that such opportunities will increase when women can dialogue further with the Holy Father. . . .
> —Sister Mary Theresa Kane, *Ms.*

◇ *Recommendation.* As far as the noun is concerned, the more dialogues the better, but we prefer to do without the verb.

diatribe. A Greek word that originally meant 'scholarly speech, learned discussion,' *diatribe* now usually means 'bitter, often violent denunciation, tirade':

> While we were waiting for Marie to come back from the market he paced back and forth, delivering a long diatribe against the gang leaders who trafficked in drugs with perfect safety.
> —Willie Sutton, *Where the Money Was*

> The gaiety and warmth of [George Sanders's] arrival evaporated after his second vodka, when he launched into a diatribe against the acting profession, which he said he considered unworthy of an intelligent man.
> —Brian Aherne, *A Dreadful Man*

dichotomy /dī-**kŏt**-ə-mē/, in Greek 'a cutting in half.' It is used to mean 'a splitting into two opposed or contrasting sections, opposition or contradiction between two elements,' or 'tension between two desires, loyalties, ideas, etc.':

> After the Persian Wars . . . the dichotomy between Hellene and barbarian becomes sharp and decisive. The Hellenes are an elect and the barbarians their inferiors.
> —Moses Hadas, *Hellenistic Culture*

> The dichotomy here [Yugoslavia] of East versus West, Serb versus Croat, even Russia versus the United States, is not new.
> —David A. Andelman, *Atlantic Monthly*

> The staff announcers had gone on strike. As a member of AFTRA, I had to observe that strike. Moreover, I was in sympathy with it. . . . At the same time there was a dichotomy in my position. I had become director of sports on the radio side and thus I was a member of the ABC executive echelon.
>
> —Howard Cosell, *Cosell*

Dictionary of American Regional English. First conceived in the 1880s and begun in earnest in 1965, the *Dictionary of American Regional English,* or DARE, is the first full-scale record of American regional dialects, based primarily on spoken instead of written language and containing maps illustrating where particular words are used in the United States. Edited at the University of Wisconsin in Madison, DARE began to appear in installments in the 1980s.

Dictionaries are word museums. The best ones contain extensive and well-displayed collections of specimens, and they try to have one of every kind. But few standard dictionaries have even tried to capture more than a small number of dialect words. This is because dialect is generally spoken and not written, and dictionaries in the past have collected samples mostly from printed sources.

DARE has also netted written and printed words, but only from dialect sources, like regional novels (by Mark Twain, William Faulkner, and others) or old diaries or local newspapers (such as the *Hungry Horse News* of Columbia Falls, Montana). But more important, it has collected words from the jungle of spoken language. Thousands of its more than 150,000 entries will be words and expressions that rarely, if ever, venture out into open print but live robustly in oral communication.

Collecting spoken words was an enormous task that took nearly 100 linguists and graduate assistants five years to complete. This was done with tape recorders and a specially designed questionnaire. The questionnaire has 1,847 questions divided into 41 categories. The B category questions ask about the weather. Question B25, for example, asks, "What joking names do you have around here for a heavy rain?" Typical dialect answers were *drencher; gusher; goose-drownder; gully-washer; toad-strangler; pour-down; chunk-floater; root-soaker;* and *dam-buster.* Question MM13 asks respondents to supply words meaning 'position' in the following sentence: "The table was nice and straight until he came along and knocked it ____." Besides such expected answers as *crooked, askew, cockeyed,* and *haywire,* there were well-known dialect responses—well-known, that is, if you live in certain regions of the country: *catawampus; antiganglin; galley-west; slaunchwise;* and so on.

The questionnaire was administered in 1,002 communities throughout the 50 states. It took anywhere from 8 to 12 hours for an informant to answer all the questions. The fieldworker read each question to the informant and then wrote the response in the questionnaire itself, often using phonetic symbols to get the pronunciation. A person qualified as an "informant" only if he or she had been born and raised in the community. This ensured a genuine and conservative sampling of the local speech.

The result was a total of more than 2.5 million responses. To handle this gigantic amount of data, a computer was used to combine and alphabetize all of the responses. With these organized data, which were supplemented with other material, a staff of editors wrote the dictionary's entries.

In addition, the computer was programmed to display on screen a U.S. map for each type of response to the questionnaire. The map pinpointed where a particular response to a particular question occurred. An X or some other symbol locating each informant on the map gave a unique image of a dialect. The map itself was distorted to reflect the relative population of each state. New York, for example, was shown to be proportionally larger in area than Utah, even though geographically Utah is larger than New York. The most interesting maps were printed in miniature in the text of the completed dictionary.

The word *bayou,* for example, has two maps, one for question C1 and one for question C14 (see maps on page 182). The map for

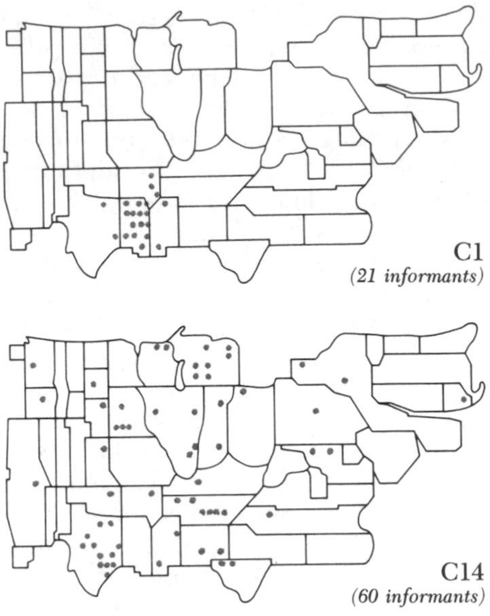

These two dialect maps, distorted to reflect the relative populations of different states, appear in the Dictionary of American Regional English. *The dots convey precise information on the use of the word* bayou. *For more details see* DICTIONARY OF AMERICAN REGIONAL ENGLISH.

question C1 ("What do you call a small stream of water not big enough to be a river?") shows that *bayou* meaning 'stream or creek' is used only in Louisiana, western Mississippi, eastern Texas, and southern Arkansas. This dialectal usage preserves the sense of the original Choctaw Indian word *bayuk* = 'river or creek.'

The second map shows that *bayou* in response to question C14 ("A stretch of still water going off to the side from a river or lake is a ____") is more widely known, though it is rarely used in the Atlantic and Pacific coastal states. *Bayou* meaning 'swamp or backwater' is a later development that spread outward from Louisiana, in the process shifting its meaning. Both definitions and maps are given in DARE.

In this book we have given extensive coverage to American regional speech. Each of the dialect areas—New England, Coastal Southern, Pacific Southwest, etc.—has a separate entry; these are surveyed and listed at REGIONAL DIALECTS OF AMERICAN ENGLISH. We also include discussions of many of the most interesting dialectal expressions, such as CATERCORNER and SHIVAREE. Most of these entries are based on materials in the files of the DARE project.

dieresis. See DIACRITICS.

differ. When the meaning is 'to be unlike (something),' the preposition is *from: The liveoak differs from the deciduous oak in several respects.* When the meaning is 'to be of another opinion, disagree (with someone),' the preposition is preferably *with: There I differ with the experts.* But *from* is also correct in this sense.

different. ***From* or *than?*** The traditional rule is that *different* should be followed by *from.* The construction *A is different from B* (or *a different A from B*) is still correct in all cases of simple comparison. But in more complex situations *different* seems to require *than* rather than *from:*

> . . . a very different Pamela than I used to leave all company and pleasure for.
>
> —Samuel Richardson, *Pamela* (1740)

> What right have you as Africans to believe anything is different than five years ago?
>
> —Andrew Young, *New York Times*

> From the middle of 1964 until 1967 the CIA quartered Nosenko in different circumstances than he now enjoys.
>
> —Kevin Buckley, *New York Times Book Review*

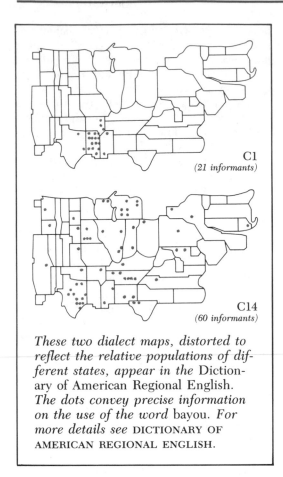

Substituting *from* for *than* in the first and third examples would produce gibberish; using *from* in the second example would sound "correct" but would otherwise not affect the sentence structure. These three examples involve *ellipsis;* that is, they omit the words that would express the idea fully—in this case the other half of the comparison. The omitted words are in italics: "a very different Pamela than *the one (that)* I used . . ."; "different than *what* (or *the way*) *it was* five years ago"; "in different circumstances than *those (that)* he now enjoys." Once the missing words have been inserted, the nature of the comparison becomes clearer and *from* becomes both possible and preferable. Some usage experts recommend revising constructions like these to express the comparison completely in order to use *from.* But this use of *different than* is an idiom that has been in continual use for the last 300 years (it was used by such writers as Addison, Steele, Coleridge, and Thackeray).

Further examples:

> . . . an old lady who seemed of quite a different class than the other passengers.
> —Willa Cather, *Katherine Mansfield*

Because the writer has used ellipsis, "class" appears to be compared with "passengers." Substituting "from" for "than" would not alter the situation. A strict traditionalist might prefer that the missing pieces be added: "a different class *from that* (or *the class*) *of* the other passengers." But Willa Cather found it natural to use the more concise construction with *than,* and her readers undoubtedly understand the intent of the sentence as she wrote it.

> Nicklaus is playing a different game than the rest of us.
> —Dave Hill, *Golf Digest*

Again because of ellipsis, this is not the simple comparison it first appears to be. Nicklaus's game is not being compared with "the rest of us." To reconstruct the sentence in order to use *from* would require "Nicklaus is playing a different game *from the one* (or *the game*) *(that)* the rest of us *are (playing).*" The idiom with *than* is simple, causes no misunderstanding, and is perfectly good English.

As a result of its success in these elliptical constructions, *different than* is frequently used where *different from* would be better:

> Yet King's case was different than Brooke's.
> —*Boston Globe*

> . . . that many mothers today have decided that they will raise their children in a different fashion than the one they learned from their own parents.
> —Richard Flaste, *New York Times*

The first example states a simple comparison in which the traditional *from* is entirely suitable: "different from Brooke's (case)." The second is part of a complex sentence in which the key words of the comparison have been expressed: "different *fashion* than *the one* [the fashion] they learned from their own parents." Whenever both sides of a comparison are so stated, *from* should be used.

Different to. This variation, clearly following the model of the word *dissimilar,* is common in British but does not significantly occur in American English.

> The first volume [of *The Lord of the Rings*] is really very different to the rest.
> —J. R. R. Tolkien (quoted), Humphrey Carpenter, *Tolkien*

Absolute Use. *Different* is sometimes used in a noncomparative sense:

> For a vacation that is truly different, try the Dominican Republic.
> —advertisement

When this use, meaning 'unusual, refreshing,' first appeared, it was regarded as slang or informal. It is now widespread, but some sensitive people still dislike it.

◇ ***Recommendation.*** In cases of simple comparison, *different from* is still preferable to *different than.* When substituting *from* for *than* would require awkward or wordy reconstruction of the sentence, *different than* is a useful and correct idiom. The absolute use of *different* to mean 'unusual' is now standard.

dilemma. In classical rhetoric a *dilemma* is an argument that maneuvers an opponent into choosing between two alternatives, either of which will disprove his position. The person trapped in this way is said to be stuck *on the horns of a dilemma*. Hence, generally a dilemma is any situation that forces a choice between two, or sometimes more, unfavorable or undesirable courses.

> He was faced with a difficult dilemma: feed them less and save coins, or continue to feed them so that they would look better at the auction in Cuba.
> —James A. Michener, *Chesapeake*

> Cabinet chiefs are publicly on both sides of the dilemma over restricting auto imports from Japan. . . .
> —*U.S. News & World Report*

The word is now also used in a looser sense, 'any difficult situation, predicament':

> . . . our most important social dilemmas get obscured and trivialized by sentimentality.
> —Gene Lichtenstein, *Atlantic Monthly*

> We face the dilemma of larger parish areas with larger populations being served by smaller numbers of priest personnel.
> —Bishop John Sullivan, *The Catholic Key*

◇ ***Recommendation.*** The less precise use of *dilemma* has been condemned by some usage experts, but it is now too well established to be regarded as an error. Nonetheless, it is best to keep in mind the horned alternatives of the true dilemma even when using the word more generally.

diplomat, diplomatist. The basic meaning of *diploma* is 'document,' especially 'public document, state paper.' But its most familiar modern meaning is 'document recording graduation from a school or college.' The adjective *diplomatic* originally meant 'relating to public documents.' In the 18th century it was applied specifically to treaties and other documents of international affairs; hence the French word *diplomatie* = 'the conduct of relations between countries,' which the English borrowed as *diplomacy*. From *diplomatie* then came the French term *diplomate* = 'person who conducts diplomacy, official employed in the foreign service,' and this came into English as *diplomat*. However, *diplomate* had been formed from *diplomatie* by *back-formation* (the making of a new word by removing a suffix from an existing one), and there used to be a feeling that this process was irregular or wrong. (For more on the whole subject, see BACK-FORMATIONS.) Accordingly, some preferred instead the word *diplomatist*, formed more regularly from *diplomatic*. To this day, old-fashioned and highly educated people, especially in Britain, and especially some who are or have been employed in diplomacy, reject the word *diplomat* altogether and insist on *diplomatist*. Regardless of all this, *diplomat* is the preferred and standard American term and is also increasingly accepted in Britain.

dis-, dys-. These are two separate prefixes. *Dis-* means 'not, un-, in reverse, against,' as in *disadvantage; disappear; disarm. Dys-* means 'bad, defective, disturbed,' as in *dysfunction* = 'malfunction'; *dyslexia* = 'impaired ability to learn to read'; *dystrophy* = 'defective nutrition or development.'

discomfit is not related to *discomfort*. The original meaning is 'to defeat, rout':

> Kings with their armies did flee, and were discomfited. . . .
> —Psalm 68, Book of Common Prayer

In modern usage *discomfit* means 'to frustrate and humiliate, embarrass acutely':

> When [George S. Kaufman] was acutely discomfited, he would try to wind his right arm twice around his head and reach back to his right ear.
> —Harpo Marx, *Harpo Speaks*

> Another drawback to the direct approach is that an explicit [sexual] suggestion requires an explicit yes or no answer, which may discomfit the partner who has been put on the spot.
> —Alice Fleming, *Reader's Digest*

The noun is *discomfiture:*

> Ted came down from the dais blushing furiously, and once back in his place he

turned a frowning, sulky face to the congratulations and sly witticisms of his friends. I minded his discomfiture and yet I enjoyed it too. . . .
—L. P. Hartley, *The Go-Between*

. . . information was available to the Senate, but Lance was never asked to explain. The question had to be answered later, to the much greater discomfiture of Jimmy Carter.
—Jack Anderson,
Savannah Morning News

discreet, discrete. These two adjectives have entirely unrelated meanings; they are occasionally confused, perhaps more by printer's error than by real mistake.

Discreet means 'sensitively restrained, tactfully unobtrusive,' especially 'keeping silence to avoid embarrassing anyone':

To my knowledge, my Hakim lover has kept silent. And so will I. Of the brothers, I considered only one a true gentleman, a feeling borne out by his discreet silence all these years.
—Veronica Lake, *Veronica*

And those who had an inkling that they were in touch with the United States government in some way, though not knowing exactly in which way, were discreet enough not to ask.
—William Colby,
Honorable Men: My Life in the CIA

Discrete means 'separate and independent':

Solti not only divides his career between three countries but also tries to keep the musical life of each country discrete. When he was musical director of Covent Garden he used English singers and conductors. . . .
—Winthrop Sargeant,
The New Yorker

As far as he could tell, an entire block of supposedly discrete four- and five-story buildings had all been connected, and housed God knew how many enterprises and people, all also somehow interconnected. —G. Gordon Liddy,
Out of Control

disembark. See DEBARK, DISEMBARK.

disinterested. (1) For many, *disinterested* means only 'free from selfish interest, uninfluenced by thoughts of personal advantage, altruistic, impartial':

. . . 'tis folly in one Nation to look for disinterested favors from another.
—George Washington,
Farewell Address (1796)

What instances must pass before them [nurses] of ardent, disinterested, self-denying attachment, of heroism, fortitude, patience, resignation—of all the conflicts and all the sacrifices that ennoble us most.
—Jane Austen, *Persuasion* (1818)

Disinterested intellectual curiosity is the lifeblood of real civilization.
—G. M. Trevelyan,
English Social History

. . . they would get some competent and disinterested person to hear him play, and if that person said he showed promise of becoming a first-rate pianist no further obstacle would be placed in his way. —W. Somerset Maugham,
The Alien Corn

Ezra [Pound] was the most generous writer I have ever known and the most disinterested. He helped poets, painters, sculptors and prose writers that he believed in and he would help anyone whether he believed in them or not if they were in trouble.
—Ernest Hemingway,
A Moveable Feast

He knew I was a disinterested party, that I was his brother, had his best interests in mind; that I had no special ax to grind, and that he couldn't really fire me. —Sam Houston Johnson,
My Brother Lyndon

Etnier . . . was not an entirely disinterested scientist when he found the snail darter. He was one of a growing number of people who opposed the dam. . . .
—Cassandra Tate, *Smithsonian*

For members of this group the word for 'not interested' is *uninterested:*

> For a long time now our society has been thoroughly uninterested in the message of the artist.
> —Henry Miller, *The Time of the Assassins*

(2) For many others *disinterested* usually or always means 'not interested, indifferent' and often 'bored':

> [Rhett Butler to Scarlett O'Hara:] "Did you ever in your novel reading come across the old situation of the disinterested wife falling in love with her own husband?" —Margaret Mitchell, *Gone With the Wind*

> Maston was waiting for him to speak, but he was tired and suddenly utterly disinterested. Without a glance at Maston he got up and walked out.
> —John Le Carré, *Call for the Dead*

> At the Tomb itself, we found a group of people snapping flashbulb pictures of their noisy, disinterested children.
> —Otto Heisig, Jr. (letter), *New York Times*

> [Ronald Reagan] guaranteed me that [Nancy Reagan] was more than disinterested in leftist causes. . . .
> —Robert Lindsey, *Book Digest*

The Controversy. The two positions seem irreconcilable and have given rise to one of the bitterest issues in English usage. Few people, if any, use *disinterested* in both senses. Those who use it to mean 'altruistic, impartial' generally use *uninterested* to mean 'not interested, indifferent.' Those who use *disinterested* to mean 'not interested' are unlikely to use it also to mean 'altruistic, impartial.' The meanings themselves are so incompatible that it seems impossible for them to coexist in the same word.

On the other hand, usage is usage. It's likely that many more speakers of English use the word in the second than in the first sense. Stylists and teachers have been trying for years to stamp out the second sense, but they haven't succeeded and obviously never will. The majority who use it are after all a vast speech community, and if that is how they perceive the word they are fully entitled to do so. They can retort that the minority are elitist and out of touch with reality.

History. Nor does the appeal to history solve the problem. As so often happens in disputed issues of usage, the more you investigate the historical background the less certain you become. But having advanced this far in discussing the word, we will pursue it to its origins. They can be simply described. The word *disinterested* was first used in the 17th century, and its first recorded meaning was—'not interested'! However, not long afterward it was also being used to mean 'not influenced by self-interest.' From the outset, in effect, it could be understood both ways. The structure of the adjective allows both, and according to context, different people found legitimate use for the two incompatible meanings, based on two of the meanings of the word *interest*. Later on, the meaning 'not interested' seems to have died out—or anyway is not found in print for a long period after 1767. The ethical meaning 'not influenced by self-interest' apparently was the only accepted meaning of the word throughout the 19th century, and the old meaning 'not interested' was marked by the great *Oxford English Dictionary* (in the 1890s) as probably obsolete. From the 1920s onward it cropped up all over again, not as any kind of conscious revival of the earlier use but as a natural enough reinterpretation of the word. This was violently denounced by the 'altruistic' party, but it continues in very widespread use and is unmistakably here to stay. History, then, does not resolve the issue. The meaning 'not interested' is both older and newer than the meaning 'impartial.'

◇ ***Recommendation.*** *Disinterested* has two meanings, the peculiarly valuable ethical one 'free from selfish interest, uninfluenced by thoughts of personal advantage, altruistic, impartial' and the less impressive but perfectly natural one 'not interested, indifferent.' The former is preferable, but both are in fact valid.

To those who prefer the ethical meaning 'altruistic' we point out that though you may dislike the other meaning, you simply can't dismiss it as an error. Far too many people use it, and in any case, in terms of the structure of the adjective and several meanings of the noun *interest*, it's entirely legitimate. To those who usually or always use *disinterested* to mean 'not interested,' we make three observations: be aware that the other meaning exists; be aware that an influential minority disapprove of the meaning 'not interested'; and notice that *uninterested*, with its clear-cut meaning, is always available.

disparate /**dĭs**-pər-ĭt, dĭs-**păr**-ĭt/. This useful word means 'strongly different, differing in real character':

> . . . the patchwork of disparate nationalities, religions and languages that make Yugoslavia the least homogeneous country in Europe.
> —*U.S. News & World Report*

> This was the ultimate team—a disparate group of men become closer than brothers through the shared ordeal of rigorous conditioning.
> —Peter Michelmore, *Reader's Digest*

disremember, a dialectal word for 'to forget,' is sometimes used by standard speakers for folksy effect; this is an informal use.

distaff. A *distaff* is a simple device for spinning thread from raw tufts of wool or flax. It consists essentially of a stick two or three feet long, with a cleft at one end on which the raw tuft is placed and through which the thread is drawn out, to be spun with the thumb and forefinger. The word is Old English and means 'flax-stick' (*dis* = 'flax' + *staff*). Before the textile industry was mechanized, spinning yarn was a constant occupation of women rich and poor. To sit at home and ply the distaff was the proverbial mark of a dutiful housewife. The word *distaff* thus became symbolic of women and their concerns and duties. The *distaff side* of a family was the female line of descent; the male line was called the *spear side*. In modern use *distaff* is most often an adjective meaning 'pertaining to women':

> When I went to Washington for a final briefing before departing for Vietnam, Kitsy accompanied me for orientation by the Department of Defense and State on distaff problems and responsibilities.
> —William C. Westmoreland, *A Soldier Reports*

> . . . some have questioned directly whether First Ladies have any right to leave the East, or distaff, Wing of the White House. —*New York Times*

> It was the first time in women's golf history that the distaff drivers would be competing for six figures.
> —Alan Ames, *Woman Golfer*

◇ ***Recommendation.*** Women are now likely to be annoyed or offended when men apply the word *distaff* to them.

distasteful, tasteless. *Distasteful* means (1) 'arousing distaste, disgusting': *a distasteful whiff of old garlic. A divorce case can be a distasteful business.* (2) 'feeling or showing distaste': *She gave a distasteful shudder.*

Tasteless means (1) 'lacking taste, savorless': *a dish of tasteless pudding* (2) 'lacking sensitive discernment, showing bad taste': *a tasteless arrangement of shoddy furniture; a tasteless and insulting remark.*

dive. The forms *dived* and *dove* for the past tense of *dive* are about equally common in standard usage.

> He must make a signal as soon as the submarine dived. . . .
> —D. A. Rayner, *The Enemy Below*

> Markham and Gargan took off their clothes and during the next 45 minutes dove again and again, endeavoring to enter the sunken car.
> —John Barron, *Reader's Digest*

In some dialects, especially General Southern, *div* is used.

◇ ***Recommendation.*** *Dived* and *dove* are equally correct.

dolphin, porpoise, dorado. (1) *Dolphin* and *porpoise* (mammals). Among the now-familiar small whales (cetaceans) there are several different kinds; some have elongated snouts almost like beaks, others have comparatively blunt rounded snouts. The true dolphins are the beak-snouted ones, and the true porpoises (also called *harbor porpoises*) are the blunt-snouted ones. However, both the name *dolphin* and the name *porpoise* are commonly applied to either kind indifferently, especially by people who are unaware that there is any distinction between the animals. This is so traditional and widespread that it can't be called a mistake; some people simply prefer the name *dolphin*, while others prefer *porpoise*.

(2) *Dolphin* and *dorado* (fish). Here there is further verbal confusion. *Dolphin* has for centuries been applied, especially by sailors, to two large sea fish of the genus *Coryphaena;* they grow to about six feet long but don't resemble the mammalian dolphins at all; they are renowned for their iridescent coloring, which changes dramatically when they have been caught and are dying. Even though it may be confusing, it is not incorrect to call these fish dolphins; but they are also known as *dorados*. However, even this alternative name doesn't solve the problem, since there is yet another, unrelated fish, of the river Plate in South America, that is also called *dorado;* it is somewhat like a salmon.

◇ ***Recommendation.*** In any context where real confusion may result from this muddle of words, the only solution is to add the scientific names at the first mention. The beaked dolphins belong to the family Delphinidae; the snub-nosed porpoises are the genus *Phocaena;* the color-changing dolphins, or dorados, are the genus *Coryphaena;* the salmonlike dorados are the genus *Salminus*.

done is the standard past participle of *do: The children haven't done their chores today*. It is widely used in dialect as the past tense of *do: He done his chores very early this morning*. This is nonstandard.

don't is the standard contracted form of *do not*. It is also used, in dialects and informally by some standard speakers, for *does not: Doris don't plan to buy a new car*. This use is comparable to *ain't;* it is clearly widespread, but it is not acceptable in formal standard speech or writing.

dorado. See DOLPHIN, PORPOISE, DORADO.

double modals. *Modals* are auxiliary verbs, such as *might, may, can,* and *should,* that indicate the speaker's *mood,* or attitude, toward the action of the main verb. Although *double modals* are generally considered nonstandard, they are used widely in the General Southern dialect, even among educated speakers, and are also heard in the German area of Pennsylvania. The commonest combinations are *might could* and *might can,* which mean 'will possibly be able to':

> Jumper's liable to throw a fit with that hide rattling along behind him, and you might not can hold him by your self.
> —Fred Gipson, *Old Yeller*

> I thought if I could get in there and people would work with me, we might could get something going.
> —*Atlanta Constitution*

The present-tense form *may can* is also commonly used for 'may be able to.'

Might would is used as an auxiliary verb to express probability or likelihood.

> De fire is most too hot for Unex, Auntie. I'm 'faid e might would catch cold.
> —Julia Peterkin, *Scarlet Sister Mary*

Might ought is also occasionally used in the South and means 'probably should or ought (to do something).' It is usually followed by an infinitive.

> I really got to thinking that I might ought to hear the good Reverend preach and—purely as an after-

thought—mention the possibility of a little horse trading some night when the meetin' was over.
—Ben Green, *Horse Tradin'*

Similar to these double modals are the verb phrases *used to could* (= 'formerly was able to'), *used to would* (= 'used to'), and *used to was* (= 'used to be, formerly was or were'). These too are nonstandard, but in the South they are common in casual speech.

Then she got to talking about . . . her relations down the river, and about how much better off they used to was.
—Mark Twain, *The Adventures of Huckleberry Finn*

She used to could smell that goat.
—*Saturday Evening Post*

double negative. The doctrine that two negatives make a positive is not a basic fact of language but a relatively recent convention. In many languages, including Shakespeare's English, two negatives can reinforce each other rather than cancel each other out (see ELIZABETHAN ENGLISH). This remains true in many present-day dialects of English, both in Britain and in America (see, for example, the discussion at BLACK ENGLISH). But in modern standard usage a double negative is permitted only as an intentional indirect affirmative. In many a dialect *I didn't say nothing* would mean 'I said nothing.' In the standard language it can only mean 'I didn't refrain from speaking, I did say something.'

◊ ***Recommendation.*** In standard usage two negatives do make a positive.

doubt. The verb *doubt* = 'to be inclined to disbelieve, think it unlikely (that something is true)' may be followed by a clause beginning with *whether, if,* or *that,* or by a clause with no conjunction.

They even came to doubt whether the *Königin Luise* would ever appear again in her previous anchorage.
—C. S. Forester, *The African Queen*

I doubt if there has ever been a time when there was so much careless use of words. . . .
—J. Donald Adams, introduction to Ivor Brown, *I Give You My Word*

But in view of the Freedom of Information Act he doubted that the government could keep his double-agentry secret. . . .
—John Barron, *Reader's Digest*

Most observers doubt the crackdown will actually occur.
—*National Fisherman*

The same applies to the adjective *doubtful.*
The noun *doubt* may also be followed by clauses like these, or sometimes by a clause with *as to whether.*

In addition, there was the gnawing doubt as to whether competition, in fact, existed.
—John Kenneth Galbraith, *The Affluent Society*

In negative statements with the verb or the noun *doubt,* the usual choice is a clause with *that,* or with no conjunction: *I don't doubt (that) it's true. There is no doubt (that) he is guilty.* The noun *doubt* with a negative may also be followed by a clause with *but that.*

The SEC investigation leaves no doubt but that bribery was corporate policy at Textron.
—William Proxmire (quoted), *Time*

◊ ***Recommendation.*** Conservative usage favors *whether* or *if* following positive statements with the noun and verb *doubt,* and *that* following negative statements. In practice, all of the above alternatives occur widely, and all are acceptable as correct.

doughnut. The recipe for *doughnuts* was first brought to America by the Pilgrims, who had learned it from the Dutch during their stay in Holland (1607–20). Originally, the doughnut (also informally spelled *donut*) resembled a "nut" because it was a small, solid ball of deep-fried sweetened dough. It wasn't until the Pennsylvania Dutch introduced their version of this pastry, which they call *fasnacht*, that the doughnut developed its now traditional hole in the middle. Fasnachts are doughnuts prepared and eaten on Shrove Tuesday, or *Fasnacht* Day, the day of merry-making that precedes the 40-day-long Lenten fast.

> Like Christmas cookies, these are made but once a year—on Fasnacht Day. . . . The most delectable of the doughnut tribe, fasnachts are very like raised doughnuts.
>
> —Frederic Klees, *The Pennsylvania Dutch*

The Pennsylvania Dutch custom of "dunking" doughnuts (from Pennsylvania German *dunken* = 'to dip') has also become an all-American custom.

The early Dutch settlers gave two other names for doughnuts, *olycooks* (from *oliekoek* = 'oil cake') and *crullers;* both are still occasionally heard in the Hudson Valley dialect.

> The table . . . was always sure to boast an enormous dish of balls of sweetened dough, fried in hog's fat, and called dough nuts, or oly koeks.
>
> —Washington Irving, *A History of New York . . . by Diedrich Knickerbocker* (1809)

> The dames of Knickerbocker proclivities . . . had added the indigestible doughnut and cruller to the dyspepsia-provoking list.
>
> —A. C. Day, *Knickerbocker Life* (1871)

Crullers (from *krulle* = 'curly cake') often have a curled or twisted shape and in the early 19th century were also known as *love knots* or *matrimony knots*. Today, they are sometimes called *twisters*.

> I had only time to drink half my coffee, to seize a perfectly unmanageable thing called a "twister" . . . and to spring aboard the train, twister in hand.
>
> —*New York Evening Post*

In New England doughnuts used to be called *cymbals* or *simballs* because they were shaped like a drum cymbal.

> The genteel form of doughnut called in the native dialect *cymbal* . . . graced the board with its plastic forms.
>
> —Oliver Wendell Holmes, *The Guardian Angel* (1867)

Also in this region they are called *boil cakes*, though the term is rarely used today.

In the Northern dialect (except for New England) *friedcake* is a commonly used term.

> The "nut-cakes" are an institution of the country. Some call 'em "dough-nuts," and some "fried cakes."
>
> —*Quinland, or Varieties in American Life* (1857)

The *bismarck* is a jelly-filled doughnut, but this name for it is used only in the Upper Midwestern and Rocky Mountain dialects:

> She placed the tray of cups . . . and a plate of sugared jelly doughnuts on the coffee table. "We still call them bismarcks, don't know why." I said, "I remember that's what they called them in Milwaukee."
>
> —Roy Winsor, *Three Motives for Murder*

Some other more humorous names for the doughnut are *belly sinkers, doorknobs, dunkers, fatcakes* (North Midland dialect), and *jumbles*.

dove. See DIVE.

doyen. See DEAN, DOYEN.

dragonfly. The colorful, predatory insect with four gauzelike wings that is known generally as the *dragonfly* has many regional names as well. In the Southern dialect, for example, it is known as the *mosquito hawk* or *skeeter hawk* because it feeds on mosquitoes, making it one of the most beneficial insects to man. (For an interesting examination of how *mosquito hawk* is identified as a Southern dialect term, see the map at REGIONAL DIALECT.) In the Chicago area the dragonfly is sometimes known as a *stinger*.

Over the centuries the dragonfly has been the object of numerous fanciful folk beliefs, which account for many of its regional names. In England and in the Northern states it is often called the *devil's darning needle* or simply (and more widely) *darning needle.* This name comes from an odd notion:

> The devil's darning needle will sew together the fingers or toes of a person who goes to sleep within its reach.
> —*Animal and Plant Lore* (1899)

Similarly, the dragonfly is known in some parts of the United States as the *sewing needle* and *ear sewer.*

Another peculiar folk belief is that this insect is a caretaker and attendant of snakes. Thus, in the Midland dialect it is called the *snake feeder.* In that same dialect, as well as in the Southern dialect, it is also widely known as the *snake doctor.*

drive. *Drive* has numerous meanings, but its basic sense is 'to force or move (something) forward' or 'to direct or control the movement of (something).' The standard past tense is *drove* and the past participle is *driven.* But several nonstandard forms are used in some dialects.

(1) *Past tense. Drave* is still used in northern England and had at one time greater acceptance than the southern English dialectal *drove.* Hence, in the King James Version of the Bible *drave* is the form used.

> And the Lord drave out from before us all the people.
> —Joshua 24:18

Driv is used in certain parts of the United States, especially in areas of the South.

> When the stage driv up she was standin' straight in the bed.
> —M. J. Holmes, *Lena Rivers* (1856)

> They say th' enemy driv' our line inteh a devil of a swamp an' took Hannises' batt'ry.
> —Stephen Crane, *The Red Badge of Courage*

Druv is not often heard but is still current in some English and American dialects.

> The devils have stripped the house of everything to eat, and druv off the cattle.
> —John Trowbridge, *Three Scouts* (1865)

> He swung the ax and druv the blade into one of the cuts.
> —William Faulkner, *Shingles for the Lord*

(2) *Past participle. Drove* was common in England until about the 19th century, when *driven* became the standard form. In the United States *drove* is widely used, though it is definitely considered nonstandard.

> Divers persons of Rhode Iland and others have from time to time drove into and Pastured their cattle and horses on the lands att Pocassett and places adjacent.
> —*New Plymouth Colony Records* (1676)

> It was drove out of my mind.
> —William Dean Howells, *The Leatherwood God* (1916)

◇ ***Recommendation.*** Except for deliberately dialectal effect, use only the standard past tense *drove* and past participle *driven.*

due to. *Due* is an adjective, and the phrase *due to* = 'caused by, resulting from' was originally used only as an adjectival phrase, directly linked to a noun: *Mud slides due to heavy rain occurred in several places. The surplus is due to a seasonal spending spree.* It is also widely used as a prepositional phrase meaning 'because of, on account of':

> Due, in whatever proportions, to the abstract principles he had formulated in himself, or in spite of them, there was the loyal conscience within him. . . .
> —Walter Pater, *Marius the Epicurean* (1885)

> During regular training, mortar crews may be permitted to fire only two live rounds due to cost constraints.
> —Ralph Kinney Bennett, *Reader's Digest*

> Due to her sex, class . . . and place of residence, she has been denied her

proper place in the near-empty pantheon of American literature.
—Gore Vidal, *Atlantic Monthly*

This use is condemned by both British and American conservatives. The British ones prefer *owing to*, which is comparatively rare in American English. American alternatives are *because of, on account of.*

◇ ***Recommendation.*** The prepositional use of *due to* = 'because of' is now natural, correct Standard American English (and probably British as well).

Dutch words. The language of the Netherlands is closely related to English; the two languages have many ancestral words in common, and many of these are easily recognized as linguistic "cousins." The Dutch and the English have also been in continuous contact throughout their history—trading, fighting, competing, exchanging ideas, and borrowing words from each other.

A selection of the many Dutch words we have borrowed, from the Middle Ages onward, is given below. A major group relates to the sea and seafaring, and another to industry, machinery, and transportation. The Dutch have been European leaders in these fields, especially in their golden age in the 15th, 16th, and 17th centuries; three-quarters of the English borrowings occurred during that period. Another interesting group of words is terms relating to painting and printmaking. Dutch-English competition went straight on in the New World. American Dutch was eventually destroyed by American English, but it has left a score of familiar words in our vocabulary.

Borrowings from the Dutch of South Africa are given at AFRIKAANS WORDS.

(1) The sea and seafaring:

boom = 'spar at the foot of a sail': Dutch *boom* = 'pole, tree' (related to English *beam*)

jibe = 'to move a fore-and-aft sail across the boat when running before the wind': Dutch *gijben* = 'to jibe'

maelstrom = (1) 'whirlpool off the coast of Norway' (2) 'any overwhelming situation': Dutch *maelstrom* = 'whirl-stream,' from *malen* = 'to whirl around' + *strom* = 'stream'

marline = 'thin cord used for bindings, etc.': Dutch *marlijn* = 'binding line,' from *marren* = 'to bind' + *lijn* = 'line'

pram = 'small, square-bowed dinghy': Dutch *prame* = 'type of flat-bottomed boat'

scow = (1) 'type of barge' (2) 'type of small, broad-beamed sailboat': Dutch *schouw* = 'type of barge or boat'

skipper = 'master of a ship, captain': Dutch *schipper* = 'shipman, shipmaster,' from *schip* = 'ship'

sloop = 'one-masted fore-and-aft-rigged sailing vessel': Dutch *sloep*

splice = 'to join (ropes) by opening up the strands and interweaving them': Dutch *splissen* = 'to splice' (related to *split*)

trawl = 'to fish by towing a net behind a boat': Dutch *traghelen* = 'to drag,' and *traghel* = 'dragnet'

yacht = (1) 'type of fast sailing ship' (2) 'any sailboat or powerboat used for pleasure': Dutch *jaght, jaghtschip* = 'pursuit-ship, type of fast sailing ship used for piracy,' from *jagen* = 'to hunt, pursue'

yawl = (1) 'type of small boat' (2) 'two-masted fore-and-aft-rigged sailing boat with a small jigger mast behind the rudder': Dutch *jol* = 'kind of ship's boat'

(2) Machinery, industry, transportation:

bush, bushing = 'metal lining or sleeve for a mechanical part': Dutch *busse* = 'box,' hence 'bushing of a wheel'

cam = 'projecting part on a wheel that rolls or slides against another part to transmit motion': Dutch *kam* = 'comb,' hence 'tooth of a cogwheel,' later 'cam'

clinker = 'hard vitreous slag formed in a coal furnace': Dutch *klinker* = 'vitrified brick,' from *klinken* = 'to clink' (since such bricks clink when struck)

drill = (1) (verb) 'to bore a hole' (2) (noun) 'tool for boring holes': Dutch *drillen* (verb) and *dril* (noun)

potash = 'potassium carbonate,' a chemical originally obtained from leached wood ash heated and dried in iron pots: Dutch *potasschen* = 'pot-ashes'

sled = 'vehicle with runners used on snow or ice': Dutch *slede* = 'sliding vehicle'

sledge = 'sled or sleigh': Dutch *sledse,* variant of *slede* = 'sled'

stoker = 'worker who tends a furnace': Dutch *stoker,* from *stoken* = 'to poke, push fuel into a furnace'

stove = 'enclosed heating or cooking apparatus,' originally meaning 'heated room': Dutch *stove* = 'heated room'

trigger = 'small catch for releasing a mechanism, firing a gun, etc.': originally *tricker,* from Dutch *trekker* = 'pull-catch, trigger,' from *trekken* = 'to pull'

wagon = 'heavy, four-wheeled horse-drawn vehicle': Dutch *wagen* = 'wagon'

(3) Painting and printmaking:

easel = 'structure for holding a painter's canvas, a photograph, etc.': Dutch *ezel* = 'ass,' hence 'easel' (as with English *clotheshorse,* the metaphor means 'thing with legs, used for bearing a load')

etch = 'to engrave metal with acid': Dutch *etsen* = 'to bite,' hence 'to etch'

landscape = 'picture of countryside': Dutch *landschap* = 'region, countryside,' hence 'picture of countryside,' from *land* = 'land' + *-schap* = suffix of condition (same as the English suffix *-ship*)

sketch = 'rough drawing or painting, preparatory design': Dutch *schets* = 'sketch'

stipple = 'to paint or engrave with dots': Dutch *stippelen* = 'to stipple, prick'

(4) Miscellaneous words:

boor = 'peasant, ill-mannered person': Dutch *boer* = 'farmer, peasant'

booze (slang) = 'alcoholic drink': Dutch *busen* = 'to drink too much'

bruin = 'a bear': Dutch *bruin* = 'brown, the brown animal,' used as the name of the bear in the medieval fable *Reynard the Fox*

bumpkin = 'rustic fool': Dutch *boomken* = 'little tree,' hence 'small, squat person,' from *boom* = 'pole, tree'

clink = 'to make a sharp but soft ringing sound': Dutch *klinken* = 'to clink'

duck = 'strong cotton or linen fabric used for sails, trousers, etc.': Dutch *dock* = 'linen cloth'

duffel = 'coarse wool cloth used for blankets, camping clothes, etc.': Dutch *duffel* = 'cloth made in Duffel' (a town near Antwerp)

foist = 'to pass off (something worthless or undesirable)'; originally gamblers' and criminals' slang, meaning 'to palm dice': Dutch *vuisten* = 'to palm,' from *vuist* = 'fist'

furlough = 'military leave of absence': Dutch *verlof* = 'leave, permission'

gherkin = 'kind of pickled cucumber': Dutch *(a)gurkje* = 'gherkin'

gin = 'grain spirit flavored with juniper juice': shortened from *geneva,* from Dutch *genever* = 'juniper,' hence 'gin'

morass = 'swamp, bog': Dutch *moerass* = 'swamp, fen'

muff = 'fur or cloth cover for keeping the hands warm': Dutch *mof,* shortened from *moffel* = 'glove'

pickle = 'cucumber, onion, etc., preserved in salt water or vinegar': Dutch *pekel,* possibly from Willem *Beukelz,* a 14th-century fisherman said to have invented pickling

serif = '(in typography) one of the fine strokes that finish off a printed letter': probably Dutch *schreef* = 'stroke, line'

skate(s) = 'footwear with blades for controlled gliding on ice': Dutch *schaats* = 'a skate'

splint = 'thin strip of wood used in bone setting, etc.': Dutch *splinte* = 'split piece'

splinter = 'split piece of wood': Dutch *splinter* = 'split piece'

split = 'to break apart, separate (wood, stone, etc.) by cleaving along the grain': Dutch *spletten* = 'to split'

(5) Words borrowed from colonial Dutch into American English (see also HUDSON VALLEY DIALECT):

boss = 'employer, chief, master': Dutch *baas* = 'master'

bowery = 'Dutch farm in New York State': Dutch *bouwerij* = 'farm, plantation'

bush = 'woodland, uncleared land, frontier land': Dutch *bosch* = 'woodland, woods'

clapboard = 'thin planks used for siding': semitranslation of Dutch *clapholt* = 'split board,' from *clappen* = 'to split' + *holt* = 'board'

* **coleslaw** = 'salad of chopped raw cabbage'

cookie = 'small, flat baked cake': Dutch *koekje* = 'small cake,' from *koek* = 'cake'

cranberry = 'tart red berry of the cranberry bush': Dutch *kranebere* = 'crane berry,' associated in some way with cranes (birds)

cruller = 'type of *doughnut': Dutch *krulle* = 'curly cake, that is, doughnut in the shape of a curl'

dope = (1) 'any thick, gluey liquid' (2) 'drug': Dutch *doop* = 'dip, sauce, gluey liquid'

hock (slang) = 'to pawn' and **in hock** (slang) = 'in pawn, in debt': Dutch *hok* = 'prison,' hence also (slang) 'debt'

pea jacket = 'short topcoat of thick cloth worn by sailors, especially in 18th-century New Jersey': Dutch *pijjekker*, from *pij* = 'kind of thick wool cloth' + *jekker* = 'jacket'

pinkie (also in Scottish, but unknown in the English of England) = 'little finger': Dutch *pink, pinkje* = 'little finger'

* **pit** = 'kernel of a peach, cherry, etc.': Dutch *pit* = 'kernel'

Santa Claus = 'mythic personification of Christmas': Dutch (dialectal forms) *Sinterklaas, Sante Klaas* = 'Saint Nicholas' (a patron saint of children), from *sint, sant* = 'saint' + *Klaas* = 'pet form of Nicholas'

sawbuck = 'carpenter's trestle on which wood is sawed': translation of Dutch *zaagbok*, from *zaag* = 'saw' + *bok* = 'buck, deer' (for a similar animal metaphor see *easel*, above)

scrod = (1) 'young cod or haddock' (2) 'slice or fillet of cod or haddock': Dutch *schrood* = 'slice'

sleigh = 'horse-drawn sledge': Dutch *slee*, variant of *slede* = 'sled' (see *sled*, above)

spook = 'ghost': Dutch *spook* = 'ghost'

stoop = '*porch with steps at the front door of a house': Dutch *stoep* = 'step, stoop'

waffle = 'crisp, flat battercake baked in a waffle iron': Dutch *wafel* = 'waffle'

*Appears as separate entry

dys-. See DIS-, DYS-.

E

each. The adjective and pronoun *each* is basically singular, referring one by one to several things or parties: *There are three apartments, and each apartment has a separate entrance. Each of them has its own private balcony. There is a smoke-detector system in each one.*

Each is also used after plural subjects. In this case the verb is always plural: *They each (of them) enjoy eating out in restaurants.* Other elements in the sentence may be plural or singular according to emphasis: *They each prefer different kinds of food. They each patronize a different Chinese restaurant.* Sometimes the singular is stressed by putting *each* after the verb; other elements in the sentence are then generally singular: *These restaurants are famous each for its own specialty.*

These are the basic formal rules, but many special circumstances occur, and in informal usage some flexibility is permissible. Errors also occur.

> Stan Altgelt . . . and Victor Regalado . . . each shot 69's and shared fourth place at 136. —*New York Times*

"Each shot (a) 69" would be correct. Also, "each . . . shared" is redundant, since both *each* and *share* contain the idea of 'the two together.' The preferable alternatives are: "Each shot 69, and they shared fourth place" (separating *each* from *shared*) and "Altgelt and Regalado shot 69's and shared fourth place" (eliminating *each*).

> Wearing . . . diamond rings on each pinkie . . . —*Time*

This should mean that the individual had several rings on each pinkie. Probably what was meant was "Wearing a diamond ring on each pinkie." If the person was really wearing more than one on each, it would be appropriate to make it explicit: "Wearing several diamond rings on each pinkie."

> In each [city] he evicted pro-Persian quislings and established Greek-style democracies.
> —Mary Renault, *The Nature of Alexander*

He might have evicted several quislings in each city, but only one democracy could be established in each.

◇ ***Recommendation.*** In respect to number, *each* often causes confusion. In formal usage the rules should be followed carefully.

each other, one another. There is a conservative rule that *each other* should refer only to two, and *one another* be applied to more than two.

> Right-wing Christian militiamen and Syrian forces accused each other today of violating the two-day truce. . . .
> —*St. Louis Post-Dispatch*

> The Swiss have never been very interested in one another's culture.
> —Jane Kramer, *The New Yorker*

◇ ***Recommendation.*** Some writers like to follow this rule strictly. In practice *each other* is used much more often than *one another,* both for two and for more than two. *One another* is also used for two as well as for more than two. All options are correct and acceptable even in formal usage.

earthworm. There are about 2,200 species of earthworm, all living underground and digesting the organic matter present in the soil. The habit of the common American earthworm of coming to the surface at night has given it its popular name *night crawler.*

> Members of the Huck Finn school of fishing . . . have been looking for some way to enliven the almost impossibly sluggish night crawler.
> —*Esquire*

Nightwalker is the New England dialect version of night crawler.

Though its most important service is aerating and mixing the soil, the earthworm is best known as fishing bait. Most of its regional names reflect this use. Throughout the Midland dialect, for example, it is called the *fishing worm.*

> A hard piece of corn-crust . . . took one of the children in the eye and curled him up like a fishing-worm.
> —Mark Twain, *The Adventures of Huckleberry Finn*

In parts of the northeastern section of the country, but especially in the Hudson Valley region, the earthworm is a *fishworm.* Ralph Waldo Emerson knew this term:

> The savant is often an amateur. His performance is a memoir to the Academy on fish-worms, tadpoles, or spiders' legs. —*Society and Solitude*

A huckster in George Barr McCutcheon's *Rose in the Ring* (1910) had an unusual use for the fishworm:

> "Say, are you goin' to learn the business? If you are, I got some fishworm

> oil that's jest the thing to limber up yer joints."

The foregoing may reflect a belief, once widespread among Algonquian Indians, that rubbing rotten earthworms on the body cured rheumatism.

Angleworm is the common term used in the Northern and Coastal Southern dialects. *Angle,* now virtually obsolete, is an old word for 'fishhook' dating back to the 9th century in England. An angleworm, then, is a worm placed on an angle for bait. In times of severe hardship the resourceful American pioneers used this creature for another purpose:

> Having no shortening they dug angleworms and crushed them up with the acorns. —Granville Stuart, *Forty Years on the Frontier* (1925)

Finally, in New England the earthworm is also called an *angledog.* This term, however, was better known in the last century.

> We pocketed the well-scoured angle-dogs, shouldered our birch fishing-rod, and sallied forth.
> —G. C. Hill, *Homespun* (1867)

economy, ecology, etc. ***Origin.*** The word *economy* comes (via Latin) from Greek *oikonomia* = 'management of a household' (*oikos* = 'house' + *-nomia* = 'control'). The word *ecology* = 'study of habitats' is a modern coinage, using Greek *oikos* = 'house,' here referring to 'habitat,' + *-logia* = 'study.'

Pronunciation. The first syllable of these words and their derivatives may be pronounced with the long vowel /ē/ or the short /ĕ/. Probably most people say /ē-**kŏn**-ə-mē/ for the noun and /ĕk-ə-**nŏm**-ə-kəl/ for the adjective; but other people pronounce both words with the long vowel or both with the short. Much the same is true of *ecology, ecological.* Both pronunciations are equally correct.

ecumenical. The pronunciation is /ĕk-yŏŏ-**mĕn**-ĭ-kəl/. This was originally a technical word used in the Roman Catholic church to mean 'worldwide.' It comes from Latin *oecumenicus,* from Greek *oikoumenē* = 'the inhabited world,' from *oikein* = 'to inhabit,' from *oikos* = 'house, dwelling place.' The word is now used mostly in reference to the movement for an *ecumenical church,* a worldwide church disregarding separate Christian denominations.

edify, edifice. The Latin verb *aedificāre* meant 'to construct a building.' It was applied by the early Christians to the spiritual improvement of the church and of the individual soul. The English form of the word, *edify,* means 'to improve (someone) morally, instruct and enlighten':

> You have often enlivened me, my dear friend, by your excellent drinking songs; in return, I beg to edify you by some Christian, moral, and philosophical reflections on the same subject.
> —Benjamin Franklin, letter (c. 1779)

> She saw herself as an entertainer; her primary motive in writing was not to edify but to delight. —David Cecil, *A Portrait of Jane Austen*

The adjective *edifying* thus means 'morally instructive':

> The superiority lies in a highly polished and poetically edifying use of the English language. . . .
> —S. M. Giovangelo, *National Catholic Reporter*

More often used is its antonym *unedifying* = 'destructive to morals':

> Versailles, in the 18th century, presented the unedifying spectacle of several thousand people living for pleasure and very much enjoying themselves.
> —Nancy Mitford, *Madame de Pompadour*

From the Latin verb came the noun *aedificium* = 'a building.' The English version *edifice* can be used literally, as a highly formal word for a building, but more often is used figuratively, to mean 'abstract construction, system of ideas, etc.'

> The art of cross-examination . . . can be constructive in that it builds an edifice out of the admissions wrung from the witness.
>
> —Louis Nizer, *My Life in Court*

> Darwin, later to erect a philosophical edifice as significant and far-reaching as Newton's . . .
>
> —A. J. Marshall, *Darwin and Huxley in Australia*

effect. See AFFECT, EFFECT.

effete. This favorite term of disparagement literally means 'worn out, exhausted' but is usually used to mean 'soft and decadent, overrefined and lacking vigor, decadently intellectual':

> He was small and stocky, somewhat effete, a senior advisor to the Regents on protocol who also had Imperial Court rank. —James Clavell, *Shōgun*

> The sports-mindedness of the rich seems to increase as one moves out of the city of New York into the less effete Middle and Far West.
>
> —Stephen Birmingham, *Panorama*

> . . . the la-de-da, effete, know-it-all textbook authors whose taste is oh, so much more sophisticated than the taste of the yahoos.
>
> —James Kilpatrick, *Brunswick News*

egregious. The etymological meaning is 'outside the flock, outstanding in any way.' The only current meaning in English is 'outstandingly bad, conspicuously deplorable.' It can be applied both to people and to things.

> Only the egregious Cohn persists in denying that Hoover gave information to McCarthy.
>
> —Arthur M. Schlesinger, Jr., *Robert Kennedy and His Times*

> There is no more egregious fallacy than the belief that order requires central direction.
>
> —Milton Friedman, *Newsweek*

Egyptian words. The ancient Egyptian language, written in hieroglyphic characters, was Hamitic, related to Berber and, more distantly, to the Semitic languages. It survives today, in greatly changed form, in Coptic, the language of the Christian Copts of modern Egypt. A few ancient Egyptian words have come into English, borrowed via Greek, Latin, and French.

- **bark** = 'sailing ship': from Egyptian *baris* = 'barge'
- **card** = 'stiff paper': from Greek *khartēs* = 'sheet of papyrus,' from an Egyptian word meaning 'papyrus' (*chart* is also from this word)
- **ivory** = 'elephant's tusk': Old French *ivoire,* from Latin *ebureus* = 'made of ivory,' from *ebur* = 'ivory,' from Egyptian *abu* = 'ivory'
- **niter** = 'saltpeter': from Egyptian *ntr-* = 'sodium carbonate'

either. The pronoun and adjective *either,* referring to one or the other of two, is singular: *Either of the two candidates is acceptable. Either alternative has one disadvantage. Either* is occasionally used of a choice of three or more; the correct word here is *any: Any of the four bridges will have heavy traffic.*

As a conjunction *either* likewise basically indicates a choice of two alternatives: *You can have either tea or coffee.* But its use for a choice of three or more is quite widespread, even among respectable writers.

> I would not have thought of eating a meal without drinking either wine or cider or beer.
>
> —Ernest Hemingway, *A Moveable Feast*

> Those who approach human contingency with Thomistic appetites to cover every situation, either exasperate, ultimately; or they end their days in futility; or they make bad law.
>
> —William F. Buckley, Jr., *Execution Eve*

◇ ***Recommendation.*** In standard usage it is a definite mistake to use the pronoun or adjective *either* of a choice of three or more; to do this with the conjunction *either* is more acceptable but is better avoided.

either-or oversimplification. See FALLACY.

elemental. While partly synonymous with *elementary,* the word *elemental* has the senses 'belonging to the basic forces of nature' and 'basic and full of power':

> The three great elemental sounds in nature are the sound of rain, the sound of winds in a primeval wood, and the sound of ocean striking beach.
> —Henry Beston, *Reader's Digest*

> Fear is the elemental alarm system of the human organism.
> —Martin Luther King, Jr., *Strength to Love*

> Mrs. Meir's call for a strong Israel . . . has to do with an elemental human right, the right to exist.
> —Julie Nixon Eisenhower, *Special People*

elite /ĭ-lēt/. It is now less often spelled *élite* /ā-lēt/. The literal meaning in French is 'the choice part, part chosen for excellence.' The basic meaning in English is 'small group of outstanding people within a particular field':

> Each honest calling, each walk of life, has its own elite, its own aristocracy based on excellence of performance.
> —James Bryant Conan, *Our Fighting Faith*

The adjective follows this primary sense and is applied especially to the military:

> . . . the 7th had destroyed the Viet Cong's elite 1st Main Force Regiment.
> —Philip Caputo, *A Rumor of War*

Outside the military the word now usually carries a more or less negative sense, an implication of social snobbishness or intellectual aloofness.

> He's in charge of a $500 elite cocktail party before the dinner. And there's a $100-a-ticket less-elite cocktail party.
> —*Boston Herald American*

> Washington reporters are increasingly conservative or apolitical, more elite and more detached from the realities of American life.
> —Ben H. Bagdikian, *Washington Post Book World*

In Black English the *elite,* often pronounced /ē-līt/ and pluralized to *elites,* are black people who have become prosperous enough to be considered bourgeois:

> Any black family that had been around Boston long enough to own the home they lived in was considered among the Hill elite.
> —Malcolm X, *Autobiography of Malcolm X*

The abstract noun *elitism* is now almost always negative:

> . . . the Nixon people had some real thematic villains. *Elitism* was one, combining social snobbery, the arrogance of wealth, and—most important—the Hamiltonian idea that some were privileged by birth and education to rule.
> —William Safire, *Before the Fall*

Likewise the derivative adjective and noun *elitist.*

> . . . in 1976 Mao, knowing his death was imminent, was afraid once more that the bureaucracy had become elitist, that revolution was an abstract idea, not a fresh memory.
> —Julie Nixon Eisenhower, *Special People*

> Object to [sloppy usage] and you are likely to be told that you are a pedant, a crank, an elitist. . . .
> —Edwin Newman, *Reader's Digest*

Elizabethan English. Queen Elizabeth I ruled from 1558 till her death in 1603; she thus lends her name to a stage of the development of the English language that is part of a longer period lasting from about 1500 to about 1660, known technically as Early Modern English. During the Elizabethan period important changes were taking place in English. Although local dialects flourished then as they do now, and although Sir Walter Raleigh "spake broade Devonshire to his dyeing day," a standard language based on that of London and the court was beginning to emerge. This was the age of the great dramatists—Shakespeare, Christopher Marlowe, Ben Jonson; but a speaker of Modern English suddenly transported to Shakespeare's Globe Theatre in the London of the 1590s would find the speech of the actors falling oddly on his ear.

Pronunciation. At the end of the Middle English period, around the last decade of the 14th century, there began a massive change in the language known as the Great Vowel Shift. The effect of this movement was to replace many of the "pure" vowels in English with diphthongs; for example, during the Middle English period, the vowel in the word *five* had a sound like Modern English /ē/, and the word rhymed more or less with Modern English *heave;* but after the Great Vowel Shift the word *five* had the sound /ī/ and rhymed with *hive.* Elizabethan English stood almost but not quite at the end of this process. The completion of the earlier stages of the Great Vowel Shift sets Elizabethan English apart from Middle English; while the completion of the final stages, together with some other changes that have happened since, distinguishes Elizabethan English from Modern English.

To a present-day visitor to Shakespeare's Globe Theatre, the most noticeable feature of the Elizabethan pronunciation of vowel sounds would be the differences in those words that now have /ī/ and /ou/, such as *fight* and *five, lout* and *loud.* The first pair would be pronounced with the sound of /əĭ/, a sound rather like that now given to *fight* (but not *five*) in Canadian English and in the speech of Martha's Vineyard and parts of eastern Virginia. Similarly, *lout* and *loud* would be pronounced with /əo͞o/, the sound given to *lout* (but not *loud*) in those same speech patterns today. Many words that now have /ŭ/, such as *blood, flood,* and *love,* and (in some dialects) /o͞o/, such as *broom, roof,* and *room,* may all have had /o͞o/ in Shakespeare's time; thus, his rhyme of *love* and *prove* in "Sonnet X" was probably a true rhyme with /o͞o/. Many words that now have /ē/ had at least an alternative pronunciation with /ā/ in Elizabethan English, so that Shakespeare's rhyme of *break* and *speak* in "Sonnet XXXIV" was probably perfect to the Elizabethan ear. In the consonants, the /k/ in *know* and the /g/ in *gnaw* were both still pronounced in educated speech, although their pronunciation may have been less definite than modern /k/ and /g/. When Kent calls Oswald "A knave; a rascal; an eater of broken meats" (*King Lear*), the speech has three /k/ sounds and not, as in Modern English, only two. Shakespeare, however, can pun on *knight* and *night*—"Come, night! come, Romeo! come, thou day in night!" (*Romeo and Juliet*)—indicating that, for some speakers at least, the initial /k/ was already lost. The letters *gh* probably still represented a spoken sound, similar to the Scottish pronunciation of *ch* in *loch,* at least for the older and better-educated speakers: the word *right* was probably /rəĭKHt/ in Shakespeare's day. The Elizabethan, finally, pronounced his *r*'s, and the modern Bostonian and Standard British pronunciations of *dark* as /dăk/ and /däk/, respectively, would have sounded as strange to him as his pronunciation /dărk/ would sound to us.

Here are the opening lines of the Lord's Prayer approximately as they would have been pronounced in Elizabethan English:

Our father which art in heaven,
əo͞or fă*th*ər hwĭch ärt ĭn hĕvən,

Hallowed be thy name.
hăləwəd bē *th*əĭ nĕm.

Thy kingdom come
*th*əĭ kĭngdəm ko͞om

Thy will be done in earth
*th*əĭ wĭl bē do͞on ĭn ĕrth

As it is in heaven.
əz ĭt ĭz ĭn hĕvən.

You may find it interesting to compare the transcription here with the transcriptions of the Lord's Prayer given at LANGUAGE CHANGE.

Grammar. The double negative was still acceptable in Elizabethan English, and Edmund Spenser could write in 1596, "Sith no redemption nigh she did not heare nor see"

(*The Faerie Queene*). The double comparative, too, was acceptable, as witness Mark Antony's "This was the most unkindest cut of all" (*Julius Caesar*). The second-person forms of address, *thou, thee*, etc., were still in common use, although there was perhaps little consistency in the way they were used.

Vocabulary. During the Elizabethan Age the English began to take an increased interest in the ideas that were circulating on the continent of Europe. At the same time a knowledge of the classical languages became much more widespread than it had been. Translations from French, Italian, and other modern languages proliferated. Literary Latin served as the standard by which these translations were evaluated. Comparing English with Latin, many of the translators (as well as other writers) found English lacking in eloquence, and so these "amenders," as they were later called, set about improving the language by wholesale borrowing from other tongues. Thus, from Greek came—each is given with the date of its first appearance in English—*anarchical* (1597), *hexahedron* (1571), *panoply* (1576), and *topic* (1568). From Latin came such words as *absorption* (1597), *adumbrate* (1581), *concatenate* (1598), *diffident* (1598), *excruciate* (1570), *imprecation* (1585), *interject* (1578), *irrelevancy* (1592), *nullify* (1595), *pantomime* (1589), *sector* (1570), and *transact* (1584); many of these borrowings from Latin are, of course, themselves borrowings into that language from Greek. From French at this time came, among others, *demolish* (1570), *exclaim* (1570), *explore* (1585), *impostor* (1586), *sanction* (1563), and *vogue* (1577). From other languages, sometimes at second or third hand, came words like *baluster* (1602), *bastinado* (1577), *battalion* (1589), *embargo* (1602), *mulatto* (1595), *palisade* (1600), *peccadillo* (1591), *renegade* (1583), and *sombrero* (1598). Of course, not all words adopted at this time remained in the language. The following, though current for a while, finally fell out of use: *assecure* (1594), 'to make secure'; *carceral* (1563), 'of a prison,' which suddenly reappeared in 1909; *deturbate* (1563), 'to drive out'; *exauctorate* (1593), 'to dismiss'; *instaurate* (1583), 'to repair'; *obsonator* (1582), 'caterer'; *peripatetician* (1559), 'peripatetic philosopher'; *quafftide* (1582), 'season for drinking'; *solutive* (1564), 'relaxative'; *splendicant* (1592), 'resplendent'; *stravagant* (1565), 'irrelevant'; and *xenagogy* (1570), 'guiding of strangers.'

Elizabethan Style. Themselves avid borrowers and also the inheritors of a long tradition of borrowing, the Elizabethans seem to have had a kind of linguistic exuberance that delighted in gorgeous language almost for its own sake. At its worst, this taste for the "magnifical" could lead to the mere bombast that Shakespeare parodies on more than one occasion; but at its best it is exemplified in a speech by the magician Prospero in the last act of *The Tempest*.

> Ye elves of hills, brooks, standing lakes, and groves;
> And ye, that on the sands with printless foot
> Do chase the ebbing Neptune and do fly him
> When he comes back; you demi-puppets, that
> By moonshine do the green sour ringlets make
> Whereof the ewe not bites; and you, whose pastime
> Is to make midnight mushrooms; that rejoice
> To hear the solemn curfew; by whose aid,—
> Weak masters though ye be—I have bedimm'd
> The noontide sun, call'd forth the mutinous winds,
> And 'twixt the green sea and the azur'd vault
> Set roaring war: to the dread-rattling thunder
> Have I given fire and rifted Jove's stout oak
> With his own bolt: the strong-bas'd promontory
> Have I made shake; and by the spurs pluck'd up
> The pine and cedar: graves at my command
> Have wak'd their sleepers, op'd, and let them forth

By my so potent art. But this rough magic
I here abjure; and, when I have requir'd
Some heavenly music,—which even now I do,—
To work mine end upon their senses that
This airy charm is for, I'll break my staff,
Bury it certain fathoms in the earth,
And, deeper than did ever plummet sound
I'll drown my book.

See also SHAKESPEARE AND THE ENGLISH LANGUAGE.

Elizabethan English in America. Most of the English settlers of America arrived before 1640, bringing with them the English language as it was spoken by Shakespeare and Queen Elizabeth. After that date only a trickle of English settlers came to the Colonies. The language of America soon grew distinct from that of the mother country. To begin with, communication between the countries was difficult. It took nearly four arduous months to cross the Atlantic Ocean. In addition, there was hardly any interchange of ideas. The famous British writers of the 18th century—Dryden, Addison and Steele, Swift, Pope—were almost unknown in America; the colonists seem to have read little except the Bible and its commentaries. In 1723 the Harvard College library had no copies of these authors' works and had only recently obtained copies of Shakespeare and Milton. Furthermore, during the 17th and 18th centuries there was a powerful movement in England to standardize English vocabulary, pronunciation, and spelling. Because the Americans were isolated from both this movement and British literature itself, their speech preserved many of the features of Elizabethan English that were dying or being forced out of British usage.

The following list is a short sample of some 17th-century terms that survived in American English but became obsolete or provincial in British English (although several words, such as *jeans*, have been readopted from American into British in recent years).

andiron
bay window
beef = 'full-grown steer, cow, etc.'
bub = 'term of address to a boy'
chinch
clodhopper
cordwood
cross-purposes
din
drouth
fall = 'autumn'
flapjack
fox fire
gotten
greenhorn
guess = 'to suppose'
homely = 'unattractive'
homespun
jeans
loophole
molasses
offal
peek (verb)
ragamuffin
shoat
stock = 'cattle'
trash
underpinning
well = 'healthy'
wilt

The speech of the southern highlands (see SOUTH MIDLAND DIALECT) has preserved even more of the Elizabethan vocabulary. The southern Appalachians and the Ozarks were settled during the 18th century by mountain folk whose speech and culture were already old-fashioned. Many of the dialectal features of this region were once common to all the American colonies. But because the mountain culture was isolated and conservative, it preserved a fair number of these old features while the rest of American society was beginning to drop them. The terms that still survive are not necessarily originally Elizabethan. Many are much older and can be found in the works of Chaucer and other Middle English authors.

The words in the following selection are obsolete in Standard British and American English but have survived in the southern highlands. More than half of these words can be found in Shakespeare's works. Today, a good many of the terms are old-fashioned, and some may also be used in other parts of the country.

admire = 'to be astonished or surprised'
afore = 'before'
bore = 'to ridicule, make fun of'
budget = 'package, bundle'
buss = 'to kiss'
care = 'to mind, object': *I don't care to do it* = 'I don't mind doing it, I have no objections.'
clever = 'generous, accommodating'
conceit = 'to imagine'
contrary = 'to contradict, antagonize'
* **disremember** = 'to forget'
feather into = 'to attack violently'
fernent, ferninst = 'adjacent, next to'
fraction = 'quarrel, fight'
funk = 'disagreeable odor'
gaum, gaumy (especially in Appalachia) = 'sticky, smeared'
generation = 'crowd, large number'
hearn = 'heard'
least = 'smallest'
look = 'to examine, inspect': *She looked the baby's head for boogers* = 'She examined the baby's head for lice.'
melt = (1) 'spleen of an animal' (2) 'courage' (3) 'recklessness'
mend (the fire) = 'to add fuel to'
mind = 'to intend'
misdoubt = 'to suspect or distrust'
misling = '(of weather) cool and foggy'
mistress = 'married woman'
nation = 'large amount'
needments = 'necessities'
pair of beads = 'necklace'
pass over one's head = 'to pass by'; used of time
preachment = 'sermon'
race = 'a root'
ramping = 'raging'
reckon = 'to suppose'
resty = 'indolent'
riddle = 'to explain, interpret'
ruinate = 'to ruin'
shift of clothes = 'change of clothes'
sleight = 'talent, knack, skill'
soon = 'early'
sorry = 'poor, inferior'
stink = 'to give off an odor without regard to pleasantness or unpleasantness'
tole = 'to entice'
use = 'to loiter or frequent a place': *Jeb's been a-usin' round Durgenville.*
ween = 'to panic, become afraid'
withouten = 'without'
wonder = 'to astonish, surprise'
zany = 'clown or buffoon'

*Appears as separate entry

Other kinds of Elizabethan speech habits are used today in parts of the United States, particularly the southern highlands. The suffix *-er*, for example, was common in Shakespeare's time. He and others used such oddities as *justicer, moraler, mediciner,* and *sworder*. Today, the Ozark hillman can sometimes be heard using *tourister* for 'tourist,' *gossiper* for 'gossip,' and *musicker* or *musicianer* for 'musician.'

The plural ending *-es* is also an older English survival in rural America in words that now take only the *-s* plural elsewhere. Such plural forms as *nestes, postes, deskes,* and *folkses* are still common in the South Midland speech region. The plural ending is pronounced, as in /**nĕs**-təz/.

Double comparatives and superlatives found widely in Shakespeare—*worser, more hotter, more better, most unkindest,* etc.—survive in many regions and in some social dialects of the United States, even though prescriptive grammarians have long since abolished them from Standard English.

emigrate, immigrate. To *emigrate* is to depart permanently *from* (one's own country); to *immigrate* is to move *to* or *into* (a new country) as a permanent resident: *My grandparents emigrated from Hungary as young children. Two of their sons immigrated to Canada.* However, this distinction is widely ignored, producing *immigrated from* and *emigrated to.* Such usage is often explained with the observation that the point of departure or destination can merely be implied: *My grandparents immigrated from Hungary* (that is, *to* some other place). *The boys emigrated to Canada* (that is, *from* some other place). Nevertheless, it is always correct to say *emigrated from* and *immigrated to,* and far less troublesome than thinking about missing words.

éminence grise. In more than one movie about the Three Musketeers, Cardinal Richelieu is shown literally as "the power behind the throne"—he stands behind young King Louis XIII's royal chair, suavely murmuring such lines as "You cannot move a finger without me, Your Majesty." If Richelieu was the power behind the throne, the power behind Richelieu was supposedly a Capuchin monk named François du Tremblay, of whom not much is known. The title of a cardinal is *Éminence.* Richelieu was known as *Éminence rouge* = 'red eminence,' his robe being red, and Du Tremblay, who was not a cardinal, was known as *Éminence grise* = 'gray eminence,' his robe being gray. This hackneyed scenario is the source of the terms *éminence grise* and *gray eminence,* favored by journalists as a fancy label for a man believed to wield much influence behind the scenes:

> [John] Mitchell was convinced that I was the source of leaks to these enterprising columnists, who painted him as the sourpussed *éminence grise* of the rise of Nixon.
>
> —William Safire, *Before the Fall*

> He had hired Clark Clifford, the gray eminence of Washington attorneys, an inside man in several administrations. . . . —James Wooten, *Dasher*

> I devoted most of my time to deepening my knowledge of and cultivating my contacts with the Saigon government and especially the triumvirate that dominated it: Diem himself, his brother and *éminence grise* Ngo Dinh Nhu, and his wife, the controversial dragon lady.
>
> —William Colby, *Honorable Men: My Life in the CIA*

enclave, exclave. An *enclave* is a piece of territory enclosed by alien territory. An *exclave* is a piece of territory cut off from the main body to which it belongs. The two words can be used of the same piece of land. Hong Kong is a British colony surrounded (on the landward side) by Chinese territory; it can be called a British *enclave* within China or an overseas *exclave* of British territory. *Enclave* is also used in social situations, of a place set apart from its surroundings, especially in a privileged sense:

> Turnberry is one of Scotland's premier resort enclaves, complete with a commodious hotel, good food, abundant sport facilities. . . .
>
> —Stephen Birnbaum, *Golf*

> . . . Lafayette Park, the Mies van der Rohe-designed set of towers that is a middle-class enclave in a troubled city [Detroit] . . .
>
> —Paul Goldberger, *New York Times*

England, English. (1) The parts of the island of Britain settled by the Angles and Saxons became known as *Engla Land* = 'Angle Land,' now *England,* and its inhabitants as *Englisc,* now *English* (see ANGLE, ANGLIA, ANGLICAN). England conquered Wales and was joined with Scotland but did not constitutionally absorb them. The combined nation was named *Great Britain* (see BRITAIN). England is still technically a separate kingdom and retains a cultural identity independent of those of Wales and Scotland. Each of them, for example, plays soccer and other international sports as a separate country. *England* and *English* are still often used for the whole nation and people. This is not correct and is likely to offend the Welsh and Scots. But the usage persists, especially among the English themselves. See also BRIT.

(2) English-speaking Canadians are now often called *English Canadians.* This seems illogical, since they are to a large extent of Scottish and other non-English descent. But the term should be understood as purely linguistic—short for *English-speaking Canadians.* Likewise *English Canada* = 'English-speaking Canada.'

> It is accepted that many English Canadians are sympathetic to French cultural aspirations. . . .
>
> —Robert Trumbull, *New York Times*

> . . . a firm reminder to English Canada that it has a choice between negotiating with Quebec, or breaking up the country.
>
> —Peter Cowan, *Winnipeg Tribune*

(3) The English language is covered historically under OLD ENGLISH; MIDDLE ENGLISH; and ELIZABETHAN ENGLISH. Its chief national varieties are covered under AMERICAN ENGLISH; AUSTRALIAN ENGLISH; BRITISH ENGLISH; CANADIAN ENGLISH; and SCOTTISH ENGLISH. See also ANGLO-SAXON.

(4) The noun *English* or *english* = 'spin given to a ball, as in pool or bowling' is an Americanism dating back to the 1880s, unknown in Britain. Its origin is obscure.

Englañol. See PUERTO RICAN SPEECH.

English. See ENGLAND, ENGLISH.

enhance in its simplest sense means 'to raise, increase':

> Modern cloud seeders . . . claim that during a growing season they can enhance rainfall by ten percent or more.
>
> —Lowell Ponte, *Reader's Digest*

Often it carries a sense of qualitative improvement, especially of making something more pleasant or enjoyable:

> . . . they motored down with us on Friday nights after a theatre in London, the journey enhanced by the inevitable flask of martinis. . . .
>
> —Cole Lesley, *The Life of Noel Coward*

> We will continue to fight for measures to enhance the well-being of older Americans.
>
> —Peter W. Hughes, *Modern Maturity*

enormity. This noun is related to the adjective *enormous.* The original meaning of *enormous* was 'abnormal, deviant,' hence also 'outrageous, wicked':

> . . . that both of them might escape the Punishment justly due to Crimes of that enormous Nature [burglary].
>
> —Benjamin Franklin, *Pennsylvania Gazette*

This use is now archaic, and *enormous* means only 'very large, huge.' But *enormity* is still used in the earlier moral sense 'outrageousness, extreme badness, wickedness':

> An outraged father called the family together and delivered a polemic on the enormity of this offense; it would get into the columns and make the family look ridiculous.
>
> —Arthur M. Schlesinger, Jr., *Robert Kennedy and His Times*

> And now the enormity of what I was doing hit me like a blow.
>
> —Daphne du Maurier, *The Scapegoat*

> The family held a meeting in the parlour, which pointed up the enormity of the offense [stealing a quarter]. . . .
>
> —Willie Sutton, *Where the Money Was*

There is a strong tradition that this is the only correct usage and that it is an error to use *enormity* to mean 'very large size, enormousness.' But the natural tendency of the language is to allow an abstract noun to be used in the same sense or senses as the adjective it is based on—unless there is some special reason against it. In the case of *enormity,* it can be argued that if it is allowed to be used as both 'hugeness' and 'outrageousness,' ambiguous situations may arise. The *Oxford English Dictionary* goes so far as to quote a joke, which must have been current in the 1890s, to illustrate the possibility:

> "You have no idea of the enormity of my business transactions," said an eminent Stock Exchange speculator to his friend. He was perhaps nearer the truth than he intended.

In fact, if you consider it carefully, you will see that the joke proves the exact opposite of what it intends. The rule is a SHIBBOLETH, a linguistic trap by which insiders, who know the rule, can detect outsiders, who have never heard of it. The stock exchange speculator is clearly an outsider, nouveau riche and not very well educated; he makes a fool of himself by unwittingly speaking of the immorality of his business transactions. Actually, since he does not subscribe to the rule, he is doing no such thing; he is simply using *enormity* in its (to him) standard sense of 'huge scale.' If the rule is ignored and both meanings are allowed, ambiguity does not in practice result.

> Meggie gave in, the enormity of her relief showing in the way she sat, loosely now, relaxed.
> —Colleen McCullough, *The Thorn Birds*

> Now I felt the responsibility not only to provide an entertaining two hours for the audience, but also to aid and support my fellow players. My eighteen-year-old mind couldn't comprehend the enormity of it all, but I felt I was on the threshold of something limitless and wonderful. . . .
> —Ricardo Montalban, *Reflections: A Life in Two Worlds*

> No effort on a village, county, or even provincial level was adequate to the enormity of the undertaking. . . .
> —Marvin Harris, *Cannibals and Kings*

> In its enormity, the federal government dwarfs every other institution in the U.S.
> —*U.S. News & World Report*

> With 16 million Americans currently using marijuana, imagine the enormity of the destruction that is taking place in this generation.
> —Peggy Mann, *Reader's Digest*

In the last two quotations the word is being used with some of the force of both of its meanings: 'awful hugeness, outrageous size.'

◇ ***Recommendation.*** Conservatives hold that *enormity* means only 'extreme badness,' never 'enormous size.' We feel that this rule is obsolete and that it is acceptable to use the word in either sense, or in both at once.

enthuse. This verb is a back-formation from the noun *enthusiasm* (see BACK-FORMATIONS). It is strongly disliked by some and found useful and harmless by others. It is used in two constructions, active and passive:

> And when Woolcott enthused, everybody else, by God, had to enthuse too.
> —Harpo Marx, *Harpo Speaks*

> Some members of the 17-man ACTU executive are not at all enthused by the prospect.
> —Malcolm Colless, *The Australian*

◇ ***Recommendation.*** *Enthuse* is still best regarded as informal.

entomology. See ETYMOLOGY.

envelop, envelope. The verb, meaning 'to enclose or surround,' is spelled *envelop* and pronounced /ĕn-**vĕl**-əp/. The noun, meaning 'an enclosing cover,' is spelled *envelope* and generally pronounced /**ĕn**-və-lōp/. The old-fashioned pronunciation /**än**-və-lōp/ is still preferred by some.

> [Uncle Matthew:] "It's a lucky thing that Fanny will have £15,000 a year of her own. . . . She'll get a husband all right, even if she does talk about lunch, and *en*velope, and put the milk in first. . . . I only say she'll drive the poor devil to drink when she has hooked him." —Nancy Mitford, *Love in a Cold Climate*

To the ferociously reactionary Uncle Matthew, the word *luncheon*, the pronunciation /än-və-lōp/, and pouring the tea before putting in the milk were acid tests of upper-class status. See also SHIBBOLETH; U, NON-U.

environment. This word clearly embodies one of the key images of our time. We now feel that nothing exists in isolation, that everything lives in an *environment*. From the ecological meaning 'conditions surrounding and affecting the growth of plants and animals,' the word has been extended to mean 'conditions surrounding and affecting the cultural life of a human community, cultural background in general':

> Golda had grown up in an environment in which the good daughter was the girl who grew up to be a good mother. . . .
> —Julie Nixon Eisenhower, *Special People*

> The daily press can be a stronger force in the year 2000 than it is today if it adapts to a changing environment.
> —Katharine Graham (quoted), *Ellsworth* (Me.) *American*

> In fact, a shrewd observation of my slum environment convinced me that the more I avoided the notice of my peers, the fewer bruises I would get.
> —Isaac Asimov, *Science Past—Science Future*

Beyond that, it is now used indiscriminately to mean 'situation, scene, mood, etc.':

> The U.S. Constitution—specifically the Bill of Rights—has operated largely within a non-electronic, paper environment.
> —*Silicon Gulch Gazette*

> Reagan, in proposing the major cuts, said that projects affected were "incompatible with the current austere budget environment."
> —*Savannah Morning News*

> A high threat environment for helicopters could exist in any intensity combat environment.
> —Capt. Carl L. Remmel, *Marine Corps Gazette*

◊ ***Recommendation.*** Fashionable clichés of one kind or another are always with us, and there is no point in getting too indignant about them. The effective writer and speaker will select them judiciously, not simply reach for them automatically.

envisage, envision. There is very little difference between these words. Theoretically, *envisage* should mean 'to look (something) in the face, confront (a situation)'; the word is from French and contains the word *visage* = 'face.'

Envision, on the other hand, was formed in English from the word *vision* and should mean 'to picture (something) as in a vision, foresee, depict vividly.' In practice *envision* is encountered more often than *envisage*, but otherwise the two words are used interchangeably, both meaning 'to imagine, suppose, foresee, predict':

> . . . have we any grounds to hope . . . that there might be changes in Russia of the kind that we are here envisaging?
> —George F. Kennan, *American Diplomacy 1900–1950*

> He envisages a new Federalism, in which national authority says to local authority, "Do it your way, but do it."
> —William Safire, *Before the Fall*

> I can envision situations where rationing might be necessary—a major supply disruption, for example.
> —Charles W. Duncan, Jr., *U.S. News & World Report*

> Some, like Sociologist Seymour Lipset, envision a "more egalitarian society" because of the computer.
> —*Time*

ephemeral /ə-fĕm-ər-əl/. This sad but appealing adjective means 'lasting or living for but a day,' and in its literal sense is applied to certain flowers and insects. It comes from Greek *ephēmeros*, from *epi* = 'on, at' + *hēmera* = 'day.' Applied to human endeavors and interests, *ephemeral* means 'passing, evanescent, short-lived, not destined to be preserved or remembered':

> He still read halfpenny papers in the train, still discussed the day's ephemeral topics, still voted at elections. . . .
> —Lord Dunsany, *The Coronation of Mr. Thomas Shap*

> Before the bier two priestlings strew tiny paper rose petals that the wind took and scattered, signifying that life was as ephemeral as a flower. . . .
> —James Clavell, *Shōgun*

> . . . an author may find his, or her, lifework reduced to a handful of paperbacks, as ephemeral as yesterday's snowflakes.
> —Pearl S. Buck, *Journey in Dialogue*

> I have been lucky enough to work in the arts—even though acting is more ephemeral than painting or poetry.
> —Rosalind Russell, *Life Is a Banquet*

> Madame de Pompadour excelled at an art which the majority of human beings thoroughly despise because it is unprofitable and ephemeral: the art of living.
> —Nancy Mitford, *Madame de Pompadour*

epistrophe. See TAUTOLOGY AND PLEONASM.

epithet. The original meaning of *epithet* is 'attributive word, adjective,' especially 'stock adjective often applied to a particular name or noun.' In Homer's poems, Odysseus is regularly called "wily" or "of many devices"; Zeus is "cloud-gathering"; the sea is "wine-dark." These repetitive adjectives are epithets. The word also means 'nickname in general,' such as the Great Emancipator for Abraham Lincoln or the Buckeye State for Ohio. Increasingly, *epithet* is now also used to mean 'disparaging term,' and especially 'term of abuse, insult' and 'profane or obscene word':

> I was on Grandpa's side, even if he *was* a failure. But I still wondered why he deserved that epithet.
> Walter Cronkite, *Reader's Digest*

> . . . Henzel, who shouted epithets all over the embassy, calling the Russians "liars," "double-crossers," and "sons of bitches" for making the Olympic deal through Bock. —Roy Rowan, *Fortune*

> I received signals from the White House that [my statement] had made me a permanent *persona non grata* and the object of the nastiest possible epithets.
> —John Dean, *Blind Ambition*

> Carole [Lombard] could lay tongue to more colorful epithets than any other woman I've ever known, and more than most men. Oddly enough, you were never shocked when she swore.
> —Bing Crosby, *Call Me Lucky*

◇ ***Recommendation.*** This use of *epithet* to mean 'disparagement, insult, swearword, etc.,' is relatively recent. It is still disliked by some, especially anyone who is familiar with the word in its classical meaning 'stock adjective.' But the new use is now also established and acceptable.

epitome /ĭ-pĭt-ə-mē/. This word comes from Greek *epitomē* = 'a cutting short, abbreviation, summary' (from *epi-* = 'on' + *tom-* = 'cut'). It is now usually used to mean 'something or someone that sums up a whole class, ideal example, perfect embodiment':

> Big occasions were supposed to be fun. . . . Your honeymoon was supposed to be the epitome of fundom.
> —Suzanne Britt Jordan, *Reader's Digest*

> Hoffa, with his dictatorial control, his high salary, his expensive suits, his Cadillacs, his manifold deals on the side, his sweetheart relations with employers, his sympathy for the Republican Party, was the epitome of business unionism.
> —Arthur M. Schlesinger, Jr., *Robert Kennedy and His Times*

Bechtel, Jr., on the other hand, is considered the epitome of the modern businessman with his engineering and Stanford MBA degrees.
—Jacqueline Thompson, *The Very Rich Book*

[Bob Jones] was simply incapable of being other than a gentleman at all times. In short, his character was the epitome of honor and integrity.
—Clifford Roberts, *The Story of the Augusta National Golf Club*

The verb *epitomize* means 'to be an epitome of, represent perfectly':

As Benjamin Braddock in *The Graduate*, Dustin Hoffman came to epitomize the unknown everyman who was the hero of the late sixties: uncertain, alienated, and, by any traditional standards, a loser. —Doris Kearns, *Lyndon Johnson and the American Dream*

The complications of modern life are epitomized in a traffic sign at an intersection of superhighways near Chicago. "To make a left turn," the sign advises, "make two right turns."
—Edwin Way Teale, *Reader's Digest*

equivocation. In its broadest meaning *equivocation* refers to any deliberate evasiveness, any deceptive statement that stops just short of outright lying. In a more specialized sense used by logicians, equivocation is a fallacious technique in which a person subtly changes the meaning of a key word in the course of presenting his case. If, for example, in the midst of a debate about the probable victor in another Middle Eastern war, someone were to say, "It's pointless to talk about who would win; in war nobody wins," the speaker would be indulging in a mild form of equivocation. Never mind that the point might bc valid; the speaker has introduced an ambiguity into the discussion, and now the word *win* must be redefined. Does it refer to triumph on the battlefield or to the long-term benefits that may or may not accrue to the participants?

Equivocation is different from AMPHIBOLOGY. Whereas equivocation usually refers to the ambiguity lurking in a single word, amphibology is the ambiguity caused by the grammatical or syntactic structure of whole phrases or sentences. See also FALLACY.

ersatz /ĕr-zäts, êr-, ər-**zäts**/ is a borrowing from German, literally meaning 'substitute, made of a substitute for the real thing.' This adjective was much used in World War II: *ersatz coffee; ersatz butter; ersatz cotton;* etc. It is now chiefly used in English to mean 'fake, spurious' or 'feebly imitative':

Exposed brick and wood and hanging plants and real or ersatz Victoriana have spread coast to coast. . . .
—Ada Louise Huxtable, *New York Times*

"The Idolmaker" would be worth seeing if only for its modesty, which is a blessing in these days of ersatz epics.
—Jack Kroll, *Newsweek*

Nor does it mean we're [women in business] all crazed ersatz-men trying to get man-sized ulcers and heart attacks. —Judith Daniels, *Savvy*

erstwhile, an old adverb meaning 'formerly,' is now most often used as an adjective meaning 'former, one-time':

The erstwhile sanction by the church of slavery, racial segregation, war, and economic exploitation . . .
—Martin Luther King, Jr., *Strength to Love*

Some of my erstwhile colleagues in the Nixon Administration, even men I had placed in their high positions, had grown more distant as the accusations increased.
—Charles Colson, *Born Again*

erudite /**ĕr**-yōō-dīt, **ĕr**-ōō-/ means 'deeply learned.' It can be used either favorably, in the sense 'admirably and genuinely learned,' or unfavorably, in the sense 'boringly full of abstruse knowledge, dry':

A cultivated and erudite man (at Harvard he majored in Romance languages and literature), he came up with brilliant pieces on Italian art and architecture whenever he could find a news peg to hang them on.
—Gary Paul Gates, *Air Time*

. . . he sat formally and talked to her in his stiff, pedantic way on cold and erudite subjects for two hours.
—William Faulkner, *Sartoris*

eschew. This word is sometimes criticized as being nothing but a fancy synonym for *avoid.* In fact, like most or all synonyms, it has its own special flavor. As the following quotations show, the verb *eschew* tends to mean 'avoid fastidiously, take conspicuous care to abstain from.' This overtone is not always strongly present but is probably the main motivation for a writer to choose *eschew* rather than *avoid* or another synonym.

. . . the original intelligence with which she ordered objects of art, or laid out her gardens, always eschewing that which seemed obvious to her in search for that which was exactly right . . .
—Nancy Mitford, *Madame de Pompadour*

There he wrote for the radio wire, which most of the senior wire-service men eschewed on the grounds that it was beneath them.
—Gary Paul Gates, *Air Time*

And yet market research for television programming . . . is one area that A. C. Nielsen scrupulously eschews.
—Ron Powers, *The Newscasters*

Although obviously Navy-oriented, [Admiral] Oley Sharp eschewed parochialism and dealt fairly with all the services.
—William C. Westmoreland, *A Soldier Reports*

From taking an occasional glass of beer as an excuse to gorge on free lunch, he had grown fond of an occasional session during which he drank quite a few glasses in a row and eschewed the food.
—Robert Lewis Taylor, *W. C. Fields*

The noun, a rather rare word, is *eschewal:*

Back in the old country one's knowledge of the Jewish law and one's eschewal of manual work had been marks of prestige. . . .
—Gerald Green, *The Last Angry Man*

Eskimo words. See INNUIT (ESKIMO) WORDS.

espouse literally means 'to take as a spouse, marry.' It is used figuratively to mean 'take up (a belief, cause, etc.), pursue, support':

More and more, the rebel army newspaper espoused the communist line.
—David Reed, *Reader's Digest*

If we are to serve as a beacon for human rights, we must continue to perfect here at home the rights and the values which we espouse around the world.
—Jimmy Carter, farewell address (1981)

I have mentioned that Ross was a consummately nineteenth-century figure in the number and variety of bigotries that he espoused and didn't hesitate to preach. . . .
—Brendan Gill, *Here at The New Yorker*

Now and then the word is mistakenly used in various other senses, such as 'to aspire' and 'to suppose.'

The noun is *espousal:*

. . . to Earlham College, a Quaker school whose espousal of social reform goes back to the 1830s.
—Bill Moyers, *Listening to America*

esquire, squire. ***Origin.*** The word *esquire,* of which *squire* is a shortened form, is from Medieval French *esquier* = 'shield bearer'; it was originally used of a man who served as armor bearer to a knight and was himself a candidate for knighthood. Later, esquire became the legal title of gentlemen ranking immediately below knights, while squire came to be used especially of country gentlemen who were landowners.

Uses. In Britain esquire is an unofficial title available to any otherwise untitled man. In practice it is used by those who consider themselves gentlemen. It is not used with any other title, such as Colonel, the Reverend, or Mr. It occurs only in legal documents and in addressing letters, usually capitalized and abbreviated and always coming after the name. A man named Richard Taylor is referred to in most formal contexts as *Mr. Taylor* or *Mr. Richard Taylor,* but letters would be addressed to *Richard Taylor, Esq.*

In the United States, Esq. is used in the English manner by some men who are anglophiles. It is also used formally by some justices of the peace and attorneys, women as well as men.

essay, assay. These two words, originally variant forms of one (French) word, are now largely distinct in use and meaning but are sometimes confused.

(1) *Essay* as a verb means 'to attempt (to do something).' It is a highly formal, sometimes mannered, synonym for *try:*

> To be candid, I essayed to persuade the last Democratic tenant of the White House to designate the senator as his ambassador to the Court of St. James.
> —Walter F. Murphy, *The Vicar of Christ*

> . . . it was getting late, and anxious not to disrupt the party, we essayed to steal out quietly through the kitchen.
> —S. J. Perelman, *Westward Ha!*

It is also occasionally used to mean 'try (something) out':

> Rand . . . decided a bath was the only way to get the dust out of his pores before essaying the motel cooking.
> —G. Gordon Liddy, *Out of Control*

As a noun, *essay* can be used to mean 'an attempt' or 'a testing, trying out,' but this is now rare. Most often it means 'a short or medium-length piece of prose writing, typically expressing personal thoughts or views rather than reporting facts.'

(2) *Assay* as a noun is primarily a technical word meaning 'chemical analysis, especially of a drug or metallic ore.' As a verb it means 'to analyze (a substance)' or, secondarily, 'to analyze or assess (a human quality)':

> You have got to draw your own conclusions when you get close to the time in which you live. You can't very well assay a man until a good deal of time has passed.
> —Harry Truman (quoted), *Truman Speaks*

> Authenticity is the innermost secret of the elusive mystique of the life of Harlem. The unforgivable sin here is to be a phony. . . . Out of the searing, age-old experience of being black in a hostile culture, an instinctual response assays in a lightning flash the true and the false.
> —Frank Hercules, *Reader's Digest*

Establishment. This first became a political term in England in the 1950s. It was said that the country was basically controlled by a few powerful and unpublicized figures independent of the elected government: this group was referred to as *the Establishment.* The term was soon taken up in the United States and now has several senses, the usual one being the supposed entrenched power structure that controls the country, as distinct from the formal government:

> President Kenneth D. Kaunda of Zambia, for instance, praised the Carter Administration's new African policies but wondered whether "the U.S. Establishment" would permit their pursuit. —*New York Times*

More generally, *Establishment* can also mean simply 'the established middle and upper classes, with their values and culture':

> He was an Establishment type from the welts of his tan cordovans to the buttoned-down collar of his Brooks Brothers broadcloth shirt. —*Harper's*

The eastern (liberal) Establishment—sometimes *Eastern,* sometimes *establishment*—

refers to the particular power structure centered in New York, wielding influence through banking, business, and the media:

> Bush got himself tagged with a charge that has proved damaging: that his background . . . made him a member of the Eastern liberal establishment. The accusation is unfair. . . . —*Time*

As the quotations show, the word is essentially a hostile one, used from the outside by critics of the status quo. Virtually every major field of human activity is now said to have its own establishment:

> The article attracted instant attention—and some criticism—from the foreign-policy "establishment."
> —*Newsweek*

> . . . detailed and often impassioned rebuttals by many of the elite of the energy establishment. —*Science*

> . . . this latter group represents only a fraction of the American medical establishment. —*Reader's Digest*

esthetic, esthetics, esthete. See AESTHETIC, ESTHETIC.

etc., et al. Both abbreviations mean 'and the rest.' *Etc.* (from Latin *et cetera* = 'and the remaining things') refers only to things. *Et al.* (from Latin *et alii, et aliae* = 'and the other people') refers only to persons. *Etc.* is pronounced in full, /ĕt **sĕt**-ər-ə, **sĕt**-rə/. *Et al.* is pronounced as an abbreviation, /ĕt **ăl**/. They are both appropriate to all but the most formal and literary style.

ethic, ethos. These two nouns started off with distinctly separate meanings but have encroached on each other.

Before discussing them we will deal with *ethics* and *ethical*. *Ethics* is the theory and practice of what is right and wrong in human behavior. *Ethical* means 'relating to ethics.' Both words are also used (like *morals* and *moral*) in the purely positive sense: *ethics* can mean 'good principles, a high standard of human behavior,' and *ethical* often means 'following good principles.' The nouns *ethic* and *ethos* /ē thŏs/, which are from the same Greek source, are colored by both of these senses but are more objective and anthropological. *Ethics* and *ethical* tend to assume that we agree about the basics of human duty and the principles of right and wrong. *Ethic* and *ethos* look at human societies more from the outside and observe different patterns of behavior with some detachment.

An *ethic* is a particular system or theory of values, priorities, drives, and morals:

> The battle lines are being drawn between . . . the Judeo-Christian ethic and atheism.
> —Homer Duncan (letter), *Smithsonian*

> There was no room in Rebekah's Protestant ethic for uncontrolled and frivolous behavior.
> —Doris Kearns, *Lyndon Johnson and the American Dream*

> The God of early Old Testament days was a tribal god and the ethic was tribal.
> —Martin Luther King, Jr., *Strength to Love*

> . . . the Irish legacy in its Kennedy form had to accommodate itself to the puritan ethic, the belief in discipline, work and achievement.
> —Arthur M. Schlesinger, Jr., *Robert Kennedy and His Times*

An *ethos* is the underlying, morally defined nature or character of a human type or group:

> The Kennedys had absorbed enough of the Boston ethos to have a certain reserve, discipline and frugality as well as a large measure of civic and intellectual aspiration.
> —Arthur M. Schlesinger, Jr., *Robert Kennedy and His Times*

> . . . we must admit that we also do not know the social and religious ethos of the megalith builders [of Stonehenge].
> —Glynn Daniel, *Scientific American*

> . . . the place was pervaded by a kind of "gentlemanly" ethos that made Merton feel crude and "colonial."
>
> —Monica Furlong, *Merton: A Biography*

> Any Christian who is an active Episcopalian . . . knows that there is a definite "in-house" Anglican ethos which permeates the Anglican community worldwide. . . .
>
> —S. M. Giovangelo, *National Catholic Reporter*

But, neat as it might be to keep these two words and their meanings separate and exclusive, we can't do so. Both words are in heavy fashionable use nowadays, and in many contexts it isn't really possible or useful to insist that one or the other would have been the only possible choice.

> According to the new charge, Harvard, ancient betrayer of Calvinism, was now betraying that religious creed's secular ghost: the ethos of capitalism.
>
> —Leonard and Mark Silk, *The American Establishment*

> Unfortunately, our society has not yet outgrown the hoodlum ethos, which admires people who get away with tax chiseling.
>
> —Jack Anderson, *Savannah Morning News*

> Musically as well as personally, the Slits embody the individualism at the heart of the original British punk ethic. . . .
>
> —Lester Bangs, *Rolling Stone*

> Among prime-time series, "Happy Days" and "Eight Is Enough" project the family ethic. . . .
>
> —Ron Powers, *The Newscasters*

ethnic. ***Origin.*** In the 1960s the words *race* and *racial* had become tainted by association with *racism,* and most people were no longer sure just what a "race" was anyway. As often happens in cases like this, the general vocabulary solved the problem by borrowing from a technical vocabulary. The word *ethnic,* from Greek *ethnikos* = 'belonging to a race,' from *ethnos* = 'race,' was used chiefly by anthropologists and sociologists. As an adjective, it meant 'relating to (a) race or culture,' and as a noun it meant 'person belonging to a particular race or culture.' (The word has also been used by Bible scholars to mean 'gentile' or 'heathen.')

Uses. Thus, *ethnic* was adopted into everyday language as a substitute for *race* and *racial:* a "race" became an *ethnic group,* and it could have *ethnic pride* without being accused of "racism."

In global or international contexts the word refers to racial or cultural identity rather than citizenship:

> In 1964, Turkey felt humiliated when President Johnson opposed Turkish intervention in Cyprus, where ethnic Turks comprise 18 percent of the population and ethnic Greeks 80 percent.
>
> —*New York Times*

> China charged that Hanoi began moving against the Chinese population in early 1977, when . . . they expelled Chinese ethnics who had settled long ago in northern Vietnam.
>
> —*Boston Globe*

In the broadest sense all human cultures are equally ethnic. But the dominant white population of the urban industrialized West seems to feel that it has somehow lost its *ethnicity,* or perhaps risen above it. In practice the word *ethnic* is mostly applied to "backward" cultures around the world and to minority cultures that have so far survived assimilation into the growing uniformity of the modern world. Suburbia, multinational companies, and Ivy League colleges, quaint though some of their folkways certainly are, are never called ethnic. Japanese traditional potters are ethnic, Japanese bankers are not. In U.S. domestic politics the word has a yet narrower application; some are more ethnic than others. Culturally speaking, American blacks, Jews, Indians, and Chinese are no more "ethnic" than White Anglo-Saxon Protestants and the Scotch-Irish. But in political reporting "the ethnics" now usually means the predominantly white and European minorities—the Italians, Hispanics, Portuguese, Poles and other Slavic groups, Germans, Hungarians, Balts, and Greeks. The inclusiveness, of course, varies from place to place and from writer to writer:

> Fishermen in the highly ethnic fleets, especially in Gloucester and New Bedford, say the logbooks are unreadable and should be translated into Italian and Portuguese.
> —*National Fisherman*

> . . . both General Mills and General Foods are moving into Mexican and other ethnic food restaurants.
> —*Business Week*

> Australia's second ethnic radio station, 3EA, will open in Melbourne at 6:30 A.M. today. . . . Each day, 3EA will broadcast in a different language—Monday in Greek, Tuesday German, Wednesday Yugoslav, Thursday Italian, Friday Spanish, Saturday Maltese and Sunday Turkish and Arabic. . . . there will be 90 per cent ethnic music of a very high quality.
> —*The Australian*

> There is a lot of talk these days about all sorts of minorities suffering discrimination equally with blacks: ethnics, Jews, immigrants and so on.
> —Anthony Lewis, *New York Times*

> . . . denounced the canonization of the Adams Family on Public TV because America's ethnics are unable to identify with such a WASP-Yankee dynasty.
> —Harriet Van Horne, *New York Post*

ethnicity. When ETHNIC became such a common word, the noun *ethnicity* was bound to follow:

> Ethnicity is also having its day this year. You have your choice [of themes on calendars] of the people of Appalachia, three centuries of the Jew in America, or Indians of the Northeast.
> —Lisa Hammel, *New York Times*

> Fifty-seventh Street is elegant; this is not the New York of ethnicity and small-scale charm.
> —Paul Goldberger, *New York Times*

ethos. See ETHIC, ETHOS.

etiolated /ē-tē-ə-lāt-əd/. This is originally a term used in botany and gardening. To *etiolate* a plant is to deprive it of sunlight so that it does not develop chlorophyll and remains white. This is regularly done with some vegetables, such as cauliflower. Figuratively, *etiolated* is used as a fancy word for 'pale and flabby, not vigorous,' sometimes 'effete':

> Philippa noticed the strong body, curiously disproportionate to the etiolated neck and the thin face.
> —P. D. James, *Innocent Blood*

> My theory is that the revolt against style has shown up an impoverished and etiolated sense of identity in the modern Western community.
> —Max Harris, *The Australian*

etymology. ***Confusion With Entomology.*** The question most often asked regarding *etymology* is, Is it about words or bugs? *Etymology* = 'word history,' and to clear up this confusion, we offer a memorizing formula with a realistic explanation. The formula: *En*tomology is *in*sect study. The explanation: Greek science was sufficiently modern to classify insects by their body structure, as 'the segmented creatures.' The word *entomon* = 'insect' literally means 'segmented thing,' from the adjective *entomos* = 'segmented, cut in pieces' (*en* = 'in' + *tom-* = 'cut'). The Romans, who took over Greek science wholesale, often translated Greek technical terms into Latin equivalents. They rendered Greek *entomon* as Latin *insectum*, likewise meaning 'segmented thing,' from the adjective *insectus* = 'segmented, cut in pieces' (*in* = 'in' + *sectus* = 'cut'). Greek *en* and Latin *in*, both meaning 'in,' are variant forms of one ancestral word. We have borrowed both Greek *entomon*, to form the word *entomology*, and Latin *insectum*, to form the word *insect*. The *en-* of *entomology* and the *in-* of *insect* are thus genuinely equivalent; the formula is not simply a coincidence.

Origin of Etymology. Words are mysterious. Some words, like *cuckoo* or *splat*, are obviously expressive of real sounds, or onomatopoeic (see ONOMATOPOEIA). The rest seem to be arbitrary symbols: there is no connection between the word *sparrow* and the bird, or between the word *beauty* and the human perceptions it refers to. Yet English-speaking children and adults alike use these words unhesitatingly and precisely. Why these words for these meanings? Where do they come from? This seems to be a universal question, asked by speakers of all human languages. The science of etymology is the attempt to answer it.

Basic words are so deeply programmed into our consciousness that they seem to have an inherent, fundamental meaning. Much of the worldwide interest in etymology takes the form of wanting to know what a word "really" means. The Greeks, following this line of inquiry in their usual logical way, felt that there must be a basic or natural language, of which their own speech was only a distorted reflection, and that underlying every actual word was an original, archetypal, word. This they called the *etymos logos* = 'true word' (*etymos* = 'true' + *logos* = 'word'), and the study of these archetypal words they called *etymologia* = 'true-word study.' The Romans adopted both the term and the concept, and we have borrowed it as *etymology*.

Modern Etymology. The Greek and Roman theory about words was, however, completely wrong. Studying the origins of words will not lead to inherent or archetypal meanings. Human language is so old (at least 100,000 years) that we have no idea how it evolved; and although we can trace many of our own words several thousand years into the past, we have no hope of reaching the true beginnings. In any case, words are created by humans for ordinary human purposes following the rules of each language; are passed on from generation to generation; are borrowed from language to language; and frequently change their forms and meanings. These processes are now accurately studied by the science of linguistics (see LINGUIST, LINGUISTICS). For us, an etymology is not the imaginary "true word" of the Greeks and Romans. It is simply the *true history* of a word as far as it has been worked out; any good modern dictionary contains etymologies for most of the words of our language.

The Etymological Fallacy. Unfortunately, the idea that origins are the key to present meanings has never quite died out. This fallacy still sometimes leads people to make imaginary rules of usage based on etymologies. The adjective *averse* = 'reluctant, opposed' is from Latin *āversus* = 'turned away, hostile' (*ā-* = 'away, from' + *versus* = 'turned'). Some people, influenced by their knowledge of this etymology, believe that *averse to* must be bad English and are careful to always use *averse from*. In fact, *averse to* is unquestionably the right idiom in English. The false usage rule results from a misunderstanding of the nature of etymology. Origins are only origins: they don't have an ongoing power over their offspring. Another example is the word *between;* its etymology reveals that it was originally—2,000 years ago, before the Anglo-Saxons settled in Britain—formed from a word related to the word *two*. Therefore, argue those who are subject to the etymological fallacy, it is now wrong to use *between* when referring to more than two items. In fact, it has correctly been used of more than two items throughout its recorded history in English. See also AVERSE, ADVERSE; BETWEEN, AMONG.

The Value of Etymology. "Languages are the pedigrees of nations," said Samuel Johnson. If etymologies don't reveal inherent meanings, what do they reveal? Merely history—sometimes illuminating, sometimes surprising, sometimes baffling or confusing. Knowledge of etymology is of little practical value. One can use a language correctly and effectively without knowing anything about etymology, just as one can live a full life without bothering about history. But to anyone who has a taste for the past and its elusive relation to the present, etymology offers insights and satisfactions. It has some advantages over old cities, tours, and historical novels. The language we use daily is both a vast museum of our culture and a living part of it, deeply stratified with layer upon layer of deposits from every age and constantly renewed, fixed up, and adapted to the environment of tomorrow. The utterances and readings of ordinary people are full of words of the most venerable antiquity mingled with the latest trendyisms, blunt Anglo-Saxonisms, suave Latinisms, Gothic words from the Middle Ages, aureate words of the Renaissance, colonial and frontier words, words borrowed into English from each of the five continents. It is easy to inform yourself about them in the most relaxed and random way, simply by looking up etymologies in a dictionary. The knowledge so gained may have little or no effect upon your speech or writing; it will certainly deepen your interest in and appreciation of your language. Every language is no doubt equally fascinating to its own speakers. English, because of its gigantic vocabulary—supposedly the largest ever accumulated and still growing fast—offers an endlessly satisfying field of etymology. This book gives wide coverage to it, both at individual words and in entries dealing with the background and historical phases of the language and with the foreign sources of much of its vocabulary, as follows. *Background and history:* INDO-EUROPEAN; GERMANIC; OLD ENGLISH; MIDDLE ENGLISH; ELIZABETHAN ENGLISH; MODERN ENGLISH. *Foreign sources:* GREEK WORDS, LATIN WORDS, FRENCH WORDS, ITALIAN WORDS, SPANISH WORDS, NORSE WORDS, DUTCH WORDS, GERMAN WORDS; PERSIAN WORDS, SANSKRIT WORDS, INDIAN WORDS (INDIA); ARABIC WORDS, TURKISH WORDS; CHINESE WORDS, JAPANESE WORDS, MALAY WORDS; INDIAN WORDS (AMERICAN INDIAN), CARIBBEAN WORDS, SOUTH AMERICAN WORDS.

euphemism. ***Taboo and Traditional Euphemism.*** Every human language contains many words that are marked as taboo—to be avoided in certain circumstances or entirely. The replacement of such words with non-taboo words is called *euphemism.* (This word comes from Greek *euphēmismos* = 'fair-speech,' a technical term in rhetoric for the substitution of a palatable expression for a bluntly accurate but offensive one.) In so-called primitive and highly traditional societies, taboo and euphemism are two sides of one coin and are essentially a social and religious control. This control survives to this day in Modern English in many forms and at many levels, especially with words relating to sex and excretion.

Stylistic Euphemism. The avoidance of straightforward language for reasons short of taboo is also called euphemism. It ranges from tactful and convenient usage to plain lying. Sensitively chosen euphemisms can serve to smooth conversation and help to keep controversy rational and polite. "I'm afraid we've got to let you go" is a polite alternative to the brutally direct "You're fired." It is no accident that euphemism is much favored in the language of diplomacy. "The talks were frank" really means "We stated our positions and failed to reach agreement." Advertising and public relations are inevitably full of euphemism.

How far to go is a matter of taste or ethics, not of usage. Some of us may be annoyed rather than mollified to hear radio and TV commercials called *messages,* or to see pornography called *adult books.* Other commercial euphemisms seem more reasonable. The *giant Japanese spider crab* was virtually unsalable in the United States; renamed the *Alaska king crab,* it was immediately recognized as a delicacy.

The cruelest euphemisms are the political ones. The epitome of these is provided by the Roman historian Tacitus, writing of the Roman conquest of Britain. In an imaginary speech made up by Tacitus, the Pictish leader Calgacus, addressing his men before their last and hopeless battle, says of the Romans, "They make a desert and call it peace." This serviceable euphemism survives in the 20th century as *pacification:*

> As for your criticism of our pacification,
> you are right that war is devastating.

> But we are doing everything we could to limit that. We rebuilt as we went along. . . .
>
> —Lyndon Johnson (quoted), Doris Kearns, *Lyndon Johnson and the American Dream*

The habit of euphemism, whether from politeness, wishful thinking, or cynical intent to deceive, is too deeply programmed into human nature to be disapproved of merely as a matter of language use. We offer a miscellany of further examples below.

> In a world of eternal blondes, brunettes and redheads there are certain women of a certain age who would rather not have what Clairol calls "a coloring experience."
>
> —Georgia Dullea, *New York Times*

> Fat is one word we'd never, never dream of using. Nor are we fond of portly, oversized or heavyset. When referring to our customers, we much prefer to say king-sized.
>
> —tailor opening an "outsize" shop, *New York Times*

> I have seen muskrats for sale in fancy butcher shops under the euphemism of marsh rabbit.
>
> —Euell Gibbons, *Stalking the Wild Asparagus*

> . . . an even larger problem—delicately called "inventory shrinkage"—that stores are facing these days. "Shrinkage" is retailer's jargon for losses to shoplifting, theft by employees, and clerical error. —*Fortune*

> . . . the President had . . . ordered Griffin Bell to "expedite" Marston, which in CIA parlance translates to "terminate with extreme prejudice."
>
> —Patrick Buchanan, *Boston Herald American*

See also JARGON; VOGUE WORDS.

euphoria is literally 'a feeling of well-being.' It is used specifically of the intensely pleasurable experiences induced by some drugs and also of psychological experiences of happiness that are so strong as to be probably irrational:

> For 15 minutes or so, a tremendous, exhilarating high fills the user. Then, when the euphoria abates, the drug must be used again, and again.
>
> —Frank Swertlow, *TV Guide*

> Many clinicians believe, as a matter of fact, that long episodes of euphoria represent what is really a flight from an underlying despair. . . . Judith Karlin, for example, was triggered into those wild destructive euphorias so easily, and by such minor life changes and stresses.
>
> —Maggie Scarf, *Unfinished Business*

More generally, *euphoria* is used of any mood or feeling of very great pleasure or happiness; but the word nearly always has a depressing edge to it, and the context reveals that this happiness is not entirely warranted by the situation—it is an unrealistic overreaction, and it is likely to vanish suddenly when the real world comes back into its usual focus.

> It was the period of all-pervading euphoria and enchantment. The skyrocket of mounting profits was lighting up the sky, emitting awesome and delightful bursts of ecstasy, and it would never come down. . . .
>
> —Roger Garis, *My Father Was Uncle Wiggily*

> In the wake of the Republican Party's sweeping victory, news items about the fate of Prime Minister Margaret Thatcher's policies in Britain may be a better guide to the next four years than the euphoria of conservatives. . . .
>
> —Paul Craig Roberts, *New York Times*

> Along came a local union clown in Cleveland to shatter the euphoria. He seized what he thought was his chance to become a big shot by threatening to keep our show off the air. . . .
>
> —Mike Douglas, *My Story*

The same applies to the adjective *euphoric*, with its adverb, *euphorically:*

> Nixon had been euphoric, filled with wonderment and the sense of history, at the prospect of going to China, but he was withdrawn and filled with a sense of caution in returning to Moscow.
>
> —William Safire, *Before the Fall*

> This feat led some American geologists to announce euphorically that earthquake prediction was now practically an accomplished fact.
>
> —Ronald Schiller, *Reader's Digest*

euphuism. See SHAKESPEARE AND THE ENGLISH LANGUAGE.

evening. In a development parallel to that of MORNING, which originally meant 'the coming of "morn" at daybreak,' *evening* took on its present-participial construction several centuries ago in signifying the coming on of "even," the time of dusk and deepening darkness at the close of day. *Evening* has since superseded *even,* which survives today chiefly as an archaic element in old poems. *Evening* now denotes the period between afternoon and night—approximately the interval between sunset and bedtime, although for many Americans, conceivably most, evening commences all through the year at 6 P.M. Figuratively, *evening* can also mean the declining period of a person's life or of anything else that can be compared to a day, such as a career or a term in public office.

An evening spent in a particular manner—entertaining friends, for example—is often called such: *an evening of cards; a gala evening.* The word figures, too, in numerous combinations: *evening gown* = 'a woman's formal dress'; *evening prayer* = 'prayer service at evening in the Anglican church'; *evening star* = 'planet that crosses the local meridian before midnight, especially Mercury or Venus when visible in the west just after sunset.' And because of the associations of hushed melancholy and resigned surrender to fate evoked by fading daylight and approaching dark, poets have long used the word to set a scene and establish a mood at the openings of poems.

> It is a beauteous evening, calm and free,
> The holy time is quiet as a nun
> Breathless with adoration.
>
> —William Wordsworth, *It Is a Beauteous Evening*

> Let us go then, you and I,
> When the evening is spread out against the sky
> Like a patient etherised upon a table.
>
> —T. S. Eliot, *The Love Song of J. Alfred Prufrock*

◇ ***Recommendation.*** To say or write *8 P.M. in the evening* is redundant. Correct forms include *eight o'clock in the evening; eight in the evening;* or simply *8 P.M.* (For the use of figures versus spelled-out numbers see NUMBER STYLE.)

every. The adjective *every* is always singular: *Every cloud has a silver lining.*

The pronouns *everybody* and *everyone* are basically singular and always take singular verbs: *Everyone was there.* Other elements in a sentence relating to *everybody* or *everyone* are usually singular but may be plural: *Everyone gets a share. Everyone collected their coats and hats and left in twos and threes.* The choice between *everybody* and *everyone* is entirely a matter of personal preference, but *everyone* is at least three times as common as *everybody.*

Every one means 'each individually,' while *everyone* means 'all people, each collectively.' *Every one* can refer to things as well as persons, *everyone* only to persons: *Pick up every one of those toys. Every one of the team got sick after the banquet. He told everyone about his new job.* As can be seen from the examples, these words are also pronounced with different stress: *every one* /ĕv-rē **wŭn**, **ĕv**-rē **wŭn**/; *everyone* /**ĕv**-rē-wŭn/.

everyone . . . he. Everyone knows that *everyone* means 'all people.' The word expresses a plural concept; but because it is singular in form, traditional usage has called for a singular pronoun: *Will everyone please take his seat.* This requirement sometimes leads to outright absurdities, as in the review of a poetry reading that ended, "When the visiting poet finished his reading, everyone in the audience stood on his feet."

Everyone . . . he constructions are painful to many people—not just to that visiting poet. To some people, they sound stiff, starchy, and unnatural; the singular pronoun does not seem to suit the plural sense. To other people, they seem to needlessly exclude women. Increasing numbers of good speakers and writers have started to use *he or she* in place of *he* alone.

An even simpler solution has been in use for quite a long time. Many writers and speakers both past and present have referred to *everyone* (or *anyone* or *someone* or *everybody*) as *they*.

> Now this king did keepe a great house, that everie body might come and take their meat freely.
>
> —Philip Sidney, *Arcadia* (1580)

> Every body does and says what they please.
>
> —Lord Byron, *Works* (1820)

> Everybody seems to recover their spirits.
>
> —John Ruskin, *Ethics of the Dust* (1866)

> Every one had made up their minds that I was to be one thing, and I came out another.
>
> —George W. Dasent, *Eventful Life* (1870)

> Everyone then looked about them silently, in suspense and expectation.
>
> —W. H. Mallock, *The New Republic* (1877)

> It's enough to drive anyone out of their senses.
>
> —George Bernard Shaw, *Candida* (1893)

In more recent years editors have diligently removed *everyone . . . they* from most books and articles. The usage has appeared in print chiefly in quotations of spoken English.

> "If someone comes here wanting to go into data processing because they think of being a keypunch operator but then change their mind, we'll find something else for them," [Herbert M.] Sussman said.
>
> —Andy Soltis, *New York Post*

Notice that Ruskin, Dasent, and Shaw treated *everybody, every one,* and *anyone* as plural, referring to "their spirits," "their minds," and "their senses." Sussman, however, employed *someone* in a singular sense, but he used "they think" instead of "he or she thinks," "their mind" instead of "his or her mind."

◇ ***Recommendation.*** Teachers and editors who still insist on *everyone . . . he* will accept *he or she, she or he* as being proper grammar. If you prefer *everyone . . . they* as being more natural, don't apologize. You will be in good company, with a long tradition to back you up. See also HE; HE OR SHE; THEY.

evince. This is a distinctly formal word meaning 'to give proof of,' especially 'to show that one possesses (a certain quality)':

> These are days when Christians must evince wise restraint and calm reasonableness.
>
> —Martin Luther King, Jr., *Strength to Love*

> Did Margery know the difference between his mother and Mrs. Hills or was she just evincing class prejudice?
>
> —Mary McCarthy, *Birds of America*

ex-, former. When the prefix *ex-* is attached to a title (as in *ex-president*) or a word expressing relationship (as in *ex-husband*), the resulting term designates the person who held the position immediately before the current holder. The term *former* should be used to refer to any previous holders of the position.

Thus, when Jimmy Carter took the oath as President, Gerald Ford became the ex-President; when Ronald Reagan was sworn in as President, Carter became the ex-President and Ford a former President.

In the same way, a man currently married to his fourth wife should not (if he wishes to be "correct") refer expansively to all his ex-wives. Only his third wife can properly be called his ex-wife; the first two are his former wives (and no doubt well rid of him).

exacerbate. The basic meaning is 'to make harsher or bitterer,' especially 'to make (a pain or diseased condition) worse' and 'to embitter (a person or human feelings)':

> But experts agree that [marijuana] may exacerbate older people's heart conditions.
> —Joyce Lowinson (quoted), *Woman's Day*

> Congressional frustration was exacerbated by the Gallup poll in January, which showed me with an approval rating at 68 percent.
> —Richard Nixon, *R.N.*

The word is now increasingly used to mean 'make (trouble of any kind) worse, aggravate (a situation)':

> Italy's present crisis has been exacerbated by a spreading plague of riots, lootings, assassinations, kidnapings and bombings. . . . —*Time*

> . . . only with extreme reluctance would they decide on measures that would further exacerbate the dollar's misfortunes. —*Boston Globe*

except. See ACCEPT, EXCEPT.

excess. See IN EXCESS OF.

exclamation point. See PUNCTUATION.

exclave. See ENCLAVE, EXCLAVE.

excoriate literally means 'to strip the skin off, flay.' It is used figuratively to mean 'condemn bitterly, denounce in scathing terms':

> He also excoriated welfare cheats, Viet Nam war protesters and the Supreme Court. —*Time*

> Erkki Haglund, our Finnish editor, cited a letter he'd received from an ardent leftist, who excoriated the magazine for accommodating what he called U.S. imperialism.
> —The editors, *Reader's Digest*

> Panama's strongman, General Omar Torrijos, as leftist and nationalist, won votes by excoriating American imperialism. —*Brunswick* (Ga.) *News*

exemplar, exemplary. An *exemplar* is something or someone so excellent as to be a good model for imitation:

> Professor Nisbet's book is by all odds the finest general account of the history of the idea of progress in any language. It is an exemplar of a well-proportioned study—compact, succinct, lucid.
> —Frank E. Manuel, *New York Times Book Review*

> Ross liked to be thought of as an exemplar of common sense, but all the evidence of his life is to the contrary.
> —Brendan Gill, *Here at The New Yorker*

The adjective *exemplary* usually means 'worthy of imitation, excellent, outstanding':

> The Prince of Wales displayed an exemplary capacity in later life for preventing mischief, and for making happy everyone by whom he was surrounded.
> —Philip Magnus, *Edward VII*

> On the other side of the coin, I have never seen a more devoted son [than Joe Namath], his manners with older women are exemplary. . . .
> —Howard Cosell, *Cosell*

> Privately run package delivery services already exist, and their performance, by contrast with that of the Post Office, is exemplary.
> —William F. Buckley, Jr., *Execution Eve*

Exemplary can also mean 'intended to serve as a warning,' as in *exemplary punishment,* and 'illustrative, typical,' as in *exemplary paragraphs*.

exigent, exigency. Referring to people, the adjective *exigent* /**ĕk**-sə-jənt/ means 'very demanding':

> If the Prime Minister was exigent, he was also thoughtful . . . having heard that excessive demands were being made upon me in Parliament. . . .
> —Anthony Eden, *The Reckoning*

Referring to situations, *exigent* means 'urgently requiring action.' The noun *exigency* /**ĕk**-sə-jən-sē, ĕk-**sĭ**-/ thus means either 'pressure urgently applied' or 'situation urgently requiring action, emergency':

> Thus have the Chinese Communists been transformed, under diplomatic exigency; so that now the polls tell us that the American people, assimilating the Nixon trip, have discovered that the Chinese enterprise is "intelligent," "progressive," and "practical."
> —William F. Buckley, Jr., *Execution Eve*

> Exposed to plunging fire from above, the feinting troops were trapped, an exigency unanticipated by their commander. —William Manchester, *American Caesar*

The plural, *exigencies*, usually means 'demanding conditions, tough requirements':

> . . . Ivar was ill prepared to meet the exigencies of the Arctic.
> —A. E. Maxwell and Ivar Ruud, *Reader's Digest*

> He was just some little crybaby from Plains, some businessman who knew nothing about the exigencies of politics.
> —James Wooten, *Dasher*

exordium. Old term for an introduction in a piece of expository writing. See EXPOSITION.

exotic. Literally, the adjective *exotic* means merely 'foreign, not native to a particular place.' In this sense it is used especially of plants. In general usage it usually means 'foreign and interesting' or 'richly strange':

> For the first time, a Muscovite tsar, the ruler of a dimly perceived, exotic land, was traveling in Europe, where he might be seen, examined, and marveled at.
> —Robert K. Massie, *Peter the Great*

> This, the true story of six young Americans, takes place in an exotic land of tinkling wind bells and clashing cymbals, half a world away—the Royal Kingdom of Laos.
> —Thomas A. Dooley, *The Edge of Tomorrow*

> . . . he was familiar with the coded whistles setting the dogs to work, and plied his whip much better than Frank, still learning this exotic Australian art.
> —Colleen McCullough, *The Thorn Birds*

> I found a gift shop loaded with elaborate boxes of exotic foods, perfect for Christmas shopping.
> —Joshua Logan, *Josh*

Exotic is also used to mean merely 'novel and unorthodox, unfamiliar':

> . . . at a time when computer analysis was still regarded as an exotic and unreliable means of projecting election results. —Gary Paul Gates, *Air Time*

> . . . speed up development of solar power, gasohol and energy from biomass and other exotic sources.
> —*U.S. News & World Report*

expect is often used to mean 'consider likely, suppose (that something is so),' without necessarily any sense of looking ahead: *I expect you're tired from the journey.*

◇ ***Recommendation.*** This use has been frowned on but is perfectly respectable and standard.

expletive as an adjective means 'serving to fill out.' An *expletive* is, first, a meaningless word used to fill out a line, or a particle used by idiom but apparently not contributing to meaning. Examples are "O" in "Green grow the rushes, O!" and *there* in *Across the street there stood a tall tree.* Second, an expletive is a meaningless exclamation or profanity, or any curse word.

> He doesn't smoke, drinks only an occasional glass of wine and seldom utters an expletive stronger than "Jiminy Criminy."
>
> —Dave Anderson, *Reader's Digest*

> They [a group of Londoners working as firemen in World War II] had few opinions on any general subject, and their conversation, with its unending string of sexual expletives, was strikingly monotonous.
>
> —Peter Quennell, *The Wanton Chase*

The word won a certain notoriety from the published transcriptions of the Watergate tapes, which contained innumerable instances of "expletive deleted." This phrase itself had a journalistic vogue.

> I like New York. I used to think it was full of (expletive deleted), but I met some real nice people.
>
> —Billy Carter (quoted), *New York Times*

exposition. Most people, if asked, would probably subdivide English prose into the categories of fiction and nonfiction. This is a perfectly reasonable subdivision, but it is essentially a classification useful to readers. People who are concerned with the nuts-and-bolts techniques of writing prose are likely to find the terms *narration, narrative, exposition,* and *expository* more to the point.

In general, *narration* and *narrative* refer to the art of telling a story; *exposition* and *expository,* to the art of conveying information. While it is true that narrative techniques predominate in fiction and expository techniques in nonfiction, there is also a great deal of crossover. The skillful report writer, no less than the skillful novelist, knows that all the techniques of prose writing may be grist for his or her mill. In this entry we shall consider some of the fundamentals of writing expository prose. The techniques of narrative prose are discussed at NARRATION.

The kinds of writing in which exposition flourishes are legion—letters (both personal and business), memos, reports, school themes, news stories, columns, magazine articles, advertising copy, essays, textbooks, biographies, and so on and on. Each form has its peculiarities, but all must obey certain common rules having to do with logic, efficiency, and the conventions of style.

Nothing is more basic to good expository prose than structure. Since the underlying object of most exposition is to inform or persuade the reader, the manner in which the writer arranges the material is all-important. The old formula that the U.S. Army used to give its prospective lecturers is, "Tell 'em what you're going to tell 'em; then tell 'em; then tell 'em what you've told 'em." Not a bad prescription to start with.

Beginnings. "Tell 'em what you're going to tell 'em" corresponds both to what ancient rhetoricians called the *exordium* /ĕg-**zôr**-dē-əm/, or introduction, and to the *propositio* /prō-pə-**sĭt**-ē-ō/, or statement of the main topic to be discussed. In the shorter forms of expository writing, the introduction and the statement of the topic are often combined. For example, a personal letter might begin:

> Dear Helen,
> The flight back from our lovely visit with you and Frank in Omaha was an absolute nightmare. When we got to the airport . . .

Here, virtually without preliminaries, the writer launches into a description of her experience. Similarly, the heading of the typical interoffice memo is designed to dispense with lengthy (or indeed any) introductory matter.

> TO: Peter Smith
> FROM: George Harper
> RE: Worsening inventory/sales ratio
> The latest Inventory Status Report shows that . . .

Major newspaper stories, though not necessarily short, also usually begin with unintroduced statements of the main topic. Here is a representative front-page story from the August 9, 1981, issue of the *New York Times:*

> Washington, Aug. 8—At a White House meeting on Thursday, President Reagan decided to go forward with the full production of neutron weapons in the face of warnings that the surprise move would lead to a storm of protest in Western Europe, Administration officials said today.
>
> —Leslie H. Gelb

The reporter used this kind of lead because newspaper reports generally try to adhere to the "pyramid style," in which exposition moves steadily from summary statements through particulars of diminishing importance. Thus, ideally, the newspaper's makeup staff can fit copy into its allotted space by cutting any news report from the bottom up, without ever damaging coherence. Thus, too, readers who may wish only to skim the first few paragraphs of a report will nevertheless be able to grasp the most important information it contains.

But though exposition obviously can take off straight from a topic statement, a well-wrought introduction—short or long—can be extremely helpful. Such an introduction can present you, the writer, to the reader; set the tone in which you intend to treat the subject; and provide useful background information about it. A skillful introduction can also capture the reader's attention and convince him that he may actually enjoy reading what follows. Sometimes such introductions even employ narrative, or storytelling, devices. Here are two other leads from the same issue of the *New York Times* that featured Leslie Gelb's neutron bomb story.

> Washington—Ten years ago this week, I hustled aboard Marine One, the Presidential helicopter, to a secret rendezvous at the Catoctin Mountain retreat named after Richard Nixon's son-in-law.
>
> "What's the big mystery?" I asked Herbert Stein. . . .
>
> —William Safire

> London, Aug. 6—From the stone portico of St. James's Palace this afternoon, a queue of people six abreast stretched down Marlborough Street and the Mall to Buckingham Palace, a 10-minute walk away. . . . —Steven Rattner

Safire's topic statement, which finally emerges in the sixth paragraph, is: "What lessons can the Reagan men draw from the stunning economic action of the Nixon men?" Rattner's subject proves, two long sentences later, to be that the public display of royal wedding presents became a major tourist attraction in London. But certainly neither piece suffers from the insertion of interesting introductory matter before the announcement of the main topic.

Middles. The army's "Tell 'em" corresponds to the presentation of the main body of information the writer wants to give the reader. How is this done best? If the writer's primary purpose is to describe, he must organize his material as coherently as possible. Some subjects lend themselves to obvious forms of organization. Historical accounts or personal experiences can often be presented in chronological order. Descriptions of physical objects usually have to be organized according to spatial or geographical relationships. Some event sequences and many idea sequences can be organized as chains of cause and effect. Action sequences—as in descriptions of how a certain object is made—usually follow a step-by-step organizational form known as *process.*

But often, in organizing exposition, we must first analyze our subject matter before we can make it coherent to the reader. We may, for example, have to define our terms.

> Wealth is never properly defined, for the purpose of economic study, by any one of the answers a person would naturally give off-hand. For instance, most people would say that a man's wealth was the money he was worth. But that, of course, is nonsense. . . .
>
> —Hilaire Belloc,
> *Economics for Young People*

Or, we may be forced to spell out certain classifications.

> The rudiments of the social state, so far as they are known to us at all, are known to us through testimony of three sorts—accounts by contemporaries of civilizations less advanced than their own, the records which particular races have preserved concerning their primitive history, and ancient law.
> —Henry Sumner Maine, *Ancient Law*

And to make our meaning clearer we may want to use examples, comparisons, and contrasts; to be more vivid we may also turn to such rhetorical devices as metaphor, simile, and understatement. Here is one of the most famous passages in English, from the King James Bible:

> For now we see through a glass, darkly, but then face to face: now I know in part; but then shall I know even as also I am known. —I Corinthians 13:12

In any case we shall certainly want to be sure that our presentation has adequately addressed itself to the six famous questions good reporters are always supposed to ask themselves: Who? What? When? Where? How? and (if possible) Why?

Persuasion. If our object, in addition to imparting information, is to persuade the reader to a particular point of view, our order of presentation is apt to be even more complicated. The introduction may have to be more informative and descriptive than it would otherwise need to be. The announcement of the main topic will also have to announce our position on the topic (unless, for tactical reasons, we decide to withhold it from the reader until a more opportune moment). And the main part of the presentation—the "Tell 'em" part—may have to blend organizational forms appropriate to both description and argument.

The elements that compose argument are simple enough in the abstract. There are really only two—what the ancients called the *confirmatio* /kōn-fər-**mät**-ē-ō/, or the presenting of evidence for your own thesis, and the *confutatio* /kōn-fo͞o-**tät**-ē-ō/, or the rebutting of actual or possible arguments against it. But in practice both elements can be broken up into parts, which can then be arranged in any number of different ways. For example, you can begin by stating all the opposing arguments, continue by disproving them one by one, and close by citing all the evidence supporting your own position. Or you may begin with the second-best argument supporting your thesis, move on to the identification and rebuttal of opposing arguments, and close by presenting your best argument.

Endings. The army prescription for conclusions—"Tell 'em what you've told 'em"—is pedagogically sound if somewhat unimaginative. Almost all formal reports, if more than about ten paragraphs long, end with summations (linked, whenever appropriate, to the author's recommendations). Indeed, any long, information-packed piece of exposition can probably benefit from a final review of salient points. Yet summary is not the only, or always the best, way to bring exposition to a close.

Short pieces, of course, do not need summary conclusions: to summarize the information that has been presented in, say, three normal-length paragraphs would obviously be silly, if not downright insulting to the reader's intelligence. Longer informal pieces, such as personal letters, essays, and magazine articles, might end with summaries, but more often they do not. And though argumentative writings sometimes use summaries in a penultimate position, they seldom conclude with them.

The trouble is that summary conclusions, even when helpful, tend to be dull. Repetition is, after all, repetition. No amount of imaginative rephrasing can entirely disguise this awkward truth. And to conclude any but the most fascinating or necessary piece of exposition in a lackluster way is to risk its being forgotten—a risk many writers prefer not to run.

Thus, the typical nonsummary conclusion (the *peroratio* /pĕr-ôr-ä-tē-ō/ to the ancients) tends to be long on rhetoric that will linger in the reader's mind—arresting images, memorable turns of phrase, ringing exhortations, thorny questions, jolting understatements. Even then, only the most skillful writers can get by on rhetoric alone. There are a number of formulas for constructing nonsummary conclusions. Perhaps the commonest are concerned with relating the central topic to some subject larger than any previously discussed. In such conclusions what might first have seemed to be a narrow issue or a purely local matter will be shown to have broader implications. For example, a letter to the newspaper complaining of exhaust fumes from metropolitan buses might end with dark warnings about the threat of global air pollution and a call for citizens to combat it by reforming their own public transport system. Sometimes even an epigrammatic generalization will suffice. Thus, in a piece edited for the Op-Ed page of the *New York Times*, a former prime minister of Jamaica made the controversial accusation that U.S. policy toward Cuba was based on ideologically inspired misconceptions, and then concluded with the plausible (though question-begging) generalization:

> A policy that flows from an analysis based on myths is likely to be crazy. Action that flows from such analysis is bound to be dangerous.
>
> —Michael N. Manley

The Structured Composition. Beginnings, middles, and ends in exposition have many variations and different orders of complexity. A full-length book of nonfiction, for instance, should have an overall structure corresponding to beginning-middle-end, but it will probably also be composed of numerous substructures (chapters), each of which will have a beginning, middle, and end of its own. Yet variation and elaboration aside, fundamental rules of composition apply in some degree to virtually all kinds of exposition. If you are interested in writing techniques, you may enjoy testing this assertion by taking a moment to analyze the structure of some of the prose that comes your way daily. Here, as an illustration, is a brief examination of a six-column article from the August 10, 1981, issue of *Newsweek*. Titled "Middle-class Junkies," the article concerns the alarming rise of heroin use in some middle-class circles. The introduction comes in the form of a "hook," or attention getter—two illustrative examples cast as narrative.

> Each morning, while her office colleagues sip coffee at their desks, she slips alone into the women's lounge for her own kind of refreshment break. Glancing furtively around, she extracts the 25-cc container. . . .

The third paragraph begins with a transition (from narration to exposition), followed by the announcement of the subject.

> Addicts like these do not fit the classic mold of the slumbound street junkie, but they are scarcely unusual. For thousands of middle-class teenagers and young adults, heroin has become the deadly new kick. . . .

The middle, or main portion, of the piece is, of course, descriptive rather than argumentative. It begins with *where* heroin is being used, moves on to some definitions and classifications of *who* is using it and *how* it is being used, and then begins to speculate about *why* it has been taken up by middle-class users. These speculations are suspended while the writers turn to consideration of some *what* and *when* background questions: What is the size and nature of the heroin business? When was heroin addiction first perceived as a major problem in the United States? What is the difference (comparison and contrast) between heroin and cocaine? The answers to these questions are given in terms of statistics, examples, illustrative anecdotes, and quotations.

Finally, the authors are ready for their transition to the conclusion. They first return to some additional speculations about the nature and motives of the typical middle-class user (*who* and *why*). From this they move smoothly to the (nonsummary) conclusion itself. Although they have already said that middle-class heroin use is national in scope, they nevertheless still want to relate their subject to an even larger context. Here is how they do it:

> In fact, the use of all drugs continues to rise among all classes of people—from alcohol and over-the-counter potions

through prescription drugs like Valium to hard drugs like heroin. Authorities fear that this is more than a problem of individual addiction. Now they worry about the graver threat of an addictive society.

Outlines and Paragraphing. If simple structural analyses such as the one above suggest anything to would-be writers, it is that outlining is indispensable for all but the shortest or most informal kinds of exposition. We have seen that within the broad framework of introduction–topic statement, main body, and conclusion, many variations are possible. But none of these variations may be random. Each must reflect the author's perception both of what the subject requires and of what the audience will respond to. An outline is an author's battle plan, a step-by-step strategy for accomplishing these twin objectives. It does not have to be written down; but if it isn't, the writer must nevertheless have it fully worked out in his head. By the same token it should never be tyrannous: if it isn't working well, change it. But at no point try to do without it. Generals without strategies are not notable for winning wars.

Paragraphs (to keep the military metaphor going) are the tactical units that are constructed from outlines. Normally, they are brief clusters of sentences grouped around a single idea. And normally they contain one topic sentence to which the other sentences in the cluster are subordinate.

Topic sentences, contrary to what some people believe, do not always have to be first in the paragraph. But wherever the topic sentence appears, it should be the focus of the paragraph, all other sentences either leading up to it or logically following from it.

There are no fixed rules about how long paragraphs may be. Short paragraphs are obviously easier for the writer to manage than long ones, but they are not necessarily better because they are short. The longer the paragraph, the more the writer must try to hold the reader's attention, by varying the form and length of sentences and by making sure that the sentences following the topic sentence don't wander so far from the subject that a new paragraph is called for.

People have, at various times, proposed many other rules about what paragraphs should and should not be, but the few precepts we have mentioned here are sufficient for most purposes. More elaborate formulas are merely apt to cause confusion. For example, the "father of modern paragraphing," the Scottish philosopher-educationist Alexander Bain, in 1866 prescribed that among other things all paragraphs must have beginnings, middles, and ends similar to those required in larger units of prose. But we no longer accept that paragraphs must be perfect minicompositions; indeed, we even consider one-sentence paragraphs permissible. And modern studies show that in even the most formal expository prose only about 23 percent of the paragraphs would come up to Bain's rigid standards for completeness. Yet modern prose is no less readable for that.

Style. Beneath the varied structures of expository prose, beneath its component paragraphs, lies the vast sea of language itself: tens of thousands of individual words that may be combined into a near-infinity of phrases and sentences. The laws of grammar, syntax, and usage govern how these combinations may be made so as to achieve order and meaning. The accomplished writer will of course be familiar with these laws; the more pressing problems relate to the elusive matter of style.

The word *style,* as applied to prose, has such a broad range of connotations that we shall have to begin by making some distinctions. At one level, the term merely refers to a set of accepted rules about such matters as spelling, punctuation, capitalization, and the formation of possessives. These subjects are exhaustively covered in standard style manuals published by, among others, the University of Chicago Press, the New York Times, and Prentice-Hall. Every serious writer should have at least one of these books in his or her library.

But though such compendiums of rules may be invaluable in helping us to write correctly, do they really tell us how to write stylishly—to make our prose as graceful, clear, and vivid as we might wish? No; the very reliability of these guidebooks precludes any such attempt. To do so they would have to leave the realm of fact and rule and enter that of opinion.

So we come to a second level of connotations associated with the term *style*. At this level we are concerned not with inflexible rules, but with commonly held views about what constitutes good writing. There are many well-known books that speak to this point, perhaps none more famous—at least in America—than William Strunk's *Elements of Style*. Originally published in 1918, it was updated and expanded some 40 years later by E. B. White, who contributed to Strunk's classic "little book" a concluding section titled "An Approach to Style." Among the 21 "gentle reminders" about style that White offers are "Place yourself in the background"; "Do not overwrite"; "Do not overstate"; "Do not explain too much"; "Do not take short-cuts at the cost of clarity"; and "Prefer the standard to the offbeat." Although nearly half of White's rules are phrased in the negative, they nevertheless are quite useful, stating, as he says, "what most of us know and, at times, forget."

The final connotation that we normally associate with the word *style* is the concept of writing that is better than good; writing that is so original, attractive, and lucid that it soars high above all prose that is merely correct and serviceable. Unfortunately, there are no how-to books that can teach us to write with this kind of style. Instead of precepts we have only examples, glittering models on every hand that make us wish, with a sort of pang, that we were their authors.

Could any of us ever aspire to write that kind of prose? The answer is yes, provided only that we care enough about words. If we are genuinely fascinated by how other people write, if we are constantly trying to find ways to improve our own writing, if we love and respect the enterprise of writing and wholeheartedly believe that

> in this way, being the response to man's organized and unceasing cravings for strength, clearness, order, dignity and sweetness, for a life intenser and more harmonious, what man writes comes to be greater than what man is.
>
> —Vernon Lee, *The Nature of the Writer*

—then anything is possible.

exquisite, a word of peculiarly delicate intensity. The pronunciation /**ĕks**-kwĭ-zĭt/ is probably preferred by most people, but /ĭk-**skwĭz**-ĭt/ is also correct.

Exquisite comes from Latin *exquīsitus* = 'searched out, chosen for excellence, elegant,' from *exquīrere* = 'to search out' (from *ex* = 'out' + *quīrere* = 'to search'). Referring to man-made objects, works of art, or human behavior or manners, or to natural objects, scenes, or creatures, *exquisite* means 'of the highest perfection, aesthetically satisfying to the highest degree':

> He promptly extracted from his mind, where he had composed and stored it away during his illness, *Eine Kleine Nachtmusik* (K. 525), a string serenade of exquisite beauty.
>
> —Marcia Davenport, *Mozart*

> I know of no other outdoor sport which can furnish me with so much pleasure as foraging wild food which can be made into exquisite dishes to share with family and friends.
>
> —Euell Gibbons, *Stalking the Wild Asparagus*

> Her hospitality was something exquisite; she had the gift which so many women lack, of being able to make themselves and their houses belong entirely to a guest's pleasure. . . .
>
> —Sarah Orne Jewett, *The Country of the Pointed Firs*

> Moments later, they came overland prior to landing, and he noted the exquisite contrast of Oahu's verdure against the now-azure sea.
>
> —Spiro T. Agnew, *The Caulfield Decision*

Likewise the adverb:

> My first wife was Jeanette Demont, an exquisitely beautiful dark brunette

> with a vibrant and magnetic personality. . . . —J. Paul Getty, *As I See It*

> They [the Neanderthals] manufactured a wide variety of exquisitely fashioned stone tools. . . . —Ronald Schiller, *Reader's Digest*

Of ideas or attainments, *exquisite* can also mean 'defined or refined to the highest level of nicety':

> . . . some highly educated people go to work, let's say, in the tax department of a large corporation, which needs exquisite intellectual skills of a certain sort. —Michael Novak, *U.S. News & World Report*

> I visualized the basic issue as pivoting on an exquisite legal conundrum: a clash between, on the one hand, a woman's supposed constitutional right to control her own body and thus to expel the fetus, and, on the other hand, the fetus's supposed right to life. —Walter F. Murphy, *The Vicar of Christ*

The word is also used of pain and other unpleasant experiences to mean 'very intense, excruciating':

> "My God, My God, why hast thou forsaken me?" Ultimate despair! Exquisite agony! —William Stringfellow, *The Witness*

> Twenty-eight members of a weight-watching club on an outing in Australia suffered the exquisite embarrassment of having their bus sink up to its axles in a tarred parking lot. —Bill Bryson, *Reader's Digest*

extra. The Latin adverb and preposition *extra* meant 'outside, outside of, beyond.' This is also the meaning of the English prefix *extra-*, as in *extraordinary* = 'beyond the ordinary' and *extraterrestrial* = 'being or originating outside the earth.' Among the meanings of *extraordinary* is 'additional,' as in *extraordinary expenses*. In this sense *extraordinary* has been clipped to form the common modern adjective *extra* = 'additional, special.' Thus, the meanings of the prefix *extra-* and the adjective *extra* form a contrast that may be somewhat confusing when considering a word like *extrasensory;* it means not 'using additional senses' but 'beyond the senses, communicated by means outside the senses.'

exurb, exurbia. An *exurb* is a residential area farther out than the contiguous suburbs of a city; in addition it is generally assumed to be more exclusive and wealthy than ordinary suburbs:

> He savors the perks [of being chairman of the First National Bank of Chicago]: the chauffeured limo that picks him up in the exurbs at 6 A.M. . . . —Marshall Loeb, *Time*

Exurbia is the world of exurbs:

> The pro-country mood is perhaps best demonstrated today by the exodus from the city to suburbia and exurbia. —Ray B. Browne, *Boston Globe*

eyrie, eyry. See AERIE.

F

fable. *Fables* are like parables in being short, fictitious tales that illustrate a moral or spiritual truth by means of similarity to something else. They differ from parables, however, in that their main characters are usually animals and their tone is often satirical. As a literary form the fable is ancient yet very much alive; a famous modern example is George Orwell's *Animal Farm* (1946), a novel based on the Russian Revolution and its aftermath. However, after Aesop—reputedly the father of fable in Western literature—probably the greatest single name associated with the genre is the 17th-century French author Jean de La Fontaine. His brilliant "The City Mouse and the Country Mouse," "The Fox and the Crow," and many other stories have delighted children and adults since first he wrote them. Here (in an English translation) is La Fontaine himself describing fable:

> Fables in sooth are not what they appear;
> Our moralists are mice and such small deer.
> We yawn at sermons, but we gladly turn
> To moral tales, and so amused we learn.

See also ALLEGORY.

fabulous, a basically evocative word, but one that is overused and thus devalued. Its literal meaning (from Latin *fābulōsus,* from *fābula* = 'story, fable') is 'belonging to fable,' implying either 'marvelous and mythical' or 'wildly impossible, elaborate and untrue':

> . . . the fishermen, at an indeterminate distance over the ice, moving slowly about with their wolfish dogs, passed for sealers or Esquimeaux, or in misty weather loomed like fabulous creatures, and I did not know whether they were giants or pygmies.
> —Henry David Thoreau, *Walden*

> He lied frequently to get himself out of scrapes and told fabulous stories.
> —Hesketh Pearson, *G.B.S.*

By legitimate extension *fabulous* means 'worthy of fable, immensely impressive, astounding, astonishing':

> Once again our fabulous American economy was in full gear, producing more than ever before, a marvel of the world, a matter of pride to every citizen. —William L. Shirer, *Midcentury Journey*

> Another fabulous coup was my acquisition of three of the world-famous Elgin marbles. —J. Paul Getty, *As I See It*

Much more often nowadays *fabulous* is used as a colorless all-purpose term of commendation, ranging in meaning from 'excellent' to 'good, nice':

> She was wearing dime-store T-shirts instead of designer clothes, but still it was a fabulous look that anyone would have wanted to have.
> —Andy Warhol and Pat Hackett, *POPism*

> Apparently George is blaming Art 'cause the pitching hasn't been so fabulous. . . .
> —Sparky Lyle, *The Bronx Zoo*

factor. In mathematics a *factor* is any of two or more numbers or quantities that by multiplication form a *product;* for example, 3 and 5 are factors of 15. This is the source of the generalized use of *factor* to mean 'any element, ingredient, fact, or consideration that contributes to a result or must be taken into account in assessing a situation':

> Even changes that seem at first glance to have nothing to do with technology can be traced back to some technological factor that made the change possible, desirable, or both.
> —Isaac Asimov, *Science Past—Science Future*

> In addition, energy shortages are a factor in holding factory operations to an estimated 70 percent of capacity.
> —*U.S. News & World Report*

Often *factor* is used unnecessarily to give a touch of precision to a statement that is not really precise:

> We could no longer film because of the lighting factor. . . . —Howard Cosell, *Cosell*

There is also the somewhat unnecessary verb *factor*, meaning 'to take (something) into account as a factor, add (something) as a factor to an assessment':

> The Russians are inevitably factoring our Cambodian intervention into their continuing appraisal of America's capabilities. . . . —George W. Ball, *Suez Is the Front to Watch*

faery, faerie. Sometimes also written *faëry, faërie,* this is an old variant of the word *fairy,* used by (among others) Edmund Spenser; it appears in his long poem *The Faerie Queene.* The word is pronounced **/fâr-ē/** or **/fā-ə-rē/**. In poetry *faery* is a romantic or elegant synonym of *fairy,* noun and adjective; as a noun it can also mean 'fairyland, place or realm of enchantment':

> The land of faery,
> Where nobody gets old and godly
> and grave. . . .
> —W. B. Yeats, *The Land of Heart's Desire*

In prose *faery* is used, while avoiding the childish associations of *fairy,* to mean 'of strange and magic-seeming beauty':

> I succumbed to [island madness] totally during a winter spent on those faery islands off the western coast of Scotland, the Hebrides.
> —James A. Michener, *Reader's Digest*

fallacy. The system of formal education that prevailed in Europe for nearly 1,500 years—from the later days of the Roman Empire until well into the Renaissance—featured seven broad areas of study. Three of them, called the *trivium,* were considered fundamental: *grammar, rhetoric,* and *logic.* The study of grammar was to provide educated persons with the essential structure underlying all language and thought. Rhetoric would teach them how to use this structure with power and grace. Logic would show them how to make of it an instrument for seeking truth.

Implicit in this curriculum was an important perception that we seem to be rediscovering today: rhetoric—the art of speaking and writing well—is not primarily concerned with truth. Its province is persuasion, and if this can be achieved by masking or distorting truth, so much the worse for truth. One of the historic functions of the study of logic has always been to help us understand and guard against the subtle seductions of rhetoric.

Logicians call any departure from the path of clear thinking a *fallacy.* A fallacy is not necessarily a complete untruth. More often it is merely an impressive statement that is less reasonable than it pretends to be, or a supposed proof that falls short of proving. This kind of fallacy permeates the rhetoric of advertising, politics, and social argument; and alas, it often infects the rhetoric we use on ourselves when we form our opinions. (As James Harvey Robinson wrote in *The Mind in the Making,* "Most of our so-called reasoning consists in finding arguments for going on believing as we already do.") In a world awash with misleading rhetoric, no intelligent person can afford to be indifferent to the subject of fallacy.

Syllogisms. The classic fallacy is the *defective syllogism.* A syllogism is a formula whereby an inescapable conclusion is derived from a set of premises, or statements. A proper syllogism would be:

> If all Riffian tribesmen have blue eyes,
> and if Ahmed is a Riffian tribesman,
> then Ahmed has blue eyes.

But this syllogism becomes a fallacy if we try to run it thus:

> If all Riffian tribesmen have blue eyes,
> and if Ahmed has blue eyes, then
> Ahmed is a Riffian tribesman.

This is a nonproof. Ahmed may be a Riff, but for all we know he is a blue-eyed Irishman with an unusual first name.

It is not hard for us to see what went wrong with our second set of statements about Ahmed. The class that comprises all blue-eyed people is much larger than the class made up of Riffian tribesmen. The smaller class can be made to fit into the larger, but not the other way around. Only if our initial premise had been "If all blue-eyed people are Riffian tribesmen," could our second set of statements have been logically consistent. Untrue, perhaps, because the premise would have been absurd, but logical nonetheless.

Verbal Tricks. The validity of our syllogism about Ahmed would also have been spoiled had we started by saying "If some Riffian tribesmen . . ." instead of "If all Riffian tribesmen. . . ." Obviously, if we admitted such a qualification into our initial premise, we would never be able to prove anything conclusive about Ahmed. So perhaps, if we nevertheless wanted to persuade a listener that we had a valid point to make, we might try some rhetorical flimflam. Perhaps we would say merely, "If Riffian tribesmen have blue eyes . . ."—without ever stating whether we meant some or all Riffs—and then surround our statement with a sea of verbiage so that the omitted qualification would go unnoticed.

It is in that "sea of verbiage" that most fallacy thrives. Simply stated syllogisms, even when they are about some subject that interests us, are fairly easy to analyze. Thus, the persuasive arguer with a shaky thesis must see to it that his syllogisms are never simply (and, if possible, never fully) stated. Unfortunately for the cause of sound logic, this is not difficult to do.

Some of the easiest weapons in the persuader's arsenal lie in the ambiguousness of language itself. For example, a statement such as "John only spoke the truth" might be interpreted as meaning "John did no more than speak the truth" or "No one but John spoke the truth" or "John just spoke the truth" (but refused to write it down?). Linguistic ambiguities often result merely in a kind of casual punning, as in the title of Maurice Zolotow's book *No People Like Show People*. But anyone who supposes that such elementary wordplay could have no role in the art of persuasion should pause to wonder why it so often turns up in print, radio, and TV advertising. Here, for example, is a typical selection of advertising headlines from a single issue of the *New York Times:*

> You've had your last dull shave
> —for a new type of shaving cream
>
> A Hole in One!
> —for a brand of cigarettes with a recessed filter
>
> Very easy to take
> —for vacations in Canada, sponsored by Atlantic Canada

Are such mild puns intended solely to capture our attention by entertaining us? Or does the advertiser also hope to implant some positive but illogical impression about the product or service in our unconscious minds? One thing is certain: none of these examples qualifies as rational argument.

Another form of verbal trickery is to attribute to things or ideas qualities that properly belong to something else. To write, as did one department store copywriter, "Dansez Mesdames! Here's Folies Bergere, the new French fragrance that's frivolous, flirtatious and full of fun!" is to accord to an inanimate object the characteristics and behavior of human beings. Editorial writers do much the same whenever they say, for instance, that today big government has a hand in everybody's pocket, or that corporations have no souls, or that the system has a vested interest in raping the environment. To personify a thing or idea can certainly make for vivid expression, but it is also a form of oversimplification that can make for bad logic. (See also PERSONIFICATION.)

Still another way to use the built-in qualities of language for nonlogical purposes of persuasion is to employ disguised qualifiers. When we read that a certain cleanser "fights stains for up to four months," may we assume that the copywriter hoped no one would notice that any span of lesser time—one day, for example—could logically fall within the definition of "up to"? And did the author of the claim that a brand of polish "keeps your no-wax floors looking better than other brands" expect us to observe that the claim failed to say "all other brands"? Or, for that matter, to tell us brands of what?

Emotion-charged Irrelevancies. A second large group of fallacies is composed of those emotion-charged irrelevancies that would-be persuaders sometimes introduce to distract us from seeing that they have not proved the point. Logicians have descriptive terms (all from Latin) for most of these fallacies of relevance: *ipse dixit; ad populum; ad baculum; ad hominem;* and others. What all these fallacies have in common is that they attempt to stimulate our emotions rather than appeal to our intellect.

Ipse Dixit. *Ipse dixit* (= 'he himself said it') is the logician's term for a tactic in argument by which the arguer quotes the opinions of some authority to support his or her position. Such "expert" opinions may certainly lend weight to an argument, but they can never, by themselves, prove its truth. Even to imply that they do is a logical fallacy.

Commercial advertisers are particularly fond of ipse dixit, usually in the form of the celebrity endorsement. Thus, we have an internationally famous actor-director, himself a kind of authority figure, rumbling:

> Experts will tell you they drink [a well-known brand of California wine] because of its full varietal aroma, brilliant color and long pleasant finish. What they mean is . . . it tastes good.

These "experts" are certainly well up on their wine connoisseur's jargon, but we are never told who they are or why we should pay the slightest attention to their opinions.

In the more heated arenas of public debate, ipse dixit may be called upon to support almost any contention no matter how unprovable. And even when there can be no expert consensus, the arguer may always resort to vague attribution, as in "All the experts agree that . . ." or (much favored by the Soviet press) "As is well known. . . ."

> I was incredulous at the consensus of Delphi poll respondents that an all-out global nuclear war would claim "only" 50 million lives. All responsible, knowledgeable articles on this subject estimate that at least a half-billion people would be killed. . . . The 50 million figure . . . obviates, a priori, *Next*'s claim that the panelists are experts.
> —letter, *Next*

The obvious rebuttal to ipse dixit—although it sometimes takes courage to assert the fact—is that so-called authorities can be wrong. For example, in *American Tongue in Cheek: A Populist Guide to Our Language*, the author Jim Quinn, arguing that popular usage is often a better test of good grammar than formal rules, points out that even Charles Dickens wrote "Nobody will miss her like I do" and Shakespeare used the solecism "between you and I" (in *The Merchant of Venice*). Undaunted by this literary heavy artillery, one reader responded to a review of the book in *Newsweek:*

> A pox on Jim Quinn. Long may John Simon, Edwin Newman and their fellow "pop grammarians" continue their struggle against the sloppiness that overtook even Shakespeare at times.

Ad Populum. *Ad populum* (in full, *argumentum ad populum* = 'argument to the people') aims at one of the popular passions, and its various forms are named accordingly. It may, for example, try to appeal to our patriotic feelings or our respect for custom, tradition, or conventional morality (*ad verecundiam* = 'to reverence for institutions, laws, etc.'); to our hostile prejudices (*ad invidiam* = 'to hatred'); or to our vulnerability to being amused or charmed by the arguer's manner (*ad captandum* = 'to the purpose of captivating').

Madison Avenue is understandably fond of ad populum. A common tactic in advertisements is to appeal to our instinct for conformity, for doing what our neighbors are doing and not being left out of the swim.

> Delizioso! Presenting the intriguing liqueur from Italy that's got everybody talking.
> —advertisement for a cream liqueur

And, of course, ad verecundiam can be used for even the most unlikely subjects:

> One American custom that has never changed: a friendly social drink.
> —advertisement for Licensed Beverage Industries, Inc.

The use of ad populum arguments in commercial advertising tends to be harmless. The same cannot always be said of their use in public controversy. Who among us has never heard an orator invoke the highest principles of patriotism, love of family, and moral duty to support some nasty racial or religious prejudice that many in the audience may secretly share?

Ad Baculum. Allied to ad populum, but more personally directed, are *ad baculum* (= 'to the stick') arguments, aimed at our private anxieties. Two classic advertising campaigns have told us of the dire social consequences of unchecked halitosis and of going to the beach if we are 97-pound weaklings. "You're on a tough course," a contemporary TV advertisement for *Fortune* magazine assures businessmen (whom the ad has just done its best to unnerve about how smart their competitors might be). "Can you afford to wait [to subscribe]?" And always good for producing a thrill of alarm in our uneasy world is an allusion to how we are doing in comparison with the Russians. This concern is not just limited to the Pentagon at appropriations time. Here, for example, is an academic writing to the *New York Times* on cuts in government funding for psychological research: "Won't our Soviet counterparts be interested to learn how much easier it is going to be for them to catch up? . . ."

Ad Hominem. The most notorious fallacy of irrelevance is *ad hominem* (= 'to the man'). At its worst it is sheer invective and can be used against anyone, without reference to ideas at all. "That dark designing sordid ambitious vain proud arrogant and vindictive knave" is how the 18th-century general Charles Lee described one of his political opponents, George Washington. But usually ad hominem seeks to discredit an idea by belittling its proponent, frequently through innuendo:

> [A prominent New York City financier] advocates a wage-price freeze, more taxes and government direction of the nation's industry. . . . [He] wants to bring to this country many of the same fascist economic ideas his parents fled when they came to the United States from Nazi-occupied France.
> —letter, *Newsweek*

This ad hominem tactic of trying to undermine an opponent's credibility is sometimes called *poisoning the well.* It can range from such mild objections as "You couldn't say the things you do if you really understood the issues" to all-out accusations that your antagonist maintains his or her position solely out of some disreputable personal interest. On the other hand, if you yourself were under attack, you might resort to *tu quoque* (= 'you too'), insisting that your accuser was guilty of the very faults he or she was attributing to you (for example, "If you think peacetime military service is such a great thing, why haven't you enlisted?").

Typically, ad hominem arguers not only make irrelevant attacks on the person representing the opposing position, but they also make equally irrelevant claims for their own authority:

> [This] article on antisubmarine warfare capabilities of the U.S. Navy is grossly misleading. . . . As a former sonar officer and an original commissioning crew member of the U.S.S. *Los Angeles* . . . I feel a bit more qualified to speak on the subject than some international-affairs major working at some egghead think tank.
> —letter, *Scientific American*

Perhaps the only positive thing to be said in favor of ad hominem is that, on rare occasions, it can be amusing. Here is a famous interchange between New York Governor Alfred E. Smith and an anonymous heckler:

> Heckler: Go ahead, Al. Tell 'em all you know. It won't take long.
> Smith: If I tell 'em all we both know it won't take any longer.

Logical Short Circuits. Fallacies of irrelevance seek to distract us from logical thought. Another large group of fallacies tries to short-circuit logical thought itself by distorting the proper relationships among the key facts in an argument. Typical of these logical short circuits is the fallacy called *petitio principii*, or *begging the question*. Here, the arguer assumes to be true the very point at issue. A simple example would be the often-heard comment, "Of course it's true. The newspaper wouldn't print it if it weren't true." Somewhat more complex is this argument, proposed by a man who was trying to collect a reward of $230,000 offered to anyone who could prove the existence of the immortal soul:

> Death is decomposition. Hence, what cannot decompose cannot die. But decomposition requires divisibility into parts. Thus what is not divisible into parts cannot die. But divisibility into parts requires matter. Hence, what has no matter in it is not divisible into parts and so cannot decompose, and so is necessarily immortal.
>
> —Dr. Richard Spurney, testimony in an Arizona court

Somehow, in all this elaborate chain of reasoning, the basic point—does the soul exist?—was never proved but was merely taken for granted. The award was given to someone else.

Question begging does not require extended argument; it can be accomplished by a single derogatory term:

> We are even hearing in other countries the contemptible slogan "Better Red than Dead" of a generation ago.
>
> —Richard V. Allen (quoted), *New York Times*

Although many people would agree with this characterization of the slogan, the rules of logical discourse oblige us to note that the speaker assumes in the single adjective "contemptible" an entire argument that remains to be proved.

The phrase "Better Red than Dead" exemplifies yet another kind of short-circuit fallacy: the *either-or oversimplification*. A spectrum of ignored possibilities lies between the two extremes of "Red" and "Dead," as it does between such rhetorical antitheses as "America: love it or leave it" and "Either you drive a Lynx, or you don't drive at all." A notorious variation of the either-or fallacy is the slogan "Guns don't kill people, people do." (Some logicians call such formulations *bifurcation*.) Obviously, the elements that go into the commission of a homicide with a deadly weapon are a good deal more complicated than the slogan implies, but many gun-control advocates have mistakenly tried to argue with this simplistic slogan on its own terms by asserting the contrary. This, in turn, has permitted such rebuttals as:

> Since "People don't kill people . . . guns do," I suggest that we free John Hinckley [would-be assassin of President Reagan] and put his gun on trial. Maybe that'll make other guns think twice before they commit such crimes.
>
> —letter, *Newsweek*

The essential silliness of such formulas is apparent when we try to apply them to ordinary, untheoretical matters:

> Some careless groundskeeper must have said at one time or other, "It wasn't the hole on the course that broke your leg, it was your stepping into it."
>
> —Dwight Bolinger, *Language—The Loaded Weapon*

Misused *generalizations* produce another kind of logical short circuitry. If, for example, we argued that Smith wouldn't mind if we gave him an exploding cigar because everyone loves a good joke, we would be guilty of (among other things) the fallacy logicians call *apriorism* or the *sweeping generalization*—that is, applying a general rule that may not fit all cases, including the one at hand. The so-called *hasty generalization* reverses the process. Here a generalization is made on the basis of insufficient evidence—for example, *All politicians are crooks. Look at how many were involved in Abscam.* The essential weakness of the misused generalization is oversimplification—a weakness that becomes more apparent the closer the argument approaches syllogistic form.

> If two men are caught breaking into a shoe store, they are tried and, if found guilty, are thrown into the clink.
>
> If two men are caught breaking into the Constitution and are found guilty, they are pardoned by President Reagan.
>
> Conclusion: the Constitution is less important than a shoe store.
>
> —letter, *New York Times*

Still other logical short circuits arise from muddling the cause-effect relationship. The fallacy known as *post hoc, ergo propter hoc* (Latin, 'after this, therefore because of this'), or simply *post hoc,* seeks to establish that because event A occurred before event B, the first event caused the second. A good many of the successes claimed for advertising campaigns probably depend heavily on post hoc reasoning. Variations of this error include all sorts of far-fetched causal relationships, and sometimes even out-and-out reversals, as when a light fixture over a dark stairway is removed on the grounds that since no one has ever fallen down the stairs, the light is unnecessary. The late Irish humorist Flann O'Brien was fond of the comic possibilities inherent in cause-effect muddles. In his novel *The Third Policeman* he wrote with mock admiration of a mad philosopher named De Selby who is something of a specialist in this form of reasoning. It is De Selby's contention, for example, that night is an "unsanitary condition of the atmosphere due to accretions of black air."

Still another fallacy, *false analogy,* can be a particularly seductive form of logical short circuitry, because it often tends to draw on the rhetorical power of metaphor and simile. When a gossip columnist describes some trivial dispute between two Hollywood celebrities as a duel of Titans or when a cosmetics firm advertises that its product is like "springtime in the windy canyons, the high clear places of the Navajo Nation," we are being asked to accept comparisons between things that are not really comparable. Even great philosophers are not immune to the temptation to use this sort of persuasion.

> And as the winds which sweep over the ocean prevent the decay that would result from its perpetual calm, so war protects the people from the corruption which an everlasting peace would bring upon it.
>
> —G. W. F. Hegel, *The Philosophy of Right* (1821)

To be sure, an analogy need not be poetic in order to be persuasive or false. We are, for example, constantly told how many people die in automobile accidents each year as a way of persuading us of the relative harmlessness of handguns, nuclear power plants, cocaine, and other potentially dangerous things. And whenever we hear someone begin a rebuttal of something we have just said with the words "That's like saying that . . ." there is a fifty-fifty chance that a false analogy is in the making.

Just as the weaknesses of either-or propositions, cause-effect confusions, faulty generalizations, and bad analogies can usually be exposed when we reduce the terms of the argument to syllogistic form, so the classically false syllogism (as in the case of blue-eyed Ahmed) may be called the ultimate form of logical short circuitry—an observation that brings us back to our starting point.

Summary. In this brief review we have looked at three main categories of fallacy—verbal tricks, emotion-charged irrelevancies, and logical short circuits—and have considered some examples of each. But the subject of fallacy is vast, and we have left out almost as much as we have included. We have not, for example, discussed those fallacies that can arise from subtle shifts of emphasis in the way we pronounce certain words, from tricks with numbers, and from errors based on misinterpretations of the laws of chance. And there are many more. So many, in fact, that they could probably be studied fully only within an academic discipline.

But we do not need to know the names and categories of every fallacy—useful though that might be—in order to set up our defenses. What is required for that is mental alertness and a dedication to clear thinking—a constant exercise of judgment in discriminating between persuasion, which is the business of rhetoric, and proof, which is the business of logic.

And along the way we should not fall into the error of denigrating rhetoric simply because it is capable of deceiving. When we are deceived by fallacies, we often have only ourselves to blame. The purposes of rhetoric are different from, and often opposed to, those of logic, but they are not necessarily less estimable. The 17th-century English writer Thomas Fuller put the matter well when he said:

> Though some condemne Rhetorick as the mother of lies, speaking more than the truth in her Hyperboles, lesse in her miosis, otherwise in her metaphors, contrary in her ironies; yet there is excellent use of all of these, when disposed of with judgement.
>
> —*The Holy State and the Prophane State* (1642)

See also BEGGING THE QUESTION; SPECIAL PLEADING.

falls. Referring to a waterfall of a river or lake, *falls* is more often used with a singular verb, sometimes with a plural.

false analogy. See FALLACY.

far from the madding crowd. See MADDING.

farrago /fə-rā-gō, fə-rä-/. In Latin this word meant 'mixed fodder, with several different kinds of grain, given to horses.' In English it means 'assortment of different elements, jumble of bits and pieces,' especially 'bewildering mixture of good and bad, true and false, etc.':

> . . . most of the stuff [news] so eagerly passed about and canvassed in the camp was a farrago of exaggeration and pure fiction.
>
> —Joseph Alsop, *Saturday Evening Post*

> Life in the fashion fast lane is a farrago of pomp and perspiration, champagne and missed meals, glamour and 18-hour workdays. —*Time*

> . . . Schorr had earned a place over the years in the farrago of Nixon villains. . . .
>
> —William Safire, *Before the Fall*

farther, further. Both as adjective and adverb these two words are used as comparatives of *far*, and everything said below applies equally to the superlative forms *farthest* and *furthest*.

(1) In the physical sense 'at or to a greater distance' *farther* is the prevailing and standard choice in American English.

> I rambled still farther westward than I habitually dwell. . . .
>
> —Henry David Thoreau, *Walden*

> You could see clusters of trees against the horizon, far away . . . and, yet farther away, the mass of Ararat.
>
> —Michael J. Arlen, *Passage to Ararat*

Further is a minority American usage in this sense (it is the majority use, however, in Standard British).

(2) In figurative senses such as 'more removed or separated (from), to a more considerable extent (than),' *farther* is also the prevailing American choice.

> . . . the opponents of Skeffington who believed him to be an avaricious man . . . could hardly have been farther from the truth.
>
> —Edwin O'Connor, *The Last Hurrah*

> . . . a goal that Ross, twenty-two years my senior, was even farther from reaching than I.
>
> —Brendan Gill, *Here at The New Yorker*

But *further* is also used in these figurative senses by substantial numbers of Americans (besides being the preferred British usage).

> If the dollar keeps getting stronger, American tourists traveling abroad will find that their money goes further. . . .
>
> —*U.S. News & World Report*

(3) In the extended sense 'additional, additionally,' with no idea of distance, *further*

is now the only standard American and British use.

> There are two further points I would make. —*National Catholic Reporter*

> Further, we evangelical Christians need a doctrine of tradition. . . .
> —*Christianity Today*

◇ ***Recommendation.*** If in doubt, follow the prevailing American usage: *farther* for the literal sense 'more distant' and for the figurative senses 'more removed, etc.' But *further* in both of these senses is still acceptable and standard American usage. In the sense 'additional(ly),' use only *further*.

fathom. The original meaning of *fathom* was 'a stretching out of both arms,' defined as a length of six feet, used especially in measuring depths at sea. The metric-system lobby is seeking to abolish fathoms, but sailing enthusiasts as well as those who appreciate English words will probably keep them alive. There are metaphorical uses, including the verb *fathom* = 'to probe into, understand' and the adjective *fathomless* = 'inexpressibly deep':

> Once in a while I still try to fathom what might have been the meaning of Kava's bizarre act. . . .
> —Isaac Bashevis Singer, *Atlantic Monthly*

> In that moment he experienced the fathomless pleasure which sailors have always felt when their vessel takes a fair breeze in effortless stride.
> —Andrew Young, *Reader's Digest*

faze. This is an American variant of the obsolete British word *feeze* = 'to drive away, put to flight.' *Faze* means 'to disconcert, bother, daunt,' almost always used in a negative sense.

> [G. B. Shaw] cut quite a figure at the Hearst ranch. Nothing about the joint fazed him. He seemed to be equally amused and offended by it.
> —Harpo Marx, *Harpo Speaks*

> The only hardwood available was teak—it took four strong men to lift one five-foot beam. That never fazed Pete.
> —Thomas A. Dooley, *The Edge of Tomorrow*

◇ ***Recommendation.*** *Faze* was formerly regarded as dialectal or slang but is now entirely standard. The spelling *phase* results from confusion with the unrelated word *phase* = 'temporary stage, appearance, etc.,' and is best avoided.

female-gender word forms. Unlike many other languages, English does not have grammatical gender. In English, nouns ending in *-er* and *-or* simply mean 'person who does something.' A *writer* is a person who writes; a *doctor* is someone who practices medicine. A tennis *instructor* or symphony *conductor* may be either a woman or a man.

Certain gender-marked French word endings have been grafted onto English words. In 1926 the British usage expert H. W. Fowler offered the opinion that "feminines for vocation-words are a special need of the future." He frowned on female writers who did not accept the label *authoress:*

> Their view is that the female author is to raise herself to the level of the male author by asserting her right to his name. —*Modern English Usage*

Today, Fowler's view that the generic word *author* should be exclusively a male name is untenable.

(1) -ess *words.* The *-ess* and *-ette* suffixes were adopted into Middle English from Old French. Some *-ess* words were applied to saints, divinities, and the nobility: *patroness; protectress; benefactress; foundress.* A duality of usage marked *-ess* words in the titles of nobility. This duality is still current. For example, the wife or widow of a duke is called a *duchess.* This is the same title for a woman who holds the rank in her own right. But a woman cannot pass on a status title to her husband as a man can to his wife. A woman who marries a prince becomes a *princess,* but the husband of a princess does not be-

come a *prince*. Titles of office once followed this same pattern. Thus, an *ambassadress* or *mayoress* might have been a woman who held the office or the wife of a man who did.

Other *-ess* words reflect the sorts of occupations that were open to women and girls in earlier times: *shepherdess; abbess; wardress; seamstress*. Specifically, an abbess or wardress presided over a group of women, as an *abbot* or *warden* oversaw a group of men. A woman who sewed for a living was originally called a *seamster*. This was the English translation of the Latin word for 'tailor,' *sartor*. But when men took up needle and thread, they took over the word *seamster*, too. Women came to be called seamstresses.

> This woman was commended to him for a very cunning seamster.
> —Francis Godwin, *Catalogue of the Bishops of England* (1601)

> To the Old Exchange, and there, of my pretty seamstress, bought four bands.
> —Samuel Pepys, *Diary* (1665)

Over time, some *-ess* words diverged in meaning from their originals. A *governor* governs a state; a *governess* teaches children in the home. But the *master* of an art or craft can be either a man or a woman:

> She [Barbara Walters] proved she is the master of body language, which has become part of her technique.
> —Julius Fast, *Boston Globe*

By contrast, its feminine form, *mistress*, now chiefly suggests 'kept woman' or 'paramour.' Like *mistress*, the words *sorceress* and *temptress* cast a woman in a purely sexual role, emphasizing her love life or allure. Like *master*, *sorcerer* and *tempter* lack this connotation. And an *adventurer* can explore the earth, but an *adventuress* seeks advantage in a world of much more limited scope.

> The odious little adventuress making her curtsey.
> —William Makepeace Thackeray, *Vanity Fair* (1847)

Here Thackeray is being ironical; he really likes his antiheroine Becky Sharp and her sex-based schemes to get on in the world. But some *-ess* words, such as *Jewess* and *Negress*, unquestionably imply inferior status. As the lexicographer Olga Coren has observed, female members of majority groups are not so designated—there is no *Christianess*, nor is there a *Caucasianess*. The originally inoffensive terms *authoress* and *poetess* have also come to imply inferiority, and we thus recommend avoiding them. (The *-ess* ending is not, however, such a deadly affront that it couldn't come in for some good-natured spoofing by women writers. For example, in 1982 the poet Alice Notley published a work titled "No Woman Is an Islandess.")

The *-ess* words are actually tending to disappear, for there is little need of them in English. Words like *instructress*, *manageress*, and *proprietress* have virtually dropped out of the language. Words like *sculptress* for *sculptor* and *murderess* for *murderer* are falling into disuse (though *murderess* is the sort of word used by sensational journalists to spice up their copy). *Stewardess* is gradually being replaced by *flight attendant;* many *actresses* now call themselves *actors;* many *hostesses* regard themselves simply as good *hosts*. However, *waitresses* do not yet answer to a call for "Waiter!" The only thing certain about language is that it changes. Most *-ess* words have gone. Others are going. *Waitress* may well be the last to go.

(2) -ette *words*. The *-ette* suffix words tend to have a minimizing or trivializing effect. The same suffix that means 'female' in *majorette* means 'small' in *kitchenette* and 'imitation' in *leatherette*. A female officer in the army may hold the rank of *major*. But a girl who twirls a baton in a marching band is not a *drum major* in a military-style uniform; she wears a miniskirt and is called a (*drum*) *majorette*. Often, the *-ette* suffix is used in the name of female auxiliaries to male organizations (*Jaycettes, Jaycees*), sometimes suggesting a status that is separate but not equal. That kind of status is reflected upon in the following editorial:

> In World War I, the Navy needed clerks so badly that it took in the first

> women ever to serve formally in the nation's military forces. "Yeomanettes" they were called. . . . All yeomen had to serve on ships but no women were permitted to do so. Necessity soon brought a solution. All 13,000 yeomanettes . . . were assigned to a tugboat buried fast in the mud of the Potomac.
> —*New York Times*

The word *suffragette* = 'woman militantly promoting voting rights for women' is another example of the belittling effect of *-ette*. An advocate of the women's vote was properly called a *suffragist*. A suffragist could be either female or male.

> I am a woman and a suffragist.
> —letter, *Daily Mail* (1914)

According to the *Oxford English Dictionary* the term *suffragette* was originally applied to a female suffragist, "esp. one of a violent or 'militant' type." In Great Britain many activists embraced the term in the years before the vote was won. In the United States, however, suffrage advocates preferred to be called suffragists. That term did not separate the women from the men who were their allies. In both nations the press played upon the word *suffragette* in a way that made the women seem unreasonable or ridiculous.

Words like *brunette* and *majorette* may be with us for a long time yet. But *-ette* words almost always signal unequal status, and most of them have become passé.

(3) -e *and* -ée *words.* Adding *-e* to form a feminine ending is another practice taken from French. For example, a man is a *blond* and a woman a *blonde,* just as a man is a *brunet* and a woman a *brunette* (see BLOND, BLONDE). A small male is *petit* in French (*mon petit fils* = 'my little son'), and a small female is *petite.* English has adopted *petite* for a small woman and for a size of clothes to fit her. However, there is no *petit* size for a small man. Nor are men designated by their hair color as often as women are.

The French feminine ending *-e* is also applied to words that have a masculine ending of *-é: fiancé, fiancée; divorcé, divorcée; protégé, protégée.* Each pair of words is pronounced alike, ending in the sound /ā/. In usage, however, the female terms in these sets occur more often than the male ones. A divorced man is seldom called a divorcé. Sometimes the accents are dropped.

> Cullen has a woman friend, a sweet-faced blonde divorcee.
> —Cynthia Gorney, *Boston Globe*

> . . . Marie M. Lambert, one of his latest [political] protegées. . . .
> —*New York Times*

The word *emigré* = 'emigrant' is usually used of both sexes:

> Mary Mead, a recent *emigré* from Dallas . . .
> —Enid Nemy, *New York Times*

In general, there is no grammatical need to maintain the *-é* and *-ée* distinctions in English. At present, the French forms are still followed, but people may begin to drop the extra *-e* just as they drop the accents.

(4) -euse *words.* Yet another set of French endings is found on the *-eur, -euse* words. In French a male may be a *danseur* (= 'ballet dancer'), a *chanteur* (= 'singer'), or a *masseur* (= 'professional who gives a massage'). A female may be, respectively, a *danseuse,* a *chanteuse,* or a *masseuse.*

> . . . the Greek chanteuse famous for her black-rimmed glasses and classically trained soprano voice . . .
> —*Maclean's*

In English, *danseur* is sometimes used as an equivalent to *ballerina* (since we do not adopt the Italian word *ballerino* for a male dancer), but a man is never called a *chanteur.* The female forms *chanteuse* and *danseuse* sound pretentious in English. Only *masseur* and *masseuse* are used as parallel terms. Even there the *-eur* term may win out. Certainly, *entrepreneur* is used for members of both sexes. No one would call a woman who started her own business an *entrepreneuse.*

◇ ***Recommendation.*** Probably the best general solution is to simplify. If in doubt, use the same term for members of both sexes.

The important thing is the function performed or designation made, not the sex of the person mentioned. See also CHAIRMAN; MAN; -MAN; MISS, MRS., MS.; PARALLEL STYLE; WOMAN, LADY, GIRL.

fewer, less. While *more* applies both to numbers and to bulk, *fewer* applies only to numbers and *less* applies primarily to bulk or quantity: *Here there are fewer farms because there is less good land.* When numbers are mentioned explicitly, the basic choice is *fewer: Fewer than ten people came. There were 23 fewer forest fires this year than last.* When numbers are used as a measure of bulk or extent rather than as an enumeration of individuals, *less* is preferred: *less than two tons of ammunition; less than five miles to go; less than a million dollars.* In many cases there is no clear-cut way of deciding which is better: *Fewer* (or *less*) *than 20,000 votes were recorded yesterday. There are less* (or *fewer*) *than 15 days left till Christmas.*

◊ ***Recommendation.*** *Fewer* should be preferred when individuals rather than quantities are compared, and with the more precise kinds of enumeration. In indeterminate cases, either *fewer* or *less* may be used.

fiction. See NARRATION.

fief, fiefdom. *Fief* /fēf/ is an old feudal term for an estate that was granted by a lord to a tenant and could be inherited by the tenant's heirs in return for continued feudal service. The holder of a fief was often virtually independent of his legal overlord. Thus, the word has been taken up in political commentary to mean 'power base, area in which a politician or bureaucrat has firm personal control':

> [Secretary Andrus] promised to end "the little fiefs that have divided Interior for years." —*Reader's Digest*

The word *fiefdom* is a modern coinage, formed by adding the suffix *-dom* = 'realm or dominion of,' as in *kingdom.* This was an unnecessary addition, since *fief* already has the sense 'estate or domain':

> Back in the thirteenth century, Osman's tribe had been granted a small fiefdom in western Asia by the dominant Seljuks.
> —Michael J. Arlen, *Passage to Ararat*

> Fiefdoms such as the Ways and Means Committee in the House and the Southern conservative minority in the Senate . . . were weakened during the tenures of Mr. Mansfield and Mr. Albert. —David E. Rosenbaum, *New York Times*

> . . . assigning a special unit to the job of riding herd on the counterintelligence fiefdoms or, when necessary, taking over for them.
> —William Safire, *Before the Fall*

◊ ***Recommendation.*** In historical contexts, as in the second quotation above, *fief* is correct and *fiefdom* is an error. But in modern political commentary *fiefdom* is so well established that it cannot be called an error; however, the historically minded writer will prefer *fief* in this context also.

figures of speech. The classification of *figures of speech* is a branch of *rhetoric.* As originally defined by the classical scholars, rhetoric was simply the art of using language to produce desired effects on a reader or listener—in short, the art of writing and speaking well. Nowadays, this term often carries the unfavorable suggestion of overblown, stereotypical language, especially political bombast. But for more than 2,000 years—roughly from Aristotle's time to the mid-18th century—the mastery of rhetoric in the original sense was considered essential for every well-educated person.

In addition to addressing broad considerations of subject matter and composition, the ancient rhetoricians identified hundreds of devices and turns of phrase by which literal meaning could be enhanced and enriched—many more than can be found in most modern dictionaries. But a fair number of these figures of speech are still used today. For discussion of some of the rhetorical devices see ANTITHESIS; HYPERBOLE; IRONY; LITOTES;

METAPHOR; OXYMORON; PUN; SIMILE; UNDERSTATEMENT; and ZEUGMA.

finalize. This verb has long been regarded by many as an archrepresentative of bad bureaucratic usage. Surprisingly, it appeared first in the 1920s in Australian English, in which it remains a standard word meaning 'to make (a negotiation or deal) final' (the spelling *finalise* following the British form):

> On the way south to Brisbane to finalise his purchase . . .
>
> —Mary Durack, *Kings in Grass Castles*

In the 1930s and 1940s, the bureaucrat-ridden era of the New Deal and World War II, *finalize* cropped up widely in the United States and Britain, whether as a borrowing from Australia or as an independent creation it's impossible to say. It was quickly identified by usage critics as a classic example of administrative jargon, an unnecessary and pseudoimpressive synonym for 'to finish, complete.' In fairness to bureaucrats, we point out that *finalize* is not necessarily synonymous with 'to finish.' Administrative procedures, as is quite well known, are slow and laborious, and many a policy or document goes through seemingly endless stages of revision and levels of approval; administrators therefore seem to find *finalize* legitimately useful to mean 'give final form or authority to':

> We made a tentative decision several weeks ago, but certain details had to be finalized before we could make the statement public.
>
> —a Missouri school board president (quoted), *St. Louis Post-Dispatch*

> Clark said he had obtained agreement in principle for the tax proposal and was to finalize it at a meeting with Alberta Premier Lougheed on Dec. 15.
>
> —*Winnipeg Tribune*

◇ ***Recommendation.*** Even though *finalize* is quite defensible in uses like those quoted above, the word has been made so notorious that we recommend avoiding it. If you do use it, you should be prepared to defend it—but some people feel so violent about it that they will condemn you anyway and will then regard the rest of your usage as tainted and suspect. Regardless of any such arguable cases, we strongly advise that *finalize* should not be used as a mere synonym for *finish* or *complete.*

fine writing. For generations, teachers of English have cautioned students against the flowery, affected style called *fine writing.* The term has actually been in use among literary people since the 18th century. Nowadays, we are used to fine writing in political speeches, travel advertisements, and the like, but do not expect to find it in such contexts as a novel, a self-help manual, a school paper, or a business letter.

But this was not always the case. An enormously popular practitioner of fine writing was the politician William Jennings Bryan (1860–1925), who combined his political career with appearances on the lecture circuit and enjoyed extraordinary success with audiences all over the United States. Here is an example of fine writing from one of Bryan's lectures:

> If matter mute and inanimate, though changed by the forces of Nature into a multitude of forms, can never die, will the spirit of man suffer annihilation when it has paid a brief visit, like a royal guest, to this tenement of clay?

There is a solemn splendor of language in the foregoing example, but the actual thought content is in fact quite skimpy. Overrich form with meager substance is the hallmark of fine writing.

flaccid is preferably pronounced **/flăk-sĭd/**, but some people say **/flăs-ĭd/**, which is also acceptable. The word means 'limp, hanging loose, flabby':

> Stage-fright was upon him now; his hands were cold and damp, his legs felt like flaccid rubber tubes filled with fine sand. . . .
>
> —Kingsley Amis, *Lucky Jim*

flair. In French the literal meaning of *flair* is 'keen sense of smell.' In English it means 'instinctive discernment, ability to make judgments without laborious analysis' or 'natural aptitude (for some skill or activity)':

> He does not seem to have had the flair, the imagination, the innovative daring one expects of an explorer.
> —Peter Forbath, *The River Congo*

> [Gracie Allen] was a big talent; she could sing, she was a great dancer, and a fine actress with a marvelous flair for comedy.
> —George Burns, *Living It Up*

flak, flack. *Flak,* a World War II borrowing from German, means 'bursting antiaircraft fire,' especially as seen from a plane under fire, often appearing as numerous exploding puffs of smoke on all sides. From this sense it is a natural extension to the informal sense of *flak,* 'hostile criticism, especially as a widespread hostile reaction to some public action or statement.' The word tends to suggest that the person receiving the flak will, like a bomber under fire, just press on regardless.

> The flak was heavy: lawsuits, mothers marching in protest and fiery legislative denunciations.
> —Eugene H. Methvin, *Reader's Digest*

Flack (preferably so spelled) is slang for 'public relations material' or, much more frequently now, 'press agent, public relations person.' It is a mildly sarcastic term, a slight disparagement.

> Jody Powell, press flack for the Top Peanut . . .
> —*Boston Herald American*

flammable, inflammable. The older word is *inflammable,* meaning 'able to be inflamed, combustible.' In technical and industrial contexts the possibility that someone might understand the word as a negative meaning 'not combustible' is too dangerous to be ignored. Accordingly, *flammable* is now generally used of highly combustible materials, and its opposite term is *nonflammable. Inflammable,* however, continues to be used in figurative senses—referring to persons, 'excitable, easily angered': *a passionate and inflammable temperament;* referring to situations, 'dangerously volatile, likely to get out of control': *an inflammable state of international tension.*

flapjack. See PANCAKE, FLAPJACK.

flaunt, flout. Old-fashioned good taste, modesty, discretion, or even common sense tends to make us keep certain things low-key or hidden. To *flaunt* something is to show it off triumphantly, boastfully, or shamelessly. Bold or brash types may prefer to flaunt such things as wealth, love affairs, or friendship with criminals. A catch phrase of the 1970s, "If you've got it, flaunt it," could refer to anything from sex appeal to commercial success.

> [Scarlett O'Hara:] "Oh—a diamond ring—and Rhett, do buy a great big one."
> [Rhett Butler:] "So you can flaunt it before your poverty-stricken friends and say 'See what I caught!'"
> —Margaret Mitchell, *Gone With the Wind*

> [In Canada in the 1950s] it took a woman a long time to be comfortable wearing a mink stole in public; aware that she could be accused of flaunting it in front of women in muskrat, she felt guilty.
> —Melinda McCracken, *Memories Are Made of This*

> . . . Pope Alexander VI, a Borgia, father of Cesare and Lucrezia, who flaunted his venality and licentiousness . . .
> —Leo Rosten, *The Joys of Yiddish*

In older English *flaunt* could be used intransitively—that is, without the direct object required by current usage:

> Fortune in men has some small diff'rence made;
> One flaunts in rags, one flutters in brocade.
> —Alexander Pope, *Essay on Man* (1734)

Flaunt can also be used without the implication of boastfulness, to mean 'wave or flutter (something) showily' or 'wear or display (something) proudly':

> It's time for witch hazel to flaunt its golden streamers in the damp woods.
> —*The Old Farmer's Almanac*

> When [Joe Namath] flaunted a mustache and long hair, he set the style for a generation of mod athletes.
> —*New York Times*

To *flout* something is to show open contempt for it. The word usually refers to blatant disregard for law or custom:

> . . . when several Protestant and Catholic churches flouted the official policy of apartheid by desegregating their schools.
> —*U.S. News & World Report*

> . . . the chicanery behind the flags of convenience which permit oil tankers to flout safety regulations.
> —Harriet Van Horne, *New York*

> . . . a continuing Israeli policy of colonization on the West Bank. In the process, Israel is flouting United Nations resolutions calling for its withdrawal. . . .
> —Edward Hughes, *Reader's Digest*

> . . . I have seldom if ever set out purposely and with malice aforethought to flout conventions and demolish icons. . . .
> —J. Paul Getty, *As I See It*

The two verbs thus have nearly opposite meanings but can occur within the same context. Someone who flaunts what should not be flaunted may be said to be flouting a convention. Those who flout authority may be said to flaunt their contempt for it. This yin-yang relationship, added to the remarkably close resemblance between the two words, sometimes leads to the accidental use of *flaunt* for *flout:*

> The last step would apply to those who persistently flaunt the fire code.
> —a fire commissioner (quoted), *Florida Times-Union*

> Prime Minister Pierre Trudeau of Canada appeared yesterday at a formal ceremony in Brasilia wearing a seersucker suit and sneakers. Diplomats are laughing at his flaunting of protocol.
> —radio broadcast

> . . . the Beatles' early flaunt-the-establishment lifestyles . . .
> —*Christianity Today*

Strangely enough, the reverse mistake, of *flout* for *flaunt,* does not seem to occur.

◇ ***Recommendation.*** The use of *flaunt* for *flout,* though rather widespread, is still a definite error. *Flaunt* means 'to show (something) off,' *flout* means 'to show contempt for (something).'

flautist. See FLUTIST, FLAUTIST.

flout. See FLAUNT, FLOUT.

flutist, flautist. Most of the terminology of classical music comes from Italian, and some flute players, especially those of European background, prefer to be called *flautists,* from Italian *flautista,* from *flauto* = 'flute.' The pronunciation of *flautist* is either /**flôt**-ĭst/ or /**flout**-ĭst/. But most English-speaking players, classical as well as nonclassical, now prefer the anglicized form *flutist,* including the dean of them all, Jean-Pierre Rampal.

folk, folks. *Folk* is the Old English (and general Germanic) word for 'separate people or race,' especially 'confederation of Germanic tribes forming a nation.' The word now has several meanings, with distinct uses of the singular and plural.

(1) *The folk* (used as either singular or plural) = 'the people of a particular country or ethnic group regarded in a basic cultural sense,' especially in terms of oral traditions, old customs and beliefs, crafts, etc., as opposed to book learning, international culture, high technology, etc.

> Folklore, by definition, is the traditional knowledge of the folk. "Folk" are

> small groups of people living in isolation who pass along by word of mouth the information and opinions that enable them to live and thrive. This material has no known author or source. It is ancient and covers a plethora of topics from myths and legends, weather and planting lore, songs and games to medicine and language.
>
> —Horace Beck, *American Folklore and Legend*

(2) *Folk* (used as plural) or *folks* = 'people of some specified kind': *country folk(s); city folk(s); plain folk(s); rich folk(s); kinfolk(s).* (3) *Folks* = 'a person's family, kin': *They always spend Christmas with his folks.*

◇ ***Recommendation.*** Be careful when you use *folks* as in the second sense above. There are cases in which the plural form with *-s* comes across as misleading or even nonstandard. Take, for example, W. E. B. Du Bois's classic title, *The Souls of Black Folk* (1903). Du Bois correctly avoided *folks*, which would have sounded inappropriately quaint or "folksy."

folk etymology. It often happens that an unfamiliar or difficult word is altered to make it resemble a familiar but unrelated word or words, as *asparagus* was altered to *sparrowgrass.* German linguistic scholars named this process *volksetymologie*, which in English became *folk etymology*. It is an unsatisfactory term, seeming to imply that such changes are ignorant distortions resulting from misunderstanding by the uneducated "folk," whereas the correct forms are known by the learned scholars who will, if possible, repair the damage. Thus, *sparrowgrass*, which in 1800 was the usual form of the word even among educated people, was condemned as a corrupt form and solemnly corrected back to *asparagus*.

Undoubtedly, the "folk" who first changed *asparagus* to *sparrowgrass*—quite likely they were the cockney greengrocers of London—knew perfectly well what they were doing. They didn't imagine that the stuff was really grass or had anything to do with sparrows; they were simply expressing a good-humored scorn for the fancy botanical name of a fancy vegetable. This cheerful irreverence is often applied to foreign personal and place names. In 1898, during the Spanish-American War, Finley Peter Dunne's Irish-American philosopher, Mr. Dooley, produced a fine specimen of the scornful folk etymology for the Cuban port *Guantánamo:*

> Th' poor tired human mind don't tumble, Hinnissy, to th' raison f'r landin' four hundhred marines at Guanotommy to clear th' forests, whin Havana is livin' free on hot tamales an' ice-cream.
>
> —*Mr. Dooley in Peace and War*

In the same spirit the British troops who restored the emperor Haile Selassie to Ethiopia in 1941 folk-etymologized his name to *High Silly Assie.*

Most of these are passing jokes, which have no serious effect on the names they satirize. But sometimes they endure. The name of the star *Betelgeuse*, which is a French form of the Arabic name, correctly pronounced /bĕt'l-zhĕz/ or /bēt'l-jĕz/, is often referred to as *Beetlejuice* by navigators and astronomers. Similarly, the *Purgatoire* River in Colorado is often known locally as the *Picketwire.*

Sometimes these changes become permanent, and as years go by their origins grow dimmer. An old Virginia square-dance song contains the puzzling line "Molly Brooks has gone to the war." This is actually a long-forgotten alteration of the 18th-century French song "Malbrouck s'en Va-t-en Guerre" (Marlborough Goes Off to War), referring to the English general the duke of Marlborough. Other cases remain speculative. There are English pubs with the baffling name *The Bag O' Nails.* It has been suggested, but can't be proved, that this is an alteration of *The Bacchanals* (= 'revelers').

The most impressive folk etymologies are those that permanently determine the form of a word. There are several well-known cases of this in the names of American plants and animals, in which words borrowed from the Indians or others have been reshaped to look like English words—usually quite irrelevant or meaningless ones. *Woodchuck* is thus a transformation of the Cree name *ochek. Cockroach* is from Spanish *cucaracha. Whisky jack* or *whisky john,* a name for the Canada jay, is from Algonquian *wiskatjân. Poor joe,* a Coastal Southern dialect name for the great blue heron, is from Gullah *pojo,* a word brought over by blacks from West Africa. Other folk-etymologized plant and animal names are *crayfish,* which is not a fish but a borrowing of French *écrevisse,* and the herb *wormwood,* which was originally *wermode* and is related to French *vermouth.*

Sometimes a folk etymology results in a permanent change in the meaning of a word or phrase. The Dutch military term *verloren hoop* means 'lost troop' and referred to a picked troop detached from an army to make an attack. In English it was rendered as *forlorn hope.* The expression, now used in the original sense only by historians, has become a generalized term meaning 'desperate undertaking' or even merely 'faint hope.'

Some terms cause needless bafflement. The *Jerusalem artichoke,* as many a cookbook rather petulantly points out, is neither an artichoke nor from Jerusalem, but is the tuber of an American sunflower. The sunflower was first grown in Europe by the Italians, who called it *girasole articiocco* = 'the sunflower artichoke' (*girasole* = 'sunflower' + *articiocco* = 'artichoke'), since the tuber tastes very like the globe artichoke. The English borrowed the name in the 17th century as *Jerusalem artichoke,* which originally was not intended to be taken literally but was an essentially humorous expression, like *Dutch courage* = 'gin' or *Welsh rabbit* = 'toasted cheese.' The latter is a particularly interesting case, in that literal-minded people, failing to see that the term is an English anti-Welsh taunt meaning 'impoverished Welshman's substitute for rabbit,' have tried to turn *rabbit* into *rarebit.* This mistaken correction is still referred to as a folk etymology, although it was made by pedantic word fanciers rather than ordinary folk, who were perfectly content with *Welsh rabbit.* Similarly, gossipy word books still repeat as historical fact the fable that Henry VIII, or James I, or Charles II, knighted a loin of beef and so created the *sirloin.* The word actually comes from French *surlonge* = 'upper loin' (*sur* = 'on, upon, above' + *longe* = 'loin'). The story doubtless originated as a pun, which was likely to have been made many a time among the sirloin-loving English: "This Sirloin is so good it deserves its knighthood"—hardly a folk story. Yet the tale may well be responsible for changing the spelling, which would otherwise probably be *surloin,* as in *surname* and *surface.*

The curious new term *cold duck* = 'cheap sparkling wine, typically made of a mixture of champagne and burgundy' seems to result from another old joke. German *kalte ende* = 'cold ends or remnants' refers to a drink made of leftovers of wine at the end of a party. Someone, perhaps in a stroke of bibulous inspiration, changed the term to *kalte ente,* which means 'cold duck.' This was taken up in the wine trade for a mixed sparkling wine and was so translated into English. The fact that it's meaningless in English doesn't bother anyone; some brands of the wine show ducks on the label, and further variations such as *cold goose* and *baby duck* have been invented.

What most of these folk etymologies have in common is a touch of humor in the deliberate distortion of a word and a liking for the apparently misleading or ludicrous result—*sparrowgrass, Beetlejuice, woodchuck, cold duck,* etc. Perhaps the term should really be "joke etymology."

football terms. Of all sports in the United States, football has expanded most in recent years, physically and linguistically. The game has seriously challenged baseball's longstanding status as our national pastime, largely because of the growth of professional football since the 1950s. The game has become highly specialized; that specialization and the consequent refinement of all techniques of play have tended to nurture "inside" terminology. This new shoptalk, however, is much more than passing jargon. Some of it has entered official rules, and knowledge of most of it is indispensable to following the sport on television or in print. A bit of the new language has been adapted for general use as well (see Section 2 below).

(1) A selection of terms specific to football:

audible = 'offensive play or defensive formation, called at the line of scrimmage, that supplants the play or formation designated in the huddle moments before'

automatic = 'audible'

blitz = 'defensive maneuver in which several backs or linebackers, anticipating a forward pass, charge through the line of scrimmage in an attempt to harry or tackle the opponents' passer'

broken play = 'improvised offensive play that supplants a play whose execution has broken down'

bump-and-run = 'legal blocking of a defensive back, consisting of one bodily contact by an eligible pass receiver at the start of the receiver's downfield run'

buttonhook = 'pass pattern in which an intended receiver runs downfield (away from the passer), then pivots abruptly and faces, or returns a few steps toward, the passer'

cheap shot (slang) = 'unsportsmanlike conduct, such as kicking or piling on a downed opponent'; usually a personal foul

completed pass = 'forward pass caught in bounds on the fly and held securely by an eligible receiver'

cover = 'to follow the movement of (any opponent, but especially an eligible pass receiver) in an attempt to disrupt a pass play or to tackle the receiver of a completed pass' See *pass coverage,* below.

crackback blocking = 'illegal, blind-side blocking of an opposing defensive back by an eligible pass receiver'

deep = 'distant from the line of scrimmage': *deep back* = 'back stationed farthest behind the line of scrimmage'; *throw deep* = 'to throw a long forward pass beyond the line'

double wing = 'offensive backfield formation with two halfbacks stationed close to the line of scrimmage and just outside the ends'

down-and-out = 'pass pattern executed by running downfield, then abruptly making a 90-degree turn and running toward a sideline'

draw = 'offensive play that culminates in a delayed run by a back after the quarterback has faked a pass to draw defensive opponents out of position'

eligible receiver = 'any of a group of offensive players (the two ends and any of the backs) who may legally catch a forward pass thrown by another offensive player'

end around = 'end run with an offensive end in the role of ball carrier'

end run = 'offensive play in which a ball carrier attempts to circle either of the flanks of the line of scrimmage'

fair catch = 'catch of a punt by a player of the nonkicking team, signaled in advance by the player's raising an arm'; the player thus forfeits a chance to run with the ball but gains exemption from being tackled

fake = 'to pretend (a pass or other maneuver) as a means of deceiving the opponents'; used of an offensive player, especially the quarterback

field goal (abbreviated *FG*) = 'score of three points resulting from a place kick or (rarely) drop kick, from scrimmage, that sends the ball over the crossbar and between the uprights of the goal posts'

first down, first-and-ten = (1) 'first in a succession of four offensive plays' (2) 'the right to begin such a succession, resulting from gains in yardage on plays in a preceding series'

flare = 'pass pattern executed by running a short distance downfield and toward one of the sidelines'

fly = 'pass pattern whose route is straight downfield'

game plan = 'a team's overall strategy for a particular game'

hang time = 'the length of time a ball is in the air after being punted'

huddle = 'on-field conference of players, between plays, in which an offensive play or defensive formation is announced by the quarterback or defensive captain'

I formation = 'offensive formation in

which the quarterback, stationed directly behind the center, and other backs form a single I-shaped file perpendicular to the line'

incomplete pass = 'forward pass that is not caught in bounds on the fly or caught securely by an eligible receiver'

intercept = 'to catch a forward pass, thrown by an opposing player, on the fly'; used of a defensive player

interference = (1) 'legal blocking that clears a path for a ball carrier' (2) 'illegal obstruction of the movement of an opponent' See *pass interference*, below.

keeper (slang) = 'offensive play in which the quarterback attempts to advance the ball by carrying it, instead of passing it or handing it off to a teammate'

key = 'to concentrate on (an opposing player, especially a running back) in an effort to contain that player'; used of defensive personnel

line = 'either of two groups of players, assembled in ranks, who face each other along and parallel to the line of scrimmage and provide the first physical contact of a play by charging at each other'; normally seven players of the offensive line and four players of the defensive line

line of scrimmage = 'imaginary line, parallel to the goal lines, on which the ball is placed to mark the offensive team's point of advance, and along which the opposing players face each other; the line that marks the start of play for any of a succession of downs'

look-in = 'pass pattern executed by a receiver who runs a short distance beyond the line of scrimmage on a diagonal course toward the center of the field'

offside = 'across the line of scrimmage before the snap of the ball that begins a play'; a violation that incurs a penalty

option play = 'offensive play for advancing the ball that gives a back the choice of either rushing or throwing a forward pass, whichever would be more favorable'

pass = 'forward or lateral throw of the ball by an offensive player who grasps it with the palm spread over the widest part and sends it on a spiral course, the ball rotating on its longitudinal axis'

pass coverage = 'defensive action designed to prevent the completion of the opposition's forward passes or to minimize gains made through completions' See *cover*, above.

pass interference = 'illegal interference with a receiver, which results in a ruling of complete pass; in general, defensive action that overtly obstructs a receiver (holding or other body contact while the ball is still in the air) as opposed to action intended only to intercept or bat down the ball'

pass rush = 'charge by defensive players intended to tackle or harry an offensive player about to throw a forward pass'

pattern = 'predetermined route followed by an offensive player, especially a pass receiver, during the execution of a play'

pit (slang) = 'area along the line of scrimmage where the two lines charge at each other'

play = 'unit of action from scrimmage, beginning with a snap of the ball and ending when the referee signals the ball as dead or when a score is made'

play book = 'collection of diagrams of a team's formations and plays'

possession = 'the fact of a team's having the ball and therefore the right to function offensively during a sequence of downs until the ball is surrendered'

prevent defense = 'defensive alignment designed to lessen the chance that a long forward pass will be completed'; it positions backs and linebackers well behind the line of scrimmage and sometimes also employs extra backs among the 11 defensive players

punt = 'kick executed by dropping the ball so that it strikes the area of the instep as the foot is swung forward and upward in an arc'

quarterback sneak = 'offensive play in which the quarterback is the ball carrier, employed as a surprise strategy'

recovery = 'act of gaining possession of a loose ball after it has been fumbled'

red dog = 'defensive maneuver by linebackers who charge at an opposing quarterback in anticipation of the quarterback's throw of a forward pass'

redshirt = 'college player who sits out a season of actual play (while practicing with a team) in order to lengthen the player's term of eligibility for intercollegiate competition'

reverse = 'offensive play that begins with the flow of action in one direction and culminates in a player's being given the ball and running with it in the opposite direction, as a deceptive maneuver'

rush = (1) 'to charge toward an offensive back in the act of preparing to throw a pass'; used of a defensive player (2) 'to carry the ball in plays designated rushing'; used of an offensive player

rushing = 'offensive play or series of plays in which the means of advance is to run with the ball from scrimmage rather than pass it'

sack (slang) = 'to tackle (an opposing quarterback) behind the line of scrimmage, while the quarterback is preparing to throw a forward pass, with a consequent loss of yardage for the offensive team'

safety valve = 'forward-pass play that gives the passer the option of throwing the ball to a secondary, or second-choice, receiver when the intended, or primary, receiver is guarded by defenders'

scrimmage = (1) 'contact between opposing lines that begins an individual play, and all the action that follows until a score results or the play ends' (2) 'a team's practice session, especially one involving body contact'

set up = 'to drop back from the line of scrimmage, after taking a snap from the center, and prepare to throw a forward pass'; used of a quarterback

signals = 'verbal code, called out by the quarterback and opposing defensive captain at the line of scrimmage, that identifies the execution of a play'

single wing = 'offensive backfield formation with one back stationed just wide of one of the ends, another just behind the guard on the same side of the line, and two others relatively deep and approximately in line with the center'

snap = (1) 'act of passing the ball, by the center to a back, that initiates each offensive play' (2) 'such a backward pass of the ball by the center in advance of a punt or place kick'

split T formation = 'variant of the T formation in which the quarterback is in motion laterally, along the line of scrimmage, after taking the snap'

Statue of Liberty = 'offensive play in which the quarterback holds the ball aloft, arm cocked as if to pass, and a back circles behind, takes the ball, and attempts to advance it by rushing'

stiff-arm (informal) = 'to straight-arm'

straight-arm = 'to extend the arm rigidly and use it to ward off (an opponent seeking to make a tackle)'; used of a ball carrier

stunting = 'predetermined movement by defensive players at or near the line of scrimmage prior to the snap'

suicide squad (slang) = 'special team employed for kickoffs' (so called because of the high risk of injury on such occasions)

tackle = (1) (noun) 'either of two members of the offensive line stationed between an end and a guard, or of the customary defensive line stationed alongside an end' (2) (noun) 'a defensive player's attempt to down an offensive opponent by grasping that player's body below the shoulders' (3) (verb) 'to down a player in this manner'

taxi squad = 'reserve members of a professional team who can be activated on short notice to replace injured players' (originally so called because reserves of the Cleveland Browns, owned by a taxicab executive, were put on the payroll of the cab company when not playing)

T formation = 'offensive backfield formation in the shape of a T, so that the quarterback, stationed just behind the center, is in turn ahead of two or more backs arranged in a rank parallel to the line of scrimmage'

three-four defense = 'variant of the standard defensive alignment, employing three defensive linemen rather than four, and four linebackers rather than three'

touch football = 'form of the game in which an offensive player's advance is terminated by tagging with the hand rather than by tackling'

trap = 'rushing play based on the strategy of creating an opening in an opponent's defense by permitting an opposing player to penetrate the offensive formation, blocking the player sidewise, and then advancing the ball through the area vacated by that player'

wishbone = 'variant of the T formation, differing in that two deep backs make up a rank behind a third (roughly in the shape of a wishbone), while the quarterback lines up behind the center and nearest the line of scrimmage'

yardage = 'yards gained or lost by a team or player, signifying the distance the ball has been advanced'

zone defense = 'defense in which a player or players are made responsible for coverage of specific areas of the field, rather than of specified opposing players'

(2) Some terms or expressions that have come into general use:

call the signals = 'to be in charge, direct an enterprise' (from the function of the quarterback)

carry the ball = 'to play the leading role, assume personal responsibility'

cheap shot = 'unsportsmanlike behavior or remark'

end run = 'stratagem, something that promotes a goal or bypasses an obstacle'

game plan = 'detailed strategy for any enterprise' (popularized by Richard M. Nixon, an ardent football fan)

huddle = (1) (noun) 'conference' (2) (verb) 'to gather for a conference'

kick off = 'to commence (an activity)'

kickoff = 'the beginning of any activity'

man in motion = 'person whose great activity is highly visible'

on the sidelines = 'not active, temporarily or permanently'

quarterback = (1) (noun) 'person who directs' (2) (verb) 'to direct (an enterprise)'

run interference = 'to clear a path for (a person with a purpose or mission), remove obstacles for'

tackle = 'to undertake (a formidable job) or take on (an opponent)'

forbid, when used with a verb, is properly constructed with *to* and the infinitive, not with *from* and the verbal noun, as in the following citation:

> Oregon now forbids the state textbook committee from approving any textbook on government history that "speaks slightingly of the founders of the republic."
> —Morton Hunt, *Reader's Digest*

This should have been "forbids the committee to approve."

former. (1) In the sense 'earlier in time' *former* contrasts with *later* or *latter: In former years the family had been prosperous; in later* (or *latter*) *times it had sunk into obscurity.*

(2) *Former* is also used to mean 'having been (so) previously': *the former Dutch colony of New Netherland, now New York; Mrs. Harold Fletcher, the former Helen McMurdo.* See also EX-, FORMER.

(3) *The former* = 'the first of two previously mentioned people or things' contrasts with *the latter.* Both are used either with nouns or absolutely: *Irish and Welsh are the chief surviving Celtic languages; the former* (*language*) *has the richer ancient literature, but the latter* (*language*) *is the living speech of many more people.* Both *former* and *latter* are properly used of only two items; if more than two are involved, *first* or *first-mentioned* and *last* or *last-mentioned* should be

used: *Last summer we visited Paris, London, and Rome; the first was my favorite.*

forms of address. The following models offer generally accepted guidelines for addressing letters to various public dignitaries, professional people, and military personnel, as well as to individuals, couples, and organizations. Along with each model an appropriate salutation is provided. When more than one salutation is given, the most formal one appears first.

Because of limited space, only masculine forms are shown in most of the following illustrations. (See also DEAR SIR OR MADAM.) When writing to a woman, make the following adjustments in the models:
(1) Replace *Sir* with *Madam.*
(2) Where *Mr.* is followed by a title (as *Mr. Ambassador, Mr. Justice*), replace *Mr.* with *Madam.*
(3) Where *Mr.* is followed by a personal name (as *Mr. Jessup*), replace *Mr.* with *Miss, Mrs.*, or *Ms.*, as appropriate.

Government Officials.

President of the United States

The President
The White House
Washington, D.C. 20500

Mr. President: *or* Dear Mr. President:

Former President of the United States

The Honorable James M. Poe
(*local address*)

Dear Mr. Poe:

Vice President of the United States

The Vice President
United States Senate
Washington, D.C. 20510
or
The Honorable Roy S. Chipps
Vice President of the United States
Washington, D.C. 20510

Sir: *or* Dear Mr. Vice President:

Cabinet Member

The Honorable Frank Russomano
Secretary of (*department*)
Washington, D.C. (*ZIP code*)
or
The Secretary of (*department*)
Washington, D.C. (*ZIP code*)

Sir: *or* Dear Mr. Secretary:

Chief Justice of the U.S. Supreme Court

The Chief Justice of the United States
Washington, D.C. 20543
or
The Chief Justice
The Supreme Court
Washington, D.C. 20543

Sir: *or* Dear Mr. Chief Justice:

Associate Justice of the U.S. Supreme Court

Mr. Justice Palmer
The Supreme Court
Washington, D.C. 20543

Sir: *or* Dear Mr. Justice:

Judge—Federal, State, or Local Court

The Honorable Homer M. Fox
(*title or name of court, or both*)
(*local address*)

Dear Judge Fox:

United States Senator

The Honorable Stephen K. Schroeder
United States Senate
Washington, D.C. 20510
or
The Honorable Stephen K. Schroeder
United States Senator
(*local address*)

Sir: *or* Dear Senator Schroeder:

United States Representative

The Honorable Victor Ruiz
House of Representatives
Washington, D.C. 20515
or
The Honorable Victor Ruiz
Representative in Congress
(*local address*)

Sir: *or* Dear Mr. Ruiz:

Governor

The Honorable Robert B. Weiss
Governor of (*state*)
(*state capital, state, and ZIP code*)

Sir: *or* Dear Governor Weiss:

State Senator
The Honorable Andrew Y. Chiverton
The State Senate
(*state capital, state, and ZIP code*)
Sir: *or* Dear Senator Chiverton:

State Assembly Member or Representative
The Honorable Tyler Godchaux
The State Assembly (*or other appropriate name*)
(*state capital, state, and ZIP code*)
Sir: *or* Dear Mr. Godchaux:

Mayor
The Honorable Jerome J. Pellegrini
Mayor of (*city*)
(*city, state, and ZIP code*)
or
The Mayor of the City of (*city*)
(*city, state, and ZIP code*)
Sir: *or* Dear Mr. Mayor:
or
Dear Mayor Pellegrini:

Diplomats.

Secretary-General of the United Nations
His Excellency Pravin Shah
Secretary-General of the United Nations
United Nations Plaza
New York, New York 10017
Excellency: *or* Dear Mr. Secretary-General:
or
Dear Mr. Shah:

Ambassador to the United States
His Excellency Rodrigo de la Cruz
Ambassador of (*country*)
(*address*)
Excellency: *or* Dear Mr. Ambassador:

Minister to the United States
The Honorable Dag Christiansen
Minister of (*department*)
(*address*)
Sir: *or* Dear Mr. Minister:

American Ambassador
The Honorable George C. Courtenay II
American Ambassador
(*foreign address of U.S. embassy*)
Sir: *or* Dear Mr. Ambassador:

American Chargé d'Affaires
The Honorable Reid Ferguson, Jr.
American Chargé d'Affaires
(*foreign address of U.S. embassy*)
Dear Sir: *or* Dear Mr. Ferguson:

Roman Catholic Clergy and Religious.

Pope
His Holiness the Pope
Vatican City
00187 Rome, Italy
or
His Holiness Pope Gregory XVII
Vatican City
00187 Rome, Italy
Your Holiness: *or* Most Holy Father:

Cardinal
His Eminence William Cardinal Dowd
Archbishop of (*diocese*)
(*address*)
Your Eminence:
or
Dear Cardinal Dowd:

Archbishop and Bishop
The Most Reverend Robert Cammarata
Archbishop (*or* Bishop) of (*diocese*)
(*address*)
Your Excellency:
or
Dear Archbishop (*or* Bishop) Cammarata:

Monsignor
The Right Reverend Monsignor John Fry
(*address*)
Right Reverend Monsignor:
or
Dear Monsignor Fry:

Priest
The Reverend Henry J. Kowalczyk
(*address*)
Reverend Father:
or
Dear Father Kowalczyk:

Brother
Brother Mark, O.S.B.
(*address*)
Dear Brother: *or* Dear Brother Mark:

Nun

Sister Ancilla Marie, S.N.D.
(*address*)
Dear Sister:
or
Dear Sister Ancilla Marie:

Protestant Clergy.

Episcopal Bishop

The Right Reverend Kelsey Phipps
Bishop of (*diocese*)
(*address*)
Right Reverend Sir:
or
Dear Bishop Phipps:

Episcopal Dean

The Very Reverend A. Kirkland Powell
Dean of (*cathedral or church*)
(*address*)
Very Reverend Sir:
or
Dear Dean Powell:

Methodist Bishop

The Reverend Wesley J. Hall, Jr.
Bishop of (*area*)
(*address*)
or
Bishop Wesley J. Hall, Jr.
(*address*)
Reverend Sir: *or* Dear Bishop Hall:

Clergyman With Doctor's Degree

The Reverend Dr. Harry F. Winger
(*address*)
or
The Reverend Harry F. Winger, D.D.
(*address*)
Reverend Sir: *or* Dear Dr. Winger:

Clergyman Without Doctor's Degree

The Reverend George G. Kenworthy
(*address*)
Reverend Sir: *or* Dear Mr. Kenworthy:

Jewish Clergy.

Rabbi With Doctor's Degree

Rabbi Bernard J. Birnbaum, D.D.
(*address*)
Dear Rabbi Birnbaum:
or
Dr. Bernard J. Birnbaum:
(*address*)
Dear Dr. Birnbaum:

Rabbi Without Doctor's Degree

Rabbi Adam Levinson
(*address*)
Dear Rabbi Levinson:

Education Officials.

President of a College or University

J. Morton Fieldston, LL.D.
President, (*name of college*)
(*address*)
or
Dr. J. Morton Fieldston
President, (*name of college*)
(*address*)
or
President J. Morton Fieldston
(*name of college*)
(*address*)
Dear Dr. Fieldston:
or
Dear President Fieldston:

Dean of a College or University

Peter S. Price II, Ph.D.
Dean, (*name of school or division*)
(*name of college and address*)
or
Dr. Peter S. Price II
Dean, (*name of school or division*)
(*name of college and address*)
or
Dean Peter S. Price II
(*name of school or division*)
(*name of college and address*)
Dear Dr. Price: *or* Dear Dean Price:

Professor

Kenneth L. Wu, Ph.D.
Department (*or* Professor) of (*subject*)
(*name of college*)
(*address*)
or
Dr. Kenneth L. Wu
Department (*or* Professor) of (*subject*)
(*name of college*)
(*address*)

or
Prof. Kenneth L. Wu
Department of (*subject*)
(*name of college*)
(*address*)

Dear Dr. Wu: *or* Dear Professor Wu:
or
Dear Mr. Wu: (*often preferred by holders of doctorates*)

Superintendent of Schools

Mr. (*or* Dr.) Harold N. Frisch
Superintendent of (*city*) Schools
(*address*)

Dear Mr. (*or* Dr.) Frisch:

Member of Board of Education

Mr. Hector S. Echavarria
Member, (*city*) Board of Education
(*address*)

Dear Mr. Echavarria:

Principal

Mr. (*or* Dr.) Milton Ungaro-Mancusi
Principal, (*name of school*)
(*address*)

Dear Mr. (*or* Dr.) Ungaro-Mancusi:

Teacher

Mr. (*or* Dr.) Wilson O. Webber
(*name of school*)
(*address*)

Dear Mr. (*or* Dr.) Webber:

Professionals.

Lawyers

Mr. Francis X. Carroll
Attorney-at-Law
(*address*)
or
Francis X. Carroll, Esq.
(*address*)

Dear Mr. Carroll:

Physicians and Others With Doctoral Degrees

Malcolm R. Kresicki, Jr., M.D.
(*address*)
or
Dr. Malcolm R. Kresicki, Jr.
(*address*)

Dear Dr. Kresicki:

Military Personnel.

Officers in the Army (USA), Air Force (USAF), and Marine Corps (USMC)

Major General (*or* Maj. Gen.) Guy Starr, USA (*or* USAF *or* USMC)
(*address*)

Sir: *or* Dear General Starr:

(*Note: The salutation* Dear General Starr *would also be used if Starr were a brigadier, a lieutenant, or full general. In the same way* Dear Colonel____ *is the salutation used for either a full or a lieutenant colonel, and* Dear Lieutenant____ *is used for a first or second lieutenant.*)

Officers in the Navy (USN) and Coast Guard (USCG)

Rear Admiral (*or* Rear Adm.) Dixon Ries, USN (*or* USCG)
(*address*)

Sir: *or* Dear Admiral Ries:

(*Note: The salutation* Dear Admiral Ries *would also be used if Ries were a vice admiral or a full admiral.*)

Commander (*or* Cmdr.) Philip Klein, USN (*or* USCG)
(*address*)

Sir: *or* Dear Commander Klein:

Lieutenant Commander (*or* Lt. Cmdr.) Gary Foy, USN (*or* USCG)
(*address*)

Dear Mr. Foy:

(*Note: From the rank of lieutenant commander down, the salutation should use the courtesy title* Mr.)

Enlisted Personnel

Private First Class (*or* Pfc.) Kit Purdy, USA
(*address*)

Dear Private Purdy:

Airman First Class (*or* A1C) Boyd Manson, USAF
(*address*)

Dear Airman Manson:

Seaman (*or* SN) Anthony C. Parillo, USN (*or* USCG)
(*address*)

Dear Seaman Parillo:

Individuals.

Man Without a Special Title

Mr. Harrison Browning
(*address*)

Dear Mr. Browning:

Woman Without a Special Title

Ms. (*or* Miss *or* Mrs.) Alison G. Marx
(*address*)

Dear Ms. (*or* Miss *or* Mrs.) Marx:

(*Note: When you know which courtesy title a woman prefers, always respect it.*)

Woman—Title Preference Unknown

Ms. Sylvia Perciatelli
(*address*)

Dear Ms. Perciatelli:
or
Sylvia Perciatelli
(*address*)

Dear Sylvia Perciatelli:

Individual—Gender Unknown

Lee Landry
(*address*)

Dear Lee Landry:

B. J. Clerihew
(*address*)

Dear B. J. Clerihew:

Individual—Gender and Name Unknown

(*title of individual, if appropriate*)
(*name of organization*)
(*address*)

Sir or Madam: *or* Madam or Sir:
or
Dear Sir or Madam:
or
Dear Madam or Sir:

Individual—Gender Known, Name Unknown

(*title of individual, if appropriate*)
(*name of organization*)
(*address*)

Sir: *or* Dear Sir:
Madam: *or* Dear Madam:

Two Individuals—Same Location

Mrs. Eileen G. Gleason
Ms. Helen R. Horowitz
(*name of organization, if appropriate*)
(*address*)

Dear Mrs. Gleason and Ms. Horowitz:

Two Individuals—Different Locations

Miss (*or* Ms.) Penelope Hodges
(*address*)

Mr. Roger Sandor
(*address*)

Dear Miss (*or* Ms.) Hodges and Mr. Sandor:

(*Note: The names and addresses in this example may be written side by side, and the man's name may precede the woman's.*)

Two Men

Mr. Frederick R. Bodoni
Mr. William L. Van Liew
(*address*)

Dear Mr. Bodoni and Mr. Van Liew:
or
Dear Messrs. Bodoni and Van Liew:
or
Gentlemen:

Two Women

Miss Gladys O. Flanagan
Miss Sarah B. Cavatelli
(*address*)

Dear Miss Flanagan and Miss Cavatelli:
or
Dear Misses Flanagan and Cavatelli:

Mrs. Rose Sanchez
Mrs. Annette Featherston
(*address*)

Dear Mrs. Sanchez and Mrs. Featherston:
or
Dear Mesdames (*or* Mmes.) Sanchez and Featherston:

Ms. Claire G. de Cuville
Ms. Jenny Palmer
(*address*)

Dear Ms. de Cuville and Ms. Palmer:
or
Dear Mses. (*or* Mss.) de Cuville and Palmer:

Miss (*or* Ms.) Holly Pinckney
Mrs. Faith Hathaway
(*address*)

Dear Miss (*or* Ms.) Pinckney and Mrs. Hathaway:

Couples.

Married Couple—Without Special Titles

Mr. and Mrs. Alfred C. Weild
(*address*)

Dear Mr. and Mrs. Weild:

Married Couple—Husband With Special Title

Prof. and Mrs. Gordon Ball
(*address*)

Dear Professor and Mrs. Ball:

Married Couple—Wife With Special Title

Dr. Catherine MacDonald
Mr. Lloyd MacDonald
(*address*)

Dear Dr. and Mr. MacDonald:

Married Couple—Both With Special Titles

Col. Benson T. Koppers
Dr. Judith M. Koppers
(*address*)

Dear Colonel and Dr. Koppers:

Unmarried Couple Living Together

Mr. Harry T. Boardman
Ms. Angela F. Curry
(*address*)

Dear Mr. Boardman and Ms. Curry:

Organizations.

Organization of Men

(*name of organization*)
(*address*)

Gentlemen:

Organization of Women

(*name of organization*)
(*address*)

Mesdames: *or* Ladies:

Organization of Men and Women

(*name of organization*)
(*address*)

Gentlemen:
or
Ladies and Gentlemen:
or
Gentlemen and Ladies:
or
Mr. Geoffrey H. Parkinson
President, (*name of organization*)
(*address*)

Dear Mr. Parkinson:
or
Chief Executive Officer (*or* President)
(*name of organization*)
(*address*)

Sir or Madam: *or* Madam or Sir:
or
Dear Sir or Madam:
or
Dear Madam or Sir:

for real. See REAL.

forte. There are two separate though related words here. The musical term meaning 'loudly' is from Italian and is pronounced /**fôr**-tā/. The word meaning 'someone's strong point' is from French and is properly pronounced /fôrt/.

> Mr. [Ray] Charles's real forte has always been live performances.
> —Robert Palmer, *New York Times*

> . . . a President like Johnson whose forte lay in one-to-one relations behind closed doors.
> —Doris Kearns, *Lyndon Johnson and the American Dream*

fortuitous. The proper meaning of this adjective is 'occurring by chance' in a purely neutral sense:

> To believe that human personality is the result of the fortuitous interplay of atoms and electrons is as absurd as to believe that a monkey by hitting typewriter keys at random will eventually produce a Shakespearean play.
> —Martin Luther King, Jr., *Strength to Love*

Likewise the adverb:

> Celebration of Kurt Gödel's work is always in order, and in this case it is

> fortuitously timely: Gödel died while this book was at press.
> —Willard Quine, *New York Times Book Review*

Naturally enough, *fortuitous* is often also used to mean 'occurring by chance' in a favorable context—'accidental but also turning out well':

> Ross's success as an editor had certain elements of the fortuitous about it; for example, it was a lucky accident that his unappeasable appetite for facts coincided with a similar appetite on the part of the public. —Brendan Gill, *Here at The New Yorker*

> . . . the research somehow determined that the colors orange and yellow were good "morning" colors—so various and sundry articles of the "AM America" set were done up in yellow and orange. These included the notebook paper for Stephanie and Bill. (Stephanie's hair, by one of those fortuitous strokes of nature, nearly matched her notepaper.)
> —Ron Powers, *The Newscasters*

By a further development, due no doubt to association with *fortunate* and perhaps also with *felicitous*, *fortuitous* occasionally is also used to mean simply 'fortunate, satisfactory, successful,' with little or no element of chance involved:

> Finding an aggressive headmaster with new ideas was far more difficult. They made a most fortuitous choice. . . .
> —David Niven, *The Moon's a Balloon*

> . . . induced CBS to send him to London. It turned out to be a fortuitous move. Going to Europe took him back to his journalistic roots. . . .
> —Gary Paul Gates, *Air Time*

◇ ***Recommendation.*** The use of *fortuitous* to mean merely 'fortunate' is an error. *Fortuitous* should primarily convey the sense 'accidental,' whether favorable, unfavorable, or neutral.

French Canadian. See CANADIAN ENGLISH; CANADIAN FRENCH; CANUCK.

French words. The French and the English have been borrowing words from each other for centuries, complaining about it all the while. The Académie Française periodically mounts public campaigns to protect the purity of classical French from the contamination of anglicisms—usually to no avail. The English and Americans have been more tolerant, not actually trying to proscribe the introduction of French words, but making each new import undergo a sort of probationary period during which it is widely said to be pretentious and quite unnecessary. In time, properly chastened, the new word generally slips into the language anyway.

Anglo-Americans do well to be tolerant. If all the words of French origin were to be subtracted from English, we would be nearly tongue-tied. English is a hybrid language, dependent on a multitude of borrowings from many sources for its enormous vocabulary and unique richness of connotation. If, in the centuries-long process of grafting foreign words onto the rootstock of the Germanic languages from which English sprang, we owe our greatest debt to the Romans (see LATIN WORDS), we certainly owe our second-greatest debt to the French.

Indeed, there was a period when English was nearly submerged in French. Until the Norman invasion of England in 1066 the exchange of words between the two countries had been minimal. But when William the Conqueror ascended the English throne, French suddenly became the language of government. Such of the Anglo-Saxon nobility as had not been killed at Hastings or in the campaigns of pacification that followed, were for the most part banished from the court, stripped of their offices, and deprived of their holdings. The new ruling elite—the king and his ministers, the great barons and prelates of the Church, the leading figures in the administrative and legal systems—were all Frenchmen. Almost overnight English had become a second-class language in its native land.

Nor did the situation improve after William's death in 1087. Like the Norman aristocracy in general, none of William's immediate successors—William II, Henry I,

Stephen, Henry II, Richard the Lion-Hearted, John, Henry III—appears even to have bothered to learn how to speak English. And for a long time there seemed no pressing need to do so. The Norman presence in England—and therefore the preeminence of French—was constantly being reinforced by waves of immigrants from the Continent. Most of these new arrivals were probably aristocrats and their retainers, but some must also have been tradesmen, for numerous anglicized proper names relating to occupations seem to have entered our language at about this time:

Barber: from Old French *barbeor* = 'barber,' from Latin *barba* = 'beard'
Butcher: from Old French *bouchier* = 'butcher,' literally 'buck slaughterer,' from *bouc* = 'male deer'
Carpenter: from Norman French *carpentier* = 'wagon maker'
Fletcher: from Old French *flechier* = 'arrow maker': from *fleche* = 'arrow'
Mason: from Old French *maçon* = 'mason,' from a Frankish word meaning 'maker,' going back to the same Germanic root from which the English word *make* derives
Taylor: from Old French *tailleur* = 'cutter'

For about 150 years after the conquest, England remained a kind of linguistic battlefield. Although French was the favored language of politics, the Church, law, scholarship, literature, science, the arts, some trades, and most refined living, the English language remained doggedly resistant to foreign influence. During this period English probably absorbed fewer than 1,000 French words into its permanent vocabulary.

The Middle Ages. It was only after the supremacy of French finally began to recede in the mid-13th century, when the acculturated descendants of the invaders at last began to think of themselves more as Englishmen than Frenchmen (and, indeed, went to war with France)—when, in short, the French language had clearly lost its battle with English in Britain—that Englishmen felt sufficiently relaxed to begin borrowing French words freely. Between 1250 and 1500 a staggering 9,000 words of French origin poured into the language, and at least 75 percent of them are still in use today.

To be sure, when we speak of "French" words, we generally mean Latin words once removed, since French is a Romance language. But questions of origins apart, there can be no doubt that the French impact on English during the Middle Ages was nothing short of massive, utterly transforming not only the way the English spoke, but probably even the way they thought.

(1) Government and politics. Most of our modern vocabulary of government and politics came into being at that time. Here is a brief sampling:

alliance = 'a joining, close association': from Old French *aliance* = 'alliance,' from *alier* = 'to join,' ultimately from Latin *ligāre* = 'to bind' (akin to the English word *ligament*)
authority = 'power, influence, self-assurance': from Old French *autorité*, from Latin *auctōritās* = 'advice, influence, command,' from *auctor* = 'master, leader'
coroner = 'public official who investigates and determines the cause of death in specific cases': from Old French *corone* = 'crown,' originally 'crowner,' from the title of a government official assigned to keep track of *crown* property; in ensuing centuries the job changed but the title remained
government = 'system of rule, administration, authority': from Old French *government*, from *governer* = 'to govern,' from Latin *gubernāre* = 'to steer (a ship)'
liberty = 'freedom': from Middle French *liberté*, from Latin *lībertās* = 'freedom, condition of a free man,' from *līber* = 'free'
mayor = 'chief governing official of a municipality': from Old French *maire*, from Latin *mājor* = 'greater,' comparative of *magnus* = 'great'
minister = 'agent, government representative, clergyman': from Old French *menistre*, from Latin *minister* = 'servant'

parliament = 'governing council, law-making body': from Old French *parlement*, originally 'speaking, talk,' from *parler* = 'to speak,' ultimately from Late Latin *parabolāre* = 'to speak in parables, speak,' from *parabola* = 'parable, speech'

public = 'of or pertaining to the people or their welfare': from Middle French *public, publique*, from Latin *pūblicus*, probably a blend of Old Latin *poplicus* = 'belonging to the people' (from *populus* = 'people') and Latin *pūbicus* = 'belonging to adults' (from *pūbēs* = 'body hair that appears at puberty, adults, people')

rebel = 'one who disregards or fights against conventional authority or rules, nonconformist': from Middle French *rebelle*, from Latin *rebellis* = 'one who makes war again, one who revolts' or 'rebellious,' from *re-* = 'back, again' + *bellum* = 'war'

revenue = 'income, return on investments, etc.': from Middle French *revenu, revenue*, past participle of *revenir* = 'to come back, return'

state = 'political entity, condition, status, etc.': from Old French *estat*, from Latin *status* = 'posture, condition, state, public affairs, etc.'

traitor = 'one who betrays country, a cause, etc.': from Old French *traître*, from Vulgar Latin *traditor* = 'betrayer,' from *trāditus*, past participle of *trādere* = 'to deliver, surrender'

treasurer = 'one who supervises the financial affairs of a group, government, etc.': from Anglo-French *tresorer*, from Old French *tresorier*, from *tresor* = 'treasure,' ultimately from Greek *thēsauros* = 'store, strongroom, safe'

treaty = 'formal agreement, pact': from Middle French *traité*, from Latin *tractatus* = 'a handling, managing, treatise,' from *tractātus*, past participle of *tractāre* = 'to handle'

(2) Religion and the law. French made an equal contribution to the language of the Church and the law. The following are just a few examples:

acquit = 'to absolve of responsibility for, exonerate, conduct (oneself)': from Old French *aquiter*, from Vulgar Latin *acquitāre*, from *ad-* + Latin *quiētāre* = 'to appease, settle'

attorney = 'lawyer,' literally 'one authorized to act for another': from Old French *atorne*, past participle of *atorner* = 'to turn to'

bail = 'money pledged for the release of an accused person from jail': from Old French *bail* = 'custody,' from *baillier* = 'to seize, carry, give,' from Latin *bājulāre* = 'to bear a burden,' from *bājulus* = 'porter'

charity = 'love, generosity, good will': from French *charité*, from Latin *cāritās* = 'affection, love'

clergy = 'persons ordained to serve as spiritual leaders': from Old French *clergie* = 'clerkship, clergy,' from ecclesiastical Latin *clēricātus*, from *clēricus* = 'belonging to the clergy, clerical'

crime = 'illegal act, offense': from Old French *crime*, from Latin *crīmen* = 'judicial decision, charge, crime'

indict = 'to formally charge with a crime, accuse': from Old French *enditer* = 'to dictate, write down, teach, prescribe,' from Vulgar Latin *indictāre* = 'to declare, proclaim in writing'

judge = 'one who decides an outcome or passes sentence, especially in legal matters': from Old French *juge*, from Latin *jūdex* = 'judge,' originally meaning 'one who shows right'

jury = 'group of persons empowered by law to decide the guilt or innocence of a party on trial': from Old French *juree* = 'oath, legal inquiry,' from *jurer* = 'to take an oath, swear,' from Latin *jūrāre*, from *jūris*, genitive of *jus* = 'right, law'

justice = 'rightness, fairness': from Old French *justice, justise*, from Latin *jūstitia* = 'justice, equity, uprightness'

larceny = 'theft of property': from Old French *larcin, larrecin* = 'theft,' from Latin *latrōcinium* = 'service of mercenaries, freebooting, robbery'

parson = 'Protestant clergyman, preacher': from Old French *persone* = 'person, parson,' from Latin *persōna* = 'mask, masked person, character, role, person'; the meaning 'parson' probably derives from the abbreviation of Latin *persōna ecclēsiae* = 'person of the church'

pastor = 'clergyman who heads a parish or congregation': from Old French *pastor, pastur,* from Latin *pāstor* = 'shepherd,' literally 'feeder'

piety = 'devotion to God, one's religion, or one's family': from Middle French *piété,* from Latin *pietās* = 'duty, dutiful conduct, devotion, tenderness,' from *pius* = 'dutiful, pious'

proof = 'something offered to verify the truth, evidence, test': from Old French *prueve, proeve,* from Late Latin *proba* = 'proof,' from Latin *probāre* = 'to prove'

religion = 'belief in divine power, organized system of belief': from Old French *religion,* from Latin *religio* = 'reverence for the gods, piety, religion'

sacrament = 'Christian rite conferring grace': from Old French *sacrement, sacrament,* from Latin *sacrāmentum* = 'oath, solemn obligation'

sanctity = 'holiness, blessedness': from Old French *sainteté, saincteté,* from Latin *sānctitās* = 'holiness, sacredness,' from *sānctus* = 'holy, sacred'

savior = 'one who saves, deliverer': from Old French *salveour, sauveour,* from Late Latin *salvātor,* from *salvāre* = 'to save'

verdict = 'decision of a jury in a trial, any judgment': from Anglo-French *verdit,* corresponding to Old French *voirdit,* from Medieval Latin *vērēdictum* = 'verdict,' from Latin *vērē dictum* = 'truly said'

So great was the influx of borrowings that sometimes the same word would be borrowed twice—that is, it would enter English in slightly different forms that corresponded to different French regional dialects; for example, *canal* and *channel, warden* and *guardian, warrant* and *guarantee.* Nor did new French words necessarily replace their Old and Middle English synonyms. Often the two would coexist—*hearty* and *cordial, yearly* and *annual, answer* and *reply, room* and *chamber, seethe* and *boil,* and so on. What is interesting about these duplications is that they gave rise to a multitude of subtle variations in connotation.

The great medieval wave of French borrowings is so distant from us today that we rarely even recognize the words in question as being derived from French. Yet our debt is truly enormous. The case was put succinctly by Prof. Albert C. Baugh of the University of Pennsylvania, whose *History of the English Language* (1957) remains a classic reference for students in the field:

> English retains a controlling interest, but French as a large minority stockholder supplements and rounds out the major organization in almost every department.

The Renaissance. If the rate of foreign borrowings tapered off somewhat during the 15th century, it sharply revived in the 16th, the century of the Tudors and the English Renaissance (see also ELIZABETHAN ENGLISH). Here are a few basic imports from French that came into English during the Renaissance:

alloy = 'mixture of two or more metals': from French *aloi,* from Old French *alei, aloi,* from *aleier, aloier* = 'to bind, combine,' from Latin *alligāre* = 'to bind to (something)'

ambuscade = 'ambush': from French *embuscade* = 'ambush,' from Italian *imboscata,* literally 'a hiding in the bush,' from Medieval Latin *imboscāre* = 'to lie in the bush'

baluster = 'upright post in a railing': from French *balustre* = 'post or support of a railing,' from Italian *balaustro,* from Latin *balaustium,* from Greek *balaustion* = 'flower of the wild pomegranate' (from the shape of the post's capital)

bizarre = 'strange, peculiar': from French *bizarre* = 'strange,' from Italian *bizzarro* = 'capricious,' from Spanish *bizarro* = 'gallant, brave,' from Basque *bizar* = 'beard'; the present sense arose from the impression of strangeness that the bearded Spanish soldiers made on the French people

comrade = 'companion, colleague, friend': from French *camarade,* from Spanish *camarado* = 'chamber fellow,' originally 'company belonging to one chamber,' from Latin *camera* = 'vault, arch'

detail = 'some usually small part of a larger work, scene, project, etc.': from French *détail,* from *détailler* = 'to cut in pieces, divide up,' from *de-* + *tailler* = 'to cut,' from Latin *tāliāre* = 'to split, cut'

equip = 'to outfit, furnish with necessary gear': from French *équiper* = 'to fit out, furnish, equip,' originally 'to fit out a ship,' from Old French *esquiper,* of Germanic origin (akin to Old Norse *skipa* = 'to fit out a ship')

***essay** = 'to try, attempt': from French *essayer* = 'to test, try, taste,' from Old French *essaier,* from Vulgar Latin *exagiāre* = 'to weigh,' from Latin *exagium* = 'a weighing,' from *exigere* = 'to weigh, measure, examine'

explore = 'to investigate, search out': from French *explorer,* from Latin *explōrāre* = 'to search out, examine, explore,' originally 'to flush (game) from cover through shouts of beaters and cries of hunting dogs,' from *ex-* = 'out of' + *plorāre* = 'to cry out, wail, lament'

probability = 'likelihood': from Middle French *probabilité,* from Latin *probābilitās,* from *probābilis* = 'that may be assumed or proved, likely, probable,' from *probāre* = 'to try, test, prove'

progress = 'a moving forward, advancement': from French *progrès,* from Middle French *progres,* from Latin *prōgressus* = 'a going forward, advance,' from *prōgressus,* past participle of *prōgredī* = 'go forward, advance'

retrench = 'to curtail expenses, activities, etc.': from French *retrancher* = 'to cut off'

surpass = 'go beyond or past, excel': from French, Middle French, and Old French *surpasser* = 'to excel'

talisman = 'object thought to bestow luck or protection': from French (and Spanish) *talisman,* ultimately—via Arabic—from Greek *telesma* = 'consecration, mystery'

ticket = 'usually small paper or card for admittance to something, label, tag': from French *étiquette,* from Middle French *estiquet, estiquete* = 'little note,' literally 'something stuck up'

troop: from French *troupe* = 'troop, flock'

trophy: from French *trophée* = 'monument or token of victory,' ultimately from Greek *tropē* = 'putting to flight, defeat'

*Appears as separate entry

The 17th and 18th Centuries. During the Renaissance new French borrowings tended to be supplementary rather than central to the English vocabulary, and a resistance grew on the part of the English to borrowings of any kind. These trends became more pronounced in the Age of Enlightenment. In the 150 years between 1650 and 1800, less than half as many French words were brought into English as had been added in the preceding 150 years, and of these a smaller proportion achieved a central position in everyday speech. Indeed, many imports of the period—such as *coiffeur, negligee,* and *soubrette*—still strike us as being faintly exotic.

The English resistance to French borrowings certainly did not stem from any decline of French as a world language. On the contrary, the prestige of French as the lingua franca of diplomacy and European culture was never higher than during the reigns of the three great prerevolutionary Bourbon monarchs (1643–1792). Nor was it a response to the political and military rivalry between England and France. Rather, the English were becoming increasingly sensitive about the deficiencies of their own language. The rules governing English grammar and spelling were still relatively chaotic, and there did not even exist a reliable source for defining the vocabulary until the appearance, in 1755, of Dr. Samuel Johnson's *Dictionary.* Besides Dr. Johnson, such literary notables as John Dryden, Daniel Defoe, and Jonathan Swift, abetted by a host of lesser lights, vigorously set to work to repair these defects, and it is largely to their efforts that we owe the formal structure of literary English as we know it today. But, preoccupied as Englishmen were with linguistic reform, this was not a time when they were likely to be very hospitable to foreign borrowings. The emphasis was on standardization, not acquisition; and the need to accommodate new words into the emerging structure was, at least for the time being, probably felt to be as much a nuisance as an enrichment.

Yet neither patriotism nor scholarly zeal could altogether staunch the time-honored flow of French into English. Here is a brief sampling of the hundreds of words that entered our language from French during the 17th and 18th centuries:

ballet	**debut**
brunette	**dentist**
burlesque	**foible**
canteen	**patrol**
cartoon	**penchant**
champagne	**publicity**
chowder	**ridicule**
cohesion	**routine**
connoisseur	**sang-froid**
coterie	**syndicate**

As this representative list suggests, the degree to which individual borrowings were assimilated into English varied considerably. For example, it does not even occur to most people today that a word like *chowder* (from *chaudière* = 'kettle') might have had a French origin, but *sang-froid* still has a distinctly Gallic ring.

During this period, and on up to the present day, French also made its mark on American English. Not only did the French give us some of our most familiar place names (*Terre Haute* = 'high ground'; *Des Moines* = 'the monks' place'; *Baton Rouge* = 'red stick'; and so on), but they also provided us with such helpful words for describing features of our landscape as *butte, bayou, sault, levee, crevasse*, and *prairie*.

Contemporary Vocabularies. It is difficult to generalize about the broader French influences on English since 1800. Certainly, the rate at which we have borrowed has increased considerably over that of the 18th century (although the rate is still only a fraction of what it was in the Middle Ages); but it is too soon to tell whether all of these comparatively recent borrowings will be permanent or, if they are, whether they will achieve central or peripheral positions in our vocabulary. Plainly, some words have made it in a big way—*restaurant, morgue, résumé, ambiance, laissez faire, gourmet, cliché, flair, détente, raconteur, prestige, attaché, liaison, dossier*, and *discothèque*, for example. The same is probably true of a number of words associated with various French products or technical innovations and applications—*garage, chassis, coupé, chauffeur, limousine, fusilage, aileron, convoy, barrage, camouflage, triage*, and so on. But it is not so clear whether words such as *accouchement*, which seems to have been imported primarily for euphemistic purposes, or *auteur*, which refers to a highly specialized and probably ephemeral concept, will ultimately stand the test of time.

What is very clear, however, is that in certain specialized contemporary vocabularies—that of ballet, for example, with its *pas de deux, pliés*, and *entrechats*—French words predominate regardless of whether they can be said to have been fully absorbed into English. This is nowhere more evident than in the vocabularies of *haute cuisine* and *haute couture*. Although some of the borrowings in these categories predate the 19th century, most have never lost their distinctly French flavor—a kind of tacit admission on the part of Anglo-Americans that in certain fields the French really are peerless. Never mind that in English such words are often misspelled and mispronounced and in many cases have perfectly serviceable Anglo-Saxon alternatives. It is not for nothing that the word *cachet* comes to us from France.

(1) Cookery. French cooking has long had supreme prestige in the Western world, and its vocabulary is internationally influential—starting with such words as *cuisine, menu*, and *restaurant*. Its influence goes beyond actual French terms and has affected even

the form of American terms such as *chicken Maryland* and *lobster Newburg*, which might more naturally have been *Maryland chicken* and *Newburg lobster*. And aside from genuinely French or French-inspired restaurants, quite ordinary eating places often put parts of their menus in French, producing such pretentious terms as *vegetable du jour*, meaning 'vegetable of the day' or, in plain English, 'only one vegetable is featured.'

The complete vocabulary of French cooking would fill a dictionary; there are several hundred named sauces alone. (Note: A dish or sauce named after a country or region does not necessarily come from that place. *Sauce béarnaise* does not come from Béarn, a former province in the foothills of the Pyrenees, but was invented in Paris and named in dedication to King Henri IV, who was also prince of Béarn. Lobster *à l'Américaine* is sautéed in olive oil and garnished with onions, tomatoes, and herbs—not a method originated in America; it was named by French restaurants in honor of American patrons who appreciated it.) Here is a selection of the more basic and familiar cooking terms:

* **à la** = 'in the manner of'

aperitif /ä-pĕr-ĭ-**tēf**/ = 'drink taken before a meal': from French *apéritif* = 'tending to open the appetite'

au gratin /ō **grät**'n/ = 'coated with bread crumbs and often grated cheese, and browned to form a crust': from French *au gratin*, literally 'with the crust'

béchamel /bā-shə-**mĕl**/ = 'spiced sauce of butter, flour, and milk or cream, used by itself or as the base for more complex sauces': after the marquis of *Béchamel*, probably the patron or employer of the chef who invented the sauce

bisque /bĭsk/ = 'rich cream soup of lobster, shrimp, crab, or vegetable': from French *bisque* (further origin unknown)

bouillon /**bōōl**-yŏn, -yən/ = 'clear broth made by boiling meat, fish, or vegetables': from French *bouillon*, from *bouillir* = 'to boil'

braise = 'to cook lightly sautéed meat and vegetables over low heat in a covered pot': from French *braiser*, originally 'to stew meat in a tightly covered pot buried in hot charcoal,' from *braise* = 'charcoal'

canapé /**kăn**-ə-pā, -pē/ = 'small piece of toast or a cracker topped with meat, fish, cheese, etc., served as an hors d'oeuvre': from French *canapé*, literally 'couch, seat'

casserole = (1) 'flameproof covered cooking pot' (2) 'dish prepared in such a pot, typically a slow-cooked mixture of meat or fish and vegetables': from French *casserole*, diminutive of *casse* = 'pan'

consommé /kŏn-sə-mā, kŏn-sə-**mā**/ = 'clear meat or vegetable soup': from French *consommé*, literally 'concentrated'

crêpe /krĕp, krāp/ = 'very thin pancake, often served rolled around a filling of cooked ham, cheese, or mushrooms or of sugared fruit': from French *crêpe*, from Old French *crespe* = 'crisp, curly'

croissant /krwä-**säɴ**/ = 'crescent-shaped roll of light pastry': from French *croissant*, literally 'crescent'

croutons /**krōō**-tŏnz/ = 'small cubes of fried bread used as a garnish for soups, etc.': from French *croûtons*, literally 'crusts'

filet mignon /fĭ-**lā** mĭn-**yŏn**/ = 'beef fillet cut from the thick end of the tenderloin': from French *filet mignon*, literally 'dainty fillet'

fines herbes /**fēn** êrbs/ = 'chopped herbs, especially parsley, or parsley, chervil, and tarragon': from French *fines herbes* = 'fine herbs'

flambé /fläm-**bā**/ = 'served with flaming liquor or liqueur': from French *flambé* = 'flamed'

fondue /fŏn-**dōō**/ = 'hot dish of Swiss origin, made of cheese, seasonings, and wine, usually dipped up with bread': from French *fondue*, literally 'melted'

gourmet /gŏŏr-**mā**/ = 'lover of fine food' See GOURMAND, GOURMET.

* **hors d'oeuvre** /ôr **dêrv**/ = 'appetizer, course of appetizers'

julienne /jōō-lē-**ĕn**/ = '(of vegetables) cut into thin strips': from French *à la julienne* = 'in the manner of Jules or Julien or Julienne' (reference unknown)

macédoine /măs-ə-**dwän**/ = 'mixture of cut-up fruits or vegetables': from French *Macédoine*, literally 'Macedonian,' the mixture of peoples in Macedonia

marinade = 'liquid made of oil and vinegar, wine, or lemon juice, seasoned with spices and herbs, used for flavoring or tenderizing raw meat or fish': from French *marinade* = 'brine pickle'

mayonnaise /**mā**-ə-nāz, mā-ə-**nāz**/ = 'sauce made by beating egg yolks in olive oil': from French (*sauce*) *mayonnaise*—origin disputed; possibly = 'sauce of Mahón' (capital of Minorca), named in honor of its capture by the French in 1756

menu = (1) 'list of dishes to be served at a formal meal' (2) 'list of all the dishes available in an eating place': from French *menu*, literally 'detailed list'

meringue /mə-**răng**/ = 'baked mixture of beaten egg whites and sugar, used as a topping': from French *meringue* (further origin unknown)

meunière /mōō-**nyâr**/ = '(of fish) lightly floured and fried in butter': from French *à la meunière* = 'in the manner of a miller's wife'

Mornay /môr-**nāy**/ = '(of seafood) smothered in a sauce of cream, eggs, and cheese': named for Philippe de *Mornay* (1549–1623), a leader of the Huguenots

mousse /mōōs/ = 'cold, sweet dessert, or light soufflélike meat or fish dish, with whipped cream, eggs, or gelatin used as the aerating agent': from French *mousse* = 'froth'

omelet, omelette /**ŏm**-lĭt, -ə-lət/ = 'dish of beaten eggs fried and folded over a filling, as of cheese, herbs, or tomatoes': from French *omelette*, literally 'thin plate'

pâté /pä-**tā**/ = 'savory mixture of ground meat or fish baked in a form and served cold': from French *pâté* = 'enclosed in pastry' (as some pâtés still are)

Provençale /prō-vən-**säl**/ = 'cooked with tomatoes and garlic and herbs': from French *à la Provençale* = 'in the manner of Provence' (region in southeastern France)

purée /pyōō-**rā**/ = (1) (noun) 'pulped raw or cooked food made by forcing it through a strainer or mashing it in a processor' (2) (verb) 'to pulp (food) in this way': from French *purée* = 'strained'

quiche /kēsh/ = 'open-faced pie with any of numerous savory fillings bound with beaten eggs': from (Lorraine dialect) French *quiche*, from German *küche* = 'pie'

roux /rōō/ = 'sauce base made of flour and butter browned together, sometimes with the addition of soup stock': from French *roux*, literally 'reddish brown'

sauté /sō-**tā**, sô-**tā**/ = (1) (adjective) 'fried quickly in a small quantity of fat, with much tossing and turning' (2) (verb) 'to fry in this manner': from French *sauté* = 'tossed'

soufflé /sōō-**flā**, **sōō**-flā/ = 'light, airy baked dish using a basic sauce thickened with flour and egg yolks, into which beaten egg whites are folded': from French *soufflé*, literally 'puffed'

tartare /tär-**tär**/ = 'a sauce for seafood, made of mayonnaise with mustard, vinegar, shallots, capers, etc.,' and **steak tartare** = 'raw chopped steak mixed with raw egg yolks, anchovies, capers, and seasonings': from French *à la tartare* = 'in the manner of the Tartars'

vichyssoise /vĭsh-ē-**swäz**, vē-shē-/ = 'cold potato and leek cream soup': from French *(crème) Vichyssoise* = '(cream soup) of Vichy' (town in central France)

*Appears as separate entry

(2) Fashion and style:

bijoux = 'jewels, gems': from Breton French *bizou* = 'finger ring,' from Celtic *biz* = 'finger'

bouffant = 'puffed out, full, as in some skirts and hair styles': from the present participle of French *bouffer* = 'to puff out'

bracelet = 'ornament for the wrist or arm':

from French, literally 'little arm,' from *bras* = 'arm' + *-elet*, diminutive suffix

camisole = 'woman's loose jacket': from Old Provençal *camisola* = 'mantle,' from Late Latin *camīsia*

chapeau = 'hat': from Vulgar Latin *capellus*, from Late Latin *cappa* = 'hood, cap, mantle'

chignon = 'coil or knot of hair worn at the back of the neck, bun': from Old French *chaignon* = 'chain, nape (of the neck),' ultimately from Latin *catēna* = 'chain'

cloche = 'close-fitting, bell-shaped hat for women': from French *cloche* = 'bell,' from Medieval Latin *clocca*

cologne = 'perfumed toilet water': from French *eau de Cologne* = 'water of Cologne,' from *Cologne* = 'Köln' (city in Germany)

cravat = 'necktie': from French *cravate*, literally 'neckcloth worn by the Croats,' from *Cravate* = 'Croat, Croatian'

culottes = 'women's or girls' trousers cut full in the legs to resemble a skirt, breeches': from French *cul* = 'bottom, posterior,' from Latin *cūlus*

décolletage = 'low neckline of a dress, gown, etc.': from French *décolleter* = 'to cut out the neck of (a dress), bare the neck and shoulders,' from *dé-* = 'away from' + *collet*, literally 'little neck,' from *col*, *cou* = 'neck'

ecru = 'light tan, yellowish color of unbleached linen': from French *écru* = 'raw, unbleached,' from *é-* = 'out of' + *cru* = 'raw,' from Latin *crūdus*

epaulet = 'shoulder ornament': from the diminutive of French *épaule* = 'shoulder,' from Old French *espalle, espalde*, from Latin *spatula* = 'broad piece,' later 'shoulder'

jabot /zhȧ-**bō**, jă-/ = 'frill of a shirt or blouse': probably related to French *gaver* = 'to cram, gorge,' from Old Provençal *gava* = 'crop, maw'

mode = 'fashion, manner, style': from French *mode*, from Latin *modus* = 'manner, mode, mood'

moiré = '(of fabric) having a watered or wavy pattern': from French *moiré*, past participle of *moirer* = 'to water (silk, etc.)'

peignoir /pĕn-**wär**/ = 'woman's loose dressing gown': from French *peigner* = 'to comb the hair,' from *peigne* = 'comb,' from Latin *pecten* = 'comb'

soigné /swȧ-**nyā**/ = 'well cared for, tidy, well-groomed': from the past participle of French *soigner* = 'to look after, take care of,' from Medieval Latin *soniare*, from *sonium* = 'care'

svelte = 'slender, lithe': from French *svelte*, from Italian *svelto*, past participle of *svegliere* = 'to pluck out,' ultimately from Latin *vellere* = 'to pluck'

vogue = 'fashion or style, mode,' literally 'a rowing, a sailing': from French *voguer* = 'to row, sail, move along,' from Italian *vogare* or Old Provençal *vogar*, of the same meaning, most likely of Germanic origin

So far, we have been talking only about individual words that either have entered or are edging their way into English. But we use an astonishing number of French phrases as well. Perhaps only a few readers will be able to translate *all* the expressions on the following list, but most of us can recognize a majority of them without difficulty.

a la carte
a la mode
amour-propre
au courant
au naturel
avant-garde
beau geste
bête noire
billet-doux
bon mot
bon vivant
bon voyage
café au lait
carte blanche
c'est la vie
cherchez la femme
chez
comme ci, comme ça
coup de grâce
déjà vu
de rigueur
eau de vie
enfant terrible
entre nous
esprit de corps
esprit de l'escalier
fait accompli
faute de mieux
faux pas
idée fixe
jeu d'esprit
joie de vivre
maître d'hôtel
mal de mer
Mardi gras
noblesse oblige

nom de guerre
nom de plume
nouveau riche
objet d'art
par excellence
pièce de résistance
pied-à-terre
prix fixe
raison d'être
roman à clef
sans souci
savoir-faire
savoir-vivre
table d'hôte
tête-à-tête
toujours l'amour
tour de force
trompe l'oeil

A few diehards might insist that they themselves would never corrupt "plain English" with any such alien expressions; but the claim would be suspect, and in any event the resisters could hardly expect to escape hearing or reading these terms. The following sentences are typical examples:

> General Moczar's partisans seized upon the pretext of student riots, which may have been instigated by agents provocateurs.
> —John Darnton, *New York Times*

> The less one sees and hears of ambassadors and ministers *en intimité*, the happier one feels.
> —Peter Quennell, *The Wanton Chase*

> [The poet Lars] Forssell was, and to an extent still is, a kind of enfant terrible of Swedish literature.
> —Peter Lennon, *Washington Post Book World*

Pronunciation. The key to French pronunciation on the opposite page is intended to enable a non-French speaker to approximate the native sound of any given French word or phrase. Remember, however, the key is only an approximation.

The Use of French Sounds in English. The question of how we should in practice pronounce French in English is a vexatious one. It is true that whenever one language finally adopts a word taken from another, the borrower is entitled to do with the word whatever it pleases. If, for example, the British want to pronounce the (originally French) proper name Beauchamps /bō-**shäN**/ as if it were spelled *Beecham*, that, presumably, is their business. But whether such latitude can be extended to the pronunciation of candidate words—words we have not yet completely admitted and still identify as more French than English—is another question, and in practice it depends on how we as native English speakers hear the sound of spoken French.

Several salient features of spoken French are likely to strike a native speaker of English: (1) It sounds as though all the words were run together, with no stress on any individual word until the final syllable of a phrase or sentence, which is often highlighted by a sharply rising pitch inflection. (2) Constant pitch variations impart to the flow of speech a singsong quality that makes English seem monotonous by comparison. (3) There are vowels and diphthongs, such as *u* and *oeu*, and consonants, such as *r*, that have no equivalents in English and are hard for an English speaker to learn. (4) The phonetics of French is heavily marked with nasality.

Bearing in mind all of the above, we do not recommend that you attempt to pronounce any of the numerous French words and phrases in English exactly as they would be pronounced in French. The most celebrated comment on the pronunciation of French in English was made by H. W. Fowler in his *Dictionary of Modern English Usage* (1926): "To say a French word in the middle of an English sentence is a feat demanding an acrobatic mouth." He concludes: "All that is necessary is a polite acknowledgement of indebtedness to the French language indicated by some approach in some part of the word to the foreign sound. . . ." The comment and the recommendation hold as true nowadays as when first written. However, the prestige of French as the language of high culture has declined over the past few generations. In the old days teachers and writers on usage cautioned against sprinkling one's speech or writing with unnecessary French expressions. The admonition is no longer needed. The French component in our vocabulary is as important as it ever was, but the ostentatious use of French words in English has long been passé in virtually all circles.

Some people will go on making an honorable effort to pronounce French words in the proper French manner, while other people,

Pronouncing French

Letter	Pronunciation
Vowels and Diphthongs	
a, à	/ȧ/
â	/ä/
e	(1) /ë/ *as in* je, me (2) /ĕ/ *as in* festin, perfidie (3) /ā/ *before a silent consonant at the end of a word, as in* filet, nez, changer (4) /ə/ *as in* regard (5) /ə/ *as in* blonde, con- [illegible] *rapid speech*
é	/ā/
è	/ĕ/
ê	*between* /ĕ/ *and* /ā/
i, î	/ē/
ie	/ē/
o	/ō/
u	/ü/
y	/ē/
au, eau	/ō/
ai	*between* /ĕ/ *and* /ā/
eu, oeu	/ë/
ou	/o͞o/
oi	/wä/
Consonants*	
ç	/s/
ch	/sh/
g	(1) /g/ *before* a, o, u, *and consonants, as in* garçon, grand (2) /zh/ *before* e, i, *as in* gendarme, gigolo
h	*not pronounced*
j	/zh/
ll	(1) /yə/ *as in* fille (2) /l/ *as in* village
q	/k/
r	*trilled on the back of the tongue*
s	(1) /s/ *in initial position* [illegible] *as in* savoir (2) /z/ *between* [illegible] *vowels* [illegible] *in* cuisine
ss	/s/
t	(1) /t/ (2) /s/ *in the combinations* -tial, -tiel, -tieux, -tion
th	/t/
x	(1) /ks/ (2) /gz/ *when initial* ex- *is followed by a vowel, as in* exister

**Final consonants are usually not sounded. The letters* b, c, d, f, l, p, v, *and* z *are the same as in English; also* m *and* n, *except when nasalized (see below). French has no* k *or* w.

Nasal Sounds

The consonants m *and* n *are nasalized at the end of a word or when followed by another consonant in a medial or final position. There are four variations of this pronunciation.*

(1) -in-, -im-, -ain-, -aim-, -yn-, -ym-, -ein- *as in* vin, impossible, main, faim, syndicat, thym, plein	/ăɴ/ *as in English* bank
(2) -an-, -am-, -en-, -em- *as in* danse, quand, tambour, enfant, tendre, centre, temps	/äɴ/ *as in English* wand
(3) -on-, -om- *as in* bon, nombre	/ōɴ/ *as in English* groan
(4) -un-, -um- *as in* lundi, parfum	*between* /ăɴ/ *and* /ŭɴ/ *as between English* hang *and* hung

perhaps regarding this task as either too demanding or too persnickety, will make every effort to anglicize them. And it is the anglicizers who will probably do the most in the long run to hasten the introduction of candidate words into mainstream English. In such matters it is impossible to talk about absolute "rights" and "wrongs."

In a larger sense, it is impossible to talk about the rights and wrongs of the English language's age-old dependence on French. Doubtless our language could have survived without its French borrowings. We could have retained from earlier times, or invented afresh, substitutes for most of the thousands of words we have taken from our French cousins. But would we be better off for having done so? It is difficult to see how.

From time to time various arbiters of English prose style advise us to compose our sentences mainly of short, simple, Anglo-Saxon words. But anyone who knows even a little about the history of our language will recognize that this is a nonsensical prescription. Not only are there not enough pure Anglo-Saxon words around to meet our needs, but who ever said that all Anglo-Saxon words were either short or simple? More to the point, those sentimental yearnings for a "pure" English diction fly in the face of a thousand years of reality. The poet Wallace Stevens was closer to the historical truth when he wrote, with pardonable exaggeration, that "French and English constitute a single language."

fruition /froo-ish-ən/. The traditional sense of this Latin-derived word is 'enjoyment,' especially 'secure possession and enjoyment of something desirable':

> I begin to look forward . . . to scenes of National happiness, which have not heretofore been offered for the fruition of the most favoured Nations.
> —George Washington, letter (1788)

Conservative usage critics have tried to limit the word *fruition* to this traditional meaning, but not many people now are even aware of it. The word has been redefined by influence of the word *fruit* and now almost always means 'a coming to ripeness or fruit, successful achievement or conclusion':

> The days at Wits were like the rich summer days of February in a good year; the enthusiasms of spring were gone, but the fruition of the ripening season was at hand.
> —James A. Michener, *The Covenant*

> Now that "The Blue Lagoon" has seen fruition, Mr. Kleiser has signed to direct the big-budget film version of the Broadway musical "Annie." . . .
> —Kirk Honeycutt, *New York Times*

◇ *Recommendation.* The use of *fruition* to mean 'enjoyment' is now old-fashioned, though still legitimate. The much commoner meaning, 'ripeness, successful achievement,' is also standard and correct.

fulminate, a resounding and satisfying word. It is from Latin *fulmināre* = 'to thunder,' used especially of Jupiter, meaning 'to blast with the *fulmen*, or thunderbolt, strike with lightning.' In the Middle Ages the pope inherited Jupiter's thunderbolt and thundered down or *fulminated* bulls of excommunication or censure on erring Christians. The verb is now used to mean 'make a severe and sonorous denunciation' and is used especially of formidable, even pontifical or Jovian, figures blasting away at mere mortals:

> Now William Randolph Hearst . . . began to fulminate against internationalism and the Wilsonians, urging instead an "America First" policy.
> —Joseph P. Lash, *Eleanor and Franklin*

> Barry Goldwater fulminated against "surrender to blackmail." . . .
> —Arthur M. Schlesinger, Jr., *Robert Kennedy and His Times*

> . . . Ayatollah Ruhollah Khomeini . . . as usual fulminating against America.
> —*Time*

So also the noun *fulmination*, meaning 'thunderous denunciation, severe outburst':

> What began in the morning as familiar Kissinger fulminations exploded by late

day into a full-scale governmental crisis. —Charles Colson, *Born Again*

Chou . . . thoroughly enjoyed the fulminations of the Soviet press against my visit. —Richard Nixon, *R.N.*

fulsome, as the form of this adjective suggests, originally meant 'very full, copious, abundant.' However, this meaning died out in the time of Shakespeare, and the word took on entirely negative senses: 'overfull, excessive, disgusting, smelly, morally repulsive.' It has been suggested, but not proved, that these connotations arose because the word was associated with *foul.*

The chief current standard use of *fulsome* is in reference to praise, and the meaning is emphatically negative: 'overdone to the point of being contemptible and revolting,' often with the implication 'insincerely and cynically flattering.'

A well-meaning journalist . . . wrote an impossibly enthusiastic piece about me, some five hundred lines dripping with fulsome praise.
—Vladimir Nabokov, *Speak, Memory*

She was aghast at Lodge's fulsome tribute to the dead president in the Senate. . . . —Joseph P. Lash, *Eleanor and Franklin*

Fulsome is also used to mean 'disgustingly insincere and cynical in general':

. . . Stalin's fulsome embrace of the German Ambassador on the railway station in Moscow with the Japanese Foreign Minister looking on.
—Anthony Eden, *The Reckoning*

Fulsome is not a very common word, and people who know nothing of its history, when meeting the stock phrase *fulsome praise* for the first time, have thought it means simply 'very full, lavish praise.' The misunderstanding has continued, and the word is now often used with little or no negative sense:

The good fellowship of the clubhouse will all seem so hearty, and the hero worship outside will grow so fulsome that the ballplayer just cannot believe they will not last forever.
—Mickey Mantle, *The Education of a Baseball Player*

Here the writer means that the hero worship is indeed excessive, too lavish, but not that it's either cynical or disgusting. This use in turn has led to an unwitting revival of the original positive meaning of the word, 'abundant, copious in general':

For the real Charley's Aunt I desperately needed someone of fulsome womanly beauty and immediately recognizable sexuality. —Joshua Logan, *Jo*[illegible]

People . . . who, by their very dress and manner and sense of fulsome consumer well-being, spoke a new national language of comfort and assurance. . . .
—Ron Powers, *The Newscasters*

This is not accepted as a legitimate use by most traditionalists. That original meaning was unquestionably dead before the *Mayflower* sailed; to use it now is not a revival but a new mistake.

◇ ***Recommendation.*** Be aware that in established current usage *fulsome* is a strongly negative term, whether applied to praise or to anything else. The new-old positive use is best avoided.

further. See FARTHER, FURTHER.

fused participle. See POSSESSIVES; VERBAL NOUNS IN -ING.

fussbudget. A person who frets or worries about small matters is known in the General Northern dialect as a *fussbudget.* This term is also used to mean 'finicky or fussy person.' As an Americanism it had the shorter, earlier noun form *fuss,* which seems to have dropped out of use.

"I hope you are not a fidget." "A what?" "A fuss then,—a person who always wants everything some other way."
—Thomas Aldrich, *The Stillwater Tragedy* (1880)

I am a fuss, and I don't deny it.
—William Dean Howells,
A Foregone Conclusion (1875)

There are numerous synonyms for *fussbudget* that use *fuss* as the root. In the Coastal Southern dialect the term is *fussbox*. In the North Midland dialect it is *fussbutton*, and in the northeastern United States, especially New York, New Jersey, Pennsylvania, and Connecticut, the term is often *fusspot*. In other parts of the country a fussbudget is known as a *fuss-cat* and as a plain old *fusser*.

Worry itself forms the root of several terms that are used interchangeably with those built on *fuss*. The best known of these is *worrywart*, which is very common throughout the United States, probably having originated here. Although *worrywart* and *fussbudget* overlap each other in meaning, the former is essentially a pessimist, someone who expects the worst, whereas the latter is a person who pays too much attention to unnecessary details, often in an irritable or peevish manner. Some other "worry" synonyms are *worry bird, worry box, worry bug, worry worm,* and the commonly used *worrier*.

A worrywart is also known as a *stewer*. To *stew* is 'to fret or worry,' and a *stewer* is one who stews about things, especially trivialities.

G

Gaelic. See IRISH WORDS; SCOTTISH ENGLISH.

gallery. See PORCH.

gambit. This is a chess term that has passed into common usage. In chess a *gambit*, or *opening gambit*, is an early maneuver in which a player exposes a pawn or pawns, intending to gain an advantage of position if the sacrifice is accepted. The word is now widely applied to sports, business, politics, etc., to mean 'move, remark, tactic, maneuver,' ranging from a trivial piece of small talk to a carefully planned stratagem:

> The opening gambit of Ehrlichman's defense backfired as his attorneys asked Sirica to call Charles Colson. . . . That allowed freer questioning and Colson promptly gave damaging testimony against Mitchell, Haldeman, and even Ehrlichman. —*Time*

> I must take credit for the most celebrated croquet shot ever made on Neshobe Island. Well—half credit, since Charlie Lederer was my partner in the game and in this particular gambit. —Harpo Marx, *Harpo Speaks*

> I've studied carefully, and I agree with the teaching of Jesus, but I don't like the idea that I've been "born again in my cell." I'm certain that people would see that as some kind of opportunistic gambit on my part.
> —Eldridge Cleaver (quoted), *Reader's Digest*

Strict constructionists would like to keep *gambit* as a precise chess metaphor, using it only of a maneuver involving the offer of a sacrifice for tactical gain.

◇ ***Recommendation.*** When the situation warrants it—for example, in a chesslike courtroom duel—*gambit* can still be used with the force of its technical meaning. But the word has been common property for too long a time to be restricted to this. For most people, and legitimately, it means simply 'move, tactic' of any kind.

gamesmanship. This word was coined in 1947 by the English humorist Stephen Potter, who defined it as 'the art of winning games without actually cheating.' Its numerous methods center on psychologically unsettling one's opponent. Potter lived to see his word adopted into the language so thoroughly that it has become the model for further coinages, most notably *brinkmanship*, which could be defined as 'the art of going to the brink of nuclear war without actually pressing the button.' Ruthless and ingenious gamesmanship now flourishes in both amateur and professional sports. The concept has passed over into the vocabulary of politics and competitive life in general:

> When they detected him, between holes, exchanging his hot ball for a chilled one from the ice bucket, there was nothing they could do about his gamesmanship except play better than he.
> —J. S. Martin, *The Curious History of the Golf Ball*

> There are very few players who use extreme gamesmanship to upset an opponent as well as Nastase.
> —John Newcombe, *New York Post*

> Larry O'Brien was one Democrat who was a grand master in the art of political gamesmanship.
> —Richard Nixon, *R.N.*

> . . . only 1.3 percent of consumers refuse payment when dissatisfied with a creditor's performance. . . . But generally you can win better service or a lower bill, provided you follow these unofficial rules of non-payment gamesmanship. . . .
> —Patricia A. Dreyfus, *Reader's Digest*

> And jobs are hard to find and when you get one it's dog eat dog and you had better read the book of Gamesmanship before you step into the office on your first day.
> —Ellen Lubin-Sherman, *New York Times*

gamut, the medieval musical term for the whole scale of notes, is used to mean 'entire sequence or range of anything, array':

> Therapists like Lipsitz have identified a gamut of phobias. The most common are fear of heights, flying, enclosed spaces, open spaces and certain animals, usually dogs, snakes or insects.
> —James C. Rogal, *St. Louis Post-Dispatch*

> Discussion flows over the gamut of frustrations and joys faced by the couples, who talk of their work drives, desire for intimacy, sexual disappointments, process of communication, and spiritual commitments.
> —Mark H. Senter III, *Christianity Today*

> Agricultural causes of fish kills run the gamut from livestock waste runoff to fertilizer spills. . . .
> —C. F. Marley, *Acres, U.S.A.*

In the last quotation *run the gamut* is used in the legitimate sense 'run through the whole range.' But this phrase has been confused by some people with the expression *run the gauntlet* = 'to go through a cross fire, be exposed to any severe experience':

> Trucks and weapons carriers in groups of two or three came roaring along at full speed with rifles and machine pistols flaring up at us as they ran the gamut.
> —Farley Mowat, *And No Birds Sang*

> But now he had to run the gamut of cross-examination.
> —Louis Nizer, *My Life in Court*

◇ ***Recommendation.*** A *gamut* is definitely not a *gauntlet,* and the use illustrated in the last two quotations above is an error. See GAUNTLET, RUN THE.

gantlet. See GAUNTLET.

gaol, British variant spelling of *jail.* Even when spelled *gaol,* it is pronounced like *jail.*

gauntlet **/gônt-lĭt, gänt-/** = 'long glove.' The variant spelling *gantlet* (pronounced the same as *gauntlet*) is now rare. Medieval knights conventionally threw down a glove as a challenge to single combat; to pick it up was to accept the challenge. Modern politicians, fond of issuing dramatic challenges, throw down many a verbal gauntlet:

> I draw the line in the dust and toss the gauntlet before the feet of tyranny. And I say, Segregation now! Segregation tomorrow! Segregation forever!
> —George Wallace (quoted), Arthur M. Schlesinger, Jr., *Robert Kennedy and His Times*

> In this second term I had thrown down a gauntlet to Congress, the bureaucracy, the media, and the Washington establishment, and challenged them to engage in epic battle.
> —Richard Nixon, *R.N.*

> Savannah Police Chief David Gellatly on Wednesday threw down the gauntlet to criminals and would-be criminals.
> —*Savannah Morning News*

gauntlet, run the. This kind of *gauntlet* (pronounced /gônt-lĭt, gănt-/), originally *gantlope,* is not related to *gauntlet* = 'long glove.' Some prefer to spell this one *gantlet,* but *gauntlet* is more usual for both.

Running the gauntlet was a punishment used in European armies, especially in Prussia, up to the 18th century. The culprit or victim, stripped to the waist, was made to walk slowly between two lines of men, each of whom struck at him with a stick or knotted rope. Similar punishments or tortures have been used elsewhere. The expression is also used figuratively in various ways.

> Then they were marched in close-rank columns to Babi Yar, a ravine just beyond the cemetery. Here they were run through a gauntlet, beaten with sticks and truncheons by *polizei* from the Western Ukraine.
> —Harrison E. Salisbury, *The Unknown War*

> Moscow police and "volunteer" auxiliaries are dispatched to form gauntlets at church entrances, where they check identity papers and otherwise harass the worshipers.
> —George Feifer, *Geo*

> "Senator Humphrey is our big rival now," Robert Kennedy said as they prepared in February to run the gantlet of the primaries.
> —Arthur M. Schlesinger, Jr., *Robert Kennedy and His Times*

Occasionally, mistakes creep into the use of this expression:

> They endured one last torment between them and the waiting Air Algérie 727—a forced march past a gantlet of militants raining kicks and curses.
> —*Newsweek*

This should have been "a forced march *through* a gantlet of militants." The mistake illustrates a problem common to many once-colorful metaphors. When the image underlying such a metaphor fades, it becomes an idiom with no literal meaning.

gay. The basic meaning of the word *gay* is 'merry, lighthearted, full of sociable fun' or 'bright, vivid.' But *gay* is now widely used to mean 'homosexual,' and as a result few people venture to use it in its original sense for fear of ridicule. This is a situation that vexes many people:

> I find it most annoying that a perfectly good old-fashioned word (and it used to be a pleasing and cheerful little word) has been taken over by one minority group as if they had invented it themselves. I have every reasonable sympathy with homosexuals . . . but I do resent their stealing the word gay from *my* vocabulary.
> —letter, Midwestern newspaper (1976)

It is not quite fair to accuse the homosexual community of having stolen the word from the general vocabulary. For more than 300 years the word *gay* has been leading a curious double life, with a cheerful role in familiar and even poetic language and at the same time with a remarkable career in more specialized contexts. A *gay man* could mean merely one who was high-spirited and fond of parties; it could also mean one who went in for violent sports, heavy drinking, and sexual adventure.

In the Victorian period *gay* became a slang code word referring to the sexual underworld from which polite society averted its eyes. This is the real reference of some apparently trite old phrases like *gay deceiver.* The code word was applied to the exploited as well as to their exploiters—for instance, a gay woman was a prostitute. To initiates *gay* meant either 'sexually adventurous' or 'sexually available,' and the gay world no doubt included the homosexual one.

In the 20th century the generalized slang usage disappeared with the Victorian underworld itself. The word *gay* was then taken up by the still-underground world of homosexuals, who applied it to themselves, again as a code word that probably would not be understood by outsiders. All this time the standard meaning of *gay* had continued in polite usage, unaffected by its secret history. With the postwar movements for homosexual liberation, the slang usage of *gay* at last emerged, proclaimed itself openly, and insisted that it had become respectable.

In addition to the adjective, *gay* has now also yielded a noun. In 1977 the mayor of Seattle could say: "If Seattle is more desirable to singles and older people, or smaller households, or gays, that is not necessarily bad." The usage may still be regarded by many as slang, but it is unmistakably on the way to becoming a part of the standard vocabulary. This may or may not be bad, but it has had the unfortunate side effect of making the original standard sense virtually unusable for the time being, to the resentment of such people as the letter writer quoted above.

See also LESBIAN.

generalization. *Generalization,* the ability to draw a broad conclusion from a group of particulars, is the most characteristically human form of reasoning. We generalize about everything, from the behavior of neutron stars and subatomic particles to ethical and political principles to baseball and the weather. Language itself is supercharged with generalizations about reality. When, for example, we refer to an object as a *chair,* we are not so much defining it as assigning it to a category of objects whose common characteristics we have generalized into the concept of "chair." In a sense we can never fully define any particular chair, not only because its attributes are probably almost infinite in number but more fundamentally because there is no way language can duplicate our direct experience of an actual object.

All generalizations, then, are defective, but some are a good deal more defective than others. From the relative logic of our soundest generalizations we have created human civilization. From the illogic of our least sound generalizations we regularly concoct those destructive errors—those intolerant orthodoxies and isms—that have been among civilization's worst enemies.

Logicians have given names to some of the more obvious ways in which our generalizations fall short of acceptability. The *sweeping generalization* assumes that what is true in many circumstances must be true in each particular circumstance. This error is very similar to what is called the *fallacy of division,* or the attempt to apply what is true of a group as a whole to each of its members indiscriminately.

The *hasty generalization* and the *fallacy of composition* do just the opposite; that is, they assume, respectively, that what is true in one set of circumstances must be true in all circumstances and that what is true of one member of a group must be true of the whole group. Here is the case for the self-conscious universe, as presented by Jose Silva:

> Can the universe think about itself? We know that at least one part of it can: We ourselves. Is it not reasonable to conclude that the whole can?
> —*The Silva Mind Control Method*

The answer to Silva's last question is, of course, that solely on the strength of the evidence offered, no, it is not particularly reasonable to conclude anything of the kind. See also FALLACY.

General Northern dialect, sometimes known as *General American.* This is the most prevalent form of American speech, spoken in nearly two-thirds of the United States. Its features are essentially those of the NORTHERN and NORTH MIDLAND dialects. Other American dialects, however, have additionally influenced the West, creating a major subdialect, WESTERN. This, in turn, has several subdivisions: the PACIFIC NORTHWEST, PACIFIC SOUTHWEST, ROCKY MOUNTAIN, and SOUTHWESTERN dialects. But these are not very distinct. Their boundaries are quite sketchy compared with the sharp lines of the older dialects of the Atlantic Coast.

Pronunciation. Words such as *ask, brass, dance,* and *path* are (except in eastern New England) pronounced with the /ă/ sound. The vowel in *hot, box, pot,* and *top* tends to be pronounced /ŏ/ instead of /ô/. The /r/ sound (except in eastern New England) is retained in all positions within a word.

Vocabulary. (1) Expressions that are old-fashioned or have decreasing use:

beanery = 'small, often poor restaurant'
beans with the bags *or* **pods open, doesn't know** = 'is ignorant, stupid'
cobble, cobblestone = 'small, generally smooth round rock'
ice-cream social = 'social gathering where ice cream is served'
piece = 'snack'
sadiron = 'nonelectric clothes iron'

(2) Chiefly rural expressions:

beet greens = 'young beet leaves used in salad'
blat = 'to bleat'; used of cows, sheep, sometimes people
bloodsucker = 'leech'
bread and milk poultice = 'folk remedy for infections'
bunter = 'goat that butts'
burrs = 'prickly seeds or cockleburs'
coboss, come-boss = 'call to cows'
gentleman cow = 'bull'

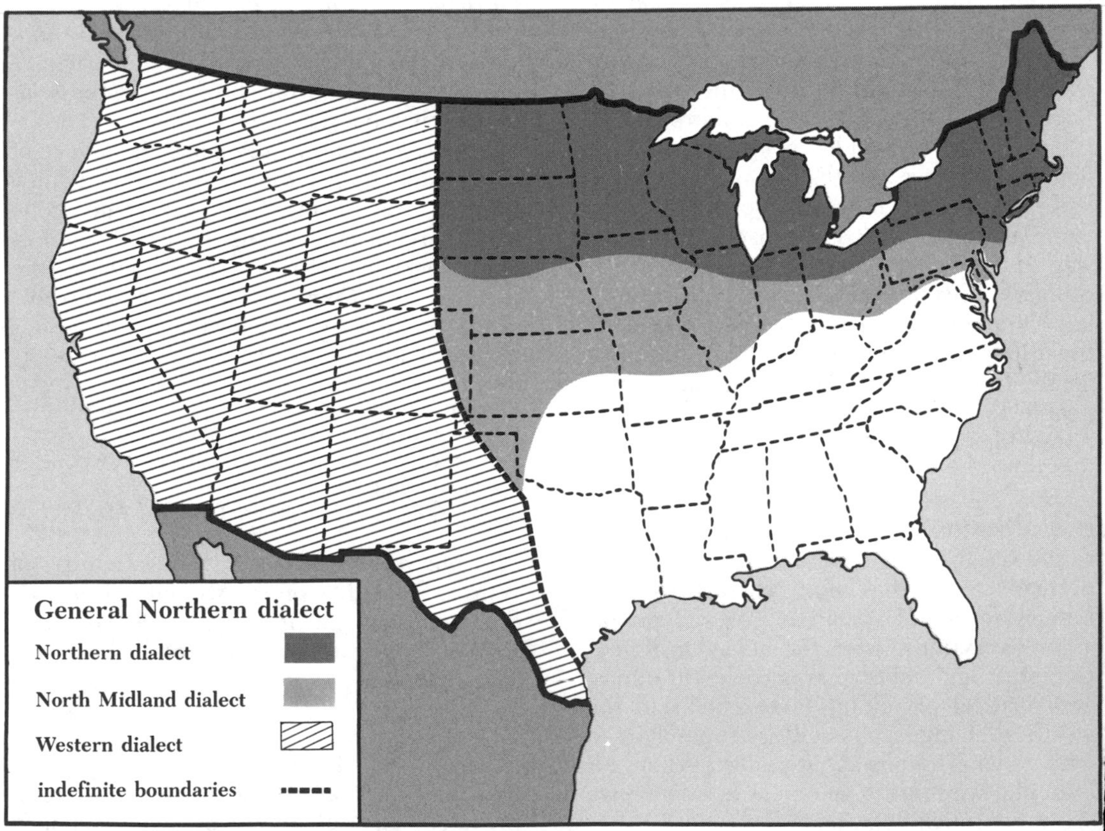

meaner than *or* **mean as dirt** = 'extremely mean'
milk snake = 'king snake'
mud wasp *or* **dauber** (also Midland) = 'wasp that builds a nest of mud'
pail = 'to milk (a cow)'

(3) Expressions of wider currency within the General Northern region:

agile = '(of an old person) lively, spry'
all-ee all-ee in free = 'call used in the game of hide-and-seek'
au revoir = 'goodbye'
belly flop = 'to land on the stomach'; used of diving or sledding
* **boughten** = 'past tense and past participle of *buy*'
buckle down = 'to get serious and do the job at hand'
bum's rush, give (someone) the = 'to get rid of summarily, brush off'
bushed = 'tired'
button, button = 'children's game'
* **Canuck** (usually derogatory) = 'a Canadian'
carmel = 'caramel'
chokecherry = 'any bitter cherry'
clunker = 'broken-down car'
crick = 'creek, *stream'
criminy, criminently = 'exclamation of surprise, anger, etc.'
crust = 'insensitive aggressiveness, nerve': *That salesclerk has a lot of crust!*
dodo, dolt = 'dull or stupid person'
donnybrook = 'fistfight, brawl'
duffer = 'old man'
eave(s) trough = '*gutter'
flighty = 'silly, lightheaded'
gesundheit = 'bless you'; said after someone sneezes
igg (used especially by black speakers) = 'to snub, ignore'
jiggers = 'chiggers'
kaput = 'broken, out of order'
mackerel sky (especially in the Northeast) = 'sky with rows of clouds'
marble orchard = 'cemetery'
meander = 'to loiter'
penuche = 'brown-sugar fudge'
pieplant = 'rhubarb'
* **pit** = 'seed of a fleshy fruit'
sick to one's stomach = 'queasy'
sword's point, swords' points, at = 'ready to quarrel, combative'

*Appears as separate entry

General Southern dialect. This dialect covers a broad area consisting largely of the former Confederate States. It also includes southern Maryland, Delaware, and West Virginia, all of Kentucky, the southernmost parts of Ohio, Indiana, Illinois, Kansas, and Missouri, and much of Oklahoma.

The same social, political, and economic forces that separated the South from the North before the Civil War were important in developing and preserving this region's unique variety of American English. Early settlement patterns also helped to establish this dialect beyond the borders of the Old South. Some of the earliest settlers came from Pennsylvania in the 1770s, such as James Harrod, who led a group of pioneers into central Kentucky to establish the first permanent settlement. In 1775 the Quaker Daniel Boone and a sizable party of pioneer families from North Carolina founded Boonesborough. Later, attracted by the fertile land and the promise of large cotton crops, the planters and hunter-farmers of Virginia, North Carolina, South Carolina, and Georgia moved west into Tennessee, Alabama, and Mississippi.

Unlike the fairly uniform General Northern dialect, the speech of the South is highly diversified, both regionally and socially. Its dialect boundaries tend to be more clear-cut, since it is a largely agricultural area that has had relatively little population movement. Geography, and the life style dictated by it, divide General Southern into two major subdivisions: the SOUTHERN and SOUTH MIDLAND dialects. The coastal lowlands and piedmont of the Atlantic and Gulf states, traditionally an area of large plantations, roughly constitute the area of the original Southern dialect; the mountainous areas of the southern Appalachians and Ozarks, with small farms and coal mines, roughly mark off the boundaries of the South Midland dialect.

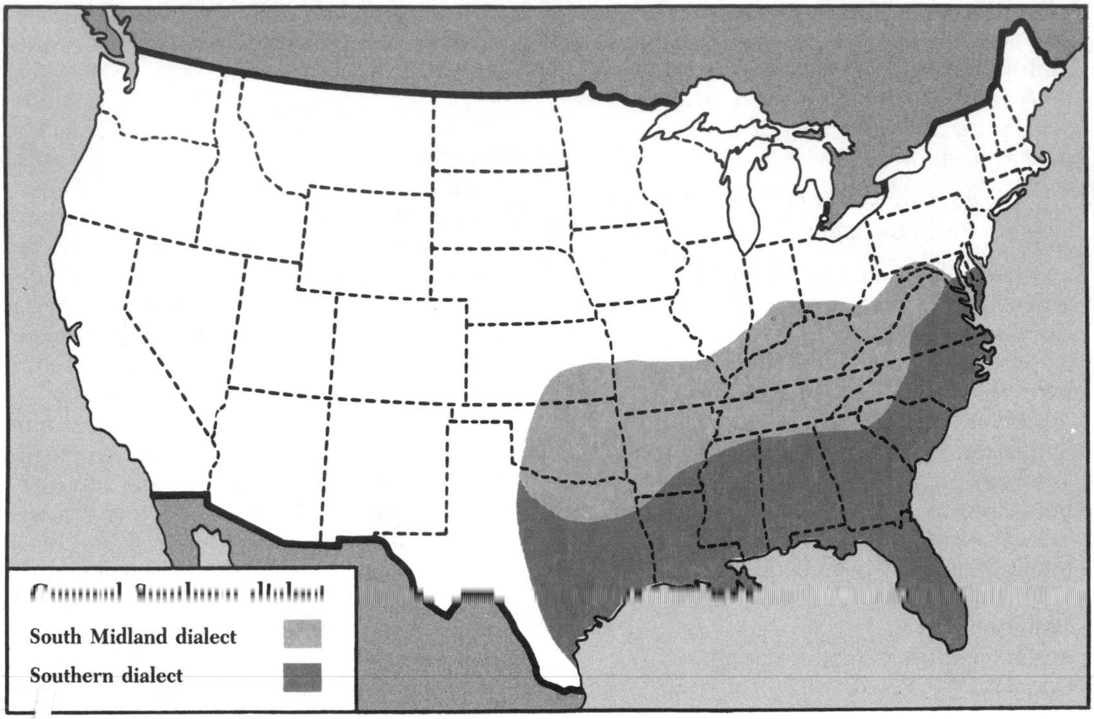

Pronunciation. One of the first things an outsider notices about General Southern is the so-called drawl, a somewhat slower manner of speaking. And there are other characteristics. The vowel /o͞o/ in such words as *due, few,* and *tune* is preceded by a "glide" /y/: /dyo͞o/, /nyo͞o/, /tyo͞on/. The vowel in such words as *time, five,* and *my* is pronounced with the /ȧ/ sound instead of /ī/: /tȧm/, /fȧv/, /mȧ/. Sometimes these words are pronounced with two vowel sounds, the diphthong /ȧə/: /tȧəm/, /fȧəv/, /mȧə/. Words like *out, plow,* and *mountain* are pronounced /ăo͞o/ instead of /ou/: /ăo͞ot/, /plăo͞o/, /**măo͞on**-tən/. Words like *class* and *yes* are often pronounced with two syllables: /**klă**-əs/, /**yĕ**-əs/.

Vocabulary. The regional vocabulary of the South is extensive and varied and is sprinkled with words of African and French origin.

(1) Culinary terms. The South is famous for its distinctive style of cooking and has many regional names for foods, especially for dishes of pork and corn—the traditional hog and hominy.

ashcake, hoecake (old-fashioned) = 'corn cake shaped by hand and baked on an open fire'
bacon = 'brine-cured bacon, salt pork'
battercake = '*pancake'
bought bread = 'store-bought bread'
breakfast bacon = 'smoke-cured bacon'
bunch bean = 'kidney bean'
butter bean = 'lima bean'
chinquapin = 'chestnut'
chitlins = 'hog intestines, chitterlings'
* **clabber** = 'curdled milk'
cobbler = 'deep-dish fruit pie with a top crust of biscuit dough'
corn dodger = 'corn dumpling or small irregular-shaped corn pone'
corn pone = 'baked or fried corn bread'
cracklin = 'crisp bits of rendered pork fat'
egg bread = 'kind of corn bread'
egg turner = 'spatula'
float an iron wedge *or* **a horseshoe, able to** = 'to be very strong'; used of coffee: *Dad's coffee could float an iron wedge.*
fritter = 'fried cornmeal cake'
hush puppy = 'deep-fried cornmeal bread'
light bread = 'white bread'
middlin(s), middlin meat = 'salt pork'

pulley bone = 'wishbone'
red-eye gravy = 'gravy made with ketchup or tomato sauce'
salad, salat = 'garden greens'
snap bean = 'string bean'
souse (also North Midland) = '*headcheese'
spoon bread = 'bread made with cornmeal'

*Appears as separate entry

(2) Rural and farm terms:

barlow knife = 'large pocketknife'
bee gum = 'hollow tree in which bees live'
corn shuck = 'corn husk'
dad-burn, dad-blast, dad-gum = 'exclamation of annoyance, anger, surprise, etc.'
dirt dauber = 'wasp'
doty = 'rotten, decayed'
durn (also occasionally Northern) = 'darn'
eye = 'round, flat iron lid on a wood-burning stove'
fox fire = 'light caused by fungi in decaying wood'
gear up (a horse) = 'to saddle and harness'
get gone = 'to leave in a hurry'
hay frame = 'hay wagon'
hay shock = 'haycock'
infidel = 'one who never goes to church'
johnny, johnny house = 'outdoor toilet'
loaf bread = 'store-bought bread'
lot, barn lot, stable lot = 'barnyard'
male cow = 'bull'
nicker = 'whinny of a horse'
paling *or* **plank fence** (also North Midland) = 'wooden or picket fence'
piece of a load = 'some part of or less than a full amount'
roastin ear (also North Midland) = 'corn ripe enough to eat'
rock fence *or* **wall** = 'wall built of unmortared stones'
rooter = 'pig's nose'
snake doctor = '*dragonfly'
whetrock = 'whetstone'

*Appears as separate entry

(3) Expressions and grammatical forms used especially by rural and blue-collar speakers:

a apple = 'an apple'
bad sick = 'extremely sick'
cuss fight = 'argument'
***disremember** = 'to forget'
div = 'past tense of **dive*'
done = 'already': *I done told you so.*
drawed (also occasionally North Midland, Inland Northern) = 'past tense of *draw*'
give-out = 'exhausted, tired'
gozzle, goozle, guzzle = 'throat'
hants, haunts = 'ghosts'
hard lick = 'hard blow'
hisself = 'himself'
hit a lick = 'to work'
holp = 'past tense and past participle of *help*'
like to = 'almost': *I like to died laughin'.*
may can = 'may be able to' See DOUBLE MODALS.
might could = 'might be able to'
mought = 'past tense of *may*'
not for sure, I'm = 'I'm not sure'
riz = 'past tense of *rise*'
taken = 'past tense of *take*'
use to could = 'used to be able to' See DOUBLE MODALS.
use to didn't = 'didn't used to'

*Appears as separate entry

(4) More widely used terms in the region:

ager, ager chills = 'chills and fever, ague'
agg (someone) on = 'to urge'
antigodlin, antigogglin, antigoslin = 'askew, slanting, awry' See CATERCORNER.
back (a letter) = 'to put a return address on'
bad man = 'the Devil'
bad place = 'hell'
before-day = 'dawn'
big = 'pregnant'
boogerman = 'bogy, hobgoblin'
branch = '*stream'
***bucket** = 'container for water'
bumfuzzled = 'confused, mixed up'
chill bumps = '*goose flesh'
chinch bug = 'bedbug'
coffee sack = 'cloth sack, *gunnysack'
coffin tack = 'cigarette'
cooter = 'tortoise, turtle'
counterpin, county pin = 'bedspread, counterpane'
creek = 'small *stream'
cut on, cut off (the light) = 'to turn on, turn off'

devilment, deviltry = 'mischievousness'
dike out = 'to dress up or adorn, deck out'
dinner-on-the-ground = 'picnic or potluck'
dipper (old-fashioned) = 'person who uses snuff'
directly = 'immediately, soon'
dirt dauber = 'wasp that makes a nest of mud'
dog drunk = 'thoroughly drunk'
dog iron, firedog = 'andiron'
earbob = 'earring'
ease = 'to move quietly'
evening = 'afternoon'
ever = 'every': *everwhere, ever direction,* etc.
fair off, fair up = 'to become sunny, clear up'
fall off = 'to lose weight'
fall out = 'to become unconscious, pass out'
fireboard = '*mantel, mantelpiece'
flying jenny = 'homemade merry-go-round'
frogstool = 'mushroom, toadstool'
frog-strangler = 'downpour, hard rain'
funky = 'smelling bad or musty'
funnel = 'to drink fast'
gallinipper = 'mosquito'
getup = 'energy'
granny woman = 'midwife'
gully washer = 'downpour, hard rain'
hamper = 'basket, especially for fruit'
harp = 'harmonica'
head rag (used especially by black speakers) = 'cloth worn on the head'
hippin = 'diaper'
ice-cream supper = 'type of social gathering where ice cream is served'
I declare (also occasionally Northern) = exclamation of surprise
jackleg (used especially by black speakers) = 'lay or unprofessional preacher or lawyer'
jake leg = 'delirium tremens'
jump the broomstick *or* **broom handle** = 'to get married'
keen-eyes = 'sharp or piercing eyes'
kinfolks = 'relatives'
king bee = 'self-important person'
laying = '(of wind) decreasing'
longhandles (also Western) = 'long underwear'
make haste (used especially by black speakers) = 'to hurry'
mammy = 'mother'
manner's piece = 'last piece of food on a plate'
mantel board = '*mantel, mantelpiece'
maypop = 'May apple'
middling = 'side of meat, usually referring to bacon'
mourners' bench = 'special front row seat in a church'
muleheaded = 'obstinate'
multiplying onions = 'variety of perennial onion'
Old Scratch = 'the Devil'
overseer = 'foreman, work superintendent'
pallet (also North Midland) = 'temporary bed on the floor'
rain frogs = 'to rain very hard'
roll the baby = 'to wheel the baby (in a carriage)'
seed (also North Midland) = '*pit of a cherry, plum, or peach'
sick at one's stomach = 'queasy'
slop bucket = 'garbage *pail'
smoothing iron (old-fashioned) = 'nonelectric clothes iron'
* **tote** = 'to carry'
woods colt (also North Midland) = '*illegitimate child'
* **you-all, y'all** = 'you'

*Appears as separate entry

generic = 'belonging to a genus or whole class, not specific.' In trademark law *generic* is used of a name or product not protected by a trademark, such as celluloid or shredded wheat (see TRADEMARKS). The word has recently been taken up in the marketing of drugs and foods, to mean 'carrying no brand name'; we can now ask for generic aspirin or generic peas. This is clearly an awkward way of talking, and there is evidence that the public doesn't like it (some, for example, tend to associate the unfamiliar word with *genetic* or *geriatric*). So far no alternative has turned up. We suggest that something along the lines of *nonbrand* or *no-name* would be an improvement.

genre /zhän-rə/, from a French word meaning 'kind, type.' In art and literary criticism it is little more than a fancy term for 'category, variety, type, style, kind': *an interesting minor genre of porcelain figurine; the romantic genre of love poetry.* In painting it also has a specific meaning: *genre painting* refers to 19th-century (and later) work that depicts everyday life more or less realistically, as opposed to earlier painting that preferred classical, historical, romantic, or other subject matter. An art critic might call Norman Rockwell a genre painter.

In its general sense 'type, style, category,' the word is now in increasingly frequent use:

> For his breakaway from public school stories was now beginning in earnest, and his genre was clearly the humorous love story.
>
> —David A. Jasen, *P. G. Wodehouse*

> [Mel] Brooks used to be a professional jazz drummer, and loves jazz of the Ellington, Armstrong, Basie genre.
>
> —Maurice Zolotow, *Reader's Digest*

> This large and handsomely illustrated volume obviously belongs to the genre of coffee table book.
>
> —O. C. Edwards, Jr., *The Living Church*

> Dodger manager Casey Stengel . . . suggested to [pitcher] Beck that he take the rest of the afternoon off. Beck's performance had been perfectly within his genre, but for some reason he was enraged at this derricking. . . .
>
> —Roger Angell, *Reader's Digest*

gentleman. The word *gentle* originally meant 'belonging to a family of noble rank.' *Gentleman* meant the same as *nobleman,* or more specifically it meant 'man who owns a coat of arms but has no title such as Sir or Lord.' This fine distinction of rank has passed away, and the word *gentleman* is left with a spectrum of meanings and uses ranging from 'upper-class man of old-fashioned courtesy and honorable character' or 'polite, considerate, and honest man' (especially 'man who is scrupulous in money matters and business ethics' or 'man who is chivalrous and protective to women'), through 'man of any type or character' all the way down to 'overrefined, prissy, snobbish man.'

> . . . the Prince held strongly at that time . . . that [Lord Randolph] Churchill had forfeited forever the right to describe himself, or to be described, as a gentleman.
>
> —Philip Magnus, *Edward VII*

> [John Hay] was a man of his time—a man of dignity and sensitivity—a great American gentleman.
>
> —George F. Kennan, *American Diplomacy 1900–1950*

> During the 1920s . . . then Secretary of State [Henry L.] Stimson had closed a code-breaking unit in his department with the righteous comment that "Gentlemen do not read each other's mail."
>
> —William Colby, *Honorable Men: My Life in the CIA*

> Since . . . I was too much of a gentleman to delegate the job to Claire, I stripped off my clothing and went diving.
>
> —Farley Mowat, *The Boat Who Wouldn't Float*

> The Get-Ready Man was a lank unkempt elderly gentleman with wild eyes and a deep voice who used to go about shouting at people through a megaphone to prepare for the end of the world.
>
> —James Thurber, *My Life and Hard Times*

> DEAR ABBY: There is this interesting-looking gentleman I see on the train on my way to work every morning. . . .
>
> —letter, *Savannah Morning News*

> [Scarlett O'Hara:] "Then why didn't Ashley do it?" "He's a gentleman," said Rhett, and Scarlett wondered how it was possible to convey such cynicism and contempt in that one honorable word.
>
> —Margaret Mitchell, *Gone With the Wind*

Gentlemen is used as the general term of polite address, both in public speaking and in business letters, whenever the addressee is not known by name. See also DEAR SIR OR MADAM; LADY.

Germanic. English belongs to the Germanic group of languages, of which the other chief members are Dutch, Flemish, and Afrikaans; Danish, Swedish, Norwegian, and Icelandic; German and Yiddish; and (extinct) Gothic. All these are descended from the language spoken by the ancient people called Germans or Teutons, living in southern Scandinavia and northern Germany from about 500 B.C. onward. Only fragments of it have survived in written form, but much of the language has been reliably reconstructed by linguistic scholars.

The Anglo-Saxons who crossed to Britain in the 5th and 6th centuries A.D. were a branch of the Germanic people, and their language, now usually called OLD ENGLISH, was a dialect of the original Germanic language. Modern English, although much altered from Old English, is inherited from it; it is thus classed as Germanic in structure, and most of our basic vocabulary is inherited Germanic vocabulary.

Throughout its later history English has also borrowed words from its Germanic cousin languages; these borrowings are covered separately at AFRIKAANS, DUTCH, GERMAN, NORSE, SCANDINAVIAN, and YIDDISH words. The ancient Germanic language was itself ultimately descended from the much earlier Indo-European language; see INDO-EUROPEAN.

German words. The Germanic languages of continental Europe excluding Scandinavia are divided into two main branches: *High German*, originally a dialect spoken in the high country of southern Germany, now the literary and official language of West Germany, East Germany, and Austria; and *Low German*, the dialects spoken in the low-lying country of Germany's western seaboard, closely related to Dutch and Flemish. The present entry is concerned with borrowings from High German, usually known simply as German. (See also GERMANIC.)

The German term for 'German' is *Deutsch* /doich/. The word *Deutsch* has been borrowed into English as *Dutch*, which formerly was applied to the speakers of High German and Low German in general but in modern usage is applied only to the people of the Netherlands. An American relic of this is the term *Pennsylvania Dutch:* the Pennsylvania Dutch people are not from the Netherlands but from Germany (see PENNSYLVANIA DUTCH).

Pronunciation. German spelling practices, not having been confused by French influence, are much more regular than those of English. As a rule, German words are pronounced exactly as they are spelled. Of course, the phonetic values are different from English, but once you know them you can hardly go wrong. Chief points of difference are covered in the table opposite.

Considering the cultural importance of the German people in Europe and the world, and the very large German immigrations into America, it is perhaps surprising to find that German borrowings have not penetrated at all deeply into the English vocabulary; they are an interesting but not profound contribution. We have arbitrarily divided the selections given below into several categories: (1) words relating to technology and science; (2) words relating to food and drink; (3) words borrowed shortly before or during World War II; (4) words borrowed from German immigrants in the United States; and (5) miscellaneous terms.

(1) Technology and science. Since the Middle Ages, German technology has been extraordinarily influential, and nowhere more than in the field of mining and related industries and sciences. The following names of minerals, first discovered or noticed by Germans, were already established in English by the 18th century or earlier.

cobalt = 'a metallic element': from German *kobalt*, originally *kobolt* = 'goblin, underground demon,' applied by early miners to cobalt ore because it seemed to maliciously spoil the purity of silver ores with which it was found

feldspar, felspar = 'type of spar or glassy mineral often found in surface outcrops, a silicate of aluminum': from German *feldspat(h)* = 'field-spar,' from *feld* = 'field' + *spat(h)* = 'glassy mineral, spar'

Pronouncing German

Letter	Pronunciation
Consonants*	
b	(1) /b/ *in initial and medial positions* (2) /p/ *at the end of a word or word element*
c	(1) /ts/ *before* e, i, ö, ä (2) /k/ *before other vowels*
ch	(1) /KH/ (2) /k/ *before* s, *as in* lachs (= *'lox'*)
d	(1) /d/ *in initial and medial positions* (2) /t/ *at the end of a word or word element*
g	(1) /g/ *in initial and medial positions* (2) /k/ *at the end of a word or word element* (3) /KH/ *at the end of a word ending in* -ig
j	/y/
qu	/kv/
r	/r/ *rolled or trilled, according to dialect and/or position in the word*
s	(1) /sh/ *before* p *and* t (2) /z/ *in initial and medial positions before vowels* (3) /s/
sch	/sh/
tsch	/ch/
tz	/ts/
v	/f/
w	/v/
z	/ts/

* *The letters* f, h, k, l, m, n, p, t, *and* x *are pronounced the same as in English.*

Letter	Pronunciation
Vowels and Diphthongs**	
a	/ä/ *or* /à/
ä	/ā/
e	/ā/, /ĕ/, *or* /ə/
i	/ē/ *or* /ĭ/
ie	/ē/ *or* /ēə/
o	/ō/ *or* /ò/
ö	/ë/
u	/o͞o/ *or* /o͝o/
ü	/ü/
y	/ü/
ai, ay	/ī/
ei, ey	/ī/
au	/ou/
äu, eu	/oi/

** *German vowels are "long" when followed by a single consonant, as in* not /nōt/ = *'need'; "short" when followed by two or more consonants, as in* Gott /gòt/ = *'God.'*

meerschaum = 'white mineral resembling hard clay, a silicate of magnesium, used for making tobacco pipes': from German *meerschaum* = 'sea-foam,' from *meer* = 'sea' + *schaum* = 'scum, foam,' referring to its creamy texture

nickel = 'a metallic element': from Swedish *nickel*, shortened from German *kupfernickel*, literally 'copper-demon,' from *kupfer* = 'copper' + *nickel* = 'demon,' applied by copper miners to nickel ore, which looked deceptively like copper ore

pitchblende = 'pitchlike uranium oxide, from which radium was first isolated': from German *pechblende*, from *pech* = 'pitch' + *blende* = 'shiny mineral, blende'

quartz = 'crystalline mineral, silicon dioxide': from German *quarz* (ultimately from Slavic)

wolfram = (1) 'a manganese compound of tungsten' (2) 'old term for the metallic element tungsten itself': from German *wolfram*, possibly meaning 'wolf-dirt,' a term applied by tin miners to the tungsten compound, which was found with tin ore and seemed to be an impurity

zinc = 'a metallic element': from German *zink*, probably from *zinke* = 'prong,' referring to the pronged shapes of smelted zinc

Other noteworthy German terms of science and technology:

Bunsen burner = 'laboratory burner using a mixture of gas and air': invented by the German chemist Robert Wilhelm *Bunsen* (1811–99)

diesel = 'internal-combustion engine that ignites by pressure rather than by spark plugs': invented by the German mechanical engineer Rudolf *Diesel* (1858–1913)

Doppler effect = 'apparent shift in sound (or other) wave frequency occurring when the source is moving toward or away from the observer': named for the Austrian physicist Christian Johann *Doppler* (1803–53)

ecology = 'science of living creatures in relation to their environment': from German *ökologie* (coined by the German biologist Ernst Heinrich Haeckel, 1834–1919) = 'habitat-study,' from Greek *oikos* = 'house,' hence 'habitat' + *-logia* = 'study'

enzyme = 'protein in living creatures acting as an agent of chemical change': from German *enzym* (coined by the German physiologist Wilhelm Kühne, 1837–1900) = 'fermenting agent,' from Greek *enzymos* = 'fermented, leavened'

ester = 'organic compound similar to an inorganic salt': from German *ester* (coined by the German chemist Leopold Gmelin, 1788–1853), a shortening of *essig-äther* = 'vinegar-ether,' from *essig* = 'vinegar' + *äther* = 'ether'

Fahrenheit = 'name of the temperature scale in which the freezing point of water is 32 degrees above zero': named for Gabriel Daniel *Fahrenheit* (1686–1736), German scientist who invented the mercury thermometer

menthol = 'an organic compound carrying a flavor of mint': from German *menthol*, from Latin *mentha* = 'mint' + the chemical suffix *-ol*

(2) Food and drink:

cold duck = 'cheap mixed wine, typically including a burgundy and a sparkling wine' See FOLK ETYMOLOGY.

delicatessen = 'shop selling a variety of prepared foods, sandwiches, etc.': from German *delikatessen* = 'delicacies'

frankfurter = 'small smoked sausage, typically made of finely ground beef and eaten in a roll'; recorded in the United States before 1900: from German *Frankfurter* = 'from Frankfurt' (German city)

hamburger = 'patty of ground beef, typically eaten in a bun'; originally *hamburg steak*, recorded in the United States before 1900: from *Hamburger* = 'from Hamburg' (German city); hence also the prolific American word element *-burger*, as in *cheeseburger*, *baconburger*, etc.

lager = 'light beer matured and clarified during storage in a cellar': from German *lagerbier* = 'storage beer,' from *lager* = 'storage' + *bier* = 'beer'

liverwurst = 'liver sausage': from German *leberwurst*, from *leber* = 'liver' + *wurst* = 'sausage'; so also other types of German sausage, such as *bratwurst, knackwurst*.

noodle = 'flat or rounded strip of dough, often served in soups, baked dishes, etc.': from German *nudel* (further origin unknown)

pretzel = 'type of hard glazed biscuit in the form of a thin rod tied in a loose knot': from German *pretzel* or *brezel*

pumpernickel = 'dark, sour, whole-rye bread': from German *pumpernickel*, literally 'fart-devil,' also 'lout, boor,' from *pumpern* = 'to fart' + *nickel* = 'devil, goblin,' said to refer to its flatulent effect

sauerkraut = 'cabbage pickled in a brine of its own juice': from German *sauerkraut* = 'sour cabbage,' from *sauer* = 'sour' + *kraut* = 'cabbage'

seltzer = 'effervescent mineral water': from German *selterswasser* = 'water from Niederselters' (place in western West Germany) See SODA POP.

wiener = 'small smoked sausage typically of finely ground beef': from German *wienerwurst* = 'Vienna sausage,' from *Wiener* = 'from Vienna' (German *Wien*)

(3) Selection of terms adopted during or shortly before World War II:

blitzkrieg = 'swift mechanized invasion': from German *blitzkrieg* = 'lightning war,' from *blitz* = 'lightning' + *krieg* = 'war'; in English shortened to *blitz*

flak = 'bursting shells from antiaircraft guns' See ACRONYMS.

Führer = 'title of Adolf Hitler as Nazi chief of state': from German *führer* = 'leader'

Gestapo = 'the Nazi secret police': from German *Gestapo*, acronym of Ge*heime* Sta*atspolizei* = 'secret state-police'

Nazi = 'belonging to the National Socialist party': from German *Nazi*, short for *Nationalsozialistische* = 'National Socialist'

panzer = 'tank': from German *panzer* = 'armor'

strafe = 'to machine-gun (ground troops, etc.) from low-flying aircraft'; originally a World War I expression meaning 'to attack or shell (the enemy) heavily,' a humorous use of German *strafen* = 'to punish,' extracted from the slogan *Gott strafe England* = 'May God punish England'

(4) Assortment of terms borrowed from German immigrants in the United States in the 19th and 20th centuries. (For words borrowed specifically from the Pennsylvania Dutch see PENNSYLVANIA GERMAN-ENGLISH.) These borrowings, some of them slang, occurred at the folk level rather than through literature, and some, though probable, are hard to prove. Among them are several "loan translations," in which the German word itself is not adopted but is translated into its English equivalent. These are especially hard to prove; there are doubtless many more of them in American English.

bum = 'social derelict, hobo': back-formation from *bummer* = 'one who begs or cadges,' used in the Civil War as a semi-official term for foragers or looters, from German *bummler* = 'loafer, time waster'

cookbook = 'book of recipes': probably translation of German *kochbuch* (replacing British English *cookery book*)

dumb = 'stupid': from German *dumm* = 'stupid'

-fest, a word element forming numerous compounds meaning 'festive gathering,' as *songfest*, or 'scene of much activity,' as *gabfest*: from German *fest* = 'festivity'

fresh = 'impertinent, sassy, cheeky': from German *frech* = 'impudent, insolent'

Gesundheit = 'health (to you),' said as a drinking toast or to someone who has sneezed: from German *gesundheit* = 'health'

glitch (slang) = 'a mechanical failure, technical problem, or mistake': from German *glitschen* = 'to slip'

hoodlum = 'professional criminal, gangster': from dialectal German *hudilump* = 'wretched person'

***hopefully** = 'it is to be hoped'

katzenjammer = (1) 'hangover or state of depression' (2) 'confused din, uproar': from German *katzenjammer* = 'lamentation of cats,' hence 'hangover'

***kitsch** = 'junk, bad art'

loaf = 'to loiter idly': back-formation from *loafer* = 'idle loiterer,' originally *landloafer*, from German *landlaufer* = 'vagabond'

nix (slang) = 'nothing': from German *nichts* = 'nothing'

spiel (slang) = 'a talk, line of talk': from German *spiel* = 'game'

*Appears as separate entry

(5) Miscellaneous German borrowings:

Bauhaus /bou-hous/ = 'influential school of design founded at Weimar in 1919, stressing functional form': from German *bauhaus* = 'architecture-house'

carouse = 'drinking bout': originally (16th

century) in the phrase *to drink carouse* = 'to drink a full draft,' translation of German *garaus trinken* = 'to drink fully,' from *garaus* = 'fully, all out'

dachshund = 'dog of a short-legged breed': from German *dachshund* = 'badger-dog,' so named probably not because it hunted badgers but because it had a heavy pointed snout and possessed powerful digging abilities

Doberman (pinscher) = 'dog of a large short-haired breed': after Ludwig *Dobermann,* who established the breed in the 19th century, + *pinscher* = 'terrier'

dollar = 'basic monetary unit of the United States, Canada, and other countries'; earlier referred to any of several large silver coins, including the Spanish peso and the German taler: from Flemish *daler*, German *taler*, a shortened form of *Joachimstaler* = 'coin from Joachimsthal' (a town in central Europe where silver was once mined)

* **ersatz** = 'artificial, substitute'

kindergarten = 'preschool for young children': from German *kindergarten,* literally 'children's garden,' a preschool as developed in the early 19th century by Friedrich Froebel

leitmotif, leitmotiv /līt-mō-tēf/ = (1) 'recurrent musical theme in Wagnerian opera, representing a particular character or element in the drama' (2) 'any recurrent theme or pattern': from German *leitmotiv* = 'leading motif or theme'

poodle = 'dog of a curly-haired breed': from German *pudel,* shortened form of *pudelhund* = 'splash-dog,' the original poodles having been bred in Germany as retrievers in marsh-bird hunting

Realpolitik /rā-äl-pō-lĭ-**tēk**/ = 'national policy based on exclusively selfish nationalism without regard to ethical considerations or the interests of other peoples': from German *realpolitik* = 'realistic or practical politics'

semester = 'one of two periods in an academic year, now (in the United States) lasting 15 to 18 weeks': from German *semester* = 'six-month period, half an academic year,' from Latin *se-mestris* = 'six-monthly'

snorkel = 'mouth-held breathing tube used in skin diving': from German *schnorchel,* literally 'a snort,' hence 'retractable breathing tube used in submarines,' and later 'mouth-held breathing tube used in skin diving'

superman = 'a man of superhuman attainment or powers': translation of German *übermensch* = 'above-man,' term used by the philosopher Friedrich Nietzsche for the superior man he considered would be the end product of human culture

swindle = 'to defraud (someone)': back-formation from *swindler,* from German *schwindler* = 'one who defrauds, cheat, confidence man,' from *schwindeln* = 'to defraud, cheat'

waltz = 'dance for couples in triple time, originating in Germany and adopted throughout Europe in the early 19th century': from German *walzer* = 'the waltz,' from *walzen* = 'to revolve, dance the waltz'

Weltanschauung /**vĕlt**-än-shou-ŏŏng/ = 'world view': from German *weltanschauung* = 'world-outlook,' from *welt* = 'world' + *anschauung* = 'outlook, view, conception'

world view = 'philosophical or cultural conception of the nature and purpose of the world': translation of German *weltanschauung* (see above)

yodel = 'to sing in a style originating in Switzerland and Tyrol, in which the voice makes smooth changes between chest voice and falsetto': from German *jodeln,* literally 'to sing the sound *jo* /yō/,' hence 'to yodel'

*Appears as separate entry

gerund. See VERBAL NOUNS IN -ING.

get, a basic verb with a huge array of different meanings and uses, most of them standard in all contexts, some of them informal, slang, or dialectal. There are two major divergences between American and British uses of *get:* American English in most senses prefers the past participle *gotten*, which in British is archaic; and British uses *have got* = 'to possess, own' as fully standard, while in American this is somewhat informal, occurring frequently in speech but less often in writing. Among the other uses that are informal are *have got to* = 'to be obliged to'; *it gets me* = 'it baffles or annoys me'; *get it* = 'to understand a problem, situation, etc.'; *get* (*someone* or *something*) = 'to defeat, destroy, or revenge oneself upon.'

ghetto. Plural *ghettos* or *ghettoes.* ***Origin.*** Jewish communities in medieval European cities were often compelled by law to live in small walled districts into which they were locked at night. In Italian cities such as Venice and Rome, these districts were called *ghettos* (for the etymology see ITALIAN WORDS). The word became known all over Europe and was later used to mean simply 'Jewish quarter of a city,' with or without walls and restrictions.

Uses. Recently the word has been extended to mean 'slum district in a modern city chiefly inhabited by people of a minority race or culture.' The implication of the word is that while modern ghetto dwellers are not confined by government decree, they are just as effectively kept in the ghetto by economic and social laws:

> The firehouse I work out of is on Intervale Avenue and 169th Street in a ghetto called the South Bronx. Of the three biggest ghettos in New York City [the others being Harlem and Bedford-Stuyvesant], the South Bronx is the least talked about.
>
> —Dennis Smith, *Report From Engine Company 82*

Perhaps inevitably, writers on the urban scene have found it necessary to coin the word *ghettoization:*

> . . . a few schools where minorities are beginning to outnumber whites. And that is accelerating some ghettoization, with middle-class movement away from the city.
>
> —Ian Menzies, *Boston Globe*

Ghetto has also been used to mean 'island of affluence in gray urban seas,' which is quite the reverse of its basic sense:

> For since the 1960s, Washington has evolved into a privileged ghetto, home of a pampered class all but immune to the disheartening tantrums of the economic weather. —*Time*

gibe. See JIBE.

girl. See WOMAN, LADY, GIRL.

gladiolus. Flowering plant of the iris family. The pronunciation is /glăd-ē-ō-ləs/, the plural *gladioli* /glăd-ē-ō-lī/ or *gladioluses.* The form *gladiola* often occurs:

> "Naturally," he said, rooting a gladiola deep into the bowl. . . .
>
> —Truman Capote, *Breakfast at Tiffany's*

To the botanist *gladiola* is an error; it should not be used in formal writing. In everyday speech it is acceptable.

golf terms. Golf originated in Scotland in the 15th century and spread to England in about the 1830s and to the United States in the 1880s. It has developed a formidable vocabulary, to which only these three countries have contributed.

(1) Original Scottish terms:

bunker = 'sandy area or pit used as a hazard'

caddie = 'person who carries a player's clubs and may give advice on play'

divot = 'piece of turf excavated by a stroke'

green = 'golf course' and **putting green** = 'closely mown ground around a hole'

links = (1) 'golf course on sandy seaside terrain' (2) 'any golf course'

putt = (1) (verb) 'to play a gentle stroke on the putting green' (2) (noun) 'such a stroke'

tee = 'small peg from which the ball is driven'

Now all but obsolete are the old Scottish names of the clubs:

baffy = 'steeply lofted wooden club, 4-wood'

brassie = 'slightly lofted wooden club, 2-wood'

cleek = (1) 'thin-bladed iron club, 1-iron' (2) 'lofted wooden club, 4-wood'

mashie = 'lofted iron club, 5-iron'

niblick = 'steeply lofted iron club, 9-iron'

spoon = 'lofted wooden club, 3-wood'

(2) Terms coined in England:

bogey = (1) 'standard amateur score for a hole, slightly easier than par' (2) 'one stroke over par for a hole'

dogleg = 'sharp turn on a fairway'

fairway = 'stretch of mown ground from tee to green'

handicap = 'number of strokes allotted to each player to allow equal competition'

par = 'standard first-class score for a hole'

rough = 'ground with long grass, bushes, or trees'

(3) Terms coined in the United States:

birdie = 'one under par for a hole'

chip = 'short lofted approach shot'

eagle = 'two under par for a hole'

Mulligan = 'unofficial free stroke'

Nassau = 'three-part bet, equal money on the first half, the second half, and the round'

wedge = 'steeply lofted iron club, 10-iron'

(4) Some golfing terms that have been adopted into general use:

one up on = 'having scored off or outsmarted (someone)'

par for the course (disparaging) = 'what one might expect, typically poor performance'

stymie = 'to block or frustrate'

teed off (slang) = 'angry'

tee off at (slang) = 'to attack (someone) verbally'

goober. This is one of several regional words for 'peanut,' used in the Midland speech region and in the South. First recorded in America in a Louisville, Kentucky, newspaper of 1833, it ultimately comes from Angola in West Africa, where the Kimbundu word *nguba* means 'peanut':

> Brer Rabbit been livin' on udder folkses' goobers en taters en things.
>
> —John B. Sale, *The Tree Named John*

> Aunt Neat, she said, held a goober-cracking last night at her house. . . . They bagged a peck and invited all the folks along the line to come in, buy a nickel bag, and crack goobers before the fire.
>
> —Ben Robertson, *Red Hills and Cotton* (1963)

good, well. In formal usage *good* is only an adjective, and its adverb is always *well.*

The verbs *seem, feel, sound, smell,* and *taste* (and a few equivalents such as *appear*) are generally followed by adjectives, not adverbs; the usage *It seems good, tastes good,* etc., is therefore correct and standard. (But note that in *All seems well* and *I feel well, well* is not the adverb but a separate adjective meaning 'satisfactory, in good health.')

In informal usage, however, *good* is widely used as an adverb:

> I had pitched good, and because we were on national television, people were beginning to notice me.
>
> —Sparky Lyle, *The Bronx Zoo*

> The lawyers coached us pretty good. We knew what to expect.
>
> —Ray LaRosa (quoted), *Reader's Digest*

◇ ***Recommendation.*** The adverbial use of *good,* natural in many people's informal speech, is not accepted as formal standard usage; *well* is always used instead.

goose flesh. The small bumps that appear on the skin usually in response to cold or a strong emotion are popularly known as *goose* *flesh.* This term, coined sometime in the 19th century, is, not surprisingly, a reference to the rough skin of a plucked goose.

> I do believe you could have grated a nutmeg on my skin, such a "goose-flesh" shiver ran over it.
> —Oliver Wendell Holmes, *The Professor at the Breakfast-Table* (1860)

Goose skin is an alternative term.

> Many a goose-skinned hour of delicious terror . . .
> —Edna Ferber, *Show Boat* (1926)

Goose bumps is another common American version of the term.

> Uncork that batch of rye and gin and chase these goose bumps from my skin.
> —*Liberty* (1928)

> I'm goosebumps all over. . . . By God, you inspire me. —J. D. Salinger, *Franny and Zooey*

Goose pimples, however, is the most commonly used term in the United States.

> I knew it, perhaps, the way animals know such things . . . the goose pimples spreading along my limbs and up the back of my neck. —*Yankee*

Some other variations used in different parts of the United States are *chill bumps, cold bumps, cold pimples*, and *duck bumps*.

gourmand, gourmet. These two words, both borrowed from French, are by origin unrelated but have come to be associated.

Pronunciation. *Gourmand* has been used in English since the 15th century and is therefore usually fully anglicized as /**gŏŏr**-mənd/. *Gourmet*, which first appeared in English during the 19th century, is still perceived as a French word and pronounced /gŏŏr-**mā**/. Because the two words are seen as a pair, the older *gourmand* is now often re-Frenchified to /gŏŏr-**mänd**/. Both pronunciations are acceptable.

Meanings. *Gourmand*, a Medieval French word, has always basically meant 'hearty eater.' It can range from 'one who is seriously interested in and knowledgeable about good food, and likes to eat well and plentifully' to merely 'one who eats a lot, glutton.' It can also be exactly synonymous with *gourmet*, meaning 'connoisseur of food,' without the implication of hearty appetite. More often, the gourmand is a hearty eater who is also a bit of a gourmet. If the two words are explicitly contrasted, the key distinguishing feature is appetite.

> He breakfasted lightly on tea and toast, for although in earlier days he had been something of a gourmand, he had of late become more prudent in his diet.
> —Edwin O'Connor, *The Last Hurrah*

> It looked like a banquet hall after the gourmands had gone home to sleep it off.
> —Robert Daley, *Reader's Digest*

> A half-million gourmands nibbled their way through the seven-hour eat-in, according to festival organizers.
> —Jennifer Dunning, *New York Times*

> It is said (variously) that I am a health-food faddist, a vegetarian, an undiscriminating gourmand, a peevish gourmet who demands that he be served only the most exotic dishes.
> —J. Paul Getty, *As I See It*

Gourmandise /**gŏŏr**-mən-dēz/ means 'the gourmand's love of and taste in food,' implying discrimination and knowledge rather than gluttony:

> . . . all masters, it seemed, of the arts of anecdote, adultery, and gourmandise.
> —Nancy Mitford, *Love in a Cold Climate*

Gourmet originally meant 'wine taster' and had no connection with food. Because the word (accidentally) resembled *gourmand*, the meaning changed to 'connoisseur of the table, expert critic of *haute cuisine*, very discriminating and knowledgeable eater.' In recent years *gourmet* has become a favorite all-purpose adjective of the prepared-food industry, including restaurants, kitchenware stores, delicatessens, cookbooks, and culinary journalists. While the noun may still be used with full understanding of its meaning 'food connoisseur,' the adjective, applied to food, often means little more than 'fancy and expensive':

> This potpourri of cookbooks posed some curious questions: In this land of instant mashed potatoes and TV dinners, are our tastebuds suddenly demanding more pampering? Are people cooking not just because they have to but for fun? Are we becoming a nation of aspiring gourmets?
> —Emily and Per Ola d'Aulaire, *Reader's Digest*

> There was nothing distinctive about Rocky Port's institutions or way of life, unless it was the frequency of gift shops selling "gourmet" foods, outsize pepper mills, "amusing" aprons and chef's costumes, bar equipment, and frozen croissants, "just like in France."
> —Mary McCarthy, *Birds of America*

> *Gourmet Equipment.* See "Housewares."
> *Gourmet Food*—Wholesl & Mfrs. See "Cheese," "Fish—Salt, Smoked, Pickled," "Food Products —Mfrs & Distrs," "Grocers—Wholesl."
> *Gourmet Shops.* . . .
> —*Manhattan Yellow Pages*

> The gourmet is a complex guy
> Who asks for "torte" when he means pie.
> —Angela Hatch, *New York Times*

> Now that the word "gourmet" has been vitiated by overuse, the new culinary status designation is "homemade."
> —Mimi Sheraton, *New York Times*

As the quotations show, many people, including serious connoisseurs of food, have become irritated by the indiscriminate use of *gourmet.* They can always fall back on *epicure* for 'food connoisseur,' with its adjective *epicurean,* and *gastronome* = 'food connoisseur,' with the adjective *gastronomic(al).*

graduate. The verb *graduate* may be either transitive, meaning 'to grant a degree or diploma to (someone), make a graduate' (*West Point graduates both men and women now*), or intransitive, meaning 'to receive a degree or diploma, become a graduate.' The following examples illustrate the intransitive use.

> Dr. Kennan graduated summa cum laude from Mount Holyoke in 1960.
> —*New York Times*

> Mrs. Kennan was graduated from Mount Holyoke College in 1960. . . .
> —*Morning Union* (Springfield, Mass.)

The passive use *was graduated* is in fact older than the active *graduated,* and many people believe it is more correct. But both are well established.

There is also another transitive use, meaning 'to receive a degree from (a university or school), become a graduate of':

> Sheldon was a childless New England bibliophile who had graduated Harvard almost a hundred years before.
> —Theodore H. White, *Boston Globe*

◇ ***Recommendation.*** The forms *He was graduated from college* and *He graduated from college* are equally correct. The form *He graduated college* is widespread but is not acceptable in formal usage. (And the same applies, with all three forms, to graduation from high schools and all other institutions.)

graffiti. Why do we use an Italian word for the writings and drawings that deface our property everywhere today? When the Roman city of Pompeii, buried by the eruption of Vesuvius in A.D. 79, was discovered preserved under the lava, the Italian excavators were fascinated to see that the ancient Romans too had the custom of writing stray, sometimes obscene, thoughts on walls—especially in disreputable places like brothels. Any such inscription is called, in Italian, a *graffito,* meaning simply 'a writing,' and the word (English pronunciation /grə-fē-tō/) came to be used by archaeologists of any informal ancient writing or drawing on a wall or hard surface. The plural is *graffiti,* in English pronounced /grə-fē-tē/. When some elements of our culture took to scrawling all over walls, statues, subway trains, etc., with aerosol spray paint and other equipment, the terms *graffito* and *graffiti* were applied to the results and so became widely familiar. They have even become quasi-literary terms, applied to the thoughts, slogans, and messages that are so written, as collected and analyzed by sociology-minded academics. The plural form *graffiti* is much more often used than the singular *graffito,* so that some people, who may never have heard or seen the singular form, use *graffiti* as a singular:

> There was *graffiti* everywhere, and instead of books students carried radios and tape players.
> —Anne Hollister, *Life*

> "Goodbye to the thieves," says this piece of graffiti on the Sun Life Building in Montreal.
> —Henry Giniger, *New York Times*

The correct singular *graffito* is still available however:

> The full impact of America's new attitudes finally reached me when I recently read this bit of graffito on a school bus: "Sheldon and Amy—for now."
> —Theodore A. Bachmann, *Reader's Digest*

◇ *Recommendation. Graffiti* is the plural form; *graffito,* an optional singular.

grammar. *Grammar,* a term derived from the Greek expression *grammatikē tekhnē* (= 'the art of reading and writing'), was once broader in meaning (see GREEK WORDS). Formerly referring to the study of language and literature together, it may now be called the study of those characteristics of a language that make it consistent enough to work. Grammar aims to examine the systems of sounds, and often merely the written representations of them, that allow the language to bear meanings more or less reliably.

The popular idea of grammar, however, stresses the presence of "rules" of vague and mysterious origin that even a native speaker is liable to violate, no matter how carefully he or she tries not to use "bad" grammar or earnestly tries to acquire "good." Grammar to many, then, is a fearsome subject, associated with reproving experts and constant threats of social, and possibly even moral, disgrace.

A sentence like *I don't got none of them there potatoes* is thoroughly grammatical in the most fundamental sense of the word. Speakers of English know it as a possible utterance of their language and can usually respond to it, whereas a reordering of the words, *There got of potatoes them I none don't,* is instantly recognized as something outside the bounds of possible English. Similarly, *Baddest doggie ated my cookie* will easily be understood as the utterance of a small child who is still learning the requirements of English but who is already showing some hold on grammar.

Syntax, Morphology, and Phonology. The child's sentence, *Baddest doggie ated my cookie,* shows in its sequence of sounds a progression of elements we can call N_1 V N_2 (noun–verb–noun) or N VT NO (noun–verb transitive–noun object). The ordering of these elements and others like them is called *syntax.* Even if we make changes or substitutions in the wording, as *The naughtiest dog ate my cookie,* we cannot improve the child's syntactical knowledge that a different arrangement of the elements—*The cookie ate my dog*—destroys her or his intended meaning.

The child's recognition that /-əd/ in *ated* is a change on the forms *eat* and *ate,* which signals completed action, shows that she or he is learning the *morphology* of the language. So also, constructing /băd/ + /-əst/ shows the child responding to the fact that various collections of sounds (words) may be manipulated according to some system in order to convey meaning. The adult who might suggest *worst* for *baddest* would be attempting to improve the child's morphological sophistication, but substituting *naughtiest* for *baddest* and *dog* for *doggie* would be, strictly speaking, not a grammatical concern at all. These are *lexical* changes, the first on behalf of precise word choice and the second, though it has the appearance of morphological change, as the preference for an adult synonym over the childish term.

Besides syntactic and morphological matters, grammar encompasses *phonology*, which deals with sounds, including such things as pitch and stress. These three—syntax, morphology, and phonology—are basic for grammarians. They represent the systems on which language is based. We are ordinarily conscious of a few of these systems; most we remain unaware of in our daily language until scholarly and scientific investigation reveals them to us. Furthermore, since language lives and changes, systems do not remain completely stable but undergo change, possibly according to laws not yet discovered. Grammar is a difficult but fascinating science, in which the basic laws of the nature of all languages are constantly being sought. Probing the grammar of even one language can carry the investigator far into philosophical and anthropological depths.

Descriptive and Prescriptive Grammar. What is traditional grammar, then, the kind that most of us are exposed to in our schooling? It seems, with its familiar rules and terminology, to be comfortably assured and authoritative. It is certainly distinct from modern scholarly and scientific grammar, which is primarily *descriptive* in its aims and is unwilling to ignore "exceptions" and difficulties. The aim of traditional grammar is *prescriptive;* that is, it tells pupils how to make choices among forms as they speak and write. Prescriptive grammarians assemble rules of thumb that try to reflect the actual current grammatical choices of the most literate and esteemed users of the language, so that pupils can have the most prestigious and thus the most practical forms available for their own use. Prescriptive grammar must be frequently updated. For example, the distinction between *I shall* (simple futurity) and *I will* (determination) was regularly taught in texts and classrooms a generation ago. Today, it is rarely to be found in either place because it is so seldom used even by the most careful speakers and writers, and it is losing force as a necessary feature of the verb system it was once a part of. (See SHALL, WILL.)

To illustrate what can happen when prescriptive grammar texts are regarded as something more than compendiums of rules of thumb, consider the familiar rule that pronouns must agree with their antecedents. In nearly all the handbooks *everyone* is identified as a singular pronoun that all other pronouns must agree with, as: *Will everyone please pass his plate.* Adhering to this requirement scrupulously will produce such a monstrosity as *When the swimming instructor said that everyone could stay in the pool an extra five minutes, he splashed and cheered in a chorus of joy.* The descriptive grammarian delights in the evidence that there are such complications for him to examine. The poor pupil hoping to improve his grammar can, if he lacks a healthy portion of common sense, be discouraged to find such "leaks" in oversimplified grammar, especially when exceptions and contradictory rules pile up. Fortunately, most current grammar books try to encourage users to regard rules as neither timeless nor absolute.

Although prescriptive grammar is a necessary tool for educating people to feel at home in their own language, it suffers from a clouded reputation because of generations of misuse. During the 18th century the overriding concern was to instruct newly literate classes of people in proper usages and, above all, to prevent a very much dreaded "decay" of language. Such a fear was based on a serious misunderstanding of the nature of language as something fixed, complete, and ideally regular. Furthermore, since grammar had for centuries been known primarily as the means to learn Latin, the grammatical systems that were appropriate to Latin were applied to English, and English was often distorted to fit those inappropriate schemes. Such difficulties did not totally thwart the growth of scientific grammar, but they did impede it very seriously—so much so that the prescriptive grammar of classrooms today uses terminology and schemes that are of little value to the scientist of languages, creating a false impression of opposition between prescriptive and descriptive grammarians. Moreover, in some quarters much of the 18th-century attitude toward language has been carried forward: that originally English was an undefiled well of regular, invariable characteristics that could be expressed by rules having the force of laws and that the faithless by their neglect have separated us from them.

Yet in some ways traditional terminology and systems have proved durable, especially as they can be taught, understood, and read by literate people who are not specialists. Dictionaries, for instance, usefully employ the *parts of speech,* although even as these are commonly known, there is no complete agreement as to how many of them there are (usually noun, pronoun, verb, adjective, adverb, preposition, conjunction, and interjection). This book frequently uses traditional terminology because it is the most widely known and therefore the most helpful to general readers. Prescriptive handbooks have almost completely abandoned awkward and stiff usages based on dead forms, so that prescribing grammatical usages is less and less likely to be seen as attempting to describe and analyze whole grammatical systems.

Standard Usages. Modern handbooks of grammar—and there are dozens in print—almost always recommend grammatical forms consistent with current *standard usage,* this being an ever-changing selection of the forms that are most widely used by good writers in formal contexts. The approach is to isolate those forms that give writers the most difficulty and then to present them with examples of standard and substandard forms, as:

Use possessive forms before a gerund.

STANDARD: I do not approve of *his* going.

COLLOQUIAL: I do not approve of *him* going.

For more information on this topic see VERBAL NOUNS IN -ING.

Grammatical topics are usually organized into categories associated with familiar terms. Because the modern handbooks are almost always written to advise writers, many topics besides grammar are included, from word choice, say, to punctuation, the preparation of manuscripts, and even matters of style. Prescriptive handbooks that give grammatical advice to speakers, as opposed to writers, have almost entirely disappeared from the market.

Advice on standard grammatical forms is frequently to be found under the following headings.

(1) *Sentences.* Writers are warned not to unknowingly use sentence fragments or fused sentences. The sentence, a unit of syntactically related words that can stand by itself as a statement, question, or command, is an extremely complicated idea for the scientific grammarian; yet recognition of its requirements, the inclusion of both subject and predicate, is still taken as essential for literate users of the language. Because the sentence is so fundamentally important to writers, as opposed to speakers, texts usually deal with sentence and nonsentence forms before any other topics are introduced. Aids are often supplied to help the unsure in recognizing essential elements. Forms are distinguished by the use of examples, as:

SENTENCE FRAGMENT: Hoping to win the prize.

CORRECTED: John hopes to win the prize.

FUSED SENTENCE: I am confused and unhappy I don't know a soul here.

CORRECTED: I am confused and unhappy, for I don't know a soul here.

CORRECTED: I am confused and unhappy. I don't know a soul here.

(2) *Modifiers.* Here the forms used to qualify the main elements of a sentence are distinguished. Frequently, the adjective forms, modifying nouns and pronouns, are confused with adverbial forms, modifying verbs, adjectives, and other adverbs:

MISUSE: The team's manager used his strategy *good.*

CORRECTED: The team's manager used his strategy *well.*

CORRECTED: The team's manager used good strategy.

Difficulties in selecting the appropriate comparative and superlative forms of adjectives (as, *good, better, best; lucky, luckier, luckiest*) can sometimes occur.

(3) *Case of nouns and pronouns.* Latin and other strongly inflected languages have an array of word endings and forms to indicate syntactic relationships. English has relatively few such indicators: for substantives (nouns and pronouns) there are three *cases* and two distinctions of *number,* singular and plural. English nouns actually alter their form in only two ways, to show possession and to show change in number: *girl, girl's; girls, girls'.* Pronouns, however, sometimes have different forms for all three cases, singular and plural: *I, my, mine, me; we, our, ours, us;* etc. The proper selection of these forms according to standard usage requires understanding of the cases. See CASE; ME.

MISUSE: Between you and I there is no real dispute.

CORRECTED: Between you and me there is no real dispute.

(4) *Verbs.* Because the forms of verbs can be varied by considerations of *voice, mood, tense, number, person,* and *aspect,* they can provide difficulty in many ways. Traditionally, students have been taught that to learn three verb forms, the *principal parts*—that is, the *infinitive, past tense,* and *past participle*—is to be able to derive all other forms. Thus, knowing the principal parts of the strong verb *ring* (*ring, rang, rung*) would allow the construction of such sentences as *Ring the bell for me. I want this bell to have been rung at least twice before sundown. Who rang?* Confusion can occur in the use of the principal parts themselves, as:

WRONG FORM: He *drunk* a glass of milk.

CORRECTED: He *drank* a glass of milk.

WRONG FORM: It's the best trick I've ever *sprang.*

CORRECTED: It's the best trick I've ever *sprung.*

Because verbs express so many varieties of meaning through changes of form, the chances of producing substandard grammar are many. A source of trouble is tense, especially when more than one verb is used in a single sentence:

MISUSE: In the snow he *traced* the marks where small rodents *have gone.*

CORRECTED: In the snow he *traced* the marks where small rodents *had gone.*

(5) *Agreement.* In choosing the correct forms of nouns, pronouns, and predicate verbs, consideration must be given as to how they relate to the forms of other words in the same sentence, especially regarding number. *Agreement,* as it is called, is required between subject and predicate verb and between pronoun and *antecedent* (the word for which it stands). Substandard grammar often violates this agreement, and the prescriptive grammarian offers corrections.

Pronoun and antecedent

MISUSE: The average *athlete* is subject to injury no matter how carefully *they train.* (singular, plural)

CORRECTED: The average *athlete* is subject to injury no matter how carefully *he or she trains.* (singular, singular)

Subject and predicate verb

MISUSE: I have no idea how *one* of those puzzles *work.* (singular, plural)

CORRECTED: I have no idea how *one* of those puzzles *works.* (singular, singular)

(6) *Traditional structure.* Most traditional grammar handbooks analyze the structure of English sentences by means of the parts of speech. The traditional system of analysis

further depends upon the ability of groups of words to perform the function of certain parts of speech, namely, of nouns, adjectives, and adverbs. These word groups are called *phrases* when the group contains no predicate verb and *subordinate clauses* when the predicate verb (and sometimes its subject) is present. Thus, an adjective function may be performed by a single word, an adjective: *I live in a* red *house*. Or by a phrase: *I live in a house* of red. Or by a subordinate clause: *I live in a house* that is red.

In this kind of analysis fundamental importance is placed on the capacity of words to combine into groups that function syntactically the way a single word does, although no one of the words within a group necessarily has the same function as the group as a whole. For example, the sentence *The children cheered the basket because they understood it to be the winning point* contains a clause, *because they understood it to be the winning point*. This clause contains no adverb, but as a whole it functions as an adverb in modifying the verb *cheered*. Thus, a terminology for such group functions emerges: *verbal, participle, gerund, nominative absolute*, and so on. Analysis of this sort appears to presume a complete descriptive grammar in which all sentences can be diagrammed by schemes and thus understood according to a regular grammatical system. The presumption is a false one, but the terminology is still used in order to recommend usages. More often than not, these have to do with punctuation and stylistic matters rather than with grammar proper. Two examples:

Use a comma after an introductory adverbial clause.

As the train came into view at last, our long month of waiting was nearly over.

Avoid dangling participial phrases.

AWKWARD: Having opened the bottle and brought it to his lips, his thirst was quenched.

REVISED: Having opened the bottle and brought it to his lips, he quenched his thirst.

See also DANGLING PHRASES.

grave accent. See DIACRITICS.

gray, grey. Nearly all Americans and some British prefer *gray*. A few Americans and most British prefer *grey*.

gray eminence. See ÉMINENCE GRISE.

grease, greasy. It has long been known, even by amateur observers of speech, that the verb *grease* and the adjective *greasy* are pronounced with /s/ or /z/ depending on where the speaker is from. This is a classic case of geographical variation; that is, the physical location of the speaker, and not social status or educational level, determines which pronunciation will be used. This /s/ versus /z/ situation is also a classic case in that it clearly divides the Northern dialect from the Southern and Midland dialects. Speakers in New England, New York, north and central Pennsylvania, Ohio, northern Indiana, Michigan, northern Illinois, Wisconsin, and most of the Western states, especially the northern ones, use /s/: /grēs/, /**grē**-sē/. South of these states the /z/ pronunciation dominates: /grēz/, /**grē**-zē/. There is a narrow region running westward through Pennsylvania, Ohio, Indiana, and Illinois, corresponding roughly to the area of the North Midland dialect, where both pronunciations are used.

The way America was settled accounts for this geographical division. The /s/ form originated in the New England colonies. Migration and settlement from this region spread the pronunciation westward throughout the northern states. The Middle and South Atlantic colonists used the /z/ form and subsequently spread this usage westward and generally south of the Ohio River.

Great Britain. See BRITAIN.

Greek words. Although the Greeks have been living in Greece continuously for about 4,000 years, their unique influence results from the very high level of civilization they attained between 500 B.C. and A.D. 200.

Transliterating Greek				
Single Letter	Name	Pronunciation	Modern	Latin
Α α	alpha	/ä/	ā	a
		/à/	a	a
Β β	beta	/b/	b	b
Γ γ	gamma	/g/	g	g
Δ δ	delta	/d/	d	d
Ε ε	epsilon	/ĕ/	e	e
Ζ ζ	zeta	/dz/	z	z
Η η	eta	/ā/	ē	e
Θ θ*	theta	/th/	th	th
Ι ι	iota	/ĭ/	i	i
		/ē/	ī	i
Κ κ	kappa	/k/	k	c
Λ λ	lambda	/l/	l	l
Μ μ	mu	/m/	m	m
Ν ν	nu	/n/	n	n
Ξ ξ	xi	/ks/	x	x
Ο ο	omicron	/ŏ/	o	o
Π π	pi	/p/	p	p
Ρ ρ	rho	/hr/	rh	rh
		/r/	r	r
Σ σ ς	sigma	/s/	s	s
Τ τ	tau	/t/	t	t
Υ υ	upsilon	/ü/	u	y
Φ φ*	phi	/f/	ph	ph

Transliterating Greek

Single Letter	Name	Pronunciation	Modern	Latin
Χ χ*	chi	/kh/	kh	ch
Ψ ψ	psi	/ps/	ps	ps
Ω ω	omega	/ō/	ō	o

Diphthong	Pronunciation	Modern	Latin
αι	/ī/	ai	ae
αυ	/ou/	au	au
ει	/ā/	ei	i
ευ	/ĕü/	eu	eu
οι	/oi/	oi	oe
ου	/o͞o/	ou	u

**Many specialists believe that these sounds were aspirated—that is, theta was pronounced /t-h/ as in* hothouse; *phi, /p-h/ as in* upheaval; *and chi, /k-h/ as in* jackhammer.

Greek ideas and insights, adopted wholeheartedly by the Romans, the Judeo-Christians, and later the Arabs, were lost sight of during the early Middle Ages and revived in the Renaissance. They are fundamental and all-pervasive in our culture to this day, and our modern vocabulary shows it.

The Greek name for Greece is *Hellas,* for the people *Hellenes,* and for the language *Hellenic.* The name *Greek* is from Latin *Graeci,* originally the name of a minor people in northwestern Hellas. The language, like Latin, is of Indo-European origin; see INDO-EUROPEAN.

Spelling and Pronunciation. The Greek alphabet differs from the Latin alphabet in several ways, and when the Romans borrowed Greek words, as they did by the thousand, they transliterated them into Latin equivalents. Most of the Greek words in English have not been taken directly from Greek but from the Latin versions (and often by way of French as well). Today, we have two systems of writing Greek words in our alphabet. For Greek words that we use in our own vocabulary, we mostly follow the Roman spelling—even if we have taken them directly from Greek. But for transliterating a Greek word as such, for example in an etymology, we use a modern spelling system. The table on these pages shows the Greek alphabet and the forms used for the two purposes.

The chief differences between the two systems are the letters kappa, chi, and upsilon and all but two of the diphthongs. Here are some examples of Greek names as they appear in the modern and Latin transliterations.

Modern	Latin
Oidipous	Oedipus
Kunikos	Cynicus
Aiguptos	Aegyptus
Kheirōn	Chiron

Note that the Romans also rendered the

Greek masculine ending *-os* as their equivalent, *-us*.

When Latin and Greek were taught as standard subjects in English and American schools, they were both at first pronounced as if they were English. By about 1850 linguistic scholars had reconstructed the correct speech sounds as used by the Greeks and Romans themselves. Since then, although not many schools now teach Greek, the restored pronunciation has been taught, as shown in the table on the preceding pages.

This, however, only applies to ancient Greek as ancient Greek. Greek words that have been borrowed into English conform to English pronunciation and generally follow the Latin spellings. Likewise the hundreds of Greek names that are familiar in English; the name of the philosopher *Sōkratēs* was pronounced **/sō-krǎ-tās/**, but in English it is spelled *Socrates* and pronounced **/sŏk-rə-tēz/**.

Vocabulary. Latin was so thoroughly permeated with borrowings from Greek that the two languages have in effect formed a fused Greco-Latin vocabulary source for European languages. Many Greek words, borrowed into Latin, have been transmitted by inheritance into Medieval French and then borrowed into Middle English. The same words have then often been adopted directly from Greek or Latin, sometimes several times over and in widely different forms and meanings. An example is the Greek word *parabolē*, literally 'something thrown alongside,' hence 'comparison, proverb, metaphor.' It was borrowed into Latin as *parabola*, keeping the Greek range of technical meanings. It then became a common word with the generalized meaning of 'speech, talk' and formed a verb, *parabolāre* = 'to talk.' This verb was inherited in French as *parler*, the everyday word for 'to talk,' from which English has borrowed such words as *parley* and *parliament*. The Latin word *parabola* in the language of the Christian church was used especially of the stories told by Jesus to illustrate his teachings. In this sense it was adopted into French as *parabole* and borrowed thence into English as *parable*. Finally, the original Greek word *parabolē* had also a technical use in geometry, and this (via Latin again) is the source of the English word *parabola;* see section 3, below.

Modern European languages including English are full of such *multiple borrowings* from Greek, and many borrowings have changed so much, like *parley*, that they are not on the face of it recognizable as Greek. In the selections given below, we have included mostly Greek borrowings that, even if they have come to us through Latin and French, remain identifiably Greek in form or meaning, or both. They are grouped as follows: (1) government and politics; (2) philosophy; (3) science; (4) medicine; (5) language and literature; (6) sports; and (7) miscellaneous words.

For a selection of Greek prefixes and suffixes used in English, see AFFIXES.

(1) Government and politics:

anarchy = absence of government: from Greek *anarkhia* = 'absence of government,' from *an-* = 'without' + *-arkhia* = 'rule, government'

aristocracy = (1) 'government by a hereditary class of nobles' (2) 'government by the best people': (via French and Latin) from Greek *aristokratia* = 'government by the best people or nobles,' from *aristoi* = 'the best people, the nobles' + *-kratia* = 'power, government'

democracy = 'government by the people': (via French and Latin) from Greek *dēmokratia*, from *dēmos* = 'the people' + *-kratia* = 'power, government'

monarchy = 'government by a single ruler': (via French and Latin) from Greek *monarkhia*, from *monos* = 'single, only' + *-arkhia* = 'rule, government'

oligarchy = 'government by a small privileged class': (via French and Latin) from Greek *oligarkhia*, from *oligoi* = 'the few' + *-arkhia* = 'rule, government'

ostracism = 'social isolation of an individual': from Greek *ostrakismos* = 'banishment of an individual by popular vote,' from *ostrakizein* = 'to write on a piece of pottery, vote,' from *ostrakon* = 'shell, tile, piece of pottery'

politics = 'the business and conduct of

government': from Greek *politika* = 'public or political affairs,' from *politikos* = 'public, relating to government, political,' from *politēs* = 'citizen'

(2) Philosophy:

Academy = 'Plato's school at Athens' See ACADEME, ACADEMIA, ACADEMY.

Cynic = 'follower of the philosopher Diogenes, practicing self-denial and rejection of convention'

ethos = 'moral code' See ETHIC, ETHOS.

logic = 'the science of accurate reasoning': (via French and Latin) from Greek *logikē tekhnē* = 'the art of discussion and reasoning,' from *logikē* = 'relating to discussion and reason' (from *logos* = 'word, reason') + *tekhnē* = 'art, craft, science'

metaphysics = 'philosophy dealing with the underlying nature of existence, or with reality beyond the physical world': (via Latin) from Greek *Ta Meta Ta Phusika* = 'the things after the Physics' (*meta* = 'after,' *phusika* = 'physics'), title of a book by Aristotle, so named because it was placed after his *Phusika* = 'Physics,' but also understood as meaning 'philosophy inquiring beyond physical realities'

philosophy = 'the pursuit of wisdom, the study of truth, underlying realities, human principles, etc.': (via French and Latin) from Greek *philosophia* = 'the activity of a philosopher, the thought or science pursued by philosophers,' from *philosophos* = 'lover of wisdom, philosopher,' from *philos* = 'loving, lover of' + *sophos* = 'wise'

* **skeptic** = 'one who doubts or denies the validity of knowledge'

sophist = 'one of a class of ancient Greek teachers who taught rules for success in life, rhetoric, and general education': from Greek *sophistēs* = 'expert, professional wise man,' from *sophizesthai* = 'to gain wisdom,' from *sophos* = 'wise'

Stoic = 'follower of the philosopher Zeno, practicing a rigorous pursuit of knowledge and virtuous behavior'

*Appears as separate entry

(3) Science:

arithmetic = 'computation of numbers': (via French and Latin) from Greek *arithmetikē tekhnē* = 'the art of numbers,' from *arithmetikos* = 'relating to numbers,' from *arithmos* = 'number' + *tekhnē* = 'art, science'

astronomy = 'the science dealing with the heavenly bodies': (via French and Latin) from Greek *astronomia* = 'the astronomer's science,' from *astronomos* = 'star-classifier, astronomer,' from *astron* = 'star' + *-nomos* = 'arranger, classifier'

atom = 'basic piece of matter constituting one of the elements, made up of a nucleus and a system of electrons': (via Latin) from Greek *atomos* = 'indivisible thing, the theoretical smallest piece of matter of which the universe is made,' from *a-* = 'not' + *tom-* = 'cut'

center = 'middle point, etc.': (via French and Latin) from Greek *kentron* = 'spike, point, pivoting point of a pair of compasses'

cone = (1) 'woody growth borne by pine trees, containing ovules' (2) 'geometric figure with a circular base and a pointed apex': (via French and Latin) from Greek *kōnos* = (1) 'pine cone' (2) 'geometric cone'

cylinder = 'geometric figure with a circular cross section': (via French and Latin) from Greek *kulindros* = 'roller, cylinder,' from *kulindein* = 'to revolve'

eclipse = 'an obscuring of the sun or moon': (via French or Latin) from Greek *ekleipsis* = 'a leaving out, a ceasing,' from *ekleipein* = 'to leave out, cease,' from *ek-* = 'out' + *leipein* = 'to leave'

ellipse = 'a specific type of plane curve': (via Latin) from Greek *elleipsis* = 'a falling short,' from *elleipein* = 'to fall short, leave within,' from *en-* = 'in' + *leipein* = 'to leave'; the geometric curve was defined as a section through a cone and was named 'the falling short' because its angle of intersection is less than (that is, falls short of) the equivalent angle for a parabola

geography = 'the science of mapping and

describing the earth': (via Latin) from Greek *geōgraphia* = 'earth-description,' from *gē* = 'earth' + *-graphia* = 'writing, description'

geometry = 'the science of spatial measurements and relationships': (via French and Latin) from Greek *geōmetria* = 'land-surveying, earth-measurement, geometry,' from *gē* = 'land, the earth' + *-metria* = 'measurement'

machine = 'device with moving parts for applying power, etc.': from French *machine,* from Latin *machina,* from (Doric) Greek *mākhanā* = 'device, machine,' variant of Attic Greek *mēkhanē,* from *mēkhos* = 'device, means'

magnet = 'piece of iron with the property of attracting other pieces': (via French and Latin) from Greek *Magnēs lithos* = 'the Magnesian stone' (name of various minerals including natural lodestones), from *Magnēs* = 'from Magnesia' (a region in Thessaly known for minerals) + *lithos* = 'stone'

mathematics = 'the science of numbers, relationships, etc.': (via French and Latin) from Greek *mathēmatika* = 'the sciences (including arithmetic, geometry, astronomy, physics),' from *mathēma* = 'learning, science,' from *math-* = 'to learn'

mechanical = 'relating to machines': (via French and Latin) from Greek *mēkhanikos,* from *mēkhanē* = 'device, machine'

parabola = 'a specific type of plane curve': (via Latin) from Greek *parabola* = 'something thrown alongside, something parallel,' from *para-* = 'alongside' + *bol-* = 'to project'; the geometric curve was defined as a conic section parallel to an element of the cone

physics = 'the science of matter, energy, etc.': (via Latin) from Greek *Ta Phusika* = 'the natural things,' title of a book by Aristotle on the phenomena of nature, from *phusikos* = 'natural,' from *phusis* = 'nature'

pi = 'the ratio of a circle's circumference to its diameter': from Greek *pi* = 'the letter π or *p*,' standing for *perimetros* = 'circumference, perimeter,' used by Archimedes for the ratio

planet = 'large heavenly body that revolves around the sun or another star': (via French and Latin) from Greek *planētēs* = 'wanderer,' from *planān* = 'to wander' (since the visible planets appear to "wander in the heavens," unlike the "fixed stars")

sphere = 'geometric body or surface formed by rotating a circle': from French *sphère,* from Latin *sphaera,* from Greek *sphaira* = 'ball, globe, geometric sphere'

tropic = 'either of two circles on the earth, 23 degrees and 27 minutes from the equator, at the northern and southern limits of the vertical noonday sun': (via Latin) from Greek *tropikos kuklos* = 'circle at the point of (the sun's) turning,' from *tropikos* = 'relating to turning' (from *tropē* = 'a turning') + *kuklos* = 'circle'

zodiac = 'the belt in the night sky containing the paths of the planets, the moon, and the sun, and the 12 original constellations': (via French and Latin) from Greek *zōdiakos kuklos* = 'circle of the constellations,' from *zōdion* = 'animal symbol, constellation symbolized as an animal' + *kuklos* = 'circle'

(4) Medicine:

anatomy = (1) 'the structure of animal bodies' (2) 'the study of this structure': (via Latin) from Greek *anatomia* = 'a cutting up, dissection of bodies,' from *ana-* = 'up, in pieces' + *tom-* = 'cut'

arthritis = 'inflammation of a joint or joints': (via Latin) from Greek *arthritis* = 'disease of a joint,' from *arthron* = 'joint'

cardiac = 'relating to the heart': (via Latin) from Greek *kardiakos,* from *kardia* = 'heart'

clinic = (1) 'class for medical students using patients in bed as case studies' (2) 'medical center serving outpatients': from French *clinique* = 'bedside teaching session,' from Greek *klinikē* = 'physician's attendance on patients in bed,' from *klinē* = 'bed'

diagnosis = 'identification and description of disease': from Greek *diagnōsis* = 'the act of discerning or distinguishing,' from *dia* = 'through, all the way through' + *gnōsis* = 'knowing'

diarrhea = 'abnormally loose or liquid excretion': from Latin *diarrhoea,* from Greek *diarrhoia* = 'a flowing through,' from *dia* = 'through' + *rrhoia* = 'flow'

diet = (1) 'controlled program of eating' (2) 'food and drink customarily eaten': (via French and Latin) from Greek *diaita* = 'way of life, controlled program of eating for athletes in training,' also 'controlled program of eating, exercise, and activity in the interests of health,' from *diaitān* = 'to control, lead one's life,' from *dia* = 'through, among' + *ait-* = 'to allot'

hemorrhage = 'heavy discharge of blood': (via French and Latin) from Greek *haimorrhagia* = 'a breaking out of blood,' from *haima* = 'blood' + *-rrhagia* = 'a bursting'

Hippocratic oath = 'oath of professional ethics sworn by newly qualified physicians': traditionally associated with the Greek physician *Hippocrates* (c. 469–399 B.C.)

pancreas = 'large gland behind the stomach secreting enzymes and insulin': from Greek *pankreas* = 'all-flesh' (presumably because it is entirely softish tissue), from *pan* = 'all' + *kreas* = 'flesh'

pharmacy = (1) 'the use of drugs in medicine' (2) 'druggist's shop': (via French and Latin) from Greek *pharmakeia* = 'medicinal drug,' also 'poison, magic charm'

* **prostate** = 'gland surrounding the male urethra next to the bladder, and secreting the seminal fluid': from Greek *prostatēs* = 'guard, one that stands in front of an entrance' (referring to the gland's position relative to the bladder), from *pro-* = 'in front' + *sta-* = 'stand'

*Appears as separate entry

(5) Language and literature:

alphabet = 'system of phonetic letters used to write a language, arranged in a customary order': (via Latin) from Greek *alphabētos,* from the first two letters of the Greek alphabet, *alpha* and *bēta*

* **dialect** = 'regional or social variety of a language'

drama = 'a play' For this and other terms of Greek drama see THEATER TERMS.

epic (poem) = 'long heroic narrative poem': (via Latin) from Greek *epikos* = 'relating to epic poetry,' from *epos* = 'word, story, epic poem'

* **epithet** = 'adjective or descriptive phrase': from Greek *epitheton* = 'something added, an attributive word or phrase,' from *epi-* = 'onto' + *the-* = 'put'

* **etymology** = 'word history'

* **grammar** = (1) 'the structure of language' (2) 'the study of this': from French *grammaire,* from Latin *grammatica,* from Greek *grammatikē tekhnē* = 'the literary art, linguistics and literary criticism, the art of reading and writing,' from *grammata* = 'letters, writing, literature' + *tekhnē* = 'art'

history = (1) 'past events' (2) 'a description of this': (via Latin) from Greek *historia* = 'knowledge gained by investigation, research, narrative, history,' from *histōr* = 'one who knows, learned man'

homonym = 'word having the same form as another but a different meaning': (via Latin) from Greek *homōnumon,* literally 'same-name,' hence 'thing having the same name,' from *homos* = 'same' + *onuma* = 'name' See HOMOGRAPH, HOMOPHONE, HOMONYM.

* **idiom** = 'an expression or usage that is traditionally correct but does not necessarily follow general rules': (via Latin) from Greek *idiōma* = 'private property, peculiar phraseology,' from *idios* = 'private'

lyric (poem) = 'poem that is typically short, divided into verses, and expressive of the poet's personal feelings': (via French and Latin) from Greek *lurikos* = 'suitable for (singing to) the lyre,' from *lura* = 'lyre'

ode = 'formal poem of lyrical type, often of rather exalted subject and feeling': from

French *ode*, from Latin *ōdē*, from Greek *ōidē* or *aoidē* = 'song, sung poem, lyric'

phrase = 'meaningful sequence of words, not forming a sentence or clause but typically substitutable for a single part of speech': (via Latin) from Greek *phrasis* = 'speech, phrase,' from *phrazein* = 'to speak'

poem = 'composition, most often written in some meter or rhythm, with or without rhyme, typically expressing imaginative, intimate, or elevated feelings': (via French and Latin) from Greek *poēma, poiēma* = 'something created, a poem,' from *poiein* = 'to make, create' See POETRY.

poet = 'writer of poems': (via French and Latin) from Greek *poētēs* = 'creator, maker,' from *poiein* = 'to make, create'

rhetoric = (1) 'the art of public speaking' (2) 'the study of effective writing': (via French and Latin) from Greek *rhētorikē tekhnē* = 'the art of public speaking,' from *rhētōr* = 'public speaker' + *tekhnē* = 'art' See FIGURES OF SPEECH.

rhythm = 'metrical pattern of language': (via French and Latin) from Greek *rhuthmos* = 'flowing movement, metrical pattern, rhythm,' from *rheu-* = 'to flow'

***synonym** = 'word that means the same thing as another': (via Latin) from Greek *sunōnumon* = 'together-word, word having the same meaning as another,' from *sun-* = 'with, together' + *onoma* = 'name'

syntax = 'the branch of grammar dealing with the grouping and ordering of words': (via Latin) from Greek *syntaxis* = 'arrangement together, ordering,' from *sun-* = 'with, together' + *taxis* = 'arrangement, rank'

*Appears as separate entry

(6) Sports:

athlete = 'person trained in sports, games, and exercises requiring physical strength, control, and skill': (via Latin) from Greek *athlētēs* = 'one who competes for a prize (in the games),' from *athlon* = 'prize'

discus = 'disk-shaped object, thrown competitively for distance in athletics': from Latin *discus*, from Greek *diskos* = 'discus, quoit,' literally 'missile,' from *dikein* = 'to throw'

gymnasium = 'room or building equipped for exercises in strength and body control': from Latin *gymnasium*, from Greek *gymnasion* = 'gymnastic school,' from *gymnazein* = 'to exercise naked, do gymnastic exercises,' from *gymnos* = 'naked'

marathon = 'footrace of 26 miles, 385 yards': introduced as a race for the first modern Olympic games in 1896, in memory of the Athenian runner who brought the news of the Battle of *Marathon* (490 B.C.) to Athens

Olympic games = 'international athletic sports held every four years since 1896': based on the *Olympian games*, a festival in honor of Olympian Zeus, held every four years from 776 B.C. to A.D. 390, and including athletic games in which the cities of Greece competed

pentathlon = 'athletic competition comprising five separate events, now either long jump, high jump, 200-meter dash, discus, and 1,500-meter run, or fencing, pistol shooting, 300-meter swim, 4,000-meter cross-country run, and 5,000-meter horse race over jumps': from Greek *pentathlon* = 'contest of five events, running, jumping, discus, javelin, and wrestling,' from *pente* = 'five' + *athlon* = 'prize, contest'

stadium = 'field for athletics and other sports, usually with tiers of seats for spectators': from Latin *stadium*, from Greek *stadion* = 'running track, typically having a circuit of about a quarter of a mile with 200-yard straights, some with stone seats for spectators'

(7) Miscellaneous words:

***aesthetic** = 'relating to perception of beauty': from Greek *aisthētikos* = 'relating to perception,' from *aisthanesthai* = 'to perceive'

anthology = 'collection of pieces or extracts of writing': from Greek *anthologia* = 'a gathering of flowers, collection of choice short poems or epigrams,' from *anthos* =

'flower' + *-logia* = 'collection,' from *legein* = 'to collect'

architect = 'professional designer of buildings': (via French, Italian, and Latin) from Greek *arkhitektōn* = 'chief builder,' from *arkhi-* = 'chief' + *tektōn* = 'carpenter, builder'

* **barbarian, barbaric, barbarous** = 'uncivilized, etc.': (via French and Latin) from Greek *barbaros* = 'non-Greek-speaking, foreign, uncivilized'

ceramic = 'relating to pottery': from Greek *keramikos,* from *keramos* = 'pottery'

chaos = (1) 'formless space existing before the universe' (2) 'extreme confusion': (via Latin) from Greek *khaos* = 'empty space'

cycle = 'period or sequence that is repeated, circular arrangement, etc.': from Latin *cyclus,* from Greek *kuklos* = 'wheel, circle, cycle'

dynamic = (1) 'relating to force in motion' (2) 'forceful, vigorous': from Greek *dunamikos* = 'forceful,' from *dunamis* = 'power'

echo = 'reproduction of a sound by reflection off a surface': (via French and Latin) from Greek *ēkhō* = 'resonant noise, echo'

eclectic = 'bringing together various elements or bits and pieces from different sources': from Greek *eklektikos* = 'choosing out,' from *eklegein* = 'to choose out,' from *ek-* = 'out' + *legein* = 'to gather, choose'

ecstasy = 'transcendent joy': (via French and Latin) from Greek *ekstasis* = 'state of being put out (of one's normal mind),' from *ek-* = 'out' + *stasis* = 'a standing, being out'

energy = 'power of action, personal vigor, etc.': (via Latin) from Greek *energeia* = 'inherent ability to operate, power of functioning,' from *energēs* = 'working within, inherently operative,' from *en-* = 'in' + *ergon* = 'work'

* **epitome** = 'brief summary, perfectly representative example (of something)'

erotic = 'relating to or arousing sexual desire': (via French) from Greek *erōtikos* from *erōt-, erōs* = 'love, sexual desire'

* **ethnic** = 'relating to a cultural group or race'

* **euphemism** = 'word or language used to avoid offensiveness or taboo'

harmony = (1) 'combination of musical notes in a chord' (2) 'agreement and integration of parts or elements': (via French and Latin) from Greek *harmonia* = a fitting together, agreement, musical harmony,' from *harmozein* = 'to fit together'

hero = 'famous or mythic warrior, admired man, champion, etc.': (via Latin) from Greek *hērō* = 'mythic personage (usually male, sometimes female) worshipped as a semidivine spirit'

hilarious = 'delightfully funny': (via Latin) from Greek *hilaros* = 'cheerful, gay'

* **hubris** = 'excessive pride, arrogance'

idea = 'concept, thought, mental picture, etc.': (via Latin) from Greek *idea* = 'form, mental form, concept'

idiot = 'fool': (via French and Latin) from Greek *idiōtēs* = 'private citizen, non-expert, lay person,' hence 'ignorant person,' from *idios* = 'private'

melody = 'sequence of musical sounds forming a tune': (via French and Latin) from Greek *melōidia* = 'choral song,' from *melos* = 'tune' + *-ōidia* = 'singing'

metamorphosis = 'transformation': (via Latin) from Greek *metamorphōsis* = 'transformation,' from *metamorphousthai* = 'to be reshaped,' from *meta-* = 'across (expressing change)' + *morphoeisthai* = 'to be shaped'

method = 'systematic way of doing something': (via Latin) from Greek *methodos,* literally 'a journey after something,' hence 'pursuit of knowledge, systematic way of investigating,' from *meta-* = 'after' + *hodos* = 'way, journey'

microcosm = 'miniature world or universe, especially human nature regarded as a miniature reflection of the universe': (via Medieval Latin) from Greek *mikros kosmos* = 'little world'

monopoly = 'exclusive control, especially of the selling of a product': (via Latin) from Greek *monopōlion* = 'sole selling (control),' from *monos* = 'only, sole' + *pōlein* = 'to sell'

music = 'the art of playing tuneful instruments, singing, etc.': (via French and Latin) from Greek *mousikē tekhnē* = 'the Muses' art,' then including poetry and literature and dance as well as music, from *mousikē* = 'relating to the Muses,' from *Mousa* = 'Muse, one of the nine goddesses presiding over the arts'

mystery = 'anything secret or inexplicable': (via French and Latin) from Greek *mustērion* = 'secret ritual, especially secret cult of Demeter at Eleusis,' from *mustēs* = 'an initiate,' from *muein* = 'to close the eyes, close the mouth, keep a secret'

myth = 'traditional story often involving forces of nature, gods, heroes, and animals, as well as mortals, and usually illustrating religious belief': (via Latin) from Greek *muthos* = 'story, myth'

nautical = 'relating to ships, sailors, or navigation': (via Latin) from Greek *nautikos* = 'relating to sailors,' from *nautēs* = 'sailor,' from *naus* = 'ship'

* **nemesis** = (1) 'a force of retribution' (2) 'avenger, inveterate rival or enemy'

nymph = 'female nature spirit': (via Latin) from Greek *numphē* = 'young unmarried woman,' hence 'nymph'

ocean = 'any of the largest bodies of sea': (via French and Latin) from Greek *Ōkeanos* = 'name of the river believed to flow continuously around the disk of the earth'

olive = 'fruit of a tree native to the Mediterranean region, used as food and as the source of an edible and flammable oil': (via French) from Latin *olīva* = 'olive, olive tree,' an early borrowing from Greek *elaiwa* = 'olive; olive tree'

organ = (1) 'keyboard instrument with pipes blown by a bellows' (2) 'part of an animal or plant regarded as a functioning unit': (via French) from Latin *organum* = 'tool,' also 'animal or plant part regarded as a tool,' also 'pipe organ,' from Greek *organon* = 'tool, instrument, animal or plant part regarded as a tool'

plastic = (1) (adjective) 'relating to modeling or sculpture' (2) (noun) 'any of numerous easily moldable organic compounds': (via French and Latin) from Greek *plastikos* = 'able to be molded,' from *plassein* = 'to mold'

psyche = 'the mind': from Greek *psukhē* = 'breath, breath of life,' hence 'soul'

school = 'place of teaching': Old English *scol,* from Latin *schola,* from Greek *skholē* = 'leisure,' hence 'leisure devoted to learning, school'

strategy = (1) 'the art of using military forces on a large scale, generalship' (2) 'planned maneuvering, as in business': from Greek *stratēgia* = 'generalship,' from *stratēgos* = 'army-leader, general,' from *stratos* = 'army' + *ēg-,* *ag-* = 'lead'

sympathy = 'fellow feeling, sensitive understanding between persons': (via Latin) from Greek *sumpathia* = 'the state of fellow-feeling,' from *sumpathēs* = 'having feelings in common,' from *sum-* = 'together' + *pathein* = 'to feel, experience'

symposium = 'academic conference': (via Latin) from Greek *sumposion* = 'drinking party,' from *sum-* = 'together' + *pos-* = 'drink'

technical = 'relating to arts, crafts, complex industrial processes, scientific or scholarly methods, etc.': from Greek *tekhnikos* = 'relating to art or craft,' from *tekhnē* = 'art, craft, skill'

theology = 'the study of the divine': (via Latin) from Greek *theologia* = 'study of the gods,' from *theos* = 'god' + *-logia* = 'study'

tone = (1) 'clear musical sound' (2) 'manner or expression, etc.': (via French and Latin) from Greek *tonos,* literally 'a stretching (of a musical string),' hence 'musical sound made by a string'

*Appears as separate entry

guerrilla. This Spanish word for 'little war' (diminutive of *guerra* = 'war') came into English during the Napoleonic Wars, when Spanish irregulars played a large part in defeating the regular French armies occupying Spain. The word is used either as an attributive (*guerrilla warfare, guerrilla forces*) or as a noun for an individual member of an irregular band (*interviewed a guerrilla in the field*). The variant spelling *guerilla* is preferred by some. We recommend *guerrilla.*

Gulf Southern dialect. This dialect is a subdivision of the SOUTHERN DIALECT. It is spoken chiefly in Alabama, Mississippi, Louisiana, southern Arkansas, and eastern Texas. In the early 19th century, as the cotton economy grew, planters and farmers from the coastal settlements of Virginia, the Carolinas, and Georgia migrated into the Gulf States, bringing with them Southern colonial English. The uniformity and stability of the migrants' farming culture helped to preserve the Southern features of this dialect.

Before the migration from the east, southern Louisiana already had a sizable population. One of its most influential groups was the Acadians, French settlers who had been deported from eastern Canada in 1755 and relocated in the New Orleans area. This French-speaking population has given many loanwords to the Gulf Southern dialect. Some of these have spread outward from the New Orleans focal area, while others have remained in southern Louisiana.

Vocabulary. (1) Some of the most commonly used words of French origin in the Gulf Southern region:

armoire = 'wardrobe'
bagasse = 'waste from sugar cane'
banquette = 'sidewalk'
bayou = 'small *stream'
bisque = 'rich soup'
boudin = 'kind of soup'
brulee = (1) 'burned clearing' (2) 'brandy drink'
cabine = 'privy'
cheniere /shĭn-ə-rē/ = 'tree-covered mound'
couche-couche /ko͞osh-ko͞osh/ = 'cornmeal dish'

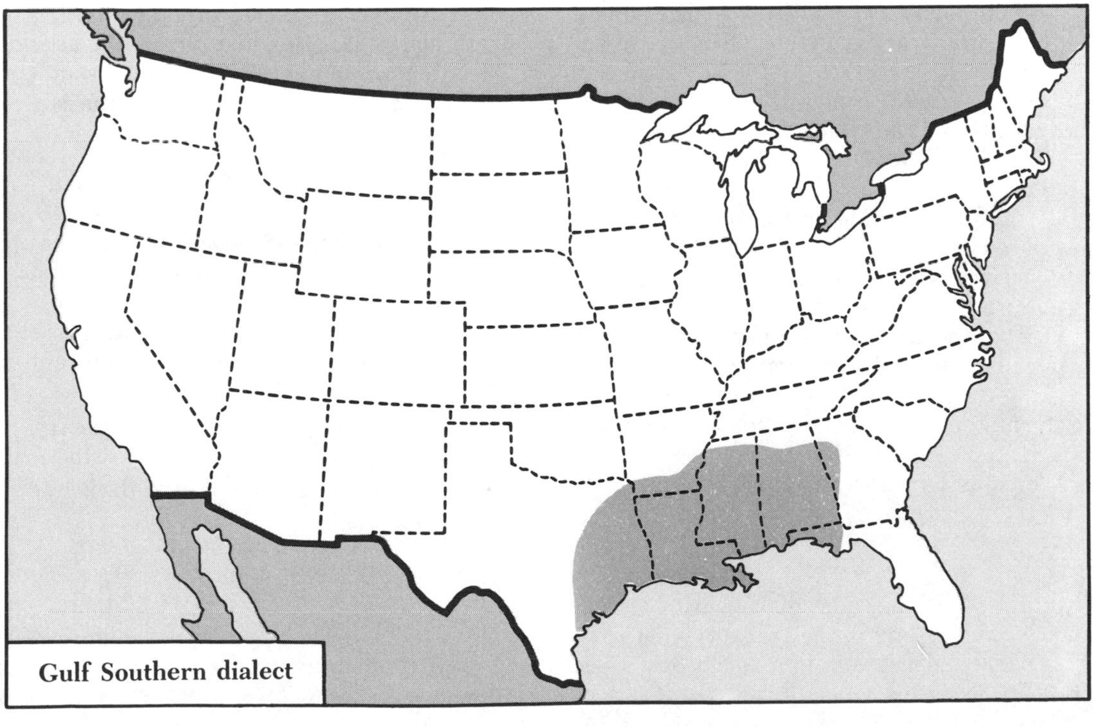

Gulf Southern dialect

coulee = 'pool'
fais-dodo = 'family party'
flottant /flō-**täɴ**/ = 'marshy prairie, bog'
galerie, gallery = '*porch'
gris-gris = 'charm, hoodoo'
jambalaya = 'rice dish'
marais /mä-**rā**/ = 'swamp'
memere /mĕ-**mâr**/ = 'grandmother'
nanan /**nä**-nă, **nä**-**năɴ**/ = 'godmother'
parrain /pä-**rā**, pä-**răɴ**/ = 'godfather'
pepere /pĕ-**pâr**/ = 'grandfather'
pirogue = 'small river boat'
poule d'eau /po͞ol **dō**/, **pooldoo** /**po͞ol**-do͞o/ = 'coot, mud hen'

*Appears as separate entry

(2) Words in more general use in the Gulf Southern region:

civet cat (also Western) = 'skunk'
clothes locker, locker = 'closet'
cream cheese = '*cottage cheese'
croker bag *or* **sack** = '*gunnysack'
dusk dark (used especially by black speakers) = 'dusk'
flitters (also South Midland) = '*pancakes'
for (a particular time) = 'at': *for eight o'clock*
French harp (also Midland) = 'harmonica'
get down (from a bus) = 'to step down, alight'
***gumbo** = 'soup containing *okra'
hydrant = 'water faucet'
kiyoodle /kī-**yo͞od**'l/ = 'worthless dog, mongrel'
lagniappe = 'bonus or present given with a purchase'
net wire fence = 'wire mesh fence'
neutral ground = 'median strip'
nit fly (also Midland) = 'horse botfly'
pecan patty (old-fashioned) = 'praline'
praline = 'candy made with pecans'
storm house (also South Midland) = 'storm cellar'
We caught rain = 'It rained'

*Appears as separate entry

Gullah. The black dialect known as *Gullah* or *Geechee* is one of the two surviving English creole languages in the United States (see PIDGIN AND CREOLE LANGUAGES). It is spoken on the Sea Islands and mainland coast of South Carolina and Georgia, from Georgetown, South Carolina, to the northern border of Florida.

The name *Gullah* itself probably derives from either of two West African tribal names—*Gola,* name of a people in Liberia, or *Ngola,* name of a people in Angola—or possibly from both. The alternative name *Geechee* is from the *Ogeechee* River in Georgia, which itself is probably named after a Liberian tribe, the *Geechee* or *Geejee.* The best-known literary rendering of this dialect is in DuBose Heyward's novel *Porgy* (1925), an authentic portrayal of Gullah life in Charleston that George Gershwin used as the basis of his opera *Porgy and Bess.*

Origin. The West African languages such as Wolof, Mende, and Yoruba, brought to America by slaves in the 18th and early 19th centuries, melded with English to form a pidgin language. During several generations of slave life on the coastal and island plantations, this synthetic language evolved into the full-fledged creole language called Gullah, which today still has many of the features of West African grammar, pronunciation, and vocabulary. The isolation of the Sea Islands from the mainland has been an important factor in preserving these African features.

Grammar. Among the most remarkable grammatical features of Gullah are the use of the verb *duh* = 'to be'; the system of comparison of adjectives; the special role of word order; and the general absence of tense, number, and the sign of the possessive.

(1) The verb *duh* /dŭ/ is used for past, present, or future meaning, with only the context showing the tense:

> "Now de cillen duh fret" = 'Now the children are fretting.'
> "I know duh Augus'" = 'I know it was August.'
> "Dey say duh gwine fall in on us" = 'They said it was going to fall in on us.'
> —from Lorenzo Turner, *Africanisms in the Gullah Dialect*

(2) The comparative and superlative degrees of adjectives are expressed with forms of the

English verb *pass* or *surpass*, or with *mo' na* = 'more than':

"'E tall pass me" = 'He is taller than I.'
"'E big mo' na una" = 'He is bigger than you.'
"Uh see uh sperrit, one big w'ite sump'n high mo' nuh dis house" = 'I saw a spirit, a big white thing higher than this house.'
—from Ambrose Gonzales, *With Aesop Along the Black Border*

(3) The word order of Gullah can be very complicated. In one of the commonest patterns, speakers begin a sentence with a subject or an object and then repeat this with a pronoun:

Two basket, what it come to? = 'What do two baskets come to?'
We what have been on de place, we save one or two = 'We who had been in the place saved one or two.'
Da gal him bin peruse 'long de road = 'The girl was sauntering along the road.'

(4) Tense or time of action is rarely indicated, though the future is sometimes marked by *gwine* or *going*, without *to:*

De deer jump out de t'icket = 'The deer jumped out of the thicket.'
Me duh gwine gone = 'I am going to go.'

The plural and singular forms of nouns are usually the same:

dem boy = 'those boys'
fi dog = 'five dogs'

Similarly, the possessive *'s* is usually omitted:

"I tek two duck, bakin, flour en' sugar en' tea, den I pit fibe dolluh een Mary lap" = 'in Mary's lap'
—from Ambrose Gonzales, *With Aesop Along the Black Border*

Pronunciation. The Gullah phonetic system is very complicated, in part because of its African sources. It has, for instance, several consonant sounds that are not found in English or any other Indo-European language. Some examples:

(1) /kp/ as in *kpakpa* = 'to pound' (from Mende)
(2) /gb/ as in *gbla* = 'near' (from Mende)
(3) /mb/ as in *Mbila*, a personal name (from Kongo)
(4) /mp/ as in *mpuku* = 'rat' (from Kongo)
(5) /nd/ as in *Ndombe*, a personal name (from Kongo, meaning 'blackness')
(6) /nt/ as in *Ntama*, a personal name (from Twi)

In addition, like many West African languages, Gullah uses variations in tone level in its pronunciations.

Some other distinctive pronunciation features:

(1) *Hair, James, raisin, give, itch, whicker* are all often pronounced with the sound /ē/: /hēr/, /jēmz/, /**rē**-zən/, /gēv/, /ēch/, /**hwē**-kər/.
(2) *Weave, screech, creek, general, deaf, January, such, put, tombstone* are often pronounced with /ĭ/: /wĭv/, /skrĭch/, /krĭk/, /**jĭn**-ər-əl/, /dĭf/, /**jĭn**-yo͞o-ĕr-ē/, /sĭch/, /pĭt/, /**tĭm**-stōn/.
(3) *Make, take, brother, shut, touch* are pronounced with /ĕ/: /mĕk/, /tĕk/, /**brĕ*th***-ər/, /shĕt/, /tĕch/.
(4) *Back, half, aunt, barn, march, calm, father* are pronounced with the vowel /ȧ/: /bȧk/, /hȧf/, /ȧnt/, /bȧn/, /mȧch/, /cȧm/, /**fȧ**-*th*ər/.
(5) *Borrow, corn, coffee, dog, wash, bundle, color* are pronounced with the sound /ȯ/: /**bȯr**-ō/, /kȯrn/, /**kȯf**-ē/, /dȯg/, /wȯsh/, /**bȯnd**'l/, /**kȯ**-lər/.
(6) *Shrimp* and *shrink* are pronounced /srĭmp/ and /srĭngk/.
(7) The sound /l/ often replaces /r/ in such words as *proud, fritter, Mary, bureau, war:* /ploud/, /**flĭt**-ər/, /**mĕl**-ē/, /**byo͞o**-lō/, /wôl/.
(8) The sound /r/ is usually dropped after vowels.

Vocabulary. (1) Africanisms. Nearly 6,000 African words have been identified in Gullah. Although most of these are in personal names, such as *Batumba* (Kongo for 'equality') and *Jala* (Vai for 'lion'), there are also many everyday words that have African origins:

be = 'to clear or clean': *Be de groun* = 'Clear the ground.' (from Wolof)
bento = 'coffin' (from Temne)
boma = 'large snake' (from Kongo)

bong = 'tooth' (from Wolof)
buckra = 'white man' (from Ibo)
det = 'a hard rain' (from Wolof)
dindy = 'small child' (from Vai)
do /dō/ = 'child' (from Mende)
duh = (1) (verb) 'to be' (from Ibo); see Grammar (1), above, (2) (preposition) 'to, in order to': *Una go duh grin' em* = 'You go to grind it.' (from Ewe)
gafa = 'evil spirit' (from Mende)
guba = 'peanut, *goober' (from Fula)
gulu = 'pig' (from Kongo)
***gumbo** = '*okra' (from Umbundu)
jamba = 'elephant' (from Umbundu)
jambi = 'red sweet potato' (from Vai)
jiga = 'insect' (from Wolof)
juju = 'magic, evil spirit' (from Hausa)
***juke** = 'disorderly, wicked' (from Wolof)
kunu = 'boat' (from Bambara)
kuta = 'tortoise' (from Bambara)
menga = 'blood' (from Kongo)
na = 'and' (from Twi)
nansey = 'spider' (from Twi, Fante)
pinda = 'peanut, pinder' (from Kongo)
pojo = 'heron, poor joe' (from Vai)
saku = '*gunnysack, crocus bag' (from Kongo)
samba = 'to dance' (from Hausa)
tawa = 'to be greedy' (from Kongo)
tot = 'to carry' (from Kongo, Umbundu)
una = 'you, your' (from Ibo)
wula = 'a heavy rain' (from Kongo)
yam, yambi = 'sweet potato' (from Mende)
ye, yeye = 'eye' (from Bambara)

*Appears as separate entry

(2) Gullah expressions not deriving from African origins, but developed from English:

alltwo = 'both'
bad mouth = 'spell, curse'
bedout = 'without, unless, except'
binnuh = 'been, was, was a': *w'en uh binnuh boy* = 'when I was a boy'
blan = 'belong'; used redundantly: *Da' dog him blan b'longs to my sistuh* = 'That dog it belongs [*or* used to belong] to my sister.'
bloodynoun = 'bullfrog'
dayclean = 'broad daylight'
enty, yenty = 'ain't it, are they not'
first dark = 'dusk, twilight'
for soul = 'very, truly'; used emphatically: *'E fat fuh soul* = 'He [*or* she] is very fat.'
for true = 'in truth, it is so'
gwine = 'going, going to'
him = 'he, she, it, his, her, its'
lawfully lady = 'wife'
lukkah = 'like, resembling'
me = 'I, my'
middleday = 'noon'
middlenight = 'midnight'
peruse = 'to saunter, walk leisurely'
quizzit = 'to ask or question'
racktify = (1) (verb) 'to break' (2) (adjective) 'broken; mentally confused'
she own = 'her own'
she-she talk = 'woman's talk, gabble'
sukkuh = 'same, same as, resembling' (contraction of *same lukkah*)
sunhot = 'sunshine, heat of the sun'
take one's foot in one's hand = 'to hasten, hurry, speed up'
toad = 'young female dog'
toad-frog = 'toad'
wedduh = 'to rain or storm': *'E gwine tuh wedduh* = 'It's going to rain [*or* storm].'
we own = 'our own, ours'
why make so = 'what makes it so, why'
yeddy, yerry = 'to hear'; used for all tenses and persons: *When Joe yeddy de woice, 'e run out* = 'When Joe heard the voice, he ran out.'

Example.

One time, Dog t'ief piece uh meat frum de Buckruh, en' run'way. 'E come to de branch, en' 'e staa't fuh cross'um 'pun de plank wuh de Buckruh hab fuh bridge. W'en de Dog git middle uh de plank, 'e look 'puntop de watuh, en' 'e see 'e shadduh, him en' de meat, alltwo. De shadduh look big, fuh true. De Dog say to 'eself, "Eh, eh! De meat wuh da' debble 'ub'uh dog got, look big mo'nuh my'own. Uh gwine graff'um, en' den Uh fuh hab two piece." 'E op'n 'e mout' fuh graff de t'odduh dog' meat, en' him own meat drap out 'e mout' en' gone'way! De Dog say to 'eself, "Uh done loss my'own, but da' t'odduh meat in de watuh, mo' bigguh. Uh fuh hab *him.*" But w'en 'e look fuhr'um, de shadduh, 'self, done gone! De Dog

> heng 'e tail, 'e tek 'e foot een 'e han' en' 'e gone home to de Buckruh' yaa'd. 'E h'aa't hebby, en' e belly light.
>
> —from Ambrose Gonzales, *With Aesop Along the Black Border*

gumbo. This word, originally Southern but now known everywhere, is borrowed from Louisiana French *gombo,* basically meaning 'okra pods' and hence also 'thick soup or stew made with okra.' The Louisiana word in turn is an Africanism from Angola, where the Kimbundu word for okra is *ochin-gombo.* The okra plant is native to West Africa, and the word *okra* itself is also of African origin. See OKRA.

gung-ho. This word was adopted from Chinese in 1942 by U.S. troops in China. As Marine Corps General Evans Carlson recalled for *Life* magazine: "I told [my men] of the motto of the Chinese Cooperatives, *Gung Ho.* It means Work Together. My motto caught on and they began to call themselves the Gung Ho battalion." In general Marine Corps usage, however, the word soon came to mean 'far too keen, dangerously aggressive':

> It bugs you worse when you can't put the guy in a neat little slot, when you know he's as likely to turn into a . . . gung ho madman as a yellow belly or a psycho case.
>
> —Walter F. Murphy, *The Vicar of Christ*

It has passed into the English language in senses ranging from the mildly apologetic (= 'terrifically keen') to the outright disapproving (= 'obnoxiously keen'):

> In Hollywood we were all very gung ho, and the day after Pearl Harbor, December 8, I was up in City Hall rolling bandages.
>
> —Rosalind Russell, *Life Is a Banquet*

> A natural question: is the "real" Dan Rather quite as gung-ho as his video persona suggests?
>
> —Ron Powers, *The Newscasters*

> I started out at K.U. as a real gung-ho Joe College. I pledged a fraternity, ran for the presidency of the freshman class, would only date the right girl. . . .
>
> —Brian Bauerle (quoted), Bill Moyers, *Listening to America*

The Mandarin term *kung-ho* or *gonghe,* literally translatable as 'work-together,' really means 'cooperative' and was not a slogan but part of the title of the wartime Chinese cooperative societies. The term still appears in the official name of the People's Republic of China, Mandarin *Chung-hua jen-min kung-ho kuo* (now rendered as *Zhonghua renmin gonghe guo*) = 'Central Flowery People's Cooperative Country' ("Central Flowery Country" being a traditional name of China). For other Chinese borrowings, and an explanation of alternate renderings like *kung-ho/gonghe,* see CHINESE WORDS.

gunnysack. This is the well-known term for the coarse, strong sack used to hold everything from potatoes to peanuts. The material itself is now usually jute. *Gunny* comes from the Hindi *goni,* which means 'sack.' It became part of the English language in the 18th century, when the British Empire embraced India. The word did not become current in America until well into the 19th century.

> She was perched high in the air, astride a pyramid of rations in a gunnysack.
>
> —DeBenneville R. Keim, *Sheridan's Troopers on the Borders* (1870)

> One had a box for a dressing-table, and covering it a gunny sack, such as the grain came in, fringed all around as a cover.
>
> —Elizabeth Custer, *Following the Guidon* (1890)

In addition to the widely used *gunnysack* and *burlap bag,* in the United States there are also a handful of regional dialect terms. *Crocus bag* or *sack* can be heard most often in South Carolina and eastern Georgia, though it is known throughout the Coastal Southern dialect region. (It is also found in JAMAICAN

ENGLISH.) The origin of *crocus* is unknown and seems to have no relation to the flower of the same name.

> James McPheeters opened a . . . grave and took therefrom the body, in order to dissect the same . . . and after doing so, did sew him up in a crokass bag and put him in the cave within mentioned.
> —*Augusta County, Virginia, Chronicles* (1790)

> As I came to the door, he held up one hand in command, unfurled a crocus sack, and with great drama rolled a large king snake onto the grass.
> —Marjorie Kinnan Rawlings, *Cross Creek* (1942)

In the Gulf Southern dialect a crocus bag is called a *croker bag* or *sack*.

> There would be frost in the air, and whole families would appear with crocker sacks slung over one shoulder—old and young would take to the cotton patch.
> —Ben Robertson, *Red Hills and Cotton* (1963)

> That spring when we found a croker sack full of turnip greens, Atticus said Mr. Cunningham had more than paid him. —Harper Lee, *To Kill a Mockingbird* (1960)

In other parts of the country the coarse, heavy-duty bag is known as a *guano bag* or *sack*, usually pronounced /**gwä**-nō/. Guano is a natural manure from sea birds that collects in great abundance on coastal islands of South America and other places. The word comes from Spanish, which adopted it from *huanu*, a term meaning 'dung' in Quechua, a South American Indian language. Guano was used as fertilizer and shipped to the United States in sacks that came to be known as guano bags or sacks.

> The State Inspector of Guano in Maryland . . . [urges] farmers to destroy or erase the marks on guano bags after emptying them.
> —*Porter's Spirit of the Times* (1856)

Another dialect term that originated in the name of the contents of the coarse sack is *coffee sack*. These sacks were used to ship green coffee. Any similar cloth sack, regardless of its original contents, is known in the General Southern dialect as a coffee sack.

> We carried charcoal from the pit to the intended "shop." With coffeesacks on our shoulders, we lifted until our appearance would have well vied with that of a city *charbonnier* [coal man].
> —Lewis H. Garrard, *Wah-to-yah and the Taos Trail* (1850)

> Now . . . he was free as the wind . . . a coffee sack across his back and a mattock in his hand.
> —Jesse Stuart, *Hie to the Hunters* (1950)

In other parts of the United States a gunnysack is called a *tow sack*. *Tow* is an old English word for 'spinning thread' but today refers to the material made from the fibers of flax, hemp, or jute.

> These mountain men . . . might stand talking an hour or better with packs on shoulders, or tow sacks of feed in hand that an outlander would drop directly, and they'd never notice.
> —Maristan Chapman, *Happy Mountain* (1928)

gutter, eaves trough, spouting. *Gutter* is the commonest term for the metal or wooden trough under the eaves of a building that carries rainwater from the roof. It has been in use since colonial times.

> If there be divers gutters to be laid, then together 13d per hundred.
> —*New Haven Town Records* (1641)

> The underwriters [suggested] that the wooden covings and gutters . . . were a dangerous and superfluous element in the construction of the roof of the factory.
> —*Century Illustrated Magazine* (1889)

Guttering and *gutter pipe* are two variant terms that have greatest currency in the Midland speech area.

In the General Northern dialect an alternative expression is *eaves* (or *eave*) *trough*, and *trough* is sometimes pronounced /trôth/ or /trôft/.

> An eave-trough and conductor has also been put on the agent's house.
> —*U.S. Bureau of Indian Affairs Report* (1878)

The Americanism *eaves* or *eave spout,* or occasionally *eaves spouting,* is another term used in the North, especially in the Northern and North Midland dialects. It also refers to the downspout.

> The water-barrel . . . stood under the eaves-spout.
> —Harriet Beecher Stowe, *House and Home* (1865)

Spout or *spouting* is used in the Midland dialect, especially the North Midland.

gybe. See JIBE.

H

haček. See DIACRITICS.

hackneyed expressions. See CLICHÉ.

haiku, a three-line poem whose lines consist of five, seven, and five syllables respectively, and whose subject matter reflects nature and the changing seasons in such a way as to trigger a flash of insight in the reader. The haiku comes from Japan and was introduced to the West during the craze for "japonaiserie" that was at its height during the 1880s and 1890s. It was a strong influence on the aesthetics of imagism as set forth by Ezra Pound, H. D., Amy Lowell, and Harriet Monroe (founder of *Poetry* magazine) on the eve of World War I. Since that time, thousands of haikus have been composed on every college campus in the English-speaking world. Here, in translation by Babette Deutsch, is a typical traditional haiku, by the 16th-century poet Moritake:

> The falling flower
> I saw drift back to the branch
> Was a butterfly.

hang. The past tense and past participle of this verb are *hung* except in the meaning 'to execute by suspending by the neck.' In this sense the predominant formal usage is *hanged*—probably, as noted by the *Oxford English Dictionary,* because English judges in pronouncing sentence preferred this relatively archaic form:

> . . . his fellow-Americans once took him for a Tory spy and nearly hanged him. —E. J. Kahn, *The New Yorker*

But in numerous dialects in England and America, *hung* has remained in use for all senses including execution; and a respectable minority of writers also prefer it, as both standard and formal:

> To one who urged that Jefferson Davis ought to be hung, he answered, "Judge not, that ye be not judged."
> —J. T. Adams, *The Epic of America*

> Stalin . . . reminded Khrushchev that in World War I a Czarist general who had led his troops into encirclement had been courtmartialed and hung.
> —Harrison E. Salisbury, *The Unknown War*

The following quotation, occurring without comment in the "How's That Again?" section of *Reader's Digest,* shows that *hung,* when applied to persons but clearly not in the sense of execution, still suggests the hangman's noose, if only at a jocular level:

> On a Redding, Calif., TV station: "Winners in the local art show will be hung in the art museum for a month after the show."

◇ ***Recommendation.*** For execution by hanging, *hanged* is definitely the preferred past tense and participle. But *hung* remains in standard use, although by a minority, and can't be dismissed as incorrect. If in doubt, use *hanged.*

hardly = 'barely, only just, almost not.' There are two deviant usages.

(1) *Can't* (or *couldn't*) *hardly* (do something). The standard construction is *can* or *could hardly.* The negative version occurs widely in dialectal and nonstandard speech. In the following passage it is used as a humorous "downward quotation"; the writer is consciously using a nonstandard form to give an effect of mock-naïve astonishment.

> Today he's in charge of two portfolios with $120 million in equities that have consistently ranked in the top 1% of the A. G. Becker rankings for the past four years. Better than that you can't hardly do. —Geoffrey Smith, *Forbes*

(2) *Hardly . . . than.* When *hardly* means 'just a very little time before, only just,' the standard construction is to use a clause beginning with *when: He had hardly walked into the room when the reporters began questioning him.* But *than* frequently occurs, even in published writings.

> Hardly had the ungainly Arvik II quit the Gulf of St. Lawrence by the Strait of Belle Isle above Newfoundland last month than those same St. Lawrence waters carried one of the newest ships afloat. —David Thomas, *Maclean's*

◇ ***Recommendation.*** *Can't hardly* is definitely nonstandard for *can hardly. Hardly . . . than* is a breach of correct idiom for *hardly . . . when.*

hark, hearken. These are two old variants of the same word meaning 'to listen,' related to *hear. Hark* in its literal sense is now obsolete except in the imperative *Hark!* = 'Be quiet and listen!' It occurs in several very familiar quotations:

> Hark! hark! The lark at heaven's gate
> sings. . . .
> —Shakespeare, *Cymbeline*

> Hark! The herald angels sing
> Glory to the newborn king.
> —Charles Wesley, *Christmas Hymn*

It also lives on in the expression *hark back to,* meaning 'to go back to an earlier point in a story or discussion' or 'to revert in thought to an earlier stage.' This idiom has its origin in the language of huntsmen shouting directions to hounds following a scent. *Hark forward!* meant 'Go on, follow the trail ahead!' *Hark back!* meant 'Come back, the fox doubled back on its trail here!'

> I must "hark back," as we say in the chase. —*Sporting Magazine* (1829)

This is a fixed idiom. *Hearken* or *harken back,* as in the next quotation, is a mistake:

> [American leaders] continually harkened back to the theme that the U.S. can and must regain its world position. —Sam Marcy, *Workers World*

Hearken is now rare and old-fashioned. It means 'to pay serious attention (to).' It has probably been kept alive by the influence of the King James Bible, in which it is the regular word for *listen,* occurring 234 times (whereas *listen* occurs only once):

> O that you had hearkened to my commandments! —Isaiah 48:18

Curiously, in the works of Shakespeare, a contemporary of the translators of the King James Bible, *listen* occurs twice as often as *hearken.*

The logical spelling *harken* has often been recommended but seldom occurs.

Hawaiian English. Hawaiian English is unique among American English dialects. It is the product of numerous European and non-European languages that came together at various times in Hawaii's history. It is also one of the youngest English dialects, having developed in about the last 150 years.

History. The Hawaiian language is Polynesian, related to Tahitian, Samoan, and Maori. English was brought to the Hawaiian Islands when Capt. James Cook landed there in 1778. This was the beginning of the shipping and whaling activities that introduced the Hawaiians to Chinese pidgin English, the lingua franca of sailors in the Pacific. In 1820 missionaries from New England arrived and began teaching English to the natives. This was encouraged by the members of the Hawaiian royal family, who were themselves the first to learn the new language. English soon acquired prestige, and by 1854 there were ten English-language schools in operation. The steady spread of English culminated in the 1890s in its being designated the official language of the government and the medium of instruction in the schools.

Great efforts were also made early on to teach the Hawaiians literacy in their own language. By the 1860s nearly all of the native people could read and write Hawaiian. That major step was necessary before English as a second language could be learned with any degree of effectiveness. This is because a knowledge of the structure of one's native language greatly influences the ease with which one learns a second language.

Hawaiian pronunciation created great obstacles in learning English. Hawaiian has only 8 consonants compared with the 24 consonant sounds of English. Hawaiian also has no consonant clusters (as in *splash* and *ghost*) and no words ending in consonants. As a result, Hawaiian speakers had great difficulty pronouncing English words. Typically, they separated the consonants of English words with vowels, substituted Hawaiian consonants, and ended words with vowels. For example, *Frank* became *Palani*, and *Bruce* became *Puluke*. Such inherent difficulties in learning the new language profoundly affected the way English came to be spoken on the Islands.

To add to the complexity of the linguistic situation, a tide of foreign immigrants and workers flooded Hawaii, their speech nearly swamping the newly established English. The first wave to hit the Islands was Chinese laborers. Then came large numbers of Portuguese and Japanese. These were followed in the first decades of the 20th century by Korean, Spanish, and Philippine immigrants.

Toward the last quarter of the 19th century, while Standard English continued to be taught in the schools, another variety of English was developing on the sugar plantations. With the conglomeration of foreign laborers came the need for a common practical language. Consequently, a new pidgin English developed to fill this need. As time passed, the children of these laborers grew up speaking the plantation pidgin, adding to it the vocabulary of the home and playground. At that point the plantation jargon became a creole, which still survives to the present day but in a decreolized form (see PIDGIN AND CREOLE LANGUAGES).

Varieties of Hawaiian English. Although Hawaiian English is a continuum ranging from remnants of early creole to educated English, at least three main varieties can be distinguished: *Hawaiian creole, nonstandard Hawaiian English,* and *Standard Hawaiian English.*

(1) *Hawaiian creole.* This variety developed (as discussed above) from the pidgin spoken on the sugar plantations in the 19th century. When the children of the pidgin-speaking parents took this language—now a creole—to school, it became the speech of the peer group. This early creole form can be heard today only in a very few isolated areas where formal schooling has had little influence.

Vocabulary. Here is a brief list of typical Hawaiian creole terms:

been = 'auxiliary to show past tense'
before = 'formerly'
broke = 'torn'
bumbye = 'in the future'
catch = 'to get'
-fellow (suffix) = 'person'
find for = 'to hunt for'
kaukau = (1) (noun) 'food' (2) (verb) 'to eat'

look-see = 'to look'
more better = 'better'
much = 'many'
no = 'not'
no can = 'cannot'
no stop = 'is not here'
number one = 'the best'
one = 'a'
pear = 'avocado'
pickaninny = 'small'
pine = 'pineapple'
plenty = 'very, much, many'
sabe, savvy = 'to know, know how to'
-side (suffix) = 'in the direction of'
stop = 'is here'
talk story = 'to tell stories'
-time (suffix) = 'at the time of'
too much = 'very, very much, very many'
wile = (1) 'to scold' (2) 'to drive away'

Example. Below is a portion of a taped interview from *Da Kine Talk* (This Kind of Talk), by Elizabeth Ball Carr. The interview is with an old woman who had almost no formal education and who lived most of her life in the remote Waipio Valley.

> Q. How many people live down in the valley now?
> A. Before, thousand—no full. No no full two hundred people down there. No much. All Kukuihaele. My family, my brother, all Kukuihaele.
> Q. Long ago there was a school there. Did you go to that school?
> A. Yeah. I went 'at school. Waipio Valley. Now, no more. They tear down. The man buy the place.
> Q. Do the children go up the trail to Kukuihaele school?
> A. Yeah. Yeah. When they been—the water been disturb—'as why they—nobody—all move Kukuihaele. Ah, the people down leave the valley go Kukuihaele. Nowdays they rent house. They go home all up there now for school day. When no school day they all go down the place. Clean taro patch—go catch fish. Hard to leave that place, very good place. If you lazy, you no more *kaukau*. You can go beach fishing, you go catch stream fishing, get taro, get *lu'au*, all kind, free.

(2) *Nonstandard Hawaiian English.* This variety ranges from the teen-age speech sometimes called *da kine talk* to the general near-standard English of a majority of Hawaii's speakers. *Da kine talk* is an outgrowth of Hawaiian creole and has many Hawaiianisms, slang terms, and foreign borrowings. It is used primarily by teen-agers, who are able to switch easily between it and Standard Hawaiian English. The following terms are used with varying degrees of frequency by speakers of Nonstandard Hawaiian English:

across = 'across from': *I waited for you across the bank.*

alphabet = 'letter': *It begins with the alphabet* d.

already = 'yet': *You been eat lunch already?*

'ass why hard = 'It's terrible, it's too bad'

attend to = 'attend': *I attended to the meeting.*

borrow = 'use': *May I borrow your phone?*

bumbye = 'after a while': *Bumbye we go movie.*

but = 'though, however': *I wen pick up my car. Nevah was ready but.*

catch = 'to get': *Us go beach—catch da tan.*

chance = 'turn': *It's my chance to hit the ball.*

clean (the yard) = 'to cut or mow the grass'

close (the light) = 'to turn out'

corns = 'corn on the cob'

down (the country) = 'to, toward'

eye-glass = 'spectacles, glasses'

find for = 'to look for': *I finding for it, but I can't see it.*

fire = 'to burn'

for = 'infinitive *to*': *I don't know what fo' cook.*

for why = 'why': *For why you tell lies?*

from before = 'before': *"You get one new car?" "No, I had 'em from before."*

from when = 'for how long': *"From when he had 'em?" "From long time."*

get = 'to have': *She gets many books.*

get down = 'to get out': *We rode the bus to the beach, then we all get down and walk.*

glass cup = 'drinking glass, water glass'

humbug = (1) (adjective) 'troublesome, naughty': *He's a real humbug boy.* (2) (noun) 'nuisance': *Your father is humbug when he stay home.*

hybolic = 'pompous, bombastic': *Don't use hybolic words here.*

junks = 'junk, things'

kine, da kine = 'this kind of'; used in many ways: (1) *Take da kine [broom] and sweep da floor.* (2) *"We goin' have one party." "Where da kine [it] goin' be?"* (3) *"You think he in love wid Alice?" "Man, he da kine [crazy] 'bout her!"*

like = 'to want to': *What you like me come out heah foah?*

mails = 'letters': *These mails need stamps.*

make = (1) 'to become': *He just made twenty-one years old yesterday.* (2) 'to behave': *No make like dat!*

meat = 'beef'

minor = 'It's nothing, don't worry': *"I forget my money." "Ah, minah! I get plenty."*

never = 'didn't, haven't': *I nevah take that picture.*

no more = 'no, not, never': *"Were you ever married?" "No more."*

on = 'in, at': *I got on the car. She sat on the table and ate lunch.*

one = 'a, each': *He eat jus' like one horse. Da candy bah cos' fi' cent one.*

open (the light) = 'to turn on'

package = 'paper sack'

pull down = 'to lose weight'

scare = 'afraid': *I scare for go on da bridge.*

shame = 'bashful, shy'

slangs = 'slang words'

sleep late = 'to go to bed late': *He's tired today 'cause he slept late last night.*

small-little = 'small'

soft = 'careful, gentle'

spark = 'to see, glimpse'

talk = 'to tell'

throw out = 'to vomit, throw up'

try = 'please': *Try give me dat paper.*

used to to = 'used to, accustomed to': *We're used to to this work.*

(3) *Standard Hawaiian English.* This dialect of American English has little trace of the New England dialect models of the 19th century. It is today essentially a part of the GENERAL NORTHERN DIALECT and most closely resembles the WESTERN DIALECT. The most distinctive characteristic of Standard Hawaiian English is its vocabulary, which has many *loanwords* (words from other languages) adopted during its melting-pot history.

The following lists of foreign borrowings are commonly used in all three varieties of Hawaiian English.

Hawaiian Loanwords. Not surprisingly, the Hawaiian language has provided the greatest number of loanwords. Many of these words have gotten into the general speech of mainland America. The pronunciation of words from the Hawaiian language tends to be anglicized, especially when these words are used on the mainland. The state name, for example, is often incorrectly pronounced /hə-**wä**-yə/. Within the state itself the preferred pronunciation is /hə-**wä'**-ē/, but also acceptable are /hä-**wī**-ē/, /hä-**vī**-ē/, and /hä-**wī**/. The following list is only a sampling of the most commonly used terms. (The apostrophe followed by a hyphen in the pronunciations indicates the *glottal stop*, which is common in Hawaiian.)

aa /'-ə'-**ä**/ = 'jagged lava'

ahahana /ä-hə-**hä**-nə/ = 'shame on you'

akamai /ä-kä-**mī**/ = 'smart, clever'

aku /**ä**-ko͞o/ = 'a fish, the bonito'

alii /ə-**lē'**-ē/ = 'chief, person of nobility'

aloha /ə-**lō**-hä/ = 'love, affection'; used as an expression of greeting, farewell, or pity

aole /'-ə'-**ō**-lā/ = 'no, not'

eleele /'-**ĕ**-lē'-**ĕ**-lē/ = 'black, dark'

hale /**hä**-lā/ = 'house, building'

hana /**hä**-nä/ = 'work, activity'

haole /**hă**-o͞o-lē/ = 'white person'

hapai /**hä**-pī/ = (1) (verb) 'to carry, lift' (2) (adjective) 'pregnant'

haupia /hă-o͞o-**pē**-ə/ = 'pudding of coconut milk'
hikiee /**hē**-kē-**ā**-ā/ = 'large couch or sleeping platform'
hilahila /**hē**-lə-**hē**-lə/ = 'ashamed, bashful'
holoku /hō-**lō**-ko͞o/ = 'gown with a long train'
hoomalimali /hō-ə-**mä**-lē-**mä**-lē/ = (1) (verb) 'to flatter' (2) (noun) 'flattery'
huhu /**ho͞o**-ho͞o/ = 'angry, offended'
hui /**ho͞o**-ē/ = 'club, association, corporation'
hula /**ho͞o**-lə/ = 'native dance'
huli /**ho͞o**-lē/ = (1) 'to turn' (2) 'to change (an opinion, one's life style, etc.)'
imu /**ē**-mo͞o/ = 'underground oven'
ipo /**ē**-pō/ = 'sweetheart'
kahuna /kə-**ho͞o**-nə/ = 'priest, expert in any profession'
kalua /kə-**lo͞o**-ə/ = 'to bake in an underground oven'
kamaaina /**kä**-mə-ī-nə/ = 'person born in Hawaii'
kanaka /kə-**nä**-kə/ = 'human being, man, person'
kane /**kä**-nā/ = 'male, husband'
kapakahi /**kä**-pə-**kä**-hē/ = 'crooked, one-sided'
kapu /**kä**-po͞o/ = 'taboo, forbidden'
kea /**kā**-ə/ = 'white, clear, fair'
kokua /kō-**ko͞o**-ə/ = 'help, cooperation'
kuleana /**ko͞o**-lā-**ä**-nə/ = (1) 'private property' (2) 'responsibility' (3) 'jurisdiction'
lanai /lə-**nī**/ = '*porch, veranda'
lani /**lä**-nē/ = (1) (noun) 'sky, heaven' (2) (adjective) 'spiritual' (3) (noun) 'high chief, royal'
lei /lā/ = 'flower wreath or necklace'
limu /**lē**-mo͞o/ = 'sea plants in general, but especially any edible seaweed'
lolo /**lō**-lō/ = 'stupid'
lomilomi /**lō**-mē-**lō**-mē/ = 'massage'
luau /**lo͞o**-ou/ = 'Hawaiian feast'
luna /**lo͞o**-nə/ = 'boss, foreman'
mahalo /mə-**hä**-lō/ = 'thank you, thanks'
maikai /mī-**kä**-ē/ = (1) (adjective) 'good' (2) (adverb) 'well' (3) (adjective) 'good-looking' (4) (noun) 'goodness'
makai /mə-**kī**/ = 'toward the sea, seaward'
make /**mä**-kā/ = (1) (verb) 'to die' (2) (verb) 'to faint' (3) (adjective) 'dead'
malihini /**mä**-lē-**hē**-nē/ = 'visitor, tourist, newcomer'
malolo /mə-**lō**-lō/ = 'flying fish'
manu /**mä**-no͞o/ = 'bird'
mauka /mä-**o͞o**-kə/ = 'toward the mountains, inland'
mauna /mä-**o͞o**-nə/ = 'mountain'
mele /**mā**-lā/ = (1) (noun) 'song, chant' (2) (verb) 'to sing'
moana /mō-**ä**-nə/ = 'ocean'
moemoe /**mō**-ā-**mō**-ā/ = 'to sleep'
moku /**mō**-ko͞o/ = (1) (noun) 'island' (2) (verb) 'to cut, sever'
muumuu /**mo͞o**-mo͞o/ = 'loose Hawaiian gown'
nani /**nä**-nē/ = 'pretty, beautiful'
niu /**nē**-o͞o/ = 'coconut'
nui /**no͞o**-ē/ = 'large, great'
okolehao /**ō**-kə-lā-**hou**/ = 'liquor distilled from ki root'
oli /**ō**-lē/ = 'chant'
ono /**ō**-nō/ = 'delicious'
opihi /ō-**pē**-hē/ = 'a small shellfish, the limpet'
opu /**ō**-po͞o/ = 'stomach, belly'
pahoehoe /pə-**hō**-ē-**hō**-ē/ = 'smooth lava'
pali /**pä**-lē/ = 'cliff'
pau /pou/ = 'finished'
pilau /**pē**-lou/ = (1) (adjective) 'rotten' (2) (noun) 'stench'
pilikia /**pē**-lē-**kē**-ə/ = 'trouble'
pio /**pē**-ō/ = 'to close, extinguish'
poho /**pō**-hō/ = 'out of luck'
poi /poi/ = 'the Hawaiian staple food made of pounded taro root'
popoki /pō-**pō**-kē/ = 'cat'
pua /**po͞o**-ə/ = 'flower'
puaa /po͞o-**ä**-ä/ = 'pig'
puka /**po͞o**-kə/ = 'hole, perforation'
punee /**po͞o**-nä'-ā/ = 'couch'
pupule /po͞o-**po͞o**-lā/ = 'crazy'
ukulele /**yo͞o**-kə-**lā**-lē/ = 'a musical instrument' (literally 'leaping flea')
ulu /**o͞o**-lo͞o/ = 'breadfruit'
wahine /wä-**hē**-nā/ = 'woman, female'
wikiwiki /**wē**-kē-**wē**-kē/ = 'quickly, in haste'

*Appears as separate entry

Japanese Loanwords. Japanese borrowings form the second-largest group (see also JAPANESE WORDS). Most of these are names of popular and useful material objects, including clothing and food dishes. Often these loanwords are compounded with English terms to create *loanblends.* Here are some of the commonest borrowings:

ajinomoto = 'monosodium glutamate'
arigato /ä-rĭ-**gä**-tō/ = 'thank you, thanks'
atsui = 'hot'
bango = (1) 'number' (2) 'identification tag'
daikon /**dī**-kən/ = 'edible root similar to a radish or turnip'
gohan = 'cooked rice'
hibachi /hĭ-**bä**-chē/ = 'portable stove for cooking'
ikebana /ē-kə-**bä**-nä/ = 'the Japanese art of flower arranging'
kamaboko = 'fish cake'
kibikaji = 'sugar-cane fire'
konnichi wa /kə-**nē**-chē wä/ = 'good day'; used as a salutation
kusa = 'weeds'
kuwa = 'hoe'
mate /**mä**-tā/ = 'to wait, stop a while'
mizu = 'water'
nagai /nə-**gī**/ = 'long'
ohayo = 'good morning'; used as a salutation
saimin = 'pork and noodle soup'
sashimi = 'raw fish'
satokibi = 'sugar cane'
sembei = 'appetizer made of crisped rice'
shibai = 'a dramatic show made to obscure an issue'; usually used in the expression *political shibai* or with reference to politics
shigoto = 'work'
shoji /**shō**-jē/ = 'lightweight sliding door covered with paper'
shoyu /**shō**-yo͞o/ = 'soybean sauce'
suki = 'plow'
tabi = 'socklike foot covering with a separate section for the big toe'
tatami /tə-**tä**-mē/ = 'mat made of woven grasses'
tempura = 'dish made of seafood and vegetables dipped in batter and deep-fried'
tofu /**tō**-fo͞o/ = 'soybean curd'
tokonoma /tō-kə-**nō**-mə/ = 'built-in niche for displaying art objects or flower arrangements'
tsunami /tso͞o-**nä**-mē/ = 'large ocean wave'
wakaru = 'to understand'
zabuton = 'large floor cushion'
zori /**zôr**-ē/ = 'grass slippers or thongs'

Philippine Loanwords

babai = 'girl, woman'
balay = 'house'
bata = 'child'
bayaw = 'brother-in-law'
dakayo = 'you (plural)'
danom = 'water'
ditoy = 'here, over this way'
ikaw = 'you (singular)'
lalaki = 'boy, man'
sabidong = 'poison'
tao = 'person, people, mankind'
tubo = 'sugar cane'

Korean Loanwords

abuji = 'father'
ajusi = 'uncle'
chun = 'pieces of meat or fish rolled in flour and fried'
kimchee = 'dish made of garlic, cucumbers, watercress, Chinese cabbage, radishes, seaweed, and mixed vegetables'
kun koki = 'beef broiled with sesame seeds, sesame oil, garlic, green onions, and hot peppers'
mandu = 'small steamed meat pie'

he. The English language lacks a third-person singular pronoun of common gender. This makes it awkward to refer to a person of unknown or unspecified sex. The traditional recommendation is to use *he*. Thus, from the womb to the work place to the nursing home the unknown human subject is made expressly masculine, as the following contemporary examples show.

> Liley finds that he can make a fetus move by tickling his fetal scalp, make him grasp by stroking his palm and bring up his toes by stimulating his sole.
> —Arthur J. Snider, *New York Post*

> In one year, the normal baby triples his birth weight.
> —Kris Hundley, *Hampshire Life*

> When the child is at the table, he should be treated with the same courtesy and attention given to adults.
>
> —Robert L. Green, *New York Times Magazine*

> The liberal arts graduate clearly has a hard fight ahead of him.
>
> —Marsha Witten, *Wisdom's Child*

> If a worker can't get to his job via a mass-transit system, he will pay for that gallon of gasoline whatever they charge, because he has no alternative.
>
> —Joel R. Jacobson, *New York Times*

> The ordinary employee works five or eight or ten years and then quits to take a better job. He loses his rights in the old [pension] plan and starts all over again in his new employer's plan. Or he is laid off in a recession. Or his firm goes bankrupt and the pension plan goes under.
>
> —William V. Shannon, *New York Times*

> Dignity lies in the patient's fight for life and in his struggle to maintain human contact, in the feeling that someone cares about him and is trying to help him.
>
> —Dr. Franklin H. Epstein, *New York Times Magazine*

These uses follow correct traditional grammar, but they carry a load of implication. The pronoun *he* is so strongly identified with males that it inevitably suggests masculinity even when the subject is supposed to be unspecified. Teaching children to use *he* in this way creates the impression that boys are the norm of humanity and girls are a secondary category or an exception. Thus, *he* is typically used to designate the homeowner, the consumer, the taxpayer, and the voter; in all such applications the word calls up the image of a male.

Considering that the other personal pronouns *(I, we, you, they)* are of common gender, some writers have wished to correct the unsymmetrical situation by creating a common pronoun for the third person singular also. Among their coinages have been *tey* (formed as a variant of *they*), *thon* (formed as a contraction of *the one*), and *(s)he* (formed as a written but unpronounceable blend of *she* and *he*). It seems obvious that such solutions cannot work. New nouns, adjectives, and verbs can be coined and are rather easily adopted into a language, but pronouns are much too basic; people will never accept planned innovations at so deep a level of language use.

For those who wish to avoid the undesirable effects of common-gender *he*, there are several alternatives. One is the scrupulous use of *he or she*, but this is not always satisfactory (see HE OR SHE). Another is the use of *they* as a singular pronoun, but many find this grammatically unacceptable (see THEY). There are also various ways of rephrasing, which we illustrate by applying them to the passages quoted above.

Some writers avoid references in which a hypothetical individual *(the student, the voter, the taxpayer, the employee)* is used to represent a group or class. Instead of generalizing in the singular, they generalize in the plural:

> When children are at the table, they should be treated with the same courtesy and attention given to adults.

Another way to rephrase is to use the handy *person who* construction instead of a conditional *if* clause:

> A worker who can't get to the job via a mass-transit system has no alternative but to pay a higher price for gasoline.

Often, judicious editing can remove superfluous pronouns:

> The liberal arts graduate clearly has a hard fight ahead.

> Dignity lies in the patient's fight for life and struggle to maintain human contact, in the feeling that someone cares and is trying to help.

A fetus or infant can be referred to as *it*:

> . . . he can make a fetus move by tickling its fetal scalp, make it grasp by stroking its palm. . . .

In one year, the normal baby triples its birth weight.
or
In one year, the normal baby's birth weight triples.

In many cases, the best solution is to start over and to express the thought in a different way. Thus, *Each worker is expected to do his job well* can become *Each worker is expected to do a good job.*

Sometimes a *he* passage can be changed by referring to the reader or listener as *you*:

> Suppose you work for one employer for ten years and then quit to take a better job. You lose your rights in the old pension plan and start all over again in your new employer's plan.

Where a subject may be a singular *he* or *she*, it may be possible to use alternating examples.

> The three-year-old, a boy for example, may begin to suck his thumb.

> Suppose the student is an 11-year-old girl. She is in the sixth grade, but tests show that she is reading at the ninth-grade level.

◇ ***Recommendation.*** *He*, referring to a person of unstated sex, has the authority of tradition and is still preferred by many conservatives. But a number of people now feel that it's inappropriate and are willing to make the effort to avoid it both in speech and in writing. We recommend doing this, using any of the alternatives described above, including *he or she* or *they* if suitable to the context.

headcheese, jellied and seasoned meat, typically made from the heads and feet of pigs and served as cold cuts. The term *headcheese* is an Americanism and may be a direct translation of the Dutch *hoofdkaas.*

> They see nothing wrong with calling something "head cheese" or "hog maw," and any outlander who can overcome a slight shuddering repugnance to taste them will wonder why he never even heard of such dishes before.
> —*Saturday Evening Post* (1948)

Scrapple is also an Americanism, used primarily in the Midland dialect. It comes from the diminutive form of the word *scrap*, since scraps of meat from the making of headcheese (plus cornmeal) are used to produce it. Scrapple is often sliced and fried.

> Bok was telling Kipling one day about the scrapple so dear to the heart of the Philadelphian as a breakfast dish.
> —E. W. Bok,
> *The Americanization of Edward Bok* (1920)

Souse is another term for headcheese. It originally meant pickled meat, especially the feet and ears of a pig, but in the General Southern and North Midland dialects it usually refers to headcheese. The related Norwegian word *sylte* or *sylteflesk*, the German *sülze*, and the Czech *sulc* can occasionally be heard in certain parts of the United States, notably Chicago. *Panhas* is the Pennsylvania German-English term for headcheese (from *pann* = 'pan' + *has* = 'rabbit'); it also appears in the North Midland dialect.

In other parts of the country, *pressmeat* or *pressed meat* is the usual term:

> My mother believed in saving everything about the hog except the squeal. . . . She [would] take the ears, feet and head of the hog and convert them into pressmeat or souse.
> —Fred Starr,
> *Good Old Days* (1967)

healthy, healthful. *Healthy* is much the commoner word. It is the only choice when applied to persons: someone in good health would be called *healthy*, never *healthful*. Referring to climate, diet, etc., as affecting human physical health, the two words are fully interchangeable. Applied to moral climate, *healthy* is more often used, but *healthful* is a possible alternative.

heap. *A heap of* is sometimes used like *a lot of* to mean 'a large amount, much':

> It takes a heap o' livin' in a house t'
> make it home. . . .
> —Edgar A. Guest, *Home*

Like *lot*, it is also used in the plural.

◇ ***Recommendation.*** This use of *heap* is informal only.

hearken. See HARK, HEARKEN.

hegemony /hə-**jĕm**-ə-nē, **hĕj**-ə-mō-nē/, from a Greek word meaning 'leadership,' is used in international politics to mean 'dominant influence or control of a powerful state over other states':

> For an increasing body of opinion, the new menace . . . was of a French Catholic hegemony in Europe.
> —Charles Wilson, *The Dutch Republic*

> Germany was now all-powerful from the North Sea to the Black Sea. She had secured the hegemony of Europe.
> —Anthony Eden, *The Reckoning*

It has become a code word of post-cold-war struggle between the United States, the Soviet Union, and China. The essential meaning is 'dominant influence or control of one of the superpowers over its satellite countries or allies.' Likewise the related adjectives *hegemonic* /hĕj-ə-**mŏn**-ĭk, hē-jə-/, *hegemonist(ic)* /hə-**jĕm**-ə-nĭst, -jĕm-ə-**nĭs**-tĭk/ = 'pursuing or supporting hegemony,' and the noun *hegemonism* /hə-**jĕm**-ə-nĭz-əm/ = 'policy of or desire for hegemony':

> Yeh Chien-ying, the 80-year-old defense minister, put it this way: "The Soviet Union and the United States are locked in an increasingly fierce struggle for hegemony."
> —Carl T. Rowan, *Reader's Digest*

> Are the Russians now to judge that they are free to pursue their hegemonic interests against the cause of human rights? . . .
> —George J. Keegan, Jr., *New York Times*

> Hsu Teh-heng, vice chairman of the fourth national committee, called for the "liberation" of Taiwan and developing an "international united front against the hegemonist powers, the Soviet Union and the United States."
> —*Boston Globe*

> Tito once ordered his armed forces to increase their vigilance against "hegemonistic" enemies—a clear reference to Russia.
> —*U.S. News & World Report*

> In the meantime, American naval power will be needed in the Western Pacific as protection against Soviet hegemonism.
> —John K. Fairbank, *New York Times*

hegira, sometimes spelled *hejira,* is usually pronounced /hə-**jī**-rə/, sometimes /**hĕj**-ər-ə/. The Hegira is the historic flight of Mohammed from Mecca to Medina on July 16, A.D. 622, considered to have been the key event in the establishment of Islam. The word is Arabic for 'departure, flight.' The Islamic world, using years of 354 or 355 days, reckons dates "from the Hegira."

Figuratively, *hegira* is used to mean 'migration, exodus' or, in a more trivial sense, 'tour, trip':

> . . . the family of 14 species of cranes—one of the most vulnerable of all groups of endangered creatures because of its small size, prominence and vast international hegiras . . .
> —S. Dillon Ripley, *Smithsonian*

> The bishop's oldest son, with the fruits of his father's relative success and influence, had left Archery as an adolescent to be educated in the North, a not uncommon hegira for the children of black status. . . . —James Wooten, *Dasher*

> The veteran rebel army from the West was now dribbling in after a heroic hegira. . . .
> —Burke Davis, *Sherman's March*

> We have released ourselves from the seasonal hegira to the mountains or the seashore.
> —Phyllis McGinley, *Reader's Digest*

height was originally *highth,* with the abstract suffix *-th* as in *width* and *breadth.* In the northern British dialects, *highth* was reduced to *height* /hīt/, and this eventually became the standard form in all English-speaking countries. However, the old pronunciation /hīth/, or sometimes /hītth/, is still used by some in southern Britain, America, and elsewhere.

> . . . with the Japs, it's all Cooperation, United Command and the Heighth of efficiency. . . .
> —Will Rogers, *Autobiography*

◇ ***Recommendation.*** Although *heighth* is both old and logically justifiable, it is now nonstandard.

help. The separate expressions *cannot help* (*doing something*) and *cannot but* (*do something*), both meaning 'unable not to, forced to,' have been combined into the illogical expression *cannot help but* (*do something*).

> Yet five weeks later Carter accepted it as a fait accompli. That couldn't help but be perceived by the Soviets as a sign of weakness. . . .
> —Gerald R. Ford, *A Time to Heal*

> Nearly six months of captivity . . . cannot help but have an impact on those detained.
> —Ned Temko, *Atlanta Constitution*

> Watching him, I couldn't help but think he was a sitting duck for a heart attack.
> —Jane E. Brody, *New York Times*

◇ ***Recommendation.*** Conservatives will continue to prefer *cannot help doing* or *cannot but do,* at least in formal usage. But *cannot help but do* is in such widespread use that we accept it as a standard idiom of the language.

he or she. For those who prefer to avoid using the masculine pronoun *he* to refer to someone of unspecified sex, the first resort is *he or she.*

> The Privacy Act empowers any U.S. citizen or resident alien to demand all information a federal agency possesses on him or her.
> —John Barron, *Reader's Digest*

The double pronoun can especially serve to underline the inclusion of women in a reference from which they are usually excluded.

> Following the Democratic convention, in all likelihood, Mr. Anderson would produce his own candidate for Vice President. . . . More important would be the stature of the person who, by agreeing to make such a hazardous race, showed that he or she considered John Anderson a serious candidate indeed.
> —Tom Wicker, *New York Times*

Although the masculine pronoun is customarily put first, note that the order of mention is not prescribed by any rule and can be alternated freely.

> . . . he challenged every individual in that audience to do some good thing for her or his nation. . . .
> —James A. Michener, *The Covenant*

Some writers attempt to shorten the dual reference by dropping the *or* and writing *he/she.* This device does not make for smoothly flowing English.

> If your fisherman is over age 70, remind him/her that she/he can receive a free fishing license. . . .
> —Betty Joyce Sheehan, *Hampshire Life*

> Nowhere is the fact that man's (or woman's) reach too often exceeds his/her grasp so dangerous as in weekend sports.
> —*Time*

The basic drawback to *he or she* as an all-purpose pronoun of common gender is that repetition of it can become laborious, awkward, or even intolerable.

> The drug patient often pays no attention to prescription instructions. He or she pops pills indiscriminately. . . . If the time comes when the doctor won't prescribe enough to satisfy the patient, he or she will go to another doctor. . . . When the physician judges that a potentially addictive drug is in order, he

> or she should ascertain that the patient is not chemically dependent. . . .
>
> —John G. Hubbell, *Reader's Digest*

This passage could be rewritten without a single use of *he or she,* for either patient or physician:

> Drug patients often pay no attention to prescription instructions. They pop pills indiscriminately. . . . If the time comes when the doctor won't prescribe enough to satisfy them, they will go to another doctor. . . . Before prescribing a potentially addictive drug, a physician should ascertain that the patient is not chemically dependent. . . .

There are also ways to avoid *he or she* when the subject has to remain singular. Consider this passage:

> Each passenger sat down in the same seat he or she had occupied before and quickly rearranged his or her face behind its previous mask of neutrality.
>
> —Vivian Gornick, *New York Times*

It could be rephrased as follows:

> Each passenger sat down in the same seat as before. Each face was quickly rearranged behind its previous mask of neutrality.

It should be noted that it does not help to throw in an occasional *he or she* if the writer continues to use the masculine pronoun in the same passage.

> The true measure of a human being is how he or she treats his fellow man.
>
> —Ann Landers, *Reader's Digest*

Here "other people" instead of "his fellow man" would solve the problem.

◊ ***Recommendation.*** As a common-gender pronoun *he or she* is partly satisfactory but will often require variation or other rephrasing as well. See also HE; THEY.

heraldic terms. Heraldry, the colorful system of graphic symbols used on shields, banners, etc., by the armored knights of the Middle Ages, is far from dead. The United States, for example, has a coat of arms (using stars and stripes), and so do the states of the Union and many American cities, universities, and other institutions. Many American families have arms inherited or brought over from Europe. One can also buy coats of arms by mail order, but these have no legitimate status. On the other hand, heraldry itself has no official standing in the United States.

In other countries, especially Britain, heraldry is going strong and has legal status—you can theoretically be prosecuted for using someone else's coat of arms without permission. The Royal College of Heralds in London presides over armorial rights and records continuing unbroken from the Middle Ages. All coats of arms are precisely described in a unique technical language derived largely from Norman French but pronounced as English. Below are some terms from this huge vocabulary; a brief explanation of its use; and a selection of heraldic expressions that have come into everyday use.

Vocabulary.

(1) General terms:

achievement = 'a person's complete armorial bearings, including shield, supporters, helmet, crest, and motto'

armorial = 'relating to heraldry and coats of arms'

arms = 'coat of arms'

badge = 'small heraldic device, separate from the coat of arms but usually extracted from it'; for example, the white rose of York or the red Tudor rose

blazon = (1) (noun) 'shield, coat of arms' (2) (noun) 'technical heraldic description of a coat of arms' (3) (verb) 'to describe (a coat of arms) in technical heraldic language'

canting arms = 'coat of arms that embodies a pun on the bearer's name'; for example, the arms of John Shakespeare (granted 1595) include a spear and those of the Scottish family Bowes-Lyon bear bows and lions

charge = 'any of the shapes or symbols borne on a shield'

coat of arms = (1) originally 'coat worn over armor and displaying the wearer's heraldic symbols' (2) 'a shield, or the heraldic symbols on a shield' (3) 'achievement'

crest = 'beast or object mounted on the top of the helmet'

escutcheon = 'shield, coat of arms'

field = 'the surface of the shield, as the background to heraldic symbols'

herald = 'officer expert in armorial bearings, formerly in charge of tournaments and the ceremonies of warfare, often employed as an ambassador; now (in Britain) in charge of state ceremonies, royal proclamations, and the recording, granting, and inheritance of coats of arms'

heraldic = 'relating to coats of arms and the system of symbols used on them'

king-of-arms = 'chief herald'; for example, *Garter King-of-Arms,* the chief herald of England; *Lyon King-of-Arms,* the chief herald of Scotland

pursuivant /**pêr**-sə-vənt/ = 'junior herald'

shield = 'portable piece of armor, typically carried on the left arm, the primary surface for displaying heraldic symbols'; numerous shapes have been used at different times, the standard shape having a straight top edge, with vertical sides curving in to a point at the bottom

supporters = 'beasts or human figures standing on either side of a shield'; for example, the lion and unicorn in the arms of Great Britain

tabard = 'herald's coat, showing the arms of his lord'

tincture = 'any of the colors used in heraldry'; technically divided into *metals, colors,* and *furs* See section (3), below.

(2) Sides and orientation:

dexter = 'right-hand side of the shield from the bearer's point of view'; thus, when you are looking at a coat of arms from the front, the dexter is on the left-hand side

sinister = (1) 'opposite of dexter' (2) '(of a charge, beast, etc.) oriented in the opposite direction to the usual'; thus *bend sinister* = 'bend running from sinister at the top to dexter at the bottom' See BAR SINISTER, BEND SINISTER.

(3) Tinctures. Whenever possible, metal is not placed against metal nor color against color.

argent = 'silver or white'
azure = 'blue'
ermine = 'white with black spots or tails'
gules /gyōōlz/ = 'red'
or = 'gold or yellow'
purpure /**pêr**-pyŏŏr/ = 'purple'
sable = 'black'
vair = 'having alternate pelts of blue and white'
vert = 'green'

(4) Some basic forms and shapes:

bar = 'broad horizontal strip across the middle of a shield'

baton /**băt**'n/ = 'bendlet with the ends cut off'

baton sinister = 'baton running from sinister at top to dexter at bottom'; used in English heraldry as a sign of royal bastardy See BAR SINISTER, BEND SINISTER.

bend = 'broad diagonal strip running from dexter at top to sinister at bottom'

bendlet = 'narrow bend'

bordure = 'solid border around the edge of a shield'

canton = 'square section in the dexter top corner of a shield'

chevron = 'broad strip in the shape of an inverted V in the middle of a shield'

chief = 'section of a shield, the top one-third of it'

cross = (1) 'broad straightedged cross from top to bottom and from side to side of a shield' (2) 'any of several hundred specific types of cross, such as the Maltese cross'

fess = 'horizontal strip, broader than a bar, across the middle of a shield'

lozenge = (1) 'charge shaped like the diamond on playing cards' (2) 'diamond-shaped shield borne by an unmarried lady or widow'

pale = 'broad vertical strip through the middle of a shield'

quarter = 'section of a shield divided horizontally and vertically through the center'

quartering = 'any of four or more sections of a shield, typically used to display several inherited sets of arms'

saltire /**săl**-tîr, **sôl**-/ = 'broad diagonal cross, Saint Andrew's cross'

Adjectives

barry = 'divided into horizontal strips'; the number of strips are specified: *barry of six* = 'divided into six equal strips'

bendy = 'divided into diagonal strips from dexter at top to sinister at bottom'

checky = 'divided into small squares of two tinctures, checkered'

dancetty = '(of a line or shape) zigzag'

flory = 'ornamented with small fleurs-de-lis'

paly /**pā**-lē/ = 'divided into vertical strips'

wavy = '(of a line or shape) undulating'

(5) Some beasts:

basilisk = 'cockatrice with a dragon's head on the end of its tail'

cockatrice = 'beast with a cock's head, a dragon's forefeet, body, and wings, and a serpent's tail with a barb'

dragon = 'well-known reptilian beast, with four feet in the form of eagle's claws, wings like a bat's, and a barbed tongue and tail'

griffin, gryphon = 'beast with the head, claws, and wings of an eagle and the body and hind legs of a lion'

leopard = 'a lion passant guardant'; for example, the three leopards on the arms of England

lion = 'the king of beasts, represented in many stylized heraldic forms'

manticore = 'beast with the head of a bearded man and the body of a lion'

martlet = 'bird like a swift, lacking feet'

pelican in her piety = 'pelican with wings raised, pecking her own breast, with her young feeding on her blood'

Talbot = 'a large English hound'

tyger = 'beast with the body of a heraldic lion, a beaked face, and small tusks'

unicorn = 'beast with the head and body of a horse, a single horn on the forehead, cloven hoofs, and a lion's tail'

wyvern = 'beast with a dragon's head, forefeet, body, and wings, and a serpent's tail with a barb'

yale = 'beast with an antelope's body and a goat's head with one horn pointing forward and the other backward'

Adjectives

couchant = 'lying down with the head raised'

couped = '(usually of a beast's head) cut off cleanly'

erased = '(usually of a beast's head) torn off leaving ragged or curling pieces'

gorged = 'wearing a collar, often in the form of a crown'

guardant = 'full-face, looking straight out of the shield'

passant = 'walking along toward the dexter, with the head in profile and the right forefoot raised'

proper = 'shown in its natural form and color'; thus, *a leopard* = 'a heraldic leopard,' that is, a lion passant guardant, but *a leopard proper* = 'drawing of a real leopard with its natural colors'

rampant = 'rearing up, facing the dexter with the left hind foot on the ground, and flourishing the other three feet'

reguardant = 'looking back over the shoulder'

Blazoning. Using this large vocabulary, of which only small selections are given above, a herald can precisely describe, or *blazon*, any of the hundreds of thousands of coats of arms that exist or may be created. The language has its own rules, even its own grammar. All words, though derived from French, are pronounced as in English. Thus, *couchant* is /**kou**-chənt/ and *argent* is /**är**-jənt/. Adjectives always come after their nouns: *lion gules* = 'red lion'; *saltire dancetty* = 'Saint

Andrew's cross with zigzag edges.' The elements of a complex coat of arms are described in a rigid sequence and style. The blazon of the arms of the city of Chicago is: "a chief azure, on a paly of 13 argent and gules, a wheat sheaf proper" (= 'the top third [of the shield] blue, on a fence of 13 silver and red stripes, and a realistic ["proper"] rendering of a wheat sheaf').

Terms in Common Use.

blazon = 'to publish and proclaim with enthusiasm'

blot on one's escutcheon = 'a cause of shame to one's reputation'

chevron = 'V-shaped stripe, used in the armed forces as the insignia of noncommissioned officers'

herald = 'someone or something that comes before and is a sign of something approaching'

rampant = 'violent, unrestrained, extravagant'

See also BAR SINISTER, BEND SINISTER.

herb. The preferred Standard American pronunciation is /ûrb/, but /hûrb/, used by a minority, is also correct. In British only /hûrb/ is accepted as standard; dropping the /h/ is considered uneducated. This is one of the many cases in which American usage is the more conservative. In Middle English the word was generally spelled *erbe,* having been borrowed from Old French *erbe.* Ultimately, the French word is from Latin *herba* = 'grass, herb.' When this fact was realized, the *h* was restored in both French and English spelling. Beginning in the 19th century, the British also began to pronounce the /h/, but most Americans continue to ignore it.

Hispanic, an adjective meaning 'Spanish-speaking, of Spanish-speaking culture,' applies to Spain, the Americas, the Philippines, and all other Spanish-settled parts.

> . . . the three civilizations of Peru—Hispanic, mestizo, Indian . . .
> —Milton Viorst, *Atlantic Monthly*

The word is also used as a noun meaning 'Hispanic person':

> Blacks and Hispanics are usually ignored [by the Moonies] because they're considered too "street-wise."
> —Charles H. Edwards, *Reader's Digest*

The formal term for U.S. citizens and residents of Hispanic descent and culture is *Hispanic-American* (adjective and noun):

> The nation's Hispanic-American population, increasing sharply in the past two decades, is approaching 20 million . . . in 1970, the Census Bureau's estimate of the number of Hispanic-Americans was 10 million.
> —*New York Times*

hisself is a dialectal and nonstandard variant of *himself.*

historic, historical. *Historical* is the basic all-purpose adjective meaning 'belonging to or concerned with history, occurring in or through history': *historical documents; a historical novel. This is now of only historical interest.*

> The . . . salmon industry got its start after mid-June and, if the historical trend were to be followed, would have peaked on July 4.
> —Robert Browning, *National Fisherman*

Historic is a more specific word, meaning 'significant in history, so important as to be a piece of history':

> An historic house was sold recently on Beacon Hill.
> —John T. Galvin, *Boston Herald American*

> Irwin signed a historic bill rescinding the sale.
> —E. J. Kahn, *The New Yorker*

But in practice each adjective is often used in either sense, and many people are frequently uncertain as to which is preferable in a given context:

> Historic data indicate . . . overfishing of the shrimp resource. . . .
> —Robert L. Dow, *National Fisherman*

> I felt that we were at a historical turning point. . . .
> —Richard Nixon, *R.N.*

Since the first syllable of *historic, historical,* and *historian* is unstressed, the /h/ sound is not always fully pronounced. When the indefinite article comes before any of these words, it sometimes appears as *an* (this does not apply to the word *history,* which is stressed on the first syllable):

> This is an historic event of the first magnitude.
> —William Randolph Hearst, Jr., *Boston Herald American*

> In the *Ninus Romance* . . . we have an "historical" element. . . .
> —Moses Hadas, *Hellenistic Culture*

This is often said to be peculiar to British usage but is also quite prevalent in the United States.

These two issues—*historic* versus *historical* and the use of *a* or *an* before the weak /h/—are common causes of doubt, and it is not surprising to find them treated inconsistently by the same person. In his book *Before the Fall* (1975) William Safire recalls President Richard Nixon saying in private conference in the White House, "This is an historic moment." But as quoted above in the second volume of his own memoirs, Nixon, referring to a similar occasion, writes of "a historical turning point." Thus, he or his editors may have reversed in print his earlier preferences in speech. Many a speechmaker and speech writer must have gone through similar hesitations and changes of mind.

◇ ***Recommendation.*** Use *historical* for 'belonging to history' and *historic* for 'significant in history.' But recognize that it is not always possible to make a clear distinction between the two. In marginal cases *historical* is the better choice. The use of *an* is regarded by some people as a Briticism, by some as an affectation. If the usage with *an* comes naturally and you like the sound of it, you are entitled to your preference. If you have no preference, use *a*.

histrionic is from Latin *histriō-* = 'actor.' It means, literally, 'belonging to actors, theatrical,' or, figuratively, 'overdramatic, emotionally exaggerated':

> Later, though still a boy, [Henry] James was taken to hear Mrs. Kemble read *A Midsummer Night's Dream* and *King Lear*. He was uplifted, as only youth can be uplifted, by the great histrionic voice and its delicate shadings, as it shifted from character to character.
> —Constance Wright, *Fanny Kemble and the Lovely Land*

> . . . [Harry] Reasoner was so amused by a baseball game argument over a close play at the plate, which featured a histrionic player dropping to his knees and pounding the turf in a paroxysm of rage and anguish . . .
> —Gary Paul Gates, *Air Time*

hockey terms. The language of ice hockey is not so much new as, for many Americans, newly discovered. Yet what was once almost exclusively a Canadian sport is now truly international and not only North American. A great impetus to the increasing interest in the game in America was the U.S. hockey team's surprising gold-medal victory in the 1980 Olympics. But, in fact, the terminology of hockey has expanded less than the sport itself.

assist = 'statistical credit for a pass or other action with the puck that immediately precedes and leads to a teammate's goal'

back-check = 'to check (an opponent) while skating backward toward the goal defended by one's team'

blueline = 'either of two bluelines, each parallel to and 60 feet from a goal line, that divide a rink laterally into three approximately equal areas'

boarding = 'illegal checking of an opponent that causes the opponent's body to strike the boards heavily'

boards = 'reinforced wooden or plastic panels that enclose the ice like a fence and separate it from the stands'

body check = 'to check (an opponent in possession of the puck) by using one's trunk or hip legally to impede the other's progress'

breakaway = 'a dash down the ice, toward the goal defended by the opponent, by a player in possession of the puck who suddenly breaks clear of surrounding players'

cage = 'the goal area as defined by four uprights with netting stretched over them'

carry = 'to advance (the puck) by sliding it along the ice while controlling it with the stick'

center = 'forward who executes face-offs'; with the two wings, primarily an offensive player responsible for attacking the goal guarded by the opponent

center ice = 'area adjoining the center of the rink, measured lengthwise, and lying between the two bluelines'

charging = 'taking a run at an opponent as a preliminary to checking, in violation of the rules'

check = 'to impede the progress of (an opponent attempting to advance the puck) with one's body or stick'

clear = 'to send (the puck) out of the area of one's goal when one or more opponents are nearby'

crease = 'rectangular area, marked off in front of the goal, that an attacking player may not enter unless the puck is also within it'

cross-check = 'to check (an opponent) illegally, by holding the stick with both hands so that no part touches the ice and thrusting it across the opponent's body'

defenseman = 'either of two members of a team, usually stationed along the blueline near the goal defended by the team and primarily responsible for protecting the goal from attack by opposition skaters'

deke (slang) = 'any act calculated to mislead an opponent, especially one by a player skating with the puck'; for example, faking a sudden change in direction or shooting the puck a split second after pretending to do so (from *decoy*)

drop pass = 'pass executed by a player who abruptly abandons possession of the puck and skates on, leaving the stationary puck in the path of a teammate coming up directly behind'

elbowing = 'using the elbows to strike an opponent, in violation of the rules'

empty-net goal = 'goal scored by shooting the puck into an unprotected goal cage when the goaltender of the team scored on has been removed in order to put an additional attacker in play'

face-off = 'play that begins a game or period or that resumes action after a goal or a halt of the action by the referee'; consists of the referee's dropping the puck to the ice between rival forwards, who vie for control of it

forecheck = 'to check (an opponent) in the area of the opponent's own goal so as to prevent the opposition from organizing an offensive move up the ice'

forward = 'any of three offensive players (center and two wings) who make up a line, primarily responsible for scoring goals'

freeze = 'to attempt to retain control of (the puck), as by holding it against an area of the boards or by falling on it and thereby stopping play'

goal = (1) 'either of two areas, at the ends of the rink and centered on the goal lines, into which players attempt to shoot the puck past the rival goaltenders'; consists of a rectangular space enclosed on the two sides and the back by netting stretched over four upright metal pipes that define the goal area, the front being open (2) 'act of shooting the puck into the cage, which results in the score of one point'

goal crease = 'crease'

goal line = 'either of two lines, extending the width of the rink and at right angles to the rink sides, that mark the front (unclosed) boundary of each goal area and over which the puck must pass in the scoring of a goal'

goaltender, goalkeeper, goalie = 'player who guards a team's goal and tries to prevent entry of the puck therein by blocking the puck with an oversize hockey stick and protective body gear'

hat trick = 'player's feat of scoring three or more goals in a single game'

high-sticking = 'making illegal contact with an opponent while holding the hockey stick above shoulder level'

holding = 'illegally obstructing an opponent by grasping the opponent's body or gear'

honest player = 'two-way player'

hooking = 'using a hooklike motion of the hockey stick to poke the puck away from the opponent who controls it'; illegal in some situations, especially when executed from behind an advancing player who thereby falls to the ice

ice time = (1) 'player's time spent in action during a game or games,' hence (2) 'opportunity to play, as opposed to being held in reserve'

icing = 'sending the puck, from behind the red line, across an opponent's goal line (but not into the cage) as a defensive attempt to keep the puck away from attacking opponents near one's own goal'; an extreme and usually illegal form of clearing that results in a face-off near the offending team's goal

interference = 'illegal bodily contact with an opponent who is not in possession of the puck or who was not the last player in possession of it at the time of the contact'

line = 'three forwards (center and two wings) considered as a performing unit, usually a threesome who play as such regularly'

National Hockey League = 'major league of professional North American hockey, composed of Canadian and U.S. teams'

nets = 'the goal (with its netting), considered as the station of a goaltender'

neutral zone = 'center ice' (so called to contrast with the areas between the bluelines and the areas nearer the goals, which are considered the zones of the defending teams)

offside = 'illegally in advance of the puck while in the zone being defended by an opponent'; so ruled when a player of the attacking side enters that zone ahead of a teammate who is skating with the puck and has not yet entered the zone

pass = 'act of tapping or otherwise striking the puck with the blade of the hockey stick so that the puck slides across the ice'

penalty = 'judgment by the referee against a team, following an infraction of the rules, that puts the offending team at a disadvantage'; usually involves removal of the player responsible for a two-minute period, forcing the team to function with five members instead of six

penalty box = 'enclosed area at rink side where a player who has committed a rules infraction must sit idly for a stipulated time while the player's team functions shorthanded'

penalty killer = 'player skilled in defensive techniques who is used especially when a team is short-handed as the result of a penalty'

penalty shot = 'shot at the goal of a team against which a serious penalty has been assessed, taken by a player who may not be obstructed by any other player of the penalized team except the goaltender'

period = 'one of three 20-minute segments making up a game'

playmaker = 'player, often a center, who is skilled in creating scoring opportunities for teammates through adroit handling and passing of the puck'

plus player = 'individual during whose ice time the opposition scores only infrequently'

point = 'a specified position (station) to the right or left of the goal, especially in the alignment of players during a power play'

poke check = 'to check (an opposing player in possession of the puck) by thrusting one's stick at the puck in an effort to dislodge it from the opponent's control'

post = 'goal post, one of two metal uprights on the goal line that define the width of the goal cage'

power play = 'procedure of play specially devised for attacking an opponent's goal when the opponent is short-handed as the result of a penalty'

power-play goal = 'goal scored on a power play by the team with the manpower advantage'

puck = 'disk of vulcanized rubber, one inch thick and three inches in diameter, that is propelled over the surface of the ice so that it will pass into the opposition's goal'

puck carrier = 'player in possession of the puck who is trying to advance it'

puck handling = 'manipulation of the puck by a player skating with it, a procedure analogous to dribbling in basketball'

rebound = 'deflection of the puck off a goaltender's stick or other equipment or off a post, immediately following a shot on the goal'

red line = 'line, parallel to the goal lines and extending the width of the rink, that divides the ice in half laterally'

roughing = 'illegal body contact that in the referee's judgment is unnecessarily and intentionally violent'

save = 'goaltender's act of blocking a shot directed at the goal cage so that the puck does not cross the goal line'

score = 'to make a goal by sending the puck over the opposing team's goal line and into the cage'

screen = 'to obstruct the view of (a goaltender) so that the goaltender cannot see the puck as it is driven toward the goal cage in question'

shift = 'span of several minutes during which a player or line is on the ice before getting a respite'

short-handed goal = 'goal scored by a team when playing without a full complement because of a penalty being served by one of that team's players'

shot, shot on goal = 'act of propelling the puck with the stick toward the opponent's goal in an attempt to score'

shutout = 'feat of keeping an opposing team scoreless throughout an entire game, credited to the goaltender of the victorious team'

skater = 'any member of a hockey club except a goaltender'

slap shot = 'shot executed by swinging the hockey stick off the ice in a wide arc comparable to the path of a golf club, rather than by using a short wrist-action stroke or a thrust of the arms'

slashing = 'illegally swinging the hockey stick, held off the ice, so that it strikes an opponent'

slot = 'unmarked area near the front of a goal cage that an attacking player seeks to occupy as a vantage during an offensive thrust'

spearing = 'illegal use of a hockey stick by thrusting its end at the body of an opponent'

stick (1) 'wooden implement by which the puck is carried, passed, and shot'; consists of a horizontal blade, about one foot long with a lower edge that can be set flush with the ice, joined to a sloping upright part about four and a half feet long that is gripped near its upper end (2) 'similar implement used by goaltenders'; consists of a blade that extends up from the ice at a slightly greater angle and has a somewhat wider upright part

stick check = 'poke check'

stickhandling = 'skillful use of the stick to keep possession of the puck, especially in heavy opposition traffic'

three-on-one = 'maneuver the same as two-on-one, but with three attacking players instead of two'

tripping = 'using the stick illegally to pull down an opponent in possession of the puck'

two-on-one = 'two attacking players in the act of advancing on the opponent's goal and confronting a single opposing defender, not counting the goaltender'

two-way player = 'one who has good skills in both offensive and defensive play, especially a forward who is also a capable checker'

wing = 'either of two forwards primarily responsible for attacking the opponent's goal while covering opposite lanes of the playing surface stretching the length of the rink'

hoi polloi. In Greek this literally means 'the many,' from *hoi* = 'the' (plural) + *polloi* = 'many' (plural). It was used as a political term meaning 'the multitude, the common people,' as opposed to *hoi oligoi* = 'the few, the aristocrats.' In English *hoi polloi* means 'ordinary people, unprivileged people,' often with a tinge of irony. Classicists used to point out that *the hoi polloi* was a redundant expression, since *hoi* already means 'the.' Not many people now know any Greek, and the idiom is firmly established in English as *the hoi polloi*:

> I have a great deal more confidence in the "hoi polloi" that are going into office on the fourth of March than I ever did in Andy Mellon and his crowd of highbinders.
>
> —Harry Hopkins (letter), Robert E. Sherwood, *Roosevelt and Hopkins*

> When she had first met him in the summer theatre he had treated her like one of the *hoi polloi,* ordering her around, criticizing the way she hammered flats, sending her on errands to the hardware store. —Mary McCarthy, *The Group*

> . . . with the $100 and $150 ticket buyers trailing up the path from their gas guzzlers side by side with the hoi polloi lugging their blankets and plastic coolers. —Linda Charlton, *New York Times*

homemaker, homemaking. The term *homemaker,* although made up of two of our most basic words, is a fairly new compound. It is used to describe a person who manages a home and family; *homemaking* is the art, business, or science of doing so. One reason for the success of the word *homemaker* is no doubt that it serves equally well for both sexes. Another reason is that it can replace the word *housewife:*

> One married woman of my acquaintance never gives her occupation as housewife, always as homemaker.
>
> —*Reader's Digest*

For more on homemaker/housewife, see HOUSEWIFE.

homograph, homophone, homonym. The meanings of these three words overlap, and it's quite a chore to unravel them. But here's the story:

A *homograph* is one of two or more words that are spelled the same way but not necessarily pronounced alike; for example, *row* (= 'series') and *row* (= 'fight'); *lead* (= 'metallic element') and *lead* (= 'to conduct').

A *homophone* is one of two or more words that sound alike but are different in meaning, derivation, or spelling; for example, *to, two,* and *too.*

A *homonym* is either of the preceding—in other words, a homograph or a homophone. In addition, however, *homonym* is used as a fancy synonym for *namesake,* one with the same name as another. (For the etymology of *homonym,* see GREEK WORDS.)

hooky. This is by far the most commonly used term in casual speech for 'staying away from school without permission.' Most often used in the phrase *play hooky,* it is an Americanism that has spread to many other English-speaking countries. It probably comes from the earlier slang term *hook,* meaning 'to leave or depart': *They hooked it for home.*

> He would not play hookey, even when his sober judgment told him it was the most profitable thing he could do.
>
> —Mark Twain, *Sketches New and Old* (1870)

> They remembered that the geography lesson was a hard one, and so they played "hookey."
> —Edward Eggleston, *The Hoosier Schoolboy* (1883)

Formerly, the expression *hook Jack* meant 'to stay out of school':

> The boy "hooked Jack" for a whole day.
> —Joseph C. Lincoln, *Partners of the Tide* (1905)

To *be* or *play truant* is also a common expression, but it is much more formal in style than *hooky* or the other synonyms discussed here. *Truant* meant in Middle English 'vagrant or beggar,' a sense that is now obsolete. By Shakespeare's time the word had acquired its modern meaning.

> Since I pluck'd geese, play'd truant, and whipt top, I knew not what 'twas to be beaten till lately.
> —Shakespeare, *The Merry Wives of Windsor*

Skip school is another common synonym for *play hooky*. It is taken from the earlier colloquial use of *skip* meaning 'to make an escape or leave hurriedly':

> All of them had used others' money in speculation . . . and then had skipped, as the newspapers said.
> —William Dean Howells, *The Quality of Mercy* (1892)

Two other more informal synonyms are *bag* or *cut (school, classes,* etc.). *Cut* is the older Americanism of the two.

> Those who cut more than one lecture or prayer in a week received a private admonition.
> —*Harvard Magazine* (1858)

> [The] course at Yale was cut with a frequency that was ridiculous.
> —*Atlantic Monthly* (1952)

Bag it is a relatively recent coinage:

> She had taught him in Sunday School, and did not report him on Sunday afternoons when he "bagged it" to go to a ball game.
> —John O'Hara, *Appointment in Samarra* (1934)

> [After my mother's death] I took to baggin' school.
> —*The New Yorker* (1950)

There are two dialect expressions that are rarely found in print. In the Coastal Southern and South Midland dialects, *lay out of school* is the common version. In the Rocky Mountain dialect to play hooky is to *slough* /slŭf/ *school* or *class*. This expression is an extension of *slough* = 'to shed, cast off, discard, abandon.'

hopefully. Before about 1960 this adverb was used only to qualify verbs and to mean 'in a hopeful manner':

> To travel hopefully is better than to arrive, and the true success is to labor.
> —Robert Louis Stevenson, *Virginibus Puerisque* (1881)

Some time around 1960 people began to use *hopefully* to qualify entire sentences or phrases, and to mean 'it is to be hoped' or 'I (we, they, etc.) hope, hoped, etc.':

> I feel sure you are still around and hopefully you will see this reply.
> —Ann Landers, *New York Daily News*

> Duffey wants Marcus in the primary, to split the race into a three-way contest and hopefully dilute the organization's unity.
> —Bill Moyers, *Listening to America*

> Unknown to Stalin and his staff, Hitler on September 6 had issued Directive 35, putting into motion *Operation Typhoon*, the plan designed to seize Moscow, crush the Soviets and, hopefully, end the war.
> —Harrison E. Salisbury, *The Unknown War*

> Now, the White House has largely left it to Senator Long, one of the most skillful tacticians in Congress, to ferry some energy tax bill through the Senate, in almost any form, hopefully within 10 days to two weeks.
> —Hedrick Smith, *New York Times*

Both the origin and the status of this innovation are disputed. One theory is that it results from a mistaken rendering of German; the German adverb *hoffentlich* means 'it is to be hoped,' and German-Americans who were less than fluent in English might have "translated" *hoffentlich* as *hopefully*. In this view the expression is ignorant and "not English," and it has been bitterly condemned by usage critics. The other view is that, on the contrary, *hopefully* = 'it is to be hoped' follows an established pattern in the English language; the adverbs *sadly, happily, mercifully*, and others are basically used to qualify verbs, in the meanings 'in a sad (happy, merciful, etc.) manner'; but they are now also used to qualify whole phrases or sentences, and to mean 'it is sad (happy, etc.) that' or 'I am sad (happy, etc.) to say that.' Those who accept this view feel that *hopefully* = 'it is to be hoped, I hope' is a natural and entirely acceptable development.

Perhaps there is some truth in both of the theories of origin.

◇ ***Recommendation.*** We feel that this innovation has proved its value and is here to stay. But many well-educated people dislike it intensely and regard those who use it as insensitive or even illiterate.

horde. Here is a word that makes etymology worthwhile.

Current Usage. *Horde* is used to mean 'a huge and threatening army of alien barbarians on the move,' as opposed to our side's civilized and essentially defensive ranks of disciplined soldiers:

> Big Brother seemed to tower up, an invincible, fearless protector, standing like a rock against the hordes of Asia. . . . —George Orwell, *1984*

> I recalled a broadcast we had heard in Berlin by the Dutch premier, De Geer, on April 9, 1940, exactly three weeks before the German hordes poured into his country, and nine days after they had overrun Denmark and invaded Norway. —William L. Shirer, *Midcentury Journey*

> . . . the primitive Red Army of World War II, with its horse-drawn cannons and hordes of foot-slogging infantrymen . . . —*Newsweek*

> Georgia lay defenseless before Sherman's horde.
> —Burke Davis, *Sherman's March*

> He did listen to her, attentively, then patiently explained that white South Africa had to protect its racial purity against the hordes that were trying to destroy it.
> —James A. Michener, *The Covenant*

Horde is also used of large groups of migrating animals:

> . . . the rolling hordes of the caribou did not deviate from their own right of way, which took precedence over man's.
> —Farley Mowat, *People of the Deer*

And it is applied to any group, gang, or crowd of people whom the speaker finds undesirable:

> It was he who arranged the financing and for the useful employment and accommodation of labourers from the great horde of Irish then pouring into the port of Boston.
> —John P. Marquand, *The Late George Apley*

> Who will provide the funds for the salaries—and the secretaries, chauffeured cars, globe-hopping junkets and other perquisites—of senators, congressmen, Members of Parliament and the bureaucratic hordes?
> —J. Paul Getty, *As I See It*

> [Vegetables you buy in stores] were harvested by migrant workers who could be suffering from any number of obnoxious diseases, handled by processors and salespeople, and picked over by hordes of customers before you bought them.
> —Euell Gibbons, *Stalking the Wild Asparagus*

> Johnson was nettled by pictures showing Bobby shooting rapids, climbing

mountains, surrounded by the horde of children he had fathered.

—Doris Kearns, *Lyndon Johnson and the American Dream*

Horde is also occasionally but persistently confused, even in respectable publications, with *hoard.* The two words are unrelated. *Hoard*, a native Old English word, means 'secret store of something, accumulation.'

Origin. The word *horde* comes to us from the tremendous migrations of the Turkic peoples. Starting from their homeland in far northeastern Asia, they moved for centuries as warrior nomads in the shifting confederacies of the steppe empires, threatening China, India, Persia, Europe. The Turkic word *ordu* means both 'camp' and 'army'—the ever-mobile army of nomadic tribes, more specifically 'large division of the nomads, individual group that travels, fights, and camps as a unit.' It was borrowed into all the languages of Europe, carrying with it an echo of terror and magnificence. In Russian the word is *ordá*, in Polish *horda*. From Polish it was borrowed into German as *horde*, thence into French as *horde*, and finally into English as *horde*—first recorded in the year 1555. The most renowned of all was the Golden Horde, a Mongol-Turkic army so named from the golden tent of its khan, who conquered Russia in the 13th century.

hors d'oeuvre. Properly speaking, this French term means 'outside (the) work, out of the ordinary,' hence 'something extra, a course of appetizers served at the beginning of a meal.' Since the usual practice is to serve a number of small items as *hors d'oeuvre*, the expression takes on a plural effect. In English it usually becomes *hors d'oeuvres* (which is not the correct French plural), and this has been so since the 18th century. The pronunciation is /ôr **dêrv, dêrvz**/.

> Well, we just had another glass of beer, and they were always passing Hors Duervs (I cant spell it but I can eat it).
>
> —Will Rogers, *Autobiography*

> In the restaurant we ordered hors d'oeuvres and beer.
>
> —Ernest Hemingway, *The Sun Also Rises*

horsemanship terms. See HORSES AND HORSEMANSHIP TERMS.

horse-racing terms. Very likely there has been racing since human beings first learned to ride horses and to bet on their performances. Since chance is such an integral part of this pastime, it is not surprising that the language of racing is a mixture of sports technicality, animal husbandry, and high (or low) finance. It is a most distinctive and colorful jargon, some of which has crossed over into the general vocabulary.

(1) Terms specific to racing:

allowance race = 'form of handicap race in which weights are varied from an established standard so as to equalize chances of winning among a field of horses that would otherwise be unevenly matched'

backstretch = 'straightaway portion on the far side of an oval racecourse, opposite the homestretch'

bookmaker = 'person who determines betting odds and accepts and pays off wagers away from the track'; illegal in most parts of the United States

brood mare = 'mare kept by a stable for breeding, especially a mare that has produced offspring'

chalk = 'latest odds, especially of a favorite in the betting' (formerly marked in chalk on an odds board)

chalk player = 'bettor who regularly wagers on favorites or other horses having short odds'

chute = 'extension of a straightaway portion of an oval racecourse, used for certain races'

daily double = 'wager based on selecting the winners of two consecutive specified races, often the first and second of a day's card'

dam = 'female parent of a horse'

dead heat = 'result of a race in which two or more mounts are judged to have crossed the finish line simultaneously in first, second, or third place'

double = 'daily double'

entry = 'two or more horses, usually of the same stable, that make up a single betting unit'

exacta = 'wager based on selecting the first- and second-place finishers in a specified race, in the proper order of finish'

field = (1) 'all the horses in a given race' (2) 'in a race with many horses, all those, in combination, other than the horses for which there are individual betting units in the operation of a parimutuel machine'

finish = 'to complete a race in first, second, or third place'

flat racing = 'competition on a course without obstacles, the commonest form of thoroughbred racing'

form player = 'bettor who regularly backs favorites or other horses at short odds on the basis of form or record of past performance'

furlong = '220 yards, or one-eighth of a mile'

futurity = 'race, customarily for two-year-olds, in which horses are entered at birth or even before'

Grand Circuit = 'association of major U.S. harness-racing tracks where the leading stakes are run'

grass course = 'racecourse consisting of natural turf rather than dirt'

handicap = 'race in which imposts are assigned according to age and past-performance records, the heavier weights to more mature and more successful members of the field, especially such a race with a field of horses of high quality'

handicapper = (1) 'track official who assigns varying imposts to a field of horses' (2) 'student of racing who selects which horses will probably finish first, second, and third in a day's program and whose selections appear in a newspaper, tip sheet, or some other publication'

harness racing = 'racing by horses specially bred for trotting or pacing, each pulling a sulky with one driver'

heat = 'one of two or more divisions of a race, especially in harness racing, each conducted separately over the distance specified for that race'

homestretch = 'portion of an oval racecourse extending from the last turn of the final curved segment to the finish line'

impost = 'assigned weight carried by a horse in a handicap race'

in the money (slang) = 'having finished first, second, or third'

length = 'unit of measure equal to the approximate extent of a horse from front to rear'; used to express the margin by which a horse leads a field or wins a race

long shot = 'horse that is held to have little chance to win a race, as calculated by most bettors and handicappers'

maiden = 'entrant of either sex that has never won a race'

meet, meeting = 'succession of daily or nightly programs at a single track, conducted over a specified period, often a month or thereabouts'

money = 'purse for a given race, divided principally among owners of the first three finishers'

morning line = 'preliminary odds for the races of a day's program, established and circulated early that day by a professional odds maker'

nose = 'approximate length of a horse's nose'; used as a measure of a very small lead or margin of victory

odds-on = 'considered a likely winner'

outsider = 'long shot'

paddock = 'enclosed area of a track where horses are saddled and mounted before parading to the starting gate'

parimutuel machine = 'electronic device that records the amounts bet on each horse in a race, determines the odds on the basis of those amounts, and calculates the payoff to backers of the first three finishers'

parlay = 'combination wager whereby the total amount won on one race is to be bet automatically on a second or more races'

perfecta = 'exacta'

photo finish = 'finish of a race so close that a photograph taken at the finish line is necessary to determine the outcome'

place = (1) (verb) 'to finish second' (2) (noun) 'a second-place finish'

pool = 'aggregate of money wagered on horses in a given race, subdivided according to amounts bet on entrants to win, to place, and to show'

post = (1) 'any of a series of stakes, perpendicular to the rail of a course, that at regular intervals serve as markers, or fractional measures, of the course' (2) 'starting point of a race or, by extension, the starting gate'

post position = 'position of a horse in the starting gate, in relation to the rail, first post position being nearest the rail'

post time = 'scheduled time of the start of a race, especially of the first race of a day's program'

rail = 'horizontal railing, supported by vertical posts, that marks the inner boundary of an oval course'

ringer = 'horse falsely entered in a race under the name of another'

router = 'horse that runs in races of more than a mile'

scratch = (1) (verb) 'to withdraw a horse from the field for a race' (2) (noun) 'horse thus removed'

scratch sheet = 'news sheet devoted to racing programs for a given day at one or several tracks'

show = (1) (verb) 'to finish third' (2) (noun) 'a third-place finish' (3) (adjective) 'pertaining to a bet on a horse to finish third or better'

silks = 'jockey's or driver's shirt and cap displaying the registered colors of the stable to which an entrant belongs'

sire = 'male parent of a horse'

stable = 'horses belonging to a single owner or group ownership, and trained and raced by such an individual or group'

starting gate = 'mechanical device for ensuring an even start in a race, consisting of a stall or some other barrier to keep each entrant in place'

steeplechase = 'event in thoroughbred racing in which horses cover a grass course provided with such obstacles as fences, hedges, and small bodies of water'

steward = 'any of several track officials who supervise the conduct of jockeys, trainers, and owners'

stretch = 'either of the straightaway portions of a course, but especially the homestretch'

string = 'stable'

studbook = 'register containing the pedigrees of racehorses'

sulky = 'very light, two-wheeled carriage pulled by a horse in harness racing'

thoroughbred racing = 'racing by fields of horses specially bred to be ridden under saddle by jockeys on flat courses or in steeplechases'

tip sheet = 'publication giving information, betting suggestions, etc., to gamblers and speculators'

totalizator, totalisator = 'parimutuel machine'

tote (informal) = 'totalizator'

turf course = 'grass course'

yearling = 'technically, a thoroughbred horse during the period between January 1 of the year following the year in which it was foaled and the next January 1'

(2) Some terms or expressions that have come into general use:

break stride = 'to hesitate or otherwise cease to function at desired speed or efficiency'

homestretch, stretch = 'final stage of a project'

horse's mouth = 'original source, best or highest authority'

long shot = 'person or thing whose chance of succeeding seems small'

nose = 'very narrow margin of victory'

off one's feed = 'not in good form, out of sorts'

parlay = 'to increase substantially the value of (something) by exploiting or transforming it'

photo finish = 'result of an cxtremely close contest'

play the field = 'to allow oneself to have a variety of activities and relationships, especially socially'

track record = 'overall accomplishments, as in a job or career'

See also HORSES AND HORSEMANSHIP TERMS.

horses and horsemanship terms. People who breed, ride, and drive horses use an enormous technical vocabulary. They have special terms for types of horses, the parts of the animal, its different colors, the equipment by which it is controlled, and the many breeds and races. Much of this vocabulary goes back to the Middle Ages and earlier. Owing to the tremendous prestige of English horse racing, breeding, and riding in the 18th and 19th centuries, English styles, methods, and terms are widely used in modern sporting horsemanship in other countries. The United States has contributed a considerable number of terms, such as *cinch, pinto,* and *mustang,* which were borrowed from Spanish in the West, and the names of American breeds such as *appaloosa, Morgan, quarter horse,* and *standardbred.*

Given below is a selection from the hundreds of technical words that are used by horse people.

(1) Types of horses:

colt = (1) 'young male horse' (2) (in racing) 'four-year-old or younger male horse'

filly = (1) 'young female horse' (2) (in racing) 'four-year-old or younger female horse'

foal = 'young horse, unweaned or less than one year old'

gelding = 'castrated male horse'

horse = (1) 'the animal in general' (2) 'adult male horse' (3) 'horse over 14 hands tall'

mare = 'adult female horse'

pony = (1) 'small horse of any breed that does not grow over 14 hands tall' (2) 'horse used in polo, up to 15 hands tall' (3) (western United States) 'any horse'

stallion = 'uncastrated adult male horse'

(2) Parts of the horse:

fetlock = (1) 'projecting part on the back of the leg above the hoof, with a tuft of hair' (2) 'the joint of the leg at this point'

forelock = 'lock of hair falling forward between the ears'

frog = 'horny pad on the sole of the foot, inside the hoof'

hand = 'the unit in which a horse's height is measured, equal to four inches'

hock = 'backward-bending tarsal joint of the hind leg'

hoof = (1) 'hard, horny covering of the foot, enclosing the toes' (2) 'the whole foot'

mane = 'growth of long hair on the ridge of the neck'

pastern = 'part of the foot immediately above the hoof'

* **withers** = 'ridge between the shoulder blades'

*Appears as separate entry

(3) Colors:

bay = 'reddish brown with black mane and tail'

chestnut = 'reddish brown with mane and tail of the same color'

dapple-gray = 'gray with dark mottlings'

dun = 'dull brown or gray'

piebald = 'black and white in patches'

pinto = 'white and another color in patches, piebald or skewbald'

roan = 'brown or black with a heavy sprinkling of white hairs'

skewbald = 'brown and white, or black and brown and white, in patches'

sorrel = 'light chestnut with light or white mane and tail'

(4) Equipment for the horse:

bit = 'steel bar held in the mouth by the bridle'

blinders, blinkers = 'leather flaps held by the bridle beside the eyes to prevent the distraction of side vision'

bridle = 'leather and metal equipment strapped to the horse's head, including headstall, bit, and reins'

cinch (especially western United States) = 'girth'

crop = 'short, stiff whip with a loop at one end for opening gates'

crupper = 'strap attached to the back of the saddle and passing around the tail'

girth = 'band attached to the saddle on both sides and strapped under the belly'

halter = (1) 'rope or strap fastened around the head, used for leading' (2) 'headstall without a bit, used for leading'

harness = 'all the equipment by which a horse is fastened to a vehicle'

headstall = 'the straps by which a bridle is fastened around the head'

martingale = 'strap attached to the girth, passing between the forelegs and attached to the reins or the bit'

rein = 'long strap attached to the bit on both sides and held by the rider or driver to control the horse's head'; usually used in the plural

rowel = 'metal wheel with sharp points in the tip of a spur'

saddle = 'the rider's seat, made of leather and wood, held on by the girth'

snaffle = 'type of bit with two or more parts flexibly jointed together'

spur = 'metal prong attached to the heel of the rider's boot, often with a rowel in the tip, for goading the horse's side'

stirrup = 'metal loop with a flat base, hung by a strap on each side of the saddle, to support the rider's foot'

traces = 'two straps or chains by which a harness is attached to a vehicle'

(5) Races and breeds:

American saddle horse = 'slender saddle horse bred in Kentucky, partly from Thoroughbreds'

appaloosa = 'strong saddle horse bred in the western United States, with black and white spotted markings on the rump'

Arab, Arabian = 'slender saddle horse bred in Arabia, the ancestor of Thoroughbreds'

bronco (chiefly western United States) = 'wild horse, mustang,' especially 'unbroken or untamable horse'

cayuse /kī-yōōs, kī-yōōs/ (western United States) = 'wild horse, mustang'

Clydesdale = 'large, heavy draft horse bred in Clydesdale, Scotland'

cob = 'stocky, short-legged horse of no particular breed'

cutting horse = 'light saddle horse bred in the United States and used especially for dividing cattle from a herd'

hack = 'hired horse,' especially 'inferior or worn-out horse'

Hackney = 'small, slender horse bred in England and trained in a very high-stepping gait'

hunter = 'strong saddle horse ridden in fox hunting and show jumping'

Morgan = 'small, versatile horse bred in the United States and descended from a stallion owned by Justin Morgan (1747–98)'

mustang = 'small wild horse of the western and southwestern United States, descended from the conquistadors' horses'

palomino = 'slender horse bred in Mexico and the southwestern United States, with a cream or golden color and blond or white mane and tail'

Percheron = 'strong draft horse bred in Perche, France'

Przevalski's horse /prĭ-zhə-văl-skēz, pər-/ = 'native horse of central Asia and Mongolia, last seen wild by Nikolai Przevalski in the late 19th century'

quarter horse = 'strong, stocky saddle horse bred in the United States'

Shetland pony = 'very small, strong pony of an old breed in the Shetland Islands'

shire = 'large, heavy draft horse bred in the Midland shires of England, the largest of all breeds'

standardbred = 'light horse bred in the United States and used in trotting races'

tarpan = 'small, stocky horse or pony of the central Asian plains'

Thoroughbred = 'slender saddle horse bred in England from Arab ancestors and always having a registered pedigree'; used in flat racing

(6) Selection of words and expressions borrowed from horse terminology into general usage:

bridle = 'to draw one's head back and upward, pulling in the chin, a motion expressing annoyance or resentment'

champ at the bit = 'to be restlessly impatient at restraint or inactivity'

cinch = (1) (verb) 'to get a firm hold on (something or someone)' (2) (noun) 'tight hold, firm grasp' (3) (noun) 'something easily done, a certainty'

hack = 'literary hireling, unambitious free-lance writer, inferior journalist'

harness = 'to control (some source of energy) and obtain work from it'

in the saddle = 'in control'

kick over the traces = 'to shake off restraint or control'

pony = 'small glass for liqueur, beer, etc.'

rein in = 'to check or restrain'

reins = 'controlling power'

spur = (1) (noun) 'a stimulus to action' (2) (verb) 'to stimulate (someone) to action'

See also HORSE-RACING TERMS.

housewife. There is a widespread feeling, not confined to extreme feminists, that a woman who performs the complex job of managing a home and family does not deserve a title that seems to suggest that she is married to her house:

> Just because the housewife is not paid a salary, no one should imagine that she is not part of the nation's economy.
> —*Reader's Digest*

On the other hand, some women both accept and defend the word:

> Why does the Women's Liberation Movement object to the word housewife? I *am* a housewife, and proud of it. . . .
> —*Reader's Digest*

History. Originally, the word *wife* meant simply 'woman.' The female head of a household was called the *hūse-wīf*, the 'house-woman,' and the male head was called the *hūsbonda*, the 'house-dweller.' Two shifts of meaning have occurred since: *wife* came to mean 'female spouse,' and *husband* came to mean 'male spouse.' This left *housewife* without a male counterpart, although the gap came to be filled during the 1970s with *househusband*. In the time of Shakespeare *housewife* began to be used scornfully, for 'immoral woman' or 'impudent girl.' This use survives in literature in the word *hussy*. Our word *housewife* is a revival of the older word.

Current Status. Whether *housewife* will live down its history, and the renewed pressure against it, remains to be seen. It is certainly receiving serious competition from the new word HOMEMAKER. Meanwhile, usage of *housewife* is entirely a matter of personal preference.

how come is a widely used interrogative expression that is equivalent to *why*. It is informal only.

hubris /hyo͞o-brĭs/. In the Greek tragedies the classic sin committed by a doomed protagonist is *hubris*, the pride or arrogance of a man who equates himself with the gods; this pride typically receives exemplary divine retribution. The word *hubris* (from Greek *hubris* = 'arrogance, insolence') is now used with this implication, 'arrogance that deserves punishment and will surely receive it, pride that comes before a fall':

> We know what happened to Adam and Eve, to Icarus, to Prometheus, to Faust. When our hubris leads us to at-

tain godlike powers, the gods will punish us.
—Albert Rosenfeld, *Smithsonian*

The CBS people headed into that year's convention with a classic case of hubris; the overweening pride of a team that has never lost, and therefore assumes it never will.
—Gary Paul Gates, *Air Time*

The sin of hubris, maybe. Me, Harold Cohen, guilty of hubris. A man who never thought of himself in an order higher than rodent, nailed for hubris?
—Woody Allen, *Side Effects*

The adjective is *hubristic* /hyōō-**brĭs**-tĭk/:

Even as I agree with such acute monitors of the controversy as James Burnham and Jeffrey Hurt who insist that science is not only hubristic but childish to the extent that it finds itself saying that the case for the harmlessness of pot is substantially established . . .
—William F. Buckley, Jr., *Execution Eve*

Hudson Valley dialect. This dialect can be heard in southeastern New York, northeastern Pennsylvania, and northern New Jersey. It is a subdivision of the NORTHERN DIALECT. Most of its distinctive regional flavor comes from the language of the colonial Dutch settlers of the Hudson River valley.

Vocabulary. (1) Words unique to the Hudson Valley region:

barrack = 'square haystack' (from Dutch *hooiberg*)
belly wop = 'to coast face down on a sled'
blickey = '*bucket, pail' (from Dutch *blikje*)
fishworm = '*earthworm'
kill = 'small *stream'; appears in place names such as *Batten Kill* and *Catskill* and in *killie fish, killifish* = 'small striped fish used for bait' (from Dutch *kil*)
skimmerton, skimmelton = 'mock serenade, *shivaree'
suppawn, spawn = 'cornmeal mush' (from Dutch *suppaen*, of Algonquian origin)

*Appears as separate entry

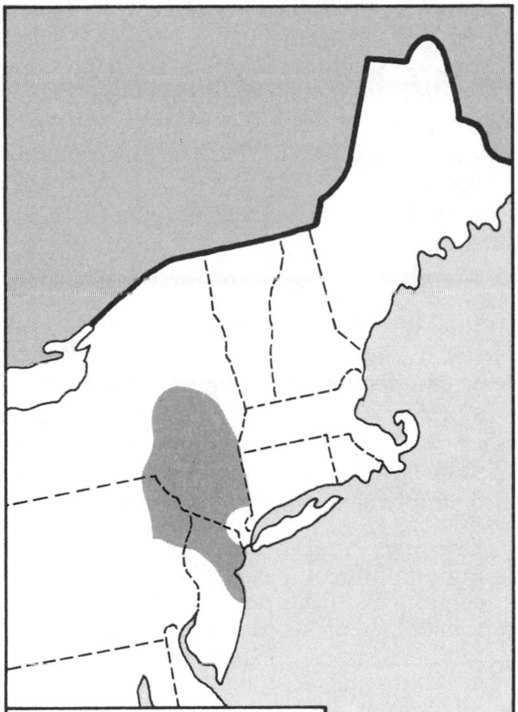

Hudson Valley dialect

(2) Farmers' calls to animals:

kees, kish = 'call to calves'
kip = 'call to chickens'
kush, kushie = 'call to cows'
so, sto = 'call to cows'
tye, tytie = 'call to cows'

(3) Food terms of Dutch origin:

cruller = 'unraised *doughnut' (from Dutch *krulle*)
olycook = '*doughnut'
pot cheese = '*cottage cheese' (from Dutch *pot kees*)
rolliche /rŏl-ĭ-chē/ = 'roulade'
thick milk = 'curdled milk, *clabber'

*Appears as separate entry

(4) Hudson Valley words that have spread to other regions:

buttonball = 'sycamore'
coal scuttle = 'bucket for coal'
loppered milk (also Inland Northern, New England) = 'curdled milk, *clabber'

sawbuck = 'sawhorse' (from Dutch *zaagbok*)
stoop = 'small *porch or a flight of steps leading to an outside door' (from Dutch *stoep*)
sugar bush, sap bush = 'sugar-maple grove'
teeter-totter = '*seesaw'

*Appears as separate entry

human, humane, etc. As a noun *human* was formerly regarded as somewhat unsatisfactory or affected—the phrase *human being* was preferred. This is no longer so. *A human* is now entirely acceptable, not only when our species is being contrasted with others but also simply as a synonym of *person:*

> Our practice of medicine was not confined to humans alone. One day a man came to Pete and presented the symptomatology of his friend [a tiger].
> —Thomas A. Dooley, *The Edge of Tomorrow*

> And, paradoxically, we creatures of mortal flesh here on earth—we humans—enjoy a dignity that no archangel or cherub, nay nor the seraphim themselves, enjoy. . . .
> —Thomas Howard, *Christianity Today*

Humane usually means 'having the gentle and civilized qualities of humans,' especially 'kindly, understanding, benevolent to other humans and to animals':

> . . . he was such an unusually humane and intelligent man for his line of work that in short order I was asking how a man like him had become a warder.
> —Willie Sutton, *Where the Money Was*

> The Chinese fly trap was designed to be humane, which was why it was so complicated. When the flies were trapped they weren't killed, or even injured.
> —Harpo Marx, *Harpo Speaks*

Humane may also mean 'relating to humanism or the humanities.'

Humanism, often with a capital *H,* refers to a cultural development in the Renaissance, when Latin and Greek literature was rediscovered, and European scholars, instead of thinking primarily in terms of religion and theology, began to think more in terms of the human mind as the defining factor of what we can know. Other uses of the word *humanism,* disregarding the Renaissance, refer to any study of or interest in human nature and capabilities, and also to the human condition in general. A *humanist* is a student of Humanism or a pursuer of (small *h*) humanism.

Humanity means, first, 'the human race collectively,' and second, 'human nature or the human condition.' It also means 'the quality of being humane,' in any of the senses of *humane,* but especially 'gentleness, kindliness.' *The humanities* are the branches of learning and study that relate to the human race, as opposed to *the sciences,* which relate to the material world and universe and to plants and animals. The humanities include psychology, history, sociology, the fine arts, linguistics, literature, philosophy, and sometimes mathematics.

Humankind means 'the human race':

> Thus there emerged a new relation between humankind and parasitic microorganisms.
> —William H. McNeill, *Plagues and People*

Origin. The word *human* is from Latin *hūmānus,* which is related both to *homo* = 'person, human being' and to *humus* = 'earth.' The underlying meaning (inherited from Indo-European) is 'earthling, creature of the earth,' as opposed to the gods who live in the heavens.

hung. See HANG.

Hungarian words. The Magyars, also known as Ugrians or Hungarians, came out of Asia in the 5th century A.D. and settled in Europe in the 9th century. Their language is Finno-Ugric, related to Finnish and, more distantly, to Turkish. For many centuries the Hungarians maintained a tradition of horsemanship deriving from their ancestral life as nomads on the central Asian plains. Among the handful of Hungarian words that have come into English, several are terms relating to horsemanship or cavalry equipment.

coach = 'four-wheeled horse-drawn carriage': (via French and German) from Hungarian *kocsi* = 'lightly built carriage with small front wheels,' from *Kocs* (a village in Hungary)

goulash /**gōō**-lăsh, -läsh/ = 'meat stew flavored with paprika': from Hungarian *gulyás hus* = 'herdsman's meat'

hussar /hōō-**zär**/ = 'light cavalry soldier wearing a uniform of ultimately Hungarian pattern': from Hungarian *huszár* = 'light cavalryman,' originally '15th-century mounted soldier of fortune'

paprika /pă-**prē**-kə/ = 'sweet or sometimes pungent powdered spice made from red bell peppers': from Hungarian *paprika* = 'Turkish pepper'

saber = 'one-edged slashing cavalry sword': (via French and German) from Hungarian *szablya* = 'sword'

shako /**shăk**-ō, **shā**-kō/ = 'soldier's hat of cylindrical shape, with a plume, a visor, and a metal plate in front': (via French) from Hungarian *czákó süveg* = 'peaked cap'

hyperbole /hī-**pêr**-bə-lē/. A figure of speech that employs deliberate exaggeration. Here is an example:

> He is so narrow minded that if he fell on a pin, it would blind him in both eyes. —Fred Allen

The term comes from a Greek word meaning 'extravagance, overshooting the mark.'

hyphen. See COMPOUND ADJECTIVES; COMPOUND NOUNS; COMPOUND VERBS.

hypostatization. See PERSONIFICATION.

I

iambic pentameter. See POETRY.

iconoclasm. The Byzantine church was notably fond of icons, or pictures of Christ, the Virgin Mary, and the saints. In the 8th and 9th centuries there was a movement and political party that opposed the use and veneration of icons and on many occasions turned out mobs to destroy icons in churches. These were the *iconoclasts,* from Greek *eikonoklastēs* = 'icon-breaker' (from *eikōn* = 'image, icon' + *-klastēs* = 'breaker'), and their movement was *iconoclasm.* In the Protestant Reformation of the 16th and 17th centuries there was a comparable movement to destroy religious paintings and statues in order to purify and simplify Christian worship. Echoing the older Byzantine movement, this Protestant movement was also called *iconoclasm:*

> Even in the earliest days of the Revolt in 1565, the mobs that destroyed statues and pictures in wild outbreaks of iconoclasm were made up of unemployed workers turned adrift in years of bad trade.
> —Charles Wilson, *The Dutch Republic*

> When the Parliamentary troops desecrated Worcester, a fury of iconoclasm and anti-popery was sweeping the south-eastern parts of the country.
> —C. V. Wedgewood, *The King's War*

In later times *iconoclasm* has been applied to any movement to 'break images,' to attack established ideas or institutions; likewise *iconoclast* = 'one who attacks established ideas,' and the adjective *iconoclastic:*

> Somebody has got to rescue us from the women's liberation movement, and if Miss Greer gets over her fundamentalist iconoclasm, she might be just the person to do it.
> —William F. Buckley, Jr., *Execution Eve*

> To many of their successors, the young iconoclasts [newsmen in Vietnam] were folk heroes whose record demonstrated that the more criticism and the more negativism, the greater the possibility of recognition and reward.
> —William C. Westmoreland, *A Soldier Reports*

> Kemp's tax-cutting efforts were refined by his economic aide, Paul Craig Roberts, an iconoclastic young economist who had rejected Keynesian orthodoxy.
> —Rowland Evans and Robert Novak, *Reader's Digest*

> Mencken, the most powerful iconoclastic journalist of the first half of this century, devoted much of his life to ridiculing patriotism, piety, pomp and "plutocrats," saying that the honorary degrees bestowed by universities were fit only for "realtors, chiropractors and Presidents of the United States."
> —Ben A. Franklin, *New York Times*

ideology /ī-dē-ŏl-ə-jē, ĭd-ē-/. This word is borrowed from French *idéologie,* which was formed from *idée* = 'idea' or its source, Greek *idea* = 'form, intellectual concept, idea.' Our word *idea* also comes from this Greek word. *Ideology* means 'system of ideas, especially political ideas.' The adjective is *ideological,* and there is also a noun *ideologue,* meaning 'person who believes in and advocates an ideology':

> The ideology of bipartisanship persuaded (or conveniently allowed) the political parties to abstain from partisan divisions on foreign policy.
> —Doris Kearns, *Lyndon Johnson and the American Dream*

> Chinese worry that the massive influx of Western ideas could undermine the Communist Party's ideological hold on China.
> —*U.S. News & World Report*

> . . . developing nations, under the influence of a few adamant ideologues . . . —*New York Times*

idiolect. See DIALECT.

idiom. This term has a specific meaning in language study, denoting an expression that is not readily understandable from its literal meaning—for example, *put up with* in the sense of 'tolerate, endure.' An example of a foreign idiom that has found a permanent place in our language is *pièce de résistance,* whose literal meaning in French is 'resistance piece.' But what on earth is a resistance piece? Not even a Frenchman could tell you for sure. The idiom sprang up in the late 1700s in the sense of 'main course of a meal.'

Here are a few examples of originally American idioms that are probably understood by English speakers worldwide:

as all get-out = 'greatly': *mad as all get-out*
be down sick = 'to be ill'
catch on = (1) 'to understand' (2) 'to become fashionable'
in the hole = 'lacking money or in debt'
pull the wool over one's eyes = 'to defraud, deceive'
run-in = 'hostile encounter'

The expression *be down sick* would be recognizable as a U.S. regionalism; it has actually been current in rural speech in various parts of the country since colonial times.

The term *idiom* may also be used more generally of the recognizable form of a given language or of that language's habit, expressiveness, or cast:

> [Anglo-Irish writers] cultivated the modified form of English spoken in Ireland, an idiom strongly colored by Gaelic constructions, as a vehicle for literary expression.
> —Margaret Schlauch, *The English Language in Modern Times*

Likewise, in this book we occasionally condemn certain expressions as unidiomatic—because they strike us as going against the grain of good English. For instance, we consider it a breach of idiom to use the word TOO as the first word in a sentence.

A perfectly acceptable further extension of the basic meaning of *idiom* is 'characteristic artistic or literary mode': *the idiom of jazz; the pianistic idiom.* (For the etymology of *idiom,* see GREEK WORDS.)

idyll /ĭd'l/, from Greek *eidullion,* literally means 'short poem, typically describing a pleasant scene of country life.' It may also, as in Tennyson's *Idylls of the King,* mean any romantic poem. It is used figuratively to mean a period or an interlude of life in which everything is happy and beautiful, and which is typically looked back on as being so good that it couldn't last:

> My existence turned into one of those Huck Finn-Tom Sawyer idylls. . . . [with] woods and mysteries, life and death among the small creatures, hunting and fishing.
> —Ronald Reagan (quoted), *Book Digest*

Or it may mean an unrealistically perfect picture of life, a scene too good to be true:

> In the 1960's there arose a widespread view of the [paleolithic] hunters' life as an idyll, free of work and want.
> —Philip Morrison, *Scientific American*

The adjective is *idyllic:*

> We spent two idyllic weeks. We swam, we fished, we walked through the woods. She loved the farm, she loved John and Alice, she was as happy as a child. —Willie Sutton, *Where the Money Was*

> . . . life in these rural towns was never as idyllic as our poets remember it.
> —Bill Moyers, *Listening to America*

> The idyllic interlude, however, was brief. Cracks appeared in our marital structure even before George was born. —J. Paul Getty, *As I See It*

if. See WHETHER, IF.

ignoble. The meaning is 'not noble, dishonorable, dishonest, contemptible':

> [Communism] enunciates movingly the theory of a classless society, but alas! its methods for achieving this noble end are all too often ignoble.
> —Martin Luther King, Jr., *Strength to Love*

> . . . Hamill has unfortunately succumbed to the ignoble television-bred myth that the public will respond positively only to recycled pulp. . . .
> —Robert Stephen Spitz, *Saturday Review*

The word is from Latin *ignōbilis* = 'not noble.' The *ig-* results from the fact that *nōbilis* = 'noble' was originally *gnōbilis* (based on the root *gno-* = 'to know'), meaning 'well-known, renowned,' used as a title of high birth. The negative form would have been *in-gnōbilis* (*in-* = 'not, un-') but was simplified to *ignōbilis.* The *ig-* of *ignorant* and *ignominious* is of similar origin.

ilk. By origin this is a Scottish pronoun meaning 'same.' It became familiar in the curious designation of some Scottish family names, in which the head of a clan with a name identical to its place of origin or seat is called *of that ilk.* Thus, the chief of the clan Ruthven, originally from a place called Ruthven, could be called Ruthven of Ruthven but would formally be called Ruthven of that ilk. Outside Scotland this peculiar formula was misunderstood as meaning 'of that family,' and thus *of that ilk* was reinterpreted to mean 'of that kind or type.' For some reason this use is often somewhat disparaging:

> . . . after 16 years of weathering the sustained attacks of Mr. Loeb and his ilk . . .
> —Thomas J. McIntyre (quoted), *Boston Globe*

> But the night before the game, Joe Frazier was to fight a college student named Terry Daniels. Like so many fights of this ilk, it was hard for me to believe that this fight could be licensed. It was a disgraceful mismatch.
> —Howard Cosell, *Cosell*

> Thundered He [Chicago's Mayor Daley]: "You and your ilk are trying to tell me you're being stepped on. As long as I am the Mayor, no one will be stepped on and that goes for you too." Yelled back [Alderman] Despres: "I don't want you or anyone else to call me an ilk." And God said, "I did not mean to call you an ilk. I meant to call you an elk." The faithful roared. Could Fred Allen have done any better?
> —Studs Terkel, *Talking to Myself*

◇ ***Recommendation.*** This use of *ilk* to mean 'sort or type,' although originally a mistake, is now established in international English. In Scotland, however, it is still frowned on.

illegitimate child. In recent times, terms that refer to a child born out of wedlock have gone out of style. But the social concept of the *illegitimate child* is an old one dating back to the time when marriage first became a legal relationship. The earliest meaning in English of *illegitimate*—which today has several other senses—referred specifically to offspring not recognized by law.

The word *bastard* has become completely pejorative and is used more often as a curse than as the legal designation it originally was. It comes from the Latin *bastardus,* a term of legal status applied to the acknowledged son of a prince or nobleman not born of the lawful wife. In the 11th century one of William the Conqueror's titles was William the Bastard, not because of his hated ruthlessness but because of his status as the illegitimate son of a prince.

The social stigma attached to the whole subject has generated many euphemisms for it. These are especially common in American folk speech and dialect. *Outside child* or *outside baby* is a Black English term used in the South and midlands, and it emphasizes the notion that the illegitimate child is outside the social and legal framework. *Love child* is an originally British euphemism now fully established in American English. In the Coastal Southern dialect *Sunday baby* or *Sunday child* is often used.

In several dialect regions the euphemism involves reference to colts, since the paternity of a colt is important in determining its value as a work or show horse. In parts of the South an *old-field* is a worn-out or overcultivated piece of land. An *old-field colt* is a colt of unknown paternity:

> I could only remember that every old field colt was a regular descendent of Eclipse.
> —*Southern Literary Messenger* (1835)

In the Virginia Piedmont dialect this term is extended further to include a child of unclaimed paternity.

In the General Southern and North Midland dialects a common euphemism is *woods colt,* a colt conceived in the anonymous cover of the forest.

> Mink and everybody else in ten miles of the Bend knew that old Will Varner was going to have to marry her off to somebody, and that quick, if he didn't want a woods colt in his back yard next grass.
> —William Faulkner, *The Mansion* (1959)

In other regions, especially the West, the corresponding term is *catch-colt* or *ketch-colt,* a colt caught or roped on the range.

illusion, allusion. See ALLUDE, ALLUSION.

imbue literally means 'to make (something) wet through, saturate' and 'to tinge (something) with a color.' It is used principally of persons, meaning 'to fill (someone) with a feeling, an attitude, a belief, etc.':

> . . . almost as soon as the boy was born, he set about to imbue the child with the religion of his New England forebears.
> —William Faulkner, *Light in August*

> Traditionally, males were indoctrinated to protect females. Like Superman, they were expected to leap tall buildings without ripping their leotards, to have a Humphrey Bogart poker face, and to be imbued with the aggressiveness of a Bengal tiger.
> —Herbert G. Zerof, *Reader's Digest*

It can also be used of objects or abstractions, meaning merely 'to fill or permeate (something) with (something)':

> The marvel was the pleasure Kermit seemed to be getting out of being able to cross his legs. That was a matter of magic—the imbuing of an inanimate object with a personality all its own.
> —John Culhane, *Reader's Digest*

> When the Germanic peoples were Christianized, English, Scandinavian and German became imbued with Christian lexicon. . . .
> —Randolph Quirk, *The State of the Language*

immigrate. See EMIGRATE, IMMIGRATE.

immune. One may have the impression that the adjective *immune* basically means 'having biological resistance to a disease' and secondarily 'not responsive to' or 'exempt from.' In fact it's the other way round. The original meaning (in Latin) was 'exempt from certain public duties,' and in law *immune* still means 'not liable, exempt' and is used with *from;* likewise the noun *immunity:*

> "Members of Congress are immune from arrest," said Donovan.
> —Fletcher Knebel, *Night of Camp David*

> The deal is that, in return for truthful testimony in Congress . . . he will win immunity from prosecution on those charges. —*Boston Herald American*

Developing from this legal sense, *immune* is used to mean 'safe from, protected from':

> The senators, of course, are not immune from political pressures.
> —Martin Tolchin, *New York Times*

> No man is immune from fear.
> —Anthony Storr, *Churchill: The Man*

> No part of America is immune from tornadoes. . . .
> —Warren H. Spencer, *Reader's Digest*

> Some 22 mobsters and fronts continued their pillage immune from investigation.
> —Lester Velie, *Reader's Digest*

The biological condition of immunity—resistance, due to the presence of antibodies, to certain diseases—was discovered in the 19th century, primarily by Louis Pasteur. In English the words *immune* and *immunity* in this medical sense were at first used with *against* or *from,* but as the condition was more and more understood as an active resistance rather than a passive protection, they came to be used primarily with *to: immune to smallpox.*

This medical use has given rise to a further generalized use of *immune,* to mean 'resistant to', or 'protected against,' but used with *to;* and similarly *immunity:*

> At this point, however, Raymond was immune to subtle looks.
> —Tom Wolfe, *The Kandy-Kolored . . . Baby*

> . . . a pampered class all but immune to the disheartening tantrums of the economic weather.
> —*Time*

> It's time for Congress to pass "catastrophic medical insurance" legislation, granting each of us immunity to devastating medical bills.
> —*Reader's Digest*

◊ ***Recommendation.*** In its legal sense 'exempt,' *immune* is always used with *from.* In its medical sense 'resistant,' it is most often used with *to.* In its various generalized senses, it may correctly be used with *from* or *against,* or with *to.* The choice probably depends on whether the speaker is thinking of protection or resistance as the underlying meaning.

imply. See INFER, IMPLY.

in, into. The preposition *in* primarily means 'located or being within' but also quite correctly means 'moving or directed inside': *going in the house; fell in the water.* In the latter meaning *into* is more specific: *looked straight into her eyes.* When the adverb *in* is followed by *to,* they are written as two words: *He walked in to the downtown area.*

in back of. See BACK OF, IN BACK OF.

in behalf. See BEHALF.

incredible is still, occasionally, used in its literal sense 'not believable':

> To Judge Boyle, Kennedy's claim also was incredible.
> —John Barron, *Reader's Digest*

Much more often it is used to mean 'amazing, remarkable':

> In some ways Burnside was about as incompetent a general as Abraham Lincoln ever commissioned, and he comes down in history looking stuffy with frock coat and incredible whiskers. . . .
> —Bruce Catton, *Glory Road*

> Computers regulate many functions, and robots at the Chrysler plant do an incredible 98 percent of the welding.
> —Ronald Schiller, *Reader's Digest*

> Still, I used to wonder how Freddy could be so talented and not be on Broadway or in a big dance company. "Can't they see how incredible he is?" I'd think to myself.
> —Andy Warhol and Pat Hackett, *POPism*

Indian. (1) The subcontinent of India includes Pakistan, Bangladesh, and Nepal as well as the Republic of India. In a geographical and cultural sense *Indian* can apply to the whole subcontinent; politically it refers only to the republic.

(2) When Columbus reached the Americas, he apparently believed that he had found an outlying part of Asia and therefore called the local inhabitants *Indios* = 'Indians.' So great has been his prestige that to this day the pre-European peoples from Tierra del Fuego to northern Canada are generally called, in Spanish, *Indios;* in English, *Indians.* (The Innuit alone are never called Indians.) This misnomer can cause real misunderstanding. If you happen to refer to "an Indian drum" or "Indian politics" without making the context clear, you may well be asked, "Indian from India or American Indian?" A partial solution is to use the compound *Amerindian* or the term *Indian American.* Some American Indians also object to being called Indians at all, preferring *Native Americans* or *Aboriginal Americans.*

◇ ***Recommendation.*** It is too late now to correct this enormous mistake. *Indian* is accepted as Standard English for 'American Indian.' But in any ambiguous situation *American Indian, Amerindian,* or *Indian American* should be used. We recommend sensitivity to the preferences of present-day Indian groups, but there is no general agreement among them.

Indian words (American Indian). Of the hundreds of different languages once spoken by the native peoples of the United States, most were never recorded and have vanished without trace. Only a few are now spoken, and most of these are destined to extinction. American English has preserved a handful of borrowed Indian words; most were picked up during the early colonial years, up and down the eastern seaboard, and nearly all come from the great Algonquian family, which includes Narragansett, Natick, Delaware, Ojibwa, Shawnee, Ottawa, and Cree. Below are virtually all of the borrowed American Indian words that are still in wide currency. In some cases the original form of the source word is available. In other cases we do not know the exact details.

(1) Plants and animals:

chipmunk = 'small striped squirrel': originally *chitmunk,* from Algonquian

hickory = 'hardwood tree bearing edible

nuts': originally *pokahickory*, from a (Virginia) Algonquian word *pawcohiccora* = 'crushed hickory nuts prepared as food'

menhaden /mĕn-**hād**'n, -**hăd**'n/ = 'very abundant small, silvery fish of the Atlantic coast': from an Algonquian word meaning 'fertilizer,' probably because European colonists taught Indians to use the menhaden as fertilizer

moose = 'very large northern deer' (in the Old World called *elk*): from Algonquian *moos*

opossum = 'tree-living marsupial animal with a gray body and white face': from Algonquian *aposum* = 'white animal'

pecan /pĭ-**kän**, -**kăn**, **pē**-kän, -kăn/ = 'type of hickory bearing much-esteemed edible nuts': from Algonquian *pakan*

persimmon = 'tree bearing edible reddish-orange fruit': from an Algonquian word meaning 'dried fruit'

quahog /**kwô**-hôg, -hŏg, **kō**-/ = 'large edible clam of the Atlantic coast': from Narragansett *poquauhock*

raccoon = 'tree-living animal related to the bear, with a black eye mask and a bushy ringed tail': from Algonquian *arathkon*

skunk = 'black and white animal related to the mink and otter, having a gland that can squirt out an intensely foul-smelling fluid': from Algonquian

squash = 'vegetable related to the pumpkin, widely cultivated by the Algonquians': from Natick *isquoutersquash*

terrapin = 'American freshwater turtle': from (Virginia) Algonquian

woodchuck = 'large, ground-living animal related to the marmot': from Cree *ocheck* (changed to *woodchuck* by FOLK ETYMOLOGY)

(2) Artifacts and Indian life:

hominy = 'hulled and dried corn kernels, often ground into small pieces, or grits, prepared as food by boiling or baking, now chiefly in the South': from an Algonquian word meaning 'prepared corn'

moccasin = 'Indian shoe of soft leather with the sole, sides, and toe formed of a single piece': from Natick *mohkussin*

powwow = (1) 'Indian medicine man or sorcerer' (2) 'Indian ceremony or festivity' (3) 'discussion among or meeting with Indians': from an Algonquian word meaning 'medicine man, sorcerer'

sachem = 'Indian chief': from Narragansett *sachim*

squaw (often used derogatorily by white speakers) = 'Indian woman or wife': from Algonquian *squa-* = 'woman'

succotash = 'corn kernels and lima beans cooked together': from an Algonquian word meaning 'cooked corn kernels'

tepee = 'cone-shaped tent of the Plains Indians': from Dakota *tipi*

toboggan = 'sled without runners, with the front end curved upward': from a Micmac word meaning 'sled made of skin'

tomahawk = 'Indian ax, used as a tool or weapon': from (Virginia) Algonquian *tamahaac*

wampum = 'beads made of shells, strung as necklaces or belts, and used as money in the early colonial period': from Narragansett *wampompeag* = 'white strings'

wigwam = 'hut used by the Indians of the Northeast and Great Lakes area, typically of rounded shape, and made of bark or hides on a pole framework': from Algonquian *wikiwam*

For words borrowed from the native languages of Mexico, the Caribbean, and South America see AZTEC WORDS; CARIBBEAN WORDS; SOUTH AMERICAN WORDS.

Indian words (India). The English began trading with India in the reign of Queen Elizabeth I, and they eventually ruled much of the country for nearly 200 years, ending in 1948. This long exposure to India's rich civilization has left a large deposit of words in the English vocabulary. Most were borrowed from Hindi, India's most widespread modern language, one of the descendants of classical Sanskrit; other words came from Marathi and Bengali, also descended from Sanskrit. Still others were taken from Tamil and Malayalam, Dravidian languages not related to Sanskrit. (Malayalam has no connection with Malay—the similarity of names is a coincidence.) Some of these Indian words are themselves of foreign origin, borrowed from Persian or Arabic, or even Portuguese.

Words borrowed from Sanskrit itself are covered separately at SANSKRIT WORDS. Set out below is a selection of the words we have taken from current Indian languages in the past 500 years.

bangle = 'bracelet, ornament': from Hindi *bangrī* = 'glass bracelet'

blighty /**blī**-tē/ (British army slang; now obsolete) = 'home, England': from Hindi *bilāyatī* = 'foreign, European,' from Arabic

bungalow /**bŭng**-gə-lō/ = 'one-story house, cottage'; in British India, a bungalow was a lightly built one-story house used by Europeans: from Hindi *bangla* = 'Bengali, house built in the style of Bengal' (now Bangladesh)

cashmere = (1) 'silky wool from the undercoat of the Cashmere goat' (2) 'fabric made of this wool, or any similar fine fabric'; the Cashmere goat, native to The Himalayas, is named for *Cashmere*, the old spelling of *Kashmir*

chapati /chə-**pä**-tē/ = 'flat, fluffy wheaten bread': from Hindi *chapati*

cheetah /**chē**-tə/ = 'large, swift-running spotted cat of Africa and southern Asia, tamed and used for hunting in India': from Hindi *chita*, from Sanskrit *citrakāya* = '(animal) with a speckled body'

cheroot /shə-**rōōt**/ = 'cigar with square-cut ends': from Tamil *shuruttu* = 'roll of tobacco, cheroot made in southern India'

chintz = 'printed and glazed cotton fabric used for upholstery': originally *chints*, plural of *chint* = 'elegant painted cotton fabric made in India,' from Hindi *chint*, from Sanskrit *citra* = 'many-colored, speckled'

chit = (1) 'check or voucher for food, drink, etc.' (2) 'short note or letter': Anglo-Indian *chitty*, from Hindi *chittha* = 'note, pass'

chukker = 'period of play in a polo match': from Hindi *chakkar* = 'circle, turn'

coir /koir/ = 'coconut fiber, used for rope and matting': from Malayalam *kāyar* = 'twisted cord'

coolie = 'Asian laborer employed by Europeans': from Hindi *kulī* = 'laborer,' originally the name of a tribe in the state of Gujarat

copra /**kŏp**-rə/ = 'dried coconut meat': (via Portuguese) from Malayalam *koppara* = 'coconut'

corundum /kə-**rŭn**-dəm/ = 'very hard mineral, occurring as gems such as rubies and emeralds; in granular form used as an industrial abrasive': from Tamil *koruntam*, probably from Sanskrit *kuruvinda* = 'ruby'

cowrie = 'shell of a small ocean mollusk, used as money in Polynesia': from Hindi *kaurī*

cummerbund = 'broad sash worn with a tuxedo'; originally a sash worn by Indian men: from Hindi *kamarband*, from Persian *kamar-band* = 'waist-band'

curry = 'cooked dish flavored with a mixture of spices, typically including turmeric, coriander, and pepper or chili': from Tamil *kari* = 'sauce'

dinghy /**dĭng**-gē/ = 'rowboat or small sailboat': from Hindi *dīngī* = 'small boat'

dungaree /dŭng-gə-**rē**/ = 'strong twilled cotton fabric, denim': from Hindi *dungrī* = 'a coarse cotton cloth'

* **Juggernaut** = 'effigy of Vishnu drawn in procession at a festival in Orissa'

jungle = 'tropical rain forest'; in India *jungle* originally meant 'waste land,' especially 'waste land covered with thick second-growth vegetation': from Hindi *jangal*, from Sanskrit *jāngala* = 'desert'

jute = 'fiber of an Asian plant, used for making sackcloth and rope': from Bengali *jhūto*

kedgeree /**kĕj**-ə-rē/ = 'British cooked breakfast dish of rice, fish, and eggs': from Hindi *khichrī* = 'cooked dish of rice, lentil sauce, and spices'

loot = 'valuables stolen in time of war or riot': from Hindi *lūt,* from Sanskrit *loptra* = 'plunder'

madras /mə-**dräs**, -**drăs**, **măd**-rəs, **mäd**-/ = 'fine cotton fabric with strong checked or plaid pattern': formerly exported from the port of *Madras* on the Bay of Bengal

Mogul /**mō**-gəl/ = (1) 'ruler of the empire in northern India founded by Mongols in the 16th century' (2) small *m* 'rich or powerful man'

mongoose /**mŏng**-gōōs/ = 'small Indian mammal that preys on snakes': from Marathi *mangūs*

mulligatawny /mŭl-ĭ-gə-**tô**-nē/ = 'soup flavored with curry': from Tamil *milagutannir* = 'pepper-water'

myna /**mī**-nə/ = 'Asian bird related to the starling': from Hindi *maina*

***nabob** /**nā**-bŏb/ = 'provincial governor or ruler in the Mogul empire'

nautch /**nôch**/ = 'dance performed by professional women dancers': from Hindi *nāch* = 'a dance'

pajamas, (British) **pyjamas** /pə-**jăm**-əz, -**jä**-məz/ = 'sleeping suit with trousers'; in India pyjamas were loose, light trousers worn especially by Muslims, adopted by English males for relaxed wear at home and then also as a sleeping garment: from Hindi *pāejāma,* from Persian *pāi-jāmah* = 'leg-garment'

***pariah** /pə-**rī**-ə/ = 'member of a low-ranking caste in southern India'

punkah = 'indoor fanning device consisting of a cloth frame hung from the ceiling, pulled to and fro with a cord by a servant': from Hindi *pankhā*

raj /**räj**/ = 'rule, especially the British rule in India': from Hindi *rāj,* from Sanskrit *rājya* = 'rule, sovereignty'

raja /**rä**-jä/ = 'king, prince': from Hindi *rājā,* from Sanskrit *rājan* = 'male ruler'

rani /**rä**-nē/ = 'queen, princess': from Hindi *rānī,* from Sanskrit *rājñī* = 'female ruler'

rupee /rōō-**pē**, **rōō**-pē/ = 'the basic Indian coin and monetary unit from the 16th century to the present day': from Hindi *rupaiya,* from Sanskrit *rūpya* = 'piece of wrought silver or gold'

sahib /**sä**-ĭb, -ēb/ = 'sir'; formerly used by Indians addressing European males: from Hindi *sāhib* = 'lord, master,' from Arabic *sāhib* = 'friend, companion (of the Prophet)'

sari /**sä**-rē/ = 'woman's dress consisting of a length of fine fabric wrapped around the body and draped over one shoulder': from Hindi *sārī*

seersucker = 'fine, light fabric woven in strips that are alternately puckered and flat': from Hindi *sirsakar,* from Persian *shīr-o-shakar* = 'milk-and-sugar'

shampoo = 'to wash the scalp and hair with special soap'; originally in India 'to massage a person's body as part of an elaborate bath': from Hindi *Chāmpō!* = 'Massage!' imperative of *chāmpnā* = 'to massage'

shawl = 'cape worn chiefly by women over the shoulders or head'; originally an expensive and decorative garment of this kind imported from India and made in Kashmir of the silky wool of a Tibetan goat: from Persian and Hindi *shāl*

sola topi /**sō**-lə **tō**-pē/ = 'pith helmet, formerly worn especially by Europeans in India': from Hindi *sholā topī* = 'pith hat,' from *sholā* = 'pith obtained from an Indian plant'

teak = 'hard wood of a southeast Asian tree': (via Portuguese) from Malayalam *tēkka*

thug = (1) 'one of an organized anti-British group of assassins and robbers in 19th-century India,' hence (2) 'strong-arm man hired to kill or beat up': from Hindi *thag* = 'robber, rogue'

toddy = (1) 'sweet, self-fermenting juice of an Indian palm tree,' hence (2) 'drink made with spirits, spices, and water': from Hindi *tārī* = 'palm juice, palm wine'

tom-tom = (1) 'type of Indian hand drum' (2) 'any small-headed, deep-bodied hand drum': from Hindi *tamtam* = 'drum' (onomatopoeic)

veranda /və-**răn**-də/ = 'roofed gallery on the front or side of a house, *porch': from Hindi *varaṇḍā*, from Portuguese *varanda* = 'gallery, porch'

wallah /**wäl**-ə/ = 'man, person in charge of something': from a Hindi suffix meaning 'one who is in charge'

*Appears as separate entry

individual. The noun *individual* basically means 'person considered as a separate entity, in contrast with a group or society.' It is often used as a pointless substitute for *person* in general or for a descriptive personal term.

> Such registrations must be given in writing to a government office so that the individual is thereby freed from paying church taxes from his other salary. —*National Catholic Reporter*

> He was soon on familiar terms with Mick Jagger, David Hockney, and Rudolf Nureyev, and . . . was among the first to see and appreciate the talents of these individuals.
> —James Danziger, *Beaton*

In the first quotation "person" would be simpler and better. In the second, "artists" would be an improvement. Following is an apt use of *individual:*

> The people are terribly disturbed across this country as to . . . whether their voices are ever going to mean anything or whether business has gotten so large, labor organizations so large, that they care nothing for the individual.
> —Robert Kennedy (quoted), Arthur M. Schlesinger, Jr., *Robert Kennedy and His Times*

◇ ***Recommendation.*** This is a matter of style. We agree with traditional criticism that *individual* is overused and is best kept for 'single person as opposed to a group.'

Indo-European. English belongs to the Indo-European language family, so named because it includes most of the languages of India and Europe. Among them are Sanskrit, Greek, Latin, Russian, and German.

A "family" is a group of languages descended from a single ancestor language. The original Indo-European was spoken by a people living north of the Black Sea around 5000 B.C. Branches of them spread southeastward into India and westward into Europe. They mixed with local peoples, and their original speech changed, splitting up into dialects that gradually became independent languages. By 2000 B.C. early forms of Sanskrit, Greek, Latin, Slavic, and Germanic had emerged. Later, as empires rose and fell, peoples migrated, and new continents were colonized, the Indo-European languages split up yet further and were spread around the world.

English, one of the members of this very large family, is thus directly descended from a language spoken 7,000 years ago. This in itself is not remarkable; all languages are descended from equally remote ancestors, and 5000 B.C. is nowhere near the beginning of human language itself (at least 100,000 years ago, possibly as much as half a million). What is remarkable is that we know so much of our own language story as far back as we do. Linguistic science has reconstructed much of the Indo-European ancestor language itself and can describe in great detail how it changed and diverged. The histories of many words can be accurately traced step by step from Indo-European to Modern English.

To take a homely example, the word *needle* was first recorded in the 8th century A.D. (Old English period) as *nǣdl*. Before that there are no records, but the linguists have deduced that the Germanic form of the word around 300 B.C. was *nēthlo-*. And the reconstructed Indo-European form of the same word, used around 5000 B.C., was *nētla-*. The methods by which such reconstructions are so confidently made are of course extremely specialized, but scholars have sound reasons for relying on them. The reconstructed forms presented in this entry are considered to be beyond serious doubt. In looking at the sequence Indo-European *nētla-* ⟶ Germanic *nēthlo-* ⟶ Old English *nǣdl* ⟶ Modern English *needle,* we are looking at a real and very long sequence of cultural life, embodied in an unbroken language tradition. Just as the use of the needle was handed down by teaching children from generation to generation, so was the word transmitted. In this and hundreds of other everyday modern words we have a living link with ancient forebears.

Not just the individual words but the language as a whole system has been inherited in this way. The grammar, the pronunciation, and the vocabulary have undergone great changes, but they remain part of a structure that continued through time.

Ancestral Indo-European, like Greek and Latin, was highly inflected; that is, grammatical relationships were expressed by a large array of different endings, or *inflections,* on nouns, pronouns, adjectives, and verbs. English has discarded the great majority of these inflections, but those we do still use—for nouns, pronouns, and verbs—are all descended from Indo-European.

Pronunciation changed systematically in the different branches of the Indo-European family. An original /p/ remained unchanged in Greek and Latin but became /f/ in Germanic and hence in English. An original /k/ also remained unchanged in Greek and Latin but in Germanic became /KH/ (approximately as in German *ich* and Scottish *loch*); but in Modern English the /KH/ has further changed to /h/ or disappeared. Some sounds, however, remained extremely stable: /s/, /m/, /n/, /r/, /l/, and /w/ mostly did not change in any of these languages. The table below sets out some of the sound changes for Greek, Latin, and Germanic.

Indo-European →	Greek	Latin	Germanic
p	p	p	f
t	t	t	th
k	k	c*	kh
d	d	d	t
g	g	g	k
bh	ph	f	b
dh	th	f	d
gh	kh	h	g

**The Latin letter* c *was pronounced* /k/.

Thus, the Indo-European word *ped-* or *pod-* = 'foot' became Greek *pod-*, Latin *ped-*, Germanic *fōt-*. And the Indo-European root *gnō-* = 'to know' appears in Greek *gnōsis* = 'knowledge,' in Latin *gnōscere* = 'to know,' and in Germanic *knowan* = 'to know.' But Indo-European *mūs* = 'mouse' remained *mūs* in all three languages.

Vocabulary. English has expanded its vocabulary enormously by borrowing words from other languages. Much of the original inherited vocabulary has been eroded and replaced over the years. As many as 80 percent of the words in a modern English dictionary are borrowings or based on borrowings. But the "core vocabulary" of the language—the words expressing the most basic conceptions and those most frequently used—remains overwhelmingly inherited and Indo-European. This includes the articles, all of the commonest prepositions, pronouns, auxiliary verbs, and conjunctions, and a majority of the most basic verbs, nouns, and adjectives.

Although English has borrowed words from all over the world, the great majority of its borrowings have been taken from French, Spanish, Italian, Norse, Dutch, and German, and from the two prestigious ancient languages Latin and Greek. All of these are Indo-European cousins of English, containing altered versions of the same original vocabulary. There are separate entries on these borrowings (see DUTCH WORDS; FRENCH WORDS; GERMAN WORDS; GREEK WORDS; ITALIAN WORDS; LATIN WORDS; NORSE WORDS) and on borrowings from yet other Indo-European sources (see IRISH WORDS; PERSIAN WORDS; SANSKRIT WORDS; WELSH WORDS). Indo-European is thus doubly represented in the mixed English vocabulary. Many Indo-European words or roots appear in both inherited and borrowed forms. Some of these are discussed at COGNATES.

Some samplings of the most ancient part of our *inherited* vocabulary follow, in eight separate sections:

(1) Common verbs, including *be, do, have,* and *make; laugh, sing,* and *weep.*
(2) Common nouns, including *friend, hearth,* and *home; sun, moon,* and *summer.*
(3) Common adjectives, including *old, new,* and *young; thick* and *thin; free* and *wise.*
(4) Tree names such as *birch, beech,* and *elm.*

(5) Animal names, including *beaver*, *otter*, and *wolf*; *cow*, *ewe*, and *mare*.

(6) Kinship terms—*father*, *mother*, *son*, *daughter*, *brother*, *sister*; *kin* and *widow*.

(7) Farming terms such as *barley* and *flax*; *acre* and *furrow*; *sow* and *harvest*.

(8) A selection of words relating to crafts, tools, artifacts, and cooking: *ax*, *saw*, and *wedge*; *spin*, *sew*, and *weave*; *door*, *roof*, and *rafter*; *brew*, *mead*, and *oven*; *yoke* and *wheel*.

In each case the Old English (A.D. c. 700–1000), Germanic (c. 300 B.C.), and Indo-European (c. 5000 B.C.) forms of the word are given. Definitions are included only when necessary. If none are given for the early forms, they are identical with that of the modern word; for example:

snow: Old English *snāw*, Germanic *snaiw-*, Indo-European *snoigwh-*

This means that the word has always meant simply 'snow.'

(1) Common verbs:

be: Old English *bēon*, Germanic *biyu-*, Indo-European *bhwiyo-*, *bheu-* = 'to be, exist'

bind: Old English *bindan*, Germanic *bindan*, Indo-European *bhendh-*

break: Old English *brecan*, Germanic *brekan*, Indo-European *bhreg-*

choose: Old English *ceōsan*, Germanic *kiusan*, Indo-European *geus-* = 'to taste, choose'

come: Old English *cuman*, Germanic *kuman*, Indo-European *gwem-* = 'to come, go'

do: Old English *dōn*, Germanic *dōn*, Indo-European *dhō-*, *dhē-* = 'to do, make'

draw = 'to pull': Middle English *drawen*, Old English *dragan*, Germanic *dragan*, Indo-European *dhregh-* = 'to pull, draw'

drink: Old English *drincan*, Germanic *drinkan* = 'to drink,' nasalized derivative of Indo-European *dhregh-* = 'to draw (in)' (see *draw*, above)

eat: Old English *etan*, Germanic *itan*, Indo-European *ed-*

fall: Old English *feallan*, Germanic *fallan*, Indo-European *pholno-*

feel: Old English *fēlan*, Germanic *fōlyan*, Indo-European *pōl-* = 'to touch, feel'

go: Old English *gān*, Germanic *gēn*, Indo-European *ghēno-* = 'to let go,' also 'to go'

grind: Old English *grindan*, Germanic *grindan*, Indo-European *gwhrendh-*

have: Old English *habban*, Germanic *habē-*, Indo-European *kapē-*, *kap-* = 'to hold, have'

hear: Old English *hīeran*, Germanic *khausyan*, Indo-European *kous-*

know: Old English *cnāwan*, Germanic *knōwan*, Indo-European *gnōw-*, *gnō-*

laugh: Old English *hliehhan*, Germanic *khlakhyan*, Indo-European *klak-*, *klag-*

make: Old English *macian*, Germanic *makōn*, Indo-European *mag-* = 'to knead, form, make'

see: Old English *sēon*, Germanic *sekhwan*, Indo-European *sekw-*

send: Old English *sendan*, Germanic *sandyan*, Indo-European *sonteyo-* = 'to cause to go, send,' from *sent-* = 'to go'

set: Old English *settan*, Germanic *satyan*, Indo-European *sodeyo-* = 'to cause to sit, put, set,' from *sed-* = 'to sit' (see also *sit*, below)

shine: Old English *scīnan*, Germanic *skīnan*, Indo-European *skīn-*

sing: Old English *singan*, Germanic *singan*, Indo-European *sengwh-* = 'to chant' (originally a technical religious word)

sit: Old English *sittan*, Germanic *sitan*, Indo-European *sed-* (see also *set*, above)

stand: Old English *standan*, Germanic *standan*, Indo-European *stand-*, *stā-*

sweat: Old English *swǣtan*, Germanic *swaidyan* = 'to sweat,' from noun *swaida-* = 'sweat,' Indo-European *swoido-* = 'sweat'

teach: Old English *tǣcan*, Germanic *taikyan* = 'to show, teach,' Indo-European *deig-*, *deik-* = 'to show, indicate,' also used in a technical sense, 'to speak solemn words, declare judgment'

weep: Old English *wēpan*, Germanic *wōpyan*, Indo-European *wābeyo-* = 'to cry, weep'

(2) Common nouns:

borough = 'self-governing town': Old English *burg*, *burh* = 'fortified town,' Germanic *burgs* = 'hill-fort, fortified town,' Indo-European *bhergh-* = 'high,' also 'high place, hill, hill-fort'

coal = (1) 'glowing ember' (2) 'natural black carbonous substance used as fuel': Old English *col* = 'glowing ember,' Germanic *kol-*, Indo-European *geul-*

fire: Old English *fȳr*, Germanic *fūri*, Indo-European *pūr-*

friend: Old English *freond*, Germanic *friyand-*, Indo-European *priyont-*, literally 'loving,' present participle of *prī-* = 'to love'

god: Old English *god*, Germanic *guda-*, Indo-European *ghuto-*, literally 'that which is prayed to,' from *ghu-* = 'to call upon, pray to'

head: Old English *hēafod*, Germanic *haubud-*, Indo-European *kaput-*

heart: Old English *heorte*, Germanic *hert-*, Indo-European *kerd-*

hearth = 'floor of a fireplace': Old English *heorth*, Germanic *herth-*, Indo-European *kert-*

heaven = (1) 'the sky' (2) 'the abode of God, or of gods': Old English *heofon*, Germanic *hibin-* = 'the sky (regarded as a huge roof or vault),' earlier *himin-*, Indo-European *kemen-* or *kamer-* = 'vault'

hell = (1) originally 'the nether world, the abode of the dead' (2) 'the place where dead sinners are punished': Old English *hell*, Germanic *khalyo* = 'the hidden place, the abode of the dead,' from *khal-* = 'to hide,' Indo-European *kel-*

home: Old English *hām*, Germanic *haim-*, Indo-European *koim-* = 'home,' from *koi-* or *kei-* = 'to lie, be in bed, be at home'

light: Old English *līht*, *lēoht*, Germanic *liukht-*, Indo-European *leuk-*

month: Old English *mōnath*, Germanic *mǣnoth-*, Indo-European *mēnot-* = 'month,' from *mēn-* = 'moon' (see *moon*, below)

moon: Old English *mōna*, Germanic *mǣnon-*, *mǣnonth-*, Indo-European *mēn-* (see *month*, above)

name: Old English *nama*, Germanic *namon*, Indo-European *nomen*

night: Old English *niht*, Germanic *nakht-*, Indo-European *nokwt-*

smoke: Old English *smoca*, Germanic *smuk-*, Indo-European *smeug-*

snow: Old English *snāw*, Germanic *snaiw-*, Indo-European *snoigwh-*

summer: Old English *sumor*, Germanic *sumar-*, Indo-European *səmar-*

sun: Old English *sunne*, Germanic *sunn-*, Indo-European *swen-*, *sun-*

water: Old English *wæter*, Germanic *watar-*, Indo-European *wodor*

weather: Old English *weder* = 'storm, wind, weather,' Germanic *wedra-* = 'wind, weather,' Indo-European *wedhro-* = 'wind,' from *wē-* = 'to blow' (see *wind*, below)

wind = 'current of air': Old English *wind*, Germanic *winda-*, Indo-European *wento-* = 'wind,' literally 'blowing,' present participle of *wē-* = 'to blow' (see *weather*, above)

(3) Common adjectives:

brown: Old English *brūn*, Germanic *brūna-*, Indo-European *bhrūno-*

cold: Old English *ceald*, Germanic *kalda-*, Indo-European *gelto-*

free: Old English *frēo*, Germanic *friya-*, literally 'dear,' hence 'belonging to the free kindred, having free legal status (as opposed to slaves),' Indo-European *priyo-* = 'dear, beloved,' from *prī-* = 'to love' (compare *friend* under Nouns, above)

full: Old English *full*, Germanic *fulla-*, *fulna-*, Indo-European *pəlno-* = 'full,' from *pel-* = 'to fill'

good: Old English *gōd*, Germanic *gōda-* = 'fitting, appropriate, satisfactory,' Indo-European *ghōdho-* = 'fitting,' from *ghedh-* = 'to fit'

green: Old English *grēne,* Germanic *grōnya-*, Indo-European *ghrōnyo-* = '(of plants) green and growing,' from *ghrē-* = 'to grow, be green'

grim: Old English *grim* = 'fierce, cruel,' Germanic *grimma-*, Indo-European *ghrem-* = 'angry'

hot: Old English *hāt,* Germanic *khaita-*, Indo-European *kaido-*

naked: Old English *nacod,* Germanic *nakweda-*, Indo-European *nogweto-*

new: Old English *nēowe,* Germanic *neuya-*, Indo-European *newyo-*

old: Old English *ald,* Germanic *alda-*, Indo-European *alto-*, literally 'grown up,' hence 'old,' from *al-* = 'to grow up, bring up'

red: Old English *rēad,* Germanic *rauda-*, Indo-European *roudho-*

right = 'correct, true, just': Old English *riht,* Germanic *rikhta-*, Indo-European *regto-*, literally 'guided in a straight line,' hence 'correct, true, just,' from *reg-* = 'to guide in a straight line, rule justly'

ripe = '(of fruit, etc.) mature, ready to be gathered': Old English *rīpe,* Germanic *rīpya-* = '(of crops or fruits) ready for reaping,' from *rīp-* = 'to reap,' Indo-European *reib-* (compare *reap* under Farming terms, below)

tame = '(of animals) domesticated': Old English *tam,* Germanic *tama-*, Indo-European *domo-* = 'tamed,' especially '(of horses) broken in,' from *demə-* = 'to tame, break in (horses)'

thick: Old English *thicce,* Germanic *thiku-*, Indo-European *tegu-*

thin: Old English *thynne,* Germanic *thunni-, thunw-*, Indo-European *tənu-*

white: Old English *hwīt,* Germanic *khwīta-*, Indo-European *kweito-*

wise = 'discerning, having a good understanding of the world': Old English *wīs,* Germanic *wissa-*, Indo-European *weidto-* = 'discerning, wise,' from *weid-* = 'to see, discern, understand'

young: Old English *geong,* Germanic *yunga-* or *yuwunga-*, Indo-European *yewnko-*

(4) Tree names:

apple: Old English *æppel,* Germanic *apal-*, Indo-European *abel-*

ash: Old English *æsc,* Germanic *ask-*, Indo-European *os-*

aspen: Old English *æspe,* Germanic *aspōn,* Indo-European *apsa*

beech: Old English *bece,* Germanic *bōkyo,* Indo-European *bhāgo-*

birch: Old English *birce,* Germanic *birkyōn,* Indo-European *bherəg-* = 'birch,' literally 'the white one'

elm: Old English *elm,* Germanic *elmo-*, Indo-European *elmo-* = 'elm,' literally 'the red or brown one'

hazel: Old English *hæsel,* Germanic *hasel-*, Indo-European *kosel-*

(5) Animal names:

beaver: Old English *befor,* Germanic *bebru-*, Indo-European *bhibru-* = 'beaver,' literally 'the brown one'

cow = 'female bovine': Old English *cu,* Germanic *kōu-*, Indo-European *gwou-* = 'bovine (of either sex)'

ewe = 'female sheep': Old English *ewe,* Germanic *awi-*, Indo-European *owi-* = 'sheep (of either sex)'

foal = 'young horse': Old English *fola,* Germanic *fulo-*, Indo-European *pulo-* = 'young animal,' especially 'young horse'

goat: Old English *gāt,* Germanic *gaita-*, Indo-European *ghaido-*

hound = 'dog,' especially 'dog of certain hunting breeds': Old English *hund* = 'dog (in general),' Germanic *hunda-*, Indo-European *kwnto-* or *kwon-* = 'dog'

mare = 'female horse': Old English *mere,* Germanic *markhyōn-* = 'female horse,' Indo-European *marko-* = 'horse (of either sex)'

mouse: Old English *mūs,* Germanic *mūs,* Indo-European *mūs*

otter: Old English *otor,* Germanic *otra-*, Indo-European *udro-* = 'water animal'

sow = 'female pig': Old English *sugu* = 'female pig,' Germanic *sū-* = 'pig (of either sex),' Indo-European *sū-* or *su-* = 'pig' (see *swine*, below)

swine = 'pig': Old English *swīn*, Germanic *swīn-*, Indo-European *suīn-* = 'pig'; related to *sū-* or *su-* (see *sow*, above)

whale: Old English *hwæl*, Germanic *khwal-*, Indo-European *kwal-* or *skwal-* = 'big fish,' probably also 'whale'

wolf: Old English *wulf*, Germanic *wulfa-*, Indo-European *wlpo-*

(6) Kinship terms:

brother: Old English *brōthor*, Germanic *brōthar-*, Indo-European *bhrāter-* = 'male belonging to the clan or family'

daughter: Old English *dohtor*, Germanic *dokhtēr*, Indo-European *dhugətēr*

father: Old English *fæder*, Germanic *fadar*, Indo-European *pətēr* = 'father as head of the family or clan'

kin: Old English *cyn*, Germanic *kunya-*, Indo-European *gənyo-* = 'family, clan'

mother: Old English *mōdor*, Germanic *mōthar-*, Indo-European *māter-* = 'mother as female head of the family or clan'

sister: Old English *swuster*, partly replaced by Old Norse *systir*, both from Germanic *swistr*, Indo-European *swesr*, *swesor* = 'female belonging to the family or clan'

son: Old English *sunu*, Germanic *sunu-*, Indo-European *sunu-*

widow: Old English *widuwe*, Germanic *widewa-*, Indo-European *widhewo-* = 'she who is cut off (from her husband),' from *weidh-* = 'to cut off, divide'

(7) Farming terms:

acre = 'measure of land, 4,840 square yards': Old English *æcer* = 'field,' also 'area plowed by a team of oxen in a day,' Germanic *akra-* = 'field,' Indo-European *agro-* = 'pasture, grazing land for cattle'

barley = 'type of cereal grain': Middle English *barrlig* = 'made of barley,' from Old English *bære* = 'barley,' Germanic *barz-*, Indo-European *bhars-*

corn (British) = 'any cereal grain': Old English *corn*, Germanic *korn-*, Indo-European *grən-* = 'grain'

flax = 'plant that yields linseed oil and a textile fiber': Old English *fleax*, Germanic *flakhs-*, Indo-European *ploks-* = 'flax,' literally 'weaving stuff'

furrow = 'trench made by the plow': Old English *furh*, Germanic *furkh-*, Indo-European *prk-* = 'furrow'

harvest = 'autumn, the season for reaping the grain crop': Old English *hærfest*, Germanic *kharbist-* = 'reaping time,' from *kharb-* = 'to reap,' Indo-European *karp-* = 'to cut down, reap'

mow = (1) 'to cut grass or a grain crop with a scythe or sickle' (2) 'to cut grass with a mowing machine': Old English *māwan*, Germanic *mǣ-*, Indo-European *mē-*

reap = 'to cut a grain crop': Old English *rīpan*, Germanic *rīpyan*, Indo-European *reib-*

scythe = 'long-bladed tool with a long curving handle, for mowing or reaping': Old English *sigthe*, originally 'sickle,' Germanic *segitho*, from Indo-European *sek-* = 'to cut'

seed = 'a plant ovule or ovules, especially as collected and propagated by farming people': Old English *sǣd*, Germanic *sēdi-*, Indo-European *sēti-* = 'seed,' literally 'that which is sown,' from *sē-* = 'to sow' (see *sow*, below)

sow = 'to plant seed in cultivated ground': Old English *sāwan*, Germanic *sēyan*, Indo-European *sēyo-* or *sē-* (see *seed*, above)

wool = 'fine hair of the sheep, used for making cloth': Old English *wull*, Germanic *wullo*, Indo-European *wləna*

yard = 'fenced area, often next to a house or farm building': Old English *geard*, Germanic *gurdya-*, Indo-European *ghorto-* = 'enclosure, fenced garden'

(8) Crafts, tools, artifacts, and cooking:

arrow = 'shaft shot from a bow': Old English *arwe*, *earh*, Germanic *arkhwo*, Indo-European *arkw-* = 'bow and arrow'

ax = 'tool with a heavy-bladed head set on a wooden handle, used for chopping wood': Old English *æx*, Germanic *akwesī*, Indo-European *agwesī*

brew = 'to make (beer) by fermenting malt in water': Old English *brēowan*, Germanic *breuwan*, Indo-European *bhreu-* = 'to boil, ferment, brew'

door = 'hinged panel for closing an entrance': Old English *dor, duru*, Germanic *dur-*, Indo-European *dhur-*

mast = 'fixed upright pole supporting the sail of a boat or ship': Old English *mæst*, Germanic *masta-*, Indo-European *mazdo-* = 'pole, mast'

mead = 'alcoholic drink made by fermenting honey in water': Old English *meodu*, Germanic *medu-*, Indo-European *medhu*

meal = 'coarsely ground grain, less fine than flour': Old English *melu*, Germanic *melwa*, Indo-European *mel-* = 'to grind,' hence also 'ground grain'

needle = 'sharp tool used for sewing': Old English *nǣdl*, Germanic *nēthlo-*, Indo-European *nētla-* = 'needle,' from *nē-* = 'to sew'

ore = 'naturally occuring substance containing a metal': Old English *ōra*, Germanic *aiz*, Indo-European *ayes* = 'copper, copper ore'

oven = 'enclosed chamber for cooking': Old English *ofen*, Germanic *ufna*, earlier *ukhwna*, Indo-European *aukwh-* = 'cooking pot,' also 'oven'

rafter = 'sloping beam supporting a pitched roof': Old English *ræfter*, Germanic *raftra-*, Indo-European *raptro-* = 'beam'

roof = 'protective covering on top of a house': Old English *hrōf*, Germanic *khrōf-*, Indo-European *krāp-*

salt = 'sodium chloride, used to preserve and to flavor food': Old English *salt*, Germanic *salt-*, Indo-European *sal-*

saw = 'cutting tool with a toothed blade': Old English *sagu*, Germanic *sago*, Indo-European *sok-* or *sek-* = 'to cut,' also 'cutting tool'

sew = 'to work on cloth with a needle and thread': Old English *seowian*, Germanic *siwyan*, Indo-European *syū-*

spin = 'to twist (a fibrous material such as wool or flax) into yarn': Old English *spinnan*, Germanic *spinnan*, Indo-European *spen-*

timber = 'wood for house building': Old English *timber*, Germanic *timr-*, Indo-European *dem-* = 'to build,' also 'house'

weave = 'to make (cloth) by interlacing yarns': Old English *wefan*, Germanic *weban*, Indo-European *webh-*

wedge = 'implement of wood or metal, tapering from thick at one end to thin at the other, used for splitting': Old English *wecg*, Germanic *wagya-*, Indo-European *wogwhni-* = 'plowshare, wedge'

wheel = 'circular piece or structure revolving on an axle, on which a vehicle runs': Old English *hweol*, Germanic *khwekhula-*, Indo-European *kwekwlo-*

yarn = 'string spun from twisted fibers, as of wool or flax': Old English *gearn*, Germanic *garno-*, Indo-European *gherno-* = 'entrail, gut,' hence also 'string'

yoke = 'wooden bar fitting over the necks of a pair of draft animals, by which they pull a vehicle or plow': Old English *geoc*, Germanic *yuka-*, Indo-European *yugo-* = 'yoke,' from *yeug-* = 'to join'

in excess of. This phrase is a fancy substitute for *more than*. It has long been denounced by writers and others concerned with usage, notably the poet William Cullen Bryant (1794–1878). During the 50 years he was editor of the *New York Evening Post*, Bryant would never allow the phrase to appear in his newspaper. However, denunciation has not killed this expression. Here is a typical modern example:

> The Wholesale Price Index increased during that time in excess of 10 percent.
>
> —Jimmy Carter, speech (1977)

◇ ***Recommendation.*** Whether or not you use the phrase *in excess of* depends on your feelings about formality and simplicity. For a similar case compare PRIOR TO.

infarction. Not a misprint for *infraction*, this word is from *infarct* = 'dead tissue resulting from a failure of blood supply,' which in turn is from Latin *infarctus* = 'crammed in, blocked up.' It is increasingly familiar as applied to a form of heart disease, in full *myocardial infarction*, a dying off of heart muscle that occurs when a coronary artery has been blocked.

infer, imply. There is no problem with the usage of *imply*, but *infer* has overlapped *imply* in two distinct senses, one of which is legitimate, while the other is questionable.

Imply. *Imply* has two basic meanings, the first primarily with personal subjects, the second primarily with impersonal subjects. (1) 'To suggest (that something is so) without directly saying so, hint': *In his history of the war he implies that the generals were incompetent. Are you implying that I haven't got a single chance?*
(2) 'To indicate (a conclusion or consequence) by logical necessity or by probability'; used of facts, situations, etc.: *The fossil evidence implies that these animals were wiped out by man. The cold war implies the permanent possibility of nuclear war.*

Infer. (1) The basic meaning of *infer*, used of persons, is 'to deduce (something) from something else' or 'to conclude from evidence or facts (that something is so), reason'; hence *inference* = 'something deduced, conclusion':

> . . . like the inference of Paley, that, if one found a watch, one inferred a maker.
> —Henry Adams, *The Education of Henry Adams*

> It is quite likely that the Americans saw smoke from the burning dumps and inferred that the town was being burnt by the grenadiers.
> —W. J. Sparrow, *Count Rumford of Woburn, Mass.*

> . . . in his final findings, Judge Boyle stated: "I infer [that] a reasonable and probable explanation of the totality of the above facts is that Kennedy and Kopechne did *not* intend to return to Edgartown at that time. . . ."
> —*Reader's Digest*

(2) A secondary meaning of *infer*, used of facts or situations, is similar to the second meaning of *imply*: 'to indicate (something) by logical necessity or by probability':

> And now, in the full conception of these facts and points, and all that they infer, pro and con . . . I proceed with my speculations. . . .
> —Walt Whitman, *Democratic Vistas*

This use is standard but now relatively rare.

(3) *Infer* is also, more problematically, used of persons in a sense close to the first meaning of *imply*: 'to argue or suggest (that something is so).'

> May I ask, Mr. Spade, if there was, as the newspapers inferred, a certain—ah—relationship between that unfortunate happening and the death a little later of the man Thursby?
> —Dashiell Hammett, *The Maltese Falcon*

> . . . engaged from the outset in a heated and interminable argument about their experiences, each plainly inferring the other was a liar.
> —S. J. Perelman, *Westward Ha!*

If you present certain facts that suggestively lead to a certain conclusion, you could be said, perhaps, to *infer* (sense one) and *imply* (sense one) at the same time. But the examples given are not so subtle as this and probably just result from confusion.

◇ ***Recommendation.*** The second sense of *infer* is legitimate, but to avoid controversy we recommend using only *imply* in this sense. The third sense of *infer* we regard as a mistake. In short, the simplest rule is to use *infer* only of persons, to mean 'deduce or conclude': *We infer from your silence that you agree.*

inferior, superior should be used with *to*, not *than*.

infixes. An *infix* is an affix inserted into the middle of a word, a regular feature of certain American Indian languages. This feature does not occur in English. See AFFIXES.

inflammable. See FLAMMABLE, INFLAMMABLE.

inflectional endings. See AFFIXES.

ingenious, ingenuous. (1) *Ingenious* is from Latin *ingeniōsus* = 'skilled, talented.' In English *ingenious* originally meant 'highly intelligent' but now has the specific meaning 'good at contriving, inventive':

> The medical supplies were uncrated, and the boys did an ingenious job of converting the empty boxes into tables and benches, and cabinets in which to store our pharmaceuticals.
> —Thomas A. Dooley, *The Edge of Tomorrow*

> New inventions, each with incalculable effects on American society, poured out of ingenious American minds.
> —Isaac Asimov, *Science Past—Science Future*

(2) *Ingenuous* is from Latin *ingenuus* = 'native, freeborn, noble, honest.' The English meaning has narrowed from 'honest' to 'innocently frank, guileless and unsophisticated':

> The officers, however, were quite entranced with the ingenuous simplicity of the islanders, their piety . . . and their anxiety not to offend.
> —H. E. Maude, *History of Pitcairn Island*

> He had a dangerous charm, on the surface so ingenuous that one thought he couldn't be aware of it.
> —Catherine Gaskin, *Edge of Glass*

Disingenuous is used as a restrained way of saying 'dishonest, deceptive, cheating':

> The President was outraged by Brezhnev's disingenuous explanations. . . .
> —*Fortune*

> I added that I didn't have the vaguest idea whether Kennedy would run. . . . Actually, I was being disingenuous, because I have heard a lot, some of it from pretty good sources, indicating that Kennedy has already begun to think seriously about 1980.
> —Richard Reeves, *Boston Globe*

The noun *ingénue* /**än**-zhə-n$\bar{\text{oo}}$, -jə-n$\bar{\text{oo}}$/ comes from a French adjective for 'innocent, unsophisticated.' It means 'inexperienced young woman,' especially as a theatrical role.

> Included in the party are Professor Aronnax . . . his daughter, a kittenish ingénue, all corkscrew curls and maidenly simpers.
> —S. J. Perelman, *The Road to Miltown*

(3) The noun *ingenuity* originally belonged to *ingenuous* but has somehow become entirely detached from it and captured by *ingenious*. Its only current meaning is 'the quality of being ingenious, resourcefulness at contrivance, inventiveness':

> The unchanging value of our principles and ideals, the stability of our political system, the ingenuity and the decency of our people . . .
> —Jimmy Carter, farewell address (1981)

As a result, the abstract noun of *ingenuous* is *ingenuousness:*

> [In the play *Dead End Kids*] Ellen McElduff portrays a variety of not-so-innocent dupes with boundless ingenuousness. . . .
> —John Simon, *New York*

-ing nouns. See VERBAL NOUNS IN -ING.

Inland Northern dialect. This subdivision of the NORTHERN DIALECT is spoken in upstate New York, western Vermont, and northern Pennsylvania. It differs very little from the speech of western New England or from the Upper Midwestern dialect. Unlike eastern New England pronunciation, Inland Northern retains the /r/ sound after vowels in such words as *horse, four, father.*

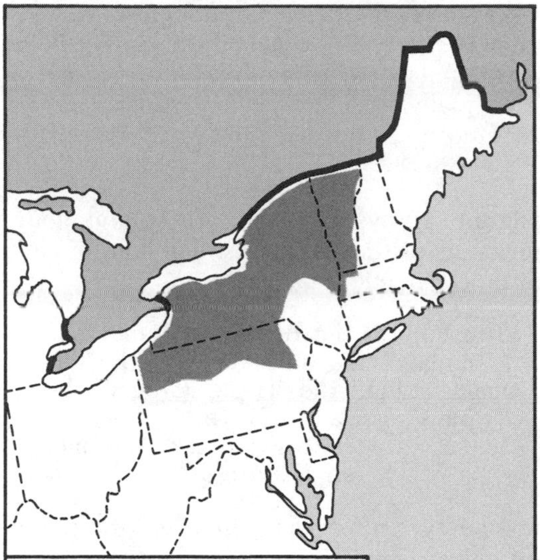
Inland Northern dialect

The following terms are typical of Inland Northern speech:

canal boots = 'unusually large or clumsy feet'

cross-lot, go *or* **cut** (also New England) = 'to take a shortcut'

drawed (also General Southern, North Midland; used especially by working-class speakers) = 'past tense of *draw*'

drawing = 'hauling or carting (wood, hay, etc.)'

Dutch cheese = '*cottage cheese'

friedcake = 'unraised *doughnut'

gathered ear (also North Midland) = 'infected, suppurating ear'

griddle = 'round cover on a wood-burning stove'

hatchway (also New England) = 'sloping outside cellar door'

horning, horning bee = 'noisy, mock serenade, *shivaree'

jacking (also New England) = 'hunting illegally at night with a spotlight'

lobbered *or* **loppered milk** (also Hudson Valley, New England) = 'sour or curdled milk, *clabber'

***mall** = 'median strip in a highway'

matterate (also New England) = 'to discharge pus, suppurate'

notch (also New England) = 'mountain pass'

stoop (also Hudson Valley) = 'small *porch, or a flight of steps leading to an outside door'

sugar bush (also Hudson Valley) = 'sugar-maple grove'

*Appears as separate entry

in medias res. Correctly, this Latin phrase means 'into the middle of things.' It is a quotation from Horace, describing one of the classical devices for starting an epic poem: instead of beginning at the beginning of the story, the poet plunges the hearer into the middle of the action and only later covers the earlier events. But now, the phrase is as often as not used to mean 'in [rather than *into*] the middle of things' and is applied to any situation, not especially narrative.

> He was always talking about what he called her "bad record," a divorce, three broken engagements, a whole series of love affairs abandoned *in medias res.*
>
> —Mary McCarthy, *The Company She Keeps*

◊ ***Recommendation.*** In its original sense this phrase is a virtually technical, and useful, literary reference. In the looser sense it offers no advantage at all; *in the middle* would do just as well.

Innuit (Eskimo) words. The name *Eskimo* comes from Greenland Danish *Eskimo,* which is from Canadian French *Esquimau.* The spelling *Esquimau* (plural *Esquimaux*), formerly used in English, is now obsolete. The name was taken by the French Canadians from the northern Algonquian Indians, who called the (unrelated) people of the Arctic various names meaning 'they who eat raw food': Cree *askimowew* = 'he eats it raw,' Micmac *eskameege* = 'to eat raw fish.'

The people themselves have never used the name Eskimo, and they dislike it. Their name for themselves is *Innuit* or *Inuit*, meaning simply 'the people,' plural of *inuk* = 'person.' *Innuit* or *Inuit*, pronounced /ĭn-o͞o-ĭt, -yo͞o-ĭt/, is the official and polite term used in Alaska, Canada, and Greenland.

An interesting handful of words has been borrowed into English from the Innuit. In the selection that follows we feel it appropriate to refer to them and their language this way. But most people outside Alaska and Canada will doubtless continue calling them Eskimos.

anorak = 'warm, insulated jacket or topcoat with a hood': from Innuit *anoraq* = 'waterproof outer sealskin coat'

husky = 'strong, heavy-coated sled dog bred by the Innuit': from Canadian *Husky*, derogatory slang for 'Eskimo'

igloo = 'Innuit house, especially the well-known domed type built of blocks of hard snow': from Innuit *iglu* = 'house'

kayak = (1) 'one-person Innuit hunting boat made of sealskins over a wooden frame, with a tight-fitting cockpit' (2) 'canvas-covered canoe modeled on the Innuit kayak': from Innuit *kayak*

malemute, malamute = 'strong, heavy-coated sled dog, generally larger than a husky, bred by the Malemute Innuit people of Alaska'

mukluk = (1) 'knee-high Innuit boot, typically of sealskin' (2) (chiefly Canadian) 'any of various warm, manufactured winter boots': from Innuit *muklok* = 'large seal'

parka = (1) 'Innuit garment for the upper body, with a hood, typically of skins with the fur side inside' (2) 'any of various warm, manufactured jackets with hoods, often furred': from Aleutian Innuit, from Russian *parka* = 'skin, pelt,' ultimately from Samoyed

umiak, oomiak = 'large Innuit boat made of skins on a wooden frame, traditionally paddled by women': from Innuit *umiak*

inside of. In general standard usage the preposition *inside* = 'in, within' is preferable to *inside of: Inside the closet were cartons of old letters.* But when the meaning is 'in less than (a stated time),' *inside* and *inside of* are equally acceptable: *I'll be back inside (of) an hour.*

insignia is by origin a Latin plural noun meaning 'distinctive marks, emblems of rank or office, heraldic badges':

> The Pope is the Bishop of Rome. The insignia of his office are the Fisherman's Ring, the Triple Crown, the Triple Cross, and the Keys.
> —Frederick W. Rolfe, *A History of the Borgias*

It is now often used as a singular, with plural *insignias*. This is condemned by some usage experts, but it has been occurring since the 18th century. Particularly when referring to such modern symbols as athletic letters, school and college emblems, or commercial marks for products or companies, *insignia* is now the usual singular form.

> Long a familiar and trusted insignia along America's highways, the AAA-in-the-oval stands for quality, comfort and service.
> —American Automobile Association

Especially, however, when referring to heraldic or military badges, the Latin singular form *insigne* /ĭn-**sĭg**-nē/ is preferred by some, keeping *insignia* strictly as a plural:

> The insigne on American aircraft was a white star set in a white bar.
> —Robert J. Donovan, *PT 109*

◇ ***Recommendation.*** *Insignia* as singular, with plural *insignias*, is now fully established and acceptable. But the Latin singular *insigne*, with plural *insignia*, is still available and is not likely to die out.

intelligentsia. The intellectuals of 19th-century Russia were seen by many as a distinct social and political subclass. The word *intelligentsia* = 'intellectuals collectively' (see RUSSIAN WORDS) was used negatively or positively according to your point of view. It could imply either 'the progressive, enlightened avant-garde, natural leadership of the culture' or 'effete, arty, arrogant intellectuals and radicals.' In English the word can have these loaded connotations or be used without comment, meaning simply 'the highly educated section of the people.'

> Anastasia Alexandrovna was by birth, circumstances and education very much a member of the intelligentsia. She lived with her husband in a tiny house near Regent's Park and here all the literary folk in London might gaze with humble reverence at pale-faced bearded giants who leaned against the wall like caryatids taking a day off; they were revolutionaries to a man and it was a miracle that they were not in the mines of Siberia.
>
> —W. Somerset Maugham, *Ashenden*

> University students [in Uganda] told of pretending to be high-school dropouts when they interviewed for jobs because they thought Amin and his henchmen were intent on eliminating the country's intelligentsia.
>
> —David Lamb, *Reader's Digest*

inter-, intra-. These two Latin prefixes are sometimes confused. Their meanings are completely different. *Inter-* means 'between or among (several things), mutually, reciprocally, shared': *international relations; interstate commerce. Intra-* means 'within, inside (one thing)': *the Intracoastal Waterway* (= 'inside the coastline'); *intramural studies* (= 'within the walls, inside a school or a university').

internecine /ĭn-tər-**nē**-sīn, -sĭn, -**nĕs**'n/. There is no real problem with this word. But it has been long and rather inconclusively discussed by dictionaries and usage experts, so for those who are interested we will go over the ground and give our verdict.

Origins. The Latin verb *internecāre* meant 'to slaughter (an enemy), kill large numbers of, exterminate.' *Necāre* means 'to kill.' The prefix *inter-* here did not have its usual meaning 'between, among' but meant 'thoroughly and destructively.' The derivative adjective *internecīnus*, referring to battles or war, meant 'to the death, aimed at exterminating the enemy rather than at strategic victory,' and when it was borrowed into English as *internecine*, the word at first kept the Latin meaning:

> . . . lawless adventurers . . . who would wage an internecine struggle with the aboriginal tribes in their neighbourhood.
>
> —George Bowen (governor, Queensland, Australia), letter (1861)

This use of the word *internecine*, formerly considered the only correct one, is now completely obsolete.

Current Uses. Since in English the prefix *inter-* always means 'between, among, mutually,' *internecine* was naturally enough reinterpreted as meaning 'causing slaughter to both sides, mutually destructive, not resulting in a clear-cut victory for either side':

> Most of the witnesses to this spell of internecine slaughter [between two feuding families] have their details in order. . . .
>
> —Virgil Carrington Jones, *The Hatfields and the McCoys*

This departure from the original Latin meaning has been frowned on by some Latin-educated authorities but was already recognized by Samuel Johnson's *Dictionary* in 1755. It is now the basic meaning of the word, with various further connotations or shades of meaning: 'pitting comrade against comrade, fratricidal' or 'causing regrettable fighting or quarreling among colleagues who ought to be working for a common cause,' or sometimes merely 'causing trouble within a group, internally disruptive.'

> The end result . . . would be an Israeli diplomatic triumph and an internecine split between Arab states. —*Time*

> And historians agree that much of the Jacobite struggle was an internecine

Scottish conflict, so that bitterness after the Forty-five would have been directed as much against the Campbells of Argyll as at the distant English King.
—Douglas Hill,
The Scots to Canada

. . . what threatened to become a dangerous internecine battle, capable of breaking up the magazine.
—Brendan Gill,
Here at The New Yorker

◇ ***Recommendation.*** All of these uses of *internecine* are correct, except the original one, which is obsolete.

into. See IN, INTO.

intransitive. See TRANSITIVE, INTRANSITIVE.

intrusive *r*. See R-LESSNESS, INTRUSIVE R.

invective. *Invective* is the "art" of directing verbal abuse against an opponent. Although the use of invective has long been recognized as the most unfair and unseemly of argumentative techniques, its history is as old as oratory itself. The Latin term *ad hominem* (= 'to the man'), which describes an argument aimed at a person rather than at his or her ideas or performance, may be taken as the basis for all invective, no matter how much its user may try to disguise the fact. As a classic example, Samuel Johnson once concluded an argument with a boatman on the Thames with the words: "Sir, your wife, under pretence of keeping a bawdy-house, is a receiver of stolen goods."

Although it is still easy to find many examples of invective in public utterances, its use nowadays is more restrained than in the past. The English critic John Ruskin, for example, wrote of a famous American painter:

For Mr. Whistler's own sake, no less than for the protection of the purchaser, Sir Coutts Lindsay [the gallery director] ought not to have admitted works into the gallery in which the ill-educated conceit of the artist so nearly approached the aspect of wilful imposture. I have seen, and heard, much of cockney impudence before now; but never expected to hear a coxcomb ask two hundred guineas for flinging a pot of paint in the public's face.
—quoted, James McNeill Whistler,
The Gentle Art of Making Enemies

(Whistler sued, appeared as his own witness, and was awarded damages of one farthing.)

Here is the way Hiram Johnson, candidate for governor of California in 1910, publicly characterized Harrison Gray Otis, publisher of the *Los Angeles Times:*

He sits there in senile dementia with gangrene heart and rotting brain, grimacing at every reform, chattering impotently at all things that are decent. . . . [He is] disgraceful, depraved, corrupt, crooked and putrescent. . . .
—quoted, David Halberstam,
The Powers That Be

If modern politicians tend to use invective somewhat more playfully—as when former Vice President Spiro Agnew called the leaders of the Vietnam Moratorium movement an "effete corps of impudent snobs"—most of us recognize that invective is rarely excusable. We even have a modern slang term for what we think of it: *cheap shot.* For more, see ad hominem argument at FALLACY.

inveigh /ĭn-**vā**/, almost always used with *against*, means 'to speak bitterly, hold forth loudly or publicly, complain':

Editors of boating magazines inveighed against the win-at-any-cost psychology, which seemed to be crowding good seamanship and sound boat handling out of the picture.
—Andrew Young, *Reader's Digest*

Inveigh is often used with a tinge of sarcasm—the inveigher is perhaps protesting too much, whether from insincerity or from self-deception:

Black nationalists in surrounding countries would publicly inveigh against

South Africa but privately see to it that planes which came flying into their airstrips were loaded with workers, for only in this way would the economies be kept afloat.
—James A. Michener, *The Covenant*

For our guests have sometimes been obviously relishing and unawarely eating food with garlic in it—while inveighing loudly against it.
—Irma S. Rombauer
and Marion Rombauer Becker,
The Joy of Cooking

Inveigh is related to the noun INVECTIVE.

inveigle. The pronunciations /ĭn-**vē**-gəl/ and /ĭn-**vā**-gəl/ are equally correct. The word was borrowed from French, and literally meant 'to make (someone) blind,' hence 'to hoodwink, beguile.' The usual meaning in English is 'to persuade (someone) by cunning and coaxing, entice, allure':

Henry later inveigled the Senate Foreign Relations Committee to certify that Kissinger had not "initiated" the taps. . . .
—William Safire, *Before the Fall*

A Texas woman revealed that her sex therapist had inveigled her into having sex relations with him.
—Donald Robinson,
Reader's Digest

It can also mean 'to obtain (something) by cunning and coaxing, maneuver, wangle':

Ashley said "Good-by," very softly, caught up from the table the wide felt hat she had inveigled from Rhett and walked into the dark front hall.
—Margaret Mitchell,
Gone With the Wind

[Cynthia Helms, as wife of the U.S. ambassador in Iran] studied Persian poetry, inveigled her way to remote areas and archeological digs. . . .
—Walter Goodman,
New York Times Book Review

ipse dixit. Old term for a form of fallacious argument. See FALLACY.

Iran, Iranian. Until recently, *Iran* was usually pronounced /ĭ-**răn**/ in English, and *Iranian* was usually pronounced /ĭ-**rā**-nē-ən/. During the 444 days of intensive media coverage induced by the hostage affair of 1979–81, most broadcast journalists changed to /ĭ-**rän**/ and /ĭ-**rän**-ē-ən/, which probably will remain the preferred pronunciations. Iran has also been known as *Persia*. For etymology, usage, and borrowed vocabulary, see PERSIAN WORDS.

iridescent /ĭr-ə-**dĕs**-ənt/. This word is sometimes misspelled *irridescent*. The word is from Greek *iris, irid-* = 'rainbow' with the Latin suffix *-escent* = 'tending toward,' as in *evanescent* and *obsolescent*. *Iridescent* means 'showing rainbowlike, shifting colors':

The bronzed grackle, a sleek, well-groomed bird, is striking in appearance when his iridescent plumage flashes its varied colors in the bright sun.
—Alfred Gross (quoted),
Arthur C. Bent,
Life Histories of
North American Blackbirds,
Orioles, Tanagers and Allies

These lights and shapes and tones of things swarmed in the boy's mind like a magic web of shifting, iridescent colors.
—Thomas Wolfe,
The Web and the Rock

Irish words. The Irish language, also known as Irish Gaelic and Erse, is one of the Celtic languages. It was first written down about A.D. 725, but its literature, transmitted orally by bards and druids, was at that time already very old. Irish invaders took the language to Scotland in the 6th century A.D.; it is the origin of Scottish Gaelic. Only a few thousand people now speak Irish as their natural language; but it is taught in the schools in Ireland, and scholarly study of it is advanced. English has borrowed several dozen words from Irish words and names, including the following.

balbriggan /băl-**brĭg**-ən/ = 'soft knitted cotton fabric used for sweaters, stockings, underwear, etc.': from *Balbriggan* (a port on the Irish Sea north of Dublin)

* **banshee** = 'female spirit who wails at night near the house to warn of a coming death in the family'

blarney = 'smooth talk and plausible lies used in flattery, coaxing, or excuses': from the legend that anyone who kisses the *Blarney* Stone at Blarney Castle, county Cork, obtains special powers of persuasion

bog = 'swamp': from Irish (and Scottish) *bogach* = 'soft ground'

bonnyclabber = 'thick curdled milk': from Irish *bainne clabair* = 'churn-milk' (This word in various forms is widespread in U.S. regional dialects. See CLABBER.)

boycott = 'to refuse to deal with (a person) or buy (goods or services) as a means of protest': first used in 1880, from the name of Charles *Boycott*, an English estate manager in county Mayo who was ostracized by tenants for maintaining high rents

brogue /brōg/ = (1) 'primitive rawhide shoe worn by Irish and Scottish Gaels,' hence (2) 'strong rural accent, especially Irish': from Irish (and Scottish) *brog* = 'shoe'

colcannon /kəl-**kăn**-ən, käl-/ = 'cooked dish of potatoes and cabbage': from Irish *cal caennan* = 'cabbage with a white head'

curragh /**kêr**-əKH/ = 'boat made of leather on a wicker frame': from Irish (and Scottish) *currach* = 'boat'; related to Welsh *corwgl* = 'boat, coracle'

donnybrook = 'riot or free-for-all': from *Donnybrook* in county Dublin, where the annual fair used to be notorious for uproars

drumlin = '(in geography) smooth ridge or hill of gravel, etc., deposited by a glacier': from Anglo-Irish *drumlin* = 'little ridge,' referring to such ridges common in Ireland, from Irish *druim* = 'ridge'

dulse /dŭls/ = 'kind of seaweed eaten as a vegetable': from Irish *duileasg* = 'seaweed'

Eire /**âr**-ə/ = 'the Irish name of Ireland': Old Irish *Ériu*, from prehistoric Celtic *Iveriu*, perhaps originally meaning 'hilly country or island'; *Erin* is another form of this name

Fenians /**fē**-nē-ənz/ = (1) 'band of hero warriors who defended Ireland in the 2nd century A.D.' (2) 'secret group of terrorist freedom fighters founded in New York about 1850 to free Ireland from the English': Old Irish *fiann* = 'followers of Fiann,' from *Fiann*, name of a hero

Gael /gāl/ = 'an Irish or Scottish Celt, especially one who speaks Irish or Scottish Gaelic': Irish *Gaedheal* /**gī**-əl/, from Old Irish *Goidel* = 'Irishman'

Ireland: Old English *Īraland*, from *Īras* = 'the Irish' + *land*

Irish: Old English *Īras* = 'the Irish,' from Old Irish *Ériu* = 'Eire'

leprechaun /**lĕp**-rə-kôn, -kŏn/ = 'small fairy or elf, sometimes a shoemaker, able to disclose buried treasure': from Irish *leipracan* = 'small body, small person'

lough /lŏKH/ = 'lake': from Old Irish *lough* = 'lake'; same word as Scottish *loch*

Mac-, Mc- = 'prefix used in surnames': from Irish (and Scottish) *Mac-* = 'son of'

machree /mə-**krē**/ = 'my darling': from Irish *mo chroidhe* = 'my heart'

mavourneen /mə-**vōōr**-nēn/ = 'my darling': from Irish *mo mhuirnin* = 'my delight'

O' = 'prefix used in surnames': from Irish *ō*, Old Irish *aue* = 'descendant, grandchild'; many Irish people prefer to write this prefix without the apostrophe: *O Connor, O Sullivan*, etc.

ogham /**ŏg**-əm/ = 'alphabet used in Ireland, Wales, and Scotland from about A.D. 350 to 600': from Old Irish *ogom* = 'writing'

poteen /pō-**tēn**/ = 'whiskey made in an illicit still': from Irish *poitin* = 'little pot,' that is, 'private and illicit pot-still'

shamrock = 'type of clover with three leaflets, the national emblem of Ireland': from Irish *seamrog* = 'clover'

shillelagh /shə-**lā**-lē/ = 'cudgel of blackthorn or oak': from *Shillelagh* (town in county Wicklow)

smithereens = 'small fragments': from Irish *smidirin* = 'small fragments'

tanistry /tăn-ĭ-strē, thô-nĭ-/ = 'the traditional Irish law of royal succession, by which the heir is elected by the people during the reigning king's lifetime from among the king's male relatives'; the heir so elected is called the *tanist* /tăn-ĭst, thô-nĭst/: from Irish *tānaiste* = 'second man,' that is, 'second-ranking man in the kingdom'

Tory = (1) 'brigand in 17th-century Ireland,' hence (2) 'British Conservative': from Irish *tōraige* = 'runaway'

***whiskey** = 'liquor distilled from barley mash': Gaelic *uisge betha* = 'water of life'

*Appears as separate entry

irony. There are several kinds of *irony*. The word is from Greek *eirōneia* = 'pretense, simulated ignorance, the saying of the opposite of what is meant.'

(1) *Socratic irony* is the device used by the philosopher Socrates of pretending to be ignorant of a truth in order to induce a pupil or an opponent to work it out and accept it for himself.

(2) *Dramatic irony* is the tense situation created in a play when the audience knows or sees that one of the characters is headed for trouble, while the character goes ignorantly on.

(3) *Irony as a figure of speech* is saying the opposite of what one means, in such a way that the hearer or reader understands the true implication. When used with strong feeling, this irony can achieve a tone of bitterness, contempt, or cynicism:

> For Brutus is an honorable man;
> So are they all, all honorable men. . . .
> —Shakespeare, *Julius Caesar*

> By spring, if God were good, all the proud privileges of trench lice, mustard gas, splattered brains, punctured lungs, asphyxiation, mud and gangrene might be his. —Thomas Wolfe, *Look Homeward, Angel*

Used gently, irony has an effect of amused mockery or mere banter:

> Mr. Richard Harvey is going to be married, but it is a great secret and only known to half the neighborhood, so you must not mention it.
> —Jane Austen, letter (1796)

> I exercise extreme self-control. I never drink anything stronger than gin before breakfast. —W. C. Fields (quoted), Robert Lewis Taylor, *W. C. Fields*

> Jimmy Two was doing magnificently in the field of fire and bomb insurance. His clients were, in the main, restaurants and taverns. One day, he met with an unfortunate accident. . . .
> —Studs Terkel, *Talking to Myself*

See also FIGURES OF SPEECH.

(4) *Irony in life* is the "mocking" effect of anything that turns out the opposite of what was expected, or anything seen as strikingly topsy-turvy or incompatible:

> Churchill High School is the ultimate Canadian irony—an American-inspired school incorporating all the glamorous extras, having a British facade by being called after a British statesman; the British identity served to conceal from people that the school was in reality American.
> —Melinda McCracken, *Memories Are Made of This*

President Jimmy Carter commented on Ramsey Clark's visit to Iran during the hostage crisis of 1979–81:

> Asked about the irony of prosecuting a former Attorney General for violating a travel ban, the President said: "The irony is apparent in a former Attorney General attending a conference to prove the criminality of his own nation." —*New York Times*

The phrase *the irony of fate* is a cliché. And journalists are perhaps too fond of perceiving ironies almost everywhere as a cheap flourish. In the following example the only point is that those who provide fuel for fires are to get less than those who put out fires—not a genuine irony:

> Irony: Government allowed 13 percent boost for miners in nationalized coal pits, more than 18 percent for firemen.
> —*U.S. News & World Report*

The adjective *ironic* or *ironical* can relate to any of the senses of the noun:

> From the very start Jane Austen was an ironist; and just as ready to be ironic about herself as about other people.
> —David Cecil,
> *A Portrait of Jane Austen*

> He waves to us, and smiles, in that ironic way that means he knows more than we do.
> —Dennis Smith,
> *Report From Engine Company 82*

irregardless. *The Reader's Digest Great Encyclopedic Dictionary* defines this as follows: "*adv.* Regardless: a nonstandard or humorous usage." Another Digest word book, *Write Better, Speak Better,* states categorically, "There is no such word as irregardless." Noting the discrepancy, an owner of both books wrote: "Now, I ask you this: Which am I to believe?" The discrepancy is only an apparent one. The dictionary writer simply describes the language as it is, good or bad. The usage writer offers judgments and recommendations, and behind statements that such words as *irregardless, normalcy,* or *hopefully* "don't exist," you must always understand an implication that in the writer's opinion they should not exist because they are bad English.

◊ ***Recommendation.*** Don't say or write *irregardless* unless you don't care what your audience may think.

irrelevancies. See FALLACY.

Italian words. The Italian language, descended from Latin, first appears in written documents in the 10th century. Modern Italian has many dialects in different parts of Italy; standard literary Italian is founded on the dialect of Florence.

Since the Italians have always been prime contributors to the civilization of Europe, innumerable Italian words have been borrowed into every European language including English. The first selections given below are arranged within three fields of culture in which Italian creativity has been conspicuously strong: the arts, warfare, and cookery. The Renaissance, which originated in Italy in the 14th century, transformed painting, architecture, literature, and all the other arts. This fact is represented in the English vocabulary by such words as *fresco* and *pastel;* by *arcade, balcony,* and *colonnade;* by *sonnet* and *scenario.* In music, Italian brilliance to the present day has been such that the entire lexicon of classical music is dominated by Italian words, including those for half the instruments, most of the musical forms, and virtually all of the stylistic directions. In the 15th and 16th centuries Italy, though fragmented politically, was a leader in the techniques of organized war. The words *battalion* and *brigade, cavalry* and *infantry,* COLONEL and *sentinel, musket* and *cannon,* were all borrowed from Italian into French and thence into English during the 16th and 17th centuries. We also have *bandit* and *brigand, duel* and *vendetta,* to remind us of other kinds of fighting. Italian cooking, already advanced before French cuisine amounted to much, has achieved a permanent place in modern kitchens and restaurants with the many forms of *pasta* as well as such contributions as *broccoli, salami,* and *zabaglione.*

And far beyond these basic pursuits of art, fighting, and cookery, much of our whole culture has been shaped and enriched by Italian style and ideas. The English vocabulary would be the poorer without *caprice* and *caress;* without *intrigue* and *incognito;* without *attitude* and *zany.* To the Italians we owe our *carnivals, casinos,* and *regattas;* both our *parasols* and our *umbrellas;* even (*dio mio!*) our very *pants, jeans,* and *wigs.*

Pronunciation. Since Italian is spelled almost entirely phonetically, Italian words present few problems to English speakers. The table on the opposite page sets forth the basics for pronouncing Italian.

A good many of the words in the following lists have come into English unchanged from the Italian. Their pronunciations, however, though generally faithful to the rules of Italian phonetics, are now anglicized.

Pronouncing Italian

Letter	Pronunciation	Letter	Pronunciation
Vowels and Diphthongs			
a	/ä/ *as in* padre	gn	/ny/ *as in* vigna
e	(1) /ā/ *as in* eco (2) /ĕ/ *as in* ecco	h	*not pronounced*
i	(1) /ē/ *as in* vino (2) /ĭ/ *as in* inferno	qu	/kw/ *as in* qui
o	(1) /ō/ *as in* cosa (2) /ô/ *as in* dolce	r	*trilled on the front of the tongue*
u	(1) /o͞o/ *as in* luna (2) /o͞o/ *as in* punto	s	(1) /s/ *in most initial positions and often between vowels, as in* così (2) /z/ *between vowels, as in* posa
ai	/ī/ *as in* mai		
au	/ou/ *as in* causa	sb, sp	/zb/, /zp/ *in initial position in certain words to avoid confusion with near-homophones*
oi	/oi/ *as in* poi		
Consonants*		sc	(1) /sh/ *before* e, i (2) /sk/ *before* a, o, u *and consonants*
c, cc	(1) /ch/ *before* e, i (2) /k/ *before* a, o, u *and consonants*	z	(1) /ts/ *as in* nazione (2) /dz/ *as in* bronzo, zero
ch, cch	/k/ *as in* chiave, occhio		
g, gg	(1) /j/ *before* e, i (2) /g/ *before* a, o, u *and consonants*		
gh	/g/ *as in* ghiro		
gl	/ly/ *as in* gli		

**The simple consonants* b, d, f, l, m, n, p, t, v *are pronounced approximately as in English. Double consonants* (cc, gg, tt, zz, etc.) *are pronounced with extra emphasis. The letters* k, w, x, *and* y *are not present in the Italian alphabet and are used only for foreign words and names.*

Vocabulary. (1) The arts:

allegro /ə-lĕg-rō/ = '(in music) fast': from Italian *allegro* = 'cheerful, lively'

arcade = 'row of arches': from French *arcade,* from Italian *arcata,* from *arco* = 'arch'

balcony = 'platform projecting from an upper window': from Italian *balcone* = 'platform, balcony'

balustrade = 'ornamental parapet of short molded columns (balusters) topped by a coping': from French *balustrade,* from Italian *balaustrata,* from *balaustro* = 'baluster'

banister = 'post supporting a handrail by a stairway' and **baluster** = 'short molded column in a balustrade'

cameo = 'gem carved with a figure or design in relief, typically in white on a colored background, in a piece of stratified onyx or shell': from Italian *cameo* (further origin unknown)

cello = 'musical instrument in the violin family': shortened from Italian *violoncello,* diminutive of *violone* = 'bass viol'

chiaroscuro /kē-är-ə-**skŏŏr**-ō, -**skyŏŏr**-ō/ = 'contrast of light and dark in a picture': from Italian *chiaroscuro* = 'light-dark,' from *chiaro* = 'light' + *oscuro* = 'dark'

cognoscente /kŏn-yō-**shĕn**-tē/ = 'connoisseur of art'

colonnade = 'row of columns': from French *colonnade,* from Italian *colonnata,* from *colonna* = 'column'

con brio /kŏn **brē**-ō, kōn/ = '(in music) with spirit and animation': from Italian *con* = 'with' and *brio* = 'sprightliness'

corridor = 'gallery, passageway': from French *corridore,* from Italian *corridore* = 'a run, runway, passage,' from *correre* = 'to run'

cupola = (1) 'dome' (2) 'small tower on top of a roof, acting as a skylight': from Italian *cupola* = 'small vault,' from Latin *cupula,* diminutive of *cupa* = 'vault'

dado = (1) 'square section of the base of a column' (2) 'bottom section of an inside wall, wainscot': from Italian *dado* = 'cube, die, square base of a column'

dilettante /**dĭl**-ə-tänt, dĭl-ə-**tänt**, -**tän**-tē/ = (1) 'connoisseur' (2) 'dabbler'

forte /**fôr**-tā/ = '(in music) loud': from Italian *forte* = 'strong, vigorous, loud'

fresco = 'watercolor painting done on moist plaster': from Italian *fresco* = 'fresh (plaster), fresco'

intaglio /ĭn-**tăl**-yō, -**täl**-yō/ = 'figure or design engraved in stone or metal': from Italian *intaglio* = 'engraving,' from *in* = 'in' + *tagliare* = 'to engrave'

miniature = 'very small painting': from Italian *miniatura* = 'illustration of medieval manuscripts,' hence also 'small painting or drawing,' from *miniare* = 'to paint with vermilion, illustrate a manuscript'

pastel = (1) 'crayon made with a paste of ground pigment' (2) 'drawing made with such crayons': from French *pastel,* from Italian *pastello* = 'paste of ground pigment'

piano = (1) /pē-**ä**-nō/ '(in music) softly': from Italian *piano* = 'softly, gently' (2) /pē-**ăn**-ō, **pyăn**-ō/ 'large musical instrument with a keyboard': shortened from Italian *pianoforte*

piazza = (1) /**pyät**-tsȧ/ 'public square in an Italian town' (2) /pē-**ăz**-ə, -**ä**-zə/ 'arcade, gallery, *porch': from Italian *piazza* = 'town square,' from Latin *platea* = 'courtyard'

picturesque = '(of scenery) suitable for a painting': from French *pittoresque,* from Italian *pittoresco* = 'in the style of a painter'

pilaster /pĭ-**lăs**-tər/ = 'flat ornamental column on a wall': from Italian *pilastro* = 'little or imitation column,' from *pila* = 'pillar, column'

portico = 'walkway or gateway with a roof supported by columns': from Italian *portico,* from Latin *porticus* = 'porch'

profile = (1) 'outline or contour of something' (2) 'picture of a human face from the side': from Italian *profilo* = 'outline picture,' from *profilare* = 'to draw in outline,' from *pro* = 'forth, out' + *filare* = 'to draw a line'

relief = (1) 'sculpture showing figures standing out to some extent from a flat background' (2) 'the effect of depth in painting or drawing': translation of Italian *rilievo* = 'a raising up, relief,' from *rilevare* = 'to raise'

***scenario** /sə-**nâr**-ē-ō, sə-**när**-/ = 'outline of a play': from Italian *scenario* = 'arrangement of scenes, scenario,' from *scena* = 'scene'

scherzo /**skêr**-tsō/ = 'typically short and lively movement in a sonata, concerto, or symphony, usually making up one of the middle sections': from Italian *scherzo* = 'joke'

sonata /sə-**nät**-ə/ = 'instrumental piece nowadays usually made up of two or more movements': from Italian *sonata* = 'loud ringing, as of a bell'

***sonnet** = '14-line poem with a special scheme of rhymes': from Italian *sonetto* = 'short poem, sonnet,' diminutive of *suono* = 'sound'

stucco = 'cement or plaster facing on

walls': from Italian *stucco* = 'facing, stucco'

vista = 'view contrived by architecture or landscaping': from Italian *vista* = 'a view'

*Appears as separate entry

(2) Warfare:

arsenal = 'storehouse or factory for arms and munitions': from Italian *arsenale*, originally Venetian *arzaná* = 'the naval dockyard of Venice,' also 'the arsenal,' ultimately from Arabic

bandit = 'member of an outlaw company of robbers, originally (16th century) in Italy': from Italian *bandito* = 'banished man, outlaw,' from *bandire* = 'to banish, outlaw'

battalion = 'unit of soldiers, now consisting of several companies': (via French) from Italian *battaglione* = 'division of an army,' augmentative of *battaglia* = 'body of soldiers, army, battle'

brigade = 'unit of soldiers, now consisting of two regiments or squadrons': (via French) from Italian *brigata* = 'company of soldiers, crew of revelers,' from *brigare* = 'to fight'

brigand = 'bandit': (via French) from Italian *brigante* = 'irregular soldier, bandit,' from *brigare* = 'to fight'

campaign = (1) 'planned movements of an army in the field' (2) 'planned political or commercial operations': (via French) from Italian *campagna* = 'the field, the countryside'; used in the 16th century of armies actively operating "in the field," as opposed to staying in winter quarters

cannon = 'large gun': (via French) from Italian *cannone* = 'large tube, barrel of a gun,' hence 'gun,' augmentative of *canna* = 'tube'

cavalier = (1) 'horseman, knight' (2) 'gallant gentleman': (via French) from Italian *cavaliere* = 'horseman, knight,' from Latin *caballārius* = 'horseman'

cavalry = 'horse soldiers collectively': (via French) from Italian *cavalleria* = 'horse soldiers,' from *cavallo* = 'horse'

citadel = 'fortress commanding a city': from Italian *citadella*, literally 'little city,' diminutive of *città* = 'city'

***colonel** = 'commanding officer of a regiment'

condottiere /kŏn-dō-**tyâr**-ā/ = 'commander of a company of mercenary soldiers in the 16th century': from Italian *condottiere* = 'commander,' from *condotto* = 'command, conduct'

duel = 'formal, prearranged armed fight between two men on a matter of honor': from Italian *duello* = 'duel,' from Latin *duellum*, old variant form of *bellum* = 'war'

infantry = 'foot soldiers collectively': (via French) from Italian *infanteria* = 'foot soldiers,' from *infante* = 'young man,' hence 'foot soldier'

musket = 'long-barreled smoothbore firearm': (via French) from Italian *moschetto*, literally 'little fly,' hence 'crossbow,' later 'firearm,' diminutive of *mosca* = 'fly'

sentinel = 'soldier on guard duty': from French *sentinelle*, from Italian *sentinella* = 'sentinel' (further origin uncertain)

squadron = 'unit of cavalry, planes, or ships': from Italian *squadrone* = 'body of soldiers drawn up as a square,' augmentative of *squadra* = 'square'

stiletto = 'short dagger': from Italian *stiletto* = 'little dagger,' diminutive of *stilo* = 'sharp instrument, dagger'

vendetta = (1) 'blood feud carried on between families' (2) 'any extended quarrel marked by hostility and revenge': from Italian *vendetta* = 'revenge,' hence 'blood feud' (especially in Corsica), from Latin *vindicta* = 'revenge'

*Appears as separate entry

(3) Food:

antipasto = 'assorted cold items eaten before the main course, hors d'oeuvres': from Italian *antipasto* = 'before the meal'

bologna /bə-**lō**-nyə, -nē/ = 'type of smoked sausage': originally from *Bologna* (city in northern Italy)

broccoli = 'variety of cabbage with a green flower head': from Italian *broccoli*, literally 'little sprouts'

canneloni /kăn-ə-**lō**-nē/ = 'large tubular noodles with a stuffing': from Italian *canneloni*, literally 'large tubes'

cappuccino /kăp-ə-**chē**-nō/ = 'espresso coffee with a topping of frothed cream': from Italian *cappuccino* = 'Capuchin friar, member of a religious order that wears a brown cape,' hence 'cup of coffee with brownish cream topping'

Chianti /kē-**än**-tē/ = 'well-known red wine': from the *Chianti* Mountains in Italy

espresso /ĕ-**sprĕs**-ō/ = 'strong coffee made in a machine that passes steam under pressure through powdered coffee beans': from Italian *caffé espresso* = 'pressed-out coffee'

fettuccine /fĕt-ōō-**chē**-nē/ = 'flat, ribbon-like noodles': from Italian *fettuccine*, literally 'little ribbons'

gelatin = 'basic jelly, glutinous substance obtained by boiling animal parts, fish, etc.': from French *gélatine*, from Italian *gelatina* = 'clear broth, gelatin,' from *gelata* = 'jelly'

lasagna /lə-**zän**-yə/ = 'wide, flat noodles cooked with layers of ground meat, cheese, and tomato sauce': from Italian *lasagna*, literally 'cooking pot'

macaroni = 'short, tubular noodles': from Italian *maccaroni*, plural of *maccarone* = 'cake, noodle'

minestrone /mĭn-ə-**strō**-nē/ = 'rich vegetable soup': from Italian *minestrone*, from *minestrare* = 'to serve out (soup)'

mozzarella /mŏt-sə-**rĕl**-ə/ = 'soft white cheese used in cookery': from Italian *mozzarella*, literally 'little slice'

Parmesan /**pär**-mə-zən, -zän/ = 'hard, dry cheese used grated for garnishing': from French *parmesan*, from Italian *parmigiano* = '(cheese) from Parma' (city in northern Italy)

pasta = 'Italian dough, the basis of numerous forms of noodles': from Italian *pasta* = 'paste, dough'

ravioli = 'flat, usually square casings of pasta stuffed with meat or cheese': from Italian *ravioli*, literally 'little turnips'

salami = 'type of spiced sausage': from Italian *salami*, plural of *salame* = 'salted pork sausage,' from *salare* = 'to salt'

spaghetti = 'long, string-shaped noodles': from Italian *spaghetti*, literally 'little strings'

vermicelli /vər-mĭ-**chĕl**-ē, -**sĕl**-ē/ = 'long, string-shaped noodles thinner than spaghetti': from Italian *vermicelli*, literally 'little worms'

zabaglione /zä-bəl-**yō**-nē/ = 'frothy dessert made of beaten eggs, wine, and sugar': from Italian *zabaglione*

(4) Miscellaneous words:

attitude = (1) 'posture of the body' (2) 'state of mind': from French *attitude*, from Italian *attitudine* = 'posture, disposition,' from Latin *aptitudo* = 'aptitude, fitness'

bronze = 'alloy of copper and tin': from French *bronze*, from Italian *bronzo* (further origin unknown)

caprice /kə-**prēs**/ = 'sudden whim, fanciful turn of mind': from French *caprice*, from Italian *capriccio*, originally 'horror,' hence 'sudden whim'

caress = 'endearment, loving touch': from French *caresse*, from Italian *carezza* = 'endearment, expression of love,' from *caro* = 'dear'

carnival = (1) 'any festival or time of revelry' (2) 'the season of feasting before Lent, including Mardi gras': from Italian *carnivale*, earlier *carnelevare* = 'giving up of meat,' from *carne* = 'meat' + *levare* = 'to raise, put away'

casino = 'public gambling house': originally 'public room or rooms for dancing and musical parties,' from Italian *casino* = 'pleasure house, summer cottage,' diminutive of *casa* = 'house'

charlatan /**shär**-lə-tən/ = 'impostor': from French *charlatan*, from Italian *ciarlatano*, probably from *ciarlare* = 'to prattle'

courtesan /**kôr**-tə-zən, **kōr**-/ = 'high-class prostitute': from French *courtesane*, from

Italian *cortigiano* = 'lady of the court, fashionable prostitute'

fiasco = 'disastrous failure': from the Italian phrase *far fiasco,* literally 'to make a bottle' (*far* = 'to make' + *fiasco* = 'bottle'), used to mean 'fail utterly' (In spite of many attempts to explain it, the reason for this expression remains unknown.)

gazette = 'news sheet, newspaper': from Italian *gazetta,* originally Venetian *gazeta de la novita,* literally 'a pennyworth of the news,' from *gazeta* = 'small Venetian coin'

***ghetto** = 'Jewish quarter of a city': from Italian *ghetto* = 'restricted Jewish quarter in medieval Rome, Venice, and other cities,' probably originally meaning 'Egypt,' from Latin *Aegyptus* = 'Egypt,' and referring to the ancient captivity of the Jews in Egypt

grotto = (1) 'cave' (2) 'artificial cave in a landscaped garden': from Italian *grotto* = 'cave'

imbroglio /ĭm-**brōl**-yō/ = 'confused situation, embarrassing entanglement': from Italian *imbroglio* = 'confusion,' from *imbrogliare* = 'to confuse, embroil'

incognito /ĭn-**kŏg**-ne-tō, -kŏg-**nē**-tō/ = 'under an assumed name to avoid publicity': from Italian *incognito* = 'unknown'

influenza = 'infectious, often epidemic, viral disease': originally used of an epidemic in Europe in 1743, from Italian *influenza* = 'influence, a flowing in, epidemic'

intrigue = 'secret scheme': from French *intrigue,* from Italian *intrigo* = 'secret scheme,' from *intrigare* = 'to scheme secretly,' from Latin *intricāre* = 'to entangle'

jean = 'strong twilled cotton cloth'; first occurring in English in the 16th century as *jene* or *gene fustian* = 'Genoa fustian': from *Genoa* (city of northern Italy from which many fabrics were exported) and *fustian,* an old word for 'coarse cotton cloth'

malaria = 'fever transmitted by a mosquito': from Italian *mal'aria* = 'bad air, swamp fever' (Swamp fevers were once believed to be caused by foul air rising from swamps.)

manifesto = 'public declaration of political principles': from Italian *manifesto* = 'a publishing, manifesting'

nepotism = 'the unfair giving of jobs to one's close relatives': from Italian *nepotismo* = 'nephew favoring,' the former practice of popes and cardinals in favoring their illegitimate sons, euphemistically called nephews, from *nepote* = 'nephew'

pantaloons = 'tight trousers of the kind that began to replace breeches in the 18th century' (hence modern *pants*): from *Pantaloon,* a character in old Italian comedy, a thin, foolish old man who wore tight trousers, from Italian *Pantaleone* = 'a Venetian,' also 'lecherous old man,' from Saint *Pantaleone,* a patron saint of Venice

parasol = 'sunshade': from Italian *parasole* = 'against the sun'

periwig = 'man's wig of the kind worn in the 17th and 18th centuries' (hence modern *wig*): originally *perwyke,* from French *perruque,* from Italian *perruca* = 'natural head of hair,' also 'wig'

regatta = 'meeting for boat races': originally an annual race of gondolas on the Grand Canal at Venice, from Venetian *Regatta*

umbrella = 'collapsible device for keeping off rain or sun': from Italian *ombrella* = 'little shade,' from *ombra* = 'shade'

volcano = 'mountain that emits lava, smoke, and flame': from Italian *volcano* = 'Vulcan,' hence 'volcano,' from Latin *Vulcanus* = 'Vulcan, god of fire'

wig See *periwig,* above.

zany = 'bizarre and crazy': from *Zany,* a character in old Italian comedy, an inept clown who mimicked the primary clown, from Italian *Zani,* originally Venetian *Zanni* = 'Johnny,' pet form of *Giovanni* = 'John'

*Appears as separate entry

(5) Words borrowed in the United States:

baloney (slang) = 'nonsense'; first recorded (1920s) meaning 'inferior boxer,' then 'stupid person' and 'nonsense': presumably from *bologna* = 'Italian sausage'

bocce /bŏch-ē/ = 'bowls played in a long narrow dirt court, usually with steel balls': from Italian *bocce,* plural of *boccia* = 'ball, bowl'

Mafia = 'large criminal organization, of Sicilian origin': from Sicilian *mafia* = 'hostility to government, general resistance to the law,' probably ultimately of Arabic origin

pizza = 'flat pie covered with a spiced filling of tomatoes, cheese, mushrooms, anchovies, etc.': from Italian *pizza,* apparently a special use of *pizza* = 'point, edge,' suggested by Greek *pitta* = 'cake, bread'

its, it's. The original neuter possessive pronoun was *his,* which was still in use as late as the time of the King James Bible (1611):

> Ye are the salt of the earth: but if the salt have lost his savour, wherewith shall it be salted? —Matthew 5:13

Around this time the new form *its* was created, leaving *his* as the exclusively masculine possessive. Although *its* was formed on the model of noun possessives like *day's,* it is not written with an apostrophe, in order to distinguish it from *it's,* the contracted form of *it is.* This is not really logical, since the same situation applies to nouns: *today's* can be the possessive of *today,* as in *today's weather,* or stand for 'today is,' as in *Today's the day.* The possessive *its* and the contracted form *it's* would be no more likely to be confused if they were both spelled the same than the two meanings of *today's.* Nevertheless, the rule is inflexible: it is incorrect to write the possessive as *it's.* See POSSESSIVES.

-ize. ***Spelling.*** In general, this verb suffix, which comes from Greek *-iz-* via French *-is-*, is spelled *-ize* in American English and *-ise* in British (but a substantial minority in Britain also prefers *-ize*). There are some exceptions or apparent exceptions.

(1) *Exorcise* is usually spelled with *s,* sometimes with *z.*

(2) There are several verbs with the French-derived suffix *-ise* that is not originally Greek: *chastise* and *franchise* are always spelled with *s; advertise* is preferably spelled with *s,* occasionally with *z.*

(3) There are also a number of French-derived verbs in which the ending *-ise* is not a suffix at all but part of the basic stem of the word. These are always spelled with *s.*

advise	exercise
circumcise	improvise
compromise	incise
despise	revise
devise	supervise
enterprise	surmise
excise	surprise

(4) *Apprise* = 'to inform' is usually spelled with *s,* sometimes with *z. Apprize* = 'to value' is the other way round.

***Proliferation of Verbs in* -ize.** The suffix originates in Greek, where new verbs could be freely created with the suffix *-iz-* (and the verb ending *-ein*). Two examples: from *Hellēn* = 'Greek' the verb *hellenizein* was formed, meaning 'to make or become culturally Greek.' The noun *ostrakon* meant 'piece of broken pottery used as a voting ballot.' Under the laws of Athens a politician could be sent into exile by popular vote; hence the verb *ostrakizein* = 'to write a man's name on a piece of pottery, send into exile.' Both of these verbs have been taken into English, as *Hellenize* and *ostracize,* and so have hundreds more.

As a result, the suffix itself has grown so familiar as a verb ending that it has become available for forming new verbs in English. It has been used since Shakespeare's time and is now more popular than ever. Just as the Greeks coined *Hellenize,* we have coined *Americanize, anglicize, Canadianize,* etc. Much like *ostracize,* we find a use for *computerize* and *containerize.*

The suffix *-ize* is now one of the most prolific word-forming elements in the language. It is almost too easy to use. Anyone can make a new verb by adding *-ize* to almost any noun or adjective. Conservative word critics such as H. W. Fowler (English) and Edwin Newman (American) have written disapprovingly of the flood of verbs created in this way, listing such examples as *accessorize, burglarize, conceptualize, decriminalize, destabilize, finalize, flavorize, funeralize, glamorize, hospitalize, inferiorize, museumize, mythicize, optimize, personalize, politicize, prioritize, privatize, radicalize, routinize, slenderize,* and *tenderize.*

Several general criticisms are made. First, some of these verbs seem unnecessary, since perfectly adequate ones without *-ize* exist already; *flavorize* is no improvement over the verb *flavor.* Many others seem to have been made up merely to avoid the effort of constructing proper sentences: *We have prioritized your request* is a pointless evasion of *We have given your request priority.* Formations of this kind are especially popular with those in commercial promotion and in the civil service — two groups widely regarded as having a disastrous influence on current usage. The suffix *-ize* seems to have a strong appeal for such people, forming verbs that sound official, technical, or somehow generally impressive but that often serve as substitutes for thought or as cover words distracting attention from trivial or unpleasant reality. The implication of a *personalized shirt* is that it has in some way been adapted to your body or personality; actually it is only a mass-produced shirt with your initials mechanically sewn on. To *tenderize* a steak stresses a desirable result, but not the fact that this may have been achieved by fiber-dissolving chemicals you wouldn't want to swallow straight. To *destabilize* a country doesn't sound too drastic, but the word is in reality a coldblooded official euphemism for secretly subverting a country's politics and economics in order to weaken or overthrow its government.

Many of these coinages in *-ize* may thus seem, to some people, unnecessary, irresponsible, or nasty. But our language is extremely democratic. No matter who first invents or promotes a word, it takes its chance on its merits and is judged by the community at large. Some new words are instantly accepted as soon as they appear. Most are not. Many a new word at first seems unnatural, ridiculous, or ugly. Hundreds of new verbs in *-ize* have quickly vanished without a trace. Others remain controversial, accepted by some and strongly disliked by others (see FINALIZE). Few now remember the word *Hooverize,* coined when Herbert Hoover was commissioner of food at the end of World War I; it meant 'to use food supplies economically.' At the birth of a new word there is no reliable way to know whether it will live or die. When *winterize* was first used by the housing industry, it was denounced by purists, but it has since become a well-established and unmistakably useful word. See also SLANG; VOGUE WORDS.

◇ ***Recommendation.*** It is reasonable to be somewhat suspicious of new verbs in *-ize.* Many of them will be unnecessary and unsatisfactory, but there is no need to condemn them out of hand, since some will certainly become permanently established in the language. The standard dictionaries will not list a new word until it has clearly entrenched itself, often allowing five years or more for this. Meanwhile, with words that are hot from the mint, you can only use your own judgment—thus participating in shaping the future of your language.

J

Jamaican English. Jamaican English is that melodious, highly intonated language of the Caribbean island. Like other English creole languages of the West Indies, Jamaican English grew out of a slavery culture that mixed West African languages with English (see PIDGIN AND CREOLE LANGUAGES). Today, the older creole survives in the hills and remote communities. But in the cities and among the middle class, Standard Jamaican English has little trace of its creole ancestry and sounds very much like an elegant and exotic version of British English.

Jamaicans have been coming to the United States for many years, and many have become citizens. Their speech, which contains fascinating echoes of the Black English of America, is becoming a permanent part of the diverse American scene, especially as reggae and other kinds of Jamaican music grow more familiar.

History. When Columbus landed in Jamaica on his third voyage to the New World, the only inhabitants were several hundred Arawak Indians. Within 100 years the Spanish had settled the island and completely exterminated the Indian population. The only linguistic evidence that the Arawaks had ever inhabited the island is in a few plant, animal, and place names, including the name of the island itself, *Xaymaca* = 'land of springs.' The Spaniards brought the first African captives to the island. Some of these escaped into the hills and established the first maroon settlements, which other runaway slaves later joined.

The British took over the island from the Spanish in 1655. Like the Arawak Indians before them, the Spanish have left only a few names as evidence that they ever occupied the island. The British began importing slaves in earnest, and by 1700 there were about 40,000 of them, mostly from the Gold Coast of West Africa. Of the 9,000 or so white settlers, most were Irish, Welsh, and Scottish. Their English dialects greatly influenced the developing creole of the slaves. This creole English became the lingua franca between whites and slaves and among the slaves themselves. By 1808, when the slave trade was banned, Southern or Standard British English became the model language toward which the Jamaican creole moved.

Today, Jamaican English is a spectrum of language varieties ranging from the British-sounding speech of the educated urban speakers to the creole folk speech of the uneducated rural population. The full flavor and distinctiveness of Jamaican English is best seen in the folk speech. For this reason the discussion that follows applies primarily to the language of the folk speakers.

Pronunciation. There is great variation in the intonation patterns of Jamaican speech. This is probably the legacy of the early West African languages, which have complex systems of stress and pitch or tone. Some of the other distinctive pronunciation features are:

(1) The sound /r/ is usually dropped after vowels.

(2) The sound /ä/ is substituted for Standard English /ă/ and /ô/. Thus, words like *rat* and *rot* are pronounced alike. But in words that have /k/ or /g/ followed by /ă/, as *cat, can't, galley,* the sound /y/ is inserted: /kyät/, /kyän/, /**gyä**-lē/.

(3) Many words with /oi/ in Standard English are pronounced with /ī/ in Jamaican. For example, *toil, loiter, oil* are pronounced /tīl/, /**lī**-tər/, /īl/.

(4) The sound /t/ replaces standard /th/, and /d/ replaces /*th*/. For example, *teeth* is pronounced /tēt/, and *other* is /**ŏ**-dər/.

(5) The sound /êr/ in the standard pronunciations of words like *bird* and *word* is pronounced /ŭ/: /bŭd/, /wŭd/.

(6) Clusters of consonants at the ends of words are reduced. *Crisp, fifths, task,* for example, are pronounced /krĭs/, /fĭf/, /täs/.

(7) The sound /s/ is dropped when it precedes /p/, /t/, or /k/. *Split, stuff, squeeze* become /plĭt/, /tŭf/, /kwēz/.

(8) When /s/ is followed by /m/ or /n/, a vowel is usually inserted. *Snake* and *smooth* become /sĭ-**nāk**/ and /sŏŏ-**mōōd**/.

Grammar. Among the many unique grammatical features of Jamaican folk speech, the formation of plurals and the use of personal pronouns are especially distinctive.
(1) In general, the *-s* suffix is not used to mark plural nouns. Instead, plurality is indicated either by a numeral or other counting word (*six hog, plenty yam*), or by the addition of *dem* (= 'them') to the noun (*de coconut-dem* = 'the coconuts').
(2) The personal pronouns in the folk speech are reduced thus:

A /ä/ = 'I': *A tink so.*

me = 'I, me, my': *Me nail dat shark tail ober me bed-head.*

you = 'you, your': *Tek you han' outa me bankra* [basket].

him = (1) 'he, him, his': *Him no da blebe me* = 'He won't believe me.' (2) 'she, her': *Miss Matty come from Kingston town/Him come back to him mammy gown.*

it = 'it, its'

we = 'we, us, our': *What you bring we? All a we frien' a come* = 'All of our friends have arrived.'

unu /**ōō**-nōō/ = 'you, your': *De judge don't know unu well. Tek unu basket.*

dem = 'they, them, their': *Dem is mekin' it dem job fe protec' we 'gains' any big-tree idea Joe have in him head.*

Vocabulary. The following is a selected list of Jamaican English terms primarily from the folk speech. Many of these are West African in origin.

aback /ä-**bäk**/ = 'ago, in the past'

a da mek /**ä dä mĕk**/, **a dat mek** /**dät**/ = 'that's why, that's the reason': *A da mek you see green-lizard always lib 'pon tree.*

baada /**bä**-dä/ = (1) 'term of respectful address to a male relative' (2) 'brother'

baba /**bä-bä**/ = 'father, grandfather'

bambai /**bäm**-bī/ = 'later, in a while'

bat /bät/ = 'large moth or butterfly'

bateau /**bä**-tō/ = 'raft'

been /bän, bĕn/ = (1) 'was, were' (2) auxiliary used to express past time: *Wha' mek you been ax me?* = 'Why did you ask me?' *Me been tell you* = 'I told you.'

before-day = 'early morning'

bickle /**bĭk**'l/, **bittle** /**bĭt**'l/ = 'food'

big-eye = 'greedy, selfish'

bill = (1) (noun) 'cutlass or machete' (2) (verb) 'to clear land by cutting down brush'

bleaky /**blē**-kē/ = '(of weather) overcast'

boasify /**bōōs**-ĭ-fī/ = (1) (adjective) 'proud, conceited' (2) (adverb) 'proudly, swaggeringly'

born-day = 'day of the week on which one was born'

born-day name, born-name = 'name given to a child, day-name'

bra /brä/ = 'mister'; used as a term of address

breshe /**brĕ**-shĕ/ = 'breadfruit'

brigin /**brī**-gĭn/ = 'haughty, proud, ostentatious'

bringle /**brĭng**-gəl/ = (1) (verb) 'to become angry' (2) (adjective) 'angry, fierce'

buckra /**bä**-krä, **bô**-krä/ = (1) 'white man or woman' (2) 'sir'; used as a term of polite address

bungay /**bông**-gē/ = 'dugout canoe, boat'

cay /kī/ = 'offshore islet'

chenk /chĕngk/ = 'small piece of something'

cockpit = 'valley with steep sides'

corn-stick = 'corncob'

crocus bag = 'bag made of hemp or jute and used to hold agricultural produce' See GUNNYSACK.

cudjoe /**kō**-jō/ = (1) (noun) 'heavy stick, cudgel' (2) (verb) 'to beat with a stick'

cunny /**kô**-nē/ = (1) (noun) 'cunning, craftiness' (2) (noun) 'a trick' (3) (adjective) 'clever, shrewd'

da = (1) (noun) 'that, that one' (2) (verb) auxiliary used to express progressive action: *As me da pass Cudjoe yard, me hear him mama da tell him . . .* = 'As I was passing Cudjoe's yard, I heard his mother telling him . . .'

day clean = 'daybreak'

day-name = 'name given to a child according to its sex and the day of the week on which it was born'; these names were of African origin but today survive only as pejorative terms

-dem /dĕm/, plural suffix: *De crab-dem bery sweet* = 'The crabs are very sweet.'

dis-ya /**dēs**-yä/ = 'this, this one'

doctor bird = 'hummingbird'

dog-driver (derogatory) = 'policeman'

don't-care = (1) (noun) 'carelessness, irresponsibility' (2) (adjective) 'indifferent, careless'

dreadlocks = 'long plaited hair, worn by men as a mark of membership in the Rastafari cult'

duppy /**dô**-pē/ = 'spirit of a dead person, ghost'

evening /**ēv**-nĭn/ = 'afternoon, from about 2 to 5 P.M.'

eye-skin /**yī-kĭn**/ = 'eyelid'

eye-water /yī-**wä**-tä/ = 'tears'

fadge = 'to manage as best one can, get on'

fi /fē, fō/ = (1) (adjective) 'belonging to, his, my, mine, etc.': *Pass me fi Leah tumpa knife* = 'Pass me Leah's short knife.' (2) 'to'; used for the infinitive: *A like fi play with me dog.* (3) (verb) 'must, should, ought to, have to'

foot = 'leg'

for true /fĭ **trōō**/ = 'truly, indeed'

god-bird /**gŏd-bôd**/ = 'hummingbird'

gombay /**gōm**-bĕ/ = 'a drum'

good-belly = 'good-natured, kindly'

grandy /**grän**-dē/ = (1) 'grandmother' (2) 'any older woman' (3) 'midwife'

gully /**gô**-lē/ = 'small stream'

guzu /**gōō**-zōō/, **guzum** /**gōō**-zōōm/ = 'an act of Obeah or witchcraft'

hand /än, hän/ = (1) 'all or any part of the arm' (2) 'the side of something'

hard Morris = 'tough guy, rough fighter'

hear-so = 'rumor, gossip'

higgler = 'itinerant peddler'

hurry-come-up = 'one who has risen rapidly in the world, usually by disreputable means'

ignorant /**ĭg**-nä-rän/ = 'angry, easily angered'

jerk-pork = 'stew made with pork and vegetables'

jumby /**jôm-bē**/ = 'ghost, especially a harmful one' (from Bantu)

junk /jôngk/ = 'lump or piece of something, chunk'

kin teet /**kĭn tēt**/ = 'to grin, laugh': *No everybody wha' kin dem teet wid you a you frien'.* (from *skin* + *teeth*)

kunu /**kōō**-nōō/ = 'fishing boat, canoe'

mad = (1) 'to make angry, astonish' (2) 'to make someone mad with jealousy, etc.'

mannersable = 'polite'

maroon = 'descendant of runaway slaves'

mash = (1) 'to strike hard' (2) 'to smash, crush' (3) 'to destroy, spoil'

masheted /mä-**shĕt**-ĕd/ = 'in bad condition'

mell = 'to annoy, interfere or meddle with'

middle-day = 'midday'

needle-case = '*dragonfly'

nof = (1) (adjective) 'many, much, great' (2) (adverb) 'plentifully'

nowherian = 'of no consequence'

nyaams /nyäms/ = (1) 'foolishness, nonsense' (2) 'silly or foolish person'

nyam /nyäm/ = (1) (verb) 'to eat, especially voraciously' (2) (noun) 'food'

Obeah /**ōō-bē-ä**, **ō-bē-ä**/ = (1) (noun) 'the practice of black magic, voodoo' (2) (noun) 'the materials with supposed magical powers intended to harm someone' (3) (verb) 'to work witchcraft against someone'

omi = 'water' (from Yoruba)

outlaw = 'indecent, outrageous'

patu /**pä**-tōō/ = (1) 'the night owl' (2) 'ugly, foolish person' (from Twi)

peel-head /**pēl-ĕd**/ = 'bald'

peeny /**pē**-nē/ = 'very small'

pickney /**pēk**-nē/ = 'child'

pickney-mumma = 'nursing mother'
pinder /**pēn**-dä/ = 'peanut' (from Kongo)
plaba = (1) 'sour milk, *clabber' (2) 'stew' (3) 'quarrel'
plenty = 'very much, many'
police = (1) 'policeman' (2) 'a variety of sweet potato'
prog = (1) 'to hunt for food' (2) 'to steal'
puss-boots = 'canvas shoes, sneakers'
quail /kwēĕl/ = (1) 'to cause to wilt' (2) 'to get rid of'
quality = 'very, extremely'
quashie /**kwä-shē**/ = (1) 'day-name for a boy born on Sunday' (2) 'peasant' (3) 'country bumpkin, fool' (from Twi)
raatid = (1) (adjective) 'angry, annoyed' (2) (interjection) used to express anger, amazement, etc.
roguing Joe = 'scrounger, pilferer'
sake /**sēĕ**-kä/ = 'because of'
sister /**sĭs**-tä/ = 'a woman'; used as a polite term of address
skin /kĭn/ = 'the body'
small-little = 'very small, tiny'
Spanish machete /**pän**-yä mä-**shēĕt**/ = (1) 'double-edged machete' (2) 'hypocrite'
stone-hole = 'cave'
stucky /**stô-kē**/ = 'sweetheart, lover'
susu /**so͞o**-so͞o/ = 'to gossip or talk behind someone's back'
sweet-mouth = (1) (adjective) 'gluttonous, greedy' (2) (noun) 'flattery, persuasiveness'
tall = (1) '(of an object) long' (2) '(of time or duration) long'
tambu = (1) 'drum' (2) 'dance or musical entertainment'
tata /**tä**-tä/ = 'father'
tea = 'any beverage usually served hot'
teeth /tēt/ = (1) 'tooth' (2) 'tine of a fork'
thunder-ball = 'thunderclap'
tief /tēf/ = 'to steal'
time = 'season': *De time is wet* = 'It's the rainy season.'
too = (1) 'very, extremely': *He too trick* = 'He's very tricky.' (2) 'too much': *You too lub chat* = 'You like to gossip too much.'
trickified = 'crafty, tricky'
ugly /**ôg**-lē/ = 'sin, wickedness'
uman /**o͞o**-män/ = 'woman'
unu /**o͞o**-no͞o/ = 'you' (from Ibo)
wa mek = (1) 'what's going on?' (2) 'why?'
warify /**wär**-ē-fī/ = 'very angry'
was-was = 'wasp, wasps'
wat-lef = 'leftover food'

*Appears as separate entry

Example. The following sample is the beginning of a folk tale transcribed by David De Camp in *Jamaican Creole* (1960):

Nou, ä o͞oōl tīm ä-nän-sē-ēn sto͞oō-rē wē gwīng ät nou. Nou wänts dĕ wäz ä o͞oōl wĭch lēĕ-dē lĭv, häd wŏn sôn, nēĕm ŏv wĭl-yəm. Wĭl-yəm wôr ēn-gyāy to͞o ä yông lēĕ-dē frŏm ä nĕks o͞oōl wĭch sĕk-shən ho͞o wäz här mä-där ēn lä. Nou dät gyôl fä-dä häd dät gyôl wēd ēz fôs wīf. Än äf-tä dē wīf dē-sēs, hē ēz mä-rē ä nĕks wo͞o-män, wĭch ēs ä o͞oōl wĭch. Än dät wo͞o-män bēĕr to͞o dä-täz bē-sīdz. Nou dē trē sēs-täz lĭv-ēng go͞od, bôt dē mä-dä ēn lä dĭd'n līk dät wŏn dä-tä ä-täl, fĭ-dē män. Hēm prĕ-fär fĭ-är to͞o. Bôt, jĕt dē trē gyôl wôr jo͞oō-bēäl wĭd wŏn ä-nä-dä. Wĕl dät wŏn gyôl frĕnz wēd dĭs yông män, nēĕm ŏv wĭl-yəm. Wĭl-yəm mä-dä ēz ä o͞oōld wĭch. Dē gyôl mä-dän-lä ēz ä o͞oōld wĭch. So͞oō, yo͞o gwīn fīn out, wä dĕ gō häp'm nou.

Translation

Now, a old-time Anancying story we going at now. Now once there was a old witch-lady live, had one son, name of William. William were engage to a young lady from a next [another] old witch's section who was her mother-in-law [stepmother]. Now that girl's father had that girl with his first wife. And after the wife decease, he is marry a next [another] woman, which is a old witch. And that woman bear two daughters besides. Now the three sisters living good [got along well together], but the mother-in-law didn't like that one daughter at all, the man's. She prefer her own two. But yet the three girls were jovial with one another. Well, that one girl was friends with this young man, name of William. William's mother is a old witch. The girl's mother-in-law is a old witch. So, you going to find out what is going to happen now.

Japanese words. The Japanese have borrowed many more words from us than we have from them. Contact dates only from 1854, when an American fleet under Cmdre. Matthew C. Perry forcibly "opened" Japan after 1,000 years of self-imposed isolation (interrupted briefly by Portuguese Jesuit missionaries in the 16th and 17th centuries). Perry's visit was one cause of the national upheaval that led to the Meiji restoration of 1868, with the abolition of feudalism and then the astonishingly swift industrialization of Japan. This transformation of Japanese life under Western influence has brought with it a great influx of words from Western languages, especially English. We meanwhile have acquired several dozen Japanese words. Most relate to purely Japanese culture: *Bushido, geisha, go, samurai, Shinto, shogun, torii.* Others reflect Japanese things and practices that the West has borrowed or imitated: *bonsai, haiku, judo, karate, origami,* and *Zen;* and there is a growing list of foodstuffs that are becoming familiar in restaurants or even in the kitchen: *miso, sake, sushi, tempura, teriyaki, tofu.* There are also a few slang words picked up by American servicemen during the American occupation following World War II and on leave in Japan during the Korean and Vietnam wars: *honcho, skosh, takusan.* So far only a handful of Japanese words have been absorbed so fully as to lose their specifically Japanese associations: *hibachi, honcho, tsunami.* With Japan's ever-growing influence in the modern world, there will certainly be more of these in the future. (See also HAWAIIAN ENGLISH.)

Pronunciation. Japanese words are easy to pronounce in English because the language has a comparatively simple sound structure. There are five vowels and seven basic consonants, including a true /r/ but no /l/. Japanese speakers of English often have difficulty hearing the difference between English /l/ and /r/ (which linguists call *liquid consonants*) and may substitute one sound for the other. Japanese writing is a hybrid, combining some Chinese characters with a phonetic script called *kana,* in which there is one character for each of the 46 syllables in Japanese.

Selected Vocabulary. (1) Japanese words in English:

banzai /**bän**-zī, bän-**zī**/ = (1) 'battle cry in honor of the emperor or another leader' (2) 'shout of congratulations, as on a birthday': literally '(May he live) 10,000 years!'

bonsai /**bän**-sī, bän-**sī**/ = (1) 'tree or shrub artificially dwarfed and growing in a pot or tray, often arranged to suggest a miniature landscape' (2) 'the technique of dwarfing such plants': literally 'tray arrangement'

Bushido /**bōō**-shē-dō/ = 'the code of the samurai, based on self-discipline, unwavering loyalty, fighting skill, and conquest of the fear of death': literally 'the way of the warrior'

daimyo, daimio /**dī**-myō/ = 'a feudal noble subject only to the authority of the shogun before 1868': literally 'great name'

dojo /**dō**-jō/ = 'classroom or practice hall in a school of judo or karate': from Japanese *dojo* = (1) 'Zen meditation hall' (2) 'practice hall for swordsmanship or other martial arts': literally 'place of the way,' a Zen translation of Sanskrit *bodhimandala* = 'place where Gautama (Buddha) attained to perfect wisdom'

Fuji /**fōō**-jī/ = 'the name of Japan's holy mountain' (Note: The correct form in Japanese is *Fujisan,* but *Fujiyama* has long been used by foreigners; *san* and *yama* both mean 'mountain.' *Mount Fuji* is the most proper form in English; *Mount Fujiyama* is definitely incorrect.)

geisha /**gā**-shə/ = 'woman trained to provide elegant and traditional entertainment for men, including music, the serving of food and drink, and conversation': literally 'artistic person' (Note: It is incorrect to apply the word *geisha* to bar girls or prostitutes.)

go /gō/ = 'game of skill for two players, played with black and white stones on a board marked with intersecting lines, the object being to capture one's opponent's pieces': of ultimately Chinese origin

* **haiku** /hī-kōō/ = '17-syllable poem': literally 'sentences for amusement'

hara-kiri /hä-rə-kîr-ē/ = 'ritual suicide accomplished by slashing open the abdomen': literally 'belly-slashing' (Note: This word is vulgar in Japanese; *seppuku* is preferred. See *seppuku,* below.)

hibachi /hĭ-bä-chē/ = 'cast-iron grill used for barbecuing': from Japanese *hibachi,* literally 'fire-bowl,' a brazier used for heating rooms (not, by the Japanese, for cooking)

honcho /hŏn-chō/ (slang) = (1) (noun) 'boss, chief' (2) (verb) 'to oversee, supervise': from Japanese *honcho* = 'squad leader'

issei /ē-sā, ē-sā/, plural *issei* or *isseis* = 'Japanese immigrant in the United States or Canada': literally 'first generation'

judo /jōō-dō/ = 'modern form of jujitsu practiced as a sport': literally 'soft path, gentle way'

jujitsu /jōō-jĭt-sōō/ = 'traditional art of unarmed self-defense using an opponent's strength and weapons against him': literally 'soft art'

Kabuki /kə-bōō-kē, kä-/ = 'the traditional popular theater of Japan, with music and dance and plays based on legendary themes': literally 'music and dance theater'

kamikaze /kä-mĭ-kä-zē/ = (1) 'suicide attack by a Japanese plane in World War II' (2) 'plane or pilot making such an attack': from Japanese *kamikaze,* literally 'divine wind,' originally applied in the 13th century to typhoons that twice sank Chinese fleets sent by Kublai Khan to invade Japan

karate /kə-rä-tē/ = 'traditional art of unarmed combat relying on the speed and concentrated force of blows struck with the hands and feet': literally 'empty hand'

kendo /kĕn-dō/ = (1) 'the traditional art of fighting with the two-handed samurai sword' (2) 'sport based on this, practiced with sticks': literally 'way of the sword'

ki /kē/ = 'spiritual energy that students of martial arts or of Zen learn to concentrate in order to achieve mastery': from Japanese *ki* = 'breath, spirit, essence,' ultimately from Chinese

kibei /kē-bā, kē-bā/, plural *kibei* or *kibeis* = 'second-generation Japanese-American or Japanese-Canadian educated largely in Japan': literally 'person who returns to America'

kimono /kə-mō-nə, -nō/ = (1) 'the traditional long robe of Japan, worn with a wide sash' (2) '(in the West) robe worn in the house, dressing gown': from Japanese *kimono* = 'clothes'

mikado /mĭ-kä-dō/ = 'term formerly used by Westerners in Japan to refer to the emperor, but not usually used by the Japanese': literally 'honorable door,' referring to the door to the throne room

miso /mē-sō/ = 'savory paste made from fermented soy, used as the base of soups': literally 'pleasant taste'

Nippon /nĭp-ŏn/ = 'the Japanese name for Japan': literally 'sun-root,' often rendered poetically as 'Land of the Rising Sun' (Note: Our word *Japan* comes from a Portuguese corruption of the Chinese pronunciation of *Nippon.*)

nisei /nē-sā, nē-sā/, plural *nisei* or *niseis* = 'second-generation Japanese-American or Japanese-Canadian': literally 'second generation'

no, noh /nō/ = 'the classical court theater of Japan, with music and dance, noted for highly stylized treatment of legendary themes': literally, 'talent'

origami /ôr-ə-gä-mē/ = 'the art of folding paper into flower and other shapes': literally 'folding paper'

sake, saki /sä-kē/ = 'rice wine (technically, a clarified beer), usually served warm': shortened from Japanese *saka-mizu,* literally 'prosperous waters'

samisen /săm-ə-sĕn/ = 'three-stringed musical instrument somewhat like a banjo': literally 'three-stringed'

*Appears as separate entry

samurai /**săm**-ə-rī/, plural *samurai* = 'man of the military ruling class abolished in 1871, owing hereditary loyalty to a daimyo and privileged to carry two swords': literally 'one who serves'

sansei /sän-**sā**, **sän**-sā/, plural *sansei* or *sanseis* = 'third-generation Japanese-American or Japanese-Canadian': literally 'third generation'

sashimi /sä-**shē**-mē, **sä**-shə-mē/ = 'sliced raw seafood served with a dipping sauce': literally 'raw fish'

satori /sä-**tôr**-ē/ = 'the enlightenment that is the goal of Zen meditation and self-discipline': literally 'sudden enlightenment'

sayonara /sä-yô-**nä**-rä, sä-yə-**när**-ə/ = 'goodbye, farewell'

sensei /**sĕn-sā**/ = 'teacher or master of any discipline, such as judo'

seppuku /sĕ-**pōō**-kōō/ = 'ritual suicide accomplished by slashing open the abdomen': literally 'stab the abdomen' (Note: *Seppuku* is the preferred form in Japanese; *hara-kiri* is considered vulgar.)

Shinto /**shĭn**-tō/ = 'the indigenous religion of Japan, emphasizing ritual purity and reverence for nature spirits and ancestors': literally 'spirit way'

shogun /**shō**-gən, -gŭn/ = 'one of the military rulers of Japan who before 1868 conducted all state business on the emperor's behalf': literally 'generalissimo'

skosh /skôsh/ (GI slang in the Vietnam War period) = 'a bit,' as *I'll have a skosh more of that, please*: from Japanese *sukoshi* /sōō-**kôsh**-ē, skôsh/ = 'a little bit'

sukiyaki /sōō-kē-**yä**-kē/ = 'thin sliced meat mixed into a vegetable stew': literally 'You'll like it broiled' (so named as part of a 19th-century drive to popularize red meat, traditionally regarded as disgusting and fit only for the lower classes)

sushi /**sōō**-shē/ = 'rolls of seaweed-wrapped rice containing raw fish, pickled vegetables, and the like': literally 'raw seafood'

takusan /**tä**-kōō-sän/ (GI slang in the Vietnam War period) = 'plenty of, a whole lot of,' as *We're going to drink takusan beer tonight*: from Japanese *takusan* = 'a great deal'

tatami /tə-**tä**-mē/ = 'woven-grass floor mat': from Japanese *tatami* = 'heavy slabs of compressed rice straw used as flooring material, on top of which woven mats are laid'

tempura /**tĕm**-pōō-rä, tĕm-**pōōr-ə**/ = 'pieces of seafood and sliced vegetables deep-fried in batter': from Portuguese *atemperar* = 'to heat, impart flavor to,' borrowed in the period of the Jesuit mission led by Saint Francis Xavier (16th and 17th centuries)

teppan-yaki /tĕp-än-**yä**-kē/ = 'cubes of beef and vegetables grilled on a hot iron slab': literally 'iron-plate grill' (more often served in the West than in Japan)

teriyaki /tĕr-ē-**yä**-kē/ = 'chicken or beef broiled with a glaze of soy sauce and mirin, a sweet rice wine': literally 'bright-broiled'

torii /**tôr**-ĭ-ē/ = 'gateway to a Shinto temple, having two uprights, an upward-curving lintel, and a straight crosspiece beneath the lintel': literally 'bird-rest'

tsunami /tsōō-**nä**-mē/ = 'ocean wave caused by an earthquake': from Japanese *tsunami* = 'harbor-wave,' borrowed from the technical vocabulary of seismologists doing research in earthquake-prone Japan, and replacing the misleading term *tidal wave*

yakitori /yä-kĭ-**tôr**-ē/ = 'chicken and scallion pieces on a skewer, dipped in a special sauce and grilled': literally 'grilled chicken'

yen /yĕn/ = 'the basic unit of Japanese currency': borrowed from Chinese *yuan* = 'round'

zaibatsu /zī-**bät**-sə/ = 'one of the famous industrial or commercial cartels, such as Mitsui, Mitsubishi, and Sumitome, forming part of the military-industrial complex up to World War II': literally 'family of property'

Zen (**Buddhism**) = 'branch of Mahayana Buddhism that relies on meditation, intuition, and self-discipline rather than words or scripture reading to achieve enlightenment': borrowed via Chinese from Sanskrit *dhyana* = 'meditation'

zori /zôr-ē/ = 'rubber beach sandals with a thong': from Japanese *zori* = 'traditional formal sandals worn by women, with platform soles'

(2) Western words in Japanese. Western travelers in Japan will encounter many words that sound strangely familiar, based on borrowings from Western languages, especially English. These are often much altered in pronunciation, and sometimes in meaning and usage as well. The visitor will stay in a *hoteru* (= 'hotel'), drink *biiru* (= 'beer') or *uisuki an za raku* (= 'whiskey on the rocks'), and have a choice of *pan* (= 'bread,' borrowed from Portuguese) or *raisu* (= 'rice,' although there is also a perfectly good Japanese word for 'rice'—*gohan*) with his meal. His Japanese friend, a *sarariman* (= 'white-collar worker,' from *salary man*) who goes to his *ofuisu* (= 'office') in a high-rise *birudingu* (= 'building'), may offer to take him for a drive in *mai-kaa* (= 'my car'). His college student son may be too busy doing *arubeito* (= 'a part-time job,' from German *arbeit* = 'work') to go along for the ride.

jargon. In recent years such guardians of correct English usage as Edwin Newman, John Simon, and William Safire have become as exercised about the flatulence of *jargon* as earlier writers had about the tedium of clichés. There is evidently more to this shift of emphasis than a mere change of fashion in the concerns of writers on usage. A certain kind of jargon does seem to be gaining ground in everyday speech and writing, often at the expense of good style and good sense. In order to understand why this is so, we must first investigate the one legitimate purpose and use of jargon.

In its narrowest definition, jargon refers to those specialized vocabularies by which members of particular arts, sciences, trades, and professions communicate among themselves—technical expressions that are understood by other members of the group and not by laypersons in general. Consider, for example, this sentence from a national computer magazine:

> The relocatable machine-code program is turned into an executable, absolute machine code by the linker, CLINK, which also merges the user's program with previously compiled program files (such as the standard C function library) if necessary.
>
> —Christopher Kern, *Byte*

However opaque this communication might seem to some of us, it represents a clear and efficient statement of facts to a computer specialist. Lawyers—especially in written documents—habitually indulge in a kind of jargon that to outsiders may seem cumbersome and repetitive, but which other lawyers know is necessary to establish exact legal definitions. Similarly, truck drivers, physicists, cooks, book publishers, dressmakers, soldiers—in fact just about everyone engaged in any institutionalized human occupation—use at least some specialized vocabulary in connection with their work.

Obviously, there is nothing much wrong with this kind of jargon, provided that its only intention is to convey meanings concisely and clearly to an expert audience. Outsiders may complain that the same meanings could be expressed in more universal terms, but the jargon users can logically reply that as long as they are addressing only their colleagues, there is no need to simplify and that to try to do so would waste time.

But is jargon, even when used only by and for members of a specialized group, always as clear and direct as it pretends to be? The answer, alas, is no—and it is by such abuse that jargon has earned its bad name. In an essay in *Harper's* in 1976, James Degnan of the University of Santa Clara described how the would-be professional is taught to use jargon while still an undergraduate. This "straight-A illiterate," said Degnan,

> learns to write gibberish by reading it and being taught to admire it. He must grapple with such journals as the *American Sociological Review*, journals bulg-

> ing with barbarous jargon, such as "ego integrative action orientation." In such journals, two things are never described as being "alike." They are "homologous" or "isomorphic." Nor are things "different." They are "allotropic." . . .

But, said Degnan, when he urged one of his own students to try to write more clearly and simply, the young man replied:

> If I followed your advice, I could never write the 5000-word term papers I am regularly assigned: I could never get a fellowship to graduate school, or a contract to do a textbook, or a decent job in business or government. . . . literacy might be okay, but I can't afford it.

Indeed, as one famous economist puts it:

> Complexity and obscurity have professional value—they are the academic equivalents of apprenticeship rules in the building trades. They exclude outsiders, keep down competition, preserve the image of a privileged or priestly class. The man who makes things clear is a scab. He is criticized less for his clarity than for his treachery. —John Kenneth Galbraith, *Wall Street Journal*

Judging by the prevalence of needless jargon in the learned professions, Professor Galbraith has a point. One might suppose that teachers of English and English literature would, of all classes of scholars, be least susceptible. But this is far from true. Academic literary criticism has long been a notorious and distinctive suburb of the jargon community; and its practitioners often take a positive delight in making simple ideas sound complicated. The following example must surely be the hard way of saying that when reading a poem, you get out of it what you put into it.

> Critical discourse gives the poem a life other than its own but cognate to its own. The power we ascribe to a poem is answered by another power, that of a reading adequate to it in principle and by intention, if inadequate to the event. —Denis Donoghue, *Raritan*

The posturings that typify much of academic criticism may only be extreme symptoms of a deeper malady. The way English composition is taught in many secondary schools and colleges may tend to foster wordiness and obscurity. On October 27, 1981, the *New York Times* reported on a six-year study conducted by Rosemary L. Hake of Chicago State University and Joseph M. Williams of the University of Chicago. In it, English teachers were asked to rate pairs of student essays on the same subject, one essay having clear and simple language and the other having flowery words, passive verbs, and complex sentence structures. The two researchers found that "teachers consistently preferred verbosity to tight writing" and concluded that many teachers were "encouraging precisely the stylistic values we claim we reject." If Hake and Williams are right, we should not be surprised if students who were trained to admire wordiness over clarity and precision eventually come to cherish jargon.

For the jargon-speaking professional it is a short (though patently downward) step from trying to impress his or her specialist colleagues to trying to impress the defenseless layperson. And when the duly impressed nonprofessional begins trying to impress other nonprofessionals by borrowing the vocabularies of the specialists, what began as a local infection can become a linguistic plague in no time.

It is no accident that among the laypersons readiest to resort to jargon are bureaucrats—people whose jobs may depend not only on their ability to impress their bosses and the public at large but also on their ability to avoid giving offense to any group that might have political power. Bureaucrats tend to shirk personal responsibility for what they have written by using verbs in the passive voice and by resorting to such impersonal statements as "a review of the available facts by the concerned governmental agencies has determined that. . . ." But such expressions merely illustrate the general tendencies of bureaucratic jargon. In practice it is a creature of fashion, its terms and phrases evolving so rapidly that they are very likely to have vanished before anyone has had time to figure out exactly what they meant. In September, 1981, for instance, the editors of the *New York Times* made a public-spirited but foredoomed attempt to keep their readers abreast of the latest Washington jargon. Here is one of the definitions they offered:

> *Minimal Prescriptiveness.* The Federal Government's phrase to explain that it wants few rules. . . .

Other items on the list included *roll, kill-jamming, time, real time,* and *real time time.* But it was hardly worth defining them. Two months later the *Times* was already reporting a new cluster of bureaucratic favorites—*mid-course correction, revenue shortfall,* and *COLA freeze*—all of which were probably so ephemeral as to be hardly worth defining, either.

Every department of government, as well as its nongovernmental counterparts, draws upon the general pool of current jargon and attempts to create terms characteristically its own. The results are often nearly unreadable. Here is an executive of a research corporation advising the Defense Department on procurement procedures:

> For each concept that is developed and demonstrated during the front end of the development/acquisition cycle, [this] methodology can be used to establish a baseline or initial set of human resources and other logistic support requirements, to target sources of high support demand ("high drivers"), and to conduct support/design trade-offs in order to ameliorate their impact.
>
> —Peter D. Weddle, *Military Science and Technology*

This example brings us to what is surely the worst abuse of jargon: using it to obscure meaning. It is bad enough when a jargoneer sacrifices clarity for the sake of pomposity. It is very much worse when he or she deliberately uses pomposity for the sake of destroying clarity. Politicians, when hard pressed to defend their actions, are notorious for using jargon in this way. One of the more celebrated examples of this occurred in the early 1970s when a White House aide announced that an earlier statement made by the administration should now be considered "no longer operative." Translation: It was a lie.

But self-aggrandizing professionals, bureaucrats, and politicians are hardly alone in using jargon to obfuscate. In any year when business profits are down, the "President's Message" that heads half the annual corporate reports in America would probably make the most seasoned bureaucrat envious. Indeed, business jargon is almost a subject in itself. On the one hand, it tends to borrow heavily from the special vocabularies of economics, finance, and technology; on the other, from the language of war, sports, and gambling. Thus, in business jargon, *bottom line, input, outlay creep, dotted-line responsibility,* and the ubiquitous *parameter* may rub shoulders with *ballpark figures, bargaining chips, cheap shots,* and *targets of opportunity.* Hyphenated all-purpose adjectives such as *-oriented, -related,* and *-intensive* are much in favor, as are such useless appendages as *situation* (*declining sales situation*), *mode,* and *system.* And business—with some help from the military—must also bear a good deal of responsibility for the current penchant for turning nouns and adjectives into verbs, as in *Let's roundtable it. How will that impact on inventory? I'll reference that to the legal department.* Soon after he became Secretary of State in 1981, Alexander Haig acquired a reputation for this kind of reckless verb making, with the inevitable result that parodists were quick to mimic his distinctive style.

> If that is how General Haig wants to nervous breakdown the Russian leadership, he may be shrewding his way to the biggest diplomatic invent since Clausewitz. Unless, that is, he schizophrenizes his allies first.
>
> —*The Guardian*

Obviously, much business jargon is intended simply to impress—to make its user sound at once knowledgeable and appropriately aggressive (as in *eye on the ball* and *hard-hitting*). But unfortunately, much of it is also valued for its inherent lack of precision. After all, like most of us, businessmen are not above wanting to sound more precise than they dare to be in fact. Our point is not that business has no legitimate specialized vocabularies of its own—plainly it has many—but rather that many businessmen regularly affect additional vocabularies and expressions that are intended to suggest quite different contexts.

And so do we all. If many junior executives strive to sound like combinations of M.B.A.'s and linebackers, likewise many psychologists try to sound like hippies, weather forecasters like astrophysicists, policemen like lawyers, advertising men like jet setters, teen-agers like film critics, and dinner party hosts like wine experts.

Here, for example, is a movie critic trying to sound like a psychotherapist:

> The fusion of conflicting tendencies in the figure of the monster in horror films has the dream process of condensation as its approximate psychic prototype.
> —Noel Carroll, *Film Quarterly*

We can only wonder if that is how a Hollywood producer would have put it.

From time to time we all play at being things we are not, borrowing words and phrases from walks of life that are not our own in an effort to spice our language and impress others with the breadth of our knowledge. But when, in the process, we blur or distort meanings, either through ignorance or intention, we do ourselves and our language a disservice.

One of the more annoying examples of how we misuse other people's jargon comes under the heading of what the author R. D. Rosen calls "psychobabble." Since gossiping about the peculiarities of our friends and neighbors is one of the enduring staples of ordinary human conversation, it was probably inevitable that the language of modern psychology would eventually begin to ooze into our everyday speech. By the 1940s many laypersons were confidently—if often inaccurately—ornamenting their speech with such Freudian terms as *complex*, *repression*, and *sublimation*. In the decades that followed, hundreds of additional psychological terms were taken over by the nonprofessionals and almost always debased in the process. The clinical term *paranoid*, for example, began to be used as a popular synonym for *suspicious* or *worried; persona* for *mannerism; schizophrenic* for *undecided;* and *syndrome* for almost any kind of consistent behavior. Then, at some point (roughly from the mid-1960s on), people began inventing their own pseudopsychological terms—*uptight; hang-up; where you're coming from; laid back;* and so on. Ironically, some professional psychologists, perhaps in an effort to "relate" better to their patients, even began to incorporate these same coinages into their own vocabularies. Thus, the wheel of jargon turned full circle, and the result, to this day, has been a victory neither for psychology in particular nor meaning in general.

To be sure, this informal history of the evolution of "pop psych" language raises a question of definition: When nonprofessionals began inventing their own psychological terms—terms that were unrelated to any existing technical vocabulary—were they, in the proper sense of the word, actually using jargon? Put more broadly, must jargon derive from specialized occupational vocabularies or can it originate in everyday speech? Is it correct to call certain speech patterns composed of common slang, vogue words, and pat phrases jargon?

Although there is no clear consensus among dictionaries and usage books on this point, we think that many such patterns deserve to be called jargon, if only because they abuse language in the same ways as do other kinds of jargon. They seek to impress rather than convey precise meanings. They tend to replace common, perfectly clear words with new expressions that seldom improve understanding. And like other kinds of jargon, these terms have about them a kind of self-congratulatory elitist or in-group quality that can be irritating.

Some particularly amusing examples of jargon-studded speech appeared in Cyra McFadden's *The Serial* (1977), a satirical novel about a group of young sophisticates who live in Marin County, an affluent suburb of San Francisco. That the inhabitants of McFadden's Mill Valley think of themselves as an elite, there is no doubt.

> They'd rapped about saunas vs. Japanese hot tubs, whether anybody really *needed* a quadraphonic stereo, whether it was sexist to vote for Barbara Boxer for supervisor. . . . Looking back on it all, Kate realized that there were all these terrifically intelligent, vital people in Marin who had practically *Renaissance* minds.

These latter-day Leonardos tend to express themselves in a style that, among other things, borrows from both psychological jargon and hip slang.

> Right away they'd flashed on how much their trips were alike, because he, too, had just split from a paranoid psychotic and was presently giving first priority to getting his head together.

The fact that popular jargon is often used to reinforce social distinctions is well illustrated in the vocabularies of that most clique-ridden of institutions, the American high school. By the early 1980s two of the best-defined social sets in nearly every high school were the "freaks" (roughly defined as descendants of the hippies of earlier decades) and the "jocks" (their more conventional counterparts). In addition to dress, mannerisms, and even accent and pronunciation, these groups sought to distinguish themselves with words. If a freak wanted to be highly approving of something, he might call it *excellent* or *radical,* whereas a jock would more characteristically call it *serious, ace, ten,* or *key.* A typical freak word of this period was *intense,* but (in almost a parody of popular jargon's usual lack of precision) the word could mean almost anything from 'great' to 'simply awful.' On and on these slang vocabularies went—*agent; that bites; like blood; wrecked; wasted; blown away*—filled with expressions unlike those that had been "in" only a few years before, expressions that were due soon to be replaced by more fashionable new slang, expressions that were deficient in meaning and had virtually no purpose other than to sound knowing and to promote social (and generational) distinctions.

As both our high school students and Cyra McFadden's fictional California suburbanites suggest, there is a considerable affinity between popular jargon on the one hand and slang and vogue words on the other. Indeed, the categories overlap to such an extent that we may say that whenever certain clusters of slang and vogue words begin to be repeated by people within any group, a kind of jargon is being created for that group.

And this, in turn, suggests what must by now be obvious—that the extent to which jargon infests our language is enormous. So enormous that it would be nearly impossible to compose a comprehensive lexicon of current jargon, and completely impossible to try to do so here. Thus, we shall have to leave it to others to make the definitive examinations of such exotica as Hollywood jargon (with its *bankable talents, nabes,* and *ozones*) or air force jargon (with its *outstandings, huds,* and *hi-lo-hi's*). Even the categories are too numerous to list.

Fortunately, we do not need to know all of jargon's manifestations in order to defend ourselves against its abuses. A few commonsense tests are sufficient to tell us whether or not most jargon words or phrases are acceptable. Are they genuinely meaningful? Could they be replaced by simpler synonyms? Are they being used for any purpose other than clear communication, and if so, are those purposes legitimate? If everyone were to apply only these simple criteria to their choice of words, 99 percent of the jargon now current would evaporate overnight.

But, of course, everyone won't. We still need paladins to fight the good fight against jargon's ceaseless encroachments. Fortunately, we have such champions not only among professional word watchers but in the journalistic grass roots as well. A case in point is the exemplary feature "Clunkers of the Month" that regularly appears in the IBM house organ *Think.* The editors invite readers to send in particularly dreadful examples of jargon they encounter in their daily work. (As the editors candidly put it: "If some IBM people are not the worst despoilers of the English Language . . . it's not for a want of trying.") Although the original sources are kept confidential, winning contributors receive copies of *On Writing Well,* by William

Zinsser. Here is a random harvest of three clunkers from "Clunkers." First we have:

> Congruent command paradigms explicitly represent the semantic oppositions in the definitions of the commands to which they refer.

And then, the mind-bending:

> In accordance with the plan, you are liable for your *actual* hypothetical tax.

And finally, the weirdly Germanic:

> Although we cannot project at this time the current eat-off because of these cuts so recent and the financial over-clearance, we will be on a continuing basis attempting to reschedule unneeded parts. . . .

See also CLICHÉ; EUPHEMISM; SLANG; and VOGUE WORDS.

jeremiad /jĕr-ə-**mī**-əd, -ăd/. The prophet Jeremiah, living in the 7th and 6th centuries B.C., rebuked the Hebrews for sinfulness, predicted the fall of Jerusalem, lived to see it taken by Nebuchadnezzar, and afterward wrote five eloquent poems of lamentations for the captive and exiled Hebrews. A *jeremiad* is a bitter and sorrowful denunciation, with predictions of doom:

> . . . it was not only the substance of his jeremiad that upset me, the blanket indictment of a whole country. It was the muddy language. . . .
> —Alistair Cooke, *The Americans*

> For a decade, Mr. Murphy, as Police Commissioner in New York, Detroit, Washington and Syracuse . . . has sounded jeremiads about the wretched and corrupt state of America's police.
> —Selwyn Raab, *New York Times*

jibe /jīb/. There are three separate words *jibe*, and two of them have spelling variants.
(1) The sailing term *jibe*, like many other nautical terms, is borrowed from Dutch. It refers to the action of a fore-and-aft sail and means 'to move from one side to the other when the vessel is sailing before the wind'—a movement that can be controlled but is often violent and even dangerous. The verb is used both intransitively and transitively, and of the vessel as well as the sail: *The mainsail jibed suddenly. He decided to jibe* or *to jibe the mainsail* or *to jibe the boat*. It is also used as a noun: *Watch out for a jibe.* The word is sometimes spelled *gybe*, but *jibe* is preferable.
(2) The verb *jibe* meaning 'to be in agreement with, harmonize,' first occurring in American English in the early 19th century, is of unknown origin. This one is spelled only *jibe*.

> It was notorious that no headquarters announcement was believed unless it jibed with what the news walkers picked up.
> —Bruce Catton, *A Stillness at Appomattox*

> . . . President Eisenhower's determination to make United States foreign policy jibe with the U.N. Charter.
> —E. B. White, *The Points of My Compass*

(3) *Jibe* or *gibe*, meaning 'to make taunting or scoffing remarks (at someone), jeer,' occurs first in the 16th century and is possibly borrowed from French. It is also a noun meaning 'a taunt, a jeer.' The spelling *gibe* is preferable, in order to distinguish it from the other two words above, but unfortunately *jibe* is also widely used for this one too:

> By the morning of November 17 Burnside's advance reached the Rappahannock River fords, and Yankee patrols went prowling down to the bank to exchange gibes with the Confederate sentries across the river.
> —Bruce Catton, *Glory Road*

> [President Johnson] jibed that I'd played football without a helmet, that I couldn't walk a straight line and chew gum at the same time.
> —Gerald R. Ford, *A Time to Heal*

jingo. This political term, nearly synonymous with *chauvinist* in its original sense, comes from a song that was popular in England in the heyday of British imperialism:

> We don't want to fight, yet by Jingo! if we do,
> We've got the ships, we've got the men, and got the money too.

It was written by G. W. Hunt in 1878, when Disraeli sent the British fleet into the Black Sea to protect Turkey from encroachment by Russia. *Jingo* became a noun meaning 'extreme and aggressive patriot,' with adjective *jingoistic* and abstract noun *jingoism*.

> Joseph Epstein . . . is clearly a raging reactionary, a zealous jingo, and a tool of the Wall Street conspiracy. . . .
> —James Hugh Toner (letter), *Harper's*

> I saw a jingoistic orator whip up a frenzy of hatred and disgust against the French because they ate frog's legs and snails.
> —Euell Gibbons, *Stalking the Wild Asparagus*

> "Do you have the impression that was a jingoistic speech?" Henry [Kissinger] asked me on the way to the Western White House one day, with a pained expression of which he was a master. "Not a bit, by jingo," I replied, figuring he had to be kidding.
> —William Safire, *Before the Fall*

John Hancock. This mildly jocular term for a signature comes from the fact that John Hancock, who later became the first governor of Massachusetts, signed the Declaration of Independence first, and with the largest and boldest of all the signatures.

> It has been 84 years since President Grover Cleveland put his John Hancock on a bill making the first Monday in September a national holiday.
> —*Boston Globe*

juggernaut, Juggernaut. One of the titles of the Hindu god Vishnu is Lord of the World, in Sanskrit *Jagannātha*. For centuries, at an annual festival in the city of Puri in Orissa, a huge effigy of the god mounted on a massive wooden vehicle has been pulled by worshippers in sacred procession. Since the Middle Ages it has been reported in the West that numerous celebrants deliberately throw themselves under Jagannātha's wheels as a form of devotion. The story is true but oversimplified. It would in fact be impossible to determine which of the deaths were deliberate acts and which were accidents caused by overcrowding. In any case, Indian newspapers to this day often contain reports of fatalities at "car festivals," as such events are called in modern India. But the accounts of these incidents caught the imagination of the West, and *Jagannātha*, altered in English to *Juggernaut* or *juggernaut*, remains proverbial for an enormous, ruthlessly crushing force, or for a person who acts like one.

> . . . the man trampled calmly over the child's body and left her screaming on the ground. . . . It wasn't like a man; it was like some damned Juggernaut.
> —Robert Louis Stevenson, *Dr. Jekyll and Mr. Hyde* (1886)

> . . . [Afghan] refugees from the town were fleeing the Soviet juggernaut.
> —*Florida Times-Union*

> At 5 p.m., on February 22, the Americans faced the perennial juggernaut of world hockey—the 20 unbeaten officers and men of the unbeaten Soviet team.
> —Peter Michelmore, *Reader's Digest*

Eighteen-wheel semitrailer container trucks are generally known as *juggernaut lorries* in England.

juke, jukebox. ***Origin.*** In Wolof, a language of The Gambia in West Africa (the presumed home of Alex Haley's ancestor Kunta Kinte), the word *dzug* means 'to misbehave, lead a disorderly life.' In another West African language, Bambara, *dzugu* means 'wicked.' One of these words (or both) is undoubtedly the source of the Gullah word *juke* or *joog* = 'disorderly, wicked,' still used by the Gullah people, descendants of slaves living on the Sea Islands on the Georgia coast.

Uses. (1) *Juke*, also spelled *jook* or *jouk*, has been used in various ways by Southern blacks generally. The earliest known written example occurs in Zora Neale Hurston's *Mules and Men* (1935):

> They talked and told strong stories of Ella, Wall, East Coast Mary . . . and lesser jook lights around whom the glory of Polk County surged.

Here the "jook lights" are prostitutes. *Juke* also came to mean 'brothel' or 'tavern or dive where moonshine could be obtained':

> These jooks are tough joints. They'll murder you, caress you, and bless you.
> —Stetson Kennedy, *Palmetto County*

This use of *juke* (also *juke-house, juke joint*) became general in the South and also spread to the North:

> [He] has no more business setting out in the woods all night than he would 'a' had setting all night in a highway juke joint.
> —William Faulkner, *Shingles for the Lord*

> Juke Operator Surrenders in Shooting Quiz
> —headline, *Chicago Daily News* (1947)

> Here on the "Gold Coast," a squalid collection of jooks and honky-tonks, liquor may be bought openly by the case.
> —*Saturday Evening Post* (1948)

In addition *juke* is used as a verb meaning 'to dance,' especially in a juke joint, and 'to drink and carouse,' all the meanings being almost puritanically faithful to the original African sense:

> "C'man gate-mouth, let's get hep and go joukin'."
> —from *American Speech* (1941)

> "I want you to go juking with me . . . that's riding and stopping to drink and dance, and riding some more and stopping to drink and dance again, and after awhile you just stop to drink . . . and sometimes you stop drinking and go to a tourist cabin [with your girl]."
> —Tennessee Williams, *Orpheus Descending*

(2) In the late 1930s the coin-operated phonograph that was frequently found in juke joints became popularly known as the *jukebox.* This is a perfectly respectable term and is known wherever American culture has spread. *Jukebox* is now also familiar in British English, in several of the languages of Europe, and even in West Africa where the word originated.

junta, junto. The Spanish word *junta* means 'committee, council.' It was first borrowed into English in the early 17th century, and in Britain has long been regarded as a fully naturalized word, pronounced /**jŭn**-tə/. In the United States the word has been in effect reborrowed from the Spanish of the Americas, and is therefore often treated as a Spanish word, pronounced /**hŏŏn**-tə/. But some Americans still prefer /**jŭn**-tə/. And others use the hybrid form /**jŏŏn**-tə/, which we don't recommend. It can mean simply 'committee, council' but most often means 'group of men, typically military officers, controlling a government by armed force without electoral sanction.' *Junto* /**jŭn**-tō/, an English variant of *junta,* means either 'small political faction' or 'secret society, group that meets clandestinely, cabal.'

K

kabala, kabbala. See CABALA, CABALISTIC.

kernel. See PIT, STONE, SEED, KERNEL.

ketchup. The original *ketchup* was a spicy Oriental sauce containing mushroom juice and walnuts, which was imported to Europe as early as the 18th century. Gradually accommodated to Western tastes, ketchup is now a thick tomato purée. The word is from Malay *kechap,* which in turn may have been borrowed from Chinese. The preferred spelling is *ketchup,* but *catsup* is also widely used.

kibosh, pronounced either /kĭ-**bŏsh**/ or /**kī**-bŏsh/ and sometimes spelled *kybosh,* is of unknown origin. It is used only in the phrase *put the kibosh on* = 'to put a decisive stop to (something), veto' or 'to give a decisive check to (someone), thwart':

> . . . one of the best ways it can put the kibosh on cranks is to apply this social boycott business. . . .
>
> —Sinclair Lewis, *Babbitt*

kidnap. This word was originally thieves' slang meaning 'to steal a child': *kid* + *nap* or *nab* = 'to steal.' It made its first appearance in the late 17th century, in England often meaning specifically 'to steal children and sell them as indentured servants for the American colonies':

> John Dykes . . . Convicted of Kidnapping, or Enticing away, His Majesty's Subjects, to go Servants into the Foreign Plantations.
>
> —*London Gazette* (1688)

Then as now the word could apply to the abduction of adults as well as children, but children have always been the easiest victims.

Dictionaries and editors are evenly divided between the spellings *kidnapped, kidnapping, kidnapper* and *kidnaped, kidnaping, kidnaper.* Both are correct, but *kidnapped,* etc., is preferable.

kilt. It is a mistake to refer to *a man wearing kilts;* the correct expression is *wearing a kilt.*

kind. (1) The commonly used phrase *these* (or *those*) *kind of,* which combines a plural pronoun (*these, those*) with a singular noun (*kind*), breaks a formal rule of grammar but has long continued to occur, both in print and in speech:

> The impertinence of these kind of scrutinies, moreover, was generally concluded with a compliment. . . .
>
> "Really," said Elinor, "I know so little of these kind of forms. . . ."
>
> —Jane Austen, *Sense and Sensibility*

> These are the kind of elements of a national health insurance important to the American people.
>
> —Jimmy Carter (quoted), *New York Times*

◇ ***Recommendation.*** In all except highly formal speech *these kind of (things)* is an acceptable idiom. In highly formal speech and all except informal writing, it should be amended either to *this kind of (thing)* or to *things of this kind.*

(2) The adverbial phrase *kind of* means 'somewhat, rather,' frequently as a mild understatement implying 'rather a lot, considerably':

> I want to say to General Sherman, who is considered an able man in our parts, though some people think [he] is a kind of careless man about fire, that from the ashes he left us in 1864 we have raised a brave and beautiful city. . . .
>
> —Henry W. Grady, *The New South* (1886)

> I guess that's why he spoke English funny—not with a foreign accent exactly, but with a different cadence, kind of like one of those light Irish brogues, going up at the end of sentences. . . .
>
> —Walter F. Murphy, *The Vicar of Christ*

◇ ***Recommendation.*** This is a well-established idiom appropriate for giving an informal touch in all but the most formal contexts.

kitsch is from a German word meaning 'trashy, slapped-together work.' In English, *kitsch* refers to objects, writings, or any other cultural products or activities that are either in ordinary cheap bad taste or in a kind of self-conscious and sophisticated bad taste that some have found amusing.

> The curios in Tucumán were versions of gaucho kitsch—sets of bolas, toy horsewhips, over-priced daggers. . . .
> —Paul Theroux, *The Old Patagonian Express*

> Americans have a friskily self-destructive habit of turning even their best impulses into junk and kitsch; a Beverly Hills hair salon lately had eight models in tank tops and khaki trousers parading around the shop carrying flags and sporting new "military" hair styles.
> —Lance Morrow, *Time*

kitty-corner. See CATERCORNER.

knot. In the days of sail the speed of a vessel through the water was measured by a device called the *log line,* consisting of a piece of wood attached to a cord with knots in it at certain intervals. The intervals were such that when the log was thrown into the water, the line would be pulled out in a period of 28 seconds to as many knots as the nautical miles per hour that the vessel was making. The speed is therefore spoken of as *X knots* rather than *X knots an hour.* However, the mistake is frequently made, and anyone who makes it can claim to be in good company—such famous sailors as Capt. Frederick Marryat and Hilaire Belloc referred to *knots an hour* in print. (A nautical mile is about 265 yards more than a statute mile.)

kola. See COLA, KOLA.

kowtow. In ordinary Chinese usage the *kowtow* (from Mandarin *k'o-t'ou/ketou* = 'head-knocking') means 'ritual bowing and touching of the head,' as by a young person to a member of the older generation on some special occasion such as New Year's. In imperial China the kowtow was a special bow to the emperor required of anyone who was granted an audience with him. Westerners greatly resented this, and their ambassadors long refused to kowtow (and were therefore refused audience). The word remains with us today as a verb meaning 'to defer obsequiously, show servile attention to (someone or something)':

> "What's wrong with you?" said Rebekah. "Why are you always kowtowing to Lyndon? Are you afraid of him or something?"
> —Sam Houston Johnson, *My Brother Lyndon*

> But he loathed playing the company game, kowtowing to superiors, and that was one of the reasons why White—for all his ability—eventually fell out of favor at CBS.
> —Gary Paul Gates, *Air Time*

kybosh. See KIBOSH.

L

la, the French feminine definite article, is applied in English to formidable women, usually with a sarcastic tinge:

> In one of the songs, *Don't Believe What You Read,* La Streisand puts journalists in their place with a flex of her mighty vocal cords. —*Time*

lackey, a borrowing from French, literally means 'male personal servant, footman, valet.' It is now only used as a term of contempt for a servile hanger-on:

> . . . increasingly, toward the end of his life, Hemingway was served by lackeys who were in fact serving themselves.
> —Brendan Gill,
> *Here at The New Yorker*

In politics *lackey* is a polemic term applied to people or institutions that are subsidiary tools or hirelings of whatever the speaker regards as the real enemy or the prime forces of oppression:

> During the last two world wars, national churches even functioned as the lackeys of the state. . . .
> —Martin Luther King, Jr.,
> *Strength to Love*

In Communist denunciations of capitalism, *lackey* is a traditional and almost technical term for low-ranking or subsidiary servants of capitalism:

> To a person, these landlords' lackeys [the Urban Affairs Task Force] have recommended that federal grants be withheld from cities that have rent control laws.
> —John Catalinotto,
> *Workers World*

laconic. In the ancient world the Spartans were admired for extremely terse and expressive utterances. When Philip of Macedon wrote to them, "If I enter your city I will raze it to the ground," their magistrates sent back the answer, "If." The usual name of the Spartans was *Lacedaemonians* or *Lacones;* this style of talking is therefore called *laconic,* and an example of it is a *laconism.* There is not much of it around nowadays. One memorable example was that of Gen. Anthony McAuliffe of the 101st Airborne Division, completely surrounded in 1944 in the Battle of the Bulge; to the German demand for surrender he replied, "Nuts." Examples of the adjective *laconic:*

> Vinny turns the radio up as the dispatcher asks Battalion 27 if the Field Communications Unit and another Battalion Chief are needed at 2737. The reply is a laconic "yes."
> —Dennis Smith,
> *Report From Engine Company 82*

> "If it ain't broke don't fix it," drawls Winegartner in the laconic accents of his native Springfield, Mo.
> —Carol E. Curtis, *Forbes*

lady. "No lady is ever a gentleman," wrote James Cabell in *Something About Eve.* At least in the usage of the words *lady* and *gentleman,* it is true that the double standard still prevails in subtle ways. In the most admiring or complimentary sense, "She's a real lady" implies a different set of qualities from "He's a real gentleman"; the lady will usually be expected to be polite, kind, and modest (or at any rate discreet), while the gentleman is supposed to be above all honest and honorable. But merely as terms of respect, without any particular implication of character, the two words are of course exact counterparts: "Will the next lady come this way, please."

Lady is also used as a genteel feminine marker with unmarked nouns of occupation, such as *lady doctor* or *lady plumber.* Many women now dislike and reject such designations. In humbler jobs for which there is no one-word job title, *lady* remains somehow more acceptable: *cleaning lady, coffee lady.* In general, *lady* is a word so full of social overtones and built-in gender assumptions that no one can prescribe rules of its usage for others. Some would like to discard the word almost entirely; for others it still has important values. See also GENTLEMAN; WOMAN, LADY, GIRL.

lama, llama. A *lama* is a Tibetan Buddhist monk or priest. A *llama* is a South American animal related to the camel. The technical name of the genus of the *llama* is, however, *Lama. Llama* is usually pronounced /**lä**-mə/, but some people prefer the more Spanish version, /**yä**-mə/.

lampoon. The original meaning of the word *lampoon,* an abusive and ribald satire directed against an individual, is betokened by its etymological origins: in French the verb *lamper* means 'to guzzle,' and in former times a rowdy drinking song was called a *lampon* or, in English, *lampoon.* But modern usage has shorn the word of most of its original biting connotations. Nowadays, the term usually refers to a kind of good-natured mockery, better described as parody than satire, that need not be directed only at people and seldom achieves the intensity of an attack. See also BURLESQUE; SATIRE; SPOOF.

language change. That our language should change as we speak it—as all living languages change, from generation to generation, from year to year, indeed from day to day—is simply inevitable. Language is the means by which we control our civilization; and if civilization develops, advances, and grows more complex, then language must change to keep pace with civilization. It would be unthinkable to try to manage a nuclear civilization with a language having no word for *fission.* Generally, however, except in certain areas such as scientific terminology, language alters so slowly that the changes are not perceived by the ordinary speaker, who perhaps never encounters those areas in which the changes occur faster. Indeed, the average speaker may deny that the language is changing in any respect at all and may even feel indignant when the fact of language change is brought to his or her attention.

Because of the relative slowness of language change, it is best examined by inspecting such changes over a comparatively long time. It is convenient to divide language into four levels: *sound, inflection, syntax,* and *vocabulary.* Change may be observed separately in each level.

Sound. At the level of sound, an English speaker living around 850 and wishing to use the word *stone* would have pronounced it rather like /stän/. Four hundred years later the sound of this same word had changed to /stôn/. Not till sometime in the 16th century did the pronunciation of the word *stone* change into its modern form /stōn/. So, too, had our speaker of 850 wished to use the word *knight,* he would have said /knĭKHt/. By Shakespeare's time the pronunciation of this same word was /knəĭKHt/. Since that time the word has lost both its /k/ and its /KH/ sounds. Nor are these two words, *stone* and *knight,* mere isolated examples. The great majority of words in the language have undergone substantial changes in pronunciation since the days of King Alfred.

Inflection. Inflection (varying the "shape" of a word) is one way of showing the relationship between one word and another; for example, in the phrase *the king's realm* we add *'s* to *king* to show that it is the king who possesses the realm, and not the other way around. Over the centuries English has so changed that there is now but little remaining of what was once a relatively rich system of inflections. For instance, around 850 the word *day* had six different forms: *dæg* = 'day'; *dæges* = 'of a day'; *dæge* = 'in or on a day'; *dagas* = 'days'; *daga* = 'of days'; *dagum* = 'in or on days.' Changes in the language have cut these down to four: *day, day's, days,* and *days'*—and the last three all sound alike. So, too, adjectives, once dowered with 36 different forms (12 in each of the three degrees—positive, comparative, and superlative), have changed, so that they now have but one form in each degree—for example, *smooth, smoother, smoothest.* Language change has reduced the English regular verb to its present four forms; 1,000 years ago the English verb had four forms in the present tense alone.

Syntax. The syntax of English (the way in which we arrange words so as to indicate meaning) has likewise changed much since King Alfred's day. Of Alfred's doings in the year 894, one of the authors of the *Anglo-Saxon Chronicle* wrote:

> Thā se cyng thæt gehīerde, thā
> *When the king that heard, then*
>
> wende hē hine west with Exanceastres.
> *turned he himself west toward Exeter.*

Loss of the Old English word endings led Modern English to establish that subjects in sentences of this type always precede their predicates and that both precede objects. This was not so in Old English, in which word order ran closer to the typical Germanic pattern, one that persists to this day in German, Swedish, and related languages. The Old English sentence quoted above could in fact be translated word for word into German with no change in order: *Da der König das gehört, da wendete er sich west gen Exeter.*

Vocabulary. It is in vocabulary that language change is most obvious, though not necessarily greatest in amount. To begin with, as the years go by, many words fall out of use; we no longer use *ānhaga* for 'solitary person,' *ār* for 'grace,' *hrēran* for 'to stir,' or *milts* for 'mercy.' Other words are borrowed into English from foreign languages. Thus, Latin gave us *mile,* Greek gave us *church,* and together they gave us *inch; steak* comes from Icelandic, *count* from French, *apartheid* from Afrikaans, *catamaran* from Tamil, and *ombudsman* from Swedish. Still other words are deliberately invented, like *kerosene* and *vaseline.* Perhaps language change can be seen most clearly in the changes in meanings of individual words. Here are some common words with their earlier meanings:

amuse = 'to bemuse'
buxom = 'lissome'
counterfeit = 'portrait'
fond = 'foolish'
knight = 'child'
lewd = 'secular, lay'
lusty = 'pleasant'
nice = 'ignorant'
prevent = 'to anticipate'
silly = 'timely'
villain = 'country dweller'

As a final illustration of language change we cite the first two sentences of the Lord's Prayer as they were in Old English (c. 850), Middle English (c. 1400), and Early Modern English (c. 1600); pronunciation is provided beneath each line.

Old English

Fæder ūre,
fădər o͞orə
thū the eart on heofonum,
tho͞o thə ăərt ŏn hĕəvənōōm,
sī thīn nama gehālgod.
sē thēn nämä yəhälgŏd.
Tōbecume thīn rīce.
tōbəko͞omə thēn rēchə.

Middle English

Oure fadir
o͞orə fädĭr
that art in hevenes
thät ärt ĭn hĕvənəs
halewid be thi name.
häləwĭd bā thē näm
Thi kyngdoom come to.
thē kĭnggdōm ko͞om tō.

Early Modern English

Our father
əo͞or fĕ*th*ər
which art in heaven
hwĭch ärt ĭn hĕvən
hallowed be thy name.
hăləwəd bē *th*əĭ nĕm
Thy kingdome come.
*th*əĭ kĭngdəm ko͞om.

Causes of Language Change. It is easy enough to identify the causes, in the broad sense, of language change. They are, for example, war, which gave the English language *blitz(krieg)* and changed the meaning of *siren;* political subjection, which led the English to dispense with *thane* and adopt *baron, duke,* etc.; trade, which led the language to adopt the measures—*inch, mile, pound*—of those with whom its speakers traded; proximity to other languages, which gave us *cache, mush, kosher,* etc.; and technological advance, which has spurred the Barnhart dictionary makers, for example, to produce since 1963 two dictionaries of new words, each containing some 5,000 entries. Moreover, a change in one level of a language often causes a change in another. Thus, the extinction of the contrasts among the unstressed vowels of English during the 9th, 10th, and 11th centuries, and the complete loss of many of these vowels during the centuries that followed, together forced another change in English grammar: the inflectional system, which had relied on such contrasts, could no longer operate when these contrasts were lost, and English had to change to a grammar that was based more upon word order.

Relating a particular change to a particular nonlinguistic phenomenon, however, is almost impossible. The word *blitz(krieg)* has survived, but *gremlin*, once common, is now little heard. English adopted *inch* and *mile* but kept the native *foot* and *yard*. It seems that the motives of people with language are too varied to admit of detailed description, at least so far.

Theories of Language Change. To some scholars language change seems random, or at best cyclic. Certainly there is some evidence for the cyclicity of language change in, for example, the alternation of periods of simple vowel sounds (*monophthongs*) and complex vowel sounds (*diphthongs*) in the history of English vowels. Other scholars, however, such as the American Edward Sapir (1884–1939), have held that language change is controlled by a "drift," that is, by a tendency of the speakers of a language to accept changes tending in one direction and to reject changes tending in another; Sapir identified a drift in English toward the nonvariable word. There is some evidence for this theory, too. Over the centuries the English adjective has changed from being a highly varying word to being, as it now is, almost completely nonvariable; and in our own times the language seems to be changing the alternative *who* and *whom* into nonvariable *who*.

See also MIDDLE ENGLISH; MODERN ENGLISH; OLD ENGLISH.

languid, languorous. *Languid* usually has negative senses—'drooping, sluggish, apathetic, lacking force or energy': *He was too languid to take any interest. The economic recovery is languid so far.* However, *languid* can also mean 'pleasantly relaxed, agreeably free from tension':

> The mood aboard the press plane was mostly muted, inquisitive in an unobtrusive way; languid like the professional athlete on the eve of protracted exertion.
>
> —William F. Buckley, Jr., *To China With Nixon*

Languorous can be synonymous with *languid* but often means 'gracefully slow-moving':

> No more beautiful people exist in the world than the languorous, able Chinese-Polynesians of the South Seas.
>
> —James A. Michener, *The Covenant*

largess and **largesse** are equally correct spellings. The prevailing pronunciation is probably /lär-**jĕs**/, but /**lär**-jĕs/ and /**lär**-jĭs/ are also common and correct. The meaning is 'generosity, bounty':

> So the sanctuary is now largely dependent on the largesse of 100 or so "wolf adopters." . . .
>
> —Bill Gilbert, *Reader's Digest*

> . . . a man preaching an anti-government philosophy while benefiting from the government's largess.
>
> —Peter W. Bernstein, *Fortune*

Latin words. In 600 B.C. Latin was an insignificant dialect spoken by a few illiterate tribes in the hills of central Italy. Like most of the languages of Iron Age Europe, it was of Indo-European origin (see INDO-EUROPEAN); it is thus related to Greek and to the Celtic, Slavic, and Germanic languages. By the time of Christ, Latin was the official language of an empire ruling the entire Mediterranean world and most of Europe. Four hundred years later the empire fell, but its language survived, both as the living speech of millions of people—splitting up and emerging as

Italian, Spanish, Portuguese, French, and Rumanian—and as the long-preserved prestige language of government, religion, and learning. Latin is the most important language in European history, with its two enormously influential roles: as the ancestor of the Romance languages and as the classical language of high culture, the equivalent of Sanskrit for India and Mandarin for China.

Our modern vocabulary everywhere displays its immense debt to Latin. English is by descent and structure a Germanic language, but for 2,000 years it has borrowed so heavily and complexly from Latin and its offspring (especially French) that it is a kind of hybrid language. More than half of the words in our dictionaries have Latin etymologies. They range from fancy and technical terms to common words indispensable to our everyday speech.

Until the 20th century Latin was one of the basic school subjects in Europe and America, but in the past two or three generations it has been sharply downgraded. Fewer than 1 in 40 American children now learn any Latin at all. In terms of the changing priorities of education, this may well have been inevitable. But for the use and appreciation of the English language, it has serious implications. Most of our vocabulary comes directly or indirectly from Latin words. Parts of our grammar have been shaped by the influence of Latin models. Many problems, real or imaginary, of modern English usage can only be understood or even described by reference to Latin details or principles.

Radicals and optimists argue that it is all to the good that the dead hand of Latin has at last been lifted, leaving our language to get on with its own development in a natural way. Think of the forbidden SPLIT INFINITIVE—a doctrine forced on us by teachers who were pedantically overawed by Latin—now increasingly abandoned by most people. But granted that English usage is in fact the better for sweeping away some of these old or artificial rules, there is no revolution around the corner; our language is not about to become radically simplified. Details, not fundamentals, are changing. The vast influence of Latin on the nature and flavor of our language is a permanently established fact, and Latin words continue to be added to the vocabulary.

English is of course an independent language, which can always be learned, mastered, and studied without reference to any other language. But for an enriched understanding of the English vocabulary, some knowledge of Latin is more than just helpful.

This entry has been divided into three main categories: English words borrowed from Latin; the pronunciation of Latin; and the influence of Latin on English. In the first main category are included terms relating to civilized life and thought and to government, politics, and law; selected nouns; selected adjectives; and selected verbs. In these samplings we have for the most part chosen words that have basically kept their Latin forms, even though many of them were brought into English through French. At the separate entry FRENCH WORDS are discussed numerous other words derived ultimately from Latin but reshaped so as to be essentially French. The same occurs at the entries ITALIAN WORDS and SPANISH WORDS. For information on Latin plurals see PLURALS. For a selection of Latin prefixes and suffixes see AFFIXES.

The second main category—the pronunciation of Latin—includes a selection of terms and phrases.

The third main category consists of a short summation of the ways in which Latin continues to shape our language.

English Vocabulary Borrowed From Latin.

(1) Words relating to civilized life, conduct, and thought:

art = 'technical skill, creative tradition, etc.': from Old French *art*, from Latin *art-*, *ars* = 'skill, ability, contrivance, art'

culture = (1) 'cultivation of land' (2) 'intellectual training' (3) 'specifically human activities generally': (via French) from Latin *cultūra* = 'cultivation of land, intellectual training,' from *cultus*, past participle of *colere* = 'to cultivate, train'

discipline = 'training, systematic behavior': from Old French *discipline*, from Latin *disciplīna* = 'teaching,' also 'military training,' from *discipulus* = 'student,' from *discere* = 'to learn'

education = 'teaching': from Latin *ēdūcātiō(n)-*, abstract noun of *ēdūcāre* = 'to bring up (a child), teach, educate,' from *ē-* = 'out' + *-dūcāre* = 'to lead, bring'

library = 'collection of books': from Old French *librairie* = 'bookshop, library,' from (unrecorded) Latin *librāria* = 'bookshop, library,' from *liber* = 'book'

literature = 'language committed to writing, creative work in prose or poetry': (via French) from Latin *literātūra* = 'writing,' from *litera, literae* = 'written symbol, written message, writing, literature'

moral = 'relating to human behavior seen in terms of right and wrong': from Latin *mōrālis,* adjective of *mōrēs* = 'customs, traditions, ethics'

science = 'knowledge, learning, systematic investigation of nature': from Old French *science,* from Latin *sciēntia* = 'knowledge,' from *scīre* = 'to know'

tradition = 'the passing of human knowledge and behavior from generation to generation': (via French) from Latin *trāditiō(n)-* = 'a handing over,' from *trādere* = 'to hand over'

(2) Words relating to government, politics, and law:

candidate = 'person seeking to be elected to public office': from Latin *candidātus* = 'man wearing a white toga' (as was the custom for those seeking office), from *candidus* = 'white'

***capitol** = 'building in which a legislature meets'

census = 'count of the population of a country': from Latin *census* = 'count and registration of Roman citizens for military service and taxation,' from *censēre* = 'to assess' See CONSENSUS.

city = (1) 'large self-governing town' (2) '(in the United States) incorporated municipality': from Old French *cité,* from Latin *cīvitās,* originally 'citizenship,' then 'the body of citizens,' hence 'incorporated town, city,' also 'sovereign state, body politic,' from *cīvis* = 'citizen'

community = (1) 'the people of a place or country' (2) 'common quality, quality shared by a group': from Latin *commūnitās* = 'common quality, shared quality,' also in Medieval Latin 'group of people as a single entity,' from *commūnis* = 'shared, held in common'

dictator = 'ruler with absolute and unconstitutional power': from Latin *dictātor* = 'special executive appointed under the republican constitution and given overriding state authority for a limited time to deal with an emergency,' from *dictāre* = 'to announce, command'

elect = 'to choose (a candidate) for public office by vote': from Latin *ēlectus,* past participle of *ēligere* = 'to choose out,' from *e-* = 'out' + *legere* = 'to choose'

emperor = 'sovereign ranking above a king or ruling a number of peoples': from Old French *emperour,* from Latin *imperātor,* originally 'commander, general,' later 'title of the rulers of the Roman Empire and of its medieval successors,' from *imperāre* = 'to command'

forum = 'public discussion': from Latin *forum* = 'marketplace, main square of a town,' especially 'the Forum at Rome, the center of political life'

judge = 'public law officer who presides over cases and trials': from Old French *juge,* from Latin *jūdic-, jūdex,* literally 'law-pronouncer,' from *jūs* = 'law' + *-dic-, -dex* = 'pronouncer, speaker'

jurisprudence = 'scholarly study of law': from Latin *jūris prūdentia* = 'skill in the law, knowledge of the law,' from *jūris,* genitive of *jūs* = 'law' + *prūdentia* = 'knowledge, prudence'

justice = 'rightness, equity, fair dealing, the rule of law as enforced by government': from Old French *justice,* from Latin *jūstitia* = 'justness,' from *jūstus* = 'just, fair, upright, according with the law,' from *jūs* = 'law'

legislator = 'lawmaker, member of a lawmaking assembly': from Latin *lēgis lātor* =

'proposer of a law,' from *lēgis*, genitive of *lēg-*, *lex* = 'law' + *lātor* = 'mover, proposer'

liberty = 'freedom, legal status of a free person': (via French) from Latin *lībertās* = 'freedom,' from *līber* = 'free, not slave, not subject'

municipal = 'relating to city government': from Latin *mūnicipālis*, adjective of *mūnicipium* = 'city with full rights under Roman rule,' from *mūniceps* = 'accepting public duties,' from *mūnia* = 'public duties' + *-ceps* = 'accepting'

nation = 'people united under one government': (via French) from Latin *nātiō(n)-*, literally 'birth,' hence 'offspring, breed of animals' and 'race of people,' from *nātus* = 'born'

orator = 'public speaker': from Latin *ōrātor* = 'public speaker,' from *ōrāre* = 'to speak publicly'

patrician = 'upper-class, aristocratic': (via French) from Latin *patricius* = 'nobleman, member of one of the families from which the Senate was originally recruited,' from *Patrēs* = 'Fathers' (collective title of the original Senators), plural of *pater* = 'father'

people = (1) 'nation' (2) 'persons': from Old French *pople*, from Latin *populus* = 'the people, the whole body of the citizens of Rome'

plebeian = 'belonging to the common people': from Latin *plēbeius* = 'belonging to the plebs,' from *plēbs* = 'the common people, all Roman people who were not patrician' (Note: The *plēbs* included both rich and poor.)

proletarian = 'belonging to the poorest class': from Latin *prōletāriī*, literally 'they who contribute only their offspring to the city,' hence 'the poorest class of Roman citizens,' from *prōlēs* = 'offspring'

province = 'administrative territory within a country, region': (via French) from Latin *prōvincia* = 'territory annexed and governed by the Romans'

public = 'relating to the people or the state': (via French) from Latin *publicus*, variant form of *poplicus*, adjective of *populus* = 'people'

republic = 'nation-state in which the people are sovereign': (via French) from Latin *rēs publica* = 'public affairs, the common good, the state,' from *rēs* = 'thing, business' + *publica* = 'public'

senate = 'highest lawmaking body in a state, such as the upper house of the U.S. Congress': from Latin *senātus* = 'supreme lawmaking council of the Roman republic,' literally 'the elders collectively,' from *senex* = 'old man, elder'

tribe = 'noncivilized social group larger than a clan and smaller than a race': (via French) from Latin *tribus* = 'one of the voting divisions of the Roman people' (In the earliest records there were 20 such.)

tribune = 'champion of popular rights': from Latin *tribūnus* = 'representative of a Roman tribe,' especially as used in the title *tribūnus plēbis* = 'tribune of the plebs, an official elected by the plebs to defend their rights against encroachment by the Senate': from *tribus* = 'tribe'

*Appears as separate entry

(3) Selected nouns:

animal = 'living creature able to move at will': from Latin *animāle* = 'thing that lives and breathes, an animal,' from *anima* = 'the breath of life'

dignity = (1) 'inherent human worthiness' (2) 'impressive comportment of a person': (via French) from Latin *dignitās* = 'worthiness, merit,' from *dignus* = 'worthy'

essence = (1) 'intrinsic quality' (2) 'concentrated extract of something': (via French) from Latin *essēntia* = 'the quality of being,' from *esse* = 'to be'

fortune = 'fate, luck, especially when prosperous': (via French) from Latin *fortūna* = 'goddess of fate, favorable fate, fate in general,' from *fort-*, *fors* = 'chance, luck'

genius = (1) 'human ability of the highest order' (2) 'person having such ability': from Latin *genius* = 'divine spirit presiding over birth,' also 'divine spirit guarding each human,' also 'individual human character, inclination, etc.,' from *gen-* = 'to be born'

glory = 'the atmosphere of human or divine brilliance produced by fame, honor, nobility, power, etc.': (via French) from Latin *glōria* = 'fame, renown, glory'

honor = (1) 'high admiration of a person' (2) 'high human quality, nobility' (3) 'high rank': (via French) from Latin *honor* = 'high reputation, quality, rank, etc.'

hospitality = 'custom of offering others welcome, shelter, and food and drink in one's own home': (via French) from Latin *hospitālitās*, from *hospit-, hospes* = 'host or guest'

luxury = 'expensive and elegant comfort': (via French) from Latin *luxūria* = 'excess, abundance, luxury'

magnitude = 'greatness': from Latin *magnitūdō* = 'greatness,' from *magnus* = 'great'

majesty = 'sovereignty, grandeur': (via French) from Latin *mājestās* = 'sovereign power, authority,' from *mājor* = 'superior, greater'

misery = 'deep distress and unhappiness': (via French) from Latin *miseria* = 'unhappiness,' from *miser* = 'wretched, unhappy'

nature = (1) 'inherent character' (2) 'living creatures collectively' (3) 'the universe': (via French) from Latin *nātūra* = 'birth, inborn character,' also 'everything that has been born, the world, the universe': from *nātus* = 'born'

quality = (1) 'characteristic feature or nature of something' (2) 'excellence, degree of excellence': (via French) from Latin *quālitās* = 'characteristic nature,' from *quālis* = 'of what kind?'

quantity = (1) 'amount' (2) 'large amount': (via French) from Latin *quantitās* = 'amount,' from *quantus* = 'how much?'

sense = (1) 'perception' (2) 'faculty of perception, such as sight or smell' (3) 'ability to think' (4) 'meaning, etc.': (via French) from Latin *sensus* = 'perception, feeling,' from *sentīre* = 'to perceive, feel'

vehicle = 'carriage, car, truck, boat, plane, etc.': (via French) from Latin *vehiculum* = 'method of transportation,' especially 'wheeled vehicle,' from *vehere* = 'to transport'

virtue = (1) 'admired personal quality, moral worth' (2) 'any good quality': (via French) from Latin *virtūs* = 'manly quality, courage,' hence also 'virtue in general'

(4) Selected adjectives:

amorous = 'relating to love, inclined to make love': (via French) from Medieval Latin *amorōsus*, from *amor* = 'love'

august = 'awe-inspiring, full of majesty and power': from Latin *augustus* = 'worthy of reverence, full of divine favor'

bellicose = 'inclined for war, aggressive': from Latin *bellicōsus*, from *bellum* = 'war'

benevolent = 'wishing others well, kindly': from Latin *benevolent-, benevolens* = 'well-wishing,' from *bene* = 'well' + *volens* = 'wishing'

bland = (1) 'mild, soothing' (2) 'lacking flavor, dull': from Latin *blandus* = 'soft, caressing, pleasant'

decent = 'following respectable morals and taste': from Latin *decēnt, decēns* = 'fitting, honorable, appropriate,' from *decēre* = 'to fit, be suitable'

divine = 'of the nature of the gods': (via French) from Latin *dīvīnus*, from *dīvus* = 'god'

* **exquisite** = 'of highest perfection and beauty'

* **fabulous** = (1) 'belonging to fable, mythical' (2) 'wonderful, remarkable'

fragile = 'easily broken, delicate': (via French) from Latin *fragilis*, from *frag-*, stem of *frangere* = 'to break'

frigid = (1) 'very cold' (2) 'lacking human warmth': from Latin *frigidus*, from *frigere* = 'to be cold'

furtive = 'done secretly with a feeling of guilt, stealthy and sly': (via French) from

Latin *furtīvus* = 'stolen, thievish,' from *fur* = 'thief'

grand = 'big and impressive, high and powerful, great': (via French) from Latin *grandis* = 'full-grown, large, grand'

grave = (1) '(of things) of serious nature, important, seriously unfavorable' (2) '(of persons) serious in character, manner, or behavior, or expressing unfavorable thoughts': (via French) from Latin *gravis* = 'heavy,' hence 'weighty, important, solemn'

illustrious = 'highly distinguished and famous, by birth or achievement': from Latin *illustris* = 'shining, eminent,' from *in-* = 'in, into, onto' + *lustrum* = 'light'

moderate = 'restrained, not extreme, middling': from Latin *moderātus* = 'restrained, controlled,' from *moderāre* = 'to keep within proper measure,' from *modus* = 'measure'

modest = (1) 'inclined to rate one's merits not very high, unpretentious' (2) 'dressing and behaving respectably' (3) 'moderate': (via French) from Latin *modestus* = 'keeping within proper measure,' from *modus* = 'measure'

mortal = (1) 'subject to death, human' (2) 'relating to or causing death': (via French) from Latin *mortālis* = 'subject to death, human' (as opposed to the gods, who are not subject to death), from *mort-*, *mors* = 'death'

noble = (1) 'very admirable in character, high-minded' (2) 'belonging to a hereditary aristocracy': (via French) from Latin *nōbilis*, originally *gnōbilis* = 'known, famous,' hence also 'admirable' and 'of aristocratic birth,' from *gnō-* = 'to know'

perfect = 'complete, flawless, absolutely excellent': from Latin *perfectus* = 'finished, complete, perfect,' from *perficere* = 'to complete,' from *per-* = 'all through, thoroughly' + *-ficere* = 'to do, make'

***pious** = (1) 'sincerely religious' (2) 'hypocritical': from Latin *pius* = 'dutiful,' especially 'doing one's duty to the gods and to one's family'

***reverend** = (1) 'worthy of deep respect' (2) 'title of clergymen': from Latin *reverēndus* = 'worthy to be revered,' from *reverī* = 'to revere'

reverent = 'feeling or showing deep respect': from Latin *reverēnt-*, *reverēns* = 'revering,' from *reverī* = 'to revere'

severe = 'harsh and unyielding in judging or punishing others': from Latin *sevērus* = 'strict in personal behavior, avoiding self-indulgence, austere'

sober = (1) 'not intoxicated' (2) 'realistic, unexaggerated, reasonable': (via French) from Latin *sōbrius* = 'not drunk,' from *se-* = 'not' + *ēbrius* = 'drunk'

solemn = (1) 'performed or undertaken with reverence and ceremony' (2) 'causing respect, impressive': (via French) from Latin *solemnis*, *sollemnis* = '(of a religious rite) performed on a fixed date,' also 'performed with reverence and ceremony'

splendid = (1) 'spectacular and beautiful' (2) 'very admirable' (3) 'fine, pleasant, enjoyable, etc.': from Latin *splendidus* = 'shining, spectacular, excellent,' from *splendēre* = 'to shine'

stupendous = 'amazingly big, impressive, extreme': from Latin *stupēndus* = 'worthy of being amazed at,' from *stupēre* = 'to be dazed, be amazed'

stupid = (1) 'dazed, stunned' (2) 'slow to understand, not clever': (via French) from Latin *stupidus* = 'dazed,' from *stupēre* = 'to be dazed'

superb = 'of the most admirable beauty, style, workmanship, quality, etc.': from Latin *superbus* = 'superior, proud, excellent,' from *super* = 'above'

vain = (1) 'useless, unproductive' (2) 'proud of one's appearance or ability': (via French) from Latin *vānus* = 'empty, useless, proud'

*Appears as separate entry

Some Formal Adjectives. English relies so heavily on Latin for its more formal vocabulary that it has created an entire class of Latin-derived adjectives that are attached to common English nouns. In many cases native English adjectives with similar meanings also exist but are used in restricted or less formal situations. For example, *father* has the English adjective *fatherly*, but *paternal* will be preferred to it in such expressions as *paternal relationships, paternal government.* English nouns can be used attributively to form adjectives, but in many cases such usage gives a distinctly less formal flavor than these Latin adjectives. *Sea,* for instance, is used attributively in the phrases *sea breeze, sea stories,* but *marine* replaces it in the phrases *marine biology, marine chart.*

arboreal = 'relating to trees, living in trees': from Latin *arboreus,* adjective of *arbor* = 'tree'

bovine = 'relating to cattle, resembling a cow or bull': from Latin *bovīnus,* adjective of *bov-, bos* = 'cow, bull'

canine = 'relating to dogs': from Latin *canīnus,* adjective of *canis* = 'dog'

dental = 'relating to teeth': from Latin *dentālis,* adjective of *dent, dens* = 'tooth'

digital = 'relating to the fingers, operated with the fingers': from Latin *digitālis,* adjective of *digitus* = 'finger'

marine = 'of or relating to the sea': (via French) from Latin *marīnus,* adjective of *mare* = 'sea'

maternal = 'relating to a mother, like a mother': from Latin *maternus* = 'motherly,' from *mater* = 'mother'

mental = 'relating to the mind': from Latin *mentālis,* adjective of *ment-, mens* = 'mind'

nasal = 'relating to the nose': from Latin *nāsālis,* adjective of *nāsus* = 'nose'

nocturnal = 'relating to night, active at night': from Latin *nocturnālis, nocturnus,* adjectives of *noct-, nox* = 'night'

paternal = 'relating to a father, like a father': from Latin *paternus,* adjective of *pater* = 'father'

rural = 'relating to the countryside': from Latin *rūrālis,* adjective of *rūr-, rūs* = 'countryside'

solar = 'relating to the sun': from Latin *sōlāris,* adjective of *sōl* = 'sun'

stellar = 'relating to a star or stars': from Latin *stellāris,* adjective of *stella* = 'star'

urban = 'relating to the town or city': from Latin *urbānus,* adjective of *urbs* = 'city'

It may be noticed that in some cases an English noun and a Latin-derived adjective are remarkably similar, as with *mind/mental, night/nocturnal, nose/nasal.* For the reason, see COGNATES.

(5) Selected verbs:

admire = (1) 'to look at with approval' (2) 'to have high respect for': (via French) from Latin *admīrārī* = 'to look at, wonder at, admire,' from *ad-* = 'at, toward' + *mīrārī* = 'to look, wonder'

create = 'to bring into existence': from Latin *creāre* = 'to cause to be born, bring forth'

crucify = 'to tie or nail (a person) to a cross as punishment or execution': (via French) from Latin *crūcifigere,* from *cruc-, crux* = 'cross' + *figere* = 'to fasten, fix'

damn = 'to judge (someone or something) as bad or guilty': (via French) from Latin *damnāre* = 'to impose loss or damage on,' from *damnum* = 'loss, damage'

edify = 'to instruct and improve (a person)': (via French) from Latin *aedificāre* = 'to build,' from *aedēs* = 'building' + *-ficāre* = 'to make'

* **fulminate** = 'to make a furious condemnation': from Latin *fulmināre* = 'to strike with a thunderbolt,' from *fulmen* = 'thunderbolt'

*Appears as separate entry

Rootlike Verbs. Latin verbs form compounds by adding prefixes such as *ab-* = 'away'; *ad-* = 'toward'; *con-* = 'together, completely'; *ex-* = 'out'; *non-* = 'not'; *sub-* = 'under, less than'; etc. The compounds often became important words in their own right, producing further derivatives, especially nouns and adjectives. In this way about 60 basic Latin verbs are the source of several thousand English verbs, nouns, and adjectives, in groups that are often complex but can still be seen to be interrelated. Some such groups are:

adduce, adducible, adduction
conduce, conducive, conduct, conductor
deduce, deduct, deductible, deduction
induce, inductive, induction
produce, product, production, productive
reduce, reduction

abstract, abstraction
attract, attraction, attractive
contract, contraction, contractor
extract, etc.
retract, etc.
subtract, etc.

Collectively these groups make up a large component of our language. One group will serve as an example.

The Latin verb *vertere* meant 'to turn.' It was both transitive (*Turn the wheel*) and intransitive (*The wheel turns*). It applied both to physical movement and to psychological actions (*Turn your mind to it*) and abstractions (*The weather turned cold*). It had many compounds, including *advertere* = 'to turn toward'; *āvertere* = 'to turn away'; *convertere* = 'to change completely'; *dīvertere* = 'to turn aside'; *invertere* = 'to turn upon, turn upside down'; *pervertere* = 'to turn (someone) around, lead astray, corrupt'; *revertere* = 'to turn back'; and *transvertere* = 'to turn across.' Among the hundred or so English words resulting from these are:

adverse = 'hostile, unfavorable' See *averse*, below.

advert = 'to call attention to': from Latin *advertere* = 'to turn (one's attention) to'

* **averse** = 'opposed, reluctant'

avert = 'to turn away, ward off': from Latin *āvertere* = 'to turn away'

converse (adjective) = 'opposite': from Latin *conversus* = 'turned around, opposite,' from *convertere* = 'to turn around completely'

convert (verb) = 'to transform (something), change (someone) deeply, as in religion': from Latin *convertere* = 'to turn (something or someone) around, change completely'

diverse = 'distinct, various': from Latin *dīversus* = 'turned in different directions,' from *dīvertere* = 'to turn aside or apart'

divert = (1) 'to turn (something) from its path' (2) 'to amuse (someone), entertain': from Latin *dīvertere* = 'to turn aside or apart'

inverse = 'backward, upside-down': from Latin *inversus* = 'turned upside down,' from *invertere* = 'to turn upon, turn upside down'

invert = 'to turn upside down': from Latin *invertere* = 'to turn upside down'

perverse = 'obstinately wrong, willfully opposed': from Latin *perversus* = 'led astray,' from *pervertere* = 'to lead astray'

pervert (verb) = 'to corrupt': from Latin *pervertere* = 'to turn (someone) around, lead astray, corrupt'

reverse (adjective) = 'backward, opposite': from Latin *reversus* = 'turned back,' from *revertere* = 'to turn back'

revert = 'to return to an earlier state': from Latin *revertere* = 'to turn back'

subvert = 'to overturn, undermine': from Latin *subvertere* = 'to overturn from below'

transverse = 'positioned crosswise': from Latin *transvertere* = 'to turn across'

*Appears as separate entry

Pronunciation. In the past, when Latin was an intimate part of their education, the English and Americans pronounced it as English. Julius Caesar's memorable message to the Senate, *Veni, vidi, vici* (= 'I came, I saw, I conquered'), was pronounced /**vē**-nī, **vī**-dī, **vī**-sī/. By 1850 linguistic scholars were able to reconstruct the actual speech sounds used by the Romans, and these differed in many ways from the English version. Caesar himself would have said, approximately, /**wā**-nē, **wē**-dē, **wē**-kē/, and he would have pronounced his own name /**yōō**-lē-ōōs **kī**-sär/. Some teachers immediately started teaching the restored pronunciation, but many disliked and distrusted it and continued to teach the traditional English way. Eventually, the authentic version prevailed, although in the meantime Latin had become a relatively unimportant subject. Most American schools that now offer Latin use the restored pronunciation or the quite similar Roman Catholic version. The table below shows some of the principal differences between the various systems of pronouncing Latin.

This sensible revolution in the teaching of a now minor subject has left the English language in a quandary. While it's obviously right to get as close to the original as possible when learning Latin itself, what about the hundreds of Latinisms used in English? Many of these have been pronounced as English for hundreds of years.

Today, the rules are in confusion. Not many people are still strong-minded enough to ignore the reformed pronunciation entirely. But not many are strong-minded enough to go all the way (in English) with the reformed style, either. Most Americans pronounce most Latinisms with an unpredictable combination of the traditional and the reformed. Lawyers, who have their own centuries-old tradition of pronouncing legal Latin emphatically as English, don't necessarily do so anymore (see LEGAL TERMS). A divorce decree *nisi* was until recently always /**nī**-sī/, but now /**nē**-sē/ is often heard in the courts. *Ultimatum,* until recently regarded as a thoroughly English word and therefore pronounced /ŭl-tə-**mā**-təm/, is now often pronounced /ŭl-tə-**mä**-təm/—a hybrid form.

◇ ***Recommendation.*** If you are confident about pronouncing Latinisms, by any system or by any feeling for language, we have no advice for you. If you are in doubt, or in search of guidelines, we offer some observations and suggestions.

(1) Latin words that have become fully English are always pronounced as English: *alibi, bonus, genius.* The same applies to names that have become part of the common stock: *Augustus, Caesar, Cicero.*

(2) Consistency is no longer important. Pronounce Latinisms in any way that seems reasonably natural.

(3) Consult dictionaries. You will find that they offer alternatives, and sometimes as many as ten possibilities for a single item. This is an accurate reflection of the present attitude—that there simply isn't any "correct" way to pronounce Latinisms in English.

(4) We list below a selection of Latinisms often encountered in English, with pronunciations that we regard as widely satisfactory. When we give two pronunciations, we express no preference between them. And we

Principal Differences in Pronouncing Latin

Letter	Traditional English	Restored Classical	Roman Catholic
ā	/ā/	/ä/	/ä/
ē	/ē/	/ā/	/ā/
ī	/ī/	/ē/	/ē/
ae	/ē/	/ī/	/ā/
oe	/ē/	/oi/	/ā/
c *before* e, i	/s/	/k/	/ch/
g *before* e, i	/j/	/g/	/j/
j	/j/	/y/	/y/
v	/v/	/w/	/v/

don't necessarily disapprove of any pronunciations not listed.

a fortiori /ā fôr-tē-**ôr**-ī/ = 'all the more so'

alias /**ā**-lē-əs/ = 'also known as'

* **alibi** /**ăl**-ə-bī/ = 'legal plea of having been elsewhere than the scene of a crime'

alumnus /ə-**lŭm**-nəs/ = 'male graduate' See ALMA MATER, ALUMNA, ALUMNUS.

apparatus /ăp-ə-**răt**-əs, -**rā**-təs/ = 'equipment'

ave /**ä**-vā, **ăv**-ā/ = 'hail'; used as a greeting on arrival

Ave Maria /**ä**-vā mə-**rē**-ə/ = 'Hail Mary' (prayer to the Virgin Mary)

* **bona fide** /**bō**-nə fīd, **bŏn**-ə/ = 'in good faith'

caveat /**kā**-vē-ăt, **kăv**-ē-ăt/ = 'word of caution, warning' (Latin, 'let him beware')

caveat emptor /**ĕmp**-tôr/ = 'let the buyer beware' (the principle that a purchaser should be careful to get good value)

credo /**krē**-dō, **krā**-/ = 'strongly held belief' (Latin *credo* = 'I believe,' the first word of the Christian creed)

cui bono /kwē **bō**-nō/ = 'who benefited?' (Latin = 'to whom [was it] an advantage?'; principle used in a criminal or some other inquiry, that whoever has benefited from what happened is likely to be responsible for it)

cum laude /ko͝om **lou**-də, -dā, kŭm **lô**-də, -dē/ = 'with distinction'; **magna cum laude** /**măg**-nə/ = 'with great distinction'; **summa cum laude** /**so͝om**-ə, **sŭm**-ə/ = 'with the highest distinction'; used for various levels of graduation from college

curriculum vitae /kə-**rĭk**-yə-ləm **vī**-tē, **vē**-tī/ = 'summary of a person's career'

* **data** /**dā**-tə, **dăt**-ə, **dä**-tə/ = 'information'

deus ex machina /**dā**-o͞os ĕks **mä**-kĭ-nä, **dē**-əs ĕks **măk**-ĭ-nə/ = '(in Greek and Roman drama) a god brought on stage by machinery'

dulce domum /**dŭl**-sĭ **dō**-məm/ = 'it is sweet to arrive home'

e pluribus unum /ē **plo͝or**-ə-bəs **yo͞o**-nəm/ = 'one from many' (U.S. motto)

* **in medias res** /ĭn **mā**-dē-äs **rās**/ = 'into the middle of the story'

in vino veritas /ĭn **vē**-nō **vĕr**-ĭ-täs/ = 'there is truth in wine'

mores /**môr**-āz, -ēz/ = 'folkways, customs'

mutatis mutandis /mo͞o-**tä**-tĭs mo͞o-**tän**-dĭs, myo͞o-**tā**-tĭs myo͞o-**tăn**-dĭs/ = 'with the appropriate changes having been made' (Latin, 'with things that have to be changed having been changed')

* **ne plus ultra** /**nē** plŭs **ŭl**-trə/ = '(go) no further beyond'

per se /pər **sā**, **sē**/ = 'in itself, as such'

prima facie /**prī**-mə **fā**-shē, -shĭ-ē/ = 'at first sight, on the face of it'

* **qua** /kwā, kwä/ = 'considered as'

* **quasi** /**kwā**-zī, **kwä**-zē/ = 'seeming, seemingly'

quid pro quo /**kwĭd** prō **kwō**/ = 'something for something, something in return for another, recompense for service'

requiescat in pace /rĕk-wē-**ĕs**-kät ĭn **pä**-chā/ = 'may he (or she) rest in peace'

sine die /**sī**-nē **dī**-ē, **sē**-nā **dē**-ā/ = 'without a specified date, indefinitely'

status /**stā**-təs, **stăt**-əs/ = 'condition, standing, etc.'

stratum /**strā**-təm, **strä**-, **străt**-əm/ = 'layer of rock, level of society, etc.'

sui generis /**so͞o**-ī **jĕn**-ər-ĭs, **so͞o**-ē/ = 'of its own kind, unlike any other, unique'

vade mecum /**vā**-dē **mē**-kəm/ = (1) 'introductory handbook to a subject' (2) 'any useful item habitually carried by someone' (Latin, 'go with me'—the author addressing the reader)

verbatim /vər-**bā**-təm/ = 'word for word, quoting literally'

via /**vī**-ə, **vē**-ə/ = 'by way of'

*Appears as separate entry

Latin and English. Not long ago, a typical piece of advice on style in English writing was to cut down on Latin-derived words and use as many Anglo-Saxon words as possible. The feeling was that short, blunt, expressive English words were being swamped by long, ornate, artificial Latin words and that simple, direct English constructions were being overwhelmed by intricate, abstract Latin constructions. There was something to it, but the advice was never easy to carry out. Few people besides specialists can tell the difference between Latinisms and Anglicisms offhand, without constant reference to historical grammars and dictionaries—clearly not the most practical way of acquiring a good straightforward style.

Today, such advice is irrelevant anyway. Latin has had its formative influence on English, and it remains an ongoing element in the language; no one now is brainwashed directly by Latinity. Some of the clearest Latin influences on our syntax are the free use of the passive, the use of ABSOLUTE PHRASES, and the difficult rules relating to the gerund (see VERBAL NOUNS IN -ING). But our most powerful single inheritance from Latin is the idea of correctness in language. In the time of Shakespeare, when classical Latin was the school-taught model of linguistic beauty and style, it was not thought necessary to have equivalent rules of correctness for English, as we can easily see in the freewheeling spelling, syntax, and usage of Shakespeare. Later, as the Latin model was gradually downgraded, the idea of rigorous and all-governing rules was transferred to English. The difference is, classical Latin (the preserved writings of a couple of dozen long-deceased masters of prose and poetry) was fixed and "dead," whereas English is a living language and, like all living languages, insists on changing and growing. (See also LANGUAGE CHANGE; SHAKESPEARE AND THE ENGLISH LANGUAGE.)

The centuries of schooling in Latin grammar have thus left the English language with a yearning for classical correctness that can never be quite satisfied. This need not be seen as a misfortune. Certain unnecessary problems of usage have resulted, but in the long run they don't do much harm. The ideal of a classical "good English," however unattainable and indescribable in detail it may be, remains beneficially with us.

The other vast legacy we have from Latin is vocabulary. The selections given above show how rich and useful, sonorous and logical, noble and reflective, it is. It still shapes our world view.

lay. The adjective *lay* = 'not belonging to the clergy' comes (via French) from Greek *laikos* = 'belonging to the people,' from *laos* = 'the people.' The derivative nouns are *layman* and *laywoman*, with the collective noun *laity* = 'lay persons in general.'

Outside the churches the first profession to start using *lay* to mean 'nonprofessional' was the law, followed by medicine and then the sciences. Now, virtually any specialized group is apt to call outsiders *lay*. We, the people, seem doomed to be patronized by self-appointed priesthoods.

> A layman who has some grasp of legal principles can avoid all sorts of expensive unpleasantness. . . .
> —*Reader's Digest*

> In the beginning, everyone was a layman, for science in the modern sense is only four hundred years old.
> —Isaac Asimov,
> *Science Past—Science Future*

> The makers of foreign policy looked with "condescending disdain on those who challenge their omniscience," supposing the layman unable to comprehend the "mystic intricacies" of diplomacy. —Arthur M. Schlesinger, Jr.,
> *Robert Kennedy and His Times*

> Many a newspaperman winces when a layman refers to him as a "writer."
> —Harry Golden, *For 2¢ Plain*

> Croquet is considered, by the lay world, to be piddling.
> —Stephen Potter, *Gamesmanship*

lay, lie. See LIE, LAY.

learn. Besides its basic sense 'to acquire knowledge,' *learn* has also been used since the 14th century to mean 'to teach (someone).' This is still used in dialect but is not accepted as standard. However, it is often used deliberately by standard speakers in the special sense 'to teach (someone) a salutary or punitive lesson.'

> The Toad . . . picked up a stout stick and swung it vigorously, belabouring

imaginary animals. "I'll learn 'em to steal my house!" he cried. "I'll learn 'em, I'll learn 'em!"

"Don't say learn 'em, Toad," said the Rat, greatly shocked. "It's not good English."

"What are you always nagging at Toad for?" inquired the Badger, rather peevishly. "What's the matter with his English? It's the same what I use myself, and if it's good enough for me, it ought to be good enough for you!"

"I'm very sorry," said the Rat humbly. "Only I *think* it ought to be 'teach 'em,' not 'learn 'em.'"

"But we don't *want* to teach 'em," replied the Badger. "We want to *learn* 'em—learn 'em, learn 'em! And what's more, we're going to *do* it too!"

—Kenneth Grahame, *The Wind in the Willows*

◊ ***Recommendation.*** We agree with the Badger and the Toad. The Rat was not only being pedantic but also missing the point.

leave, let. In dialect, *leave* has encroached on various uses of *let*, notably in *leave (someone* or *something) be* and *leave (someone* or *something) go.* But *leave (someone* or *something) alone* = 'not to interfere with' is also accepted in standard usage. Another nonstandard use of *leave* is expressed in the following imperative: *Leave us begin;* correctly: *Let us begin.*

legal terms. Mr. Bumble the beadle came right to the point:

> . . . the law is a ass, a idiot.
> —Charles Dickens, *Oliver Twist*

And the impassioned Eloisa, thinking of Abelard, wrote:

> Curse on all laws but those which love has made! —Alexander Pope, *Eloisa to Abelard*

And Dick Butcher, addressing his comrades, moved beyond feelings to a call for action:

> The first thing we do, let's kill all the lawyers!
> —Shakespeare, *Henry VI, Part II*

It is reasonable to conjecture that this long-established tradition of animosity toward lawyers and the law can be traced not only to what lawyers have said but also to the way in which they have said it.

The language of law, as it presents itself to us today, is a mixture of Latin phrases (*nolle prosequi, nolo contendere, subpoena duces tecum*), Medieval French and English terms (*culprit, curtesy, escheat, fee simple, replevin*), and ordinary English words so loaded with special meaning as to trap the uninitiated. Giving adequate *consideration* in a contractual matter does not mean taking lots of time to think things over, as a legal innocent might reasonably infer. And the legal definition of *assault* is strikingly different from its meaning in common usage. See both of these words below.

A healthy movement is afoot these days to compel the authors of consumer sales agreements, leases, and similar documents to write these agreements in language that a layperson can understand. However, it is certain that the special vocabulary of the law will manage to endure. Hence the need to come to grips with the terms most likely to survive. The following glossary has been prepared in spite of this warning of Dr. Samuel Johnson's:

> It is one of the maxims of the civil law, that definitions are hazardous.
> —*The Rambler*

administrator (masc.), **administratrix** (fem.) = 'person appointed by a court to handle a deceased person's estate'; usually named when the deceased person has failed to name a competent executor in his or her will or has simply failed to leave a will—compare *executor,* below

adverse possession = 'act of occupying another person's land and claiming it as one's own' If the true owner fails to assert his property rights, then the occupant may legally obtain title to the property after a certain period of time (fixed by law) has elapsed—usually 10 to 20 years.

amicus curiae /ə-mī-kəs **kyŏŏr**-ĭ-ē/ = 'a person with special expertise, who seeks to advise the court on a particular case (typically at his or her own initiative), even though not a party to that case' (Latin, 'friend of the court')

assault = 'threat to inflict physical harm on another person, with the apparent capacity to carry it out' Compare *battery,* below.

assignment = 'transfer of some or all of the rights under a contract'; for example, the party who is to be paid for performing a certain act may assign the right to receive payment to a third party, the person transferring the right being the *assignor,* the person obtaining the right the *assignee*

attachment = 'legal process whereby all or part of a person's property is seized and held so that it will be available if needed to satisfy a legal claim or judgment against that person'

bailment = 'legal relationship between the owner of certain personal property who as *bailor* temporarily transfers possession (but not ownership) of that property to a second person, known as the *bailee*' A *bailment* exists whenever personal property is (1) lent or rented, (2) left off for repair or storage, or (3) pledged as security for a debt.

battery = 'the unlawful inflicting of physical harm on another person' Compare *assault,* above.

beneficiary = 'person named to receive the proceeds from an insurance policy or the income from a trust'

bequeath = 'to give personal property by will' Compare *devise,* below.

bequest = 'gift of personal property by will'

breach = 'the breaking of a contract or the violation of a law'

brief = 'document prepared by an attorney, intended to provide an overview of the client's case and the points of law on which the case rests'; in view of the actual length of many legal briefs, the term is often unintentionally humorous in effect

caveat emptor /**kā**-vē-ăt **ĕmp**-tôr, **kăv**-ē-ăt/ = 'principle of common law holding that if purchased goods later turn out to be defective, the buyer has no recourse against the seller in the absence of warranties expressly given by the seller (or implied by law) that the goods are free of such defects' (Latin, 'let the buyer beware')

certiorari /sêr-shē-ə-**râr**-ē/ = 'a writ from a higher court to a lower court, asking for the lower court's records on a certain case so that the proceedings can be reviewed for legality' (Latin, 'to be made more certain, be informed')

chattel = 'item of personal property'; in the days of slavery, slaves and bondsmen were considered chattel (from Middle English *chatel* = 'property'; *cattle* has a similar derivation, and both are from Medieval Latin *capitāle* = 'property')

codicil = 'legal document that adds to or changes the terms of an existing will'

. . . Learn to give
Money to colleges while you live.
Don't be silly and think you'll try
To bother the colleges, when you die,
With codicil this, and codicil that,
That Knowledge may starve while Law
  grows fat;
For there never was pitcher that
  wouldn't spill,
And there's always a flaw in a donkey's
  will.

—Oliver Wendell Holmes,
Parson Turell's Legacy

common law = 'body of law developed by judicial decisions and based largely on custom and precedent' Compare *statutory law,* below.

. . . nay, the common law itself is nothing else but reason. . . .

—Sir Edward Coke,
First Institute

competence = 'the legal or mental capacity for entering into a valid contract or will' For example, a minor lacks legal capacity and cannot be held liable for most of his or her contracts if he or she chooses to break them. An insane person is considered to lack mental capacity and therefore cannot be bound to most of his or her contracts.

consideration = 'a promise to do something, or to refrain from doing something, in exchange for another person's promise; a quid pro quo' Consideration is an essential element of a valid contract; a person who promises to do something for nothing cannot be legally required to carry out the promise.

contract = 'legally enforceable agreement between two or more people to perform certain actions' In order for a contract to be considered valid and thus enforceable in court, it must meet five criteria: (1) The parties to the contract must freely come to mutual agreement on the terms, without duress or undue influence. (2) The parties must each have the legal or mental competence to enter a contract. (3) The parties must exchange adequate consideration. (4) The subject matter of the contract must be legal. (5) The contract must conform to any legal requirements concerning the form in which the contract is expressed. See also *competence; consideration,* above, and *duress; undue influence,* below.

conversion = 'the illegal holding of someone else's personal property' Conversion is a kind of *tort* and may also be considered a *crime* (see both below).

crime = 'wrongful act considered to injure society as a whole' A crime often involves a wrongful act against an individual or a private organization (see *tort,* below). Thus, a drunken driver who crashes into another car may be the defendant in two kinds of lawsuits: (1) a criminal action, where the government is the plaintiff and the defendant is charged with an act damaging to the community at large, and (2) a civil action, where the plaintiff is the driver or owner, or both, of the struck car, who is suing for bodily injuries or damage to the car.

curtesy = 'widower's life interest in his wife's real property' See also *dower,* below.

deed = 'legal document that, when delivered to the buyer of real property and filed with the appropriate government office, formally transfers title (ownership) to the property from the seller to the buyer'

defendant = 'person or persons required to make answer to charges in a lawsuit' See also *plaintiff,* below.

devise = (1) (verb) 'to give real property (as opposed to personal property) by will' (2) (noun) 'the real property so given' Compare *bequeath,* above.

devisee = 'person who receives real property by will' Compare *heir; legatee,* below.

double indemnity = 'provision in an insurance policy under which the insurer promises to pay twice the face value of the policy in the event that the insured person meets with accidental death'

dower = 'widow's life interest in her husband's real property' See also *curtesy,* above.

duress = 'set of circumstances involving threatened or actual violence under which a person is forced to do something against his or her will' Compare *undue influence,* below.

easement = 'irrevocable right to go over, under, or above someone else's land'; the term applies to such acts as lawfully driving over someone else's property, laying pipe under the property, or stringing transmission wires over it

embezzlement = 'theft of money by someone entrusted with it by the rightful owner'

eminent domain = 'right of a governmental body to take private property for public use, such as the construction of a highway or a governmental building'

equity = 'set of general rules and procedures, based on judicial discretion, that supplement common and statutory law with the aim of ensuring that those who have suffered some legal injury receive fair treatment and adequate remedies'

escheat /ĕs-chēt/ = 'the transfer of ownership of private property to the state government in the absence of lawful heirs'

escrow = 'funds, documents, or property entrusted to a disinterested party and ultimately intended for delivery to someone else as soon as certain acts are performed or conditions are met'

executor (masc.), **executrix** (fem.) = 'person named by the testator to carry out the provisions of a will and settle the testator's estate' Compare *administrator, administratrix,* above.

fee simple = 'total ownership of real property without restrictions'; in feudal law *fee* refers to an estate in land, and *simple* in this context means 'unconditional, unlimited, unrestricted'

felony = 'crime sufficiently serious to generally require, at a minimum, imprisonment for more than a year' Compare *misdemeanor,* below.

fixture(s) = 'personal property regarded as real property because it has become permanently attached to the land or affixed to a building'

garnishment = 'legal proceedings designed to ensure that a creditor or a plaintiff in a legal action will receive payment due from a debtor or a defendant' A court directs a *garnishee* (a person such as an employer, who holds money or property belonging to the debtor or the defendant) to withhold some or all of that money or property for the benefit of the *garnishor* (the creditor or the plaintiff).

goods = 'tangible personal property'

grand jury = 'investigative body consisting traditionally of 12 or more people who examine evidence of crime and decide whether or not to issue indictments against those charged with the crime'

grantor = 'one who gives something, such as the maker of a trust'

habeas corpus /**hā**-bē-əs **kôr**-pəs/ = 'court order requiring that a person currently being detained or imprisoned be brought into court so that the legality of the detention or imprisonment can be determined' (Latin, 'that you have the body')

heir = specifically 'person who receives real property from someone who dies intestate'; broadly used to designate a person who receives real or personal property from a deceased person, with or without a will—see also *next of kin,* below

holographic will = 'will done entirely in the handwriting of the person making the will'

indictment /ĭn-**dīt**-mənt/ = 'formal document accusing one or more persons of having committed a crime'

infant = 'minor'

injunction = 'court order that usually directs someone to refrain from acting in a certain way'

intangible personal property = 'right to hold property in the form of stocks, contracts, mortgages, etc.'

intestate /ĭn-**tĕs**-tāt/ = 'without a will'; a person is said to "die intestate" if he or she does not leave behind a valid will

landlord = 'owner of real estate, lessor'

larceny = 'form of theft that does not involve actual or threatened violence or unlawful entry into the building where the theft occurs' Compare *robbery,* below.

lease = 'contract under which the owner of real estate permits another person to occupy it for a period of time' See *landlord,* above, and *lessee; lessor,* below.

legacy = 'gift of personal property by will, bequest'

legatee = 'person who receives personal property by will' Compare *beneficiary; devisee,* above.

lessee = 'one who pays rental on real property'

lessor = 'owner of real estate who rents it to another, landlord'

libel = 'defamatory remarks about a person in writing' Compare *slander,* below.

* **lien** /lēn/ = 'legal claim that a creditor may hold against a debtor's real or personal property until the debt is repaid or otherwise satisfied'

L.S. = *locus sigilli,* 'place of the seal'; abbreviation used on many contracts in lieu of an actual seal

*Appears as separate entry

mandamus /măn-**dā**-məs/ = 'court order that calls for the performance of some public act or duty by a public official' (Latin, 'we command')

metes and bounds /mēts/ = 'measurements and boundaries'; used to refer to the dimensions of a piece of real property

minor = 'person who has not yet reached the age of legal majority (18 or 21 in most states), infant'

misdemeanor = 'crime less serious than a felony, generally requiring a sentence no greater than one year's imprisonment' Compare *felony*, above.

mortgage = literally 'dead pledge,' specifically 'legal document by which the *mortgagor* (the owner of certain property) transfers the property to the *mortgagee* (a lender or creditor) as security for the repayment of borrowed money or for the performance of some specified act'

necessaries = 'things such as food, clothing, lodging, and medical attention that a person needs to sustain himself' The definition of necessaries for each person will vary according to the person's age and station in life. While minors and others with limited legal or mental capacity can avoid liability for most of their contracts, they usually cannot avoid responsibility on contracts under which they have purchased necessaries.

negligence = 'failure to exercise a reasonable degree of care, thereby causing injury to someone else or damage to his or her property'

next of kin = 'those people who receive personal property from someone who dies intestate' See also *heir*, above.

nolle prosequi /nŏl-ē **prŏs**-ə-kwī/ = 'decision made by a prosecutor in a criminal action or by a plaintiff in a civil action to drop the case in whole or in part' (Latin, 'to be unwilling to pursue'); the derivative English verb *nol-pros* /nŏl-**prŏs**/ means 'to discontinue a legal action'

nolo contendere /**nō**-lō kən-**tĕn**-də-rē/ = 'plea of no defense made by a defendant in a criminal action that does not admit guilt but leaves the defendant open to conviction' (Latin, 'I do not wish to contend')

nuisance = 'the use of one's own property, or someone else's, in a way that interferes with the rights of others' A *private nuisance* (like loud music coming through the wall from an adjacent apartment) affects only a few individuals and is considered a tort. A *public nuisance* (like dirty emissions from a smokestack) affects the community as a whole and is considered a crime. An *attractive nuisance* (for example, an easily accessible swimming pool in a neighbor's yard) is a potentially dangerous situation that attracts children; the person who maintains an attractive nuisance may be held liable for injuries suffered by others, even though they did not have permission to enter the owner's property. See also *crime*, above, and *tort*, below.

perjury = 'lying under oath'

personal property = 'all property that is movable and may be legally taken from place to place by the owner' *Tangible personal property* (also called *goods*) consists of articles that are manufactured (like clothing, jewelry, furniture, automobiles), grown (like harvested crops), raised (like farm animals), or extracted (like minerals removed from the land); *intangible personal property* consists of the right to hold property (in the form of contracts, mortgages, stocks, bonds, etc.) rather than the property itself.

petit jury /**pĕt**-ē/ = 'group traditionally consisting of 12 people chosen to hear a case and make decisions about the facts at issue in it'

plaintiff = 'a person who files a complaint or initiates a lawsuit against a defendant'

power of attorney = 'legal document that authorizes one person to act for another in certain situations' The person who acquires this power does not have to be literally an attorney; any legally competent adult can be named.

prima facie (evidence) /**prī**-mə **fā**-shē, -shĭ-ē/ = specifically 'of or concerning evidence sufficiently strong to establish the facts of a situation' If the opposing party cannot disprove this evidence, the first party is said to have a *prima facie case,* one that will support a finding in that party's favor. (Latin, 'at first view')

probate = 'to submit a will to a court to prove the validity of the document and get legal authority to carry out its terms'

pro bono publico /prō **bō**-nō **pŭb**-lĭ-kō/ = 'for the common or public welfare'; often used of legal work taken on by an attorney as an act of public service, rather than for profit (Latin, 'for the public good')

proxy = (1) 'special type of power of attorney, by which one person authorizes another to vote on his or her behalf, usually at a meeting of corporate stockholders' (2) 'the document of such authorization' (3) 'the person so authorized to act'

public domain = (1) 'land owned by the government' (2) 'property rights unprotected by copyright or patent'

quash = 'to nullify or cancel'; usually done by a judge who may quash an indictment

real property *or* **estate** = 'land and the things that are attached to or part of it, such as timber, minerals in the soil, buildings, walls, and fences' Items of personal property that become permanently attached to the land or affixed to a building are called *fixtures* and are regarded as part of the real property.

replevin /rĭ-**plĕv**-ĭn/ = 'process of recovering personal property that has been wrongfully taken or illegally withheld'; *replevy* means 'to recover such property by means of a writ of replevin'

robbery = 'act of theft that involves threatened or actual violence' Compare *larceny,* above.

slander = 'defamatory remarks about a person that are made orally' Compare *libel,* above.

stare decisis /**stä**-rē dĭ-**sī**-səs/ = 'policy of following legal precedents established in previous judicial decisions' (Latin, 'to stand by decided matters')

statute of limitations = 'law that fixes the time within which a person can pursue legal remedies for a complaint or a claim'; once the time limit has been exceeded, no legal action can be initiated

statutory law = 'body of laws or statutes enacted by a legislature' Compare *common law,* above.

sub judice /sŭb **jōō**-dĭ-sē/ = 'under consideration by a judge or court but not yet decided' (Latin, 'under judgment')

subornation = 'act of persuading or bribing someone to commit an illegal act, especially perjury'

subpoena, subpena /sə-**pē**-nə/ = 'document ordering a person to appear in court under the threat of a penalty for failing to do so' (Latin, 'under penalty'); a *subpoena duces tecum* /**dōō**-kās **tā**-kəm/ (= 'under penalty you shall bring with you') orders a person to appear in court along with certain documents

tangible personal property = 'personal property such as clothing, furniture, crops, and minerals; goods'

testator (masc.), **testatrix** (fem.) = 'person who makes a will' Compare *intestate,* above.

title = 'legal ownership'

tort = 'a wrongful act committed against an individual or a private organization, civil wrong' Compare *crime,* above.

trust = 'legal arrangement under which the maker of the trust (*grantor*) transfers certain property to a *trustee,* who is to hold the property for the benefit of someone else (*beneficiary*)'

undue influence = 'the improper exercise of influence over the mind of another person so as to cause that person to act in a way that he or she otherwise might not' Undue influence is much like duress but works not because of threatened or actual violence but because of blind trust or confidence or lack of mental capacity. Compare *duress,* above.

venue /**vĕn**-yōō/ = (1) 'the place where a trial takes place' (2) 'the area from which members of a jury are selected'; a *change in venue* is a change in the location of a trial, usually authorized so that a jury can be selected from a group of people less familiar with the details of a given case

warranty = 'statement of fact (as opposed to a statement of opinion or puffery) made by the seller of goods, which the buyer relies on in deciding to purchase the goods'

will = 'legal document that indicates how a person wants his or her property disposed of, minor children cared for, and estate administered after death' See also *holographic will,* above.

writ = 'formal court order'

legion. The peculiar usage *They are legion* = 'they are very numerous' results from a slight distortion of the eerie story of the Gadarene swine, in which Jesus exorcised a man possessed by a multiple devil:

> And Jesus asked him, "What is your name?" He [the devil] replied, "My name is Legion: for we are many."
> —Mark 5:9

It is rather surprising that the proverbial expression that resulted is now used not only of undesirables but freely of anyone or anything, without stigma:

> Whatever his defects as a hedonistic vulgarian—and they were legion, simply legion—he was loyal to Walsh and his lady.
> —Walter F. Murphy, *The Vicar of Christ*

> For those of us who remember—and we are legion, Catholic, Protestant, Jew, Moslem and those of no recognized faith—Archbishop Sheen's own story is "must-reading."
> —Jane Quinn, *The Catholic Key*

For more examples of common expressions from the Scriptures see BIBLE.

lend. See LOAN.

lesbian. This word is derived from the proper adjective *Lesbian* = 'belonging to the island of Lesbos' and has acquired its present-day sense by association with the poet Sappho. Sappho was born on Lesbos about 612 B.C. Most of her works have been lost, but the ones that remain are rated with the finest Greek lyric poetry, especially remarkable for intensity of feeling. Nearly all of these poems treat of erotic love and are focused upon the young women who were part of her circle. But Sappho was not exclusively homosexual, and was married and had a child. The word *lesbian* was formerly applied to homosexual women as a cover word or euphemism, but it is now widely accepted as the term preferred by homosexual women themselves:

> All of us millions of lesbians and gay men were once American children.
> —Jean O'Leary and Bruce Voeller, *New York Times*

The original sense ('from Lesbos') has fallen out of use. See also GAY.

less. See FEWER, LESS.

lesser. The adjective *lesser* is the comparative of *less.* It has a number of different uses.

(1) In phrases: *the lesser of two evils.*

(2) With numerical quantities: *the lesser number* (but this would be more likely to have *smaller* or *lower*); *X or Y, whichever is (the) lesser* (which could equally well have *less* or *smaller*).

(3) In compound adjectives: *lesser-known* (equally often *less-known*).

(4) In the names of plants and animals that are the smaller of two similar species: *the lesser celandine; the lesser spotted woodpecker.*

(5) In a few geographical names: *Lesser Antilles; Lesser Slave Lake.*

lest. The conjunction *lest,* meaning 'for fear that' or 'so that not,' is always followed by a verb in the subjunctive mood, with or without *should:*

> Be careful when riding a saddle horse through a gate, lest he brush too closely to the post and bang your knee.
> —Chet Huntley, *The Generous Years*

> . . . Richard Nixon is given to suggesting that history follows him about with a Polaroid camera, lest history miss something.
> —William F. Buckley, Jr., *Execution Eve*

let. See LEAVE, LET.

lexicon. This term, borrowed from Greek, is first a synonym of *dictionary*. From it come the words *lexicographer* = 'compiler of dictionaries' and *lexicography* = 'the occupation or craft of compiling dictionaries.'

Lexicon is also used in a technical sense in linguistics to mean 'the whole vocabulary, the stock of words or meaningful units in a language.' This is understood in an abstract sense, regardless of the existence or coverage of dictionaries. Thus one can speak of the lexicon of an unwritten language such as that of the mountain peoples of Vietnam; or one can say that the total lexicon of English has never yet been recorded in even the biggest dictionaries and is now so vast that it cannot be known to any one person. Lexicon is contrasted by the linguists with grammar and pronunciation. While the grammar and sound pattern of a language are structures—closed systems of rules that can be learned once and for all and can then be applied to an infinite number of possible utterances—the lexicon is not a structure but an infinitely extensible list or collection of unique items. The lexicon of a language is perpetually changing—by loss or deletion of words, by change of the use and meaning of words, and by addition of new words. It is the way in which language handles culture. As culture changes, lexicon changes. It is a mirror of human thought and behavior.

liable is originally, and still, a legal term, meaning 'obligated by law, responsible' and 'subject to (laws, penalties, duties, etc.).' It is also used in a generalized sense that is largely synonymous with *apt* or *likely* but has a special quality of its own. The use of *liable* often signals that the thing likely to happen involves undesirable consequences or is merely odd, ridiculous, or unexpected in some way; it can thus have the effect of a faint smile or a subliminal exclamation point.

> A fellow who has grown up far from the sprawling vines of a watermelon patch is liable to commit the basic error of cutting the melon indoors.
> —Jo Northrop, *Southern World*

> . . . Mrs. Braddocks, who in all the excitement of talking French was liable to have no idea what she was saying.
> —Ernest Hemingway, *The Sun Also Rises*

> He made no secret of his false teeth, told anybody who was interested all about them, and was liable to take out his plate to show you how splendid it was.
> —Cole Lesley, *The Life of Noel Coward*

See also APT; LIKELY.

lie, lay. The verbs *lie* and *lay* have been closely related throughout their history and are in fact ultimately variant forms of a single ancestral root. In many regional and social dialects of both American and British English, *lay* is used for *lie* and, occasionally, *lie* is used for *lay*. But in Standard English they cannot be so used. *Lay* is purely transitive, meaning 'to cause (something) to lie, put,' with only two special exceptions: a hen can be said to *lay*, without mentioning eggs, and in nautical usage *lay* can mean simply 'to go,' as in *The ship began to lay forward*. Conversely, *lie* is only intransitive, meaning 'to be in, or move into, a reclining position, or on or onto a flat surface,' and there are no exceptions. This rule is clear and definite for Standard English and often causes trouble for speakers of nonstandard dialects. The past tense and past participle of *lay* are both *laid*. The past tense of *lie* is *lay*, and its past participle is *lain*. Typical examples of errors:

Nonstandard	Standard
Let it lay.	Let it lie.
He laid down on the grass.	He lay down.

Lie the book down flat.	Lay the book down.
Your papers have laid there for days.	The papers have lain there.
When were the trolley tracks lain?	When were the tracks laid?

lien. This legal term, meaning 'a claim on property as security for a debt,' is pronounced either /lēn/ or /lē-ən/.

like. In Standard English *like* is primarily an adjective meaning 'the same, similar' and a preposition meaning 'similar to, similarly to, the same as, etc.' *Like* has also a strong tendency to be used as a conjunction meaning 'as, as if, such as, etc.'; but this and some other uses are, in varying degrees, inappropriate in formal usage.

As a Conjunction. (1) Meaning 'as, in the same way as, in the way that,' followed by a clause:

> He was finally persuaded, and he sang it like nobody ever will again.
> —Bob Hope, *Reader's Digest*

> Mr. Carter yearns for his windfall bill like Faust yearned for Helen of Troy.
> —James J. Kilpatrick, *Savannah Morning News*

> Evans' sales volume isn't growing like it was a decade ago. . . .
> —Kathleen K. Wiegner, *Forbes*

> Some Chiefs direct fire operations the way NASA control directs moon shots—calmly, and with great self-assurance. Others . . . lead their men like Leonard Bernstein conducts the New York Philharmonic in a Stravinsky symphony—with frenzy, and great excitement. —Dennis Smith, *Report From Engine Company 82*

(2) Meaning 'as,' followed by a phrase (representing a clause from which the verb has been dropped):

> . . . they conjured up ever more lurid pictures of the Matson children going through their money like Sherman to the sea. . . .
> —Dorothy Parker, *Little Curtis*

> Step backwards, looking intently at the roots of the girl's hair, like in the films.
> —Stephen Potter, *Anti-Woo*

(3) Meaning 'as if':

> . . . he went on preaching every Sunday like nothing had happened. . . .
> —William Faulkner, *Light in August*

> It was like we had hit twelve home runs in Yankee Stadium.
> —Mary Martin (quoted), *Time*

(4) Meaning 'as if,' following certain verbs, including *look, feel,* and *sound:*

> Humphrey was closing the gap in the polls and it looked like the campaign of '68 would be another cliffhanger.
> —William Safire, *Before the Fall*

> "You make me feel like I'm back in the campaign," Jimmy Carter laughingly told a woman in Los Angeles last week.
> —*Time*

> Tully, sounding like he was still campaigning, pressed his query at a City Council meeting.
> —*Springfield* (Mass.) *Morning Union*

(5) Meaning 'as,' in the phrase *like I said* and variations of it:

> [Question:] "When you got that job as you call it in the White House, you didn't really have any time to sit around and find out what it was all about." [Harry Truman:] "No, no. Like I told you, I was sworn in one night, and the next morning I had to get right on to the job at hand."
> —Merle Miller, *Plain Speaking*

> Like Noel Coward said, only mad dogs and Englishmen go out in the midday sun, and, brother, was he right.
> —S. J. Perelman, *Vinegar Puss*

◇ ***Recommendation.*** The first four of these conjunctional uses are very widespread in speech and are becoming more and more so in writing, in the areas of journalism, politics, business, and fiction. Many people feel that these uses are entirely natural, and they would find it unnatural and irksome to be required to reword with *as, as if,* etc. Some others tend to use *like* in these situations when they wish to give a relaxed, informal, or sometimes emphatic tone, but they would use *as, as if,* etc., in formal contexts. Still others prefer to avoid these uses of *like* entirely, even in speech. In most informal kinds of speech or writing, therefore, we simply advise you to follow your own instincts in choosing among these positions. But in highly formal contexts, such as ceremonial or major speeches, historical narrative, or belles-lettres, the use of *like* as a conjunction is still not acceptable as standard.

The last conjunctional use, the phrase *like I said,* is an established colloquial idiom, often used for emphasis. It is appropriate only in clearly informal contexts.

In Prepositional Phrases. Prepositional phrases beginning with *like* sometimes are used in a "dangling" way, so that the phrase does not relate appropriately to the rest of the sentence:

> Like other ethnic groups in America before them, the act of preserving a culture has to be worked at assiduously.
> —Jon Nordheimer, *New York Times*

> Like all true prophets, his words seem to be timeless.
> —Louis Nizer, *My Life in Court*

> Tolkien . . . is not much involved with his college, and like all professors his first responsibility is towards his Faculty. —Humphrey Carpenter, *Tolkien*

◇ ***Recommendation.*** This use comes naturally in speech and is harmless in most situations. In formal contexts, we advise that *like* be replaced by *as with* or *as for,* or else that the sentence be reconstructed in one way or another: "like all professors he owes a first responsibility"; "his words, like those of all true prophets"; etc.

As an Unattached Adverb. *Like* is used as an unattached adverb mostly in speech, sometimes meaning 'for example' or 'as it were,' often merely as a meaningless filler:

> Like, my dad when he was growing up in Sedamsville used to get with other guys and they'd swim naked in the Ohio River. . . . Like, he used to steal tomatoes from a farmer who lived across the river in Kentucky.
> —Pete Rose, *The Pete Rose Story*

> . . . we rode uptown with them to the Warwick Hotel where there were hundreds of girls all lined up in front screaming, like, very insane.
> —girl (quoted),
> Andy Warhol and Pat Hackett, *POPism*

◇ ***Recommendation.*** Although this use has been documented for nearly 200 years, many consider it vulgar.

like for. The verb *like,* meaning 'wish or want (someone) to do (something),' is often used with *for* instead of a direct object:

> I would like for the people of Georgia to know . . .
> —William V. Tyson, Jr. (letter), *Savannah Morning News*

> I would like for you to have prepared . . . a study of where we are to go with regard to the admission of Red China to the UN.
> —memorandum,
> Richard Nixon, *R.N.*

◇ ***Recommendation.*** To the many people who use it, this construction is a natural and correct way of expressing a polite request or wish. We believe there's nothing wrong with it, but many others regard it as incorrect.

likely, primarily an adjective, is used also as an adverb meaning 'probably.' Many people always qualify it with another adverb such as *quite, very, more,* or *most.* But it is also correctly used alone:

> The report foreshadows what likely will be a long and bitter debate over rewriting the clean air law. . . .
> —*Savannah Morning News*

> He isn't the first foreign-born to become a Canadian bank president . . . but he is likely the most surprised at his own success.
>
> —Roderick McQueen, *Maclean's*

Likely can be used as a synonym for *liable.* See also APT; LIABLE.

limerick. This is a humorous or nonsensical verse of five anapestic lines that rhyme *aabba,* the first, second, and last containing three feet and the others two. Popularized by Edward Lear in his *Book of Nonsense* (1846), it derived its name much later from the refrain "We'll all come up, come up to Limerick," sung by merrymakers whenever one of them improvised and sang such a verse. Modern limericks tend to be ribald. Here is a nonribald one by Morris Bishop:

> A ghoulish old fellow in Kent
> Encrusted his wife in cement;
> He said, with a sneer,
> "I was careful, my dear,
> To follow your natural bent."

See also POETRY.

lingua franca. See PIDGIN AND CREOLE LANGUAGES.

linguist, linguistics. The earlier meaning of *linguist* is 'someone who can speak several languages,' typically implying great skill and fluency. This meaning is still current, but the word now also means 'student or specialist in *linguistics.*' Linguistics is the science of language, the study of all aspects of human language in general—its system of sounds (*phonology*), its system of word-formation (*morphology*), the relationships of words within sentences (*syntax*), and the nature and structure of meanings (*semantics*). There are many specialized areas within the linguistic field, such as the psychological aspect of language (*psycholinguistics*), the study of regional and social variations within one language (*dialectology*), and the study of language change (*historical linguistics*). See also DIALECT; GRAMMAR; LANGUAGE CHANGE.

litany, liturgy. These are two unrelated Greek-derived words that in religion have similar but not identical meanings and are also used in distinct metaphorical senses.

(1) *Litany,* in Greek meaning 'supplication, prayer,' is the form of public prayer used in churches in which the clergy lead and the people respond; it may be sung, chanted, or spoken. There are various traditional or official litanies in the different churches; they chiefly consist of expressions of penitence and prayers for forgiveness.

Figuratively, *litany* is used in two ways. Most often it means 'a dreary, much-repeated recitation of errors or troubles':

> The news in the *Pacific Stars and Stripes* and on the armed forces radio network was a litany of defeats: outposts overrun, relief columns ambushed, airfields raided and shelled.
>
> —Philip Caputo, *A Rumor of War*

> The litany of U.S. economic woes at times seems endless.
>
> —George M. Taber, *Time*

It is also used in a metaphor that evokes the repetitive sequences and responses of the Christian litany:

> He was still twenty feet away when they began their litany.
>
> "Mr. Vice President, over here, please, sir."
>
> "Mr. Vice President, are you splitting with administration policy?"
>
> —Spiro T. Agnew, *The Caulfield Decision*

> Spent cartridges tinkled brightly on deck like a thousand fairy bells. The bow gun fired in steady rhythm: breech slam . . . *bark!* . . . shell clatter on deck. *Thud* . . . *thud* . . . *thud,* the Chinese guns responded. It was a joyous litany.
>
> —Richard McKenna, *The Sand Pebbles*

(2) *Liturgy,* in Greek meaning 'service to the people,' also 'service to God, divine service,' was at first a more general term. It primarily means 'public worship, prescribed form of religious ritual,' referring to Christian or

other religions. In Christianity (especially in the Orthodox churches) the liturgy is the Eucharist, or service of Holy Communion.

As a metaphor, *liturgy* is commonly used to mean 'ritualistically repeated and unchanging praise':

> The aristocracy of Charleston is a hermetically sealed tribe that worships the severe goddess of the city's history and will go to any ends to preserve the structure of the liturgy dedicated to her. —Pat Conroy, *Geo*

> But in the liturgy of the conventional wisdom, the praises of price competition are still vigorously sung.
> —John Kenneth Galbraith, *The Affluent Society*

literally means 'in literal truth, without exaggeration, not metaphorically speaking.'

> Co had literally grown up in the army, having been an "enfant de troupe" (a homeless child adopted by the troops) with the French army.
> —William C. Westmoreland, *A Soldier Reports*

But people with an insatiable craving for emphasis can't resist using *literally* as a mere verbal bludgeon.

> But there was a change in Gatsby that was simply confounding. He literally glowed; without a word or a gesture of exultation a new well-being radiated from him and filled the little room.
> —F. Scott Fitzgerald, *The Great Gatsby*

> She went reluctantly to parties. Indeed, she had literally to be dragged to them by her parents.
> —John Anthony Scott, *Fanny Kemble's America*

> Congressman Sanders literally yanked me through the telephone wire.
> —Sam Houston Johnson, *My Brother Lyndon*

◇ ***Recommendation.*** There are innumerable ways of achieving emphasis or vividness. Abuse of *literally* is not one of the good ones.

litotes /lī-tə-tēz, lī-**tō**-tēz/ is a figure of speech in which an idea is expressed by the denial of its opposite. It is a special type of UNDERSTATEMENT, intended to convey a shade of modesty, judiciousness, or irony:

> Paul replied, "I am a Jew from Tarsus in Cilicia, a citizen of no mean city."
> —Acts 21:39

> Death closes all: but something ere the end,
> Some work of noble note, may yet be done,
> Not unbecoming men that strove with gods.
> —Alfred, Lord Tennyson, *Ulysses*

> You were for years engaged in a reasonably legitimate form of illegality, but now you appear to have started stealing things outright from other people and I cannot call this an improvement.
> —Judge Martin J. Erdmann (quoted), *New York Times*

> He said that Brezhnev would not look unkindly on receiving a new car for his collection of luxury automobiles.
> —Richard Nixon, *R.N.*

Litotes is often, however, used mechanically, merely to avoid a positive statement, and without any stylistic point:

> [Theodore Dreiser] blasts his way through his interminable stories by something not unlike main strength.
> —H. L. Mencken (quoted), Alistair Cooke, *The Vintage Mencken*

The foregoing is at least clear; however, another danger inherent in litotes is that it can lead to ambiguity, as in the following example from Jane Austen:

> When Mr. Collins said anything of which his wife might reasonably be ashamed, which certainly was not unseldom . . . —*Pride and Prejudice*

liturgy. See LITANY, LITURGY.

loan. *Lend* is the primary verb meaning 'to allow (someone) the temporary use of (something).' *Loan* is primarily a noun, but it is also used as a verb meaning 'lend':

> . . . any general, so long as he had a few troops to spare and was willing to loan a few of them to help open a vital railway line.
> —Bruce Catton, *Mr. Lincoln's Army*

> He wanted me to read the new book, *The Great Gatsby,* as soon as he could get his last and only copy back from someone he had loaned it to.
> —Ernest Hemingway, *A Moveable Feast*

◇ ***Recommendation.*** The use of *loan* as a verb is well established and can't be classed as an error. But *lend* is still preferable.

loathe, loathsome, loath. *Loathe* /lōth/ is an even stronger verb than *hate.* It means 'to feel deep and uncontrollable dislike and disgust for':

> [My brother] loathed, as much as I do, bullfighting.
> —Vladimir Nabokov, *Speak, Memory*

The meaning of the adjective *loathsome* /**lōth**-səm, **lōth**-/ corresponds exactly to that of the verb, 'arousing deep disgust':

> I think corrupt public officials are an especially loathsome form of life. . . .
> —Meg Greenfield, *Newsweek*

But the adjective *loath* /lōth, lōth/ has a milder meaning, 'reluctant, unwilling':

> Starting out in high gear, Willkie's campaign quickly lost speed. He waffled on the issues and seemed loath to offend the isolationists and party conservatives. —Ronald Speed, *Book Digest*

> By the final day, the swamp had made its mark on us and we were loath to break its spell.
> —Jean George, *Reader's Digest*

The set phrase *nothing loath* means 'not reluctant, quite willing':

> The *Spray* neared Cape Pillar rapidly, and, nothing loath, plunged into the Pacific Ocean at once, taking her first bath of it in the gathering storm.
> —Joshua Slocum, *Sailing Alone Around the World*

The adjective *loath* has a spelling variant *loth,* which is acceptable though chiefly British. The spelling *loathe* for the adjective, however, is a mistake.

lobby has a remarkable history. It was originally a technical term in monastic architecture (Medieval Latin *lobium*) that meant 'cloister or covered walkway in a monastery.' It came to be used of buildings in general, meaning 'corridor, passageway' and 'anteroom, small waiting room attached to a large room or hall.' As early as the 17th century it was used specifically of an anteroom in the House of Commons in London where private citizens could talk with Members of Parliament, and hence was used of similar anterooms in legislative buildings in Colonial America. By 1850 the verb *lobby,* a political Americanism, emerged, meaning 'to try to influence (legislators) to vote for a particular piece of legislation' and 'to promote a particular policy or interest by influencing legislators.' Hence also, the noun *lobby* means 'political organization that promotes a special interest by influencing legislators.' A far cry from the monastic cloister.

locate. In the intransitive sense 'to settle in a place, take up residence,' *locate* is an Americanism, first recorded in Virginia in the 17th century. It is fully correct and standard (though unfamiliar in British). Also standard is *relocate* = 'to move one's residence.'

logical short circuits. See FALLACY.

lollygag. This American word (also spelled *lallygag*) first appeared more than 100 years ago, from unknown origins. It belongs to the fanciful language known as *tall talk.* The original meaning was 'to flirt.' The present meaning is 'to fool around, waste time':

> This is the first full month of summer

> and a proper time to be lollygagging on a friendly beach. . . .
>
> —James K. Page, Jr., *Smithsonian*

Hence the noun *lollygagger* (or *lallygagger*):

> Whatever his failings as a writer, Sheldon is no lollygagger. His research is extensive.
>
> —Peter Andrews, *New York Times Book Review*

loose, lose. These, with their distinctive pronunciations, respectively /lo͞os/ and /lo͞oz/, are never confused in speech or meaning but are sometimes confused as to spelling. *Loose,* basically the adjective meaning 'not tight,' is also a verb meaning 'to let loose, release':

> He hath loosed the fateful lightning
> of His terrible swift sword. . . .
>
> —Julia Ward Howe, *Battle Hymn of the Republic*

Lose is only a verb meaning 'to fail to find, be deprived of, etc.'

Louisiana French. There are three basic varieties of French currently being spoken in southern Louisiana. Although each one has a different history and form, outsiders frequently confuse them.

There is the *provincial French* spoken by a handful of the descendants of the elite French settlers in and around New Orleans. It is a variety of Standard French that preserves a few archaic features. Basically identical with the French of the mother country, it has virtually no currency as a form of everyday speech. The descendants of the old French-American upper classes no longer exist as a distinct cultural group.

Cajun French is the speech of the descendants of the Acadian refugees of the 1760s. Its speakers are predominantly of white stock and use a dialect of French that developed out of the 17th-century folk speech. Cajun French varies somewhat from parish to parish within Louisiana.

Louisiana French Creole is very different from the other two varieties. It is the language of the descendants of plantation slaves and is closely related to the French creoles of the Caribbean. Louisiana Creole and the creole languages of Haiti, the Lesser Antilles, Trinidad, and French Guiana are essentially mutually intelligible.

The relationship between English, Cajun, and Creole is a complex one. Most speakers in southern Louisiana today are at least bilingual. If we were to overhear a conversation among these bilingual and sometimes trilingual speakers, we would notice that the participants occasionally switched back and forth from Cajun to English, or Creole to Cajun, and so on, depending on the situation.

In general, English has the most social prestige, followed by Cajun and then by French Creole. Aware that English is the coin of the "outside" world, parents ordinarily talk to their children in English. It is not unusual to hear adults speak Cajun or Creole among themselves and then switch to English to reprimand a misbehaving child.

Despite the pressures of the English-speaking world, the prestigious language within the local adult community is Cajun French. But when speakers know both Cajun and Creole, they tend to use Creole as the language of intimacy. Husband and wife, for example, often switch to Creole when alone or when exchanging remarks during the course of a group conversation in Cajun.

Cajun French. The story of the Louisiana Cajuns begins in Nova Scotia. In the early 17th century, France established a colony on the peninsula of Nova Scotia, at that time called *Acadia,* a name the French borrowed from the Indians. The Micmac word was *aquoddianke* or *aquoddie* and meant 'pollack,' an important and esteemed food fish. The French colonists were known as *Acadians.* Over time the pronunciation of *Acadian* /ə-**kā**-dē-ən/ was altered to /**kā**-jən/, which then produced the spelling *Cajun.*

During the 18th century, France and England fought several wars over this Canadian territory. Acadia was shuffled back and forth between the two sides until 1713, after the final British victory. In that year the Treaty of Utrecht formally ceded Acadia to England. Because the Acadians were still French and sympathetic toward the mother country, in 1755 the British began to expel them from their homeland. Some 10,000 unarmed Acadians were loaded on ships and deported, to be scattered all along the Atlantic coast. This sad event is memorialized in Longfellow's poem *Evangeline*.

It was not until 1765 that the first Acadians (about 650 of them) arrived in hospitable New Orleans. Later, others poured into the region and established settlements along the Mississippi River and adjoining bayous. Today, the descendants of these settlers, the Cajuns, are concentrated chiefly in southeastern Louisiana, in St. James Parish (a parish being a political unit in Louisiana similar to a county).

Cajun French differs from Standard French in several details of pronunciation and in numerous vocabulary items. It has preserved a few of the archaic features of the rural 17th-century French of Acadia. Unlike Standard French, Cajun has a few Spanish loanwords borrowed during the brief Spanish rule in the early history of Louisiana. Cajun French has also adopted several French Creole expressions, such as *mon gardemanger* = 'my stomach'; *mon tendé* = 'my ear'; *mon senti* = 'my nose'; and *mon oi clair* = 'my eye.'

Cajun also often uses the third-person pronoun *on* (= 'one') for the first person *je* (= 'I'), saying, for example, *on va* instead of Standard French *je vais* for 'I go.' Other instances in which Cajun uses a different form from Standard French are:

haler la porte = 'to shut the door' (Standard French *tirer la porte*)

il est paré = 'he [*or* it] is ready' (Standard French *il est prêt*)

il mouille = 'it's raining' (Standard French *il pleut*)

le désert = 'field or open country' (Standard French *le champ*)

In addition, the Cajun French of each parish has its own set of unique features. Nevertheless, a Cajun speaker from Thibodaux in Lafourche Parish would easily be able to understand a speaker from St. Martinville in St. Martin Parish, and both would be able to converse with a Parisian, though perhaps with some difficulty.

Louisiana French Creole. Although the Creole spoken in southern Louisiana is basically French, it is substantially different from the other varieties of Louisiana French. Like all pidgins and creoles, it developed out of the contact between two distinctive cultures: that of the West African slaves and that of the French settlers and plantation owners of colonial Louisiana (see PIDGIN AND CREOLE LANGUAGES). Since the two groups had no language in common, they developed a pidgin. French, the base language, was greatly simplified, down to only one or two hundred words. This vastly altered version of French was the mother tongue of the second-generation slaves. At that point it became a creole language, evolving into a more complex form to meet the need for broader, more sophisticated communication. After several generations of speakers this creole had greatly expanded its vocabulary and become a full-fledged language, moving ever closer to the base language, French.

Today, it retains its simplified or reduced pronunciation and grammar. It has, for example, seven basic vowels: /ē/, /ā/, /ĕ/, /ä/, /ȯ/, /ō/, and /o͞o/. And in general it does not have the tense or rounded vowels of Standard French. Other differences in pronunciation can be seen in the following list, which gives the Standard French term with its Creole pronunciation.

aimer /lĕN-mĕN/ = 'to like, care for'
beaucoup /bo͞o-ko͞o/ = 'much, a great deal'
beurre /bĕ/ = 'butter'
cercle /sĕk/ = 'circle'
chambre /shȯNm/ = 'room'
cheval /shwäl/ = 'horse'
coeur /chĕ/ = 'heart'
connaître /kȯN-nĕN/ = 'to know'
cuit /chwē/ = 'cooked, baked'
déjeuner /dā-zhĕN-nĕN/ = 'lunch'
Dieu /jā/ = 'God'
dîner /dē-nĕN/ = 'dinner'
dormir /drō-mē/ = 'to sleep'

fermer /frĕN-mĕN/ = 'to close, shut'
galerie /gär-lē/ = 'gallery'
gardienne /gä-jĕN/ = 'guardian, keeper'
guerre /jĕ/ = 'war'
monsieur /mē-shā/ = 'sir'
oiseau /zō-zō/ = 'bird'
oublier /bē-lyā/ = 'to forget'
queue /chā/ = 'tail, end'
raconter /kȯN-tā/ = 'to tell'
soeur /sĕ/ = 'sister'
térébenthine /tā-lā-bȯN-tēn/ = 'turpentine'
tranquille /trȯN-kēn/ = 'calm, still'
tuer /chwā/ = 'to kill'

An article or a final consonant preceding a noun is usually permanently attached to the noun in Creole. For example, French *la table* (= 'the table') is in Creole *latab*. Thus, French *une table* (= 'one table, a table') is in Creole *une latab* /ĕN lä-täb/. French *un homme* (= 'one man, a man') is in Creole *un nomme* /ĕN nȯNm/.

The personal pronouns in Creole are *mo, to, li, nous, vous, ye* (= 'I, you [*sing.*], he [she, it], we, you [*pl.*], they'), instead of French *je, tu, il/elle, nous, vous, ils/elles*.

Creole frequently uses uninflected verbs. For example, the Standard French verb *aller* (= 'to go') is conjugated *je vais, tu vas, il va, nous allons*, etc. (= 'I go, you go, he goes, we go,' etc.). The Creole simplifies this by using only the infinitive form, *aller* /ä-**lā**/, usually written *alé*. When used with personal pronouns, the vowel of the pronoun is dropped: *m'alé, t'alé, l'alé, n'alé*, etc.

Here are some examples illustrating the differences between the two ways of saying the same thing. The Standard French is given first, followed by the Creole version and its pronunciation, and then the English translation.

L'homme et la femme sont arrivés hier.
Nomme-la et fomme-la rivé hié.
nȯNm-lä ā fȯNm-lä rē-vā yĕ
The man and woman arrived yesterday.

Les miens ne sont pas bons.
Moquennes-ye pas bons.
mō-kĕNn-yĕ pä bȯn
Mine are not good.

Il a deux chaises dans sa maison.
Li gain dé lachaises dans so lamaison.
lē gĕN dā lä-shāz dȯN sō lä-mĕ-zȯN
He has two chairs in his house.

la hache avec laquelle tu as coupé l'arbre
lahache-là 'vec ça to coupé narb-là
lä-äsh-lä vĕk sä tō ko͞o-pā näb-lä
the hatchet with which you have chopped the tree

M

machinate. To *machinate* is to contrive devious and malignant maneuvers. The word is preferably pronounced /**măk**-ə-nāt/, though /**măsh**-ə-nāt/ is possible. The noun is *machination*, often used in the plural: *defeated by her own political machinations*.

macho, machismo. These terms, now universally familiar, first came into English in the 1960s. In Spanish, *macho* is basically an adjective meaning 'masculine, manly' and secondarily a noun meaning 'male.' *Machismo* is an abstract noun meaning 'masculinity.' The two words are used of the special qualities often attributed to Latin American males, including conspicuous virility, pride, and courage, occasionally carried to aggressive levels. Borrowed into English, *macho* /**mä**-chō/ and *machismo* /mä-**chēz**-mō/ mean the same as in Spanish but have also developed further connotations and uses.

(1) *Macho* primarily means 'swaggeringly male' or 'a man who is macho':

> The macho cowboy still does about everything from roping a steer to busting a bronco while tugging on a Marlboro. —*Reader's Digest*

> Al Pacino might be the original lovable macho.
> —Jonathan Mandell, *Boston Globe*

Secondarily, *macho* means 'politically aggressive, culturally tough':

> Khrushchev knew he was behind and therefore had to put on this big bravado act or the big macho act to prove that he was ahead of everybody and everything.
> —Richard Nixon (quoted), *New York Times*

> In the 50's and 60's, there was Brutalism . . . a macho flexing of architectural muscles in reinforced concrete, with fiercely articulated joints and great rough slabs. . . .
> —Ada Louise Huxtable, *New York Times*

(2) *Machismo* similarly means, first, 'male swagger, he-man behavior' and second, 'political aggressiveness, cultural toughness':

> Producers and moviegoers discovered that Pacino's innately lovable characters made machismo palatable.
> —Jonathan Mandell, *Boston Globe*

> The Premier of Queensland demonstrates his machismo by threatening our major trading partner. . . .
> —Evan Whitton, *National Times* (Australia)

(3) Increasingly, *macho* is also used as an abstract noun in the same senses as *machismo:*

> Liberals seem to earn their macho sneering at our reverence for work, family, home, neighborhood, discipline and responsibility.
> —Barry Farber, *New York Times*

(4) And *machismo* is often used attributively to mean, in effect, the same as *macho:*

> Lyndon Johnson, the grand champion machismo politician of all time . . .
> —Ron Powers, *The Newscasters*

◇ *Recommendation.* It is best not to mix up the grammatical functions of these two words, but to keep *macho* as the adjective (and noun meaning 'a man who is macho') and *machismo* as the abstract noun meaning 'the quality of being macho.'

mad. In many people's speech *mad* is the usual word for 'angry.' This once was considered unsuitable for formal usage but is now so widespread and natural that we regard it as standard and acceptable in all contexts.

madding. From an old verb, *mad,* meaning 'to rush around insanely, act as if mad,' *madding* was immortalized in this line by the English poet Thomas Gray in 1749:

> Far from the madding crowd's ignoble strife . . .
> —*Elegy in a Country Churchyard*

Later Thomas Hardy used the quotation for the title of his novel *Far From the Madding Crowd* (1874), which is set in the rural calm of the west of England. Thus *madding,* preserved by one accidentally memorable phrase, is all we have left of an otherwise obsolete verb. It is not surprising that it is often "corrected" to *maddening:*

> . . . he had gone so far as to speak with a certain dreaminess of the joys of retirement, of the quiet time of withdrawal which would follow a lifetime spent in the service of the public. "Far from the maddening crowd," he had said, gazing at the reporters expressionlessly. . . .
> —Edwin O'Connor, *The Last Hurrah*

◇ *Recommendation.* Don't use this phrase. It is a cliché. If you must, however, at least use the correct word, *madding.*

maelstrom. In Dutch this means 'rotating stream, whirlpool,' from *malen* = 'to grind, rotate' + *strom* = 'stream.' It was the name given by sailors to a specific famous whirlpool in the sea off the coast of Norway. Edgar Allan Poe's story "The Descent Into the Maelstrom" (1844) helped to popularize the name as a general term for 'whirlpool, any dangerous rough waters.'

> We heard the heavy, sullen roar of a big rapids, and went ashore to have a look before proceeding into the maelstrom.
> —Farley Mowat, *People of the Deer*

Maelstrom is also used as a metaphor for any situation that tends to overwhelm:

> The distinguished guests were engulfed in a maelstrom of boots, spurs, ten-gallon hats, six-foot men.
> —Edna Ferber, *Giant*

> For decades, I have bobbed like a cork, cheekily unsinkable, in a maelstrom of loans, mortgages, liens. . . .
> —Brendan Gill, *Here at The New Yorker*

malapropism. Captain Absolute, Lydia Languish, Sir Lucius O'Trigger—most of us would probably have difficulty recognizing these as characters in Richard Brinsley Sheridan's 1775 play *The Rivals*. But one character in *The Rivals*—the redoubtable Mrs. Malaprop—is known to nearly every literate person, even if he or she has never read the play. Indeed, Mrs. Malaprop, via the term *malapropism*, has become a fixture in our language.

Mrs. Malaprop's problem is that the reach of her linguistic pretensions exceeds the grasp of her vocabulary. She is always trying, as another character in the play remarks, "to deck her dull chat with hard words she don't understand." The result is that Mrs. Malaprop's speech is filled with words that may sound vaguely like the words she wants but are nevertheless totally and amusingly wrong. Thus, she can speak airily of "an allegory on the banks of the Nile," describe a person as a "progeny of learning," or mystify everyone around her with a sentence (defending her own use of language) such as "Sure, if I reprehend anything in this world, it is the use of my oracular tongue, and a nice derangement of epitaphs!" Ever since Mrs. Malaprop's debut, the terms *malaprop* and *malapropism* have been used to describe not only the wrong use of individual words but also, by extension, mangled quotations and sayings as well as impossible or ludicrously mixed metaphors.

Unfortunately, the English language contains enough tricky sound-alike words—*fortunate* and *fortuitous*, for example, or *aural* and *oral, turbid* and *turgid, factious* and *fractious*—to make malapropisms fairly common in everyday speech. Thanks to alert copy editors, they occur less often in print, but as magazines such as *The New Yorker* and *Verbatim* never tire of reminding us, copy editors cannot catch everything. The following three citations appeared as filler paragraphs in *The New Yorker:*

> Well known Museum needs an all around assistant to work in the Director's office. Deal with infamous people in the Art World.
> —advertisement, *New York Times*

> "Another criterion was whether viewers emphasized with portrayed characters," Robinson said. "We might assume that viewers cannot emphasize if distracted by inconsistent or incredible details."
> —*Register-Guard* (Eugene, Oreg.)

> Shakespeare didn't have television in mind when he warned about the ideas of March. —*Television/Radio Age*

Borrowed foreign words and phrases are fraught with danger for the inept. In addition to being mispronounced or misspelled, they can also produce full-blown malapropisms:

> [Actress Isabelle] Huppert, with the freckled enigmatic face of a sullen schoolgirl, is a *tabula rosé* on which other directors have written personality. —*Time*

Because malapropisms can be so amusing, they continue to be staples of comedy:

> "Well, Miss 'Lame Brain,'" he retorted sardonically, "maybe you had better

stop galvanizing around nights and pay attention." —S. J. Perelman, *Crazy Like a Fox*

One well-known modern Mrs. Malaprop was Jane Ace, wife of comedy writer Goodman Ace, on the old radio program "The Easy Aces." Here are some of Jane's better-remembered forays into the mysteries of vocabulary:

We are all cremated equal.

Explain to me in words of one cylinder.

In all my bored days.

And Jane's fractured rendition of an old saying became something of a radio classic: "Time wounds all heels."

Although it is easy to make fun of malapropisms because they are both obvious and absurd, they are by no means the worst of verbal sins. Anyone who is trying to enlarge his or her working vocabulary may occasionally commit a malapropism. But it is not a sin of bad taste, bad logic, or bad intentions, only of bad memory. If it is the price we must all sometimes pay for trying to speak better, it is a reasonable one.

Malay words. The Malays are the dominant people of the Malay Peninsula and the huge archipelago south and southeast of it, divided between the nations of Malaysia and Indonesia. Collectively their various languages and dialects are called Malay; this is the sense of the term as used in the word histories given below. In a narrower definition the Malay language is the official language of the 10 million people of Malaysia. The Indonesian official language (known as Bahasa Indonesia) is a closely related form, as are such dialects as Javanese, spoken by the 70 million people of the island of Java, and Balinese, spoken by the 2 million people of Bali.

Malaya is the old name of the Malay Peninsula south of Thailand. Malaysia is the nation comprising Malaya and the northern parts of Borneo. The word *Malay* is pronounced /**mā**-lā/ or, especially by the British, /mə-**lā**/.

Europeans have been trading with the Malays for more than 400 years, and the Dutch and British established colonial rule over them, which ended only in the 1950s. These long contacts have left a considerable number of Malay words in the English vocabulary, mostly denoting plants, animals, and products.

* **amok, amuck** /ə-**mŭk**/ = 'in a wild or crazed state': from Malay *āmoq* = 'in a state of homicidal frenzy'

bamboo = 'giant grass with hollow wooden stems, used for building, furniture, etc.': from Dutch *bamboes*, from Portuguese *mambu*, from Malay *mambu* = 'bamboo'

batik /bə-**tēk**/ = 'technique of dyeing cloth in complex patterns': from Javanese *mbatik* = 'writing, drawing'

camphor /**kăm**-fər/ = 'aromatic white oil obtained from several Indonesian trees': entered English in the 14th century via Old French, Latin, and Arabic, probably ultimately from Malay *kāpūr*

cockatoo = 'large parrot of Indonesia and Australia': from Dutch *kakatoe*, from Malay *kakatua*

* **compound** = 'enclosed private estate with several buildings'

dugong /**dōō**-gŏng/ = 'large, plant-eating tropical sea mammal': from Malay *dūyong*

gamelan /**găm**-ə-lăn/ = 'orchestra comprising bamboo xylophones and other percussion instruments, flutes, etc.': from Javanese *gamelan* = 'bamboo xylophone, orchestra'

gingham /**gĭng**-əm/ = 'cotton cloth typically woven in plaid or check patterns of white with one color': from Dutch *gingang*, from Malay *ginggang* = 'striped'

gong = 'hanging bronze disk with a turned-back rim, giving a resonant boom when struck with a soft mallet': first recorded in English in 1600, from Malay *gōng* (onomatopoeic)

gutta-percha /gŭt-ə-**pêr**-chə, -kə/ = 'rubbery substance obtained from the sap of several Indonesian trees, formerly used for making golf balls': from Malay *getah percha*, from *getah* = 'sap' + *percha* = 'name of one of the trees used for this purpose'

kapok **/kā-pŏk/** = (1) 'fine cottonlike fiber obtained from the seeds of an Indonesian tree' (2) now usually 'similar fiber obtained from a tropical American tree, used for stuffing mattresses, life jackets, etc.': from Dutch *kapok,* from Malay *kāpoq*

*__ketchup, catsup__ = 'thick, spicy sauce'

kris **/krēs/** = 'Malay dagger, typically with a blade of forged steel with wavy edges': from Malay *keris* = 'dagger'

launch = (1) '(in the days of sail) the largest boat carried by a warship' (2) 'large, usually open powerboat for carrying passengers': sense one first recorded in English as *lanch* in the 17th century, from Portuguese *lancha* or *lanchara,* from Malay *lancharan* = 'type of fast sailing boat' (The change of spelling in English from *lanch* to *launch* is an example of FOLK ETYMOLOGY.)

orangutan **/ə-răng-ə-tăn/** = 'large, tail-less ape living in rain forest in Borneo and Sumatra': from Malay *orang utan* = 'man of the woods'

paddy = 'heavily irrigated rice field,' originally 'rice as harvested, before removal of straw and husks': from Malay *pādī* = 'rice in the husk'

rattan **/ră-tăn/** = 'stems of several vinelike Indonesian palms, used in house building, furniture, basketwork, etc.': from Malay *rōtan*

sago **/sā-gō/** = 'starch obtained from the pith of several Indonesian palm trees': from Malay *sagu*

sarong **/sə-rŏng/** = 'long skirt, tightly wrapped at the waist, worn by Malay women and men': from Malay *saroeng* = 'sheath, sarong'

*Appears as separate entry

male chauvinism. See CHAUVINISM.

mall. ***Origin.*** Our latest version of the traditional marketplace is the enclosed shopping center, or *mall.* The word has a curious history. In the 17th century the Italian game of *pallamaglio* = 'mallet-ball' (*palla* = 'ball' + *maglio* = 'mallet') became fashionable all over Europe. It was played with boxwood balls and springy-shafted mallets or clubs, in specially made alleys bounded by low walls. The ball could be hit several hundred yards at a stroke, and the object was to drive it through a metal hoop suspended above the ground. It was a city game, played by the upper classes; most cities had alleys, and these were meeting places of fashionable society. The game itself was called in English *pall-mall* **/pĕl-mĕl/** or *mall* /môl/, and both terms were applied to the alley as well.

The first pall-mall in London, running eastward from St. James's Palace, was turned into a street, still named Pall Mall, about 1660. It was then replaced by a new alley in the fields to the south, called the Mall. In the 18th century the game of pall-mall disappeared, and the long alleys were generally turned into walks where fashionable strollers still met and mingled. In London, Pall Mall became famous for exclusive men's clubs, while the Mall was made into a tree-lined parade leading up to Buckingham Palace. *Mall* became a general term for 'a tree-lined walk in a town'; by 1800 both Boston and New York had their malls.

After World War II, architects and planners revived the idea of streets to be used exclusively by pedestrians, as an escape from automobiles; such streets, often landscaped, either for shopping or among public buildings, were called malls. By about 1970 this idea had evolved into the fully enclosed suburban shopping center, a complex often covering several acres, with interior landscapes and walkways winding through the shops. While these are generally known in the trade as malls, they are widely known to the public as shopping centers. In the present state of suburban development they are serious competition to downtown shopping areas and are clearly here to stay.

Pronunciation. The old game pall-mall is pronounced **/pĕl-mĕl/**, **/păl-măl/**, or **/pôl-môl/**. Pall Mall, the street in London, is always pronounced **/pĕl-mĕl/**; but the brand of cigarettes named after it is pronounced **/pôl-môl/** in the United States. The other street in

London, the Mall, is pronounced /môl/, like the word *mall.*

Note. The word *pell-mell* = 'headlong, at a furious pace' or 'confused, disordered' is not related; it is from Old French *pesle mesle,* originally *mesle mesle* = 'mixed up, helter-skelter.'

man. In Modern English the word *man* has been endowed with three major meanings. Everyone knows that a man is an adult male human being. In this sense, a man is not a woman, and a woman is not a man. But earlier meanings of *man* are still around to create confusion. Sometimes, dictionaries tell us, a *man* may be any human being, regardless of sex. *Man* without an article before it is also used collectively to mean human beings or the human race. When Neil Armstrong set foot on the moon on July 20, 1969, he said, "That's one small step for a man, one giant leap for mankind." Did he mean one small step for a human being or one small step for a human male?

In earlier periods of the English language, the situation was simpler and more straightforward. In Old English *man* meant 'human being' and was applied to members of both sexes. It corresponded to the Latin *homo,* 'human being.' There were separate words for males and females. *Wer* meant 'male human being,' also 'husband.' *Wīf* meant 'female human being,' also 'wife.' Over the years the general word *man* came to be applied to the male specifically, as well as to the species as a whole. Meanwhile the female came to be called *wīfmann* or *wimman* or *wummon* or *woman.*

In the 16th century the word *man* was still sometimes used to include both sexes. In 1597, for example, a writer observed of Adam and Eve that "the Lord had but one paire of men in Paradise." Even so, the meaning of *man* had already shifted. When Shakespeare had Hamlet exclaim, "What a piece of work is a man," he seemed to mean a human being, as distinguished from a lower animal. But at the end of that same speech, he narrowed the meaning down to the male sex, as distinguished from the female.

> What a piece of work is a man, how noble in reason, how infinite in faculties, in form and moving, how express and admirable in action, how like an angel in apprehension, how like a god! the beauty of the world; the paragon of animals; and yet to me what is this quintessence of dust? Man delights not me—nor women neither. . . .

This masculinizing of the word *man* is also evident in Shakespeare's "seven ages of man" speech from *As You Like It.* There, all the men and women may be players, but life is seen in terms of a purely male progression from infant to schoolboy to lover "with a woeful ballad/Made to his mistress' eyebrow" to soldier to justice to pantaloon (old man).

By the 18th century, writers were having to specify when they meant *man* or *men* to include both sexes.

> There is in all men, both male and female, a desire and power of generation. . . .
>
> —David Hume,
> *Political Discourses*

> Such a deplorable havoc is made in the minds of men (both sexes) in France. . . .
>
> —Edmund Burke, letter

Words change in meaning depending on how they are used. *Girl* originally meant 'young person of either sex'; it eventually came to mean 'young female.' Like *girl, man* has narrowed in meaning. Today, its primary use is to designate a male as distinct from a female.

Can the same word, *man,* distinguish males from females in one context and include both males and females in another? Some usage experts insist that it can. Other writers and speakers disagree. They feel that the conflicting meanings of *man* create needless ambiguity.

> The generic singular *man* sometimes means both sexes (God made the country, and man made the town) and sometimes only one (Man is destined to be a prey to woman). . . . This is decidedly a defect in the English language, and the tendency recently has been to use unambiguous, if clumsy, expressions

like *a human being*. . . .

—Otto Jespersen,
The Philosophy of Grammar

Many writers have continued to use *man* as though its masculine connotations presented no problem. However, even the best sometimes slip up and make an incompatible switch in midsentence from *man* the human being to *man* the male:

> As for man, he is no different from the rest. His back aches, he ruptures easily, his women have difficulties in childbirth, all because he has struggled up upon his hind legs without having achieved a perfect adjustment to his new posture.
>
> —Loren Eiseley, *Natural History*

Apparently, the writer balked at saying of man that "*he* has difficulties in childbirth." But if *man* and *he* were truly inclusive words, that statement would sound natural and correct. Consider how the sentence might change if it were written from a female human being's point of view: "Her back aches, she has difficulties in childbirth, her men rupture easily."

Do most people think of the word *man* as embracing all the members of the human race? In the Schneider-Hacker study at Drake University in 1972, students were asked to find pictures to illustrate chapter titles in a sociology book. One set of students were given titles such as "Urban Man," "Economic Man," and "Political Man." They brought back pictures that focused on males, especially on white males of high status. Another set of students were given titles such as "Urban Life," "Economic Behavior," and "Political Behavior." Those students turned in a significantly higher proportion of pictures showing men, women, and children. The word *man* had caused students to visualize males.

In an experiment at a junior high school in Ridgewood, New Jersey, 100 seventh-graders were asked to find the books on early humans in the school library. Ninety-nine reported that there were no books on early humans. One student asked the teacher if early humans were included in books on "early man." As a result, the library changed its categories of classification.

When *man* is used to mean 'a person' or 'the human race,' it is used with the masculine pronoun *he*. The *man . . . he* style of writing carries with it strong male connotations. Consider this quotation:

> The American once was a man bound to his country and his fellows by a common belief in something, not yet realized, that he loved. Now he is a man—or there are those who tell him he is a man—bound to his country and the rest by a common hatred of something looming that he fears.
>
> —Archibald MacLeish,
> *Atlantic Monthly*

Would a female reader feel included in this reference? No one tells a woman she is a man. Presumably, MacLeish does not mean to imply that all Americans are men. But some writers, apparently, have gotten—and given—that impression.

> Americans of higher status have more years of education, . . . less divorce, lower mortality, better dental care, and less chance of having a fat wife.
>
> —Theodore Caplow,
> *Elementary Sociology*

When the word *man* is used as part of a job title, it does not specify the nature of the work performed. Does a *fireman* stoke fires or put them out? On the other hand, it is clear what a *firefighter* does. The tendency now is to use job titles that specify function rather than gender—for example, *police officer; mail carrier; milk deliverer; insurance agent; flight attendant*.

Given the changes in usage, when is a woman a man and when is she not a man? Some may call her a "craftsman," but would anyone think of her as "the working man"? She may be the victim of "manslaughter," but is she the typical person we visualize when we say "the man in the street"? A woman might still sometimes be called the "chairman" of a committee, but would anyone refer to her as "a local businessman"? If she is not a man on board, how can she be a "man overboard"?

To avoid ambiguity, refer to humans as *human beings, the human race, the human species, people, men and women,* or *women and men.* An unspecified individual might be *the average person, the working person,* or *the ordinary citizen.* To keep from overusing *man* in other contexts, specify the work or function being performed; for example, *advertising agent* or *copywriter* or *account executive* instead of *advertising man; business person* or *owner* or *manager* or *executive* instead of *businessman; ten-member committee* instead of *ten-man committee; worker-hours* instead of *man-hours; workers' compensation* instead of *workmen's compensation;* and, instead of *manpower,* words like *workers, work force, staff,* or *personnel.*

Man is also used in many familiar phrases, such as *one man, one vote.* An alternative to this phrase was found by a federal judge:

> . . . the present equal apportionment of at-large seats in the New York City Council violates the "one person, one vote" principle embodied in the equal protection clause of the 14th Amendment. . . .
>
> —Edward R. Neaher, *New York Times*

The easiest way to change a *man . . . he* passage is to pluralize. The MacLeish passage quoted above could be recast to read:

> Americans once were bound to their country and to one another by a common belief in something, not yet realized, that they loved. Now they are—or are told that they are—bound to their country and the rest by a common hatred of something looming that they fear.

A *man . . . his* passage can also be recast:

> Man is continuously influenced by his surroundings or environment. Man and his behavior have been affected by the changing environment.

We . . . our will work as well:

> We are continuously influenced by our surroundings or environment. Humans and human behavior have been affected by the changing environment.

The *-man* in the word *human* has nothing to do with the English word *man; human* is from Latin *hūmānus,* originally meaning 'earthling,' from *humus* = 'earth.' And the idea that the syllable *man-* in such words as *manager* and *mandate* is the same as the word *man* is a fantasy or joke invented by feminist writers to draw attention to the real problems of bias in language. This *man-* comes from Latin *manus* = 'hand.' Likewise, the suggestion that *history,* on the principle of equal time, be changed to *herstory* should be taken as an amusing taunt rather than a serious proposal; *history* is from Greek *historia* = 'inquiry, narrative, information,' based on a word meaning 'to know.'

In attempting to be inclusive, writers do not have to be ridiculous. As one commentator noted:

> [No one] seriously suggests that the word "person" be substituted for "man" or "woman" in every instance. It's unlikely that you'll ever get stung by a Portuguese person-of-war. You'll never land on the Isle of Person. You'll never tell time with your grandperson clock. And the story of Watergate will never be known as the saga of Haldeperson, Ehrlichperson, Mitchell, and Dean.
>
> —Elsa Goss, *Philadelphia Inquirer*

See also CHAIRMAN; DEAR SIR OR MADAM; EVERYONE . . . HE; HE; HE OR SHE; -MAN; PARALLEL STYLE; THEY.

-man. Should words ending in the suffix *-man* be applied to women? Some *-man* words, such as *businessman, policeman,* and *fireman,* were until recent times clearly male identified. Others, such as *craftsman* and *freshman,* seem more inclusive, if only because they have long been applied to women as well as men. Even so, *craft worker* and *craftsperson*—and even *freshperson*—have been introduced as substitutes.

With the language in transition from one set of rules to another, many speakers and writers have been left in a no man's land. They find themselves on shifting sands of usage where it is hard to get a firm footing. They may want to be inclusive and fair, but at the same time they do not want to sound ridiculous. When even the experts often disagree, what is the best thing to do?

Many *-man* words are used in organizations and in politics—for example, *alderman; chairman; committeeman; congressman; foreman* (of a jury); *layman;* and *spokesman.* These compounds were formed at a time when only males held such positions or performed such functions. In an age when women take an active part in public life, *-man* titles strike many people as inappropriate. However, some speakers and writers continue to use them as though no change had taken place.

> . . . the jury foreman, Miss Kucharski, notified the judge by note that a verdict had been reached.
> —Martin Arnold, *New York Times*

◇ ***Recommendation.*** There are at least three acceptable ways to avoid *-man* suffix words:
(1) Let the suffix suit the object of the reference: *Selectman Tom Brown; Alderwoman Alice Bowen; Congresswoman Shirley Chisholm; Democratic committeemen and committeewomen; a real estate saleswoman.*

> Sybil Kucharski, the 21-year-old forewoman of the Mitchell-Stans jury . . .
> —Marvin Smilon and Robert Garrett, *New York Post*

(2) Use the suffix *-person* in place of *-man* or *-woman;* for example, *spokesperson.* If a *-person* word is used, it should be applied to men as well as women. If a female is a *spokesperson* but a male is still a *spokesman,* the whole effect of the gender-free term is lost. Appending *-person* is not a panacea, however; it suits some words better than others. Different solutions can frequently be found. Sometimes, no suffix is necessary; the root word can stand alone: *the chair of the committee; a lay* (instead of *layman's*) *point of view.*
(3) Use a different gender-free title when one is available: *a real estate agent; Representative Shirley Chisholm; Democratic Committee members; members of Congress.* Such usage can make a real difference, not just a cosmetic one, as the following attests:

> The [Los Angeles city] council approved a recommendation by the personnel department of a plan to abolish the posts of "policeman" and "policewoman," replacing them with the classification "police officer." The action makes women officers eligible for promotion to ranks for which they were ineligible in the past.
> —*New York Times*

See also CHAIRMAN; FEMALE-GENDER WORD FORMS; MAN; PARALLEL STYLE.

mandarin. The first Europeans to reach the Far East, in the 16th century, were the Portuguese. Unable or unwilling to learn the many languages of the area, they used a simplified trade language or pidgin, containing a mixture of elements from various languages including their own (see PIDGIN AND CREOLE LANGUAGES). In Indonesia they picked up the Malay word *menteri,* meaning 'councilor, minister of state,' and reshaped it to *mandarim* or *mandarin,* under the influence of the Portuguese verb *mandar* = 'to command.' When they reached China, they came into contact with the highly educated civil servants of the Chinese empire, whose title in Chinese was *kuan.* There were nine ranks of them, each rank wearing a distinctive button in the hat. The Portuguese, failing to learn Chinese, applied to these scholarly bureaucrats their all-purpose word for 'Oriental official,' *mandarin.* This word was later adopted into other European languages including English, and *mandarin* has remained the Western term although it was never used in China.

The official standard dialect of Chinese is (in the West, not in China) called *Mandarin* or *Mandarin Chinese.* For further details see CHINESE WORDS.

Mandarin is also used allusively of high-ranking civil servants in Western countries. The word suggests 'aloof, powerful nonelected official, often of old-fashioned education and outlook':

> . . . [Rockliffe Park in Ottawa] where most of the foreign ambassadors and top-ranking civil servants—called "man-

darins"—have their luxurious homes.
—Robert Trumbull, *New York Times*

Washington is full of power-hungry mandarins and bureaucrats. . . .
—S. I. Hayakawa, *Harper's*

manner. The expression *to the manner born* originates in Shakespeare, meaning 'accustomed from birth to this practice':

But to my mind—though I am native here,
And to the manner born—it is a custom
More honour'd in the breach than the observance.
—*Hamlet*

(1) As a catch phrase it means '(as if) naturally talented in some demanding activity,' often 'with impressively natural ease of manner in a position of social prominence':

When he writes badly, he writes like a lecturer. But in the last two months of 1939, like a man bewitched, he wrote five poems in heroic couplets as though to the manner born.
—Sylvia Townsend Warner, *T. H. White*

I was glad, therefore, when Lady Blandford assured me that I had carried it off in the manner born, adding, "I must tell you that no one would take you for an American."
—Consuelo Vanderbilt Balsan, *The Glitter and the Gold*

(2) The variant form *to the manor born* is taken as 'born to inherit a manor house or mansion' and is thus used to mean 'of upper-class birth, of superior breeding':

. . . Kay, according to her, should have got married quietly in City Hall, instead of making Harald, who was not to the manor born, try to carry off a wedding in J. P. Morgan's church.
—Mary McCarthy, *The Group*

And why did he have to fire that nice General MacArthur? The general was a man she could have felt socially at ease with; for one thing, he was a gentleman to the manor born.
—Merle Miller, *Plain Speaking*

mantel, fireboard, etc. In the United States the most general term for the shelf over a fireplace is *mantel,* used all over the country. *Mantelpiece* is also widely known, but its use is commonest east of the Mississippi River. In New England this shelf is sometimes called a *manteltree* or *manteltree piece.* In the South, especially in the southern Appalachians and Ozarks, it is frequently called a *fireboard* and sometimes a *man tel board.*

For the social-class usage of *mantelpiece* versus *chimney piece* in British English see U, NON-U.

Maritimes dialects. The Maritime Provinces of Canada, usually known simply as *the Maritimes,* are three: New Brunswick, Nova Scotia (which includes Cape Breton Island), and Prince Edward Island. (When Newfoundland is included, the four provinces are known as the *Atlantic Provinces.*) See the map at CANADIAN ENGLISH.

For such a relatively small area, the settlement pattern is quite complex. Even before the Loyalist influx in 1783, there were some thousands of English-speaking inhabitants in the area, living mostly in isolated settlements, notably at the mouth of the St. John River in New Brunswick, in the Annapolis Valley and Halifax in Nova Scotia, and around Charlottetown and Summerside in Prince Edward Island. In Lunenburg County in Nova Scotia, a settlement of German speakers was established as early as 1753. The arrival of the Loyalists in 1783 doubled the English-speaking population of the Maritimes almost overnight. In New Brunswick the settlement at St. John became an "instant city," and English-speaking settlers, originally from New York, New Jersey, Pennsylvania, Maryland, etc., pushed up the river as far as Woodstock. In Nova Scotia existing settlements were reinforced and new settlements were begun, notably at Shelburne and Sydney. Later immigration has brought Scots and Irish to New Brunswick and Prince Edward Island and Yorkshiremen to the Chignecto isthmus, which joins New Brunswick to Nova Scotia; and Gaelic speakers, who keep their language alive to this day, have settled along the northern coast of Nova Scotia and in Cape Breton Island. Later movement within what is now Canada has added more complication by bringing to the area round Sydney, Nova Scotia, immigrants from Newfoundland whose descendants still speak an English very closely resembling that of Newfoundland. It is little wonder that modern Canadian dialect study began in the Maritimes, with the work of Henry Alexander (who was then a professor at Dalhousie University, Halifax) in the late 1930s and early 1940s.

Pronunciation. In many ways Maritimers share the pronunciation habits of other Canadians: they rhyme *greasy* with *fleecy;* they pronounce *cot* and *caught* identically; they give to *knives* and *knife* their own diphthongs, as they do to *loud* and *out;* and they pronounce their /r/ sounds. However, this last habit does not apply everywhere in the Maritimes: many inhabitants of the island of Grand Manan, New Brunswick, speak a dialect in which /r/ before a consonant and final /r/ are not pronounced; and in Lunenburg County, although the /r/ is usually pronounced, it is given a pronunciation not found elsewhere in Canada.

But if the Maritimers use for the most part the same sounds that other Canadians use, they do not always use them in the words in which other Canadians would use them. To begin with, a Maritimer may well call himself a *Marintimer* or even a *Marimtimer*. Many Maritimers still pronounce an /f/ in *lieutenant,* and the word *aunt* is often pronounced with /ä/, especially in New Brunswick, where this pronunciation is common enough almost to serve as a dialect marker. In Nova Scotia and Prince Edward Island the word *almond* is often pronounced with /l/. In Nova Scotia the words *calm* and *father* frequently used to be heard with a pronunciation rather like /ă/; nowadays, however, a pronunciation with /ä/, like that heard elsewhere in Canada, seems to be spreading in both words. In Lunenburg County /d/ and /t/ are often used where the rest of Canada, including the Maritimes, has /th/ and /th/; and at the ends of words the sounds /p/, /t/, and /k/ often replace /b/, /d/, and /g/, respectively. In and around North Sydney, Nova Scotia, immigration from Newfoundland has produced a group of speakers who, native Nova Scotians though they be, frequently use /ī/ where their fellow Nova Scotians use /oi/. In Prince Edward Island the word *vase* is most commonly pronounced /vās/, in contrast with the situation in the other two Maritime Provinces, where the most common pronunciation is /väz/. Finally, there is some evidence for the existence in Prince Edward Island of the substitution of /oi/ for /ī/ in words such as *nice, fine,* and *tide.*

Grammar and Syntax. In the Maritimes dialects you will hear many of the nonstandard morphological and syntactic usages common elsewhere in Canada. A Maritimer is just as ready as any other Canadian to tell you that she *swum* the river or *clum* the tree, or that he *has drank* a glass of rum, but there seems to be no recognizable dialectal distribution of these features. However, a few features of morphology and syntax do appear to have Maritime associations. The use of *some, right,* and to a lesser extent *real* as adverbs—*It's some cold. You're right welcome. It's real hot*—does appear to be commoner in the Maritimes than elsewhere in Canada. In Nova Scotia the verb *happen* can be followed directly by a pronoun, without the intervention of a preposition: *This might happen you tomorrow* might well be a Nova Scotian's warning of trouble to come. Finally, although the use of *wore* for *worn,* as in *I'm wore out,* is certainly not unknown in other parts of Canada, it seems to be more popular in Prince Edward Island than elsewhere.

Vocabulary. Naturally, the Maritimes share much of the vocabulary of the rest of Canada (see CANADIAN ENGLISH). Some words, of course, common in English in all areas, have a special Maritime sense. Thus, in British Columbia *the Island* is Vancouver Island; but in southern New Brunswick it is the island of Grand Manan, while elsewhere in the Maritimes it is Prince Edward Island.

(1) Some words, though they circulate in other parts of Canada, are especially characteristic of Maritime speech. Among such are:

bogan /bō-gən/ = 'backwater, narrow, usually quiet stretch of water'
brook = 'small freshwater *stream'; elsewhere in Canada often *stream*
frosting = 'hard sugar on top of a cake'; now giving place to *icing*
jill-poke = 'log with one end lodged on the bank or bottom of a stream'
pung = 'low sled with box seats'
shiretown = 'county town'
station, bus station = 'bus terminal'

*Appears as separate entry

(2) Some terms are shared by two of the three Maritime Provinces. Among these are:

Boston states, the Boston states (New Brunswick, Prince Edward Island) = 'New England'
caribou (New Brunswick, Nova Scotia) = 'large North American reindeer'
lender(s), linder(s) (New Brunswick, Prince Edward Island) = 'men's long woolen underwear'
longers (Nova Scotia, Prince Edward Island) = 'the horizontal parts of a post-and-rail fence'
smelt storm (Nova Scotia, Prince Edward Island) = 'storm in late spring'; *robin storm* is common elsewhere in Canada

(3) Some terms seem to belong particularly to one province; among such are:

aftergrass (New Brunswick) = 'second crop of hay, etc.'
jag (Nova Scotia) = 'maximum load of wood that a wagon can transport'
napkin (New Brunswick) = 'small square of cloth or paper for wiping the hands during a meal'; *serviette* is more popular elsewhere in Canada
salute (Nova Scotia) = 'rough, usually derisory serenade'; **shivaree* is used elsewhere in Canada
stand (Nova Scotia) = 'a farm and its outbuildings'
stick (Nova Scotia) = 'length of lumber'

*Appears as separate entry

(4) Some words recall the settlement history of the province to which they belong:

clart (Prince Edward Island) = 'slovenly woman'; commonest among islanders of Irish descent (probably of Irish origin)
coal scuttle (New Brunswick) = 'fireside container for coal' (British in origin, but probably came with the Loyalists from New York and New Jersey)
comfortable (New Brunswick) = 'thick quilt' (probably of Loyalist origin)
double-runner (New Brunswick) = 'bobsled'; links New Brunswick speech with the NEW ENGLAND DIALECT
foother (Prince Edward Island) = 'to trifle, act ineffectually'; use and origin similar to *clart*, above
kist (Prince Edward Island) = 'chest, box'; common among islanders of Scots descent (originally from Scots)

(5) Some words belong specifically to Lunenburg County. They include terms showing the German influence on the area's speech:

cellar porch = 'roofed entrance to an outside cellarway'
Daks Day = 'Groundhog Day'
handkase = '*cottage cheese'
snits = 'dried apple slices'
winkelaize = 'three-cornered rip in cloth'

*Appears as separate entry

(6) One expression originating in New Brunswick has spread across all of Canada:

main John = 'superintendent, boss' (after the logging baron *John* B. Glasier, 1809–94, of York County, New Brunswick)

(7) The Maritimer's language is enriched by numerous picturesque idioms that are not necessarily peculiar to the Maritimes dialects. For example:

big as a barn door (Nova Scotia) = 'very large'
climb fool's hill (New Brunswick) = 'to commit the follies of youth'
flying ax-handles (Nova Scotia) = 'diarrhea'
one-lunger (Nova Scotia) = 'boat powered by a single-cylinder engine'

maxim. Insofar as a *maxim* is a short, pithy statement expressing a general truth, it is much the same as an aphorism, an adage, or a saying. It has been observed that if the term has any distinguishing characteristic, it is that a maxim should go beyond mere expression of truth and give advice either implicitly or explicitly. By this strict definition La Rochefoucauld's famous statement that "a gentleman in love is permitted to behave like a madman, but not like an ass" would definitely qualify as a maxim. But since most of the other statements in La Rochefoucauld's great *Maxims* probably would not, it might be prudent not to insist too much on the definition. Presumably, anyone who can write as well as La Rochefoucauld is free to call his aphorisms by any name he wants. See also APHORISM; APOTHEGM; PROVERB.

may. See CAN, MAY.

may be = 'can possibly be' is spelled as two words: *Next Tuesday's performance may be sold out.* As an adverb *maybe* is fully standard and interchangeable with 'perhaps': *Maybe the rain will hold off till tomorrow.* The spelling *mebbe* represents dialectal or informal speech, as in the phrase *mebbe so, mebbe not.* (Will Rogers preferred *maby* or even *mabe.*)

may can. See DOUBLE MODALS.

me. The rule is that *I* is the subjective form and *me* the objective form, but there are certain exceptions.

(1) Some people are still punctilious in always saying *It is I, It's I, It was I.* But probably most of us now find this use a bit unnatural, even pretentious, and say *It is me,* etc.

> A rush of people, maybe 300 in all, pressed forward. Was this me standing there among them?
>
> —Peter Gorton Jenkins, *Reader's Digest*

Notice that in the case of *That's me,* the alternative *That's I* is almost impossible.

◇ ***Recommendation.*** Those who prefer *It is I* are of course impeccably correct. But we now regard *It is me* as acceptable in virtually all situations.

(2) *Me,* often coupled with a noun or name, is often used informally as a straight subject.

> Or, me and some guys my age were up on the steep Ohio hillside. . . .
>
> —Pete Rose, *The Pete Rose Story*

Although this subjective use of *me* occurs widely in informal speech, it is not acceptable as standard. It can be used to give a consciously casual or folksy effect, as in the quotation above.

(3) *Between you and I* was used by Shakespeare and was in reputable use into the 18th century, so that some modern observers have defended it. We regard it as a definite error; *between you and me* is the only correct form, at least in formal contexts.

media. This plural is showing strong signs of turning into a singular. When the different forms or systems of news dissemination are considered separately, the newspapers, for example, are one *medium,* and magazines, radio, and television are other *media*; or they may be divided into only two, *the print medium* and *the broadcast* (or *electronic*) *medium.* Collectively, they are *the media.* But the entire news world or industry is now often referred to as an undifferentiated mass: *good media coverage; everyone who works in media.* From this it is a short step to making the word a true singular: *The media reflects its own values. Does media cause violence?*

◇ ***Recommendation.*** This evolution seems natural enough and may soon establish itself. But it is still too new to be acceptable as good usage. We advise keeping *media* as a plural and using *medium* for the singular.

medias res. See IN MEDIAS RES.

medium. See MEDIA; PLURALS.

mention. See ALLUDE, ALLUSION.

metaphor. A *metaphor* is an implied comparison. When, for example, we say of someone that "he's a real weasel," we are speaking metaphorically. We do not mean to be taken literally; what we are suggesting is that the person in question has certain qualities we associate with weasels—furtiveness, perhaps, or untrustworthiness, or even opportunism. Like most other metaphors, what this comparison loses in precision, it hopes to gain in vividness and immediacy. Concepts, qualities, and actions, as well as people and objects, can be compared metaphorically.

If, as it is commonly defined, metaphor is merely one among a large number of figures of speech, it is certainly a whale among minnows. We virtually swim in a sea of metaphor. (Alert readers will note that our whale has now become a sea: we shall turn to the question of mixed metaphor shortly.) Metaphor is the basis of everything that is figurative, allusive, and poetic in our language. Indeed, it may be central to our very thought processes. Nearly 100 years ago the great American philosopher William James observed: "Pure similarity must work before the abstraction can work which is based upon it. . . . [Thus] the primeval man will say, not 'the bread is hard' but 'the bread is stone.'" In our own day numerous writers have speculated that the penchant for metaphorical thinking may be an inherent feature of the human brain structure.

Be that as it may, our everyday speech is more heavily encrusted with metaphor than most of us realize. Thousands of common English words are the burned-out embers of forgotten metaphors—the *head* of a bed, for example, or the *arms* of a chair or the *leg* of a piano. Battalions of Greek- and Latin-derived words have entered the English language metaphorically changed from their original meanings. Thus, to *suspect* derives from the Latin *suspicere* = 'to raise one's head'—hence, by progressive stages, 'to take notice of, wonder about, look askance, doubt, distrust.'

If these are "dead" metaphors (as the usage expert H. W. Fowler called them), many others might be described as "half-dead." These are the clichés or slang expressions that have so lost their original savor that we recognize them as metaphors only when we stop to think about them. *Game plan; gimlet-eyed; breathing down the neck of; hawks and doves; off the wall; financial liquidity; Madison Avenue* (the advertising business); *open-and-shut case; blockbuster novel*—the list could be multiplied almost indefinitely.

Although the mortality rate among metaphors is high, the supply seems inexhaustible. We can hardly pick up a book, magazine, or newspaper without being exposed to a shower of new metaphors. Thus, a film critic laments the appearance of Laurence Olivier in a movie the critic doesn't like:

> No amount of actorish busy-ness can hide the fact that this great man is marooned in the middle of an empty parking lot of a movie.
> —Vincent Canby, *New York Times*

Or a former President, perhaps drawing on an image from a popular film about a killer shark, reflects on the Watergate scandal:

> Two *Washington Post* reporters had been instrumental in toppling a President; other "investigative" journalists smelled blood in the water and . . .
> —Gerald R. Ford, *A Time to Heal*

Insofar as metaphors can be classified, the most important subcategories are SIMILE, *metonymy*, and *synecdoche*. For most practical purposes, simile and metaphor are the same, the technical distinction being that metaphor implies a comparison, whereas simile expresses it using *like, as*, or *as if*. For the most part, similes tend to be a little weaker than pure metaphors, but they can nevertheless be used to considerable effect:

> In a community [Hollywood] where facial tics were commonplace, his were exceptional; they literally pursued each other across his face like snipe.
> —S. J. Perelman,
> *Baby, It's Cold Outside*

> He came back softly, holding his pork pie under his arm, debonair as a French count in a college play.
> —Raymond Chandler,
> *Farewell, My Lovely*

> Listening to Britons dining out is like watching people play first-class tennis with imaginary balls.
> —Margaret Halsey, *With Malice Towards Some*

Metonymy refers to that group of metaphors in which a word or phrase is replaced by something usually associated with it—*Rome*, for example, instead of *the papacy*. Metonymy is a favorite, if sometimes rather tiresome, device of journalists:

> The Pentagon could save more than $400 million a year, for example, if Congress. . . —*Newsweek*

Synecdoche is a refinement of metonymy, in which a word or phrase is replaced by something referring to one of its parts. Thus, in describing a regatta we might speak of a squadron of *20 sail* when we meant *20 sailboats*. Similarly, there was a point in the evolution of teen-age slang when clothes could only be called *threads* and cars *wheels*.

Metaphors (or similes) are also familiar ingredients in many other features of style. When a metaphor is considerably extended—say, beyond the confines of a few sentences or paragraphs—it may develop into one of the literary forms known as *parable*, FABLE, or ALLEGORY. While there are some technical distinctions among these forms, they all tell stories or present situations meant to be taken at face value *and* to be understood in terms other than those actually described. Sometimes the literal aspect of such works proves so entertaining that the underlying sense tends to be ignored. Thus, Jonathan Swift's masterpiece, *Gulliver's Travels*, the adventures of a shipwrecked Englishman among giants, diminutive people, and other fantastic creatures, has often been regarded as merely a charming tale with special appeal for children. But the mature reader will find, beneath Swift's beguiling metaphorical surface, a dark subtext satirizing nearly every human folly and vice.

The eternal quest for metaphor is not without its perils. The most famous of these is the dreaded *mixed metaphor*, a figure in which unrelated images are slapped together often to the point of absurdity. The mixed metaphor has long been a favorite of humorists:

> This is playing with fire, old chap. Keep your nose clean; you are treading on dangerous ground.
> —S. J. Perelman, *Crazy Like a Fox*

Unfortunately, mixed metaphors are likely to spring more from carelessness than from any conscious desire to amuse:

> Each used the referendum as simply another stick to beat the government and to ride particular political hobby horses. —*Winnipeg Tribune*

Perhaps the British writer George Orwell had the last word on mixed metaphors. They are, he observed, "a sure sign that the author is not interested in what he is saying."

Extended metaphors can also be troublesome. Used with taste, an extended metaphor can be a powerful rhetorical device:

> Most people, and Christians in particular, are thermometers that record or register the temperature of majority opinion, not thermostats that transform and regulate the temperature of society. —Martin Luther King, Jr., *Strength to Love*

> If we can stand up to him [Hitler], all Europe may be free and the life of the world may move forward into broad sunlit uplands. But if we fail, the whole world . . . will sink into the abyss of a new Dark Age, made more sinister, and perhaps more protracted, by the lights of a perverted science.
> —Winston Churchill, *Their Finest Hour*

But, carried too far, an extended metaphor can easily begin to sound like self-parody:

> However, all of this, though close to the "heart," is nonetheless merely a leaf on the activist artichoke. There are other, tender leaves—federal judges who prefer intellectual gymnastics. . . . The very heart of the artichoke is the nonsensical concept of the corporation as being entitled to all of the legal protections afforded human beings under the Constitution.
> —letter, *New York Times*

And, at worst, an extended metaphor can simply get out of hand:

> "We are out on a limb," he said. "It was cut off by the Supreme Court. We don't know whether we are up in the air, or whether we will be able to tape the limb back on, but we are in limbo."
> —*New York Times*

It would be convenient if we could set down precise rules as to what constitutes a mixed or an overextended metaphor, but in many cases the only sure guide is the sensitivity of the metaphor user. It is, for example, certainly permissible for an orator to change metaphors in the course of a speech. Doing so will produce a mixed metaphor only when the dissimilar images are placed too close together. But when the speech is being prepared, what constitutes "too close together" is something that only the orator can determine—at his or her peril.

By the same token, some metaphors that are neither mixed nor overextended can nevertheless be inept.

> . . . the Russians have every expectation of soon . . . neutralizing the large submarine . . . yet we are proceeding willy-nilly to put all our deterrent eggs in few and fewer underwater baskets.
> —George J. Keegan, Jr., *New York Times*

As usual, it is the skill of the metaphor user that finally determines whether a metaphor is weak or strong, foolish or illuminating.

Yet perhaps the greatest peril lies not in the abuse of metaphor but in its uncritical acceptance. We must constantly remind ourselves that even the best metaphors are likely to be inexact—that, for the sake of richness and power, they regularly blur or ignore distinctions that may be important. When we indulge in the undeniable pleasures of figurative speaking, we owe it to ourselves never to lose touch with literal thinking.

For all its implicit dangers, metaphor nevertheless remains one of the glories—perhaps the paramount glory—of our language. Any sampling of the world's most famous quotations will run overwhelmingly to metaphor. Here is one such collection of quotations. See how many of the sources you can identify (answers at the end of this entry):

1. Ye are the salt of the earth
2. the wine-dark sea
3. the slings and arrows of outrageous fortune
4. She walks in beauty, like the night
5. I should have been a pair of ragged claws/Scuttling across the floors of silent seas
6. The fog comes/on little cat feet
7. No man is an island
8. A foolish consistency is the hobgoblin of little minds
9. As idle as a painted ship/Upon a painted ocean
10. I am become as a sounding brass, or a tinkling cymbal
11. Ah, but a man's reach should exceed his grasp
12. Life's but a walking shadow, a poor player/That struts and frets his hour upon the stage

Such quotations, cherished ornaments of our language, remind us that at the heart of metaphor lies something profoundly mysterious. If we were asked to say what makes a good metaphor, we might be tempted to reply, "Aptness." But on reflection, we would have to admit that some of the most powerful metaphors are not, in the normal sense, apt at all:

> The woods decay, the woods decay and fall,
> The vapours weep their burden to the ground.
> Man comes and tills the field and lies beneath,
> And after many a summer dies the swan.
> —Alfred, Lord Tennyson, *Tithonus*

Commenting on these lines, the author Aldous Huxley (who would later use this haunting image of the swan as the title of one of his novels) asked:

> Why the swan? Heaven knows. The swan is a luminous irrelevance, sailing for a moment into the picture with all its curves and its whiteness and its

> mythologies, and sailing out again to the strains of a defunctive music, fabulously mournful. Tennyson knew his magician's business.
>
> —*Texts and Pretexts*

Magic. That may be as close as we can get to explaining the mystery. Some metaphors simply seem to have in them a strange evocative power that can transport our senses and emotions far beyond the frontiers of ordinary meaning. It is the business of poetry to explore the uses of this magical power, but probably no poet will ever fully understand the mystery itself—its (to borrow a famous Shakespearean metaphor) "glassy essence."

(**Answers:** 1. Bible, Matthew 5:13; 2. Homer, *The Iliad;* 3. Shakespeare, *Hamlet;* 4. Lord Byron, *She Walks in Beauty;* 5. T. S. Eliot, *The Love Song of J. Alfred Prufrock;* 6. Carl Sandburg, *Fog;* 7. John Donne, *Devotions XVII;* 8. Ralph Waldo Emerson, *Self-Reliance;* 9. Samuel Taylor Coleridge, *The Rime of the Ancient Mariner;* 10. Bible, 1 Corinthians 13:1; 11. Robert Browning, *Andrea del Sarto;* 12. Shakespeare, *Macbeth*)

metonymy. See METAPHOR.

Middle English. ***Origin.*** Even before 1066 and the Norman Conquest of England, a radical change was under way in the English language. In common with their Germanic relatives on the Continent and in Iceland, the Anglo-Saxons spoke a language with many word endings, three genders (masculine, feminine, and neuter), and the characteristically convoluted sentence pattern still found in more conservative Germanic languages, such as German and Icelandic. Sometime around the year 1000, however, for reasons impossible to determine, the English language began to simplify. Words started to drop their inflectional endings, the old three-gender system began to yield to the all-purpose "natural gender" that we have in Modern English, and the old Germanic word order gave way to a word order similar to that of English today.

With the conquest of 1066, English ceased to be the officially recognized language of government and high culture. Norman French replaced it as the prestige language for the next 200 years. Englishmen went on speaking English, however, and the conservative restraints that had slowed the language's evolution before the conquest were now gone. Reduced to the status of a vernacular of the have-nots, English evolved very rapidly. Tendencies that had been there before 1066 now came to the fore; and as the enforced cohabitation of conquered with conquerors wore on from decades into centuries, the language received so many new words from French that by 1400 more than half of its total vocabulary consisted of French imports. From the 100 percent Germanic tongue that it had been before 1066, English became a hybrid reflecting the bilingual situation in which its speakers lived. Middle English was born—the language as spoken between roughly 1200 and 1500, marking the transition between Old and Modern English.

Nowhere was the seesaw situation between English and French more evident than in the schoolrooms of 14th-century England. As the century began, French was still the only language of instruction. An Englishman writing in 1327 complains:

> Children in scole agenst the usage and manere of alle othere naciouns beeth compelled for to leve hire owne langage, and for to construe hir lessouns and here thynges in Frensche, and so they haveth seth the Normans come first in to Engelond. Also gentil men children beeth itaught to speke Frensche from the tyme that they beeth irokked in here cradel, and kunneth speke and playe with a childes broche; and uplondisshe men wil likne hymself to gentil men, and fondeth with greet besynesse for to speke Frensche, for to be itolde of.
>
> **Translation**
> Children in school against the usage and manner of all other nations are compelled to leave off their own language and to construe their lessons and their subjects in French, and so they have since the Normans came first into England. Also gentlemen's children are taught to speak French from the time that they are rocked in their cradle, and

> can speak and play with a child's brooch [teething ring?]; and upland [rustic] men will liken themselves to gentlemen and try with great busyness to speak French, so as to be talked about.

A comment on the foregoing, inserted in the text a couple of generations later, about 1385, shows that by that time English in the form we call Middle English had regained primacy as the national language of England:

> This manere was moche iused tofore the firste moreyn and is siththe sumdel ichaunged; for Iohn Cornwaile, a maister of grammer, chaunged the lore in gramer scole and construccioun of Frensche in to Englische; and Richard Pencriche lerned that manere techynge of hym and othere men of Pencrich; so that now, the yere of oure Lord a thowsand thre hundred and foure score and fyve, and of the secounde kyng Richard after the conquest nyne, in all the gramere scoles of Engelond, children leveth Frensche and construeth and lerneth an Englische, and haveth therby avauntage in oon side and disavauntage in another side; here avauntage is, that they lerneth her gramer in lasse tyme than children were iwoned to doo; disavauntage is that now children of gramer scole conneth na more Frensche than can hir lift heele, and that is harme for hem and they schulle passe the see and trauaille in straunge landes and in many other places. Also gentil men haueth now moche ileft for to teche here children Frensche.

> **Translation**
> This system was much used before the first murrain [the Black Death, 1348] and since then has somewhat changed; for John Cornwaile, a grammar school master, changed the teaching in grammar school and the construing of French into English; and Richard Pencriche learned that system [of] teaching from him and other men from Pencrich; so that now, the year of our Lord a thousand three hundred and four score and five [1385], and of the second king Richard, after the conquest the ninth, in all the grammar schools of England, children abandon French and construe and learn in English, and have thereby advantage on one side and disadvantage on another side, their advantage is, that they learn their grammar in less time than children were wont to do; [the] disadvantage is that now grammar school children know no more French than their left heel knows, and that is harm for them if they shall pass the sea and travel in foreign countries and in many other places. Also, gentlemen have now much neglected to teach their children French.

In only 60 years the tables had been completely turned, and the situation of English speakers vis-à-vis the French language was by 1400 already exactly what it is today, with the majority knowing "no more French than their left heel knows." The return of English to the classroom paralleled its comeback in the courtroom and at court. Poets and other writers arose on all sides, and the race was on to shape and polish the vernacular into a literary tongue rivaling French and Italian. A great variety of material has survived, written in various dialects of Middle English, and much of it is high-quality writing.

Chaucer. Regional differences in Middle English were sharper than they are in the present-day language. It was inevitable that a single prestige dialect should emerge that would be the Middle English ancestor of our modern literary language. The dialect spoken in and around London came out on top, partly because then as now London was the political and commercial capital of the land, and partly because of the genius of one man, Geoffrey Chaucer (c. 1340–1400), the most important writer of the entire Middle English period. His *Canterbury Tales,* translated into many languages including Modern English, delights audiences to this day. Chaucer's language represents a masterly blend of the Romance and the Germanic. A high proportion of the poet's vocabulary derives from French, Italian, and Latin. Chaucer spent several years in Italy and France and translated major contemporaries of both countries, including Dante, Boccaccio, and Jean de Meung—consequently enriching our language with many personal borrowings and also introducing numerous French and Italian poetic forms, which have been with us ever since. At the same time, Chaucer's idiom exhibits a vigorous earthiness reflecting the older Anglo-Saxon word stock, the traditional taste for alliteration, and the bumpier cadence characteristic of Germanic. Chaucer created the pattern for all of literary English down to the present time, and his influence on our language ranks with that of Shakespeare and the King James Bible. Here is a passage (with translation) from the celebrated "Prologue" to *The Canterbury Tales:*

With us ther was a doctour of physik,
With us there was a doctor of physic [physician],
In al this world ne was ther noon him lyk
In all this world there was none like him
To speke of phisik and of surgerye,
To speak about medicine and surgery,
For he was grounded in astronomye.
For he was grounded in astrology.
He kepte his pacient a ful greet del
He kept his patient to a large extent
In houres, by his magik naturel.
In hours [alive], by means of his natural magic.
Wel coude he fortunen the ascendent
Well could he give a good fortune to the ascendant
Of his images for his pacient.
Of his [the patient's] constellations for his patient.
He knew the cause of everich maladye,
He knew the cause of every illness,
Were it of hoot or cold, or moiste, or drye,
Were it of hot or cold, or moist, or dry,
And where engendred, and of what humour;
And where engendered, and of what humor;
He was a verrey parfit pratisour.
He was a truly perfect practitioner.
The cause y-knowe, and of his harm the rote,
The cause and root of his [the patient's] harm being known,
Anon he yaf the seke man his bote.
Anon he gave the sick man his remedy.
Ful redy hadde he his apothecaries
Full ready had he his apothecaries
To sende him drogges and his letuaries
To send him drugs and his electuaries [remedies]
For ech of hem made other for to winne;
For each of them [doctor and pharmacist] made the other profit;
Hir frendscipe nas nat new to beginne.
Their friendship was not newly begun.
Wel knew he th'olde Esculapius
Well knew he the ancient Aesculapius
And Deiscorides, and eek Rufus,
And Dioscorides, and also Rufus,
Old Ypocras, Haly, and Galien;
Old Hippocrates, Hali, and Galen;
Serapion, Razis, and Avicen;
Serapion, Rhazes, and Avicenna;
Averrois, Damascien, and Constantyn;
Averrhoës, Damascene, and Constantine;
Bernard, and Gatesden, and Gilbertyn.
Bernard, and Gatesden, and Gilbert.
Of his diete mesurable was he,
Of his diet moderate was he,
For it was of no superfluitee,
For it was of no superfluity,
But of great norissing and digestible.
But of great nourishment, and digestible.
His studie was but litel on the bible.
His study was but little on the Bible.
In sangwin and in pers he clad was al,
All in blood-red and sky blue he was clad,
Lyned with taffata and with sendal;
Lined with taffeta and with thin silk;
And yet he was but esy of dispence;
And yet he was but moderate in spending;
He kepte that he wan in pestilence.
He kept what he earned in plague time.
For gold in physik is a cordial,
For gold in medicine is a cordial,
Therfore he lovede gold in special.
Therefore he loved gold especially.

Reading a Middle English Text Aloud. The question of how Middle English sounded is

Pronouncing Middle English

Letter	Pronunciation
Vowels and Diphthongs	
a	(1) /ä/ *as in* March (2) /ȧ/ *as in* Aprille
ai, ay	/ī/ *as in* gay
au, aw	/ô/ *as in* straunge, Caunterbury
e	(1) /ĕ/ *as in* vertu (2) /ə/ *as in* ende /**ĕn**-də/; *occurs mostly at the ends of words and is often either dropped or elided with a following vowel* (3) /ā/ *as in* clene (4) /ē/ *as in* swete
ei, ey	/ī/ *as in* wey
i	(1) /ĭ/ *as in* bidde (2) /ē/ *as in* ire
y	/ē/ *as in* melodye /mā-lō-**dē**-ə/ (= *'melody'*)
ie	/ē/ *as in* mischief
o	(1) /ô/ *as in* botme (2) /o͞o/ *as in* love (3) /o͞o/ *as in* sote
o, oo	/ō/ *as in* stoon
ou, ow	/o͞o/ *as in* flour
ogh	/ouKH/ *as in* y-nogh

Letter	Pronunciation
ough	/o͞oKH/ *as in* thoughte
u	(1) /ŭ/ *as in* cut (2) /ü/ *as in* just; *in many words a drawn-out sound, as in* nature /nȧ-**tü**-rə/
we	(1) /wə/ *as in* arwes /**är**-wəz/ (= *'arrows'*) (2) /o͞o/ *as in* halwes /**hȧl**-o͞oz/ (= *'shrines'*)
Consonants* Consonants are pronounced as in Modern English, with the following exceptions.	
gh	/KH/ *as in* droghte
gn	(1) /gn/ *in originally Germanic words, as* gnow /gno͞o/ (= *'gnawed'*) (2) /n/ *in words borrowed from French, as* digne /**dē**-nə/ (= *'worthy, honorable'*)
kn	/kn/ *as in* knotte /**knôt**-tə/ (= *'knot, gist of a story'*)
ng	/ngg/ *as in* thing /thĭngg/; *like* /ngg/ *in Modern English* finger
r	*trilled, especially in initial positions*

**In older English spelling (c. 1200–c. 1600)* v *is frequently used for* u, *and vice versa; also,* i *often appears for* j.

of more than academic interest. To teach yourself Old English pronunciation so as to read a masterpiece like *Beowulf* out loud, you almost have to be a linguist with good control of another Germanic language such as Norse. This isn't true of Middle English, however, and the rewards of learning how to pronounce it are considerable—you can read without too much difficulty and with reasonable correctness such marvelous works as *Sir Gawain and the Green Knight, Piers Plowman, Pearl, Everyman,* and *The Voyage of Sir John Mandeville,* as well as *The Canterbury Tales.* It is of course impossible to read Middle English verse smoothly unless you learn the pronunciation. The chart above provides a basic outline—it approximates the dialect spoken in London around 1400.

The most famous of all Middle English texts is the opening of Chaucer's *Canterbury Tales.* We give the text here, with pronunciation and a word-for-word translation. Don't worry about where the verse accents fall. If you read it over and over, Chaucer's language will soon come naturally to you.

When that Aprille with his shoures sote
hwȧn *th*ȧt ȧ-**prĭl**-lə wĭth ĭz **sho͞o**-rəz **so͞o**-tə
When April with his showers sweet

The droghte of Marche hath perced to the rote,
*th*ə droukht ôv märch hȧth **pĕr**-səd tō *th*ə **ro͞o**-tə
The drought of March has pierced to the root,

And bathed every veyne in swich licour,
ȧnd **bä**-*th*əd **āv**-rĭ vīn ĭn swĭch lĭ-**ko͞or**
And bathed every vein in such liquor,

Of which vertu engendred is the flour;
ôv hwĭch vĕr-**tü** ĕn-**jĕn**-drĕd ĭz *th*ə flo͞or
By whose power the flower is generated;

Whan Zephirus eek with his swete breeth
hwȧn **zā**-fĭ-rəs āk wĭth ĭz **swē**-tə brāth
When Zephyr also with his sweet breath

Inspired hath in every holt and heeth
ĭn-**spē**-rəd hȧth ĭn **ēv**-rĭ hôlt ȧnd hāth
Has quickened in every holt and heath

The tendre croppes, and the yonge sonne
*th*ə **tĕn**-drə **krô**-pəz ȧnd *th*ə **yo͝ong**-gə **so͝o**-nə
The tender crops, and the young sun

Hath in the Ram his halfe cours y-ronne,
hȧth ĭn *th*ə Räm hĭz **hȧl**-fə ko͞ors ĭ-**ro͞o**-nə
Has in the Ram run one half of his course,

And smale fowles maken melodye,
ȧnd **smȧ**-lə **fo͞o**-ləz **mȧ**-kən mā-lō-**dē**-ə
And small birds make melody,

That slepen al the night with open yë,
*th*ȧt **slā**-pən ȧl *th*ə nĭkht wĭth **ō**-pən **ē**-yə
That sleep all the night with open eye,

(So priketh hem nature in hir corages):
sō **prĭ**-kəth ĕm nȧ-**tür** ĭn ĭr ko͞o-**rä**-jəz
(*Thus nature pricks them in their dispositions*):

Than longen folk to goon on pilgrimages
*th*ȧn **lông**-gən fôlk tō gōn ôn pĭl-grĭ-**mä**-jəz
Then people long to go on pilgrimages

(And palmers for to seken straunge strondes)
ȧnd **päl**-mĕrz fôr tō **sā**-kən **strôn**-jə **strän**-dəz
(*And palmers to go seeking foreign shores*)

To ferne halwes, couthe in sondry londes;
tō **fĕr**-nə **hȧl**-o͞oz ko͞oth ĭn **so͝on**-drĭ **lôn**-dəz
To distant shrines well known in sundry lands;

And specially, from every shires ende
ȧnd **spā**-sē-ȧ-**lē** frôm ā-vrĭ **shē**-rəz **ĕn**-də
And especially, from every shire's end

Of Engelond, to Caunterbury they wende,
ôv **ĕng**-gə-lônd tō **kôn**-tər-brĭ *th*ī **wĕn**-də
Of England, to Canterbury they wend,

The holy blisful martir for to seke,
*th*ə **hō**-lē **blĭs**-fŭl **mär**-tîr fôr tō **sā**-kə
In order to seek out the holy blessed martyr,

That hem hath holpen, whan that they were seke.
*th*ȧt ĕm ȧth **hôl**-pən hwȧn *th*ȧt *th*ī wĕr **sā**-kə
Who has helped them when they were sick.

Midland dialect. The Midland speech area is a large central section of the United States between the Northern and Southern dialect areas. The dialect itself is divided into NORTH MIDLAND and SOUTH MIDLAND.

Pronunciation. The /r/ sound is seldom dropped after vowels but is frequently added to words such as *wash* and *Washington:* /wärsh/, /**wärsh**-ĭng-tən/. The /ĕ/ sound is used in words such as *Mary* and *dairy:* /**mĕr**-ē/, /**dĕr**-ē/. *With* is regularly pronounced /wĭth/ not /wĭ*th*/.

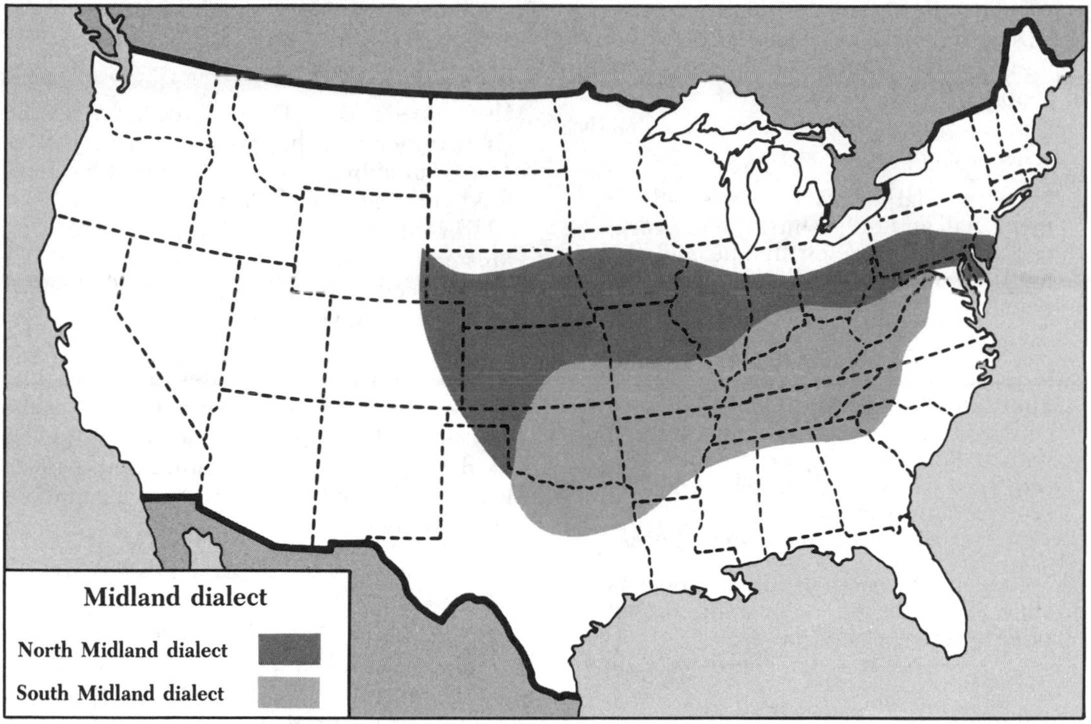

Vocabulary.

blinds = 'window shades'
clum = 'past tense of *climb*'
dip (especially North Midland; old-fashioned) = 'syrup'
draggy = 'lethargic, restless'
fishing worm = '*earthworm used as bait'
fourteen-day pickles = 'kind of pickles'
fox fire = 'light caused by fungi in decaying wood'
French harp (also Gulf Southern) = 'harmonica'
* **goober** = 'peanut'
green beans = 'string beans'
guttering, gutter pipe = '*gutter'
hull (peas *or* **beans)** = 'to shell'
johnboat = 'small rowboat'
keen, king (used especially by black speakers) = '(of shoes) having sharply pointed toes'
later (used especially by black speakers) = 'goodbye, farewell'
little piece = 'short distance'
mango, mango pepper = 'sweet or bell pepper'
medium, medium strip = 'median strip of a highway'
mud dauber (also General Northern) = 'wasp that builds a nest of mud'
nit fly (also Gulf Southern) = 'horse botfly'
outside baby *or* **child** (used especially by black speakers) = '*illegitimate child'
poke = 'bag, sack'
rick (of hay) = 'pile of hay stored outdoors'
rid *or* **red (the table) off** = 'to clear or clean after a meal'
scrapple (especially Central Atlantic States) = '*headcheese'
skillet = 'frying pan'
snake feeder = '*dragonfly'
sook = 'call to cows'
spouting, spout = 'eaves trough, *gutter'

*Appears as separate entry

might can, might could, etc. See DOUBLE MODALS.

mighty. As an adverb meaning 'very,' *mighty* has a long history in both British and American English but is now primarily American. It is regarded by some conservatives as unacceptable in written use. But there are plenty of people who like to use it for its special flavor of emphasis, which can't be exactly matched by any other word.

> He [my father] was six-feet-three inches tall and rather husky, and everyone around town knew that he could be mighty rough when the occasion demanded.
> —Sam Houston Johnson, *My Brother Lyndon*

> He deserved to have a secret hideout, considering all we made him put up with at the villa. We were mighty curious, nevertheless, about where his secret hideout was.
> —Harpo Marx, *Harpo Speaks*

> We're seven back. If Boston doesn't start losing a few, it's going to get mighty tense around here.
> —Sparky Lyle, *The Bronx Zoo*

◇ ***Recommendation.*** If not quite suitable for the most ceremonial of formal contexts, the adverb *mighty* is Standard American English in all others.

militate against means 'to operate or work against': *The strikers' attitude militates against an early settlement.* Many people say *mitigate against,* but this is an error. See MITIGATE.

minuscule originally refers to a small, cursive script used in the Middle Ages; it can also mean 'lower-case letter.' Its opposite number is *majuscule* = 'large script, upper-case letter.' *Minuscule,* under the influence of *mini-* and *miniature,* is often misspelled *miniscule.* The word is generally used to mean 'very small, trivial, negligible':

> . . . almost all the impact of war must fall on France. We lamented our minuscule contribution on land.
> —Anthony Eden, *The Reckoning*

◇ ***Recommendation.*** The meaning 'very small' is fully established and correct, but the spelling *miniscule,* though widespread, is still an error.

Miss, Mrs., Ms. These three titles are all abbreviations of the word *mistress,* just as *Mr.* is an abbreviation of *master.* Five hundred years ago a male head of household was addressed as Master, a female as Mistress. *Master* came to be abbreviated as *Mr.* and pronounced **/mĭs-tər/.** *Mistress* was abbreviated in two ways: as *Mrs.,* pronounced **/mĭs-ĭz/,** and as *Miss.*

Mrs. had two different uses in the 17th and 18th centuries. It was used before the name of a married woman, as it is today. It was also used to distinguish an unmarried woman from a child. Witness the conflicting citations from the period:

> . . . Just as a woman is not called Mrs. until she is married.
> —Horace Walpole, letter

> Mrs. Veal was a maiden gentlewoman.
> —Daniel Defoe, *The History of Colonel Jack*

> His only sister Mrs. Grizzle . . . was now in the thirtieth year of her maidenhood.
> —Tobias Smollett, *Peregrine Pickle*

By contrast, *Miss* was applied to female babies and young girls:

> Little Miss Davis did dance a jigg after the end of the play.
> —Samuel Pepys, *Diary*

> Enter Miss Hoyden, and Nurse.
> —John Vanbrugh, *The Relapse*

At the same time, *miss* had the less innocent meaning 'prostitute or concubine':

> She being taken to be the Earle of Oxford's Misse (as at this time they began to call lewd women).
> —John Evelyn, *Diary*

The full word *mistress* was also used of both married and unmarried women:

> *Mistress* was then the style of grown up unmarried ladies, though the mother was living; and, for a considerable part

> of the [18th] century, maintained its ground against the infantine term of *miss.* —Henry J. Todd, editor, *A Dictionary of the English Language by Samuel Johnson* (1818)

It was not until the 19th century that *Miss* and *Mrs.* were strictly distinguished in meaning and used as marks of marital status:

> The Miss Gaskells were staying with them. —George Eliot, *George Eliot's Life. . . in Her Letters and Journals*

> Mrs. This and Mrs. That . . . approved of the . . . friends of their respective husbands. —Mary Bridgman, *Robert Lynne*

The 20th century brought yet another change in courtesy titles for women. A third abbreviation of *mistress* was introduced: *Ms.*, pronounced /mĭz/. Like *Mr.*, *Ms.* abbreviated its parent word by first and last letters only. Also like *Mr.*, *Ms.* did not indicate marital status.

Ms. may have been first introduced as early as the 1930s. It was mentioned in the 1949 edition of Mario Pei's *Story of Language*, but it was dropped from the 1965 revision. However, with the advent of computerized mailing lists, *Ms.* filled a real need. Some early computers were programmed to combine *Mrs.* and *Miss* when they encountered a woman's name without a title. Thus, some women received mailings addressed to *Mrss.* Other computers telescoped the title to *Ms.* Then, in March, 1971, a congressman from New York began actively promoting the use of *Ms.*:

> "Is that Miss or Mrs.?" A routine question, perhaps, but many women don't see any reason why they should have to divulge their marital status to a salesclerk or business associate. And neither do I. I suggest that all women refer to themselves as "Ms." . . . The use of Ms. as a neutral form of salutation is not new. Some stenographer's manuals have long suggested it. And in my Congressional office we had independently adopted this same solution some time ago. —Jonathan Bingham, *McCall's*

By October, 1971, the use of *Ms.* had become a subject of controversy. "Ms Isn't Sweeping the Nation," the *New York Times* headlined. Voting for *Ms.* were Bella Abzug, Helen Gurley Brown, Bess Myerson, Eleanor Holmes Norton, and women like the one quoted below:

> "Why should I be asked if I am Miss or Mrs. in almost every application when a man, married or single, simply designates himself Mr.?" asked one young woman. "When you circle 'Miss' on an application form, it's an automatic strike against you." —Enid Nemy, *New York Times*

Voting against *Ms.* were Mrs. Jacob K. Javits, Mrs. John V. Lindsay, Mrs. Richard M. Nixon, and Mrs. Harding Lawrence.

> "I'm much prouder of being Mrs. Harding Lawrence than I was of being Miss Mary Wells," said the woman considered to be one of the leading advertising executives in the country. —Enid Nemy, *New York Times*

In December, 1971, the preview issue of *Ms.* magazine was published. *Ms.* provided this rationale for the new title:

> For more than 20 years, *Ms.* has appeared in secretarial handbooks as the suggested form of address when a woman's marital status is unknown; a sort of neutral combination of *Miss* and *Mrs.*
>
> Now *Ms.* is being adopted as a standard form of address by women who want to be recognized as individuals, rather than being identified by their relationship with a man. After all, if *Mr.* is enough to indicate "male," then *Ms.* should be enough to indicate "female."

In 1972 *Ms.* entered *The American Heritage School Dictionary*. It also entered the world of limericks:

> Mr., Mrs., Miss, Ms.—it's a mess
> Like the argument: Pants vs. Dress.
> Since the genders converge
> In a unisex surge,
> Let's use M.—and have *everyone* guess!
> —Charlotte Curtis, *New York*

By 1973 the battle lines were drawn. Opponents of *Ms.* did not want to guess—they wanted to *know* a woman's marital status:

> If you use Ms. for a female, please indicate in parentheses after the Ms. whether it's Miss or Mrs.
> —notice to Pennsylvania public information officers (quoted), *Ms.*

Others insisted on the traditional titles as a matter of personal preference:

> . . . at the outset, I stipulate that if our correspondence is to continue, I must henceforth be saluted as *Miss* Stafford if the subject at hand has to do with me and my business or as *Mrs.* Liebling if inquiries are being made about my late husband.
> —Jean Stafford, *New York Times*

Not long after, the managing editor of the *New York Times*, A. M. Rosenthal, held that "even convicted criminals remain entitled to the dignity connoted by 'Mr.'" However, he would not allow the title *Ms.* for women who preferred it, arguing, "We can't call everybody what they want to be called." Despite this dictum, *Ms.* was already being used in an extended sense:

> May Hugh Hefner publish *Playboy* from Chicago, where Mr. or Ms. Average finds no objection, and sell it in Indianapolis, where Ms. or Mr. Average may tomorrow say it is porn?
> —Eleanor Jackson Piel, *New York Times*

Today, many people would still agree with the writer who observed:

> Almost no one is neutral about the neutral Ms. It provokes sharp reactions, pro and con.
> —Fern Marja Eckman, *New York Post*

However, in recent years *Ms.* has gained wider acceptance, particularly with younger women. A 1979 study of Smith College graduates from the classes of 1949, 1959, and 1969 revealed:

> Almost half of the youngest group of women preferred to be addressed as Ms., compared with less than 7 percent in the class of '49.
> —Leslie Bennetts, *New York Times*

◇ ***Recommendation.*** The courtesy title *Ms.* was proposed to solve a problem. However, it has compounded the problem. Instead of replacing *Miss* or *Mrs.*, *Ms.* has become a third option. It seems likely that all three titles will continue in use for some time. Thus, usage must depend on circumstance. If you address others with courtesy and respect for their feelings, you may make an occasional misstep—who could avoid it?—but you will not go far wrong. Here are some suggestions and observations.

(1) Always use the title a woman prefers if you know her preference. To do otherwise is to use courtesy titles in a discourteous way.

As a rule of thumb, a woman who identifies herself primarily as a wife and mother will usually prefer the title *Mrs.* before her husband's full name or her first name and his last name: *Mrs. John L. Karney, Mrs. Alice A. Karney.*

A woman who uses her own name, whether married or not, may prefer either *Miss* or *Ms.* as a courtesy title; or, she may prefer no title before her name at all.

Some husbands and wives use both first names instead of *Mr.* and *Mrs.*: *John and Alice Karney.* Some wives keep their own last names, too: *Alice Reed and John Karney.* And some families form new hyphenated names: *John and Alice Reed-Karney.*

When a woman is divorced, she usually returns to the use of her own first name. She may prefer to continue using her ex-husband's last name: *Mrs. Alice A. Karney.* Or, she may return to her own last name: *Ms. Alice Reed.*

(2) If you do not know a woman's preference, you can avoid titles altogether. For example, a letter can be addressed to *Alice Karney*, with the salutation *Dear Alice Karney.*

(3) Some publications, like the famous entertainment trade paper cited below, have adopted a last-name-only style for women as well as for men:

> After 67 years of referring to females as Miss (or, where known, as Mrs.), VARI-

ETY is abandoning chivalry and henceforth will treat ladies the same as men in news copy and reviews, by last name only, without designations of Miss, Mrs., or Ms.—except where absolutely necessary, as in Mrs. John Doe. Thus a Helen Hayes or Lucille Ball will, after introduction by full name, be referred to as Hayes or Ball. It is believed that no sex designation is a higher form of heightened consciousness than the compromise, "Ms."

The *Los Angeles Times* uses this style for women who are being written about for their own accomplishments. It reserves the *Mrs.* for women being written about, or identified, as wives. Thus, Eleanor Roosevelt is called "Roosevelt," but Nancy Reagan is "Mrs. Reagan."

Here are some examples of *Times* usage:

> Secretary of State March Fong Eu . . . filed the required papers Tuesday to run for a third term. . . . Democrat Eu is primarily responsible for managing statewide elections (her office counts the vote). . . .
>
> If this is to be public broadcasting's last stand, Sharon Rockefeller is ready for the fight. Rockefeller, chairman of the Corporation for Public Broadcasting, came out swinging here this week. . . .
>
> For an initially shy person, Roosevelt led an extraordinarily public life. Part was of her own choosing. . . .
>
> —Laura Green
>
> . . . a birthday party honoring Jean (Mrs. Douglas C.) Liechty.

(4) Don't use *Ms.* for historical personages who have long been titled *Mrs.* For example, Elizabeth Barrett Browning should remain *Mrs. Browning.* To dub her retroactively *Ms. Browning* would create an undesired comic effect because anachronistic.

See also CHAIRMAN; FEMALE-GENDER WORD FORMS; MAN; -MAN; PARALLEL STYLE; WOMAN, LADY, GIRL.

mitigate is often mistakenly used in the phrase *mitigate against* to mean 'have an adverse effect on, work against':

> Timing mitigates against the appearance of front-line American pros on the Asia circuit.
>
> —Mark McCormack, *Golf Annual*
>
> . . . the three-dimensional quality of the image on the Shroud. . . . This, too, mitigates against any hypothesis that the image was painted. . . .
>
> —Barbara J. Culliton, *Science*

This mistake is undoubtedly caused by confusion with *militate.* The correct meaning of *mitigate* is 'to soften the effect of, reduce the severity of':

> To the ordinary man, in fact, the pealing of bells is a monotonous jangle and a nuisance, tolerable only when mitigated by remote distance and sentimental association.
>
> —Dorothy L. Sayers, *The Nine Tailors*
>
> . . . hoping that his own agony and depression might mitigate his brother's suffering and loss.
>
> —Monica Furlong, *Merton: A Biography*

◊ ***Recommendation.*** The use of *mitigate against* is a definite malapropism.

modals. See DOUBLE MODALS.

Modern English. When we speak of "modern English," we are usually talking about present-day language as opposed to, say, Victorian English. In discussions of the history of the language, however, the term *Modern English* (capital *M*) has a special technical sense: 'English since 1500.' This term serves to distinguish the "later" language from its predecessors, MIDDLE ENGLISH and OLD ENGLISH. For the changes, mainly of sounds and word endings, that transformed Middle English into Modern English, see ELIZABETHAN ENGLISH. For a detailed description of the two leading branches of Modern English, see AMERICAN ENGLISH; BRITISH ENGLISH.

moot. The original *moot,* in Anglo-Saxon England, was a meeting of freemen to settle disputes. The word is now used of a debate or mock court in which law students or lawyers argue cases. This use has given rise to a verb and an adjective. The verb means 'to debate (a case or an issue) in a moot,' hence 'to propose (a plan), consider (a possibility)':

> . . . such a remote eventuality had never even been mooted at Alconleigh.
> —Nancy Mitford, *The Pursuit of Love*

The adjective has two distinct meanings: 'debatable, open to question, unresolved' and 'no longer of practical importance, academic':

> Just where Hopkins saw evidence of a dramatic change in American public opinion, so serious as to affect American foreign policy, is moot.
> —Charles L. Mee, *Meeting at Potsdam*

> Whether the North Vietnamese came as units or as individuals was soon moot.
> —William C. Westmoreland, *A Soldier Reports*

more than. See IN EXCESS OF.

morning. Rather surprisingly for a word that rarely causes confusion in its use, *morning* has no single meaning but several. Originally, it meant 'the approach or beginning of "morn"'—that is, the period extending from shortly before sunrise to shortly after it. The term *morn* is now largely confined to poetry of a traditional kind. *Morning* retains its original sense in some rural parts of the country, where the word *forenoon* is then used to designate the period from about 8 A.M. till noon (though *forenoon* in general usage now covers the time from daybreak to noon).

Far more commonly, however, *morning* signifies the entire early part of the day, ending at noon; but depending on what the speaker or writer has in mind, this period may begin at midnight, dawn, or sunrise. To complicate matters further, mornings are not considered to be over in some regions before the hour of the midday meal. Thus, in some cities a receptionist in an office may continue to greet callers with "Good morning" until 1 P.M. or even later.

Figuratively, *morning* can mean the beginning or early part of anything that can be likened to a day: *life's sweet morning; the morning of the king's reign.* The time between midnight and noon is specified by putting after a given hour or hour and minutes the phrase *in the morning* or the abbreviation A.M. (representing the Latin words *ante meridiem* = 'before the meridian, before noon'). *Morning* occurs in idiomatic adverbial phrases like *morning and evening* and *morning, noon, and night* (= 'all the day, incessantly'), and in various adjectival uses: *morning dress* = 'clothes worn in the morning, especially formal men's wear of cutaway coat and striped trousers'; *morning sickness* = 'nausea that affects a pregnant woman in the morning'; *morning star* = 'planet visible in the east before sunrise, especially Venus.'

◇ ***Recommendation.*** The expression *8 A.M. in the morning* is redundant and should be avoided. Instead, you should say or write *8 A.M.* or *eight in the morning* or *eight o'clock in the morning.* (For the use of figures versus spelled-out numbers see NUMBER STYLE.)

Moslem, Muslim, an adherent of Islam. In general, the two forms are equally correct, and each has wide support among publishers, journalists, and teachers. The earliest spelling of the word, when it entered English in the 17th century, was *Moslem,* from Arabic *muslim* = 'one who surrenders (to God).' By the mid-20th century preference in both British English and in English-language publications emanating from the Islamic world had shifted to the spelling *Muslim.* Much U.S. usage has held to the earlier *Moslem,* a choice backed up by the *New York Times,* for example, and by such sources as *Webster's New World Dictionary,* which serves as dictionary of first reference to the *Times.*

◇ ***Recommendation.*** We recommend the spelling *Muslim* because it is preferred by Muslims themselves and is the only form used by the Nation of Islam, or Black Muslims. If you choose to write *Moslem,* you are technically (and conservatively) correct, but some people might not like it; whereas if you use *Muslim,* the choice is both technically and politically unexceptionable.

most, as a shortened form of *almost,* has long been familiar in American English, though rare in British and other English dialects.

> Smiley said all a frog wanted was education, and he could do most anything—and I believe him.
> —Mark Twain, *The Celebrated Jumping Frog of Calaveras County*

There are modern usage critics who disapprove of it strongly in written usage, and even in speech. This is probably because they associate it with rustic or uneducated people. But in fact *most* is in wide reputable use, in writing as well as in speech.

> Lyndon and my sisters would come in with my mother and we would all sit around the kitchen talking about most anything.
> —Sam Houston Johnson, *My Brother Lyndon*

> Most everyone [on the Amazon frontier in Brazil] has a gun at home, and at night groups of pioneers with shotguns across their shoulders wander from one saloon to another.
> —Jonathan Kandell, *New York Times*

> In most any other industry, a company with a gain like Texaco's would probably hail it with trumpets. —*Fortune*

◇ ***Recommendation.*** *Most* = 'almost' is actually good American English but is simply not accepted as such by a large body of opinion. If you want to be on the safe side, don't use it in formal writing; if, on the other hand, you feel strong-minded about it, it's perfectly justifiable. But even in a formal context, as the quotations show, this usage does give a mildly informal flavor.

muchly is occasionally used for the adverb *much;* it is nonstandard, or archly humorous.

mufti /mŭf-tē/, a peculiar term for civilian dress worn by military officers off duty:

> Even when he [Admiral Stansfield Turner] is in mufti, his erect military bearing is obvious. —*Time*

The word first turned up in the early 19th century, apparently a transferred use of Arabic *mufti,* the title of a Muslim judge or jurist. But no convincing explanation for the English meaning has been found.

Muslim. See MOSLEM, MUSLIM.

mutual. The underlying meaning of *mutual* is 'exchanged, done by way of equal exchange.' It applies primarily to relations between two (people, parties, or things) and means that their feelings or actions are the same in both directions.

> We were made joyful by their evident mutual happiness, since it was obvious that each had brought to the other the qualities which . . . they needed and appreciated.
> —Brian Aherne, *A Dreadful Man*

> Literary intellectuals at one pole, at the other scientists. . . . Between the two a gulf of mutual incomprehension.
> —C. P. Snow, *The Two Cultures*

> . . . the remarkable mutual respect and friendliness of the Canadian and American NORAD personnel.
> —*Winnipeg Tribune*

Naturally enough, the word is also used of relations among more than two parties, and of friends, activities, property, etc., held or done in common by two or more.

> A zeal for different opinions concerning religion, concerning government, and many other points . . . an attachment of different leaders . . . have . . . divided mankind into parties, inflamed them with mutual animosity. . . .
> —James Madison, *The Federalist* (1787)

> 14. A general association of nations must be formed . . . for the purpose of affording mutual guarantees of political

> independence and territorial integrity to great and small states alike.
> —Woodrow Wilson, address to Congress (1918)

> The mutual confidence on which all else depends can be maintained only by an open mind and a brave reliance upon free discussion.
> —Learned Hand, speech (1952)

> Of course [Howard Hughes and I] had—and still have—many mutual friends and acquaintances, but our own direct, personal acquaintance is virtually nil. —J. Paul Getty, *As I See It*

An important current use of the word is in insurance, in which *mutual* means precisely 'held in common and involving equal exchange among a group'; the policyholders own the association that insures them, and share both profits and liabilities.

Usage critics tend to have a craving for simplicity, a feeling that everything would be better if words were limited to primary meanings. *Mutual* is a classic example of this. Many an expert has laid it down that *mutual* should refer only to reciprocal relations between two parties; or anyway, that it would be nice if it did. As the quotations show, it simply isn't so and hasn't been so for a long time. The primary meaning coexists perfectly well with the secondary and equally useful meanings.

◇ ***Recommendation.*** There is no problem with the word *mutual*. All of its meanings are valid and correct.

myself. Some usage critics have strongly condemned the use of *myself* as a substitute for *I* or *me* in compound subjects or objects. They are irritated, presumably, by the kind of person who says "My wife and myself thank you for your invitation" or "The decision will be taken by the senior vice-president, the sales managers, and myself." Certainly, the pronoun can acquire a pompous or self-dignifying character in this way, and *I* or *me* might well be preferable in such cases. But it depends considerably on the context, and on the manner and tone of voice the person uses. There is nothing inherently wrong with the usage itself, as some of the critics have claimed. Shortly before the Battle of Waterloo someone asked the duke of Wellington what he thought the outcome would be. He replied, "By God! I think Blücher and myself can do the thing." In fact, *myself* is regularly used like this, to give a touch of objectiveness: the speaker is seeing himself from the outside. There need not be anything pretentious about it.

> The next day a dogged and worried Maisky came to a meeting with the Chiefs of Staff and myself.
> —Anthony Eden, *The Reckoning*

> No longer were Price, Buchanan, and myself part of the innermost circle. . . .
> —William Safire, *Before the Fall*

> We had been heading down Alabama country road 117 at our customary speed: three miles an hour. *We* means my dog, Cooper-Half-Malamute, and myself.
> —Peter Gorton Jenkins, *Reader's Digest*

◇ ***Recommendation.*** By all means avoid pompous or pretentious uses of *myself* for *I* or *me*, but there is no need to throw out the entire usage. It is a matter of taste rather than correctness.

myth. In its primary meaning the term *myth* refers to a traditional story by which a primitive society seeks to explain either natural phenomena or its own particular beliefs, practices, and institutions. Creation myths, for example, explain how the universe came into being and how the human race was established. Other common myths characterize divinities and their relationships, explain the change of the seasons, and describe how certain tribes or clans originated.

In the societies that create them, such myths are meant to be taken literally, and they have the authority of religious conviction. But myths appear different to believers and nonbelievers. What may be an article of faith to one may seem merely a charming fiction to another. Plato is often credited with being the first to describe traditional myths as allegories of philosophical concepts, though other Greek thinkers preceded him in this. Whatever its origin, this change of perception produced a secondary definition of the term that has given rise to a certain amount of confusion. In this second meaning, myth is treated as a deliberate artifice, almost the reverse of the original concept.

Some anthropologists and sociologists have extended this secondary definition to popular fragments of folklore and systems of belief that exist within relatively sophisticated modern societies. Thus, they may speak of the myth of the Western cowboy hero, or the myth of Aryan superiority, or even the "instant" myths of Madison Avenue, such as Mr. Clean and the White Knight. By the same token, critics are apt to label new books, plays, or paintings that are heavily freighted with symbolism as "modern myths," "myth making," or "mythopoeic." Whether such extended applications of the term are as meaningful as they sound is debatable. See also ALLEGORY.

N

nabob. The governor of a province in the Mogul empire in India had the title *Nawwāb* = 'viceroy,' which the English rendered as *Nabob* /**nā**-bŏb/. This became a scornful or resentful nickname for a man who returned to England with a huge fortune amassed in India:

> I regretted the decay of respect for men of family, and that a Nabob would carry an election from them. Said Mr. Johnson: "The Nabob will carry it by means of his wealth in a country where money is highly valued . . . but if it comes to personal preference, the man of family will always carry it."
>
> —James Boswell, *Journal* (Aug. 25, 1773)

The word (spelled with a small *n*) is now used more generally, but still somewhat scornfully, of any man of wealth or power:

> In the United States today, we have more than our share of the nattering nabobs of negativism.
>
> —Spiro T. Agnew, speech (written by William Safire)

> In preparation for Gough Whitlam's visit to Washington, his advice men and the White House nabobs were drawing up briefing papers. . . .
>
> —*National Times* (Australia)

naïve. The French adjective *naïf* (masculine form), *naïve* (feminine form) means 'natural, ingenuous, artless' and is ultimately a variant of *natif, native* = 'native.' It was borrowed into English both as *naïf* /nä-**ēf**/ and *naïve* /nä-**ēv**/, but the form *naïve* has generally prevailed, no doubt because of the many other adjectives and nouns ending in *-ive* (*captive, relative*, etc.). Curiously, *naïve* continues to be treated as a semiforeign word. It is most often written with the dieresis, in all forms, and the abstract noun *naïveté* /nä-ēv-**tā**/ is almost always written with the acute accent (though some prefer the anglicized version *naïvety* /nä-**ēv**-tē/). *Naïve* is occasionally written in italics, but we don't recommend this.

A few people still use *naïf* for the adjective, especially when clearly referring to a nonfeminine subject. There is also a noun meaning 'a naïve person'; this is almost always *naïf*, regardless of gender.

The meaning ranges from 'unaffected, guileless, innocent' to 'simple-minded, ignorant of the world, overly credulous.'

(1) *Naïve* (adjective):

As the colonel put it, "My son thinks nations can solve political disputes around the peace table, and I think he's naïve. But," he beamed, "if the world had more people like Bob, there'd be no need for war." —*Reader's Digest*

Politically, Reagan is straightforward, uncomplicated, and even naïve, though, as with Ike, there can be guile behind his seemingly artless ways.
—Hedrick Smith, *Book Digest*

(2) *Naïf* (adjective):

. . . the later eighteenth century saw the life of the country gentry noticeably more civilized than that of their grandparents. Gone were the *naïf*, ignorant Squire Sullens and Squire Westerns of sixty years earlier, with their rustic accents and oafish manners. . . .
—David Cecil,
A Portrait of Jane Austen

(3) *Naïf* (noun) = 'naïve person':

Like many a militant leftist who turned to antiwar violence in the faraway '60s, Jane Alpert was a model student, a troubled romantic and a political naïf.
—*Time*

(4) *Naïveté* = 'the quality of being naïve':

There was a certain naïveté, almost adolescent in tone, in that celebration of America.
—Michael Novak,
U.S. News & World Report

More than anything else, however, we need an end to naïveté in our dealings with Cuba.
—David Reed, *Reader's Digest*

narration. The hero of Molière's play *Le Bourgeois Gentilhomme* is astonished to learn that for more than 40 years he has been speaking prose without knowing it. Many of us feel a little that way about EXPOSITION. Since the great preponderance of what we write has to do with conveying information, most of us have absorbed at least the rudiments of writing expository prose without quite knowing when or how we did it.

The same can hardly be said of *narration* (or *narrative*), the art of storytelling. We have all read plenty of narrative prose, but anyone who has ever tried to write it for the first time would agree that it is a very different proposition from writing exposition. Not more difficult, necessarily, but certainly less familiar, if only because many of the most important considerations in narration are minor in, or even absent from, exposition.

In this entry we shall take a brief look at some of the fundamentals of writing narrative prose. We do not imagine that anyone, solely as the result of reading what is written here, will become an accomplished writer of narrative—a little talent and a lot of practice are needed for that—but we shall at least try to touch on some general points that may prove helpful both to would-be writers and to their readers. This entry is divided into two main sections: Narrative Technique and Narrative Tradecraft. Under Narrative Technique you will find subsections devoted to point of view; plot; elements of narrative prose; and characterization. Under Narrative Tradecraft come subsections on dialogue; openings, transitions, and pacing; information; and style, tone, and voice.

Narrative Technique. The special domain of narrative is fiction. To be sure, narrative techniques may often be used to advantage in various kinds of nonfiction—in personal letters, for instance, or in history, biographies, or essays—just as expository techniques are often used in fiction. But it is in plays, short stories, and novels that we find not only the best and most varied examples of narrative technique but also the best illustrations of how special considerations can affect both structure and style. These considerations include point of view, plot, the elements of narrative prose, and characterization.

Point of View. In exposition, *point of view*, or POV, seldom refers to anything much more than the author's personal attitude toward his or her subject. But in narration, POV has an important technical meaning. Briefly, it refers to the relationship of the *narrator* both to the actual author and to the characters in the story.

The actual author has a wide range of choices in setting up this relationship. Suppose that our narrator is completely identified with one of the characters in the story—so identified that he not only speaks with the character's voice but even shares his innermost feelings and semiconscious thoughts. In such a case the narrative will take the form of *stream of consciousness*. Here is James Joyce's character Leopold Bloom contemplating a shelf of delicatessen items in a Dublin pub:

> Sardines on the shelves. Almost taste them by looking. Sandwich? Ham and his descendants mustered and bred there. Potted meats. What is home without Plumtree's potted meat? Incomplete. What a stupid ad! Under the obituary notices they stuck it. . . .
>
> —*Ulysses*

Still closely identified with a fictional character, but a little less deeply embedded in his psyche, is the narrator who appears in the first person present tense. In this situation the narrator delivers a kind of running commentary on the story's action for the benefit of the reader:

> The old ram stands looking down over rockslides, stupidly triumphant. I blink. I stare in horror. "Scat!" I hiss. "Go back to your cave, go back to your cowshed—whatever." He cocks his head like an elderly, slow-witted king. . . .
>
> —John Gardner, *Grendel*

As a rule, neither stream-of-consciousness nor first-person present-tense narrative can be sustained for very long. The POV is so sharply restricted with respect to both time and space that it is difficult for an author to present a complex plot; and because it is no easy job trying to live deep inside someone else's head, the reader may find these narrative POV's exhausting. For these reasons by far the most favored first-person narrative form is cast in the past tense. Here the effect is of a reminiscence. The narrator can modulate time and space at will; and (to the relief of many readers) nothing prevents him from speaking in complete sentences.

> In those days cheap apartments were almost impossible to find in Manhattan, so I had to move to Brooklyn. This was in 1947, and one of the pleasant features of that summer which I so vividly remember was the weather, which was sunny and mild, flower-fragrant. . . .
>
> —William Styron, *Sophie's Choice*

Before we move on from first-person narrative forms we should note one important fact about them—that the narrator need not be the protagonist or even one of the central characters in the story (see PROTAGONIST). "Call me Ishmael" are the opening words of what may be America's greatest novel. Yet the narrator, Ishmael, soon proves to be more an observer than a leading actor in Herman Melville's tale of the mortal struggle between Captain Ahab and his mysterious nemesis, the white whale called Moby-Dick.

Once the narrative form changes from first person to third person, the POV is no longer exclusively tied to the thoughts and perceptions of a single character in the story. But this does not necessarily mean that the point of view automatically becomes that of the author. Even though the narrator may now exist as a kind of disembodied voice separate from the characters, able at once to read their thoughts and to know things they do not, the narrator may nevertheless follow so closely the fortunes of one or more of the characters that, in effect, he places arbitrary limits on what might otherwise be his omniscience. The narrator does not anticipate what will happen to these characters but rather seems to share their feelings of surprise, triumph, or frustration as the story unfolds.

Indeed, it is a mistake to call all third-person narration omniscient, as some textbooks do. The completely omniscient narrator is a rarity in fiction, for such a narrator may seem to the reader altogether too godlike and remote, too obviously able to manipulate at will all the characters and events in the story. The object of most fiction, after all, is to involve readers, not in the mind of the storyteller, but in the story itself. Thus, though the narrator may in some cases come close to being identified with the author, the identification is absolute in very few cases. Instead, the third-person narrator's POV is more likely to lie somewhere between what the author does know and what one or more of his characters can know.

Here are a few examples of how differently the POV can be positioned in third-person narration. In the following example the ostensible narrator is remote and impersonal, recording action and dialogue but not presuming to reveal much about what is going on inside the minds of either the characters or the author:

> The waiter . . . put down the saucer and poured a glass full of brandy.
>
> "You should have killed yourself last week," he said to the deaf man. The old man motioned with his finger. "A little more," he said. The waiter poured on into the glass so that the brandy slopped over and ran down the stem into the top saucer in the pile. "Thank you," the old man said.
>
> —Ernest Hemingway, *A Clean Well-Lighted Place*

John Updike, on the other hand, positions his third-person narrator firmly inside the consciousness of one of his characters:

> Caldwell turned and as he turned his ankle received an arrow. The class burst into laughter. The pain scaled the slender core of his shin, whirled in the complexities of his knee, and swollen broader, mounted into his bowels. His eyes were forced upward to the blackboard where he had chalked the number 5,000,000,000, the probable age in years of the universe.
>
> —*The Centaur*

In the next example C. S. Forester deliberately obscures his POV: Is it the author, the character Horatio Hornblower, or a disembodied narrator whose thoughts are being presented to us here?

> It was then that Hornblower could allow himself to draw breath and relax. The captain of a ship that is no ship, but only a mere hulk, helpless in a land-locked inlet, cannot feel a moment's peace. A heretic in an inquisitor's dungeon is happy compared with him. There is the menacing land all about him, the torment of helplessness. . . .
>
> —*Beat to Quarters*

One of the rare cases in modern fiction in which a novelist comes close to intruding on his own story occurs when John Fowles (or at any rate a narrator who is very much like him) suddenly steps forward to propose two alternative endings to *The French Lieutenant's Woman*. Up to this point we have been enthralled in the story itself; now, abruptly, we are asked to consider the mechanics of storytelling. Usually a risky business, but Fowles carries it off brilliantly. The last chapter of the book begins:

> It's a time-proven rule of the novelist's craft never to introduce any but very minor characters at the end of a book . . . but the extremely important-looking person that has, during the last scene, been leaning against the parapet of the embankment across the way from 16 Cheyne Walk . . . may seem at first sight to represent a gross breach of the rule. I did not want to introduce him; but . . .

The novelist John Barth may have had something approaching the last word on the mysteries of narrative POV when he permitted the disembodied narrator of his short story "Autobiography" to characterize himself in the first person:

> My situation appears to me as follows: I speak in a curious, detached manner, and don't necessarily hear myself. I'm grateful for small mercies. Whether anyone follows me I can't tell. Are you there? If so I'm blind and deaf to you, or you are to me, or both're both. . . . first person, tiresome. Pronoun sans ante or precedent, warrant or respite. Surrogate for the substantive; contentless form, interestless principle; blind eye blinking at nothing. Who am I. A little *crise d'identité* for you.
>
> —*Lost in the Funhouse*

So far we have been discussing the intricacies of POV only in its most important context—that of fiction. But considerations of POV do not altogether vanish when we turn to narrative nonfiction. Obviously, in first-person nonfiction there is no problem: the ostensible narrator *is* the author. But in some third-person nonfiction narratives—such as biographies that imaginatively re-create scenes from their subjects' lives—POV may not be so clearly defined. Unless the author is careful, the point of view in such narratives may tend to become that of the subjects themselves. At some indeterminate point fact may slide over into "faction"—the re-creation of actual events using techniques of fiction; for example, Truman Capote's *In Cold Blood*—and eventually into outright fiction. No clear-cut rules state how far writers of nonfiction may legitimately go in this direction; but if they want to be fully believable, they should always try to maintain a distance between themselves and the people, things, or ideas they are writing about.

Two final points about POV are worth noting. The first is that POV need not be fixed within a given narrative. A single story may be told by several first-person narrators or by a combination of first-person and third-person narrators. Nor is the positioning of a third-person narrator necessarily constant: like a camera, such a narrator may shift his POV many times, now moving close to the characters and the action, now pulling back, detaching himself from the story and commenting on it from a distance.

The reference to cameras brings us to our last point. Most of the things we have so far been discussing about POV refer to literary fiction, to novels and short stories. Drama is another matter. In drama the point of view is almost always confined to multiple first-person narrative—to what the various characters say and do in the course of the play. Throughout history dramatists have chafed at this constraint, and some have tried to find ways around it. In classical times playwrights often resorted to the device of the chorus, a group of actors who stood apart from the events and commented on them. Today, in film, the same function is sometimes performed by a voice-over narrator. But such techniques are seldom very satisfactory because they tend to break the mood created by drama. Thus, apart from the (sometimes considerable) effects that may be achieved by stage lighting or camera positioning, manipulation of the POV in drama remains sharply restricted.

Plot. Extended exposition is logically structured into beginnings, middles, and ends. So is narration. But there, for most practical purposes, the comparison stops.

The distinctive feature of narrative structure is the requirement of "story," a sequential description of events involving (usually) imaginary people, places, and things. Unless the story forms a meaningful pattern—unless it goes somewhere or has a comprehensible point—we are not likely to find it satisfying. There are several names for such patterns—*scenario, story line,* and the like—but for the sake of simplicity we shall here use the all-embracing word *plot* to refer to any coherent narrative pattern, whether simple or complex.

Why do almost all readers like their stories to have plots? No one knows for sure. Perhaps one reason is that all of us have an instinctive craving for order and purpose that goes largely unsatisfied in everyday life. Narrative can create an imaginary world of experience in which plot harmonizes events into sequences leading to a clearly understood destination. In this sense the main object of plotted narrative is to give experience purpose. Thus, anyone who scorns plot on the grounds that it is an artifice, that it isn't "true," is ipso facto missing the point.

To be sure, some experimental modern writers, feeling that the requirement of plot inhibits pure expression, have attempted to do without it. The results have seldom been widely popular, and the technique has brought mixed reactions even from reviewers who ordinarily encourage experiment.

> Donald Barthelme may have influenced the short story in his time as much as Hemingway and O'Hara did in theirs. They loosened the story's grip on the security of plot, but he broke it altogether. . . . [But] toward the end of [Barthelme's] "Sixty Stories," one becomes aware of a feeling of strain. . . . It may be that without ordinariness, without plot or character in the usual sense, there is too little

> rest, or pace, or breathing room in some of the stories. And then readers are cozy creatures who are hungry for homey things like empathy and Mr. Barthelme is not.
>
> —Anatole Broyard, *New York Times*

There are several different sorts of plots. Let us examine the most familiar, the so-called dramatic plot, which is the structural basis for the great majority of novels and plays.

The standard dramatic plot concerns a protagonist in conflict. The protagonist is a central character with whom the reader is supposed to sympathize and, if possible, identify. The protagonist either wants something that is hard to get or is menaced by something that is hard to counter—or both. Along the way toward solving the problem, the protagonist may encounter any number of complications, make surprising discoveries, and experience unexpected reversals of fortune; but all of these must be so orchestrated that they lead inexorably to a climax in which the protagonist either succeeds or fails. What happens constitutes the resolution of the conflict.

The major elements in a dramatic plot can be graphed like a fever chart of the protagonist's fortunes. Here, for instance, is how a typical heroic melodrama, such as a good espionage thriller, would unfold.

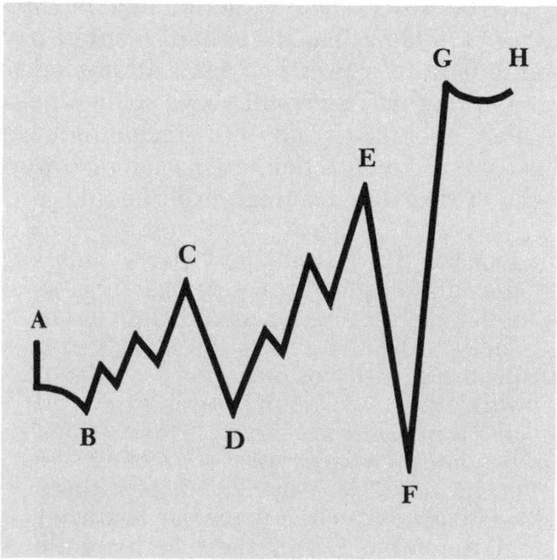

Point A represents an attention-grabbing opening scene. The action from A to B represents establishment of the setting, introduction of the major characters, and definition of the problem. The line dips down because as the problem's dimensions become clearer, it seems increasingly unlikely to the reader that the protagonist will ever be able to solve it. But then, at B, the protagonist begins to try to cope. Fighting his or her way up through thickets of complications, the protagonist reaches the minor promontory of C, and we begin to think that maybe the problem can be solved after all. Then comes the first major reversal; something goes seriously wrong, and the protagonist, worse off than ever, falls into the pit of D. Another hard climb follows, and eventually the protagonist achieves the high summit of E. The solution is almost in sight. But now comes the second reversal, far more catastrophic than the first, and the protagonist is hurled down into the horrendous abyss of F. A tragic drama might end here, but since this is a heroic plot, there is more to come. By almost miraculous fortitude, ingenuity, and luck the protagonist recovers and soars back up to G, solving the problem once and for all. Should any loose ends remain, the author may dispose of them—briefly—in the short tailpiece that runs from G to H, the end.

Like most plot designs, this one seems obvious almost to the point of simple-mindedness. Yet for a thriller writer as accomplished as, say, John Le Carré it could easily form the basis for a gripping and satisfying story. Plot is only a scaffolding on which the other elements of narrative can be built.

In the simplest kind of plot—found in many short stories—neither the protagonist nor the nature of the conflict is likely to be as clear-cut as in the dramatic plot. Indeed, the whole action of the story may be confined to a single episode. Here, the point is not so much to find out whether a protagonist succeeds or fails but rather to provide the reader with an insight into the people or situation described. James Joyce, who was adept at writing this kind of story, called such revelations "epiphanies." In a typical Joyce story ("A Little Cloud") a man meets a journalist for a big London newspaper. He is envious; long ago he had wanted to be a journalist himself. When he returns home, his wife, as usual, bullies him. Suddenly, the extent of his disappointed hopes and diminished manhood seems unbearably clear to him.

More complex is the episodic, or picaresque, plot. Here the protagonist moves through a series of loosely connected adventures—miniconflicts, all of about the same interest and intensity—toward goals that may be only vaguely defined. Henry Fielding's *Tom Jones* and James Clavell's *Shōgun* are representative of this kind of episodic plotting in novels. Since picaresque plots lack the unity conferred by the central conflict of dramatic plots, the protagonist becomes the main unifying element. In no other narrative structure is the reader's identification with the protagonist so nearly indispensable.

Some complex structures use two or more major plot lines that may or may not intersect at various points in the story but that usually mesh at the end. So-called disaster novels, for example, often tell us stories about several groups of unrelated characters who come together, and whose individual problems are resolved (for better or worse), only after the hotel catches fire, the ship founders, the hurricane strikes, or some other cataclysm produces the climax. The difficulty with such structures, apart from wear and tear on the author's imagination, is that the reader's interests and sympathies may become dissipated by all the characters and conflicts, rather than being concentrated on the problems of a single protagonist. First-class writers may be able to surmount this problem, but in most multiple-plot narratives one character and his or her particular story will tend to engage the reader's imagination over all the others. This may not necessarily have been the intention of the author, but it is a nearly inevitable consequence of the way we read stories.

This brings us to another major consideration in plotting: the use of *subplots*, or secondary plots, that the author deliberately makes subordinate to the main plot. Subplots have several uses. They can, for example, be a fruitful source of those complications needed to plague the protagonist in his or her efforts to solve the major problem. They can also give secondary characters things to do. And they can add richness and variety to a story that might otherwise have been too narrowly focused.

There are two main classes of subplots—those in which the protagonist becomes involved in a secondary problem and those in which secondary characters become involved in major problems of their own. In practice the classes are often blended, the major problem of a secondary character becoming a secondary problem for the protagonist, or the protagonist's efforts to solve his or her major problem radically affecting the fortunes of secondary characters. Whenever subplots involving secondary characters are allowed to have little or no bearing on the main plot, the overall story may be edging close to a multiple-plot narrative structure, thus threatening to weaken the reader's interest in the protagonist's problem.

Plots, whether simple or complex, and their interweaving subplots really have only one objective: to help create suspense in the mind of the reader. Not necessarily suspense in the sense of a fearful dis-ease, but at least an unremitting curiosity about what is going to happen next. While it is true that plots tend to try to reshape disorderly experience into meaningful patterns, skillful narrators seldom let their readers know the full shape of the pattern until close to the last page.

Elements of Narrative Prose. The oft-repeated formula, "Exposition tells, whereas narrative shows," is both a cliché and such an oversimplification as to be virtually useless to the writer. In fact, only drama is exclusively concerned with showing. Most narrative prose is composed of three main elements—*action*, *summary*, and *description*—and in some perfectly effective narratives action is the least of the three.

The special province of action in narration is the *scene*. In a scene some event occurs that moves the story dramatically forward. Time and geography come into narrow focus, and the narrative point of view tends to move close to that of one or more of the participating characters. The action that constitutes the event may be physical, may be expressed in dialogue, or may take place (usually in the form of a realization or a decision) only in the mind of one of the characters. In effect, the scene attempts to re-create the quality of immediate experience. In purpose, it attempts to advance the narrative along some important segment of the plot line.

To be effective a scene need not require the active participation of the protagonist; its mere existence may be enough. For example, in the climactic scene of one of H. P. Lovecraft's most famous horror stories the narrator-protagonist is merely a witness, but what he sees confirms the suspicions he has formed about who—or what—the secret denizens of the decaying seaport of Innsmouth may really be:

> It was the end, for whatever remains to me of life on the surface of this earth, of every vestige of mental peace and confidence in the integrity of nature. . . . And yet I saw them in a limitless stream—flopping, hopping, croaking, bleating—surging through the spectral moonlight in a grotesque saraband. . . . Some of them had tall tiaras of that whitish-gold metal . . . and some were strangely robed . . . and one, who led the way, was clad in a ghoulishly humped black coat and striped trousers, and had a man's felt hat perched on the shapeless thing that answered for a head.
>
> —*The Shadow Over Innsmouth*

Scenes may be the highlights of narrative prose, but they are seldom its only elements, any more than highlights are the only elements of paintings. By definition a highlight must have a background; and scenes must have a context. Some of the context for any given scene will usually have been provided by earlier scenes (whether they occur in natural sequence or in the form of flashbacks) or, less frequently, by subsequent scenes. But most context in narrative prose is supplied by summary.

The primary purpose of summary is not to show but to tell—to sketch the pattern of events that either precede a scene or separate one scene from another. Since summaries open up enlarged vistas of time and space and, even in first-person narrative, tend to be somewhat detached from the events they describe, they rarely create the dramatic impact of scenes. Nor, for the most part, do they aspire to. Orchestrating the contrast between the relative calm of summary and the intensity of scene is an important feature of the art of pacing.

In first-person narrative, summary necessarily takes the form of personal reminiscence, but in third-person narrative the job of summarizing usually falls to the voice of the disembodied narrator. In such cases narrative becomes, for all practical purposes, exposition.

Nineteenth-century novelists in general, and perhaps Henry James in particular, were so enamored of summary that they sometimes wrote relatively few scenes. Here is a characteristic Jamesean opening summary:

> It was one of the secret opinions, such as we all have, of Peter Brench that his main success in life would have consisted in his never having committed himself about the work, as it was called, of his friend Morgan Mallow. This was a subject on which it was, to the best of his belief, impossible with veracity to quote him, and it was nowhere on record. . . . —*The Tree of Knowledge*

Description, the third major element of narrative prose, is also a standard feature of exposition. In narration, description performs the indispensable function of permitting the reader to *sense*—to see, smell, hear, feel, or taste—what is happening in the story.

Amateur writers sometimes scant description; descriptive passages are, after all, passive, and they interrupt the flow of action. But every experienced narrator knows that well-handled description can be one of his or her most potent weapons. If a reader can, through the power of description, be made to believe in the reality of, say, a place or a set of characters, the writer may then be able to move on to a narration of events that could otherwise strike the reader as quite incredible. Stephen King, the best-selling author of such supernatural horror novels as *Salem's*

Lot, *Carrie*, and *The Shining*, is meticulous about establishing a sense of place through detailed description. King knows that if he can succeed in making us believe in, for example, the mythical Maine town of Salem's Lot—in making us know exactly how it looks, how it sounds, smells, and functions—we will be that much readier to suspend disbelief when he begins afflicting Salem's Lot with vampires.

Descriptions have a unique capacity for drawing us into a story, and for this reason they are often used for openings, even when the people, places, or things described are not central to the story itself. Note the economy and rhetorical vividness with which Josephine Tey opens her mystery novel *The Singing Sands:*

> It was six o'clock of a March morning, and still dark. The long train came sidling through the scattered lights of the yard, clicking gently over the points. Into the glow of the signal cabin and out again. Under the solitary emerald among the rubies on the signal bridge. On towards the empty grey waste of the platform that waited under the arcs.
>
> The London mail at the end of its journey.

Since description does, in fact, interrupt action, it should never be permitted to run overlong. At best, it should be concise and evocative, drawing on metaphor and concentrating on significant details that will imply a host of other, unspecified details. In short, hard writing.

Characterization. Some writers argue that characterization is the single most important consideration in narrative—more important than theme or governing idea, more important than plot. Indeed, some writers insist that character *is* plot. Here is how William Faulkner described his method of writing a novel: "It begins with a character, and once he stands on his feet and begins to move, all I can do is trot along behind him with a paper and pencil trying to keep up long enough to put down what he says and does."

To debate the relative importance of plotting and characterization may be, in Shakespeare's phrase, to consider too curiously. Both are indispensable to a finished narrative, no matter how they are arrived at. Yet there is no denying that good characterization is harder to arrive at than good plotting. The rules of plotting are comparatively simple and straightforward; there are hardly any rules at all for creating interesting fictional characters. Few aspects of narrative are more dependent on the quality of the writer's native talent.

Fictional characters can, of course, never be fully dimensional in the same way as living persons. Their appearance, their manners, the depth and complexity of their personalities, can only be implied through the presentation of carefully selected traits. In this sense they are caricatures. Yet, mysteriously, such confections can sometimes create an illusion of reality more powerful than that created by living, breathing human beings. It is said that when Charles Dickens finally killed off Little Nell in his original serialized version of *The Old Curiosity Shop*, readers in England and America wept publicly. And are not many of us secretly convinced that we know Sherlock Holmes better than we know most of our business acquaintances?

Within the limits imposed by point of view, characterization may be accomplished through action, summary, or description, but it is in action that character is most clearly and vividly revealed—to the reader and sometimes to the character himself. Aristotle said that the climax of all well-wrought narratives should involve the protagonist's learning something about himself. This may fall short of being a universal rule, but it does correctly suggest that progressive revelation (or self-revelation) of character can be an important element in the unfolding of plot.

Fictional characters, of course, do not usually exist in a social vacuum, and how a writer sets up the relationships among his characters can be as important as any of his individual characterizations. Such relationships may be formed into such a vast number of patterns that we could not possibly begin to discuss them all here. Instead, let us look briefly at only one—a pattern of great antiquity that has done yeoman service in countless dramatic narratives. In addition to any number of minor characters, it consists of five major characters, designated hero, heroine, confidant(e), villain, and fifth business.

Normally, either the hero or the heroine is the protagonist, the other falling into a slightly subordinate role. The fates of heroine and hero, who are almost always romantically involved, are closely linked, but this may not prevent them from sometimes operating at cross-purposes (usually through misunderstanding), thus creating useful plot complications. The villain is simply the embodiment of the conflict over which the hero and heroine must jointly triumph.

The confidant(e), the protagonist's faithful companion, serves as a foil for the protagonist's personality, is someone to whom the protagonist can reveal his or her innermost thoughts, and runs helpful errands. The confidant(e), often amusing and always likable, is thus firmly positioned on the protagonist's side of the conflict.

Not so the fifth business. He or she may be positioned anywhere with respect to the other four principals and to the central conflict. Indeed, a certain detachment is desirable, for it is the task of the fifth business to act as a kind of catalyst, to precipitate events that propel the other major characters toward failure or success.

Taking only these five stock roles, let us consider how their formal relationship might affect their characterization. The triumphant hero (or heroine) must, in this kind of grouping, be admirable and must represent someone with whom the reader can identify. These requirements are not entirely synonymous. If the hero is too competent, the reader may not only subconsciously resent him but may also not take his central problem seriously enough. On the other hand, if the hero has too many vulnerabilities, too many human frailties, the reader may have difficulty empathizing with him. Therefore it is generally best to limit the hero's weaknesses to those that are universal, or are worthy of sympathy, or, if possible, are even possessed of a certain charm.

Ian Fleming's James Bond exemplifies the near-perfect hero: no wonder the challenges Agent 007 has to face are seldom less than global in scope. The hero of J. R. R. Tolkien's *The Hobbit*, Bilbo Baggins, has the universal vulnerability of the small and the weak, of the perennial child cast adrift in a menacing and wholly mysterious sea of adult perils. (But, in accordance with the fantasies of childhood, Bilbo also has a magical compensation for his weakness and small size: the ring of invisibility.) George Smiley, hero of *Call for the Dead*, *Smiley's People*, and *Tinker, Tailor, Soldier, Spy*—three popular John Le Carré espionage novels—is riddled with vulnerabilities. He is fat, middle-aged, not very attractive, a bit dull, more than a little disillusioned, and forever the victim of an unfaithful wife, treacherous colleagues, and conniving bureaucrats. Yet however much we are invited to pity Smiley, there is never any question of our scorning him. Indeed, his hard-won triumphs, we feel, serve as a kind of retribution on those characters in the story who do scorn him.

It is usually only in the untriumphant or tragic heroes that we find vulnerabilities so serious that we cannot entirely forgive them—the intemperate jealousy of Othello, the foolish, egocentric romanticism of Emma Bovary, or the self-destructiveness of all those burnt-out cases who populate Joseph Conrad's novels. To this extent, at least, characterization in fiction tends to moralize.

Certainly, it tends to moralize about villains. It is rare that we are ever permitted to like a villain. It is even harder for a writer to create a fully human villain than to create a fully human hero. But by the same token it is probably easier to create an interesting villain than an interesting hero. Whereas the hero's character must have in it numerous recognizable traits of common humanity, the villain operates under no such constraint: the uncommoner he is, the better. His quirks may be legion, and none has to be endearing. He may be compounded of any and every kind of vice or folly, save one: he may never be incompetent. Except in comedy, a consistently ineffectual villain can have no place in the repertoire of plot. If nothing else, he must be a credible threat.

The French philosopher Simone Weil made

an interesting point about villainy in fiction. "Imaginary evil," she wrote, "is romantic and varied; real evil is monotonous, barren, boring. Imaginary good is boring; real good is always new, marvelous, intoxicating. 'Imaginative literature,' therefore, is either boring or immoral, or a mixture of both."

Because it is difficult to give (nontragic) heroes and heroines fully human dimensions, and because no one really wants villains to be unduly human, writers may be tempted to lavish characterization on confidant(e)s. This can be dangerous. The history of literature is strewn with nurses, mentors, and boon companions who are more real to us than the people they serve. In Miguel Cervantes' *Don Quixote,* for example, the squire Sancho Panza is a far more human figure than his master, Don Quixote. He was meant to be, of course, since the Don is a figure of satire. Yet Cervantes ran a considerable risk in making Sancho such a rounded character. Toward the latter part of the novel our sympathies are precariously divided between the two. Is it the Don's story we are following, or Sancho's? Most writers have preferred not to take such chances. Dr. Watson may have been the ostensible first-person narrator of the Sherlock Holmes stories, but never for a moment do we doubt who the real protagonist is, or that Watson's role is solely that of the Great Man's confidant.

The same considerations apply to the fifth business as to all noncentral characters. Whenever characterization begins to interfere with function or assigned role, plot may be the loser. Shakespeare's *Henry IV, Part I* is a case in point. Sir John Falstaff is surely one of Shakespeare's most memorable creations, far more vivid in our imagination than Prince Hal. Yet the story is meant to be about Hal—about how he attains maturity, setting aside his dissolute ways and becoming a responsible heir to the throne. Formally, Falstaff stands in relationship to Hal as part confidant, part fifth business, and perhaps, in a very minor way, part villain. Yet his characterization is so strong that he comes close to overwhelming Hal and, in the process, hopelessly distorting the basic story. The problem is compounded by the fact that several other characters, including Hotspur, Hal's enemy, also seem much more vital than Hal. Even though *Henry IV, Part I* has a perfectly sound and serviceable plot, it somehow strikes people as being a weak story. The very power of its secondary characterizations, along with its striking scenes and dazzling language, obscures its essential narrative structure. *Henry IV, Part I* is a masterpiece, but an unbalanced one.

Yet this is not to imply that plot is more important than characterization. As we said at the beginning of this section, both are indispensable. Just as a plot without characters would be a poor thing, so characters ungoverned by any plot or central idea can seldom produce satisfactory narrative. The writer's problem is to harmonize the two, so that each serves the other's ends. Any writer who begins with the idea that one must predominate over the other is simply asking for trouble.

So far, we have been talking mostly about how external considerations may modify characterization and have been avoiding the more difficult question of what constitutes really good characterization. Since there are no formal answers to this question, no rules that do not have their roots in the mysterious ground of the writer's innate talent and sensibility, we can only end by suggesting a few guidelines.

In the first place a good character should be both an individual and a type. If nothing about him conforms to any recognizable human type, he may appear to us as a lunatic or a monster, but we shall neither learn anything from him nor care much about him. If, on the other hand, everything about him is ordinary and commonplace, we are still not likely to learn from him or care about him.

An underlying consistency is a second hallmark of good characterization. The character must respond to events in a way that the reader sees as "right" for that character, even when the "rightness" may not always be apparent until later in the story.

This requirement does not mean that a character must be uncomplicated. The heroine of Muriel Spark's much-dramatized novel *The Prime of Miss Jean Brodie* is as quirky as they come—silly, inspiring, arrogant, loving, maddeningly blind toward some things and enchantingly insightful about others. Indeed, so fascinating is Jean Brodie that the novel's plot is almost entirely—but appropriately—taken up with exploring the many facets of her personality. But at no time is Jean untrue to herself. Any apparent inconsistencies in her behavior derive absolutely from the unchanging bedrock of her character. In the end it is our attitude toward her, rather than Jean herself, that may prove the more inconsistent, for we are hard put to know whether she leaves us more admiring or infuriated.

Nor does the requirement for consistency mean that a character may not change during the course of a story. As we have seen in the case of *Henry IV, Part I,* this kind of character transformation may even be a key element in the plot structure. But the change must never be arbitrary. It must always spring from some potential we perceive in the character's basic personality. It may surprise us at first, but in the long run we must recognize it as an organic growth—good or bad—and never as something contrived by the writer.

Finally, a good character must be thoroughly and sympathetically understood by his creator. *"Madame Bovary, c'est moi!"* ("Madame Bovary is *me*!") cried Gustave Flaubert of the title character of his famous novel. No matter that Louise Colet, and perhaps every other woman Flaubert had ever met, served in some way as a model for Emma Bovary. Ultimately, it was only because Flaubert had reached a point where he could imaginatively coexist with Emma, could share her every thought and feeling, that she was able to step onto the stage of world literature as one of the most brilliantly realized characters in narrative history.

Narrative Tradecraft. Point of view, plot, prose forms, characterization—these are only the most basic considerations in narrative. Beneath them lies a host of lesser concerns that range from technical tricks of the trade to matters so abstruse that they are hard even to define. In this section, rather than trying to cover them all, let us touch on only a representative few.

Dialogue. Dialogue (which includes monologue, interior or exterior) is one of the most important subdivisions of the narrative prose form we have called action. Many scenes are composed almost exclusively of dialogue, and it is certainly one of the most effective vehicles for establishing character. Yet most authors would agree that writing good dialogue is always exceptionally difficult.

The reason for this is clear. Anyone who has ever had to read a written transcript of his own spoken words probably knows the meaning of shame. When we talk we all ramble, explain overmuch and not well, make errors of grammar and syntax, leave sentences unfinished, use clichés and euphemisms, and generally commit most of the verbal sins we take such pains to avoid in writing. To try to duplicate this kind of oral expression in narrative dialogue would be both confusing and boring.

So the writer—of literary fiction, certainly, but also of drama—must perform a kind of conjuring trick. He must suggest not only the structure of spoken language but even its intonation and accent; yet at the same time he must produce written dialogue that is markedly cleaner, more pointed, and swifter-moving than anything we are likely to overhear in real life. He achieves this—as he achieves his most effective descriptions and characterizations—through selection of significant detail. Into dialogue whose primary purpose is simply to advance the story, he will seed certain carefully chosen words and phrases indicative of the speaker's characteristic style and present mood. Not so many that they blunt the dialogue's pace or purpose, but enough to feed the reader's imagination, enough to make him feel that he is hearing actual speech, even though at some level of intellect he knows he is not. It is the old business of persuading the reader to enter into a state of willing suspension of disbelief, to become the writer's accomplice in the construction of an illusion. This, of course, is the essence of all narrative art, and it is no easier to achieve an illusion of the ear than of the eye or the mind.

Openings, Transitions, and Pacing. Plot defines only the general architecture of narrative. It tells the writer what has to be built but not how to build it. How, for example, should the writer begin his story? How will he move smoothly from one scene to another, or from a scene to summary or description and then back again? Should he subdivide his story into chapters or acts, and if so, how? What rules should he follow for sequencing passages of action, summary, and description?

Plot outlines merely hint at the answers to such nuts-and-bolts questions. Ultimately, the writer will discover the best answers in his own common sense and personal taste; but there are nevertheless some established conventions of the narrative craft that he should take into account while he is searching for solutions.

Most writers agree that the way a story begins is crucial. It is here that the reader makes his first decision about whether he will or won't become involved in the author's imaginative enterprise. For obvious reasons, therefore, the jargon term for the commonest kind of narrative opening is the *hook.*

What constitutes an effective hook? To begin with, it must be an attention grabber. Hooks composed solely of extended summary are the hardest to make effective. Descriptions—of a vividly realized setting or an intriguing character—are better; and exciting action is best of all. The classic hook, then, may start with a brief introductory summary or description, or both, but usually soon develops into a strong opening scene.

Here are two representative openings: the first, an intriguing summary-cum-description; the second, a scene of violent action.

> The book of ballads published by Von Humboldt Fleisher in the Thirties was an immediate hit. Humboldt was just what everyone had been waiting for. Out in the Midwest I had been waiting eagerly, I can tell you that. An avant-garde writer, the first of a new generation, he was handsome, fair, large, serious, witty, he was learned. The guy had it all. . . .
>
> —Saul Bellow, *Humboldt's Gift*

> The gale tore at him and he felt it bite deep within and he knew that if they did not make a landfall in three days they would all be dead. . . .
>
> —James Clavell, *Shōgun*

What should the opening accomplish? First, it should rivet the reader's attention. Second, it should fill his mind with enough unanswered questions to make him want to read on. Finally, it should relate directly to what the reader will eventually perceive as the central conflict.

The hook may or may not introduce the reader to the protagonist, but in any case this introduction must not be delayed for too long a time, lest the reader's natural inclination to identify with someone in the story lead him to the wrong person. When they occur, such misidentifications are astonishingly hard to undo.

Once past the hook, both reader and writer can relax a little. The dominant POV can be established, and the whos, whats, whens, wheres, and whys of the story itself can be sketched in with summary, description, and not-overdramatic scenes.

The next major scene should present either the event that precipitates the major conflict or, if this has already been done in the hook, the first major complication. If the story is to be divided into chapters, this is a logical place to end the first one.

As the story progresses, the writer must shuttle constantly among the three narrative prose forms available to him. Since summary and description are less dramatic than action, he must rely mainly on scenes to make his most important advances in plot; but he must also be wary of bunching highly dramatic scenes too close together. Sustained highs can fatigue readers and diminish their emotional responses. Well-placed intervals of summary, description, or weak action can thus be welcome relief. Nor should the writer unleash his best dramatic scenes too early: the story must constantly build, and no earlier scene should be more powerful than the climax.

Transitions between summary and scene are usually relatively easy, often requiring nothing much more than a space break. Transitions from description to scene can be a little harder, the commonest technique being to open the scene with a character's acting on the thing, or within the place, just described. Transitions from scene to scene require the most care. Abrupt shifts set a jarring, staccato pace that may be useful when action and suspense are entering high gear, but they can also be confusing and wearing on the reader's nerves. Normal interscene transitions are more considerate. One type of transition has a character in a scene think about what he or she is going to do next, thus setting up the locale and premise of action for the following scene. Another common transitional technique is to have a new scene begin with a statement of time or location that fixes it in relation to the preceding scene ("The flight from La Guardia to Logan took 50 minutes. Belov was waiting for me in the airport lounge. 'I see you haven't brought the manuscript,' he said . . .").

Whatever else may be said of transitions, it is generally true that they should be brief and efficient. Inexperienced writers sometimes waste much space in introducing their characters to one another, getting them in and out of buildings, accounting for their irrelevant activities during weeks or months of telescoped time, and so on. It is always better to risk an abrupt transition than a boring one.

Information. Woe to the author who permits a reader to think the reader knows more about the subject at hand than the author does himself. Nothing can break the narrative spell—the reader's willingness to suspend disbelief—faster. A writer must be as accurate or plausible in all his circumstantial details as he is in the delineation of his characters' psychology.

That is one reason why most novelists are so addicted to research. They know that they cannot afford to be caught referring to the (nonexistent) cocking hammer of a Luger or locating Botticelli's *Primavera* in the Louvre (it's in the Uffizi Gallery in Florence) or having the gallant captain rush from the quarterdeck to the masthead by scampering up a bowline. Precisely because they are dealing in the larger untruth of fiction, writers depend on being believed in all lesser things, at least for the duration of the story.

In typically wry fashion, novelist Vladimir Nabokov put the matter this way:

> Some of you may still wonder why I and Tolstoy mention such trifles [historical data contemporary with the time in novels]. To make his magic, fiction, look *real,* the artist sometimes places it, as Tolstoy does, within a definite, specific historical frame, citing facts that can be checked in the library—that citadel of illusion.
>
> —*Lectures on Russian Literature*

Some writers, in an effort to establish their authority over detail, go beyond the strict requirements of accuracy, showering readers with information on all manner of arcane subjects. The mystery writer John D. MacDonald, for example, is prone to tell us more than we really need to know both about the complexities of Florida real estate dealings and the art of maintaining houseboats. And perhaps the most fondly remembered scene in Sir Arthur Conan Doyle's great chivalric romance, *Sir Nigel,* occurs when young Squire Nigel, come a-courting the lady Edith, is catechized by her father, Sir John Buttesthorn. Sir John speaks:

> "Answer me now, lad, how would you say if you saw ten badgers in the forest?"
>
> "A cete of badgers, fair sir."
>
> "Good, Nigel—good, by my faith. And if you walk in Woolmer Forest and see a swarm of foxes, how would you call them?"
>
> "A skulk of foxes."
>
> "And if they be lions?"
>
> "Nay, fair sir, I am not like to meet several lions in Woolmer Forest."
>
> "Aye, lad, but there are other forests besides Woolmer. . . . A huntsman would have said that he had seen a pride of lions, and so proved that he knew the language of the chase. Now had it been boars instead of lions?"
>
> "One says a singular of boars."
>
> "And if they be swine?"
>
> "Surely it is a herd of swine."
>
> "Nay, nay, lad, it is indeed sad to see how little you know. . . . No man of gentle birth would speak of a herd of swine. . . ."

A few writers tell us more than we can know, confronting us with impressive chunks of information that is both uncheckable and essentially bogus. It is not only science fiction writers who do this: Richard Condon's learned disquisitions on posthypnotic suggestion, complete with citations, in his novel *The Manchurian Candidate* are mostly playful nonsense.

But whether or not we need this gratuitous information, do we want it? Surprisingly often, the answer is yes. We may have no earthly use for detailed information about the structure of prewar Singapore society, or even for up-to-the-minute lore about buying and selling condominiums, but if this kind of esoterica is presented to us properly—in context, vividly described or dramatized, and neither overlong nor too abstract—it will probably fascinate us.

Why? Any answer would be speculative, but then writers don't really need to know the right answer. The important thing is that it works.

Style, Tone, and Voice. In our entry on exposition we noted that the word *style*, as applied to writing, had many different connotations. Sometimes style means merely those universal rules of punctuation, grammar, spelling, and the like that govern all English prose. At other times style refers to widely accepted conventions of composition and usage that are thought to produce superior writing. And sometimes the term indicates a characteristic or highly individual way in which a particular author writes.

If the word *style* is ambiguous, words like *tone*, *texture*, and *voice* are equally so. It would be convenient if we could ignore such words entirely, but we cannot. However inexact they may be, these terms nevertheless suggest concepts important to both writers and readers. They refer to qualities in writing that lie either at the outermost fringes of or completely beyond technical proficiency. A writer of narration may have mastered plot, characterization, dialogue, and all the rest and may still never achieve genuine style, tone, or voice.

Does this imply that style, tone, and the rest are innate and therefore unteachable? That depends on what we mean by each word; and, as we have seen, what we mean must be pretty much what we say we mean. For argument's sake, then, let us take only three words—*style*, *tone*, and *voice*—define them more or less arbitrarily, and see whether we can get closer to the concepts they represent.

By style we shall mean only the sum of an author's skills and talents in using language—his or her ability always to find the right word to convey the meaning, to know when to be eloquent and when not to be, to understand the resonances and melodies that inhere in certain words or phrases and to sense accurately how these will affect the reader, and so on. Although no one has yet succeeded in writing down very many of the rules that confer style on the writer, it is nevertheless a subject that can, up to a point, be learned. In his autobiography, *The Summing Up*, W. Somerset Maugham describes how he taught himself to write well. He began by copying down passages written by writers he admired and then trying to rewrite them from memory. From this he graduated to writing original passages in the characteristic styles of his favorite authors. Finally, he went on to develop a narrative style of his own, not imitative of anyone in particular but in subtle ways derived—through a process of acceptance or rejection—from many models.

Maugham's case is hardly unique. Hundreds of other writers have used the same technique, and indeed, it is recommended in some textbooks on creative writing. That we cannot precisely specify what Maugham learned is irrelevant. The point is, it was learnable; that is, it was—and is—there to be learned.

Closely related to style is tone. By tone we mean those ways in which a writer conveys an attitude toward the subject matter of the narrative. Modulated through point of view, the writer's attitude may run the gamut—involved or detached, admiring or contemptuous, sympathetic or derisive. But whatever it is, it is probably an attitude that the writer wants the reader to share. Tone may be set via plot, characterization, or other basic elements of narrative form, but primarily it is conveyed through the use of language—in the most obvious way, by direct comment. Consider, for example, the famous ending of Aldous Huxley's satirical 1928 novel, *Point Counter Point*. In this scene the hypocrite Burlap and his mistress are getting ready for bed. Huxley's loathing for Burlap and all he represents is expressed in a tone of savagely explicit irony:

> That night he and Beatrice pretended to be two little children and had their bath together. Two little children sitting at opposite ends of the big old-fashioned bath. And what a romp they had! The bathroom was drenched with their splashings. Of such is the Kingdom of Heaven.

Subtler tones may be established through general style. Both William Faulkner and Thomas Wolfe, for example, tended toward a somewhat overstated or hyperbolic style. The characteristic effect was a tone that was emotional, intense, sometimes impressionistic, always deeply involved in the feelings of the characters or the mood of the story itself. Ernest Hemingway, on the other hand, preferred understatement, a style of laconic detachment that seemed to express no attitude whatever toward the people and events in the narrative. But this was an artful illusion, for Hemingway was really relying on the reader's imagination to make the judgments and form the attitudes that he seemed not to be supplying. Against this background, on the rare occasions when Hemingway did permit himself to make a more or less direct comment, the effect could be devastating. The novelist R. V. Cassill neatly describes this technique with a boxing simile.

> The stylist who employs understatement works like a boxer who feints in order to draw a punch from his opponent. Then, if he is a real stylist, like Hemingway, he counterpunches.
>
> —*Writing Fiction*

When a writer sets a tone to his narrative, he may do so deliberately or unconsciously—or both. As a rule, the closer his discernible attitude is to his true feelings, the less artifice he needs to use in setting tone.

Still further removed from ordinary technique is voice. According to the definition we shall use, if tone conveys an author's specific attitude toward the story, voice conveys his or her general personality; lets us know, in effect, what kind of person is addressing us.

Since personalities can be either genuine or assumed, voice may at times be something of a contrivance, leading us toward a persona rather than a real person. But authentic voice is never an artifice—rather, it is a distillation, the character of the author shining through a façade of words. Here is Anatole Broyard on voice (using, incidentally, the term *tone* in its more ordinary sense):

> Pressed for a definition, I would say that voice is the sound of conviction, of a writer finding the truth of his experience. It is not eloquence, but the best personal tone a writer can produce, a tone very close to the one he uses when he is alone and talking to himself.
>
> —*New York Times Book Review*

Authentic voice is not what makes writing great. There is no guarantee that by coming to know a writer through his writing we shall like either the writer or his work any better. But by the same token, voice is almost never absent from truly great writing. It is an elusive but potent quality that lets us make a leap from a literary creation into the mind of its creator. And if that mind happens to be a particularly fine one, the experience can be singularly affecting.

There is, of course, much more to the enterprise of writing narrative prose than the things we have written here. More, indeed, than has ever been written anywhere. For written narrative is an art—at its best, unsurpassed by any other. Radically different from sculpture, poetry, music, painting, acting, singing, or dancing, it nevertheless shares with all other arts one common bond: in the end, its capacity to move us so profoundly is wholly mysterious. An art of words, narrative—and what finally and truly makes it work—is beyond words.

nauseous /nô-shəs, -zē-əs/. Usage conservatives insist that the only correct meaning of *nauseous* is 'arousing nausea,' either literally or figuratively:

> The odour of Zanzibar Aloes is strong and characteristic, and its taste nauseous and bitter.
> —M. Grieve, *A Modern Herbal*

> The nomination was greeted with universal disapproval. The *New York Herald Tribune* called it "nauseous."
> —Arthur M. Schlesinger, Jr., *Robert Kennedy and His Times*

In the 17th century the word was also used to mean 'feeling nausea.' This meaning died out in the 18th and 19th centuries but has cropped up again in the 20th century:

> . . . and even as his heart and bowels sickened with their nauseous disbelief of recognition, he knew it, lived it, breathed it utterly to the last remotest degradation of its horror.
> —Thomas Wolfe, *The Web and the Rock*

> Ochiba felt faint and nauseous and she wondered if it was her *karma* to be buried in the rubble today.
> —James Clavell, *Shōgun*

Probably, in fact, the commonest use of the word in today's American speech is simply as a synonym for 'sick to the stomach.'

◇ ***Recommendation.*** To some, *nauseous* means only 'arousing nausea, disgusting'; to others it means only 'feeling nausea, sick to the stomach.' Both usages are legitimate. Anyone who wants to avoid the issue entirely can abandon *nauseous* and use the unequivocal words *nauseated* and *nauseating*.

Negro. See BLACK, COLORED, NEGRO.

neither /**nē**-*thər*, **nī**-/. (1) As a pronoun or an adjective, *neither* means 'not either'; it is singular, not plural.

> Yet valid and useful as these [two] inventions are, neither represent the true stature of the man whose name they bear.
> —Alfred Friendly, *Beaufort of the Admiralty*

This should be "neither represents the true stature of the man whose name it bears" (plural verbs and pronoun changed to singular forms). Alternatively, the word *neither* could be eliminated and the plural sense retained: "they do not represent the true stature of the man whose name they bear."

(2) As a conjunction, *neither* means 'not one or the other'; it is followed by *nor*, not *or*.

> My best chance would be to rap the ball so firmly that neither the left or right break could really take effect.
> —Jack Nicklaus, *The Greatest Game of All*

Here, "or" should be "nor." Also, it is best to keep the items parallel: "neither the left nor the right break" or, alternatively, "neither left nor right break."

(3) When the items introduced by the conjunction *neither* are singular, a singular verb follows.

> . . . there's no question in my mind that neither Haldeman or Ehrlichman are guilty. —Richard Nixon, *R.N.*

This should be "that neither Haldeman nor Ehrlichman is guilty." (It is a quotation from an informal diary, not a piece of edited prose.) Naturally, if items introduced by *neither . . . nor* are themselves plural, a plural verb will follow: *Neither the Jets nor the Steelers are playing this weekend.* If the items are a mixture of singular and plural, the number of the verb is governed by the item nearest the verb: *Neither the characters nor the plot is convincing.*

(4) As a conjunction, *neither* usually introduces two items, but it may also be used to introduce more than two.

> Her daughter enjoyed a most uncommon degree of popularity for a woman neither young, handsome, rich, nor married.
> —Jane Austen, *Emma* (1816)

> Neither Kennedy nor Markham nor Gargan has ever been compelled to answer that question.
> —John Barron, *Reader's Digest*

◇ ***Recommendation.*** As pronoun or adjective, *neither* is singular and takes a singular verb. As conjunction, it is followed by *nor*. Singular items introduced by *neither . . . nor* take a singular verb. These rules, though often broken, are still standard; to break any of them is a definite error. See also EITHER.

nemesis /nĕm-ə-sĭs/. The Greeks held that human sin, especially the sin of arrogance, or HUBRIS, would inevitably be punished by divine retribution, or *nemesis*. The word comes from the name of the goddess Nemesis, from *nemein* = 'to allot.' It is now used in several derived senses.

(1) 'Inevitable, quasi-divine punishment':

> In darkness the Van Doorns sat silent, contemplating the nemesis that seemed at times to hang over their nation: a splendid patriot assassinated. . . .
> —James A. Michener, *The Covenant*

(2) 'Person who seems destined to act as an agent of punishment':

> Who was sitting there, waiting for us, but my old nemesis, Judge McDevitt. We had been indicted for prison breach, he informed us. "And," he said, "we'll go to trial immediately."
> —Willie Sutton, *Where the Money Was*

(3) 'Relentlessly hostile person, persistent enemy':

> At the White House we considered him our arch nemesis, and I once proposed an investigation of [Jack] Anderson.
> —Charles Colson, *Born Again*

(4) 'Longstanding and formidable opponent':

> Harvey's golf nemesis was a fellow named Hank Baldwin. . . . It's my guess that throughout the years he's beaten Harvey nine-tenths of the time and accumulated a nice little savings account in the process.
> —Bing Crosby, *Call Me Lucky*

(5) 'Longstanding source of trouble, bugbear':

> The new boom in electronic equipment also promises to make a big dent in the old nemesis of every office—paper work. —*U.S. News & World Report*

ne plus ultra. According to fable the Latin motto *Ne plus ultra* was inscribed on the Pillars of Hercules at the western extremity of the Mediterranean Sea. The meaning is '(Go) no farther beyond' or 'Thus far and no farther'—a warning to Roman navigators not to venture out into the Atlantic Ocean. In English it is used to mean 'ultimate achievement, the highest possible form (of something)':

> The combination of brown eyes and gold hair was the Elizabethan *ne plus ultra* of womanly beauty.
> —Mary McCarthy, *The Group*

The emperor Charles V (1500–1558), as king of Spain, alluding to Spanish conquests in the Americas, adopted the motto *Plus ultra*, meaning '(Spain has gone) farther beyond.' *Plus ultra* is thus occasionally used to mean 'superultimate achievement.'

New England dialect. The speech of New England, especially that of the southeastern section, has for many years had a prestige that no other American dialect can claim. Among the reasons for this prestige are the wealth and literary interests of Boston, the academic influence of Harvard University, and the fact that Boston speech in some ways resembles polite Southern British. Historically, New England speech is the general source of the NORTHERN DIALECT and is now one subdialect of it. Within the New England dialect there are two major subdivisions, which fall roughly east and west of the Connecticut River.

Eastern New England speech has for centuries been dominated by the upper-class speech of the Boston area. Its pronunciation is one of the most distinctive in the United States, and its vocabulary contains many local expressions and relic words that have died out elsewhere. (For more details see BOSTON URBAN DIALECT.) Western New England speech was carried westward as far as the upper Midwest and has contributed more to the dialects of the North than has eastern New England speech. For this reason it is much less unusual, both in pronunciation and in vocabulary.

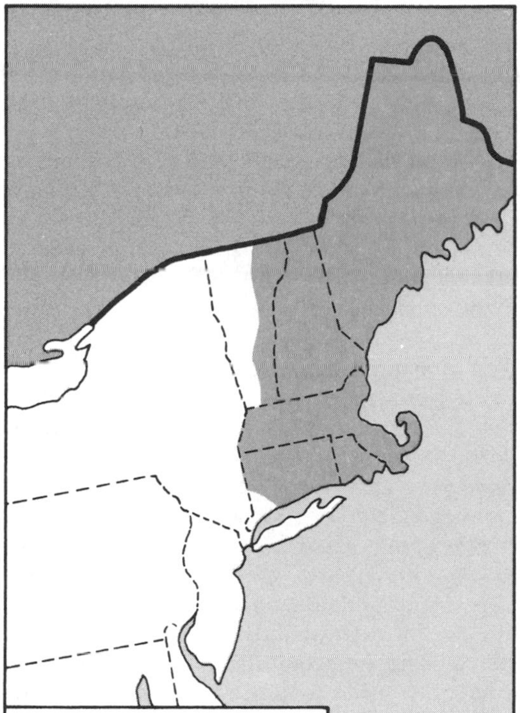

New England dialect

Pronunciation (Eastern New England). The /r/ sound is regularly omitted in such words as *barn, four, Thursday, horse, father:* /bȧn/, /fō/, /**thŭz**-dā/, /hōs/, /**fȧ**-*th*ə/. The /r/ sound is commonly added to words ending with vowels: *law, idea, saw* are pronounced /lär/, /ī-**dîr**/, /sär/. It would not be at all unusual to hear a sentence such as *It's against the* /lär/ *to* /pȧk/ *the* /kȧ/ /rĭn/ *the* /yȧd/ (It's against the law to park the car in the yard). See R-LESSNESS, INTRUSIVE R.

Words that in most American speech have the /ă/ sound, such as *glass, bath, France, aunt, afternoon,* are often pronounced with an /ȧ/ sound: /glȧs/, /bȧth/, /frȧns/, /ȧnt/, /ȧf-tə-**nōōn**/. This pronunciation is almost invariably a feature of cultivated speech, and it is especially common in the southeastern part of New England.

Vocabulary. (1) Eastern New England:

apple dowdy = 'deep-dish apple pie'
belly bumper, belly bunt = 'to ride face down on a sled'
blart = 'blat or bawl of a calf'
bonnyclabber, bonnyclapper = 'curdled milk, *clabber'
breeze up *or* **on** = 'to become windy'
buttonwood = 'sycamore'
culch, sculch = 'rubbish, trash'
double-runner (also Maritimes) = 'bobsled'
fritter = '*pancake'
northeaster, norwester = 'wind blowing from the northeast or northwest'
pigsty = 'pigpen'
sour milk *or* **curd cheese** = '*cottage cheese'
spindle = 'top of the cornstalk'
tilt, tilting board, tilter, tiltering board = '*seesaw'
whicker = 'whinny'
white bread = 'wheat bread'

(2) Western New England:

angledog = '*earthworm'
callithump = 'noisy mock serenade, *shivaree'
ivy = 'mountain laurel'
tinter, teenter = '*seesaw'
topgallant = 'top of the cornstalk'

(3) General New England:

creek = 'saltwater inlet'
cross-lot, go *or* **cut** (also Inland Northern) = 'to take a shortcut'
dropped egg = 'poached egg'
flea in (someone's) ear, put a = 'to hint or suggest'
frankfurt = 'hot dog, frankfurter'
grinder = 'large sandwich made with a roll or bun, hero sandwich'
hatchway (also Inland Northern) = 'sloping outside cellar door'
Indian pudding = 'baked dessert made with cornmeal, molasses, etc.'
jacking, jacklighting (also Inland Northern and in eastern Pennsylvania) = 'hunting illegally at night with a spotlight'
lobbered *or* **loppered milk** (also Hudson Valley, Inland Northern) = 'sour or curdled milk, *clabber'
matterate (also Inland Northern) = 'to discharge pus, suppurate'

*Appears as separate entry

nightwalker = '*earthworm'
notch (also Inland Northern) = 'mountain pass'
open-and-shut day = 'day when the clouds come and go continually'
penuche (also General Northern) = 'homemade brown-sugar fudge'
piazza (also Coastal Southern) = 'covered *porch'
pieplant = 'rhubarb'
pop lash = 'ox whip'
pung = 'sleigh or sled used for hauling loads'
rotary = 'traffic circle'
rowen = 'stubble field left for cattle to graze on'
sick to one's stomach = 'queasy'
spider = 'cast-iron frying pan'
tonic = '*soda pop'

*Appears as separate entry

Newfoundland English. Nominally part of Canadian English only since Newfoundland joined the Confederation in 1949, Newfoundland English is an independent branch of the language, resulting from the island's early settlement and long isolation from the Canadian mainland. See the map at CANADIAN ENGLISH.

History. To begin with, many of Newfoundland's original English settlers were from the English West Country, that is, from Devon and Cornwall, while most of mainland Canada's early settlers were Loyalists whose ultimate origins lay in the East, the Midlands, or the North of England. The dialect of the West Country was, and is, derived from pre-Conquest West Saxon, while the dialect of the rest of England derives from pre-Conquest Anglian. In addition, Newfoundland experienced a heavy influx of Irish settlers, whose influence in the sparsely populated island was proportionately much greater than it would have been in a more densely populated area. Until Confederation, Newfoundland was relatively isolated, both economically and culturally, from the rest of Canada. Because of variations in the influence of English West Country speech and Irish speech in different parts of the island, and because of the interface between these two influences, Newfoundland English has formed eight major dialect areas, all of them affected by the relative isolation of the outposts.

Not all dialects of Newfoundland share all of the following characteristics of pronunciation, grammar, and vocabulary, but on the whole these characteristics will give some idea of the qualities of the English spoken in Newfoundland.

Pronunciation. The influence of the English West Country appears in the voicing of initial fricatives common in Newfoundland. Thus, *feet*, *finger*, and *fire* are pronounced /vēt/, /**vĭng**-gər/, and /**vī**-ər/; *said* and *see* are pronounced /zĕd/ and /zē/; and *things* and *three* are pronounced /*th*ĭngz/ and /*th*rē/. Alternatively, other parts of Newfoundland substitute a special dental /d/ and /t/ for /*th*/ and /th/, giving, for example, /dăt/ for *that* and /trē/ for *three*. The Newfoundland use of "clear" /l/ (that is, /l/ made with the tip of the tongue on the teethridge) in words like *looking* may originate with the English of Ireland. The Newfoundland pronunciation of a strong retroflex /r/, however (that is, /r/ made with the tip of the tongue pointed up and back), though often thought to be Irish, is probably not of this origin at all, and some other features of Newfoundland English are likewise of debatable or unknown origin. The sound /h/ is unstable, resulting in /**hăf**-tər/ for *after* but /**ăr**-ĭ/ for *Harry*. The sounds /oi/ and /ī/ are often not distinguished, so that such pairs as *boy* and *bye*, *toy* and *tie*, become homophones: /bī/, /tī/. So, too, many Newfoundlanders make no distinction between /ē/ and /ā/, so that *speak* rhymes with *break*; and they make no distinction between /ô/ and /ä/, so that *born* rhymes with *barn*.

Grammar. Probably the single most striking feature of the grammar of Newfoundland English is its treatment of the verb *be*. In some parts of Newfoundland, the entire present tense of *be* is expressed by *is: I is, you is, he is, we is*, etc. Alongside this, and expressing the same meaning, is the form *'m: I'm, you'm, he'm*, etc. Both usages are paralleled in the English West Country. Beside both is a third form, *bees,* which is often used to express habitual or continuous action (*I bees sick, you bees sick,* etc., that is, continuously), as opposed to *is,* which expresses merely present time. The same verb *be* has *idden* and *wooden* as forms alternative to the usual *isn't* and *wasn't,* and its form *been* is sometimes used to replace *have,* as in *I been cut more wood.* This last and the following features of verb usage in Newfoundland may have no specifically West Country associations, though they vary quite widely from usage in mainland Canada.

In some parts of Newfoundland, *-s* is added to make all the present-tense forms: *I gives, you gives, he gives,* etc.; the form without *-s* is used to express past time: *I give, you give, he give,* etc., meaning 'I gave,' 'you gave,' 'he gave.' In a similar way, many verb forms strong elsewhere are made weak in Newfoundland; for example, *throwed* for *threw, rised* for *rose, blowed* for *blew.* Pronouns in some versions of Newfoundland again show a West Country inheritance, especially in the use of *I, he,* etc., in the emphatic final position in the sentence: *He gave it to we.* The same is true of the use of *'n* as a general pronoun to replace *him, her, it,* or *them;* for example, *He got'n* for *He got it.*

Vocabulary. Like the other features of Newfoundland English, the vocabulary mirrors the settlement history of the province and its economy; it also adds a new dimension to Newfoundland English, namely its testimony to the linguistic inventiveness of Newfoundlanders. The fact that the Portuguese were among the earliest fishermen to visit the island is mirrored in *baccalao* = 'codfish,' while French fishermen gave its name to the *capelin,* a small edible marine fish, often used as bait by cod fishermen. The early days of the province are recalled by *planter* = originally 'resident settler' and *liveyer* = 'fisherman permanently resident in Labrador' (as opposed to a *visiting fisherman*).

(1) West Country terms. The connection between Newfoundland and the English West Country appears in:

bangbelly = '*pancake'
figgy-pudden = 'pudding containing raisins'
flanker = 'spark'
linhay = 'shed'

*Appears as separate entry

(2) Earlier English terms. The same connection is shown by many other words that were current in Shakespeare's day but have since been lost from Standard English, to survive only in the West Country and in Newfoundland. Among these are:

bavin /bă-vən/ = 'brush faggot'
bawn /bôn/ = originally 'cattle enclosure,' now 'foreshore where fish are dried'
brewis /**broo**-ĭs/ = 'stew of ship's biscuit, cod, etc.'
dean /dēn/ = 'valley'
dout = 'to extinguish'
droke /drōk/ = 'narrow lane through a valley'; can also have other meanings
felon = 'sore on the finger'
glaum /gläm/ = 'to snatch suddenly'
janney = 'disguised Christmas visitor'
lightsome = 'cheerful'
more /mär/ = 'tree root'

(3) Irish Gaelic terms. Newfoundland's Irish inheritance is most clearly apparent in the use by some Newfoundlanders of Irish Gaelic words, such as:

bresney = 'pile of firewood'
omadawn, omadhaun /ä-mə-*th*ôn/ = 'foolish person'
sleeveen = 'rogue'
starrigans = 'small sticks or trees'
stookawn = 'simpleton'

(4) Fishing terms. The fishing and marine economy of Newfoundland is mirrored in:

ballycaters = 'ice floes rafting to the shore'
barbel, barvel = 'fisherman's apron'
brichins = 'cod roes'
flake = 'platform for drying fish'
flirrup = 'large lamp used on fishing wharves'
fresh fish = 'fish caught in fresh water, regardless of age and condition'
growler = 'small iceberg'
grump-head = 'post on a wharf for receiving lines from vessels, bollard'

handyan = 'fingerless glove worn by fishermen when hauling lines'
nippers = 'mittens worn by fishermen to protect the palms of their hands'
oil clothes = 'oilskin garments'
scrod = 'small cod, slightly dried'
spudgel = 'large, long-handled bailing scoop'
strouters = 'perpendicular supports at the front of a wharf'

(5) Topographical terms. Newfoundland's topography is reflected in:

knap /năp/ = 'small hill'
mish = 'low-lying area, usually damp, but drier than a swamp'
tolt /tōlt/ = 'small hill'

(6) Inventive terms. The linguistic inventiveness of Newfoundlanders is shown by:

barber = 'early morning fog over water'
copying (various forms) = 'leaping from ice floe to ice floe'
crackie = 'small, noisy dog'
dally = 'lull in the wind during a snowstorm'
gaze = 'hide or blind used in hunting'
rattle = 'river rapids'
steady = 'wide, placid stretch in a river'
tickle = 'narrow strait'

(7) Idioms. Newfoundland can lay claim to a number of idioms that, if not entirely peculiar to the province, do something to mark its English. The use of *some* and *right* as adverbs, as in *It's some hot* and *It's right flat*, it shares with the rest of Atlantic Canada. The expression *stomach-sick* for *sick in/at/to the stomach* is about three times as popular in Newfoundland as it is elsewhere. Some idioms—for instance, *belly and back* = 'odd gloves,' *go dog for* = 'to accompany as a helper,' and *hat of woods* = 'low growth of trees on a hilltop'—may be current in Newfoundland English only.

news, tune, duke, etc. One of the oldest contrasts between Southern and Northern speech lies in the pronunciation of the vowel in words like *news, tune,* and *duke.* Southern speech has retained the older /yo͞o/ sound—/nyo͞oz/, /tyo͞on/, /dyo͞ok/—whereas Northern speech has dropped the /y/ and pronounces these words as /no͞oz/, /to͞on/, and /do͞ok/. (See GENERAL NORTHERN DIALECT; GENERAL SOUTHERN DIALECT.)

In Middle English these vowels were usually pronounced /ēo͞o/ until as late as the 16th century. Then this changed to a pronunciation with what linguists call a "glide," the /y/ sound before a vowel. When the /yo͞o/ pronunciation was brought to Colonial America, it continued to be used in the South and in rural New England but gradually disappeared in the Northern and North Midland dialect regions.

But this old distinction between the two major dialects is dying out. At one time /yo͞o/ was pronounced after the consonants /ch/, /j/, /r/, /l/, /s/, and /sh/, as in *chew, jewelry, rude, lewd, soon,* and *shoe.* Now this pronunciation has almost totally disappeared. The glide remains only after /t/, /d/, and /n/, and even that situation is changing.

When the words are infrequently used terms, such as *tutor, tunic, neutron, nutrient, duel,* and *dune,* young Southern speakers tend to pronounce them the same way as Northern speakers—with /o͞o/. In more commonly used words, such as *Tuesday, new,* and *during,* Southern speakers use the glide about half the time, sometimes saying /**tyo͞oz**-dā/, /nyo͞o/, and /**dyo͝or**-ĭng/, and sometimes /**to͞oz**-dā/, /no͞o/, and /**do͝or**-ĭng/. It is likely that in 50 years or so the /yo͞o/ pronunciation will no longer be a characteristic of Southern speech.

Newspeak /**no͞o**-spēk/. Those who feel that the English language is going to the dogs are fond of referring darkly to *Newspeak,* the loathsome official language used for political thought control in George Orwell's novel *1984.* Are we in fact degrading our language in the direction of Newspeak?

In the year 1984 (according to the book) bureaucratic lexicographers were still working on the official Newspeak dictionary, but the language itself was not yet in everyday use. It was planned to replace *Oldspeak* (the Newspeak term for Standard English) by about 2050. Newspeak itself was derived from Oldspeak by a process of narrowing, simplification, and redefinition. Unlike other languages, Newspeak was to drop (rather than add) vocabulary items every year.

Many words like *justice, morality,* and *science* were simply abolished. Other basic Oldspeak words like *free* were retained, but their meanings were restricted to simple and unpolitical senses. *Free* meant only 'not affected by something,' as in *This field is free from weeds;* its political senses were eliminated. Synonyms, near-synonyms, and metaphors were also abolished.

The political vocabulary of Newspeak consisted of newly coined compound words:

doublethink = 'the ability to believe key contradictions laid down by the party'; for example, *War is peace. Ignorance is strength.*

goodthink = 'correct political belief'

prolefeed = 'low-quality news and entertainment provided for the proles' (the uneducated 85 percent of the population outside the party)

unperson = 'political offender condemned by the party and subsequently defined as never having existed'

The grammar of Newspeak was highly simplified and regular. All nouns could function as verbs and vice versa. All verbs were inflected with *-ed, -ing.* Adjectives were formed with the suffix *-ful,* adverbs with the suffix *-wise.*

goodthink = (1) (noun) 'correct political belief' (2) (verb) 'to be politically orthodox'

goodthinkful = 'naturally orthodox, incapable of thinking a bad thought'

goodthinkwise = 'in a politically correct manner'

Another feature of Newspeak was that names of institutions, doctrines, etc., were coined as easily pronounced words made up from simple or reduced syllables:

Ingsoc = 'English Socialism' (the party ideology)

Minipax = 'the Ministry of Peace' (the war department)

Minitrue = 'the Ministry of Truth' (the department of news, entertainment, education, and the fine arts)

Pornosec = 'the Pornographic Section of the Ministry of Truth' (producing pornography for the proles)

In our real English-speaking world, Oldspeak is alive and well. Whatever else big government may have been doing, it has not been taking control of the language. Dictionaries have no official status but are compiled by reasonably independent editors and published by fiercely competitive commercial firms. Correctness is not imposed by a ruling elite but emerges from actual usage, with its numerous levels of social prestige, literary convention, and the never-ceasing innovations of a living language. Bureaucrats and businessmen as always display a fatal hankering for a few individual features of Newspeak (see ACRONYMS; JARGON), but they are no more of a general threat than they were in Orwell's day. The notorious suffix *-wise*—as in *saleswise, demographic-profile-wise*—was, in fact, already in commercial fashion before *1984* was written and is now if anything somewhat dated. The mass media may be doing a fine job of turning out prolefeed, but at least we proles still have the option of turning to Station OFF.

It is something worth reflecting on, our freedom from language control. If Orwell was right in suggesting that thought control cannot be enforced without language control, then the English-speaking peoples have done remarkably well for themselves in instinctively resisting attempts at language legislation. The huge vocabulary at their disposal continues to grow, and their freedom to use it as they wish is unrestricted. This freedom may be valuable enough to put alongside the other great freedoms.

Meanwhile, it is amusing to note that a few Newspeak words have been absorbed into the general vocabulary, but not necessarily in the forms and meanings endorsed by Orwell's all-seeing, inescapable Big Brother.

Doublethink is often used, not so much in the official Newspeak sense defined above, but meaning merely 'muddled or self-contradictory thinking, especially by bureaucrats, politicians, etc.'

Double talk is a word not actually reported by Orwell but impeccably formed according to the rules of Newspeak; it has two meanings: (1) 'muddled and often self-contradictory language, especially as used by bureaucrats, politicians, etc.' (2) 'improvised and boldly meaningless verbiage.' Here is an example of the second kind of double talk:

> We put a couple bucks into it [a 25-year-old refrigerator] every four or five years for a new frammis gasket or a whatzis foonjib. . . .
> —Jerome Brondfield, *Reader's Digest*

Doublespeak is an equally correct variant of *double talk.*

Prole, a shortening of *proletarian,* is used chiefly in a humorous or sarcastic vein:

> The important thing about Las Vegas is not that the builders were gangsters but that they were proles. . . . Because it is prole, it gets ignored. . . .
> —Tom Wolfe, *The Kandy-Kolored . . . Baby*

> This is arrogant moviemaking: its assumption is that the proles will buy their tickets and march unprotestingly through the fun house no matter how evident is the contemptuousness of the barkers. —John Skow, *Time*

The word *unperson* is used in the true Newspeak (or *goodthinkful*) sense, 'political offender condemned to nonexistence by a totalitarian regime':

> . . . a law [in South Africa] that would make it a crime to publish the name of anyone arrested under the security laws. Those arrested would just disappear: become unpersons.
> —Anthony Lewis, *New York Times*

Nonperson is a frequent variant of *unperson* (but is not strictly correct Newspeak, in which *un-* is the sole negative prefix); *nonperson* is sometimes used in a humorous political sense, 'someone who has lost all political status':

> . . . when Democratic Chairman Leonard Kramp, a Kennedy fan, was stripped of control over hiring local census workers, he was told by Regional Census Director Manker Harris: "You're a nonperson. You decided to back the wrong man for President. . . ."
> —*Time*

New York City dialect. New York City speech is unique among URBAN DIALECTS. Most large cities predominantly use the dialect of their general region. Boston speech, for example, is essentially an urbanized form of the NEW ENGLAND DIALECT, which is a division of NORTHERN DIALECT. New York City speech, on the other hand, is a dialect in its own right, a separate Northern dialect.

Vocabulary and Speech Patterns. New York is the largest and most densely populated city in the United States, with some seven million residents in 1980. The Dutch were the first to settle in the region, establishing New Amsterdam on the tip of Manhattan Island in 1624. Relics of their language are still present in the city's dialect. By 1700 the dominant settlers were English, coming primarily via New England. In fact, up until about 1900, New England contributed the largest number of white lifetime settlers. As a result, there are several New England speech patterns in New York City's dialect. After 1900 most in-migrants were from the Middle Atlantic States.

As the traditional gateway of foreign immigration, New York City has the highest percentage of foreign-born citizens of any U.S. city. As late as 1930, 33 percent of its population was born outside the United States. Today, almost every national and racial group in the world is represented among the city's inhabitants. There are especially large communities of Italian-, German-, and Yiddish-speaking citizens. New York also has the largest Puerto Rican population of any city in the world. This influx of foreign culture and language, however, has had little direct influence on the city's dialect, except perhaps to enlarge its vocabulary. The Jewish culture especially, because it plays such a prominent everyday role in the life of the city, has contributed many words to its general vocabulary. Most of these words are Yiddish in origin and have been fully adopted into the dialect (see YIDDISH WORDS).

New York City is made up of five boroughs, each having its own cultural and economic characteristics. *Manhattan,* whose name comes from the Algonquian Indian word meaning 'hill island' (*manah* = 'island' + *atin* = 'hill'), is the cultural and commercial heart of the city. *The Bronx* (originally *the Broncks,* referring to the family of Jonas *Bronck,* a Dane who had a farm just north of the Harlem River) is chiefly a crowded, residential borough. *Queens,* the largest of the five boroughs in area, is industrialized and has many railroad yards but has several residential communities as well. *Brooklyn* (originally *Breuckelen,* named after a town in the Netherlands) is a residential and industrial area, having the largest population of the five boroughs. *Staten Island* (named in honor of the *Staten,* or 'Estates,' the parliament of the Netherlands) is the least populated and has only recently lost its semirural character.

These five boroughs and the communities within them have their own characteristic speech patterns. This is the result of many complex factors, and location within the city is only one of them. Probably the most important consideration when talking about the difference, say, between the speech of the Lower East Side (Manhattan) and Astoria (Queens) is social and economic status.

New York City speech is a complex mixture of SOCIAL DIALECT as well as REGIONAL DIALECT. Even so, the distinctions between the way the residents talk in Forest Hills (Queens), Flatbush (Brooklyn), and Washington Heights (Manhattan) are more a matter of the frequency of certain features than of actual differences in features. All three of these communities have the same basic speech characteristics, but in varying proportions. Generally then, New York City can be considered a single speech community.

Pronunciation. It is especially in the proportions of pronunciation features that we hear the difference between the speech of a Brooklyn cabdriver, for example, and a downtown Manhattan executive.

(1) R-*lessness.* Like the speakers of the New England, Virginia Piedmont, and Coastal Southern dialects, New Yorkers often drop the /r/ after a vowel (see R-LESSNESS, INTRUSIVE R). This was especially true in the past. When /r/ is dropped at the end of a word, it is usually replaced with the unsyllabic vowel sound /ə/. Thus, *beard, poor, care, four* are often pronounced /bĭəd/, /po͞oə/, /kĕə/, /fôə/.

The dropping of /r/ is a good indicator of social class. This fact was first observed by William Labov in 1962 in his innovative survey of Manhattan department-store employees. For the top, middle, and bottom levels on a price and fashion scale, Labov chose Saks Fifth Avenue, Macy's, and S. Klein (now defunct). The employees of these stores, he reasoned, would be representative of the three major social-class divisions. Armed with pad and pencil, he would ask a sales clerk the whereabouts of an item that he knew was on the fourth floor. When he got the expected answer, "Fourth floor," he would lean forward and say, "Excuse me?" The clerk would then repeat the phrase in a careful or more emphatic style. In this way he was able to record both a spontaneous pronunciation and a more careful pronunciation of words in which /r/ followed a vowel. Labov soon discovered that Saks employees pronounced the /r/ in these words more often than Macy's employees and considerably more often than S. Klein employees. The dropping of /r/, then, is commoner among speakers of the working class than of the middle and upper-middle classes. For this reason the pronunciation of /r/ after vowels has come to have prestige. Consequently, the dropping of /r/ as a feature of New York pronunciation is beginning to die out.

(2) As in the New England dialect, an intrusive, or extra, /r/ is frequently added to words ending in a vowel, such as *china, law, vanilla:* /**chī**-nər/, /lär/, /və-**nĭl**-ər/. The /r/ is nearly always added to words ending in a vowel when they precede another word that begins with a vowel. The three examples above would nearly always be pronounced with the additional /r/ sound in the phrases *china and glass, the law of the land, vanilla ice cream.*

(3) One of the best-known and most satirized

New York pronunciations is the substitution of the vowel sound /oi/ for the sound /êr/ in words like *bird, thirty-third, girl:* /boid/, /thoi-dē-**thoid**/, /goil/. (The first or beginning sound of the diphthong /oi/ is actually pronounced more like /ə/ or /ŭ/.) This makes words like *coil* and *curl, loin* and *learn* homophonous, that is, identical in sound. Although this is a stereotyped characteristic of "Brooklynese," it has, in fact, for generations been a feature of working-class speech throughout New York City. The television character Archie Bunker, for example, who was depicted as a resident of Queens, regularly used this pronunciation.

(4) Sometimes the previous substitution works in reverse: some words that have the /oi/ diphthong, like *oil, oyster, toilet,* are pronounced with the sound /êr/: /êrl/, /**êr**-stər/, /**têr**-lət/. This is an example of *hypercorrection,* the mistaken application of a speech change that is correct in one situation to a situation where it is unsuitable.

(5) The vowel in words like *father, palm* is usually the sound /ȯ/: /**fȯ**-*th*ər/, /pȯlm, pȯm/. This feature is characteristic of all classes of New York speakers.

(6) The consonant sounds /th/ and /*th*/ as in *throw, with, this* are often pronounced /t/ and /d/: /trō/, /wĭd/, /dĭs/. This feature, however, is beginning to die out in New York speech.

(7) Vowels in general, but especially the vowel /ă/, are often strongly nasalized.

(8) An extra /g/ sound is occasionally added to words that have the /ng/ sound followed by a vowel. *Singing, singer, Long Island,* for example, are often pronounced /**sĭng**-gĭng/, /**sĭng**-gər/, /lông **gī**-lənd/. This feature is especially characteristic of speakers from many foreign or ethnic communities.

(9) The sound /t/ when it occurs in the middle of a word is often pronounced with a glottal stop. As in British cockney, such words as *metal, bottle, kitten, button* are pronounced /**mĕ′**-l/, /**bŏ′**-l/, /**kĭ′**-n/, /**bŭ′**-n/. This pronunciation is heard primarily among working-class speakers.

These nine features, along with several others, make up a pronunciation style that is generally regarded as having low prestige. Recent detailed studies show that not only do non–New Yorkers consider this to be a relatively nonprestigious dialect but that New Yorkers themselves also show a general distaste for their speech. As a result, most white middle-class New Yorkers tend to avoid this dialect as much as possible. The fact that New York City speech has not spread very far even into the metropolitan suburbs would seem to confirm this.

nice. Its underlying senses are '(of persons) finely discriminating, judicious, fastidious' and '(of things) finely discriminated, delicately balanced':

> They are the brave, free, joyful, hope-inspiring fellows who are not too nice and dainty and who have no sneers.
>
> —Thomas Wolfe, *The Web and the Rock*

> Furnished . . . with Academies of Science, with nice instruments and the Spirit of Experiment . . .
>
> —Benjamin Franklin, *Autobiography*

These meanings are still current, and old-fashioned critics have tried to persuade people not to use the word in other senses. But *nice* is now used as an endlessly varied term of moderate approval. It ranges in meaning from 'kindly, good,' 'attractive, pleasing in manner,' and '(of young, unmarried women) sexually modest' to 'satisfactory, cheerful, pleasant, congenial':

> [Harpo] was worth all the wonderful adjectives that were used to describe him. He was a nice man in the fullest sense of the word.
>
> —Groucho Marx, *The Groucho Letters*

> She was the first "nice" girl he had ever known.
>
> —F. Scott Fitzgerald, *The Great Gatsby*

> We passed lots of Basques, with oxen, or cattle, hauling carts along the road, and nice farm houses, low roofs, and all white-plastered.
>
> —Ernest Hemingway, *The Sun Also Rises*

It would be nice to report that Congress showed some concern. . . .
—Gerald R. Ford, *A Time to Heal*

I think it was Li'l Abner's Mammy Yokum who used to say, "Good is better than evil because it's nicer."
—James Hitchcock, *St. Louis Review*

◊ ***Recommendation.*** There is no problem about *nice*. It is natural for certain words to be taken up as all-purpose value terms. (Just the same, we could wish that people would go easy on "Have a nice day.")

nicety takes its meanings not from the common meanings of *nice* ('kind, pleasant, etc.') but from its underlying meanings 'finely discriminating, delicately balanced.' *Nicety* usually means 'fastidiousness,' 'delicate balance,' or 'fine detail':

. . . watched her as she walked primly away across the square, holding her skirts at the curbs with ladylike nicety.
—Thomas Wolfe, *Look Homeward, Angel*

The scales of justice are maintained in balance by a sensitive mechanism, adjusted with such nicety that they record the minutest evidentiary weight.
—Louis Nizer, *My Life in Court*

Kennedy, who could not imagine letting legal niceties halt the search for a kidnapped child, grew heated.
—Arthur M. Schlesinger, Jr., *Robert Kennedy and His Times*

Niceties often means 'polite formalities':

"I shall be brief and to the point," Rand said, and those around the table noticed that he remained standing and omitted such prefatory niceties as the word "Gentlemen."
—G. Gordon Liddy, *Out of Control*

nohow, meaning either 'in no way, not at all' or 'in no particular way, anyhow,' has formerly been in good usage but is now rare except in dialect or when deliberately used in informal speech for emphasis.

none. The pronoun *none*, a contraction of *no one*, is originally singular but has for centuries been used also as a plural.

The grave's a fine and private place,
But none, I think, do there embrace.
—Andrew Marvell, *To His Coy Mistress* (1681)

In modern formal usage there is a tendency to make *none* singular wherever it can logically be construed as being singular.

. . . wrote innumerable stories and a few novels, none of which was published.
—Brendan Gill, *Here at The New Yorker*

None of the elected officials has indicated he would object.
—*Atlanta Constitution*

◊ ***Recommendation.*** There is some merit in making *none* singular when possible. But it is by no means a binding rule. The first modern example above would be equally correct with *none* as a plural.

non-U. See U, NON-U.

no place. Also spelled *noplace*, this adverb, meaning 'nowhere,' is not accepted in formal use.

no question. See QUESTION.

normalcy. The suffix *-cy* occurs primarily in abstract nouns formed from nouns or adjectives ending in *-t* or *-te*: *infant* forms *infancy; confederate* forms *confederacy*. It is also used with some nouns not ending in *-t* or *-te*: *chaplain* forms *chaplaincy; colonel* forms *colonelcy*. It is almost never used with adjectives ending in *-al*, which regularly form abstract nouns in *-ality: final, finality; legal, legality; normal, normality;* etc. Thus *normalcy*, first recorded in 1857, is an exception, perhaps a unique formation. It remained a rare word until 1920, when President Warren G. Harding called for a return to normalcy in his presidential campaign. The word immediately became either familiar and acceptable or notorious and unacceptable, according to taste—and some people have doubtless been more influenced by their feelings about Harding than by their feeling for words.

> . . . since Caspey has more or less returned to normalcy . . .
> —William Faulkner, *Sartoris*

> . . . [American English's] daring experiments lie in the grand tradition of English, and are signs of its incurable normalcy and abounding vigor.
> —H. L. Mencken (quoted), *Reader's Digest*

◊ ***Recommendation.*** The regular and impeccable abstract noun from *normal* is *normality. Normalcy* is somewhat deviant in its formation, but our language abounds in such oddments and alternatives. This one does no harm and now has a long history of standard usage. Anyone who dislikes it is entitled to avoid it but can't expect to stamp it out.

Norse words. Vikings first raided Britain in A.D. 787. Coming from Norway and Denmark, they were a Germanic people closely related to the Anglo-Saxons, who had originally lived just south of them on the Continent. Their language, known as Old Norse, was very similar to Old English; the two peoples could understand each other quite well, and many of their individual words (such as Old Norse *systir*, Old English *sweoster* = 'sister' and Old Norse *skyrta*, Old English *scyrte* = 'shirt') were easily recognizable as variants. (For an investigation of the later development of *skyrta* and *scyrte* see COGNATES.)

Large parts of England and Scotland settled by Vikings remained bilingual for several centuries. The English element eventually prevailed, and the descendants of the Vikings forgot Norse and spoke English. But a real fusion of peoples and cultures had occurred; hundreds of words, including many basic and everyday ones, were permanently absorbed into the English vocabulary, often displacing original English ones. The enduring image of the Vikings as bloodthirsty and destructive savages, as vividly depicted in the *Anglo-Saxon Chronicle*, is strikingly belied by the hoard of indispensable words they have bequeathed us. Among them are the nouns *skill* and *law, husband* and *sister, leg* and *skin;* the pronouns *both* and *they;* the verbs *get* and *take;* and the adjectives *flat, happy,* and *ill.*

After the Norman Conquest, French became the overwhelming influence on English, pouring thousands more words into the vocabulary than Norse had; but neither French nor any other language has ever scored as high as Old Norse as a transfusion of fundamental high-frequency words, which to this day are in our mouths every hour. The fraternal Norse ingredient thus provides one of the most interesting in the vast smorgasbord of our speech. (Later borrowings from the modern Scandinavian languages, though also interesting, supplied no basic words; these borrowings are discussed separately at SCANDINAVIAN WORDS.)

(1) Pronouns:

both: from Old Norse *bāthir* = 'the two'

their: from Old Norse *theira* = 'of them'

they, them: from Old Norse *their, them* (replacing Old English *hī, hīe*)

(2) Basic verbs:

call = 'to cry out': from Old Norse *kalla* = 'to shout, to name'

cast = 'to throw': from Old Norse *kasta* = 'to throw'

die = 'to cease to live': from Old Norse *deyja* = 'to die' (replacing Old English *steorfan*, originally 'to die,' later 'to die of hunger, starve')

gasp = 'to draw in the breath sharply': from Old Norse *geispa* = 'to yawn'

get = 'to obtain': from Old Norse *geta* = 'to obtain, beget'

happen = 'to occur': from *hap* = 'chance, luck,' from Old Norse *happ* = 'good luck'

hit = 'to strike': from Old Norse *hitta* = 'to come upon, meet with' (replacing Old English *slēan*, originally 'to strike,' later 'to kill, slay')

lift = 'to elevate': from Old Norse *lypta* = 'to elevate'

raise = 'to elevate, build up': from Old Norse *reisa* = 'to elevate'

scare = 'to frighten': from Old Norse *skirra* = 'to frighten'

scrape = 'to take off the top layer of something, especially by abrasion': from Old Norse *skrapa* = 'to scratch'

take = 'to get hold of, seize': from Old Norse *taka* = 'grasp, touch' (replacing Old English *niman* = 'to take')

want = 'to lack, wish for': from the noun *want* = 'lack, deficiency,' from Old Norse *want* = 'lack'

(3) Basic nouns:

awe = 'dread': from Old Norse *agi* = 'dread'

axle = 'shaft on which wheels revolve': earlier *axletree*, from Old Norse *öxull-trē* = 'axle-pole'

bag = 'container made of flexible material': from Old Norse *baggi* = 'sack'

ball = 'round object': from Old Norse *ball* = 'round object'

bank = 'ridge of earth': from Old Norse *banki* = 'ridge'

bark = 'skin of trees': from Old Norse *börkr* = 'bark' (replacing Old English *rind*, originally 'bark')

cake = 'flat loaf, piece of rich bakery': from Old Norse *kaka* = 'cake, biscuit'

club = 'heavy stick used as a weapon': from Old Norse *klubba* = 'club'

dirt = 'filth, mud': from Old Norse *drit* = 'filth'

dregs = 'sediment of beer, etc.': from Old Norse *dregg* = 'sediment'

gear = 'equipment': from Old Norse *gervi* = 'equipment'

leg = 'limb used for walking': from Old Norse *leggr* = 'limb' (replacing Old English *sceanca* = 'leg, shank')

link = 'loop of chain': from Old Norse *hlenkr* = 'link'

root = 'part of a plant growing in soil': from Old Norse *rōt* = 'root'

scrap = 'piece, fragment': from Old Norse *skrap* = 'scraps, bits and pieces'

seat = 'thing to sit on': from Old Norse *saeti* = 'seat'

sister = 'female sibling': from Old Norse *systir* (replacing the Old English equivalent *sweoster*)

skill = 'trained ability, knowledge and understanding': from Old Norse *skil* = 'discernment, knowledge'

skin = 'tissue covering flesh': from Old Norse *skinn* = 'skin'

window = 'opening, originally unglazed, to admit air and light to a building': from Old Norse *vind-auga* = 'wind-eye' (replacing Old English *eag-duru* = 'eye-door')

(4) Basic adjectives:

flat = 'level': from Old Norse *flatr* = 'flat'

happy = 'fortunate, prosperous,' later 'contented': from *hap* = 'chance, luck,' from Old Norse *happ* = 'good luck'

ill = 'bad, badly': from Old Norse *illr* = 'bad'

loose = 'not tied': from Old Norse *louss* = 'not tied'

low = 'not high': from Old Norse *lāgr* = 'low-lying'

odd = (1) '(of numbers) not even' (2) 'strange, peculiar': from Old Norse *oddi* = 'point of a triangle, third part, odd number'

rotten = 'decayed': from Old Norse *rotinn* = 'rotted'

tight = 'dense, firmly fixed, watertight': earlier *thyght*, from Old Norse *thehtr* = 'close-textured, watertight'

ugly = 'unpleasant-looking,' originally 'horrible, frightful': from Old Norse *uggligr* = 'frightful,' from *uggi* = 'fear'

wrong = 'not right, evil,' originally 'twisted, deviant': from Old Norse *wrangr* = 'unjust, awry'

(5) Birds, fish, animals, farm terms:

auk = 'large northern sea bird': from Norse *alk* = 'auk'

bat = 'nocturnal flying mammal': earlier *bakke*, from Old Norse *backe*, originally *ledhr-blaka* = 'leather-flapper'

booth = 'stall, hut': from Old Norse *bōth* = 'hut'

down = 'soft feathers of young birds': from Old Norse *dūnn* = 'down'

egg = 'oval reproductive capsule laid by a bird': from Old Norse *egg* = 'egg' (replacing Old English *ey* = 'egg')

eider = 'northern sea duck with very soft plumage': from Norse *aethr* = 'eider'

filly = 'young female horse': from Old Norse *fylja* = 'female foal'

fulmar = 'large northern gull': from Old Norse *fūl-mār* = 'foul-smelling gull,' from *fūl* = 'foul' + *mār* = 'gull'

geld = 'to castrate': from Old Norse *gelda* = 'to castrate'

gill = 'fish's breathing organ': from Old Norse *gil* = 'gill'

girth = 'strap around the belly of a saddle horse': from Old Norse *györdh* = 'belt, girdle'

kid = 'young goat,' later also 'child': from Old Norse *kidh* = 'young goat'

loon = 'large diving bird of northern waters': from Old Norse *lomr* = 'loon'

midden = 'dung heap': from Old Norse *myki-dyngja* = 'muck-heap'

skate = 'flat-bodied sea fish related to the ray': from Old Norse *skata* = 'skate'

skua = 'large predatory northern gull': from Old Norse *skūfr* = 'skua'

slaughter = 'the killing of meat animals': from Old Norse *slātr* = 'slaying'

snipe = 'small, large-billed moor bird': from Old Norse *myri-snipa* = 'moor-snipe'

stack = 'pile, haystack': from Old Norse *stakkr* = 'haystack' (replacing Old English *hrēac* = 'haystack, rick')

tern = 'slender, fork-tailed sea bird': from Old Norse *therna* = 'tern'

wing = 'bird's limb for flying': from Old Norse *vaengir* = 'wings' (replacing Old English *feathra* = 'feathers, wings')

(6) The sea, shipping, and weather:

billow = 'wave': from Old Norse *bylgja* = 'wave'

bulk = 'ship's cargo, heap, mass': from Old Norse *bulki* = 'cargo'

gale = 'strong wind': originally *gale wind*, from Norse *galen* = 'bad weather'

gust = 'sudden blast of wind': from Old Norse *gustr* = 'gust'

keel = (1) 'basic timber of a boat, to which the ribs are fastened' (2) later 'flat structure projecting below the hull': from Old Norse *kjölr* = 'keel'

lee = 'side away from the wind': partly from Old English *hlēo* = 'shelter' and partly from Old Norse *hlē* = 'lee of a ship'

muggy = 'warm and humid': from *mug* = 'drizzle, Scotch mist,' from Old Norse *mugga* = 'drizzle'

raft = 'logs fastened together for transportation in water,' later 'flat floating platform': originally 'beam, log,' from Old Norse *raptr* = 'rafter, beam'

sky = 'the heavens as seen from Earth': originally 'cloud,' from Old Norse *skȳ* = 'cloud'

stern = 'back end of a boat': from Old Norse *stjōrn* = 'steering, rudder, stern'

(7) Society:

fellow = 'associate, member of an institution, person': originally 'business partner,' from Old Norse *fē-lagi* = 'fee-layer, person who lays down money or makes an investment'

husband = 'male spouse': originally 'master of the household,' from Old Norse *hūs-bonda* = 'house-dweller, head of the house'

hustings = 'political campaigning or the scene of a campaign speech': from Old Norse *husthing* = 'house-assembly, meeting of the king's household' (as opposed to the public *thing*, or parliament of all the people), from *hus* = 'house' + *thing* = 'assembly'

law = 'codified rule enforced by custom or authority': from Old Norse *lagu* (plural) = 'things laid down' (replacing Old English *dom* = 'sentence, decision, law')

* **ombudsman** = 'citizens' representative'

outlaw = 'person declared outside the protection of the law': from Old Norse *ūtlagr*, from *ūt* = 'out' + *lagu* = 'laws'

*Appears as separate entry

(8) Miscellaneous words:

anger = 'to make angry': originally 'to distress,' from Old Norse *angra* = 'to grieve'

freckles = 'brown spots on the skin': earlier *frekens*, from Old Norse *freknur* = 'freckles'

lass = 'girl, young woman': earlier *lasce*, probably from Old Norse *laskwa* = 'unmarried woman' (*Lad* is probably also of Norse origin.)

meek = 'gentle, kind, humble': from Old Norse *miukr* = 'soft, gentle'

nay (archaic) = 'no': from Old Norse *nei* = 'never,' from *ne* = 'not' + *ei* = 'ever'

ransack = 'to search and plunder (a place)': from Old Norse *rannsaka* = 'to make a legal search of a house for stolen goods,' from *rann* = 'house' + *saka* = 'seek'

***scathe** = 'harm, injury': from Old Norse *skadhi* = 'injury'

snub = 'to treat with contempt, put (a person) down': from Old Norse *snubba*, probably originally 'to thumb one's nose at'

steak = 'thick slice of meat': from Old Norse *steik* = 'piece of meat roasted on a skewer or stick'

*Appears as separate entry

(9) Some Norse words that have remained localized or dialectal in Britain:

beck (chiefly Northern) = 'stream, brook': from Old Norse *bekkr* = 'stream'

firth (Scottish) = 'arm of the sea, estuary of a river': from Old Norse *fjördhr* = 'arm of the sea, fiord'

garth (Northern) = 'house yard, garden': from Old Norse *gardhr* = 'yard' (competing with Old English *geard* = 'yard')

gate (Northern and Scottish) = 'street' (as the *Canongate*, a street in Edinburgh): from Old Norse *gata* = 'path, street'

kirk (Scottish) = 'church': from Old Norse *kirkja* = 'church' (competing with Old English *cirice* = 'church')

***riding** = 'one of the three divisions of Yorkshire'

*Appears as separate entry

northerly, etc. In nautical usage a northerly current is one flowing from south to north, but a northerly wind is one blowing from north to south.

> . . . a tempestuous sea brewed that evening from a hard extemporaneous northerly (that is, a wind that comes from the north) battering against a hard northerly current (that is, a current that flows out of the south—I know, I know) . . .
>
> —William F. Buckley, Jr., *Airborne*

This paradox applies equally to all the other points of the compass. The explanation is this. Orientations and courses in general are naturally referred to by the direction *toward which they face* (or are thought of as facing): *a northerly flight of birds. The view from the house was northerly. They set a northerly course. The Gulf Stream flows northerly up the Florida coast.*

Winds are an exception, because a seaman (or anyone else for that matter) gauging the direction of a wind *faces into it*, and therefore names it by the direction *from which* it blows.

Northern dialect. Historically, the Northern speech area is the result of the westward migration of settlers from New England. The Dutch settlers of the Hudson Valley were also important in the formation of this dialect. Its southern boundary runs through central New Jersey and northern Pennsylvania and on through northern Ohio, Indiana, Illinois, and Iowa, where it begins to lose its sharp definition.

The subdivisions of the Northern dialect are the HUDSON VALLEY, INLAND NORTHERN, NEW ENGLAND, NEW YORK CITY, and UPPER MIDWESTERN dialects. Together with the NORTH MIDLAND DIALECT, the Northern dialect is the source of the much larger GENERAL NORTHERN DIALECT.

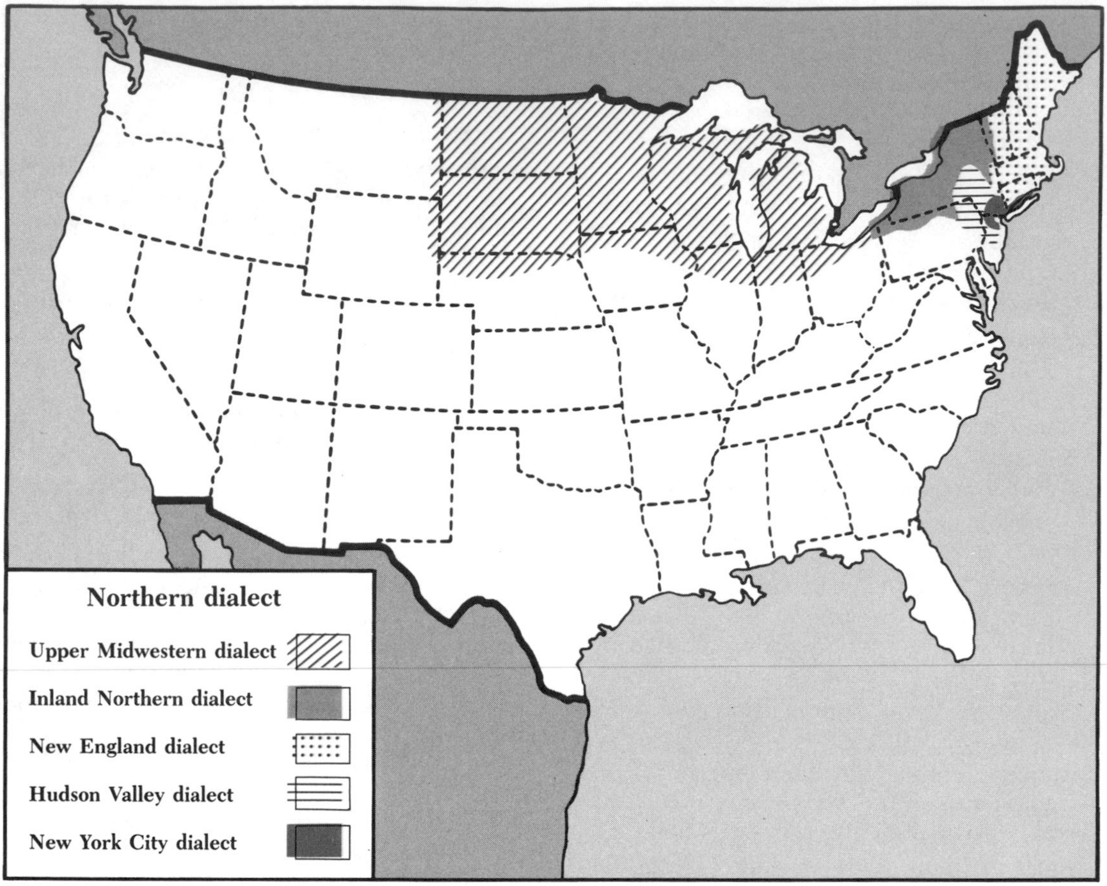

Pronunciation. When they come before /r/, the sounds /ō/ and /ô/ distinguish certain pairs of words:

morning /**môrn**-ĭng/, **mourning** /**mōrn**-ĭng/
hoarse /hōrs/, **horse** /hôrs/
fourteen /fōr-**tēn**/, **forty** /**fôr**-tē/

With is regularly pronounced /wĭth/, not /wĭth/. *Greasy* is pronounced /**grē**-sē/, not /**grē**-zē/. *Roots* is pronounced /ro͞ots/, not /ro͝ots/.

Vocabulary.

angleworm = '*earthworm'
* **boughten** (also North Midland) = 'purchased in a store'
brook = '*stream'
buttons, not have all one's = 'to be eccentric or crazy'
cabbage salad = '*coleslaw'
clapboards = 'finished siding'
clear = '(of tea) without milk or lemon'
clobber *or* **clobbered milk** = 'curdled milk, *clabber'
cowboy (especially in the East) = 'reckless or wild driver'
dog's age (especially in the East; old-fashioned) = 'very long time': *We haven't seen her in a dog's age.*
douse the glim = 'shut off the light'
duck bumps = '*goose flesh'
durn (also General Southern) = 'darn'
eave(s) spout *or* **spouting** = '*gutter'
farmer matches (also North Midland) = 'wooden striking matches'
-fest = 'celebration, gathering': *talkfest, summerfest,* etc.
four corners (also Western) = 'crossroads'
friedcake (except New England) = '*doughnut'
fritz, on the = 'broken, out of order'

galley-west (old-fashioned) = 'awry, askew' See CATERCORNER.
get a wiggle on (also North Midland) = 'to hurry, make haste'
gooms (also Western) = 'gums'
hardhead, hardhead stone = 'stone that is large and smooth'
hitch = 'to be friendly, get along with'; used negatively: *Their in-laws don't hitch.*
hoity-toity (also North Midland) = 'haughty, patronizing'
I declare (also General Southern) = 'exclamation of surprise'
jamboree (old-fashioned) = 'social gathering for talk, gabfest'
johnnycake = 'corn bread'
Judas Priest = 'exclamation of surprise or anger'
kittens, kitties = 'dust balls'
kitty-corner (also Western) = 'in a diagonal position, *catercorner'
later (used especially by black speakers) = 'goodbye, farewell'
murphies (also North Midland) = 'potatoes'
nana (especially in the Northeast) = 'grandmother'
no-see-um (also Pacific Northwest, Pacific Southwest, and Canadian) = 'stinging gnat'
pail = '*bucket'
pea beans (especially in the Northeast) = 'small, white dried beans'
***quite** = 'very, extremely'
rubber ice = 'ice that bends without cracking'
shuck (peas *or* **beans)** = 'to shell'
shuck = 'walnut shell'
sill cock = 'water tap, faucet'
spider (especially New England and Inland Northern) = 'heavy iron skillet'
stick *or* **tap of work** = 'least amount of work'; used negatively: *He hasn't done a stick of work all day.*
stone = 'seed of a fruit, *pit'
stone wall = 'wall built of unmortared stones'
stump fence (rural and old-fashioned) = 'fence made of uprooted tree stumps'
swill = 'garbage'

*Appears as separate entry

North Midland dialect. This dialect is spoken in southern New Jersey, northern Delaware and Maryland, and most of Pennsylvania; in northwestern West Virginia; in the southern half of Ohio, Indiana, Illinois, and Iowa; and westward into the plains states. For the most part, it is the result of the westward migration of settlers from Pennsylvania. Among these settlers the English Quakers, the Palatine Germans (who came to be known as the Pennsylvania Dutch), and the Scotch-Irish were particularly influential. The North Midland dialect is a transitional dialect between Northern and General Southern. On the one hand, with the speech of the South, North Midland forms part of the MIDLAND DIALECT; on the other hand, and in a larger sense, it belongs with the speech of the North and the West within the GENERAL NORTHERN DIALECT.

Pronunciation. The pronunciation features of North Midland speech do not differ much from those of the Northern dialect. Two exceptions: the vowel sounds in pairs of words such as *morning, mourning* and *horse, hoarse* are not distinguished and *creek* is usually pronounced /krĭk/.

Vocabulary. (1) As indicated below, many North Midland words are shared with other regions either to the north or to the south. Those borrowed from Scotch-Irish and PENNSYLVANIA DUTCH are so indicated.

***boughten** (also Northern) = 'purchased in a store'
callithump = 'noisy mock serenade, *shivaree'
clook = 'setting hen' (from Pennsylvania Dutch)
crudded *or* **cruddled milk** = 'curdled milk, *clabber'
dornick = 'hand-sized stone suitable for throwing' (from Scotch-Irish)
drawed = (also General Southern, Inland Northern; used by rural and working-class speakers) = 'past tense of *draw*'
eave(s) spout *or* **spouting** = '*gutter'
farmer matches (also Northern) = 'wooden striking matches'
fatcake = '*doughnut' (from Pennsylvania Dutch)

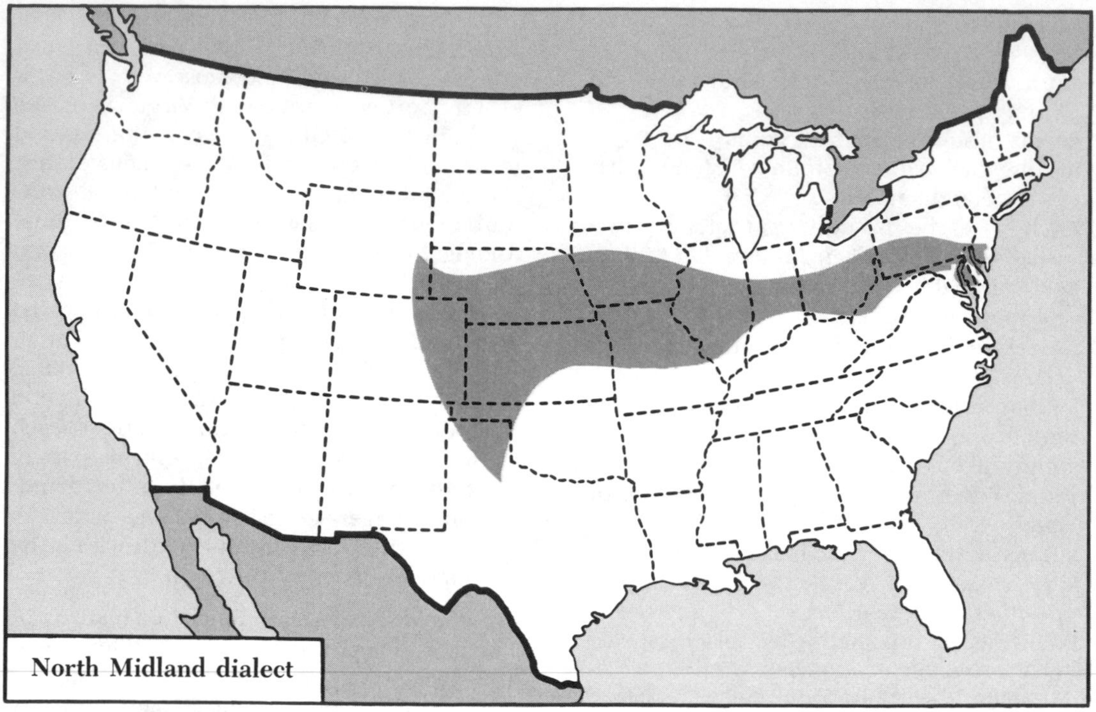

fresh-fried potatoes = 'French-fried potatoes'
fussbutton = 'fussy person, *fussbudget'
gathered *or* **gathering ear** (also Inland Northern) = 'infected, suppurating ear'
get a wiggle on (also Northern) = 'to hurry, make haste'
hoity-toity (also Northern) = 'haughty, patronizing'
murphies (also Northern) = 'potatoes'
outen (the fire *or* **light)** (also Coastal Southern) = 'to put out, shut off'
paling fence (also General Southern) = '*picket fence'
pallet (also General Southern) = 'temporary bed on the floor'
panhas = 'scrapple or *headcheese' (from Pennsylvania Dutch)
peanut heaven (especially in Pennsylvania and Ohio) = 'upper theater balcony'
red *or* **rid up (a room)** = 'to clean or tidy'
roastin' ears (also General Southern) = 'corn ripe enough to eat'
run = '*stream'
seed (also General Southern) = 'stone of a plum, cherry, or peach, a *pit'
smearcase, shmearcase = '*cottage cheese' (from Pennsylvania Dutch)
snits = 'dried fruit' (from Pennsylvania Dutch)
souse (also General Southern) = '*headcheese'
splinter = 'rain trough or spout'
spouting, spout = 'eaves trough, *gutter'
stone fence (**rock fence** or **wall** in the South, **stone wall** in the North) = 'wall built of unmortared stone'
thick milk = 'curdled milk, *clabber' (from Pennsylvania Dutch)
woods colt (also General Southern) = '*illegitimate child'

*Appears as separate entry

(2) Words confined to the Susquehanna and Delaware valleys, the latter dominated by Philadelphia:

baby coach = 'baby carriage'
flannel cake = '*pancake'
pavement = 'sidewalk'
sick on one's stomach = 'queasy'
till = 'until': *till the time I get there*

*Appears as separate entry

(3) Words confined to western Pennsylvania, dominated by Pittsburgh and Wheeling, West Virginia, pre–Revolutionary War outposts that later became centers of trade. This area forms a kind of buffer zone between the area east of the Alleghenies and the rest of the North Midland region. Most words are rural and now old-fashioned:

baby cab = 'baby carriage'
barn burners = 'wooden matches'
carbon oil = 'kerosene'
caretaker = 'road maintenance superintendent'
cruds = 'curdled milk, *clabber' (from Scotch-Irish)
grinnie = 'chipmunk'
gum band = 'rubber band'
hap = 'comforter' (from English dialect)
haydoodle = 'haycock'
sugar camp = 'sugar-maple grove'

*Appears as separate entry

nostalgia. The old German word *heimweh,* literally 'home-sadness,' means 'the yearning to return to one's home.' Early Swiss medical writers, interested in the psychology of this feeling, translated the word into medical Latin as *nostalgia* (from Greek *nostos* = 'homecoming, a return home' + *algia* = 'pain, sickness'). The underlying meaning of *nostalgia* is thus 'homesickness.' In English the primary meaning is 'a yearning to return to a happy past time in one's life':

> Tolkien had long dreamt of returning to Oxford. Throughout his war service he had suffered an ache of nostalgia for his college, his friends, and the way of life that he had led for four years.
> —Humphrey Carpenter, *Tolkien*

Often it means 'sentimental admiration for a past time that one may never have experienced and that may not have existed as one imagines it':

> There was in the culture of the sixties a romantic nostalgia for the era of the Old West, the simple life, the life of adventure.
> —Doris Kearns, *Lyndon Johnson and the American Dream*

The adjective is *nostalgic* = 'full of nostalgia, yearning for home or the past':

> Back in Bus 4, a pretty Philippine tour guide named Lulu led her Americans in nostalgic songs of the '40s: "Paper Doll," "You Are My Sunshine."
> —Charles N. Barnard, *Reader's Digest*

The original German word *heimweh* was also separately translated into English as *homesickness. Homesickness* and *nostalgia* are thus in a sense COGNATES, with the former keeping the original meaning and the latter taking on derived meanings.

not about to. See ABOUT.

notorious, ultimately from Latin *nōtus* = 'known,' means simply 'well-known, being a matter of common knowledge':

> It is notorious that the savages knew nothing of agriculture.
> —Washington Irving, *A History of New York . . . by Diedrich Knickerbocker* (1809)

Most often, the word means 'noted for some bad quality or reason,' whether 'famous for cruelty, crime, or immorality' or merely 'all too well-known,' with a mildly negative or apologetic tinge:

> The Mafia is notorious for its use of violence—murdering or intimidating into silence any witnesses against it.
> —*U.S. News & World Report*

> . . . Charlie and I put on white tie and tails, as was the custom in thirty-one, and started for Berlin's most elegant and notorious nightclub. . . .
> —Joshua Logan, *Josh*

> *New Yorker* editors have always been notorious for preoccupying themselves with punctuation.
> —Brendan Gill, *Here at The New Yorker*

The noun is *notoriety:*

> One party gave me undesired notoriety when Lee Udall, the wife of the Secre-

tary of the Interior, pushed me fully clothed into the swimming pool as I stood on the edge. . . .

—Arthur M. Schlesinger, Jr., *Robert Kennedy and His Times*

no way. (1) The old adverb *noway*, spelled as a single word and pronounced with stress on the first syllable, /**nō**-wā/, means 'not at all, by no means.' It is now rare in standard usage but survives in some regional dialects.

(2) In the 1960s the phrase *no way*, pronounced either with equal stresses, /**nō wā**/, or with rising stress, /nō **wā**/, suddenly came into fashion. Its primary use is as an emphatic negative reply or interjection:

> My boys—Ben, 15, Luke, 14, and Felix, 12—declined the invitation to join us. They loved the water. But go swimming with your old man and little sister? No way!
>
> —Brian Davies, *Reader's Digest*

It is also used in the construction *There's no way* (followed by a clause) = 'It's impossible, it's out of the question (that)':

> I saw people already trapped by the flames. I knew they'd never get out, and I knew there was no way they were going to put that fire out.
>
> —Ralph Graves (quoted), *New York Times*

(3) Another version of the constructions above drops the word *there's*, keeping the clause in the standard subject-verb order:

> "The trouble is these shell creatures are from British Columbia, 550 million years ago," he says. "No way they're from around here."
>
> —Sidney Horenstein (quoted), *New York Times*

(4) A further construction, probably developed from the first rather than the second version above, is *no way* followed by a clause with inversion of the subject-verb order:

> Personally I have all the confidence in the world that no way is he going to sell out the philosophies and the ideals which we stand for. . . .
>
> —Thomas P. O'Neill, Jr. (quoted), *New York Times*

Note. The sudden emergence of *no way*, with almost instantaneous diffusion all over the English-speaking world, is one of the most conspicuous innovations in the recent history of English. It is still distinctly informal and not yet suitable for formal written usage. Like most innovations, it is disliked by many conservative speakers; but it is unmistakably here to stay.

nuclear. Those who shift a consonant in this word, producing /**nōōk**-yə-lər/, aren't committing a grievous sin against the language; they are doing what comes naturally. The phenomenon is technically known as *metathesis*—the transposing of two sounds in a word. For example, the Romans rendered the name of the Greek hero *Herakles* as *Hercules*. And Old English *wæps* became Modern English *wasp*. Nevertheless, *nuclear* is pronounced /**nōōk**-lē-ər/.

number. The conventions of English usage relating to grammatical number—the use of singular and plural forms—are more complex and flexible than might be expected. Rather than attempt to analyze the underlying rules in all their permutations, we shall cite some typical examples of correct, debatable, and wrong or awkward choices, and follow each one with brief comments.

(1) *Collective nouns.*

> The new cabinet, as individuals, were not hostile.
>
> —Henry Adams, *The Education of Henry Adams*

The specification "as individuals" forces the choice of the plural verb.

> I think the Parliament of Great Britain hath no more right to put their hands into my pocket, without my consent, than I have to put my hand into yours for money. . . .
>
> —George Washington, letter (1774)

If the parliament is to be singular, as is indicated by "hath," it should have only one collective thieving hand (a pickpocket picks only one pocket at a time).

> . . . the Spanish government was coming around very rapidly . . . to the sort of attitude and action we had been demanding of them.
> —George F. Kennan, *American Diplomacy 1900–1950*

Either "the government were . . . them" or "the government was . . . it."

> In recent years advertising has recognized that the scientific community are the people with status, and has tried to borrow some of their luster by aping their language.
> —Theodore Bernstein, *The Careful Writer*

Some would balk at "the community are," but it's a defensible choice and the plurality is properly maintained through the rest of the sentence by the pronoun "their."

> The crew has been advised to lower their helmet visors.
> —NBC commentator

"The crew has" is initially a correct choice but turns out to be incompatible with the plurality of the action involved. Either "The crew have . . ." or "The members of the crew have. . . ."

(2) *Multiple subjects.*

> The depth of Johnson's feelings, and the distance between the different views, was brought home to me. . . .
> —Doris Kearns, *Lyndon Johnson and the American Dream*

Each of the two subjects, "depth" and "distance," is singular; despite the intervening punctuation, the two together require a plural verb.

> Nor does Secretary Vance and his traveling party look all that professional this week.
> —William Safire, *New York Times*

Since the auxiliary verb "does" occurs before the plurality of the subject has been revealed, initially it causes no problem. But "Secretary Vance" and "party" are the subjects of the sentence. This particular situation could have been saved by changing "and" to "with"; otherwise the verb must be the plural "do."

> The card and pencil has tended to supersede the spirit of match play. . . .
> —T. Simpson, *Golf Architecture*

The real subject here is "the card and pencil," meaning the system of scoring by strokes instead of holes; the singular verb is definitely correct.

(3) *Multiple complements and antecedents.*

> She had the sort of figure and posture that makes inexpensive clothes look good.
> —Eric Ambler, *The Schirmer Inheritance*

If the antecedent of the relative clause "that makes . . . good" is "the sort," the singular verb can be justified; but some would prefer to ignore "sort" and regard "figure and posture" as the antecedent, thus requiring a plural verb.

> On the left wing of the Royalist army opposite Fairfax was George Goring, Sir Charles Lucas and the Northern Horse.
> —C. V. Wedgwood, *The King's War*

The plural verb is definitely required.

(4) *Various examples of "attraction," hesitation, or change of mind.*

> The evidence, in the form of forced confessions, other documents and photographs, were recently made available to the Western media. . . .
> —Jim Graves, *Soldier of Fortune*

The verb has been "attracted" into the plural by the plural phrase intervening between it and the subject, "evidence"; but the subject is singular and the verb must be singular.

> How does a couple make sure they want children?
> —letter to columnist Ann Landers, *Florida Times-Union*

Here the writer has hesitated between undesirables: "how do a couple" and referring to a couple as "it." One or the other must be accepted; alternatively, the dilemma can be avoided by using "can" instead of "does."

> An average of 400 people has participated in the weekend searches. . . .
> —*Savannah Morning News*

Probably the writer considered "have" but edited it to "has"; this is strictly correct but "have" is more natural and equally correct.

> . . . human rights . . . have long been at the center of international politics. . . . Human rights has nothing to do with our innocence or guilt as a civilization.
> —Ardis Whitman, *Reader's Digest*

"Human rights" would normally be plural but can quite correctly be construed as singular if understood as "the issue of human rights" or "the human rights issue." Each sentence is correct, but it would be better to be consistent throughout one short article.

number style. The key question here (which many people cheerfully neglect to ask) is whether to express a number in figures or in words. Many writers simply follow their whims; there is no pattern and no coherence to the way they treat numbers. However, even professional copy editors who care about such things—when confronted with a style decision in this area—have been known to become paralyzed. Some simply turn numb. (Some even turn number.)

There is a simple way to come to terms with number style. Keep in mind the basic distinctions between the two forms. Numbers expressed in figures stand out; numbers spelled out in words recede into the middle ground, along with all the other words in a sentence. Figures are emphatic; their spelled-out equivalents are not. Figures give the appearance of being precise, accurate, crisp, even informal. Numbers expressed in words convey an air of approximation or of verbal formality.

To dramatize these distinctions, visualize a company memo announcing a staff meeting and an engraved invitation to a church wedding. The company memo might set the meeting at *10:30 A.M. on 7/27/83;* the invitation would set the wedding ceremony at *half after ten on the twenty-seventh of July in the year of Our Lord one thousand nine hundred and eighty-three.* If you look again at these two expressions of time and date, you will see the extreme limits of number style. Most of the action, however, occurs somewhere in between.

There are virtually as many number styles as there are style books, but allowing for variations, you will find that they fall into two camps: figure style and word style.

Figure Style. This is the style used in business and technical writing and in journalism, since most of the numbers in this material represent important information that should stand out. Here are the key rules:
(1) Spell out numbers from 1 through 10, but use figures for all numbers above 10: *About 75 people attended the introductory lecture, but only 23 signed up for the course.*
(2) If a sentence or paragraph contains related numbers and some are above 10 and some below, put all the related numbers in figures: *All we need are 10 to 15 volunteers to keep the three day-care centers operating during the summer months.* (*Three* stays spelled out because it is not related to *10 to 15 volunteers.*)
(3) Large numbers over a million can be expressed all in figures (*6,800,000, 3,250,000,000*) or in a mixed form (*6.8 million, 3¼ billion*).

Word Style. This style is used in writing that is formal, literary, or nontechnical, where not many numbers are used and where figures might look distractingly obtrusive.
(1) Spell out numbers from 1 through 100.
(2) Spell out round numbers above 100 that can be written in one or two words. A hyphenated compound like *thirty-eight* is considered one word; thus *thirty-eight thousand* or *thirty-eight billion* falls within the two-word limit.
(3) Large numbers over a million that would require more than two words if spelled out can be expressed all in figures or in the mixed form shown at Figure Style, above.

(4) Treat related numbers the same way within the same context. Thus, a number that can be spelled in two words should be expressed in figures if related to a number that has to be in figures: *Despite predictions that we would sell more than 3,000,000 units, we sold only 1,682,544.*

Which Style to Use? Once you consider the difference between numbers expressed in words and those expressed in figures, the choice between using the word style or using the figure style is not especially difficult—or even momentous. As you approach a particular piece of writing, simply size up the situation and determine the effect you are trying to achieve. Will the material contain numbers that should stand out for emphasis or easy reference? If so, choose the figure style. Are the numbers not especially significant and is the writing somewhat formal? If so, the word style is the obvious choice.

Once you've made a basic style decision for a given piece of writing, the important thing is to let that decision guide you toward some sensible pattern of consistency throughout that material. Thus, if you have chosen the figure style for a particular occasion, you will choose *the 15th of May* over *the fifteenth of May;* both forms are "correct," but the former is more appropriate, given your basic style decision. And if you have elected to follow the word style in another piece of writing, you will prefer *eleven o'clock* over *11 o'clock.* Again, both forms are correct, but one is more appropriate to the word style.

Some number expressions call for special handling, regardless of which basic style you have chosen. The following guidelines will show you how to deal with these expressions.

Mostly Figures. Even if you are following a word style, certain number expressions almost always require the use of figures. In such cases even the numbers from 1 through 10 are expressed in figures.

(1) Use figures in the following expressions of *dates:*

October 7, 1978	(form commonly used in the United States and Canada)
7 October 1978	(standard form in many countries, optional in the United States and Canada)
10/7/78	(U.S. number style)
7/10/78	(Canadian number style, equivalent to the British 7.10.78, both of which stand for *7 October 1978*)

Note that the U.S. style for dates expressed totally in figures gives month-day-year, whereas the Canadian and British styles give day-month-year. We suggest that you use number style (shown in the last two examples above) only in informal situations and where space is limited and that you avoid it wherever possible, because the number sequence could lead to confusion and error.

When the day precedes the month, two forms are correct (as previously noted): *the 17th of March* (number or emphatic style) and *the seventeenth of March* (word or formal style). And in ultraformal situations both the day and the year may be spelled out. You may also encounter the style *October 7th, 1978,* which is common in England and some parts of the British Commonwealth. There is nothing wrong with your using this style, but bear in mind that it is not standard for formal writing in the United States and Canada.

(2) Use figures to express amounts of *money: $2; $24.50; about $600; $37.5 million; 50 cents' worth; 50¢ worth* (in statistical or informal material). Use words to express *indefinite amounts (millions of dollars)* and *isolated references* where figures would be too strong *(not worth two cents).*

(3) Use figures to express *percentages, ratios, measurements,* and *proportions: an 8.4 percent increase; a 60–40 split of the profits; a surcharge on packages over 10 pounds; 6 parts of gin to 1 part vermouth.*

(4) Use figures with *abbreviations* and *symbols: 7 A.M.; 4 × 6 ft.; No. 1; 25°C.*

(5) Use figures to express *scores, votes,* and *numbers used as numbers: an 8-to-5 victory; a majority of only 559 votes; count backward from 10 to 1; multiply by 3.14159; divide by 2.*

Mostly Words. Some types of number expressions almost always require the use of words (even if you have chosen to follow a figure style).

(1) Spell out a number *at the beginning of a sentence,* as well as any related numbers that follow it. *Ten to fifteen percent of the voters don't know any of the candidates' names.* If the spelled-out number requires more than two words or if figures are preferable, reword the sentence: *Between 10 and 15 percent. . . .*

(2) Spell out *indefinite numbers: hundreds of men; thousands of women; millions of children; billions of dollars.*

(3) Spell out most *fractions that stand alone* (without a whole number preceding them): *one-half the usual time; three-quarters of the student body,* but *3/4-inch pipe* (a technical measurement); *multiply by 3/8* (a number used as a number). When a fraction is preceded by a whole number, put the entire expression in figures: *We've had less than 1½ inches of rain this summer.*

(4) Except for such things as year dates, generally spell out numbers *in dialogue* or *direct quotations*: *"He was earning forty-five thousand dollars annually in 1955," she exclaimed.*

Expressing Numbers in Figures and Words. Here are a few technical guidelines that can perhaps help you express numbers in the proper form.

(1) When expressing numbers in figures, use commas to set off thousands, hundreds of thousands, etc., in numbers that run to more than three digits: *1,435,647.* The comma is now often omitted in a four-digit number *(1250)* unless it is used together with a larger number that takes commas. But never use commas in page numbers *(page 1518),* year numbers *(2001),* or similar expressions.

(2) When expressing whole dollar amounts *($56)* or time on the hour *(7 P.M.),* don't bother adding zeros to account for cents or minutes except when these elements are combined with figures that do express them, as in a column of numbers where a consistent appearance is important:

$56.00	7:00 P.M.
$27.25	8:15 A.M.

(3) To form the plurals of figures, just add *-s*: *during the 1980s, the '80s, the 80s; temperature in the 20s.* It is also permissible to use the apostrophe and *-s*: *1860's; in the low 90's.* The form without the apostrophe is probably being used more frequently nowadays. In any case, whichever style you choose, be consistent.

(4) When expressing numbers in words, hyphenate all compound numbers between 21 and 99, whether they stand alone *(twenty-five)* or are part of a larger number *(twenty-five hundred).* However, do not hyphenate other parts of a spelled-out number: *sixty million; eighty-five billion.*

(5) When spelling out numbers, choose the shortest form that is available; for example, *fifteen hundred* rather than *one thousand five hundred.*

(6) To form the plurals of spelled-out numbers, follow the standard rules for adding *-s* or *-es*: *ones; twos; sixes; eighths; twenties; hundreds; millions.*

(7) In expressions such as *twenty 8-page brochures* and *six 4-room condominiums,* put one of the numbers in words and the other in figures for the sake of clarity. Ordinarily, spell the first number (as shown above) unless the second number will make a much shorter word: *2,000 eight-page brochures.*

(8) In a sequence of numbers *(during the years 1980–1985, on pages 348–356),* a hyphen (sometimes, in print, an *en dash,* slightly longer than a hyphen) may be used to replace the word *to.* However, if the sequence begins with the word *between,* use *and* rather than a hyphen *(between 1980 and 1985,* not *between 1980–1985).* If the sequence begins with the word *from,* use *to* rather than a hyphen: *from page 348 to page 356,* not *from page 348–page 356.*

O

O, oh. These are variant spellings of the same interjection, but they are used somewhat differently. *O*, always capitalized, is used for the archaic vocative:

> To your tents, O Israel!
> —1 Kings 12:16

> O God! O Montreal!
> —Samuel Butler

Oh, not necessarily capitalized, is much the commoner spelling in all modern uses. It may represent a separate exclamation of any intensity from rage or terror to the mildest surprise, or it may represent a noncommittal or questioning reply:

> "The coffee's cold."
> "Oh."

> "I'm leaving right away."
> "Oh?"

When it is used to address someone, with a name, or as part of an expletive, it may or may not be followed by a comma:

> "Oh, Miss, could I have the check, please?"

> "Oh Mr. Johnston!"

> "Oh, my goodness."

A few modern writers prefer to use *O* in some or all cases, but the great majority use *oh*.

oblige, obligate. These two closely related verbs overlap each other's meanings at several points, but each also has uses of its own. The origin is Latin *obligāre*, meaning 'to bind,' especially in law 'to bind (someone) by oath'; the word is related to *ligature* = 'a binding, surgical thread.' In French *obligāre* became *obliger*, which was then borrowed into English as *oblige*. The Latin word was later separately borrowed directly into legal English as *obligate*.

(1) Both *oblige* and *obligate* are used in the legal sense 'to require or compel (someone to do something) by the force of law':

> A city law [in Sian, China] obliges every healthy adult to personally deliver close to one ton of night soil to the countryside each year.
> —Anthony M. Paul, *Reader's Digest*

> So there we would be . . . in allegedly complete control of Georges Bank and still obligated to give away half of the catch.
> —Tim Sullivan, *National Fisherman*

Of the two, lawyers prefer *obligate*.

(2) Both *oblige* and *obligate* are also used to mean 'to require (someone to do something) by social convention or personal duty.' But *obligate* is much commoner in this sense:

> In principle, he was obligated to devote all his time to *The New Yorker*, but he figured out a means of getting around this difficulty. . . .
> —Brendan Gill, *Here at The New Yorker*

> . . . every Christian minister should feel obligated to speak to his people on this controversial theme.
> —Martin Luther King, Jr., *Strength to Love*

(3) *Oblige*, but not *obligate*, is used to mean 'to compel (someone to do something) by logic, circumstances, or physical force':

> If you want to fix something you are first obliged to understand, in detail, the whole system. . . .
> —Lewis Thomas, *The Medusa and the Snail*

> President George N. Shuster of Hunter College testified for Ridder and was obliged to stand a withering cross-examination.
> —Louis Nizer, *My Life in Court*

(4) Both *oblige* and *obligate* can be used to mean 'to do (someone) a favor that puts him or her under a debt of gratitude':

> He liked to wield power mildly and to cast bread on the waters: in a world as

> unstable as the one he lived in it paid off more handsomely in the long run to oblige people than to jail them.
> —J. Christopher Herold, *Mistress to an Age*

> It is one thing to obligate fifty or sixty Democratic senators by the delivery of services; it is quite another to obligate the entire government establishment.
> —Doris Kearns, *Lyndon Johnson and the American Dream*

(5) *Oblige*, but not *obligate*, is further used in several milder senses derived from sense four above, such as 'to do (someone) a modest favor without entailing any serious debt of gratitude' and 'to go along with, humor':

> He expected recognition, and I didn't mind obliging him, it was all right by me, except I'd never heard of O. J. Berman.
> —Truman Capote, *Breakfast at Tiffany's*

> The White House has asked Culver . . . to delay action on Stevenson's proposal . . . and Culver has obliged by scheduling a hearing.
> —Elizabeth Drew, *Senator*

Oblige is also used in various formulas of rather old-fashioned courtesy and politeness: *I'm much obliged to you* = 'Thank you'; *Could you oblige me* = 'Would you do me a favor.'

oblivion, oblivious. The noun *oblivion* literally means 'forgetfulness' or 'the state of being forgotten':

> The Qin terra-cotta figures are the earliest large-scale sculptures yet known in China. . . . As for the First Emperor, his terra-cotta army is bringing him back out of oblivion at last, to the immortality he craved.
> —Maxwell K. Hearn, *Reader's Digest*

More often, it means either 'unconsciousness' or 'death':

> She tried hard to stay awake, but it was difficult. Despite her efforts, she would feel herself drifting into oblivion.
> —Philip Yancy, *Reader's Digest*

> Soon both headlights spotlighted the unstoppable horror of two giant locomotives rushing to oblivion.
> —Raymond Schuessler, *Modern Maturity*

The adjective *oblivious* originally meant 'forgetful' and was used only with the preposition *of.* Some usage authorities would still like to restrict the word to this meaning. But the word is now quite rare in this sense. It now almost always means either 'unconscious' or 'unaware, ignorant, paying no attention.' It is usually used with *to:*

> A great artist is a great performer, and he is great because he is oblivious to everything except that which he is performing. —Pearl S. Buck, *For Spacious Skies*

> And they were oblivious to the first portents of the changes that were destined to shatter that pattern of security.
> —George F. Kennan, *American Diplomacy 1900–1950*

It is also, though less often, used with *of:*

> Since the end of the French and Indian War in 1763, colonial society had advanced with startling rapidity—a fact of which the mother country was oblivious. . . . —Thomas Fleming, *Reader's Digest*

◇ ***Recommendation.*** The use of *oblivious* to mean 'unconscious, unaware, paying no attention,' with either *to* or *of,* is fully established and correct.

of. (1) *Of* is sometimes deleted after nouns of quality or degree and such words as *couple:*

> With the tournament offering that size purse . . . —Gordon S. White, Jr., *New York Times*

> There is Mayor Beame in a subway station, swearing in a couple dozen new Transit police officers. . . .
> —Steven R. Weisman, *New York Times*

◇ ***Recommendation.*** This is widespread in informal speech but is not acceptable as standard in speech or writing.

(2) *Of* is wrongly inserted after some adjectives when used with adverbs of degree:

> It was too good of a shot.

> "I need a roll of paper tape."
> "How big of a roll?"

◇ ***Recommendation.*** This use is nonstandard in both speech and writing.

(3) *Of* is used as a spelling of unstressed *have,* used as a modal auxiliary (it is actually pronounced /əv/):

> "If we'd had a few more like Quantrill, we'd of won the War Between the States," the old man said.
> —Merle Miller, *Plain Speaking*

◇ ***Recommendation.*** This is acceptable as a rendering of dialectal speech; alternatives to *could of, we'd of,* etc., are *could've, we'd've,* etc. The spelling *of* in such cases should not be mistaken for any kind of use of the preposition *of.*

off of. This is widely used in speech for *off,* both by standard speakers and dialect speakers. It sometimes appears in writing:

> He would give you the shirt off of his back.
> —William Faulkner, *Sartoris*

> We wouldn't tear down the library because someone tried to jump off of it.
> —Dick Janssen, *Massachusetts Daily Collegian*

◇ ***Recommendation.*** *Off of* is not acceptable in standard writing except for a deliberately folksy effect, which is probably the case in the first quotation above. In speech it is informal or dialectal at best, and many would regard it as definitely nonstandard.

O.K., OK, okay. ***History.*** This, probably the most famous of all Americanisms, originated as political slang in Boston in the 1830s, when there was a vogue for humorous code words expressed by initials. At the outset, *O.K.* seems to have stood for *oll korrect,* used as a general boosting slogan, but it was soon reinterpreted as *Old Kinderhook,* a cryptic reference to Martin Van Buren, who was born in Kinderhook, New York. Subsequently, *O.K.* took off and established itself in the general vocabulary of American and worldwide English, as an interjection, a noun, a verb, an adverb, and an adjective, in various meanings that are universally familiar today.

Spelling. The spellings *O.K., OK,* and *okay* are preferred by different publishers; they are equally correct and acceptable. If *O.K.* or *OK* is used, the inflections are usually spelled with apostrophes: *O.K.'s, OK'ing,* etc. *Okay* has the advantage of being spelled as a full-fledged word with normally spelled inflections: *okays, okayed, okaying.*

Usage. Some conservatives still regard *okay* as slang, to be avoided in speech and never to be used in writing. But the great majority of people use it freely in speech on all but ceremonial occasions and in any writing that is less than highly formal. It is widely used in business correspondence, for example, but would be out of place in historical narrative. Some newspapers and magazines forbid it in copy; others allow it.

> . . . Andrus okayed the plant's construction.
> —James Nathan Miller, *Reader's Digest*

◇ ***Recommendation.*** We prefer the spelling *okay* and favor a reasonably relaxed attitude toward using the word.

okra /ō-krə/. This is a plant related to the marsh mallow. It is native to tropical West Africa, where it has long been cultivated for its green pods or fruits, which are full of a sweet mucilage. The English introduced okra to Jamaica more than 200 years ago, recording its name as *okro* or *okra,* based on the West African name. The exact original is not known but would have been similar to *nkru,* the word for okra in Twi (a language of Ghana). Green okra pods are eaten as a side vegetable, but their most celebrated use is to thicken the soups or stews known as *gumbos*. The word GUMBO is also of African origin. See also AFRICAN WORDS.

Old English. By King Alfred's time, about A.D. 850, the descendants of the Germanic folk—Angles, Saxons, Jutes, and others—who had settled in Britain during the 5th century A.D. were referring to themselves and their language as *English*. Their form of English, now designated Old English, was so different from the English we speak today that we have to study it like a foreign language in order to make sense of it; nevertheless, our modern speech is a direct though altered continuation of Old English, and most of our most familiar words are of Old English origin.

Old English was greatly enriched during the 8th and 9th centuries by the closely related Norse vocabulary of the invading Vikings (see NORSE WORDS). Though the Norman Conquest of 1066 marked the beginning of the end for Old English, its native speakers resisted the linguistic influence of the French-speaking invaders for nearly two centuries, and by 1250 the descendants of the Norman settlers had taken to speaking English. In the process it became transformed into a new language (now called MIDDLE ENGLISH), which is the immediate parent of our own MODERN ENGLISH.

Old English Versus Anglo-Saxon. It was long customary to refer to Old English as *Anglo-Saxon* and to its speakers as the *Anglo-Saxons*. Many scholars and writers prefer Anglo-Saxon even today, although a majority of academics over the past 100 years have elected to follow the lead of the *Oxford English Dictionary* and call the language *Old English* and its speakers the *English* or the *Anglo-Saxons*, according to the context. This is purely optional—the choice is yours. It isn't advisable, however, to call Old English *Saxon* or *Old Saxon*, as you will sometimes see in popular writings. This usage, although somewhat uncouth nowadays, has a venerable ancestry, going back to the Celts who were pushed out of Britain by the original Anglo-Saxons in the 5th century A.D. Their historians referred to this traumatic event, or series of events, as the *adventus Saxonum*, or coming of the Saxons. Historical writers throughout the Middle Ages followed this usage, and it was perpetuated by novelists like Sir Walter Scott and authors of storybooks of the Robin Hood type. For such contexts *Saxon* is fine, but if you are talking about the actual people and their language, it is better to use *Anglo-Saxon* and *Old English*. See also ANGLO-SAXON.

Vocabulary. Although the English language has been transformed since the Old English period, and its vocabulary has been invaded by hordes of borrowed words, especially from French and Latin, the Old English core has endured. Most of our fundamental, everyday words have come down to us by unbroken inheritance (though with considerable change of form) from the pre-Norman speech of the Anglo-Saxons.

Pronouns.

I, me, mine: from Old English *ic, mē, mīn*

we, us, our: from Old English *wē, ūs, ūre*

thou, thee, thine: from Old English *thū, thē, thīn*

ye, you, your: from Old English *gē, ēow, ēower*

he, him, his: from Old English *hē, hine, his*

she, her: from late Old English *sēo* (replacing earlier *hēo*), *hira*

it: from Old English *hit*

Basic Verbs.

break: from Old English *brecan* = 'to break, take (a fortified place) by storm'

bring: from Old English *gebringan* = 'to bring, bring forth'

drink: from Old English *drincan* = 'to drink'

eat: from Old English *etan* = 'to eat'

fly: from Old English *flēogan* = 'to fly'

go: from Old English *gān* = 'to go'

have: from Old English *habban* = 'to have, take, get'

heal: from Old English *haelan* = 'to heal, cure, save'

know: from Old English *cnāwan* = 'to know'

lay: from Old English *lecgan* = 'to lay'

learn: from Old English *leornian* = 'to learn'

lie = 'to recline': from Old English *licgan* = 'to lie down, be located'

love: from Old English *lufian* = 'to love'

meet: from Old English *gemētan* = 'to meet'

offer: from Old English *geoffrian* = 'to offer, sacrifice,' from Latin *offerre* = 'to present in sacrifice'

own: from Old English *āgan* = 'to own'

play: from Old English *plegan, plegian* = 'to play'

ride: from Old English *rīdan* = 'to ride'

set: from Old English *gesettan* = 'to set'

tie: from Old English *tīegan* = 'to tie'

win: from Old English *gewinnan* = 'to win'

work: from Old English *gewyrcan* = 'to work'

Basic Nouns. (1) Nouns relating to human affairs:

answer: from Old English *andswaru* = 'reply,' literally 'back-swearing'

book: from Old English *bōc* = 'book,' ultimately from a Germanic word meaning 'beechwood' (because the earliest writing by the European ancestors of the Anglo-Saxons was done on sticks or boards of beechwood, or possibly on beech bark)

craft: from Old English *cræft* = 'strength, art, skill, cunning'

deed: from Old English *dǣd* = 'deed'

earl: from Old English *eorl* = 'nobleman'

England: from Old English *Englaland* = 'England, land of the Angles' See ENGLAND, ENGLISH.

English: from Old English *Englisc* = 'English, the English language'

errand: from Old English *ǣrende* = 'message, errand'

fee: from Old English *feoh* = 'cattle, money, property'

fiend: from Old English *fēond* = 'enemy'

***folk:** from Old English *folc* = 'people, nation'

friend: from Old English *frēond* = 'friend'

Gospel: from Old English *godspell* = 'Gospel'; originally *gōdspell* = 'good news,' but confusion arose between *gōd-* = 'good' and *god-* = 'God-, divine,' and the word was understood in the sense of 'divine story'

headman: from Old English *hēofodmann* = 'ruler, captain, headman'

heathen: from Old English *hæthen* = 'pagan,' literally 'heath dweller'

home: from Old English *hām* = 'home'

house: from Old English *hūs* = 'house'

king: from Old English *cyning* = 'king'

lord: from Old English *hlāford*, originally *hlāf-weard* = 'bread-keeper' (that is, the giver of sustenance to his servants and dependents)

love: from Old English *lufu* = 'love'

need: from Old English *nīed* = 'necessity'

queen: from Old English *cwēn* = 'queen'

ship: from Old English *scip* = 'ship'

shire: from Old English *scīr* = 'province, county'

sledge: from Old English *slecg* = 'hammer,' from *slēan* = 'to strike, smite, slay'

sleep: from Old English *slæp* = 'sleep'

speech = 'language': from Old English *spēc* = 'speech'; earlier and commoner form *sprǣc* (thus, *sprecan* = 'speak' and *sprǣc* = 'speech,' corresponding to Modern German *sprechen, sprache*)

strength: from Old English *strengthu* = 'strength'

thane = 'clan chief, warrior companion of a king': from Old English *thegen* = 'servant, retainer, thane'

token: from Old English *tācen* = 'sign, token, miracle'

Viking: from Old English *wīcing* = 'Viking,' probably from *wīc* = 'dwelling, camp' (because the Vikings camped out wherever they went raiding)

wall: from Old English *weall* = 'wall,' ultimately from Latin *vallum* = 'defensive stockade' (This word was doubtless in the language of the Anglo-Saxons' European ancestors, a borrowing from the time of contact with Roman legions in Germany.)

wight = 'person, creature': from Old English *wiht* = 'creature, thing'

*Appears as separate entry

(2) Nouns relating to the family:

bairn = 'child': from Old English *bearn* = 'child,' literally 'born-one'

bride: from Old English *brȳd* = 'bride'

bridegroom: from Old English *brȳdguma* = literally 'bride-man'

brother: from Old English *brōthor* = 'brother'

child: from Old English *cild* = 'child'

daughter: from Old English *dohtor* = 'daughter'

elder: from Old English *ieldra* = 'older' (*ieldran* = 'ancestors')

father: from Old English *fæder* = 'father'

kin: from Old English *cynn* = 'family, race, people, class, kind'

* **man:** from Old English *mann* = 'human being, person, man'

mother: from Old English *mōdor* = 'mother'

name: from Old English *nama* = 'name'

offspring: from Old English *ofspring* = 'offspring'

son: from Old English *sunu* = 'son'

wife: from Old English *wīf* = 'woman' See HOUSEWIFE.

* **woman:** from Old English *wīfmann* = 'woman,' literally 'female person'

* Appears as separate entry

(3) Nouns relating to the body:

arm: from Old English *earm* = 'arm'

blood: from Old English *blōd* = 'blood'

body: from Old English *bodig* = 'body'

ear: from Old English *ēare* = 'ear'

eye: from Old English *ēage* = 'eye'

foot: from Old English *fōt* = 'foot'

hand: from Old English *hand* = 'hand'

head: from Old English *hēofod* = 'head'

heart: from Old English *heorte* = 'heart'

mouth: from Old English *mūth* = 'mouth'

nail: from Old English *nægel* = 'fingernail or toenail,' hence also 'metal spike used in carpentry'

(4) Nouns relating to food and drink:

ale: from Old English *ealu* = 'ale'

beer: from Old English *bēor* = 'beer'

egg: from Old English *ǣg* = 'egg'

food: from Old English *fōda* = 'food'

honey: from Old English *hunig* = 'honey'

milk: from Old English *meolc* = 'milk'

wine: from Old English *wīn* = 'wine,' ultimately from Latin *vīnum* = 'wine'

yolk: from Old English *geolca* = 'egg yolk'

(5) Nouns relating to farming:

acre: from Old English *æcer* = 'field'

barn: from Old English *bern* = 'barn'

field: from Old English *feld* = 'field'

meadow: from Old English *mǣd* = 'meadow'

sheep: from Old English *scēap* = 'sheep'

(6) Nouns relating to nature and the world in general:

adder: from Old English *nǣdre* = 'adder, snake'

day: from Old English *dæg* = 'day'

deer: from Old English *dēor* = 'wild animal'

dune: from Old English *dūn* = 'hill, down'

earth: from Old English *eorthe* = 'earth' (pictured in the Old English epic *Beowulf* as 'a shining plain encircled by ocean')

* **evening:** from Old English *æfen* = 'evening'

fish: from Old English *fisc* = 'fish'

God: from Old English *god* = 'God,' ultimately from an Indo-European root meaning 'one called upon, invoked, or spoken to'

heaven: from Old English *heofon* = 'heaven, sky'

hue: from Old English *hīw* = 'appearance, shape, color'

moon: from Old English *mona* = 'moon'

mouse: from Old English *mūs* = 'mouse'

night: from Old English *niht* = 'night'

snow: from Old English *snāw* = 'snow'

sound = 'long, narrow body of water': from Old English *sund* = 'swimming'

sparrow: from Old English *spearwa* = 'sparrow'

star: from Old English *steorra* = 'star'

stead = 'place': from Old English *stēde* = 'place'

sun: from Old English *sunne* = 'sun'

water: from Old English *wæter* = 'water'

worm: from Old English *wyrm* = 'serpent'

* Appears as separate entry

Examples. The following passage comes from a short epic poem, *The Battle of Maldon*, composed in A.D. 991 shortly after the event, to commemorate a brave last stand against invading Vikings by the East Saxon chief Brihtnoth and his followers. Brihtnoth was one of the three richest men in England—his widow Æthelflæd's will is extant, and in it she distributes no fewer than 142 manors to her heirs. The Vikings carried off Brihtnoth's head as a trophy. Æthelflæd buried him with a ball of wax to replace the head and wrought his deeds in tapestry. She probably also commissioned this poem. Here Byrhtwold, a companion of the fallen chief, exhorts his surviving comrades to fight to the death.

Byrhtwold mathelode, bord hafenode,
Byrhtwold spoke, shield [board] lifted,

sē wæs eald genēat, æsc ācwehte,
who was old companion, spear [ash] shook,

hē ful baldlīce beornas lǣrde:
he full boldly men exhorted:

"Hige sceal thē heardra, heorte thē cēnre
"Mind shall the harder, heart the keener,

mōd sceal thē māre, thē ūre mægen lȳtlath. . . .
Courage [mood] shall the more, as our strength [main] lessens ["littleth"]

Ic eom frōd fēores: fram ic ne wille
I am experienced of life: hence I will not [go]

ac ic mē be healfe mīnum hlāforde
but I me beside my lord

be swā lēofan men licgan thence."
by such a beloved man to lie down think."

Translation
Byrhtwold spoke up, lifted his shield—he was an old companion—shook his spear, and full boldly exhorted the men: "Mind shall be the harder, heart the keener, courage the more, as our strength lessens. . . . I am a veteran in life; I will not go away from here; instead, I intend to lay me down next to my beloved lord."

By contrast with the formality of Old English poetry, the language of prose was straightforward. Word order was similar to that of Modern English. Departures from our present-day word order are those characteristic of other Germanic languages and tally closely with the kind of inversions that typify traditional "poetic" style. The following recipe, dealing with the medicinal uses of the herb betony, dates from about A.D. 1000.

Thēos wyrt, the man betonican nemneth, hēo
This plant which people betony call, it

bith cenned on mǣdum and on clǣnum dūnlandum
is produced in meadows and in clean downlands

and on gefrithedum stōwum. Sēo dēah gehwæther
and in sheltered places. It is useful both

ge thæs mannes sāwle ge his līchoman. Hīo
for the person's soul and for his body. It

hyne scyldeth with unhȳrum nihtgengum and with
him shields against monstrous night prowlers and against

egeslicum gesihthum and swefnum; and seo wyrt
dreadful visions and dreams; and the plant
byth swȳthe hāligu. And thus thū hī scealt
is very sacred. And thus thou it shalt
niman on Agustes mōnthe būtan īserne; and
gather in August's month, not with iron; and
thonne thū hī genumene hæbbe, āhrys e thā
when thou it gathered have, shake the
moldan of, thaet hyre nānwiht on ne clyfie,
dirt off, so that on it no whit cleave on,
and thonne drīg hī on sceade swȳthe thearle,
and then dry it in the shade very thoroughly,
and mid wyrttruman mid ealle gewyrc tō dūste. . . .
and with roots and all work into a powder. . . .
Gif mannes hēafod tobrocen sȳ, genim thā
If a person's head broken be, take the
ylcan wyrte betonican, scearfa hȳ thon ne
same plant betony, shred it then
and gnīd swȳthe smale tō dūste. Genim
and knead very fine to powder. Take
thonne twēga trymessa wǣge, thige hit
then two dram's weight, drink it
thonne on hātum bēore. Thonne hāleth
then in hot beer. Then heals
thæt hēafod swȳthe hrāthe æfter thām
the head very rapidly after the
drince. With ēagena sār, genim thære
drink. Against eyes' soreness, take of the
ylcan wyrte wyrttruman, sēoth on wætere
same plant the roots, seethe [boil] in water
tō thriddan dǣle, and of thām wætere
to the third part, and from the water
betha thā ēagan; and genim thære sylfan
bathe the eyes; and take of the same
wyrte lēaf and brȳt hȳ, and lege ofer
plant's leaf and crush it, and lay over
thā ēagan on thone andwlitan. With
the eyes on the face. Against
ēarena sār, genim thære ylcan wyrte lēaf
ears' soreness, take the same plant's leaf
thonne hēo grēnost bēo, wyl on wætere
when it greenest be, boil in water
and wring thæt wōs, and siththan hyt
and extract the ooze [juice], and after it
gestanden bēo, dō hit eft wearm and thurh
has stood, make it again warm and through
wulle drype on thæt ēare.
wool drip into the ear.

The Pronunciation of Old English. Linguists have reconstructed the approximate sound of Old English. There were at least a half-dozen different dialects at any given time during the language's 600-year span. Old English was extremely rich in vowels and diphthongs and had more consonant sounds than Modern English. To present Old English pronunciation in detail would be outside the scope of this book, but a few points are worth noting here. Old English had several letters—some of them derived from older Germanic runes—that no longer exist in the Modern English alphabet. Here are the names, graphic shapes, and sound values of the two most important ones.

Name	Shape	Sound
edh	ð	/th/
thorn	þ	/th/

To make it easier for you to read the Old English texts in this entry, we have represented these letters by their closest modern equivalents.

Here are the opening lines of *The Battle of Maldon* and the medicinal recipe quoted above, together with approximate pronunciations, just to give you an idea of how our ancestor tongue may have sounded:

Byrhtwold mathelode, bord hafenode,
bürkнt wôld mȧ thĕ lō dĕ **bôrd** hȧ vĕ nō dĕ
sē wæs eald genēat, æsc ācwehte,
sā wăs **ĕəld** yə-**nā**-ət **ăsh ä-kwā**-kнtĕ
hē ful baldlīce beornas lǣrde . . .
hā **fo͝ol bäld**-lē-chĕ **bĕôrn**-əs **lăr**-dĕ . . .
Thēos wyrt, the man betonican nemneth, hēo
thāəs würt, thə mȧn bā-**tō**-nĭ-kən **nĕm** nəth, hāə
bith cenned on mǣdum and on clǣnum dūnlandum
bĭth **kĕn**-əd ŏn **măd**-o͞om ənd ŏn **klăn**-o͞om **do͞on**-lȧnd-o͞om
and on gefrithedum stōwum. . . .
ənd ŏn yə-**frĭth**-ĕd-o͞om **stō**-o͞om. . . .

Old English Versification. The cadence of the foregoing lines, like that of all Old English poetry and much of the closely related Norse epic material, is jerky and bumpy to an ear attuned to the measured cadences we inherited from French and Italian during the Middle English period. The actual delivery by minstrels in the lord's hall, who accompanied themselves with chords struck on the harp, was doubtless much smoother than we can guess from looking at the text. The rhythm was syncopated, reflecting normal Germanic speech cadence—an anticipation by 1,000 years of the "sprung rhythm" proclaimed in the 19th century by the English poet Gerard Manley Hopkins and used ever since by virtually all poets departing from the classic measured forms. (For more on poetic measure see POETRY.)

The basic unit of all Old English verse is the half line—each full line consists of two half lines, and the full line contains at least three strongly accented syllables. Two or three of the accented syllables begin with the same consonant, consonant cluster, or any combination of vowels. The unaccented syllables are irregular in number. This made for great freedom and fluidity, and—as the verses rolled on, like waves beating against some northern coast—for an overall pattern of consistency and power.

Oldspeak. See NEWSPEAK.

ombudsman /**ŏm**-bədz-mən/, a product of Scandinavian democracy. In Norway and Sweden the *ombudsman* (from Old Norse *umboths-mathr* = 'title of an official in medieval Norway representing the king,' from *umboth* = 'administration' + *mathr* = 'man') is a high-ranking official appointed by the government with the power to investigate private citizens' complaints against the government or civil service. During the 1960s and 1970s, New Zealand, Britain, Australia, and Canada adopted the idea and appointed ombudsmen or ombudswomen of their own. (The form *ombudsperson* also became current during the 1980s.) The U.S. government considered and rejected the concept, but it has caught on at lower levels; some states and cities have commissioners for consumer affairs who are known as ombudsmen. And journalists specializing in citizens' rights or consumer complaints now sometimes call themselves ombudsmen.

omen. An *omen* is an event considered as a sign of the future, either by superstition or by rational prediction. It may be good or bad.

> It's a beautiful morning. I wonder if that's an omen.
> —Colleen McCullough, *The Thorn Birds*

> I was going to tell you also now rice is very expensive and that's a bad omen.
> —James Clavell, *Shōgun*

The adjective form *ominous*, however, is always negative, meaning either 'being a bad omen' or merely 'threatening, disturbing, sinister':

> A third warning went out at 10:45 and it was very ominous indeed: "Southwest severe gale Force 9, increasing to storm Force 10."
> —Andrew Jones, *Reader's Digest*

> An ominous, buzzing sound came from the cellar when I entered the farmhouse kitchen in Somesville late one night last week.
> —Dick Saltonstall, *Bar Harbor Times*

Compare AUGER, AUGUR; AUSPICES, AUSPICIOUS; PORTEND, PORTENT, PORTENTOUS.

on account of. See DUE TO.

on behalf. See BEHALF.

one. When the pronoun *one* meaning 'a person, anyone' is repeated in a passage, it may be repeated either as *he* (or *he or she*) or as *one*. In American usage, *one . . . he* is more traditional.

> However, if one designs to construct a dwelling house, it behooves him to exercise a little Yankee shrewdness. . . .
> —Henry David Thoreau, *Walden*

> Maycomb's proportion of professional people ran high; one went there to have his teeth pulled, his wagon fixed, his heart listened to, his money deposited, his soul saved, his mules vetted.
> —Harper Lee, *To Kill a Mockingbird*

Some Americans may feel that *one . . . one* is affectedly British (it is the only choice in British). But *one . . . one* is as correct as *one . . . he* in American usage and has also the advantage of avoiding problems of gender, especially the possible repetition of *he or she*.

> But one's first impression of a slightly simian likeness in the man was quietly forgotten as one came to know him.
> —Thomas Wolfe, *The Web and the Rock*

> One put one's family and one's friends off the track because one was afraid that the affair might not come out right. . . .
> —Mary McCarthy, *The Company She Keeps*

But to alternate *one* with *you*, although often done, is much less desirable.

> One can be sure only of one thing, and that is that [human nature] will never cease to have a surprise in store for you.
> —W. Somerset Maugham, *A Man With a Conscience*

> While one may argue gently about the beguiling dissidence of such metrics, you have to agree at the very worst they can't be bad.
> —Theodore Levitt, *New York Times*

◇ ***Recommendation.*** It is equally correct to follow the indefinite pronoun *one* with *he*, with *he or she*, or with repeated *one*. It is better not to follow it with *you*. See also EVERYONE . . . HE; THEY; YOU.

one another. See EACH OTHER, ONE ANOTHER.

only. It is a traditional maxim of style that the adverb *only* is best placed immediately before the word or phrase it qualifies:

> If the U.S. tightens its money supply and raises interest rates, it's a signal Canada can ignore only at its peril.
> —Anthony Whittingham, *Maclean's*

> The White House announced the plan . . . explaining that the system would cost only \$2.8 billion more. . . .
> —Kenneth Y. Tomlinson, *Reader's Digest*

It may well be true that these sentences would be less effective if *only* were placed before the verbs: "a signal Canada can only ignore at its peril"; "that the system would only cost \$2.8 billion more." It is sometimes claimed, however, that such a placement of *only* would cause it to qualify the verbs (*ignore* and *cost*) and thus make nonsense of the sentences. This is not true. As a matter of natural grammar or correct syntax, *only* can refer forward in a sentence, and most often is in fact placed next to the main verb without necessarily qualifying it.

> . . . we only need to see a person do any one of these things to know how great a sensualist he is.
> —Henry David Thoreau, *Walden*

> This direct conflict of opinions . . . could only be settled, if at all, between the President and myself.
> —Winston Churchill, *Triumph and Tragedy*

> Mike had a bottle of Fundador. I only took a couple of drinks.
> —Ernest Hemingway, *The Sun Also Rises*

Certainly, there are cases in which the placement of *only* affects the intended meaning. *She is doing only what's necessary* is quite different from *Only she is doing what's necessary.* Such a difference is straightforward and obvious; the meaning of the second example ('no one else is doing it') cannot be conveyed clearly if *only* is moved to another place in the sentence.

◇ ***Recommendation.*** The placement of *only* immediately before the element it qualifies is usually a matter of style and preference, not of grammar or correctness. Do it if you like the effect, but don't feel you have to do it unless a real change in meaning would otherwise occur.

onomatopoeia /ŏn-ə-măt-ə-**pē**-ə, ŏn-ə-mät-/, Greek for 'word making,' means the formation of words that to some extent imitate sounds. Linguists generally prefer to call such words *echoic, imitative,* or *expressive,* but *onomatopoeia* remains the traditional noun, with the adjective preferably *onomatopoeic* but sometimes *onomatopoetic.*

All languages contain considerable numbers of onomatopoeic words and continue to create new ones. Some English examples are *bleep, boom, buzz, click, crunch, fizz, hiss, hum, jingle, meow, peep, ping, plunk, pop, quack, screech, thud, tinkle, toot, whiz,* and the names of birds such as *bobwhite, cuckoo, whippoorwill.*

Writing that suggests sounds is also called onomatopoeic. It is done both in poetry and in prose.

> Rend with tremendous sounds your ears asunder,
> With drum, gun, trumpet, blunderbuss, and thunder.
> Then all your muse's softer art display.
> Let Carolina smooth the tuneful lay. . . .
> —Alexander Pope, *Satire*

> Soothe! Soothe! Soothe!
> Close on its wave soothes the wave behind.
> —Walt Whitman, *The Brown Bird*

onto, on to. The preposition *onto* means 'to a position upon': *fell down the steps and onto the sidewalk.* It is also used in the sense of attaching: *glue the rearview mirror onto the windshield.* In addition, there is a slightly informal use, 'in contact with, actively aware of': *I think I'm really onto something.*

Many British people still prefer to write *on to,* even when it is clearly functioning as a single preposition and is pronounced as a single word. In American usage *onto* is completely established, and *on to* is considered a mistake for the preposition.

On and *to,* however, can often occur together without forming a single preposition: *On to victory! They went on to win.* All such cases can be judged both by function and by pronunciation. *On* functions either as an adverb meaning 'further, continuously' or as part of a phrasal verb such as *come on,* and *to* has some separate function. The two words are also pronounced as such, not as the single word *onto* /**ŏn**-to͞o/ or /**ŏn**-tə/.

oregano. Although many people pronounce the word /ôr-ə-**găn**-ō/, it is from Spanish *orégano,* and the best pronunciation is /ô-**rĕg**-ə-nō, ə-**rĕg**-/. This fragrant herb is the same as wild marjoram.

orient, orientate, orientation. The verb *orient* originally meant 'to place (something) so as to face east,' especially 'to build (a church) facing east.' It now has a range of meanings, including 'to get (one's own) bearings, guide (someone) toward a goal':

> After getting ourselves oriented we made a quick descent, then pushed through the massed alders and thick grasses that had overgrown the canyon access track.
> —Paul Bratton, *Sierra*

The adjective *oriented* means 'directed, inclined (to a specified interest or character)':

> Mainstream liberally oriented churches have lost millions of members in the last two decades.
>
> —*Christianity Today*

The variant form *orientate* sometimes occurs but is more British than American.

> The fact that Britain is a member of the EEC for national and practical reasons does not mean that the people are any more emotionally or culturally orientated toward Europe.
>
> —Duke of Edinburgh (quoted), *U.S. News & World Report*

Orientate enjoyed a vogue for more than 50 years, well into the 20th century, and H. W. Fowler's *Dictionary of Modern English Usage* predicted that it would prevail over *orient*. The reverse turned out to be the case in American English, and it is much commoner usage nowadays to speak of getting *oriented*; even to a purist's ear *orientated* sounds somewhat odd and old-fashioned.

Orientation, familiar to us in the expression *orientation session*, was borrowed into English from French in the sense of 'determination of bearings' roughly 100 years ago. In the older sense of 'adjustment (of a building) relative to direction,' it has been in English since the 1830s.

orotund, a peculiar adjective, formed in English as a blend of the Latin phrase *ōre rotundō* = 'with round mouth.' Primarily it refers to a style of speech and means 'sonorous and artificially enunciated in the manner used by old-fashioned public speakers.' It may also refer to writing, meaning 'highly rhetorical,' often 'pompously rhetorical.'

> During an interview she is anything but relaxed and chatty, and has a tendency to speak with the same orotund phrases that she uses before an audience.
>
> —Irwin Ross, *Reader's Digest*

> Churchill turned out an orotund obituary in which he said of [Rupert] Brooke, "He advanced toward the brink in perfect serenity."
>
> —Anatole Broyard, *New York Times*

ostentatious, ostensible. Both of these adjectives derive from the Latin verb *ostendere* = 'to show, display.' *Ostentatious* means 'displayed very openly, pointedly conspicuous':

> . . . that fear of seeing a revolution provoked by the ostentatious frivolity and extravagance of the higher classes . . .
>
> —Philip Magnus, *Edward VII*

Ostensible means 'displayed as a deception to conceal the real fact.' Its adverb *ostensibly* is much commoner than the adjective.

> The ostensible purpose of the meeting was to plan how the campaign for the last three weeks would be handled and that was hardly discussed at all.
>
> —Arthur M. Schlesinger, Jr., *Robert Kennedy and His Times*

> American pilots could provide air support only with a Vietnamese pilot aboard, ostensibly executing a training mission.
>
> —William C. Westmoreland, *A Soldier Reports*

owing to. See DUE TO.

oxymoron /ŏk-sĭ-**môr**-ŏn/, a combination of words that gains force and point from a seeming paradox or absurdity: *cruel kindness*. A stock phrase cited by ancient Roman writers on style was *strenua inertia* (= 'strenuous idleness'). *Oxymoron* is one of the most effective of all the figures of speech and works especially well in poetry, humorous writing, and political rhetoric. It is basically poetic, however, because the flash of insight a good oxymoron gives must come from the unconscious, not the rational part of the writer's mind; and like all poetic devices, it appeals to the reader's unconscious responses, not his or her reason. The term comes from the Greek word *oxumōros* = 'pointedly foolish,' but the Greeks used the neuter form of that word, *oxumōron*, in the same sense that we do—to designate a wittily paradoxical turn of phrase. Quite a few clichés in everyday language are oxymorons, such as the now old-fashioned genteelism *frightfully amused*.

P

Pacific Northwest dialect. This dialect, a subdivision of the WESTERN DIALECT, is spoken in Washington, Oregon, western Idaho, and northwestern Montana. The area was settled primarily by immigrants from New England, the Midwest, and to a lesser extent the Old South. There were also considerable numbers of Canadian, German, Scandinavian, and British settlers. As a result, the speech of the Pacific Northwest region most closely resembles the old Northern dialect, although Oregon favors the Midland dialect somewhat.

Vocabulary. Though not very distinct from other varieties of Western dialect, this subdialect has a handful of special terms, many of them borrowed from the Indian languages of the region (see also CHINOOK JARGON):

butte = 'flat-topped hill'
catty-corner (also Coastal Southern, Pacific Southwest) = 'in a diagonal position, *catercorner'
cayuse = 'wild horse'

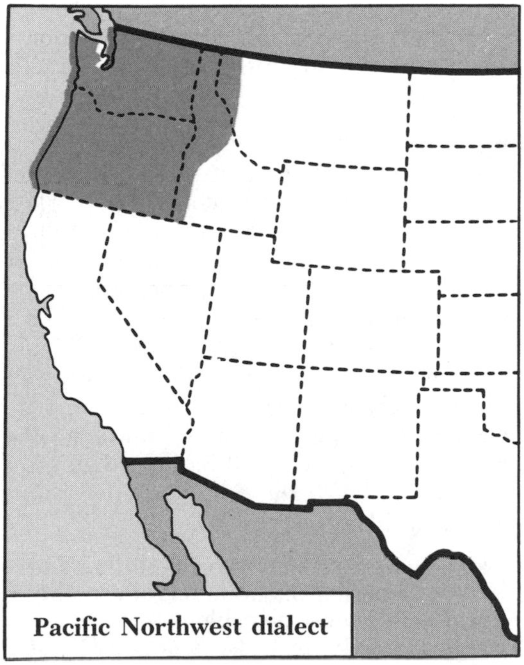
Pacific Northwest dialect

cayuse wind = 'cold east wind'
chinook = 'warm, inland-blowing wind'
chuck, salt chuck = 'salt water'
coulee = 'deep, dry-wash ravine'
ear sewer = '*dragonfly'
granger = 'farmer'
muckamuck = 'food'
no-see-um (also Northern, Pacific Southwest, and Canadian) = 'stinging gnat'
potlatch = 'festive celebration'
saddle band = 'herd of gelding horses, remuda'
skid road = (1) 'a trail for skidding newly cut logs' (2) 'a skid row' (altered form of *skid road*)
skookum = 'big'

*Appears as separate entry

Pacific Southwest dialect. This dialect, a division of the WESTERN DIALECT, is spoken in most of California and Nevada, though it is almost impossible to draw definite boundaries for it. Most of the region's English speaking settlers, who began arriving in 1841, came from the Northeast and the Midwest, particularly from New York, Missouri, Ohio, and New England. Settlement of this region, as well as of the West as a whole, was greatly accelerated by the discovery of gold in California in 1848 and of silver and gold in the Comstock Lode in Nevada some ten years later. The various dialects of these settlers soon blended into a subdialect that for the most part resembles the Northern and North Midland dialects. Today, the urban dialects of Los Angeles and San Francisco exert a shaping and diversifying influence on the speech of the area as a whole (see SAN FRANCISCO URBAN DIALECT; SOUTHWESTERN DIALECT).

Vocabulary. This region has a lively and in many ways experimental culture, which is constantly inventing new words and phrases. Most of these, as in current speech everywhere, are short-lived or are slang and do not become fully established.

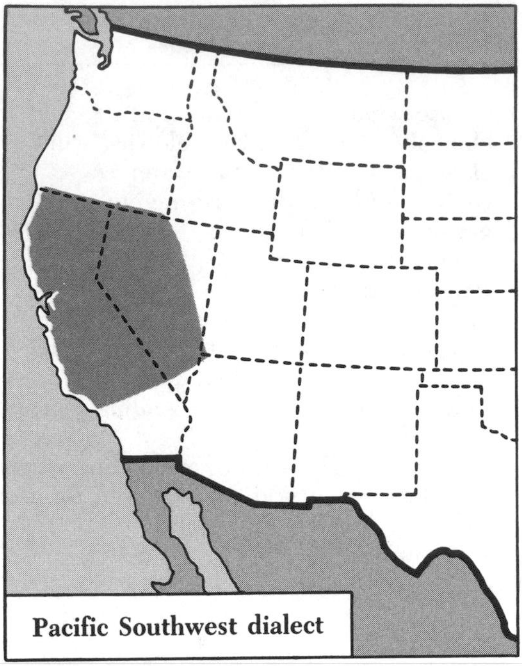

Pacific Southwest dialect

(1) Some established forms that are unique or special to this region:

barley sack = 'burlap bag'
bayos /bī-ōz/ = 'pinto beans'
catty-corner (also Coastal Southern, Pacific Northwest) = 'in a diagonal position, *catercorner'
cayuse = 'wild or unbroken horse'
chinas /chē-nəz/, **chinies** /chē-nēz/ = 'marbles'
cranberry beans = 'pinto beans'
dobies /dō-bēz/ = 'marbles (usually made of clay)'
ear sewer = '*dragonfly'
lanai /lə-nī/ = 'patio, covered walk'
lass *or* **lasso rope** = 'rope with a loop in it' See SPANISH WORDS.
leppy = 'maverick calf'
no-see-um (also Northern, Pacific Northwest, and Canadian) = 'stinging gnat'
pogonip = 'frozen winter mist or fog'
rustic = 'clapboard siding'
sanky = 'irrigation ditch'
Santa Ana, Santana (in southern California) = 'very dry inland wind blowing from the interior deserts into coastal valleys'

*Appears as separate entry

(2) Words that were originally used by gold miners:

alkali water = 'water containing alkaline salts'
chispa = 'speck or small nugget of gold'
crowbait = 'worthless horse or other type of animal'
dead water = 'stagnant or foul water'
dig out (a mine site) = 'to exhaust'
dry gulch = 'dry riverbed or ravine'
dry up = 'to shut up, stop talking'
gas = 'to talk idly or excessively, gossip'
gold dust = 'granulated gold used as currency'
goner = 'marked or doomed person, loser'
living water = 'pure, running water'
make the riffle = 'to succeed'
outfit = 'clothes'
pan = 'bread'
pan out = 'to succeed, turn out'
pay dirt = 'any useful or valuable discovery or attained object'
prairie feathers = 'grass'
swipsy = 'tipsy, drunk'
Taos lightning = 'whiskey'
toad-striker = 'knife'
yellow = 'gold'

pail. See BUCKET, PAIL, BLICKEY.

palpable. Latin *palpāre* means 'to stroke or caress,' and *palpating* or *palpation* is that technique of medical examination in which the physician feels or presses parts of the patient's body with the hands. *Palpable* thus literally means 'touchable, perceptible to touch,' hence figuratively 'real, not imaginary' and 'easily perceptible, considerable, obvious.' The word is now almost always applied to abstractions, qualities, etc. If the writer is thinking of the literal sense 'touchable,' the abstraction will be described as *almost palpable.* If the fully figurative senses are used, *almost* is omitted.

> When he smiles—exuberantly and often—he sets off vibrations of geniality that are almost palpable.
> —Irwin Ross, *Reader's Digest*

> We examined the drawings, which, incidentally, happened to be the most palpable forgeries, and clucked dutifully.
> —S. J. Perelman, *Westward Ha!*

> But there is something else in the McGovern Spirit, and it is quite palpable here in Miami. It is the sense of absolute, total self-righteousness.
> —William F. Buckley, Jr., *The New Religion*

panacea /păn-ə-**sē**-ə/ is from a Greek word meaning 'medicine that cures all diseases, universal remedy.' It is used to mean 'something that removes all troubles' or more narrowly 'something that fully solves a complex and longstanding problem.' It is almost always used with a negative or sarcastic implication; the speaker is saying that there's no such thing as a cure for all evils, or that someone claiming to have a solution for some well-known intractable problem is being naïve or deceptive.

> [George Washington] advocated no sure cure for all the sorrows of the world, and doubted that such a panacea existed.
> —H. L. Mencken, *Pater Patriae*

> Khrushchev returned from his 1959 visit to the United States persuaded that corn represented a panacea for Soviet agricultural problems.
> —John Barron, *Reader's Digest*

> The Friedmans are full of advice. For just about every difficulty, the panacea is a free market.
> —Peter W. Bernstein, *Fortune*

panache /pə-**năsh**/, from French, literally means 'plume of feathers worn as a crest on a helmet or hat.' It has become an abstract noun meaning 'bold and stylish brilliance' or 'skill displayed with a dramatic flourish':

> Frank Sinatra sings these songs with effortless panache. . . .
> —Tom Carson, *Rolling Stone*

> Nixon looked forward to a sudden announcement of summit in Peking, ripping off a national blindfold with daring and panache, dumbfounding critics by leapfrogging what seekers of drip-by-drip détente might have tried.
> —William Safire, *Before the Fall*

pancake, flapjack, etc. There are different types of pancakes, and there are also numerous different words for them, some used in different parts of the country. For a flat cake made of thin batter fried in a pan, *pancake* is the oldest and commonest term. *Flapjack* is also common and has in America two variants: *flatjack* and *slapjack* (a *jack* being a lad or fellow). Nathaniel Hawthorne, in his *Notebooks* (1842), was the first writer to record the latter variant:

> We had a splendid breakfast . . . of flap-jacks or slap-jacks, and of whortleberries.

Hot cake is also a widely used term and may have entered English as a translation of the Dutch word for pancake, *heetekoek*. Originally, a hot cake was a baked corncake:

> Their entertainment was . . . twenty bucks, with hot cakes of new corn.
> —William Penn, *Selected Works* (1683)

Later, the word *hot cake* came to refer only to a pancake:

> The usual settlers' dinner of fried bacon, venison cutlets, hot cakes, and wild honey, with some tolerable tea and Indian sugar . . . was soon placed before us.
> —Charles Hoffman, *A Winter in the West* (1835)

The American expression *to sell* (or *go*) *like hot cakes*, meaning 'to sell or be taken rapidly, be in great demand,' first came into use in the 1830s. It was already established as a common phrase by 1860; an observer of the Civil War in the South wrote in his journal that "revolvers and patent fire-arms are selling like hot cakes," and a senator from the North observed in 1879 that "four per cent bonds . . . go off like hot cakes." Still in use today, this phrase has become a cliché.

The common term *griddle cake* is also an Americanism, with the old-fashioned variant *griddle:*

> My woman wants to set some griddles and she took a notion she must have risin' ["rising," or leavening] to put in 'em.
>
> —Caroline Kirkland, *Forest Life* (1842)

In addition to these widely used terms, there are several regional dialect versions. The word *fritter* generally means 'deep-fried pastry often filled with fruit,' but in the North and New England it may mean 'pancake':

> Fine Corn flour . . . being fried in the fresh bear's oil makes very good hot cakes or fritters.
>
> —William Bartram, *Travels* (1791)

In the Gulf Southern and South Midland dialects a pancake is often called a *flitter.*

In the North Midland dialect pancakes are also known as *flannel cakes.* This term was originally the Scotch-Irish word *flannel* or *flannen,* which referred to a coarse oatcake. But after *flannen* arrived in America, it was altered to the more refined *flannel cake:*

> A very delicate species of food, which I tasted then for the first time, called flannel cakes.
>
> —H. Franco, *Tripping Tom Pepper* (1847)

Battercake is the General Southern dialect term:

> It was hard to make batter cakes over an open fire without the proper hanging griddle.
>
> —*Harper's Magazine* (1880)

In various parts of the country pancakes are also known as *buckwheat cakes, flippumjacks, flittercakes, gandies, jumpovers, leatherbread, splatterdabs,* and *stack cakes.*

pandit. See PUNDIT, PANDIT.

panoply /păn-ə-plē/. The word is from Greek *panoplion* = 'complete set of arms and armor,' from *pan* = 'all' + *hoplon* = 'weapon.' The *panoply* of a classical Greek warrior consisted of helmet, breastplate, greaves, shield, spear, and sword.

> Over [the coffin] was spread a pall of gold-embroidered purple, on which was displayed Alexander's panoply of arms.
>
> —Mary Renault, *The Nature of Alexander*

The word is also used of any military display of weapons and equipment, and of other impressive ceremonial arrays:

> A cloud of dust swept toward us from far down the line, and out of it gradually emerged a great number of field and staff officers, their horses galloping rapidly. At the head rode Maj.-Gen. George B. McClellan, and at his side a civilian dressed in black and wearing a high silk hat. The contrast between the latter and those attired in all the glittering panoply of war was striking.
>
> —quoted in Rufus Rockwell Wilson, *Intimate Memories of Lincoln*

> At about 4.30 p.m. the Queen reentered the state coach in full panoply, wearing the Crown, attired in robes of purple velvet, carrying the sceptre in her right and the orb in her left hand. . . .
>
> —Cecil Woodham-Smith, *Queen Victoria*

Figuratively, the word is used to mean 'formidable array of power':

> . . . a class of people of status, education, income and adversarial intent, with an extraordinary panoply of state power at their beck and call.
>
> —Michael Novak, *U.S. News & World Report*

> If we don't have a new levy, the resultant inflation will bring on a World War II-like panoply of controls.
>
> —Malcolm S. Forbes, Jr., *Forbes*

parable. A short tale illustrating some spiritual truth. See ALLEGORY.

paradigm /păr-ə-dīm, -dĭm/, an almost indispensably fashionable term in psychology, the social sciences, and related journalism. It means 'pattern, example, model,' in any of several senses.

(1) 'Typical example':

> Though she is a minor figure in the rise and fall of the New Left, her career is a paradigm of the retreat from politics to more personal concerns.
>
> —*Time*

(2) 'Excellent example, model to be imitated':

> Baines, a lawyer, educator, and lay preacher in the Baptist church in Blanco, Texas, was seen by his devoted daughter as the paradigm of religious ideals, moral thought, and civic duty.
>
> —Doris Kearns, *Lyndon Johnson and the American Dream*

(3) 'Theoretical model, theory of an underlying pattern':

> . . . the idea that frustration leads to aggression. This paradigm of human behavior, now so familiar, simply was not to be encountered prior to the publication of "Frustration and Aggression" in 1939. . . .
>
> —Daniel Patrick Moynihan, *New York Times Book Review*

(4) 'Structure or pattern of behavior':

> *Aptic structures* are the neurological basis of aptitudes that are composed of an innate aptic paradigm plus the results of experience in development.
>
> —Julian Jaynes (footnote), *The Origin of Consciousness in the Bicameral Brain*

The adjective is *paradigmatic* /păr-ə-dĭg-**măt**-ĭk/:

> . . . narcissism is increasingly a core problem. He [Heinz Kohut] calls it today's "paradigmatic" complaint.
>
> —Susan Quinn, *New York Times Magazine*

◊ ***Recommendation.*** If you crave to be seen at the cutting edge of today's progressive thought and writing, use *paradigm* on all possible occasions. Otherwise, go easy on it.

paragon. Greek *parakonē* meant 'abrasive stone used for sharpening blades, whetstone.' The word was borrowed into Medieval Italian as *paragone,* with the specialized meaning 'touchstone,' that is, a type of stone used for testing gold, silver, and alloys. The metal was rubbed lightly, or "touched," with the stone; the appearance of the metal trace left on the blackish surface of the stone indicated the metal's purity. In English *paragone* became *paragon;* both *paragon* and *touchstone* were used to mean 'any test or standard by which excellence is judged.'

> Freedom of religion; freedom of the press; and freedom of person under the protection of the *habeas corpus.* . . . They should be . . . the touchstone by which we try the services of those we trust.
>
> —Thomas Jefferson, first inaugural address (1801)

By a further development *paragon* specifically came to mean 'pattern or model of excellence,' especially 'something or someone regarded as perfect or supreme in merit':

> An attempt was made to mould him, in isolation from his contemporaries, into a moral and intellectual paragon.
>
> —Philip Magnus, *Edward VII*

> . . . when it comes to pure native intelligence, both [cat and dog] are completely overshadowed by that barnyard paragon, the pig.
>
> —Kent Britt, *Reader's Digest*

parallel style. *Parallelism* is the use of comparable words, phrases, or structures when writing about two or more thoughts, objects, etc. In speaking of language style that strives to be unbiased, we use *parallel style* to refer to the matching of the various terms for males and females. The following pairs of words are parallel: *women/men; girls/boys; ladies/gentlemen; sir/ma'am.* These pairs are not parallel: *men/girls; men/ladies; sir/honey.*

Society calls a male of 18 or 21 a *man,* but it has been traditional to call a female of 18 or 21—or even 62—a *girl* or *lady* rather than a *woman.* As a plant manager in St. Louis observed in 1979, "We just had a party for a girl who was retiring after forty years."

Many women still feel flattered at being called girls, because the word implies that they are young and attractive. Other women feel that since they have reached adulthood and assumed adult responsibilities, they should be called by an adult term. They are proud to be women, just as men are proud to be men. The word *lady*, like *gentleman*, emphasizes polite social behavior and suits formal or social occasions.

With shifting and changing usage, many people simply do not know how to address women in speech. Consider this dialogue between a middle-aged woman (MW) entering an office and a younger woman (YW) working there. The time is January, 1982.

> YW *(noticing MW and addressing a colleague):* Mrs. Jones, would you help this . . . this . . .
> MW *(coming to the rescue):* Woman.
> YW *(recovering):* This young lady.
> MW: *Woman* will do nicely.

In that case "lady" alone would also have been a good choice, as YW would probably have said of a man, "Would you help this gentleman?"

Similar situations often arise on airplanes, as in this exchange involving a flight attendant (FA), a male passenger (MP), and a female passenger (FP).

> FA *(to MP):* Sir, excuse me, sir, what would you like to drink, sir?
> FA *(to FP):* What would *you* like?

The parallel term to *sir* is *ma'am*. In Great Britain *ma'am* is used in addressing the queen or a royal princess. In the United States it was once widely used as a title of respect for any adult woman. Now this usage has all but disappeared except in the South. Many women would like to revive *ma'am*. Otherwise, lacking a title, they find themselves being called *honey, dear, darling,* or *sweetie* by salesclerks, vendors, counter attendants, and other strangers.

In the use of names and courtesy titles, some publications deliberately avoid parallel style. For example, some use last-name-only style for men but insist on courtesy titles for women, as in this headline:

> Moynihan Edges Out Mrs. Abzug . . .
> Badillo, Mrs. Chisholm Winners
> —*New York Times*

Parallel style is also violated when women are called by their first names and men by their last. In each of the following citations the flippant tone of the headline is at odds with the serious nature of the story.

> Golda and Kissinger Meet Again
> Secretary of State Kissinger met until early this morning with Israeli Prime Minister Golda Meir.
> —*New York Post*

> Sister Golda via Ma Bell
> Premier Golda Meir told her sister here in a brief telephone call Monday that Israel had the war under control.
> —*New York Times*

Parallel style implies equal respect, as former Rep. Shirley Chisholm once pointed out in the House Rules Committee:

> Rep. James Delaney . . . addressed each of the panel's congressmen as "Mr." but called the Brooklyn Congresswoman by her first name. The third time this happened, she turned angrily towards Delaney and snapped: "Will you please call me Ms. Chisholm."
> Red-faced, Delaney said sheepishly: "But we're both from New York, Shirley."
> "Yes, but the public doesn't know that, *Jim*," she shot back.
> —*New York Post*

Publications can follow parallel style in a variety of ways. They can refer to both women and men by their first names ("Golda and Henry Meet Again"), by their last names ("Meir and Kissinger Meet Again"), or by their titles and names.

> Rep. Holtzman Democratic Victor
> In the Democratic primary, Representative Elizabeth Holtzman defeated three Democratic rivals. . . .
> —Frank Lynn, *New York Times*

The way women are written about frequently violates parallel style. Women and men may be in comparable positions, doing equal work, but they are often described quite differently:

> In particular, textbooks that teach journalistic writing imply that men "do" while women "appear." It is not surprising that reporters describe appearance more often for women than for men, since a textbook once taught them to write this lead. "Pretty in skirts and pert in slacks—that's Mildred Miller, size 12, mezzo-soprano with the Metropolitan Opera Co."
>
> —Dr. Matilda Butler and Dr. William Paisley (quoted), *Media Report to Women*

This story on female traffic police in 1973 illustrates the problem further.

> City Traffic Cop Takes on a New Image: Small, Friendly and Curvy
>
> . . . on the first day, the girls—oops, the officers, that is—were working closely with regular men traffic officers. . . . Much, but not all, of their equipment was diminutive. . . . And Officer Ethel Cunningham, at Fifth Avenue and 57th Street, was also equipped with miniature gold earrings. . . . At Herald Square, the tiniest of the new officers, Mrs. Annmarie Butler, 5 feet 5 and 115 pounds, was fulfilling a nine-year-old dream to be on the police force. The women officers are all professional in appearance. But a passing male chauvinist . . . saw one tuck the bulky, unfeminine-looking summons book in her belt. . . .
>
> —Edward C. Burks, *New York Times*

Such a description gives the impression that the women are not regular officers but little girls pretending to be traffic police. It is funny, but the humor is achieved by trivializing the women and making them appear unfit for their jobs. Another example of female stereotyping is this story on Jane Byrne when she won the Democratic nomination for mayor of Chicago. A story on a male politician who had defeated a powerful political machine would have been written quite another way.

> Jane Byrne strolled down victory lane today, down the Magnificent Mile, the fashionable shopping stretch of Michigan Avenue. . . . and her bright red lipstick flashed like a Christmas wreath around her winner's smile. Other, shocked Chicagoans were still awakening to the fact that their next Mayor, all but certainly, will be a person who visits a beauty parlor.
>
> —William Robbins, *New York Times*

Wit, flavor, and variety do not have to be sacrificed to achieve parallel style. Parallel style is simply a way of saying in words that equal treatment is important.

See also FEMALE-GENDER WORD FORMS; GENTLEMAN; LADY; MISS, MRS., MS.; WOMAN, LADY, GIRL.

parameter. Not to be confused with *perimeter,* this once obscure mathematical term has risen to celebrity. Technically, a *parameter* is one of the measurable quantities or factors that determine a system or event. Thus, among the parameters affecting the flight of a Frisbee are launch speed, spin, and wind. Suddenly, parameters are everywhere. The usual meaning is 'relatively fixed or known factor in a complex or fluid situation,' and especially 'defining element, limiting factor':

> Infectious disease . . . will last as long as humanity itself, and will surely remain, as it has been hitherto, one of the fundamental parameters and determinants of human history.
>
> —William H. McNeill, *Plagues and Peoples*

> . . . during their first year or so on the Court, most justices feel their way around the parameters of the institution, writing for the Court mostly on relatively trivial issues. . . .
>
> —Walter F. Murphy, *The Vicar of Christ*

> [Alexander] Haig told me that Richardson had suggested as an alternative to firing Cox, putting what he called "parameters" around him. . . . The pa-

rameters could include an instruction that he was forbidden to sue for any further presidential documents.
—Richard Nixon, *R.N.*

◇ ***Recommendation.*** Parameters no doubt have their place in genuinely technical usage. Otherwise we can easily do without them. In the first quotation above, "parameters and" can simply be deleted without loss of meaning. In the second, "limits and possibilities" would be an improvement. In the third, the word is a political euphemism for "restraints."

paramount, from a Norman French word meaning 'above, superior,' means 'supreme in importance or power, outranking all others':

My paramount object in this struggle is to save the Union, and is *not* either to save or destroy slavery.
—Abraham Lincoln, letter (1862)

Dominating the daily lives of his countrymen with iron-willed ruthlessness, [the Shah] works hard and openly to make himself a paramount figure in world affairs.
—Carl T. Rowan, *Reader's Digest*

paranoia, paranoiac, paranoid. To the professional psychologist *paranoia* is a diagnosable psychosis or mental disorder; the patient typically has serious delusions of being persecuted or threatened. Outside the profession, many of us recognize that the term *paranoia* offers a valuable insight into the everyday human condition, diagnosable or not. Since it is often hard to be sure whether we are really being threatened and persecuted or are merely worrying about things, we freely accuse ourselves and others of paranoia. The word has thus become a common term applied to almost any level of suspiciousness, distrust of others, self-doubt, or worry, even though such feelings may well be quite "normal" or at least inevitable. Of the two adjectives *paranoiac* and *paranoid*, the latter is much more popular.

Mekhlis was another of the police generals whose paranoia, vindictiveness and inefficiency marked their every assignment. —Harrison E. Salisbury, *The Unknown War*

"Am I paranoiac about hating people and trying to do them in?" And the answer is: at times, yes. I get angry at people, but . . . I believe that an individual must never let hatred rule him.
—Richard Nixon (quoted), *New York Times*

Since the Soviets are notoriously paranoid about their satellites dealing with the West . . . —*Time*

San Francisco, of course, cheered me up; it is the most gorgeous city in America, if also the most culturally paranoid.
—Eliot Fremont-Smith, *Village Voice*

parentheses. See PUNCTUATION.

pariah. The pronunciation is /pə-rī-ə/, sometimes (chiefly British) /păr-ē-ə/. The Pariahs are a low-ranking caste in southern India; the name is Tamil for 'drummers,' referring to members of the caste who act as hereditary drummers at religious festivals. The British (inaccurately) used the name for low castes throughout India, including those regarded by higher castes as untouchables. Hence the figurative use of *pariah* for anyone who has been rejected socially or politically.

"You're going to the Embassy? That's never been done before, they don't have actresses."

Rosalind, the social pariah, didn't care. I put on my long white gloves and off I sailed. —Rosalind Russell, *Life Is a Banquet*

. . . in 1935, when the Nuremberg Laws made Jews into German pariahs . . . —Jim Miller, *Newsweek*

Moreover, if he backed Carter, Young knew he stood a good chance of becoming a pariah not only among blacks but among white liberals as well.
—James Wooten, *Dasher*

parish, parochial. The earliest Christians called themselves, in Greek, *paroikoi*, literally 'sojourners, expatriates,' meaning that during life on earth they were exiles from their true country, the kingdom of heaven. Hence, *paroikia* = 'community of Christians, individual church with its congregation.' Greek *paroikia* became Latin *parōchia*, then Old French *paroisse*, and finally English *parish*. The Latin adjective *parōchiālis* = 'relating to a parish' was taken directly into English as *parochial*. Thus, the noun *parish* and its adjective *parochial* are exact cognates although they don't look like it; for similar situations, such as *bishop* and *episcopal*, see COGNATES.

In the Catholic and Episcopal churches a parish is a subdivision of a diocese, with its own church and priest. A parish is also a district of local government in England, and in Louisiana it is the equivalent of a county. *Parochial* means (1) 'relating to or belonging to a parish,' as in *parochial school*, a school run by a parish, and (2) 'concerned only with local interests, ignorant of the outside world.'

> American newspapers . . . have always been parochial in outlook: published, edited, and written by people who have made a long-term commitment to the city they cover. . . .
> —Ron Powers, *The Newscasters*

> Over and over again I would discover how parochial were the values and axioms I had learned from my limited environment. . . .
> —Shirley MacLaine, *Don't Fall Off the Mountain*

> It is indeed an irony . . . that the Japanese, while possessing the world's most global economy, should at the same time be among its psychologically most parochial peoples.
> —Edwin O. Reischauer (quoted), *Science News*

parody. See SATIRE.

paronomasia. See PUN.

participial phrases. See ABSOLUTE PHRASES; DANGLING PHRASES.

pastiche /păs-tēsh/. The word comes from French *pastiche*, which is from Italian *pasticcio* = 'hodgepodge, medley.' There are two kinds of pastiche. The first is a musical or literary composition made up of bits and pieces, often (but not necessarily) from different composers or writers:

> He was making an album, *I Am the Greatest*, a long pastiche of poems and skits composed wholly in terms of his impending fight with Sonny Liston.
> —Tom Wolfe, *The Marvelous Mouth*

The second kind is a literary work that obviously imitates the style of a known writer:

> I won a prize for writing a long narrative poem in what everyone must have seen was a pastiche of Frost.
> —Brendan Gill, *Here at The New Yorker*

Pastiche can also be used figuratively of any close but inferior imitation:

> To many, Dutch society seemed a clumsy bourgeois *pastiche* of French culture.
> —Charles Wilson, *The Dutch Republic*

pathetic fallacy. See PERSONIFICATION.

patriate is a word created by a peculiarity of constitutional history. The original charter of Canada's national existence was, though basically drawn up by Canadians, passed into law as an act of the British Parliament and entitled the British North America Act of 1867. The document itself was and still is kept in the parliamentary archives in London. More than 100 years after its passage, Canadians decided that they ought to have a totally Canadian constitution, spontaneously enacted as law in Canada and physically residing in Canada. The movement to achieve this was at first referred to as "repatriating the Constitution," until it was pointed out that *repatriate* means 'to bring (someone or something) back home,' which was inappropriate to something that had never been in Canada in the first place. Accordingly, the infinite resources of the language soon yielded the new word *patriate,* which could be defined as 'to bring (something) to the home it always should have had but never did.' Thus the constitution was *patriated* in 1982. And, as is often the way with unique new coinages, it caught the imagination and quickly began to find new applications. In the following, *patriate* means 'to give (people) something they always should have had':

> What galvanized CBC management into fully supporting the project, however, was the need for a last-ditch stand to—in [CBC President Al] Johnson's words—"patriate Canadian audiences to quality Canadian programming."
> —*Maclean's*

peer. A *peer* is an equal, a person of equal rank or standing. The word was originally a legal term, taken from Old French *per* and Latin *par* = 'equal.' The Magna Carta established that "no man shall be imprisoned but by the lawful judgment of his peers." The word now has several distinct uses.
(1) As a high-sounding or poetic word for a person of equal virtue or prowess. Tennyson's Ulysses boasts that he has

> . . . drunk delight of battle with my peers
> Far on the ringing plains of windy Troy.

This sense often occurs in negative expressions, of someone who has no equal, that is, is *peerless:*

> For Lycidas is dead, dead ere his prime,
> Young Lycidas, and hath not left his peer.
> —John Milton, *Lycidas*

(2) In England and other feudal kingdoms the *peers* were the small group of the highest-ranking noblemen, who were legally equal among themselves and to no others. The 12 peers of France were the 6 temporal and 6 spiritual lords of the kingdom, supposedly inheriting their rank from the 12 companions of Charlemagne. In Britain today the peers are the members of the House of Lords, now made up partly of hereditary nobles and partly of distinguished persons appointed for life (called *life peers*). A *peerage* is the rank or title of a peer; *the peerage* is the body of peers collectively.
(3) In sociology one's *peer group* or *peers* are one's equals within the community in age or status. This is now the common use:

> . . . I have learned from hearing my own children's conversations that SAT scores have now become one of the peer group measuring devices. . . .
> —Frank Bowles (quoted), *Atlantic Monthly*

> Yet the 515 students at this virtually all-black parochial school far outpace their public-school peers.
> —Mark Frazier, *Reader's Digest*

Peking, capital of China. The name is from Mandarin *Pe Ching* or *Beijing* = 'northern capital' (as opposed to *Nanking* = 'southern capital'). The name has several variant forms.
(1) *Pekin* is a spelling borrowed from the French version, *Pékin.* In English it is now obsolete for the city but remains standard for a kind of striped silk fabric and for the familiar breed of white duck, which is of Chinese origin. The word *Pekinese* is also obsolete as an adjective but is still sometimes used as a noun for the breed of dog. *Pekingese,* however, is the preferred spelling for the dog, although it is usually pronounced /pē-kə-**nēz**/.
(2) *Beijing* /**bā-jĭng**/ is the new Pinyin spelling recommended by the Chinese government since 1979 (see the section on writing and pronunciation at CHINESE WORDS). This spelling and pronunciation are now used by some Western newspapers and broadcasters. (In 1980 in New York City there was one restaurant called The Peking Duck and another called The Beijing Duck.)
(3) *Peiping* /**bā-pĭng**/ is a different name for the same city; it represents Mandarin *Pei-p'ing* or *Beiping* = 'peace in the north' and was used during the early Ming dynasty (1368–1644), when the capital of China was Nanking. In 1927, when the Nationalists made Nanking their capital, Peking was again

called Peiping. This continued until the proclamation of the People's Republic in 1949, when the "northern capital" became once more the capital of China and reverted to Peking. But the U.S. State Department and the news media continued to call it Peiping throughout the cold war period, and the government of the Republic of China in Taiwan still does so.

◇ ***Recommendation.*** The traditional form *Peking* is still the preferred one. *Pekin* and *Peiping* are both obsolete. *Beijing* is correct and is used by some news media and China specialists, but is not yet widely established.

Pennsylvania Dutch. The language popularly known as *Pennsylvania Dutch* is not Dutch at all but a dialect of German. *Dutch* stands for the old pronunciation of *Deutsch*, which means 'German.' This dialect, also called *Pennsylvania German*, is spoken by upward of 300,000 people concentrated primarily in the south-central and southeastern areas of Pennsylvania. But it is also spoken in Rowan and Cabarrus counties in North Carolina; in parts of the Shenandoah Valley in Virginia; in western Maryland and eastern West Virginia; and in scattered areas of the Midwest. It can be heard too in Perth and Waterloo counties of Ontario.

From 1683 to the Revolutionary War great numbers of German immigrants settled in Philadelphia and then moved into the fertile valleys of southeastern Pennsylvania. Most of these German settlers came from Switzerland and central and southern Germany, particularly the Palatinate. These early settlers belonged to various strict religious sects, most notably the Mennonites, Amish, Dunkards (Church of the Brethren), Schwenkfelders, and Moravians. Once established, they used their various German dialects for everyday speech. Over time, a leveling and blending process produced the relatively uniform dialect heard today.

Not only is Pennsylvania Dutch a spoken language; it is also a written one. Since the middle of the 19th century a sizable body of folk literature has been written, and since the 1920s many poems, novels, short stories, and essays have been published. For a discussion of the American dialect that has been influenced by Pennsylvania Dutch, see PENNSYLVANIA GERMAN-ENGLISH.

Pennsylvania German-English. The Pennsylvania Dutch (or German) dialect of parts of Pennsylvania has had a profound influence on the English spoken in these regions. (For the history of this dialect see PENNSYLVANIA DUTCH.) Pronunciation, vocabulary, and grammar have all been affected.

Pronunciation. (1) Certain pairs of consonant sounds are usually not distinguished. These include /b/ and /p/, /d/ and /t/, and /g/ and /k/. Thus, a speaker may give the same pronunciation for *bet* and *pet*, for *wed* and *wet*, and for *egg* and *eck* (= 'corner').
(2) Because the /th/ sound does not occur in Pennsylvania Dutch, it is often pronounced /s/. Thus, *souse* and *south* may be pronounced as /sous/, *sick* and *thick* as /sĭk/, and *sought* and *thought* as /sôt/.
(3) No distinction is made between /w/, /v/, and /hw/. *Wine*, *vine*, and *whine* are pronounced alike.
(4) The /z/ sound is usually pronounced /s/. Thus, *use* (noun) and *use* (verb) are both pronounced /yo͞os/.

Vocabulary. (1) The English spoken in the Pennsylvania Dutch region inevitably has numerous words taken from that dialect. Many are connected with the home and farm. Here are some commonly used terms:

alter /äl-tər/ = 'old man'; used as a term of endearment
blotz /blŏts/ = 'to bounce, bump': *Don't blotz me around so.*
dapp /däp/ = 'to walk clumsily or awkwardly'
dappi /däp-ē/ = 'clumsy'
fasnacht /fäs-näk/ = 'molasses or honey *doughnut'
fress /frĕs/ = 'to eat excessively or like an animal'
greissel /grī-səl/ = 'to nauseate, sicken'
hammi /hä-mē/ = 'little calf'
hutschi /ho͞ot-shē/, **hutschli** /ho͞ot-shlē/ = 'little horse or pony'

kluck /klo͝ok/ = 'setting hen'
kotz /kôts/ = 'to vomit'
panhas /**pän**-häs/ = '*headcheese or scrapple'
rutsch /ro͞och/ = 'to move restlessly'
rutschi /**ro͞och**-ē/ = 'fidgety'
schnitz and knepp /shnĭts ən **knĕp**/ = 'dish made of boiled ham, dried apples, and dumplings'
schussel /**sho͞o**-səl/ = 'to hurry'
smearcase /**smîr**-kās/ = 'creamy *cottage cheese'
smutz /smo͞ots/, **schmutz** /shmo͞ots/ = 'to kiss or caress'
speck /spĕk/ = 'the fat of meat'
specki /**spĕk**-ē/ = 'fatty'
spritz /sprĭts/ = 'to squirt or sprinkle'
struwli /**stro͞o**-lē/ = '(of hair) disheveled, unkempt'
toot /to͞ot/, **tut** /to͞ot/ = 'paper bag'
verhuddelt /fər-**ho͞o**-dəlt/ = 'mentally confused'
wutzi /**wo͞ot**-sē/ = 'little pig'
zidderli /**zĭ**-dər-lē/ = 'souse'

*Appears as separate entry

(2) There are also many terms that are not German in origin but are peculiar usages of certain English words:

all = 'all gone'
butterbread = 'bread and butter'
cook = 'to boil': *a soft-cooked egg*
dare = 'may': *Pop, dare I go uptown with George?*
dumb = 'stupid'; never used to mean 'silent' or 'unable to speak'
from little up = 'from the time that one was small or little'
ground = 'soil, earth, dirt'
It looks for rain = 'It looks as though it is going to rain'
jellybread = 'bread and jelly'
keep up = 'to detain'
loan = 'to borrow'
lock open = 'to unlock'
make out = 'to plan'
reach = 'to be enough': *The apples won't reach.*
shell = 'skin (of a fruit), peeling'
sneaky = 'persnickety, fussy in eating'
so = 'unchanged, plain': *I don't want no butter on my bread; I'll eat it so.*
tie loose = 'to untie'
till, until = 'by, before, by the time that'
towards = 'in comparison with': *I am nothing towards him.*
want = 'to forecast': *The newspaper wants rain.*
what for = 'what kind of'
with = 'along': *He always came with.*
wonder = 'to cause to be surprised, amazed, puzzled, etc.'; usually used in the expression *It wonders me* (or *him, her,* etc.)
wonderful = 'exceedingly, very'

Grammar. (1) The impersonal construction is commonly used: *It wonders me how he found that out. I'll take the apples out of the refrigerator so it gives room for other stuff. It has people like that* (There are people like that).
(2) The reflexive construction is also used more than in Standard American: *Eat yourself done* = 'Finish eating.'
(3) *Already, once* or *oncet,* and *yet* are often used redundantly: *He has lost his respect for her long already. Let me see that oncet. And then your mother was with yet.*
(4) The verb *make* has a wide range of uses: *Make the door open. Make the bucket empty. Make the fire out.*
(5) *Would* is used almost exclusively in place of the subjunctive *were: If I would be you, I wouldn't do that. If he would be here, we'd go to Sunbury.*
(6) *Let* and *leave* are commonly confused: *Leave me go. I left him do it. School has just left out. I'll let my tools here.*

per. The preposition *per* = 'in or for each' occurred first in Latin phrases like *per annum* = 'each year' and *per centum* = 'in each hundred.' It was then transferred to expressions such as *miles per hour* and *pounds per square inch.* As a freely available English preposition, *per* is most appropriate to numerical and quantitative contexts, such as business communications, books on economics, or history. It does not occur very often in literary writing.

per cent, percent, percentage. *Per cent* originated as an abbreviation of the Latin phrase *per centum* = 'per hundred.' In British and more conservative American usage it is still regarded as an adverbial phrase and is written as two words: *ten per cent* or *10 per cent.* Current U.S. usage treats it as a single-word adverb: *ten percent* or *10 percent.* (For the use of figures versus words see NUMBER STYLE.) The percent symbol (%) is usually reserved for scientific, technical, tabular, or other specialized matter, and it is always used with a figure: 22%.

The formal noun meaning 'a proportion of something considered in hundredths' is *percentage: This year saw a high percentage of new-business failures. Percentage* is also used to mean simply 'some unstated proportion of anything': *Of these ancient and corny jokes, a percentage will still get laughs.* But *percent* is now widely used as a noun in both of these senses.

> As to values, the percent saying it is very important that a home have plenty of books, magazines, and other reading material increased from 79 percent in 1972 to 82 percent in 1977.
> —*Christian Science Monitor*

> A system that moves in secret, then winds up disciplining a minuscule percent of those whose conduct is complained about, can be neither effective nor credible.
> —report of a legal grievance committee (quoted), *Reader's Digest*

Percent is now sometimes further used as a noun meaning 'one percent':

> Government regulations add about three quarters of a percent annually to the rate of inflation.
> —Barry Bosworth, *U.S. News & World Report*

◇ ***Recommendation.*** In formal usage *percentage* is still preferable both for 'proportion considered in hundredths' and for 'unquantified proportion.' The noun *percent* seems to be gaining acceptability, but we advise avoiding it except in informal contexts. We likewise consider that *one percent* is preferable to *a percent.*

period. (1) A rare example of a spoken word arising from a piece of graphic punctuation. (For the use of the mark itself see PUNCTUATION.) *Period* is used as an emphatic interjection, by which the speaker either refuses any further discussion or rejects any change in or addition to the preceding statement.

> Minnie, at fifteen, had announced to us what her future was going to be, in no uncertain terms. She was going to marry a guy who raised horses. Period.
> —Harpo Marx, *Harpo Speaks*

> Some opponents don't want any radioactive materials used in their neighborhood, period.
> —*Bar Harbor* (Me.) *Times*

> When you're playing baseball, you're playing baseball—*period.* That's why I'm not one of these "business" ballplayers.
> —Pete Rose, *The Pete Rose Story*

Some Southerners, instead of saying *period,* say *dot.*

(2) *Period* is also used as a somewhat old-fashioned synonym of *periodic sentence,* that is, a complex sentence with the main clause at the end and no grammatical elements trailing it. The "periodic style" inherited from ancient Latin writers was the basis of much high-flown writing in all the Western languages, including English, between the Renaissance and the end of the 18th century. The following citation (the original sentence is too long to be quoted in full) is a typical 17th-century period:

> . . . about two hours before supper, they [public-school boys] are by a sudden alarum or watch word, to be called out to their military motions, under sky or covert, according to the seasons, as was the Roman wont; first on foot, then as their age permits, on horseback, to all the art of cavalry; that having in sport, but with much exactness, and daily muster, served out the rudiments of their soldiership in all the skill of

embattailing, marching, encamping, fortifying, besieging and battering, with all the helps of ancient and modern stratagems, tactics and warlike maxims, they may as it were out of a long war come forth renowned and perfect commanders in the service of their country.

—John Milton,
Of Education:
To Master Samuel Hartlib

The foregoing is by no means an extreme example; however, no one writes in this fashion nowadays—such a sentence in a present-day context would probably work only if clearly humorous in intent. But in former times the period was much admired for the "flow and variety" that were its principal charm in the hands of a skilled writer, like Milton. To the brevity and directness characteristic of most good modern style, the periodic style was diametrically opposed. This opposition goes back to ancient times, as the following discussion of the historians Thucydides and Sallust makes clear.

> Thucydides, although he brings forward only the principal idea, and discards what is collateral, yet frequently employs long and involved periods. Sallust, on the other hand, is abrupt and sententious, and is generally considered as having carried this sort of brevity to a vicious excess. . . . Lord Monboddo calls his style incoherent, and declares that there is not one of his short and uniform sentences which deserves the name of a period; so that, supposing each sentence were in itself beautiful, there is not variety enough to constitute fine writing.
>
> —Charles Anthon,
> *Life and Writings of Sallust* (1833)

Interestingly, the very features that for the older critics constituted a drawback (abruptness, brevity) are features that we would praise today. Note also that "fine writing" for the above-quoted critic was the opposite of what we mean by FINE WRITING.

peripatetic /pĕr-ĭ-pə-**tĕt**-ĭk/. The followers of the philosopher Aristotle used a building in Athens that had a covered walkway or cloister, called in Greek *peripatos,* from *peripatein* = 'to walk about.' For this reason their school became known as the Peripatetic School, meaning 'the school with the walkway.' Later, it was alleged that Aristotle had walked up and down while lecturing and that this accounted for the name, which would mean 'the walking-up-and-down school.' But there is no evidence for this. Nonetheless, the word *peripatetic* has come to mean 'walking around' or 'moving from place to place.' It is a somewhat pedantic word (unless used humorously).

> John James Audubon . . . was the most peripatetic of men. For more than 30 years he tramped forests and meadows, scoured marshes and bayous, navigated rivers. . . .
>
> —Albert Maisel,
> *Smithsonian*

> The business of commercial fishing must be conducted by peripatetic entrepreneurs moving, like their quarry, without regard for state boundary lines.
>
> —Thurgood Marshall (quoted),
> *New York Times*

peroratio. Old term for the *peroration,* or conclusion, in a piece of expository writing. See EXPOSITION.

perpetrate is essentially a formal legal verb meaning 'to commit (a crime or other offense).' Even when *perpetrate* is not used in a legal context, its object should be something undesirable, such as a mistake, or something at least humorously deplorable, such as a hoax or a bad joke. The word occasionally used to mean 'preserve, continue'; this is a mistake for *perpetuate.*

Persian words. (1) *Iran* and *Persia* are two names for the same country. It was founded before 1500 B.C. by a branch of the Aryan people who also conquered northern India; its original name was *Iran* /ĭ-**rän**/ = 'Aryan land.' Persis (now called Fars) was one of the ancient kingdoms or provinces within Iran, in the south. Around 550 B.C. Cyrus the Great of Persis conquered the whole of Iran, and his large empire became known to the Greeks as *Persia.* Europeans continued to call the country Persia until 1935, when it officially readopted its ancient name of Iran. See also IRAN, IRANIAN.

◊ ***Recommendation.*** *Iran* is now the only correct name for the modern nation and is also acceptable in historical contexts back to the foundation. *Persia* remains preferable for all periods from the reign of Cyrus to 1935. The adjectives *Iranian* and *Persian* overlap in the same way, except that *Persian* is the more usual cultural term: *Persian architecture; Persian carpets.*

(2) The Persian (or Iranian) language belongs to the Indo-European family, most closely related to Sanskrit and other languages of India and more distantly to English (see INDO-EUROPEAN). It is now written chiefly in the Arabic script, but the language is not related to Arabic. From ancient times and throughout the Middle Ages, Persian civilization has been influential. Already in the time of Cyrus, the Greeks and Hebrews were borrowing Persian words and concepts. The English vocabulary has a noteworthy collection of Persian words, borrowed mostly through Arabic, Turkish, Greek, Latin, and other European languages.

angel = 'an immortal being acting as an agent or messenger of God': (via French and Latin) from Greek *angelos* = 'messenger,' from a Persian word meaning 'courier, messenger'

arsenic = 'poisonous metallic element used in insecticides, glass, etc.': (via French and Latin) from Greek *arsenikon* = 'arsenic trisulfide,' from Syriac *zarnikā,* from a Persian word meaning 'yellow substance, arsenic trisulfide'

azure /**ăzh**-ər/ = 'clear light blue': from French *l'azur,* from Arabic *(al-)lazaward* = '(the) lapis lazuli,' from Persian *lāzhward* = 'lapis lazuli, a blue or green gemstone'

baksheesh /băk-**shēsh**/ = 'charitable gift, tip, bribe': from Persian *bakshīsh* = 'gift'

bazaar /bə-**zär**/ = 'Middle Eastern market': (via Italian and Turkish) from Persian *bāzār* = 'market'

caravan = 'company of merchants and others traveling together over long-distance trade routes': (via French and Italian) from Persian *kārwān*

chess = 'ancient board game for two players': from Old French *esches* = 'the game of chess,' plural of *eschac* = 'check in chess,' (via Arabic) from Persian *shah* = 'king'

dervish = 'member of a Muslim religious order practicing self-denial and contemplation': from Turkish *dervish,* from Persian *darvīsh*

divan /**dĭ**-văn, **dī**-văn/ = 'long seat, backless couch': from Turkish *divān* = 'cushioned seat, law court, business office,' from Persian *dīwān* = 'account book,' hence 'accounting office or law court with a long cushioned seat against one wall,' hence also 'cushioned seat'

jasmine /**jăz**-mĭn/ = 'Asian shrub with fragrant white flowers': (via French and Arabic) from Persian *yasmīn*

julep /**jōō**-ləp, -lĭp/ = 'cold drink made with bourbon and mint,' originally 'nonalcoholic syrupy drink': from French *julep,* from Arabic *julāb,* from Persian *gulāb* = 'rose water'

lilac /**lī**-lək, -lăk/ = 'shrub with clusters of fragrant pale-violet flowers': (via French and Spanish) from Arabic *līlak,* from Persian *līlak* = 'lilac,' variant of *nīlak* = 'bluish'

Magi See *magus,* below.

magic = 'art of controlling natural events by supernatural means': (via French and Latin) from Greek *magikē tekhnē* = 'the sorcerer's art,' from *magos* = 'sorcerer, magus'

magus /**mā**-gəs/ = 'sorcerer, magician' and (plural) **Magi** /**mā**-jī/ = 'the wise men from the East who brought gifts to the child Jesus': from Latin *magus* (singular) and *magī* (plural), from Greek *magos* = 'Persian priest, sorcerer,' from Persian *magush* = 'member of an order of Zoroastrian priests'

paradise = (1) 'the Garden of Eden' (2) 'heaven, bliss': (via French and Latin) from Greek *paradeisos* = 'garden,' originally 'walled garden or park of a Persian noble or king,' from Persian *pairi-daēza* = 'walled garden or park,' from *pairi* = 'around' + *daēza* = 'wall'

peach = 'sweet fruit of a tree native to China': from Old French *peche*, from Latin *persica* = 'Persian fruit,' from *Persicus* = 'Persian'

pistachio /pĭ-**stăsh**-ē-ō, pĭ-**stäsh**-/ = 'nut of a tree native to the Middle East': Italian *pistachio* (via Latin and Greek), from Persian *pistah*

rice = 'cereal grass native to Asia': (via French, Italian, and Latin) from Greek *orȳza*, from Persian *vrīz*

* **satrap** = 'ruler of a province in the ancient Persian Empire': (via French and Latin) from Greek *satrapēs*, from Persian *khshathra-pāvan* = 'kingdom-protector'

scimitar /**sĭm**-ə-tər, -tär/ = 'curved Oriental sword': from Italian *scimitarra*, from Persian *shimshīr* = 'sword'

shah = 'Persian king': from Persian *shāh*, from Old Persian *khshāyathiya* = 'ruler, king'

talcum = 'powder for the skin, made from a soft mineral compound of magnesium': from Latin *talcum*, from Arabic *talq*, from Persian *talk*

tiara /tē-**är**-ə, -**ăr**-ə/ = (1) 'the triple crown of the pope' (2) 'jeweled headpiece worn with formal dress by women': from Latin *tiāra*, from Greek *tiāra* = 'headpiece worn by Byzantine emperors,' originally 'conical hat or crown worn by Persian kings,' from a Persian word meaning 'crown'

tiger = 'large Asian cat with an orange coat striped with black': (via French and Latin) from Greek *tigris*, from Persian *tigra* = 'sharp'

tulip = 'bulb of the lily family, native to Asia, with strongly colored cup-shaped flowers': from Persian *dulband* = 'turban'

turban = 'Oriental headdress made of a strip of cloth wound around the head, or around a cap': (via French) from Italian *turbante*, *tolipante*, from Persian *dulband* = 'turban'

zircon = 'brown to grayish mineral compound from which a brilliant blue-white gem is obtained': from German *zirkon* (via French and Italian), from Arabic *zarqūn*, from Persian *zargūn* = 'gold-colored mineral'

*Appears as separate entry

person, chairperson, spokesperson, etc. See CHAIRMAN; FEMALE-GENDER WORD FORMS.

persona, personage, personality. It seems deeply right in psychological terms that the basis of these quite different words is a Latin word (*persona*) that first meant 'mask used by an actor,' then 'part played by an actor,' and only finally 'human individual, person.' (1) Our term *persona* was coined by the psychologist Carl Jung to mean 'the outward role assumed by a person in order to function in society':

> . . . to lay the burden of individuality down, to be washed clean of the persona we hold together, to shed the character we have constructed for a lifetime . . .
> —Sam Keen, *Psychology Today*

Persona is now also a popular mass-media term for 'characteristic role played or projected by a well-known figure, public image':

> In his 25 years at CBS . . . Cronkite has had the luck, or the genius, to personify the prototypical Middle American. This persona is crucial to his success.
> —Ron Powers, *The Newscasters*

> In these interviews . . . Vidal is always on stage, perpetuating a persona that crosses Will Rogers with Oscar Wilde.
> —Michael Dirda, *Washington Post Book World*

(2) *Personage*, an older word, means 'genuinely eminent person, person of real distinction':

> Colonel the Honourable George Napier and his wife Lady Sarah Lennox were two remarkable personages. The one a tall and majestic soldier, probably the finest specimen of military manhood then in the service of King George the Third, the other a lady of such beauty, wit, and grace that her fascination had induced the same King George to offer her all his heart and half his throne.
> —William Butler, *Sir Charles Napier*

> Political personages frequently joined us; and one night, after a dinner party, I remember seeing Winston Churchill . . .
> —Peter Quennell, *The Wanton Chase*

(3) First, *personality* means 'the distinctive character of a person, the aggregate of features that make an individual unique':

> "Bobby and Jack," said Bill Lemmings, who loved them both, "had very different personalities and really different interests outside of politics. . . ."
> —Arthur M. Schlesinger, Jr., *Robert Kennedy and His Times*

Second, *personality* has also come to mean 'attractive or remarkable personal quality': *As a performer she really has personality.* Finally, *personality* is another mass-media word, meaning 'well-known media figure who is not famous for anything in particular and probably lacks real talent':

> In Chancellor's lingo a "hot dog" is a phony—a TV personality masquerading as a newscaster.
> —Theodore H. White, *Panorama*

personification. As it is most commonly used, the word *personification* is simply a synonym for *embodiment* or *incarnation,* as in *Karen was the personification of Nordic good looks.* More strictly defined, the word, like the term *anthropomorphism,* refers to the act of attributing personal or human qualities to nonhuman subjects.

One well-known category of personification is *pathetic fallacy* (personifying inanimate nature): *the laughing brook; a threatening storm; a noble tree; "April is the cruellest month . . ."* (T. S. Eliot, *The Waste Land*). Another is *hypostatization* (personifying concepts or ideas): *England expects every man to do his duty.* See also FALLACY.

phenomenon, phenomenal. As a philosophical term *phenomenon* means 'something that appears, an event as perceived by the senses.' In general usage it usually means 'a remarkable, puzzling, or significant event or effect':

> . . . warts can be ordered off the skin by hypnotic suggestion. Generations of internists and dermatologists, and their grandmothers, for that matter, have been convinced of the phenomenon.
> —Lewis Thomas, *The Medusa and the Snail*

> The overbuilding of fishing fleets is a worldwide phenomenon that no single nation has been able to solve. . . .
> —Bruce J. Cole, *National Fisherman*

Often the meaning is intensified to 'sensational event, person of the utmost fame, or dazzling commercial success':

> The abrupt downfall of one of the most powerful and respected labor leaders in the country made the Rackets Committee overnight a national phenomenon.
> —Arthur M. Schlesinger, Jr., *Robert Kennedy and His Times*

> For Paramount, which had made the better offer, he now began the string of pictures that was to build him into a national phenomenon.
> —Robert Lewis Taylor, *W. C. Fields*

The preferred plural is *phenomena,* but *phenomenons* is probably commoner in the last sense. *Phenomena* is often used as a singular; this is a definite error.

The basic meaning of the adjective *phenomenal* as a term of philosophy is 'perceived by the senses,' as opposed to 'existing in absolute reality.' But in everyday use it follows the last sense of the noun, meaning 'remarkable, amazing, sensational':

For the next hour we stayed there, and for an hour the half-mile-wide river of caribou flowed unhurriedly north in a phenomenal procession, so overwhelming in its magnitude that I could hardly credit my senses.
—Farley Mowat, *People of the Deer*

Prizefighters are known to have phenomenal memories for faces, maybe because our trade demands that we keep our eyes fixed, studying the face of the opponent.
—Muhammad Ali, *The Greatest*

All through the decade of the Vietnam war, the population grew at the phenomenal rate of 3 percent a year.
—Marvin Harris, *Cannibals and Kings*

pidgin and creole languages. Some ten million people around the world speak pidgin and creole languages. Until very recently these language varieties were considered merely corruptions of European languages (including English). But in fact they are languages in their own right, all having rule-ordered grammars, pronunciation systems, and vocabularies. They also all have similar characteristics. Polynesian pidgin, Haitian creole, and Afrikaans, for example, have features in common even though they are based on English, French, and Dutch, respectively. All pidgins and creoles are the result of contact between two or more groups of speakers of different languages.

Lingua Franca. Often when people do not speak each other's language, they communicate through a third language spoken by both. This "adopted" language is called a *lingua franca*. For instance, in the Philippines, when an Ilocano speaker and a Tagalog speaker converse in Spanish, Spanish serves as their lingua franca. Visitors to a foreign land may use as their lingua franca whatever language they have in common. This would be the case if, on a train in France, travelers from, say, Sweden, Japan, and Hungary discovered that they all spoke English.

Pidgin. *Pidgin* is a lingua franca that is drastically simplified and restructured. The pronunciation and grammar of the base language, the lingua franca, are reduced to the simplest forms possible. For example, pidgins based on European languages commonly eliminate the verb inflections. The English verb *go* has two inflected forms in the present tense: (*I, you, we, they*) *go;* (*he, she, it*) *goes*. English-based pidgins, such as Cameroon or Melanesian, reduce these to one form: *go*. This form is also used in all tenses, whereas English has two other forms: *went* and *gone*. In Cameroon pidgin English, for example, this is the way *go* is used. (Note: Most pidgins and creoles are not written. Thus, it is easier and more accurate to follow the practice of linguists and use pronunciation symbols instead of traditional spellings.)

ē gō mäkĕt = 'She goes to market.'
ē dē gō mäkĕt = 'She is going to market.'
ē bēn gō mäkĕt = 'She went to market.'
ē dông gō mäkĕt = 'She has gone to market.'
ē gō gō mäkĕt = 'She will go to market.'

A pidgin is a marginal language native to no one. It is used for certain restricted needs, usually for communication in trade and commerce. The term *pidgin* probably derives from the 19th-century Chinese pronunciation of the English word *business*. Chinese pidgin English was primarily the means of communication between European and Chinese traders and merchants. In this language *pidgin* also had the broader meaning of 'affair,' as in dăt blông yo͞o pĭjĭn = 'That's your affair'—still occasionally heard in British English as "That's your pigeon, old boy."

Pidgins range from limited to extended forms. Korean "bamboo" English is an example of a limited, short-lived pidgin. It had restricted use, filling minimal communication needs between Koreans and Americans in the Korean War. A similar temporary pidgin developed in Vietnam. On the other hand, West African and several Pacific pidgins are well established and widely used. In polyglot New Guinea, for example, Melanesian pidgin, or Neo-Melanesian, is used in the schools and the national parliament; it is officially called *Niugini*.

Creole. A *creole* is a pidgin that has become a native language. When the children of pidgin-speaking parents grow up using the pidgin as their first language, a creole is established. The same simple grammar and pronunciation are carried over into the creole. But because a native language must express the human experience more fully, its vocabulary, or LEXICON, is greatly expanded. This process is called *relexification*. Sometimes a more elaborate syntax also evolves.

The vocabulary of a creole, though taken primarily from the base language, is a mixture drawn from all the various languages in contact with it. The base language of Papiamento, the creole of Curaçao, West Indies, is Spanish. But Papiamento contains many Portuguese and Dutch borrowings, as well as words from the native West African languages of the blacks brought to the West Indies.

Varieties. Over the centuries, wherever traders, colonists, or rulers came into contact with native peoples, a pidgin or creole language was likely to form. Many such languages were the result of the expansion of European trade, commerce, and slavery after the 15th century. The oldest known pidgin is a specific language called *lingua franca* (the term now also used to indicate any "adopted" common language). Based on French and Italian, it was used in the Middle Ages by traders and crusaders in the eastern Mediterranean countries.

European-based pidgins and creoles, particularly English ones, fall into two major classes: Atlantic and Indo-Pacific. Each has its own distinguishing grammatical and historical connections. The Atlantic varieties have historical roots in the slave trade. Consequently, their syntax and vocabulary are marked by the influence of the coastal languages of West Africa. Here are the major pidgin and creole languages of the world.

(1) English-based:

Language	Area
ATLANTIC	
*Gullah	South Carolina and Georgia coasts
Jamaican creole	Jamaica
Bahama creole	Bahama Islands
Lesser Antilles creole	Virgin Islands, Antigua, Grenada, Tobago, Trinidad, etc.
Guyana creole	Guyana
Djuka	Surinam
Sranan (Taki-Taki)	coastal Surinam
Krio	Sierra Leone
Liberian English	Liberia
Cameroon pidgin	Cameroon and eastern Nigeria
INDO-PACIFIC	
Australian pidgin (several varieties)	Australia
Melanesian pidgin (Neo-Melanesian, or Niugini)	New Guinea
Hawaiian creole	Hawaii

*Appears as separate entry

(2) French-based:

Language	Area
ATLANTIC	
Louisiana Creole	eastern Louisiana, eastern Texas
Haitian creole	Haiti
Lesser Antilles creole	St. Thomas, Dominica, Martinique, etc.
Guyane creole	French Guiana
pidgin French	North Africa
INDO-PACIFIC	
Mauritian creole	Mauritius
Reunion creole	Reunion
Seychellois creole	Seychelles

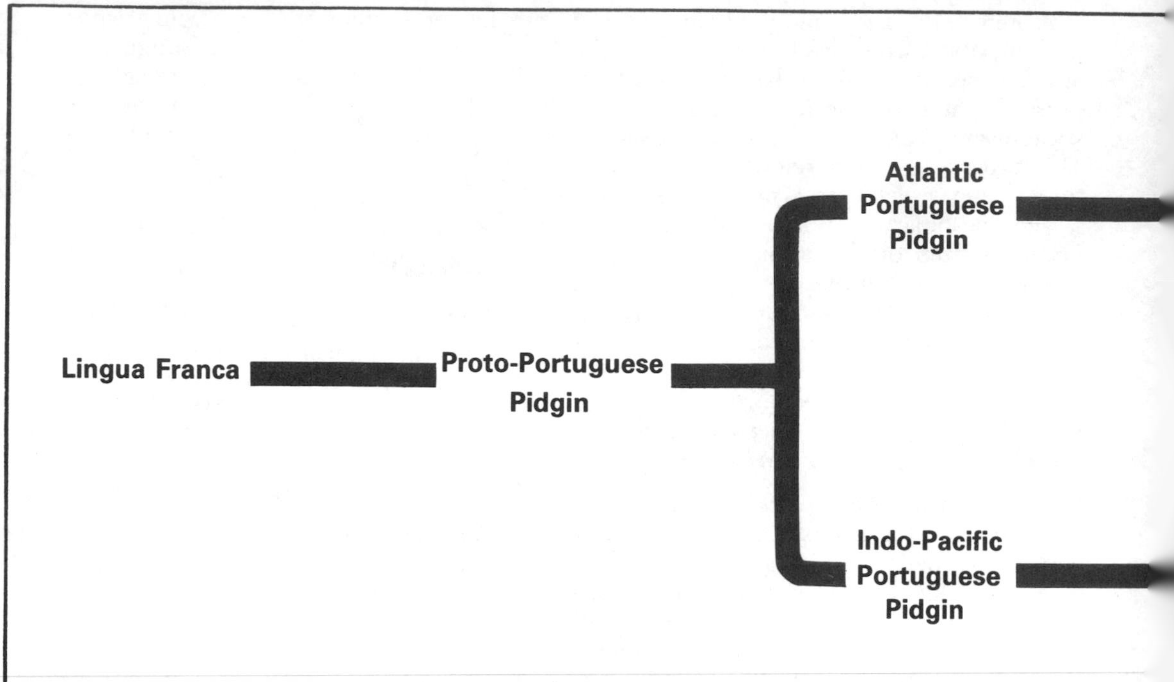

The Family of European-Based Pidgins and Creoles

(3) Spanish-based:

Language	Area
ATLANTIC	
Papiamento	Curaçao
INDO-PACIFIC	
Chabakano	Philippines

These are a few of the many pidgin and creole languages based on English, French, and Spanish. (For more on Jamaican creole, see JAMAICAN ENGLISH; Hawaiian creole, see HAWAIIAN ENGLISH; French Creole, see LOUISIANA FRENCH.) In addition, there are many pockets around the world of pidgins and creoles based on Portuguese, Dutch, Italian, German, and a few Slavic languages.

There are also many non-European-based pidgins and creoles. Here are a few.

(1) Chinook jargon—a pidgin based on several Pacific Northwestern American Indian languages. (See CHINOOK JARGON.)

(2) Bazaar Malay—a pidginized variety of Malay spoken throughout Malaysia and Indonesia.

(3) African-based:

Language	Area
Swahili pidgins and creoles	East and Central Africa
Sango	Central African Republic
Fanagalo (pidginized Zulu)	Southeast Africa
Mbugu	Tanzania

Origin. Among European-based pidgins and creoles there are striking similarities in grammar and vocabulary. For example, nearly all contain some Portuguese-derived words. Of those pidgins and creoles that are not actually based on Portuguese, some have only a few Portuguese terms in their vocabulary, while others are up to 30 percent Portuguese. Vir-

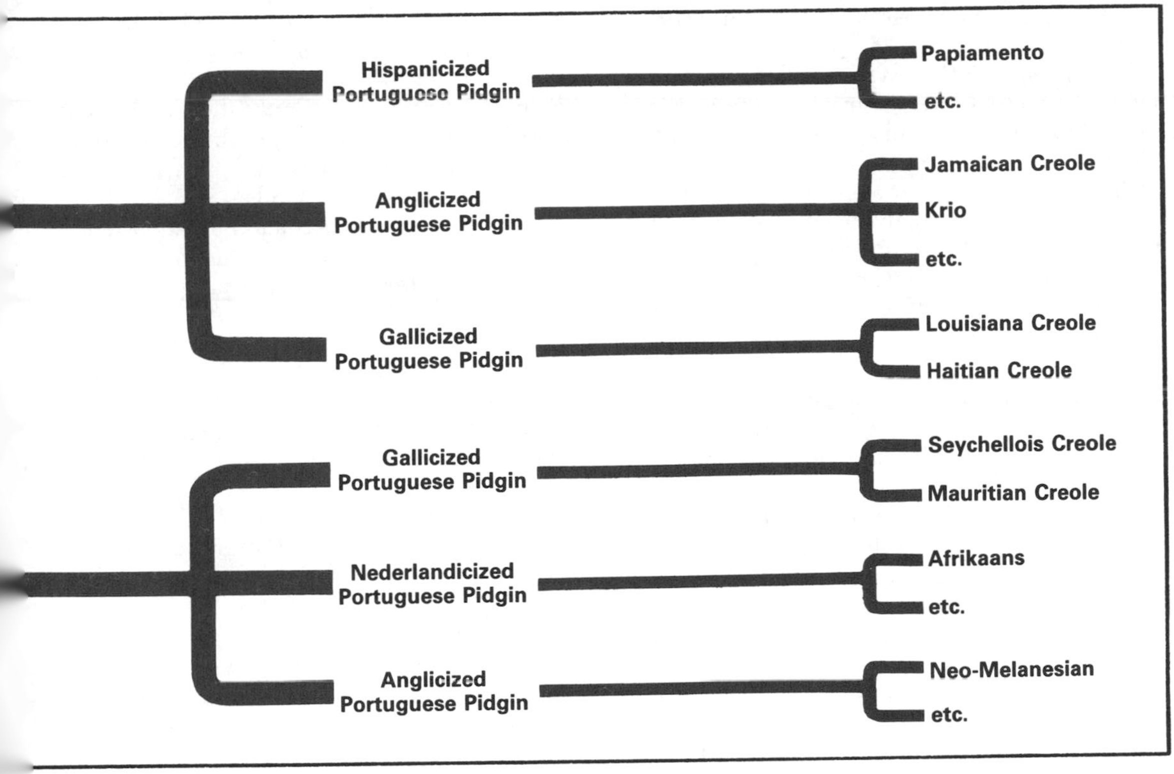

tually all European-based pidgins and creoles have the words *pikin* or *pikinini* (= 'small, little' or 'child') and *savi* or *sabi* (= 'to know'), derived, respectively, from Portuguese *pequeno* = 'little' and *sabir* = 'to know.' (See SAVVY.)

These and other common features have led some linguists to develop the following theory. All European-based pidgins and creoles derive from a 15th-century Portuguese pidgin, which in turn evolved from the Mediterranean pidgin, lingua franca, used by medieval traders and crusaders. When the Portuguese sailed along the western coast of Africa, and then to India and the Far East, they naturally used their contact language, the Portuguese form of lingua franca. Even though by the 17th century the Portuguese were no longer a world power, they had thus established their (pidgin) language in both the Atlantic and the Pacific.

The speakers of this pidgin then drew on the vocabulary of the later arriving European traders. The languages of the new maritime powers—English, Spanish, French, and Dutch—subsequently altered the original Portuguese pidgin. By this theory, then, it is more accurate to call a French creole a gallicized pidgin Portuguese or an English creole an anglicized pidgin Portuguese. The chart above is a simplified family tree of European-based pidgins and creoles.

Pronunciation. In the process of simplifying the base language, pidgins and creoles usually change the vowels to a broader form. In Haitian creole, for example, the French vowels /ü/ and /ë/ are simplified to /ē/ and /ā/. French *l'heure* /lër/ (= 'the hour') is in Haitian creole /lā/ (= 'hour, time'). French *la rue* /là rü/ (= 'the street') is /là rē/ in Haitian creole, and *du feu* /dü fë/ (= 'some fire') is /dē fā/.

Many combinations of consonants present in European languages are absent in pidgins and creoles. Melanesian pidgin, for example, frequently has a vowel inserted to break up such consonant clusters as /kl/, /st/, and /sp/. *Clear* is /kəlîr/, *stone* is /sētōn/, and *spear* is /sēpēə/. In Jamaican creole initial /s/ is frequently dropped altogether: /plĭt/ for *split*, /kwēz/ for *squeeze*.

The pronunciation system of the native language tends to determine how the words of the base language will be pronounced. The English consonant sounds /*th*/ and /th/ are rare in the world's languages. Since these sounds do not occur in the native languages of New Guinea or West Africa, for example, they are regularly replaced by /d/ and /t/, respectively. In Neo-Melanesian, *think* is /tĭngk-tĭngk/. *This* becomes /dēsē/ in Sranan and /dĭs/ in Gullah.

Vocabulary. At its earliest stages a pidgin permits only limited communication between two or more groups of speakers. Its vocabulary is so restricted that gestures must usually be used to convey even the simplest ideas. Because this marginal pidgin is inadequate for full communication, it eventually either dies out or expands into a more complex and useful form. In expanding, it increases its vocabulary in several ways.

(1) The most important way is simply by borrowing words from the base language. Most of the vocabulary of a pidgin or creole—up to 80 percent—comes from the base language. Often the original meanings of the borrowed words are kept, but in many cases meanings are extended in different directions. For example, in many English-based pidgins *grass* refers not only to the plant but also to anything growing outward from a surface. Thus, *hair* is *grass-belong-head*, and *beard* is *grass-belong-face*.

(2) Another but less important source of vocabulary is the native language. The vocabulary of most pidgins and creoles has fewer than 15 or 20 percent native words. For the most part, these are terms for local flora and fauna, such as Neo-Melanesian ko͞orētä = 'octopus,' and kēou = 'egg.' Occasionally, there are other terms of native origin, such as the West African (Twi) words in Jamaican creole for 'food,' nyăm, and for 'a kind of bag or sack,' kōtōko͞o.

(3) Another important way that pidgins and creoles expand their vocabularies is by *reduplication*, the doubling or repetition of a word to make a new form. Through this device the meaning can be extended or intensified. For example, in Atlantic English-based pidgins, *ben* = 'bend,' *benben* = 'crooked'; in Pacific English-based pidgins, *bik* = 'big,' *bikbik* = 'very big.' Reduplication also distinguishes words that sound the same but have different meanings, as in (Atlantic) *san* = 'sun,' *sansan* = 'sand.'

(4) Word compounding is another important way that pidgins and creoles increase their vocabularies. Here are some examples.

Atlantic English-based

bĭgī = (1) (noun) 'greed' (2) (adjective) 'greedy' (*big* + *eye*)
bĭgmăn = 'important person' (*big* + *man*)
bo͞oshbēf = 'wild animal, game' (*bush* + *beef*)
dīmăn = 'corpse' (*die* + *man*)
swētmŏt = (1) (verb) 'to flatter' (2) (noun) 'flattery' (*sweet* + *mouth*)

Pacific English-based

bĭgmous = 'conceited' (*big* + *mouth*)
bĭgsŏndē = 'feast day' (*big* + *Sunday*)
bo͞oshnīf = 'machete' (*bush* + *knife*)
dīmăn = 'corpse' (*die* + *man*)
kloudĭbrōk = 'thunder, cloudburst' (*cloud* + *broke*)

All four methods of vocabulary expansion can be seen in the following representative lists.

Neo-Melanesian

bəgərəpĭm = 'to ruin, wreck' (*bugger* + *up* + *him*)
bĭgfĕlə = 'big' (*big* + *fellow*)
bĭgmous = 'insolent person' (*big* + *mouth*)
bĭlông = 'of, for' (*belong*)
blăkfĕlə = 'black' (*black* + *fellow*)
blăkfĕlə măn = 'dark-skinned person'
dĭsfĕlə = 'this' (*this* + *fellow*)
fītĭm = 'to strike, beat' (*fight* + *him*)
härdwŏk = 'to work hard' (*hard* + *work*)
kăləbo͞os = 'jail' (Spanish *calabozo*)
mē = 'I, me'
mēfĕlə = 'we, us'
nădərfĕlə = 'another' (*another* + *fellow*)
ôlgādər = 'all' (*altogether*)
ôlsām = 'thus, so' (*all the same*)
plĕntē = 'many' (*plenty*)
rous = 'to get out'; used as a command (German *raus*)

skrōō bĭlông lĕg = 'knee' (*screw* + *belong* + *leg*)
tälə-tälə = 'Protestant' (Polynesian, 'friend')
tămbōō = (1) (noun) 'prohibition' (2) (adjective) 'forbidden' (*taboo*)
tĭngk-tĭngk = 'opinion, thought' (*think*)
tŏk = 'talk'
tŏkĭm = 'to speak to, address'

Chinese pidgin

chouchou = 'to eat'
dăt = 'that'
dĭstīm = 'now' (*this* + *time*)
dlĭngkē = 'drink'
dŏksīd = 'at the docks' (*dock* + *side*)
fōrpēsē = 'four' (*four* + *piece*)
hwŭttīm = 'when' (*what* + *time*)
kĭlē = 'to kill'
kōlō = 'cold'
lōōksē = 'to look' (*look* + *see*)
mō = 'more'
tōōpēsē = 'two' (*two* + *piece*)

Sranan

älätə = 'rat'
älətĕn = 'always, all the time'
ängrē = (1) (adjective) 'hungry' (2) (noun) 'hunger'
bäsē = 'boss'
bĭgēfăsē = 'pride, haughtiness' (*big* + *fashion*)
bōōsēmĕtē = 'wild game' (*bush* + *meat*)
dätrə-drĕsē = 'medicine' (*doctor* + *dressing*)
fēsē = 'fish'
jărōōsōō = 'jealous'
kĕ = 'care': *mē nō kĕ* = 'I don't care.'
kŏkrŏntō = 'coconut'
săfōō = 'soft': *wŏn săfōō ĕksē* = 'one soft [soft-boiled] egg'
täkē = 'talk'
tēfē = 'teeth'

Haitian creole

ăgyō = 'goodbye' (French *adieu*)
blā = 'blue' (French *bleu*)
blēā = 'to forget' (French *oublier*)
bôɴ = 'good' (French *bon*)
bōōlā = 'to burn' (French *brûler*)
bōōrĕk = 'donkey' (French *bourrique*)
găsôɴ = 'young man' (French *garçon*)
kēltē = 'cultivation' (French *culture*)
kētā = 'to leave' (French *quitter*)
kō = 'body' (French *corps*)
läsā = 'to go away' (French *laisser*)
lē = 'he, him, she, her, it' (French *lui*)
mwā = 'I, me' (French *moi*)
pētēt = 'child, children' (French *petite*)

Examples.

(1) *Neo-Melanesian*. A section of the autobiography of a work boy, Chavi, collected by Margaret Mead in the 1930s.

> Nou mē stŏp räboul. mē stŏp lông bĭglīn, mē kŭtĭm kōprä. nou wənfĕlə măstər bĭlông kəmpənē ĕm ē-kĭchĭm mē, mē kōōk lông ĕm gĕn. măstər kĭng. mē stŏp. nou ôl măstər ē-kĭk, nou ôl ē-kĭkĭm ĕm, nou läg bĭlông ĕm ē-swĕləp. ôl măstər täsôl ē-kĭk, nou ôl ē-kĭkĭm ĕm. nou ĕm ē-gō lông sĭdnē lông hous sĭk. mē wənfĕlə mē stŏp lōōkoutĭm hous bĭlông ĕm. ôltəgĕdər səmtĭng mē lōōkoutĭm, mē stŏp. ôrīt, nou păs ē-kəm. nou kēäp ē-lōōkĭm, ē-tôk: "ō, măstər bĭlông yōō ē-nō kăn kəm băk."

Translation

Then I stayed in Rabaul. I was in the work-group, cutting copra. Then a white man from the company took me as a cook again. Mr. King. I stayed there. Now all the white men were playing football, and they kicked him, so that his leg swelled up. The white men were just kicking, and kicked him. So he went to Sydney, to the hospital. I stayed alone to look after his house. I looked after everything, and stayed there. Very well, then a letter arrived. Then the government official looked at it, and said: "Oh, your master cannot come back."

(2) *Chinese pidgin*. A dialogue dictated to Robert A. Hall in 1944 by a native of China. The dialogue is between a lady and her tailor.

> MISTRESS: tälər, mī hăv kăchē wənpēsē plēntē hănsəm sĭlkä. mī wônchē yōō mākē wən nīs ĭvnēng-drĕs.
> TAILOR: mĭsē hăv gŏt bōōk?
> MISTRESS: mī nō hăv kăchē bōōk. pāmē sē yōō bōōk.
> TAILOR: mī bōōk blông tōō ōlə.

MISTRESS: măskē, yo͞o pāmē lo͞oksē. mī lĭvē sĭlkä *th*ĭssīd, səpōs mī kəm to͞omôrə nĕks dā.
TAILOR: ôrīt, mĭsē, to͞omôlō nĕks dā kăn do͞o. mī mākē vĕrē pôpä fô yo͞o.

Translation
MISTRESS: Tailor, I have a very fine [piece of] silk. I want you to make a nice evening dress.
TAILOR: Has missy a [fashion] book?
MISTRESS: I haven't brought a book. Let me see your book.
TAILOR: My book is too old [out of date].
MISTRESS: Never mind, let me see it. I'll leave the silk here, and possibly I'll come day after tomorrow.
TAILOR: Very well, missy, day after tomorrow is all right. I'll make it just right for you.

(3) *Sranan*. The beginning of a Surinam folk tale recorded in 1936.

Wŏn kōndā bān dā, ān wŏn fōro͞o bān dā bärē. āf ä-bär sō, nä hār kōndrā ā tro͞obo͞o. kōno͞o pōt täkē, wŏn so͞omä kĭr nä-fōro͞o, ä-sä-trō nängä wŏn o͞omän pēkĭn fō-āng. änänsē yĕrē. ä-gō tīg kōno͞o täkē, āng sä-kĭrē nä-fōro͞o. māk kōno͞o gĭ-ām mōnē ān bī sänē, dän āng sä-gō kĭr āng. dē änänsē gō, ä-tän to͞o wĭkē.

Translation
There was once a kingdom, and there was a bird which screeched. If it screeched so, the whole kingdom was disturbed. The king announced that the person who killed the bird would marry a daughter of his. Anansi heard this. He went to tell the king that he would kill the bird. Let the king give him money to buy things, then he would go and kill it. When Anansi went, he remained away two weeks.

(4) *Haitian creole*. The beginning of a folk tale.

lēōɴ äk-bo͞orēk. lōɴ-täɴ lēōɴ tā-pā bo͞orēk, päskā lē tā-wā bo͞orēk tā-pē-grō nāg päsā lē. no͞o zho͞o lēōɴ dē: "bo͞orēk, mōɴ shā, äɴn-älā fā yo͞o tē-prōmnäd." yō pätē, yō rēvā bō yo͞o dlō. lēōɴ fā yo͞o sāl bōɴ, lē trävāsā dlō-ä.

Translation
The Lion and the Donkey. A long time [ago], the lion was afraid of the donkey, because he saw the donkey was a bigger man than he. One day the lion said: "Donkey, my dear chap, let's go take a little walk." They set out, [and] they came to the edge of a stream. The lion gave a single leap, [and] he crossed the stream.

pious, piety. The unfashionable word *pious* basically means 'dutiful.' In religion, to be pious is to be sincere in belief and scrupulous in observance:

> "Blessed be thou," say pious Jews whenever they encounter some small happiness—the good sleep, the loving friend, the sky full of stars, the clarity of a good mind.
> —Ardis Whitman, *Reader's Digest*

Pious also means 'respectful and dutiful to one's parents and family or to others whom one owes respect':

> We wish that this column [part of the Bunker Hill Monument] . . . may contribute to produce in all minds a pious feeling of dependence and gratitude.
> —Daniel Webster, address (1825)

But *pious* is now much more often used negatively to mean (1) 'naïvely believing'; (2) 'hypocritically parading religion'; (3) 'conventional and insincere':

> Perhaps since the start of the Christian Era, if not before, pious people have hoped that the timbers of the ark could be found somewhere on those slopes [of Mount Ararat]. —*Scientific American*

> Far from being the pious injunction of a Utopian dreamer, the command to love one's enemy is an absolute necessity for our survival.
> —Martin Luther King, Jr., *Strength to Love*

> There has been enough of emitting little squeaks of pious horror and collecting United Nations resolutions and other valueless pieces of paper.
> —Alex McColl, *Soldier of Fortune*

Piety also basically means 'dutifulness,' either in religion or toward parents and others:

> Let them learn first to show piety at home, and to requite their parents.
> —1 Timothy 5:4

But nowadays the word is seldom used except to mean 'old-fashioned and outmoded belief' or 'pretended devoutness, hypocritical parade of religion':

> . . . he was voicing the accepted pieties of his day and place—the small-town Texas where success was a reward for virtuous effort, ambition was an admired good, and there was little room for cynicism.
> —Doris Kearns, *Lyndon Johnson and the American Dream*

> His "Checkers speech" defense saved his political life in 1952 but sickened Democratic partisans, who liked neither his pitch nor his piety.
> —William Safire, *Before the Fall*

The depreciation of the meaning of a word in this way is called *pejoration*.

pit, stone, seed, kernel. These terms all refer, in different parts of the United States, to the hard central portion of fleshy (drupaceous) fruits, such as cherries, plums, peaches, apricots, and olives. *Pit* is an Americanism (not related to *pit* = 'hole') adopted from the Dutch settlers (from *pit* = 'kernel'). Today, it is very common in the General Northern dialect.

> You put an apple-seed or a peach-pit into the ground and it springs up into the form of a miniature tree.
> —G. Bush, *Anastasis* (1841)

> One man may suck an orange and be choked by a pit, another swallow a penknife and live.
> —W. Mathews, *Getting On in the World* (1873)

> In California, peach pit fuel is on the market. —*Democrat* (1947)

Stone is used in scattered areas throughout the country but is especially common in the Northern dialect. *Seed,* on the other hand, when used to refer to the hard center of peaches, cherries, etc., has the greatest general currency of any of these terms, except in the Northern dialect. (A *pip* is also a seed, but usually a small one in fruits having many seeds, as oranges, apples, and pears. *Pip* is much commoner in British than in American English.)

Kernel is usually used today to mean either 'a whole grain of wheat or other cereal' or 'the edible part of a nut or of the hard seed of a peach, etc.' But in the Coastal Southern dialect and in certain British dialects it also means 'a whole fruit seed.'

plausible. See SPECIOUS, PLAUSIBLE.

plenty is a noun, basically meaning 'fullness, plenitude, abundance, sufficiency': *We have plenty of food. There was plenty of work to do.* It is also used as an adjective. When the adjective is used predicatively, after the verb *be* or an equivalent, it is standard:

> Now the heroes were plenty and well
> known to fame
> In the troops that were led by the Czar.
> —*Abdullah Bulbul Amir*

Used directly with a noun, *plenty* occurs in speech but is not accepted as standard: *I have plenty problems.* It is also nonstandard as an adverb: *It was raining plenty.*

◇ ***Recommendation.*** In standard speech and writing, *plenty* should be used only as a noun or as a predicate adjective.

pleonasm. See TAUTOLOGY AND PLEONASM.

plethora /plĕth-ə-rə/. From a Greek word meaning 'fullness, repletion,' *plethora* is an old medical term for a bodily condition in which the flesh is distended by an excess of blood. The word is now used chiefly to mean 'abundant supply of anything, profusion,' especially 'overabundant supply, embarrassingly large amount':

> English has many more prepositions than Chinese has, and I have never quite grown used to such a plethora of

prepositions, each so exact in its use.
—Pearl S. Buck, *For Spacious Skies*

Consumption of the plethora of consumer goods churned out by affluent economies is itself a time-absorbing activity.
—E. J. Mishan, *The Economic Growth Debate*

The adjective *plethoric* /plə-**thôr**-ĭk/ may mean simply 'abundant, overabundant' but can also mean 'unhealthily fat, bloated':

The British and American communities in Hong Kong had once been rather plethoric and overfed, but now there were gaunt faces everywhere in the camp.
—Joseph Alsop, *Saturday Evening Post*

ploy. This was originally a Scottish word, a shortening of the noun *employ*, and it meant 'occupation, pastime, amusement,' later also 'trick, stunt.' It was popularized by the English humorist Stephen Potter, who used it to mean 'a basic move in social competition or gamesmanship.' The word has now entered the language of politics, meaning 'deceptive maneuver':

[Stalin] devised sets of diplomatic ploys to test whether the Americans were naive, or determined ideological crusaders, or had some ulterior motive.
—Charles L. Mee, *Meeting at Potsdam*

Sadat interpreted the measure as an Israeli ploy to keep the subject of Jerusalem's future out of the talks. —*Time*

plurals. Forming the plural of most English nouns is a straightforward matter of adding *-s* or *-es* to the singular; to put it another way, most English nouns form their plural regularly. Yet the application of that simple formula can often seem anything but simple. Because there are a fair number of words in English whose plurals are irregular, have varying forms, are the same as the singular, or otherwise exhibit special features, a basic question arises: Which words form regular plurals and which do not? This entry deals with that question.

Regular Plurals. All the words in the following categories add *-s* or *-es* to form the plural.

Common Nouns. (1) *Nouns ending in a consonant or silent* e. Typical of these are:

truck, trucks	buzz, buzzes
hose, hoses	dress, dresses
window, windows	rebuff, rebuffs
watch, watches	tonic, tonics
box, boxes	gas, gases
bush, bushes	menorah, menorahs
bath, baths	value, values

Words ending in *-y* vary. If the *-y* is preceded by a vowel, only *-s* is added:

day, days	honey, honeys
decoy, decoys	foray, forays
guy, guys	

Exceptions:
colloquy, colloquies
obloquy, obloquies
soliloquy, soliloquies
money, moneys *or* monies

Words ending in *-y* preceded by a consonant change *-y* to *-i* before adding the plural *-es*:

candy, candies	mercy, mercies
country, countries	jealousy, jealousies
duty, duties	story, stories
navy, navies	rarity, rarities

Nouns ending in *-f, -ff,* or *-fe* form their plurals variously. Some just add the regular ending:

oaf, oafs	fife, fifes
cuff, cuffs	belief, beliefs

Others undergo a spelling change before adding the regular ending:

half, halves	life, lives
elf, elves	wife, wives
wolf, wolves	thief, thieves

A few others do both (preferred forms are given first):

calf, calves *or* calfs
loaf, loaves *or* loafs
roof, roofs *or* rooves
scarf, scarves *or* scarfs
wharf, wharves *or* wharfs

The word *staff* takes either *staffs* (preferred) or *staves* for the sense 'pole, rod, etc.,' but only *staffs* for the sense 'personnel, assistants, etc.'

Also regular are some words of Latin origin ending in *-us*:

census, censuses
prospectus, prospectuses
hiatus, hiatuses
sinus, sinuses

But see also Foreign Words under Irregular and Special Plurals, below.

(2) *Nouns ending in a vowel other than silent* e.

In *-i*:

alibi, alibis
ski, skis
mini, minis
rabbi, rabbis
spaghetti, spaghettis

Exceptions:
alkali, alkalies *or* alkalis
taxi, taxis *or sometimes* taxies

In *-o*. Some of these add only *-s*; typically, words ending in *-o* preceded by a vowel and words ending in *-oo*:

patio, patios
studio, studios
ego, egos
radio, radios
cameo, cameos
piano, pianos
kangaroo, kangaroos
tattoo, tattoos

Some add *-es*:

hero, heroes
echo, echoes
tomato, tomatoes

Some add either *-s* or *-es* (preferred forms are given first):

cargo, cargoes *or* cargos
halo, halos *or* haloes
tornado, tornadoes *or* tornados
motto, mottoes *or* mottos
banjo, banjos *or* banjoes
zero, zeros *or* zeroes
mosquito, mosquitoes *or* mosquitos

In *-ee, -ie, -a,* and *-u*:

jamboree, jamborees
menagerie, menageries
freesia (*and other flowers*), freesias
area, areas
menu, menus

Proper Nouns. With very few exceptions, proper names form regular plurals:

Todd, Todds
Harris, Harrises
Knox, Knoxes
Lenz, Lenzes
Mancini, Mancinis
McGuinness, McGuinnesses
Leto, Letos
Moreau, Moreaus
Rose, Roses

Names ending in *-y* add *-s* without any change in spelling:

Germany, Germanys
Gilroy, Gilroys
Kansas City, Kansas Citys

Exceptions:
Allegheny Mountains, Alleghenies
Rocky Mountains, Rockies
Sicily, Sicilies
Ptolemy, Ptolemies
Mercury, Mercuries

When two or more persons share a name and a title, pluralize either the title or the name, but not both: *the Misses Halliday* or *the Miss Hallidays.* When two or more persons share a title but not a name, pluralize the title once or repeat the singular title with each name: *Messrs. Farnham and Scott* or *Mr. Farnham and Mr. Scott.* The plural name with the singular title (*Miss Hallidays*) and the repeated name with the singular title (*Mr. Farnham and Mr. Scott*) are less formal yet may be used appropriately in almost any circumstances. Other plural titles include:

Mmes. (*plural of* Mme. *and* Mrs.)
Mss. *or* Mses. (*plural of* Ms.)
Drs. (*plural of* Dr.)

Irregular and Special Plurals. The following examples include (1) nouns that do not add *-s* or *-es* to form the plural, or, if they do, may also have another plural form with a different meaning or use; (2) nouns whose regular plural form may be seldom used; and (3) nouns with one form only.

Spelling Changes or Irregular Endings. These nouns form the plural with *-en*, sometimes also undergoing a spelling change:

ox, oxen
brother, brethren
child, children

Brother has a regular plural, *brothers.* The form *brethren* is now used chiefly in formal reference to members of the same sect, organization, society, etc., and often conveys a sense of spiritual relationship.

The following nouns undergo an internal spelling change:

foot, feet (*hence* forefoot, forefeet; tenderfoot, tenderfeet *but also* tenderfoots)
goose, geese (*but* mongoose, mongooses)
man, men (*hence* alderman, aldermen, etc.)
mouse, mice (*hence* titmouse, titmice)
woman, women (*hence* chairwoman, chairwomen, etc.; but see CHAIRMAN)

Foreign Words. The following sampling includes words from foreign languages that are assimilated into English and have usually acquired a regular plural while retaining their original plural as well.

(1) *French words.* In French, words ending in *-eu* and *-au* add *-x* to form the plural. Preferred forms are given first.

adieu, adieus *or* adieux
beau, beaux *or* beaus
bureau, bureaus *or* bureaux
chateau, chateaus *or* chateaux
trousseau, trousseaux *or* trousseaus

(2) *Italian words.* In Italian, words ending in *-o* and sometimes *-e* change the vowel to *-i*. Preferred forms are given first.

concerto, concerti *or* concertos
dilettante, dilettantes *or* dilettanti
graffito, graffiti (*no English plural*)
libretto, librettos *or* libretti
palazzo, palazzi *or* palazzos

(3) *Latin words.* These include words whose singular ends in *-a, -um, -us,* or *-x*. Preferences and special uses are indicated; otherwise both forms are equal.

	English plural	**Latin plural**
alga	*none*	algae
antenna	antennas (*usual form used of radio, TV apparatus*)	antennae (*form for sense organs of insects, etc.*)
apparatus	apparatuses	apparatus (*preferred*)
appendix	appendixes (*preferred*)	appendices
*aura	auras (*preferred*)	aurae
bacterium	*none*	bacteria
cactus	cactuses	cacti (*preferred*)
datum	*none*	*data (*sometimes construed as singular*)
formula	formulas (*preferred*)	formulae
fungus	funguses	fungi (*preferred*)
genus	*none*	genera
index	indexes	indices (*preferred for mathematical symbols*)
medium	mediums (*only form for spiritualist*)	*media (*usual form for radio, TV, etc., and laboratory culture*)
opus	opuses	opera (*preferred*)
radius	radiuses	radii (*preferred*)
stadium	stadiums (*sports arenas*)	stadia (*Greek and Latin senses*)
stratum	stratums	strata (*preferred*)
vertebra	vertebras	vertebrae (*preferred*)

*Appears as separate entry

(4) *Greek words.* Many Greek nouns have a singular form ending in *-is* or *-on*. Words with *-is* have only the Greek plural:

analysis, analyses
crisis, crises
ellipsis, ellipses
nemesis, nemeses
oasis, oases
parenthesis, parentheses
synopsis, synopses

Words ending in *-on* have both a Greek and an English plural. The Greek is formed by dropping *-on* and adding *-a*; the English, by adding *-s* to the *-on* ending. The preferred form is given first.

automaton, automatons *or* automata
criterion, criteria *or* criterions
phenomenon, phenomena *or* phenomenons

(5) *Miscellaneous words.* The Hebrew words *seraph* and *cherub* have the Hebrew plurals *seraphim* and *cherubim* and the English plurals *cherubs* and *seraphs; kibbutz* has only Hebrew *kibbutzim.* Arabic *fellah* is *fellahin* in the plural.

Plural Same as Singular. These include (1) animal names; (2) names of nationalities, tribes, and races; (3) singular forms used as plurals; and (4) nouns with one form only.
(1) *Animal names.* Many animal names form regular plurals with *-s* and are always used so. The following are among those that have only one form for the singular and plural; this is called the *zero plural.*

bison	moose
cattle	salmon
deer	sheep
grouse	swine

The following sampling covers names for which the zero plural is preferred, especially by hunters. These names are sometimes used with a regular *-s* or *-es* plural, especially by people who are nonhunters or are opposed to hunting.

antelope	partridge
bear	quail
buffalo	shrimp
caribou	stag
elk	tiger
fish	trout
flounder	tuna

The following quotation demonstrates how variously animal names can be used in the same context:

> [The Yukon Flats land] is also a prime salmon fishing area as well as habitat for 37 mammal species, including 5,000 moose, 140,000 caribou in migration, 900 black bears, 450 grizzly bears, wolves, porcupines, and many muskrat and beaver. —*Audubon*

The word *fish* is used in its (regular) plural form *fishes* when the reference is to different species or classifications: *development of the ganoid fishes.* The names of specific fish are often used this way: *All the mackerels belong to the family Scombridae.*
(2) *Names of nationalities, tribes, and races.* Names ending in *-ese* that are derived from place names stay the same in the plural; for example:

Balinese	Maltese	Senegalese
Japanese	Portuguese	Taiwanese

Names of Indian tribes and other peoples preferably take the zero plural, although the regular plural is also used, often when referring to individuals: *two Apaches; a band of Cherokees.* Typical of these are:

Bantu	Innuit
Chippewa	Navaho
Dakota	Zuñi
Eskimo	

The names *Sioux* and *Norse* have only the zero plural.
(3) *Singular form as plural.* A few words with a regular plural also have a zero plural used equally in all senses or only with a certain sense. Among those used equally are *dozen, pair,* and *youth.*

> How many dozen of the brown eggs were ordered?
> New memberships are coming in by the dozens.
>
> Three pairs of gloves were lying on the counter.
> He owns two pair of silver candlesticks.
>
> Several youths began to scuffle.
> Black youth are looking vainly for work.

The zero plural *head* is customarily used only with unit counts, as of domestic animals: *Disease claimed 500 head of cattle and sheep.*
(4) *Words with one form only.* Although the form may look plural, some words are singular or plural depending on the intended sense, and others are almost always taken in only one way (but occasionally both ways).

The following selection may be singular or plural depending on use:

corps	offspring
congeries	remains
proceeds	scissors

goods	species
means	series

See also UNITED STATES.

Such words as the following are plural in form but are used as a singular:

news	whereabouts
mumps	works

Has the news about the settlement been released?

Mumps is usually accompanied by fever.

His whereabouts was known to a few close friends.

The steelworks is reopening soon.

Words ending in *-ics* vary; for example:

Always or usually singular

Geriatrics includes the study of hygiene and nutrition.

Mathematics was my best subject.

Possible: The mathematics [calculations] in this survey do not prove out.

Singular or plural

Politics was her life.
Office politics are ruining the project.

Gymnastics is the most popular activity in school.
Gymnastics have improved Eddie's physique.

Always plural

Theatrics haven't helped the situation so far.

Compounds. The plural of hyphenated and phrasal compounds (including military terms) is most often formed by pluralizing the key noun.

brothers-in-law	maids of honor
men-at-arms	ladies-in-waiting
major generals	hangers-on
consuls general	goose steps

Note: man-child, men-children; candle-foot, candle-feet

Some hyphenated compounds, especially those without nouns in them, add *-s* to the final element:

shut-ins	forget-me-nots
face-offs	will-o'-the-wisps
step-downs	

Solid compounds, including words ending in *-ful,* add the plural to the end of the word:

journeymen	armfuls	throwbacks
stepchildren	cupfuls	footcloths
icehouses	turncoats	goosefoots

Note: Manservant, womanservant *become* menservants, womenservants.

Foreign phrases follow the rules of the source language:

mot juste, mots justes
beau geste, beaux gestes
ignis fatuus, ignes fatui

Numbers, Letters, Words as Words, Abbreviations, and Symbols. Figures and abbreviations form the plural in two ways. The traditional way is by the addition of *'s;* the current trend is toward the addition of *-s* only:

count by 5's *or* 5s
knew his ABC's *or* ABCs
in the 1960's *or* 1960s
appointed two VP's *or* VPs

When numbers are written out, they form their plurals regularly: *How many sevens did you score?*

The plural of letters, words as words, and symbols is rendered by *'s;* the first two items are also preferably rendered in italics (or underscored) to distinguish their use:

crossing my *t*'s
too many *that*'s in the sentence
carved X's on the stone
a series of #'s

plus has long been used as a preposition (*price plus sales tax*), as an adjective (*This is a plus factor*), and as a noun (*That was a real plus*). These uses are established and standard. *Plus* is now also used, especially in speech and informal writing, as a conjunctive adverb meaning 'and furthermore':

> Any ideas or help of any kind would be greatly appreciated, plus I'd just plain enjoy hearing from you.
> —Ann Lewis, *Countryside*

> They were playing catch-up ball in that respect, which is dangerous. Plus there was a very high turnover in personnel.
> —John McGinnis (quoted), *Forbes*

◇ ***Recommendation.*** The use of *plus* as a conjunctive adverb may one day establish itself, but it is not yet acceptable in standard usage.

poetess. There is now general agreement that a woman who writes poetry should be called a *poet*. There is one traditional exception: Sappho, the Greek lyricist of the 6th century B.C., is often referred to as the Poetess of Lesbos. We recommend *poet* in all cases, including even Sappho. See FEMALE-GENDER WORD FORMS.

poetry. English discourse is broadly divided into prose and poetry. Elsewhere, at EXPOSITION and NARRATION, we have discussed the major subdivisions of prose. Here we shall examine poetry.

It is harder to talk about poetry than about prose. Someone once said that poetry is best appreciated by children, barbarians, and the very old, which is another way of suggesting that its most characteristic elements are either too simple or too complicated to be easily defined. At its best, poetry is the highest, most intense use that we can make of language. Language, the essential human medium of communication, is after all only a set of symbols that we recombine continually in order to tell each other about our experience of reality. How efficiently we use language is directly proportional to how much meaning we can make our symbols carry, how well we can infuse words with a vivid, accurate sense of our perceptions and feelings. The best poetry is an unceasing effort to refine this process. It seeks not only to find ways to say "what oft was thought but ne'er so well express'd," but to break new ground, to communicate what was perhaps never expressed before, possibly not even thought of.

In this sense, writing poetry can be the most daring enterprise of language. Like every other venture into the unknown, it is cursed with a high failure rate. But its intermittent successes advance the sum of human awareness and understanding just as surely as do the breakthroughs of science or the hard-won insights of philosophy.

Here is the great 20th-century Welsh poet Dylan Thomas describing the experimental nature of his art in a letter to an inquiring student:

> To your third question . . . yes. I am a painstaking, conscientious, involved and devious craftsman in words, however unsuccessful the result so often appears. . . . I use everything and anything to make my poems work and move in the direction I want them to: old tricks, new tricks, puns, portmanteau-words, paradox, allusion, paranomasia, paragram, catachresis, slang, assonantal rhymes, vowel rhymes, sprung rhythm. Every device there is in language is there to be used if you will.

Some people say they find poetry uncongenial. One often-heard objection is that it is too abstract and ethereal. This attitude is the result, perhaps, of overexposure in school to certain (mostly 19th-century) poets who mistakenly equated the ethereal with the exalted. Much poetry is—or tries to be—just the opposite, aiming for the most concrete, immediate, powerful, and direct form of communication possible. Ezra Pound's advice to young poets was, "Go in fear of abstractions."

Harder to rebut is the claim that much poetry is too difficult to be read easily or pleasurably. There is some truth in this, but it cuts both ways, as much a reproach to the reader as to the poet. We always have difficulty adjusting to something genuinely new. If a poet has succeeded in finding a new way to say something, or a way to say something new in itself, should he or she be blamed if we turn a deaf ear? We owe it, not to poets, but to ourselves, to cultivate an openness to linguistic innovation. Such receptivity may come naturally to children and barbarians, but unfortunately the rest of us have to make an effort most of the time.

Have we said anything, so far, about poetry that could not be said of prose? No, but what we have said cannot be said equally of prose. Pushing against the frontiers of language is not the business of most prose; it is, however, the main business of most poetry. Yet at its most creative, prose is indistinguishable from poetry. In this sense poetry is not so much a category of writing as an objective, an ideal, of language.

It is, of course, a category as well, informed by many traditions, conventions, and rules, some useful and some not. If, in the following pages, we seem to dwell on the formal aspects of poetry, it is only because it is always easier to talk about attributes than essences. But bear in mind that form is merely accessory to poetry, a matter of convenience (and sometimes inconvenience), not the thing itself. True poetry would as soon make form as obey it.

Classes of Poetry. Being compositions, poems ought to be classifiable, but attempts to classify poetry have never been very satisfactory. Throughout the ages, categories such as epic, heroic, didactic, and satiric have been used. Nowadays, most scholars are content to choose one of three rather elastic general headings when characterizing a given poem: *dramatic*, *narrative*, or *lyric*. These categories are only mildly helpful. The distinction between dramatic and narrative poetry is often fuzzy enough; but according to this system, not only would the overwhelming majority of the world's poetry be classified as lyric, almost *no* poetry could be said to be without strong lyric elements. In fact, what most people mean when they speak of poetry at all is lyric poetry. For these reasons we shall concentrate mainly on lyric poetry.

Originally, in ancient Greek poetics, lyric poetry was poems sung or intoned to the accompaniment of a lyre. This implication of a melodic quality is the chief characteristic of what today we call lyric poetry. Unlike narrative or dramatic poems, which tend to develop in progressive, sequential, or argumentative ways, lyric poems are usually self-enclosed, sometimes even emphasizing repetition and circularity of form. Lyric poetry also favors a unity of mood, often expressed in tones of exclamation, invocation, or meditation (as opposed to argument, storytelling, dialogue, or exposition), and it relies heavily on the use of symbols and metaphors. Above all, it seeks to make use of the inherent musical components of language itself: *rhythm*, *rhyme*, and *refrain*.

Rhythm. All spoken language contains rhythmic qualities based on how we choose to stress or accent syllables; on how long it takes us to articulate syllables; and, more generally, on how fast we speak and how we alter the volume and pitch of our voices. The rhythms of natural speech are so complex, and vary so much with our intentions and meanings, that they virtually defy analysis. One of the objectives of lyric poetry—or perhaps we should say, of the lyric aspect of all poetry—is to shape this complexity into recognizable patterns that share some of the qualities of song.

Historically, this end has been accomplished by poetic *meter*, the arrangement of syllables in certain orderly ways in lines of verse. Every line is broken up into *feet*, that is, sequences of two or three syllables with a characteristic pattern of accents. The commonest foot is the two-syllable *iamb*, consisting of an unstressed syllable followed by a stressed one. A conventional notation for this is ˘ –. The reverse of the iamb is the *trochee*, – ˘. Among other metrical feet are the *anapest*, ˘ ˘ –; the *dactyl*, – ˘ ˘; and the *spondee*, – –.

The foregoing symbols, inherited from the notation of Latin and Greek meters, have also been traditional in the analysis of poetic measures in the modern languages over the past few hundred years. They are best confined to abstract representations of the various measures. In the analysis of an actual English text, it is simpler and more convenient to mark only the stressed syllables with an oblique stroke (´). The analyses that follow will provide a demonstration of how the simplified system works.

The metrical arrangement of a poem is identified by the number and type of feet in a single verse line; for example, the *iambic trimeter* (three sets of iambs) of Greek tragedy, the *iambic pentameter* (five sets of iambs) of most classical English verse, and the *dactylic hexameter* (six sets of dactyls) of Greek and Latin epic poetry. The analysis of the rhythmic pattern of verse is called *scansion;* to analyze a line of verse for its pattern is to *scan* it.

The counting of iambs, dactyls, spondees, and the like is by no means the merely mechanical exercise it might seem to someone unfamiliar with the techniques of poetry. Of the iamb, for example, the poet George Bowering has written: "The iamb is the representation of the human heart beat in poetry. . . . Although the poem might waver all over the page during flights of brainy fancy, when it gets to the pressure of the human heart it will settle into a strong series of iambs." The opening lines of Thomas Carew's "To My Inconstant Mistress" are made up of four iambs each:

When thóu, | poor éx | commú | nicáte
From áll | the jóys | of lóve | shalt sée

The effect is to underlay the words with a sweet, simple, regular pulse. A tetrameter of clattering anapests in Robert Browning's "How They Brought the Good News from Ghent to Aix" is intended to create a headlong rhythm like hoofbeats:

Not a wórd | to each óth | er; we
képt | the great páce |
Neck by néck, | stride by stríde, |
never cháng | ing our páce. |

But not all verse lines are regular. Some of the best rhythmic effects come from making occasional variations on a rhythmic theme. A simple variation on an iambic theme appears in the old ballad that goes:

There líved | a wífe | at Úsh | er's
Wéll |
And a wéalth | y wífe | was shé |

A more complicated variation may be seen in this line by Dylan Thomas:

Dóubled | the glóbe | of déad |
and hálved | a cóuntry |

In addition to the metrical patterns indicated by sequences of feet, verse rhythm makes use of various kinds of pauses—not only at the ends of lines, but sometimes within the lines. In this line from Milton's "Lycidas,"

Blínd móuths! | that scárce | them-
sélves | know hów | to hóld |

the exclamation mark clearly indicates a pause longer than anything suggested by mere division between the feet. In fact, even without punctuation marks, most lines of verse contain a slight pause somewhere. Called a *caesura* /sĭ-zhŏŏr-ə/, this pause is usually marked by double lines in standard poetic notation:

Yet áll | expér | íence || is an árch |
wherethró |

Prosody—the technical name for the art of formal versification—contains many more definitions and precepts relating to the role of meter; but perhaps these few fundamentals are enough to suggest the salient point about meter: that it produces rhythms that are unlikely to occur in ordinary speech. Whenever we read poetry aloud, it is possible—even likely—that we shall speak many verse lines in such a way that their theoretical meter will be altered or suppressed. For example, in *An Approach to Poetry* Wayne Shumaker points out that the famous opening line of Shakespeare's "Sonnet XXX" may be scanned quite differently by different readers. In theory the line consists of five iambs:

When tó | the sés | sions óf | sweet sí |
lent thóught |

But to read it so would produce an artificial singsong. A more natural reading might be:

Whén to | the sés | sions óf | sweet sí |
lent thóught |

Or perhaps some readers might even prefer:

Whén to | the sés | sions of | swéet si |
lent thóught |

The sometimes considerable difference between natural and metrical rhythms has always bothered, as well as attracted, poets. Certainly, there are long passages in the works even of such classical poets as Shakespeare, Milton, and Dryden that seem so lacking in any obvious metrical signature that they could only be described as being of *mixed meter*, a clear attempt to get closer to the rhythms of ordinary speech. Yet the authority of meter was not openly questioned until the 19th century. A preliminary challenge came from the poet Gerard Manley Hopkins, who proposed a system that he called *sprung rhythm*, which projected a heightened reflection of the syncopated ("sprung") rhythms of natural speech. Other poets were quick to carry what Hopkins had started to its logical conclusion and to declare poetry free of all metrical restrictions. Lines could contain any number of feet of any kind in any order. Such liberated poetry was called *free verse* (a term translated directly from the French *vers libre*, which properly refers only to French versification).

Conservatives denounced free verse, saying that it deprived verse of one of its most important constituents, substituting mere chaos for an ideal of order. The Irish poet William Butler Yeats went so far as to declare: "If I wrote of personal love or sorrow in free verse . . . amid all its accidence, I would be full of self-contempt because of my egotism and indiscretion, and foresee the boredom of my reader." Meter, the conservatives argued, was never intended to dominate the reading of poetry. It existed to imply pattern rather than impose it. Like a sometimes inaudible base beat beneath a melody, it was meant to create a counterpoint or tension between natural and artificial rhythms. Its object was not, as the critic I. A. Richards expressed it, to lead us "to our perceiving pattern in something outside us, but to our becoming patterned ourselves."

Free-verse partisans said such arguments were beside the point. Regular meter, some claimed, contributes about as much to poetic rhythm as a metronome does to musical rhythm. Just the way subtle but important musical rhythms arise from balances of whole phrases, so balances of speech phrases, called *cadences*, can constitute the true rhythmic element in poetry. The purpose of free verse, its champions maintained, was not to remove rhythm from poetry but to enhance it by making it more flexible and less mechanical.

The debate continues to this day, though in muted form, since the concept of free verse is now established and accepted. And in any case, the terms of the debate were probably always overstated by both sides. Meter is not lock step, free verse is not license; and the essential nature of poetry inheres in neither. T. S. Eliot put the matter in perspective:

> As for "free verse" . . . no verse is free for the man who wants to do a good job. . . . only a bad poet could welcome free verse as a liberation from form. . . . Forms have to be broken and remade: but I believe that any language, so long as it remains the same language, imposes its laws and restrictions and permits its own license, dictates its own speech rhythms and sound patterns. . . . The [only] liberties that [a poet] may take are for the sake of order.
>
> —lecture (1942)

Rhyme. Next to rhythm, the most obvious musical component of poetry is *rhyme*, the correspondence or repetition of similar sounds in words, usually at the ends of lines. Yet rhyme is not nearly so important a component as many people think. Old English verse was based not on rhyme but on ALLITERATION, or phonic similarities at the beginnings of words. Verse without end rhyme, called *blank verse*, has been a staple of English poetry since the 16th century. Most of Shakespeare's poetry is blank verse; though, to be sure, the term is most closely associated with Milton, who wrote a spirited defense of "English Heroic verse, without Rime" in his preface to *Paradise Lost*. Certainly, the overwhelming majority of 20th-century poetry is unrhymed.

Nevertheless, since end-rhyming schemes define many of the most important categories of classical poetry, they can hardly be ignored. In conventional poetic notation, rhyme schemes are indicated by lower-case letters starting with *a*, each letter representing a specific sound. The simplest rhyme scheme is the *couplet,* a set of two rhymed lines. A scheme of couplets would be rendered *aabbcc.* . . . Here is an example:

True ease in writing comes from art, not chance,
As those move easiest who have learn'd to dance.
'Tis not enough no harshness gives offence,
The sound must seem to echo to the sense. . . .

—Alexander Pope,
An Essay on Criticism

Lines of poetry may be arranged in patterned groups called *stanzas.* Individual couplets may function as two-line stanzas or as parts of larger stanzas.

A *tercet* is a trio of lines all with the same rhyme, and it usually forms a stanza. Thus, a three-stanza poem composed of tercets might be represented by the notation *aaa, bbb, ccc.* More complex is the *quatrain,* a four-line stanza (or poem) that may employ any of a number of rhyme schemes: *aabb; aaba; abcb;* etc. Longer stanza or poem units are ranked numerically: *quintain* (five lines); *sestet* (six lines); *septet* (seven lines); and *octave* (eight lines).

Throughout poetic history certain rhyme schemes have been so much preferred over others that they have become known by special names. For example, a quatrain consisting of alternate four- and three-foot lines and rhymed *abcb* is known as a *ballad* or *hymnal* stanza. Quatrains rhymed *abab* are sometimes called *elegiac* stanzas. A septet composed entirely of lines in iambic pentameter with the rhyme scheme *ababbcc* is known as a *rhyme royal.* An iambic pentameter octave with an *abababcc* rhyme scheme (much favored by Lord Byron) is called an *ottava rima.* A nine-line stanza, eight lines in iambic pentameter and the last in iambic hexameter, rhymed *ababbcbcc,* is called a *Spenserian.* A well-known combination of rhyme scheme and stanza length is the *terza rima,* used by Dante in his *Divine Comedy*—a succession of three-line stanzas that rhyme progressively *aba, bcb, cdc, ded,* and so on. For another type of poetic "architecture" see SONNET.

Rhyming is not quite so simple a matter as it might at first appear. Ordinarily, end rhymes are made from identical stressed final vowel sounds, plus identical following consonant sounds, if any (*cat, hat, rat,* but not *map*). Two words that sound the same but are spelled differently (*sea, see*) make a permissible rhyme that goes by the technical name of *rime riche* or *perfect rhyme.* One-syllable rhymes are called masculine, two-syllable (*breezy, wheezy*) are called feminine; rhymes of three or more syllables are, quite logically, called rhymes of three or more syllables. For some unknown reason the more syllables to a rhyme, the funnier it is likely to sound, a truth not lost on limerick writers:

A tiger, by taste anthropophagous,
Felt a yearning within his esophagus. . .

All sorts of internal end rhymes are also available to poets; for example:

At Flores in the Azores Sir Richard Grenville lay,
And a pinnace, like a fluttered bird, came flying from far away:
"Spanish ships of war at sea! We have sighted fifty-three!"
Then sware Lord Thomas Howard: " 'Fore God I am no coward;
But I cannot meet them here, for my ships are out of gear. . . ."

—Alfred, Lord Tennyson,
The Revenge

Besides such internal "eye" rhymes as "Flores/Azores" (spelled but not pronounced alike), Tennyson's poem also uses patterned internal rhymes that in effect divide some lines into trimetric couplets.

Ever since end rhyme took its place in English poetry, it has had to contend with much the same sorts of objections raised against regular meter—that it is essentially artificial and thus remote from normal speech. No less a poet than Shakespeare's great contemporary Ben Jonson proposed that whoever invented meter and rhyme should be damned:

He that first invented thee,
May his joints tormented be,
Cramp'd forever.

Still may syllables jar with time,
Still may reason war with rime,
Resting never.
—*A Fit of Rhyme Against Rhyme*

But of course Jonson did not mean to be taken altogether seriously. He knew as well as anyone that all poetry—indeed, all literary composition—is based on artifice. Poetry is not like ordinary speech precisely because it tries to do what ordinary speech cannot do. By the same token the convention of end rhyme in poetry cannot be criticized on the ground of its artificiality, but only in terms of its success or failure in producing meaningful effects. Thus, there are good rhymes and bad; but rhyme, as a category, is no more to be condemned than are such categories as television, novels, plots, landscape painting, or poetry itself.

When some of the subtleties of alliteration are applied to end rhyme, the result is called *slant rhyme*. Much favored by modern poets, some slant rhymes are merely orthographic—spelled similarly but pronounced differently—while others are related only in that they end with the same consonants, or with the same vowels (followed by different consonants), or even with different but equally stressed vowels. Such devices, especially when joined to recognizable metrical rhythms, can be remarkably effective in suggesting conventional end rhyme without ever resorting to it.

Refrain. Of all the songlike qualities in poetry, *refrain*—or repetition—is the simplest and most obvious. But it is hardly to be despised on that account. Repeated words, phrases, or lines appear in some of the greatest poems of every age, often enhancing both melody and meaning.

The commonest form of refrain consists of a repeated line, or lines, at the end of each stanza. Here, for example, is the best-known stanza of the six that make up a famous Renaissance poem (for illustrative purposes we have italicized its one-line refrain).

Beauty is but a flower
Which wrinkles will devour;
Brightness falls from the air;
Queens have died young and fair;
Dust hath closed Helen's eye;
I am sick, I must die——
Lord, have mercy on us!
—Thomas Nashe,
In Time of Pestilence

But not all the stanzas in a poem need be regular or end identically in order to set up a refrain. For example, William Butler Yeats's "Easter 1916" is made up of four stanzas, the first and third of 16 lines, the second and fourth of 24. The first, second, and fourth stanzas all end with the line "A terrible beauty is born" (the last word of the preceding line, in every case, being "utterly"); but the end of the third stanza bears no relation at all to this repetitive scheme. The effect is certainly musical, but it is more muted and freer than if each stanza had been of equal length and had ended identically.

In fact, repetitions may occur anywhere in a poem. In some forms of Renaissance verse the rules governing repetition were almost impossibly elaborate. For instance, in the *triolet*, an eight-line poem rhymed *abaa, abab*, the fourth line had to be a repetition of the first, and the seventh and eighth lines a repetition of the first and second. Amid the daily horrors of life in the trenches in World War I, a much-decorated young American Marine tried to hang on to his sanity by composing humorous triolets on scraps of cigarette paper. Here is one of his efforts:

The triolet grows
On a cigarette paper.
Concise, like a rose,
The triolet grows.
While voluminous prose
Is obscure in its vapor,
A triolet grows
On a cigarette paper.
—John Culnan, *Semper Fidelis*

There are, to be sure, some kinds of repetition much subtler than anything discussed so far—repetitions of phrases, words, or sounds at intervals so irregular that it is difficult to define their pattern. Some scholars prefer to call these irregular repetitions *repetends*, rather than refrains, but however they are named, they perform the same musical function as their more regularly patterned cousins. Consider, for example, the various deliberate word and sound repetitions in this translation by the 19th-century poet Dante Gabriel Rossetti of a lyric composed by the 6th-century B.C. poet Sappho:

> Like the sweet apple which reddens upon the topmost bough,
> A-top on the topmost twig,—which the pluckers forgot, somehow,—
> Forgot it not, nay, but got it not, for none could get it till now.
> —*Beauty: A Combination From Sappho*

Never mind how the original may have sounded: Rossetti's version is a tour de force in its own right.

Sound and Sense in Poetry. We have been speaking mostly about the music of poetry, but what about its meaning? As one of our greatest contemporary poets points out, we should be wary of drawing too sharp a distinction between these two qualities.

> But I would remind you, first, that the music of poetry is not something which exists apart from the meaning. Otherwise, we could have poetry of great musical beauty which made no sense, and I have never come across such poetry. . . . If we are moved by a poem, it has meant something, perhaps something important, to us.
> —T. S. Eliot, *The Music of Poetry*

How this interrelationship can work in practice may be seen in a short poem called "Faintheart in a Railway Train":

> At nine in the morning there passed a church
> At ten there passed me by the sea,
> At twelve a town of smoke and smirch,
> At two a forest of oak and birch,
> And then, on a platform, she:
>
> A radiant stranger, who saw not me.
> I said, "Get out to her do I dare?"
> But I kept my seat in my search for a plea,
> And the wheels moved on. O could it but be
> That I had alighted there!
> —Thomas Hardy

In what ways does the music of this poem relate to its sense? Here is one example. As the poet-critic Ambrose Gordon has noted, if the next to the last line is read normally, it consists of an anapest, a spondee, an iamb, and an anapest; whereas the final line, despite its exclamation mark, seems to lapse into a resigned, somehow diminishing, rhythm. Gordon suggests that the anapest-spondee formula of "And the wheels moved on" perfectly represents the inexorable surging turn of the locomotive wheel as the train gathers speed. The period represents a caesura pause, over which we make a slight leap forward in time. The remaining iamb-anapest combination at the end of the line, joined with staccato alliteration ("but be"), suggests both the clicketyclack of the train now beginning to move rapidly over the rails and the tumult in the narrator's mind. But in the last line the train is fairly on its way; the moment has passed; the narrator's emotions have subsided into regret; the trochaic rhythm of the last line now imposes a steady, faintly mocking beat that will carry us even farther away from what might have been.

If the analysis is correct, the music of this poem not only exists for itself but also reflects the physical action described in the poem, the narrator's successive emotions, and finally the poet's ironic conclusion—quite a lot to pack into a couple of lines. In short, the full meaning of the music depends on the presence of other meanings: those supplied by language.

Poetic Language. Musical considerations apart, poetic language differs from ordinary language mainly in vividness and compression. Admittedly, these differences can sometimes raise formidable barriers to understanding; but since no genuine poet ever wants to be misunderstood, we must always assume that any poem intends to convey a set of specific meanings.

At the most elementary level the language of poetry simply consists (as does any other language) in choosing the right words. In poetry "right" very often refers to words that contribute to the construction of an *image,* a term defined by Cleanth Brooks and Robert Penn Warren in their influential book *Un-*

derstanding Poetry (1950) as "the representation in poetry of any sense experience."

Most poets aim to communicate with the greatest possible directness and immediacy; and images, based as they are on the fundamental sensations of touch, taste, smell, sight, and sound, go right for the jugular. They serve what the American poet Wallace Stevens called the "pure" purpose of poetry, to "give a sense of the freshness and vividness of life."

Words relating to sound are much favored by poets, since they draw on both the inherent music of verse and the clicks, buzzes, and squawks of ONOMATOPOEIA. Words evocative of the taste of honey, the feel of velvet, the smell of incense, and the like can be used with equal effect. But most of all the imagery of poetry refers—even when other senses are involved—to the master sense, sight. It is rare to find a poem that is not rich in visual imagery. Illustrations of this truth could fill many volumes; here is just one example, in which a 17th-century poet finds the perfect word to create a striking image:

> Whenas in silks my Julia goes,
> Then, then (methinks) how sweetly flows
> That liquefaction of her clothes.
> —Robert Herrick,
> *Upon Julia's Clothes*

Herrick's "liquefaction," a metaphor, suggests the tremendous importance of figurative language in the creation of poetic imagery. Poetic diction is filled not just with straightforward descriptions, but with metaphors, similes, hyperboles, pathetic fallacies, metonymies, oxymorons, and every other imaginable figure of speech. These verbal figures not only contribute to the conciseness of poetic imagery (and therefore to the intensity of its effect), but they also capture shades of meaning unavailable to ordinary language. Why, for example, does nearly everyone respond to the Homeric epithet "the wine-dark sea"? Sea water and wine have little in common, but such logical objections are futile. In some zone of consciousness beneath (or above) reason we acknowledge the mysterious rightness of the image.

At a level slightly more complex than figurative language is *symbolism,* in which a poetic image, action, or idea is meant to represent both itself and something else. "Three trees on the low sky" may, in a poem by T. S. Eliot, represent the three crosses on Golgotha; a phoenix in a poem by John Donne may stand for the way love renews itself after each consummation; Byzantium, in William Butler Yeats's "Sailing to Byzantium," has little to do with an actual place and much to do with an aesthetic ideal. Sometimes the things represented by a symbol are so complex that they cannot be easily defined. And sometimes they are inherently ambiguous, perhaps as much a mystery to the poet as to the reader. In such cases the symbol may be understood as a kind of groping for meaning, an attempt to find hidden correspondences between something known and something not yet quite grasped.

If poetic metaphors and symbols can sometimes tax a reader's powers of comprehension, so can poetic syntax—and for roughly the same reasons. Poets want to endow their sentences, no less than their words, with strongly communicated meanings; and to this end they tend to condense sentences and to arrange word clusters in unusual ways. Generally, through *ellipsis*—the omission of words or normal punctuation that must be inferred by the reader—they can bring images and ideas closer together, thus enhancing the intensity of their effect. In addition, by playing with the order in which such images and ideas would customarily occur in prose, poets can often find surprising new shades of meaning.

Consider, for example, how hauntingly this short 16th-century poem by an unknown hand seems to draw its meanings from the curious sequence of its expressions and ideas, as though it were saying almost as much in its silences as in its words.

> Western wind, when wilt thou blow,
> [That] The small rain down can rain?
> Christ, if my love were in my arms,
> And I in my bed again!

Poetic Meaning. Throughout this discussion of the attributes of poetry—its music, its images, its figurative language, its dislocated syntax—we have freely spoken of "meaning." Yet how do we define the term? If we cannot even begin to suggest an answer, we shall not be able to respond to the next logical question: "What good is poetry?"

Since the meaning of meaning, like the nature of truth, is a matter that has eluded philosophic definition for centuries, we should avoid approaching this problem on too high a level of abstraction. Instead, perhaps we should do better to concentrate on how poetry relates to the ways in which we habitually think and communicate.

Much 20th-century poetic theory has concentrated on the importance of the image, since thinking in images represents a more primitive and basic form of mental activity than does conceptualizing or verbalizing. To the extent that words can be used to create images, poets have argued that verbal communication, especially on the level of feeling, is most immediate. Yeats made one of the earliest formulations of this thesis:

> All sounds, all colours, all forms, either because of their preordained energies or because of long association, evoke indefinable and yet precise emotions, or, as I prefer to think, call down among us certain disembodied powers, whose footsteps over our hearts we call emotions. —*Ideas of Good and Evil*

In a less mystical vein, T. S. Eliot named these emotional triggers "objective correlatives," by which he meant "a set of objects, a situation, a chain of events which shall be the formula [for evoking a] *particular* emotion." One of the objectives of poetry, then, is to determine which images provoke which emotions.

Yet purity of communication on the emotional plane, while doubtless one measure of meaning, is hardly the only one. Ideally, images and their associated emotions ought not to exist solely for themselves, but should be capable of giving us significant new perceptions of reality.

Even though poetry is an art of words, it aspires to transcend the conventional limits of words.

> There is a poetic language in which words are no longer the words of free practical usage. They are no longer held together by the same attractions; they are charged with . . . different values operating simultaneously and of equivalent importance.
> —Paul Valéry, *A Course on Poetics*

Although some readers might feel that such statements smack too much of mysticism and illogic, contemporary research into the functioning of the human brain lends powerful support to the notion that not only creative thinking, but indeed most thinking, is not formally logical.

> Cognitive scientists have . . . cogent reasons for thinking that logic is not the normal mode of human thought. . . . Most of our plausible reasoning relies on the intuitive recognition of similarities or analogies between two things.
> —Morton Hunt, *New York Times*

Many poets nowadays would not find such conclusions especially surprising. Years ago Wallace Stevens wrote, "We never arrive intellectually; but emotionally we arrive constantly." Although most contemporary poets reject the notion that poems should be flat-footedly preachy, few would agree with Archibald MacLeish's oversimplification, "A poem should not mean/But be" ("Ars Poetica"). Of course, poems should have meaning, but of a special kind. They should, in Robert Frost's words, begin in delight and end in wisdom.

pogrom /pō-grŏm, pə-, pō-grəm/ = 'a massacre of Jews in czarist Russia, carried out by the people of a community, often with the approval or connivance of the government.' The Russian word *pogrom* literally means 'devastation as if by a thunderbolt,' from *po-* = 'like' + *grom* = 'thunder.' The word has also been applied to comparable acts of mass murder of ethnic minorities elsewhere, such as the massacres of Armenians by the Turks.

The word is sometimes used with loose exaggeration by political writers referring to general racial oppression or mere backlash:

> Every reassurance that comes from the camp of the president-elect seems only to be taken as confirmation that a pogrom is about to be visited upon Black America.
>
> —Patrick Buchanan, *Savannah Morning News*

◇ ***Recommendation.*** Anyone who is aware of its historical background should use the word *pogrom* carefully.

poisoning the well. See FALLACY.

political terms. Like poets, politicians have coined some of our most colorful and descriptive word usages. The irreverence and colloquial nature of political vocabulary may have much to do with its wide appeal. *O.K.*, which had its roots in American politics, is known in virtually every part of the world (see O.K., OK, OKAY). *Bunk* is another term with wide currency. Americans have also coined unique senses of borrowed terms. The British LOBBY has acquired special usage on these shores, and CONSENSUS has American overtones that are almost technical.

The listing that follows includes lesser-known items, together with notes on some of the origins and historical backgrounds.

advice and consent = 'U.S. Senate's role in reviewing appointments of the President, as outlined in the Constitution'; more often employed as a verb phrase: *advise and consent* (originally British, in use for more than 1,200 years)

backlash = 'adverse reaction or resistance to something that has advanced the status of a certain group'; used widely in the 1964 presidential campaign as the supposed reaction of white voters antagonistic to social gains by blacks

balanced ticket = 'political slate that includes nominees with appeal to a wide number of ethnic or religious groups and regions'; a practice now less common than in the past

bandwagon = 'effect created by a party or cause that appears to be on the ascent and is thus desirable to join or support' (very likely from circus usage, when a parade wagon carried musicians through the streets to attract audiences and children were encouraged to jump on for the ride)

barnstorming = 'making appearances in rural areas in behalf of one's candidacy or that of a fellow party member'

bipartisan = 'supported by two parties'; applied especially to foreign policy

bleeding heart (derisive) = 'one who is excessively sympathetic toward a supposedly oppressed person or group'

bloody shirt = 'symbol of reproach flaunted at an opponent, especially in the role of warmonger'; found at least as far back as the writings of Philip Sidney, and popularized in post–Civil War America in reference to the Republican party's record of saving the Union as contrasted with the Democratic party's initial lack of enthusiasm for the war

* **boondoggle** = 'wasteful or useless scheme or project'

boss = 'leader of a political machine, usually viewed as corrupt and manipulative'

brain trust = 'intellectuals and political theorists in the early years of Franklin D. Roosevelt's administration' (originally *brains trust,* credited to James M. Kieran of the *New York Times*)

brinkmanship = 'willingness to go to the brink of war if necessary, as a means of attaining an end in foreign policy' (coined by critics of Secretary of State John Foster Dulles in the 1950s) See GAMESMANSHIP.

buck stops here, the = 'ultimate duty or accountability' (adage often miscredited to Harry S Truman, who had the motto mounted on his desk as a reminder of presidential responsibility)

bunk = 'empty talk, something said for the benefit of one's constituents' (originally *buncombe,* later *bunkum;* inspired by a speech "for Buncombe" delivered in the Capitol in 1820 by Rep. Felix Walker, whose district included *Buncombe* County, North Carolina)

Camelot = 'imaginative name for President John F. Kennedy's administration' (from the legendary locale of King Arthur's court)

carpetbagger = originally 'self-seeking Northerner who went to the South during Reconstruction,' now 'any nonresident opportunist who hopes to profit at a locality's expense and then move on' (from *carpetbag*, type of luggage once carried by such persons)

caucus = 'convocation of party leaders or members to deal with policy, choose a candidate, etc.' (probably from an Algonquian word for 'counselor')

change horses in midstream = 'to withdraw support from an incumbent or administration during a critical period'

chicken in every pot = 'a state of prosperity and security' (from a campaign slogan of the Republican party in 1928)

Christmas tree (bill) = 'proposed legislation with riders favoring special interests not related to the subject of the bill'

cloture /klō-chər/, closure = 'the termination of debate by a call for an immediate vote on the matter under discussion' (from French *clôture* = 'closure of debate')

clout = 'power or influence' (perhaps from other senses of the term: 'powerful blow' and 'long hit in baseball')

coattails, ride someone's = 'to be elected to office on the strength of the candidate who leads the political slate' (probably from Victorian romping games, in which a man played the horse and a child held on to or rode on his *coattails*)

cold war = 'a state of hostility without open warfare, especially the tension between the Soviet bloc and the Western powers after World War II' (coined by the American editor Herbert Bayard Swope in 1945 and used shortly thereafter by Bernard M. Baruch)

* **consensus** = 'agreement of the majority'

Copperhead = 'Northerner sympathetic to the South during the Civil War' (first political use said to have been in the *Cincinnati Gazette*, July 30, 1862)

credibility gap = 'the difference between what a public official says and what is widely believed' (coined during the mid-1960s)

creeping socialism = 'policies of the Franklin D. Roosevelt years viewed by some as encroaching on free enterprise'

cronyism = 'the practice of appointing persons to governmental positions on the basis of friendship rather than ability'

cross of gold = 'gold viewed as an arbitrary monetary standard' (from the conclusion of a speech delivered by William Jennings Bryan at the Democratic National Convention of 1896: "You shall not crucify mankind upon a cross of gold")

dark horse = 'seemingly unpromising candidate who wins nomination, sometimes as a compromise'

* **détente** = 'the relaxation of hostile relations'

Dixiecrat = 'member of the States Rights party, Southerners who bolted the Democratic party in 1948 as a protest against President Truman's civil rights policy'

dollar diplomacy = 'policy of furthering U.S. business and political interests in foreign countries through economic aid'

do-nothing Congress = 'the Republican-dominated 80th Congress' (so identified by President Truman during his 1948 whistle-stop campaign)

dove = 'one who advocates nonmilitant solutions'

egghead = 'someone thought to be highly intelligent and learned, an intellectual, especially one who is self-satisfied and patronizing'; used of Adlai E. Stevenson in the 1952 presidential campaign

Fair Deal = 'policy of Harry S Truman's administration regarding the government's responsibility to citizens'

fat cat = 'generous contributor to a political party, wealthy patron'

favorite son = 'candidate who has local

* Appears as separate entry

support but usually does not expect or intend to be nominated for a higher office'

filibuster = (1) (verb) 'to speak at great length in order to delay or block the passage of legislation' (2) (noun) 'the obstruction of legislation by long speeches, digressions, etc., or one who does this' See SPANISH WORDS.

Foggy Bottom = 'Department of State' (from the name of part of the District of Columbia along the Potomac where department headquarters are located)

front-porch campaign = 'political campaign in which a candidate stays close to home instead of traveling widely'

-gate = 'suffix associated with scandal or questionable conduct' (from *Watergate*, apartment complex in Washington, D.C., where the first events of the Nixon administration scandal took place)

gerrymander = 'to divide a political unit into districts whose voting pattern will favor one party over another' (coined in 1811 by the editor Benjamin Russell, as a fanciful combination of *salamander* and the name of the governor of Massachusetts, Elbridge *Gerry*)

gobbledygook = 'pompous bureaucratic jargon' (coined by Rep. Maury Maverick in the early 1940s, possibly referring to the sound made by a turkey)

GOP = 'the Republican party' (standing for Grand Old Party)

grass roots = (1) 'the local level of political organization' (2) 'the common people, especially those outside urban and industrial areas'

hat in the ring, throw one's = 'to announce one's candidacy for political office'; especially associated with Theodore Roosevelt (originally the convention by which an amateur made his challenge in a prizefight)

hawk = 'one who advocates militant solutions'

high muckamuck = 'someone of great importance or authority, especially one who is self-satisfied or pompous' (from CHINOOK JARGON)

Hill, the = literally 'Capitol Hill in Washington, D.C., the site of the Capitol,' figuratively 'Congress'

horse trading = 'political bargaining in which the stakes are openly acknowledged and the dealing is firm and unsparing'

hundred days = 'figurative period of time in which a new administration implements its programs' (in America, from the *100 days* in 1933 in which the 73rd Congress enacted President Roosevelt's programs)

hustings = (1) 'the platform or scene of a campaign speech' (2) 'the act of campaigning' See NORSE WORDS.

iron curtain = 'figurative partition separating the Soviet bloc countries from the West' (coined in that sense by Winston Churchill and used in an address in Fulton, Missouri, in 1946)

kingmaker = 'someone who successfully guides another into office or some other powerful position'

kiss of death = 'endorsement for a candidate that is viewed as ruinous'

kitchen cabinet = 'unofficial presidential advisers, thought to be more influential than regular cabinet members'; first used of Andrew Jackson's administration

knee-jerk = 'responding automatically and predictably, without thought or discrimination': *knee-jerk liberals*

know-nothing = 'an anti-intellectual, or someone highly intolerant of minorities, foreigners, etc.' (from *Know-Nothings*, collective name for members of various mid-19th-century parties promoting so-called native-born-American interests)

lame duck = 'incumbent officeholder in the interval between an election that produces a successor and the end of the incumbent's term, or officeholder nearing the end of a nonrenewable term'

***lobby** = 'to try to influence (legislators) or promote one's interests by such influence'

logrolling = 'the trading of favors by politi-

*Appears as separate entry

cians, especially of votes by legislators in order to ensure passage of bills, etc.'

low profile = 'deliberate inconspicuousness, behavior intended to avoid attention'

machine = 'the well-developed, highly disciplined, often very powerful organization of a political party, frequently seen as detrimental to the common welfare'

Manifest Destiny = '19th-century doctrine asserting the right, and duty, of the United States to expand throughout North America and even beyond'

maverick = 'one who is independent and often disregards party affiliations' (from the sense 'unbranded, usually stray range animal,' from Samuel *Maverick,* 19th-century Texas rancher who would not brand his cattle)

McCarthyism = 'the practice of making reckless charges of disloyalty, of browbeating the targets of investigations, and of generally creating a climate of fear' (probably coined by the political cartoonist Herblock in 1950, referring to tactics of Sen. Joseph *McCarthy* in pursuing alleged Communists in government)

middle of the road = 'moderate course'; often identified with Dwight D. Eisenhower's administration

muckraker = 'reformer who exposes corruption, usually a journalist who makes accusations in print'; popularized by Theodore Roosevelt (from an allusion to a character in Bunyan's *Pilgrim's Progress*)

mugwump = originally 'Republican who rejected James G. Blaine as the party's presidential candidate in 1884,' later 'one who is politically independent' (from an Algonquian word for 'chief')

New Deal = 'policies and programs of Franklin D. Roosevelt's administration, especially early ones dealing with economic recovery'; used by Roosevelt in accepting nomination in 1932

New Federalism = 'system that recognizes the sovereignty of a central authority while broadening the responsibility and options of state and municipal governments in carrying out national policies'

New Frontier = 'the policies and goals of John F. Kennedy's administration'

Oval Office = literally 'the White House office occupied by the President,' figuratively 'presidential authority and power'

palace guard = 'those with ready access to a President of the United States, usually viewed as having influence'

plank = 'one of the issues or articles that make up a party's platform'

platform = 'the statement of principles, issues, and goals to which a party and its candidates are committed'

pork barrel = 'project or scheme funded by the government and serving chiefly as a source of patronage'

sachem = originally 'a leader of Tammany Hall,' later 'a party leader' (from a Narragansett word meaning 'chief')

scalawag = originally 'white Republican resident of the South during Reconstruction,' later 'devious, rascally person'

silent majority = 'rank-and-file citizens regarded as silent supporters of a leader'; used by Richard Nixon in 1969, referring to his Vietnam War policies

smoke-filled room = 'now mostly figurative place where political deals are made' (supposedly coined by Harry M. Daugherty, campaign manager for Warren G. Harding in 1920)

spoiler = 'candidate who is unlikely to win but who draws enough support to ruin an opponent's victory'

spoils system = 'the practice of distributing the patronage benefits of an election to the party faithful' (from the expression *to the victor belong the spoils,* used in a speech by William L. Marcy in 1832)

steamroller = 'high-pressure political methods for defeating the opposition, gaining control of a convention, etc.'

stump = 'to travel throughout (an area) for the purpose of making political speeches' (from the early days of American politics, when tree stumps in frontier settlements served as platforms for speakers)

Tammany, Tammany Hall *or* **Society** =

'once-powerful New York City Democratic organization, dating from 1789' (from *Tamanend,* name of a Delaware Indian chief)

ticket = 'list, or slate, of party candidates in an election'

tinhorn politician = 'politician who is showy and boastful but has no influence and little ability' (coined by William Allen White in 1901, possibly suggested by the earlier *tin horn gambler*)

Uncle Sam = 'cartoon figure representing the United States or its government, a tall, thin, goateed man in a high hat and a suit with the motif of the American flag' (from the abbreviation *U.S.*, possibly also from the nickname of Samuel Wilson, a government inspector during the War of 1812; first appeared in 1813)

wheelhorse (sometimes disparaging) = 'party loyalist, one who has worked long and dependably'

whistle stop = 'brief appearance by a political candidate at a town on the campaign trail, especially in the days of railroading'

pontiff. Perhaps the only occurrence of this word in everyday life is when a newspaper uses it as a cliché synonym for *pope.* In such a context the first mention uses *pope*; the next reference appears as *pontiff,* more often than not with age specified, as in the following example (in which, strictly speaking, the word *pontiff* is misused):

> . . . the first visit to the North American continent of a reigning Coptic Pope, His Holiness Pope Shenouda III. The 53-year-old pontiff, spiritual leader of more than 22 million Coptic Christians . . .
>
> —*New York Times*

The Roman Catholic pope alone inherits the title *pontifex maximus* = 'supreme pontiff,' from the high priest of pre-Christian Rome. (*Pontifex* means 'bridge-builder' in Latin, but the word is really an Etruscan word probably meaning simply 'priest.') Several Eastern churches have popes of various rank, but none of them is a pontiff.

poorly. The adverb meaning 'in a poor manner' is standard: *I thought the band played poorly.* The adjective *poorly,* meaning 'being in poor health, rather sick,' is considered informal or nonstandard by some: *He's still feeling poorly. He's poorly again today.*

◇ ***Recommendation.*** This adjectival use is not very formal but perfectly standard.

porch. *Porch* (from Latin *porticus, porta* = 'gate') in England is primarily an architectural term for a covered entranceway to a building, especially a church or large house. In Scotland and northern England it refers to a side chapel or transept. As an open portico or veranda attached to the exterior of a house, and usually roofed and sometimes partly enclosed or screened, *porch* is an American English term. In America one of the amenities of homeownership is sitting on the porch and enjoying the evening air. For as Donald G. Mitchell put it in *Rural Studies* (1867): "A country house without a porch is like a man without an eyebrow."

Veranda or *verandah* (from Hindi *varaṇḍā* and Portuguese *varanda* = 'railing, porch, balcony') has become slightly old-fashioned in America and is used much less often today than *porch.*

There are numerous dialect synonyms for *porch.* In the Hudson Valley and Inland Northern dialects the early Dutch settlers left the term *stoep,* which was a porch with seats or benches; in English this became *stoop.* Today, the stoop has shrunk considerably and is any entrance stairway or platform to a house, such as the typical front stairway to a New York City brownstone. In the Chicago area this is known as the *landing.*

Most other dialect synonyms refer to a more spacious structure or area where one can barbecue steaks, lie in the sun, or sit sipping a mint julep. In the Gulf Southern dialect a veranda or porch is often called a *gallery* or *galerie.*

> The dwelling House is to be 36 feet by 24, with a gallery of 7 feet on each side of the house.
>
> —George Washington, *Diaries* (1784)

He had been cultivating it for forty-five years . . . (or maybe not even doing that, maybe sitting through a whole morning on his front gallery).
—William Faulkner, *Go Down, Moses*

In the New England and Coastal Southern dialects *piazza* has currency, though the original Italian meaning of 'town square or open market square' has been changed.

[It was] one of those spacious farmhouses . . . the low projecting eaves forming a piazza along the front, capable of being closed up in bad weather.
—Washington Irving, *The Legend of Sleepy Hollow*

What gives Charleston its peculiar character, however, is the verandah, or piazza, which embraces most of the houses on their southern side.
—Basil Hall, *Travels in North America* (1829)

The piazza politician, sipping his toddy, spreading his legs, and discussing constitutional questions on the spacious verandahs of open-air Virginia.
—J. A. Harrison, *George Washington* (1906)

In the Southwest there are *patios* instead of galleries and piazzas. In its purest Spanish form the patio is an inner walled garden and courtyard open to the sky.

The houses present to the street a blank wall of stone without windows, and one large portal, which leads to the patio . . . around which are the rooms.
—George Ruxton, *Adventures in Mexico and the Rocky Mountains* (1847)

Today, especially in the West, a patio is also a paved open area adjoining a house where families can play and dine out-of-doors.

Another, more exclusively Southwestern dialect term is *ramada*, which is an arbor or arborlike structure. This is also a Spanish word that referred to an improvised shelter made of tree branches with the leaves left on (*rama* = 'branch, limb').

I paid them a dollar for my bath, at the rustic bathing establishment they have constructed, consisting of two goods' boxes sunk in the ground, sheltered by a *ramada.*
—Benjamin Hayes, *Pioneer Notes* (1869)

The family was already breakfasting . . . under the ramada, or brush-roofed shed, which is the general living-room during the hot months.
—J. Smeaton Chase, *California Desert Trails* (1919)

More recently, *ramada* is used to refer to any kind of open porch.

In Hawaiian English the Hawaiian word *lanai* is often used to refer to an open veranda. Originally, it was a living room that opened to the outdoors or an outdoor terrace used as a living room.

pore. As a verb, *pore* means 'to read intently and exhaustively.' It is occasionally confused with *pour;* in fact, *pore* is probably related to the verb *peer. Pore* is now usually used with *over* or *through: poring over the account books; pored through the immigration records.*

porpoise. See DOLPHIN, PORPOISE, DORADO.

portend, portent, portentous. The Latin verb *portendere* was a technical term in magical divination, meaning 'to be a sign of a future event, presage.' In English *portend* may have this superstitious sense, but more often it refers to logical assessment or projection of the future.

He considered that the folly of his German nephew portended war, and that the weakness of his Russian nephew portended revolution.
—Philip Magnus, *Edward VII*

The so-called leading economic indicators, which seek to portend future business trends . . . —*Time*

The derivative Latin noun *portentum* meant 'natural or supernatural event or thing, considered to indicate a future event.' English *portent* may also have this meaning or may additionally mean 'sign symbolically foreshadowing the future' or simply 'any indication of future events.' The kind of future indicated by a portent is nearly always dire or at least worrisome.

> The V sign is the symbol of the unconquerable will of the occupied territories, and a portent of the fate awaiting the Nazi tyranny.
> —Winston Churchill, speech (1941)

> The younger man, the heavyweight champion of the world, fixed his opponent with eyes so baleful they seemed to carry portents of pain and death.
> —Robert Lipsyte, *Reader's Digest*

The adjective *portentous* basically means 'indicative of a worrisome future, ominous':

> I was thirty. Before me stretched the portentous, menacing road of a new decade.
> —F. Scott Fitzgerald, *The Great Gatsby*

Portentous may also mean 'stupendous, prodigious, awesome':

> "Portentous and mysterious" was how Herman Melville described the great whales, and so they remain today for most people.
> —James C. Simmons, *Reader's Digest*

More often, *portentous* means 'self-important, pompous':

> A remote, portentous figure who entered and left his office by a private door, he was rarely seen except by other senior partners.
> —Eric Ambler, *The Schirmer Inheritance*

> He takes ragtime seriously without becoming solemn and portentous. . . .
> —Rudi Blesh, *Scott Joplin*

Portuguese words. Portuguese is the language of Brazil, Portugal, and the remnants of Portugal's far-flung empire in Africa and Asia. After opening the trade routes to the Far East around the Cape of Good Hope, the Portuguese became the chief participants in the slave trade between Africa and the Americas. Their language consequently served as the vehicle for the penetration of certain exotic Asian and African words into English and was the source for a number of terms associated with slave culture (see also PIDGIN AND CREOLE LANGUAGES). More recent loanwords have been related to food and culture, coming from both the motherland and her former African colonies. During the 20th century large immigrant groups, mainly from the Azores, have established themselves in New England and California, but their presence has had only local linguistic effects.

The following terms have entered English from Portuguese:

albatross = 'large web-footed ocean bird with very large wingspread, native to the South Seas': from Portuguese *alcatraz* = 'pelican,' perhaps blended with *albo* = 'white'

albino = 'animal or plant lacking normal pigmentation': Portuguese *albino*, originally applied to white Negroes in West Africa

auto-da-fé /ô-tō-də-fā/ = 'ceremonious punishment of heretics by the Inquisition': Portuguese *auto-da-fé*, literally 'act of faith'

caste = 'hereditary social class in India': Portuguese (*raça*) *casta* = 'pure (race)'

cobra = 'venomous snake able to form a flattened hood with the skin of its neck': Portuguese *cobra* (*de capelo*) = '(hooded) snake'

creole = 'person of European descent born in the Americas'; used especially of the French of Louisiana: the ultimate source is Portuguese *crioulo* = 'Negro born in Brazil,' transmitted via Spanish (*criollo*) and French (*créole*)

dodo = 'large flightless bird of the island of Mauritius, now extinct': Portuguese *doudo*, variant of *doido* = 'simpleton, fool'

jaguar = 'large spotted cat of tropical America' See SOUTH AMERICAN WORDS.

madeira /mə-dîr-ə/ = 'dessert wine produced on the island of Madeira'

***mandarin** = 'high public official in imperial China'

molasses = 'thick syrup produced in refining sugar': Portuguese *melaço*

pagoda = 'Oriental temple': Portuguese *pagode*, of Dravidian origin

palaver /pə-lăv-ər/ = 'idle talk,' earlier 'conference, parley': Portuguese *palavra* = 'word, discourse'

pickaninny (derogatory) = 'black child': from Portuguese *pequenino* = 'wee one,' diminutive of *pequeno* = 'little'

port = 'sweet wine of Portugal': originally *port wine*, from the Portuguese place name *Oporto*, literally 'the port'

samba = 'lively Brazilian dance' See AFRICAN WORDS.

veranda = 'long covered *porch' See *veranda* at INDIAN WORDS (INDIA).

yam = 'sweet potato': Portuguese *inhame*, of undetermined West African origin

zebra = 'striped African animal related to the horse': Portuguese *zêbra*

*Appears as separate entry

possessives. ***Formation.*** In English the possessive case of nouns is shown by an apostrophe, often followed by *-s* but sometimes not. The possessive case of the personal and relative pronouns involves a change in form that sometimes includes the letter *s* but without the apostrophe. The following guidelines consider these issues.

Nouns. (1) *Common nouns.* The possessive of singular nouns that do not end in *-s* is easy to form; just add *'s* to the word: *My sister's apartment has two fireplaces. Did you bring the baby's toys? Solemnly he shook the woman's hand.* Singular nouns ending in *-ss* may also form the possessive with *'s: my boss's attitude; the seamstress's thimble; an actress's photograph.* This spelling reflects the pronunciation of the form itself. Some writers prefer to use only the apostrophe following *-ss: the witness' statement; the duchess' jewels.* This is still an acceptable form.

By convention, words that end in *-s* or the sound of *-s*, when followed by the word *sake* form the possessive by adding only the apostrophe: *for goodness' sake; for appearance' sake; for convenience' sake;* etc.

Forming the possessive of a plural noun sometimes gives trouble. The simplest approach is first to determine what the plural of the word is and then to add the sign of the possessive to it. To form the possessive of a noun with a *regular plural* (ending in *-s* or *-es*), add only an apostrophe after the *-s*. In the following list the last three examples show words that undergo a spelling change when forming the plural. But as long as the plural ends in *-s*, the rule applies.

Singular	Plural
my uncle's birthday	my uncles' advice
a waitress's voice	the waitresses' tips
the fox's ears	the foxes' barking
the lady's concern	the ladies' gowns
the secretary's book	the secretaries' pens
his wife's joy	the wives' response

To form the possessive of a noun with an *irregular plural* (one not ending in *-s*), add *'s* to the plural.

Singular	Plural
the man's role	the men's competition
a child's kiss	the children's library

(2) *Proper nouns.* Names that do not end in *-s* form possessives in the ordinary way, by adding *'s* to the singular and just the apostrophe to the plural: *Bob's music group; Nancy's opinion; the Bradburys' garage; the Ferraras' party.*

Names that end in *-s* or *-ss* form the singular possessive like common nouns ending in *-ss*, with either *'s* or just the apostrophe: *Moss's, Moss'; Davis's, Davis'.* The spelling with *'s* represents the way most of us would tend to pronounce the form.

Names ending in *-s* or *-ss* form their plural regularly, by adding *-es;* thus, they form the plural possessive regularly, with the apostrophe after the final letter: *Walter found Mr. Gross's briefcase* (singular). *The Grosses' dog chases cars* (plural).

By convention, certain names take only the apostrophe in the possessive case. In this category are *Jesus, Moses,* and classical and mythological names ending in *-s* or *-es: Jesus' disciples; Moses' brother; Eos' torch; Praxiteles' sculpture.*

Names ending in an *-x* or *-z* that is pronounced form regular possessives, both singular and plural: *Jim Fixx's running book, the Fixxes' schedule; Mrs. Ramirez's profile, the Ramirezes' income.* The same is true of names with final *-s, -x,* or *-z* that is not pronounced: *Malraux's novels; Buloz's review.*

A proper name retains the singular possessive form when used with *Mr. and Mrs.,* etc.: *I bought Mr. and Mrs. Cass's tickets.* Without the title the plural form is required: *The Casses' tickets have been paid for.*

(3) *Compounds.* The singular possessive of compound words is formed in the regular way, by adding *'s* to the end of the word: *secretary-general's announcement; father-in-law's office; attorney general's report.* If a compound forms its plural by adding *-s* to the last word, the possessive is regular, adding only the apostrophe after the *-s: the major generals' quarters; the mother superiors' conference.* If a compound does not form its plural by adding *-s* to the final word, the possessive is formed by adding *'s* to the last word: *the mothers-in-law's complaints; the chiefs of staff's verdict.* (Note: Such possessive forms are cumbersome. It is better to rewrite so that the possessive is indicated by a prepositional phrase: *complaints of the mothers-in-law; verdict of the chiefs of staff.*)

Some compounds have possessives already in them, and these forms are singular: *debtor's prison; widow's walk; adder's-tongue; fool's paradise; baker's dozen.* When a logical plural can be found for such compounds, the possessive term does not have to be changed: *debtor's prisons; widow's walks; adder's-tongues.*

Pronouns. (1) *Personal and relative pronouns.* In the sentence *I told Jim to write to me at my new address,* there are three personal pronouns: *I,* subjective (or nominative) case; *me,* objective case; and *my,* possessive case (*the new address belonging to me*). The personal pronouns besides *my* that indicate possession are *mine, your, yours, his, her, hers, its, our, ours, their,* and *theirs.* The possessive form of the relative pronoun *who* is *whose: Whose scarf is this?* Not one of the preceding forms has an apostrophe in it, and that is the simple rule to follow when forming the possessive of personal and relative pronouns: Never use an apostrophe.

A number of common contractions sound like possessive pronoun forms: *it's* (= 'it is, it has'); *who's* (= 'who is, who has'); *there's* (= 'there is'); *you're* (= 'you are'); *they're* (= 'they are'). Interchanging the possessive form and the sound-alike contraction is without doubt one of the commonest mistakes in our written language:

> Packed in it's own juice. No sugar added. —label, canned fruit

It's is always a contraction; substituting *it is* or *it has* in the example given above makes the statement unintelligible. The word needed, of course, is *its* ("Packed in its own juice"—that is, in juice natural to it). See also ITS, IT'S.

In a certain sense this type of mistake is a logical error, because the apostrophe followed by *-s* is the expected sign of the possessive. The idea that a possessive form must have *'s* is undoubtedly what leads some writers into the misspellings *her's, their's, your's,* and *our's.* These forms are wrong. The possessive form of the personal and relative pronouns never takes an apostrophe.

> . . . I happened to be wearing orchids. And so Lila said oh, weren't they lovely and all, and who sent them to me. . . . So I thought, well, it will just do you good, and I told her Cousin Larry did. I told her it was a sort of a little anniversary of ours. . . .
> —Dorothy Parker, *Cousin Larry*

(2) *Indefinite pronouns.* Indefinite pronouns—*one, anyone, anybody, everyone, everybody, no one, someone, another, other, either, neither*—form the possessive the regular way, with *'s: one's reputation; everyone's idea; no one's sympathy; one another's eyes.* Of these, only *other* has a possessive plural: *the other's motives* (singular); *the others' motives* (plural). *Each* is not rendered in the possessive: *the treasures of each,* not *each's treasures.*

When the indefinite pronoun is used with *else,* the sign of the possessive goes with *else: someone else's turn; no one else's approval.*

The form *oneself* is now preferred over *one's self.*

Usage. (1) *Animate versus inanimate nouns.* The possessive case is used of both animate and inanimate nouns: *our landlord's property; the sailors' duties; haven't seen him in a dog's age; got her heart's desire; the razor's edge; the ocean's roar; state's evidence; New Year's Day.* Frequently, however, the possessive construction with an inanimate noun is awkward and should be avoided: *a clock's hands; the ladder's rung.* These sound better as *the hands of a clock* and *the rung of the ladder.* (By the same token, turning the possessive of an animate noun into an *of* phrase produces a similar awkwardness: *the boots of your son* for *your son's boots.*)

In some well-established expressions with an inanimate possessive, the possessive is singular or plural as necessary: *a month's vacation, two months' vacation; a dollar's worth, five dollars' worth; an hour's delay, four hours' delay.* (Alternatively, in some of these expressions a compound modifier may be substituted for the possessive construction: *a one-hour delay, a four-hour delay.* Using both the possessive and the hyphen is unacceptable: *a four-hours' delay.*)

(2) *Possession by more than one.* When the thing possessed belongs jointly to two or more individuals, the sign of the possessive goes with the last word only: *Mary, Peggy, and Kit's project; the joggers and bikers' route.* When the thing possessed belongs separately to two or more persons, the sign of the possessive goes with each owner: *Roger's and David's experiments; the dancers' and the singers' costumes.* (Note that the plural form of the noun being possessed also establishes separate ownership, as does repeating *the,* although it is not necessary to do so.)

(3) *Prepositional phrases.* As noted above, the prepositional phrase with *of* is useful for eliminating clumsy possessives with inanimate nouns: *the back of the chair,* not *the chair's back.* The *of* construction also avoids the double possessive and long possessive phrases before a noun: *the rent board's secretary's report; the manufacturer of the electronic components' instructions.* These are better as *the report of the rent board's secretary* (or *the rent-board secretary* or *the secretary of the rent board*) and *the instructions of the manufacturer of the electronic components.* However, brief phrasal titles are customarily used with the possessive: *the queen of England's visit.*

A noun or pronoun in an *of* construction may express the possessive when the thing possessed is taken to be only one among others: *a classmate of Jennifer's; a friend of the Williamses'.*

> . . . Jefferson not only had an opinion on everything but was driven to express it. Indiscreet letters of his will one day delight and trouble unborn historians.
>
> —Gore Vidal, *Burr*

A common error with this construction, probably heard in everyday speech more than seen in writing, is the redundant *I have a friend of mine who. . . .* Since the verb *have* already indicates possession, there is no need to use the *of* phrase too. Say either *I have a friend* or *A friend of mine.*

(4) *Gerunds.* A long-standing rule in English is that a gerund—a verbal noun ending in *-ing*—must be modified by the possessive case: *Do you recall his promising to return?* The gerund *promising* is the direct object of the verb *do recall,* and *his* modifies it. But this can be a hard rule to follow, especially in spoken English. And it is certainly violated often in print:

> Home fires and burn injuries are often the result of children playing with matches and careless handling of matches by adults.
>
> —American Red Cross,
> *Standard First Aid*
> *and Personal Safety*

Strictly, in the above example "children" should be "children's," since it modifies "playing," one of the two gerunds that are the direct objects of the preposition *of* (the other is "handling"). This combination of a gerund with a noun or pronoun not in the possessive case has been called by usage experts the *fused participle.*

However, the presence of an *-ing* form in a text does not automatically demand the possessive modifier. For example, in the sentence *She fears anyone's asking her a question,* the fear is of *asking* (that is, she fears being asked a question). If the wording were *She fears anyone asking her a question,* the fear would be of *anyone* (that is, she would fear anyone who asked her a question). Thus, depending on the intended meaning, the possessive may or may not be suitable. If the *-ing* form is the logical subject of the verb or the intended object of the verb or a preposition, then the noun or pronoun that precedes it takes the possessive form. If the *-ing* form and the words that follow it can be turned into a dependent clause (as could be done with the second example above, *She fears anyone who asks her a question*), then the possessive is not needed. See also VERBAL NOUNS IN -ING.

◇ *Recommendation.* In formal writing it is still best to try to apply the rule about using the possessive with the gerund. If the construction sounds ponderous with or without the possessive, rewrite the offending text. Such a sentence as *Mrs. Fanning thinks that the members of the welcoming committee('s) not mingling properly made the party break up early* can be improved thus: *Mrs. Fanning thinks the party broke up early because the members of the welcoming committee didn't mingle properly.*

(5) *Appositives.* Constructions that combine an appositive with a possessive are treated in two ways. If the appositive itself falls last in the sentence (or independent clause), the sign of the possessive is added to the noun to which the appositive refers and not to the appositive: *Of all the illustrations I've seen, I still prefer Tenniel's, the original illustrator.* If the appositive falls anywhere else, then it gets the possessive sign: *Will we meet with the manager, Mr. Landau's representative before dinner?* The second comma normally used with an appositive is omitted here. A construction such as the preceding example is at best an ambiguous one and can usually be rewritten for greater clarity: *Will we meet with the representative of the manager, Mr. Landau, before dinner?*

post hoc. *Post hoc,* short for the Latin phrase *post hoc, ergo propter hoc* (= 'after this, therefore because of this'), refers to a common logical fallacy in which event B is claimed to be the result of event A simply because event A came first. For example, it might be argued that diesel-engine buses should be banned from the streets because no sooner had they been introduced into the local transit system than the number of respiratory complaints began to rise. There could well be a connection between the two events, but until cause and effect have been established, the argument is merely a post hoc conclusion. See also FALLACY.

practicable, practical. These two adjectives are partly synonymous. *Practicable* chiefly means 'able to be put into practice': *a practicable solution.* It can also mean 'able and suitable to be used, usable': *a practicable implement for the purpose. Practical* can be used in either of these senses, but it also has a much wider spread of meanings, including 'relating to practice or action in general': *practical experience;* 'applied to useful (as opposed to theoretical) purposes': *practical mathematics;* and '(of persons) able and inclined to act effectively and sensibly': *She was certainly more practical than he was.*

precipitate, precipitation. The basic meaning of the verb *precipitate* /prĭ-sĭp-ə-tāt/ is 'to hurl down from a height' or 'to launch or propel violently':

> The river . . . does not merely *fall;* it is precipitated downwards.
> —Peter Forbath, *The River Congo*

> . . . he paused suddenly and precipitated himself across the room.
> —Thomas Wolfe, *Look Homeward, Angel*

The secondary meaning is 'to cause (something) to happen suddenly, bring on':

Russian bad faith and aggression had precipitated an outbreak of war between the Russian and Japanese empires in February 1904. . . .
—Philip Magnus, *Edward VII*

Far from mollifying the press, the statement precipitated a hail of questions.
—John Barron, *Reader's Digest*

Early chemists, impressed by the suddenness of certain reactions that cause a solid to be separated out of a solution, used the word *precipitate* to describe this process:

. . . we can say that light can cause a colorless solution of a certain type to precipitate tiny black granules.
—Isaac Asimov, *Science Past—Science Future*

Later, the term was taken over into meteorology and used of the action of cold in causing water to be condensed out of vapor in the air and thus to fall as rain or snow. This is the origin of the irritating expression used by some weather forecasters, "Precipitation probability X percent." When they're talking to the public, it would be nice if they'd use plain language.

precipitate, precipitous. These two adjectives have sometimes been used interchangeably, but they are clearly distinct in good current usage. Their origin is Latin *precipit-*, literally meaning 'headfirst' (from *pre* = 'before' + *caput* = 'head'), hence meaning 'plunging down headfirst' or 'rushing violently along' and '(of terrain) extremely steep and dangerous.'

(1) *Precipitate* /prĭ-**sĭp**-ə-tāt, -tĭt/ primarily means 'rushing at violent or reckless speed, going pell-mell':

With professional interest we examined the armored vehicles and guns the enemy had abandoned in his precipitate retreat.
—Farley Mowat, *And No Birds Sang*

Secondly, it means 'sudden, abrupt':

The pain was minimal, the ordeal so quickly over it might hardly have been; in spite of the stitches she had to have because his entry into the world had been so precipitate, Maggie felt wonderful.
—Colleen McCullough, *The Thorn Birds*

Thirdly, *precipitate* means 'too hasty, without due consideration, rash':

It is impossible to estimate how much revenue the Getty interests lost because of my precipitate decision.
—J. Paul Getty, *As I See It*

(2) *Precipitous* primarily refers to terrain, meaning 'extremely steep and dangerous':

For the next two years he would be campaigning in rough country, against tribesmen familiar with it, and often established in precipitous strongholds.
—Mary Renault, *The Nature of Alexander*

It may also refer to physically falling or plunging down a steep place:

. . . the plunge [of the river] would occur in a single, albeit dreadfully precipitous fall. . . .
—Peter Forbath, *The River Congo*

Figuratively, *precipitous* is used of dramatic, often disastrous declines or plunges; the adverb, *precipitously*, is most likely to occur in this sense:

. . . the network's profits have dropped precipitously during the last three years, from $122 million in 1978 to an estimated $70 million for 1980.
—Tony Schwartz, *New York Times*

◇ ***Recommendation.*** A historical argument can be made that the two words have been interchangeable; and each is still sometimes used in some of the other's senses. But the strong tendency of the best modern usage is to keep them distinct. We advise using them exactly as shown above.

prefer. When *prefer* is used to make an explicit comparison between two things, the best linking conjunction is *to*. It may sometimes seem reasonable to use *than*, which is the conjunction used in most comparisons;

but this is a matter of idiom or convention, not logic.

> Stolen art is sometimes used to extort money from insurance companies, which may prefer paying for recovery of a work than meeting the full insured cost.
> —Nathan M. Adams, *Reader's Digest*

Here there are two simple alternatives: "may prefer paying . . . to meeting" or "may prefer paying . . . rather than meeting." It is also possible to use *instead of* or *over* in place of *rather than.* But if infinitives were used instead of *-ing* forms, only *rather than* would be possible: "may prefer to pay . . . rather than to meet."

When the adjective *preferable* is used in straightforward comparisons, the same applies: "may find paying . . . preferable to meeting" or "may find it preferable to pay . . . rather than to meet."

There is also a tendency to use *more* with *preferable.*

> Perhaps violent sports were necessary and more preferable than the other things human beings could do to each other.
> —Shirley MacLaine, *Don't Fall Off the Mountain*

This is considered redundant, since *preferable* is already a kind of comparative. This passage should be: "Perhaps violent sports were necessary and preferable to the other things. . . ."

◇ ***Recommendation.*** Comparisons with *prefer* and its derivatives should not be made with plain *than.* The best construction is with *to;* when this is not possible, *rather than* is usually the alternative.

prefixes. See AFFIXES.

pretty. The adverb *pretty* = 'rather, somewhat, quite' is fully standard and appropriate to formal usage.

> It is pretty difficult to imagine a single person having, simultaneously, the characteristics of the serpent and the dove, but this is what Jesus expects.
> —Martin Luther King, Jr., *Strength to Love*

principal, principle. The traditional confusion between these two still sometimes occurs in print, doubtless as a mere lapse rather than a serious misunderstanding.

> Skeffington was the principle subject of discussion.
> —Edwin O'Connor, *The Last Hurrah*

(1) *Principal* is first an adjective meaning 'ranking first in importance, chief': *His principal supporter was Governor Brown. The principal export is coffee.* Second, *principal* is a noun with several meanings, including 'person of chief or leading rank': *The heads of some schools are called principals;* 'person of primary responsibility in legal matters'; and 'basic capital part of a payment such as a debt.'

(2) *Principle* is exclusively a noun meaning either 'fundamental truth': *the principles of mathematics;* or 'standard or rule of moral conduct or justice': *She was willing to fight for a principle.*

Principled is an adjective meaning 'based on or guided by principle': *Disregarding the publicity, he took a principled stand.*

prior to. This is a legal phrase that provides a fancy Latinate synonym for the plain English word *before.* It has long since entered the mainstream of general written usage:

> Prior to leaving for the Coast, Chris promised to write or call every few weeks.
> —Charles H. Edwards, *Reader's Digest*

The author quoted above was writing in an everyday context and had no special need for an elevated style. Nonetheless, he used *prior to* instead of *before,* and the editors did not presume to correct him—a sign that the phrase *prior to* is now acceptable at all levels of usage. For a similar case, compare IN EXCESS OF.

program. The inflected forms of the verb may be spelled *programmed, programming* or *programed, programing;* the former is preferable. The British spelling of *program* is *programme.* The pronunciation /**prō**-grăm/ prevails, but /**prō**-grəm/ is also used.

propositio. Old term for the *proposition,* or statement of the main topic, in a piece of expository writing. See EXPOSITION.

prostate, prostrate. The word *prostate* is often confused with *prostrate* in speech, and sometimes even in writing and print. They are completely unrelated. *Prostrate* means 'lying face downward on the ground,' and hence also 'exhausted.' It is from Latin *prōstrātus* = 'thrown forward, thrown down, lying down.' The *prostate* is a gland in male mammals that secretes the seminal fluid; it is situated in front of the bladder and surrounds the urethra. It was given its name by the ancient Greek anatomists; for its etymology, see GREEK WORDS.

protagonist. In a Greek tragedy there is theoretically always one leading character on whom the whole play centers, called the *prōtagonistēs,* literally 'first actor' (from *prōtos* = 'first' + *agonistēs* = 'actor'). This is still the proper meaning of the word *protagonist,* whether referring to Greek or other drama, or to real people:

> I brought it on myself like the tragic protagonist of a Greek play.
> —Woody Allen, *Side Effects*

> *Little Orphan Annie* was the only subteenage protagonist ever to be successful as an adventure character on radio.
> —Jim Harmon, *The Great Radio Heroes*

The word is also more loosely used to mean 'one of two opposed leading characters or rivals' or 'one of several principal characters,' either in drama or in dramatic scenes in life:

> Philip was caught on the wrong foot while fuddled with wine; Alexander acted like Alexander; it was one of those situations where hidden fires, which the protagonists have been containing, are released by shock.
> —Mary Renault, *The Nature of Alexander*

In yet looser usage, *protagonist* is often qualified by *chief, main, principal,* etc.:

> . . . he had resolved to take the chief protagonists across the sea towards the West at the end of the book. . . .
> —Humphrey Carpenter, *Tolkien*

> [This story] is based on information from sources close to the principal protagonists in Washington, Panama, Miami and other cities.
> —Tad Szulc, *Florida Times-Union*

Some critics insist that the classical usage is the only correct one; that there can be only one protagonist in any one drama or situation; and that to qualify the word with *chief, main, principal,* etc., is redundant and therefore an error.

Protagonist is further often used to mean 'supporter or champion.' This use probably arose because the word seems to contain the prefix *pro-* = 'for, in behalf of' (although, as indicated above, etymologically it doesn't); also because *protagonist* seems to be the opposite of ANTAGONIST (but actually the two are not a matching pair). This use too is condemned as an error by purists. But it has been occurring for a long time and is now in wide use by respectable writers:

> The birthplace of these ideas was nineteenth-century England, and their principal source and protagonist was Herbert Spencer.
> —John Kenneth Galbraith, *The Affluent Society*

> For a time I was canvassed to be the first Secretary-General at the United Nations. . . . Mr. Trygve Lie was an enthusiastic protagonist on my behalf.
> —Anthony Eden, *The Reckoning*

> What the protagonists of tradition forget is that the 1662 Prayer Book was the third Prayer Book in English.
> —Arthur Thompson, *Winnipeg Free Press*

◇ *Recommendation.* To those who have read Greek plays or studied the history of drama, the meaning of *protagonist* is classical and fixed; it means solely the single leading character, typically a tragic hero struggling against his destiny. But the classicists don't have exclusive rights over the word. Those who take little interest in Greek drama are entitled to use the word in its other established meanings, 'any of several leading characters' and 'champion or supporter'—but they should be aware that some purists will wince and groan to hear them do so.

protean /prō-tē-ən/. In Greek myth Proteus was a sea god, associated with Egypt. He was the herdsman of sea creatures and could change his own shape at will. Hence, *protean* (sometimes capital *P*) means 'able to change, able to assume different roles':

> . . . the Protean figure of the confidence trickster, ever ready to change his personality and his part to suit the present situation. . . .
> —Gamini Salgado, *Coney-Catchers and Bawdy Baskets*

> Lover, killer, funnyman, slob—this protean perfectionist with a thousand faces [Walter Matthau] can play them all.
> —Maurice Zolotow, *Reader's Digest*

proverb. The terms *proverb* and *adage* are synonyms for a particular class of aphorisms. Like aphorisms in general, they are short, succinct statements expressing general truths, but they are distinctive in both their antiquity and their commonality. The special province of the proverb is everyday experience and observation, and its favored (although by no means exclusive) form is the metaphor. Thus, stitches in time save nine; rolling stones fail to gather moss; and so on. The typical proverb seems to have been around forever and to be known by everyone. A wit may coin an aphorism, but only his descendants will know if he coined a proverb. See APHORISM; APOTHEGM; MAXIM.

provided, providing. As conjunctions meaning 'on condition (that),' both *provided* and *providing* are correct and standard. *Provided* is the commoner, especially in American usage.

> . . . his host promised to send a couple of bottles around to the manse provided the reverend gentleman acknowledge the gift in the parish newsletter.
> —Sylvia L. Boehm, *Reader's Digest*

> Her own authorization to lend money extended to a million dollars in any one instance, providing two other officers in the branch concurred.
> —Arthur Hailey, *The Moneychangers*

◇ *Recommendation.* If you are in doubt, use *provided.*

publishing terms. The publishing world has long been viewed by the general public as one inhabited by gentle, professorial types—an ivory tower. It is perhaps in reaction to this oversimplified conception that people in publishing have, over the years, developed a professional jargon of a peculiarly violent cast.

One begins with relatively harmless maritime images—of galleys and mastheads, of rivers and casting off—but before long one encounters broadsides, sinkage, and widows.

Back on shore there are dummies and nuts running around, armed with bullets and slugs, and other inferior characters (some with bastard titles) on the skids and running ragged in gutters. There are linecuts and bleeds, cropping and blind stamping. Operative terms in this world include *kill, delete,* and *blow up.* Chase leads to crash and lockup, and then inexorably to hanging heads and dead matter. For the doubtful, there is foul proof. But for the truly fortunate, there is perfect binding.

The following list will give you a quick overview of this language of violence. Once you have probed the real significance of this terminology, you may return (in circular fashion) to the conviction that the publishing world is, indeed, chiefly populated by quiet, bookish, emotionally serene individuals.

AA's = 'author's alterations, made after the manuscript has been set and sometimes charged against royalties'

back matter = 'material, such as the index, glossary, and bibliography, that follows the last chapter of the text'

bastard title = 'the half title when it precedes the title page'

battered type = 'type damaged so as to produce an imperfect impression'

binding = (1) technically 'the gathering together and fastening of the pages of a book, traditionally in sewn signatures' (2) in general nontechnical use 'the material in which a bound book is encased, typically either of cardboard covered with cloth or leather, or of coated paper'; in the book trade called *case* or *cover*

bleed = 'an area of plate or print that extends to one or more of the outside edges of a page after trimming'; such an area is said to *bleed off*

blind folio = 'page number not printed on the page but counted in the numbering sequence'

blind-stamp = 'to imprint a design on a cover or some other surface without using ink or foil'

blow up = 'to enlarge photographically'

blurb = 'promotional copy on a jacket'

boldface (type) = 'type that prints darker than the normal text face'; for example, the entry words on this vocabulary list

broadside = 'a large sheet, folded for mailing'

bullet = 'a centered dot (•) used as an ornament, to introduce items in a list, etc.'

caps, all caps = 'capital letters'

caps and small caps (abbreviated *c&sc*) = 'typographical instruction to set copy in small capital letters with full initial capitals'; for example, SUCCESS WITH WORDS

caption = 'descriptive material that typically appears above a table, illustration, etc.'; often used interchangeably with *legend* (see below)

caret = 'the symbol (∧) used to indicate the point where copy or other matter is to be inserted'

case = 'binding'

cast off = 'to estimate from manuscript or galley proof the number of printed pages the material will occupy'

chase = 'the frame in which letterpress type is positioned firmly, or locked up, prior to printing'

composition = 'the process of setting a manuscript into type' See *compositor; printer*, below.

compositor = 'the person or establishment that sets type'

cover = 'binding'

crash = 'strip of cloth pasted around the spine of a book to strengthen the binding'

crop = 'to trim one or more sides of an illustration before it is reproduced to improve its composition or eliminate details'

cut = literally 'engraving or etching of an illustration,' now 'any printed illustration, even one photographically reproduced from a drawing or photograph'

dead matter = 'proofs returned by the printer after a book is printed'

delete = 'to take out, remove'

drop folio = 'page number positioned at the foot of the page'

dummy = (1) 'galley proofs and other materials pasted down to show how final pages will look' (2) 'blank pages bound to suggest the size of the finished product'

EA's = 'editor's alterations, made after the manuscript has been set'

edition = 'all copies of a book prepared from the same plates or the same typeset material'; additional printings with minor corrections are still considered part of the same edition, but when a book is substantially revised before a new printing, it is said to go into a new edition

em = 'unit of measurement relative to the type size being used'; for example, in 10-point type an em measures 10 points

en = 'unit of measurement one-half the width of an em'

endpaper = 'folded sheet of paper at the front and back of a book that attaches the book to its covers'

extract = 'quotation, example, etc., usually set in smaller type and often on a narrower measure than the regular text'

flush = 'without indention'; copy set *flush left* aligns at the left margin, *flush right* at the right margin

flyleaf = 'blank page or sheet at the front or back of a book'; not to be confused with *endpaper* (see above)

folio = 'page number'

foreword = 'introduction to a book, often written by someone other than the author and considered part of the front matter'

foul proof = 'proofs containing corrections that have already been incorporated in a new set of proofs'

front matter = 'material, such as the title page, table of contents, and preface, that precedes the text and carries its own sequence of numbers (usually lower-case Roman numerals)'

galley = (1) 'long narrow tray that holds lines of hand- or machine-set type when first set' (2) 'galley proof' (see below)

galley proof = (1) 'a copy or impression of the material contained in a galley' (2) 'any proof of typeset material, usually before it has been sectioned into pages'

gutter = 'the white space formed by the inside margins of facing pages'

half title = 'page containing only the title of the book, included in the page numbering when it precedes the first page of the text' (see *bastard title*, above)

halftone = (1) 'photograph or similar illustration that for printing purposes has been converted into a set of dots that can produce tonal gradations found in the original' (compare *linecut*, below) (2) 'process by which such a photoengraving is made'

hanging head = 'heading that extends beyond the left or right margin of the text material to which it relates'; for example, the title of this entry, *publishing terms*, is a hanging head

hanging indention = 'an arrangement in which the first line of a paragraph or other text begins flush left and runs the full width of the measure and all successive lines are indented'; for example, the entries on this list

head, heading = 'phrase or other text that serves as a title or description of the material it introduces'; a head may be *free-standing* (set on a line by itself) or *run-in* (starting on the first line of a paragraph)

inferior characters = 'subscripts'

italic type, italics = 'a slanting type style used for emphasis and differentiation from regular text'; in this book, non-English words are in italics, as are words such as *italics* when referred to as words

jacket = 'the paper cover wrapped around a hard-bound book'

justify = 'to set type so that all full lines end evenly at the right margin'

kill = 'to delete material, remove standing type or stored text'

leaders = 'a sequence of dots used in tables, programs, etc., to direct the reader's eye across the same row'

leading /lĕd-ĭng/ = 'extra space (measured in points) between lines of type'

leaf = 'one sheet of paper in a publication, consisting of two sides (pages)'

legend = 'descriptive material that typically appears below a table, chart, or illustration'; often used interchangeably with *caption* (see above)

letterpress = 'method of printing in which metal type is inked and comes in direct contact with paper'

linecut = originally 'engraving consisting entirely of black and white areas, without any gradation in tone,' now 'any illustration with only black and white areas'

lock up = 'to secure lines of type firmly in a chase before printing'

lower-case = 'designating uncapitalized letters' (from the arrangement of old-style type cases, in which the uncapitalized letters were kept in the lower sections of the case) See *upper-case*, below.

makeup = 'the positioning of all the elements (text, illustrations, folios, etc.) that belong on each page'

margins = 'the white space that frames the typeset material'; referred to individually as the *top* or *head margin*, the *bottom* or *foot margin*, the *outside margin*, and the *inside* or *back margin*

masthead = 'the listing in a newspaper, magazine, or other publication of key editorial and administrative personnel'

measure = 'the width established for a full line of type on a page or in a column'; usually expressed in picas

mechanicals = 'the final set of proofs with all elements typically in place, pasted up on forms by hand and ready to serve as camera copy'

nut = 'an en'

offset = 'method of printing in which the inked plate does not come in direct contact with the paper, the image being transferred to a rubber blanket that in turn transfers the image onto paper'

OP = 'out of print, no longer available'

OP/OS = 'permanently out of print after the current inventory is exhausted'

OS = 'out of stock, temporarily unavailable'

page = 'one side of each sheet or leaf within a book'

perfect binding = 'binding process in which the backs of signatures are trimmed and held together by adhesive'

PE's = 'printer's (that is, compositor's) errors, corrected at no charge to the publisher or author'

photocomposition, phototypesetting = 'any of a number of processes in which manuscript is set by projecting characters photographically, without casting metal'

pica = 'unit of measurement containing 12 points and equivalent to about 1/6 inch'

point = 'unit of measurement equivalent to about 1/72 inch and used to identify type sizes'; for example, this book is set in 10-point Caledonia typeface

printer = 'the person or establishment that does the printing of text and other matter, and usually the binding'

proof = 'a copy of typeset material, illustrations, etc., presented before manufacture so that errors can be corrected by editors'

recto = 'a right-hand page, whose folios are odd numbers'

river = 'irregular stream of white space that appears to flow down between the words on consecutive lines'

roman type = 'the straight-up-and-down style of type normally used for text matter'; for example, the words of this definition are in roman type

rule = 'any printed line, straight or ornamental, of varying thickness and design'

running head *or* **foot** = 'descriptive line that appears at the top or bottom of most pages and carries the folio, chapter title, pronunciation guide, or other information'

run ragged, rag right = 'to typeset material without justifying each line'

sheet = 'leaf'

signature = 'printed sheet folded one or more times so that when trimmed at the top, outside, and bottom it will resemble a small unbound pamphlet, with a specific number of pages'; for example, a single fold will produce a signature of 4 pages, four folds will produce 32 pages (standard signature for most books)

sinkage = 'the insertion of extra space between the normal top margin of a page and the first line of type'

skids = 'pallets on which printed sheets, bound books, and the like are stacked'

slug = (1) 'a piece of metal used as spacing material between lines of type' (2) 'a line of type cast in metal on a Linotype or similar machine'

spread = 'facing pages viewed as a whole'

stet = 'standard instruction signifying that a change previously indicated should not be made and that the original or an earlier version should remain as it was' (Latin, 'let it stand')

stripping = '(in photocomposition) the process of assembling elements of film to make up pages'

subhead = 'any head within a chapter or a particular span of text that is preceded or embraced by a more inclusive head'

subscripts = 'letters or figures that hang below the normal base of a line of type'; for example, in the formula $C_{12}H_{22}O_{11}$ (sucrose), the figures 12, 22, and 11 are subscripts

superscripts = 'letters or figures that rise above the normal base of a line of type'; for example, in the equation $4^2 = 16$, the figure 2 is a superscript

trim size = 'the final dimensions of a page after the edges have been trimmed'

type page = 'the area framed by the four margins of a page, within which all text and usually the illustrations are expected to fall'

typo = 'typographical error'

upper-case = 'designating capitalized letters' (from the arrangement of old-style type cases, in which the capitalized letters were kept in the upper sections of the case) See *lower-case*, above.

verso = 'a left-hand page, whose folios are even numbers'

widow = 'line of type much shorter than the full width of the type page'; considered poor page makeup when it appears as the first line at the top of a page

Puerto Rican speech. Puerto Ricans live in two worlds. One is the world of Spanish colonial tradition that most Puerto Ricans proudly want to preserve. The other is the modern American industrial world whose politics and economy dominate the island of Puerto Rico. Its languages reflect this complex mixture of the traditional and modern. Both Spanish and English are official languages. English is a required subject from the first grade through college. But since 1950 Spanish has been the medium of instruction in all public and many private schools. Puerto Rico's desire to preserve its Hispanic cultural heritage has made language, especially in the schools, a controversial issue. Numerous officials, educators, and professionals insist on keeping the Spanish language pure and free of all English influence. But in reality this has not happened. The close contact between Puerto Rican Spanish and American English since the turn of the century has created two new and independent varieties of speech known as *Spanglish* and *Englañol.* The term *Spanglish* has achieved widespread currency within the Puerto Rican community and is commonly pronounced /spän-gwĭsh/.

Spanglish. This is a hybrid language spoken primarily in the metropolitan areas that has relatively low prestige. It is the result of several social and economic factors, the most important being (1) the reimmigration of "Newyorricans" (New York Puerto Ricans) to the island to live; (2) the large English-speaking population such as military personnel, non–Puerto Rican residents, and tourists; (3) the English names of the all-pervasive American-made products; and (4) the geographical isolation of Puerto Rico from other Spanish-speaking areas.

As a result of the intense contact between the two languages, Puerto Rican Spanish (which is itself a unique variety of Spanish) has absorbed many American English words. The English loanwords are fully adopted but are modified by Spanish pronunciation and are used only in Spanish contexts. This situation is very similar to that in England during the Middle Ages, when thousands of French words became a naturalized and enriching part of the English language.

In some cases English words are substituted for Spanish equivalents. For example:

Hágalo anyway = 'Do it anyway [*de todas maneras*].'

La gente de mi building vive del welfare = 'The people living in my building [*edificio*] are on welfare [*bienestar público*].'

El boss dijo que había que trabajar overtime este weekend = 'The boss [*jefe*] said that we had to work overtime [*extra*] this weekend [*fin de semana*].'

In many other cases the English borrowings have no Spanish equivalents. For example:

El beisbol es mi hobby favorito = 'Baseball is my favorite hobby.'
Amplio parking gratis = 'plenty of free parking'

The vocabulary of American merchandising with its varied messages and snappy slogans is a common sight in Spanglish advertisements. For example:

Sears de Puerto Rico: Use nuestro plan de compra Lay-Away.
Use el plan Easy Payment de Sears.
Use el plan Revolving Charge de Sears.
—signs in a Sears, Roebuck department store

Marco Discount House: Cabecera con frame, 2 mesas de noche, 1 triple dresser con 2 espejos. Fibra lavable, 2 corner bed y ottomon en azul. Elegante sofa-cama.
—newspaper advertisement

In Spanglish speech the English loanwords are usually altered to conform to Spanish pronunciation and spelling. Nouns are given articles that agree in gender and number: *el rufo* (= 'the roof'); *la bosa* (= 'female boss'); *el bos* (= 'male boss'). Following the pattern of Spanish words, often a final vowel is added to an English loanword. In multisyllable words the stress is also shifted to the next-to-last syllable. For example:

carpeta /käl-**pā**-tä/ = 'carpet'
caucho = 'couch'
factoría /fäk-tō-**rē**-ä/ = 'factory'
furnitura /fo͞ol-nē-**to͞o**-rä/ = 'furniture'
ganga = 'gang'
grocería /grō-sĕ-**rē**-ä/ = 'grocery'
marqueta /mäl-**kā**-tä/ = 'market'
norsa = 'nurse'

Initial /s/ followed by a consonant is often changed to /äh/; note that the letter *h* is aspirated, as in the English word *hat*. For example, *street, switch, slip* become /äh-**trē**/, /äh-**wēch**/, /äh-**lēp**/.

When /r/ occurs after a vowel in an English borrowing, it is changed to /l/, as in *army* /**äl**-mē/, *freezer* /**frē**-sĕl/, *foreman* /**fōl**-män/, and *mister* /**mēh**-tĕl/.

Final /m/ is usually changed to /ng/, as in /ro͞ong/ for *room* and /ō-bĕl-tīng/ for *overtime.*

English verbs adopted by Spanglish are conjugated according to the regular Spanish pattern. Some typical Hispanicized English verbs are:

bakear = 'to bake'
batear = 'to bat in baseball'
bowlear = 'to bowl'
catchear = 'to catch'
chequear = 'to check'
clipear = 'to clip'
flipear = 'to flip'
flirtear = 'to flirt'
foolear = 'to fool'
freezear = 'to freeze'
hitear = 'to hit'
mopear = 'to mop'
parquear = 'to park'
taipear = 'to type'
vacuunear = 'to vacuum'

There are many others, and new ones are being created all the time.

Englañol. Unlike Spanglish, Englañol has prestige. Englañol is a hybrid variety of English spoken by educated bilingual adults whose first language is Spanish. Unlike Spanglish, versions of which are spoken in the American Southwest and in Florida, Englañol is limited to Puerto Rico. Where Spanglish is Spanish modified primarily by English loanwords, Englañol is English modified by the structure of Spanish. The Spanish patterns of pronunciation, inflection, and word order are carried over into English. This is a process of analogy. The logic of the argument goes something like this: "Since Spanish says it this way, then English must also say it this way."

Englañol may be spoken with little or no Spanish accent. Even so, Spanish influences the pronunciation of cognates (English words that come from the same source as the Spanish words). Spanish vowels, for example, are often carried over into English, as in *culture* /**ko͞ol**-cho͞or/; *color* /**kō**-lōr/; *famous* /**fā**-mōs/; *typical* /**tē**-pē-kəl/.

Consonants in the middle of words are often dropped, changed, or added: *demon-*

stration /dě-mō-**strā**-shən/; *interrupted* /ĭn-tĭ-**rŭm**-təd/; *cemetery* /**sĕ**-mĕn-tĕr-ē/; etc.

Spanish /y/ replaces English /j/, as in *project* /**prŏ**-yĕkt/ and *major* /**mā**-yōr/.

And final /m/ is pronounced /n/, as in *minimum* /**mĭn**-ə-mən/; *maximum* /**măk**-sə-mən/; and *aluminum* /ə-**lōō**-mə-nən/.

The inflections of Spanish are also carried over into English. This is especially noticeable with the formation of plural compound nouns: *salads dressing* (*salsa para ensaladas* = 'sauce for salads'); *children discipline* (*disciplina de los niños* = 'discipline of children'); and so on.

The idiomatic singular or plural of certain Spanish nouns is usually retained for the corresponding English word(s). For example:

at your *services* [*a sus órdenes*]
I am taking my *vacations* [*vacaciones*] next week.
I will give you *a good advice* [*un consejo*].
This is *a nonsense* [*una tontería*].

As in Spanish, the definite article *the* is used in Englañol much more often than it is in Standard English. For example:

The French [*el francés*] is a melodious language.
Is money really so important in *the life* [*la vida*]?

Spanish word order plays a major role in Englañol. This is especially apparent in the placement of adverbs. For example:

Buy *today* your luxurious apartment.
You can have *there* a wonderful time.
This affects *directly* my work.

Finally, the Englañol speaker frequently uses Spanish-English cognates that have different meanings in the two languages. This can create some startling sentences. Here are some commonly used deceptive cognates:

She was *molested* [*molesta* = 'annoyed'].
We should *pretend* [*pretender* = 'to try'] to work carefully.
My skin is very *sensible* [*sensible* = 'sensitive'].
He *compromised* [*hacer compromiso* = 'to promise'] me.
There are many *marginal* [*marginal* = 'fringe'] benefits.
The government has helped other *entities* [*entidad* = 'organization'].
The *New York Times* is *finished* [*finito* = 'sold out'].
There is too much *competence* [*competencia* = 'competition'] between nations.
There are serious *lagoons* [*laguna* = 'gaps'] in our education.
It's a *disgrace* [*disgracia* = 'pity'] you lost the address.

pun. "A play on words, similar in sound but different in meaning." That is how the writer who described himself only as B. E. Gent. (meaning 'B. E., Gentleman') defined the word *pun* in his *New Dictionary of the Canting Crew*, published around 1696. The word had evidently entered English well before B. E. Gent.'s time, possibly as a contraction of the Italian word *puntiglio* = 'small point, quibble'; and equally evidently, the idea of punning goes back at least to classical times (the ancient Greeks called this minor verbal art form *paronomasia*) and doubtless to the prehistoric origins of language itself.

Yet for all its antiquity, the pun seems to have always existed on the borderline of respectability, the subject of both ardent defense and virulent attack. Some people can't abide puns. Alexander Pope, for example, wrote that "he that would pun would pick a pocket." Oliver Wendell Holmes compared punsters to "wanton boys who put coppers on the railroad tracks," and the lexicographer Noah Webster dismissed the pun as "a low species of wit" (to which definition Oscar Levant later added "—when you don't think of it first").

The defenders of puns—among whom have been such notables as Joseph Addison, James Boswell, and Edgar Allan Poe—have tended to be equally firm but more moderate. An exception was one of punning's greatest champions, the English essayist Charles Lamb. "A pun is a noble thing, *per se*," he wrote in 1810. "It fills the mind; it is as perfect as a sonnet; better!" To be sure, pun haters might point out, Lamb also confided to his friend Robert Southey, "Anything awful makes me laugh; I misbehaved once at a funeral." But as we shall see, that may just be the central issue in the debate.

Among "awful" puns there are also intentionally cynical or macabre ones, designed to get a grim chuckle rather than a laugh. In the Civil War, Gen. Hugh Kilpatrick, Sherman's cavalry commander, sent a message to Sherman from the town of Barnwell, South Carolina: "We have changed the name of Barnwell to Burnwell." Kilpatrick himself, notorious for recklessness, was known as General Kill-cavalry. Names are often punned on in this way. When Ulysses S. Grant took over the Army of the Potomac, one officer remarked that only time would tell whether Grant's first name was Ulysses or Useless.

H. W. Fowler, the authority on British English usage, dismissed critics of puns thus:

> The assumption that puns are *per se* contemptible . . . is a sign at once of sheepish docility and a desire to seem superior. Puns are good, bad and indifferent, and only those who lack the wit to make them are unaware of the fact.
>
> —*A Dictionary of Modern English Usage*

But here Fowler may be missing—or at any rate, glossing over—a key point: in the world of puns, "badness" may actually be the main criterion of "goodness." In precisely the measure that a pun is outrageous and far-fetched, the pun connoisseur may treasure it. Thus, different people may find awful, in either the pejorative or the admiring sense, such elaborate foolishness as S. J. Perelman's comment on the commercial value of impressionist paintings:

> "Money makes the mare go," I said, "but Monet makes the van Go."
>
> —*Baby, It's Cold Outside*

Not all puns, of course, go to such lengths. Many are merely small embellishments used to enliven what might otherwise be routine prose. Such minor punning, not unexpectedly, is often favored by journalists.

> I realized that I had lost interest in that particular stretch of beach. (And if the surf hath lost its savor, wherewith shall we be surfeited?)
>
> —E. B. White, *The Points of My Compass*

A *Newsweek* story on Ernest Lefever's preparations for his Senate confirmation hearings for the post of Assistant Secretary of State was headlined "The Importance of Briefing Ernest." In the *New York Times* Marvin Frankel wrote of tax shelters, stock options, deductible yachts, and "other artifacts to succor the rich and sucker the poor." On CBS radio Charles Osgood summed up the decision of the New York Department of Corrections to auction off an original painting by Salvador Dali, discovered on a wall of the Riker's Island prison, with the words: "Goodbye, Dali." And from the most inveterate journalistic punster of them all, the *New York Times* columnist William Safire, comes a virtually endless stream of confections, such as *interreaganum* (to describe the period between President Ronald Reagan's election and swearing in) and *Haigravations* (to describe former Secretary of State Alexander Haig's sometimes eccentric use of English).

A good source of illustrations of how puns can be derived from formulas are the verbal competitions that have been run in *New York* magazine. Once contestants were asked to take a famous quotation, delete one letter from one word in it, and ascribe the result to a well-known person. One of the more amusing submissions was: "'Frankly, my ear, I don't give a damn.'—Rhett Van Gogh."

In some ways it is the punning shaggy-dog story that is most likely to separate pun lovers from pun haters. The whole point of such a joke is to cap an elaborate circumstantial buildup with a profoundly silly pun. An example, abbreviated to its barest bones, is the story of the Indian brave who, suffering from chronic indigestion, applies to the tribal shaman. The shaman prescribes a short, thin strip of magical leather, a little bit of which the ailing brave is to chew off each day until he is cured. Weeks later, when the shaman asks how the cure has worked, the brave replies gloomily, "The thong is ended, but the malady lingers on."

But whatever your tolerance for the worst of awful and contrived puns, we consider it definitely deplorable to commit a pun and then draw attention to it by adding "no pun intended":

> . . . sales on fancy cuts of beef are—no pun intended—rare.
> —Lawrence Van Gelder, *New York Times*

If the pun was accidental, it is preferable either to delete it or to let it stand and speak for itself.

The 19th-century English writer Sydney Smith made a good point about puns when he wrote: "They are exactly the same to words which wit is to ideas, and consist in the sudden discovery of relations in language." Thus, it is no wonder that people who insist upon looking to puns for insight or instruction are bound to come away disappointed and probably scornful. Puns have very little to do with ideas and much to do with the charm of words and the humor of outrageous nonsense—with that "anything awful" that always made Charles Lamb laugh. That is why they will always have a literate and unrepentant constituency.

punctuation. The most important fact about punctuation is that it gives order and clarity to the written or printed word. The omission, overuse, or careless placement of punctuation marks can sabotage the meaning of a text and, at the very least, frustrate and confuse us, its readers. Ultimately, the successful use of punctuation depends on a solid grasp of sentence structure. Recognizing sentences, clauses, and phrases determines where and how we will place periods, commas, semicolons, colons, dashes, and parentheses. Although the use of the more "mechanical" marks—quotation marks, question marks, exclamation points—is a matter of remembering a few basic conventions, the conventions themselves rest firmly on the syntax of the sentence.

Modern newspaper style favors a more streamlined type of punctuation, typically in the dropping of commas and the conservative use of the semicolon and the colon. Literary and scholarly works still rely on the full range of punctuation marks, though perhaps using the comma less often than in the past. Despite the traditional "rules" and suggestions about punctuation, many times the choice of which mark to use—a comma or a semicolon; a semicolon or a colon; parentheses or dashes—comes down to what the writer intends to suggest by one mark rather than another or simply prefers for no easily explainable reason.

It is safe to say that some form of punctuation will be with us as long as language is written down. The following guidelines cover the basics of using the common punctuation marks in English.

Period. The period is often regarded as a "strong" punctuation mark because it indicates the end of a sentence or a thought that is treated like a sentence for emphasis:

> Three o'clock. Half past three. Four o'clock. Sisters Ursule and Jane, Solomon, Gulab and the cart had not come in. Mother Morag had been up since midnight. . . .
> —Rumer Godden, *The Dark Horse*

One of the commonest trouble areas in written English is the *run-on sentence* (also called *fused sentence*), in which two or more independent thoughts are combined without intervening punctuation: *In the morning they decided to swim across the lake their bathing suits were locked in the trunk of the car however they tried to pick the lock they couldn't get it to open.* Several interpretations are possible as to the exact sense of such a jumble of information, and the following could be one of them: *In the morning they decided to swim across the lake. Their bathing suits were locked in the trunk of the car. However they tried to pick the lock, they couldn't get it to open.*

Another common mistake in this area is to punctuate a run-on sentence with a comma instead of a period: *We're planning a surprise party for the twins, Saturday is the only day we can have it.* The better choice is a period after *twins*.

Semicolon. The semicolon (;) is probably the most sophisticated of all the punctuation marks. Like the period, it strongly separates word groupings. Yet it also keeps these groupings closely linked in the same sentence. The semicolon functions in various ways.
(1) To separate the independent clauses in a compound sentence: *My parents are coming up for the weekend; they expect to arrive late Friday afternoon.* Although the two statements could easily be written as two sentences, the close connection of the thoughts makes the semicolon appropriate. The semicolon usually takes the place of the coordinate conjunction (traditionally preceded by a comma) that would otherwise join two independent clauses: *I forgot to mail your letter, but I'll do it first thing tomorrow.* With the semicolon: *I forgot to mail your letter; I'll do it first thing tomorrow.* When at least one of the independent parts of a compound sentence has a subordinate clause in it, both the conjunction and the semicolon may be used: *It was raining when the game started; but by halftime the sky had begun to clear.*

When the second clause of a compound sentence is introduced by *moreover, however, that is, furthermore,* etc., the conjunction is customarily followed by a comma:

> The charge [by many critics] is that the characters of both novelists [Henry James and Virginia Woolf] do not experience the range of life as it is really lived; moreover, they seem to inhabit worlds in which questions of social strife, of evil and suffering, of religious doubts, even of something so necessary to life as work, are ignored.
>
> —Joyce Carol Oates, *New Heaven, New Earth*

(2) To separate parallel clauses or strings of phrases, especially when they have subordinate clauses in them:

> The task here undertaken . . . seeks to show that what we have all this time called "human nature" and deprecated, was in great part only male nature, and good enough in its place; that what we have called "masculine" and admired as such, was in large part human, and should be applied to both sexes; that what we have called "feminine" and condemned, was also largely human and applicable to both.
>
> —Charlotte Perkins Gilman, *The Man-Made World* (1904)

The following made-up example shows how the rule works in practice:

> There were muddy paw prints on the front porch; in the hallway, where the new pale-blue runner lay; in the parlor, with its Aubusson rug that only the housekeeper was allowed to vacuum; in the kitchen, its linoleum freshly scrubbed and waxed.

The semicolon may also be used to separate an independent clause from a phrase or a dependent clause introduced by an adverbial construction: *He has sung major roles in musical comedy; for example, Billy Bigelow in* Carousel.

Comma. This mark (,) serves a number of purposes.
(1) To set off introductory words, including terms of direct address, and phrases: *Ladies and gentlemen, we have a winner.*

> Gropingly, Willy looked towards the sound of the voice, and dimly in the desert brightness he made out two nattily dressed strangers and a vague form that might have been Cynthia.
>
> —Walt and Leigh Richmond, *Shortstack*

> With the affluence of the last twenty-five years, dependency became a systemic disease in America.
>
> —Gail Sheehy, *Passages*

(2) To set off words and phrases in series: *Today's special includes soup, a sandwich, a beverage, and dessert. You can park the car on the street, in the driveway, or in the garage.* In these examples the comma before the conjunction is called the *series comma.* In modern American usage it is often omitted:

> Be sure swimming, boating, water skiing and other water activities are supervised at all times by a qualified person who holds a current instructor's certifi-

cate from the Red Cross, Y or Boy Scouts. —*Changing Times*

◇ *Recommendation.* Dropping this final comma can sometimes cause confusion. Keeping the comma leaves no room for misinterpretation.

(3) To separate two independent clauses when the conjunction is expressed or to set off a series of short or simple independent clauses:

> His mind leaped from one interest to another almost too swiftly, and yet the average man understood and liked him.
> —Theodore Dreiser, *Peter*

> Transporting the stone when it was once broken was comparatively simple. The horses carried it off in cart-loads, the sheep dragged single blocks, even Muriel and Benjamin yoked themselves into an old governess-cart and did their share.
> —George Orwell, *Animal Farm*

(4) To set off dependent clauses that precede the main clause. Such clauses are introduced by *when, if, although, after, where,* and other subordinate conjunctions.

> When all the converging factors are toted up, it is no wonder that a woman begins to feel the change to a midlife perspective at 35.
> —Gail Sheehy, *Passages*

> If you continue to follow the techniques of this 9-day money management program, you are going to eventually begin to accumulate surplus money.
> —H. Stanley Judd, *Think Rich*

When such clauses are short, the comma is sometimes omitted: *If you join I'll join. After she died he sold the house.*

◇ *Recommendation.* When in doubt, use the comma in a sentence of this type. It may look slightly fussy and old-fashioned, but at least it's clear.

(5) To set off dependent clauses within a sentence, interpolated expressions, and words and phrases in apposition: *He expected, for the most part, that his decision would be approved. The desk clerk, who always greeted them by name, handed over the key in silence.*

> Van, her personal secretary, had, among other duties, the privilege of decoding certain top-secret documents Madame Ngha would show to no one else.
> —Pierre Boulle, *Ears of the Jungle*

(6) To indicate the omission of words in sentences containing independent clauses. In the following quotation the comma after the names Sid and Leanne indicates that the auxiliary verb *was* has been omitted.

> Sally looked around at them all. Derek was sitting silently on the sandy floor, his best spear in his hand; Sid, lying beside his feverish brother; Leanne, sitting cross-legged, rocking slightly to and fro. —Gabrielle Lord, *Fortress*

(7) To set off the words that introduce or identify the speaker of a quotation from the quotation itself: *"The prognosis," he announced cheerfully, "is very favorable indeed."* See Quotation Marks, below, for more details.

Colon. The chief use of the colon (:) is to introduce text that explains or amplifies what has just been said.

> The dispute involved serious issues: titles, boundary lines, right of way, and the status of tenants.

> She had made up her mind to reveal the truth: why she had left; why she had come back; why, finally, she stayed.

When a full sentence follows a colon, it may or may not be capitalized, depending on the writer or the style preferred by the publishing house:

> A fertilized egg differs from an asexually reproducing cell in one fundamental respect: it contains a newly assembled mixture of genes.
> —Edward O. Wilson, *On Human Nature*

When a motto, an adage, or a slogan follows a colon, the first word is capitalized:

> My father had a favorite saying: A man convinced against his will is of the same opinion still.

For more details on how to capitalize following a colon, see CAPITALIZATION.

In the following quotation the novelist V. S. Naipaul has deftly balanced a clause and a long series of phrases by using an unusual combination of colons and dashes (see Dash, below). Much information and atmosphere are conveyed here, yet the effect is smooth and remarkably simple.

> At lunch in their flat one day—a good lunch: they had gone to a lot of trouble: silver and brass polished, the curtains drawn to keep out the glare, the three-stemmed standard lamp lighting up the Persian carpet on the wall—Shoba asked Indar, "Is there any money in what you do?"
>
> —*A Bend in the River*

The colon is often used to introduce longer quotations or those not preceded by *said*, *remarked*, etc.

> It was an emotional moment for Washington, as his diary reveals: "About ten o'clock I bade adieu to Mount Vernon, to private life, and to domestic felicity; and, with a mind oppressed with more anxious sensations than I have words to express, set out for New York. . . ."
>
> —Richard M. Ketchum, *The World of George Washington*

Dash. This is a punctuation mark that should be used carefully. A dash (—) is a device for separating some portion of a text from the words around it, usually as a means of explaining something. Any text set off by dashes is likely to be read with a sense of emphasis. When used too freely, the dash soon loses its power to emphasize. And a piece of writing that is thick with dashes can seem hasty and disjointed.

The text to be set off must be preceded and followed by a dash unless that text ends or begins a sentence. It is important to place the dashes correctly. In the first quotation below, the dashes enclose a noun phrase with its own dependent clause.

> The party was rather large, as it included one other family—a proper unobjectionable country family, whom the Coles had the advantage of naming among their acquaintances—and the male part of Mr. Cox's family, the lawyer of Highbury.
>
> —Jane Austen, *Emma*

> Miss Amelia was left with everything that Marvin Macy had ever owned—his timberwood, his gold watch, every one of his possessions.
>
> —Carson McCullers, *The Ballad of the Sad Café*

> A customer in a shop, a client in an office, a group of guests in the home of their hosts—these persons put on a performance and maintain a front, but the setting in which they do this is outside of their immediate control. . . .
>
> —Erving Goffman, *The Presentation of Self in Everyday Life*

In modern usage the dash is not combined with the comma, semicolon, or colon, but in writings of an earlier age such combinations are found.

> His strength had been weakened,—his blows could not tell at such a distance,—he was obliged to fling himself at his adversary, and could not strike from his feet. . . .
>
> —William Hazlitt, *The Fight* (1821)

Question marks and exclamation points should be retained within the text set off by dashes: *The day after graduation—didn't I predict it?—Sally and Victor eloped. The entire clan—what an uproar they made!—gathered in the glen.* (Note that the matter enclosed by the dashes is not capitalized, though each text is a full sentence.)

The dash is also used to indicate incomplete sentences and breaks in thought. When so used, it is not followed by any punctuation except quotation marks if appropriate.

> "And about the funeral," he said softly. . . .
>
> Josephine and Constantia got up too. "I should like it to be quite simple," said Josephine firmly, "and not too ex-

pensive. At the same time I should like—"

"A good one that will last," thought dreamy Constantia, as if Josephine were buying a nightgown.

—Katherine Mansfield,
The Daughters of the Late Colonel

Laurie smiled. "I'm sure Mrs. Reilly will let us have her station wagon."

"Why should Mrs. Reilly— What do you mean, us?"

They were in the kitchen, where Laurie had found her mother unloading bags of groceries when she came in from school. "I mean me and Chris."

—Frances Rickett and
Steven McGraw,
Totaled

Parentheses and Brackets. Traditionally, these marks, ( ) and [ ], have been reserved for text that in some way explains or adds to the main text.

(1) Parentheses usually enclose commentary or elaboration by the writer of the material in which they appear. Such matter is usually not essential to the structure of the sentence, but its presence may be an important ingredient in the writer's style or handling of the subject. In the following, the parenthetical text could be left out of the sentence without altering its structure or basic message.

The sun can do three things: increase your sex appeal (many men find a tan attractive), increase your authority (having a tan is part of the executive mystique), and (according to medical research) increase your chances of getting skin cancer.

—John T. Molloy,
The Woman's Dress for Success Book

In the above example the first two parenthetical texts are complete sentences. When a declarative sentence is enclosed in parentheses within a sentence, it does not take an initial capital or end punctuation. However, the first word of adages, mottoes, etc., is frequently capitalized, though the period is dropped: *She embroidered her favorite saying (Well begun is half done) on a pillow.* When the text inside the parentheses is a question or has an exclamation point, no capital is used but the end punctuation is retained: *He wrote the play (have you ever seen it?) in three days. Connie took over the job (she's such a good sport!) when Ann caught the flu.*

It is important to distinguish between a full parenthetical sentence within a sentence, as described above, and an independent sentence that happens to be set in parentheses. An independent sentence in parentheses has an initial capital and end punctuation that must fall inside the closing parenthesis: *Each side blamed the other for not having bargained in good faith. (This came as no surprise to the press corps.)*

Parentheses also contain references to pages, chapters, illustrations, and so on.

(2) Brackets enclose information supplied by an editor or author for a text written by someone else. These devices are likely to be needed where a quoted text has been shortened; where it contains unfamiliar or difficult terms, misspellings, incomplete identifications, references not readily understood, etc.; or when the editor or author wishes to stress, by means of italics or underscoring, a part of the quotation not emphasized by the original author. In the following example the literary scholar Bernard Spivack quotes three lines from a 15th-century English morality play and translates one of the words.

What ys yt xall make me clene?
Put yt, Lorde, in-to my thowte!
Thi olde mercy, let me remene [remember].

—*Shakespeare and the Allegory of Evil*

Misspellings, on the other hand, are indicated by the word *sic,* usually in italics (underscored in the typescript), and editorial emphasis by the words *emphasis added, italics mine,* or something similar (usually in roman type). Stage directions are often put in brackets, especially in Shakespeare's plays.

Quotation Marks. These marks are used to enclose the exact words or thoughts of an individual, to set off expressions that require emphasis for various reasons, or to designate the titles of certain literary and artistic works.

Quotation marks are in American usage a pair of small symbols (". . ."), in British usage often a single symbol ('. . .'), put at the beginning and end of the quoted text. In American style the single quotation mark is used most often to set off anything quoted within a quotation: *"Remove the plastic cover," the sign read, "and turn the 'Magnadial' to 'start.'"* (Note that the period ending the sentence falls inside the single quotation mark.) In British style it is the opposite: double quotation marks within the single marks. (The British term for quotation marks is *inverted commas.*)

The single quotation mark may also be used in place of the double mark for special purposes, as in newspaper headlines or in a work on philosophy or language that must define many terms precisely. This book has chosen to use the single quotation mark this way, wherever English and foreign words are defined, explained, or translated; for example, at PUNDIT, PANDIT we state that *pandit* is from Sanskrit *pandita* = 'wise man, scholar.'

The placement of quotation marks themselves is not usually a difficult matter, so long as you know the extent of the quotation. But combining quotation marks with other marks can often be troublesome. Here is how to use quotation marks with other punctuation.

With the Period. The period is always placed inside the closing quotation marks: *I heard Aunt Zelda call, "When you come up, turn off the porch light."*

> On the hearth, in front of a back-brand to give substance, blazed a fire of thorns, that crackled "like the laughter of the fool." —Thomas Hardy, *The Three Strangers*

In British usage the period is placed outside the closing quotation mark. In the quotation above, from an English writer, the punctuation has been Americanized.

With the Comma. The comma, which separates the quoted text from the words that introduce or surround it, must always fall inside the closing quotation marks: *"It's annoying," he grumbled, "how many of our calls are wrong numbers." Across the top of the page were penciled the comments "intelligent," "original," "articulate."*

With the Semicolon. The semicolon is always placed outside the closing quotation marks: *According to the manager, "We've sold every candle in the store"; she hadn't looked in the stockroom. He wanted a tonic for his "nerves"; for his "blue spells"; for what his wife called "the cranks."* The period that normally ends a full-sentence quotation (as in the first example) is omitted when the quotation is followed by a semicolon.

With the Colon. Like the semicolon, the colon falls outside the closing quotation marks: *"A song," he cried, "our old school song": the very song he had never bothered to learn. The recipe called for fresh "parshey": it was the only ingredient I understood.* When a full-sentence quotation is followed by a colon, the period for that sentence is omitted: *"Exhale and let the tension out": the professor always began this way.*

With the Dash. Unlike the colon and the semicolon, the dash may fall within the closing quotation marks, provided it is part of the quotation. A typical instance of this is when the dash is used in dialogue or other quoted text to indicate choppiness, abruptness, or an incomplete thought.

> "If I did not sell love potions," said the old man, reaching for another bottle, "I should not have mentioned the other matter to you. . . ."
>
> "And these potions," said Alan. "They are not just—just—er—"
>
> "Oh, no," said the old man. "Their effects are permanent. . . ."
>
> —John Collier, *The Chaser*

Punctuation is not used after a dash that ends a quotation, even if the quoted matter is a complete sentence itself or it falls at the end of a full sentence:

> "The superintendent just called—"she interrupted.
>
> "The school budget was voted down," he replied, "and it looks like a fight—" He banged his fist on the table.

When the dash is not part of the quotation, it falls outside the quotation marks: *"If you can hear me"—it was my father's voice—"tug on the rope."* The comma that would ordinarily fall after *me ("If you can hear me, tug on the rope")* has been omitted because of the dash.

With the Question Mark. Like the dash, the question mark falls inside the quotes when it is part of the quoted text, outside them when it is not: *"Who gets the spare-ribs?" the waitress asked. What Victorian poet celebrated "success in failure"?*

With the Exclamation Point. As with the question mark, the exclamation point goes inside the quotes when it is part of the quoted text, outside them when it is not: *"Stop!" the witness cried. We heard the congregation shout, "Glory be!" He had forgotten the meaning of "sea smoke"!*

In the first example no other punctuation is needed after the exclamation point; but if it were not used, the quoted text would be followed by a comma inside the quotation marks: *"Stop," the witness cried.* Note that in the second example the exclamation point serves as the end punctuation of the sentence, even though the mark applies only to the quotation.

***Exclamation Point* (or *Mark*).** This mark (!) is used to express a high degree of emotion, emphasis, or excitement. Like the dash and italics, it can lose its effect rather fast if applied to a text too liberally. The exclamation point is considered somewhat stronger than the question mark, so that when both would be appropriate in a text, it is generally better to omit the question mark in favor of the exclamation: *Who was the first man to shout out "Vengeance!"*

The exclamatory *oh* may be followed by an exclamation point or a comma (but sometimes neither), depending on the degree of emphasis desired; the *O* of direct address should stand without punctuation: *Oh! You startled me! Oh, let's forget the whole thing!*

> O powerful western fallen star!
> O shades of night—O moody, tearful
> night!
>
> —Walt Whitman,
> *When Lilacs Last in the Dooryard Bloomed*

See also O, OH.

Question Mark. This mark (?) is probably, next to the period, the most straightforward punctuation mark in English, because it follows a direct question. Yet there are several situations where its use can pose problems.
(1) Within a declarative sentence. A question should be punctuated within a sentence that is not itself a question: *Why did I agree to meet him? I asked myself.* (Note that quotation marks may be omitted in constructions involving unspoken questions, interior monologues, etc.) *In answer to the question Why did you leave your station? he merely bowed his head.* (Note that no punctuation is needed following the question mark.)
(2) With a series of questions within the same sentence. The question mark should be repeated with each change of phrase: *What time will you leave the office? catch the train? reach Washington?*
(3) With indirect questions. No question mark is used with the indirect question: *He asked her why she was a vegetarian. Mr. Simpson wondered what he would do without his car.*
(4) With the polite request or suggestion. The polite request, although it sounds like a question, ordinarily takes the period, not the question mark: *May I recommend the veal Marsala for the main course.* At the writer's discretion, however, such sentences can be punctuated as questions, depending on the context and the emphasis desired.

For the use of the apostrophe see POSSESSIVES. For the use of the hyphen see COMPOUND ADJECTIVES; COMPOUND NOUNS; COMPOUND VERBS.

pundit, pandit. In India a *pandit* /pŭn-dĭt/ is a scholarly Hindu of the Brahmin caste, expert in the Sanskrit scriptures. The word is from Sanskrit *pandita* = 'wise man, scholar.' Europeans were first taught Sanskrit, and Indian culture in general, by pandits:

> All our great Sanskrit scholars used to work with a Pandit at each elbow, instead of the grammar and dictionary.
>
> —Max Müller,
> *Chips From a German Workshop* (1862)

It is also used as an honorary title for a wise and learned man, such as *Pandit Nehru*. The British in India, taking the old-fashioned spelling *pundit*, used the word humorously for anyone setting up as an expert on anything. It has passed into American usage in this slightly mocking sense:

> Nelson Rockefeller and William F. Buckley laugh it up at a party at the Waldorf. The encounter between the former Vice President and the conservative pundit . . . —*New York Post*

> For months, planners, pundits and assorted experts had been predicting [the Bicentennial celebration] would be a disaster.
> —Thomas Fleming, *Reader's Digest*

> [John] Anderson, virtually ignored by the pollsters and pundits, provided the shocker. . . . —*Florida Times-Union*

purposely, purposefully. These are not entirely synonymous. *Purposely* means 'on purpose, deliberately': *It was clear that the fire had been started purposely. Purposefully* means 'with conscious purpose, in a highly deliberate manner': *He purposefully set about eliminating the opposition.*

Pyrrhic victory /pîr-ĭk/. Pyrrhus (c. 319–272 B.C.), king of Epirus in northwestern Greece, spent most of the 25 years of his reign fighting wars to enlarge his kingdom and eventually died in combat. He won nearly all of his battles, including one against the Romans at Asculum in 279 in which he lost most of his army. Hence, a *Pyrrhic victory* is a success won at too high a price:

> To win the nomination under these circumstances would have been—though possible—a Pyrrhic victory. It would have torn the nation apart.
> —Doris Kearns, *Lyndon Johnson and the American Dream*

> Considering its costs, the settlement seems a Pyrrhic victory for the major oil company. —*Business Week*

Q

qua /kwā, kwä/ = 'when considered merely as.' It is often written in italics.

> *Qua* work of art, the work of art cannot be interpreted; there is nothing to interpret; we can only criticize it according to standards, in comparison to other works of art. . . .
> —T. S. Eliot, *Essays*

> . . . the shrinking in the number of those who engage in work *qua* work is something to be regarded . . . with positive approval.
> —John Kenneth Galbraith, *The Affluent Society*

quasi /kwā-zī, kwä-zē/. Originally a Latin conjunction meaning 'as if,' *quasi* is used either adverbally or adjectivally, usually as a kind of prefix and often attached with a hyphen to the word it qualifies. Its meaning ranges from 'sort of, more or less, almost' to 'virtually, virtual, to all intents and purposes' and 'pseudo-, so-called.'

(1) As an adverb:

> Margaret came in. She was wearing the green Paisley frock and the quasi-velvet shoes. —Kingsley Amis, *Lucky Jim*

> . . . the Christian League of South Africa, a quasi-religious, political organization that has been financed by the former South African Department of Information.
> —Karin Johansson, *Christianity Today*

(2) As an adjective:

> There is no mention of the proposed English Prayer Book of 1928. Presumably, it ceases to have whatever quasi-authority it may have had.
>
> —Massey H. Shepherd, Jr., *The Living Church*

> . . . by providing destroyers to England, Roosevelt was placing the United States in a state of quasi belligerence, since the sale of destroyers was seen as an act of war.
>
> —Doris Kearns, *Lyndon Johnson and the American Dream*

question. The expression *There is no question* is used as a strong affirmation of something, that a statement or situation is true or effective *beyond question.* There is evidently some hesitation about the logic involved, of just what it is that can't be questioned, since the key clause can be introduced with several different constructions. The chief alternatives are *no question that* and *no question but that;* others are *no question but* (without *that*) and *no question but what.*

> If we went into a nuclear war today there is practically no question that the Russians would win that war and the U.S. would cease to exist.
>
> —Edward Teller (quoted), *Forbes*

> There is no question but that boredom is the commonest complaint sex therapists now hear.
>
> —Robert Reitman (quoted), *Reader's Digest*

> No question but we have had enough of it.
>
> —Benita Sanders (quoted), Brian Aherne, *A Dreadful Man*

> There is hardly any question but what Jones had become a threatening menace to the pros.
>
> —H. B. Martin, *Fifty Years of American Golf*

◇ ***Recommendation.*** Any of these constructions is acceptable. The prevailing one in current good usage is *no question that.* If in doubt, use this one.

quick. The original meaning of *quick* is 'living,' preserved in a famous passage of the King James Bible: ". . . the Lord Jesus Christ, who shall judge the quick and the dead at his appearing . . ." (2 Timothy 4:1). The noun *quick,* literally 'living flesh,' refers to the soft and sensitive flesh under a fingernail or toenail, or under a corn or callus. Hence the expressions *cut, hurt, stung, wounded,* etc., *to the quick.*

> Had it been reported that we had thrown away one single fish, every inhabitant in the settlement would have been hurt to the quick, and we would have become virtual pariahs. . . .
>
> Shaken to the quick, I headed the vessel back toward the centre of the harbour. . . .
>
> —Farley Mowat, *The Boat Who Wouldn't Float*

The first example is fine, but the second is presumably a mistake for *shaken to the core.*

The adjective *quick* developed a further range of meanings, 'lively, full of life, active, mobile' and eventually 'fast-moving, swift,' whereupon the original meaning was lost. *Quick* has long been used also as an adverb, synonymous with *quickly,* and this use is fully standard and correct.

quid pro quo. This Latin phrase means 'something in exchange for something.' It may refer to an honest trade-off, to a secret deal or bribe, or to retaliation.

> Aware that he had not invited some of our relatives, I decided to ask for a *quid pro quo.* "Okay, Lyndon," I said, "I'll come, but I think you ought to invite all our kinfolk."
>
> —Sam Houston Johnson, *My Brother Lyndon*

> He agreed that the contractors were all well qualified and that there had been no quid pro quo involved.
>
> —Richard Nixon, *R.N.*

> It had been awhile in coming, but if Murrow could take a slap at the corporate power of CBS, then CBS could take a slap at Murrow. *Quid pro quo.*
>
> —Gary Paul Gates, *Air Time*

quintessence. The ancient and medieval philosophers believed that the cosmos is composed of four basic elements—earth, air, fire, and water—and a fifth and highest element, sometimes called *ether,* of which the planets and stars are made. This was called, in Latin, the *quinta essentia* = 'fifth essence,' becoming *quintessence* in English.

> Swift to their several quarters hastened then
> The cumbrous elements, earth, flood, air, fire;
> And this ethereal quintessence of heaven
> Flew upward, spirited with various forms
> That rolled orbicular, and turned to stars
> Numberless. . . .
>
> —John Milton, *Paradise Lost*

Quintessence is now used to mean 'the purest form of anything, the perfect example':

> . . . he was by Soviet definition the quintessence of the New Communist Man.
>
> —John Barron, *Reader's Digest*

> All my life, while my musical taste and capacity have widened, I have found in Mozart's music the quintessence of all that I feel most keenly in mind and in emotion.
>
> —Marcia Davenport, *Mozart*

The adjective *quintessential* means 'perfect and typical, representing something in its purest form':

> That idea—humankind's inalienable right to life, liberty and the pursuit of happiness, coupled with a system for protecting human rights—was and is the quintessential American dream.
>
> —John Gardner, *Reader's Digest*

> Tom has the most common pattern, what is known—especially to derisive outsiders—as the quintessential Jersey accent.
>
> —Paul Bradley, *New Jersey Monthly*

quisling. During the German occupation of Norway in World War II the puppet government was headed by the Norwegian Nazi official Vidkun Quisling. He was executed in 1945. His name has a suggestively contemptible flavor in English, and it was adopted as a permanent term meaning 'traitor who governs his own country for a foreign power.'

> In each he evicted pro-Persian quislings and established Greek-style democracies.
>
> —Mary Renault, *The Nature of Alexander*

> . . . the CIA's almost legendary Ed Lansdale identified Magsaysay as a decent and honest alternative to Communists on the left and corrupt quislings on the right. . . .
>
> —William Colby, *Honorable Men: My Life in the CIA*

quit has the variant forms *quitted* and *quit* for the past tense and past participle. Both are correct, but *quit* is much more often used when the sense is 'to resign (from a job)' or 'to leave off (doing something).' In the various other senses *quit* and *quitted* are used about equally in American English, but only *quitted* is used in British.

> He quit one Saturday night without warning, after almost three years. . . .

> . . . the house which he had quitted not six hours ago.
>
> —William Faulkner, *Light in August*

> But before that book was published, he had quitted the army.
>
> —J. H. Plumb, *Churchill: The Historian*

quite. The adverb *quite* is used in two curiously different senses: 'fully, entirely' and 'moderately, somewhat.' On the face of it this would seem to lead to ambiguity, but in practice it seldom does. The context nearly always makes it clear which one is meant, and in speech emphasis and intonation also play a part. *He's quite happy,* with strong stress on *quite* and equally strong or nearly as strong stress on *happy,* means 'He's entirely happy.' *He's quite happy,* with strong stress on *quite* and little stress on *happy,* means 'He's moderately happy.' The sense 'entirely' is the original and basic one, but both senses are fully standard and acceptable in formal usage. *Quite a,* in expressions such as *quite a few* and *quite a day,* is a little less formal but still standard.

quixotic. The British feel free to anglicize foreign names that they have known familiarly for hundreds of years; just as they pronounce Don *Juan* as /**jōō**-ən/, so they pronounce Don *Quixote*—from Cervantes' novel about the impractical, gallant, and romantic knight first published in 1605—as /**kwĭk**-sət/. The name is now written in Spanish as *Quijote,* pronounced /kē-**hō**-tā/—also the current Standard American pronunciation of the name. The adjective *quixotic* /kwĭk-**zŏt**-ĭk/ means 'romantically enthusiastic or exciting but somewhat impractical':

> John James Audubon, quixotic, charming, driven, remains something of a mystery to the end.
> —Albert Meisel, *Smithsonian*

> . . . the legend of Prester John crystallized and took such hypnotic hold on the medieval imagination that it was to persist unshakably for nearly 500 years and set off a quest—as romantic and quixotic and rich in consequence as the search for the Golden Fleece or the Holy Grail or the Fountain of Youth.
> —Peter Forbath, *The River Congo*

quondam is a Latinism meaning 'one-time, having been so once but being so no longer.' The word is pronounced /**kwŏn**-dəm/.

> For years, with the irreconcilable hatred of the musical Establishment, [ragtime] was countenanced even by its quondam partisans, the public, only in the nightclubs' broad and belittling burlesque.
> —Rudi Blesh, *Scott Joplin*

quotation marks. See PUNCTUATION.

R

rack. See WRACK, RACK, WRECK.

raise. See RISE, RAISE.

ramada. See PORCH.

rationale is from Latin and was formerly pronounced with four syllables, /răsh-ə-**nä**-lē/ or /răsh-ə-**nā**-lē/. It is sometimes (wrongly) thought to be French, like *morale,* and therefore pronounced /răsh-ə-**näl**/. All three pronunciations, though perfectly acceptable, are now less common than /răsh-ə-**năl**/, which makes no particular assumptions about origin. To anyone in doubt, we recommend this last pronunciation.

The word basically means 'the rational basis of something, the underlying reasons':

> Although in some states life sentences are administered consecutively, in New York they are not, the rationale being that a defendant has, in fact, only one life.
> —Anna Quindlen, *New York Times*

It is also used to mean 'rational explanation, reasoning produced to justify something':

> [Geraldo] Rivera understands all this. He has a ready rationale for his seemingly contradictory status as superstar spokesman for the teeming masses.
> —Ron Powers, *The Newscasters*

rationalize literally means 'to make (something) rational, explain in terms of reason.' Much more often it is used in senses that originated in a technical concept of psychology, according to which the mind frequently devises "rational" explanations and justifications for the person's irrational actions and buried motivations. Thus, *rationalize* often means 'to explain away, make a plausible version of something undesirable':

> Interviews . . . revealed that the Vietnam failure has been effectively rationalized in that bureaucracy as an accident of history and geography.
> —Richard J. Barnet, *The Security of Empire After Vietnam*

> . . . my foreknowledge that the elegance of his prose and the apparent solidity of his reasoning united to form a mere facade to rationalize the specific public policy that he wished, at the moment, to fasten upon the nation.
> —Walter F. Murphy, *The Vicar of Christ*

It is also used with a clause, meaning 'to deceive oneself into believing (that), reason falsely (that)':

> . . . the former President rationalized that the so-called Huston plan to spy on dissidents . . . had been [a] logical extension of Presidential authority to maintain internal order.
> —James M. Naughton, *New York Times*

> In short, I went along with the whole scheme, rationalizing that God takes care of children, drunks, and singing talk show hosts named Douglas.
> —Mike Douglas, *My Story*

real is widely used in informal speech as an adverb meaning 'very.' This is not appropriate to formal writing but can be used to give a colloquial or folksy effect.

> Eddie Popowski was the manager of Pittfield. He had ulcers, used to get real sick, and he had an alarm watch that was always going off to remind him to take his medicine.
> —Sparky Lyle, *The Bronx Zoo*

> This struck me as a real chatty letter.
> —E. B. White, *The Points of My Compass*

The phrase *for real* = 'in earnest, serious' also has an informal flavor but is perhaps coming into more general use.

> Some commentators were not yet convinced I was for real, and hopefully predicted I would be a flop against any "real professional" fighter.
> —Muhammad Ali, *The Greatest*

> The one man in the world whom Stalin trusted was not bluffing. This was for real.
> —Harrison E. Salisbury, *The Unknown War*

reason . . . because. The word *because* obviously contains the word *cause;* therefore, to say, for example, *The cause of the accident was because the brakes failed* would clearly be redundant. The simplest definition of the conjunction *because* is 'by reason that'—that is, the word *because* contains the idea of 'reason'; therefore, it is argued, to say *The reason for the accident was because the brakes failed* is just as redundant as the first example. The nonredundant alternatives are *The reason for the accident was that the brakes failed* and *The accident occurred because the brakes failed.*

Nonetheless, while almost no one says or writes *the cause is because,* people often say *the reason is because.* Evidently, the redundancy of the first is obvious and unacceptable, whereas the redundancy of the second is not felt to be so strong, for *the reason is because* occurs not only in speech but in perfectly respectable writings.

> The reason why "South" *seems* such a wonderful word is because we had the word "North" to begin with. . . .
> —Thomas Wolfe, *The Web and the Rock*

> The reason that Cicero . . . hated Epicureanism was because it questioned the supernatural basis of authority.
> —Moses Hadas, *Hellenistic Culture*

> The reason we exalt common sense is because it results chiefly from the training school of experience which all of us attend.
> —Louis Nizer, *My Life in Court*

Several of the best dictionaries now recognize that the conjunction *because* can mean simply 'that,' making the examples given above acceptable and correct.

When the phrase *because of* is used as a preposition, much the same applies: it can be argued that *the reason is because of* is redundant, but it is in respectable use.

> West German officials say the main reason that they changed the rules on visas was because of the number of Turks requesting political asylum.
> —Marvine Howe, *New York Times*

◇ ***Recommendation.*** There is a case, based on widespread actual usage, for abolishing the rule that *the reason is because* is redundant and incorrect. But it's an old and well-established rule and is still observed by most good writers. We advise observing it; rewrite *the reason is because* as either *the reason is that* or *this occurred because.*

receipt, recipe. *Receipt* /rĭ-**sēt**/ is still an acceptable synonym for *recipe* /**rĕs**-ə-pē/ when meaning 'instructions and ingredients for preparing food'; but *recipe* is now commoner in this sense. In the figurative sense 'sequence or set of events or policies likely to produce a certain result,' as in *This plan is a recipe for unemployment and recession,* only *recipe* is used. *Recipe* was originally medical Latin, used at the beginning of prescriptions and meaning 'Take (the following materials)'; the symbol ℞ does not, as is often supposed, stand for *Rx* but is the old-fashioned handwritten abbreviation for *Recipe.*

Received Standard. See BRITISH ENGLISH.

recidivism /rĭ-**sĭd**-ə-vĭz-əm/ is from a Latin word meaning 'one who falls back or relapses into sin, backslider.' *Recidivism* usually refers to the tendency to relapse into crime or destructive behavior such as drug addiction, especially as reflected in the proportion of convicted criminals who after serving a sentence commit further crimes and come before the courts again.

> Of the 77 released inmates the society has had contact with in the one-to-one programs, only five have returned to prison, an improvement over the national recidivism rate of at least 25 percent.
> —*Reader's Digest*
> (from the *Eagle,* Reading, Pa.)

By analogy with drug addiction *recidivism* and *recidivist* are now often applied to backsliding by would-be dieters.

> A recidivist at 37, one of those hopeless failures, never to succeed at thinking thin.
> —Madeline Lee, *Ms.*

reckon, in the sense 'to suppose, figure, think,' occurs in dialects and in informal speech: *I reckon I'm as good as he is.* It is not considered acceptable in standard use.

redoubt, redoubtable. The adjective *redoubtable* is from an obsolete verb, *redoubt,* meaning 'to fear, regard with awe,' which is related to the verb *doubt. Redoubtable* means 'worthy of serious respect or fear, formidable':

> Rupert had wanted to know where Cromwell was stationed so that he could make dispositions to deal with this redoubtable leader of cavalry.
> —C. V. Wedgewood, *The King's War*

> Redoubtable as it seems on paper, however, the Soviet Army remains a polyglot conscript force with almost no combat experience.
> —*Newsweek*

The noun *redoubt,* an old term in fortification that means 'small defensive wall or earthwork,' is from Italian *ridotto* and is completely unconnected to *doubt.* The *b* was inserted in English by people who wrongly assumed that the two words were related. *Redoubt* is now usually used to mean 'defensive political stronghold':

> So long as the white redoubt in southern Africa [Rhodesia and the Portuguese colonies] held firm, South Africa presented no pressing problems for American policy.
> —George W. Ball, *Reader's Digest*

Red River dialect. This unique frontier language was spoken in the 19th century in the Red River valley, north of Winnipeg, Manitoba. Its speakers were mostly half-breeds, descended from Gaelic-speaking Scots from the Orkney Islands and Cree-speaking Amerindians, neither side having English as a first language.

Pronunciation. The Red River dialect is supposed to have lacked /l/ and /r/ as a result of the Cree's alleged difficulty with these two sounds. Other features of this dialect were (1) instability of /s/ and /sh/, as in *story* /**shtôr**-ē/, *smoked* /shmōkd/, and *sniffing* /**shnĭf**-ĭn/ and in *bush* /bo͞os/, *she's* /sēz/, and *sharp* /särp/; (2) /ts/ for /ch/, as in *church* /tsêrch/ and *chair* /tsâr/; (3) /dz/ for /j/, as in *just* /dzŭst/ and *jumped* /dzŭmpd/; (4) /är/ for /êr/, as in *burned* /bärnd/ and *nervous* /**när**-vəs/.

Grammar. The use of auxiliaries in this dialect was unusual in two respects: *am* was often used for *have*, and *will* was used before *can*, as in *I'm got to get home* and *It'll not can meet* (= 'It [a blouse, for example] is not able to meet [close]'); this latter feature is still found in some Scottish dialects. Also, an extra, appositional *it* was often found before a direct object, as in *I'm just slocked it the light* (= 'I have just doused the light').

Vocabulary. (1) The dialect made some use of Cree and Ojibwa words. The following list is a sampling of these words:

apeechequanee = 'upside down'
chimmuck = 'all of a sudden'
kaykatch = 'nearly'
keeyam = 'no matter, forget it'
neechimos = 'sweetheart'
neepinans = 'high-bush cranberry'
rogan = 'basket'

(2) Some words show the influence of the Scots. Among these are:

bannock = 'unsweetened oatmeal cake'
byre /bīr/ = 'cow stable, shed for cattle'
make tea = 'to prepare tea'
message = 'errand'
slock = 'to douse'
wife = 'any woman, married or not'

(3) Words such as the following show a little of the dialect's linguistic color:

belly = 'stomach'
calling = 'screaming'
coal oil = 'kerosene'
full race = 'at full tilt, at full speed'
long piece = 'a long distance'
on topside = 'on top of'
spell = 'a while'
upset = 'beside': *upset the hotel* = 'beside the hotel'

redundancy. See TAUTOLOGY AND PLEONASM.

refer. See ALLUDE, ALLUSION.

regional dialect. There are two major divisions of DIALECT: social and regional. A SOCIAL DIALECT is a language variety of a particular social group. A *regional dialect* is a language variety of a particular region of a country. Strictly speaking, these two types of dialects do not exist in isolation; the separation is a convenient fiction that makes it easier for linguists to study the continuum of language.

A *sociolinguist* is interested primarily in the social variables of dialect. A *linguistic geographer* is concerned mainly with the geographical distribution of a dialect. Neither can ignore the work of the other.

Linguistic geography, the older of the two scientific approaches to language, began in the late 19th century with the work of the German linguist Georg Wenker. Wenker sent a list of sentences to thousands of teachers throughout Germany and asked them to translate these items into their local speech. With this information he was able to tell which words were used where.

In France, Jules Gilliéron improved on Wenker's method by sending a fieldworker out with a questionnaire of 2,000 items requesting such specific information as the names of activities, objects, and social relationships. When an informant or native speaker answered a question, the fieldworker was thus able to get the folk and dialect terms with their pronunciations.

This interview method is still followed today, its thoroughness and accuracy being much improved by the use of the tape recorder. A project of this type has been under way in the United States since the early 1930s. Its findings are being published in a series known as *The Linguistic Atlas of the United States*. To date, the volumes covering New England and the upper Midwest, and parts of the volumes for the South Atlantic and Gulf states, have been published.

Dialect Boundaries. Once the field data are collected, linguists plot them on maps to discover the regionally distributed features and vocabulary. A line called an *isogloss* is drawn around the outer limits of each term's spread. As an example, the map on this page shows how the terms *mosquito hawk* and *rain frog* occur throughout the South.

By charting many features the linguist can compare various isoglosses on a given map. When several isoglosses approximately coincide, they reveal a dialect boundary that defines a dialect region. This method enables linguistic geographers to define the major and minor dialect areas of a country (see REGIONAL DIALECTS OF AMERICAN ENGLISH).

Origins of Regional Dialects. General dialect

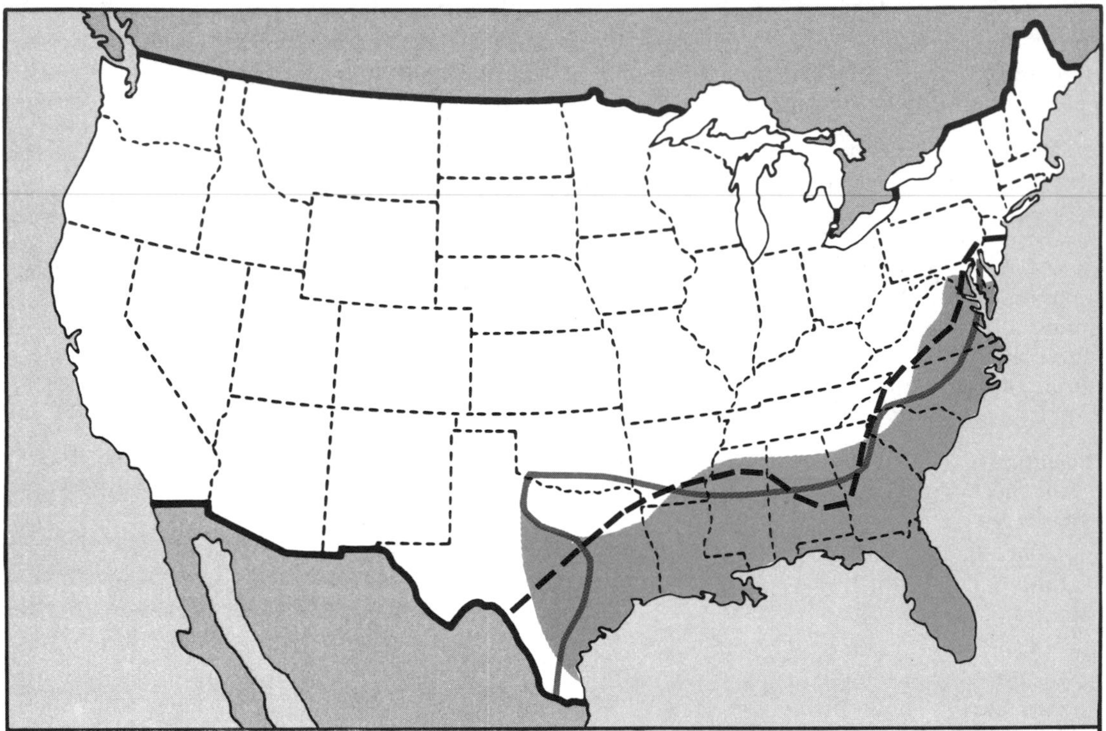

The tinted area represents the boundary of the Southern dialect. The two lines are isoglosses, based on data collected for the Dictionary of American Regional English. Mosquito hawk = *'dragonfly' is used primarily by people living south of* – – – – – – *and* rain frog = *'small frog, spring peeper' by people living south of* ———— . *Many other Southern features show similar but not identical patterns. By combining a large number of such distribution lines, dialectologists are able to define the boundaries of the major dialects of American English. For more information see* REGIONAL DIALECT. *See also* DICTIONARY OF AMERICAN REGIONAL ENGLISH; REGIONAL DIALECTS OF AMERICAN ENGLISH.

regions are the result of the interaction of various historical forces. The most important of these are (1) the speech of the original settlers; (2) the routes of migration and communication; (3) the restrictions imposed by physical barriers such as mountains and rivers; (4) long-established political boundaries; (5) economic patterns of an area; (6) the domination of an area by a cultural and political center; (7) later foreign immigration. When these forces are balanced with the social factors, a complete picture of language variation can be seen.

regional dialects of American English.

This entry consists of two main parts: the historical development of American dialects and present-day dialect divisions. The latter includes a breakdown of the major dialect areas with their subdialects.

Historical Development

Of the complex social, cultural, and economic forces that shaped the regional varieties or dialects of American English, the most important is the settlement pattern of the country. Three general settlement periods have influenced the development of the American language.

The Colonial Period: 1607–1790. From the immigration patterns of this period three major sections can be identified in the strip of land along the Atlantic coast from Maine to Georgia: New England, the Middle Atlantic colonies, and the South Atlantic colonies.

New England. The first settlers colonized the Massachusetts Bay area and from there moved into Connecticut, Rhode Island, and the Maine coastal area. Nearly all of these colonists were from England. To this day the New England dialect resembles in many ways the Southern British speech of its first settlers.

Middle Atlantic Colonies. New York was first settled by the Dutch, whose influence still survives in the Hudson Valley dialect. New Jersey, although almost wholly English, was a mixture of New England colonists, Quakers, and settlers from Yorkshire and London. Pennsylvania was a mixture of Quakers, Welsh, Scotch-Irish, and Germans, all of whom left their mark on the language. From about 1720 one of the most important groups of settlers to the developing American dialects migrated from Ulster (northern Ireland) to Pennsylvania. Many did not remain there long, however, but moved southwest down the mountain valleys and later pushed westward. The language of these vigorous Scotch-Irish frontiersmen was important in the development of the Midland dialect.

South Atlantic Colonies. The Tidewater region of Virginia was the focal point of this colonial area, attracting English settlers from a wide range of social classes and regions. The blended social and regional speech of this early miscellaneous group constituted the roots of the Virginia Piedmont dialect. From this area the colonists moved into North and South Carolina. (In the latter colony they were joined by French settlers.) These colonists established the early forms of the Coastal Southern dialect.

The Period of Expansion: 1790–1850. By 1790, 95 percent of the population of the United States still lived east of the Appalachian Mountains. After this date settlement of the regions west of the Appalachians was rapid. In general, migration took a westward direction to the Mississippi River. The country north of the Ohio River was settled mainly by people from western New England and Pennsylvania. Kentucky is an extension of Virginia, and Tennessee is an extension of western North Carolina; but both also have a strong Scotch-Irish representation from Pennsylvania. Alabama and Mississippi were settled largely from the Coastal Southern states. This general east-to-west migration is reflected in today's ribbonlike pattern of dialects east of the Rocky Mountains: the Northern, North Midland, South Midland, and Southern dialects.

The Modern Period: 1850–Present. This period is characterized by the rapid expansion of the Far West and a great tide of European immigration.

The Far West. With the discovery of gold in California in 1848 the Far West saw an

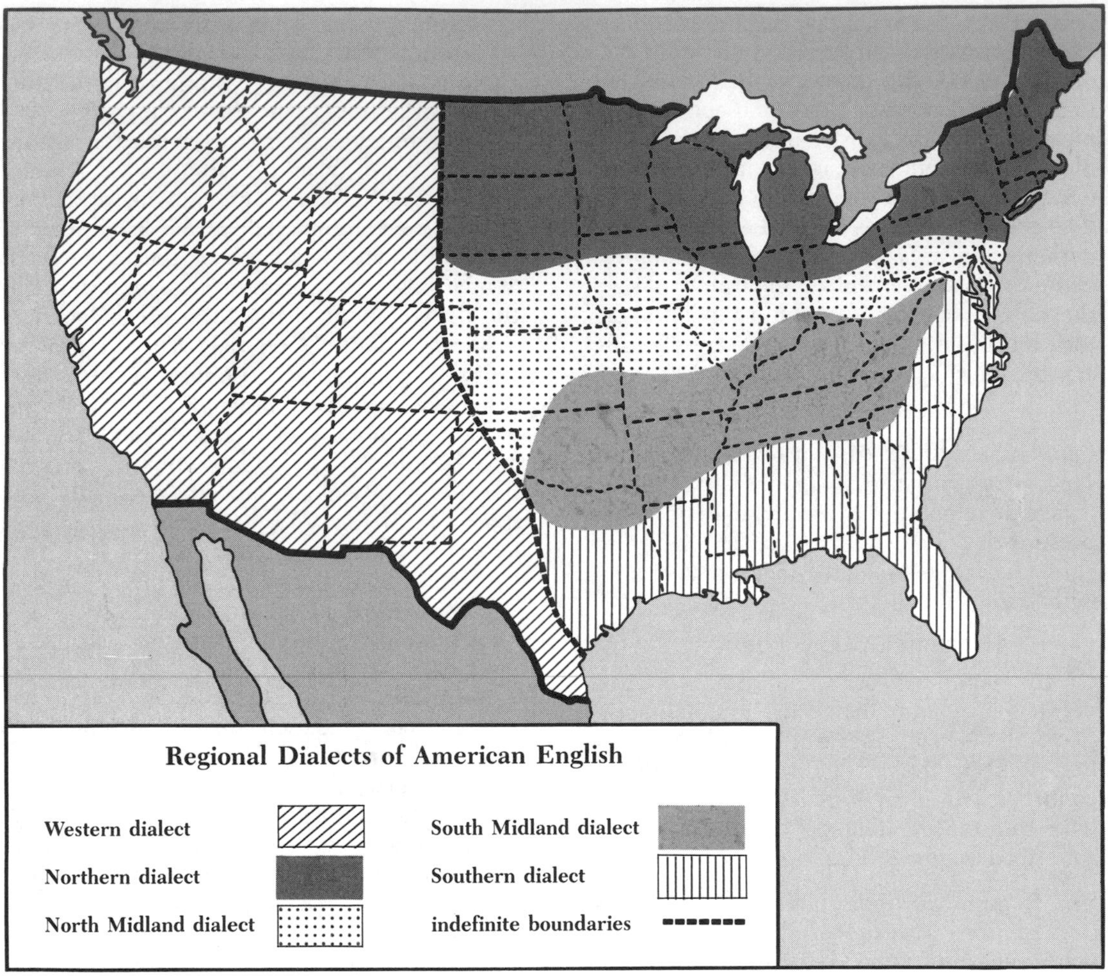

explosion of immigration from nearly every part of the country. Most of the settlers of this vast territory were from the North and the North Midlands speech area, though substantial numbers came from Kentucky, Tennessee, and especially Missouri. There were, however, relatively few settlers from the Coastal and Gulf Southern speech regions; this for the most part accounts for the generally Northern character of the Western dialect. Again, the predominantly Northern and Midland migration westward beyond the Rockies is reflected in the geographical pattern of today's General Northern dialect.

European Immigration. There were massive influxes of non-British immigrants to this country from the mid-19th century onward. Most notable of these were the (southern) Irish and German immigrations in the 1850s, the Scandinavian immigration in the 1870s, and the great southern European and Slavic immigrations after about 1890. This enormous surge of new peoples, however, has probably had a greater influence on American culture, especially urban culture, and the American language as a whole than it has on regional American dialect divisions.

Dialect Divisions Today

As much as we might wish it, dialects do not fall neatly into well-defined geographical regions. There is always overlapping and blurring of boundaries. This is especially true of a "young" language like American English. At best, dialect boundaries can only be approximated; but as soon as a line is chosen, it inevitably distorts the true picture. Dialects are fluids—blending, mixing, eddying.

American English can be divided into two very broad sections: the General Northern and General Southern dialects (see the maps on pages 272 and 274). This division expresses cultural and economic regionality as well as linguistic regionality. Though on the maps the dividing line between the two meanders distinctly westward through West Virginia, Ohio, and on into Kansas, then due south through Oklahoma and Texas, in reality the line is quite vague. We can think of these two very general dialects as hot and cold water; where they meet they mix, creating warm water—the Midland dialect.

This same metaphor can be applied to all adjoining dialects and subdialects. With this qualification in mind, it is possible to divide the entire country into a mosaic of dialect regions. Most of the larger divisions are plotted on the map on page 574. Each of the following dialects has a separate entry devoted to it and is accompanied by a map. This list is arranged to show the major dialect areas with their subdialects.

GENERAL NORTHERN
- NORTHERN
  - HUDSON VALLEY
  - INLAND NORTHERN
  - NEW ENGLAND
  - NEW YORK CITY
- NORTH MIDLAND
- WESTERN
  - PACIFIC NORTHWEST
  - PACIFIC SOUTHWEST
  - ROCKY MOUNTAIN
  - SOUTHWESTERN

GENERAL SOUTHERN
- SOUTHERN
  - VIRGINIA PIEDMONT
  - COASTAL SOUTHERN
  - GULF SOUTHERN
- SOUTH MIDLAND

There is also a separate entry on the MIDLAND DIALECT.

For further details about U.S. dialects and language consult the following entries:

ALASKAN ENGLISH
AMERICAN ENGLISH
BLACK ENGLISH
BONAC
BOONTLING
BOSTON URBAN DIALECT
CHICAGO URBAN DIALECT
DICTIONARY OF AMERICAN REGIONAL ENGLISH
ELIZABETHAN ENGLISH IN AMERICA
GULLAH
HAWAIIAN ENGLISH
PENNSYLVANIA GERMAN-ENGLISH
SAN FRANCISCO URBAN DIALECT

renege. Despite the spelling, the usual pronunciation is **/rĭ-nĭg/** or **/rĭ-nĕg/**, sometimes **/rĭ-nēg/**. The meaning is 'to deny, renounce, break one's word, back out of an agreement.' It is often used with *on*.

> Of course, nations don't literally renege on their debts; they either postpone them indefinitely by borrowing from Peter to pay Paul, or else pay them off in depreciated currency.
> —Roger W. Bridwell, *Book Digest*

> Stalin had plainly reneged on the Yalta Agreements and was aggressively pushing his ambitions in much the way Hitler had done a decade before.
> —William Colby, *Honorable Men: My Life in the CIA*

> Our priority is how the music is played; we would never renege on it for the sake of commercialism.
> —Paddy Moloney (quoted), *Rolling Stone*

In the last quotation above the use of "renege" may at first sight appear strained; but its reference is to "priority" in the sense 'personal commitment,' and the use is in fact quite legitimate.

resin, rosin. *Resin* is the wider and more general term. Resins are substances exuded by trees, typically yellow or brown and translucent, sticky when soft and shiny and brittle when hard. There are many different kinds. They are used in the manufacture of varnish and adhesives and in a wide range of other industrial applications. The word *resin* is now also applied to synthetic substances, such as epoxy, that are somewhat similar to natural resins. *Rosin* is itself one type of resin, obtained from pine tree resin by removing the turpentine. Chemical derivatives of it are used as waterproof sealants with fiberglass coatings and for rubbing on violin bows to give suitable friction. The word *rosin* is a medieval variant of the word *resin.*

reverend. By origin this title for a minister of religion is an adjective meaning 'worthy of much respect.' In the more conservative churches, such as the Protestant Episcopal church, the only correct forms are *the Reverend John Smith* or *the Reverend Mr.* (or *Dr.*) *Smith.* The forms *the Reverend Smith* and *Reverend Smith* are considered incorrect, and it is also considered wrong to address a minister as *Reverend* or to use *Reverend* as an independent noun. In other churches, however, such as many of the Southern Baptist and independent churches, *Reverend* is used freely in all these ways, including as a polite form of address (*Good morning, Reverend*) and as a noun (*I saw the Reverend this morning*).

◊ ***Recommendation.*** Among the churches, as among other divisions of society, there is no single standard of correctness. Usage varies; if in doubt, consult your clergyman.

rhetoric. See FALLACY; FIGURES OF SPEECH.

riding. In Canadian usage a *riding* is an electoral district.

> He intends to leave provincial politics and seek the nomination for the federal riding of Halifax. —*Winnipeg Tribune*

In England *riding* is an archaic Norse term peculiar to the three ancient divisions of the large county of Yorkshire, the *North Riding,* the *East Riding,* and the *West Riding.* The word was originally *thriding,* from Old Norse *thrithjungr* = 'third part.' It is recorded in the Domesday Book and presumably goes back to the independent Norse principality of York founded in the 9th century A.D.

Colonial Yorkshiremen occasionally created new ridings in various parts of the world—including Long Island, New York (where, in the 17th century, Suffolk and Nassau counties were East Riding and West Riding, respectively). The original ridings of Yorkshire were abolished by the British government in the 1970s, but the term continues in official use in Canada and in a similar use in New Zealand. Thus, an archaic word often survives only at a great distance from its place of origin.

right has long been in standard use as an adverb in many senses, including (1) 'directly, straight': *keep right on;* (2) 'immediately, right away': *I'll be right down;* (3) 'entirely, absolutely': *took it right off;* (4) 'according to right, rightly': *do it right.*

In the sense 'very much, very' it is now mostly archaic or dialectal. This sense has been preserved in the British title *the Right Honourable* (given to members of the Privy Council) and in the church title *the Right Reverend* (given to Anglican and Episcopal bishops and to some Roman Catholic prelates). In everyday speech *right* = 'very' is still widely used, especially by Southerners, but some others consider this nonstandard.

> And that was a right interesting experience.
> —Jody Powell (quoted), *Boston Globe*

> It was "right nice" of Mayor Beame, one oilman said, to offer New York City as an onshore base of operations. . . .
> —*New York Times*

◊ ***Recommendation.*** In the speech of anyone to whom it comes naturally, *right* = 'very' is correct and respectable. It is not appropriate in formal standard writing.

rigmarole, rigamarole. The story behind this excellent word is itself—the word is inescapable—an absolute rigamarole. A peculiar game of chance was played in medieval Europe, with a rolled-up scroll on which various slogans or lots were written, each with a string attached to it. Each player chose a string and received the indicated lot; the game was used for serious gambling, to the extent that it was forbidden by law under penalty of a fine. It was called *Ragman*, apparently after *Rageman* or *Ragman*, the (French) name of a character who featured in one of the lots, and the scroll was called the *ragman's*, or *ragman, roll*. Subsequently, *ragman roll* became a term for any document with seals hanging down on strips of parchment, hence also for various particular legal documents, and generally for a long list or catalogue. Eventually, in the 18th century, the expression surfaced in the altered form *rigmarole*, meaning 'long rambling story, a lot of meaningless talk,' later also 'sequence of pointless activities.' The form *rigamarole* is probably the preferred form in American English nowadays. (The first example quoted below dates from the 19th century.)

> What's the good of studying Latin and Greek, and all that rigmarole?
> —Horatio Alger, *Risen From the Ranks*

> The blunt fact is that a foreign government on American shores is preying on American citizens. And notwithstanding the niceties of diplomatic immunity and extraterritoriality and rigamarole, the response should be equally blunt.
> —editorial, *New York Times*

> . . . during spring training the management said, "We're going to be a family. Nobody's going anywhere, 'cause that's the best way to play." Lee said, "They give you all this rigamarole and then they traded Carbo to Cleveland."
> —Sparky Lyle, *The Bronx Zoo*

> My few visitors had to go through a security rigamarole—like gun molls visiting their husbands at Sing Sing.
> —Sam Houston Johnson, *My Brother Lyndon*

rile. See ROIL, RILE.

rise, raise. ***Standard Usage.*** *Rise* is an intransitive verb; *raise* is transitive. *Rise* means 'to get up, go upward, increase'; *raise* means 'to cause (something or someone) to rise.' The past tense of *rise* is *rose*, and its past participle is *risen*. The past tense and past participle of *raise* are both *raised*.

Dialect Usages. In widespread American dialects, including General Northern and South Midland, *raise* is often used intransitively: *The dough raised quickly in the warm room.* This usage is not dying out but is in fact becoming commoner in informal speech even among well-educated speakers:

> I said, "Jimmy, one of these days you're just going to have to raise up on your hind legs and tell 'em you're fixin' to run." . . . and I believe it wasn't long after that that he did. Just raised up and did it.
> —Charles Kirbo (quoted), *New York Times Magazine*

There are several variant inflections. In the Southern dialect among older, less-educated speakers, *rose* is often used as the past participle of *rise: When the dough had rose enough, she put it in the oven.*

Rised as the past tense and past participle of *rise* is common throughout the country among older working-class speakers: *He rised before dawn.*

Riz is an old-fashioned form of the past tense and past participle of *rise* and is still occasionally used in the General Southern dialect by older speakers. It is also heard in rural New England, along with the terms *riz bread, riz dough*, and *riz biscuit.*

> They'll bring him back all right, but don't you think she'd be afeared 'ut he might be took up in the New Jerusalem when it riz ag'in?
> —William Dean Howells, *The Leatherwood God* (1916)

> First we kneeled down and then the Pope come in an' I riz up an' I said, "Pope . . . your time is nigh."
> —Carl Carmer, *Stars Fell on Alabama* (1934)

> The entire Jennings family joined in the feast of cold chicken, jelly, pickles, "riz" biscuits, dried beef, apple pie, cake, and cheese.
>
> —Hamlin Garland, *Boy Life on the Prairie* (1899)

Raise, Rear. The older term for 'to bring up (children)' is *rear*, and this is still standard. In American usage *raise* is also standard in this sense (it is no longer standard in British).

Self-rising, Self-raising. Referring to commercial preparations of flour to which a fermenting agent has been added, *self-rising* is the Standard American term, *self-raising* the Standard British. The former is understood as intransitive, 'rising by itself,' the latter as transitive, 'raising itself, causing itself to rise.'

The Nouns. *Rise* is the general noun meaning 'something that rises, upward movement, increase, piece of rising ground, etc.' But in Standard American usage *raise* is the noun used for 'an increased bet in poker' and for 'an increase in wages or salary.' In British *rise* is used for the latter.

◇ ***Recommendation.*** In case there is any doubt, we advise that the intransitive use of *raise*—as in *The dough is raising*—belongs to dialect (though perfectly respectable dialect). In standard usage *raise* is only transitive: *Please raise the window shade*. The other variant usages covered above are interesting but present no problems.

r-lessness, intrusive *r*. The letter *r* symbolizes in the European languages at least six different kinds of pronunciations, depending on the way you analyze the sound. American English has basically one /r/ sound, which is either *voiced* (pronounced with the vocal cords vibrating), as in *dread, red,* and *arrow*, or *unvoiced*, as in *prim* and *creep*. Unlike British English and its Northern dialects, American English has no *trill*, or rolled /r/.

One of the most noticeable features of several American regional and social dialects is the dropping of the /r/ sound in words that historically have it (see REGIONAL DIALECT; SOCIAL DIALECT). This occurs only with *postvocalic* r; that is, with an *r* that follows a vowel. For example, in those dialects both /r/'s in *farmer* are usually dropped, /**fä**-mə/, and the second one in *rare* is omitted, /rāə/. When postvocalic *r* is dropped at the end of a word, it is usually replaced by /ə/: *door* /dōə/, *care* /kāə/.

The loss of postvocalic *r* in a stressed syllable first occurred about 1300 in some but not all British dialects. Today, *r* loss is a feature of Standard British English, or Received pronunciation. In America *r*-lessness is a dialect feature and is characteristic only of the speech of eastern New England, New York City, the South, and certain social dialects.

Social Dialect* R*-lessness. Whether /r/ is pronounced or dropped depends in part on the social class, sex, and ethnic background of the speaker and in part on the prestige attached to the pronunciation. In England accents without postvocalic *r* have more prestige than accents with it. In New York City just the reverse is true. Dropping of postvocalic *r* has lower status and is a feature of the working-class dialect (see NEW YORK CITY DIALECT).

R loss is also a distinctive feature of BLACK ENGLISH. But the frequency with which a given black speaker pronounces /r/ depends on such social factors as class and sex. In a study of black speech in Detroit, researchers found that upper-middle-class speakers pronounced postvocalic *r* twice as often as upper-working-class speakers and that the women of both classes used postvocalic *r* one and a half to two times more often than the men of the same classes.

In working-class black speech *intervocalic* r—the *r* that comes between vowels—is often lost: *Carol* /**kĕ**-əl/, *Paris* /**pĕ**-əs/. Also among these speakers, /r/ is occasionally dropped after initial consonants: *from* /fŭm/, *protect* /pə-**tĕkt**/.

***Regional Dialect* R*-lessness and Intrusive* R.** Northern *r*-lessness (eastern New England, New York City) differs from Southern in two important ways. Like Standard British English, the Northern *r*-less areas have *linking* r.

This only occurs under one condition. When a word ending in *-r* precedes a word beginning with a vowel, the *r*—the linking *r* is preserved. Thus, *your boat* is pronounced /yōə bōt/, but *your aunt* is pronounced /yōər änt, ănt/. In the South, however, *your* in both cases is usually pronounced without the /r/.

Another kind of linking *r* common to both Standard British and the Northern *r*-less areas is *intrusive* r—an additional /r/ sound inserted at the end of a word that normally has no final *-r*. This occurs only when a word ending in a vowel sound is followed by a word beginning with a vowel sound. For example, *law and order* /lôr ənd **ôd**-ə/; *ma and pa* /mär ən pä/; *Martha and I* /**mä**-thər ənd ī/. Again, the South does not usually have intrusive *r*. Southern *r*-lessness, then, is a unique innovation in the English language.

Another kind of intrusive *r* occurs in the South Midland dialect among old and rural speakers. This is the /ər/ sound added to the ends of words that have the final vowel sound /ō/. Thus, *hollow, meadow,* and *fellow* are pronounced /**hŏl**-ər/, /**mĕd**-ər/, and /**fĕl**-ər/.

Finally, in the Midland dialect a *medial intrusive* r can often be heard in the word *wash*. Thus, *wash* and *Washington* are pronounced, respectively, /wärsh/ and /**wärsh**-ĭng-tən/. Occasionally *mush* and *mushroom* also follow this pattern: /mêrsh/, /**mêrsh**-ro͞om/.

Rocky Mountain dialect. A subdivision of the WESTERN DIALECT, Rocky Mountain dialect can be heard in Utah, Colorado, Wyoming, eastern Nevada, eastern Idaho, and Montana. To date, the details of the speech of this area are not well analyzed. In general, based on the settlement patterns, Rocky Mountain is an extension of the Northern and North Midland dialects. Following the primary settlement of this territory, after about 1890, a blending of vocabularies took place, largely as the result of the reversed movement of migration. During the development of the West, population movement proceeded generally nonstop from the Midwest to the Far West. But around the turn of the century, large numbers of Pacific coast resi-

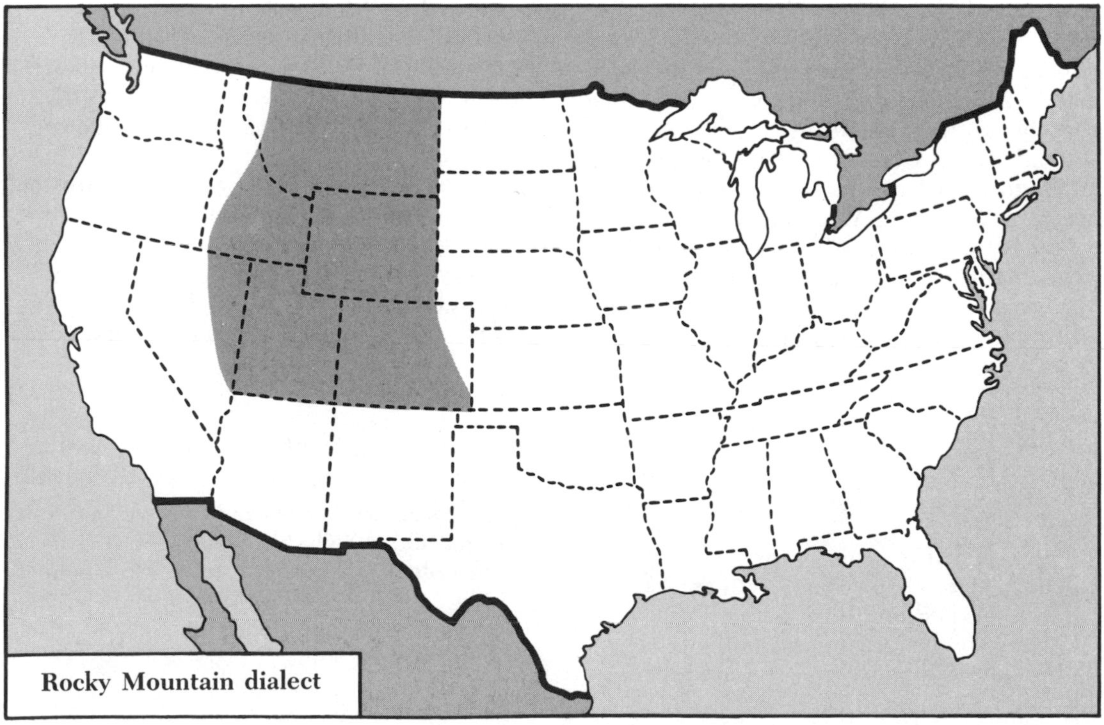

dents reversed the tide and began to move inland, changing and complicating the speech patterns of the region.

Vocabulary. (1) *Mormon influence.* Besides the frontier and range life style, which profoundly influenced the Western dialect as a whole, the Mormons and their culture have had a strong impact on this region, particularly in Utah, eastern Nevada, southern Idaho, and southwestern Wyoming. Settling in the 1850s and 1860s, the Mormons, or Latter-day Saints, brought with them the specialized vocabulary of their church. These are some of the more widely known terms:

apostatize = 'to voluntarily leave the Mormon church'
bishop = 'the religious leader of a ward'
Gentile = 'a non-Mormon, outsider'
stake = 'unit made up of several wards'
ward = 'the basic unit of church and social organization'
ward *or* **church house** = 'building for religious services'
ward teacher = 'church member who visits each home of a ward to ask after the welfare of the family and give a brief scriptural lesson'

(2) Wyoming, one of the most sparsely populated states in the country, was settled largely by immigrants from the Northeast and later from Utah. However, a large group of English coal miners settled in the southwestern corner of Wyoming in the 1880s. Because this group was relatively isolated, its speech remained distinct and has formed a dialect relic area. Some of the colorful words of this now fading language are:

apanchion, apansion = 'small pan used to wash dishes'
chine = 'choice cut of pork'
clarry, clary = 'dressing for bread, such as butter, jam, or honey'
clen = 'to clean'
dag = 'small portion'
dout (**a fire**) = 'to douse, extinguish'
hillins = 'bedding, bed clothing'
kittern = 'cornerwise, across the corner of a room': *She placed the piano kittern.*
laden = 'dipper, cup, spoon, ladle'
marb = 'to growl or grumble'
mauey, mowy = '(of someone's speech) rambling, mumbling, evasive'
mugs (used especially by children) = 'to choose': *I mugs first shot.*
piggle at = 'to pull or tug nervously': *The baby kept piggling at my ear.*
sempt, semt = 'past tense of *seem*'
siden (**a table** *or* **room**) = 'to straighten up or tidy'
slithery = 'sloppy, careless'
slop = 'any loose work coat or jacket'
spit = 'image, likeness': *He's the spit of his father.*
teem, past tense **tempt** = 'to pour from one vessel into another': *He tempt the milk into the trough.*
tempid = 'tepid, lukewarm'
thoud, thould = 'small camp stove'
tret = 'past tense of *treat*': *He tret me fine.*
wed = 'past tense of *weed*': *I wed three rows of turnips this morning.*

(3) Some of the more generally known words of the Rocky Mountain dialect are:

barrow pit = 'roadside ditch'
bushed = 'tired, exhausted'
cache = 'hiding place'
cut a shine = 'to perform an antic thought clever'
heintz (rare) = 'friend' (from Shoshone)
kick off = 'to die'
pothole = 'small land basin or depression'
pull a face = 'to grimace'
silk = 'barbed wire'
skate = 'worthless horse'
slough school /slŭf/ = 'to play *hooky'
squaw man = 'white man married to an Indian'
up the country = 'in the vicinity'

(4) Terms shared with the Upper Midwestern dialect:

American fries = 'hashed brown potatoes'
bismarck = 'jelly-filled *doughnut'
box-elder bug = 'red and black sap-sucking bug'
canyon = 'steep-sided valley' See SPANISH WORDS.

*Appears as separate entry

catch-rope, throw rope = 'long rope used in roping horses and cattle, lariat'
corral = 'fenced-in area for horses' See SPANISH WORDS.
cowhand, cowpoke = 'ranch employee, cowboy'
grazing land = 'pasture'
gulch = 'small valley with steep slopes'
hay bunch = 'small pile of hay in a field, haycock'
hay flats *or* **land** = 'low-lying grassland, meadow'
soogan (old-fashioned) = 'saddle roll, wool-filled comforter'
thicket = 'small clump of trees'

roil, rile. The old verb *roil,* of unknown origin, basically means 'to stir up (water), make cloudy with sediment':

> I had dug out the spring and made a well of clear gray water, where I could dip up a pailful without roiling it. . . .
> —Henry David Thoreau, *Walden*

> Unlike the common [carp], the grass carp does not roil the waters.
> —Wesley Marx, *Smithsonian*

It may also be intransitive, meaning 'to be stirred up':

> Broken power lines in Hilo flicked lethal shocks into the roiling waters.
> —Leonard Bickel, *Reader's Digest*

Hence the adjective *roily:*

> The waves came in roily or silken, gray or cobalt or silver.
> —Joan Mills, *Reader's Digest*

Roil is also used in the extended sense 'to stir up (persons or personal feelings), irritate, exacerbate, annoy':

> . . . what Allnutt felt more keenly still was Rose's presence, and her manner of ignoring him. That roiled him inexpressibly.
> —C. S. Forester, *The African Queen*

> An equally explosive issue that is certain to roil relations between the two nations is the support that Mexico fears [President] Reagan intends to give to military dictatorships in Central America.
> —*U.S. News & World Report*

The variant form *rile,* originally a dialectal pronunciation, is also well established in the meanings 'to irritate, exacerbate, annoy,' although it is regarded by some as undesirable or informal: *Putting up the screens always gets Uncle Joe riled.*

◇ ***Recommendation.*** Both *roil* and *rile* are correct and standard in American English.

Roman numerals. Throughout classical antiquity there were two prevailing systems of number writing—one based on the Roman and the other on the Greek alphabet—in use in the western and eastern halves, respectively, of the Roman Empire. The system we use today, Arabic numerals (they are actually from India, and medieval Arabs called them Hindu numerals), did not come into general use in the West until the late Middle Ages. To the present time we retain Roman numerals for such specialized purposes as dates on monuments, chapter and section headings in lengthy works, subdivisions in outlines or long enumerations, and designations of persons or entities whose names recur serially (*Louis XIV, Trac II*).

The table on the following page sets forth the Roman numerals with their Arabic equivalents. When a letter representing a lower numerical value precedes a letter of higher value, it subtracts from the latter's value; when a letter representing a lower value follows one of higher value, it adds to it; and a bar over a letter multiplies the value of the letter by 1,000. Lower-case numbers (*v, vi, xii, xlii,* etc.) are customary for pagination, as in the front part of this book. You will notice that in older books the final *i* in such numbers is often written *j* (*vij, xlij,* etc.).

Roman numerals actually go back to a system predating the existence of the Latin alphabet, and the correspondence between the shapes of the numerals and certain Latin letters is accidental. For example, the V that represents 5 was not a V originally but half of X, or 10. Likewise, M, or 1,000, was not M for *mille* (= 'one thousand') but in fact a graphic simplification of the sign CIↃ, which in turn arose from a more ancient Tuscan numeral of roughly the same shape.

rout, route. There are several unrelated words spelled *rout.* The two most important are the noun meaning (1) 'total defeat' (2) 'riot' (3) 'rabble' and the verb (a variant of *root*) meaning 'to dig.' The word *route* = 'highway, course, itinerary' is pronounced /rōōt/ or /rout/. Both are correct; but /rōōt/ is perhaps preferable at least in the general senses, while /rout/ is more widely used of newspaper and other delivery courses and /rout/ is standard in the military for *route march, route step,* etc. The phrase *en route,* pronounced /än **rōōt**/, means 'on or along the way'; it is sometimes anglicized to *on route,* with the same pronunciation. Finally, *route* is often spelled *rout,* but we recommend keeping it as *route.*

rub. In Shakespeare's day, bowls (lawn bowling) was popular at every level of society, and metaphors from the game abound in the literature of the period. The noun *rub* is one of them. In bowls a rub was something that stopped or deflected a running bowl (the usage is from the verb *rub* in the sense 'to chafe, irritate, hinder'). The rule was that the player had to accept the rub, without compensation. Thus, *rub* came to be used figuratively to mean 'obstacle, difficulty, snag,' any of the minor but inevitable problems of life. Hamlet's "Ay, there's the rub" is the most famous occurrence of this sense. Here is another instance:

> Surely there are in every man's life certain rubs, doublings and wrenches which pass awhile under the effects of chance, but at the last well examined prove the mere hand of God.
>
> —Thomas Browne, *Religio Medici* (1643)

Roman Numerals

Arabic	Roman	Arabic	Roman
1	I	40	XL
2	II	50	L
3	III	60	LX
4	IV *or* IIII	70	LXX
5	V	80	LXXX
6	VI	90	XC
7	VII	100	C
8	VIII	200	CC
9	IX	300	CCC
10	X	400	CCCC
11	XI	500	D (*in old books* IↃ)
12	XII	600	DC
13	XIII	700	DCC
14	XIV	800	DCCC
15	XV	900	DCCCC *or* CM
16	XVI	1,000	M (*in old books* CIↃ)
17	XVII	1,995	MCMXCV
18	XVIII	2,000	MM
19	XIX	2,001	MMI
20	XX	4,000	M$\overline{V}$
30	XXX	5,000	$\overline{V}$

Rub in Hamlet's sense is still in use:

> In four years, Joe Schneider has adopted and resettled no fewer than 3,000 dogs. The rub is that, in the matter of dogs, people are more willing to give than to receive.
> —*Daily Hampshire Gazette*

The word has also happened to survive in golf, which in its early days in Scotland was played, like bowls, on rough common ground by the seaside (*links*). The golfers adopted *rub* and defined it as 'any accident, good or bad, that happens to a ball in play,' and they also adopted the rule that the player must accept it without compensation. There were no "winter rules" and "preferred lies" in those days; the fundamental rule was, "Play it where it lies." The full term *rub of the green*, still enshrined in the rules of golf, was first recorded in 1812. Golfers should note that *green* here is used in the Scottish sense of the whole golf course, not the putting green; a *rub of the green* is, literally, an accident of the course. (See also GOLF TERMS.)

run the gamut, run the gauntlet. These expressions are often confused. See GAMUT; GAUNTLET, RUN THE.

Russian words. Russian, first written down in the 11th century, is one of the Slavic languages. It is written in the Cyrillic alphabet. Russian words first came into English in the reign of Elizabeth I, through trading contacts. No basic words have been contributed, only words for things that are specifically or originally Russian (except *intelligentsia, mammoth, parka,* and *sable*). Some of these words were originally borrowed into Russian from Turkic or Tatar (Mongolian) peoples.

(1) Words predominantly Russian:

balalaika /băl-ə-**lī**-kə/ = 'guitarlike instrument with three strings and a triangular body': from Russian *balalaika*

beluga /bə-**lo͞o**-gə/ = 'sturgeon of the Black and Caspian seas, the source of the most expensive caviar': from Russian *byeluga* = 'white (animal)'

blini /**blē**-nē/ = 'buckwheat pancakes, served with caviar or sour cream': from Russian *blini,* plural of *blin* = 'pancake'

borsch /**bôrsh**/, **borscht, borsht** /**bôrsht**/ = 'beet soup': from Russian *borshch* = 'parsnip' (the original ingredient)

borzoi /**bôr**-zoi/ = 'slender hunting dog with a silken white coat': from Russian *borzoi* = 'swift'

boyar /bō-**yär**/ = 'nobleman of medieval Russia': from Russian *boyarin* = 'lord,' ultimately from Turkic

Cossack = 'one of a people of Turkic origin living in south Russia, famous as cavalrymen': from Russian *Kozak, Kazak,* from Turkic *kuzzāk* = 'nomad, freebooter'

***czar, tsar** /**zär**/ = 'Russian emperor': from Polish *czar* and Russian *tsar,* both from Old Russian *tsisari,* from Gothic *kaisar,* from Latin *caesar* = 'emperor,' originally the family name of the first dynasty of Roman emperors

dacha /**dä**-chə/ = 'country house, vacation home': from Russian *dacha,* literally 'land grant, estate given by a feudal lord'

droshky = 'open horse-drawn carriage': from Russian *drozhki*

***intelligentsia** = 'intellectuals collectively': from Russian *intelligentsiya,* from Polish *inteligencja,* from Latin *intelligentia* = 'intelligence'

kopeck /**kō**-pĕk/ = 'coin worth one one-hundredth of a ruble': from Russian *kopeika*

kremlin = 'fortress commanding a city, citadel,' especially 'the citadel of Moscow,' hence, as *the Kremlin,* 'the Russian or Soviet government': from Russian *kreml'* = 'fortress,' originally a Tatar word

mammoth = (1) 'extinct elephant found preserved in frozen earth in Russia,' hence (2) 'anything very large': from Russian *mammot',* from Yakut *mamma* = 'earth,' since it was at first supposed that the mammoth was an underground burrowing animal

parka = 'hooded jacket': from Russian

*Appears as separate entry

parka = 'parka, skin, pelt,' ultimately from a Samoyed word for 'animal skin'

ruble, rouble = 'the basic monetary unit of Russia and the Soviet Union': from Russian *rubl,* originally 'silver bar'

sable = (1) 'the northern marten, a small animal of the Arctic and sub-Arctic, with dark-brown fur used for clothing and paintbrushes' (2) 'black': from Old French *sable,* from Medieval Latin *sabelum,* from Russian *sobol* (or another related Slavic word)

samovar /săm-ə-vär/ = 'tea urn': from Russian *samovar* = 'self-boiler'

steppe /stĕp/ = 'grassland plain': from Russian *step*

ukase /yōō-kās, yōō-**kās**/ = (1) 'law proclaimed by the imperial government, royal decree' (2) 'any command or decree issued by mere authority, especially in an imperious manner': from Russian *ukaz* = 'decree'

vodka = 'clear alcoholic liquor distilled from grain mash': from Russian *vodka* = 'little water,' originally a translation of Latin *aqua vitae* (see WHISKEY).

(2) Words, mostly political, that have been borrowed since the Revolution of 1917 or that are associated with the revolutionary movement:

* **apparatchik** = 'political worker, member of the Communist party machine'

Bolshevik /**bōl**-shə-vĭk, **bŏl**-/ = 'original member of the Russian Communist party, in particular one who took part in the Revolution of 1917': from Russian *Bol'shevik* = 'majority-person,' originally one of the left-wing majority that followed Lenin in 1903

commissar = 'high official of the Communist party responsible for political discipline': from Russian *komissar* = 'commissioner'

cosmonaut = 'astronaut': from Russian *kosmonavt,* literally 'cosmos-sailor'

politburo /pə-**lĭt**-byŏŏr-ō, **pŏl**-ĭt-/ = 'ruling political committee of a Communist party': from Russian *Politburo,* shortened from *politicheskoe buro* = 'political bureau or office'

* **soviet** /sō-vē-ĕt, -ĭt/ = 'council, committee'

sputnik /**spŏŏt**-nĭk, **spŭt**-/ = (1) capital *S* 'the first artificial earth satellite, launched by the Soviet Union on October 4, 1957' (2) 'any of the first generation of Soviet earth satellites': from Russian *sputnik zemlyi* = 'fellow traveler of the earth'

Stakhanovite /stə-**kä**-nə-vīt/ = (1) 'Soviet worker who voluntarily exceeds production quotas' (2) 'workaholic': after Aleksei *Stakhanov* (born 1905), a Russian miner who in the 1930s pioneered an ethic of spontaneous overproduction

*Appears as separate entry

S

said. The participial adjective *said* = 'previously mentioned' is a legalism. It is occasionally used for mildly humorous effect: *Pour a substantial measure of brandy. Take the said brandy in the right hand and raise it smartly to the lips.*

same. (*The*) *same* is used in legalistic and commercial documents as an absolute pronoun meaning 'the thing or person previously mentioned': *When he shall have performed this service, he shall receive compensation for the same. We stock a full line of writing paper with matching envelopes for same.* This is occasionally found in ordinary usage, usually with jocular intent.

sanctimony, sanctimonious. *Sanctimony* once meant 'real holiness or saintliness'; now it means only 'affected holiness, hypocrisy':

> Meanwhile Mr. Nixon's critics, always willing to believe the worst about him, took the curdling sanctimony of his speech as a personal challenge to uproot any scintilla of evidence linking the President to Watergate. . . .
> —William F. Buckley, Jr., *Execution Eve*

> In the face of the sanctimony that greeted my May 22 statement, I decided that I wanted all the wiretaps of previous administrations revealed.
> —Richard Nixon, *R.N.*

The adjective *sanctimonious* likewise means 'affecting holiness, hypocritical':

> How can a business executive who cheats on his expense account to buy himself a hundred-dollar call girl get so sanctimonious about Adam Clayton Powell?
> —Sam Houston Johnson, *My Brother Lyndon*

> . . . the church . . . too often has been content to mouth pious irrelevancies and sanctimonious trivialities.
> —Martin Luther King, Jr., *Strength to Love*

sanction originates as a term in church law, meaning 'the action of making something sacred or inviolable, an official decree.' In this legal sense, a *sanction* generally carries both rewards for obeying it and penalties for disobeying it. The same applies to *moral sanctions,* the practical motives that tend to enforce moral laws of conduct.

> . . . an upbringing in many ways typical of the youth of Western societies in the 1930s—rootless because the old orders of society and the old sanctions of religion had broken down . . .
> —Monica Furlong, *Merton: A Biography*

In general current use, the noun *sanction* has two contrasting senses; first, 'official, or quasi-official, approval or permission':

> Senn was not satisfied with this outcome, and he has been fighting ever since to win some kind of official sanction.
> —Marvin Stone, *U.S. News & World Report*

Second, *sanction* can mean 'official, or quasi-official, disapproval or punishment':

> This is not to say that rewards were never dispensed to faithful Congressmen, nor that sanctions were never imposed on those who opposed the administration's programs.
> —Doris Kearns, *Lyndon Johnson and the American Dream*

This sense is used especially of economic embargoes imposed by a group of nations to coerce or punish a nation that is following some disapproved policy:

> Once when Vwarda's representative at the United Nations was addressing the Security Council and asking for sanctions against South Africa . . .
> —James A. Michener, *The Covenant*

As a verb, however, *sanction* has only the positive sense, 'to approve, either morally or officially':

> He could not believe that there was any legal basis for such an action or indeed that English law sanctioned the owning of slaves in England at all, and it was on this basis that he set about bringing a challenge to slavery in the courts.
> —Peter Forbath, *The River Congo*

> A weary world, pleading desperately for peace, has often found the church morally sanctioning war.
> —Martin Luther King, Jr., *Strength to Love*

San Francisco urban dialect. San Francisco speech is essentially an urbanized form of the NORTHERN and NORTH MIDLAND dialects with a few variations. Just as with all dialects, the settlement patterns of San Francisco have to a great extent determined its speech patterns. The city's settlement was quite different from that of California as a whole. In the first half of the 20th century, most of the many migrants to California from Missouri, Kentucky, Arkansas, Oklahoma, and Texas settled in the southern and rural areas of the state; very few settled in San Francisco. As a result, San Francisco speech has virtually none of the Southern and South Midland dialect features that tint the rest of California's language.

Out-of-staters and foreigners have always far outnumbered persons born in San Francisco. The earliest influx of settlers into the city after the 1849 gold rush was primarily from the coastal Northeast, especially New England, New York, and New Jersey. In 1870, 34 percent of the interstate migrants were from New York, especially New York City. Hints of their dialect survive today among San Francisco's older and less educated speakers. Most notably, these speakers tend to drop their /r/'s.

The next large wave of migrants came from the Midwest, bringing with them the western or inland variety of the Northern and North Midland dialects. In 1940 more than 40 percent of the interstate migrants to the city were from the north-central states, especially the Great Lakes area. Most of the city's residents, the younger, educated middle class, speak this variety of American English (see UPPER MIDWESTERN and INLAND NORTHERN dialects).

Like most major cities, San Francisco has a large foreign population. The early immigrants were predominantly Irish and German. There were also significant numbers of English, Italian, and Chinese immigrants. The languages they brought with them, however, have had very little influence on the general speech of the city.

The city's residents have long observed a subdialect they call Mission dialect. It is spoken primarily by Irish Catholics born and raised south of Market Street, and it resembles working-class New York City speech. Two distinct features are especially noticeable—the use of the glottal stop instead of /t/ in words like *bottle* /bŏʼ-l/ and the use of /oi/ or /əĭ/ instead of /êr/ in words like *nurse* /nəĭs/ and *bird* /bəĭd/. Because of its lower prestige, this subdialect seems to be dying out.

sanguinary, sanguine. These two adjectives are based on Latin *sanguis* = 'blood' but have almost entirely separate meanings. *Sanguinary* refers only to bloodshed, literally meaning 'covered with blood' but more often either 'involving heavy slaughter' or '(of persons) bloodthirsty, eager for slaughter':

> Yet another sanguinary battle was fought on the 28th of July, before Atlanta. . . .
>
> —B. J. Lossing, *History of the Civil War*

> He was . . . like all other lawless barbarians, prone to be cruel and sanguinary whenever he might safely vent his evil humor.
>
> —Peter Forbath, *The River Congo*

Sanguine refers, first, to the human complexion, meaning 'showing the color of the blood vessels, ruddy'; it can also be used to mean 'blood-colored' in general, as of a sunset. Much more often *sanguine* is used in meanings developed in medieval physiology. It was believed that different human temperaments resulted from the predominance and mixture of four bodily fluids, or *humors:* blood; phlegm; yellow bile, or choler; and black bile, or melancholy. A cheerful and bold person with a ruddy complexion was supposed to have a predominance of blood over the other humors and was called sanguine. Applied to persons the word now means simply 'confident and hopeful':

> He had a sanguine nature; and doubt, anxiety, and self-mistrust seemed entirely foreign to his disposition.
>
> —Peter Quennell, *The Wanton Chase*

Applied to hopes, plans, etc., *sanguine* means 'optimistic':

> The sanguine hopes, which I had not shared, that Germany would collapse before the end of the year, failed.
>
> —Winston Churchill, *Triumph and Tragedy*

sans /sănz/ is an old borrowing of French *sans* = 'without.' It is chiefly kept alive by the famous speech on the seven ages of man from Shakespeare's *As You Like It*, in which the character Jaques describes extreme old age as being "sans teeth, sans eyes, sans taste, sans everything." *Sans* is best used with a mocking allusion to this passage.

> . . . [for white Rhodesians] to face the prospect of starting life afresh in some harsher, colder country, sans servants, sans swimming pool, sans sunshine, sans supremacy.
>
> —Jan Morris, *Rolling Stone*

Sanskrit words. Sanskrit, one of the Indo-European family, descends from the language of the Indo-Aryans, a nomadic people skilled in warfare and poetry who came from central Eurasia and entered India between 2000 and 1500 B.C. (see INDO-EUROPEAN). As the language of much of the sacred literature of Hinduism and Buddhism, Sanskrit has been preserved with very little change over the past 2,000 years. Written in Devanagari (= 'divine city script') characters, it is used to this day by learned Hindus and has a classical status like that of Latin in Europe. The word *Sanskrit* means 'perfected, refined.' The pronunciation /**săn**-skrĭpt/, influenced by the word *script*, is a mistake.

The vocabulary of Sanskrit has been enormously influential throughout the Old World and has made a deep imprint on the English language.

(1) A number of Sanskrit words relating to religion and mystic philosophy have been borrowed into English since about 1800, when Europeans first began to translate the Hindu scriptures. Americans—from Ralph Waldo Emerson and the transcendentalists to the millions who today turn to meditation and yoga—have welcomed India's spiritual heritage with open arms.

ahimsa /ə-**hĭm**-sä, -sə/ = 'nonviolence': from Sanskrit *a-* = 'without' + *himsa* = 'injury'

ashram /**äsh**-rəm, **ăsh**-/ = 'religious commune or retreat': from Sanskrit *āśrama* = 'religious community and retreat in the forest, at the core of which is a spiritual teacher together with his students'

atman /**ät**-mən/ = (1) 'self' (2) capital A 'supreme soul,' the Hindu equivalent of 'the ground of existence, or kingdom of heaven within you': from Sanskrit *ātman* = 'breath, spirit, soul'

avatar /**äv**-ə-tär/ = 'an incarnation of a god': from Sanskrit *avatāra* = 'descent'

Brahmin = 'member of the Hindu priestly caste'

dharma /**där**-mə/ = 'law, justice, the nature of the universe': from Sanskrit *dharma* = 'law'

dhyana /dē-**ä**-nə/ = 'deep meditation': from Sanskrit *dhyāna* = 'thought'

guru /**goo͝**-ro͞o/ = 'spiritual teacher': from Sanskrit *guru* = 'heavy,' hence 'venerable, revered'

kama /**kä**-mə/ = 'love, sexual desire' and **Kamasutra** = 'Aphorisms About Love' (title of the classic Hindu love manual): from Sanskrit *kāma* = 'desire'

karma /**kär**-mə/ = 'a person's actions and destiny as determined by those actions'

mahatma /mə-**hăt**-mə/ = 'title for a wise or holy person held in special reverence, such as Mohandas Gandhi': from Sanskrit *mahātman* = 'great soul'

mandala /**mŭn**-də-lə/ = 'geometric pattern used as an aid to meditation'

mantra /**mŭn**-trə, **män**-/ = 'mystic word or syllable used as an aid to meditation'

maya /**mä**-yə/ = 'illusion, the seeming reality of the world': from Sanskrit *mayā* = 'magic, illusion'

moksha /**mōk**-shə/ = 'liberation from the cycle of birth and death, final salvation': from Sanskrit *mokṣa* = 'release'

nirvana /nîr-**vä**-nə, nər-/ = 'extinction of self-will, enlightenment'

om, aum /ōm/ = 'the sacred syllable, used as a mantra'

* **pundit, pandit** = 'learned man'

raga /**rä**-gə/ = (1) 'musical scale' (2) 'piece of music based on one of the scales': from Sanskrit *rāga* = 'color, redness, inflammation, passion, musical note or scale'

*Appears as separate entry

rishi /rĭ-shē/ = 'inspired sage': from Sanskrit *ṛṣi* = 'seer, sage' (title of the authors of the Hindu scriptures)

sutra /sōō-trə/ = (1) 'aphorism, short sentence' (2) 'book of aphorisms': from Sanskrit *sutra* = 'thread'

swami /swä-mē/ = 'title of respect for a Hindu teacher'

swastika /swäs-tĭ-kə/ = 'mystic symbol in the form of a cross with bent arms' (The symbol of Nazism was adopted, via Western books on "Aryan" things, from the Hindu swastika.)

tantra /tŭn-trə, tän-/ = 'esoteric doctrine, that is, an esoteric meditative or sexual religious practice': from Sanskrit *tantra* = 'system, book of esoteric formulas'

yoga /yō-gə/ = (1) 'Hindu spiritual discipline' (2) 'system of exercises, postures, and meditative breathing exercises': from Sanskrit *yoga* = 'yoke, discipline'

(2) Several more Sanskrit words have come into English via long chains of borrowing over the centuries, through Persian, Greek, Latin, Arabic, the various European languages, and even Japanese:

ginger = 'tropical Asian plant with a pungent-tasting root used as a delicacy and a spice': (via Old French and Latin) from Greek *zingiberis*, from Sanskrit *shringavera* = 'horn-shaped (root)'

orange = 'citrus tree native to China': from French *orange*, from Arabic *nāranj*, from Persian *nārang*, from Sanskrit *nāranga* = 'orange'

pepper = 'pungent spice made from the ground dried fruits (peppercorns) of an Indian plant': Old English (via Latin and Greek) from Sanskrit *pippalī* = 'peppercorn'

sugar = 'sweet extract of the juice of the sugar cane, native to Asia': (via Medieval French, Italian, and Latin) from Sanskrit *sharkarā* = 'gravel, granulated sugar'

Zen = 'Japanese and Chinese school of Mahayana Buddhism stressing meditation': from Japanese *zen*, from Chinese *ch'an-na*, from Sanskrit *dhyāna* = 'meditation' See *dhyana*, above.

(3) Sanskrit in India is like Latin in Europe, preserved as a classical and scholarly language and remembered as the ancestor of modern everyday languages. Among these are Hindi, Urdu, Bengali, and Marathi, each spoken by millions of people today. Many more words have been borrowed into English from these languages, and many of those came in during the period of British rule in India. A selection of them is given at INDIAN WORDS (INDIA).

sardonic, sarcastic. (1) *Sardonic.* In the range of human responses to the world, one reaction is that of bitter humor. Things are bad; the sardonic person chooses to find them amusing. The sardonic attitude toward incurable folly or misery that cannot be helped is expressed by an acrid smile.

> The mood was sardonic, fatalistic, and melancholy. I could hear it in our black jokes: "Hey, Bill, you're going on patrol today. If you get your legs blown off can I have your boots?"
>
> —Philip Caputo, *A Rumor of War*

> Implicit in the *Times*'s attack on Robert Kennedy's appointment was the notion that nepotism was a wicked thing. Robert Kennedy took sardonic pleasure in observing the retirement of Arthur Hays Sulzberger as publisher of the *Times* and his replacement by his son-in-law Orville Dryfoos, with Arthur Ochs (Punch) Sulzberger standing next in line.
>
> —Arthur M. Schlesinger, Jr., *Robert Kennedy and His Times*

Etymologically, *sardonic* is a suitably nasty combination of bitterness and laughter. It started out as Greek *sardanios* = 'derisive, contemptuous' but was altered to *sardonios* by association with *Sardonion* = 'Sardinian plant,' the name of an herb native to Sardinia that was supposed to cause facial contortions resembling convulsive laughter and then death. To this day the Latin medical term for the ghastly grin characteristic of facial spasm in tetanus is *risus sardonicus* = 'the sardonic smile.'

(2) *Sarcasm, sarcastic.* Greek *sarkasmos* and Latin *sarcasmus* literally meant 'a tearing of flesh with the teeth,' hence 'extremely cutting speech.' Properly, *sarcasm* is any speech that is intended to wound as deeply as possible, generally achieving this by mockery or wit. *Sarcastic* is thus not the same as *ironic,* although it frequently overlaps with it (see IRONY).

> It is an old saying, "A blow with a word strikes deeper than a blow with a sword." . . . for many are of so petulant a spleen, and have that figure *sarcasmus* so often in their mouths, so bitter, so foolish, as Balthasar Castilio notes of them, that "they cannot speak but they must bite."
>
> —Robert Burton, *The Anatomy of Melancholy*

> It seemed to her that she was forever quivering under Sister Agatha's sarcastic comments or flushing bright red because the rest of the class was laughing at her.
>
> —Colleen McCullough, *The Thorn Birds*

Typically, sarcasm does employ irony, or the stating of something other than what is actually meant:

> Mr. Lackaye had not been working for some time. A sarcasm he had hurled in regard to a certain theatrical manager's lack of culture brought about his unemployment. When asked, "Do you think so-and-so will ever produce *Les Misérables*?" he had replied, "Produce it! Hell, he can't even pronounce it!"
>
> —Gene Fowler, *Good Night, Sweet Prince*

A key element in sarcasm is scathing personal bitterness, sometimes carried to the level of cruelty. An example:

> Many in Hollywood attribute their third false start to the news that leaked two months earlier that Kathryn had ordered a wedding gown from designer Danny Lawson . . . when a reporter asked about the gown, Bing denied that he was marrying Kathryn or anyone else. As to the wedding gown, Bing said, "I hope she gets a chance to use it."
>
> —Donald Shepherd and Robert F. Slatzer, *Bing Crosby: The Hollow Man*

Rhetoricians used to regard sarcasm as irresponsible, because it could do harm and the subject of it could not refute it. We conclude with a moral suggestion:

> Sarcasm I now see to be, in general, the language of the Devil; for which reason I have, long since, as good as renounced it.
>
> —Thomas Carlyle, *Sartor Resartus*

satire. Terms such as *lampoon, parody, burlesque, sendup, pastiche, takeoff, spoof,* and *satire* are often used so loosely in everyday speech that it is difficult to distinguish among them. This is a pity, because some distinctions do exist, and they are worth preserving for the sake of clarity both in our language and in our thinking.

Perhaps the key terms in the above group are *satire, parody,* and *pastiche.* Of these, satire is the most important and the hardest to define. Satire is a form of moral criticism, a denunciation—explicit or implicit—of human vice or folly, delivered with humor. Balancing the disparate elements involved makes it one of the most difficult of all literary forms to master. It must be at once serious and funny. Its targets must be worthy, its criticism must be both trenchant and just, and its expression must be imaginative and amusing. By means of such devices as exaggeration, irony, parody, and reduction to the absurd, satire can illuminate both the silliness of our vices and the viciousness of our silliness. But excellence of execution is everything: let satire become too soft and it slips into good-natured parody; let it become too harsh and it degenerates into mere jeering and insult; let it fix on an unworthy or innocent target and it becomes pointless and offensive. That is why so many of the literary (or TV or movie) efforts that call themselves satire are undeserving of the name.

The art of satire was defined—if not invented—by the Romans, its most famous practitioners being Lucilius, Horace, and Juvenal. Perhaps the greatest Renaissance satire, Shakespeare's *Troilus and Cressida*, a bitterly sardonic comment on human motivation, is based on a parody of the *Iliad*. The 18th century, the golden age of satire, produced such masters of the form as John Dryden, Alexander Pope, Jonathan Swift, and Voltaire. In our own day such writers as Evelyn Waugh (*Decline and Fall, Scoop, The Loved One*), Mary McCarthy (*The Groves of Academe*), and Jerzy Kosinski (*Being There*) have ably upheld the satiric tradition. Arguably the best satire written today is in the pages of the British magazine *Private Eye*, which savagely and brilliantly ridicules established journalism, politics, and mores. The success of real satire can always be measured by the response of those who are satirized. The Roman poet Horace received serious threats from some of his targets; *Private Eye* is constantly being sued for libel.

Parody. Parody may be one of the weapons of satire, but it is, in itself, less than satire. Properly speaking, parody has to do with imitating (and subtly distorting) some well-known literary, musical, or artistic style for comic effect. Lacking any moral point, parody tends to be gentler than satire; and although it can be equally amusing, it is less thought-provoking. As commonly used, the terms *sendup, burlesque, lampoon, spoof,* and *takeoff* almost always refer to parody.

An immensely popular form of humor, parody can be found today in virtually every medium of communication, from Oliver Jensen's famous magazine essay "Eisenhower's Address at Gettysburg" (beginning, "I haven't checked these figures, but eighty-seven years ago, I think it was, a number of individuals . . .") to Sid Caesar's hilarious renditions of grand opera on TV's "Your Show of Shows." One of the most prolific contemporary sources of parody has been Harvard's venerable humor magazine, *The Lampoon*. At one time or another the irreverent Cantabrigians have produced elaborate parody editions of the *New York Times, Time, Newsweek, Life, Cosmopolitan, The Lord of the Rings*, and others too numerous to mention.

Pastiche. Pastiche is just the same as parody, with one important difference: it is not meant to be funny. It is an *admiring* imitation of someone else's style. Thus, the early 20th-century horror-story writer H. P. Lovecraft wrote admiring pastiches in the style of Edgar Allan Poe, and the contemporary best-selling horror novelist Stephen King has written pastiches in the manner of H. P. Lovecraft. For more see PASTICHE.

See also BURLESQUE; LAMPOON; SPOOF.

satrap. This was the title of the rulers of provinces in the ancient Persian Empire. They were not constitutionally appointed governors but loosely subordinate kings who accepted the great king or emperor as their overlord. For the etymology, see PERSIAN WORDS. The word is pronounced /**săt**-răp/ or /**sā**-trăp/. It is now used metaphorically to mean 'man wielding great personal power over an area or a department, either in government or in business life.' The domain of a satrap is a *satrapy* /**săt**-rə-pē, **sā**-trə-/.

> [During the reconstruction period after the Civil War, when the South was ruled as a conquered country] she even wrote asking the help of General Meade, the satrap of Georgia, Florida, and Alabama. . . .
>
> —Constance Wright, *Fanny Kemble and the Lovely Land*

> In order to return "power to the people," Nixon had first to wrench it out of the hands of the satraps [Federal bureaucrats] that had controlled it for generations.
>
> —William Safire, *Before the Fall*

> What he does not know about the various satrapies of New York publishing is not worth hearing.
>
> —Paul Gray, *Time*

Saudi. The most accurate pronunciation is /sä-**o͞o**-dē/, but /**sou**-dē/ is the usual version in English and is fully acceptable. Less acceptable is /**sô**-dē/. Saudi Arabia is named after its founder, King Abdul-Aziz ibn-Saud /sä-**o͞od**/, who reigned from 1932 to 1953.

save. As a preposition and conjunction, *save* is a slightly self-conscious synonym for *except* or *but*. It seldom occurs in speech, but it is used in certain kinds of writing.

> In *The Cabala* [a novel by Thornton Wilder], the several heroes of the several episodes seem at first to have nothing in common save the accident of all being observed by the American who is telling the story. . . .
> —Edmund Wilson, *A Literary Chronicle of the Twenties and Thirties*

> I can remember little save that when I got home late that afternoon I went at once to bed. . . .
> —Brendan Gill, *Here at The New Yorker*

Like *except, save* is generally used with the objective form of pronouns, but there is also good historical precedent for using the subjective form, as in the following:

> . . . nothing in all that vast world moved or lived save we three intruders and a white-winged gull.
> —Farley Mowat, *People of the Deer*

savvy originates in the pidgin language used for centuries by sailors, traders, and explorers as an all-purpose system for communicating with people of the Third World (see PIDGIN AND CREOLE LANGUAGES). It is based on Spanish *sabe usted* = 'you know' or 'do you know.' *Savvy* was at first a verb meaning 'know, understand':

> Pat savvies Italian like a native, so we do pretty well.
> —Farley Mowat, *And No Birds Sang*

> . . . when she was on the range she showed that she not only could ride the rough string but that she could savvy cattle.
> —Louis L'Amour, *The Sky-Liners*

The verb remains slang, but recently *savvy* as an adjective and noun has virtually entered the general vocabulary, tending to lose the slang marking. The adjective means 'knowledgeable, knowing and effective':

> I'm a successful, savvy woman, and by now the very thought of the ERA exhausts me. —Jane O'Reilly, *Savvy*

> There is also hope that medically savvy patients will be more inclined to follow their doctors' advice.
> —Robert C. Yeager, *Reader's Digest*

The noun means 'experience, effectiveness, know-how':

> A real nice guy from Wichita, they called him the Big Dee and listen, that guy had plenty of baseball savvy.
> —Pete Rose, *The Pete Rose Story*

> Vincent has the kind of savvy and conviction that leave no doubt he will make good on all his wild promises.
> —Janet Maslin, *New York Times*

scallop = 'shellfish with two ribbed and fan-shaped shells.' The usual pronunciation is **/skäl-əp/**, but **/skăl-əp/** is also correct. The spelling *scollop* is now obsolete.

Scandinavian words. Scandinavia proper is the peninsula occupied by Norway and Sweden. Culturally, Denmark and Iceland are also included under the term. The Scandinavian languages—Norwegian, Swedish, Danish, and Icelandic—constitute the northern branch of the Germanic group. The earliest recorded form of Scandinavian is Old Norse. The Viking settlements in England in the early Middle Ages left hundreds of Old Norse words in the English vocabulary; these are discussed at NORSE WORDS.

A selection of the words borrowed into English from the modern Scandinavian languages is given below.

aquavit **/ăk-wə-vēt/** = 'clear grain- or potato-based liquor flavored with caraway': from *akvavit* (in all the Scandinavian languages), from Latin *aqua vitae* = 'water of life, alcohol' See WHISKEY.

Celsius **/sĕl-sē-əs/** = 'the centigrade scale of temperature': after Anders *Celsius* (1701–44), Swedish astronomer

fjord, fiord **/fyôrd/** = 'long inlet of the sea on the Norwegian coast, typically between cliffs or steep slopes': from Norwegian *fjord*, from Old Norse *fjördhr* = 'inlet,' originally 'crossing, place that must be crossed' (Scottish *firth* is also a borrowing of this word; see NORSE WORDS.)

geyser /gī-zər/ = 'hot spring that sends up a column of water and steam': from Icelandic *Geysir* = 'Gusher' (name of a particular hot spring in Iceland), from *geysa* = 'to gush'

gremlin = 'mythical gnome or imp of World War II that caused mechanical failures in airplanes': probably from Danish *gräm* = 'demon'

lemming = 'small Arctic rodent famous for occasional mass migrations in which many are drowned': from Norwegian *lemming*

litmus = 'substance extracted from a lichen, which turns red in acid solution and blue in alkaline': from Old Norwegian *litmosi* = 'dye-moss,' from *lit* = 'dye, color' + *mosi* = 'moss'

mink = 'small aquatic mammal related to the weasel, with soft shiny fur': from Swedish *menk* = 'mink'

narwhal /**när**-wəl/ = 'large sea mammal of the Arctic with a single sharp, straight tusk': from Norwegian *narhval* = 'corpse-whale,' supposedly because it can look like a human corpse floating in the water, from *nar* = 'corpse' + *hval* = 'whale'

* **ombudsman** = 'official who investigates private citizens' complaints against government': from Norwegian and Swedish *ombudsman* = 'commissioner, representative'

rug = (1) (British) 'lap robe, travel wrap' (2) 'floor covering, carpet'; originally 'kind of thick, coarse wool cloth': from Norwegian (dialectal) *rogga*, *rugga* = 'coarse coverlet, shaggy cloth'

rutabaga /rōō-tə-**bā**-gə/ = 'turniplike root of a variety of cabbage, used as a vegetable': from Swedish *rotabagge*, from *rot* = 'root' + *bagge* = 'bag'

saga /**sä**-gə/ = 'an early medieval Norse history': from Icelandic *saga* = 'saying, tale, history'

ski /skē/ = 'footgear for gliding over snow': from Norwegian *ski* /shē/ = 'ski,' originally 'split piece of wood'

skoal /skōl/ = 'a drinking toast'

slalom /**slä**-ləm/ = 'competitive ski run down a zigzag course between pairs of markers': from Norwegian *slalom*, from *sla* = 'slope' + *lom* = 'path'

walrus /**wôl**-rəs/ = 'large marine mammal of northern seas, related to the seal': from Dutch *walrus*, probably borrowed from a lost Scandinavian word similar to Old Norse *hrossvalr* = 'horse-whale, walrus,' but with the elements reversed, from *hross* = 'horse' + *valr* = 'whale'

*Appears as separate entry

scarcely = 'only just, almost not, hardly' is sometimes followed by *than: Scarcely had the unemployment rate been brought down to a reasonable level than inflation went over 10 percent.*

◇ ***Recommendation.*** This is definitely a breach of idiom. Use *when*, not *than*.

scarify /**skăr**-ə-fī/ has nothing to do with *scare*. It means 'to make lacerations or scars in.' Literally, this can refer to making ceremonial tribal scars, performing surgical procedures such as inoculations, or breaking up compacted topsoil with a harrow. Figuratively, *scarify* means 'to criticize mercilessly, tear (someone) to shreds' or 'to cause severe pain to, traumatize':

> People said that with her scarifying wit she had actually whiplashed the timorous Karfrey into marrying her.
>
> —Edna Ferber, *Giant*

> Cunningham was raised a devout Catholic, so the divorce of her mother from her amiable but drunken father was scarifying.
>
> —James McKinley, *National Catholic Reporter*

scathe, from an Old Norse word meaning 'to injure, harm,' is now a rare word, but its derivatives *scathing* and *unscathed* are in common use. The verb *scathe* originally meant 'to injure physically,' especially 'to blast or scorch.' It is still occasionally used in the transferred sense 'to blast (someone) verbally, speak with harsh and devastating effect':

> . . . a man whose mirth was of the heartiest, but whose tongue could scathe.
> —George Seaver, *Edward Wilson of the Antarctic*

The adjective *scathing* similarly refers to harsh condemnation, whether expressed verbally or in other ways.

> . . . after having his ears blistered by the scathing invective of which Mrs. Hopper was the complete mistress . . .
> —Thomas Wolfe, *The Web and the Rock*

> Paddy's fierce blue gaze beat him down, contemptuous and scathing. . . .
> —Colleen McCullough, *The Thorn Birds*

Unscathed, on the other hand, retains the original sense of *scathe,* meaning either 'not physically injured, unhurt,' or 'undamaged, unharmed in any way':

> Swift rapids carried me downstream into a pool, from which I emerged unscathed, but without my ski poles.
> —Galen Rowell, *Sierra*

> But [Secretary of State Alexander Haig] emerged unscathed, with his reputation for steely toughness further enhanced.
> —*U.S. News & World Report*

scenario, like some other theater terms, is an Italian word, originating in the old comedies (the commedia dell'arte) featuring stock characters such as Harlequin and Punchinello. The *libro scenario,* literally 'stage book' (from *scena* = 'scene, stage'—see ITALIAN WORDS), was a brief plot outline from which the actors improvised both the action and the dialogue. In modern stage usage a scenario is a narrative synopsis of a play or an opera; in cinema and television it is the detailed script or screenplay for a film or TV story, or for any feature including news or a commercial.

In the late 1960s *scenario* was rather suddenly adopted into the vocabulary of journalism and politics. Since then it has passed into wide general usage and is now one of the unmistakable signature words of our period. It has an interesting range of distinct meanings. In politics, strategic planning, economics, etc., it usually means 'projection of a possible sequence of future events.' The key notion here, following the film or television metaphor, is that the events are seen as following each other in a particular sequence like the sequence of scenes in a shooting script; these events are outside the actors' control, but planners must try to guess how the story will turn out (though one wonders who is supposed to be writing the script).

> The basic scenario for war in Europe envisages a Soviet armored blitzkrieg advancing under cover of tens of thousands of surface-to-air missiles. . . .
> —Drew Middleton, *New York Times*

> The following chilling scenario ["The Day San Francisco Is Hit"] is based on studies of possible damage, should a similar cataclysmic quake occur today at the worst possible hour.
> —Martin Koughan, *Reader's Digest*

Scenario is also used in science and related fields to mean 'theoretical chain of events or effects, which may have happened in the past or may happen in the present or future':

> The fashionable new environmental worry is acid rain. If we burn more coal—so the scenario goes—sulfur and nitrogen emissions from electric power plants turn into acid in the atmosphere.
> —Ann Hughey, *Forbes*

> The classic scenarios for the development of life on other planets . . .
> —Richard C. Hoagland, *Star and Sky*

In contrast with the previous two uses, which picture sequences of events that humans may seek to deduce, anticipate, or respond to, *scenario* is also used to mean 'planned or proposed sequence of actions' or, in a more general sense, 'plan, proposal, tactic, maneuver.' Here the planners are in control of their own script.

> . . . Haldeman told me about the latest ideas for dealing with the Watergate matter. Liddy was going to write a "scenario" that would tie together all the loose ends: he would take responsibility for planning the entire Watergate operation and say that no one higher up had authorized it.
>
> —Richard Nixon, *R.N.*

Finally, *scenario* has become a term used in popular psychology in a different extended sense: 'fantasized situation or sequence of actions' or simply 'fantasy.' This use of the word seems to relate not so much to the script behind the film or television presentation as to the viewer's response to the finished product.

> Nowadays many men and women are seduced out of marriage by images, dreams and scenarios of divorce lifestyles modeled in the media by prominent figures in entertainment, sports and popular culture.
>
> —Louise Montague, *Reader's Digest*

Scot, Scotch, Scots, Scottish. The correct Scottish use of these words is not necessarily followed by non-Scots.

Scottish Usage. A native of Scotland is a *Scot.* The title of the sovereign is king or queen *of Scots,* not *of Scotland.* There are two standard adjectives, *Scottish* and *Scots. Scottish* is the all-purpose word: *Scottish architecture; a Scottish face; the Scottish economy. Scots,* a variant form of the word *Scottish,* is rarer but equally correct in all contexts. It is also used exclusively with some words and names: *the Scots Guards,* an infantry regiment; *Scots law,* the legal code of Scotland, based (unlike English law) on Roman law. Hence also the nouns *Scotsman* and *Scotswoman.*

The adjective *Scotch,* an old but normal variant form of *Scottish,* is now generally accepted only for a limited range of things, such as food and drink. Most Scots strongly resent the use of the word *Scotch* for people or institutions. This objection has arisen only within the past 100 years or so, apparently as a reaction to insulting uses of the word by English people. Nonetheless, a minority of Scottish people have ignored the taboo and continue to call themselves *Scotch;* this usage can be found in the writings of Thomas Carlyle, Robert Louis Stevenson, Sir James Barrie, Sir James Murray (editor of *The Oxford English Dictionary*), A. J. Liebling, and others to the present day.

Non-Scottish Usage. The English have long been aware that most Scots dislike being called *Scotch.* Although some English people persist in it, on the grounds that it is traditional and that they mean no harm by it, the majority now say *Scottish* instead.

The situation in North America is rather different. The earlier migrants from Scotland mostly called themselves *Scotch* and, having left the English behind, never had any objection to the word. Nearly all the pioneering golf professionals, for example, used it. Golf itself is often called the Scotch game, and in the United States the traditional form of match is always called *Scotch foursomes* (in Scotland simply a *foursome*). The Protestant Scots who settled in northern Ireland, many of whom later went to the United States and Canada, are generally known as the Scotch-Irish. Thus, Americans, and to a lesser extent Canadians, have generally continued, without rancor, to use the adjective *Scotch* in all applications; in American English it is standard and correct. But if Americans use it freely when visiting Scotland, they must expect to be corrected rather sharply.

◇ ***Recommendation.*** If in doubt, use the adjective *Scottish.* In the following terms, however, *Scotch* is correct:

Scotch broth = 'mutton soup thickened with vegetables and barley'

Scotch eggs = 'hard-boiled eggs encased in pastry'

Scotch grain = 'coarse finish for leather'

Scotch mist = 'heavy, rainlike mist'

Scotch pebble = 'kind of quartz found in Scotland'

Scotch pine, Scots pine = 'the tree *Pinus sylvestris*'

Scotch salmon

Scotch tape (trademark)

Scotch verdict = 'jury verdict of Not Proven, allowed under Scots law'

Scotch, Scotch whisky = 'smoky-flavored whiskey made from malted barley'; usually just *whisky* in Scotland

Scotch woodcock = 'a savory dish of scrambled eggs on toast topped with anchovy fillets'

scotch. Use of this rather rare verb stems entirely from a passage in *Macbeth:* "We have scotch'd the snake, not kill'd it." It is not related to *Scotch* = 'Scottish' but is probably a variant of the verb *score* or perhaps *scorch.* The original meaning was 'to wound and disable, render harmless for the time being.' The usual current meaning is 'to put a decisive stop to (a plan, rumor, idea, etc.)':

> How neatly Melanie had scotched the scandal, keeping Scarlett at her side all through the dreadful evening.
>
> —Margaret Mitchell, *Gone With the Wind*

> Energy Secretary James Schlesinger . . . is trying to scotch a scheme that would reduce U.S. dependence on Arab oil. . . .
>
> —Jack Anderson, *Daily Hampshire Gazette*

Scottish English. The term *Scottish English,* also as a noun *Scottish* or *Scots,* refers to the branch of the English language spoken in Scotland. Already by A.D. 700, Anglo-Saxons were settled throughout Lowland Scotland. Up to the time of Mary, Queen of Scots (16th century), Scottish English, with a rich literature, was the official language of the kingdom of Scotland, very different from the English of southern England. If Scotland had remained an independent country, its form of English would by now be a separate language, mostly incomprehensible to other modern English speakers. But the crowns of Scotland and England were by 1707 united, and the much wealthier and more populous southern partner to a large extent imposed its standard language on the Scots. Fervent nationalists have sought to revive a form of Scottish and make it the official language again, especially the dialects known as *Broad Scots* or *Lallans* (= 'Lowland speech'), and a trickle of literature, especially poetry, continues to be written in it. The actual usage of most Scottish people is now quite similar to Standard British English. But several varieties of the broad dialect survive, divided into regional types such as *Southern Scots,* spoken in the border country, and *East Mid Scots,* spoken around Edinburgh.

Note. Scottish Gaelic, or Gaelic for short, is an offshoot of Old Irish, introduced in Scotland by Celts from Ireland sometime around A.D. 600. Gaelic and Irish did not diverge as separate tongues until after 1600. Like its sister languages Irish and Welsh, Gaelic was officially discouraged in favor of English until recent times but survived in western Scotland. With the rise of 20th-century Scottish nationalism, Gaelic has won a small place in the public school curriculum. The special flavor of Scottish English owes a good deal to a sprinkling of words borrowed from Gaelic over the past 1,000 years.

Pronunciation. Some of the characteristic sounds of Scottish English can be suggested by a selection of Scottish words that are pronounced (and traditionally spelled) strikingly differently from their southern English and American counterparts.

Scottish	Standard English
auld	*old*
ba	*ball*
bluid /blüd/	*blood*
ca	*call*
coo	*cow*
din	*done*
dinna	*don't, didn't*
gie	*give*
guid /güd/	*good*
hame	*home*

himsel	*himself*
hoose	*house*
licht	*light*
sae	*so*
sair	*sore*
twa	*two*
wha	*who*

Vocabulary. (1) Scottish still has a large amount of unique vocabulary, much of it surviving from Anglo-Saxon or Scandinavian origins and some coming from Gaelic and French:

birk = 'birch tree'
crack = 'chat'
dominie = 'schoolmaster'
doot = 'to think probable'
douce = 'respectable'
dreich /drēk/ = 'dreary'
ettle = 'aim'
feart = 'afraid'
gey = 'very'
greet = 'to weep'
jigot = 'leg of mutton'
kirk = 'church'
laverock = 'lark'
loon = 'boy, young man'
lum = 'chimney'
mind = 'to remember'
neb = 'nose'
outwith (preposition) = 'outside'
policies = 'estate grounds'
procurator-fiscal = 'public prosecutor'
reek = 'smoke'
stance = 'standing place'
writer to the signet = 'lawyer'

(2) A large number of Scottish words have been taken into international Standard English—far more than from Welsh and Irish together. Among the many Scotticisms familiar all over the English-speaking world are:

bog = 'waterlogged ground, swamp'
cairn = 'heap of stones, marker'
canny = 'shrewd, careful, wise'
eerie = 'supernaturally strange'
fey = 'half-crazed, touched'
flat = 'apartment' (originally a one-floor apartment in certain buildings in Edinburgh)
glamour = 'enchantment'
glen = 'valley'
golf = 'game with club and ball' See also Scottish words at GOLF TERMS.
gruesome = 'horrifying'
heckle = 'to harass with interruptions'
loch = 'lake'
outcome = 'that which comes out, result, consequence'
pet = 'animal kept for companionship'
pony = 'horse of a small breed'
raid = 'a riding forth, punitive expedition'
rampage = 'to behave wildly'
relevant = '(legally) pertinent'
slogan = 'war cry, motto'
stalwart = 'strong and valiant'
weird = (1) (noun) 'fate, destiny' (2) (adjective) 'magical, unearthly, strange'
whisky = 'liquor distilled from barley mash' See WHISKEY.

scuttlebutt. In the days of sail, ships carried their fresh water in *butts,* or large barrels. The daily supply of drinking water for the crew was kept in a butt with a square opening cut in it. This was called the *scuttled butt* or *scuttlebutt, scuttle* being an old nautical term for 'small hatchway or opening.' We have evidence that long before office workers lingered at the water cooler, sailors were deliberately wasting time at the scuttlebutt. In the following quotation the writer is describing how a sailor feeling ill used by his officers in a 19th-century American merchant ship would loiter around the ship to shirk duty.

> He must not refuse his duty, or be in any way disobedient, but . . . every man who has been three months at sea knows how to "work Tom Cox's traverse"—"three turns round the longboat, and a pull at the scuttled butt."
> —Richard Henry Dana,
> *Two Years Before the Mast*

To "work Tom Cox's traverse" evidently meant 'to work an idle passage'; *traverse* meant 'passage, voyage on a ship,' but who the eponymous Tom Cox was is lost to history. To this day, drinking fountains on modern ships are known as scuttlebutts, and no doubt sailors are still taking very leisurely pulls at them and exchanging ship's gossip while waiting their turn. All this is the background to the American term *scuttlebutt* meaning 'rumor, gossip.' (The first quotation below refers to members of the crew of a U.S. Navy ship.)

> Scuttlebutt sprang up that Holman and Chien were feuding.
> —Richard McKenna, *The Sand Pebbles*

> This is the latest fascinating piece of scuttlebutt out of Canberra.
> —Jeremy Salt, *Nation Review* (Australia)

seed. See PIT, STONE, SEED, KERNEL.

seesaw. *Seesaw* and *teeter-totter* are the two commonest terms for 'board or long plank balanced on a central fulcrum so that persons, usually one on each end, can ride up and down.' Both are reduplicated forms. They contain two word elements, one of which is a slightly altered version of the other: *see* of *saw; totter* of *teeter* or *titter.*

Seesaw is by far the more popular word. It was originally part of a rhythmic jingle sung by sawyers in the 17th century and by children imitating the sawyers at work. Nursery rhymes then adopted the nonsense sound: "See saw, Margery Daw, Jackey shall have a new master." In the 18th century the expression referred to a child's amusement at moving up and down on a balanced board. By the early 19th century *seesaw* referred to the plank itself.

Teeter-totter was originally the 16th-century British dialect term *titter-totter.* In certain British dialects to *titter* is 'to move unsteadily, totter or sway.' In America the seesaw itself was first known as a *teeter-board.* The term soon became widespread and was often used in political contexts.

> We were having a grand time with our "teeter-boards" up on the highest fence. —*Knickerbocker* (1855)

> We [in the United States] are not on a teeter-board and have no need to be incessantly concerned about the balance of power.
> —*Chicago Advance* (1897)

In some parts of the country a teeter-totter is a *teeter-tooter* or just a *teeter.* In western New England it is also called a *tinter* or *teenter;* in eastern New England, a *tilt, tilting board, tilter,* or *tiltering board.*

> As I was playing a childish play on a tilter with one Power Merit . . . I fell.
> —John Comer, *The Diary of John Comer* (1727)

In the Coastal Southern dialect a seesaw is often called a *hickey-board* or *hickey-horse.*

semi-. See BI-, SEMI-.

senior citizen. To those who accept and use the term *senior citizen,* it may come as a surprise to hear that some people violently dislike and reject it.

> . . . this paper, by a college professor, employs the illiterate term "ageism" (What does it mean? Adherence to the writings of James Agee?) on top of the unsavory euphemism "senior citizens." . . . —John Simon, *Esquire*

The argument is that people should not be ashamed to be called *old, elderly,* or *retired* if that is what they are, and that to be called *senior citizens* is an evasion invented by bureaucrats that is really more insulting than the use of plain language. Should the young therefore be called *junior citizens*? No, because our culture admires youth; whereas, according to the theory of *ageism* (a perfectly legitimate term), it tends to despise age and to discriminate against it. But even if this grim and simplified view were true, it is still unlikely that a label like *senior citizen* is really going to inculcate respect in anyone who doesn't already practice it.

It is interesting that the Latin word *senex,* meaning 'old' or 'old person,' carried a definite marking of respect. This is clearly seen in the derivative word *senātus* = 'the assembly of the old men,' the supreme council or parliament of the Roman Republic (which we of course have adopted as *senate*). *Senior,* basically the comparative of *senex* and meaning 'older,' was also used as a noun meaning 'an older person, an elder.' It too implies respect, as in our use of the word *senior* to mean 'high-ranking, higher-ranking.' It was no doubt intended that these connotations would be present in the new term *senior citizens,* sometimes alternatively *seniors;* and apparently for many people it works. Others indignantly repudiate the title precisely because the connotations are unacceptable—so-called senior citizens are not, in general, of especially high rank or status in the culture, so why pretend that they are?

This is a classic instance of EUPHEMISM—the avoidance of words or names felt to be dangerous or tainted—as in the way the Greeks often called the *Erinyes,* terrible goddesses of retribution, by the placatory name *Eumenides* = 'the kindly ones.' Euphemism is a universal device or tendency in languages and evidently serves real needs. Whether you subscribe to any particular instance of it is a matter of personal preference. *Senior citizen* is in very wide use, both officially and in everyday speech and writing.

> A senior-citizen friend, on vacation in the Deep South . . .
> —Wyn Esselborn, *Reader's Digest*

◇ ***Recommendation.*** The underlying respect due by nature to old people or senior citizens is more important than the words by which you choose to express it.

sensual, sensuous. In the ascetic or spiritual view of life, the senses and the appetites they serve are considered to distract the proper functioning and development of the pure spirit or intellect. Opposed to this are materialistic, biological, and aesthetic views, that the senses are all we have for perceiving the world and that it is natural and healthy to enjoy and cultivate them. The adjectives *sensual* and *sensuous* are used with various connotations between these two points of view. In spite of attempts to separate the words, they are to most intents and purposes synonymous. Both can mean simply 'related to the senses or to sensation,' 'gratifying to the senses,' or '(of persons) devoted to gratifying the senses.' Both can have negative implications: 'self-indulgent,' especially 'too fond of sex, food, or luxury'; or positive implications: 'healthily or beautifully arousing and satisfying the appetites of the senses' or '(of persons) healthily interested in sexual or aesthetic pleasure.'

(1) *Sensual:*

> In the autumn of the year he dwelt upon boyhood and death and pleasures of a harsh, sensual nature.
> —Joyce Carol Oates, *A Sentimental Education*

> Marriages may then be regarded as provisional and sex becomes less sacred, more sensual.
> —Albert C. Outler, *Christianity Today*

> The man was tall and fair, and his face was striking—the planes sharp, the mouth a straight deep line, but sensual. . . .
> —Catherine Gaskin, *Edge of Glass*

> The light was amber-brown in vast, dark chambers shuttered from young light, where, in great walnut beds, the glorious women stirred in sensual warmth their lavish limbs.
> —Thomas Wolfe, *The Web and the Rock*

(2) *Sensuous:*

> After a partial cessation of his sensuous life, the soul of man, or its organs rather, are reinvigorated each day. . . .
> —Henry David Thoreau, *Walden*

> . . . refused to give up alcohol and tobacco, which had become his only sensuous pleasures.
> —Peter Quennell, *The Wanton Chase*

> Naturally, I did not succumb, but I confess that rolling the temptation around in my mind created a fair amount of sensuous pleasure.
> —Walter F. Murphy, *The Vicar of Christ*

> Hollywood is good at doing that sort of thing. Its proficiency at transforming little Connie Ockleman of Brooklyn into sultry, sensuous Veronica Lake was proved by the success of the venture.
> —Veronica Lake, *Veronica*

Some usage experts allot *sensual* more to sexuality and *sensuous* more to aesthetic pleasure, and some individual writers may prefer to observe such distinctions. In general usage the words are usually interchangeable.

◊ ***Recommendation.*** In choosing between *sensual* and *sensuous* we can only suggest that you follow your own instincts. But note that *sensory* means only 'relating to the senses' in a purely neutral or physical sense: *sensory stimulation; sensory organs.*

serendipity = 'the ability or fact of making fortunate discoveries unintentionally.' The word was coined by the 18th-century English writer Horace Walpole, after a Persian fairy tale, *The Three Princes of Serendip,* who "were always making discoveries, by accidents or sagacity, of things they were not in quest of." *Serendip* is an Arabic name for Sri Lanka (Ceylon).

> Almost by serendipity, Piaget was stimulated to investigate the origins of knowledge in infancy and the stages through which children passed. . . .
> —Howard Gardner, *New Boston Review*

The adjective is *serendipitous.*

> Sixty-five million years ago, more than three-quarters of plant and animal species disappeared from the earth. . . . A serendipitous trail of discoveries led scientists to speculate about asteroids. "We started out looking for one thing; we ended up finding something far more interesting," explains Luis Alvarez. . . .
> —Terence Dickinson, *Maclean's*

set. In dialects, both British and American, the verb *set* is used intransitively to mean 'be seated, sit':

> [Servant in an English university:] "I ask your pardon, sir, for taking such a freedom as to set down."
> —M. R. James, *The Mezzotint*

> The old man seated alone at the table spoke up then. . . . "I'm Cap Rountree. . . ." "Heard you spoken of," Galloway said. "Come on over and set."
> —Louis L'Amour, *The Sky-Liners*

◊ ***Recommendation.*** *Set* for *sit,* though widespread in dialect, is not accepted in standard usage.

Shakespeare and the English language. There is the old story of the woman whose only complaint about Shakespeare was that the man seemed addicted to clichés. She had a point, albeit a not very logical one. Hundreds of Shakespearean words and phrases are such a part of everyday speech that we might well call them clichés if it weren't for the fact that they are almost too familiar even for that. It would probably be kinder and more accurate to say that most of them have long since become legitimate English idioms.

We have made Shakespeare required reading in our schools. We measure our greatest actors by how well they speak Shakespeare's poetry. We use Shakespearean lines for the titles of books, plays, and movies, and we pepper our conversation and writing with Shakespearean allusions. For a crude measure of Shakespeare's influence on our language, just look at any standard dictionary of quotations. First, you will find that the entry headed "Shakespeare" is by far the longest in the book—probably about twice the length of the next longest entry, "The Bible." Second, you will probably find that you recognize many more of the quotations than you supposed you would. And finally, you will almost certainly be astonished to discover how many of the ordinary expressions most people never think of as being Shakespearean come in fact from the pen of this extraordinary man. Try to name the plays in which these phrases appear (answers below): (1) "I'll tell the world"; (2) "It was Greek to me"; (3) "bag and baggage"; (4) "something in the wind"; (5) "at one fell swoop."

How did this one man come to exert such a profound influence over the way we speak, write, and even think today? The easiest (and no doubt best) single answer is simply to say

(**Answers:** 1. *Measure for Measure*; 2. *Julius Caesar*; 3. *As You Like It*; 4. *The Comedy of Errors*; 5. *Macbeth*)

that he was a genius. But there are some other points that are also worth noting about Shakespeare's peculiar relation to the English language.

There is little evidence that Shakespeare did much to shape the language of his contemporaries. Although he was popular enough, most Elizabethans considered Ben Jonson by far the better playwright; at death Jonson was widely eulogized and Shakespeare was hardly mentioned. Of Shakespeare, Jonson himself said, on being told that Shakespeare never blotted out a line he had written, "Would he had blotted a thousand."

Nor did Shakespeare's critical reputation improve much in the 150 years that followed his death. Milton, Dryden, and Pope were all critical both of his use of language and of what they considered to be his uncertain grasp of the dramatist's craft; and Dr. Samuel Johnson's dismissive comment to his biographer, James Boswell, is famous: "Shakespeare never has six lines together without a fault. Perhaps you may find seven, but this does not refute my general assertion." Indeed, it was not until the 19th century that Shakespeare's reputation among the most influential critics shifted from that of interesting playwright to universal genius.

Yet perhaps more significant than what critics thought of Shakespeare during the 17th and 18th centuries is the fact that his works, unlike those of many of his contemporaries, continued to be performed and were thoroughly enjoyed by playgoing audiences. Whatever else anyone might have said, Shakespeare's language was beginning to cast a spell over posterity.

Was there anything special about the language of Shakespeare's time that might have attracted (or repelled) later generations? Possibly. During the 16th century, English vocabulary underwent an explosive growth. Torrents of new words—perhaps 10,000—poured in on a wave of borrowings from Latin, Greek, French, Spanish, and Italian (see also ELIZABETHAN ENGLISH). Shakespeare, more than any poet of his time, seems to have reveled in this linguistic enrichment. In his works many of the newly imported words appear in print for the first time. In all, his vocabulary ran to about 20,000 words, more than that of any other Elizabethan writer, certainly more than that of any of his predecessors, more even than that of a good many subsequent writers. (Geoffrey Chaucer, for example, used only about 8,000 words; Milton, only about 11,000.)

To be sure, total vocabulary is hardly a definitive measure. Today, the average American adult has an operative vocabulary of about 30,000 words, and highly literate people may recognize—if not always understand, or use—more than 100,000 words. But that doesn't make them Shakespeares.

Obviously, it was not so much the size of Shakespeare's vocabulary that counted; it was how he used it. Still setting aside the matter of native talent, is there anything we can say about that? The massive infusions of new words into 16th-century English produced a kind of word intoxication among Elizabethan writers. They were inebriated by this sudden advent of novel sounds and meanings, and more especially by the effects that could be created when new words were mingled with old. A typical example is Macbeth's guilt-ridden lament:

> Will all great Neptune's ocean wash this blood
> Clean from my hand? No, this my hand will rather
> The multitudinous seas incarnadine,
> Making the green one red.

The rumbling Latinisms of the third line are cut off, in the fourth, by sharp Anglo-Saxon words as though by the stroke of a knife—or a pang of the heart.

Since many of the new words were not yet fully assimilated into the language, either grammatically or even in terms of precise definitions, writers felt an uncommon freedom to use them in highly imaginative ways, a license they extended to their use of older words as well. Shakespeare, for example, had no compunction about changing individual words into almost any part of speech that suited his purpose (as in "stranger'd with an oath") or about using a term like *humorous* to mean, variously, 'damp,' 'capricious,' or 'peevish' (all potentially derivable from the word's root meaning). As one noted historian of language put it, when Shakespeare wrote this way,

> he was fitting the language to his thought, rather than forcing his thought to the mould of conventional grammar. This was in keeping with the spirit of his age. It was in language, as in many other respects, an age with the characteristics of youth—vigor, a willingness to venture, and a disposition to attempt the untried. The spirit that animated Hawkins, and Drake, and Raleigh was not foreign to the language of their time. —Albert C. Baugh, *A History of the English Language*

This exhilarating new freedom inevitably seduced many Elizabethan writers into excess. From John Lyly's 1579 book *Euphues, the Anatomy of Wit* we get the word *euphuism* /**yōō**-fyōō-ĭz-əm/, a high-spirited, fast-talking style that literary historians have characterized as tedious, absurd, and overblown (when in fact it is no more so than much of Jack Kerouac or Tom Wolfe). Elizabethan readers found Lyly's book hilariously entertaining, and it was a best seller. In the following typical passage Euphues is trying to seduce a young lady named Lucilla. He succeeds but is soon jilted:

> Though the stone cylindrus at every thunderclap roll from the hill, yet the pure sleek stone mounteth at the noise, though the rust fret the hardest steel, yet doth it not eat into the emerald, though polypus change his hue, yet the salamander keepeth his color, though Proteus transform himself into every shape, yet Pygmalion retaineth his old form, though Aeneas were too fickle to Dido, yet Troilus was too faithful to Cressida, though others seem counterfeit in their deeds, yet, Lucilla, persuade yourself that Euphues will be always current in his dealings.

The boundary that separates a euphuistic style from a truly poetic style consists only of discipline and intention. The central defect of euphuism is not that it tries to bend language to serve thought, but that it bends both language and thought to serve mere words. Understanding euphuism helps us to see how the best and worst of much Elizabethan writing—and of Shakespeare's writing in particular—sprang from a common ground. Shakespeare was perfectly capable of lapsing into euphuism; we do not honor him for that, only for the times he soared above it. But the point is that the 16th century, with its linguistic turmoil, may have provided conditions more favorable to the writing of poetry, good and bad, than any other period in the history of our language. That a man like Shakespeare should have been born into such an age was a stroke of luck from which, happily, we continue to benefit.

It is easier to understand Shakespeare's debt to language than it is to understand language's debt to him—another way of saying that we still cannot explain his genius. His influence, since his death, has been continuous. Few of his most vociferous critics have found him wholly without virtue; few of his most ardent admirers have found him wholly without fault; and at no time have people been able to ignore or forget him.

Just as the line between euphuistic excess and effective lyricism is sometimes hard to draw, so it is hard—or, at any rate, rash—for us today to try to draw up a definitive balance sheet of what is good and bad in Shakespeare. The only worthwhile thing is to let Shakespeare do what he has always done with such incomparable effectiveness: speak for himself. The mini-anthology that follows makes no pretense at being comprehensive. It may, however, at least suggest some categories of ways in which Shakespeare affects contemporary language.

Best-known Speeches. Many of the great speeches and memorable lines that most of us know by heart come from three plays—*Julius Caesar*, *Hamlet*, and *Macbeth*. In each of the following quotations we have omitted the final word or phrase; most readers will have little, if any, difficulty in supplying the missing parts.

> To be, or not to be: that is . . .
> —*Hamlet*

. . . the play's the thing
wherein I'll catch the conscience of the . . .
—*Hamlet*

Beware the ides of . . .
—*Julius Caesar*

This above all: to thine own self . . .
—*Hamlet*

Friends, Romans, countrymen, lend me your . . .
—*Julius Caesar*

There are more things in heaven and earth, Horatio,
Than are dreamt of in your . . .
—*Hamlet*

All the world's a stage,
and all the men and women merely . . .
—*As You Like It*

Double, double toil and . . .
—*Macbeth*

Nor set down aught in malice: then, must you speak
Of one that loved not wisely but too . . .
—*Othello*

A horse! a horse! my kingdom for . . .
—*Richard III*

The quality of mercy is not . . .
—*The Merchant of Venice*

I come to bury Caesar, not to . . .
—*Julius Caesar*

Recognizable Passages. The second category consists of passages we may not be able to quote from memory but nevertheless immediately recognize, even if we cannot always tell which play or poem they come from. Obviously, the line that separates the first category from the second is indistinct, since it is slightly different for every reader. Here is a brief selection of quotations we think many people might consign to the second grouping.

This royal throne of kings, this scepter'd isle . . .
This happy breed of men, this little world,
This precious stone set in the silver sea . . .
This blessed plot, this earth, this realm, this England . . .
—*Richard II*

The lunatic, the lover, and the poet,
Are of imagination all compact. . . .
—*A Midsummer-Night's Dream*

But, soft! what light through yonder window breaks?
It is the east, and Juliet is the sun.
—*Romeo and Juliet*

What's in a name? That which we call a rose
By any other name would smell as sweet.
—*Romeo and Juliet*

Then come kiss me, sweet and twenty,
Youth's a stuff will not endure.
—*Twelfth Night*

Child Rowland to the dark tower came,
His word was still,—Fie, foh, and fum,
I smell the blood of a British man.
—*King Lear*

As flies to wanton boys, are we to the gods;
They kill us for their sport.
—*King Lear*

Age cannot wither her, nor custom stale
Her infinite variety. . . .
—*Antony and Cleopatra*

O brave new world,
That has such people in't!
—*The Tempest*

Shall I compare thee to a summer's day?
Thou art more lovely and more temperate. . . .
—*Sonnet XVIII*

When to the sessions of sweet silent thought
I summon up remembrance of things past . . .
—*Sonnet XXX*

Let me not to the marriage of true minds
Admit impediments. . . .
—*Sonnet CXVI*

Words and Phrases in Everyday Use. The third category is composed of words and phrases that we might or might not recognize as coming from Shakespeare, but that are, in any case, firmly embedded in contemporary speech. Interestingly, several of these quotations, divorced from their original contexts, have acquired different meanings. What ideas do you normally associate with "If music be the food of love, play on" and "Now is the winter of our discontent"? Listen to these expressions in context:

If music be the food of love, play on;
Give me excess of it, that, surfeiting,
The appetite may sicken, and so die.
—*Twelfth Night*

Now is the winter of our discontent
Made glorious summer by this sun of York. . . .
—*Richard III*

The following selections represent the merest fraction of the great volume of everyday language from Shakespeare.

I cannot tell what the dickens his name is.
—*The Merry Wives of Windsor*

Well said: that was laid on with a trowel.
—*As You Like It*

The livelong day . . .
—*Julius Caesar*

But love is blind. . . .
—*The Merchant of Venice*

He hath eaten me out of house and home. . . .
—*Henry IV, Part II*

True is it that we have seen better days. . . .
—*As You Like It*

. . . brevity is the soul of wit. . . .
—*Hamlet*

It did me yeoman's service. . . .
—*Hamlet*

As good luck would have it.
—*The Merry Wives of Windsor*

But I will wear my heart upon my sleeve. . . .
—*Othello*

O, that way madness lies. . . .
—*King Lear*

Fight till the last gasp.
—*Henry VI, Part I*

. . . laugh yourselves into stitches. . . .
—*Twelfth Night*

. . . I will tell you my drift.
—*Much Ado About Nothing*

My salad days
When I was green in judgment . . .
—*Antony and Cleopatra*

. . . It beggar'd all description.
—*Antony and Cleopatra*

I bear a charmed life. . . .
—*Macbeth*

'Tis neither here nor there.
—*Othello*

Best-loved Passages. The final category is the hardest to define, but it may be the most important of all. Made up of those passages that each of us personally loves best, it represents a private communication between poet and reader through the magical intermediary of language. Such a selection is never the same for any two people; your favorites will not—and doubtless should not—be exactly the same as ours. In offering you a few of our selections we mean only to remind you of your own. Here is a lovely quartet about sunsets and sunrises:

Night's candles are burnt out, and jocund day
Stands tiptoe on the misty mountain tops.
—*Romeo and Juliet*

The glow-worm shows the matin to be near,
And 'gins to pale his uneffectual fire. . . .
—*Hamlet*

The gaudy, blabbing, and remorseful day
Is crept into the bosom of the sea.
—*Henry VI, Part II*

But, look, the morn, in russet mantle clad,
Walks o'er the dew of yon high eastward hill. . . .
—*Hamlet*

Some of Shakespeare's greatest lyrics appear in *The Tempest.* Here are two passages, the first from act 1 and the second from act 4, that familiarity never seems to dull:

Full fathom five thy father lies;
Of his bones are coral made;
Those are pearls that were his eyes:
Nothing of him that doth fade
But doth suffer a sea-change
Into something rich and strange.

These our actors,
As I foretold you, were all spirits and
Are melted into air, into thin air;
And, like the baseless fabric of this vision,
The cloud-capp'd towers, the gorgeous palaces,
The solemn temples, the great globe itself,
Yea, all which it inherit, shall dissolve
And, like this insubstantial pageant faded,
Leave not a rack behind. We are such stuff
As dreams are made on, and our little life
Is rounded with a sleep.

Some passages are able to convey a philosophic point of view with astonishing pungency, whereas others charm us with their simplicity. What cat fancier could resist "a harmless necessary cat" (*The Merchant of Venice*)?

Many of Shakespeare's best-loved verses cannot, of course, be separated from the dramatic context in which they appear. For example, the poignancy of Hotspur's death in battle at the hands of Prince Hal in *Henry IV, Part I* comes largely from our understanding of the characters of the two men—Henry Percy, known to everyone as Hotspur, the perfect knight, afire with his own vision of honor and justice; and Hal, apparently weak and dissolute, trying only to become a man and to do his duty. When in the end it is Hal who delivers the mortal blow, both men are shocked.

Hotspur: O, Harry, thou hast robb'd me of my youth!
I better brook the loss of brittle life
Than those proud titles thou hast won of me;
They wound my thoughts worse than thy sword my flesh:
But thought's the slave of life, and life time's fool;
And time, that takes survey of all the world,
Must have a stop. . . . Percy, thou art dust,
And food for—— [*Dies*]

Hal: For worms, brave Percy: fare thee well, great heart!
Ill-weaved ambition, how much art thou shrunk!
When that this body did contain a spirit,
A kingdom for it was too small a bound;
But now two paces of the vilest earth
Is room enough. . . .

Playgoers with long memories may recall Laurence Olivier's outstanding performance as Hotspur for England's Old Vic Theatre Company in 1946. Olivier deliberately gave the character a stammer, so that Hotspur died in the midst of struggling to pronounce the word *worms.*

But if Shakespeare depends on story, poetry, and performance to move us, in order to create his greatest effects he depends most of all on his uncanny ability to enlist our imaginations. In *Henry V* the character Chorus explicitly asks us to transcend the limitations of the Elizabethan stage and "eke out our performance with your mind."

Suppose that you have seen
The well-appointed king at Hampton pier
Embark his royalty; and his brave fleet
With silken streamers the young Phoebus fanning:
Play with your fancies . . . behold the threaden sails,
Borne with the invisible and creeping wind,
Draw the huge bottoms through the furrow'd sea,

Breasting the lofty surge: O, do but think
You stand upon the rivage and behold
A city on the inconstant billows dancing. . . .

In this, as in so many other passages, we may wonder whether Shakespeare was not, after all, transcending language itself.

shall, will. In conservative standard usage the rule is that simple future is expressed by *I shall, you will, he/she/it will,* but intention, determination, or command is expressed by *I will, you shall, he/she/it shall.* The distinctive use of *shall* in the third person is shown in the following:

> . . . that ten thousand engineers are busy making sure that the world shall be convenient even if it is destroyed in the process.
>
> —E. B. White,
> *A Slight Sound at Evening*

> Our mother nurtured these hopes. . . . Finish high school with good grades. Then there will be a way to go to college. There *shall* be a way.
>
> —James A. McCracken,
> *Reader's Digest*

Guardians of usage have for years claimed that this distinction between *shall* and *will,* together with many other more subtle ones, is of vital importance.

> The Scots and the Irish, even of the first rank, generally use *will* for *shall* in the first person; by which means, they substitute a promise for an intended prediction. Several errors of this kind have escaped the notice of the most celebrated writers.
>
> —Noah Webster,
> *Dissertations on the English Language* (1789)

The favorite example traditionally given is the alleged cry of an Irishman struggling in the river: "I will drown and no one shall save me!" A grammarian standing on the bank comments, rather coldbloodedly, that if the Irishman means what he says, he intends to drown and forbids anyone to save him; but if the fellow really means that he is about to drown (he fears) and no one is willing to save him, he should say, "I shall drown and no one will save me!"

The truth is that most people—including the English, the Irish, the Scottish, the Americans, and all other English speakers—do not consistently observe these distinctions and have never done so. In current usage *will* is simply far commoner than *shall* with all three grammatical persons and in all shades of futurity, intention, etc. The distinctive choice of *shall* varies very widely in different places, among different social groups, from person to person within them, and even in most people's usage from day to day.

◇ ***Recommendation.*** The choice between *shall* and *will* is made at such a deep level of linguistic instinct that any native speaker's usage must be regarded as acceptable and correct.

shambles. A *shamble* or *shambles* was originally a butcher's shop or a slaughterhouse. This sense is obsolete, but the word *shambles* is still sometimes used figuratively to mean 'scene of blood and slaughter':

> The roundhouse was like a shambles; three were dead inside, another lay in his death agony across the threshold; and there were Alan and I victorious and unhurt.
>
> —Robert Louis Stevenson,
> *Kidnapped*

> It was not hard to imagine what the Germans might do to any Canadians they captured—once they had seen the shambles we had made of their lorried infantry.
>
> —Farley Mowat,
> *And No Birds Sang*

Much more often *shambles* is used without reference to bloodshed, meaning 'state of great disorder or hopeless disorganization':

> Our U.S. Army is in a shambles when one compares our discipline to that of Israel or the U.S.S.R.
>
> —George W. Arruda (letter),
> *Soldier of Fortune*

> His game was a shambles; he seemed to be doing everything wrong—slicing off the tee, choking on his downswing, forcing putts.
> —Kathleen Maxa, *Esquire*

shan't as a contracted form of *shall not* is less common in American English than in British. It is somewhat informal but standard.

she. In a secondary sense *she* has often been applied to collective entities (the church, the nation), abstractions (liberty, justice), things in nature (the moon), and inanimate objects (a ship, a plane, a car).

> Summer is when the lake most strikingly displays her moods to those whose lives are entwined with hers.
> —William K. Stevens, *New York Times*

> . . . The tanker Mobil Aero sailed from Beaumont, Tex., with a load of gasoline for storage tanks in three cities in Florida. But she was not able to unload all of her cargo because the storage tanks were full, so she returned to Texas with 132,000 gallons still in her hold.
> —Martin Tolchin, *New York Times*

Interestingly enough, the pronoun *his,* now exclusively masculine, was once used in a similar way. Thus, "the earth brought forth his fruit" (1405), "the gunpowder lost his strength" (1644), and "famine raged in all his horrors" (1818). With the disappearance of grammatical gender, people felt that the foregoing usage was no longer appropriate. So the possessive pronoun *its* came into currency around the end of the 16th century. Shakespeare was the first author of note to use the form, which in his day retained a strong colloquial flavor. This is why *its* doesn't occur in the King James Bible of 1611.

Many women today do not want their pronoun used for natural forces, organizations, abstractions, and machines. Many such usages arise in areas from which women are excluded. They can be a way of seeming to include the female principle while actually limiting participation to males.

> They are sad because they disclose a great nation being led by men unworthy of her and her history.
> —Tom Wicker, *New York Times*

◇ ***Recommendation.*** Instead of personifying an object and thus being tempted to use a feminine pronoun, a writer can often avoid biased usage by ascribing action to the people who performed it. Here is how two of the preceding examples can be restated, using the genderless *its* or the plural pronoun:

> But the crew could not deliver all the cargo [*or,* But dock workers did not unload all the cargo] because the storage tanks were full, so the ship returned to Texas with 132,000 gallons still in its hold.

> They are sad because they disclose a group of leaders unworthy of their great nation and its history.

shibboleth. Language defines people, and individual words can even mean life or death. In a war between two of the ancient tribes of Israel, the Gileadites defeated the Ephraimites. After the fighting, Ephraimite refugees trying to cross the Jordan were arrested by the Gileadites, and if they denied their nationality were subjected to a linguistic test—the pronunciation of the Hebrew word *shibboleth* (it means 'ear of grain,' also 'steam'—but the meaning is unimportant). Anyone who pronounced it *sibboleth* was immediately recognized as an Ephraimite and was executed. For the original Biblical quotation see the section Enduring Language From the King James Bible at BIBLE.

From this ruthless exploitation of speech variety, the word *shibboleth* is used to mean 'any speech sound or language usage by which a person's social background or native region can easily be recognized':

> . . . we will avoid forms like *I seen him, he don't* because they are shibboleths, disregard of which may lead to unfortunate results for us in our living and relations with others.
> —Robert A. Hall, Jr., *Linguistics and Your Language*

The prolonged /ä/ of such words as *far, farm, farther, calm,* and *Harvard* is perhaps the most striking feature of the regional type, the shibboleth by which the outsider recognizes the Eastern New Englander.

—C. K. Thomas, *Phonetics of American English*

Secondly, *shibboleth* can mean 'an old slogan or belief that is often repeated but has lost relevance or meaning':

I knew too that I was flouting the shibboleth of avoiding a ground war in Asia. . . .

—William C. Westmoreland, *A Soldier Reports*

His words are worth noting since they provided a strong counterpoint to the conservative shibboleths of contemporary Republican politics.

—Walter Shapiro, *Atlantic Monthly*

shivaree, callithump, skimmerton, etc. This peculiar group of words refers to old-fashioned country customs of holding mock parades with raucous "music" for various satirical purposes, especially relating to weddings and marriages. Such customs exist in many European folk traditions and were variously brought to America from colonial times onward. The American terms are especially interesting for both their variety and their regional distribution.

(1) *Charivari* and *shivaree.* In France a *charivari* (from a Medieval Latin word meaning 'headache') was a noisy mock serenade lampooning an unpopular marriage, such as that of a widow who married too soon after her husband's death. The word *charivari* /shə-rĭv-ə-**rē**, shĭv-ə-**rē**/ is still used in parts of Louisiana. *Shivaree* /shĭv-ə-**rē**, **shĭv**-ə-rē/, a distortion of *charivari,* is the most basic and widespread American term and is found in Canadian English as well. It is used both as a verb and a noun for a relatively good-humored hazing of newlyweds, who are usually expected to provide refreshments or other placating compensation to silence the "serenaders." The first passage below describes one such occasion:

Among the manly recreations which they have proposed to themselves is that of shivareeing "that Dutchman, Gus Wehle." It is the solemn opinion of the whole crowd that "no Dutchman hadn't orter be so lucky as to git sech a beauty of a gal and a hundred acres of bottom lands to boot."

The members of the party were all disguised. . . . The instruments provided by this orchestra were as various as their musical tastes. . . . Bob Short had a dumb-bull, a keg with a strip of raw-hide stretched across one end like a drum-head, while the other remained open. A waxed cord inserted in the middle of the drumhead, and reaching down through the keg, completed the instrument. The pulling of the hand over this cord made a hideous bellowing, hence its name. Bill Day had a gigantic watchman's rattle, a hickory spring on a cog-wheel. . . . Then there were melodious tin pans and conch-shells and tin horns. But the most deadly noise was made by Jim West, who had two iron skillet-lids . . . which, when placed face to face, and rubbed . . . made a sound discordant and deafening. . . . That serenade! Such a medley of discordant sounds. . . . But [Gus Wehle's] house remained quiet. Once Bill Day thought that he heard a laugh within. Julia [Gus's wife] may have lost her self-control. She was so happy, and a little unrestrained fun was so strange a luxury!

At last the door . . . was suddenly opened, and Julia, radiant as she could be, stood on the threshold with a candle in her hand. "Come in, gentlemen." . . . They followed [her] into the room. . . . A smell of hot coffee and the sight of a well-spread table greeted their senses.

—Edward Eggleston, *The End of the World* (1872)

We kids would "shivaree" at the neighborhood weddings until the bridegroom tossed us coins with which to buy treats.

—*Chicago Tribune* (1946)

Shivaree has also been used for harsher social purposes:

> The head of the procession . . . was a drabbled and weeping trollop who was being "Chivareed" out of town.
> —Jerome Hart, *Vigilante Girl* (1910)

And the word can also be used to mean simply 'a loud, confused din':

> I started such a rattling "shivaree" down below as never had astounded an engineer in this world before.
> —Mark Twain, *Old Times on the Mississippi* (1876)

(2) *Callithump.* This term originates in the west of England. In 18th-century Devon and Dorset *gallithumpian* meant 'one who makes loud disturbances at parliamentary elections.' In America, *callithump* or *callathump* is used in the New England and North Midland dialects with the same meaning as *shivaree.* But it is also used without reference to weddings. A *callithumpian band* is a noisy band of intentionally discordant instruments, and to *callithump* is 'to caterwaul, make raucous discordant music':

> The call [on the exchange] lasts ten or fifteen minutes, and occasionally has the accompaniment of callithumpian discord. —*Harper's Magazine* (1886)

(3) *Belling* is the term used in Indiana, Ohio, western Pennsylvania, West Virginia, northern Maryland, and southern Michigan. It comes from *bell* = 'to ring a bell,' perhaps referring to wedding bells. This term is reserved only for weddings and is closer to the notion of a wedding reception.
(4) *Horning* or *horning bee* is an Inland Northern dialect term. Like *shivaree,* its earliest meaning is 'the noisy harassment of someone':

> "Horning" is peculiar to Dartmouth, and is much in the line of hazing. Feb. 1 the sophomore class howled beneath the windows of Professor Foster's study and hurled snowballs and coal at them, breaking the glass.
> —*Chicago Record* (1896)

(5) *Skimmerton* or *skimmelton* is the term used in the Hudson Valley dialect, and it comes from the rural English *skimmington,* which was a boisterous procession ridiculing an unfaithful husband or a shrewish wife, often including effigies and a mock serenade. Today the skimmerton has also been toned down and is usually a good-natured hazing of newlyweds.
(6) *Tin-panning* is also a shivaree. This term is rarely used today except in a few scattered places in the Middle Atlantic States, but it is probably the origin of the expression *Tin Pan Alley* = 'the world of commercial popular music.'

shrift. The archaic verb *shrive,* used of a priest, means 'to absolve (a penitent) of sins after hearing confession.' The noun *shrift* means 'confession and absolution,' and *short shrift* was the brief time customarily allowed to a condemned person for confession before being executed. The expression *short shrift* is now used to mean either 'swift and ruthless treatment' or, less violently, 'abrupt and unsympathetic dismissal.'

> Now in the death agonies of the Third Reich Vlasov and his men found themselves in Czechoslovakia. They knew that if they fell into Russian hands it would be short shrift—the firing wall or a quick bullet in the head beside the road.
> —Harrison E. Salisbury, *The Unknown War*

> My father, had he still been alive, would have given short shrift to my petulant questioning.
> —Christiaan Barnard, *Reader's Digest*

Related to *shrive* is the *shrove* in *Shrove Tuesday,* literally 'confession Tuesday,' the last day before the beginning of Lent.

silicon, silicone. Nontechnical people often fail to distinguish between these two very different substances. *Silicon* is a hard, nonmetallic element that is used (among other purposes) as a semiconductor in transistors, computer chips, etc.; hence the slang name *Silicon Valley* for the heartland of the microelectronics industry in Santa Clara and San Mateo counties, California.

Silicone is an organic compound of silicon and oxygen; there are various types of it, used in lubricants, artificial limbs, and many other applications. The way to remember the difference between the two is by the suffixes: the *-on* of *silicon* denotes an element, as in *carbon, neon,* etc.; the *-one* of *silicone* denotes a compound that contains oxygen, as in *acetone, ketone,* etc.

simile. Whereas metaphor is usually defined as an implied comparison made between one object, concept, quality, or action and another, *simile* is that same comparison made explicit. If, for example, John Donne had said "No man is like an island" instead of "No man is an island," he would have been using simile instead of metaphor. But once that technical distinction has been acknowledged, it is clear that simile is nevertheless no more than a subclass of metaphor. See also FIGURES OF SPEECH; METAPHOR.

simplistic is sometimes used as if it were a synonym for *simple.* This is a mistake. *Simplistic* means 'unrealistically limited, oversimplified':

> TV news tends to be . . . unrealistically tied to available news pictures, under-researched, predictable, and simplistic.
> —Ron Powers, *The Newscasters*

> Air-bag benefits were derived from laboratory tests that were simplistic versions of real-life accidents.
> —Earl and Miriam Selby, *Reader's Digest*

In the latter sentence "simplified" would have been better.

sine qua non, Latin for '(thing) without which not,' may be pronounced /sĭn-ā kwä **nōn**/ or /sī-nē kwā **nŏn**/. The expression means 'absolute prerequisite, indispensable condition or feature':

> For these reasons it is a *sine qua non* of successful dealing with Russia that the foreign government in question should remain cool and collected. . . .
> —George F. Kennan, *American Diplomacy 1900–1950*

> Almost from the beginning of organized government the balanced budget or its equivalent has been the *sine qua non* of sound and sensible management of the public purse.
> —John Kenneth Galbraith, *The Affluent Society*

> Her brief tenure as president of the University of Chicago has even included a major confrontation with protesters, surely a sine qua non in the rite of passage for anyone inheriting the mantle of campus leadership.
> —Gene I. Maeroff, *New York Times*

As can be seen from the above quotations, this expression is sometimes italicized and sometimes not. Since it is a phrase well-assimilated into English, it need not be set off from the surrounding text. (For more on pronouncing Latin expressions see LATIN WORDS.)

sinister. See BAR SINISTER, BEND SINISTER.

Sisyphus /sĭs-ə-fəs/, in Greek myth, was a wicked king of Corinth who was condemned to a unique punishment in Hades; he had to roll a heavy stone to the top of a hill, only to have it roll back to the bottom again. His name remains proverbial for any endlessly, often hopelessly, renewed task or effort. The adjective is either *Sisyphean* /sĭs-ə-**fē**-ən/ or *Sisyphian* /sĭ-**sĭf**-ē-ən/, preferably the former.

> [Jimmy] Carter's attempt to stem the world's arms traffic may be the labor of Sisyphus. —*Time*

> . . . the Sisyphean aspects of golf . . .
> —George Plimpton, *The Bogey Man*

> For highway departments it is the time to undertake the Sisyphean task of repairing the potholes of winter. . . .
> —James K. Page, Jr., *Smithsonian*

sit. See SET.

skeptic. The British spelling *sceptic* is sometimes used in the United States, but *skeptic* is very much commoner. Greek *skēptikos* means 'thoughtful, reflective.' The original Skeptics were philosophers who held that it is impossible to observe reality and that there is no such thing as objective knowledge. They therefore suspended judgment on everything and cultivated a state of imperturbable calm. Modern skeptics don't generally go that far but are those who habitually doubt or challenge accepted beliefs or idealism.

> . . . Miller, like many contemporary skeptics, is suspicious of the very idea of greatness and passion.
> —Jack Kroll, *Newsweek*

Skepticism is the attitude or practice of doubting or disbelieving.

> To most people, of course, the sudden popularity of religion in a town like Washington remained a matter for skepticism.
> —Charles Colson, *Born Again*

The adjective *skeptical* can mean either 'inclined to doubt' or 'systematically challenging assertions in order to arrive at truth.'

> Kennedy was skeptical. He doubted whether the Government Operations Committee had jurisdiction; trade union affairs belonged to the labor committees.
> —Arthur M. Schlesinger, Jr., *Robert Kennedy and His Times*

> Skeptical scrutiny is the means, in both science and religion, by which deep insights can be winnowed from deep nonsense.
> —Carl Sagan, *Reader's Digest*

Skeptical is now also used with clauses introduced by *that*, merely meaning 'doubtful, inclined to disbelieve':

> Culver is skeptical that the reorganization will lead to a resolution of questions of strategy and policy.
> —Elizabeth Drew, *Senator*

skimmerton. See SHIVAREE, CALLITHUMP, SKIMMERTON.

slang. American slang is one of the success stories of the English language. There are probably some 35,000 expressions that are, or once were, American slang. Along with baseball, apple pie, supermarkets, and jeans, our slang seems to symbolize America, and some of its most popular terms have spread around the globe. Yet, many people aren't exactly sure what slang is, where it comes from, when it first appeared, or even who uses it and why. In fact, many Americans aren't sure whether, or when, slang can be used as an acceptable part of their speech, whether they will be criticized for using it, or whether it might not indeed threaten the language and its clarity.

Most of our talk is spontaneous; if we stopped to analyze every word, we would never get anything said or done. Only when we pause to think about it, look into a usage book, use a dictionary, or hear a teacher or critic talk about language do we become actively conscious that there are different types of words and vocabularies. Slang is but one of several usage levels into which scholars, dictionary makers, and the general public divide the language. These levels are, in descending order of acceptability, (1) *standard* or *formal;* (2) *informal;* (3) *slang;* (4) *cant* (the technical vocabulary or shoptalk of any group); (5) *jargon* (the informal vocabulary of any group); (6) *argot* (the combined cant and jargon of criminals); (7) *nonstandard* or *substandard* (words like *ain't* and *irregardless*); (8) *taboo* or *vulgar* (terms taking the name of God in vain or referring too bluntly to sex, body waste, or the parts of the body having to do with them).

Standard and informal words are those used and accepted by the general public all across the nation. Cant, jargon, and argot are in-group terms known and used by workers, hobbyists, or others with a common occupation, interest, or concern. Nonstandard and taboo terms, though widely known, are often restricted in use by those who don't want to be considered illiterate or vulgar.

From standard through taboo, each succeeding level of usage has fewer words in it, and even those words are less frequently used. For example, there are many more standard words than cant words, and more people use them more often. The specific in-groups or cultural subgroups that use cant, jargon, and argot can be large or small, educated or uneducated, rich or poor. They can be members of specific occupations, such as automobile workers, atomic scientists, coal miners, farmers, taxi drivers, soldiers, teachers, accountants, doctors, politicians, or pickpockets. They can be cultural subgroups that share certain viewpoints, experiences, or activities, such as baseball players and fans, poker players, art lovers, teen-agers, jazz enthusiasts, antiques collectors, film buffs, computer users, motorcyclists, gourmets, or vegetarians.

The Nature and Function of Slang. All words are born equal, and labeling a word slang—or anything else—comes after the fact of its use. No word or word use is slang until linguists, dictionary compilers, teachers, critics, or—most important of all—the general public decides it is. This decision has nothing to do with spelling, pronunciation, or etymology. You could not tell whether the isolated words *dough, bread, grass,* and *pot* were standard or slang merely by looking at or saying them or by knowing their origins. Only usage would give the clue to their meanings and thus their status. The first two, *bread* and *dough,* have standard use as food terms, but slang use meaning 'money'; the last two, *grass* and *pot,* also have standard or formal use meaning, respectively, 'type of plant life' and 'cooking utensil,' but slang use meaning 'marijuana.' With *dough, bread,* and *grass,* the slang sense is etymologically the same as the standard sense; the cooking *pot,* however, comes from Old English *pott,* whereas the marijuana *pot* is considered by some experts to come from a completely different word, the Mexican Spanish *potaguaya* = 'marijuana.'

Much slang, then, is created by changing or extending the meaning of existing words. But some slang words are new coinages altogether. *Moolah* and *gage,* for example, are also slang for 'money' and 'marijuana,' respectively, but are not new uses of old standard words.

To say that slang is more colorful, blunt, or hard-working than more formal English doesn't define or describe slang and isn't fair to Standard English. Some slang is indeed earthy, or at least down-to-earth, and some people claim that it avoids pretensions; is "language that rolls up its sleeves" and gets to work. Slang words, however, like all other words, can also be dull, euphemistic, vague, or so overworked as to seem mere mutterings. In fact, all language, not just slang, can roll up its sleeves and get to work; much standard terminology is pertinent and can be sharp, fresh, and even memorable. To call a person a *windbag* or a *blowhard* is slangy and does give us a colorful image, but to call someone a *fool* in Standard English is just as much to the point. In fact, the standard word *fool* also calls a person a windbag, or at least a bellows, because our English word *fool* comes to us via Middle English and Old French from Late Latin *follis,* which meant 'bellows or bag' and is akin to Latin *flare* = 'to blow'—exactly the same image as *windbag* and *blowhard.* The difference is merely one of time. *Fool* has been filtered through several languages and many centuries, so that its original image of a windbag or blowhard has been obscured or forgotten; but the word is as vivid, blunt, and precise as the more recent slang terms.

Slang seems to stand between the general words—the standard and informal ones available to everyone—and the in-group words—the cant, jargon, and argot associated with, or most available to, specific segments of the population. As a matter of fact, slang is the dividing line. It is the meeting place or interface of the general and the specific in-group vocabularies.

Many words do enter the general vocabulary from specific groups. It is often a special-interest group that first develops or encounters a new object, idea, concept, or attitude. The group names the new entity or creates a vocabulary for it; then later the general public may adopt the new word or words and meanings. *Atomic bomb, carburetor, cinematographer, movie, phone, squeeze play*—even *baseball, supermarket,* and *jeans*—were all terms originally used by insiders, and most of these terms quickly spread into formal or informal speech and writing. Some terms, however, don't make this leap from group use to general use all at once. Some, like *movie* for 'motion picture' and *phone* for 'telephone,' seem so new, startling, or eccentric, or carry so many connotations of their original in-group use, that they do not get completely accepted or assimilated into formal or informal use. These words become slang.

Thus, slang appears to serve as a barrier or a strainer between specific in-group use and general use—a holding area or proving ground for some in-group words that seem to be trying to filter into the general language.

Some words that enter slang from cant, jargon, etc., sooner or later make it into the standard or informal general vocabulary; others never make it but are screened out, to disappear or drop back into restricted in-group use; still others seem destined to remain in the halfway house of slang forever. For instance, the standard words *blizzard, goodbye, mob, racketeer,* and the aforementioned *movie* and *phone* were once considered slang (*O.K.* was labeled slang in most dictionaries until the mid-1960s but is now considered informal or even standard by many). On the other hand, such once-popular slang expressions as *lucifer* for 'match,' *tomato* for 'young woman,' and *fab* and *gear,* both meaning 'fabulous, wonderful,' have dropped out of use, for the time being at least, and are seldom heard on any usage level. As to those words that seem to remain slang forever, *bones* = 'dice' has been slang for at least 600 years, since Chaucer used it in the 14th century; *beat it* = 'to go away' has been slang for some 400 years, since Shakespeare used it in the 16th century; and *dough* = 'money' has been American slang for more than 130 years.

Regardless of what happens to a word that becomes slang, knowing where slang originates tells us what slang is. Slang, as we have said, comes from in-groups or cultural subgroups. All subgroups, including the most educated, can contribute slang. Obstetricians gave us *preemie* = 'premature baby' (though this word is now considered informal); astronauts gave us *A-OK* = 'functioning very smoothly'; law enforcement gave us *OD* = 'overdose'; union organizers gave us *fink* = 'informer, odious person'; and Treasury Department officials long ago gave us *greenback* = 'U.S. bank note.'

Though slang comes from many such groups, high and low, it does seem that from time to time a particular group emerges to attract the popular imagination or attention. Words from such groups become widely known, even faddish for a while. During Prohibition we took much slang from bootleggers and organized crime, such as *hijack; Jake* = 'liquor made from Jamaican ginger'; *pineapple* = 'hand grenade'; *torpedo* = 'gunman, thug'; and *take for a one-way ride.* Beginning around 1915 we began to pull much slang from sports terms, as *KO* = 'knockout'; *take it on the chin* = 'to receive punishment, harsh criticism, etc.'; *go to bat for* = 'to defend or support'; *play ball* = 'to cooperate.' During wartime we take much slang from our military forces, such as *lobsterback* = 'British soldier, redcoat' (American Revolution); *leatherneck* = 'Marine' (War of 1812); *AWOL* = 'absent without leave' and *skedaddle* = 'to hurry off' (Civil War); *boot* = 'new recruit' and BOONDOCKS = 'distant, unpopulated place' (Spanish-American War); *civvies* = 'civilian clothes,' *doughboy* = 'U.S. foot soldier,' and *Jerry* = 'German soldier' (World War I); FLAK = 'antiaircraft fire,' *GI* = 'U.S. soldier,' and GUNG-HO = 'extremely enthusiastic' (World War II); *chopper* = 'helicopter' and *honcho* = 'man in charge' (Korean War); *hack it* = 'to be able to do' and *Nam* = 'Vietnam' (Vietnam War).

The flappers and sheiks of the Roaring Twenties caught the popular interest and produced such slang expressions as *jazz up, Oh yeah, nerts,* and *the cat's pajamas.* Swing musicians and enthusiasts of the 1930s provided *hep, cat* = 'person,' and *groovy;* in the 1950s cool jazz and its followers gave us *cool, beat, out of sight, real gone,* and *shades* = 'dark glasses.' During the 1960s and 1970s we took much slang from the drug culture, as *downer, high, pot,* and *rush* = 'thrill, feeling of excitement.'

The Origins of Slang. New words have, of course, been entering language ever since man began to speak. Hundreds, and perhaps thousands, of new words and uses come into the English language every year. At the same time that new words are entering the language, old words are changing in status. Thus, slang enters the language continually. More than 2,000 years ago both Plato and Aristotle referred to cultural subgroup vocabularies in Greek, and Plato (c. 427–347 B.C.) even complained that the ruling classes were using words once associated with slaves, soldiers, and artisans—in other words, that the standard or formal Greek of his day was absorbing some slang from cant, jargon, and nonstandard speech.

When then did slang come to America? It arrived with the earliest Spanish, French, Dutch, and Italian explorers and settlers. English slang came on the *Mayflower* and before. *Goodbye* was a fairly new and breezy form of *God be with you* in the early 17th century, and settlers in Virginia and the Plymouth Colony may well have criticized their younger, breezier members for using it. Our patriots and soldiers used slang before, during, and after the Revolutionary War. For example, though the word *say*, meaning 'to speak or utter,' is more than 1,000 years old, it is still considered slang by many when used at the beginning of a sentence to get the listener's attention, as in "Say, isn't it a great day!" In 1814 this slangy use appeared in a patriotic poem by Francis Scott Key, which opened with the words "Oh, say, can you see, by the dawn's early light," making our national anthem the only one that begins with a slang expression.

Despite its existence some 2,000 years ago, slang did not begin to grow rapidly in Europe until the establishment of the large medieval cities; its growth accelerated during the Renaissance. Though farming centers and crossroads towns may have existed before the medieval period, few people met or mingled frequently with others of different areas or backgrounds. Noblemen and peasants had little conversation together. Although a royal chef, tutor, or armorer might move from one castle to another, and although there were a few wandering peddlers, soldiers, monks, and scholars, most people lived all their lives in one place and with one small group of family and neighbors, speaking with a few people who shared the same limited occupations, concerns, beliefs, and vocabulary. With the growth of the city, however, people increasingly began to move, from countryside to town and from town to town. Instead of doing everything for themselves, people began to concentrate on one occupation and to turn to other specialists—farmers, blacksmiths, carpenters, tailors, butchers, bakers, merchants—to supply the rest of their needs. With the growth of such occupations came in-group cant and jargon, which might then spread from the group into the general vocabulary. Society had begun to fragment; and as the centuries passed, there came circus roustabouts, oilfield workers, railroad men, hot rodders, atomic physicists, prizefighters, surfers, astronauts, pop-music fans, computer programmers, stamp collectors, cardiologists, TV actors—all of them potential contributors to slang.

The term *slang* itself didn't appear until 1756. It was first used to refer to the vocabulary of people of low or disreputable character; by 1802 people were applying it to the cant and jargon of a class or profession and by 1818 to mean new words, and the new meanings of old words, that seemed extremely informal or especially rakish. The word *slang* is of somewhat obscure origin. Authorities formerly believed it came from Scandinavian *slenge* or *slengje* = 'sling,' found in the Scandinavian terms for 'new word' and 'nickname.' More recent scholars lean toward the belief that *slang* comes from the French *langue* = 'language' with a gliding *s-* prefixed to it, while others wonder whether it might not have developed from our own word *language* by the blending and shortening of such phrases as *thieves' language* or *beggars' language*.

The Uses of Slang. All nations have slang. North American English seems to have the most slang, with Russian and Spanish not too far behind. Quite simply, North America has more slang than anywhere else because we embrace two of the most diverse, most technically advanced democracies in the world. We have the most in-groups, the best communications and transportation, and the freedom to move, meet, and say and write not only what we please but how we please. Yet, as individuals we do tend to restrict our language. Many of us know levels of speech and specific words that we prefer not to use, at least in certain situations. We all know the nonstandard *ain't,* but many of us use it only for humorous effect because we have been taught that it is inelegant and illiterate. We avoid certain taboo words: some of us, because we feel such words offend God or morality; others, because such words might brand us as vulgar; still others, because we might shock or embarrass people. At times we may not use our own in-group words with outsiders because they may not understand them or because we want to keep this part of our lives to ourselves, to share it only with colleagues and close friends.

Similarly, our use of slang is also a matter of choice and circumstances. Many people may not know or care whether a word is nonstandard, slang, cant, jargon, or even taboo. They may not care for such fine distinctions, or they may maintain that the unacceptability of a word is in the mind of the listener. Many of us, however, do know about usage levels and treat words, if not by concepts of morality, at least by the codes of etiquette. For many educated speakers language levels are akin to dress. We wear a suit or dress to the office; sport coat and trousers or skirt and blouse or pant suit on less formal occasions; jeans or shorts and a T-shirt in very casual circumstances. Likewise, we use standard formal speech, informal speech, and slang depending on the degree of formality of the occasion or situation and on the people we are with and our relation to them.

Almost everyone uses some slang sometimes, and some people use a lot of slang often. Those who don't go to offices or seldom find themselves in formal situations, those who spend more time with close friends than with business associates and mere acquaintances, use the most slang. Some students and young people may also use slang abundantly because they are receptive to new ideas, concepts, and words; because some old ideas and concepts seem new to them and hence call forth new words; and, of course, because they may want to establish their individuality and independence by using terminology that older people have not yet adopted.

People of all ages use slang to appear "with it." Most adults don't want to be considered old fogies; and both young and old like to be recognized as people with an awareness of the latest ideas, attitudes, and fads. Many older people have, or at least want others to think they have, a youthful outlook, so some older people may use much new slang too. This projection of personality, of appearances, is an important part of language. In our speech we not only tell others what we think and feel but also who we are—our social status, our in-group connections, our unique feelings and attitudes. Thus, we sometimes pepper our speech with our group's cant or jargon or with the slang taken from it. We use slang then primarily because it is a natural part of our vocabulary, and it indicates that we feel relaxed and are among friends; because we want others to know that we are up-to-date and reasonably broad-minded; and because we want the world to see that we have a background, personal interests, and in-group sympathies and position.

Slang has been used for hundreds, and even thousands, of years. It is created by the converging of in-groups and their words with the general public and its standard vocabulary. Like the clothes in our closets or the rest of the words in our vocabularies, it can be ignored on the one hand and overused on the other. Nearly everyone uses some slang, and some of us use a lot. For those who listen carefully, slang reveals much about its users. For those who care about words and meaning, the division of language into levels of acceptability is a fascinating topic. The labeling of words need carry neither praise nor condemnation. A true word lover could honestly say, "I never met a word I didn't like," because each word has its own compelling history, connotations, and use. Words are tools, and each, whether standard, slang, or any other level, has its proper function and occasion. Using the right tool—the right word at the right time—is the only way to achieve clarity or strive for beauty.

See also AIN'T; CLICHÉ; EUPHEMISM; IRREGARDLESS; JARGON; O.K., OK, OKAY; REGIONAL DIALECTS OF AMERICAN ENGLISH; VOGUE WORDS.

Slav, slave. The original homeland of the Slavs was probably in what is now the northern Ukraine. Their original name for themselves seems to have been *Slověne;* its literal meaning is not known with any certainty. The name *Slav* is now the most general of several related ethnic names, embracing the Russians, the Ukrainians, the Bulgarians, the Serbs, the Croats, the Czechs, the Poles, and a number of smaller groups. The *Slovaks* are one of the peoples of Czechoslovakia, the *Slovenes* are a people of Yugoslavia. The name *Czechoslovakia* means 'land of the Czechs and Slovaks,' and *Yugoslavia* means 'land of the South Slavs.' The adjective *Slavonic* refers to the culture or character of the Slavs in general. *Slavic* refers especially to their languages.

In the early Middle Ages the Slavs expanded westward into Europe as conquerors, and the Byzantine Greeks recorded their name as *Sklabenoi* or *Sklaboi,* which became *Sclavi* in Latin. By the 9th century some groups of Slavs in eastern Europe had been reduced to serfdom. Thus, the ethnic name *Sclavus* was used to mean, first, 'Slavic person who is a serf' and then simply 'serf.' It was borrowed into French as *esclave* and into English as *slave.*

slough. In its literal sense *slough* is usually pronounced /sloo͞/ in the United States, but sometimes /slou/; and it is sometimes spelled *slue* or *slew.* It means different things in different terrain; it may be a patch of muddy ground, a small swamp, a swampy pond, or a swampy backwater off a larger channel (see also SWAMP, MARSH, BOG). In British the only pronunciation is /slou/. The word was given its figurative sense 'state of hopeless dejection' by John Bunyan's allegory *Pilgrim's Progress* (1678), in which the Slough of Despond is a deep mudhole or swamp representing the tendency to despair.

> Some indicators [of inflation] are headed up again, throwing economists into sloughs of despond.
> —*New York Times*

In its figurative use the word is usually pronounced /slou/ in the United States as well as in Britain.

The word *slough* /slŭf/, meaning 'to shed a skin, get rid of something unwanted,' is completely unrelated.

slow, slowly. In adverbial use, in most cases *slowly* is the only correct choice; in some instances either *slowly* or *slow* is possible; and in a few situations *slow* is the preferable or even the only choice. When a complete action or process is described, only *slowly* is usually possible: *Slowly he woke up. He sat down slowly. The water evaporated slowly. Slow* can be used only after the verb it qualifies. When a continuing action or process is described, and the adverb follows the verb, either *slow* or *slowly* may be used: *The fire was burning slowly* (or *slow*) *and quietly. Move as slow* (or *slowly*) *as you can.* When straightforward motion through space is involved, *slow* is often the idiomatic choice: *He was driving quite slow. Go slow around the corner.*

so. Clauses with *so that* express either purpose or result. Purpose: *He got the gas tank filled so that he wouldn't have to stop on the way.* Result: *There had been a hard frost, so that the roads were dangerously icy.* In either case *that* is often omitted. *So that* has a slightly more formal effect, but *so* alone is also correct and standard. In clauses of result, *so (that)* should always be preceded by a comma.

social dialect. There are two major divisions of DIALECT: regional and social. A REGIONAL DIALECT is a speech variety unique to a particular region of a country. A *social dialect* is a speech variety used by speakers of a particular social group.

Sociolinguistics, which grew out of the urban dialect studies of the 1960s (see URBAN DIALECT), is the study of social dialects. It describes language variation primarily in terms of such social factors as sex, age, ethnic group, and class. It uses many of the theories and field methods of sociology.

Even though sociolinguistics has only recently been established as a field of scientific inquiry, the relationship between language diversity and social status has long been recognized. The ancient Romans, for example, were well aware of the difference between "vulgar" Latin (from *vulgus* = 'people, crowd'), the speech of the peasants and the lower classes, and "classical" Latin, the language of the aristocracy and of poets and orators.

Language differences reflect social differences. Everyone knows this at least intuitively. We constantly make judgments about people based on how they talk. With little information besides a person's pronunciation, grammar, and choice of words, we readily form an opinion about his or her education, ethnic background, and social status. Just as we can often recognize that someone we've just met speaks with a dialect, such as New England or Southern, we may also recognize whether his or her speech is perhaps an ethnic or a working-class dialect.

Standard and Nonstandard Dialects. Generally speaking, a dialect is any systematic speech variety of a single language. This includes the varieties of both Standard and Nonstandard English. A popular view of nonstandard speech is that it is deficient, somehow inferior as a form of communication; there is also a widespread belief that it is a corruption of, or a deviation from, some higher form of language.

For linguists, all language varieties are different but equal; all are systematic and ordered, including nonstandard varieties. There is nothing inherently inferior in Nonstandard English. It is wholly adequate as a system of communication. Moreover, Nonstandard English has its own history and has evolved in an orderly way.

Whether someone's speech is "good," "bad," "correct," or "pure" is a social, not a linguistic judgment. Within any given social group, there are implicit rules about good and bad language usage. Usually, these reflect the rules of standard speech—the prestige dialect sanctioned by the schools, the media, and the government. Value judgments about language are built into the social structure itself. The speech of a socially stigmatized group will be considered stigmatized, while the speech of a socially prestigious group will be considered highly prestigious.

In England, for example, upper- and middle-class speakers drop /r/ after vowels. Consequently, dropping this /r/ (*postvocalic* r) has prestige; it is the so-called Received pronunciation of educated English speech (see BRITISH ENGLISH). But the opposite is true in certain parts of the United States. In New York City, for example, pronouncing *cart* or *car* without /r/ is a speech characteristic of the working classes. *R*-lessness has come to be stigmatized (see R-LESSNESS, INTRUSIVE R; NEW YORK CITY DIALECT). These are opposite and strictly arbitrary judgments. Obviously, there is nothing inherently good or bad, correct or incorrect, cultivated or uneducated, about postvocalic *r*. Social structure, the layering of society into classes, then, has a direct bearing on the way we speak and the way we perceive the speech of others.

The interaction of five main variables accounts for most social dialects. These variables are social status, sex, age, ethnicity, and speech style.

Social Status. This is perhaps the most important factor in any account of social dialects. The stratification of a society is mirrored in its language. The concept of "social class" itself is controversial, especially in the United States, where a strong democratic, Populist tradition tends to play down class distinctions. Even sociologists disagree on how to define social class.

Nearly any evaluation of social status, however, takes into account occupation, education, income (or source of income), and sometimes house type and dwelling area (the overall conditions of the neighborhood). Based on these criteria, two major class divisions are usually distinguished: middle class and working class. Most American sociolinguists break these into four subclasses: upper and lower middle class and upper and lower working class. British sociolinguists tend to make even finer class distinctions: upper, middle, and lower middle class, etc.

Like regional dialects, social dialects are not distinct entities. Instead, they overlap and merge with each other, forming a continuum; there are no sharp dividing lines. However, the greater the distance between two dialects, whether that distance is geographical or social, the clearer the distinction between them. Nearly 1,000 miles separate the regions of the very different Gulf Southern and New England dialects, whereas the regions of the almost indistinguishable North and South Midland dialects border each other. Likewise, the difference between the upper-middle-class and lower-working-class dialects of New York City, for example, is much greater than the difference between upper-working-class and lower-working-class speech.

Any linguistic feature that is used more often by one social group than another is said to be *socially diagnostic*. For example, the dropping of the final consonant sound of words that are followed by words beginning with a vowel is a socially diagnostic feature. The pronunciations /ēs ĕn/, /bĕs ăp'l/, and /kōl ĕg/ are acceptable renderings of *east end, best apple*, and *cold egg* in Black English and probably other nonstandard dialects. Most socially diagnostic features have to do with pronunciation and grammar. Vocabulary differences are less reliable as features of social-class dialects.

A social-dialect feature can be either general or regional. A feature is general when it is socially diagnostic throughout the country and regional when socially diagnostic only in a particular area of the country.

In the North, for example, certain Southern dialect features have social significance. This is the result of the large influx of blacks from the South into the urban North in the last 50 years or so. Given the social and economic realities of the typical black community, this immigration has transformed many of the standard Southern dialect features into class and ethnic patterns. In Detroit and Chicago three features in particular have been shown to be socially diagnostic; that is, they have taken on social significance in these Northern cities even though in the South they are not features of any single ethnic group or social class. These features are:

(1) The dropping of postvocalic *r*.

(2) The pronunciation of the diphthong /ī/ as the single vowel, or monophthong, /ȧ/. *Time*, for example, is usually pronounced /tȧm/.

(3) The elimination of the contrast between /ĭ/ and /ĕ/ before the nasal consonants /n/, /m/, and /ng/. Thus, words like *pin* and *pen* are pronounced in the same way.

Many linguistic features have social significance regardless of locale. Three general nonstandard dialect features that are socially diagnostic throughout the country are:

(1) The absence of the third-person-singular present-tense *-s: He like her a lot. She walk to work every day.*

(2) The use of *be* as a main verb: *She be here tomorrow. Sometime' he be busy.*

(3) The use of multiple negation: *He doesn't know nothin'. The movie wasn't no good.*

Nonstandard-dialect speakers use these features some of the time, in some cases most of the time. Even standard-dialect speakers may occasionally use these features. But what differentiates the various social-class dialects—say, the lower-middle-class from the lower-working-class dialect—is the frequency with which these features are used. In other words, language correlates with social class in terms of the frequency of particular features. Nonstandard speakers, for example, use multiple negation in their speech more often than standard speakers do.

Sometimes the difference in the frequency of such usage from one social class to the next is sharp and apparent. This is the case for most grammatical usage, such as the dropping of -*s* on verbs in the third person singular of the present tense: *She work every day. It move very fast.*

In a study of black speech in Detroit, researchers discovered from hundreds of taped interviews and questionnaires that in upper-middle-class speech the third-person-singular verbs were missing the *-s* about 1.5 percent of the time. The lower-middle-class speakers dropped the *-s* about 10 percent of the time. But among upper-working-class speakers the frequency rose sharply to 57 percent, while lower-working-class speakers dropped the *-s* 72 percent of the time. These usage percentages (1.5 and 10 percent versus 57 and 72 percent) reveal a sharp boundary between middle-class and working-class speech.

Usually, dialect contrasts are not so distinct. Grammatical features like the absence of the third-person *-s* typically show a sharper stratification than do pronunciation features. In other words, grammatical features are more socially diagnostic.

In the same Detroit study, researchers found a gradual increase in the number of times /r/ is dropped the farther down the social scale one goes. The percentages of time for dropped /r/ in the four main classes are:

upper middle class—21 percent
lower middle class—39 percent
upper working class—61 percent
lower working class—72 percent

Even though this feature distinguishes the four dialects, it does so in a less clear-cut way than does the grammatical feature of *-s* absence in the third-person-singular verb. This gradient pattern tends to be the rule for the pronunciation features of social dialects.

Sex. Just as social status is reflected in language, so the social roles assigned to men and women take slightly different linguistic forms. This is especially evident in certain cultures where sex roles are more sharply defined. In several American Indian languages men pronounce most words in one way, while women and children pronounce the same words in a different way.

In the English-speaking countries the speech of men and women differs in at least one striking way. Women consistently avoid stigmatized forms and generally use language that tends to be closer to the standard or prestige dialect. In Detroit researchers compared the frequency with which males and females used multiple negation (as, *They don't want none*). In all social classes the researchers found that women use this nonstandard form considerably less than men do.

The same results held true for pronunciation features. In Detroit again, the women used the prestige pronunciation of postvocalic *r* much more often than did the men. And in a study done in Norwich, England, the women of any given social class consistently chose the standard dialect /ĭng/ form (for example, *walking* instead of *walkin'*) more often than did the men. A South African study revealed similar differences in speech between boys and girls.

In general, women are more responsive to prestige norms than men are. This probably reflects the role expectation that women are supposed to have the more "correct" social behavior. In the opposite way, nonstandard or working-class speech can have a positive value for males. It has connotations of masculinity and toughness. There is a macho stereotype of the football player or boxer who uses ungrammatical street talk, employing slang freely, clipping his words, but getting his message across.

As a result, women tend to be responsible for language change. With their sensitivity to "correct" speech they readily adopt a new prestige variant in a given locale. They are also the ones who tend to transmit the prestige norms to the next generation.

Age. The stages in an individual's life are partially defined by certain types of behavior, such as dress style, social interactions, and speech. Vocabulary is one readily noticeable difference between age groups. Teen-agers, for example, freely use slang and the jargon of their peer group. Their speech is considered inappropriate for a middle-aged person to use, even on an informal level. In general, the vocabulary items that characterize adolescent speech are very transient and are usually obsolete within a few years.

Vocabulary differences between generations tend to be fairly superficial markers of age dialects. Of a more substantial nature is the correlation between age and stigmatized pronunciation and grammar. Adolescents from about 10 to 17 years old use stigmatized forms considerably more often than do adults. This is true regardless of social class. But as adolescents approach adulthood, exposure to a wider range of social classes and hidden pressures to speak the more prestigious upper-middle-class dialect move their speech patterns away from the stigmatized vernacular forms.

Up to about the age of six, children learn the main rules of language and acquire a major portion of their lifetime working vocabulary. After that age they learn the local dialect of their peers. Peer influence on a child's speech is much greater than the language spoken at home or in the classroom. One study of Puerto Rican teen-agers in New York City's East Harlem showed that peer contact with black speakers resulted in their speaking authentic Black English, despite parental and school pressures.

Each generation tends to hang onto the language patterns it learned early in life. Older speakers who grew up with an icebox still use that term even though electric refrigerators have long since replaced iceboxes. In New York City the dropping of postvocalic *r* by speakers over 50 years old is not socially diagnostic, because that was the pronunciation everyone of their generation learned. But for younger speakers, dropping one's /r/'s is a feature of lower-class speech. Such observable differences in the speech from one generation to the next are the smallest units of language change.

Ethnic Group. There is no inherent or necessary link between language and race. But language is often an important part of ethnic identification. The degree to which ethnicity influences language depends on the relative isolation of the ethnic group. For example, the Italian community of a large city will show some differences in speech from other groups, but the differences will not be so great as those found in the black community because of its historically greater isolation.

It follows, then, that the greater the contact an ethnic speaker has with another social group, the less distinctive will be his or her ethnic speech. For example, the Detroit study found that those blacks who had extensive contact with whites tended to use considerably fewer Black English or nonstandard features than those speakers who had extensive contacts primarily with other blacks. Similarly, in New York City those Puerto Ricans who had extensive contact with blacks used Black English features more frequently than those who had only limited contact with black speakers.

Of all the ethnic dialects in America, Black English is the most distinctive and the most studied. It has its own grammatical rules, pronunciation, and vocabulary. The Jewish and Italian speech communities in the large cities also have their own sets of characteristic pronunciation and vocabulary.

Like social-class dialects, ethnic speech is characterized by the frequencies with which certain features are used. Although any given group of ethnic speakers may use a particular feature much or even most of the time, they almost never use it all of the time. The features themselves are often the indirect result of the continuing effect of the language of the forebears, the first-generation immigrants. Often, for the second generation the old language—General Southern dialect, perhaps, or Yiddish or Italian—is in effect a stigmatized language. Consequently, the second generation may go out of its way to avoid pronunciations that resemble the old language. In New York City, for example, second-generation Italians, in an attempt to avoid the common Italian vowel /à/, have unconsciously selected other similar vowels when pronouncing words like *bad* and *bag*. This has contributed to the general New York City dialect tendency to use the vowel combination /āə/ or /ĕə/ when pronouncing words like *bad, cab,* and *dance:* /bāəd/, /kāəb/, and /dāəns/. Speakers of Italian heritage show a greater tendency to use these vowels than any other ethnic group.

Many urban Jewish speakers, on the other hand, tend to pronounce the vowel /ô/ in *off, lost, dog* as /o͞oə/: /o͞oəf/, /lo͞oəst/, /do͞oəg/. This too may be the result of trying to avoid a foreign accent, in this case Yiddish. Yiddish speakers who have learned English don't tend to distinguish between /ô/ and /ŭ/, so that *coffee cup* /kô-fē kŭp/ may be pronounced /kŭ-fē kŭp/. In a deliberate effort to avoid this pronunciation characteristic, second-generation speakers may have exaggerated the difference between these two vowels, pronouncing the /ô/ as /o͞oə/. This pronunciation was then passed on to succeeding generations.

Speech Style. Any given speaker has considerable flexibility in his or her use of language. The way we speak to friends is usually quite different from the way we speak to our pastor or employer. Even the way we speak to our friends may differ in the locker room, at a cocktail party, and at work. The social context of the speech act—to whom we are speaking and where—largely determines the stylistic choice.

Another way of looking at style is to see it as varying according to how self-conscious we are about our speech in any given situation. The more attention we pay to our speech, the more formal our style.

Style variation is a spectrum ranging from informal or casual speech to formal or careful speech. As one moves from informal to formal styles, the frequency of stigmatized features decreases and that of prestigious features increases. In a study of New York City speech, this was shown to be true for the pronunciation of *th* as in *the, then, that.* As the style became more formal, the frequency of the stigmatized pronunciation, /d/, decreased, while the frequency of the pronunciation /th/ increased. This was true of all social classes. For the lower classes the shift in frequency was quite dramatic, since they use the /d/ pronunciation in casual speech much more often than do the upper classes.

Even though we can talk about such categories as the working-class dialect or the male or female dialect or the black dialect, these social-dialect divisions are only conceptual conveniences, theoretical figments. In reality, speech is the result of a complex interaction of regional influences and the five main social factors: status, sex, age, ethnicity, and style.

soda pop. Naturally effervescent spring water, for centuries valued for its therapeutic and refreshing qualities, was the ancestor of today's carbonated beverages. Niederselters, in the former state of Prussia, was especially famous for its natural springs. From the place name, Germans called the bubbly mineral water *selterswasser,* which produced the word *seltzer,* a term still used today for unflavored, unsweetened carbonated water. By the latter half of the 18th century, European chemists discovered the technique for making artificially carbonated water. Originally, sodium bicarbonate was used, but around 1780 methods for charging water with carbon dioxide were developed. By 1810 there were numerous factories and bottling plants in Europe and America. At about this time *soda water* was the most commonly used term for the man-made mineral water.

> Let us have wine and women, mirth
> and laughter,
> Sermons and soda-water the day after.
> —Lord Byron, *Don Juan* (1819–24)

> The reputation of the Powders, as the most convenient and best method of making Soda Water, is becoming well established.
> —*Columbian Centinel* (1820)

During the 1830s *soda fountains* sprang up everywhere. Flavorings and sweeteners were added to the treated water, creating such favorites of the time as *birch beer, ginger ale, ginger champagne, ginger pop* (the first use of *pop*), *root beer,* and *sarsaparilla soda.*

Soda pop is today a common term for any flavored carbonated drink, but in the 1920s it was considered slang.

> Such imps as the beloved demon rum, the comforting demon nicotine, and the flapper demon soda-pop. . . .
> —*The Nation* (1923)

> It was run over by a soda-pop truck when he was playing baseball in the street. —*Chicago Tribune* (1950)

Today, the individual words *soda* and *pop* are each more commonly used (especially the latter term) than the compound *soda pop.*

Soft drink is also a very common generic term, but it differs from the others in that it refers to nearly all sweet nonalcoholic beverages, including noncarbonated drinks.

> Each regiment had a "canteen" of its own, where the men could buy . . . soft drinks. —*Outing* (1894)

In 1886 in Atlanta, Georgia, the pharmacist John S. Pemberton invented a syrup made with the flavoring of the cola nut, which he added to carbonated water. It caught on with the local customers, and in 1893 Pemberton had the name Coca-Cola registered as the trademark of what was to become one of the most popular beverages ever concocted. In the Coastal Southern dialect Coca-Cola (or Coke, another trademark) is called *dope.*

> Drink Coca Cola. They say he stole the formula from old mountain woman. $50,000,000 now. Rats in the vats. Dope at Wood's better. Too weak here.
> —Thomas Wolfe,
> *Look Homeward, Angel* (1929)

> "You want a dope?" She nodded. He . . . fished in his pocket for a dime for the two bottles of Coca Cola.
> —Marjorie Kinnan Rawlings,
> *South Moon Under* (1933)

Dope may derive from the Dutch word *doop,* which means 'sauce.' In the past dope usually referred to a cola, especially one prepared at a soda fountain, or *dope shop.* But more recently it is sometimes used to refer to any carbonated soft drink.

In other parts of the South *cold drink* refers to soda pop, even if it's at room temperature. The inelegant, somewhat jocular *bellywash* is another synonym.

In the New England dialect, especially around the Boston area where it originated, *tonic* is a common term for soda pop. Originally a trade word, it seems to be spreading outside the New England region.

solecism /sŏl-ə-sĭz-əm, sō-lə-/ is a mistake in language, or a usage considered substandard. The word is from Greek *soloikismos,* after *Soloi,* a city in Asia Minor where Athenian colonists spoke a dialect considered corrupt by the standards of Athens. Compare MALAPROPISM.

solon. This term for a legislator is from *Solon,* an Athenian statesman who about 575 B.C. rewrote the constitution of Athens. The term is always used ironically:

> . . . Concord, where New Hampshire's solons spent several months intensely debating the question of whether they had any reason to be in session at all.
> —*Time*

some is often used as an adverb meaning 'to some extent, somewhat':

> The fire in front of us has darkened down some, the flames have disappeared into the building.
> —Dennis Smith,
> *Report From Engine Company 82*

> The quality of the American soldier may have deteriorated some over the years. . . .
> —Ron Wiginton,
> *Savannah Morning News*

◇ ***Recommendation.*** The use of *some* to mean 'to some extent' is a well-established American idiom that retains a slightly informal flavor. It is not appropriate to highly formal usage.

someplace. See ANYPLACE, SOMEPLACE.

somewheres is a dialectal and nonstandard variant of *somewhere.*

sonnet. A sonnet is a poem of 14 lines, usually of iambic pentameter and rhyming according to a fixed rhyme scheme, in which a single idea or sentiment is developed. (For the etymology of the word see ITALIAN WORDS; for more details on poetic structure see POETRY.) Typically, the theme of the sonnet is set forth in the opening eight lines (the *octave*) and resolved in the closing six (the *sestet*). The sonnet's tight structure might make it seem artificial, but its iambic cadences echo those of speech, while its 14-line span functions as a kind of natural frame, affording just the right amount of space within which to examine and dispose of virtually any topic. The sonnet has been one of the most important of the traditional poetic forms ever since Elizabethan times, and it remains so today.

The sonnet originated in 13th-century Sicily at the court of the Holy Roman emperor Frederick II. It evolved out of Sicilian folk songs and was later taken up by Italian poets, among them Dante, Petrarch, and Tasso. It spread to Spain, Portugal, France, and, in the 16th century, England. The octave of the sonnet rhymed *abbaabba* and its sestet either *cdecde* or *cdcdcd*. This type of sonnet is known as the Italian or Petrarchan form; an English example from the early 19th century is John Keats's "On First Looking Into Chapman's Homer":

> Much have I traveled in the realms of gold,
> And many goodly states and kingdoms seen;
> Round many western islands have I been
> Which bards in fealty to Apollo hold.
> Oft of one wide expanse had I been told
> That deep-browed Homer ruled as his demesne;
> Yet did I never breathe its pure serene
> Till I heard Chapman speak out loud and bold:
> Then felt I like some watcher of the skies
> When a new planet swims into his ken;
> Or like stout Cortez when with eagle eyes
> He stared at the Pacific—and all his men
> Looked at each other with a wild surmise—
> Silent, upon a peak in Darien.

While English is rich in words, it has fewer words than Italian that end in the same sounds. Soon after the sonnet was introduced into England, English poets therefore devised a version calling for only one rhyme for each line ending instead of two or three. So arose the second of the two main types of sonnet in English, the Elizabethan or Shakespearean. It consists of three quatrains and a couplet, and it rhymes *abab, cdcd, efef, gg.* Here is a Shakespearean sonnet by one of its ablest practitioners, Shakespeare himself:

> Shall I compare thee to a summer's day?
> Thou art more lovely and more temperate:
> Rough winds do shake the darling buds of May,
> And summer's lease hath all too short a date:
> Sometime too hot the eye of heaven shines,
> And often is his gold complexion dimm'd:
> And every fair from fair sometime declines,
> By chance, or nature's changing course untrimm'd;
> But thy eternal summer shall not fade,
> Nor lose possession of that fair thou ow'st,
> Nor shall death brag thou wander'st in his shade,
> When in eternal lines to time thou grow'st;
> So long as men can breathe, or eyes can see,
> So long lives this, and this gives life to thee.

sort of. (1) The hybrid plural *those* or *these sort of thing(s)* is clearly illogical but has an enduring tendency to crop up in at least conversational speech.

> . . . it is three o'clock, and your sister is not used to these sort of hours.
> —Jane Austen, *Mansfield Park*

> It is best to leave those sort of people out of serious matters.
> —W. Somerset Maugham, *Ashenden*

◇ ***Recommendation.*** This is a harmless idiom in conversational speech. In formal writing it should be corrected. For most purposes *this* or *that sort of* is sufficiently plural. *These* or *those sorts of* will only be necessary if several distinct categories are present.

(2) *Sort of*, like *kind of*, is often used as an adverb meaning 'in a way, somewhat, to some extent':

> . . . the Speaker let fly with some remarks about his chief Republican tormentor, Bruce Caputo of New York, for which he sort of apologized to the House last week.
> —Joseph Kraft, *Boston Globe*

> Mr. Corcoran and his longtime friend Anna Chennault . . . were sort of mentors for Tongsun Park.
> —Marjorie Hunter, *New York Times*

◇ ***Recommendation.*** In spite of the two quotations from serious reportage, we regard this usage as informal.

South American words. Nearly all the words we have acquired from the native languages of South America have been borrowed into English through Spanish, the chief language of most of the continent, and Portuguese, the chief language of Brazil.

The native peoples of South America speak hundreds of different languages, grouped in several scores of unrelated language families. Of these, only a handful have supplied words that have reached English. Quechua /**kĕch**-wə/, the language of the ruling caste of the Inca empire, which was destroyed by the Spanish in the 1530s, is still spoken in Peru, Chile, and Ecuador. Tupi /**tōō**-pē/ is a widespread language of the Amazon basin in Brazil. Aymara /ī-mə-**rä**/ is spoken in Bolivia and Peru, and Araucanian /ăr-ô-**kä**-nē-ən/ is a language family of Argentina and southern Chile. The Cariban language family is in northern South America and Central America as well as some of the Caribbean islands (see also CARIBBEAN WORDS).

alpaca /ăl-**păk**-ə/ = 'Peruvian animal related to the llama, with long, silky wool used in textiles': Spanish *alpaca*, from Aymara *allpaca*

cashew = 'nut of the cashew tree of tropical South and Central America': Portuguese *cajú, acajú*, from Tupi *acajú*

coca = 'leaves of the coca plant, of the Andes region, chewed by Andean people as a stimulant and exported commercially as the source of cocaine': Spanish *coca*, from Quechua *kúka*

cougar /**kōō**-gər/ = 'American mountain lion': French *couguar*, from Portuguese *cuguardo*, from Tupi *suasuarana* = 'deerlike animal'

coypu /**koi**-pōō/ = 'large freshwater-living South American rodent': Spanish *coipú*, from Araucanian *kóypu*

curare /kōō-**rär**-ē, kyōō-/ = 'poisonous or medicinal extract obtained from several South American trees': Spanish *curare*, from Cariban *kurari*

guanaco /gwə-**nä**-kō/ = 'South American animal related to the llama': Spanish *guanaco*, from Quechua *huanaco*

guano /**gwä**-nō/ = 'bird droppings used as fertilizer': Spanish *guano*, from Quechua *huanu* = 'dung'

guava /**gwä**-və/ = 'fruit of the guava tree of tropical America': Spanish *guava, guayaba*, from Tupi *guayava*

jacaranda /jăk-ə-**răn**-də/ = 'tropical American tree with pale-purple flowers': Portuguese *jacarandá*, from Tupi *yacarandá*

jaguar = 'large wildcat with spotted markings, of tropical America': Portuguese *jaguar*, from Tupi *jaguara*

llama /**lä**-mə, **yä**-mə/ = 'large South American animal distantly related to the camel, domesticated as a beast of burden and valued for its wool': Spanish *llama*, from Quechua *llama*

maraca /mə-**rä**-kə/ = 'gourd filled with beans or pebbles, used as a rhythm instrument': Portuguese *maracá*, from Tupi *maraca*

maté /**mä**-tā/ = 'tea made from the leaves of the maté tree': Spanish *maté*, from Quechua *mate*

pampa = 'grassland plain in South America': Spanish *pampa*, from Quechua and Aymara *pampa*

petunia = 'flowering South American plant, related to the tobacco plant': from

French *petun* = 'tobacco,' from Tupi *petyn*

piranha /pĭ-**rän**-yə/ = 'small, fierce South American freshwater fish': Portuguese *piranha,* from Tupi *piranha* = 'fish with teeth'

poncho = 'woolen cape or cloak with a hole for the head': Spanish *poncho,* from Araucanian *pontho* = 'wool fabric'

puma /**pyoo̅**-mə, **poo̅**-/ = 'American mountain lion': Spanish *puma,* from Quechua *puma*

tanager /**tăn**-ə-jər/ = 'small American bird': Portuguese *tangara,* from Tupi

tapioca = 'starchy pudding made from cassava root': Portuguese *tapioca,* from Tupi *tipióca* = 'pounded cassava'

tapir /**tā**-pər, tə-**pîr**/ = 'forest-living hoofed animal of South America and Southeast Asia': Spanish *tapir,* from Tupi *tapiira*

toucan /**too̅**-kăn/ = 'brightly colored tropical American bird with a large bill': French *toucan,* from Portuguese *tucano,* from Tupi *tucana*

vicuña /vĭ-**koo̅n**-yə/ = 'small Andean animal related to the llama, with silky wool used for textiles': Spanish *vicuña,* from Quechua *wikuña*

Southern dialect. Historically, the Southern dialect originated in the speech of the colonial settlements of Virginia, the Carolinas, and Georgia. This speech, dominated by the prestigious cities of Richmond, Charleston, and Savannah, spread into the Gulf States as people sought to develop new land for plantations there at the end of the 18th century. Today, the Southern dialect, with its so-called drawl, is spoken in southern Delaware and Maryland, the warm coastal lowlands and piedmont of Virginia, North and South Carolina, and Georgia; in Florida, Alabama, Mississippi, Louisiana, and the southernmost part of Arkansas; and in eastern Texas. Southern and the inland and later-developing South Midland dialect form the GENERAL SOUTHERN DIALECT; the features common to both are discussed at that entry. The Southern dialect has three major subdivisions: the COASTAL SOUTHERN, GULF SOUTHERN, and VIRGINIA PIEDMONT dialects. Each of these subdivisions has characteristic speech patterns and vocabulary, which are discussed at the separate entries. Pronunciations and vocabulary belonging specifically to the Southern dialect are covered below. (For vocabulary items shared with the SOUTH MIDLAND DIALECT see that entry.)

Pronunciation. As in eastern New England, /r/ is usually dropped except before a vowel. *Letter,* for example, is pronounced /**lĕt**-ə/ or /**lĕd**-ə/, but in *literal* the /r/ is pronounced. The intrusive, or extra, /r/ found in South Midland (as /**wĭn**-dər/ for *window*) and New England (as /lär/ for *law*) is very rarely heard in the Southern dialect.

The vowel in words like *carry* and *dairy* is frequently pronounced /ā/.

Vocabulary. (1) Terms used chiefly in farming and rural areas:

bellowsed = '(of a horse) short of breath'
bray = 'whinny of a horse'
butt-headed = '(of a cow) hornless'
co-wench = 'call to cows'
dogged /dôgd/ = 'darned': *Well, I'll be dogged.*
drop (**a crop**) = 'to plant'
grind rock = 'whetstone'
lightwood /**līd**-əd/ = 'kindling wood'
middlebuster = 'kind of plow'
potato bank = 'vegetable bin or cellar'
sling blade = 'sickle or scythe'
turn of wood = 'armload of wood'

(2) Expressions and grammatical forms used especially by working-class speakers:

all both, all two = 'both'
belongs = 'ought': *She belongs to be careful.*
do = 'does': *He do fine baking.*
gwine = 'going'
heern tell = 'hear tell'
make = 'makes': *What make you do it?*
on account of = 'because': *I like her on account of she's so funny.*
outn = 'out of': *He fell outn the bed.*
wan't = 'wasn't'

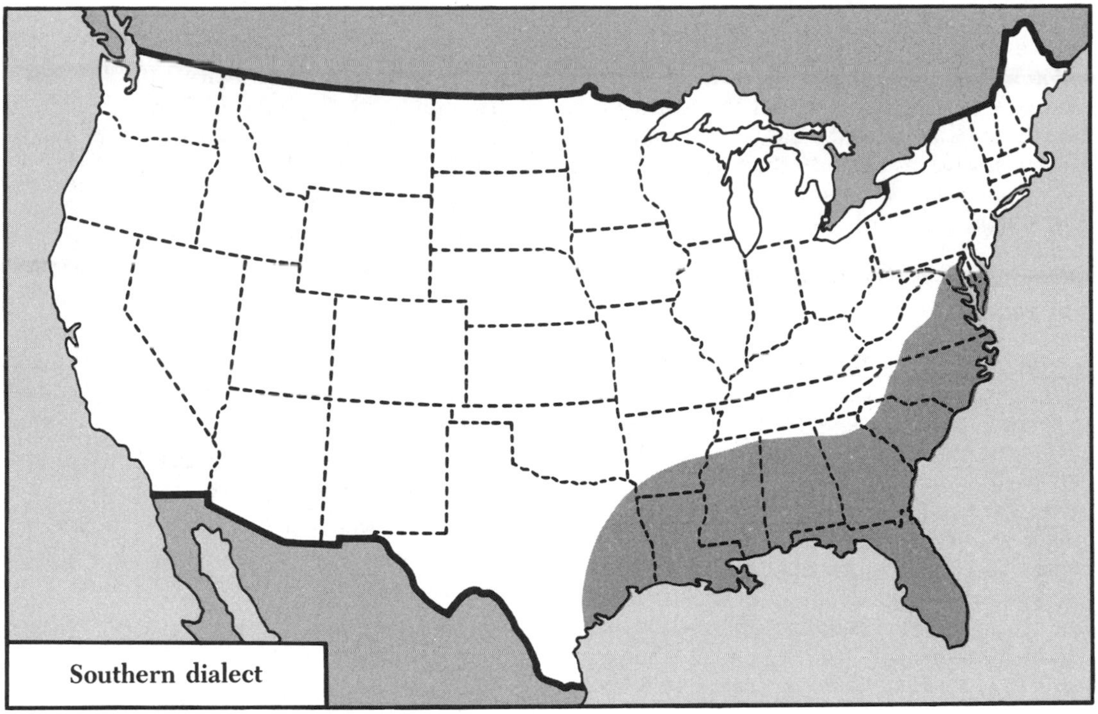

(3) More widely used terms in the Southern region:

big daddy = 'grandfather'
big mamma = 'grandmother'
carry (a person) = 'to take, escort'
cat squirrel = 'common squirrel'
chunk = 'to throw'
clearseed *or* **clearstone peach** = 'variety of peach'
coachwhip snake = 'colubrid snake'
Confederate War = 'the Civil War'
cooter = 'turtle'
curd = '*cottage cheese'
fire ant = 'stinging ant'
fix, out of = 'broken, out of order'
fixing to = 'going to': *It's fixing to rain.*
fix (the table) = 'to set'
gall shirt (used chiefly by black speakers) = 'shirt-length undergarment'
***goober** = 'peanut'
harp, mouth harp = 'harmonica'
hasslet = 'edible inner organs of a pig'
hey = 'hi, hello'
***juke** = 'to carouse'
jumped the broom = 'got married'
keen, king (used especially by black speakers) = '(of shoes) having sharply pointed toes'
mosquito hawk = '*dragonfly'
mulligrubs = 'melancholy or ill-tempered mood'
outside baby *or* **child** (used especially by black speakers) = '*illegitimate child'
pinder = 'peanut'
press peach = 'clingstone peach'
rain frog = 'small frog, spring peeper'
safe = 'container for storing bread or pastry'
shed room = 'storage room'
storm pit = 'underground storm shelter'
suck-egg dog = 'worthless dog, mongrel'
wiggler, Georgia wiggler = 'bait worm'

*Appears as separate entry

South Midland dialect. This dialect is spoken from the southern Appalachians through the states westward to parts of Kansas, Oklahoma, and Texas, but is especially concentrated in the Ozarks. The South Midland region was settled relatively late by such groups as the PENNSYLVANIA DUTCH and the Scotch-Irish, migrating both southward from the North Midland area and westward from the Virginia Piedmont area. Consequently, it is a transitional region, sharing words and pronunciation features with its neighbors to the north and south. South Midland can be considered on the one hand part of the MIDLAND DIALECT, and on the other hand part of the GENERAL SOUTHERN DIALECT.

Pronunciation. South Midland pronunciation, occurring most distinctively in the speech of working-class people, has much in common with the Southern dialect. The following are some of its notable features. The sound /t/ is often added to such words as *once, twice, across, cliff:* /wŭnst/, /twīst/, /ə-**krôst**/, /klĭft/. This feature is probably related to the earlier British development of such words as *amidst* from *amid* and *amongst* from *among*. As in Black English, the /th/ sound at the end of a word or syllable is occasionally pronounced /f/: *mouth, with, booth, birthday* become /mouf/, /wĭf/, /bo͞of/, /**bêrf**-dā/. As in Southern dialect, the vowel in such words as *time, pie, wide, sky* is pronounced with the /ȧ/ sound: /tȧm/, /pȧ/, /wȧd/, /skȧ/. The vowel in *boil* and *oil* is sometimes pronounced /ô/: /bôl/, /ôl/. The /ō/ sound of the unstressed final syllable of certain words is frequently pronounced /-ər/. Thus, *window, yellow, tobacco, hollow* become /**wĭnd**-ər/, /**yĕl**-ər/, /tə-**băk**-ər/, /**hŏl**-ər/.

Grammar. The verb form *are* following a pronoun *(we, you, they)* is often deleted: *We interested in huntin'. You just dreamin'. They afraid to drive there.* This deletion is similar to the deletion of forms of the verb *be* in Black English, but unlike Black English, the South Midland dialect almost never deletes the singular form *is*. The prefix *a-*, usually pronounced /ə/, is often added to the beginning of present participles: *He come a-runnin'. The dog kept a-beggin' and a-cryin' and a-wantin' to get out.* (For more background on this prefix see A-.)

Vocabulary. Contrary to popular belief, South Midland, even in the highlands of the Appalachians and Ozarks, has relatively few expressions that are uniquely its own, but shares most of its vocabulary with the Southern and North Midland dialects.

(1) Some characteristic terms found in the South Midland dialect:

dusky dark = 'sunset, twilight'
fernent, ferninst = 'adjacent, next to' (from Scottish)
flitter (also Gulf Southern) = '*pancake'
gaum, gaumy (especially in Appalachia) = 'sticky, smeared'
hidy = 'hello, howdy'
jarfly = 'cicada'
lay out (of school) (also Coastal Southern) = 'to play *hooky'
main = 'very, extremely'
make against = 'to injure, work against'
master = 'very, extremely'
open-stone peach (especially in Appalachia) = 'freestone peach'
pieplant (also General Northern) = 'rhubarb'
salt shake = 'saltshaker'
storm house (also Gulf Southern) = 'storm cellar'

(2) Common South Midland terms shared with the Southern dialect:

ambeer = 'tobacco spittle'
antick = (1) (adjective) 'playful, rambunctious' (2) (noun) 'clown, buffoon'
baby-trough = 'cradle, playpen'
biddable = 'good-natured, docile'
blackguard, blaggard = 'to swear, curse'
bobble, misbobble = 'error, mistake'
* **bodacious** = 'outright, bold'
bogue = 'to move slowly or aimlessly'
booger = 'louse, usually head louse'
bore (someone) for the simples = literally 'to make a hole in the skull'; used to indicate a person's stupidity (from the idea that the hole might let some of the foolishness, or "simples," out)
brickle = 'brittle, crisp'
bust middles = 'to plow or break up the earth between rows'

*Appears as separate entry

chap = 'small child'
confidence = 'to trust': *I couldn't confidence a person who lied.*
cribber = 'horse'
dauncy = 'lacking an appetite, fastidious about food'
dido = 'prank, caper'
disencourage = 'to discourage'
durgen = 'awkward, uncouth person, lout'
gaum = 'mess, muddle, poor job'
goozle = 'throat'
heap = 'large amount'
hipped = 'seriously injured, disabled'
hog molly = 'fish, spotted sucker'
jibble = 'to cut into small pieces'
june = 'to hurry, move quickly'
light a shuck = 'to leave quickly'
mallyhack = 'to cut up, beat severely'
mother wit = 'common sense'
noodle-hook = 'fishhook'
passel = 'large number or quantity'
piedy = 'spotted'
pod = 'belly, paunch'
right smart = 'considerable amount'
scrooge, scrooch = 'to squeeze or crowd'
set a spell = 'to visit'
shuckle = 'to hurry, bustle about'
slicker = 'to beat or thrash'
smidgin = 'small amount'
squander = 'to scatter, disperse'
swoggle = 'to dip, stir'
tetchous = 'sensitive, tender'
trotter = 'foot, leg'
whack = 'to exaggerate'
work-brickle = 'industrious'

Southern Appalachia. It is not yet clear to linguists how Appalachian speech differs from the rest of the South Midland dialect. But because southern Appalachia has other distinctively regional characteristics, such as its mining, lumbering, and farming economy and its basically rural population, it is likely that its language is also regional and forms a subdialect.

The Ozarks. The Ozark Mountains are a relatively isolated region where a colorful variety of South Midland dialect can be heard. The backwoodsmen are the direct descendants of pioneers from the southern Appalachians.

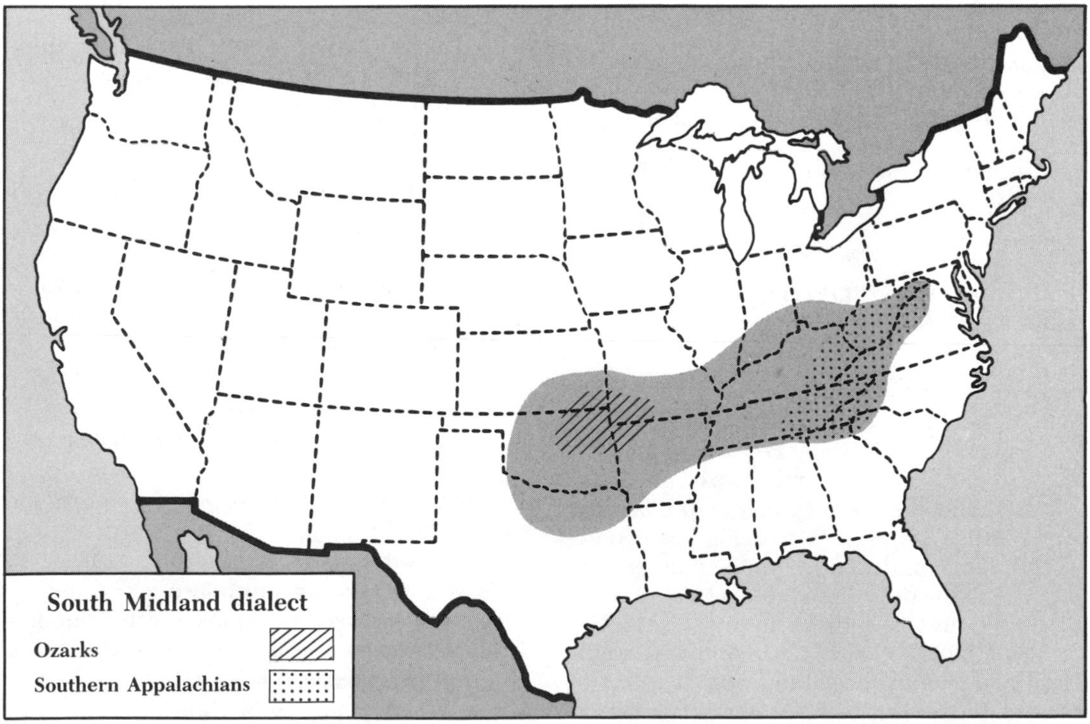

Largely for this reason, the speech here does not differ substantially from that of northern Georgia, western North and South Carolina, eastern Tennessee and Kentucky, western Virginia, and southern West Virginia.

Example. Here is a sampling of old-fashioned Ozark speech (see preceding vocabulary list):

> Lee Yancey allus was a right work-brickel feller, clever an' biddable as all git-out, but he aint got nary smidgin' o' mother-wit, an' he aint nothin' on'y a tie-whackin' sheer-crapper noways. I seed him an' his least chaps a-bustin' out middles down in ol' man Price's bottom t'other ev'nin', a-whoopin' an' a-blaggardin' an' a-spewin' ambeer all over each an' ever', whilst thet 'ar pore susy hippoed woman o' hisn was a-pickin' boogers out'n her yeller tags, an' a-scrunchin' cheenches [chinches] on th' punch'on 'ith a antiganglin' noodle-hook. D'reckly Lee he come a-junin' in all narvish-like [nervous] an' tetchous, an' rid th' pore ol' trollop a bug-huntin'—jes' plum bodacious hipped an' ruinated her. They never did have nothin' on'y jes' a heap o' poke sallat an' a passel o' these hyar hog-mollies, but he must a got hisse'f a bait o' vittles some'ers, 'cause come can'le-light he geared up his ol' piedy cribber an' lit a shuck fer Gotham Holler. The danged ol' durgen—he should orter be bored fer th' simples!
>
> —Vance Randolph, *American Speech* (1929)

For additional history and vocabulary see ELIZABETHAN ENGLISH IN AMERICA.

Southwestern dialect. This dialect is a division of the WESTERN DIALECT. The large arid section of the country where it is spoken includes southern California, Arizona, New Mexico, and the western half of Texas. Like the West in general, this region has experienced rapid and recent population growth and economic development. Its large volume of immigrants has come from all over the United States, making the Southwest a cultural and linguistic melting pot. Because of the relatively recent settlement of the area, however, this dialect is not as distinct and clear as the dialects of the Atlantic seaboard. Even so, the Mexican-Spanish influence has marked the speech of the region with a character of its own.

Spanish-English Vocabulary. Occupied by the Spanish for nearly two and a half centuries, by 1821 New Mexico had ninth- and tenth-generation Spaniards, and California and Texas had fourth- and fifth-generation descendants. Today, New Mexico's legislature is still bilingual, and Los Angeles is second only to Mexico City in number of Mexican residents. Arizona and Texas also have large Spanish-speaking populations. The following list is a selection of the commoner terms of Spanish origin that are used in everyday English in the Southwestern region (for more details on the origin of some terms see SPANISH WORDS).

acequia /ə-**sā**-kē-ə/ = 'irrigation ditch'
alabado /ăl-ə-**bä**-dō/ = 'hymn'
alameda /ăl-ə-**mē**-də/ = 'area where alamos or poplar trees grow'
arroyo /ə-**roi**-ō/ = 'creek, narrow gorge, gully'
baile /**bī**-lā/ = 'a dance, especially under Mexican or mixed sponsorship'
barranca /bə-**răng**-kə/ = 'ravine'
batea /bə-**tē**-ə/ = 'shallow pan used in panning gold'
borracho /bə-**ră**-chō/ = 'drunkard'
borreras /bə-**rār**-əs/ = 'sheep'
bosque /**bōs**-kā/ = 'clump or grove of trees'
* **bracero** /brə-**sâr**-ō/ = 'immigrant worker'
brasado /brə-**sä**-dō/ = 'brush country'
caballero /kăb-ə-**lâr**-ō, -əl-**yâr**-ō/ = 'gentleman'
cabron /kə-**brōn**/ = 'outlaw'
calaboose /**kăl**-ə-bo͞os/, **calabozo** /kăl-ə-**bō**-zō/ = 'jail'
campanyero /kăm-pən-**yâr**-ō/ = 'companion, friend'
cantina /kăn-**tē**-nə/ = 'tavern'
casita /kə-**sē**-də/ = 'outhouse'
charco /**chär**-kō/ = 'pool of water, puddle'
cholo /**chō**-lō/ (derogatory) = 'a Mexican'
cienega /**syā**-nə-gə/ = 'swamp'
comun /kə-**mo͞on**/ = 'outhouse'

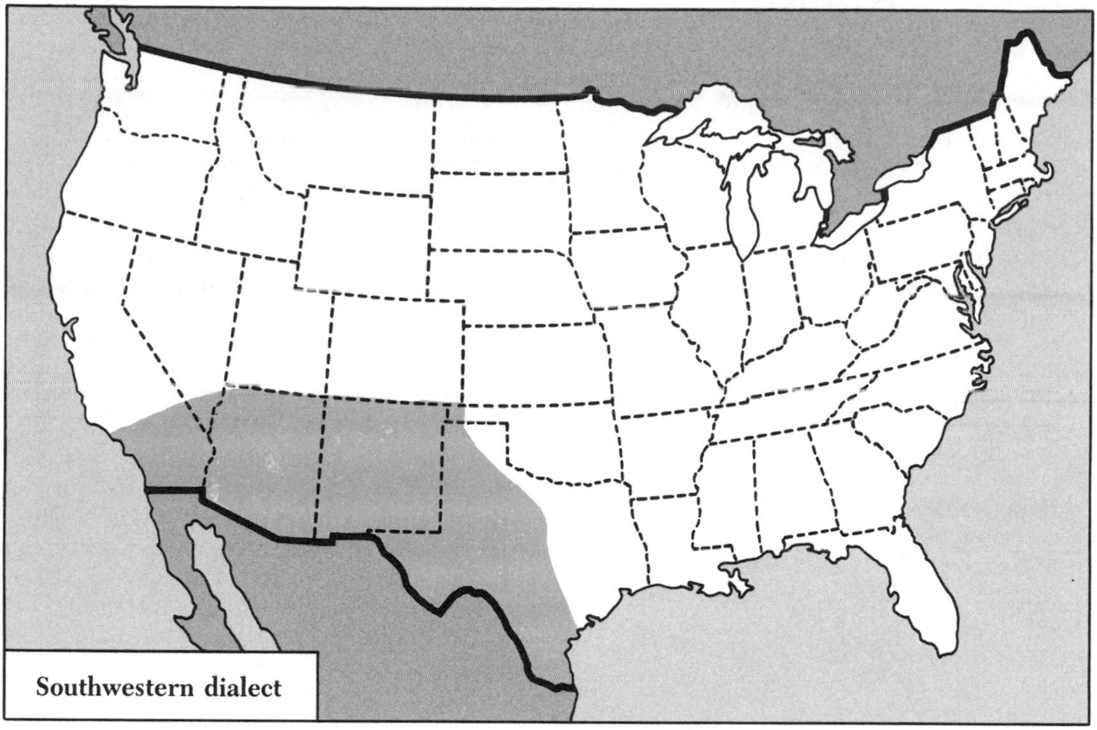

Southwestern dialect

corral /kə-**răl**/ = 'cow barn, cow yard'
dulce /**dōōl**-sā/ = (1) 'affectionate term for a girlfriend or sweetheart' (2) 'sweetmeat, candy'
embarcadero /ĕm-bär-kə-**dâr**-ō/ = 'wharf'
frijoles /frē-**hō**-lēz/ = 'beans, especially kidney beans'
hoya /**hoi**-ə/ = 'park'
langosta /lăng-**gŏs**-tə/ = 'crawfish'
latigo /**lăd**-ə-gō/ = 'girth, cinch'
madre /**mä**-drā/ = 'mother'
malpais /mäl-pä-**ēs**/ = 'badland, lava mesa'
mesa /**mā**-sə/ = flat-topped hill, high plateau'
morrall /mə-**răl**/ = 'nose bag, feed bag for a horse'
nana /**nä**-nə/ = 'grandmother'
padre /**pä**-drā/ = 'father, priest'
paisano /pī-**sä**-nō/ = (1) 'person of Mexican ancestry' (2) (derogatory) 'peasant' (3) 'compatriot'
patio /**pä**-dē-ō/ = 'front *porch, back porch'
plaza /**plä**-zə/ = 'town square'
potrero /pə-**trĕ**-rō/ = 'meadow, pasture, park'
ramada /rə-**mä**-də/ = '*porch, covered walk'
ranchero /răn-**châr**-ō/ = 'cowboy'
reata /rē-**äd**-ə/ = 'rope, lariat'
rincon /rĭng-**kōn**/ = 'secluded valley, park, bend in a river'
Santa Ana /**săn**-tə **ăn**-ə/ = 'warm, dry wind'
tata /**tä**-tə/ = 'grandfather'
toro /**tōr**-ō, **tô**-rō/ = 'bull'
tortilla /tôr-**tē**-yə/ = 'flat cake made of cornmeal'
vaca /**vä**-kə/ = 'cow'
vaquero /və-**kâr**-ō/ = 'cowboy'

*Appears as separate entry

soviet /**sō**-vē-ĕt, -ĭt/. The Russian word *sovyet* means 'council, committee.' During and after the Revolution of 1917, local groups of workers, soldiers, and farmers elected *soviets* to express their political views, and grass-roots soviets of many kinds are still an everyday part of modern political life in the U.S.S.R. Constitutionally, the U.S.S.R. is a union (federation) of 15 states called soviet socialist republics—republics headed by Communist councils; hence the formal title Union of Soviet Socialist Republics, informally the Soviet Union. The federal parliament of the nation is the Supreme Soviet, composed of two equal-ranking houses, the Soviet of the Union (elected by proportional representation) and the Soviet of the Nationalities (elected by each of the ethnic-national groups, from Russians to Chukchis).

Soviet is also used, in English, as an adjective: *the new Soviet citizen; Soviet ambitions in the Middle East.* In the plural it is now also widely used by journalists to mean 'the people of the Soviet Union': *The Soviets believe that the Chinese are their inveterate enemies.*

◇ ***Recommendation.*** The adjective *Soviet* = 'relating to the U.S.S.R.' is entirely correct. *The Soviets* = 'the people of the U.S.S.R.' is still not formally correct, since it conflicts with the primary meaning of *soviet* = 'council, committee'; but in general nonscholarly use it is acceptable.

Spanglish. See PUERTO RICAN SPEECH.

Spanish words. Spanish, the language of Spain and the Spanish-American republics, is also spoken in the United States where Hispanic communities have survived since the days of the Spanish empire (Louisiana and New Mexico) and where more recent immigrants have congregated (Mexicans in the Southwest, Puerto Ricans in New York City, Cubans in Miami).

Intense and often hostile contact between Spain and Great Britain began soon after the discovery of the New World. During the three centuries that followed Columbus's voyages, numerous Spanish words entered the English language, in particular those that designated physical and cultural objects first encountered by Europeans in the Americas. Such *loanwords* most often originated in native American languages but usually passed into English through the medium of Spanish, and are not peculiar to American English.

National and religious rivalries were carried over to North America by the three great colonizing powers—Spain, France, and Great Britain. The English-speaking settlers won control first over the French colonies (by 1763) and then, between 1803 and 1853, conquered or purchased the Spanish domains of Florida, Louisiana, and the Southwest (a territory of independent Mexico since 1820).

In Florida and Louisiana the Spanish-speaking population was small and had little impact on the English of the newcomers. In the Southwest, however, the English-speaking settlers found an established culture from which they learned a great deal, borrowing numerous words and expressions in the process. Even at present, one of the chief distinguishing traits of the American English spoken in the Southwest is the relatively frequent use of words of Spanish origin. Many became clichés popularized in Western fiction and film, thereby reaching a wider audience in the rest of the United States.

The Spanish influence on American English was strongest in such cultural areas as the names of states, towns, mountains, rivers, and every sort of geographical feature; the terminology of cattle raising; and the names of Southwestern plants and animals. A few everyday phrases picked up in direct interaction with speakers of Spanish were adopted, sometimes with remarkable changes in meaning and usage.

In the 20th century three great Hispanic immigrations have increased the number of Spanish-speaking residents of the United States many times over. The troubled times in revolutionary Mexico (1910–20) combined with the great expansion of U.S. agriculture in the 1920s brought many Mexicans to this country in search of economic opportunity. After World War II there began a considerable migration of Puerto Ricans from their island to New York City (see PUERTO RICAN SPEECH), and in the wake of the Castro revolution (1958) many Cubans took refuge in Miami. It is difficult to assess the impact these immigrations may have had on American English, but it is likely that except for possible local influences, the English spoken by most of the population has taken very little from the 20th-century Spanish immigrants.

The situation became somewhat different in the decades of the sixties and seventies,

Pronouncing Spanish

Letter	Pronunciation
Vowels	
a	/ä/
e	/ā/
i	/ē/
o	/ō/
u*	/o͞o/
y	/ē/ *as in* y (= *'and'*)

The* u *in the syllables* -gue-, -que-, -gui-, -qui-, *and the like is silent. In the handful of words where this* u *is pronounced, it is marked with a dieresis,* ü, *as in* argüir /är-go͞o-ēr**/ (= *'to argue'*).

Letter	Pronunciation
Consonants**	
c	(1) *Castilian* /th/, *Latin American* /s/ *before* e, i, *as in* centro /**thān**-trō, **sān**-/ (2) /k/ *before* a, o, u, *as in* cabeza
ch	/ch/
g	(1) /h/ *before* e, i, *as in* giro (2) /g/ *before* a, o, u, *as in* ganar
h	*not pronounced*
j	/h/ *as in* jugo
ll	/ly/ *as in* llano
ñ	/ny/ *as in* cañón
q	/k/ *as in* queso
r	*trilled on the front of the tongue*
y	/y/ *as in* yerba
z	*Castilian* /th/, *Latin American* /s/ *as in* azúcar /ä-**tho͞o**-kär, ä-**so͞o**-/

***The consonants* b, d, f, l, m, n, p, s, t, v, *and* x *are pronounced approximately the same as in English. Spanish has no* k *or* w.

since the civil rights movement brought about a heightened awareness of minorities as distinct cultural entities. Certain Spanish terms, rather heavily charged with cultural and political overtones, have recently established themselves in American English.

This entry covers Spanish loanwords that are, by and large, known in general American English. Some of these, plus others not included here, are used primarily in the West. See the PACIFIC SOUTHWEST, ROCKY MOUNTAIN, SOUTHWESTERN, and WESTERN dialects.

Pronunciation. Compared with that of other European languages, the Spanish vowel system is a simple one, consisting of five basic sounds. Speakers of Spanish are conscious of this simplicity, and often describe their native vowels as having a "clear quality" or "purity." Many consonants are pronounced approximately the same as in English. The letter *y* is both a vowel and a consonant, and the letters *c* and *z* have special variations. For these and other fundamental features of Spanish pronunciation, see the table above.

Word stress is completely predictable in the Spanish writing system. If a word ends in *n, s,* or a vowel, the next-to-last syllable is stressed: *caballero* /kä-bä-**lyā**-rō/. If a word ends in a consonant (other than *n* or *s*), the last syllable is stressed: *corral* /kō-**räl**/. All exceptions are marked with an accent: *término* /**tār**-mē-nō/; *piñón* /pē-**nyōn**/.

Vocabulary. (1) Words borrowed from Spanish during the colonial period (16th to 18th centuries):

alligator = 'large reptile of the crocodile family': Spanish *el lagarto* = 'the lizard'

anchovy = 'small fish of the herring family': Spanish *anchova, anchoa*

armada = 'fleet of warships': Spanish *armada* = 'fleet, navy,' originally *flota armada* = 'armed fleet'

armadillo = 'burrowing animal covered with bony armor, of South America and the southern parts of North America': Spanish *armadillo* = 'armadillo,' literally 'little armored one,' from *armado* = 'armored'

avocado = 'pear-shaped fruit of the avocado tree' See AZTEC WORDS.

banana = 'fruit of a tropical tree' See AFRICAN WORDS.

barbecue = 'grill for roasting meat' See CARIBBEAN WORDS.

barracuda = 'voracious tropical fish': Spanish *barracuda* (of uncertain origin)

binnacle /bĭn-ə-kəl/ = 'box containing a ship's compass,' earlier *bit(t)acle*: from Spanish *bitácula*

bonito = 'striped tuna': Spanish *bonito*, literally 'pretty (one)'

booby, (shortened form) **boob** = 'dolt, simpleton': Spanish *bobo*

bravado = 'swaggering show of courage': Spanish *bravata* = 'arrogant, boastful threat,' from *bravo* = 'fierce'

cannibal = 'human who eats human flesh' See CARIBBEAN WORDS.

canoe = 'light, narrow paddle boat' See CARIBBEAN WORDS.

chocolate = 'drink or candy made from ground cacao beans' See AZTEC WORDS.

cockroach = 'common insect pest,' earlier *cacarootch*: from Spanish *cucaracha* = 'cockroach'

doubloon = 'Spanish gold coin': Spanish *doblón*

hammock = 'swinging bed made of netted string' See CARIBBEAN WORDS.

hurricane = 'tropical cyclone' See CARIBBEAN WORDS.

maize = 'corn' See CARIBBEAN WORDS.

mosquito = 'bloodsucking winged insect': Spanish *mosquito*, from *mosca* = 'fly'

mulatto = 'person of mixed white and black ancestry': Spanish *mulato* = 'mulatto,' literally 'young mule,' with reference to the mule's mixed parentage, from *mulo* = 'mule'

Negro = 'person of black race': Spanish *negro* = 'black (race and color)'

potato = 'tuberous plant': Spanish *patata, batata* = 'sweet potato,' from Taino

quadroon = 'person of one-quarter black ancestry': Spanish *cuarterón*, probably via French

tapioca = 'starch obtained from cassava roots': Spanish *tapioca*, from Tupi-Guaraní

tobacco = 'plant whose leaves are used for smoking': Spanish *tabaco* (of uncertain origin)

tomato = 'plant bearing edible red fruit,' earlier *tomate*: Spanish *tomate*, from Nahuatl *tomatl*

tornado = 'destructive funnel-shaped column of rotating air associated with violent thunderstorms': Spanish *tronada* = 'thunderstorm'

(2) Words borrowed from Spanish during the westward expansion of the United States (19th century):

abalone /ăb-ə-lō-nē/ = 'large, edible marine gastropod with a highly prized shell': Mexican Spanish *abulón*

adobe /ə-dō-bē/ (Western) = 'sun-dried brick of clay and straw': Spanish *adobe*, from Arabic *aṭ-ṭūb* = 'the bricks'

alfalfa = 'cultivated forage plant': Spanish *alfalfa*, ultimately from Arabic

arroyo /ə-roi-ō/ (Southwestern) = 'gulley, dry wash': Spanish *arroyo* = 'stream'

bonanza = 'rich vein of precious metal': Spanish *bonanza* = 'fair weather'

bronco (Western) = 'wild, unbroken horse': Spanish *bronco* = 'coarse, rough'

* **buckaroo** /bŭk-ə-ro͞o, bŭk-ə-ro͞o/ (Western) = 'cowboy': possibly from Spanish

* Appears as separate entry

vaquero = 'cowboy,' from *vaca* = 'cow'

burro /bêr-ō, in the Southwest **bōō**-rō/ (Western) = 'small donkey': Spanish *burro*

caballero /kăb-ə-**lâr**-ō, -əl-**yâr**-ō/ (Southwestern) = 'horseman': Spanish *caballero* = 'horseman,' also 'gentleman,' from *caballo* = 'horse'

calaboose (Southwestern) = 'jail': Spanish *calabozo* = 'dungeon'

canyon (Rocky Mountain, Upper Midwestern) = 'deep gorge, defile': Spanish *cañón* = 'gorge, tube, pipe, cannon'

chaps /chăps, shăps/ = 'leather trousers without a seat, worn by cowboys over work pants': abbreviation of Mexican Spanish *chaparreras*, from *chaparro* = 'scrub oak'

chili = 'hot pepper' See AZTEC WORDS.

cinch = 'strap to secure a saddle,' figuratively 'sure thing': from Spanish *cincha*

corral (Rocky Mountain, Southwestern, and Upper Midwestern) = 'fenced-in area for horses, cattle, etc.': Spanish *corral*, related to *correr* = 'to run'

* **coyote** /kī-**ō**-tē, **kī**-ōt/ = 'small American wolf' See AZTEC WORDS.

dago /**dā**-gō/ (derogatory) = 'Italian person'; originally applied to Spaniards: from Spanish proper name *Diego*

desperado /dĕs-pə-**rä**-dō/ = 'outlaw, badman': pseudo-Spanish formation from English *desperate*

enchilada /ĕn-chə-**lä**-də/ = 'rolled tortilla stuffed with meat, chili, cheese, spices, etc.': Mexican Spanish *enchilada*, from *chile* = 'chili pepper'

fandango /făn-**dăng**-gō/ = 'lively dance': Spanish *fandango*

fiesta /fē-**ĕs**-tə/ = 'celebration, festival': Spanish *fiesta*

filibuster = originally 'U.S. citizen engaged in insurrectionary activities in Central America,' now 'tactic for blocking legislation': probably from Spanish *filibustero*, distantly related, via French and Dutch, to English *freebooter*

frijoles /frē-**hō**-lās, -lēz/ (Southwestern) = 'beans': Spanish *frijoles*

garbanzo /gär-**băn**-zō/ = 'chickpea'; often heard in the (redundant) phrase *garbanzo bean*: Spanish *garbanzo*

gringo /**grĭng**-gō/ (derogatory) = 'U.S. citizen of non-Hispanic European descent': Mexican Spanish *gringo* = 'American or English person,' specialized meaning of general American Spanish *gringo* = 'foreigner,' variant of *griego* = 'Greek,' that is, 'one who speaks an unintelligible language'

hacienda /ä-sē-**ĕn**-də, hä-/ = (1) 'large ranch or plantation' (2) 'the chief dwelling on such an establishment': Spanish *hacienda* = 'farmstead, country property'

hombre /**ŏm**-brā, -brē/ = 'man, guy': Spanish *hombre* = 'man'

incommunicado /ĭn-kə-myōō-nə-**kä**-dō/ = 'prevented from communicating with friends, counsel, etc.': Spanish *incomunicado*

jerky = 'dried beef preserved in thin strips': Spanish *charqui*

lariat (Western) = 'long rope with running noose': Spanish *la reata* = 'strap used to keep animals in single file'

lasso (Western and Pacific Southwest) = 'long rope with running noose, lariat': Spanish *lazo* = 'snare'

loco (Western) = 'crazy,' specifically 'poisoned by locoweed': Spanish *loco* = 'mad, insane'

mesa (Western and Southwestern) = 'flat-topped mountain with steep sides': Spanish *mesa* = 'table'

mosey = 'to amble along, dawdle,' earlier 'to hurry away, skedaddle': the earlier meaning suggests a relationship with *vamoose* = 'let's get out of here, beat it' (see *vamoose*, below)

mustang (Western) = 'wild horse': Mexican Spanish *mesteño*, originally an adjective referring to livestock held in common by the *mesta* = 'association of livestock raisers'

patio (Southwestern) = 'interior courtyard': Spanish *patio*

peon /pē-ŏn/ = 'unskilled agricultural laborer': Spanish *peón* = 'indentured laborer'

piñon, pinyon /pĭn-yən, -yōn/ = 'edible seed of certain pine trees': Spanish *piñón*

pinto = 'piebald horse': Spanish *pinto*, related to *pintar* = 'to paint'

placer /plăs-ər/ = 'sandy alluvial deposit containing valuable minerals': Mexican Spanish *placer*, in Standard Spanish 'shoal, sandbank,' apparently a Catalan loanword derived from *plaça* = 'public square'

plaza (Southwestern) = 'public square': Spanish *plaza*

poncho = 'blanketlike cloak with a hole in the center for the head' See SOUTH AMERICAN WORDS.

pronto (Western) = 'soon, right away': Spanish *pronto*

pueblo = 'Hopi Indian village': Spanish *pueblo* = 'village'

quirt /kwêrt/ = 'riding whip': probably from Spanish *cuerda* = 'rope, cord'

ranch = 'large farm for raising livestock': Mexican Spanish *rancho*, from earlier meaning 'encampment, field mess'

rodeo /rō-dē-ō, rō-dā-ō/ = (1) 'cattle roundup' (2) 'public exhibition of riding, roping, etc.': Spanish *rodeo* = 'surrounding,' from *rodear* = 'to surround'

***savvy** = 'practical knowledge, know-how'; earlier used as a tag question, *savvy?* = 'you know?': Spanish *¿sabe?* = 'you know?' from the verb *saber* = 'to know'

sierra = 'mountain range with an irregular, jagged contour': Spanish *sierra* = 'mountains or hills having a saw-toothed appearance,' from the basic meaning 'saw'

sombrero = 'wide-brimmed Mexican hat': Spanish *sombrero* = 'hat,' from *sombra* = 'shade'

stampede = 'wild charge of frightened livestock': American Spanish *estampida* = 'stampede,' from Spanish *estampido* = 'explosion, report (of a gun)'

stevedore = 'longshoreman': Spanish *estibador*, from *estibar* = 'to stow'

tamale = 'Mexican dish consisting of cornmeal, chopped meat, and peppers, wrapped in a corn husk': Mexican Spanish *tamal*, plural *tamales*, from Nahuatl *tamalli*

tortilla /tôr-tē-yə/ = '(in Mexican cuisine) flat unleavened flour or cornmeal pancake': Mexican Spanish *tortilla*, from *torta* = 'cake'; not to be confused with the Standard Spanish *tortilla* = 'potato omelette'

vamoose /vă-mōōs/ = 'to leave,' from the exclamation *vamoose* = 'let's go, scram, beat it': Spanish *Vamos!* = 'Let's go!' first person plural imperative of the verb *ir* = 'to go'; possible source of English *mosey* (see above)

vigilante = 'member of a self-appointed committee formed to execute summary justice on suspected criminals': Spanish *vigilante* = 'watchman, guard'; like English *desperado* (see above), *vigilante* may be no more than a partial Hispanization of English *vigilant*

wrangler = 'cowboy who tends saddle horses': Mexican Spanish *caballerango* = 'cowboy'

(3) Words borrowed in the 20th century, including sociopolitical terms:

boricua /bôr-ē-kwə/ = 'a Puerto Rican,' specifically 'one who resists assimilation to Anglo-American culture and speech': Spanish *boricua* = 'native inhabitant of Borinquén' (Puerto Rico)

***bracero** /brə-sâr-ō/ (Southwestern) = 'migrant agricultural worker'

cafeteria = 'self-service restaurant': Spanish *cafetería* = 'coffee shop,' from *café* = 'coffee' (This word has given rise to an enormous number of commercial derivatives ending in *-teria.*)

chicano /chĭ-kä-nō/ = 'U.S. citizen of Mexican descent'; generally designates someone more committed to minority causes and more determined to resist cultural assimilation than the neutral Mexican American: originally a derogatory nickname for Spanish *mexicano* = 'Mexican'

conga /kŏng-gə/ = 'dance in which partici-

*Appears as separate entry

pants form a line': Spanish *(danza) conga* = '(dance) from the Congo'

*** macho** = 'aggressively, belligerently male'

marijuana, marihuana = 'euphoria-inducing herb, *Cannabis sativa*': Spanish *marihuana, mariguana*

pachuco /pə-**chōō**-kō/ (derogatory) = 'Mexican American juvenile'; refers particularly to those who knew Southwestern Spanish slang *(caló)* and wore zoot suits in the 1940s: Southwestern Spanish *pachuco,* derogatory and humorous nickname for residents of El Paso, Texas, where the pachucos supposedly originated

palomino = 'horse with a golden coat and silvery-white mane': Mexican Spanish *palomino,* from *paloma* = 'dove'

peyote /pā-**ō**-tē/ = 'drug obtained from the mescal cactus': Spanish *peyote,* from Nahuatl *peyotl*

pinto bean = 'string bean with mottled seeds': Mexican Spanish *(frijol) pinto*

rumba /**rōōm**-bə, **rŭm**-/ = 'dance with characteristic Latin beat': Cuban Spanish *rumba*

siesta = 'nap taken after the midday meal': Spanish *siesta*

taco = 'baked cornmeal tortilla, filled with meat, cheese, lettuce, tomato, etc.': Mexican Spanish *taco*

*Appears as separate entry

special pleading. *Special pleading* is one of those terms whose meaning has grown increasingly fuzzy. Originally, in logic, the term simply referred to a one-sided argument—one in which inconvenient facts or opposing points of view are ignored because, presumably, to acknowledge them would weaken the arguer's own case. Meanwhile, in law, special pleading came to refer to a courtroom tactic in which an attorney, rather than merely denying matter pleaded by the opposition, alleges the existence of new, previously unintroduced matter that will offset the opposition's contention. But while both definitions still exist, current usage has tended to give yet another meaning to the term, that of "ax grinding," or trying to find general arguments for or against some position in which the arguer has a lively (if not always apparent) personal interest. Given the incompatibility of these definitions of special pleading, it is probably wise to avoid using the term unless the context defines precisely what is meant by it. See also FALLACY.

species, specie. The Latin word *species* means 'class, kind, type.' As a modern biological term, pronounced /**spē**-shēz/ or /**spē**-sēz/, it means 'the most basic category of plants or animals': *Canis familiaris* is the species of domestic dogs; this species is a subdivision of the genus *Canis* (which includes also the wolves and jackals). The plural of *species* is *species: There are at least six species of American wren.*

In legal Latin the phrase *in specie* means 'in a stated kind, of a stated type.' The phrase was formerly often used of money payments that were made in actual coin of a stated type. Subsequently, *specie* /**spē**-shē/ or /**spē**-sē/ became an independent noun meaning 'money in coin.'

> . . . the effects of a paper currency are substantially the same, whether it be convertible into specie or not.
> —John Stuart Mill,
> *Principles of Political Economy* (1848)

Specie is occasionally used as if it were the singular of *species.* This is a mistake.

specious, plausible. These two subtly overlapping adjectives belong to an elusive area of meaning, full of debatable truths and human deviousness. Both words are two-faced: they refer to such things as reasoning, interpretation of fact, excuses, and lies, and they describe them, in varying degrees, as apparently convincing or valid but actually either doubtful or false. On the whole *specious* is the more hostile and assertive word. To call something specious is to state that it's definitely invalid and that its superficial validity is a deception. *Plausible,* on the other hand, refers first to the apparent validity, then casts some level of doubt on it but does not necessarily label it false.

(1) *Specious:*

> It took some time to discover the specious denials the defendant was making. —Louis Nizer, *My Life in Court*

Here the lawyer is telling us that the denials were lies, smoothly told. If he had called them *plausible,* he would be doubting that they were accurate, but leaving the possibility open.

> His voice was still soft and filled with specious humility.
> —Margaret Mitchell, *Gone With the Wind*

The humility was entirely fictitious and had no sincere basis.

(2) *Plausible, plausibility:*

> True or false, a rumor is hard to bury if it has a certain plausibility.
> —Roy Rowan, *Reader's Digest*

All that matters is whether the rumor is reasonably convincing on the face of it, regardless of underlying truth.

> Even where we know, from a comparison with other sources, that Snorri Sturluson's facts are considerably inaccurate, his account is always eminently plausible.
> —Magnus Magnusson, introduction to *King Harald's Saga*

Here the underlying facts are wrong, but the story as told is plausible—coherent and credible when taken by itself. *Specious* could not have been used here.

The next quotation refers to the apparent pain suffered by a mouse being killed by a cat.

> There are now some plausible reasons for thinking that it is not like that at all.
> —Lewis Thomas, *Reader's Digest*

The scientist goes on to explain that there is a theory that certain painkilling hormones are released by the brain. But it's only a plausible theory that has not yet been proved or disproved, and he is content to suspend judgment.

> I found him a plausible, attractive rogue, all nervous energy and wit.
> —Thomas Flanagan, *The Year of the French*

Applied to persons, *plausible* means 'superficially impressive but arousing one's suspicions that the individual is putting on an act.'

split infinitive. In most cases the infinitive of an English verb is preceded by the word *to,* as in *To err is human* or *I want to go.* Historically, this *to* started life as the preposition *to* = 'toward, in the direction of' followed by a verbal noun, forming sentences such as *I went to finding my father.* Eventually, the *-ing* dropped away: *I went to find my father.* This use of *to* then ceased to be felt as a preposition and became a meaningless adjunct or marker of the infinitive. As a result grammarians (probably influenced by Latin, in which an infinitive is a single word) got the idea that the *to* of the infinitive is virtually part of the verb itself; that *to err* in effect forms a single word that should never be "split."

In most situations no one wants or tends to split infinitives anyway, so the "rule" is unnecessary. But in at least one common type of sentence, the rule comes up against a general and natural tendency of English—the tendency to place adverbs, especially emphatic ones, immediately before the verbs they modify, including infinitives. *I want to really understand this* is the natural order for that sentence. *I want really to understand this* is an unnatural order, forced on the sentence by an unnatural rule.

For generations this rule has been taught in most schools, and it is still supported by many teachers and stylists. Historical surveys have shown that numerous great writers accepted it as binding and left few if any split infinitives in their work. But an equally formidable list can be made of eminent writers who have ignored the rule. The issue can't be settled by counting famous heads.

In the late 20th century the rule is unmistakably weakening. More and more editors, publishers, journalists, and teachers have abolished the taboo entirely.

> The Boston Red Sox drafted him to eventually replace an injured relief pitcher on a farm team.
> —Bill Surface, *Reader's Digest*

> Congressional leaders had to nearly dragoon members into serving on the Senate and House ethics committees this year.
> —*U.S. News & World Report*

> . . . a new method of carrying out carbon-14 dating of archeological and paleontological specimens that promises to more than double the time span from which ancient organic objects can be dated.
> —Boyce Rensenberger, *New York Times*

> There are no votes in doing those things, and it takes some strength . . . to resist the pressures to almost never do them. —Elizabeth Drew, *Senator*

In some of these cases it actually changes the meaning, or at least the emphasis, of the sentence if the adverb is moved from where it truly belongs, immediately before the verb.

But many still prefer to obey the rule, even at the cost of sacrificing the natural flow of a sentence.

> It was the time formally to open the campaign for the forthcoming elections.
> —*Time*

> . . . a militant anti-communist . . . willing openly to threaten the use of nuclear weapons.
> —Richard H. Ullman, *New York Times Book Review*

> People have really to feel deeply about something or somebody before a tragedy like Pop's death could turn into a comedy like his funeral.
> —Billie Holiday and William Duffy, *Lady Sings the Blues*

In the last example we feel sure it was the coauthor, not Ms. Holiday, who moved *really* from its natural place.

In the final two examples the adverb has been moved to a position between the verb and its direct object—an even more unnatural sentence order.

> Mr. Carter was said to have decided . . . to proceed with a request for authority to increase automatically the Federal tax on gasoline. . . .
> —*New York Times*

> I strongly felt that I could not allow [Archibald] Cox to defy openly a presidential directive.
> —Richard Nixon, *R.N.*

◊ ***Recommendation.*** We are on the side of those who feel free to utterly disregard the rule against split infinitives. But if you have been conditioned to the rule, and feel bound to eliminate any split infinitive that may rear its harmless head, it is better to rewrite the sentence in some way than unnaturally to distort its structures.

spoof. To the extent that its meaning can be pinned down, the term *spoof* generally refers to making good-natured fun of someone or something. In fact, *spoof* is still too new a word to have acquired a completely precise definition or set of firmly established connotations. The word was coined by an early-20th-century British comedian named Arthur Roberts, who used it for the name of a tricky game he had invented. At first—used mostly as a verb—*spoof* meant 'to hoax or deceive.' Later, when it also began to be used as a noun, it acquired the now dominant meaning of 'gentle ridicule or parody.' Whether *spoof* has found its final resting place in meaning or will evolve still further, only the lexicographers of the future will know for certain. See also BURLESQUE; LAMPOON; SATIRE.

spoonerism. The Reverend William Spooner (1844–1930) was an Oxford scholar who taught philosophy and theology. He had a tendency to accidentally transpose initial sounds in adjacent words, producing such examples as "Kinquering kongs their titles take" and "The Lord is a shoving leopard." This tendency is in fact very widespread, and almost everyone does it at times. The technical linguistic term for it is *metathesis,* but admirers of Dr. Spooner named it the *spoonerism,* an expression that has passed into popular usage. Dr. Spooner himself is said to have taken to perpetrating spoonerisms on purpose. No one has ever improved on his alleged reproof to an undergraduate, "You have hissed all your mystery lectures and completely tasted two whole worms." But perhaps his supreme achievement, which we dearly hope is not apocryphal, involved the transposition of whole word elements in separate sentences. Going into a stationery store he asked, "Have you any signifying glasses?" The salesperson retired baffled, conferred with a colleague, refused to admit defeat, and claimed to have just run out of them. "Never mind, it really doesn't magnify," said Dr. Spooner.

squire. See ESQUIRE, SQUIRE.

stalagmite, stalactite. The American pronunciations are /stə-**lăg**-mīt/, /stə-**lăk**-tīt/. The British pronunciations are /**stăl**-əg-mīt/, /**stăl**-ək-tīt/. Assuming that it really matters which hangs down and which grows up, the two words were coined in a hopelessly confusing way: from Greek *stalaktos* = 'dropping, dripping'; and Greek *stalagma* = 'drop, drip.' But here are two mnemonics that solve the problem quite reliably: the stalactite has to hold on *tight* so as not to fall off; the stalagmite, if it kept on growing long enough, *might* reach the roof of the cave. Or, the *c* in *stalactite* is for *ceiling;* the g in *stalagmite* is for *ground.*

staple. In medieval Europe a *staple* was a commercial market or export center, often with a monopoly for the export of certain products. A *staple commodity,* also shortened to *staple,* was one of the products exported in this way; for years the chief staple of England was wool.

Nowadays, *staple (commodity)* means 'any of the chief commodities produced or sold in a place' or 'any large-scale, long-established product.' This is the origin of the word *staple* meaning 'basic element, preoccupying theme, favorite topic.' It is sometimes confused with *stable,* which is a completely unrelated word.

> You could not open an illustrated paper without seeing in it a portrait of her, and her mad pranks were a staple of conversation.
> —W. Somerset Maugham, *The Human Element*

> People in the News. Faces and Places. Personalities. These became the new staples of the local newscast. . . .
> —Ron Powers, *The Newscasters*

stem-winding. In the old days, before digital watches, not only was your watch powered by clockwork, but you used a tiny key to wind it up. The key was often attached to the other end of the watch chain adorning your vested Victorian frontage. Then the ever-innovative watch industry came up with a watch with a built-in winding contraption—a stem topped with a knurled knob. Suddenly everyone had to have one of these state-of-the-art stem-winders; by the 1890s *stem-winder* was also slang for a top-quality person: *My boss is a real stem-winder!*

Time, and many generations of innovative timepieces, have passed since those days. But the adjective *stem-winding* has acquired a specialized use, evoking the rhetorical style of the American politician of the age of the stem-winding watch. It means, approximately, 'sonorously eloquent, speaking with forceful sincerity':

> He was a man of swift intelligence, immense sympathy and great gusto, a stem-winding orator in the style of mid-western populism. . . .
> —Arthur M. Schlesinger, Jr., *Robert Kennedy and His Times*

> On those occasions when he takes to the Senate floor for a major speech, it is an event; he lets go in a stem-winding style that one associates with the Senate of a hundred years ago.
> —Elizabeth Drew, *Senator*

stone. See PIT, STONE, SEED, KERNEL.

stream, branch, creek, brook, etc. *Stream* is the universal term in English for a body or channel of running water, especially one smaller than a river. Because streams come in all sizes and shapes, and because of their historical importance to settlement and economics, the word *stream* has numerous synonyms. Many of these are unique to certain regions of the country, and many have subtle differences in meaning.

The English word *branch* = 'bough' took on a new meaning when transplanted to America. By analogy, it very early referred to any stream that separated from, or "branched off," a larger one.

> Here doth the river divide it selfe into 3 or 4 convenient branches.
>
> —John Smith, *The Generall Historie of Virginia, New-England, and the Summer Isles* (1624)

Before long any small stream came to be known as a *branch*, though this use of the word exists today primarily in the General Southern dialect:

> The swamp dipped to a running branch no broader than a fence post.
>
> —Marjorie Kinnan Rawlings, *The Yearling*

> They take the pride of a connoisseur in their water. . . . If it is branch water they drink, it must come from some stream running in laurel and rock . . . achingly cold in its purity.
>
> —Roderick Peattie, *The Great Smokies and the Blue Ridge*

Like *branch*, the word *creek* developed a new meaning in America. In Britain it referred to a long, narrow arm of the sea extending into the land, up which boats could travel a short distance:

> They had made a harde voiage, had they not mett with a Canoa coming out of a Creeke, where their Shallop could not goe.
>
> —*Virginia Colony Journal* (1619)

The inlets on the coast of Virginia are still called creeks. But it was not long before the colonists began calling the minor tributaries of rivers creeks.

> The stage . . . made the trip . . . when the creeks were not up and there was no other preventing providence.
>
> —Thomas Robley, *History of Bourbon County Kansas* (1894)

Creek is used throughout the United States, though it has much less currency in New England. The pronunciation /krēk/, however, is commoner in the General Southern dialect than elsewhere, whereas /krĭk/ is the usual pronunciation in the General Northern dialect, often with the spelling *crick*.

> He wer aimin fur the swimin hole in the krick.
>
> —G. W. Harris, *Sut Lovingood* (1867)

> I will open that crick bottom, and then I shall make some money.
>
> —Edward Eggleston, *The Circuit Rider* (1874)

Brook is chiefly a Northern dialect term brought to America from England where it meant 'torrential stream.' Today, a brook is a stream that babbles rather than roars along.

> It is impossible for a brook of this size to be modelled into more diversified, or more delightful, forms.
>
> —Timothy Dwight, *Travels in New England and New York* (1821)

Kill is a Hudson Valley dialect term for a rivulet or brook, but it is no longer used much except in certain place names—for example, the Beaverkill, a famous trout stream in New York. The term is a relic of the Dutch settlement of the region and derives from *kil*, which referred to a watercourse or channel:

> Some Familyes from Maryland may have liberty to come and settle upon ye Kill below Apoquenimi.
>
> —*New York Colonial History Documents* (1669)

> There was an old hunter camped down
> by the kill,
> Who fished in this water and shot on
> that hill.
>
> —Charles Hoffman, *Greyslaer, a Romance of the Mohawk* (1839)

Kill is also used locally in New York as the name for a strait; the straits separating Staten Island from New Jersey are the Arthur Kill and the Kill van Kull.

> The number of vessels plying through the Kills is annually increasing. . . . There are ten thousand vessels employed in the Arthur Kill traffic.
> —Congressional Record (1886)

A *bayou* is widely known as a swampy area having stagnant bodies of water. But in the Gulf Southern dialect the earliest meaning is still commonly used, 'side stream or tributary having little or no observable current.' The term comes from Choctaw *bayuk* = 'river or creek,' which the French Americans (Cajuns) adopted and gave to later English arrivals. (For an illustration of how *bayou* is used locally, see DICTIONARY OF AMERICAN REGIONAL ENGLISH.)

> The hired men . . . wandered among the swamps and bayous of the Mississippi, till they and their horses had nearly perished.
> —*Missionary Herald* (1822)

> The term *Bayou* is understood here [in Louisiana] to mean an alluvial stream with but little current, and sometimes running from the main river, and connected with it again, as a lateral canal.
> —Timothy Flint, *Recollections* (1826)

Run is a North Midland dialect term for a small stream and was probably brought to America by settlers from northern Britain, where the term is still occasionally used.

> There is no body's of Flat rich Land to be found—till one gets far enough from the River to head the little runs and drains.
> —George Washington, *Diaries* (1770)

subjunctive. The term *subjunctive* serves as a general label for verbs representing an action that could or should happen. In the following sentence the word *go* is subjunctive: *I insist that he go home.* In the parlance of grammarians the clause *that he go home* is in the subjunctive mood. (Some say *mode* for *mood* in this sense; both are correct.) The other two moods are the *indicative (He goes home)* and the *imperative (Go home!).* In the following sentence the verb "impose" is in the subjunctive:

> President Carter stuck to his insistence that the UN impose economic sanctions. —*Winnipeg Tribune*

In the next example "remain" is subjunctive:

> I am not suggesting that anyone remain in a dreadful marriage.
> —Louise Montague, *Reader's Digest*

Sentences like the foregoing make up most of our everyday uses of the subjunctive. Next commonest in usage is the so-called contrary-to-fact condition: *if I were you.* Many people say *if I was you,* and in British English this is considered a correct alternative; but in North American English it is felt to be strongly colloquial, if not entirely wrong. The issue has been a live one in the English-speaking New World for the past 200 years. Noah Webster wrote in 1789:

> Writers and grammarians have attempted for centuries to introduce a subjunctive mode into English, yet without effect; the language requires none, distinct from the indicative; and therefore a subjunctive form stands in books only as a singularity, and people in practice pay no regard to it. The people are right.

In matters of language the people are indeed right, but in this case Webster was wrong. Sentences like the ones quoted earlier come naturally to any native user of the language; they were not imposed by schoolmasters. However, there are cases where you have a choice; there are borderline cases; and finally, there are cases where use of the subjunctive would be old-fashioned.

Here is a colloquial use in which the author might just as well have used the indicative and written "was":

> She asked if I were looking forward to boarding the Blue Express.
> —Truman Capote, *The Muses Are Heard*

Here is another case in which "was" would be equally correct:

> If the hall were a landmark and it could prove it was not getting a 6 percent return on its operations, it could apply for a tax abatement. . . .
> —Fred Ferretti, *New York*

In the following sentence the subjunctive is obligatory; "as though he was" would be incorrect in standard usage.

> The purchaser then slid open the window and tossed the radio into the street, as casually as though he were flipping a cigarette butt.
> —Herb Caen, *Reader's Digest*

Here is a case in which the writer could have used the subjunctive and written "unless the government were," but did not:

> She would not travel first class, unless the government was paying for it.
> —Mary McCarthy, *Birds of America*

In the following instance the subjunctive is obligatory—the verb has to be "quit" in both clauses:

> Her husband was called into the dean's office and given an ultimatum: either his wife quit or they both quit.
> —Janet Battaile, *New York Times*

Here is a sentence in which the writer could not have done without the subjunctive:

> With lobsters, as with crabs, the most important thing about them is that they be alive.
> —Mimi Sheraton, *New York Times*

If the writer had used indicative "are" instead of subjunctive "be," the sentence would have meant something else.

Old-fashioned Uses of the Subjunctive. Until the end of the 19th century, sentences like the following one were common in formal writing:

> These voyages are so prolonged, and the shore intervals at home so exceedingly brief, that if the captain have a family . . . he does not trouble himself much about his ship in port.
> —Herman Melville, *Moby-Dick*

Modern usage would require "if the captain has," of course, but you will occasionally encounter this old-fashioned kind of subjunctive in present-day writing. It is not a mistake, but the writer must be skilled enough to make it work and not sound oddly obsolete or pedantic. It has been a very long time since the old-fashioned subjunctive was fully colloquial, as in the following sentence from Samuel Pepys's *Diary* of 1663:

> I wish it [card playing] do not lose too much of my time.

Yet present-day descendants of the same construction are very much alive. Compare the following sentence from a recent issue of *Reader's Digest* with the previous one cited by Pepys:

> In return, they ask that Israel withdraw from the occupied territories.
> —William E. Griffith

◇ ***Recommendation.*** Let your native ear be your guide. Or, if you aspire to write mannered literary prose, read the older stylists such as Herman Melville and Edgar Allan Poe. Learn from them how the subjunctive can sometimes lend greater elegance and precision to an already well-turned sentence.

suffixes. See AFFIXES.

suspicion is used in dialect as a verb meaning 'to suspect (that something is so).' This is not accepted in standard usage.

swamp, marsh, bog, etc. *Swamp* and *marsh* are both common terms for 'low-lying, soft or spongy land, usually saturated or partially covered with water.' However, in a number of places a strict distinction is carefully observed—a swamp is always fresh water; a marsh is always salt water. This distinction, however, is not present in the following sentence from a description of the early settlement of Virginia; here the marsh has got to be fresh water.

> In the low Marishes, growe plots of Onyons containing an acre of ground or

more in many places.

—John Smith,
A Map of Virginia: with a Description of the Countrey (1612)

Bog, which entered English from the Irish or Gaelic *bogach* with the same meaning, was until this century a primarily Northern usage. It too has been used in America since colonial times.

> The Creeks are rather useful, than noisome; and no Bogs have been seen here by any.
>
> —Virginia House of Burgesses, *Journals* (1623)

A *swale* also refers to 'low-lying wetland.' In England it was a dialect term probably adopted from an early Scandinavian word, such as Old Norse *svalr* = 'cool.' Today, it is only occasionally used in the North.

> South of the hill, in a low, sheltered swale, surrounded by a mulberry hedge, was the orchard.
>
> —Willa Cather, *O Pioneers* (1913)

Slough /slo͞o/ is also synonymous with *swamp* and *marsh*. It has been used in English since the Old English period and has considerable currency throughout America today; see SLOUGH. The term has the additional sense in America of 'backwater or narrow sluggish channel or inlet.' Except for the northeastern section of the country, this sense is widespread.

> At 11:57 a.m. on New Year's day, I saw my first robin, near Katydid slough at Willow Springs.
>
> —*Chicago Tribune* (1950)

Bayou, from the Choctaw word *bayuk* = 'river or creek,' is used synonymously with both senses of *slough*. In the Gulf Southern dialect a bayou is a backwater or side stream (see STREAM, BRANCH, CREEK, BROOK; DICTIONARY OF AMERICAN REGIONAL ENGLISH). Its commoner meaning, however, is 'marsh or swamp.' This meaning is especially well known in the Mississippi and Missouri river valley regions of the country.

A *tule* is either of two common large bulrushes found in swampy areas of the United States. It is a loanword from American Spanish, which in turn took it from the Nahuatl Indian word *tollin* = 'rush.' In the West, especially the Southwest, *tule* also refers to the region or tract of wetland where these bulrushes grow.

> They . . . held on down through the low reach of tulles and sand-dunes that stretch between the barracks and the old red fort.
>
> —Frank Norris, *Blix* (1900)

More recently, the plural *tules* has been extended to mean 'out-of-the-way place or rural area,' synonymous with *boondocks* and *sticks*.

In North Carolina and Virginia *pocosin* /pə-**kō**-sən/ is the term often used for a marsh or swamp. It is a colonial borrowing of the Delaware Indian word *pakwesen*.

> The drive is one of the large pocosons so common in the lower pine country.
>
> —*Outing* (1893)

> The Indians called these queer round swamps pocosins. The white hunters and woodsmen, differentiating them sharply from the more typical swamps of irregular shape along the creeks and rivers, called them bays . . . perhaps because the bay tree or shrub abounds in them.
>
> —*Saturday Evening Post* (1944)

swashbuckler. Such a fellow is so named not because he buckles a swash but because he swashes a buckler. The original *swashbuckler* was an Elizabethan type, a swearing, brawling, hard-drinking braggart, armed and looking for mayhem. To *swash* was to make a clashing noise with a sword, and the *buckler* was a small round shield or guard used to ward off sword blows. The word *swashbuckler* thus means 'one who clashes sword on buckler'; this could refer either to actual fighting or to clashing one's sword on one's own buckler to make a noise.

The cinematic swashbuckler typified by Douglas Fairbanks and Errol Flynn is a swaggering but chivalrous and well-mannered hero. The word is also used of real-life fighting soldiers of the more daredevil kind—perhaps closer to the Elizabethan original.

The adjective *swashbuckling* and even the verb *swashbuckle* are also used and are good examples of BACK-FORMATIONS.

syllogisms. See FALLACY.

syndrome. In medicine and psychology a *syndrome* is a set of distinct symptoms that typically appear together and are taken as indications of one underlying disease or condition. The word has become a superstar of popular culture, meaning, approximately, 'set of ideas, type of behavior':

> I wanted to go beyond the Beautiful People Peace and Protest syndrome to a campaign concerned with the distribution of wealth in this country. . . .
> —Rev. Joseph Duffey (quoted), Bill Moyers, *Listening to America*

> . . . many of them found themselves in the trapped-housewife syndrome.
> —Judith Krantz, *Book Digest*

> Caught in the toils of the Soviet spiderweb, the people have become largely apathetic and have succumbed to the nothing-can-be-done-anyway syndrome.
> —Jack Anderson, *Savannah Morning News*

synecdoche. See METAPHOR.

synonym, a word having the same meaning as another word. Some pairs of synonyms are *link* and *connection; wisely* and *sagely; candid* and *frank.* It has often been observed that there are no true synonyms. Each word has its own individual shade of meaning and feeling, its own special flavor. The ability to use the aptest word in a given context, out of a cluster of possible synonyms or near-synonyms, is a hallmark of the good writer, one whose language has distinction.

In the past the quest for *le mot juste* ('the precise word') was carried to extremes by such stylistic precisionists as Flaubert and Henry James. There is nothing wrong with such a quest nowadays. Beauty is difficult and so is good writing—and the latter comes chiefly from what the great French stylist Louis-Ferdinand Céline once called "the mania to perfect." Whether your personal writing goals of the moment are ambitiously literary or are on a more modest, everyday level, you might consider using a thesaurus to expedite the search for the right synonym. Thesauruses (or thesauri—either plural is correct) may be arranged alphabetically or by topics. The Reader's Digest *Family Word Finder* is an alphabetical thesaurus. The classic topical thesaurus is *Roget's*. The modern thesaurus concept was invented by the English physician Peter Mark Roget (1779–1869), and present-day topical thesauruses in English are all rewrites of Roget's original work, first published in the mid-19th century.

syntax, the arrangement of words or word groups to generate sentences. See GRAMMAR; LANGUAGE CHANGE.

T

taboo. See EUPHEMISM.

take. See BRING, TAKE.

tall talk. See REGIONAL DIALECTS OF AMERICAN ENGLISH.

tantamount. From an Old French phrase meaning 'to amount to as much' (*tant* = 'so much'), *tantamount* is an adjective. It means 'equivalent, coming to the same thing.' It is used only predicatively, as *This is tantamount to that*, and cannot go directly with a noun (as *a tantamount quantity*). It is always used with *to:*

> None of us said a word, for we all three were sure a descent into the valley would be tantamount to suicide.
> —Farley Mowat, *And No Birds Sang*

> Acceptance of a work at the museum can be tantamount to establishing the reputation of a young artist.
> —*U.S. News & World Report*

tasteless. See DISTASTEFUL, TASTELESS.

tautology and pleonasm. *Tautology* is repetition or redundancy. The term commonly signifies a stylistic fault, since it is usually defined as a needless reiteration of words or ideas. But the adjective *needless* requires qualification. A repetition that may be unnecessary for a speaker who merely wishes to convey meaning can be thought essential by a speaker who is looking for ways to emphasize what he or she is saying.

There comes a point, however, when the deliberate use of tautology can irritate the reader or listener. Exactly where that point lies is difficult to define. Here, for example, is a cluster of tautologies that appear in four successive paragraphs of David Halberstam's *The Powers That Be* (1979). In the first paragraph Halberstam says that in the 1950s *New York Times* reporter James Reston "had become the symbolic journalistic figure of the city [Washington] and that generation." In the second paragraph he informs us:

> Reston was the dominant Washington journalist of the fifties. For slightly more than a decade James Reston owned the town. . . . He had become, by the early fifties, the journalist that all young reporters admired . . . a symbol of journalism to be. . . . He seemed to represent what journalism might become.

In the following paragraph we are told that "even more than Lippman, [Reston] was far more the role model for working reporters." In the fourth paragraph Halberstam states that "his power in Washington in the fifties was unique" and that "the *Times* owned the town." And, lest anyone miss the point, when Halberstam returns to the subject of Reston about 20 pages later, he reminds us that "he had become, like Walter Lippman, a symbolic figure in Washington" and that "he profoundly affected the thinking of other working reporters."

Obviously, David Halberstam used a good many more words than were necessary to make his points. But did he gain anything from his insistent repetitions—sonority, emphasis, a structural looseness reminiscent of conversation? That is a question his readers may fairly dispute.

A subclass of tautology is *pleonasm*, the joining together of virtual synonyms—*cruel and inhuman; limited only to; a positive step in the right direction;* and the like. As with tautologies in general, most pleonasms are inadvertent and, by any standard, unnecessary:

> He had a mercurial changeable temperament. . . .
> —David Cecil, *A Portrait of Jane Austen*

> The events in the wake of the rescue mission to Iran that failed are stunningly shocking.
> —*Savannah Morning News*

But sheer production alone seldom satisfies. . . . —*Smithsonian*

If some forms of tautology can occasionally be justified, in good speaking or writing the same can almost never be said of pleonasm.

Still another form of tautology is the pointless abstract appendage. Thus, for example, meteorologists (presumably because they think it somehow sounds more important) may speak not of the weather, but of *weather conditions;* not of showers, but of *shower activity.* Similarly, marriage counselors may talk of *divorce situations;* educators of *subject areas;* economists . . . but the list is endless.

tawdry, a favorite example of how odd and unpredictable some word histories can be. Saint Audrey, an Anglo-Saxon queen who founded Ely cathedral in East Anglia, died in the year A.D. 679 of a tumor in the throat. She chose to regard the affliction as punishment for having been fond of wearing magnificent jeweled necklaces as a young woman. For centuries afterward her feast day (October 17) was celebrated with a fair at Ely, where the country women would buy "Saint Audrey's laces," which were narrow bands of silk or lace worn around the throat, cheap if colorful substitutes for real necklaces. *Saint Audrey's lace* was gradually altered to *Tawdrey-lace;* and later (17th century) the word *tawdry* was extracted from this and used to mean 'cheap and showy, gaudy.'

The tawdry dancing hall faded from around them.
—Pearl S. Buck, *Hearts Come Home*

By a further development *tawdry* now often means 'morally cheap, sordid':

Exactly a week after Jenkins' arrest, United Press International sent the entire tawdry story over the wires. . . .
—Sam Houston Johnson,
My Brother Lyndon

teeter-totter. See SEESAW.

terrible, terrific. A striking case of divergence. Both words begin by meaning 'causing terror, extremely frightening.' Both are extended to mean 'very great, intense, severe,' as *a terrible mistake; a terrific amount of work.* Then finally in informal use they are extended in exactly opposite directions, *terrible* to mean 'extremely bad' (*The performance was terrible*) and *terrific* to mean 'extremely good' (*The performance was terrific*).

than. In theory *than* is only a conjunction. Therefore, when it is used to make a comparison between two elements, of which the first is in the subjective case and the second is a pronoun, that pronoun must be in its subjective form.

Harold, being so much younger than we, took little part in our games.
—Consuelo Vanderbilt Balsan,
The Glitter and the Gold

The Japs knew these waters better than we.
—James J. Fahey, *Pacific War Diary*

But *than* is unmistakably becoming also a preposition. Such changes generally start in the informal levels of the language and work their way through to the more formal levels, often meeting with stubborn resistance. In everyday speech most people would say *He was younger than us* and *They knew the waters better than us.* (Of course, if the second element is a fully expressed clause, the pronoun automatically becomes subjective: *He was younger than we were. They knew the waters better than we did.* But this presents no problem.)

The tendency of *than* to become a legitimate preposition is confirmed by the fact that when it is used with *who,* the pronoun takes the objective case: *than whom.* But this is a construction that is used only in highly formal speech and writing; most people would never use it in everyday speech, if at all.

. . . Beelzebub . . . than whom,
Satan except, none higher sat.
—John Milton, *Paradise Lost*

It was a pleasure to hear Canon Liddon, than whom, in his day, there

was no finer preacher.
—from H. W. and F. G. Fowler, *The King's English*

It is true that *who* is in several other respects unique among the pronouns; but if *than* is officially allowed to be a preposition with *whom*, and is obviously trying to be a preposition in general, it's hard to see why it shouldn't.

◇ ***Recommendation.*** Only an old-fashioned minority now say *You're no better than I* or *He's older than she* in their natural everyday speech. If, like most people, you naturally say *You're no better than me* and *He's older than her*, don't correct yourself. But the change is not yet complete. In highly formal, and especially written, usage, *than I, than she*, etc., are still preferred.

that. (1) *That* versus *which* and *who.* Relative clauses may be restrictive or nonrestrictive. A restrictive clause is seen in *The family that prays together stays together;* the clause *that prays together* restricts the main statement to a limited class of family. A nonrestrictive clause is seen in *The family, which is the basic unit of human society, is weakening;* the clause *which . . . society* gives information applying to the family without any restriction. Most often, nonrestrictive clauses are set off by commas, representing pauses in speech, while restrictive clauses are not set off by commas or pauses.

Nonrestrictive clauses are also nearly always introduced by *which* (with impersonal antecedents) or *who* (with personal antecedents). With restrictive clauses the choice is not so clear. Those with impersonal antecedents are preferably introduced by *that;* but in actual usage, both written and spoken, *which* is very often used and cannot be called incorrect. *The family that prays together* is preferable, but *The family which prays together* is also possible. Restrictive clauses with personal antecedents are now usually introduced by *who:*

> Scott had always had some friend whom he considered his mentor. . . .
> —Nancy Milford, *Zelda*

But historically, and in much well-known literature, restrictive personal clauses are often introduced by *that:*

> He that hath ears to hear, let him hear.
> —Matthew 11:15

And this continues to occur in ordinary current usage:

> He helped poets, painters, sculptors and prose writers that he believed in.
> —Ernest Hemingway, *A Moveable Feast*

Furthermore, it must be recognized that there are relative clauses that are not clearly restrictive or clearly nonrestrictive, and that anyway there are many exceptions to the rule. When the relative pronoun is governed by a preposition, *that* cannot be used; *of which, to whom,* etc., are the only choices. If one antecedent is followed by a restrictive clause and then by a nonrestrictive clause, it may often seem awkward to use *that* for one and *which* or *who* for the other. And the juxtaposition of the demonstrative pronoun *that* and the relative pronoun *that* is avoided by using *that which: We ate that which was set before us* (instead of *We ate that that was set before us*).

◇ ***Recommendation.*** It is a good general precept, but not a binding rule, to prefer *that* for impersonal restrictive clauses whenever possible.

(2) Omission of the conjunction *that.* In both speech and writing, *that* is very often omitted after verbs like *say, think,* and *feel.*

> . . . he thought there was no one in the world who believed him.
> —Thornton Wilder, *The Bridge of San Luis Rey*

But in a clause remote from the verb, *that* will be included even if it has been omitted in an earlier parallel clause.

> . . . but Robert . . . said he could not bear to part with the boy, and that the pair of them would lodge with Monsieur and Madame Fiat. . . .
> —Daphne du Maurier, *The Glass-Blowers*

If any kind of ambiguity would result from omitting *that,* it must be retained. *He said several times he had lost hope* is ambiguous; it requires *that,* either before or after *several times.*

◇ ***Recommendation.*** In highly formal usage some people still prefer to retain conjunctive *that* in all situations. The option of omitting it, however, is entirely standard and acceptable unless ambiguity results.

(3) Adverbial *that.* A fully standard use of *that* is to qualify adjectives in the specifically demonstrative sense 'as that, to that degree or amount': *A car that old is a bad risk. If it costs that much, I won't buy it.* Somewhat less formal is the usually negative construction with *that* or *all that,* meaning 'not very':

> The French are not that devoted to foreigners. . . .
> —Brian Aherne, *A Dreadful Man*

> If Mullincaux and Crandall were not all that surprised when the activity on St. Helens began, most Americans presumably were.
> —P. F. Kluge, *Smithsonian*

◇ ***Recommendation.*** *Not that* and *not all that* = 'not very, not especially' are standard but informal.

theater, theatre. Although the spelling *theater* accords with the regular American treatment of similar French-derived words (like *meter, center*), many people in the theatrical world prefer *theatre;* this is also the official spelling used for many establishments.

theater terms. Western theater was originated by the Greeks, and a number of their theatrical terms are still in use. Their plays were originally part of religious festivals in honor of the god Dionysus. The theater was open-air and had a semicircular auditorium, often cut into the side of a hill. The actors wore formal masks, and there was little or no scenery. As the selection of terms below shows, the original meanings of the words have often changed considerably.

(1) Greek-derived terms:

chorus = (1) '(in Greek drama) group of dancers and singers who sang odes between sections of the play and also played a collective role in the drama' (2) 'group of singers who sing together in unison or harmony' (3) 'supporting group of dancers and singers in opera, musical comedy, etc.': from Latin *chorus,* from Greek *khoros* = 'dancing ground, dance, dramatic chorus'

comedy = 'play aimed at hilarity, and typically having a happy ending': from Latin *cōmoedia,* from Greek *kōmōidia,* literally 'revel-singing,' hence 'comic drama,' from *kōmos* = 'drunken revel' + *-ōidia* = 'singing'

drama = (1) 'a play' (2) often with *the* 'theater as an art': from Greek *drāma* = 'action, acting, drama'

orchestra = (1) '(in the Greek theater) circular floor in front of the proscenium, where the chorus danced and sang' (2) '(in modern theaters) first floor seating in a theater' (3) 'large group of musicians playing string, woodwind, brass, and percussion instruments': from Latin *orchēstra,* from Greek *orkhēstra* = 'dancing floor, orchestra in a theater,' from *orkheisthai* = 'to dance'

proscenium /prō-**sē**-nē-əm/ = (1) '(in a Greek theater) the main stage, where the acting occurs' (2) '(in a modern theater) the part of the stage in front of the curtain, the apron': from Latin *proscēnium,* from Greek *proskēnion* = 'place in front of the *skēnē,*' from *pro-* = 'in front of' + *skēnē* = 'back wall of the stage' See *scene,* below.

***protagonist** = 'the leading actor in a drama'

scene = (1) 'section of a play in which the action is continuous without change of place' (2) 'painted hanging or structure used on stage to represent a place': from Latin *scēna,* from Greek *skēnē,* originally 'tent, hut, room used by actors, in front of which the play was played,' hence 'ma-

*Appears as separate entry

sonry structure behind the proscenium, including the back wall of the stage'

***theater, theatre** = (1) 'unroofed Greek stage and auditorium' (2) 'modern building containing a stage and an auditorium' (3) often with *the* 'the drama as an art and an industry': from French *theatre,* from Latin *theatrum,* from Greek *theatron* = 'place for viewing (plays),' from *theasthai* = 'to view, watch'

tragedy = (1) '(in Greek drama) play typically concerning the protagonist's struggle against destiny or gods, culminating in his death or ruin' (2) 'play or book having an unhappy moral or ending': from Latin *tragoedia,* from Greek *tragōidia,* literally 'goat-singing, early form of drama involving men dressed as satyrs or goat men,' hence later 'tragic drama,' from *tragos* = 'goat' + *-ōidia* = 'singing'

*Appears as separate entry

(2) Selection of theater terms, some of which have spread into everyday use:

ad-lib = 'to improvise words or actions'

angel = 'person who provides money to produce a play'

Annie Oakley = 'complimentary ticket' (because a prepunched free ticket looked like one of the small targets hit by the sharpshooter *Annie Oakley* in vaudeville shows and distributed to the audience)

apron = 'that part of the stage in front of the main curtain'

backdrop = 'curtain or screen hung at the back of the stage'

backstage = (1) (adverb) 'behind the stage, in the wings, dressing rooms, or storage rooms' (2) (adjective) 'relating to the personal lives of people in the theater'

bit part = 'very small role'

block = 'to plan actors' movements and actions throughout a play'

boards = (1) with *the* 'stage of a theater'; often used in *tread the boards* = 'to act on a stage' (2) 'theater posters'

bomb = (1) (noun) 'play that is a failure' (2) (verb) 'to fail'

break = 'to miss a cue, forget lines, or laugh at the wrong time on stage because of being provoked or teased by another actor'

bus and truck = 'tour of a show in which the performers go by bus and the sets by truck'

business = 'actions of performers used for a particular effect or when there is no dialogue'

call = 'notice for a performer to appear, especially for an audition or a rehearsal'

callback = 'request for a performer to return for another audition'

callboard = 'backstage notice board for rehearsal times, instructions, changes, etc.'

cattle call = 'audition at which a large number of performers are seen very briefly'

cue = (1) (noun) 'last line or words of a speech, a few notes of music, or any action or event that signals an actor to speak, make an entrance or exit, etc.' (2) (verb) 'to signal an actor to begin performing or to make an entrance or exit'

dark = '(of a production or theater) giving no performance'

downstage = 'toward the front of the stage'

fabulous invalid = 'the theater' (because of recurrent reports that the legitimate theater is about to perish)

flat = 'upright frame covered with canvas, usually painted or decorated as background for a scene'

fourth wall = 'imaginary wall separating the performer from the audience'

freebies = 'free tickets'

go up = 'to forget one's lines'

greenroom = 'room or area in a theater where performers can gather before or between appearances on stage'

gypsy = 'chorus dancer in a musical, who moves from job to job'

head shot = 'photograph of a performer usually showing just the face and shoulders'

house = (1) 'theater in which a play is performed' (2) 'the audience'; often used in the expressions *capacity house* = 'all seats filled'; *bring down the house* = 'to get an enthusiastic, often prolonged response from an audience'

ice = (1) 'commission charged on a ticket bought from a ticket agent' (2) 'illegal payment made to a theater management by a ticket broker'

lay an egg = 'to fail completely before an audience, flop'

limelight = 'brilliant light created by directing an oxyhydrogen flame against lime, formerly used in theaters to light the stage'

nut = 'total weekly operating expenses of a show'

off (the) book = 'able to rehearse or perform without using a script'

on its feet = '(of a play in rehearsal) showing vitality and coherence because the actors are beginning to perform'

paper the house = 'to fill a theater by giving away free tickets'

pony = 'smallest girl in a chorus line'

prop = 'any article besides costumes and scenery, often one that can be carried or moved and is part of the actor's stage business'

provinces = 'any location outside New York City'

quick study = 'actor or actress who learns lines quickly and seemingly without effort'

role = 'character played by an actor or actress, part'

run-through = 'rehearsal of a play from beginning to end, without interruption'

scalper = 'person who buys theater tickets at regular or discount prices and sells them for much higher amounts'

showcase = 'production intended to display talents of the participants for agents, producers, and directors and often involving little or no pay'

sightlines = 'lines of vision from seats in various positions of a theater'

slow study = 'actor or actress who has to work hard and long to learn lines'

smash = 'successful show'

Spelvin, George *or* **Georgina** = 'fictitious name traditionally used in theater programs to conceal the identity of an actor or actress who is playing more than one role in a production'

S.R.O. = 'standing room only'

standby = 'understudy who has no role in a production but is ready to go on at each performance if needed'

step on (someone's) lines = 'to begin speaking before another actor has completed his or her lines'

swing boy *or* **girl** = 'chorus dancer or singer who has learned all the other chorus parts and can fill in when needed'

turkey = 'play or production that is a failure'

twofer = 'ticket that allows a person to buy two tickets for the price of one'

typecast = (1) 'to hire (an actor or actress) because he or she is similar to a character in looks or personality' (2) 'to cast (an actor or actress) repeatedly in the same kind of part'

understudy = 'actor or actress in a production who learns another performer's role and is prepared to replace him or her when necessary'

upstage = (1) (adverb) 'toward the back of the stage' (2) (verb) 'to draw audience attention from (another performer) by gestures, movements, etc., or by maneuvering him or her into an unfavorable position'

walk-on = 'very small, usually nonspeaking role'

walk through = 'to rehearse by reading from a script while adding movements'

wings = 'areas to the left and right of a proscenium stage, out of sight of the audience'

(3) Theater terms having universal currency. The observation "All the world's a stage" was already old when Shakespeare made it, and theater terms have long been used as meta-

phors in daily life. Among the many are:

comedy = 'hilarious event'
drama = 'tense and exciting sequence of events'
limelight = 'public attention'
scene = 'any episode or place of human actions and interactions'
tragedy = 'sad or disastrous event'
upstage = (1) 'to snub (someone), treat haughtily' (2) 'to take attention away from (someone or something)'

them is widely used in dialects for the adjective *those: Get up them stairs.* This is a nonstandard use.

there. In *There are apples in the basket, There was a loud noise, There came a time,* etc., *there* is sometimes regarded as an adverb and sometimes as a kind of pronoun. It is simpler to call it a meaningless "function word" and to regard the noun that follows the verb as the subject of the sentence. The verb therefore generally takes its number from the noun. With several subjects, each singular, the verb may be singular or plural: *There is* (or *are*) *an apple and a pear.* The same is true with several subjects of which only the first is singular: *There is* (or *are*) *an apple and two pears.* In dialects and casual speech *there is* or *there's* is often used with plural subjects: *There's four of them at home.* This is not acceptable in formal usage.

these kind of, those kind of. See KIND.

they. The pronoun *they,* basically plural, has long been used also with singular antecedents. In one type of usage, it follows words that are singular in form but often plural in implication, such as *each, any, everyone, someone,* and *nobody.*

> Each of them should . . . make themself ready.
> —William Caxton, *Sonnes of Aymon* (1489)

> Now leaden slumber with life's strength doth fight,
> And every one to rest themselves betake. . . .
> —Shakespeare, *The Rape of Lucrece* (1594)

> Every body fell a laughing, as how could they help it.
> —Henry Fielding, *Tom Jones* (1749)

> Now, nobody does anything well that they cannot help doing.
> —John Ruskin, *The Crown of Wild Olive* (1866)

In another kind of usage *they* refers to words like *person* that can apply to either sex. It replaces *he or she.*

> If a person is born of a gloomy temper . . . they cannot help it.
> —Lord Chesterfield, letter (1759)

> Little did I think . . . to make a . . . complaint against a person very dear to you . . . but don't let them be so proud . . . as to make them not care how they affront everybody else.
> —Samuel Richardson, *Pamela* (1740)

> A person can't help their birth.
> —William Makepeace Thackeray, *Vanity Fair* (1847)

Today, many or most people use *they* in this way when speaking, because it seems easy and natural. Some also use it in writing.

> If that person gets sick . . . they are in the hospital for more than two weeks. . . .
> —John F. Kennedy, *New Republic*

> Many a person now a victim of dyspepsia might trace their trouble to those nursery meals. . . .
> —Sheila Hutchins, *New Statesman*

> Your child should ask about financial-aid application procedures at the same time they ask about admission.
> —*New York Post*

When both sexes are mentioned, it sounds particularly odd to use the masculine pronoun only.

> She and Louis had a game—who could find the ugliest photograph of himself.
> —Joseph P. Lash,
> *Eleanor and Franklin*

One usage expert even used *he* with a plural antecedent, which seems unnatural.

> Our public schools have therefore held to the ideal that every boy and girl should be so equipped that he shall not be handicapped in his struggle for social progress and recognition. . . .
> —C. C. Fries,
> *American English Grammar* (1940)

When two or more subjects are connected by *or* instead of by *and*, they are traditionally considered to be a singular subject, not a plural one. However, Doris Lessing's plural solution seems much more satisfactory than the awkward *him or her*:

> . . . a man or a woman would come in here, glance around, find smiles and pleasant looks waiting for them, then wave and sit down by themselves. . . .
> —*Ms.*

◇ ***Recommendation.*** The case against using *they* as a singular pronoun is based on rigid adherence to the rule that a plural pronoun must refer exclusively to plural antecedents. As a language evolves and adapts, such rules are often modified; the pronoun *you*, originally plural only, has long since been used and accepted also as singular. There is a clear tendency for *they* to follow suit, in order to function as a singular and indefinite pronoun of common gender. Conservatives do not yet accept this development. We approve of it and think it's already on the way to full acceptance. See also HE; HE OR SHE.

this here, that there. In widespread dialects, British as well as American, *this here* and *that there* have long been used as somewhat emphatic demonstrative pronouns: *This here coffee's cold. That there dog has fleas.* This usage seems entirely natural and logical (and is exactly parallel to the French pronouns *celui-ci, ceci* and *celui-la, cela*). However, it is not accepted in Standard English, although *this coffee here* and *that dog there* are accepted.

thou is the original English pronoun for addressing a single person (exactly cognate with German *du*, French *tu*, and equivalents in the other Indo-European languages). From the late Middle Ages, the plural pronoun *ye* or *you* was increasingly used for formal and respectful address to one person; *thou* was increasingly reserved on the one hand for familiar address (as to a child or a social inferior) and on the other hand for poetry and archaic usage, including prayers to God.

Thou has its own archaic verb inflections, ending in *-est, -st,* or *-t: thou art, hast, dost, wilt, shalt, comest, goest,* etc. The objective form of *thou* is *thee,* and the possessives are *thy* and *thine.*

Thou long survived in everyday use in rural dialects, chiefly for addressing equals and intimates. In many cases the objective form *thee* came to be used interchangeably with *thou,* and the old verb inflections were often replaced by the ordinary third-person inflections. In the 17th century the Friends (or Quakers) deliberately adopted this rural plain folks' usage as the only form by which they would address a fellow mortal, considering all to be equal before God. This use is shown in a letter from Abdel James to Benjamin Franklin, quoted by Franklin in his *Autobiography:*

> . . . in hopes it may be a means, if thou continued it up to a later period, that the first and latter part may be put together; and if it is not yet continued, I hope thee will not delay it.

Thou and *thee* now remain in tenuous and fast-dwindling use in certain British dialects, by some Friends, and by churches that still use the older forms of prayer and liturgy. They are seldom used in writing poetry any more; but they are of course permanently enshrined in a large array of familiar literature from the King James Bible and the works of Shakespeare onward:

> A Jug of Wine, a Loaf of Bread—and Thou
> Beside me singing in the Wilderness. . .
> —Edward FitzGerald,
> *The Rubaiyat of Omar Khayyam*

through. The shortened spellings *thro* and *thro'* are archaic or poetic. The phonetic spelling *thru*, often used on signs and notices, and sometimes in informal writing such as letters or breezy journalism, is not accepted in formal prose. The adjective *thorough* = 'fully done, complete,' also 'careful and painstaking,' is by origin a variant of *through*, but the two words are now entirely distinct.

thusly. *Thus* is an adverb and only an adverb, meaning 'in this way, like this, as follows.' *Thusly* is a consciously deviant form used by some journalists to achieve a certain archly humorous effect.

> Kris Kristofferson describes her thusly: "She's still sexy in a strange way. . . ."
> —*Boston Herald American*

> After Christmas, the governor responded thusly to a letter of thanks from the boy's mother. . . .
> —Helene Von Damm, *Sincerely, Ronald Reagan*

◇ ***Recommendation.*** Do not use *thusly*.

tilde. See DIACRITICS.

till, until. *Till* is not a shortened form of *until;* it's the other way around—*until* is a compound meaning 'up till.' So the spelling *'til* is unnecessary; the proper spelling is *till*. *Till* and *until* are equally standard and correct at all levels of usage including the most formal:

> . . . to love and to cherish, till death do us part.
> —Solemnization of Matrimony, Book of Common Prayer

> Until the day breathes, and the shadows flee. . . .
> —Song of Solomon 2:17

In most current formal writing, *until* is often preferred to *till;* but this is a tendency, not a rule. *Until* is especially likely to be chosen when the clause precedes the main verb.

◇ ***Recommendation.*** In choosing between *till* and *until*, follow your inclination.

tongue twisters. Elocutionists claim that mastery of certain *tongue twisters* can help to eliminate particular speech defects or improve pronunciation of difficult words. Some actors, singers, and broadcasters tune up their speech organs with favorite tongue twisters, especially if they have trouble with individual sounds such as /r/, /th/, or /s/. Tongue twisters have also been used to test sobriety. The following selection, mostly classics, may be mined for any of these useful purposes.

> Betty bought a bit of butter,
> But it was a bitter bit;
> But a better bit of butter
> Betty never bit.

> If Peter Piper picked a peck of pickled peppers, where's the peck of pickled peppers Peter Piper picked?

> A flea and a fly fled into a flue.
> Said the flea, "Let us fly,"
> Said the fly, "Let us flee,"
> And they flew through a flaw in the flue.

> Round the rugged rocks the ragged rascal ran.

> (*many times, fast*)
> Red leather, yellow leather

> A literary library literally littered with literature.

> Many a mini-anemone mimes an enemy mini-anemone.

> My sister Cecilia is a thistle sifter, and she sifts a sieve of unsifted thistles through a sieve of sifted thistles, since she is an official thistle sifter.

> A tittering titular tutor toted a tubular teeter-totter.

> Tidy Dottie dated heated Teddy.

> Wise women whistle while weaving white woolly waistcoats.

> Woman to wayside tinker:
> "Are you copper-bottoming 'em, my man?"
> Tinker to woman:
> "No ma'am, I'm aluminuming 'em, ma'am."

> The Leith police dismisseth us.
>
> (*many times, fast*)
> Toy boat, toy boat, toy boat, toy boat

too. (1) The rule is that *too,* as an adverb meaning 'in addition, also,' cannot stand first in a sentence. This never happens in standard spoken English but has begun to appear in some journalistic writing.

> . . . applications for accident and health insurance to pay off debt . . . are not showing any increase. Too, delinquencies and losses were still at historic low percentage levels. . . . —*Forbes*

> A large and growing concentration of lower-income citizens . . . are increasing the cost of city services. . . . Too, there is a growing "skills mismatch." . . .
> —Wayne King, *New York Times*

> Some say that Circus Maximus should not have sailed at all, crewed as it was with too few people. Too, the crew were unfamiliar with the way of the 12-ton, light-displacement racer.
> —Bill Tuttle, *Soundings*

◇ ***Recommendation.*** This is an unacceptable breach of idiom. Either rewrite, placing *too* after the opening phrase (as in the third quotation, "The crew, too, were unfamiliar . . ."), or, if that seems inappropriate or awkward, as in the two other quotations, substitute *furthermore, moreover, in addition,* etc.

(2) *Too* is used in juvenile, or mock-juvenile, altercations, as *"I'm not." "You are too."* This use is occasionally mimicked in descriptive sentences, with humorous effect.

> He would begin patiently enough, explaining how anybody can see through a microscope, but he would always end up in a fury, claiming that I could *too* see through a microscope but just pretended I couldn't.
> —James Thurber,
> *My Life and Hard Times*

torturous, tortuous. These can be confused. *Torturous* means 'like torture, agonizing, grueling':

> . . . he was virtually always the first to arrive on the set and the last to leave. His torturous schedule . . . may have cost him a couple of marriages. . . .
> —Ronald Reagan, *Reader's Digest*

Tortuous literally means 'twisting and turning,' and figuratively 'not straightforward, involved and difficult to follow,' as *a tortuous argument; a tortuous way of looking at it.* The following quotation uses the metaphor of a winding road representing a career full of turns and difficulties:

> The tortuous road which has led from Montgomery to Oslo is a road over which millions of Negroes are traveling to find a new sense of dignity.
> —Martin Luther King, Jr.,
> Nobel Prize acceptance speech

In the next quotation *torturous* might mean 'agonizing, agonized' but could also be construed as a mistake for *tortuous,* meaning 'involved and difficult to follow.'

> The Secretary of War had by this time taken both sides of nearly every question that had come to his attention; and still his mind would not stop churning the same points over and over. Stimson's torturous arguments with himself were at last mercifully put to rest. . . .
> —Charles L. Mee,
> *Meeting at Potsdam*

◇ ***Recommendation.*** If ambiguity, or even the appearance of ambiguity, arises with pairs of closely similar words like these, it is best either to make the context clearer or to pick another word.

tote. Noah Webster wrote in 1789: "*Tote* is local in Virginia and its neighborhood. In meaning it is nearly equivalent to *carry.* I have taken great pains to discover the etymology of the local terms used in the United States; but this word has eluded my vigilance." Webster's failure is not surprising. It is now known that the word was brought to Virginia by captive Africans from Angola or western Congo, where the word *tota* or *tuta* still means 'to carry.' It quickly became a part of white American speech, for in the colonial records of Gloucester County, Virginia, there is this 1677 entry:

> [Armed men] were by Beverly commanded to goe to work, fall trees and mawle and toat rails. . . .

Tote remained a Southern word until less than 100 years ago. Mark Twain used it figuratively in *Life on the Mississippi:*

> You've got to admire men that deal in ideas that size and can tote them around without crutches.

Strangely enough, the best-known use of the word—"Tote dat barge,/Lift dat bale," in Jerome Kern's "Ol' Man River"—is a misuse (*tote* is not a synonym for *tow*). In New England and parts of the Midwest a *tote road* is a logging road. The newest use of the word is in *tote bag*, current since the 1960s and now also shortened to *tote.*

to the manner born. See MANNER.

trademarks. A *trademark* is a word, name, symbol, or device adopted by a manufacturer or merchant to identify his goods or services and distinguish them from those manufactured or sold by others. Trademark words and names present a unique linguistic situation. They are words in our language, but they are legally owned by individuals or companies. Their owners generally do everything they can to encourage us to use these words—but (in most cases) only in an artificially limited form of usage. No other words in the language are subject to this form of restriction. Trademarks virtually constitute a special part of speech, and dictionaries do in fact label them as if they were. However, trademarks are always trying to escape into the general vocabulary, and although their owners are bound to keep trying to stop them, some of them do gain their freedom.

History. Trademarks have been used for thousands of years. The first ones, which predate the alphabet, were symbols used by potters in ancient Egypt and Sumer to mark their wares. As early as the 5th century B.C. the Romans were using trademarks on wine bottles, ornaments, cloth, and even bricks and tiles. The trademark was a means of identifying and locating the maker. If the merchandise turned out to be unsatisfactory, the maker was either punished or forced to leave the city.

The use of trademarks died out during the Dark Ages and was not revived until the 12th century, when the great craft guilds emerged and began to flourish. The goods they produced were marked with a symbol of the guild and of the individual artisan. Guild members had to meet certain standards. If they did not, they were subject to penalties.

Trademarks underwent a change in the 18th and 19th centuries in England. An expanding population, as well as a wealthier one, began to demand more and better goods. As a result of the development and growth of factories and large-scale machine production during this period, many companies began to manufacture similar goods. Trademarks served to distinguish a particular product from another of the same type.

Today, there are four types of trademarks: *brand names* that identify goods and products; *service marks*, which are used in the sale or advertising of services; *collective marks,* which are used by members of a collective group or organization; and *certification marks*, which certify that goods or services meet certain standards. Technically, the term *trademarks* refers to brand names, but it is also a term generally applied to all four categories.

Legal Requirements. Trademarks are often used improperly in both spoken and written language. A trademark identifies a product or service. As such, it is a proper adjective and must be spelled with a capital letter. A trademark is always meant to be used with the generic, or common, name of the product or service. It is not meant to be used as a noun, verb, or modifier (*put tabasco in the soup; vaselined his hair; sleeping on a dacron pillow*), or in the plural (unless the trademark itself ends in *-s,* such as Keds sneakers). A trademark should not qualify nouns other than generic terms: *Pyrex brand glass,* not *pyrex dish.*

Trademark owners carefully guard their trademarks. A trademark is a property right; it can be protected by law and transferred. However, if the public begins to use a trademark as a noun, a possessive, or a verb, there is a possibility that the trademark will eventually become a generic term and the owner will then lose exclusive rights to it. Generally speaking, the position of the U.S. courts has been that a trademark ceases to be such when it is principally understood by the public to be synonymous with the nature of the item.

Aspirin, for example, was once a brand name for acetylsalicylic acid. Apparently, acetylsalicylic acid was too much of a tongue twister for customers: they simply asked their druggists for "aspirin." Eventually, it became a generic term, and today a customer may ask for a specific aspirin, such as Bayer.

Many trademark owners prefer that their marks be written or published with all capital letters or with italics or quotation marks. This is not always practical, however. It would look out of place in a novel if a character said, for example, "Please hand me a KLEENEX." In such a case an initial capital is sufficient. An easier alternative would be to use the generic term *tissue* without the brand name.

Trademark owners often prefer that a trademark notice follow the trademark. If a trademark is registered with the United States Patent and Trademark Office, either the symbol ® may be used after the trademark or an asterisk and the phrase "Registered U.S. Patent & Trademark Office." (This phrase is frequently abbreviated: "Reg. U.S. Pat. & Tm. Off.") If a trademark is not federally registered, then the letters TM should follow closely after the trademark or an asterisk and the phrase "A Trademark of ——— Company." This is a notification that the user claims trademark rights or that a trademark application is pending, or both.

Some companies use the word *brand* after their trademarks as further protection. An example is Scotch brand cellophane tape. The use of *brand* means that "scotch" tape is not a generic type of tape, such as masking tape, but that Scotch is a trademark.

Owners spend millions of dollars protecting their trademarks. Some companies have employees whose main function is to check magazines, books, and newspapers for possible misuse of their firm's trademarks. Other companies wage aggressive advertising campaigns to educate the public on the correct use of their marks. Johnson and Johnson, maker of adhesive bandages and other products, has advertised in trade magazines asking writers not to use such expressions as *band-aid diplomacy;* Band-Aid is a Johnson and Johnson trademark. A Xerox Corporation advertisement states that its trademark "shouldn't be used when referring to anybody else's copier, duplicator, paper, or whatsoever. (Let them use their own name.)"

A few companies are confident enough of their trademark that they themselves use it in ads without the generic term. This is especially true of car and cigarette manufacturers. There is little danger that the trademark Cadillac will ever become a generic term for automobile, so strongly is it associated with one particular automobile.

Some Etymologies. Many trademarks have interesting backgrounds. The Sanka trademark for caffeine-free coffee comes from a contraction of the French term *sans caféine* (= 'without caffeine'). Aunt Jemima pancake mix is named from an old vaudeville song, "Aunt Jemima." Shell motor oil got that name because the founder of the company originally had a small shop in which he sold shell-covered boxes made by his children. Listerine mouthwash comes from the name of Joseph Lister, who founded antiseptic surgery. Miltown tranquilizers were named after Milltown, New Jersey, which was near the laboratory where the tranquilizers were developed. One *l* was dropped so that the trademark could not be classified as a geographical term.

Consumers are responsible for the Coke trademark. The Coca-Cola Company originally marketed its soft drink under the Coca-Cola trademark. But when people ordered the beverage at soda fountains or in stores, they repeatedly asked for Coke. To no avail the company waged an advertising campaign to persuade the public to ask for a Coca-Cola soft drink. The word *Coke* began to be used by other soft-drink companies, but in 1920 a Supreme Court decision ruled that the term meant "a single thing coming from a single source." The Coca-Cola Company then registered the word as a trademark.

Dictionaries. Some owners of popular trademarks have constant problems with dictionaries. Some dictionary entries for trademarks list the trademark first, as a proper adjective, and then also list it as a common noun, without an initial capital. Trademark owners feel that the dictionary should represent correct usage; most dictionary editors prefer to report language as it is being used. The misuse of a trademark in the dictionary does, however, pose potentially serious legal problems for a company in defending and maintaining the protectability of its mark. At least one current dictionary, *Webster's New Collegiate Dictionary* (eighth edition), acknowledges the complexities of the trademark situation: "Those entries known to be trademarks or service marks are so labeled and are treated in accordance with a formula approved by the United States Trademark Association. No entry in this dictionary, however, should be regarded as affecting the validity of any trademark or service mark."

◇ ***Recommendation.*** Two strong social forces are here in conflict—the force of law and the force of language usage. Neither can be ignored. In all public, formal, and commercial speaking and writing, the law must be complied with, and it can be enforced. Theoretically, you can also be legally restrained from using trademarks as generic words even in private conversation or letters. But it's impossible to police everyday language to that extent. We give below a selection of well-known trademarks as they are legally required to be used; that is, as proper adjectives qualifying generic nouns. The resulting phrases are cumbersome. The natural tendency of the language is to use trademarks as nouns, and these particular trademarks are often so used.

ALKA-SELTZER brand effervescent antacid tablets
ANACIN analgesic tablets
BAGGIES plastic bags
CHAP STICK lip balm
COCA-COLA soft drink
DACRON polyester fiber (*polyester* is a coined generic term)
DICTAPHONE dictating machine
DRAMAMINE antinauseant (DRAMAMINE dimenhydrinate)
FIG NEWTONS cakes
FORMICA laminated plastic
FRIGIDAIRE appliances
JELL-O brand gelatin dessert
KODAK photographic film, cameras, etc.
KOOL-AID brand soft drink mix
LEVI'S jeans and sportswear
LIBRIUM tranquilizer (LIBRIUM chlordiazepoxide)
MAALOX antacid liquid
MASONITE hardboard products
NAUGAHYDE vinyl coated fabrics
NOVOCAIN local anesthetic (NOVOCAIN procaine)
PAMPERS disposable diapers
PERRIER sparkling mineral water
PLEXIGLAS acrylic plastic
Q-TIPS cotton swabs and cotton balls
SANKA brand decaffeinated coffee
SARAN WRAP brand of plastic film
SWEET'N LOW sugar substitute
TABASCO brand pepper sauce
TANG brand instant breakfast drink
TEFLON fluorocarbon resins
VASELINE petroleum jelly, hair tonic, etc.
XEROX copiers, duplicators, etc.

Some Escapees. The following words were once trademarks but are now generic terms:

cellophane	mimeograph
celluloid	raisin bran
escalator	shredded wheat
kerosene	thermos
lanolin	trampoline
linoleum	yo-yo
milk of magnesia	zipper

transitive, intransitive. A transitive verb is one that takes a direct object: *God created* *the world in six days.* An intransitive verb is one that does not take a direct object: *The plane arrived on time.* Many verbs may be used both transitively and intransitively: *He left the lecture. He left quietly.* In the first sentence *left* is used transitively; in the second sentence it is used intransitively. This may seem to be a simple-minded distinction, but it is in fact indispensable to the description of verbs and the various ways they function in sentences.

transpire. The underlying meaning is 'to leak out imperceptibly like vapor from the pores of a plant.' Referring to facts or information, it means 'to come out into the open, become known':

> But when I asked specific questions, it transpired she had never seen Jackson.
> —Nicholas Rhea, *Reader's Digest*

> In fact, it transpires, the CBS–AFTRA contract lapsed last week. . . .
> —William F. Buckley,Jr., *Execution Eve*

When referring to events, 'to become known' can mean just the same as 'to turn out, come about,' and if *transpire* is used, it's often impossible to tell whether the writer was thinking specifically of one meaning or the other.

> But I was long gone from Italy when all these events transpired.
> —William Colby, *Honorable Men: My Life in the CIA*

As a result *transpire* is also widely used to mean simply 'happen,' without any sense of becoming known.

> You can still see bullet-holes where those troops fought, and then Quantrill, William Quantrill, came up, and he saw what was transpiring.
> —Mrs. W. L. C. Palmer (quoted), Merle Miller, *Plain Speaking*

> The nation . . . sold its products to the entire world, but otherwise it largely ignored what transpired beyond its borders. —J. Paul Getty, *As I See It*

This last development occurred in America in the early 19th century. It is accepted in Webster's *American Dictionary* of 1828 and was used by Henry David Thoreau and Nathaniel Hawthorne and also by Charles Dickens. But it is now widely condemned by American as well as British usage experts, partly because it is an unnecessary synonym for *happen, occur, take place,* etc.

◇ *Recommendation. Transpire* has been used to mean 'happen' for so long that we can't regard it as a mistake. But we agree that if you mean 'happen,' 'occur,' or 'take place,' it's much better to use one of the simpler terms and to keep *transpire* for 'to become known.'

trauma. This word is pronounced either /**trou**-mə/ or /**trô**-mə/. In common usage the plural is *traumas,* in technical usage usually *traumata.* It is from a Greek word meaning 'a wound,' and the basic medical sense of the word is 'an injury to the body caused by external violence, including flesh wounds, fractures, and concussion.' In psychology *trauma* means 'an injury to the mind caused by an emotionally shocking experience, or the shocked state resulting from this.' In popular usage the word is widely used to mean 'any severely unpleasant or difficult experience, or the resulting unhappy human situation.'

> . . . tributes to the importance of the parish's dealing with the central traumas and crises of people's lives.
> —Bishop John Sullivan, *The Catholic Key*

> Two days later the country [Italy] suffered a second trauma when the head of the joint chiefs of staff, the highest ranking officials of the financial police and three secret service organizations were put on temporary leave. . . .
> —Theodora Lurie, *Maclean's*

The adjective *traumatic* means 'causing trauma, being or resulting from a trauma':

> At nine he had already adjusted to the traumatic loss of his mother. . . .
> —Monica Furlong, *Merton: A Biography*

The related verb *traumatize* means 'to cause trauma to':

While the U.S. remains traumatized by the Three Mile Island incident, other industrialized nations are moving rapidly in the field of nuclear power.
—*Time*

trek. The Boers of South Africa, who originally settled at the Cape of Good Hope, began to make organized migrations northward into unoccupied country, in ox-drawn wagons, as early as the 17th century. The Afrikaans verb *trekken* means 'to draw (in wagons), travel,' specifically 'to make an organized migration,' and the noun *trek* means 'an organized migration.' These *treks* continued into the late 19th century. Both noun and verb were then borrowed into English as *trek,* first in the South African senses, sometimes applied to American pioneering in the West, then also in the further senses '(to make) a long, tiring walk' and '(to make) any long, difficult journey.'

. . . she had the inner toughness of pioneer ancestors who had trekked to Missouri in covered wagons.
—Peter Gorton Jenkins, *Reader's Digest*

. . . the average [Soviet] housewife, loaded down with packages, normally faces a long, tiring trek home on crowded buses and trains.
—Jean Knight, *U.S. News & World Report*

As I prepared to get the expansion bill started on the long trek through bureaucracy . . .
—William C. Westmoreland, *A Soldier Reports*

trendy, an adjective coined in London in the 1960s, from *trend* in the sense of 'the latest social fashion.' *Trendy* almost always carries some negative comment. It means 'following the more pointless and passing styles' or 'thoughtlessly going along with the newest social mores, mindlessly fashionable.'

One-inch ties and shallow collars are what the trendy people are wearing.
—*Boston Globe*

More and more people are today opting for this trendy life-style [unmarried living together].
—*Reader's Digest*

The plots of the five-nights-a-week serial throb with trendy themes: the occult, nuclear waste, ESP, jogging, the Oedipus and military-industrial complexes, the high cost of breakfast and where to eat lunch.
—Harry F. Waters, *Newsweek*

trivial, trivia. The source is Latin *trivium,* literally 'three-roads,' hence 'place where three roads meet or where a small road meets a main road' or, loosely, 'crossroads.' Its adjective *triviālis* meant 'such as you might meet at the crossroads, everyday, ordinary.' This is the original sense of the English word *trivial:*

In our most trivial walks, we are constantly, though unconsciously, steering like pilots by certain well-known beacons and headlands. . . .
—Henry David Thoreau, *Walden*

Trivial now means, more narrowly, 'unimportant, insignificant, pointless':

But it made you seem sorrowfully trivial, and the creature of a day, and such a short and paltry day, too.
—Mark Twain, *The Mysterious Stranger*

The Pacific crossed, Magellan himself perished on Asia's outer islands in a trivial feud.
—Maurice Shadbolt, *Reader's Digest*

In Latin *Trivia* meant 'she of the crossroads'; it was a title of the underworld goddess Hecate, to whom crossroads, and especially places where a small road met a main road, were sacred. In the 18th century the poet John Gay wrote a poem that he humorously dedicated to her as goddess of the commonplace things that might happen to one at the crossroads:

Thou, Trivia, Goddess, aid my song,
Thro' spacious streets conduct thy bard
along.
—*Trivia: or, the Art of Walking the Streets of London* (1716)

Echoing this, the American belletrist and philologist Logan Pearsall Smith used the title *Trivia* for a best-selling collection of miniature essays or paragraphs on miscellaneous topics that was published in 1918. The name *Trivia* then seems to have been mistaken for a Latin plural meaning 'trivial things or topics.'

Regardless of its muddled origin, *trivia* now exists as a plural or collective noun meaning 'trivialities':

> The new Legal Services Corp. has just taken over responsibility for federal support of civil legal services to the nation's poor. Some contend that the LSC clutters the courts with trivia.
> —Jerrold K. Footlick, *Reader's Digest*

> He knew all the Hollywood trivia, all the character actors, all the obscure scenes in all the obscure movies that all the big stars had been in.
> —Andy Warhol and Pat Hackett, *POPism*

troglodyte /**trŏg**-lə-dīt/. The Greeks knew of a primitive people of Ethiopia whose name was *Trogodytes.* They altered the name to *Troglodytes,* which made it seem, in Greek, to mean 'cave dwellers' (from *trōglos* = 'opening, cave' + *dutēs* = 'enterer'), although the actual Trogodytes did not live in caves (this is an example of FOLK ETYMOLOGY).

In English *troglodyte* has several meanings. The first is 'cave dweller, member of a people living in caves':

> . . . towns [in eastern Turkey] founded by troglodytes still hugged cave-ridden hillsides.
> —Maurice Shadbolt, *Reader's Digest*

Secondly, *troglodyte* is used to mean 'uncouth, brutish person':

> She is beautiful, Kugelmass thought. What a contrast with the troglodyte who shared his bed!
> —Woody Allen, *Side Effects*

Thirdly, there is a sarcastic metaphor referring to the popular idea of cave men as the ancestors of modern man; in this connection *troglodyte* is used to mean 'extremely old-fashioned or politically ultraconservative person'; the adjective is *troglodytic* /trŏg-lə-**dĭt**-ĭk/.

> . . . he [William Simon] was characterized by one journalist as Washington's "resident troglodyte." . . .
> —Ralph Kinney Bennett, *Reader's Digest*

> . . . the mere accident of starting a twentieth-century career from a nest of associations so colonial—so troglodytic—as the First Church, the Boston State House, Beacon Hill, John Hancock, Mount Vernon Street and Quincy . . .
> —Henry Adams, *The Education of Henry Adams*

> . . . the daily battering he took from publisher William Loeb's troglodytic Manchester Union-Leader.
> —*Newsweek*

trooper, trouper. *Troop* and *troupe* are the same word by origin, both coming from French *troupe* = 'company of people, body of soldiers.' But in English *troop* means primarily 'body of soldiers' and *troupe* means 'company of actors.' *Trooper* thus means 'cavalryman, policeman,' while *trouper* means 'actor.' A *(good) trouper* also means 'experienced and professional actor who can surmount difficulties' or, figuratively, 'member of a group who keeps things going gamely, person who doesn't let the side down.'

> . . . Gladys [Cooper] could not learn her words and her part was enormously long. . . . Good trouper that she was she rose word-perfect to the occasion of the first night. . . .
> —Cole Lesley, *The Life of Noel Coward*

> As Election Day approached, Smith's defeat seemed likely, but Eleanor was a good trooper and sought to counteract a mood of defeatism.
> —Joseph P. Lash, *Eleanor and Franklin*

In the second quotation *trooper* is a mistake for *trouper.*

tropic, tropical. *Tropical* is the general-purpose adjective meaning 'relating to the tropics, typical of the tropics.' *Tropic* is a poetic or somewhat romantic synonym, evoking images of lushness, splendor, etc. In the following quotation, both are used.

> On a deep-black sea, under the stars of a tropic sky, seven men cling to a swamped and slowly sinking boat. . . .
>
> . . . The quick tropical dusk came, then dark. . . .
> —Maurice Shadbolt, *Reader's Digest*

truculent. The original meaning of this adjective was 'fierce, cruel, deadly,' but the word now means 'aggressively assertive, pugnaciously defiant.' The related noun is *truculence;* the adverb, *truculently.*

> Kissinger stayed at the table, but the North Vietnamese remained truculent and on December 13 Henry broke off negotiations. . . .
> —Charles Colson, *Born Again*

> With increasing truculence, Maloney took to boasting of how many hundreds of thousands of words—indeed, how many millions of words—he had written for *The New Yorker.*
> —Brendan Gill, *Here at The New Yorker*

> Fists pounding the lectern, he truculently declared: "Your President has come here to ask you people . . . to join us in a total national effort to win the war."
> —Doris Kearns, *Lyndon Johnson and the American Dream*

try and. This idiom is a little more casual and a little more optimistic than *try to.* It is used only with the form *try,* never with *tries, tried,* or *trying.* It is fully standard and acceptable in all contexts.

> To try and cheer her up, the King now put in hand a scheme . . . for a little country house in the gardens of Trianon.
> —Nancy Mitford, *Madame de Pompadour*

> . . . the Dutch example stimulated seventeenth-century English economic thinkers to try and emulate the results (which the Dutch had achieved by the spontaneous operation of enterprise) by means of state action.
> —Charles Wilson, *The Dutch Republic*

In each of the examples *try and* suggests probable success; *try to* would stress the attempt slightly more than the outcome. But the difference is very small.

tu quoque. See FALLACY.

turgid /têr-jĭd/. Literally, *turgid* means 'swollen, distended.' It is most often used in the figurative sense 'puffed up with self-importance, pompous':

> MacArthur's turgid communiques, and his love of braid and ceremony, evoked malicious laughter all across the Pacific.
> —William Manchester, *Reader's Digest*

> Spare me, I pray, your turgid rhetoric and bootlicking protestations. . . .
> —S. J. Perelman, *The Road to Miltown*

Turkish words. In the time of the Turkish (or Ottoman) Empire (about 1300–1918), numerous Persian and Arabic words were transmitted to the West through the medium of Turkish; but we have in our language today only a handful of original Turkish words. The Turks came to the Mediterranean from remote parts of central Asia. Their language is not related to Persian or Arabic. It is now written in roman script.

*__horde__ = (1) 'tribe of warrior nomads in central Asia' (2) 'throng or crowd of people': Polish *horda,* from Turkish *ordu* = 'camp, army'

odalisque = 'Oriental concubine': French *odalisque,* from Turkish *odalik* = 'room-servant, chambermaid,' from *oda* = 'room'

*Appears as separate entry

ottoman = 'cushioned couch': French *ottomane* = 'sofa, Turkish seat,' from *Ottoman* = 'Turkish,' from Arabic *Othmānī* = 'Turkish,' from Turkish *Osman,* name of the founder of the Turkish or "Ottoman" Empire (reigned about 1299–1326)

pilaf = 'dish of rice and meat, etc.': Turkish *pilāw* or *pilav* = 'rice dish'

yogurt = 'milk fermented by certain bacteria': Turkish *yogurt, yōurt* = 'yogurt'

-type has become a common suffix forming adjectives. It can be added to proper names, nouns, or adjectives. The resulting adjectives are of several kinds.

(1) Adjectives meaning 'of a certain general kind, but not identical to, not a normal example of':

> Each had big saddle bags . . . a lariat rope and a fifteen-foot Australian-type bullwhip.
>
> —R. G. Tonkin, *Saturday Evening Post*

> As American forces increased, I established three corps-type headquarters with boundaries corresponding to those of the Vietnamese corps.
>
> —William C. Westmoreland, *A Soldier Reports*

> Another fellow sharpened knives. He rode a bicycle-type conveyance with a grindstone between his knees. . . .
>
> —Harry Golden, *For 2¢ Plain*

(2) Adjectives meaning simply 'similar to.' When these are formed with long proper names they are noticeably awkward.

> We are not talking about a World War II-type situation or a World War I-type situation.
>
> —Harold Brown (quoted), *U.S. News & World Report*

> He wondered aloud whether people really wanted to read a *National Geographic* type publication about wooden boats.
>
> —Jon Wilson, *Wooden Boat*

> . . . the court took a step backward to a King George's Star Chamber-type system that would permit secret deals. . . .
>
> —Jack Anderson, *Florida Times-Union*

(3) There is also a use of *-type* in which it is placed after an existing adjective or attributive without altering the meaning.

> . . . the plan of developing as many original type golf holes as the terrain and surroundings might make possible.
>
> —Clifford Roberts, *The Story of the Augusta National Golf Club*

> Before the award, the skipper and crew of the Cape Upright wondered if anyone, anywhere, recognized the yeoman-type work the vessel had been doing.
>
> —C. E. McClaurin, *Savannah News-Press*

(4) Finally, *type* is attached to adjectives, as a substitute for *type of.*

> This type approach will allow the private sector to catch up with the excessive government overspending. . . .
>
> —James L. Self (letter), *Florida Times-Union*

◇ ***Recommendation.*** While this suffix is undoubtedly here to stay, and can be useful, we don't much like it in any of its uses, although some are more justifiable than others. The first two classes above seem legitimate and relatively acceptable, but in formal contexts we advise rewriting even these: "a bullwhip of Australian type"; "three headquarters resembling corps"; "a conveyance that was partly a bicycle"; etc. This applies more strongly to the cumbersome adjectives formed with proper names: rewrite as "a situation like World War II"; "a system like King George's Star Chamber"; etc. The third category is entirely unacceptable and unnecessary—either *type* should not appear at all, or it should appear as *type of:* "as many original golf holes" or "types of golf holes"; "the yeoman work." The fourth category is also substandard; write *type of.*

U

U, non-U. British language labels meaning 'upper-class' and 'non-upper-class.' In the late 1950s it was claimed that the British upper class had lost nearly all of its traditional privileges. In terms of wealth, political clout, education, clubs, clothes, and appearance, you could hardly tell the difference between an upper-class person and a middle-class person. Had the small old ruling class then simply been merged into a large middle class? Not at all. Its members could still infallibly recognize each other and detect outsiders, by means of a code of words and usages. A professor of sociology named Alan Ross termed the upper-class usages *U* and the non-upper-class usages *non-U* (the professor himself, like Professor Higgins in *My Fair Lady,* was, at least apparently, upper-class):

U	non-U
How d'you do.	Pleased to meet you.
(*in social drinking*) *no remark*	Cheers!
What? *or* What did you say?	Pardon? *or* Beg pardon?
sofa	couch, divan
drawing room	living room, sitting room
chimney piece	mantelpiece
luncheon	lunch
napkin	serviette
mamma, pappa (*with variations*)	mum, dad (*with variations*)
Could I have the pepper?	Pass the pepper (please).
false teeth	dentures
loo, lavatory	toilet, W.C.
girl /gĕl/	girl /gêrl/
golf /gŏf/	golf /gŏlf/
riding	horseback riding
rich	wealthy
writing paper	note paper

Publication of these code usages caused some excitement. The labels *U* and *non-U* were themselves taken into everyday use for referring not just to language but to people, places, clothes, etc.: *Ascot is utterly non-U these days. How can the queen be U, she has corgis and wears a babushka?* In the swinging sixties some young upper-class types confused the issues by making it chic to be non-U in certain social areas. In the further social turmoil of the seventies, the old upper class seemed to have shed yet more of its traditions and preferences, including even some of the usages set out above. But with subtle changes that will always baffle outsiders, the code goes on.

ubiquitous /yo͞o-**bĭk**-wə-təs/. The source is Latin *ubīque* = 'everywhere.' *Ubiquitous* literally means 'existing everywhere, all-pervasive' or 'occurring virtually throughout and all the time':

> The virus of lymphocytic choriomeningitis is ubiquitous among mice.
> —Lewis Thomas, *The Medusa and the Snail*

> Indeed, these films . . . reflect a world view in which evil is the dominant force in life and violence is as ubiquitous as it is purposeless.
> —Paul Leggett, *Christianity Today*

More often (by hyperbole) *ubiquitous* means 'seen at every turn, very widespread' or 'appearing so often as to be disconcerting, busying oneself everywhere':

> Then I travelled through Germany. Military uniforms were ubiquitous.
> —J. Paul Getty, *As I See It*

> Perhaps Bill [Rogers] was also concerned that there were too many references to the ubiquitous Dr. Kissinger in the speech.
> —William Safire, *Before the Fall*

Likewise the noun *ubiquity* /yo͞o-**bĭk**-wə-tē/ means either 'the fact of existing everywhere, omnipresence' or 'the fact of seeming to be everywhere':

In college we were taught the ubiquity of God. But to see God in all things when you are plunged into bleating materialism is sometimes hard.
—Thomas A. Dooley, *The Edge of Tomorrow*

The eternal model of the English butler, which he kept before his eyes, even in his moments of relaxation and on his day off, required that he have the attributes of omniscience and ubiquity. . . .
—Mary McCarthy, *The Group*

U.K. See UNITED KINGDOM.

umbrage in its original sense, 'shadow, shade,' is all but obsolete.

. . . sought protection from the solar ray beneath the umbrage of densely foliaged apple trees . . .
—Allan Cunningham (quoted), H. S. Russell, *The Genesis of Queensland*

It was later used figuratively, to mean 'a shadow of suspicion,' but this too is virtually obsolete, and the only widely current use is in the expression *to take umbrage* = 'to take offense, be resentful,' which usually carries a suggestion of annoyance or sulkiness rather than deep anger.

An actor or author may take umbrage at some comparatively minor criticism, while being impervious to the larger expressions of disapproval.
—Louis Nizer, *My Life in Court*

The patient who sees "SOB" on his chart should not take umbrage, as it is usually intended to mean "short of breath."
—William Safire, *New York Times Magazine*

The adjective *umbrageous* /ŭm-**brā**-jəs/ survives marginally in the literal sense 'shadowy, shady' and is also occasionally used to mean 'touchy, likely to take offense.'

umlaut. See DIACRITICS.

unbeknown, unbeknownst. The reason for the *-st* of *unbeknownst* has not been satisfactorily explained. The two forms are equally correct, but *unbeknownst* is now the commoner. They are used with *to* in adverbial clauses meaning 'without the knowledge of.'

Unbeknown to the shopper, the checkout computer also logs out each outgoing item against inventory. . . .
—*Time*

After a dozen years of gazing idly at the passing show, I have assembled, quite unbeknownst to them, a cast of characters that I depend on.
—E. B. White, *The Points of My Compass*

unction literally means 'anointment,' especially ceremonial anointment with holy oil. As a Christian metaphor *unction* refers to the outpouring of God's healing influence on humans; hence also to strong spiritual feeling and manner, as in prayer, by an individual. (In Roman Catholicism the sacrament now called the Anointing of the Sick was formerly known as *extreme unction.*)

The word *unction* is also applied to insincere and overdone exhortation of a self-righteous kind, as by clergymen. This use results from combining the sense 'strong spiritual feeling and manner' with an ironical interpretation of the original sense of the word, 'anointment': hence 'oiliness, greasiness.'

That clerical unction which in a vulgar nature so easily degenerates into greasiness.
—James Russell Lowell, *Among My Books* (1870)

Unction now most often means 'offensive sham benevolence of manner':

And as Mag, bridling and ludicrously humble, advanced to the pulpit after the preacher's harangue, he would bend with greased unction over her hand, saying: "And how is the good woman today?"
—Thomas Wolfe, *The Web and the Rock*

Individuals, most notably the great television and radio commentators, make

> a profession of knowing and saying with elegant unction what their audience will find most acceptable.
> —John Kenneth Galbraith, *The Affluent Society*

Similarly, the adjective *unctuous* literally means 'oily, rich with fats':

> On the regular menu there is an unctuous combination of poached egg, smoked salmon, and sauce mousseline. It is an unusual mixture that blends well. . . . —*New Jersey Monthly*

By the religious metaphor it means 'blessed by God's anointment, full of true spiritual feeling.' But the commonest use of *unctuous* is in the negative senses 'offensively self-righteous' and 'full of sham benevolence':

> . . . his voice had changed from rasping efficiency to an unctuous familiarity with sin and with the Almighty.
> —Sinclair Lewis, *Babbitt*

> . . . with unctuous rectitude *The Times* expressed a wish that the Prince of Wales would sign a pledge never again to play cards for money.
> —Philip Magnus, *Edward VII*

understatement. *Understatement* has the same purpose as exaggeration, or *hyperbole:* to enhance the impact of a statement or description by deliberately not giving a straightforward or literal version of the facts. By taste or temperament, many people prefer understatement to exaggeration, and it can be highly effective. A classic example is the description of the chaotic and terrifying evacuation of an army of 350,000 men from the beaches of Dunkirk in 1940, attributed to an anonymous British officer who was there: "My dear fellow—the noise, the confusion, and the *people!*"

This conveys the essential strategy of well-judged understatement: it maneuvers the listener or reader into painting the true picture from his or her own general knowledge and imagination. In the following example, the people concerned are safe in an American jail after a murderous rampage; instead of spelling out what might have been their fate elsewhere, the writer leaves the reader to think about the possibilities:

> If the Hanafi Muslims had played out their recent adventure in a Muslim land such as Iraq or Syria instead of Washington, D.C., they would certainly be much less comfortable today.
> —Walter Goodman, *New York Times*

Understatement can also be used simply to impart a certain wryness or irony:

> Still, the band manages to eke out a living. Gross revenues . . . for 1979 have been estimated as high as $4 million.
> —Ben Fong-Torres, *Rolling Stone*

Finally, a favorite type of understatement is purely humorous:

> He was a big man but not more than six feet five inches tall and not wider than a beer truck. —Raymond Chandler, *Farewell, My Lovely*

This last one is virtually an example of a special type of understatement, the denial of the opposite. See LITOTES. Compare HYPERBOLE.

under the auspices of. See AUSPICES, AUSPICIOUS.

under way. The nautical term *under way* refers to a vessel that is moving through the water freely, or at least is not anchored or moored; it is especially used in the expression *to get under way,* meaning 'to begin moving forward, start a voyage.' Like many nautical terms it is borrowed from Dutch: *onderweg,* from *onder* = 'under, in course of' + *weg* = 'way, motion.' The spelling *under weigh* is often used and has been since the 18th century; it is a FOLK ETYMOLOGY, based on the expression *to weigh anchor* = 'to pull up the anchor and start a voyage,' so that *under weigh* would mean 'having weighed anchor.'

> Bildad had told them that no profane songs would be allowed on board the Pequod, particularly in getting under weigh. . . . —Herman Melville, *Moby-Dick* (1851)

I guess we can get underway now, sir.
—Richard McKenna, *The Sand Pebbles*

The term has since passed into common usage meaning 'having started off, moving, in progress' and often spelled *underway*:

Once [the book] really gets under weigh the steady upward slope of grandeur and terror . . . is almost unequalled in the whole range of narrative art known to me.
—C. S. Lewis, letter to J. R. R. Tolkien (1949)

The Oregon shrimp fishery got underway in 1957 with seven vessels. . . .
—*National Fisherman*

There are already four separate investigations underway. . . .
—*Boston Herald American*

◇ ***Recommendation.*** *Under weigh* is a venerable mistake. *Under way* is the traditional nautical form, but *underway* is now frequently used. But note that *anchors aweigh,* meaning 'with anchors pulled up,' is correct nautical usage, while *anchors away* is considered a lubberly error.

uninterested. See DISINTERESTED.

unique. It is possible to argue about degrees of uniqueness as a matter of logic or philosophy, but in terms of the word *unique* there are two main levels of usage: the absolute and the nonabsolute.

(1) The absolute meaning of *unique* is 'being the only one of its kind or the only example or occurrence of something within a particular field':

. . . SRI, a California research firm, has tested the ink and recommended that the Postal Service Laboratory take out a patent on it because it is unique.
—*St. Louis Post-Dispatch*

This unique color photograph of Leo Tolstoy was taken by Prokudin-Gorskii in 1908.
—Robert A. Allshouse, *Photographs for the Tsar*

Since 1979, when Quebec's Consumer Protection Act banned advertising directed at children under 13—a move unique in North America . . .
—Larry Black, *Maclean's*

He greatly admired Jesus, particularly his Sermon on the Mount, but strenuously denied that he was unique.
—John R. W. Stott, *Christianity Today*

Obviously, in this absolute sense something cannot be *more unique* than another, nor *the most unique* of several. It can, however, approach uniqueness and can thus reasonably be called *almost unique.*

(2) The nonabsolute meanings of *unique* range from 'unequaled, unparalleled, standing apart from all others' down through 'exceptional, outstanding, special, remarkable.' The exactness of meaning is often debatable. When you say that something is "in a class by itself," you aren't expected to be making a statement of mathematical precision; usually all you mean is that it's the best, worst, most amazing, etc., thing of its kind that you can think about just now. So with *unique.*

Wild food is used at our house in a unique method of entertaining. Our "wild parties," which are dinners where the chief component of every dish is some foraged food, have achieved a local fame.
—Euell Gibbons, *Stalking the Wild Asparagus*

A unique faith in the trustworthiness of humanity was another of my father's traits.
—Roger Garis, *My Father Was Uncle Wiggily*

On March 2, 1904, I first experienced the unique thrill of being on the scene when a drilling crew reaches pay sand and strikes oil.
—J. Paul Getty, *As I See It*

In many of these less-than-absolute senses *unique* can be qualified by most adverbs of degree, including *more* and *most.*

When you are visiting the beauty spots of this country, don't overlook Frank

> Phillip's ranch and game preserve at Bartlesville, Okla. It's the most unique place in this country. Got everything but reindeer.
>
> —Will Rogers, *Autobiography*

> Of all the military services of the United States, the Marine Corps is the most unique.
>
> —Lt. Gen. Thomas H. Miller, Jr., *Marine Corps Gazette*

> . . . a 90-second, animated commercial that Robert L. Bunting, the company's manager of product marketing, humbly calls "the most unique commercial ever made for writing instruments."
>
> —*New York Times*

Even when it is used in a less-than-absolute sense, the word *unique* retains a strong flavor of its basic and absolute meaning. It is a powerful and satisfying word. To apply it so freely that it loses its flavor seems hamfisted. There is something especially clumsy about *more unique, most unique, very unique, rather unique,* etc., even if they can be defended on grounds of logic and frequent occurrence. Usage experts have often condemned these uses; in our opinion, rightly so.

(3) The nature of uniqueness. In terms of human perceptions, there are indeed degrees of uniqueness. A postage stamp of which there is only one copy is unique—but it is also a member of the huge class of postage stamps, so that nonphilatelists may feel that its uniqueness is rather trivial. For most purposes our planet is unique, and very importantly so, but to an astronomer, and especially one like Carl Sagan who is sure there are many inhabited planets, Earth is only provisionally unique, until its peers are found. Each human individual, each plant and animal, is unique, but we can't be equally impressed by each.

> Uniqueness is so commonplace a property of living things that there is really nothing at all unique about it.
>
> —Lewis Thomas, *The Medusa and the Snail*

Words are likewise unique; there are no clones among them, no absolute synonyms. The word *unique* has its own individual vibrations, which no other word can duplicate.

◇ *Recommendation. Unique,* like any other word, is freely available to all for use as a sharp or blunt instrument. We would like to see it kept sharp, used either in its absolute sense, or in the upper ranges of its nonabsolute senses. The best rule is never to qualify it with any adverb. There is, after all, a large vocabulary of adjectives conveying innumerable shades and degrees of remarkableness from *outstanding* to *impressive.*

United Kingdom. Its components are the kingdom of England, the principality of Wales, the kingdom of Scotland, and the six counties of Northern Ireland. Its full name is *the United Kingdom of Great Britain and Northern Ireland.* It is usually shortened to *the United Kingdom* or *the U.K.* This name is used in formal political contexts, as at the United Nations, and whenever the constitutional unity of the nation is being stressed. In most other contexts the country is known as *Britain* or *Great Britain.* See BRITAIN.

United States. The abbreviations *U.S.* and *U.S.A.* (now often written without periods) are chiefly appropriate to informal writing and speaking, to texts in which space is a serious consideration, and to postal addresses. In most other situations, the proper form of the name is *the United States,* spoken or written out in full. For the adjective, *United States* is still the most formal version, but *U.S.* is also widely acceptable.

In the early days of the nation, it was unclear just how united the 13 sovereign ex-colonies were going to be, and *the United States* was very often regarded as a fully plural name requiring a plural verb.

> The United States were settled by emigrants from different parts of Europe. . . .
>
> —Noah Webster, *Dissertations on the English Language* (1789)

It is now exclusively singular, except in the expression *these United States,* which has no official standing and which usually stresses the diversity of the country.

unscathed. See SCATHE.

until. See TILL, UNTIL.

upon. Except in a few set expressions, such as *once upon a time, upon* is interchangeable with the preposition *on* in virtually all of its senses. The only difference is that *upon* has a slightly more formal tone.

Upper Midwestern dialect. This dialect can be heard in North and South Dakota, Minnesota, Wisconsin, and Michigan and in the northern portions of Nebraska, Iowa, Illinois, Indiana, and Ohio. The speech unique to this region is largely the result of the westward migration in the 19th century of speakers from New England and New York State; it is thus basically an extension of the NORTHERN DIALECT. Yet other factors in the settlement of the region have made the Upper Midwestern dialect less homogeneous than is popularly thought. The most significant of these are the Mississippi River, the economy, and immigration.

The Mississippi River. The Mississippi allowed south-to-north in-migration. Many settlers from the midlands who reached the Mississippi at St. Louis traveled up the river and dispersed into Iowa, western Wisconsin, Minnesota, and the Dakotas. Consequently, this important waterway roughly divides the upper Midwest into eastern and western sections. The eastern section speaks a more distinctly Northern dialect, while the western section has elements of the Midland dialect in its speech. Here are some of the Midland features that are used more frequently in this region the farther west one goes (especially along the southern border):

(1) *Pronunciation.*

The /ou/ sound in words like *flower, ours* is often pronounced /äər/: /**flä**-ər/, /äərz/.

Rinse is pronounced /rĕns/ or occasionally /rĕnch/.

Keg is often /kăg/.

Roof and *root* are often pronounced with /o͞o/ rather than /o͝o/.

Yolk is often /yĕlk/.

Water, daughter are often /**wôr**-tər/, /**dô**-tər/.

Wash is often /wôrsh/.

(2) *Vocabulary.*

caterwampus, cattywampus = 'askew, diagonal' See CATERCORNER.
draw = 'dry ravine or watercourse'
ground squirrel = 'gopher'
parking = 'strip of grass between the sidewalk and the street'
roasting ears = 'corn on the cob'
slick = '(of a road) slippery'
snake feeder *or* **doctor** = '*dragonfly'

*Appears as separate entry

The Economy. The different economies of the two subsections of the upper Midwest have also helped to make their speech more distinctive. The western section is dominated by a rural economy typified by "bonanza farms" and cattle ranches. It is also thinly populated, having only about 5 percent of the U.S. population but about 10 percent of the land area. The eastern section, though it has some farming, is largely industrial and commerical with such major manufacturing and trade centers as Detroit, Cleveland, Akron, Milwaukee, and Chicago.

(1) *Rocky Mountain terms.* Many of the terms common in the western portion of the upper Midwest are also shared with the Rocky Mountain dialect, and most are related to the ecology and economy of those regions:

American fries = 'hashed brown potatoes'
bismarck = 'jelly-filled *doughnut'
box-elder bug = 'red and black sap-sucking bug'
canyon = 'steep-sided valley' See SPANISH WORDS.
catch-rope, throw rope = 'long rope used in roping horses and cattle, lariat'
corral = 'fenced-in area for horses' See SPANISH WORDS.
cowhand, cowpoke = 'ranch employee, cowboy'
grazing land = 'pasture'

*Appears as separate entry

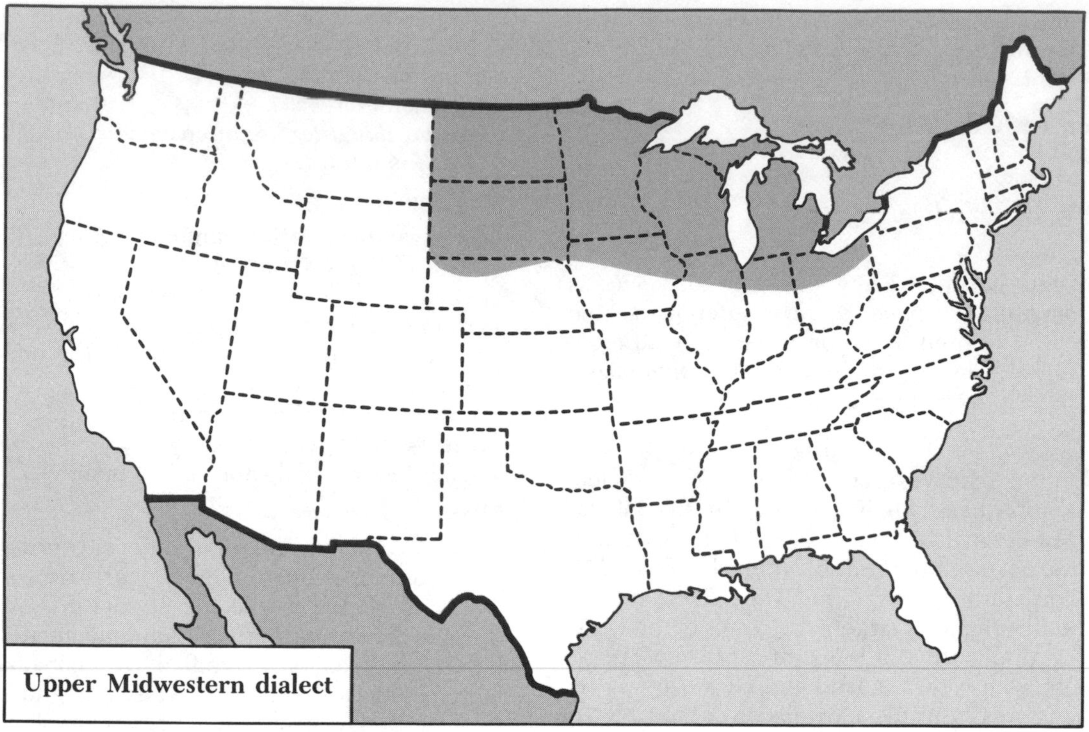

gulch = 'small valley with steep slopes'
hay bunch = 'small pile of hay in a field, haycock'
hay flats *or* **land** = 'low-lying grassland, meadow'
soogan (old-fashioned) = 'saddle roll, wool-filled comforter'
thicket = 'small clump of trees'

(2) *Other terms.* The following words are usually found only in the western section of the Upper Midwestern speech region:

berm = 'strip of grass and trees between the sidewalk and the street'
gab = 'the mouth'
honyocker (old-fashioned) = 'homesteader'
jack-pine *or* **cedar savage** = 'less affluent person'; used pejoratively
rubber binder (especially in the Minneapolis area) = 'rubber band, elastic'
tarvia, tarvy = 'macadamized road'
tote road (also New England) = originally 'logging road,' now 'any rural or back road'
tote wagon = 'wagon used especially for hauling wood'

Immigration. The many German and Scandinavian communities scattered throughout the region also account for some of the diversity of the Upper Midwestern dialect. Canadian speech as well has spilled over into the region, especially in the northern bordering states.

(1) *Pronunciation.* Although the foreign languages brought to the region have had almost no influence on the dialect as a whole, second and third generations of Scandinavian immigrants occasionally, but inconsistently, use the following:

The sound /y/ instead of /j/ in *jag, generally:* /yăg/, /**yĕn**-rə-lē/.

The sound /w/ instead of /v/ in such words as *cultivated, vegetable, vomit:* /**kŭl**-tĭ-wā-tĭd/, /**wĕj**-tə-bəl/, /**wŏm**-ĭt/.

(2) *Idioms.* Some occasional idiomatic carry-overs:

cut it over = 'to cut something in half' (Danish)
pick eggs = 'to gather eggs' (Norwegian)
put down fruit = 'to can or preserve fruit'

the headache, the sore throat = 'a headache, a sore throat': *I've got the headache this morning.* (Finnish)

(3) *Canadian words.* Words of Canadian origin used occasionally in the bordering northern states:

bluff = 'clump of trees on the open prairie'
booya /bōō-yə/ = 'stew, soup'
chesterfield = 'sofa, couch'
hatcher, hatching hen = 'setting hen'
perambulator, pram = 'baby carriage'
piggery, pig stable = 'shelter or enclosure for hogs or pigs'
quoits = 'game of horseshoes'
stook (old-fashioned) = 'shock of corn or wheat'

urban dialect. The notion of an *urban dialect* is a new one, and no study has yet conclusively shown that there are consistent or universal features common to the speech of the major U.S. cities. Broadly speaking, the big cities use the general dialect features of their region. Chicago, Boston, and Detroit, for example, are in varying degrees varieties of the Northern dialect. Even so, each urban speech differs in several ways from the dialect of its encompassing region. The speech, say, of Charleston, South Carolina, is not simply Coastal Southern dialect, but a complicated species of that dialect; likewise, San Francisco speech is a unique brand of Pacific Southwest dialect.

Urban speech can be considered distinctive because it arises out of an unusually complex environment; inevitably, the language of the city reflects its complexity. Unlike small towns and rural areas, which have a relatively homogeneous social structure, large cities have a multilayered society. For this reason, the city's location, its region, is often less important to its language than the social factors are—the economic, occupational, ethnic, and religious especially. For an understanding of the speech of a large city, its social dialects are probably more important than its regional dialect. (See REGIONAL DIALECT; SOCIAL DIALECT.)

The speech of a big city, then, is an urbanized form of the dialect of its general region with a wide range of social dialects. There are also various other subdialects that have regional boundaries within the city itself.

One community's speech may differ from another's because each has different features of pronunciation, grammar, and even vocabulary. This is the case with ethnic neighborhoods. The English spoken in the Puerto Rican, Jewish, and black communities in New York City differs because each has slightly different sets of features. But even if two communities of the same ethnic and social class have the same set of pronunciation and vocabulary features, their speech may still differ. Different subdialects may use the same features but with different frequencies. For example, middle-class white Protestant speakers in Brooklyn drop /r/ after vowels more often than do speakers in Staten Island.

The pronunciation style of urban dialects also seems to have relatively low prestige. This is especially noticeable in the attitude toward the New York City dialect among New Yorkers and nonresidents alike. Such an attitude is probably related to the fact that Americans have generally distrusted the city. (See also BOSTON, CHICAGO, NEW YORK CITY, and SAN FRANCISCO urban dialects.)

us has an informal use as subject of a sentence that is not quite paralleled by any of the other personal pronouns. It is used with an appositive noun or noun phrase to make highly informal, sometimes emphatic, declarations.

> Of course, we all had problems, but us boys never talked about them. . . .
> —Scotty Beaulieu (quoted), *Jack's Book*

> "Us middle income people, we're taxed right up to here!" Charlie's hand sliced at his neck. —a taxpayer (quoted), *Boston Herald American*

This use is strictly informal.

used to could, used to would, etc. See DOUBLE MODALS.

V

vagary. The older pronunciation is /və-**gâr**-ē/, but /**vā**-gə-rē/ is now commoner; both are correct. The word is usually used in the plural. The meaning is 'unpredictable change or fluctuation' or 'whimsical or eccentric action or idea':

> Still, Holiday Inns is not without a hedge against the vagaries of driving trends. —Carol E. Curtis, *Forbes*

> The Comte de Charolais was a ripsnorting oddity; he dressed like a gamekeeper and ordered his coachman to run over any monks he might see on the road, but he could afford such vagaries as he was a cousin of the King's.
> —Nancy Mitford, *Madame de Pompadour*

vehicle. The standard and best pronunciation is /**vē**-ĭ-kəl/. Many people now like to pronounce the *h*: /**vē**-hĭ-kəl/; this is also acceptable but unnecessary. It is less acceptable to stress the middle syllable: /vē-**hĭk**-əl/.

venal, venial. These words are unrelated. *Venal* basically means 'for sale.' Referring to people it means either 'motivated primarily by money, greedy for money' or 'open to bribery, corrupt.' Referring to politics, justice, etc., it means 'operating by bribery, corrupt.'

> . . . a charming boy with a great love of beauty and of luxury, a little venal perhaps (but which of us is not if we get the opportunity to be?) . . .
> —Nancy Mitford, *Love in a Cold Climate*

> He came to see its [the Georgia legislature] members, for the most part, as venal, incompetent hacks.
> —James Wooten, *Dasher*

> Under Genoese rule justice had been venal, so the Corsicans had taken the law into their own hands and evolved a kind of barbarian justice: revenge.
> —Vincent Cronin, *Napoleon*

Venial refers to sins or offenses, and means 'forgivable, not grave':

> She was a flop at cooking and sewing, detested cleaning and spent money carelessly. In the circumstances the sins were venial. They could afford cooks, maids and extravagance.
> —Arthur M. Schlesinger, Jr., *Robert Kennedy and His Times*

venison = 'the meat of wild animals, especially deer,' is hardly an everyday word. Most people other than hunters will encounter it only on unusual menus or in literature. The standard American pronunciation follows the spelling and gives three syllables, /**vĕn**-ə-sən/ or /**vĕn**-ə-zən/. But in various dialects, especially among people who hunt deer, and especially in the South, the middle syllable is dropped: /**vĕn**-sən/ or /**vĕn**-zən/.

> . . . git a gobbler in thutty minutes. And a ven'son ham in a hour mo'.
> —William Faulkner, *Sartoris*

This is interesting because in Britain the standard upper-class pronunciation is /**vĕn**-zən/. Presumably, this is kept alive by the archaic upper-class English pursuits of stag hunting and deer stalking.

veranda. See PORCH.

verbal nouns in -ing. English verbs form nouns with the suffix *-ing*, which are thus identical to their present participles: *the coming of spring* (noun); *spring was coming* (participle). These nouns are in traditional (Latin-based) grammar called *gerunds*; we prefer to call them simply *verbal nouns.*

The underlying subject of a verbal noun is, in traditional usage, put in the possessive case.

> Elinor was prevented from making any reply to this . . . by the door's being thrown open, the servant's announcing Mr. Ferrars, and Edward's immedi-

ately walking in.
—Jane Austen, *Sense and Sensibility*

It struck him that his being in boarding-school just now was a great convenience for his mother.
—Mary McCarthy, *Birds of America*

But, as a doctor, I see nothing noble in a patient's thrashing around in a sweat-soaked bed, mind clouded in agony.
—Christiaan Barnard, *Reader's Digest*

Despite its being a cold and drizzly April day . . .
—Steve Wissink, *Reader's Digest*

But increasingly, many such phrases are structured in a different way, with the subject simply governing the verbal noun without being put in the possessive, so that the verbal noun is halfway to functioning as a participle.

. . . his visits were conditional upon the *African Queen* being fit to travel. . . .
—C. S. Forester, *The African Queen*

The indications seem to me to point to the Government appealing to the country in November. . . .
—Anthony Eden, *The Reckoning*

The rage and uproar over me becoming a Muslim was still at a fever pitch.
—Muhammad Ali, *The Greatest*

Conservatives, rallying behind the authority of the great usage expert H. W. Fowler, regard this ambivalent noun-participle usage (which Fowler labeled the *fused participle*) as unacceptable. C. S. Forester should have written "the *African Queen*'s being fit"; Sir Anthony Eden, "the Government's appealing"; and Ali, "my becoming a Muslim." However, the fused participle has evolved naturally within the structure of English. It occurred as early as the 18th century, and it is now almost universal in everyday speech and very widespread in writing (unless edited out by conservative copy editors). Hardly anyone nowadays would go all the way with Jane Austen's string of meticulously repeated possessives (nor, probably, would Miss Austen herself if she were writing today). See also POSSESSIVES.

◇ ***Recommendation.*** The traditional construction of possessive plus verbal noun still has a serious place in English usage. It gives full play to the verbal noun *as a noun*, casting its underlying subject in a somewhat subordinate role. This tends to make rather strong, well-structured sentences. We recommend this construction, especially in formal contexts. But we don't believe in being fanatical about it. In any sentence in which the possessive seems awkward, even in formal contexts but more so in informal ones, we fully accept the fused participle.

verbal tricks. See FALLACY.

very. Some adverbs can qualify adjectives, adverbs, verbs, and even whole sentences, while others can qualify only adjectives and adverbs. In general, *very* is used only with adjectives and adverbs: you can say *The rain was very heavy* or *It rained heavily*, but not *It very rained* or *It rained very*.

The past participle of a verb is to some extent a verb and to some extent an adjective. The more it is felt to be functioning as a verb, the less likely it is to be qualified directly by *very*. The more a participle is felt to be used as a full adjective, the more easily can *very* be applied to it. Compare *He was very changed by the experience* with *He is a very changed man*. Conservatives regard both as wrong, and instead of *very* would use *much, very much,* or another adverb such as *deeply*. Moderates would accept *a very changed man*, regarding *changed* in this position before its noun as a full adjective, but would reject *He was very changed by the experience* on the grounds that *changed* in this case is simply the participle of the verb, forming the passive past tense *was changed*. Others, and not necessarily radicals, regard both sentences as perfectly natural and acceptable.

◇ ***Recommendation.*** The clear tendency of the language is to make virtually any participle into an adjective on occasion and to use *very* freely with participles in any case. We fully accept *He was very changed by the experience*, but point out that many people prefer *very much changed.*

vice. This prefix, meaning 'in place of,' is used before a title to designate a deputy to the person who holds the full title (without qualification). While the more traditional practice is to insert a hyphen between *vice* and the title to which it relates, the current trend is to drop the hyphen and treat the title as one or two words. But the fact is, any survey of leading dictionaries will reveal that there can be much inconsistency in the way this prefix is attached to words; for example, *Webster's Third New International Dictionary* gives *vice-regent,* while the original *American Heritage Dictionary* has *vice regent* and *Webster's New World Dictionary* gives *viceregent.* Moreover, even though some dictionaries still show the form *vice-president,* the practice in Washington, D.C., is to refer to the second in command as the *Vice President.* In business organizations (where hyphens tend to be detested almost as much as semicolons) the style most commonly seen is *vice president.*

By the same token, titles such as *vice admiral, vice chancellor,* and *vice consul* are now increasingly written as two separate words (although the forms *vice-admiralty, vice-chancellor,* and *vice-consul* show up in the dictionaries). Words like *viceroy* (= 'deputy to or representative of the king') and *vicereine* (= 'wife of a viceroy') are written solid.

◇ ***Recommendation.*** Choose one dictionary as your authority and follow its spellings on a word-by-word basis.

victuals is pronounced /vĭt-əlz/. Such is the result of tinkering with the language by classicists. The pronunciation represents the earlier forms *vittles* and *vitailles.* The word was borrowed from French and ultimately goes back to Latin *victuālia* = 'provisions'; when the classicists realized this, they officiously "corrected" the modern spelling to *victuals.* The old spelling *vittles* was then ruled illiterate, but it persisted as a rendering of working-class speech.

> No, Ed, you says, a milk punch is too much like vittles and I can't stand the idea of vittles.
> —Don Marquis, *The Old Soak* (1921)

More recently, some down-to-earth types have tried to revive it.

> Just think how thrifty you'll feel (and be) when you've created delectable winter vittles . . . from stuff most folks throw away nowadays.
> —Mary-Bet West, *Countryside*

It would be convenient if everyone started spelling the word *vittles* again; the odd spelling is, however, firmly entrenched.

Virginia Piedmont dialect. This is a subdivision of the SOUTHERN DIALECT. The piedmont (literally 'foothills') of Virginia is a highly distinctive speech area. The four old seaports of Alexandria, Fredericksburg, Richmond, and Petersburg form the cultural and linguistic focal point of this region. From these cities the dialect area radiates westward to the Blue Ridge Mountains, southward into the piedmont of North Carolina, and northward to Baltimore.

Pronunciation. The pronunciation features of this area are highly distinctive and complex.

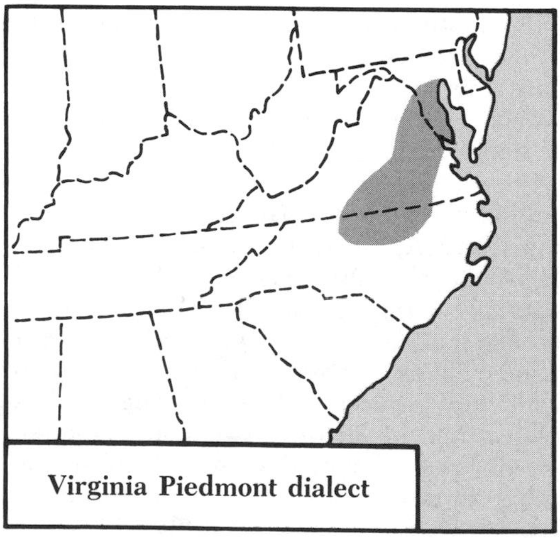

Virginia Piedmont dialect

Here are a few of them. The sound /r/ is dropped after vowels and usually replaced by the sound /ə/. *Beard, stairs, four, wire* are commonly pronounced /bēəd/, /stăəz/, /fōə/, /wīə/. The /ou/ sound before a voiced consonant in words like *loud* and *down* is pronounced /ăōō/: /lăōōd/, /dăōōn/. The vowel in *law, frost, dog* is often pronounced with a back glide: /läô/, /fräôst/, /däôg/.

Vocabulary. (1) Rural and farm terms unique to this area:

cornhouse = 'corn crib'
cuppin = 'cowpen'
hoppergrass = 'grasshopper'
hovel, hover = 'chicken house or roost'

(2) Terms that have more general currency in the Virginia Piedmont region:

batter bread = 'spoon bread, soft corn bread'
croker *or* **crocus sack** = 'burlap bag'
guana *or* **guano sack** = '*gunnysack'
lumber room = 'storeroom'
old-field colt = '*illegitimate child'
school breaks up = 'school lets out'
snake doctor (also in eastern Pennsylvania) = '*dragonfly'
turn of wood (also Coastal Southern) = 'armload of wood'
weskit (old-fashioned) = 'man's vest' (from *waistcoat*)

*Appears as separate entry

vogue words. H. W. Fowler, the famous British expert on usage, preferred the term *vogue words* to the more limiting *catchwords* when he meant to signify those words and phrases that suddenly—and often inexplicably—become fashionable. Most modern lexicographers have agreed with Fowler. The term is a good one, useful and largely self-explanatory. It will almost certainly outlast *buzz words,* its modern counterpart.

The typical vogue word seems to sprout as quickly and mysteriously as mushrooms after a summer rain. Formerly, it either didn't exist or was no more remarkable than any other word. Then, apparently overnight, it is everywhere. You have the oppressive feeling that if you attend a dinner party or business meeting or listen to a TV talk show, you will almost certainly hear the word at least once and probably several times. Your only consolation is that since everybody seems to be using the word so much, it will quickly be regarded as a cliché and then begin to fade away. Less consoling is your near-certainty that by the time it fades, it will have been replaced by a new vogue word.

The verb *relate* is a case in point. The older, standard senses of this word are 'to give an account of,' 'to apply retroactively,' and 'to establish a logical or causal connection between.' But at some point around the mid-20th century the word began to be used in the specialized vocabularies of psychologists and sociologists in the more general senses of 'to have a relationship with' and 'to respond favorably to.' Then, during the 1960s, for reasons that probably no one will ever be able to establish precisely, this psychological-sociological use of the verb hit the streets, and *to relate to* became one of the great vogue phrases of the decade. People were no longer merely interested in things or attracted to them: people *related.* They related to other people, to ideas, to folk music, to natural foods, to plants, to . . . you name it. In time, the constant use of *to relate to*—often in ways noticeably deficient in meaning—began to grate on people's nerves, and by the mid-1970s the term's popularity had declined. Today, although far from dead, this voguish use of *to relate to* can hardly be considered a fashionable locution. Indeed, it has about it a faint aura of nostalgia, a reminder of a tumultuous bygone decade when a youthful generation could "relate" passionately to a variety of attitudes and aspirations that ran the gamut from noble to perverse.

This informal history of the fortunes of *relate* illustrates one way in which vogue words are born. In this case a standard word was picked up, given a fresh connotation, and used to replace synonyms that, although more exact, were somehow perceived to be less forceful.

Indeed, a certain imprecision of meaning seems characteristic of many vogue words, since it permits them to be used in a wide variety of contexts. This is especially apparent in those vogue words borrowed from the special vocabularies of technology, science, and the learned disciplines. In such cases the original meaning of the word may be all but obliterated in popular usage. In the 1960s and 1970s, for example, the word *parameter* enjoyed a certain vogue in business and bureaucratic circles. In popular use the term was often employed as a near-synonym of *perimeter*, somewhat vaguely suggesting boundaries, confining limits, or configuration (usually of a concept). In fact, the word was originally a highly technical mathematical term (see PARAMETER).

Public rhetoric—politicians' phrases, advertising slogans, lines from current books, movies, or plays, and the like—provide another source of vogue words. Until nearly the end of the 1950s, for example, it was still possible to borrow Secretary of State John Foster Dulles's phrase "agonizing reappraisal" without feeling that it had become a hopeless cliché. Again, in the early 1980s some people apparently still felt that there was something fresh and original about paraphrasing out of context the sales pitch for a movie about man-eating sharks; thus, a June, 1981, *New York Times* story on the collapse of Democratic opposition to President Reagan's budget began: "Just when [House Speaker] Tip O'Neill thought it was safe to go back in the water. . . ."

Perhaps some other vogue words owe their brief popularity to rhetorical appeal or to sheer exoticism, but it must be admitted that for a great many, there can be little explanation save the vagaries of fashion itself. Why did *manipulate* suddenly become popular, for example, or *tacky* or *meaningful relationship* or *chic*? (See also CHIC.)

Are slang words vogue words? In a way, but for our purposes it is more convenient to keep the categories separate, letting the term *slang* refer to brand-new coinages and *vogue words* refer to old words suddenly made popular in new settings. Similarly, there is a distinction to be made between vogue words and *jargon*, for while jargon is often awash in vogue words, it is nevertheless possible to speak jargon without resorting to any but the stalest of old words. (See JARGON; SLANG. See also EUPHEMISM.)

Are vogue words clichés? Here the answer must be a qualified yes. Vogue words may not start out as clichés, but they always end up as such—so rapidly, in fact, that they almost qualify as "instant clichés." Yet if all vogue words end as clichés, not all clichés are vogue words; and so, once again, the categories must be kept separate. (See CLICHÉ.)

Finally, are vogue words, as such, bad? To the extent that they sometimes distort meanings and always qualify soon as public nuisances, they are of course deplorable. But during the brief periods when they are coming into flower, they can also sometimes enrich our vocabulary, enliven our conversation, and even extend our perceptions. They are rather like uninvited houseguests: however glad we may be to get rid of them, we may occasionally look back on their visits as having been something less than a total loss.

W

waive, wave. The legal verb *waive* means 'to voluntarily give up (a legal right),' also 'to postpone or set aside (something) for the time being.' It is not related to *wave.* But since the action of *waiving* may often have a sense of dismissing something with a wave of the hand, *waive* is often confused with the verb *wave,* as:

> He was full of good humor and waived aside my apology for imposing on him when ill.
> —Louis Nizer, *My Life in Court*

◇ *Recommendation.* Although this confused use occurs quite often and is accepted by one major dictionary, we regard it as a mistake. You may *waive* something or *wave it aside,* but you may not *waive it aside.*

wake. This basic verb for a basic human act has a remarkable number of variations.

(1) *Forms and inflections.* The simple verb *wake* itself has past tense *woke* or *waked* and past participle *woken* or *waked. Woke* and *woken* are somewhat commoner.

Waken has past tense and past participle *wakened.*

Awake has past tense *awoke* and *awaked* and past participle *awoken* or *awaked. Awoke* and *awoken* are much commoner.

Awaken has past tense and past participle *awakened.*

(2) *Meanings.* All four verbs can be intransitive, meaning 'to come out of sleep' (*When you wake, give me a call*), or transitive, meaning 'to arouse (someone) from sleep' (*The wail of a siren awakened the baby*). *Wake* is used about equally in both ways. *Waken* and *awake* are chiefly intransitive. *Awaken* is used both ways, but more often transitively. (See TRANSITIVE, INTRANSITIVE.)

All four verbs are also used figuratively, meaning 'to become aware and alert' and 'to make (someone) aware and alert.' *Awaken* is so used more often than the others: *The accident awakened the community to its environmental neglect.*

(3) *Up. Wake* is as often as not used with *up,* both transitively and intransitively, and figuratively as well as literally. *Waken* is sometimes used with *up.* The other two are not.

◇ *Recommendation.* There are no problems among all these permutations. Whatever choice your instinct suggests is almost sure to be right. If in doubt for stylistic reasons, use the simple verb *wake* whenever it seems appropriate, with or without *up,* and preferably inflect it *woke, woken.* But don't let this advice override your own preferences.

wane. See WAX, WANE.

want. (1) *Want for.* This phrasal verb is standard when meaning 'to lack,' typically used in the negative: *We wanted for nothing.* It is also used to mean 'wish (someone to do something)':

> I think he wanted very much for me to go, but he said nothing.
> —Catherine Gaskin, *Edge of Glass*

◇ *Recommendation.* This is an informal idiom. We advise against using it in formal speech or writing. Standard usage is "he very much wanted me to go."

(2) *Want in, out,* etc. The expression *want in* = 'to want to go inside' seems to have risen from the strange pidgin lingo habitually used by many people to their dogs and cats: *Does 'oo want in, then?* It has become an accepted, if still somewhat informal, phrase among hard-nosed businessmen, meaning 'to want to get in on a group, situation, etc.,' along with its opposite, *want out,* and variations such as *want off.*

> My sources tell me an emotional Yablans said at one point that he "wants out" of his contract.
> —Dan Dorfman, *New York*

> Although he wanted off the Cronkite show, Leiser did not want to lose

ground in the overall pecking order of CBS News.
—Gary Paul Gates, *Air Time*

warts and all = 'without flattery, not glossing over faults, hiding nothing.'

. . . the role of the eternally flighty Billie Burke in a warts-and-all film about Florenz Ziegfeld . . .
—Guy Flatley, *New York Times*

The warts themselves may be singled out:

True, the picture of Warren E. Burger, the Chief Justice, is unflattering in the extreme, and there is no attempt to paint over the warts on the other justices. . . . —Jethro K. Lieberman, *Business Week*

The origin of this expression is the instruction given by Oliver Cromwell to the portrait painter Peter Lely (reported in Horace Walpole's *Anecdotes of Painting in England*):

Mr. Lely, I desire you would use all your skill to paint my picture truly like me, and not flatter me at all. But remark all these roughnesses, pimples, warts, and everything as you see me, otherwise I will never pay a farthing for it.

watershed. This word, borrowed from German *wasserscheide* = 'water-separation,' is a geographical term meaning 'line or area dividing two natural drainage areas'; it is typically a ridge of high ground from which runoff flows in opposite directions into separate river systems. The word is used figuratively to mean 'time or event that marks a turning point in political history':

The years 1822–32 are a watershed in the history of Southern ideas about slavery. —Samuel Eliot Morison, *The Oxford History of the American People*

The President seemed to take the Afghanistan incursion as a highly personal affront—and a watershed in his feelings about the Soviet Union.
—*Newsweek*

wave. See WAIVE.

wax, wane. These two verbs are felt as a matched pair because of their similar sound, but they are unrelated. Their classic reference is to the moon as it grows apparently larger and smaller.

Nothing that is can pause or stay;
The moon will wax, the moon will wane,
The mist and cloud will turn to rain. . . .
—Henry Wadsworth Longfellow, *Keramos*

Both verbs are also used of days, seasons, and years as they progress and as they draw to an end:

. . . myriad odors of the waxing spring and the drowsy humming of insects . . .
—William Faulkner, *Sartoris*

. . . in the waning days of 1938 . . .
—Brendan Gill, *Here at The New Yorker*

Wax has the general meaning 'to grow stronger or larger':

In the twenty years after it joined the revolt . . . the economic power of Amsterdam waxed exceedingly.
—Charles Wilson, *The Dutch Republic*

More particularly, *wax* is used with adjectives, meaning 'to grow (strong, healthy, etc.)' and especially 'to become (active, angry, etc.)':

Perhaps villagers do not wax eloquent on political affairs. . . .
—Thomas A. Dooley, *The Edge of Tomorrow*

Even on the air, [Harry Reasoner] frequently waxed snappish and scornful of Walter's remarks.
—Ron Powers, *The Newscasters*

Wane in general means 'to diminish, grow weaker':

After about an hour, Kunta's excitement had waned almost as much as his pace. —Alex Haley, *Roots*

. . . it was clear that the Church's political power was waning [in Italy]. . . . —William Colby, *Honorable Men: My Life in the CIA*

On the wane means 'growing weaker, approaching an end':

He claimed that capitalism was on the wane as a way of life in the world. . . . —Spiro T. Agnew, *The Caulfield Decision*

way. The American adverb *way* = 'away, a long way,' is a shortening of *away*. It has been spelled *'way* and considered informal or folksy. The following quotations from a book published in the 1950s show editorial hesitation about the spelling, probably indicating a change in the status of the word:

. . . a look about the eyes as of a man who had come way up from very far down . . .

. . . Much time and money had been spent on [the defenses of Washington], beginning 'way back in the McClellan era. . . . —Bruce Catton, *A Stillness at Appomattox*

◇ ***Recommendation.*** It is time to dispense with the apostrophe and recognize *way* as an independent adverb, suitable for use in all but the most formal contexts.

Webster, Noah. Noah Webster was born in Connecticut in 1758 and was at Yale during the Revolutionary War. Intensely patriotic, he marched with the student militia but never saw combat, just missing the Battle of Saratoga. In the new republic freed from British rule, young Noah Webster, with no authority but unlimited nerve, took on a staggering task. He would establish American English as the national standard language, able to take its own course and independent of British usage. The birth of a nation provided a unique opportunity to shape and guide a language. Webster believed that the English of Americans was already better than that of the British, because it was more conservative and democratic, uncorrupted by fashionable novelties and snobbish values. He planned to purify it further, impose a standard pronunciation and a phonetic spelling, and fix it for the future: ". . . within a century and a half, North America will be peopled with a hundred millions of men, *all speaking the same language*." He even hoped that it would become an independent language, "as different from the future language of England, as the modern Dutch, Danish and Swedish are from the German."

Webster himself was unimpressive, pedantic, humorless, and obsessed with his self-appointed mission. Benjamin Franklin gave him some encouragement, but in general the Establishment of his day never accepted him or his right to legislate their language. His revolutionary vision of its future turned out to be exaggerated, and he himself was willing to revise both his vision and his goals as he went along, eventually realizing that American English was not destined to move very far apart from British English.

Nonetheless, Noah Webster put his mark on American English more clearly than anyone else before or since. His enormous influence was exerted through two books: a "speller," first published in 1783, and a dictionary, published in 1828. His speller included pronunciation drills, usage rules, and moral precepts as well as spellings. It was America's basic elementary textbook for much of the 19th century, eventually selling more than 80 million copies. His *American Dictionary of the English Language*, carrying 70,000 entries, was a clear improvement over all British predecessors; the tradition and excellence of American dictionary making stem from this pioneer work. It is appropriate that the name *Webster* remains partly synonymous with *dictionary*.

Most of the American spellings that systematically differ from British are directly due to Webster's choices and improvements. The most important of these are the change of *-our* to *-or* in *color, honor, labor*, etc.; the change of *-re* to *-er* in *center, meter, theater;* the change of *-ce* to *-se* in *defense* and *offense;* the change from British *travelled,* *traveller,* to American *traveled, traveler,* and similar words; and the preference for *-ize* over *-ise* in verbs like *baptize.* He is also responsible for such isolated improvements as *ax* for *axe* and *draft* for *draught.* In pronunciation he established the American forms of *lieutenant* and *schedule,* and it is his decision that gives us *aluminum* instead of *aluminium.* Many of his planned improvements were never accepted. Among them are *groop* and *soop; tung* and *yung; deserv, primitiv,* and *twelv; haz, iland, thum, wimmen,* and *zink.*

Webster was interested in regional Americanisms but had a strong tendency to prefer the usage of New England, specifically that of the ruggedly individual small farmers. He was "democratic" enough to support the correctness of such usages as *you was, it is me, them horses,* and *who she is married to.* But his most enduring influence on usage was in putting across a concept of a single, correct, national Standard American English, to be learned by children in school.

weird. This universally familiar adjective has an appropriately strange history. Old English *wyrd* was a noun meaning 'fate, destiny.' It was used specifically of the Norns, the three Germanic fate goddesses who controlled the destinies of men. The three "weird sisters" in Shakespeare's *Macbeth* are described as witches, but they are really the Norns, able to reveal the future to Macbeth. In the phrase *weird sisters,* the word *weird* is used attributively; the meaning is either 'the sister Fates' or 'the fate-controlling sisters.' The modern use of *weird* as an adjective results entirely from this attributive use by Shakespeare in one of his most familiar plays.

In the early 19th century, when the romantic cult of Gothic horrors was at its height, *weird* was extracted from *weird sisters* and reinterpreted to mean 'unearthly, belonging to witchcraft, and menacing.'

> From a weird clime that lieth, sublime,
> Out of Space—out of Time . . .
> —Edgar Allan Poe, *Dreamland*

It has since become a favorite all-purpose term with a range of meanings from 'supernaturally and evilly mysterious' through 'indefinably strange, uncanny' and 'hauntingly strange, fey' to 'odd, irrational, eccentric, unconventional, disagreeable, nasty.'

> Bending his head and flapping his cloak in weird, vampiric fashion he would slowly cavort around a lugubrious aspen.
> —Vladimir Nabokov, *Speak, Memory*

> It was a musical, with a little story to it, and it gave me a chance to sing a song—a real weird and pretty blues number.
> —Billie Holiday and William Duffy, *Lady Sings the Blues*

> Everyone on the club thinks Rawly is weird because he buys *Rolling Stone* magazine. Everybody else reads the *Sporting News.*
> —Sparky Lyle, *The Bronx Zoo*

Welsh words. Welsh, also known as Cymric /**kĭm**-rĭk/, is the most vigorous surviving Celtic language. There are still several hundred thousand people in Wales who speak Welsh in preference to English. But the English, who conquered the Welsh in the Middle Ages, have borrowed only a handful of Welsh words and names.

Avalon = 'island in the west to which King Arthur and other heroes went after death': from Welsh *Ynis yr Afallon* = 'Isle of Apples'

coracle = 'leather boat on a wicker framework': from Welsh *corwgl* = 'boat'; related to Irish *currach* = 'boat, curragh'

corgi = 'short-legged dog originally used as a watchdog': from Welsh *corgi* = 'dwarf-dog'

cromlech /**krŏm**-lĕk/ = 'ancient monument of massive stones supporting a capstone': from Welsh *cromlech* = 'arched stone'

crowd = 'medieval Welsh stringed instrument': from Welsh *crwth* /kro͞oth/

cwm /ko͞om/ = 'steep-walled hollow at the head of a mountain valley, sometimes containing a lake': from Welsh *cwm* = 'mountain valley, coomb'

eisteddfod /ī-**stĕth**-vŏd, -vôd/ = 'meeting of Welsh bards, annual competition of Welsh musicians and poets': Welsh *eisteddfod* = 'a sitting, session'

flannel = 'loosely woven woolen fabric': from Welsh *gwlanen* = 'woolen garment,' from *gwlan* = 'wool'

metheglin /mə-**thĕg**-lĭn/ = 'drink made from fermented honey and water with herbs': from Welsh *meddyglyn* = 'medicinal drink'

pendragon /pĕn-**drăg**-ən/ = 'title of the war leader of the British after the departure of the Romans in the 5th century A.D.': from Welsh *pendragon* = 'chief dragon' (figures of mythic beasts, including dragons, were carried on poles as battle standards)

penguin = 'flightless marine bird of the cold Southern Hemisphere': first recorded in the 16th century, applied by English explorers to the great auk in Newfoundland and later transferred to the penguin; early accounts claim that the name was given by Welsh sailors on the English ships; if so, it is from Welsh *pen gwyn* = 'white head'

Western dialect. The vast region of the United States where this dialect is spoken is made up of the states in and west of the Rocky Mountains. Western, which is a subdivision of GENERAL NORTHERN, has yet to be thoroughly studied. Several projects to examine this and other dialects are under way as part of the countrywide study *The Linguistic Atlas of the United States*. To date, however, little has been published on the Western dialect or its subdivisions: the PACIFIC NORTHWEST, PACIFIC SOUTHWEST, ROCKY MOUNTAIN, and SOUTHWESTERN dialects. This situation is compounded by the newness of the language itself. Because dialects take some time to develop and become distinct, the speech of this newest American region is more homogeneous than the older dialects of the Atlantic seaboard. In addition, the development and population growth of the West have been so enormous that speech patterns have not yet stabilized. Nevertheless, the unique history of this region sets it apart from the rest of the country in many respects.

The large volume of migration mainly from the old Northern and North Midland speech regions established a kind of "base" language. In time, this base language absorbed many elements of the languages previously existing in the region, most notably Spanish and to a lesser extent the native Indian languages. The economy of the region was also very influential. Specifically, fur trading, farming, cattle raising, mining, and lumbering have enriched the language and stamped it with its own character.

Vocabulary. (1) Terms of Spanish origin (for more details on the origin of some words see SPANISH WORDS):

adios /ä-dē-**ōs**/ = 'goodbye'
adobe /ə-**dō**-bē/ = 'sun-baked clay and straw mixture used as a building material'
amigo /ə-**mē**-gō/ = 'friend, good fellow'
andale /**än**-də-lā/ = 'to hurry up'; usually used as a command
aparejo /ăp-ə-**rā**-hō, äp-/ = 'packsaddle'
bronco = 'unbroken horse'
***buckaroo** = 'cowboy'
burro = 'donkey'
chaparral /**shăp**-ə-răl/ = (1) 'dense thicket of shrubs and small trees' (2) 'country where these grow'
hoosegow /**hōōs**-gou/ = 'jail'
ladino /lə-**dē**-nō/ = (1) 'outlaw cow' (2) 'any vicious animal'
lariat = 'rope used for lassoing'
lasso /**lăs**-ō, lă-**sōō**/ = (1) (noun) 'rope with a noose used for catching cattle' (2) (verb) 'to rope an animal with a lasso'
lobo = 'timber wolf'
loco = 'crazy, foolish'
manada /mə-**nä**-də/ = 'herd of mares'
mesa /**mā**-sə/ = 'flat-topped hill'
mustang = 'wild horse'
parada /pə-**rä**-də/ = 'main herd of cattle'
partida /pär-**tē**-də/ = 'herd of cattle'
poco = 'little, small in amount'
pronto = 'quickly, soon, in a hurry'
reata /rē-**äd**-ə/ = 'rope, especially leather rope'
tapadera /tăp-ə-**dâr**-ə/ = 'leather covering on the front and sides of a stirrup'

*Appears as separate entry

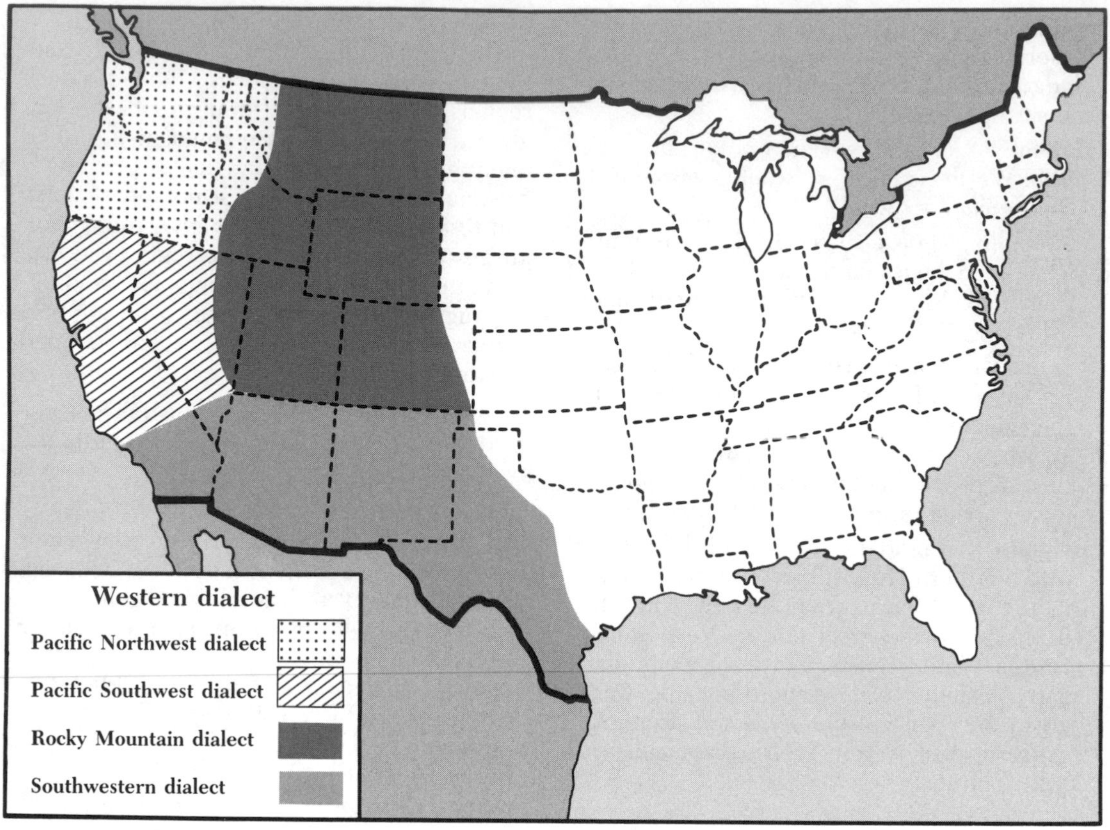

(2) Some range and cowboy terms that are or have been used in the West:

acorn calf = 'runt calf, weakling'
air the lungs = 'to curse'
air the paunch = 'to vomit'
Arizona nightingale = 'donkey'
Arkansas toothpick = 'large knife or dagger'
barefoot = '(of a horse) unshod'
base burner = 'whiskey'
bedded = '(of an animal) roped and thrown to the ground'
belly up = (1) (verb) 'to stand at a bar and drink' (2) (adjective) 'drunk' (3) (adjective) 'dead'
bobtail flush = '(in five-card poker) four to a flush (a valueless hand)'
bobtail straight = '(in five-card poker) four to a straight (a valueless hand)'
bog rider = 'cowboy working to get bogged cattle to dry ground'
bone orchard, boneyard = 'cemetery'
booger (an animal) /bo͝og-ər/ = 'to scare'
Boston dollar = 'penny'
brand artist *or* **blotter** = 'cattle thief who alters brands'
buck-nun = 'recluse'
buck out = 'to die'
buffaloed = 'confused, baffled'
bulldog = 'to trip and throw a steer'
bull-necked = 'headstrong'
burro milk! = 'nonsense!'
cahoots = 'partnership, collusion'
calf around = 'to loaf'
caught in one's own loop = 'having failed through some fault of one's own'
chew the cud = (1) 'to carry on a long conversation' (2) 'to argue'
chuck wagon = 'wagon with cooking equipment and provisions'
cowpuncher = 'cowboy'
dancing devil = 'whirling desert sandstorm'

dauncy = 'moody, melancholy'
desert canary = 'donkey'
dodge out = 'to separate calves from a herd'
dogie /dō-gē/ = 'scrubby maverick calf'
dough belly, puncher, *or* **roller** = 'cook'
fag = 'to leave in a hurry'
feathered out = 'dressed up'
fence lifter = 'a very heavy rain'
fill a blanket = 'to roll a cigarette'
flannelmouth = 'braggart, one who talks nonsense'
forefoot (an animal) = 'to rope by the forefeet'
frothy = 'angry'
goosey = 'nervous, touchy'
greenhorn = 'novice'
grit = 'courage'
grubstake = 'supplies, provisions'
gulch = 'ravine, gully'
gunsel = 'novice'
hayburner = 'horse'
hightail = 'to depart suddenly'
kack = 'saddle'
larrup = (1) (noun) 'molasses' (2) (verb) 'to strike or thrash'
line rider = 'cowboy who patrols boundaries'
lone ranger = 'bachelor'
lump oil = 'kerosene'
maverick = 'unbranded, motherless calf' See POLITICAL TERMS.
motte = 'clump of trees'
muley = 'hornless cow'
Oklahoma rain = 'dust storm'
out-coyote = 'to outsmart'
plant = 'to bury'
plow chaser = 'farmer'
pony-express *or* **running mount** = 'the mounting of a running horse without touching the stirrups'
prairie lawyer = 'coyote'
punch the breeze = 'to depart in a hurry'
ranahan, ranny = 'top cowhand, efficient cowboy'
ride herd on = 'to guard, supervise'
roostered = 'drunk'
roundup = 'the herding together of cattle'
rustler = 'cattle thief'
sag = 'slope'
salty = 'good, exceptional'
scorcher = 'branding iron'
short-aged = '(of cattle) less than three years old'
silver thaw = 'freezing rain'
sin buster *or* **twister** = 'preacher'
slick up = 'to dress up'
smooth mouth = 'old horse'
snake poison *or* **water** = 'whiskey'
snorty = 'high-spirited, easily angered'
snubbed = 'dehorned'
sop = 'gravy'
sourdough = 'cook, bachelor'
squaw wood = 'dried cow chips or dry sticks used for fuel'
strawberries = 'beans, especially pintos'
straw boss = 'ranch foreman'
stretch the blanket = 'to exaggerate, lie'
sull = 'to sulk'
tinhorn = 'flashy, pretentious gambler'
underwears = 'sheep'
unshucked = 'naked'
water hole = 'saloon, tavern'
wet herd = 'herd of milk cows'
wingding = 'party, social'
wrangle (horses *or* **cattle)** = 'to round up'
yack = 'stupid person'
yamping = 'petty theft'

(3) Some more generally known terms:

barrow pit, bar pit, bar ditch = 'roadside drainage ditch'
bear claw (also Upper Midwestern) = 'kind of pastry'
beer bust = 'noisy party at which there is considerable drinking'
box canyon = 'gorge or canyon with only one opening'
bunkhouse = 'living quarters for the hired men on a ranch or farm'
cat and mouse = 'the game of tick-tack-toe'
catch-colt, ketch-colt = '*illegitimate child'
chukar = 'Indian rock partridge'
civet cat (also Gulf Southern) = 'skunk'
corral /kə-răl/ = 'enclosure or pen for livestock' See SPANISH WORDS.
corrugate = 'to make small irrigation ditches in a field'
four corners (also Northern) = 'crossroads'
frontage road = 'road running parallel to

*Appears as separate entry

an expressway and providing access to stores and businesses isolated from the expressway, service road'

gnat's eyebrow = 'the last detail': *They had it planned out down to a gnat's eyebrow.*

gooms (also Northern) = 'gums'

kitty-corner (also Northern) = 'in a diagonal position, *catercorner'

longhandles (also General Southern) = 'long underwear'

pourdown = 'heavy, short-lasting rain'

*Appears as separate entry

Example. The colorful language of the Western cowhand was generously sprinkled with imaginative, sometimes outrageous, hyperbole. Here is a typical example of the Western dialect as spoken by one of its chief representatives, a cowboy:

> Holdin' a herd on a dark and stormy night was a job for a man with fur on his brisket. If the weather was good and ever' hoof had a paunchful of grass and water, all was quiet. But if a storm blowed up and the weather got wholesale, the cattle were mighty apt to be so restless you'd have to ride a mile to spit. Maybe it was so dark you couldn't find your nose with both hands. That was when you had to do some real singin'—maybe till you was plumb tired of it. You might be cussin' the very steers you was ridin' herd on, but as long as you did it to a tune that had that soft accompaniment of squeakin' saddle leather and the tinkle of bridle chains, it was mighty soothin' to a spooky longhorn.
>
> —Ramon F. Adams, *The Old-Time Cowhand*

whether, if. The conjunction *whether* basically means 'which of two.' Used to begin clauses after verbs like *ask, discover, see, wonder*, it was originally always used with *or not: I asked whether or not he was coming.* But *or not* is now optional and may be omitted. It is also correct to use *if* instead of *whether.* Some authorities consider *as to whether* redundant; they recommend simply *whether.* See also DOUBT.

whiskey. The art of distilling pure alcohol from wine or beer was probably discovered in the 12th century, by alchemists working with monks in Italy. Believing that the volatile new liquid was a somewhat miraculous substance, the discoverers named it, in Latin, *aqua vitae* = 'water of life.' Liqueurs in small quantities were made in some monasteries, but the technique of distilling remained a closely guarded secret throughout the Middle Ages. Between 1500 and 1550, hundreds of monasteries were broken up in the Protestant Reformation, and the secret of aqua vitae was spread by ex-monks all over Europe.

In the Scandinavian countries the product is still called *aquavit.* In Russia the term was partly translated, as *vodka* = 'little water.' In Ireland and Scotland *aqua vitae* was fully translated into Gaelic as *uisge betha* = 'water of life.' The Irish and Scottish liquor, made from barley mash (the latter flavored by the smoke of the peat fires used in its production), came to the notice of the English in the reign of Elizabeth I; they borrowed the Gaelic name as *usquebaugh,* pronounced /ŭs-kwĭ-bô/. This was later changed to *whiskybae* and then shortened to *whisky.* In North America, Scotch-Irish immigrants used corn mash or rye instead of barley, but the results were still acceptable. The usual Irish and American spelling is *whiskey;* the usual Scottish and Canadian spelling is *whisky.*

For *aquavit* see SCANDINAVIAN WORDS; for *vodka* see RUSSIAN WORDS.

white-collar. See BLUE-COLLAR, WHITE-COLLAR.

who. (1) *Whom.* In traditional formal usage the objective form of the interrogative and relative pronoun *who* is *whom.* This applies both when the pronoun is the direct object of a verb, as *Whom did you see?* and *the man whom you saw,* and when it is governed by a preposition, as *For whom did you vote?* and *the man for whom you voted.* The rule has been eroding, but it is still observed in most formal writing and by a minority of people in everyday speech.

> Who is proving what to whom?
> —editorial, *New York Post*

> Whom does the Transit Authority think it's kidding when it claims that it seriously tries to schedule these buses?
> —I. M. Walker (letter), *New York Times*

> I am intrigued by waiters and waitresses who instinctively know to whom to give the check.
> —Erma Bombeck, *Boston Globe*

To most people nowadays the use of *whom* in speech has an emphatically formal or even artificial ring.

> This fellow came on very strong [on the telephone]. He started to sing "Happy Birthday to you," taking his time. . . .
> "To whom am I speaking, please," I asked rather formally.
> "Bing Crosby. Happy birthday, Jack."
> —Jack Nicklaus, *The Greatest Game of All*

> [Archie Goodwin:] ". . . hearsay."
> [Nero Wolfe:] "Whom did you hear say what?"
> I have tried to talk him out of that "whom." Only highbrows and grandstanders and schoolteachers say "whom," and he knows it. It's the mule in him.
> —Rex Stout, *All in the Family*

In everyday speech most people say *Who did you see?* and *the man (who) you saw; Who did you vote for?* and *the man (who) you voted for.* This is a natural and increasing development in the language and is frequently done in writing.

> . . . and I thought who is calling who a lost generation?
> —Ernest Hemingway, *A Moveable Feast*

> . . . the French couple—who he disliked on sight . . .
> —Mary McCarthy, *Birds of America*

> In the lane, the children tried to make the chauffeur tell them who he worked for.
> —John Le Carré, *Tinker, Tailor, Soldier, Spy*

> Last night, the 52-year-old bachelor, who most regard as liberal, but who thinks of himself as a centrist . . .
> —*New York Times*

◇ ***Recommendation.*** Neither conservatives nor progressives need advice from us. The former scrupulously use *whom* in all situations including casual conversation. The latter have abolished it entirely. The most comfortable position, which is what we recommend, is that of the double standard: use *whom* in highly formal contexts such as academic theses and ceremonial speeches, but ignore it in everyday talk. Where you draw the line in, say, business correspondence or reportage is a matter of personal style.

(2) *Hypercorrection.* Anxious not to miss a single *whom,* people very often put it in where it doesn't belong. This usually occurs where the relative clause depends on a noun that is, or seems to be, the object of a verb.

> . . . the collective attitude of the freed hostages, Americans whom their captors had said were enjoying themselves while imprisoned.
> —Tom Coffey, *Savannah Morning News*

> We requested the opportunity to deliver personally letters of greeting from my father to Chairman Mao and, if his health permitted, Premier Chou En-lai, whom we had heard was suffering from cancer.
> —Julie Nixon Eisenhower, *Special People*

The test is, What is the role of the relative pronoun *within the clause that it introduces*? If it is the subject of the clause, the form must be *who,* regardless of the structure of the rest of the sentence. In the quotations above, the relevant clauses are "who (*their captors had said*) were enjoying themselves" and "who (*we had heard*) was suffering from cancer." The clauses shown here in parentheses are literally parenthetical expressions that do not affect the construction of the relative clauses introduced by the pronoun.

◊ *Recommendation.* This hypercorrected use of *whom* is a definite mistake.

(3) *Whose.* Normally, *who* is used only with antecedents that are personal nouns or (like nations) are personified. *Which* is used with impersonal antecedents. But the form *of which,* when followed by a noun phrase beginning with *the,* is often felt to be unacceptably awkward; *whose* is then used instead.

> . . . a chopping-block across which lay an ax whose helve had been mended with rusty wire . . .
> —William Faulkner, *Sartoris*

> . . . a credit to a game whose traditional manners are undermined by increasing rudeness . . .
> —George Feifer, *Reader's Digest*

◊ *Recommendation. Whose* is a fully standard alternative to *of which the.*

(4) *Whoever.* The objective form of *whoever* is *whomever,* and just the same rules and attitudes apply to it as to *who* and *whom.* Many people now prefer to boycott *whomever,* but the impeccable *whom*-user does not flinch at *whomever.*

> As everyone knows, reporters drink deeply wherever, whatever, however and with whomever they can.
> —Jack Thomas, *Boston Globe*

> Who the hell am I to be telling whomever whom to vote for?
> —George C. Scott (quoted), *New York Times*

As a forceful example of the very rare double *whom,* the second quotation commands our admiration.

will. See SHALL, WILL.

window. This is perhaps the most striking metaphor that has so far entered the general vocabulary from the jargon of space exploration. The original meaning is 'period of time during which the relative orbital position of the moon or planets is favorable to the launch of a particular mission':

> For a brief period of time (the familiar "window" of all interplanetary missions) there exists an opportunity to send a single spacecraft to *all* the giant planets in the outer solar system. . . .
> —Richard C. Hoagland, *Star and Sky*

Window is now used to mean 'limited favorable period' or sometimes 'limited area,' in any number of different applications.

> The Soviets will soon be entering a period of about five to eight years of military and naval superiority. This is the "window" of time that U.S. strategists dread: the period in which the Soviet military will have great freedom of action . . . with a new generation of laser weaponry.
> —William Safire, *New York Times*

> In the East, the law meant the foreigners could be driven entirely from the waters of New England and confined tightly to fishing "windows" in the mid-Atlantic where fisheries were allowed to continue for some so-called underutilized species.
> —*National Fisherman*

withers. This is a very curious word, used chiefly by people interested in horseflesh or literature (or both):

> Now he weighs 1,145 and measures 16 hands 2 inches at the withers.
> —Red Smith, *New York Times*

The *withers* are the slightly projecting ridge of muscle between the shoulder blades of a horse. The height of horses is always measured to the withers (and always in *hands,* units of four inches). The horse has only one withers, but nonetheless the word is plural. Its origin is obscure.

An ill-fitting saddle or collar is apt to bruise, or gall, the horse's withers. The old term for this was *wring the withers,* used metaphorically by Shakespeare:

> Let the galled jade wince, our withers are unwrung.
> —*Hamlet*

This means, approximately, 'If you're hurt you complain, but I have no problem.' Mostly because of Shakespeare's example, the expression remains in occasional use:

> Here was President Roosevelt, his withers still wrung with the Hearst yoke. . . .
>
> —Alva Johnston, *Saturday Evening Post*

This means that Roosevelt was feeling political pain from the burden of Hearst's support. For other terms related to horses, see HORSES AND HORSEMANSHIP TERMS.

woman, lady, girl. There is no question as to what an adult male human being should be called. He is a *man*. A *boy* has always increased his status when he became a *man*. But for a *girl*, becoming a *woman* traditionally meant not a gain but a loss—a loss of the youthfulness for which she was valued. She was taught to cling to girlhood as long as she could. Then, she could become a *lady*, a title that implied possession of refinement and good manners. The one word everyone shrank away from was *woman*. One meaning of *woman* was 'a female human being of a class or character lower than that of a lady.' *Woman* in general was also assigned a number of negative attributes. *Woman* was fickle, fearful, and foolish. *Woman* was cowardly, tearful, and weak. All the admirable qualities of adults—courage, strength, fortitude, determination, vigor—were assigned solely to men. Although both males and females possessed these good qualities, they were called *manly*, not *womanly*, virtues. It was little wonder, then, that girls did not look forward to being *women* the way boys looked forward to becoming *men*.

> The boys endured their punishment like men and Christians.
>
> —Robert Wodrow, *History of the Sufferings of the Church of Scotland* (1721)

> Teach her to subdue the woman in her nature.
>
> —Sir Henry Taylor, *Philip van Artevelde* (1834)

To make a *man* of someone meant to make that individual strong and self-reliant. To make a *woman* of someone meant to bring that person into submission.

> We conquer'd You, we made Women of you.
>
> —*Colonial Records of Pennsylvania* (1742)

Therein lay the problem. *Woman* was being defined from a male, not a female, point of view. *Woman* was not defined as the ideal adult model of human nature to which girls should aspire. It was defined as the negative opposite of *man*. Now women have reclaimed their own word and rehabilitated it. *Woman* has become the preferred designation for 'adult female human being.'

The problem with the word *girl* was somewhat different. In business, *girl* took on the meaning of 'secretary or assistant.' This usage tended to stereotype young women in low-level clerical positions. It also tended to close such entry-level positions to young men. Some industries joined with women in objecting to the usage. In 1979 United Technologies published this declaration in such papers as the *Wall Street Journal:*

> Wouldn't 1979 be a great year to take one giant step forward for womankind and get rid of "the girl"? Your attorney says, "If I'm not here just leave it with the girl." The purchasing agent says, "Drop off your bid with the girl." A manager says, "My girl will get back to your girl." *What* girl? Do they mean Miss Rose? Do they mean Ms. Torres? Do they mean Mrs. McCullough? Do they mean Joy Jackson? "The girl" is certainly a woman when she's out of her teens. Like you, she has a name. Use it.

The following citation is in a similar vein:

> . . . didn't everybody say "boiler-room girls" in 1969, referring to the persons who *man* the telephones in a political campaign? "You could say 'girls' in 1969," she responded, "but not in 1979." She has a point. . . . women who are secretaries resent their bosses' saying, "Talk to my girl about that," especially when girlhood is long gone, and the self-description of a group of

> women as "the girls" seems to be on the wane.
>
> —William Safire, *New York Times Magazine*

The parallel term to *man* is *woman*, not *girl* or *lady*. *Lady* once implied a superior social position. It still has that connotation.

> . . . a lady loses her dignity when she condescends to be useful.
>
> —Washington Irving, *Salmagundi* (1807–8)

Later, *lady* came to be used of any woman, as a courtesy. It now implies a certain standard of refined manners and polite behavior. In all these usages it is akin to *gentleman*.

Woman, *lady*, and *girl* have all been used as modifiers, as in *woman driver*, *lady lawyer*, or *girl reporter*. Such usages imply that a driver, lawyer, or reporter is assumed to be male unless specified to be female. This kind of usage is frowned upon now. *Girl* (for an adult) and *lady* should never be used in this way. When modifiers must be used, *female* is the proper parallel term to match *male*, as in *male and female police officers*. Still, *woman* is preferred by many. It is almost always used to designate single-sex groupings, such as *women artists* and *women poets*.

See also FEMALE-GENDER WORD FORMS; MISS, MRS., MS.; PARALLEL STYLE.

wont. This rather archaic word is variously pronounced /wōnt/, /wônt/, /wŏnt/, and /wŭnt/; all forms are correct. As an adjective it means 'accustomed, in the habit of':

> . . . he learned after resigning that Mr. Kissinger was wont to make occasional disparaging remarks about him.
>
> —James M. Naughton, *New York Times*

As a noun it means 'usual practice, habit':

> As was his wont when his superior raved, Farington became even more unemotional in reply.
>
> —G. Gordon Liddy, *Out of Control*

woods. Referring to a tract of forested land, whether wilderness or planted, or to a stand of trees, *woods* takes either a singular or a plural verb; the plural is the more usual choice: *The woods are scary tonight.*

word division. The following rules and guidelines are designed for material that is to be typed or handwritten. (For material that is to be set in type, some rules are occasionally relaxed because of the need to maintain an even right margin.)

(1) Avoid word division whenever you can. These breaks at the end of a line can distract and even confuse your reader; and to divide correctly often requires a time-consuming look in the dictionary.

(2) If you must divide a word, divide only between syllables. Syllabification is typically based on pronunciation, but since authorities often disagree on how a word is syllabified, the safest course is to choose one dictionary and follow it consistently.

(3) Don't divide one-syllable words (*through, rhythm, prism*). Be especially careful with words ending in *-ed;* many of them (like *watched, skimmed, strained*) are one-syllable words and can't be divided.

(4) It's not worth dividing a word unless you can leave at least a two-letter syllable on the upper line and carry over a three-letter syllable to the line below. Thus, you can divide the word *undue* (*un-due*) but not the word *undo* (*un-do*). You can divide the three-syllable word *radio* (*ra-di-o*) as *ra-dio* but not as *radi-o*, even though *-o* is a syllable. But you shouldn't touch a three-syllable word like *alibi* (*a-li-bi*) since the first possibility (*a-libi*) would leave only one letter on the upper line and the second possibility (*ali-bi*) would carry over only two.

(5) If you have to divide a solid compound word, try to divide between the parts of the compound rather than within one of the parts: *tender-hearted* rather than *ten-derhearted.* By the same token, if you must divide a hyphenated compound word, try to do it at the point of the hyphen rather than adding another hyphen to the word: *middle-aged* rather than *mid-dle-aged.*

(6) Divide a word after a prefix or before a suffix rather than within the base word or

within the prefix or suffix: *extra-curricular* rather than *ex-tracurricular* or *extracur-ricular*. However, avoid breaks that can mislead the eye; for example, *super-lative* or *extra-ordinary*. In such cases, *extraor-dinary* or *su-perlative* would be preferable.
(7) When a one-letter syllable falls within a word (*sep-a-rate, pen-e-trate, rad-i-cal*), divide after it rather than before it: *sepa-rate*, not *sep-arate; pene-trate*, not *pen-etrate; radi-cal*, not *rad-ical*.
(8) When two adjacent vowels are pronounced separately, divide between them: *re-address* rather than *read-dress; soci-eties* rather than *socie-ties; gradu-ation* rather than *gradua-tion*.
(9) When a word ends in double consonants before a suffix is added (for example, *recall*), you can safely divide after the double consonants if the suffix represents another syllable. Thus, you can divide *recalling* as *recall-ing*, but you cannot divide *recalled* after the double *l* because the addition of the suffix *-ed* does not create a new syllable.
(10) When the final consonant of a base word is doubled because a suffix is added, you can safely divide between the double consonants provided the suffix represents a syllable. Thus, you can divide *deterrent* as *deter-rent*, but you can't divide *deterred* between the double *r* since the addition of *-ed* does not create another syllable.
(11) When double consonants appear within a base word, you can safely divide between them: *suf-fer; bab-bled; hap-pens*.
(12) Don't divide abbreviations or acronyms, even when they contain more than one syllable: *estab.; prelim.; ASCAP; UNESCO*. By the same token, don't divide contractions: *haven't; wouldn't; o'clock*.
(13) Don't divide a number unless it's extremely long—a billion (1,000,000,000) at a minimum. As a rule of thumb, leave at least four digits on the upper line (dividing after the comma, naturally) and carry over at least six digits to the line below. Thus, if it was absolutely necessary, you could divide 3,564,203,100 as 3,564-203,100.
(14) For appearance' sake, try not to end more than two consecutive lines with a hyphen. For the same reason, try not to divide a word at the end of the first line or the last full line of a paragraph.
(15) For your reader's sake, try not to divide the last word at the bottom of a page.
(16) A dash should preferably fall at the end of a line, not at the beginning of the next:

> Let's plan a follow-up meeting—
> next week if possible.
> *Not:* Let's plan a follow-up meeting
> —next week if possible.

(17) Try not to split up phrases that need to be grasped as a whole. Here are some typical cases:

Title and surname:	Ms. Feltrinelli
Surname and abbreviation:	Roy Menck, Jr.
Month and day:	February 26
Month and year:	October, 1988
Page and number:	page 1214
Number and abbreviation:	10:30 A.M.

In longer phrases, where a break may be unavoidable, look for the division point that produces the most intelligible grouping of words.

Full name:	Mary C./Feeney *Not:* Mary/C. Feeney
Full date:	August 31,/1989 *Not:* August/31, 1989
Street address:	43 Kent/Parkway *Not:* 43/Kent Parkway
City address:	Montclair,/N.J. 07042 *Not:* Montclair, N.J./07042

(18) Try not to divide within a proper name. However, if a break is unavoidable, follow the general principles given above. For example: *Mrs. Eleanor F. Franken-heimer; Bob Tol-liver; Missis-sippi; Walling-ford; Mine-ola.*

word elements. ***Definition.*** Word elements are meaning-bearing pieces of words that do not stand alone but are combined to form whole words. They are also called *combining forms* or *bound forms* (*bound* = 'compounded' as opposed to *free* = 'standing alone').

Word elements are either prefixal, forming the beginnings of words, as *micro-* = 'small,' or suffixal, forming the ends of words, as *-scope* = 'optical instrument.' But we distinguish between word elements and AFFIXES, because although the difference isn't hard and fast, it's convenient; affixes modify meaning and function, while word elements contain as much meaning as independent words.

Most word elements are in effect adjectives, as *micro-*, or nouns, as *-scope;* but some are verbs, as *-fy* = 'to make, cause to be.' Many suffixal word elements have a range of related forms giving different functions, as *-fy* (verb), with *-fic* (adjective), *-ficity*, *-fication* (noun).

Selection of Word Elements. Most English word elements are based on borrowings from Greek and Latin.

(1) Prefixal word elements:

Anglo- = 'English (and)': *Anglo-American; Anglo-French*

bi- = 'two': *bicolored; bimonthly*

bio- = 'life': *biology; bioluminescent*

crypto- = 'hidden, secret': *cryptography; cryptophyte*

Euro- = 'European (and)': *Eurocrat; Eurodollar*

Franco- = 'French (and)': *Francophile; Franco-Prussian*

Judeo- = 'Jewish (and)': *Judeo-Christian*

macro- = 'big, large-scale': *macroeconomics; macrohabitat*

mega-, megalo- = 'big': *megabuck; megalomania*

micro- = 'small': *micrometer; microscope*

mono- = 'single, only': *monopoly; monorail*

neo- = 'new': *neoclassical; neolithic*

proto- = 'first, earliest': *Proto-Germanic; protoplasm*

Sino- = 'Chinese (and)': *Sino-Soviet; Sino-Tibetan*

theo- = 'god': *theocentric; theology*

tri- = 'three': *tricycle; tripartite*

(2) Suffixal word elements:

-burger = 'edible patty': *steakburger; fishburger*

-crat = 'person of power': *Eurocrat; technocrat*

-ectomy = 'surgical removal': *hemorrhoidectomy; tonsillectomy*

-ferous = 'bearing, yielding': *carboniferous; diamondiferous*

-fy = 'to make, cause to be': *beautify; solidify*

-graph = 'something written, instrument for communicating': *autograph; telegraph*

-graphy = 'writing, field of study': *calligraphy; geography*

-ish = 'like, near, tending to, about, etc.': *roguish; pinkish; sevenish*

-itis = 'inflamed condition': *appendicitis; laryngitis*

-logy = 'field of study': *archaeology; biology*

-mat = 'automatic machine, establishment with automatic machines': *vendomat; laundromat*

-osis = 'abnormal increase, diseased condition': *fibrosis; tuberculosis*

-phone = 'instrument for transmitting sound, person who speaks a language': *gramophone; Francophone*

-stomy = 'surgical operation to make an opening': *colostomy; tracheostomy*

-thon = 'large-scale contest or fund-raising event': *telethon*

-tomy = 'surgical incision': *lobotomy*

wrack, rack, wreck. Several different words are involved:

(1) The verb *wrack* means 'to inflict pain on (someone), cause agony to.' This is a variant of *rack* = 'to stretch on the rack, torture.' Of the two spellings, *rack* is probably the commoner, but *wrack* is fully standard and is preferred by some in the figurative sense 'to cause pain and suffering to.'

> The intensely patriotic Sherman loved the South . . . but was emotionally wracked by the collapse of the Union.
> —Burke Davis, *Sherman's March*

> Scorched by the sun, wracked by the wind and rain of the monsoon, fighting

in alien swamps and jungles, our humanity rubbed off us. . . .
—Philip Caputo, *A Rumor of War*

(2) The verb *wrack* means 'to batter destructively.' This is related to both *wreck* and the noun *wrack*, below. But it is an independent word, not merely a variant or equivalent. When applied to ships, it is a somewhat more emotive word than *wreck*. *Wreck* means 'to cripple and usually sink (a vessel) in any way'; *wrack* means 'to batter and smash (vessels, etc.) with great violence,' not necessarily resulting in sinking.

. . . a rescue boat was washed off a causeway into the storm-wracked harbor early yesterday morning.
—Michael Kenney, *Boston Globe*

A greater hazard than pirates, however, were the storms and reefs that wracked the ships as they passed the Caribbean islands. . . .
—Joseph P. Blank, *Reader's Digest*

(3) The noun *wrack* means 'destruction' and is related to the second verb *wrack*, above. The noun is used chiefly in the phrase *wrack and ruin*, for which *rack and ruin* is the slightly commoner spelling.

wreak /rēk/. This Old English verb originally meant 'to punish, inflict vengeance on,' also 'to avenge.' It now sometimes means 'to turn or unleash (anger, hatred, etc.) on someone.'

That I might wreak the utmost of my anger upon his head.
—Mary Shelley, *Frankenstein*

Much more often *wreak* means 'to inflict (pain, damage, confusion, etc.) on.' By far the commonest thing that is wreaked is *havoc* (= 'devastation, destruction').

Few had believed that a tsunami could speed through the sea and still wreak havoc.
—Leonard Bickel, *Reader's Digest*

But a treaty of the kind they wanted would have wreaked havoc among our NATO allies in Europe.
—Richard Nixon, *R.N.*

wreck. See WRACK, RACK, WRECK.

wrong is used as an adverb, often in preference to *wrongly*, when coming after the verb it qualifies.

In other ways, too, the generals had been brought up wrong.
—Bruce Catton, *A Stillness at Appomattox*

In all other situations, only *wrongly* is possible: *They were wrongly brought up. Wrongly, they decided to attack.*

wrought /rôt/ is the old past tense and participle of the verb *work*. It is used in a few limited ways.

(1) Referring to skillfully done work:

Typically, Culver worked toward a solution that could win a consensus in the committee, and it has come to the Senate floor with the committee's unanimous approval. Now he must try to preserve the compromise he has wrought.
—Elizabeth Drew, *Senator*

(2) Referring to change, damage, etc.:

The film's inner movement is the change that is wrought in the behavior and character of the single parent. . . .
—Gene Lichtenstein, *Atlantic Monthly*

There was too much damage wrought by that last weekend in the summer of 1977 to be repaired easily. . . .
—James Wooten, *Dasher*

(3) The first telegraph message, sent by the inventor Samuel Morse from Washington to Baltimore in 1844, quoted from the Book of Numbers 23:23: "What hath God wrought!" This famous quotation is occasionally echoed, as in the title of an article in *Time* magazine: "What Hath Xerox Wrought!"

(4) Designating a relatively soft type of iron used for forging as opposed to casting: *wrought iron*.

(5) Referring to certain emotional states: *wrought up* = 'extremely agitated'; *overwrought* = 'excessively agitated.'

XY&Z

X, x. The use of the letter *x* to denote 'unknown quantity' goes back to the French philosopher-mathematician René Descartes, who introduced *x, y, z,* and the like into the mathematical discourse proceeding from an originally Arabic paradigm. By the 18th century the usage was extended from math to everyday language, and *X* in the sense of 'unknown person' has been with us ever since. *X-rays,* likewise, were so named by their discoverer, Wilhelm Roentgen, because their nature and source were unknown.

xenophobia, literally 'fear of strangers,' means 'fear or dislike of foreigners or foreign influences.' Its adjective is *xenophobic.*

> A complicated impulse has stirred in Americans' thinking about their country and its place in the world. Patriotism has reappeared, along with its scruffy little half brothers, xenophobia and chauvinism.
>
> —Lance Morrow, *Time*

> Having undergone long foreign occupations—Chinese, French, Japanese—the [Vietnamese] people are strongly xenophobic.
>
> —William C. Westmoreland, *A Soldier Reports*

Xmas. This abbreviation for 'Christmas' is one of the oldest informalities of our language—in its Old English form it occurs in the *Anglo-Saxon Chronicle.* The *X* stands for the Greek letter *chi,* the initial in the name *Χριστός* (*Khristos* = 'Christ').

◇ ***Recommendation.*** Don't use this abbreviation in formal writing. Many people consider it to be in bad taste—commercial, offensive to the Christian religion, or the like. This feeling may have arisen from a confusion of *X* in the sense of 'Christ' with *X* meaning 'unknown person or quantity.'

yahoo. This name was coined by Jonathan Swift in his satirical novel *Gulliver's Travels* (1726). The often-shipwrecked Englishman Lemuel Gulliver is at one point marooned in the country of the *Houyhnhnms* /**hwĭn**-ĭmz/, a race of civilized horses, and finds that human beings in that country are a degraded and disgusting race of animals:

> The master horse ordered a sorrel nag, one of his servants, to untie the largest of these animals, and take him into the yard. The beast and I were brought close together, and our countenances diligently compared, both by master and servant, who thereupon repeated several times the word *Yahoo.* My horror and astonishment are not to be described, when I observed in this abominable animal a perfect human figure. . . .

The word *yahoo* is now used to mean 'ignorant barbarian,' usually referring either to bad manners and general uncouthness or to extremely reactionary political views:

> For over a century club owners have turned a deaf ear to the yahoos in the bleachers or press box who yelled, "Kill the umpire."
>
> —Peter Seitz (quoted), *New York Times*

> . . . he tried to have it both ways: to attract both liberals and conservatives . . . Eastern sophisticates and Oklahoma yahoos.
>
> —James Wooten, *Dasher*

The word is often used attributively:

> [Sen. Joseph McCarthy's] real constituency was almost a mirror-image of the Yahoo coalition that opposed Al Smith in 1928.
>
> —John Roche, *Boston Herald American*

> Mr. Hunt has done his share . . . to give capitalism a bad name . . . by his eccentric understanding of public affairs, his yahoo bigotry and his appallingly bad manners.
>
> —William F. Buckley, Jr., *Execution Eve*

Yiddish words. Yiddish is the language of the Jews of eastern Europe and their descendants worldwide. Originally a dialect of Middle High German, it has about 15 percent Hebrew words and some smaller percentages from other languages. It is written in Hebrew letters.

Selected Vocabulary. A good many Yiddish words have been borrowed into English. Some have become Standard English, while others have retained a slangy flavor.

bagel /**bā**-gəl/ = 'hard doughnut-shaped bread roll'

bialy /**byä**-lē/ = 'flat bread roll often sprinkled with chopped onions': from *Bialystok*, city in Poland

blintz = 'thin pancake filled with cream cheese, berries, etc.'

borsht, borscht, borsch = 'hot or cold beet soup'

* **chutzpah** /**hŏŏts**-pə, **KHŏŏts**-/ = 'extreme effrontery, audacity'

goy = 'Gentile': from Hebrew *goy* = 'nation'

kibitz /**kĭb**-ĭtz/ = 'to look on at (a card game or the like) and give advice,' especially 'to give unwanted advice, meddle'

klutz = 'clumsy, stupid person'

knish /kə-**nĭsh**/ = 'baked dough roll stuffed with potato'

kosher /**kō**-shər/ = 'proper to eat under Jewish dietary laws'

lox = 'smoked salmon'

matzo /**mät**-sə/ = 'thin, flat, unleavened bread, similar to crackers'

mensch /mĕnsh/ = 'person worthy of respect, admirable human being'

-nik (suffix) = 'person who is (something)': *kibbutznik* = 'member of a kibbutz'

nosh = (1) (noun) 'snack' (2) (verb) 'to eat between meals, snack'

schlemiel /shlə-**mēl**/ = 'bungling and unlucky person'

schlep, shlep = 'to carry (something burdensome)'

schlock, shlock = 'trashy, shoddy product or performance'

schmaltz, schmalz, shmaltz /shmältz/ = 'maudlin sentimentality'

schmuck, shmuck (vulgar slang) = 'idiot, jerk, contemptible person'

shtick, shtik = 'contrived piece of acting, special talent, etc.'

*Appears as separate entry

you is used as an indefinite personal pronoun in two distinct ways.

(1) As an equivalent of *one*, but giving a less abstract effect, as of a speaker directly addressing an audience.

> You cannot stop the spread of an idea by passing a law against it.
> —Harry Truman (quoted), Eldorous L. Dayton, *Give 'em Hell, Harry*

(2) In autobiography or a fictionalized equivalent of it, giving a more intimate effect than *one* or *I*. This use of *you* sets up an unstated sympathy between the writer and the reader.

> One of the advantages of being born in the ghetto of the Lower East Side is that you are born an "adult."
> —Harry Golden, *For 2¢ Plain*

> . . . at Auteil it was beautiful to watch each day they raced when you could be there and see the honest races with the great horses, and you got to know the course as well as any place you had ever known. You knew many people finally. . . .
> —Ernest Hemingway, *A Moveable Feast*

> Teachers were never interested in finding out that you couldn't concentrate because you were so hungry, because you hadn't had any breakfast.
> —Dick Gregory, *Nigger*

See also ONE.

you-all. This shibboleth of Southern speech means 'you' in addressing one, two, or more persons. It can be distinguished from the standard *you all*, which means 'all of you,' by the placement of the stress. The Southern *you-all* has the stress on the first word: /**yōō**-ôl/; in speech it is often collapsed into one syllable, /yôl/, written *y'all.* The non-Southern and standard *you all* has the stress on *all* and is rarely contracted into one syllable; it refers only to three or more persons.

Much has been written about the origin of the Southern expression. Some scholars argue that it may have come to the South directly from the English of Shakespeare's time (see ELIZABETHAN ENGLISH IN AMERICA).

> O spite! O hell! I see you all are bent
> To set against me for your merriment.
> —Shakespeare,
> *A Midsummer-Night's Dream*

Others challenge this view. It is also possible that the expression is indigenous to the United States, perhaps originating in the creolized English of the slaves.

> They [Virginians] say . . . madam and mistress, instead of our abbreviations. Children learn from the slaves some odd phrases; as, every which way; will you *all* do this? for, will *one* of you do this?
> —Arthur Singleton,
> *Letters From the South and West* (1824)

You-all is also used possessively as *you-all's*:

> I saw you-all's wagon go on down the road till it got round and a sight littler and seemed like anybody's wagon a-goen anywheres.
> —Elizabeth Roberts,
> *The Time of Man* (1926)

> "Reckon we might as well begin," said the preacher. "We are honored to have you-all's company."
> —Carl Carmer,
> *Stars Fell on Alabama* (1934)

zed. This is the British name for the letter *z*, shortened from *zeta*, the name of the Greek letter originally representing the sound /dz/ (see GREEK WORDS). This letter was introduced into English to render the anglicized forms of numerous Latin and Greek words. However, it has always been regarded as something of an interloper in the English alphabet, so much so that the term *zed* could be applied contemptuously to a useless person: "Thou whoreson zed! thou unnecessary letter!" (Shakespeare, *King Lear*). In the American South *z* was called *zed* until well past the Civil War, long after the rest of the country had adopted the name *zee* for the last letter of our alphabet.

zeugma /**zōōg**-mə/. This is a figure of speech in which a single word is related to two or more other words in a sentence in such a way that the construction is not parallel: *She checked out of the hotel with a head cold and a Gideon Bible.* Here, *with* is used to apply both to the person's condition (head cold) and to what she was carrying (Bible). There is an incongruity about zeugmas that almost always strikes a native speaker of a language as a defect of construction. Used carelessly or unconsciously, zeugma can be awkward, even embarrassing; used deliberately for comic effect, it is one of the most enjoyable devices a writer can employ.